MediaShare for Business offers a curated collection of business videos that provide customizable, auto-scored assignments. MediaShare for Business helps students understand why they are learning key concepts and how they will **apply** those in their careers.

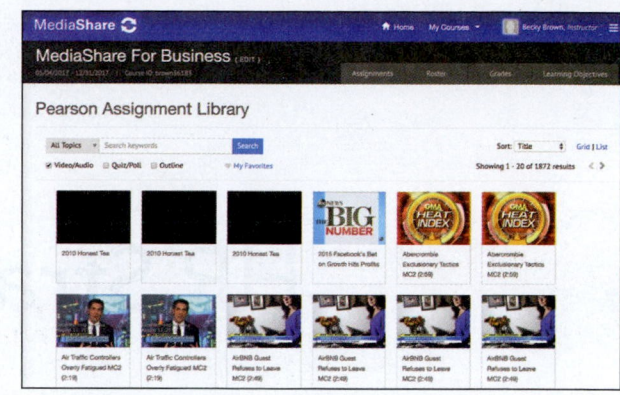

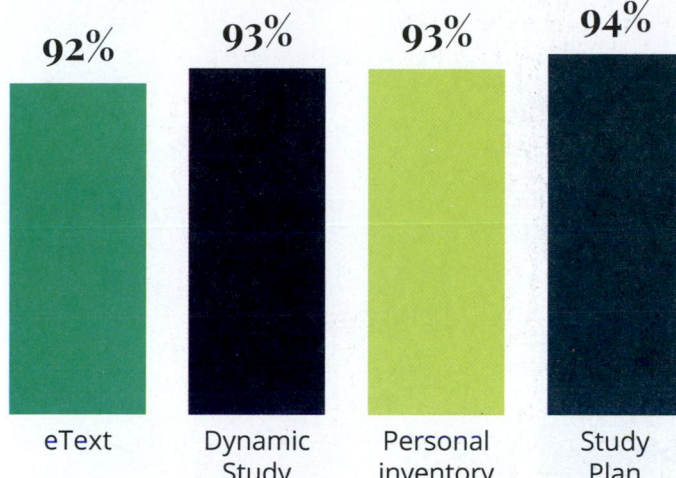

92%	93%	93%	94%
eText	Dynamic Study Modules	Personal inventory assessment	Study Plan

% of students who found learning tool helpful

Pearson eText enhances student learning—both in and outside the classroom. Take notes, highlight, and bookmark important content, or engage with interactive lecture and example videos that bring learning to life (available with select titles). Accessible anytime, anywhere via MyLab or the app.

86%

of students would tell their instructor to keep using MyLab Management

The **MyLab Gradebook** offers an easy way for students and instructors to view course performance. Item Analysis allows instructors to quickly see trends by analyzing details like the number of students who answered correctly/incorrectly, time on task, and median time spend on a question by question basis. And because it's correlated with the AACSB Standards, instructors can track students' progress toward outcomes that the organization has deemed important in preparing students to be **leaders.**

"I was able to find myself actually learning at home rather than memorizing things for a class."
— Katherine Vicente, Student at County College of Morris

For additional details visit: www.pearson.com/mylab/management

HR Strategy Model

The HR Strategy Model in the Part openers illustrates the basic idea behind strategic human resource management, which is that *in formulating human resource management policies and practices, the aim must be to produce the employee competencies and behaviors that the company needs to achieve its strategic goals.*

FIFTH EDITION

Fundamentals of
Human Resource Management

Gary Dessler

Florida International University

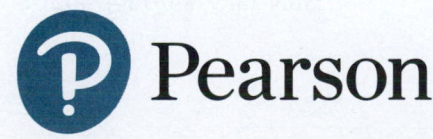

New York, NY

This book is dedicated to Taylor

Vice President, Business, Economics, and UK Courseware: Donna Battista

Director of Portfolio Management: Stephanie Wall

Development Editor: Kerri Tomasso

Editorial Assistant: Linda Siebert Albelli

Vice President, Product Marketing: Roxanne McCarley

Product Marketer: Kaylee Carlson

Product Marketing Assistant: Marianela Silvestri

Manager of Field Marketing, Business Publishing: Adam Goldstein

Field Marketing Manager: Nicole Price

Vice President, Production and Digital Studio, Arts and Business: Etain O'Dea

Director of Production, Business: Jeff Holcomb

Managing Producer, Business: Melissa Feimer

Content Producer: Yasmita Hota

Operations Specialist: Carol Melville

Design Lead: Kathryn Foot

Manager, Learning Tools: Brian Surette

Content Developer, Learning Tools: Lindsey Sloan

Managing Producer, Digital Studio and GLP, Media Production and Development: Ashley Santora

Managing Producer, Digital Studio: Diane Lombardo

Digital Studio Producer: Monique Lawrence

Digital Studio Producer: Alana Coles

Project Manager: Ann Pulido, SPi Global

Interior Design: Laurie Entringer, SPi Global

Cover Design: Laurie Entringer, SPi Global

Cover Image: David Trood/Getty Images

Printer/Binder: LSC Communications, Inc./Owensville

Cover Printer: Phoenix Color/Hagerstown

ISBN 10:   0-13-474021-1
ISBN 13: 978-0-13-474021-8

BRIEF CONTENTS

CONTENTS

PREFACE

New To This Edition

Today managers—not just HR managers—need a strong foundation in HR concepts and techniques like interviewing and appraising to do their jobs. You'll therefore find an emphasis here on practical material you need to perform your day-to-day management responsibilities, even if you never spend one day as a human resource manager.

At the heart of the book is the practical skills-oriented material woven into almost every paragraph—into the book's DNA—plus special "how-to" features.

HR management is changing fast. For example, Accenture Consultants estimates that social media tools like LinkedIn will soon produce up to 80% of new recruits.

New **Trends Shaping HR** features highlight how managers today accomplish their HR tasks.

Building Your Management Skills features show how to apply what you've learned, such as how to conduct effective employment interviews.

Know Your Employment Law features show the practical implications of the employment laws that apply to each chapter's topics, such as recruitment.

HR as a Profit Center features show how to use HR methods to cut costs and improve performance.

Special "how-to" Features for Building Your Work Skills and Employability

HR Tools for Line Managers and Small Businesses show how managers, supervisors, and small businesses use practical HR tools such as work sampling tests to improve performance.

HR in Practice features show how managers and companies such as **Zappos** actually implement their HR practices.

TRENDS SHAPING HR: *Digital and Social Media*

USING LINKEDIN Sometimes the easiest way to unearth job titles and duties is just to use social media like LinkedIn. For example, to paraphrase what someone who recruits for open positions in his company posted on LinkedIn: I hope some of you IT recruiters out there can help me to better understand what I need to put into the job descriptions that I'm writing for the developers and development managers I'm recruiting for. The first of many replies listed 12 tasks including: (1) Do technical skills match the desired job? (2) What technical problems were solved by the job seeker? and (3) Did job seeker know about Cloud Deployment?[31]

TRENDS SHAPING HR: *Digital and Social Media*

SOME SOCIAL MEDIA HR PROS AND CONS Widespread use of social media presents challenges to employers. Some employees use Facebook-type accounts to bully coworkers. Here, employers must distinguish between illegal online harassment (applying to race, religion, national origin, age, sex/gender, genetic information, and disability discrimination) and common personality conflicts. Employers at least need a zero-tolerance policy on bullying.[89]

Of course, social media has been great for staffing. It's easy for employers to find applicants on LinkedIn, for instance. However, viewing an applicant's social media profile may reveal information on things like religion, race, and sexual orientation.[90] Some states therefore forbid employers from requesting employees' or applicants' passwords. At a minimum, implement policies restricting who can check out candidates online. Supervisors should generally not do such checking themselves.

About 25% of today's workers don't have "regular" jobs. Instead, they're independent or "gig" workers—that's about 60 million gig workers in the USA alone.

New **HR and the Gig Economy** features show how companies manage gig workers' HR needs, for example how to recruit, train, and manage the safety of gig workers.

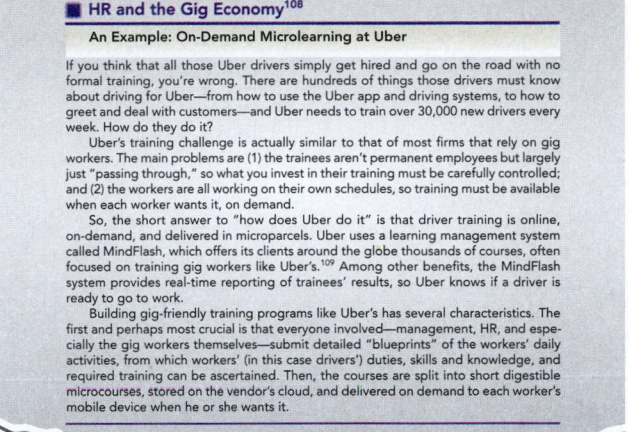

■ HR and the Gig Economy

Do Gig Workers Need Job Specifications?

Hiring gig workers doesn't mean the employer doesn't need job descriptions and job specifications. With respect to job descriptions, the prudent employer will still want to list at least the main duties it expects the worker to do. And job specifications are surely required, because the employer must ensure that the people doing its work at least fit certain minimum requirements.

For example, both Lyft and Uber list "driver requirements," which are essentially job specifications.[46] Although driver requirements vary somewhat by location, both Uber and Lyft require drivers to be at least 21, have a Social Security number and in-state driver's license (at least one year old), have in-state insurance, and undergo both DMV and national and county-wide background checks. For Uber, the background check also means for the past 7 years no DUI or drug-related offenses, or incidents of driving without insurance or license, or fatal accidents, or history of reckless driving, and no criminal history. And there are other requirements, including that your car pass muster. As a partial list, it must be a four-door sedan, seat four or more (excluding driver), be 2001 or newer, have in-state plates and be currently registered, and pass Uber's vehicle inspection.

☆ Talk About It– 2

If your professor has chosen to assign this, go to **www.pearson.com/mylab/ management** to discuss the following questions. Based on your experience, what other human requirements would you say there are to be a good Uber or Lyft driver? Should the companies add these as requirements? Why?

■ HR and the Gig Economy[108]

An Example: On-Demand Microlearning at Uber

If you think that all those Uber drivers simply get hired and go on the road with no formal training, you're wrong. There are hundreds of things those drivers must know about driving for Uber—from how to use the Uber app and driving systems, to how to greet and deal with customers—and Uber needs to train over 30,000 new drivers every week. How do they do it?

Uber's training challenge is actually similar to that of most firms that rely on gig workers. The main problems are (1) the trainees aren't permanent employees but largely just "passing through," so what you invest in their training must be carefully controlled; and (2) the workers are all working on their own schedules, so training must be available when each worker wants it, on demand.

So, the short answer to "how does Uber do it" is that driver training is online, on-demand, and delivered in microparcels. Uber uses a learning management system called MindFlash, which offers its clients around the globe thousands of courses, often focused on training gig workers like Uber's.[109] Among other benefits, the MindFlash system provides real-time reporting of trainees' results, so Uber knows if a driver is ready to go to work.

Building gig-friendly training programs like Uber's has several characteristics. The first and perhaps most crucial is that everyone involved—management, HR, and especially the gig workers themselves—submit detailed "blueprints" of the workers' daily activities, from which workers' (in this case drivers') duties, skills and knowledge, and required training can be ascertained. Then, the courses are split into short digestible microcourses, stored on the vendor's cloud, and delivered on demand to each worker's mobile device when he or she wants it.

SHRM—the Society for Human Resource Management administers a certification program for HR professionals. This 5th edition addresses SHRM's functional knowledge areas, with Knowledge Base icons call-outs and a SHRM knowledge overview and group activity questions in the accompanying MyLab Management.

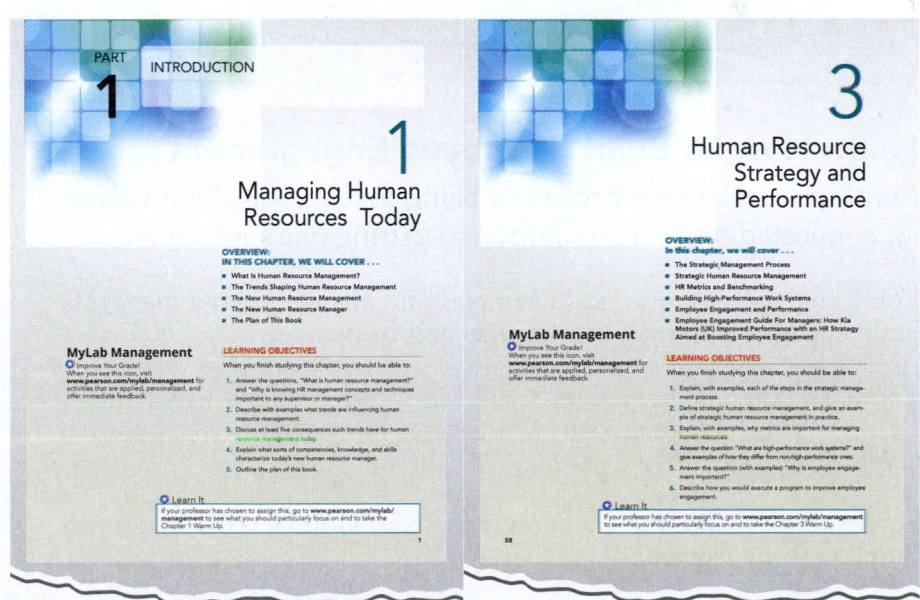

Solving Teaching and Learning Challenges

A Focus on Building Your Management Skills

One of the best ways to get and keep a job is to show that you can do the job and do it well.

That's why every single edition of this book has had the same aim: to provide all managers—not just HR managers—with the practical skills and knowledge you need to perform your day-to-day management responsibilities. For example, you'll learn about:

Ch2: How to deal with a charge of discrimination

. . . You turn down a member of a protected group for a job. This person believes he or she was discriminated against due to being in a protected class, and decides to sue . . . What should you do?

Ch 4: How to write a job description

. . . A job description is a written statement of what the worker actually does, how he or she does it, and what the job's working conditions are. This information is in turn . . .

Ch 6: How to interview job candidates

. . . First make sure you understand the job and its human requirements. Then compose questions based on actual job duties from the job description. . . . Examples include (1) situational questions like "Suppose you were giving a sales presentation and a difficult technical question arose . . .

Ch 12: How to discipline an employee

. . . Make sure the evidence supports the charge of employee wrongdoing. (Arbitrators often cite "the employer's evidence did not support the charge.") . . . Make sure to protect the employees' due process rights . . .

Learn How to Build Employee Engagement

Employee engagement refers to being psychologically involved in, connected to, and committed to getting one's jobs done.

You'll find specific practical examples and advice on how managers build engaged employee work teams and companies.

Employee Engagement Guide for Managers sections in Chapters 1–14 show how managers use human resource activities to improve employee engagement.

For example, Chapter 3's show how Kia Motors (UK) improved Employee Engagement.

BUILDING YOUR MANAGEMENT SKILLS
How to Execute an Employee Engagement Strategy

Actually executing Kia UK's employee engagement HR strategy involved six steps (and these provide a roadmap for any such endeavor). First, Kia UK set *measurable objectives* for the program. These objectives included improving by at least 10% survey feedback scores for line managers' behaviors, in terms of communication, the quality of appraisal feedback they gave their direct reports, the recognition of work done, and the respect between manager and employee.[76] Other objectives included reducing employee turnover employment costs (e.g., recruitment costs) by at least 10% per year.

Second, Kia UK held an extensive *leadership development* program. For example, they sent all managers for training to improve their management skills. They then tested the new skills with "360-degree" assessment tools (these basically meant having managers' bosses, peers, and subordinates rate the managers' new leadership skills).

Third, Kia UK instituted new *employee recognition programs*. These included, for instance, giving "Outstanding Awards" to selected employees quarterly, and "Kia thank you" cards for jobs well done.[77]

Fourth, Kia UK *improved internal communications*. For example, they instituted quarterly employee briefings, more extensive use of performance appraisals, and launched a new corporate intranet called Kia Vision (this provided key business information and other useful communiqués to all employees). Based on employee feedback, Kia UK also decided, as part of the enhanced communications, to institute an *employee forum*. This consisted of one representative from each department; the forum in effect empowered and involved employees by enabling them to express opinions, suggestions, and concerns about their jobs.

Fifth, they instituted a new *employee development program*. This involved using the company's appraisal process to identify employees' training needs. Kia then created training plans for each employee. They based these plans on Kia's needs and on the employee's stated career aspirations.

Sixth, Kia UK made a number of changes to its *compensation and other policies*. For instance, they eliminated bonuses and substituted fixed-rate percentage-based salary increases. They also rewrote the entire employee handbook and all HR policies and procedures "to ensure they were aligned with [Kia UK's new] cultural values."[78]

Unique to this book: New **HR and the Gig Economy** features show how to recruit, train, and manage the safety of gig workers.

And our unique **Strategy Model** helps provide you with a "big picture" view:

Strategic human resource management means formulating and executing human resource policies and practices that produce the employee competencies and behaviors the company needs to achieve its strategic aims.

Our model illustrates this idea and follows this three-step sequence:

- *Set* the firm's strategic aims,
- *Pinpoint* the employee behaviors and skills we need to achieve these strategic aims, and then
- *Decide* what HR policies and practices will enable us to produce these necessary employee behaviors and skills.

MyLab Management suggested activities

Learn It

Students can be assigned the Chapter Warm-Up before coming to class. Assigning these questions ahead of time will hopefully help ensure that students come to class prepared.

> ⭐ **Learn It**
>
> If your professor has chosen to assign this, go to www.pearson.com/mylab/management to see what you should particularly focus on and to take the Chapter 1 Warm Up.

> ⭐ **Watch It**
>
> How does a company actually go about putting its human resource philosophy into action? If your professor has chosen to assign this, go to **www.pearson.com/mylab/management** to watch the video Patagonia Human Resource Management and then answer the questions to show what you would do in this situation.

Watch It

Recommends a video clip that can be assigned to students for outside classroom viewing or for in-classroom use.

Try It

Recommends a mini-simulation that can be assigned to students as an outside classroom activity or that can be done in the classroom.

> ⭐ **Try It**
>
> How would you do applying the concepts and skills you learned in this chapter? If your professor has chosen to assign this, go to **www.pearson.com/mylab/management** and complete the Human Resource Management simulation.

> ⭐ **Talk About It – 3**
>
> If your professor has chosen to assign this, go to **www.pearson.com/mylab/management** to discuss the following questions: Go to one or more sites like these. If you were a programming manager for a company, could you use the site to find and hire a new employee directly? If not, what else might you need?

Talk About It

These are discussion-type questions that can be assigned as an activity within the classroom.

Assisted-Graded Writing Questions

These are short essay questions that the students can complete as an assignment and submit to you, the professor, for grading.

> **MyLab Management**
>
> If your instructor is using MyLab Management, go to www.pearson.com/mylab/management for Auto-graded writing questions as well as the following Assisted-graded writing questions:
>
> 1-16. How do today's HR managers deal with the trends and challenges shaping contemporary HR management?
>
> 1-17. Discuss some competencies HR managers need to deal with today's trends and challenges.

MyLab Management

Reach every student by pairing this text with MyLab Management MyLab is the teaching and learning platform that empowers you to reach *every* student. By combining trusted author content with digital tools and a flexible platform, MyLab personalizes the learning experience and improves results for each student. Learn more about MyLab Management at www.pearson.com/mylab/management.

Deliver trusted content You deserve teaching materials that meet your own high standards for your course. That's why we partner with highly respected authors to develop interactive content and course-specific resources that you can trust—and that keep your students engaged.

Empower each learner Each student learns at a different pace. Personalized learning pinpoints the precise areas where each student needs practice, giving all students the support they need—when and where they need it— to be successful.

Teach your course your way Your course is unique. So whether you'd like to build your own assignments, teach multiple sections, or set prerequisites, MyLab gives you the flexibility to easily create *your* course to fit *your* needs.

Improve student results When you teach with MyLab, student performance improves. That's why instructors have chosen MyLab for over 15 years, touching the lives of over 50 million students.

Developing Employability Skills

Trends Shaping HR: Digital and Social Media Career sites make the inner workings of employers more transparent. Sites such as Glassdoor, CareerBliss, CareerLeak, and JobBite let members share insights into hundreds of thousands of specific employers, including specific company-by-company commentaries, salary reports, and CEO approval ratings . . . .

HR as a Profit Center contains actual examples of how human resource management practices add value by reducing costs or boosting revenues.

HR and the Gig Economy features show how companies manage gig workers' HR needs, for example, how to recruit, train, and manage the safety of gig workers

HR Tools for Line Managers and Small Businesses explains that many line managers and entrepreneurs are "on their own" when it comes to human resource management and describes work sampling tests and other straightforward HR tools that line managers and entrepreneurs can create and safely use to improve performance.

Know Your Employment Law features within each chapter discuss the practical implications of the employment laws that apply to that chapter's topics, such as the laws relating to recruitment (Chapter 5), selection (Chapter 6), and safety (Chapter 14).

Diversity Counts features provide **practical** insights for managing a diverse workforce, for instance, regarding gender bias in selection decisions, bias in performance appraisal, and "hidden" gender bias in some bonus plans.

Improving Performance Through HRIS are embedded features that demonstrate how managers use human resource technology to improve performance.

HR Practices Around the Globe

Applying Equal Employment Law Abroad

The Civil Rights Act of 1991 marked a big change in the geographic applicability of equal rights legislation. Congressional legislation generally only applies within U.S. territory unless specifically stated otherwise.[85] However, CRA 1991 specifically expanded coverage by amending the definition of "employee" in Title VII to mean a U.S. citizen employed in a foreign country by a U.S.-owned or controlled company.[86] At least theoretically, therefore, *U.S. citizens* now working overseas for U.S. companies enjoy the same equal employment opportunity protection as those working within U.S. borders. (Title VII does not apply to foreign operations not owned or controlled by a U.S. employer, however.)

However, two factors limit the widespread application of CRA 1991 abroad. First, there are numerous exclusions. For example, an employer need not comply with Title VII if compliance would cause the employer to violate the law of the host country (for instance, some foreign countries have statutes prohibiting women in management positions).[87]

Another problem is the practical difficulty of enforcing CRA 1991 abroad. For example, the EEOC investigator's first duty in such a case is to analyze the finances and organizational structure of the respondent (employer). But in practice few investigators are trained for this duty, and no precise standards exist for such investigations.[88]

HR Practices Around the Globe

Applying Equal Employment Law Abroad Expanding abroad complicates complying with equal employment laws. For example, Dell announced big additions to its workforce in India. Are U.S. citizens working for Dell abroad covered by U.S. equal opportunity laws? In practice, the answer depends on U.S. laws, international treaties, and the laws of the host country.

Instructor Teaching Resources

This program comes with the following teaching resources.

Supplements available to instructors at www.pearsonhighered.com	Features of the Supplement
Instructor's Manual authored by Carol Heeter, Ivy Tech Community College	• Chapter-by-chapter summaries and interesting issues on related topics • Additional assignments and activities not in the main book • Teaching outlines • Teaching tips • Solutions to all questions and problems in the book
Test Bank authored by Susan Leshnower, Midland College	More than 1,500 multiple-choice, true/false, short-answer, and graphing questions with these annotations: • Difficulty level (1 for straight recall, 2 for some analysis, 3 for complex analysis) • Type (Multiple-choice, true/false, short-answer, essay • Skill (Application or concept) that is needed to answer the question • Learning outcome • AACSB learning standard, where applicable (Written and Oral Communication; Ethical Understanding and Reasoning; Analytical Thinking; Information Technology; Interpersonal Relations and Teamwork; Diverse and Multicultural Work; Reflective Thinking; Application of Knowledge)
Computerized TestGen	TestGen allows instructors to: • Customize, save, and generate classroom tests • Edit, add, or delete questions from the Test Item Files • Analyze test results • Organize a database of tests and student results.
PowerPoints authored by Dan Morrell, Middle Tennessee State University	Slides include applicable graphs, tables, and equations in the textbook. PowerPoints meet accessibility standards for students with disabilities. Features include, but not limited to: • Keyboard and Screen Reader access • Alternative text for images • High color contrast between background and foreground colors

ACKNOWLEDGMENTS

I am indebted to many people for their assistance in creating this book. I appreciate the conscientious and useful suggestions from the reviewers of the previous editions of *Fundamentals of Human Resource Management*.

Samuel Todd, Georgia Southern University/UMASS Amherst
Dale J. Dwyer, The University of Toledo
Melissa L. Gruys, Wright State University, Ohio
John H. Stern, Darla Moore School of Business, University of South Carolina
Dan Morrell, Middle Tennessee State University
Marie D. K. Halvorsen-Ganepola, University of Notre Dame
Howard J. Klein, The Ohio State University
Paul W. Mulvey, Poole College of Management, North Carolina State University
Gary Stroud, Franklin University, Ohio

I am very grateful to our supplements authors, Carol Heeter, Ivy Tech Community College and Dan Morrell.

At Pearson, I thank the *Fundamentals of Human Resource Management*, 5th edition team including Stephanie Wall, Editor in Chief; Daniel Tylman, Acquisitions Editor; Melissa Feimer, Managing Producer for Qualitative Disciplines; Yasmita Hota, Content Producer; Linda Siebert Albelli, Editorial Assistant; Ann Pulido, Project Manager; and Kerri Tomasso, Development Editor. Thanks to the world-wide Pearson sales team, without whose hard work this book might just languish on a shelf.

At home, I want to thank as always my wife Claudia for her support, my son Derek for his advice, and of course, Lisa, Samantha, and Taylor.

ABOUT THE AUTHOR

Readers worldwide use Gary Dessler's *Fundamentals of Human Resource Management, Human Resource Management*, and *Framework for Human Resource Management* in a total of more than 10 languages and international editions, including Russian, Spanish, French, Arabic, Thai, Greek, and Chinese. Dr. Dessler's other books include *Winning Commitment: How to Build and Keep a Competitive Workforce*, and *Management: Modern Principles and Practices for Tomorrow's Leaders*. He has published articles on employee commitment, leadership, supervision, human resource management practices in China, and quality improvement in journals including the *Academy of Management Executive, SAM Advanced Management Journal, Supervision, Personnel Journal*, and *International Journal of Service Management*.

Dr. Dessler served for many years as a Founding Professor in Florida International University's College of Business teaching courses in human resource management, strategic management, and management. For the past few years, he has focused on his textbook writing, research, and consulting and on giving lectures, seminars, and courses around the world on modern human resource management methods, maintaining positive employee relations and employee engagement, strategic management, leadership development, and talent management.

Dr. Dessler has degrees from New York University, Rensselaer Polytechnic Institute, and the Baruch School of Business of the City University of New York.

PART 1 INTRODUCTION

1 Managing Human Resources Today

OVERVIEW:
IN THIS CHAPTER, WE WILL COVER . . .

- **What Is Human Resource Management?**
- **The Trends Shaping Human Resource Management**
- **The New Human Resource Management**
- **The New Human Resource Manager**
- **The Plan of This Book**

MyLab Management

⭐ Improve Your Grade!
When you see this icon, visit
www.pearson.com/mylab/management for activities that are applied, personalized, and offer immediate feedback.

LEARNING OBJECTIVES

When you finish studying this chapter, you should be able to:

1. Answer the questions, "What is human resource management?" and "Why is knowing HR management concepts and techniques important to any supervisor or manager?"

2. Describe with examples what trends are influencing human resource management.

3. Discuss at least five consequences such trends have for human resource management today.

4. Explain what sorts of competencies, knowledge, and skills characterize today's new human resource manager.

5. Outline the plan of this book.

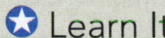 ⭐ Learn It

If your professor has chosen to assign this, go to **www.pearson.com/mylab/management** to see what you should particularly focus on and to take the Chapter 1 Warm Up.

INTRODUCTION

During her senior year at State University Mira was a merchandising intern for TJX, which owns TJ Maxx and Marshalls, and after graduating joined its Store Leadership Pathway program for intensive training; now she's one week into her first management job, as Assistant Store Manager for a TJ Maxx store on the East Coast. "How did your week go?" asked Gladys, her Store Manager and mentor, over coffee. "I love it!" Mira said. "I guess the only surprise is that I thought I'd spend almost all my time on merchandising tasks like setting up displays to give our customers that real 'treasure hunt' experience. But I've actually been spending over a third of my time on "HR" tasks like interviewing prospective associates, training them, and letting them know how they're doing." "Get used to that" said Gladys. "My experience was about the same, and now as Store Manager I find I spend almost half my time on such tasks—including mentoring!"[1]

Source: stylephotographs/123RF

organization
An organization consists of people with formally assigned roles who work together to achieve the organization's goals.

manager
Someone who is responsible for accomplishing the organization's goals, and who does so by managing the efforts of the organization's people.

managing
To perform five basic functions: planning, organizing, staffing, leading, and controlling.

management process
The five basic functions of planning, organizing, staffing, leading, and controlling.

What Is Human Resource Management?

To understand what human resource management is, we should first review what managers do. The TJ Maxx store is an *organization*. An **organization** consists of people (in this case, people like sales and maintenance employees) with formally assigned roles who work together to achieve the organization's goals. A **manager** is someone who is responsible for accomplishing the organization's goals and who does so by managing the efforts of the organization's people.

Most writers agree that **managing** involves performing five basic functions: planning, organizing, staffing, leading, and controlling. In total, these functions represent the **management process**. Some of the specific activities involved in each function include the following:

- **Planning.** Establishing goals and standards; developing rules and procedures; developing plans and forecasts
- **Organizing.** Giving each subordinate a specific task; establishing departments; delegating authority to subordinates; establishing channels of authority and communication; coordinating the work of subordinates
- **Staffing.** Determining what type of people should be hired; recruiting prospective employees; selecting employees; setting performance

standards; compensating employees; evaluating performance; counseling employees; training and developing employees
- **Leading.** Getting others to get the job done; maintaining morale; motivating subordinates
- **Controlling.** Setting standards such as sales quotas, quality standards, or production levels; checking to see how actual performance compares with these standards; taking corrective action as needed

human resource management (HRM)
The process of acquiring, training, appraising, and compensating employees, and of attending to their labor relations, health and safety, and fairness concerns.

In this book, we will focus on one of these functions—the staffing, personnel management, or *human resource management (HRM)* function. **Human resource management** is the process of acquiring, training, appraising, and compensating employees, and of attending to their labor relations, health and safety, and fairness concerns. The topics we'll discuss should therefore provide you with the concepts and techniques you'll need to perform the "people," or personnel, aspects of management. These include

- *Conducting job analyses* (determining the nature of each employee's job)
- *Planning labor needs* and *recruiting* job candidates
- *Selecting* job candidates
- *Orienting and training* new employees
- *Managing wages and salaries* (compensating employees)
- *Providing incentives and benefits*
- *Appraising performance*
- *Communicating* (interviewing, counseling, disciplining)
- *Training employees*, and *developing managers*
- *Building employee relations and engagement*

And what a manager should know about:

- Equal opportunity and affirmative action
- Employee health and safety
- Handling grievances and labor relations

Why is Human Resource Management Important to All Managers?

Why are the concepts and techniques in this book important to all managers? Perhaps it's easier to answer this by listing some of the *personnel mistakes you don't want to make* while managing. For example, you don't want to

- Have your employees not doing their best
- Hire the wrong person for the job
- Experience high turnover
- Have your company in court due to your discriminatory actions
- Have your company cited for unsafe practices
- Let a lack of training undermine your department's effectiveness
- Commit any unfair labor practices

Carefully studying this book can help you avoid mistakes like these.

Improving Profits and Performance More important, it can *help ensure that you get results—through people.*[2] Remember that you could do everything else right as a manager—lay brilliant plans, draw clear organization charts, set up modern assembly lines, and use sophisticated accounting controls—but still fail, for instance, by hiring the wrong people or by not motivating subordinates. On the other hand, many managers—from generals to presidents to supervisors—have been successful even without adequate plans, organizations, or controls. They were successful because they had the knack for hiring the right people for the right jobs and then motivating, appraising, and developing them. Remember as you read this book that *getting results* is the bottom line of managing and that, as a manager, you will have to get these results through people. This fact hasn't changed from the dawn of management. As one company president summed it up:

For many years it has been said that capital is the bottleneck for a developing industry. I don't think this any longer holds true. I think it's the workforce and the company's inability to recruit and maintain a good workforce that does constitute the bottleneck for production. I don't know of any major project backed by good ideas, vigor, and enthusiasm that has been stopped by a shortage of cash. I do know of industries whose growth has been partly stopped or hampered because they can't maintain an efficient and enthusiastic labor force, and I think this will hold true even more in the future.[3]

At no time in our history has that statement been truer than it is today. As we'll see in a moment, intensified global competition, technological advances, and economic upheaval have triggered competitive turmoil. In this environment, the future belongs to those managers who can improve performance while managing change; but doing so requires getting results through engaged and committed employees.

Human resource management practices and policies play a big role in helping managers do this. For example, we'll see that one call center averaged 18.6 vacancies per year (about a 60% turnover rate). The researchers estimated the cost of a call-center operator leaving at about $21,500, making the estimated total annual cost of agent turnover about $400,000. Cutting that rate in half through improved recruiting and testing would save this firm about $200,000 per year.[4]

You May Spend Some Time As An HR Manager Here is another reason to study this book: *you might spend time as a human resource manager*. For example, about a third of large U.S. businesses surveyed appointed non-HR managers to be their top human resource executives. Thus, Pearson Corporation (which publishes this book) promoted the head of one of its publishing divisions to chief human resource executive at its corporate headquarters. Why? Some think these people may be better equipped to integrate the firm's human resource activities (such as pay policies) with the company's strategic needs (such as by tying executives' incentives to corporate goals).[5] Spending some time in HR can also be good for a manager. For example, one CEO served a three-year stint as chief human resource officer on the way to CEO. He said the experience was invaluable in learning how to develop leaders and in understanding the human side of transforming a company.[6]

However, most top human resource executives do have prior human resource experience. About 80% in one survey worked their way up within HR. About 17% had the HR Certification Institute's Senior Professional in Human Resources (SPHR) designation, and 13% were certified Professional in Human Resources (PHR). Many others carry the SHRM Certified Professional (SHRM-CP) or Senior Certified Professional (SHRM-SCP) designations from the Society for Human Resource Management (SHRM). SHRM offers a brochure describing alternative career paths within human resource management.[7] Find it at www.shrm.org.

HR for Small Businesses And here is one final reason to study this book: *you may well end up as your own human resource manager*. About half the people working in the United States today work for small firms.[8] Small businesses as a group also account for most of the 650,000 or so new businesses created every year.[9] Statistically speaking, therefore, most people graduating from college in the next few years either will work for small businesses or will create new small businesses of their own. If you are managing your own small firm with no human resource manager, you'll probably have to handle HR on your own. To do that, you must be able to recruit, select, train, appraise, and reward employees. There are special HR Tools for Line Managers and Small Businesses features in most chapters. These show small business owners how to improve their human resource management practices.

Line and Staff Aspects of HRM

All managers are, in a sense, human resource managers because they all get involved in activities such as recruiting, interviewing, selecting, and training. Yet most firms also have a separate human resource department with its own human resource manager. How do the duties of this departmental HR manager and his or her staff relate to line managers' human resource duties? Let's answer this by starting with short definitions of line versus staff authority.

Line versus Staff Authority

authority
The right to make decisions, direct others' work, and give orders.

line manager
A manager who is authorized to direct the work of subordinates and is responsible for accomplishing the organization's tasks.

staff manager
A manager who assists and advises line managers.

Authority is the right to make decisions, to direct the work of others, and to give orders. In management, we usually distinguish between line authority and staff authority. Line authority gives managers the right (or authority) to issue orders to other managers or employees. It creates a superior–subordinate relationship. Staff authority gives a manager the right (authority) to advise other managers or employees. It creates an advisory relationship. **Line managers** have line authority. They are authorized to give orders. **Staff managers** have staff authority. They are authorized to assist and advise line managers. Human resource managers are staff managers. They assist and advise line managers in areas like recruiting, hiring, and compensation.

In practice, HR and line managers share responsibility for most human resource activities. For example, human resource and line managers in about two-thirds of the firms in one survey shared responsibility for skills training.[10] (Thus, the supervisor might describe what training she thinks the new employee needs, HR might design the training, and the supervisors might then ensure that the training is having the desired effect.)

Line Managers' Human Resource Management Responsibilities

The direct handling of people always has been an integral part of every line manager's responsibility, from president down to the first-line supervisor. For example, one company outlines its line supervisors' responsibilities for effective human resource management under the following general headings:

1. Placing the right person in the right job
2. Starting new employees in the organization (orientation)
3. Training employees for jobs that are new to them
4. Improving the job performance of each person
5. Gaining creative cooperation and developing smooth working relationships
6. Interpreting the company's policies and procedures
7. Controlling labor costs
8. Developing the abilities of each person
9. Creating and maintaining departmental morale
10. Protecting employees' health and physical conditions

In small organizations, line managers may carry out all these personnel duties unassisted. But as the organization grows, line managers need the assistance, specialized knowledge, and advice of a separate human resource staff.[11]

The Human Resource Department

In larger firms, the *human resource department* provides such specialized assistance.[12] Figure 1.1 shows human resource management jobs in one organization. Typical positions include compensation and benefits manager, employment and recruiting supervisor, training specialist, and employee relations executive. Examples of job duties include the following:

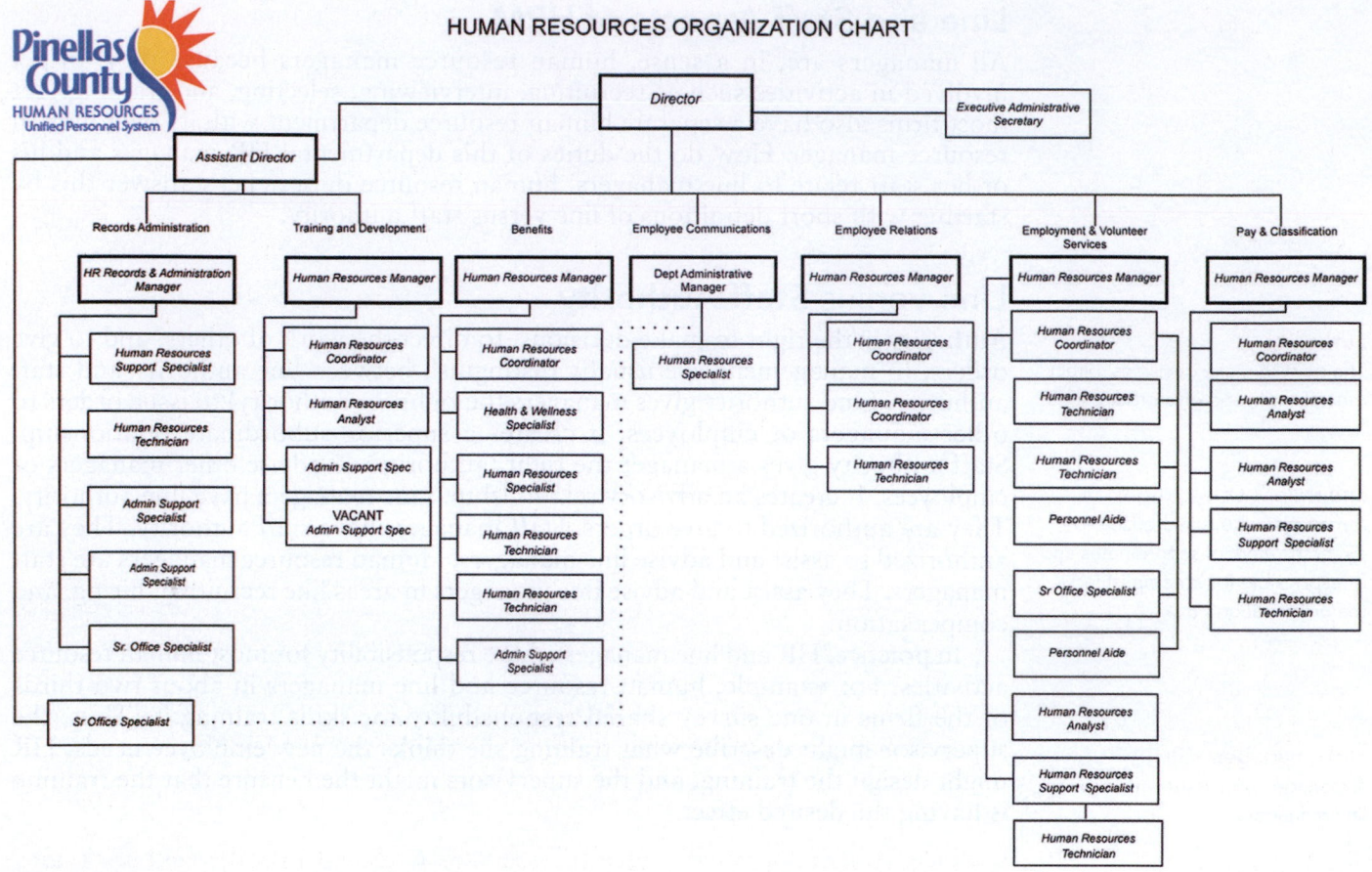

Figure 1.1

Human Resource Department Organization Chart Showing Typical HR Job Titles

Source: "Human resource development organization chart showing typical HR job titles," www.co.pinellas.fl.us/persnl/pdf/orgchart.pdf. Courtesy of Pinellas County Human Resources. Reprinted with permission.

Recruiters: Maintain contacts within the community and perhaps travel extensively to search for qualified job applicants.

Equal employment opportunity (EEO) representatives or affirmative action coordinators: Investigate and resolve EEO grievances, examine organizational practices for potential violations, and compile and submit EEO reports.

Job analysts: Collect and examine detailed information about job duties to prepare job descriptions.

Compensation managers: Develop compensation plans, and handle the employee benefits program.

Training specialists: Plan, organize, and direct training activities.

Labor relations specialists: Advise management on all aspects of union–management relations.

New Approaches to Organizing HR However, many employers are revamping how they organize their human resource functions.[13] For example, most plan to use technology to institute more *"shared services"* arrangements.[14] These create centralized HR units whose employees are shared by all the companies' departments to obtain advice on matters such as discipline problems. The shared services HR teams use intranets or centralized call centers to provide managers and employees with specialized support in day-to-day HR activities (such as discipline problems). Others use technology to *"distribute"* HR, for instance, by enabling store managers to use online interviewing tools to recruit and select their own employees. You may also find specialized *corporate HR teams* within a company. These assist top management in top-level issues such as developing the personnel aspects of the company's long-term strategic plan. *Embedded HR teams* have HR generalists (also known as "relationship managers" or "HR business partners") assigned to functional departments like sales and production. They provide the selection and other assistance the departments need. *Centers of expertise* are like specialized HR consulting firms within the company. For example, one center might provide specialized advice in organizational change to all the company's various units.

LEARNING OBJECTIVE 2
Describe with examples
what trends are
influencing human
resource management.

The Trends Shaping Human Resource Management

Working cooperatively with line managers, human resource managers have long helped employers hire and fire employees, administer benefits, and conduct appraisals. However, trends are occurring in the environment of human resource management that are changing how employers get their human resource management tasks done. These trends include workforce trends, trends in how people work, technological trends, and globalization and economic trends.

Workforce Demographics and Diversity Trends

The composition of the workforce will continue to change over the next few years; specifically, it will continue to become more diverse, with more women, minority group members, and older workers in the workforce.[15] Table 1.1 offers a bird's-eye view. Between 1992 and 2024, the percent of the workforce that the U.S. Department of Labor classifies as "white" will drop from 85% to 77%. At the same time, the percent of the workforce that it classifies as "Asian" will rise from 4% to 6.6%, and those of Hispanic origin will rise from 8.9% to 19.8%. The percentages of younger workers will fall, while those over 55 years of age will leap from 11.8% of the workforce in 1992 to 24.8% in 2024.[16] Many employers call "the aging workforce" a big problem. The problem is that there aren't enough younger workers to replace the projected number of baby boom–era older workers (born roughly from 1946–1964) who are retiring.[17] Many employers are bringing retirees back (or just trying to keep them from leaving).

Table 1.1 Demographic Groups as a Percent of the Workforce, 1992–2024

Age, Race, and Ethnicity	1992	2002	2012	2024
Age: 16–24	16.9%	15.4%	13.7%	11.3%
25–54	71.4	70.2	65.3	63.9
55+	11.8	14.3	20.9	24.8
White	85.0	82.8	79.8	77.0
Black	11.1	11.4	11.9	12.7
Asian	4.0	4.6	5.3	6.6
Hispanic origin	8.9	12.4	15.7	19.8

Source: U.S. Bureau of Labor Statistics Economic News Release, www.bls.gov/news.release /ecopro.t01.htm, accessed December 19, 2013, and https://www.bls.gov/news.release /ecopro.t01.htm, accessed April 16, 2017.

With not enough younger workers to replace retirees, many employers are hiring foreign workers for U.S. jobs. The H-1B visa program lets U.S. employers recruit skilled foreign professionals to work in the United States when they can't find qualified American workers. U.S. employers bring in about 85,000 foreign workers per year under these programs, although such programs face opposition.[18] Under the Trump administration the Department of Justice and the immigration services began enforcing H-1B rules more forcefully.[19]

Some employers find millennial employees (those born roughly between 1980 and 1997) a challenge to deal with, and this isn't just an American phenomenon. For example, China's senior army officers are having problems getting millennial-aged volunteers and conscripts to shape up.[20] "Intergenerational consultants" help employers deal with what they say are millennials' unique needs. For example, they say millennials want meaningful work and frequent feedback.[21] And while many employees spend about an hour per workday on their social media, millennials spend more.[22] On the other hand, millennials grew up with smartphones and social media and are experts at collaborating online. "Generation Z" (born 1994–2010), having seen their millennial predecessors struggle to find jobs, are reportedly "not willing to settle" and "extremely self-motivated."[23]

Trends in How People Work

At the same time, work has shifted from manufacturing to service in North America and Western Europe. Today, over two-thirds of the U.S. workforce is employed in producing and delivering services, not products. By 2024, service-providing industries are expected to account for 129 million out of 160 million (81% of) wage and salary jobs overall.[24] So in the next few years, almost all the new jobs added in the United States will be in services, not in goods-producing industries.[25]

■ HR and the Gig Economy

On-Demand Workers

For many people today Upwork (www.upwork.com)[26] symbolizes much of what's new in human resource management. Millions of freelancers from graphic designers to translators, accountants, and lawyers register on the site. Employers then use Upwork to find, screen, hire, and pay the talent they need, in more than 180 countries.[27] Workers like these are part of a vast workforce comprised of contract, temp, freelance, independent contractor, "on-demand," or simply **"gig" workers**. Such workers may comprise half the workforce in the next 10 years.[28]

Anyone using Uber already knows about on-demand workers.[29] At last count, Uber was signing up almost 30,000 new independent contractor drivers per week, a rate that was increasing fast.

Today, many workers aren't employees at all, but are freelancers and independent contractors who work when they can on what they want to work on, when the company needs them.[30] So, for example, Airbnb can run in essence a vast lodging company with only a fraction of the "regular" employees Hilton Worldwide would need (because the lodgings are owned and managed by the homeowners themselves). Other sites tapping on-demand workers include Amazon's Mechanical Turk, TaskRabbit, and Handy (which lets users tap Handy's thousands of freelance cleaners and furniture assemblers when they need jobs done).[31]

Similarly, more employers use contractors for their jobs. Before it combined with Alaska Air Group, Virgin America used contractors rather than employees for jobs including baggage delivery, reservations, and heavy maintenance. A trucking

gig workers
The large and growing workforce comprised of contract, temp, freelance, independent contractor, "on-demand," or simply "gig" workers.

company supplies the contract workers who unload shipping containers at Walmart warehouses. And even Google's parent, Alphabet Inc., has about the same number of outsourced jobs as full-time employees.[32] We'll see in this text that companies that rely on freelancers, consultants, and other such nontraditional employees need special HR policies and practices to deal with them.

Gig economy work has detractors.[33] Some people who work in such jobs say they can feel somewhat disrespected. One critic says such work is unpredictable and insecure. An article in the *New York Times* said this: "The larger worry about on-demand jobs is not about benefits, but about a lack of agency—a future in which computers, rather than humans, determine what you do, when and for how much."[34] Some Uber drivers sued for the right to unionize.

Globalization Trends

Globalization refers to companies extending their sales, ownership, and/or manufacturing to new markets abroad. Thus Toyota builds Camrys in Kentucky, and Apple assembles iPhones in China. Free trade areas—agreements that reduce tariffs and barriers among trading partners—further encourage international trade. The North American Free Trade Agreement (NAFTA) and the European Union (EU) are examples.

Globalization has boomed for the past 50 or so years. For example, the total sum of U.S. imports and exports rose from $47 billion in 1960, to $562 billion in 1980, to about $5.0 *trillion* recently.[35] Changing economic and political philosophies drove this boom. Governments dropped cross-border taxes or tariffs, formed economic free trade areas, and took other steps to encourage the free flow of trade among countries. The fundamental economic rationale was that by doing so, all countries would gain, and indeed, economies around the world did grow quickly until recently.

More globalization meant more competition, and more competition meant more pressure to be "world class"—to lower costs, to make employees more productive, and to do things better and less expensively. As multinational companies jockeyed for position, many transferred operations abroad, not just to seek

Anyone using Uber already knows about on-demand workers. It is signing up tens of thousands of new independent contractor drivers per week, a rate that is doubling fast.

Source: Pressmaster/Shutterstock.

cheaper labor but to tap new markets. The search for greater efficiencies prompted some employers to *offshore* (export jobs to lower-cost locations abroad). Some offshore even highly skilled jobs such as radiologists.[36] We'll see that a loss of jobs and growing income inequities are prompting some to rethink the wisdom of globalization.[37]

Economic Trends

Although globalization supported a growing global economy, the past 15 or so years were difficult economically. As you can see in Figure 1.2, gross national product (GNP)—a measure of the United States of America's total output—boomed between 2001 and 2007. During this period, home prices (see Figure 1.3) leaped as much as 20% per year. Unemployment remained docile at about 4.7%.[38] Then, around 2007–2008, all these measures fell off a cliff. GNP fell. Home prices dropped by 10% or more (depending on city). Unemployment nationwide soon rose to more than 10%. Some economists called it the "Great Recession."

Why did all this happen? It's complicated. Many governments stripped away rules and regulations. For example, in America and Europe, the rules that prevented commercial banks from expanding into new businesses such as investment banking were relaxed. Giant, multinational "financial supermarkets" such as Citibank emerged. With fewer regulations, more businesses and consumers were soon deeply in debt. Homebuyers bought homes with little money down. Banks freely lent money to developers to build more homes. For almost 20 years, U.S. consumers spent more than they earned. The United States became a debtor nation. Its balance of payments (exports minus imports) went from a healthy *positive* $3.5 billion in 1960, to a huge *minus* (imports exceeded exports) $497 billion deficit more recently.[39] The only way the country could keep buying more than it sold from abroad was by borrowing money. So, much of the boom was built on debt.

Around 2008, all those years of accumulating debt ran their course. Banks and other financial institutions had trillions of dollars of worthless loans. Governments stepped in to prevent their collapse. Lending dried up. Businesses and consumers stopped buying. The economy tanked.

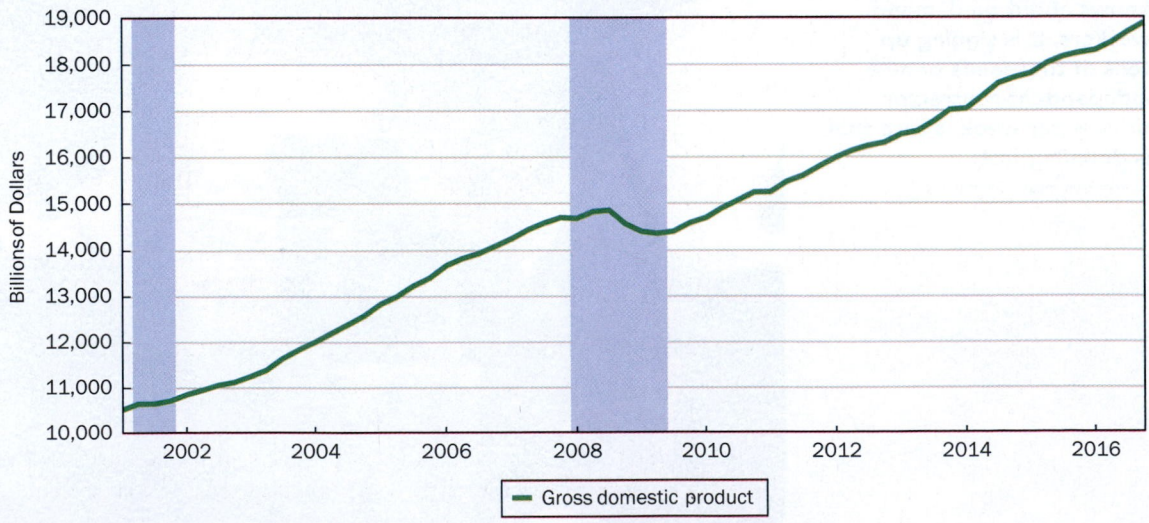

Figure 1.2

Gross National Product, 2000–2016

Source: St. Louis Federal Reserve Bank, https://fred.stlouisfed.org/ accessed April 16, 2017.

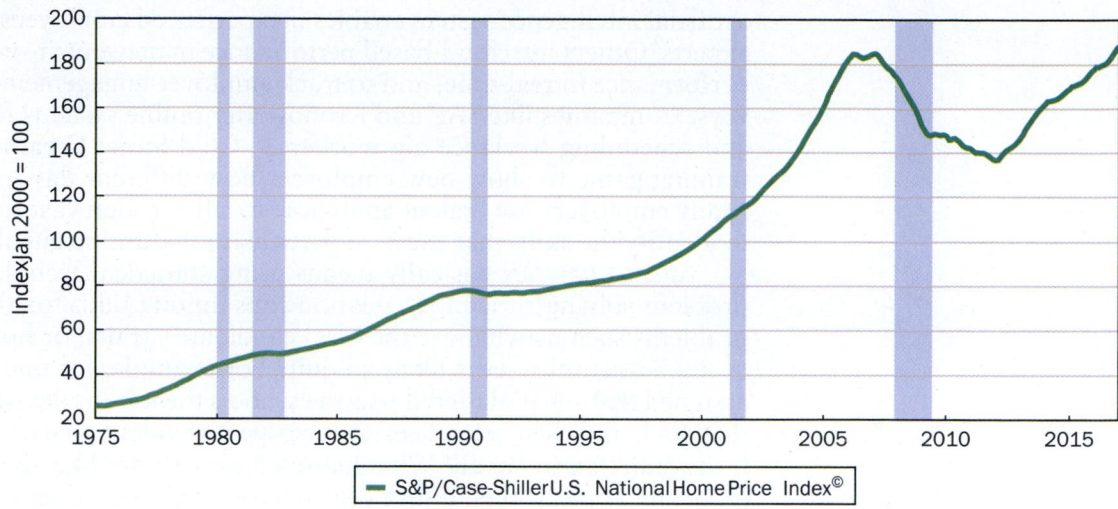

Figure 1.3

Case-Shiller Home Price Indexes 1975–2016

Source: St. Louis Federal Reserve Bank, https://fred.stlouisfed.org/ accessed April 17, 2017.

Today, economic trends are pointing up, and hopefully they will continue to do so. For example, by 2017, the unemployment rate had fallen from a high of more than 10% to around 4.5%.

However, that doesn't necessarily mean clear sailing for the economy. For one thing, after seeing the economy tank in 2007–2008, many companies became hesitant to expand factories and equipment. With their credit card and tuition loan debts still hanging over them, and many still without good jobs, consumers are understandably wary about pulling out all the stops on spending.[40] At the same time, productivity growth is slowing, which may further retard economic growth.[41] And after what the world went through in 2007–2009, it's doubtful that the deregulation, leveraging, and globalization that drove economic growth for the previous 50 years will continue unabated.

Labor Force Trends Complicating all this is the fact that the labor force in America is growing more slowly than expected (which is not good, because if employers can't get enough workers, they can't expand). To be precise, the Bureau of Labor Statistics projects the labor force to grow at 0.2% per year from 2015 to 2025, compared with an annual growth rate of 0.7% during the 2002–2012 decade.[42] Why? Mostly because with baby boomers aging, the "labor force participation rate" is declining—in other words, the *percent* of the population that wants to work is declining.

Add it all up, and the bottom line looks to be slower economic growth ahead. The Bureau of Labor Statistics projects that gross domestic product (GDP) will increase by 2.6% annually from 2012 to 2022, slower than the 3% or higher that more or less prevailed from the mid-1990s through the mid-2000s.[43]

Technology Trends

Technological change is also reshaping human resource management.[44] Just over half of companies in one survey were using digital and mobile devices to "redesign HR." For example 41% were designing mobile apps to deliver human resource management services, and about a third were using artificial intelligence.[45] For instance, Accenture estimates that social media tools like Facebook and LinkedIn will soon produce up to 80% of new recruits—often letting line managers bypass HR and do their own recruiting.[46] At a large insurance firm in Japan, IBM's Watson artificial intelligence system enables inexperienced employees to analyze claims like experts. Others use cloud-based performance management systems to monitor team performance in real-time, and to track employee engagement via quick weekly surveys. Companies like SAP and Kronos offer online systems for in-taking, tracking, and scheduling freelance gig workers.[47] Cold Stone Creamery Inc. uses a digital training game to show new employees how different flavors "scoop" differently. Many employers use "talent analytics" to sift through vast reams of employee data to identify the skills that excel on particular jobs, and to cut absences and accidents.

Talent analytics basically means using statistical techniques, algorithms, and problem solving to identify relationships among data for the purpose of solving problems such as what are the ideal candidate's traits, or how can I predict which of my best employees is likely to quit? For example, for many years one employer assumed that what mattered was the schools the job candidates attended, the grades they had, and their references. A retrospective talent analytics study revealed these traits didn't matter at all! What mattered were things like: their résumés were grammatically correct, they didn't quit school until obtaining some degree, they were successful in prior jobs, and they were able to succeed with vague instructions.[48]

Technology is also affecting the nature of work.[49] "Tech jobs," no longer just mean jobs at Apple and Google. For example at Alcoa's Davenport Works plant in Iowa, a computer at each workstation helps employees control their machines.

Human Capital One big consequence of globalization and of economic and technological trends is that employers are more dependent on their workers' knowledge, education, training, skills, and expertise—on their "human capital."

Jobs like consultant and lawyer always required education and knowledge. Today, even production assemblers as well as bank tellers, retail clerks, and package deliverers need a level of technological sophistication they wouldn't have needed a few years ago. The point is that in our knowledge-based economy, ". . . the acquisition and development of superior human capital appears essential to firms' profitability and success."[50]

The challenge for managers is that they have to manage such workers differently. For example, empowering them to make decisions presumes you've selected and trained them to make more decisions themselves.[51] The accompanying HR as a Profit Center feature illustrates how one employer took advantage of its human capital.

Technology changed the nature of work and therefore the skills that workers must bring to their jobs. For example, many factory jobs today require special technology skills and training.

Source: Suwin Puengsamrong/123RF.

■ HR as a Profit Center

Boosting Customer Service

A bank installed special software that made it easier for its customer service representatives to handle customers' inquiries. However, the bank did not otherwise change the service reps' jobs in any way. Here, the new software system did help the service reps handle more calls. But otherwise, this bank saw no big performance gains.[52]

A second bank installed the same software. But, seeking to capitalize on how the new software freed up customer reps' time, this bank also had its human resource team upgrade the customer service representatives' jobs. This bank taught them how to sell more of the bank's services, gave them more authority to make decisions, and raised their wages. Here, the new computer system dramatically improved product sales and profitability, thanks to the newly trained and empowered customer service reps. Value-added human resource practices like these improve employee performance and company profitability.[53]

✪ Talk About It–**1**

If your professor has chosen to assign this, go to **www.pearson.com/mylab/management** to discuss the following: Discuss three more specific examples of what you believe this second bank's HR department could have done to improve the reps' performance.

LEARNING OBJECTIVE 3
Discuss at least five consequences such trends have for human resource management today.

The New Human Resource Management

For much of the 20th century, "personnel" managers focused mostly on day-to-day activities. In the earliest firms, they took over hiring and firing from supervisors, ran the payroll department, and administered benefits plans. As expertise in testing emerged, the personnel department played a bigger role in employee selection and training.[54] New union laws in the 1930s added "Helping the employer deal with unions" to its duties. With new equal employment laws in the 1960s, employers began relying on HR for avoiding discrimination claims.[55]

We've seen that today's employers face new trends and challenges. Demographic trends make finding and hiring employees more difficult and managing diversity more important. Employers must also address the equal employment laws that diversity has engendered. Technology trends mean employers must manage their employees' knowledge, skills, and expertise, and also that they can use new digital and social media tools to do so.[56] A slower-growing economic pie means more pressure on employers to get the best efforts from their employees. Employers expect their "people experts"—their human resource managers—to deal with such challenges. This has prompted several changes in human resource management.

Distributed HR and the New Human Resource Management

Perhaps the most important change is that more human resource management tasks are being redistributed *from* a central HR department *to* the company's employees and line managers, thanks to digital tools like mobile phones and social media.[57] For example, at Google, when someone applies for a job, his or her information goes into a system that matches the recruit with current Google employees based on interests and experiences. In a process Google calls "crowdsourcing," Google employees then get a big say in whom Google hires.

Some experts say that many aspects of HR (such as recruiting, selecting and training) will become "fully embedded ["distributed"] in how work gets done throughout an organization, thereby becoming an everyday part of doing business."[58] So, somewhat ironically, we may be shifting in some respects back toward the time before the first personnel departments, when line managers did more of the personnel tasks themselves. As an example, Hilton Worldwide is placing more HR activities in the hands of employees, while redirecting the savings to building up the more strategic aspects of what its human resource managers do.[59] In the following chapters, we'll use Trends Shaping HR features like the accompanying one to present more examples.

TRENDS SHAPING HR: *Digital and Social Media*

Digital and Social Media Tools and the New Human Resource Management
Digital and social media tools are changing how people look for jobs and how companies recruit, retain, pay, and train employees. In doing so, they've transformed human resource management and created, in a sense, a new human resource management.

For example, career sites like Glassdoor, CareerBliss, CareerLeak, and JobBite let members share insights into hundreds of thousands of employers, including commentaries, salary reports, and CEO approval ratings.[60] One report says 48% of job seekers surveyed report using Glassdoor during their job search, including checking before applying for employment at a company.[61] Such transparency prompts sensible human resource managers to redouble their efforts to ensure their internal processes (such as promotion decisions, pay allocations, and performance appraisals) are fair, and that their recruitment processes are civil by responding to rejected job candidates and giving them some closure.

As another example, talent analytics algorithms help employers improve employee retention. They do this, for example by identifying the factors (such as experience, career advancement, performance reviews, compensation, and even a surge in activity on social media sites) that flag high-potential employees who are more likely to leave.

HR and Performance

Employers expect their human resource managers to help lead their companies' performance-improvement efforts.[62] Today's human resource manager is in a powerful position to do this and uses three main levers to do so. One is the *HR department lever*. He or she ensures that the human resource management function is delivering its services efficiently. For example, this might include outsourcing certain HR activities such as benefits management to vendors, controlling HR function headcount, and using technology to deliver its services more cost effectively.

The second is the *employee costs lever*. For example, the human resource manager takes a prominent role in advising top management about the company's staffing levels and in setting and controlling the firm's compensation, incentives, and benefits policies.

The third is the *strategic results lever*. Here the HR manager puts in place the policies and practices that produce the employee competencies and skills the company needs to achieve its strategic goals. For example (see the HR as a Profit Center feature on page 13) a bank's new software helped its customer service reps improve their performance, thanks to new human resource training and compensation practices.

HR and Performance Measurement Improving performance requires being able to measure what you are doing. For example, when IBM's former HR head needed

$100 million to reorganize its HR operations several years ago, he told top management, "I'm going to deliver talent to you that's skilled and on time and ready to be deployed. I will be able to measure the skills, tell you what skills we have, what [skills] we don't have [and] then show you how to fill the gaps or enhance our training."[63]

Human resource managers use performance measures (or "metrics") to validate claims like these. For example, median HR expenses as a percentage of companies' total operating costs average just under 1%. On average, there is about 1 human resource staff person per 100 employees.[64]

HR and Evidence-Based Management Basing decisions on such evidence is the heart of *evidence-based human resource management*. This is the use of data, facts, analytics, scientific rigor, critical evaluation, and critically evaluated research/case studies to support human resource management proposals, decisions, practices, and conclusions.[65] Put simply, evidence-based human resource management means using the best-available evidence in making decisions about the human resource management practices you are focusing on.[66] The evidence may come from *actual measurements* (such as, how did the trainees like this program?). It may come from *existing data* (such as, what happened to company profits after we installed this training program?). Or, it may come from published *research studies* (such as, what does the research literature conclude about the best way to ensure that trainees remember what they learn?).

Sometimes, companies translate their findings into what management gurus call *high-performance work systems,* "sets of human resource management practices that together produce superior employee performance."[67] For example, at GE's assembly plant in Durham, North Carolina, highly trained self-directed teams produce high-precision aircraft parts. We'll discuss performance measurement and high-performance work systems in Chapter 3.

HR and Adding Value The bottom line is that today's employers want their HR managers to *add value* by boosting profits and performance. Professors Dave Ulrich and Wayne Brockbank describe this as the "HR Value Proposition."[68] They say human resource programs (such as screening tests) are just a means to an end. The human resource manager's ultimate aim must be to add value. *Adding value* means helping the firm and its employees improve in a measurable way, as a result of the human resource manager's actions. We'll see in this text how human resource practices do this, for instance with HR as a Profit Center features like the one on page 13.

The accompanying HR in Practice feature raises a related issue.

■ HR in Practice

Does Performance Trump Equity?

Can too much productivity and performance be bad? Many would say "yes." In brief, they would argue that what they'd consider an excessive drive for performance can cost workers their jobs and lead to growing inequities between a highly paid and skilled elite and ordinary workers.

For example, in an episode made famous by then-presidential candidate Donald J. Trump, a Carrier Corporation executive was videotaped telling workers in Indianapolis that Carrier was moving 1,400 of their jobs to Mexico, putting them out of work. On the tape he calls it "just a business decision." (Carrier's Midwest workers earn about $15–$26 per hour, while those in Mexico earn about $9.50–$19 *per day*).[69] Similarly, Toys "R" Us hired a staffing/outsourcing company from abroad. Toys "R" Us then brought in a number of the staffing company's employees using temporary worker visas. These employees spent four weeks sitting with selected Toys "R" Us employees learning every detail of their jobs. The staffing company employees then returned to their country, where they trained local employees to take over the Toys "R" Us workers' jobs.[70] Automation plays a role too. For example, "machine learning"—sophisticated algorithms that can learn, for instance, which types of employees are best for which jobs and can therefore gradually replace, say, human resource recruitment and selection employees—are replacing even higher-level jobs with automation.[71]

For whatever reason, a big gap has emerged between what *The Economist* newspaper calls a skilled elite and ordinary workers. Since the Great Recession of 2007–2009, incomes have risen, but almost only for those in the very highest income brackets. Good jobs, to paraphrase the *Harvard Business Review*, are disappearing, often replaced by relatively insecure and lower paid jobs.[72] Inequities are rising. Even some economists who once believed that globalization and technological advances could always be counted on to boost demand and hiring are now rethinking their theories.[73] This was the environment that prompted 2016 presidential candidate Hillary Clinton to call for a "fairer, more equal, just world,"[74] and candidate Donald Trump to demand that Carrier bring the jobs back to America.

✪ Talk About It–2

If your professor has chosen to assign this, go to **www.pearson.com/mylab/management** to discuss the following question: Do you think an employer can achieve high performance while preserving jobs and minimizing these sorts of inequities? Give examples of why or why not.

HR and Employee Engagement

employment engagement
The extent to which an organization's employees are psychologically involved in, connected to, and committed to getting their jobs done.

Employee engagement refers to being psychologically involved in, connected to, and committed to getting one's jobs done. Engaged employees "experience a high level of connectivity with their work tasks," and therefore work hard to accomplish their task-related goals.[75]

Employee engagement is important because it drives performance. For example (as we will discuss in Chapter 3), based on one Gallup survey, business units with the highest levels of employee engagement have an 83% chance of performing above the company median; those with the lowest employee engagement have only a 17% chance.[76] A survey by consultants Watson Wyatt Worldwide concluded that companies with highly engaged employees have 26% higher revenue per employee.[77]

The problem for employers is that, depending on the study, only about 21–30% of today's employees nationally are engaged.[78] In one survey, about 30% were engaged, 50% were not engaged, and 20% were actively disengaged (anti-management).[79]

We will see in this text that managers improve employee engagement by taking concrete steps to do so. For example, a few years ago, Kia Motors (UK) turned its performance around, in part by boosting employee engagement.[80] As we will discuss more fully in Chapter 3, it did this with new HR programs. These included *measurable objectives*, new *leadership development* programs, new *employee recognition* programs, improved *internal communications* programs, a new *employee development* program, and new *compensation and other policies*. We use special Employee Engagement Guide for Managers sections in most chapters to show how managers use human resource activities such as recruiting and selection to improve employee engagement.

HR and Strategy

Strengthening organizational performance and building engaged work teams puts a company's human resource managers in a more central role. This means they tend to be more involved today in the company's strategic planning.[81]

Most companies have a strategic plan, a plan for how it will balance its internal strengths and weaknesses with external opportunities and threats to maintain a competitive advantage. Traditionally, developing such a plan is a job primarily for the company's operating (line) managers. Thus, company X's president might decide to enter new markets, drop product lines, and embark on a five-year cost-cutting plan. Then the president would more or less leave the personnel implications of that plan (hiring or firing workers, and so on) to the human resource manager.

strategic human resource management

Formulating and executing human resource policies and practices that produce the employee competencies and behaviors the company needs to achieve its strategic aims.

Today, human resource managers often get much more involved in both developing and implementing strategic plans. Chapter 3 (Human Resource Management Strategy and Analysis) expands on this. In brief, we will see there that **strategic human resource management** means *formulating and executing human resource policies and practices that produce the employee competencies and behaviors the company needs to achieve its strategic aims*. The basic idea behind strategic human resource management is this: In formulating human resource management policies and practices, the manager's aim should be to produce the employee skills and behaviors that the company needs to achieve its strategic aims. So, for example, when Yahoo's CEO wanted to improve her company's innovation and productivity a few years ago, she turned to her new HR manager (a former investment banker). Yahoo then instituted many new HR policies. It eliminated telecommuting to bring workers back to the office where they could continuously interact, and adopted new benefits (such as 16 weeks' paid maternity leave) to lure new engineers and to make Yahoo a more attractive place in which to work.[82]

We will use a model starting with Chapter 3 to illustrate this idea, but in brief, the model follows this three-step sequence: *Set* the firm's strategic aims, *Pinpoint* the employee behaviors and skills we need to achieve these strategic aims, and *Decide* what HR policies and practices will enable us to produce these necessary employee behaviors and skills.

HR and Sustainability

In a world where sea levels are rising, glaciers are crumbling, and increasing numbers of people view financial inequity as outrageous, more and more people say that businesses can't just measure "performance" in terms of maximizing profits. They argue instead that companies' efforts should be "sustainable," by which they mean judged not just on profits, but on their environmental and social performance as well.[83] We've just seen that *strategic human resource management* means putting in place the human resource policies and practices that produce the employee skills and behaviors that are necessary to achieve the company's strategic goals. When those strategic goals include sustainability issues, then it follows that human resource managers should have HR policies to support these goals.

For example, PepsiCo wants to deliver "Performance with Purpose," in other words financial performance while also achieving human sustainability, environmental sustainability, and talent sustainability. PepsiCo has goals to measure financial performance, for instance in terms of shareholder value and long-term financial performance. Its goals for human sustainability include providing clear nutrition information on products. Environmental sustainability goals include protecting and conserving global water supplies. Talent sustainability goals include respecting workplace human rights and creating a safe and healthy workplace.[84]

PepsiCo's human resource managers can help the company achieve these goals.[85] For example, it can use its *workforce planning* processes to help determine how many and what sorts of environmental sustainability ("green") jobs the company will need to recruit for. It can help top management institute *flexible work arrangements* that help sustain the environment by reducing commuting. It can change its employee *orientation* process to include socializing new employees into PepsiCo's sustainability goals. It can modify its *performance appraisal* systems to measure the extent to which managers and employees are achieving their individual sustainability goals. It can put in place *incentive systems* that motivate employees to achieve PepsiCo's sustainability goals. It can institute *safety and health* practices aimed at eliminating unsafe conditions and improving worker safety. It can make Talent Sustainability part of the company's *HR Philosophy*, for example, by fostering a respectful work environment.[86] And it can institute *employee relations* programs aimed at maintaining positive employee relations and ensuring that employees have a safe, fulfilling, and respectful tenure at the company. With such actions, HR can play a central role in supporting a company's sustainability efforts.

HR and Ethics

ethics
The principles of conduct governing an individual or a group; specifically, the standards you use to decide what your conduct should be.

Regrettably, news reports are filled with stories of otherwise competent managers who have run amok. For example, prosecutors filed criminal charges against several Iowa meatpacking plant human resource managers who allegedly violated employment law by hiring children younger than 16.[87] Behaviors like these risk torpedoing even otherwise competent managers and employers. **Ethics** means *the standards someone uses to decide what his or her conduct should be.* We will see in Chapter 12 that many workplace ethical issues—workplace safety and employee privacy, for instance—are human resource management related.[88]

LEARNING OBJECTIVE 4
Explain what sorts of competencies, knowledge, and skills characterize today's new human resource manager.

The New Human Resource Manager

When asked, "Why do you want to be an HR manager?" many people basically say, "Because I'm a people person." Being sociable is certainly important, but as we've seen in this chapter it takes much more. Tasks like formulating strategic plans and making data-based decisions require new competencies and skills.

What does it take to be a human resource manager today? The Society for Human Resource Management (SHRM) has a "competency model" (called the SHRM Body of Competency and Knowledge™); it itemizes the competencies, skills, knowledge, and expertise that human resource managers need. Here are the behaviors or competencies (with definitions) SHRM says today's HR manager should be able to exhibit:

- Leadership and Navigation: The ability to direct and contribute to initiatives and processes within the organization.
- Ethical Practice: The ability to integrate core values, integrity, and accountability throughout all organizational and business practices.
- Business Acumen: The ability to understand and apply information with which to contribute to the organization's strategic plan.
- Relationship Management: The ability to manage interactions to provide service and to support the organization.
- Consultation: The ability to provide guidance to organizational stakeholders.
- Critical Evaluation: The ability to interpret information with which to make business decisions and recommendations.
- Global & Cultural Effectiveness: The ability to value and consider the perspectives and backgrounds of all parties.
- Communication: The ability to effectively exchange information with stakeholders.

SHRM also says HR managers must have the basic knowledge of principles and practices of the basic functional areas of HR, which include the following:

- Functional Area #1: Talent Acquisition and Retention
- Functional Area #2: Employee Engagement
- Functional Area #3: Learning and Development
- Functional Area #4: Total Rewards
- Functional Area #5: Structure of the HR Function
- Functional Area #6: Organizational Effectiveness and Development
- Functional Area #7: Workforce Management
- Functional Area #8: Employee Relations
- Functional Area #9: Technology and Data
- Functional Area #10: HR in the Global Context
- Functional Area #11: Diversity and Inclusion

- Functional Area #12: Risk Management
- Functional Area #13: Corporate Social Responsibility
- Functional Area #14: U.S. Employment Law and Regulations
- Functional Area #15: Business and HR Strategy

HR and the Manager's Skills

This text aims to help all managers develop the skills they'll need to carry out the human resource management–related aspects of their jobs, such as recruiting, selecting, training, appraising, and incentivizing employees and providing them with a safe and fulfilling work environment. Building Your Management Skills features in each chapter cover matters such as how to interview job candidates and train new employees. HR Tools for Line Managers and Small Businesses features aim to provide small business owners and managers in particular with techniques they can use to better manage their small businesses. Know Your Employment Law features highlight the practical information all managers need to make better HR-related decisions at work. Employee Engagement Guide for Managers features show how managers improve employee engagement.

HR Manager Certification

Many human resource managers use certification to demonstrate their mastery of human resource management knowledge and competencies. Managers have, at this writing, at least two testing processes to achieve certification.[89]

The oldest is administered by the HR Certification Institute (HRCI), an independent certifying organization for human resource professionals (see www.hrci.org). Through testing, HRCI awards several credentials, including Professional in Human Resources (PHR) and Senior Professional in Human Resources (SPHR). Managers can review HRCI's Knowledge Base and take an online HRCI practice quiz by going to www.hrci.org and clicking on Exam Preparation and then on Sample Questions.[90]

Starting in 2015, SHRM began offering its own competency and knowledge-based testing and certifications, for SHRM Certified Professionals, and SHRM Senior Certified Professionals, based on its own certification exams.[91] The exam is built around the SHRM Body of Competency and Knowledge™ model of functional knowledge, skills, and competencies.

A summary of the SHRM and the HRCI knowledge bases is available to your instructor as appendices titled "HRCI PHR® and SPHR® Certification Body of Knowledge" and "About the Society for Human Resource Management (SHRM) Body of Competency and Knowledge™ Model and Certification Exams." Your instructor can obtain these appendices from the Pearson Instructor Resource Center and pass them onto you. One covers SHRM's functional knowledge areas (such as employee relations). The other covers HRCI's seven main knowledge areas (such as Strategic Business Management, and Workforce Planning and Employment). This also lists about 91 specific HRCI "Knowledge of" subject areas within the seven main topic areas with which those taking the test should be familiar.

You'll find throughout this book special Knowledge Base icons, starting in Chapter 2, to denote coverage of SHRM and/or HRCI knowledge topics.

HR and the Manager's Human Resource Philosophy

People's actions are always based in part on the basic assumptions they make; this is especially true in regard to human resource management. The basic assumptions you make about people—Can they be trusted? Do they dislike work? Why do they act as they do? How should they be treated?—together comprise your philosophy of human resource management. And every personnel decision you make—the people you hire, the training you provide, your leadership style, and the like—reflects (for better or worse) this basic philosophy.

How do you go about developing such a philosophy? To some extent, it's pre-ordained. There's no doubt that you will bring to your job an initial philosophy based on your experiences, education, values, assumptions, and background. But your philosophy doesn't have to be set in stone. It should evolve as you accumulate knowledge and experiences. For example, after a worker uprising in China at the Foxconn plant owned by Hon Hai that assembles Apple iPhones, the personnel philosophy at the plant softened in response to its employees' and Apple's discontent.[92] In any case, no manager should manage others without first understanding the personnel philosophy that is driving his or her actions.

One of the things molding your own philosophy is that of your organization's top management. Although it may or may not be stated, it is usually communicated by their actions and permeates every level and department in the organization. For example, here is part of the personnel philosophy of the founder of the Polaroid Corp., stated many years ago:

> To give everyone working for the company a personal opportunity within the company for full exercise of his talents—to express his opinions, to share in the progress of the company as far as his capacity permits, and to earn enough money so that the need for earning more will not always be the first thing on his mind. The opportunity, in short, to make his work here a fully rewarding and important part of his or her life.[93]

Current "best companies to work for" lists include many organizations with similar philosophies. For example, the CEO of software giant SAS has said, "We've worked hard to create a corporate culture that is based on trust between our employees and the company... a culture that rewards innovation, encourages employees to try new things and yet doesn't penalize them for taking chances, and a culture that cares about employees' personal and professional growth."[94]

✪ Watch It

How does a company actually go about putting its human resource philosophy into action? If your professor has chosen to assign this, go to **www.pearson.com/mylab/management** to watch the video Patagonia Human Resource Management and then answer the questions to show what you would do in this situation.

After a worker uprising in China at the Foxconn plant owned by Hon Hai that assembles Apple iPhones, the personnel philosophy at the plant softened in response to its employees' and Apple's discontent.

Source: Dmitry Kalinovsky/123RF.

LEARNING OBJECTIVE 5
Outline the plan of this book.

The Plan of This Book

This book has two main aims: to provide all future managers, not just HR managers, with the practical human resource skills (for instance how to interview, train, engage, and appraise employees) they need to produce an engaged and high-performing workforce, and to cover SHRM's and HRCI's bodies of knowledge in a relatively compact and economical 14-chapter soft cover format. Special main features—Employee Engagement Guide for Managers, Building Your Management Skills, HR Tools for Line Managers and Small Businesses, HR and the Gig Economy, HR as a Profit Center, and Know Your Employment Law—help illustrate important points.

The Chapters

We've organized the book as follows:

Part 1: Introduction (Chapters 1, 2, 3)

1. **Managing Human Resources Today**
2. **Managing Equal Opportunity and Diversity** What you need to know about equal opportunity laws as they relate to human resource management activities such as interviewing, selecting employees, and evaluating performance.
3. **Human Resource Strategy and Analysis** What is strategic planning, strategy formulation and execution, and evidence-based management?

Part 2: Staffing: Workforce Planning and Employment (Chapters 4, 5, 6)

4. **Job Analysis and Talent Management** What is talent management? How to analyze a job and how to determine the job's requirements, specific duties, and responsibilities, as well as what sorts of people need to be hired.
5. **Personnel Planning and Recruiting** Workforce planning and techniques for recruiting employees.
6. **Selecting Employees** What managers should know about testing, interviewing, and selecting employees.

Part 3: Training and Human Resource Development (Chapters 7, 8, 9)

7. **Training and Developing Employees** Providing the training and development necessary to ensure that your employees have the knowledge and skills required to accomplish their tasks.
8. **Performance Management and Appraisal Today** Techniques for managing and appraising performance.
9. **Managing Careers** Causes of and solutions for employee turnover, and how to help employees manage their careers.

Part 4: Compensation and Total Rewards (Chapters 10, 11)

10. **Developing Compensation Plans** How to develop market-competitive pay plans.
11. **Pay for Performance and Employee Benefits** Developing total reward programs, including incentives and benefits plans for employees.

Part 5: Employee and Labor Relations (Chapters 12, 13, 14)

12. **Maintaining Positive Employee Relations** Developing employee relations programs and employee involvement strategies; ensuring ethical and fair treatment through discipline and grievance processes.
13. **Labor Relations and Collective Bargaining** The relations between unions and management, including union-organizing campaigns, negotiating and agreeing on collective-bargaining agreements between unions and management, and managing the agreement.
14. **Improving Occupational Safety, Health, and Risk Management** The causes of accidents, how to make the workplace safe, and laws governing your responsibilities in regard to employee safety and health.

Part 6: Special Issues in Human Resource Management (Modules A, B)

Module A: Managing HR Globally Applying human resource management policies and practices in a global environment.

Module B: Managing Human Resources in Small and Entrepreneurial Firms Special HRM methods small business managers can use to compete more successfully.

Review

MyLab Management

If your instructor is using MyLab Management, go to **www.pearson.com/mylab/ management** to complete the problems marked with this icon ⭐.

Summary

1. Staffing, personnel management, or human resource management includes activities such as recruiting, selecting, training, compensating, appraising, and developing. Human resource management is the process of acquiring, training, appraising, and compensating employees, and of attending to their labor relations, health and safety, and fairness concerns. The HR manager and his or her department provide various staff services to line management, including assisting in the hiring, training, evaluating, rewarding, promoting, disciplining, and safety of employees at all levels. HR management is a part of every line manager's responsibilities. These responsibilities include placing the right person in the right job and then orienting, training, and compensating the person to improve his or her job performance. Reasons every manager needs HR expertise include avoiding HR mistakes (such as high turnover); getting results; spending time as an HR manager; and being in a small business where the owner needs to do most HR tasks him or herself.

2. Trends are requiring HR to play a more central role in organizations. These trends include workforce diversity, technological change, the expanding use of social media and digital tools, globalization, and economic challenges.

3. These trends are helping to shape a new human resource management, one characterized by more emphasis on distributed HR, as well as on performance and evidence-based management, employee engagement, strategy, sustainability, and ethics.

4. As a result, any manager responsible for managing human resources today will need competencies, (such as in relationship management and in the ability to manage interactions), practical skills (for instance in using new tools for selecting employees), a consciously thought through "HR philosophy," and skills, knowledge, and competencies tested through certification.

5. This text aims to help managers develop the skills they'll need to carry out the human resource management-related aspects of their jobs, such as recruiting, selecting, training, appraising, and incentivizing employees, and providing them with a safe and fulfilling work environment. There is a special emphasis on building skills and in fostering employee engagement. Special Building Your Management Skills features in each chapter cover matters such as how to interview job candidates and train new employees.

Key Terms

organization 2	line manager 5
manager 2	staff manager 5
managing 2	gig workers 8
management process 2	employment engagement 16
human resource management (HRM) 3	strategic human resource management 17
authority 5	ethics 18

 Try It

How would you do applying the concepts and skills you learned in this chapter? If your professor has chosen to assign this, go to **www.pearson.com/mylab/management** and complete the Human Resource Management simulation.

Discussion Questions

1-1. What is human resource management?

1-2. Explain with at least five examples why "a knowledge and proficiency in HR management concepts and techniques is important to all supervisors or managers."

1-3. Explain with examples what we mean by "the changing environment of human resource management."

1-4. Give examples of how the HR manager can support a company's sustainability goals.

⭐ 1-5. Discuss with examples four important issues influencing HR management today.

⭐ 1-6. Explain HR management's role in relation to the firm's line management.

1-7. Compare the authority of line and staff managers. Give examples of each.

Individual and Group Activities

1-8. Working individually or in groups, contact the HR manager of a local bank. Ask the HR manager how he or she is working as a strategic partner to manage human resources, given the bank's strategic goals and objectives. Back in class, discuss the responses of the different HR managers.

1-9. Working individually or in groups, interview an HR manager. Based on that interview, write a short presentation regarding HR's role today in building competitive organizations.

1-10. Working individually or in groups, bring several business publications such as *Bloomberg Businessweek* and *The Wall Street Journal* to class. Based on their contents, compile a list entitled "What HR Managers and Departments Do Today."

1-11. Based on your personal experiences, list 10 examples showing how you used (or could have used) human resource management techniques at work or school.

1-12. Laurie Siegel served as senior vice president of human resources for Tyco International from 2003 to 2012. She took over her job just after numerous charges forced the company's previous board of directors and top executives to leave the firm. Hired by new CEO Edward Breen, Siegel had to tackle numerous difficult problems starting the moment she assumed office. For example, she had to help hire a new management team. She had to do something about what the outside world viewed as a culture of questionable ethics at her company. And she had to do something about the company's top management compensation plan, which many felt contributed to the allegations by some that former company officers had used the company as a sort of private ATM.

Siegel came to Tyco after a very impressive career. For example, she had been head of executive compensation at AlliedSignal, and was a graduate of the Harvard Business School. But, as strong as her background was, she obviously had her work cut out for her when she took the senior vice president of HR position at Tyco.

Working individually or in groups, conduct an Internet search and library research to answer the following questions: What human resource management–related steps did Siegel take to help get Tyco back on the right track? Do you think she took the appropriate steps? Why or why not? What, if anything, do you suggest Tyco's HR head do now?

1-13. Working individually or in groups, develop a list showing how trends such as workforce diversity, technological trends, globalization, and changes in the nature of work have affected the college or university you are now attending or the organization for which you work.

1-14. Working individually or in groups, develop several examples showing how the new HR management practices mentioned in this chapter (using technology, and supporting sustainability efforts, for instance) have or have not been implemented to some extent in the college or university you are now attending or in the organization for which you work.

1-15. For this activity, you will need the documents titled (1) "HRCI PHR® and SPHR® Certification Body of Knowledge, and (2) "About the Society for Human Resource Management (SHRM) Body of Competency & Knowledge® Model and Certification Exams." Your instructor can obtain these two documents from the Pearson Instructor Resource Center and pass them on to you. These two documents list the knowledge someone studying for the HRCI or SHRM certification exam needs to have in each area of human resource management (such as in Strategic Management, and Workforce Planning). In groups of several students, do four things: (1) review the HRCI and/or SHRM documents; (2) identify the material in this chapter that relates to HRCI's or SHRM's required knowledge lists; (3) write four multiple-choice exam questions on this material that you believe would be suitable for inclusion in the HRCI exam and/or the SHRM exam; and, (4) if time permits, have someone from your team post your team's questions in front of the class, so that students in all teams can answer the exam questions created by the other teams.

MyLab Management

If your instructor is using MyLab Management, go to **www.pearson.com/mylab/management** for Auto-graded writing questions as well as the following Assisted-graded writing questions:

1-16. How do today's HR managers deal with the trends and challenges shaping contemporary HR management?

1-17. Discuss some competencies HR managers need to deal with today's trends and challenges.

APPLICATION EXERCISES

HR IN ACTION CASE INCIDENT 1

Jack Nelson's Problem

As a new member of the board of directors for a local bank, Jack Nelson was being introduced to all the employees in the home office. When he was introduced to Ruth Johnson, he was curious about her work and asked her what her machine did. Johnson replied that she really did not know what the machine was called or what it did. She explained that she had been working there for only two months. She did, however, know precisely how to operate the machine. According to her supervisor, she was an excellent employee.

At one of the branch offices, the supervisor in charge spoke to Nelson confidentially, telling him that "something was wrong," but she didn't know what.

For one thing, she explained, employee turnover was too high, and no sooner had one employee been put on the job than another one resigned. With customers to see and loans to be made, she explained, she had little time to work with the new employees as they came and went.

All branch supervisors hired their own employees without communication with the home office or other branches. When an opening developed, the supervisor tried to find a suitable employee to replace the worker who had quit.

After touring the 22 branches and finding similar problems in many of them, Nelson wondered what the home office should do or what action he should take. The banking firm was generally regarded as a well-run institution that had grown from 27 to 191 employees during the past eight years. The more he thought about the matter, the more puzzled Nelson became. He couldn't quite put his finger on the problem, and he didn't know whether to report his findings to the president.

Questions

1-18. What do you think is causing some of the problems in the bank's home office and branches?

1-19. Do you think setting up an HR unit in the main office would help?

1-20. What specific functions should an HR unit carry out? What HR functions would then be carried out by the bank's supervisors and other line managers?

Source: "Jack Nelson's Problem," by Claude S. George, from *Supervision in Action: The Art of Managing Others,* 4th ed., 1985. Copyright © 1985 by Pearson Education, Inc. Reprinted with permission.

HR IN ACTION CASE INCIDENT 2
Carter Cleaning Company

Introduction

A main theme of this text is that HR management—activities like recruiting, selecting, training, and rewarding employees—is not just the job of a central HR group but rather a job in which every manager must engage. Perhaps nowhere is this more apparent than in the typical small service business. Here the owner/manager usually has no HR staff on which to rely. However, the success of his or her enterprise (not to mention his or her family's peace of mind) often depends largely on the effectiveness through which workers are recruited, hired, trained, evaluated, and rewarded. Therefore, to help illustrate and emphasize the front-line manager's HR role, throughout this book we will use a continuing case based on an actual small business in the southeastern United States. Each chapter's segment of the case will illustrate how the case's main player—owner/manager Jennifer Carter—confronts and solves personnel problems each day at work by applying the concepts and techniques of that particular chapter. Here is background information you will need to answer questions that arise in subsequent chapters. (We also present a second, unrelated case incident in each chapter.)

Carter Cleaning Centers

Jennifer Carter graduated from State University in June 2013 and, after considering several job offers, decided to do what she really always planned to do—go into business with her father, Jack Carter.

Jack Carter opened his first laundromat in 2001 and his second in 2004. The main attraction of these coin laundry businesses for him was that they were capital intensive rather than labor intensive. Thus, once the investment in machinery was made, the stores could be run with just one unskilled attendant and have none of the labor problems one normally expects from being in the retail service business.

The attractiveness of operating with virtually no skilled labor notwithstanding, Jack had decided by 2003 to expand the services in each of his stores to include the dry cleaning and pressing of clothes. He embarked, in other words, on a strategy of "related diversification" by adding new services that were related to and consistent with his existing coin laundry activities. He added these in part because he wanted to better utilize the unused space in the rather large stores he currently had under lease. But he also did so because he was, as he put it, "tired of sending out the dry cleaning and pressing work that came in from our coin laundry clients to a dry cleaner 5 miles away, who then took most of what should have been our profits." To reflect the new, expanded line of services, he renamed each of his two stores Carter Cleaning Centers and was sufficiently satisfied with their performance to open four more of the same type of stores over the next five years. Each store had its own on-site manager and, on average, about seven employees and annual revenues of about $700,000. It was this six-store cleaning centers chain that Jennifer joined upon graduating from State University.

Her understanding with her father was that she would serve as a troubleshooter and consultant to the elder Carter with the aim of both learning the business and bringing to it modern management concepts and techniques for solving the business's problems and facilitating its growth.

Questions

1-21. Make a list of five specific HR problems you think Carter Cleaning will have to grapple with.

1-22. What would you do first if you were Jennifer?

Experiential Exercise

HR and "The Profit"

Purpose: The purpose of this exercise is to provide practice in identifying and applying the basic concepts of human resource management by illustrating how managers use these techniques in their day-to-day jobs.

Required Understanding: Be thoroughly familiar with the material in this chapter, and with at least one or two episodes of CNBC's *The Profit* with Marcus Lemonis (www.tv.com/shows/the-profit/watch/). (Access a library of past episodes at URLs such as www.cnbc.com/live-tv/the-profit.)

How to Set Up the Exercise/Instructions:

- Divide the class into teams of several students.
- Read this: As you may know by watching billionaire Marcus Lemonis as he works with actual small businesses in which he's taken an ownership share, human resource management often plays an important role in what he and the business owners and managers need to do to be successful. For example, at Grafton Furniture, a lack of clarity about who does what (a lack of up-to-date job descriptions) leads to inadequate supervision of some ongoing orders and to lower profit margins. Questions also arise at Grafton about, for instance, the effectiveness of the training that some managers (including the owner's son) have received.
- Watch several of these shows (or reruns of the shows), and then meet with your team and answer the following questions:

1-23. What specific HR functions (recruiting, interviewing, training, and so on) can you identify Mr. Lemonis addressing on this show? Make sure to give specific examples based on the show.

1-24. What specific HR functions can you identify as being problematical in this company? Again, please give specific answers.

1-25. In terms of HR functions (such as recruiting, selection, interviewing, compensating, appraising, and so on), what exactly would you recommend doing to improve this company's performance?

1-26. Present your team's conclusions to the class.

2

Managing Equal Opportunity and Diversity

OVERVIEW:
In this chapter, we will cover . . .

- Equal Employment Opportunity Laws
- Defenses Against Discrimination Allegations
- Building Your Management Skills: Illustrative Discriminatory Employment Practices
- The EEOC Enforcement Process
- Diversity Management and Affirmative Action

MyLab Management

⭐ Improve Your Grade!
When you see this icon, visit
www.pearson.com/mylab/management for
activities that are applied, personalized, and
offer immediate feedback.

LEARNING OBJECTIVES

When you finish studying this chapter, you should be able to:

1. Summarize the basic equal employment opportunity laws and how each impacts HR functions such as recruitment and selection.

2. Explain the basic defenses against discrimination allegations.

3. Give examples of what employers can and cannot legally do with respect to recruitment, selection, and promotion and layoff practices.

4. Explain the Equal Employment Opportunity Commission enforcement process.

5. List five strategies for successfully increasing diversity of the workforce.

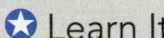 Learn It

If your professor has chosen to assign this, go to **www.pearson.com/mylab/management** to see what you should particularly focus on and to take the Chapter 2 Warm Up.

Source: Monkey Business Images/Shutterstock.

INTRODUCTION

HR AND THE GIG ECONOMY: A CASE OF DISCRIMINATION?

Earnest was sure his carpentry skills would get him plenty of gigs and help pay for college, but he didn't count on getting bad reviews. Now his gigs are few and far between, and he's wondering if being African American might be prompting the bad reviews.

He may be right. Most traditional-economy companies use recruiters, supervisors, and/or HR professionals to do their hiring, so if an applicant suffers discrimination, it's usually pretty clear who did it.[1]

But what do you do when you're a gig worker, doing work through a gig economy company like Uber, Task Rabbit, or Fiverr? Here the people doing the "hiring" are usually Task Rabbit, Uber, or Fiverr users, and they're making their decisions based on reviews compiled from previous users, or from photos in your profile. What stops them from illegally discriminating?

Unfortunately, as Earnest is finding, the answer may be, "not much." For example, in one study of labor markets like Task Rabbit and Fiverr, minority service providers got more negative reviews than white ones. Because most such services use algorithms to rate service providers partly based on prior customers' reviews, the minority service providers were then usually less likely to get new gigs. As you read this chapter, think about what you'd tell Earnest about dealing with this problem.

LEARNING OBJECTIVE 1
Summarize the basic equal opportunity laws and how each impacts HR functions such as recruitment and selection.

Equal Employment Opportunity Laws

Abercrombie & Fitch rescinded its "look policy" after a Muslim applicant won a judgment from the U.S. Supreme Court. The Court held that A&F should have accommodated her for religious reasons by letting her wear her headscarf.[2]

Hardly a day goes by without equal opportunity lawsuits like this.[3] One survey of corporate general counsels found that such lawsuits were their biggest litigation fears.[4] Performing supervisory tasks like hiring and appraising employees without understanding these laws is fraught with peril. We'll look at what managers should know about these laws in this chapter.

Background

Legislation barring discrimination is nothing new. The Fifth Amendment to the U.S. Constitution (ratified in 1791) states that "no person shall . . . be deprived of life, liberty, or property, without due process of the law."[5] Other laws as well as various court decisions made discrimination against minorities illegal by the early 1900s, at least in theory.[6]

But as a practical matter, Congress and presidents avoided dramatic action on implementing equal employment until the early 1960s. At that point, "they were finally prompted to act primarily as a result of civil unrest among the minorities and women" who eventually became protected by the new equal rights legislation and the agencies created to enforce it.[7]

Equal Pay Act of 1963

Equal Pay Act of 1963
The act requiring equal pay for equal work, regardless of sex.

The **Equal Pay Act of 1963** (amended in 1972) was one of the first new laws Congress passed. This made it unlawful to discriminate in pay based on sex when jobs involve equal work—equivalent skills, effort, and responsibility—and are performed under similar working conditions. (Differences in pay do not violate the act if the difference is based on a seniority system, a merit system, a system that measures earnings by quantity or quality of production, or a differential based on any factor other than sex.)

Title VII of the 1964 Civil Rights Act

Title VII of the 1964 Civil Rights Act
The section of the act that says an employer cannot discriminate on the basis of race, color, religion, sex, or national origin with respect to employment.

Title VII of the 1964 Civil Rights Act was another of the new laws. Title VII (amended by the 1972 Equal Employment Opportunity Act) says an employer cannot discriminate based on race, color, religion, sex, or national origin. Specifically, it states that it shall be an unlawful employment practice for an employer:[8]

1. *To fail or refuse to hire or to discharge an individual or otherwise to discriminate against any individual* with respect to his or her compensation, terms, conditions, or privileges of employment, because of such individual's race, color, religion, sex, or national origin.
2. *To limit, segregate, or classify his or her employees or applicants for employment* in any way that would deprive or tend to deprive any individual of employment opportunities or otherwise adversely affect his or her status as an employee, because of such individual's race, color, religion, sex, or national origin.

Equal Employment Opportunity Commission (EEOC)
The commission, created by Title VII, empowered to investigate job discrimination complaints and sue on behalf of complainants.

Title VII established the **Equal Employment Opportunity Commission (EEOC)**. It consists of five members, appointed by the president with the advice and consent of the Senate. Each member serves a term of five years. The EEOC has a staff of thousands to assist it in administering the Civil Rights law in employment settings.

The EEOC receives and investigates job discrimination complaints. When it finds reasonable cause, it attempts (through conciliation) to reach an agreement. If this fails, the EEOC has the power to go to court. Under the Equal Employment Opportunity Act of 1972, discrimination charges may be filed by the EEOC on behalf of an aggrieved individual, as well as by the individuals themselves. We explain this procedure later in this chapter.

Executive Orders

Office of Federal Contract Compliance Programs (OFCCP)
The office responsible for implementing the executive orders and ensuring compliance of federal contractors.

Under executive orders that U.S. presidents issued over the years, most employers who do business with the U.S. government have an obligation beyond that imposed by Title VII to refrain from employment discrimination. Executive Orders 11246 and 11375 don't just ban discrimination; they require that contractors take *affirmative action* to ensure equal employment opportunity (we explain affirmative action later in this chapter). These orders also established the **Office of Federal Contract Compliance Programs (OFCCP)**, which is responsible for ensuring the compliance of federal contracts.[9]

Age Discrimination in Employment Act of 1967

Age Discrimination in Employment Act (ADEA) of 1967
The act prohibiting arbitrary age discrimination and specifically protecting individuals over 40 years old.

The **Age Discrimination in Employment Act (ADEA) of 1967**, as amended, makes it unlawful to discriminate against employees or applicants for employment who are 40 years of age or older, effectively ending most mandatory retirement.[10] Plaintiffs' lawyers like the ADEA. It allows jury trials and double damages to those proving "willful" discrimination.[11] In a case called *O'Connor* v. *Consolidated Coin Caterers Corp.*, the U.S. Supreme Court held that employers can't circumvent the ADEA by simply replacing employees over 40 years of age with those who are "significantly younger" but also over 40.[12]

Yet age discrimination still occurs. For example, Staples recently fired a 64-year-old man for allegedly stealing a bell pepper. He sued for age discrimination. It transpired that a Staples facility manager had told other managers there to "take a closer look at the older people" and "write them up and get rid of them." The terminated employee won his case (for $16 million), and an appeal.[13] As another example, recruitment ads routinely use phrases like "applicants should have received their degrees 2012–2016," or "applicants should have 4–6 years' experience;" "although not always illegal, these are sometimes just code words for if you're over 40, don't bother to apply."[14]

Vocational Rehabilitation Act of 1973

Vocational Rehabilitation Act of 1973

The act requiring certain federal contractors to take affirmative action for disabled persons.

The **Vocational Rehabilitation Act of 1973** requires employers with federal contracts over $2,500 to take affirmative action for the employment of disabled persons. The act does not require hiring an unqualified person. It does require that an employer take steps to accommodate a disabled worker unless doing so imposes an undue hardship on the employer.

Pregnancy Discrimination Act of 1978

Pregnancy Discrimination Act (PDA)

An amendment to Title VII of the Civil Rights Act that prohibits sex discrimination based on "pregnancy, childbirth, or related medical conditions."

Congress passed the **Pregnancy Discrimination Act (PDA)** in 1978 as an amendment to Title VII. The act prohibits using pregnancy, childbirth, and related medical conditions for discrimination in hiring, promotion, discharge, or any other term or condition of employment. Basically, the act says that if an employer offers its employees disability coverage, then pregnancy and childbirth must be treated like any other disability and must be included in the plan as a covered condition.

Court decisions and more working mothers are prompting more (and more successful) PDA claims.[15] For example, a Chipotle Mexican Grill restaurant let go a pregnant employee. She told the jury that despite a history of positive performance feedback, her manager allegedly began harassing her when she said she was pregnant. For example, she was made to announce bathroom breaks to coworkers, and told she couldn't leave early for doctors' appointments. The jury agreed with her. It awarded her actual losses plus $500,000 in punitive damages.[16] The bottom line is that managers should base "any [such] decision on whether an employee can do the job on medical documentation, not on a manager's interpretation."[17]

Federal Agency Uniform Guidelines on Employee Selection Procedures

The federal agencies charged with ensuring compliance with the aforementioned laws and executive orders—the EEOC, Civil Service Commission, Department of Labor, and Department of Justice—have adopted uniform guidelines for employers.[18] These guidelines explain, for instance, how to validate a selection procedure.[19] The OFCCP has its own guidelines. The American Psychological Association published its own (nonlegally binding) *Standards for Educational and Psychological Testing*.[20]

Selected Court Decisions regarding Equal Employment Opportunity (EEO)

Several early court decisions helped to form courts' interpretive foundation for EEO laws.

Griggs v. Duke Power Company

Supreme Court case in which the plaintiff argued that his employer's requirement that coal handlers be high school graduates was unfairly discriminatory. In finding for the plaintiff, the Court ruled that discrimination need not be overt to be illegal, that employment practices must be related to job performance, and that the burden of proof is on the employer to show that hiring standards are job related.

Griggs v. Duke Power Company *Griggs v. Duke Power Company* (1971) was a landmark case because the Supreme Court used it to define unfair discrimination. In this case, a suit was brought against the Duke Power Company on behalf of Willie Griggs, an applicant for a job as a coal handler. The company required its coal handlers to be high school graduates. Griggs claimed that this requirement was illegally discriminatory because it wasn't related to success on the job and because it resulted in more blacks than whites being rejected for these jobs.

Griggs won the case. The decision of the Court was unanimous, and in his written opinion, Chief Justice Burger laid out three crucial guidelines affecting equal employment legislation. First, the court ruled that discrimination on the part of the employer need not be overt; in other words, the employer does not have to be shown to have intentionally discriminated against the employee or applicant—it need only be shown that discrimination took place.

Second, the court held that an employment practice (in this case requiring the high school diploma) must be shown to be *job related* if it has an unequal impact on members of a **protected class**.

In the words of Justice Burger:

> The act proscribes not only overt discrimination but also practices that are fair in form, but discriminatory in operation. The touchstone is business necessity. If an employment practice which operates to exclude Negroes cannot be shown to be related to job performance the practice is prohibited.[21]

Third, Burger's opinion placed the burden of proof on the employer to show that the hiring practice is job related. Thus, the *employer* must show that the employment practice (in this case, requiring a high school diploma) is needed to perform the job satisfactorily if it has a disparate impact on members of a protected class.

Albemarle Paper Company v. Moody In the *Griggs* case, the Supreme Court decided that a screening tool (such as a test) had to be job related or valid—that is, performance on the test must be related to performance on the job. The 1975 *Albemarle* case is important because it helped to clarify what the employer had to do to prove that the test or other screening tools are related to or predict performance on the job. For example, the Court ruled that before using a test to screen job candidates, the performance standards for the job in question should be clear and unambiguous, so the employer can identify which employees were performing better than others (and thus whether the screening tool was effective). In arriving at its decision, the Court also cited the EEOC guidelines concerning acceptable selection procedures and made these guidelines the "law of the land."[22]

The Civil Rights Act of 1991

Subsequent Supreme Court rulings in the 1980s had the effect of limiting the protection of women and minority groups.[23] In response, President George H. W. Bush signed into law the new **Civil Rights Act of 1991** (CRA 1991). This act rolled back the clock to where it stood before the 1980s decisions and actually placed more responsibility on employers.

For example, CRA 1991 addressed *burden of proof*. Today, after CRA 1991, the process of filing and responding to a discrimination charge goes something like this. The plaintiff (say, a rejected applicant) demonstrates that an employment practice (such as a test) has a disparate impact on a particular group. **Disparate impact** means "an employer engages in an employment practice or policy that has a greater adverse impact [effect] on the members of a protected group under Title VII than on other employees, regardless of intent."[24] Requiring a college degree for a job would have an adverse impact on some minority groups, for instance.

The plaintiff need not prove discriminatory intent. Instead, he or she must show that an apparently neutral employment practice, such as "be able to lift 100 pounds," is causing the disparity.[25] Once the plaintiff shows such disparate impact, the *employer* has the *burden of proving* that the challenged practice is "job related."[26] For example, the employer has to show that the business could not run efficiently without the 100-pound requirement—that it is a business necessity.

CRA 1991 also makes it easier to sue for *money damages*. It provides that an employee who is claiming *intentional discrimination* (called **disparate treatment**) can ask for both compensatory damages and punitive damages, if he or she can show the employer engaged in discrimination "with malice or reckless indifference to the federally protected rights of an aggrieved individual." Finally, CRA 1991 also addresses so-called "mixed motive" cases. Here employers claim that although

protected class

Persons such as minorities and women protected by equal opportunity laws, including Title VII.

Civil Rights Act of 1991 (CRA 1991)

The act that places burden of proof back on employers and permits compensatory and punitive damages.

disparate impact

An unintentional disparity between the proportion of a protected group applying for a position and the proportion getting the job.

disparate treatment

An intentional disparity between the proportion of a protected group and the proportion getting the job.

their actions were discriminatory, other factors, such as perhaps the employee's poor performance, made the job action (such as dismissal) acceptable. Under CRA 1991, if *there is any such discriminatory motive, the practice may be unlawful.*[27]

The Americans with Disabilities Act

Americans with Disabilities Act (ADA)

The act requiring employers to make reasonable accommodations for disabled employees; it prohibits discrimination against disabled persons.

The **Americans with Disabilities Act (ADA)** of 1990 prohibits employers with 15 or more workers from discriminating against qualified individuals with disabilities with regard to hiring, discharge, compensation, advancement, training, or other terms, conditions, or privileges of employment.[28] And it requires employers to make "reasonable accommodations" unless doing so imposes an "undue hardship" on the business.[29]

The ADA does not list specific disabilities. However, EEOC guidelines say someone is disabled when he or she has a physical or mental impairment that "substantially limits" one or more major life activities. Impairments include any physiological disorder or condition, cosmetic disfigurement, or anatomical loss affecting one or more of several body systems, or any mental or psychological disorder.[30] The act specifies conditions that it does *not* regard as disabilities, including homosexuality, bisexuality, voyeurism, compulsive gambling, pyromania, and certain disorders resulting from the current illegal use of drugs.[31] The EEOC's position is that the ADA prohibits discriminating against people with HIV/AIDS.

Mental disabilities account for the greatest number of ADA claims.[32] "Mental impairment" includes "any mental or psychological disorder, such as . . . emotional or mental illness." Examples include major depression, anxiety disorders, and personality disorders. The ADA also protects employees with intellectual disabilities, including those with IQs below 70–75.[33] Employers should be alert to the possibility that behaviors normally regarded as undesirable (such as chronic lateness) may reflect mental impairments. Reasonable accommodation might then include providing room partitions or other barriers between work spaces.

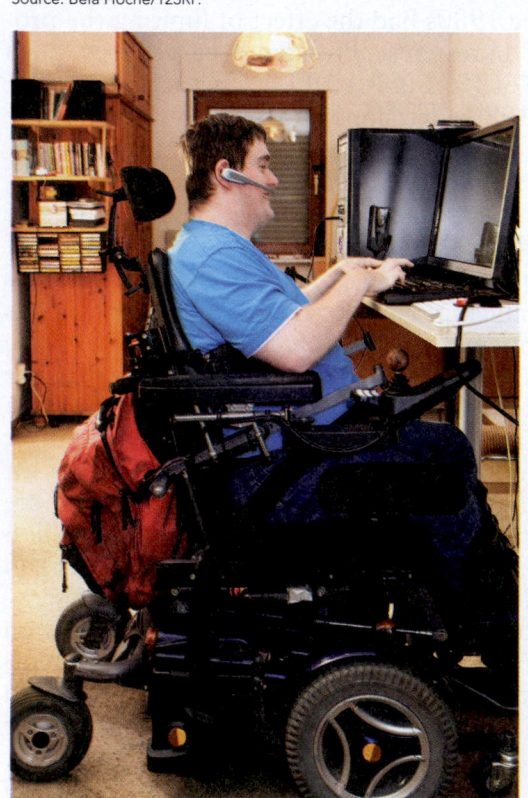

Technological innovations make it easier today for employers to accommodate disabled employees.
Source: Bela Hoche/123RF.

Qualified Individual   Just being disabled doesn't qualify someone for a job, of course. It only prohibits discrimination against *qualified individuals*—those who, with (or without) a reasonable accommodation, can carry out the *essential functions* of the job. The individual must have the requisite skills, educational background, and experience. A job function is essential when, for instance, it is the reason the position exists, or it is so highly specialized that the employer hires the person for his or her expertise or ability to perform that particular function. For example, when a worker had a seizure, his driver's license was suspended, and the employer fired him. The court ruled that he had no ADA claim because he couldn't perform the essential functions of the job (driving).[34]

Reasonable Accommodation   If the individual can't perform the job as currently structured, the employer must make a "reasonable accommodation" unless doing so would present an "undue hardship." Reasonable accommodation might include redesigning the job, modifying work schedules, or modifying or acquiring equipment or other devices (such as adding curb ramps and widening door openings).[35] For example, by one estimate about 70% of working-age blind adults are unemployed or underemployed, although they are educated and excellent employees.[36] Existing technologies would enable most of them to work successfully in numerous jobs. For example, a program called Jaws converts text from a computer screen into Braille and speaks it.[37]

Attorneys, employers, and the courts continue to work through what "reasonable accommodation" means.[38] In one classic case, a

Figure 2.1

Familiar Tools Aid Impaired Employees

- Voice recognition software, for employees with impairments.
- Real-time translation captioning lets employees participate in meetings.
- Vibrating phones notify employees when messages arrive.

Walmart door greeter with a bad back asked if she could sit while on duty. The store said no, and she sued. Walmart said door greeters must act in an "aggressively hospitable manner," which can't be done sitting on a stool.[39] Standing was an essential job function. The federal court agreed with Walmart. As in Figure 2.1, you can use technology and common sense to make reasonable accommodations.

Traditional Employer Defenses and the "New" ADA Employers used to prevail in about 96% of federal appeals court ADA decisions.[40] A U.S. Supreme Court decision typifies why. An assembly worker sued Toyota, arguing that carpal tunnel syndrome prevented her from doing her job.[41] The Court ruled that the ADA covers such disabilities only if her impairments affect (were "central to") not just her job performance but also her daily living activities. The employee admitted that they were not, in that she could perform personal chores such as fixing breakfast.[42]

However, the ADA Amendments Act of 2008 (ADAAA) made it much easier for employees to show that their disabilities *are* influencing one of their "major life activities," such as reading and thinking.[43] Employers must therefore redouble their efforts to ensure they're complying with the ADA.[44]

Many employers simply take a progressive approach. For example, Walgreens tries to fill at least one-third of its large distribution center jobs with people with disabilities.[45] Common employer concerns about people with disabilities (for instance, that they are less productive) are generally baseless.[46]

Figure 2.2 summarizes some important ADA guidelines for managers and employers.

Uniformed Services Employment and Reemployment Rights Act

Under the Uniformed Services Employment and Reemployment Rights Act (1994), employers are generally required, among other things, to reinstate employees returning from military leave to positions comparable to those they had before leaving.[47]

Genetic Information Nondiscrimination Act of 2008

The Genetic Information Nondiscrimination Act (GINA) prohibits discrimination by health insurers and employers based on people's genetic information. It prohibits using genetic information in employment decisions, prohibits the intentional acquisition of genetic information about applicants and employees, and imposes strict confidentiality requirements.[48]

Figure 2.2

ADA Guidelines for Managers

- *Do not* deny a job to a disabled person if he or she is qualified and able to perform the job's essential functions.
- *Make* a reasonable accommodation unless that would result in undue hardship.
- In general, you may *not* make preemployment inquiries about someone's disability before making an offer. However, you *may* ask about the person's ability to perform essential job functions.
- *Itemize* essential job functions on the job descriptions.
- *Do not* accept misconduct or erratic performance (including absences and tardiness), even if linked to a disability.

State and Local Equal Employment Opportunity Laws

In addition to federal laws, all states and many local governments prohibit employment discrimination. Many cover employers (like those with under 15 employees) not covered by federal legislation.[49] In Arizona, for instance, plaintiffs can bring sexual harassment claims against employers with even one employee. Some bar discrimination against not only those over 40, but also those under 17. (Here, for instance, it might be illegal to advertise for "mature" applicants.)[50] Managers use manuals such as *HR Compliance Basics: Your State and Federal Employment Law Manual* (available from the SHRM) to understand local EEO requirements.

State and local agencies (often called "human resources commissions" or "fair employment commissions") play a role in equal employment compliance. When the EEOC receives a discrimination charge, it usually defers it for a time to the state and local agencies that have comparable jurisdiction. If that doesn't achieve satisfactory remedies, the charges go back to the EEOC for resolution.

Religious and Other Types of Discrimination[51]

The EEOC enforces laws prohibiting discrimination based on age, disability, equal pay/compensation, genetic information, national origin, pregnancy, race/color, religion, retaliation, sex, and sexual harassment. The Commission has also argued that sexual orientation claims by lesbian, gay, bisexual, and transgender individuals alleging sex-stereotyping have a sex discrimination claim under Title VII.[52]

Religious discrimination involves treating someone unfavorably because of his or her religious beliefs. The law protects not only people who belong to traditional religions such as Buddhism, Christianity, Hinduism, Islam, and Judaism, but also others who have sincerely held religious, ethical, or moral beliefs. Unless it would be an undue hardship for the employer, an employer must reasonably accommodate an employee's religious beliefs or practices. This applies to schedule changes or prayer breaks, as well as to such things as religious dress or grooming practices. These might include, for example, wearing particular head coverings or other religious dress (such as a Jewish yarmulke or a Muslim headscarf), or wearing certain hairstyles or facial hair. Religious discrimination claims are increasing.[53]

One question is how far the employer must go to reasonably accommodate the employee's religious practices. For example, Muslim workers have sued employers alleging that the employers should have accommodated their need for periodic prayer breaks. Here what is "reasonable" depends partly on how disruptive the accommodation would be for the employer. For example, such breaks might be too disruptive for those working on high-speed continuous production lines.[54]

Trends in Discrimination Law

Some trends are broadening the impact of equal employment laws, while others are forming new headwinds.

In terms of the former, the U.S. Supreme Court held that the Federal Defense of Marriage Act's exclusion of state-sanctioned, same-sex marriages was unconstitutional.[55] In a guidance from the Department of Labor (DOL), the DOL said that under the Employee Retirement Income Security Act (ERISA), "The term 'spouse' will be read to refer to any individuals who are lawfully married under any state law, including those . . . who are [now] domiciled in a state that doesn't recognize such marriages."[56] In 2014, then-President Obama signed an executive order barring federal contractors from discriminating against lesbian, gay, bisexual, and transgender employees, for instance in terms of benefits.[57] In 2017, a federal appeals court ruled that the Title VII ban on sex discrimination means employers cannot discriminate against lesbian and gay workers based on sexual orientation.[58] The DOL passed regulations requiring that federal contractors employ a minimum (7%) of disabled workers or face penalties, possibly including loss of their contracts unless they take immediate remedial actions.[59]

Other recent decisions may produce headwinds. The U.S. Supreme Court upheld a Michigan constitutional amendment banning affirmative action in

TABLE 2.1 Summary of Selected Equal Employment Opportunity Actions*

Action	What It Does
Title VII of 1964 Civil Rights Act, as amended	Bars discrimination because of race, color, religion, sex, or national origin; instituted EEOC
Executive orders	Prohibit employment discrimination by employers with federal contracts of more than $10,000 (and their subcontractors); established OFCCP.
Federal agency guidelines	Promulgate policies covering discrimination based on sex, national origin, and religion, as well as on employee selection and other procedures such as test validation
Supreme Court decisions: *Griggs* v. *Duke Power Company, Albemarle Paper Company* v. *Moody*	Ruled that job requirements must be related to job success; that discrimination need not be overt to be proved; that the burden of proof is on the employer to prove the qualification is valid
Equal Pay Act of 1963	Requires equal pay for men and women for performing similar work
Age Discrimination in Employment Act of 1967	Prohibits discriminating against a person 40 or over in any area of employment based on age
State and local laws	Often cover organizations not covered by federal laws
Vocational Rehabilitation Act of 1973	Requires affirmative action to employ and promote qualified disabled persons and prohibits discrimination against them
Pregnancy Discrimination Act of 1978	Prohibits discrimination in employment against pregnant women, or related conditions
Vietnam Era Veterans' Readjustment Assistance Act of 1974	Requires affirmative action in employment for Vietnam War era veterans
Americans with Disabilities Act of 1990 and ADA Amendments Act of 2008	Strengthens the need for most employers not to discriminate and to accommodate disabled employees at work
Civil Rights Act of 1991	Reverses several 1980s Court decisions; places burden of proof back on employer and permits compensatory and punitive money damages for discrimination
Genetic Information Non-Discrimination Act of 2008 (GINA)	Prohibits discrimination by health insurers and employers based on people's genetic information

*The actual laws (and others) can be accessed via a search at www.usa.gov/Topics/Reference-Shelf/Laws.shtml, accessed January 24, 2017.

admissions to the state's public universities. This may allow voters in other states to eliminate affirmative action–based admissions to their public universities.[60] And in two other decisions, the Court made it more difficult for someone to bring a retaliation claim against an employer; it also more strictly defined "supervisor," reducing the likelihood someone could show that an employer was responsible for a "supervisor's" harassing behavior.[61] With its stated goal of reducing regulations, the Republican administration could possibly be less supportive of equal employment regulations (and regulations in general).

Table 2.1 summarizes selected equal employment opportunity laws, actions, executive orders, and agency guidelines. The accompanying HR Tools feature provides some guidance for small business managers.

■ HR Tools for Line Managers and Small Businesses

The U.S. Equal Employment Opportunity Commission (EEOC) administers Title VII of the Civil Rights Act of 1964 (Title VII), the Age Discrimination in Employment Act of 1967 (ADEA), Title I of the Americans with Disabilities Act of 1990 (ADA), and the Equal Pay Act of 1963 (EPA). For managers or small business owners with a question, the site www.eeoc.gov provides small business owners with practical advice. For example, click that URL and then go to Employers, and then to Small Business FAQ.[62] The EEOC provides small business liaisons to answer questions, as well as standard answers such as

- What should I do when someone files a charge against my company?
- How do I determine if my business is covered by EEOC laws?
- Who may file a charge of discrimination with the EEOC?
- Can a small business resolve a charge without undergoing an investigation or facing a lawsuit?[63]

⭐ Talk About It – **1**

If your professor has chosen to assign this, go to **www.pearson.com/mylab/management** to discuss the following question. Check with the EEOC's website and compile a list of the three biggest sources of complaints in 2017. What were they, and why do you think those elicited the most complaints?

Sexual Harassment

Under Title VII, conduct based on sex generally qualifies as **sexual harassment** when such conduct has the purpose or effect of substantially interfering with a person's work performance or creating an intimidating, hostile, or offensive work environment. CRA 1991 also permits victims of intentional discrimination, including sexual harassment, to have jury trials and to collect compensatory damages for pain and suffering, and punitive damages in cases where the employer acted with "malice or reckless indifference" to the person's rights.[64] The Federal Violence against Women Act of 1994 provides another path women can use to seek relief for violent sexual harassment. It provides that someone "who commits a crime of violence motivated by gender and thus deprives another" of her rights shall be liable to the party injured.

Under EEOC guidelines, employers have an affirmative duty to maintain workplaces free of sexual harassment and intimidation. The U.S. Supreme Court held (in *Oncale* v. *Sundowner Offshore Services Inc.*) that same-sex sexual harassment is also actionable under Title VII.[65] In one recent year, the EEOC received 6,758 sexual harassment charges, 16.6% of which were filed by men.[66]

Minority women are most at risk. One study found "women experienced more sexual harassment than men, minorities experienced more ethnic harassment than whites, and minority women experience more harassment overall than majority men, minority men, and majority women."[67]

What Is Sexual Harassment? EEOC guidelines define sexual harassment as unwelcome sexual advances, requests for sexual favors, and other verbal or physical conduct of a sexual nature that takes place under any of the following conditions:

1. Submission to such conduct is made either explicitly or implicitly a term or condition of an individual's employment.
2. Submission to or rejection of such conduct by an individual is used as the basis for employment decisions affecting such individuals.
3. Such conduct has the purpose or effect of unreasonably interfering with an individual's work performance or creating an intimidating, hostile, or offensive work environment.

Proving Sexual Harassment There are three main ways someone can prove sexual harassment.

1. **Quid pro quo.** The most direct is to prove that rejecting a supervisor's advances adversely affected what the EEOC calls a "tangible employment

Sexual harassment is unwelcome sexual advances, requests for sexual favors, and other verbal or physical conduct of a sexual nature, including creating an intimidating, hostile, or offensive work environment.
Source: Tom Wang/Shutterstock.

action" such as hiring, firing, promotion, demotion, and/or work assignment. In one case, the employee showed that continued job success and advancement were dependent on her agreeing to the sexual demands of her supervisors. Courts generally require that the behavior be pervasive or severe. In one case, the court ruled that although the supervisor had touched the employee's shoulder twice as he drove her back from work and also mentioned that she "owed him" for hiring her, she did not have a trial-able sexual harassment claim.[68]

2. **Hostile environment created by supervisors.** One need not show that the harassment had tangible consequences such as demotion. For example, in one case the court found that a male supervisor's sexual harassment had substantially affected a female employee's emotional and psychological ability to the point that she felt she had to quit her job. Therefore, even though the supervisor made no direct threats or promises in exchange for sexual advances, his advances interfered with the woman's performance and created an offensive work environment. That was sufficient to prove sexual harassment. Courts generally do not interpret as sexual harassment sexual relationships that arise during the course of employment but that do not have a substantial effect on that employment.[69] The U.S. Supreme Court also held that sexual harassment law doesn't cover ordinary "intersexual flirtation."[70]

3. **Hostile environment created by coworkers or nonemployees.** The questionable behavior doesn't have to come from the person's supervisor. For example, one court held that a mandatory sexually provocative uniform led to lewd comments by customers. When the employee said she would no longer wear the uniform, they fired her. The employer couldn't show there was a job-related necessity for requiring the uniform, and only female employees had to wear it. The court thus ruled that the employer, in effect, was responsible for the sexually harassing behavior. Such abhorrent client behavior is more likely when the clients are in positions of power, and when they think no one will penalize them.[71] EEOC guidelines also state that an employer is liable for the sexually harassing acts of its nonsupervisor employees if the employer knew or should have known of the harassing conduct.

WHEN IS THE ENVIRONMENT "HOSTILE"?   Hostile environment sexual harassment generally means that the intimidation, insults, and ridicule were sufficiently severe to alter the working conditions. Here, courts look at several things. These include whether the discriminatory conduct is *frequent* or *severe*; whether it is *physically threatening* or *humiliating*, or a mere offensive utterance; and whether it unreasonably *interferes* with an employee's work performance.[72] Courts also consider whether the employee subjectively *perceives* the work environment as being abusive. For example, did he or she welcome the conduct or immediately show that it was unwelcome?[73]

SUPREME COURT DECISIONS   The U.S. Supreme Court used a case called *Meritor Savings Bank, FSB* v. *Vinson* to endorse broadly the EEOC's guidelines on sexual harassment. Two other Supreme Court decisions then further clarified sexual harassment law. In the first, *Burlington Industries* v. *Ellerth*, the employee accused her supervisor of quid pro quo harassment. She said her boss propositioned and threatened her with demotion if she did not respond. He did not carry out the threats, and she was promoted. In the second case, *Faragher* v. *City of Boca Raton*, the employee accused the employer of condoning a hostile work environment. She said she quit her lifeguard job after repeated taunts from other lifeguards. The Court ruled in favor of the employees in both cases.

The Court's written decisions in the latter cases have two implications for employers. First, in quid pro quo cases it is *not* necessary for the employee to suffer a tangible job action (such as a demotion) to win the case; just the threat may be sufficient.

Second, the Court laid out an important defense against harassment suits. It said the employer must show that it took "reasonable care" to prevent and promptly correct any sexually harassing behavior *and* that the employee unreasonably failed to take advantage of the employer's policy. The implication is that an employer can defend itself against sexual harassment liability by showing two things:

- First, it must show "that the employer exercised reasonable care to prevent and correct promptly any sexually harassing behavior."[74]
- Second, it must demonstrate that the plaintiff "unreasonably failed to take advantage of any preventive or corrective opportunities provided by the employer." The employee's failure to use formal reporting systems would satisfy the second component.

Prudent employers promptly took steps to show they did take reasonable care.[75] Steps to take include:[76]

- Take all complaints about harassment seriously.[77]
- Issue a strong policy statement condemning such behavior. Describe the prohibited conduct, assure protection against retaliation, include a confidential complaint process, and provide impartial investigation and corrective action.
- Take steps to prevent sexual harassment. For example, communicate to employees that the employer will not tolerate sexual harassment, and take immediate action when someone complains.
- Train supervisors and managers to increase their awareness of the issues, and discipline managers and employees involved in sexual harassment.

Diversity Counts

In Sexual Harassment   There is virtually no doubt that certain behaviors constitute sexual harassment. For example, behavior of the "quid pro quo" variety (in which, say, the supervisor tells a subordinate that the person either performs a sexual favor or is terminated) is clearly sexual harassment. But where the behaviors are not so blatant (but may still foster a sexually hostile environment) defining how a reasonable person would interpret the behavior becomes more complex.

One problem is that there are gender-based differences in how men and women view various behaviors. In one study, about 58% of employees reported experiencing potentially harassment-type behaviors at work. Of these, about 25% found it flattering and about half viewed it as benign. But on closer examination, about *four times more men than women* found the behavior flattering or benign.[78] (One Silicon Valley commentator supposedly explained the scarcity of women in the industry by saying he'd hire more women but his wife feared he would sleep with them, and that he probably would.)[79] Based on studies, females are much more likely than males to report that they experienced unwelcome sexual attention and to define more social sexual behaviors as sexual harassment than do males. Similarly, males are less likely to attribute responsibility for sexual harassment to the alleged harasser than are females, and men are more likely to place blame on the female target than are females.[80] Sexual harassment training programs (for instance, to explain these differences to male employees) and antiharassment policies can reduce this problem.[81]

A second problem is that employees often won't complain. For example, two Air Force generals appeared before the U.S. Congress' House Armed Services Committee to explain how 23 instructors at an Air Force base could engage in unprofessional relationships or sexual assaults against 48 female trainees. The Air Force blamed both a climate of fear among female personnel (who believed that reporting the offenses to superior officers would be futile or counterproductive) and "a weak command structure."[82] The solution is to execute zealously antiharassment policies like those mentioned earlier.

What Can the Employee Do? First, as noted previously, the employee should remember that courts generally look to whether *the harassed employee used the employer's reporting procedures to file a complaint promptly.* Generally, this duty is *not* fulfilled if the employer had an effectively communicated complaint procedure and the victim did not utilize it, or if the victim did make a complaint but then refused to cooperate in the investigation.[83] Steps an employee can take include the following:

1. Speak with the harasser and his or her boss, stating that the unwanted overtures should cease.
2. Inform your own supervisor.
3. If the problem does not cease, file written reports regarding the unwelcome conduct and unsuccessful efforts to get it to stop with the harasser's manager and/or the human resource director.
4. If these do not suffice, the accuser may file a claim with the EEOC. In serious cases, the employee can also consult an attorney about suing the harasser for assault and battery, intentional infliction of emotional distress, injunctive relief, and to recover compensatory and punitive damages.[84]

The HR Practices Around the Globe and the Trends Shaping HR features address some special issues in equal empolyment.

⭐ Watch It

How does an employer actually deal with problems such as sexual harassment? If your professor has chosen to assign this, go to **www.pearson.com/mylab/management** to watch the video UPS Equal Opportunity Employment, and then answer the questions to show what you would do.

◼ HR Practices Around the Globe

Applying Equal Employment Law Abroad

The Civil Rights Act of 1991 marked a big change in the geographic applicability of equal rights legislation. Congressional legislation generally only applies within U.S. territory unless specifically stated otherwise.[85] However, CRA 1991 specifically expanded coverage by amending the definition of "employee" in Title VII to mean a U.S. citizen employed in a foreign country by a U.S.-owned or controlled company.[86] At least theoretically, therefore, *U.S. citizens* now working overseas for U.S. companies enjoy the same equal employment opportunity protection as those working within U.S. borders. (Title VII does not apply to foreign operations not owned or controlled by a U.S. employer, however.)

However, two factors limit the widespread application of CRA 1991 abroad. First, there are numerous exclusions. For example, an employer need not comply with Title VII if compliance would cause the employer to violate the law of the host country (for instance, some foreign countries have statutes prohibiting women in management positions).[87]

Another problem is the practical difficulty of enforcing CRA 1991 abroad. For example, the EEOC investigator's first duty in such a case is to analyze the finances and organizational structure of the respondent (employer). But in practice few investigators are trained for this duty, and no precise standards exist for such investigations.[88]

✪ Talk About It – **2**

If your professor has chosen to assign this, go to **www.pearson.com/mylab/management** to discuss the following questions. If you were running a China-based unit of an American company, would you work hard to follow U.S. EEO laws? Why?

TRENDS SHAPING HR: *Digital and Social Media*

SOME SOCIAL MEDIA HR PROS AND CONS Widespread use of social media presents challenges to employers. Some employees use Facebook-type accounts to bully coworkers. Here, employers must distinguish between illegal online harassment (applying to race, religion, national origin, age, sex/gender, genetic information, and disability discrimination) and common personality conflicts. Employers at least need a zero-tolerance policy on bullying.[89]

Of course, social media has been great for staffing. It's easy for employers to find applicants on LinkedIn, for instance. However, viewing an applicant's social media profile may reveal information on things like religion, race, and sexual orientation.[90] Some states therefore forbid employers from requesting employees' or applicants' passwords. At a minimum, implement policies restricting who can check out candidates online. Supervisors should generally not do such checking themselves.

Defenses Against Discrimination Allegations

To understand how employers defend themselves against employment discrimination claims, we should first review some basic legal terminology.

Discrimination law distinguishes between disparate *treatment* and disparate *impact*. Disparate treatment means intentional discrimination. It "requires no more than a finding that women (or protected minority group members)" were intentionally treated differently because they were members of a particular race, religion, gender, or ethnic group.[91] Having a rule that says "we do not hire bus drivers over 60 years of age" exemplifies this.[92]

Disparate impact means that "an employer engages in an employment practice or policy that has a greater adverse impact (effect) on the members of a protected group under Title VII than on other employees, regardless of intent."[93] A rule that says "employees must have college degrees to do this particular job" exemplifies this (because more white males than some minorities earn college degrees).

Disparate impact claims do not require proof of discriminatory intent. Instead, the plaintiff must show that the apparently neutral employment practice (such as requiring a college degree) creates an **adverse impact**—a significant disparity—between the proportion of (say) minorities in the available labor pool and the proportion you hire. So, the key here is to show that the employment practice caused an adverse impact. If it has, then the employer will probably have to defend itself (for instance, by arguing that there is a business necessity for the practice).

adverse impact
The overall impact of employer practices that result in significantly higher percentages of members of minorities and other protected groups being rejected for employment, placement, or promotion.

The Central Role of Adverse Impact

Showing an adverse impact therefore plays a central role in discriminatory practice allegations. Employers may not institute an employment practice that has an adverse impact on a particular class of people unless they can show that the practice is job related and necessary.[94] Under Title VII and CRA 1991, a person who believes that (1) he or she was a victim of unintentional discrimination because of an employer's practices need only (2) establish a prima facie case of discrimination. This means showing, for instance, that the employer's selection procedures (like requiring a college degree for the job) did have an adverse impact on the protected minority group.[95] Then the burden of proof shifts to the employer.

So, for example, if a minority applicant feels he or she was a victim of discrimination, the person need only show that the employer's selection process resulted in an adverse impact (significant disparity) on his or her group. (For example, if 80% of the white applicants passed the test, but only 20% of the black applicants passed, a black applicant has a prima facie case proving adverse impact.) Then the burden of proof shifts to the employer. It becomes the employer's task to prove that its test (or application blank or the like) is a valid predictor of performance on the job (and that it applied its selection process fairly and equitably to both minorities and nonminorities).

In practice, an applicant or employee can use one of the following methods to show that an employment procedure (such as a selection test) has an adverse impact on a protected group.

Disparate Rejection Rates The plaintiff shows *disparate rejection rates* by comparing rejection rates for a minority group and another group (usually the remaining nonminority applicants).[96]

Federal agencies use a "4/5ths rule" to assess disparate rejection rates: "A selection rate for any racial, ethnic, or sex group which is less than four-fifths or 80% of the rate for the group with the highest rate will generally be regarded as evidence of adverse impact, while a greater than four-fifths rate will generally not be regarded as evidence of adverse impact." For example, suppose the employer hires 60% of male applicants, but only 30% of female applicants. Four-fifths of the 60% male-hiring rate would be 48%. Because the female hiring rate of 30% is less than 48%, adverse impact exists as far as these federal agencies are concerned.[97]

The Standard Deviation Rule Similarly, courts may use the *standard deviation rule* to confirm an adverse impact. (The standard deviation is a statistical measure of variability. Suppose we measure the heights of every person in your management class. In simplest terms, the standard deviation helps to describe, among other things, how wide a range there is between the shortest and tallest students.) In selection, the standard deviation rule holds that, as a rule of thumb, the difference between the numbers of minority candidates we *would have expected* to hire and whom *we actually hired* should be less than two standard deviations. (Please see the accompanying HR in Practice for an example.)

■ HR in Practice

How to Use the Standard Deviation Rule in Practice

Here's how the standard deviation rule works in practice. Suppose 300 applicants apply for 20 openings; 80 of the applicants are women and the other 220 are men. We use our screening processes and hire 2 females and 18 males. Did our selection process have adverse impact? To answer this, we first calculate the standard deviation (see Figure 2.3). It is 1.977, or about 2.

In our example, women are 26% (80/300) of the applicant pool. We should therefore *expect* to hire 26% of 20 or about 5 women. We *actually* hired 2 women. The difference between the numbers of women we would expect to hire and whom we actually hired is 5 − 2 = 3. We can use the standard deviation rule to gauge if there is adverse impact. In our example, the standard deviation is 1.977. Again, the standard deviation rule holds that, as a rule of thumb, the difference between the numbers of minority candidates *we would have expected to hire* and whom *we actually hired* should be less than two standard deviations. Two times 1.9777 is about 4. Because the difference between the number of women we would have expected to hire (5) and actually hired (2) is 3, the results suggest that our screening did not have adverse impact on women. (Put another way, in this case, hiring just 2 rather than 5 is not a highly improbable result here.)[98]

✪ Talk About It – 3

If your professor has chosen to assign this, go to **www.pearson.com/mylab/management** to discuss the following: if you are an employer, do you think you're better off using the standard deviation rule or disparate rejection rates? Why?

Figure 2.3

Calculating Our Standard Deviation

$$SD = \sqrt{\frac{(\text{Number of minority applicants})}{(\text{Number of total applicants})} \times \frac{(\text{Number of nonminority applicants})}{(\text{Number of total applicants})} \times (\text{Number of applicants selected})}$$

In our case:

$$SD = \sqrt{\left(\frac{80}{300} \times \frac{220}{300} \times 20\right)} = \sqrt{(0.2667 \times 0.7333 \times 20)}$$

$$= \sqrt{3.911} = SD = 1.977$$

Restricted Policy The restricted policy approach means demonstrating that the employer's policy intentionally or unintentionally excluded members of a protected group. Here the problem is usually obvious—such as policies against hiring bartenders shorter than 6 feet tall. Evidence of restricted policies such as these is enough to prove adverse impact and to expose an employer to litigation.

Population Comparisons This approach compares (1) the percentage of minority/ protected group and white workers in the organization with (2) the percentage of the corresponding group in the labor market. The EEOC usually defines labor market as the U.S. Census data for that Standard Metropolitan Statistical Area.

"Labor market," of course, varies with the job. For some jobs, such as secretary, it makes sense to compare the percentage of minority employees with the percentage of minorities in the surrounding community, because they will come from that community. But for jobs such as engineer, recruiting may be nationwide. Determining whether an employer has "enough" black engineers might thus require knowing the number available nationwide, not in the community.

Employers use *workforce analysis* to analyze the data regarding the firm's use of protected (minority or women) versus nonprotected employees in the company's various job classifications. *Utilization analysis* is the process of comparing the percentage of minority employees in a job (or jobs) at the company with the number of similarly trained minority employees available in the relevant labor market.

McDonnell Douglas Test Lawyers in disparate impact cases use the previous approaches (such as population comparisons) to test whether an employer's policies or actions have the effect of unintentionally screening out disproportionate numbers of women or minorities. Lawyers use the McDonnell Douglas test for showing (intentional) disparate *treatment*, rather than (unintentional) disparate *impact*.

This test grew out of a case at the former McDonnell Douglas Corporation. The applicant was qualified but the employer rejected the person and continued seeking applicants. Did this show that the hiring company intentionally discriminated against the female or minority candidate? The U.S. Supreme Court set four rules for applying the McDonnell Douglas test:

1. That the person belongs to a protected class.
2. That he or she applied and was qualified for a job for which the employer was seeking applicants.
3. That, despite this qualification, he or she was rejected.
4. That, after his or her rejection, the position remained open and the employer continued seeking applications from persons with the complainant's qualifications.

If the plaintiff meets these four conditions, then a prima facie (basically, obvious at first sight) case of disparate treatment is established. At that point, the employer must articulate a legitimate nondiscriminatory reason for its action and produce evidence but not prove that it acted based on such a reason. If it meets this relatively easy standard, the plaintiff then has the burden of proving that the employer's articulated reason is merely a pretext for engaging in unlawful discrimination.

KNOW YOUR EMPLOYMENT LAW
Dealing with a Charge of Discrimination

Assume you turn down a member of a protected group for a job with your firm. You do this based on a test score (although it could have been interview questions or something else). Further, assume that this person believes he or she was discriminated against due to being in a protected class, and decides to sue your company.

Basically, all he or she must do is show that your human resource procedure (such as the selection test) had an adverse impact on members of his or her minority group. The plaintiff can apply several approaches here, such as disparate rejection rates, the standard deviation rule, restricted policy, or population comparisons. Once the person proves adverse impact (to the court's satisfaction), the burden of proof shifts to the employer. The employer must defend against the discrimination charges.

Note that there is nothing in the law that says that because one of your procedures has an adverse impact on a protected group, you can't use the procedure. In fact, it may well happen that some tests screen out disproportionately higher numbers of, say, blacks than they do whites. What the law does say is that once your applicant has made his or her case (showing adverse impact), the burden of proof shifts to you. Now you (or your company) must defend use of the procedure.

There are then two basic defenses employers use to justify an employment practice that has an adverse impact on members of a minority group: the bona fide occupational qualification (BFOQ) defense and the business necessity defense. We'll look at these next. ■

Bona Fide Occupational Qualification

bona fide occupational qualification (BFOQ)
Requirement that an employee be of a certain religion, sex, or national origin where that is reasonably necessary to the organization's normal operation. Specified by the 1964 Civil Rights Act.

One defense is to claim that the employment practice is a **bona fide occupational qualification** (BFOQ) for performing the job. Title VII provides that "it should not be an unlawful employment practice for an employer to hire an employee . . . on the basis of religion, sex, or national origin *in those certain instances where religion, sex, or national origin is a bona fide occupational qualification* reasonably necessary to the normal operation of that particular business or enterprise."

However, courts usually interpret the BFOQ exception narrowly. It is usually a defense to a disparate *treatment* case based on direct evidence of *intentional* discrimination, rather than to disparate impact (unintentional) cases. As a practical matter, employers use it mostly as a defense against charges of intentional discrimination based on age. The Age Discrimination in Employment Act (ADEA) permits disparate treatment in those instances when age is a BFOQ.[99] For example, age is a BFOQ when the Federal Aviation Administration sets a compulsory retirement age of 65 for commercial pilots.[100] Actors required for youthful or elderly roles suggest other instances when age may be a BFOQ. Employers who use the BFOQ defense admit they base their personnel decisions on age. However, they seek to justify them by showing that the decisions were reasonably necessary to normal business operations (for instance, a bus line arguing its driver age requirement is necessary for safety).[101]

Religion as a BFOQ Religion may be a BFOQ in religious organizations or societies that require employees to share their particular religion. For example, religion may be a BFOQ when hiring persons to teach in a religious school. However, remember courts construe the BFOQ defense very narrowly.

Gender as a BFOQ Gender may be a BFOQ for positions like actor, model, and restroom attendant requiring physical characteristics possessed by one sex. However, for most jobs today, it's difficult to claim that gender is a BFOQ. For example, gender is not a BFOQ for parole and probation officers.[102] It is not a BFOQ for positions just because the positions require lifting heavy objects. A Texas man filed a discrimination complaint against Hooters of America. He alleged that one of its franchisees would not hire him as a waiter because it " . . . merely wishes to exploit female sexuality as a marketing tool to attract customers and insure profitability."[103] Hooters defended its right to hire only women before reaching a confidential settlement.

National Origin as a BFOQ A person's country of national origin may be a BFOQ. For example, an employer who is running the Chinese pavilion at a fair might claim that Chinese heritage is a BFOQ for persons to deal with the public.

Business Necessity

Business necessity is a defense created by the courts. It requires showing that there is an overriding business purpose for the discriminatory practice and that the practice is therefore acceptable.

It's not easy to prove business necessity.[104] The Supreme Court made it clear that business necessity does not encompass such matters as avoiding an employer inconvenience, annoyance, or expense. For example, an employer can't generally discharge employees whose wages have been garnished merely because garnishment (requiring the employer to divert part of the person's wages to pay his or her debts) creates an inconvenience. The Second Circuit Court of Appeals held that the practice "must not only directly foster safety and efficiency" but also be essential to these goals.[105] Furthermore, "the business purpose must be sufficiently compelling to override any racial impact . . . ."[106]

However, many employers have used the business necessity defense successfully. In an early case, *Spurlock* v. *United Airlines*, a minority candidate sued United Airlines. He said that its requirements that pilot candidates have 500 flight hours and college degrees were unfairly discriminatory. The court agreed that the requirements did have an adverse impact on members of the person's minority group. But it held that in light of the cost of the training program and the huge human and economic risks in hiring unqualified candidates, the selection standards were a business necessity and were job related.[107]

In general, when a job requires a small amount of skill and training, the courts closely scrutinize any preemployment standards or criteria that discriminate against minorities. There is a correspondingly lighter burden when the job requires a high degree of skill and when the economic and human risks of hiring an unqualified applicant are great.[108]

Attempts by employers to show that their selection tests or other employment practices are *valid* are examples of the business necessity defense. Here the employer must show that the test or other practice is *job related*—in other words, that it is a valid predictor of performance on the job. Where the employer can establish such validity, the courts have generally supported using the test or other employment practice as a business necessity. In this context, validity means the degree to which the test or other employment practice is related to or predicts performance on the job; Chapter 5 explains validation.

Building Your Management Skills: Illustrative Discriminatory Employment Practices

Federal laws like Title VII usually don't expressly ban preemployment questions about an applicant's race, color, religion, sex, or national origin. In other words, "with the exception of personnel policies calling for outright discrimination against the members of some protected group," it's not the questions but their impact.[109] So, illustrative inquiries and practices like those that follow are not illegal per se. For example, it isn't illegal to ask a job candidate about her marital status (although such a question might seem discriminatory). You can ask. However, be prepared to show either that you do not discriminate or that you can defend the practice as a BFOQ or business necessity.

But in practice, there are two strong reasons to avoid asking questions such as "What is your marital status?" First, although federal law may not bar such questions, many state and local laws do. Second, the EEOC has said that it will disapprove of such practices, so just asking the questions may draw its attention. Such questions become illegal if a complainant can show you use them to screen out a greater proportion of his or her protected group's applicants, and you can't prove the practice is required as a business necessity or BFOQ.

As a rule, therefore, it's not just foolish but quite risky to ask questions like these. Let us look more closely at some examples of the potentially discriminatory practices the manager will want to avoid.[110]

Recruitment

Word of Mouth You cannot rely on word-of-mouth dissemination of information about job opportunities when your workforce is all (or substantially all) white or all members of some other class such as all female, all Hispanic, and so on. Doing so might reduce the likelihood that others will become aware of the jobs and thus apply for them.

Misleading Information It is unlawful to give false or misleading information to members of any group or to fail to refuse to advise them of work opportunities and the procedures for obtaining them.

Help Wanted Ads "Help wanted—male" and "Help wanted—female" advertising classifieds are violations of laws forbidding sex discrimination in employment unless sex is a BFOQ for the job advertised.[111] Similarly, you cannot advertise for a "young" man or woman.

Selection Standards

Educational Requirements An educational requirement may be held illegal when (1) it can be shown that minority groups are less likely to possess the educational qualifications (such as a high school diploma), and (2) such qualifications are also not required to perform the job.

Tests According to former Chief Justice Burger:

> Nothing in the [Title VII] act precludes the use of testing or measuring procedures; obviously they are useful. What Congress has forbidden is giving these devices and mechanisms controlling force unless they are demonstrating a *reasonable measure of job performance.*

> Thus, tests that disproportionately screen out minorities or women *and are not job related* are deemed unlawful by the courts.

Preference to Relatives You cannot give preference to relatives of your current employees with respect to employment opportunities if your current employees are substantially nonminority.

Height, Weight, and Physical Characteristics Maximum weight rules for employees don't usually trigger adverse legal rulings. "Few applicants or employees will be able to demonstrate an actual weight-based disability" (in other words, they are 100% above their ideal weight or there is a physiological cause for their disability).

However, managers should be vigilant against stigmatizing obese people.[112] First, you may adversely impact minority groups, some of whom have a higher incidence of obesity.[113] And, studies leave little doubt that obese individuals are less likely to be hired, and more likely to receive poor customer service as customers.[114]

Health Questions Under the ADA, "Employers are generally prohibited from asking questions about applicants' medical history or requiring preemployment physical examinations." However, such questions and exams can be used once the job offer has been extended to determine that the applicant can safely perform the job.[115]

Arrest Records Unless the job requires security clearance, do not ask an applicant whether he or she has been arrested or spent time in jail, or use an arrest record to disqualify a person automatically. Due to racial and ethnic disparities in arrest and prison rates, both the EEOC and the OFCCP have guidance discouraging employers from using blanket exclusions against individuals with criminal records.[116]

Application Forms Employment applications generally shouldn't contain questions pertaining, for instance, to applicants' disabilities, workers' compensation history, age, arrest record, marital status, or U.S. citizenship. Instead, collect personal information required for legitimate reasons (such as whom to contact in case of emergency) after the person has been hired.[117]

Sample Discriminatory Promotion, Transfer, and Layoff Procedures

Fair employment laws protect not just job applicants but also current employees.[118] Therefore, any employment practices regarding pay, promotion, termination, discipline, or benefits that (1) are applied differently to different classes of persons, (2) have the effect of adversely affecting members of a protected group, and (3) cannot be shown to be required as a BFOQ or business necessity may be held to be illegally discriminatory. For example:

Uniforms When it comes to discriminatory uniforms and/or suggestive attire, courts frequently side with employees. Thus requiring female employees (such as waitresses) to wear sexually suggestive attire as a condition of employment has been ruled as violating Title VII in many cases.[119]

Tattoos and Body Piercings About 38% of millennials in one survey had tattoos, and about 23% had body piercings. One case involved a waiter with religious tattoos on his wrists at a Red Robin Gourmet Burgers restaurant. The company insisted he cover his tattoos at work; he refused. Red Robin subsequently settled a lawsuit after he claimed that covering the tattoos would be a sin based on his religion.[120]

Management Malpractice and Retaliation The human resource manager helps the company navigate problems like these, but the supervisor usually triggers the problem. Even telling a female candidate you'd be concerned about her safety on the job after dark might trigger a claim. The supervisor—not just the employer—may suffer legal consequences. *Management malpractice,* and *retaliation* are two big potential problems.

Management malpractice is aberrant conduct on the part of the manager that has serious consequences for the employee's personal or physical well-being, or which "exceeds all bounds usually tolerated by society."[121] In one outrageous example, the employer demoted a manager to janitor and took other steps to humiliate him. The jury subsequently awarded the former manager $3.4 million. Supervisors who commit management malpractice may be personally liable for paying some of the judgment.

Second, retaliation is illegal under equal rights laws. The EEOC says, "[R]etaliation occurs when employers treat applicants, employees or former employees, or people closely associated with these individuals, less favorably for: reporting discrimination; participating in a discrimination investigation or lawsuit (for example, serving as a witness), or; opposing discrimination (for example, threatening to file a charge or complaint of discrimination)."[122] Retaliation charges are the most common charges filed with the EEOC.[123]

The EEOC Enforcement Process

If someone does file a charge, the EEOC will get involved. There are several steps in the EEOC enforcement process.

Processing a Discrimination Charge

Filing of Claim The EEOC enforcement process begins with someone filing a charge (see the EEOC's charge handling flowchart at www.eeoc.gov/employees/upload/charge_status_flow_chart.pdf).[124] Under CRA 1991, the discrimination claim must be filed within 300 days (when there is a similar state law) or 180 days (no similar state law) after the alleged incident took place (two years for the Equal Pay Act).[125] The filing must be in writing and under oath, by (or on behalf of) either the aggrieved person or by a member of the EEOC who has reasonable cause to believe that a violation occurred. In practice the EEOC typically defers someone's charge to the relevant state or local regulatory agency; if the latter waives jurisdiction or cannot obtain a satisfactory solution to the charge, they refer it back to the EEOC. The EEOC recently received 91,503 private-sector discrimination charges in one fiscal year.[126]

EEOC Investigation After a charge is filed (or the state or local deferral period ends), the EEOC has 10 days to serve notice of the charge on the employer. Attorneys advise against submitting lengthy statements in response to receiving a charge. Instead, provide a concise explanation describing why the actions were lawful.[127] The EEOC next investigates the charge to determine whether there is reasonable cause to believe it is true; it is expected to make this determination within 120 days. EEOC attorneys urge cooperating with the EEOC during this investigation.[128]

If no reasonable cause is found, the EEOC must dismiss the charge, in which case the person who filed the charge has 90 days to file a suit on his or her own behalf. If reasonable cause for the charge is found, the EEOC must attempt to conciliate. If this conciliation is not satisfactory, the EEOC may bring a civil suit or issue a notice of right to sue to the person who filed the charge. Figure 2.4 summarizes important questions to ask after receiving notice from the EEOC of a bias complaint. Some employers obtain employment practices liability insurance (EPLI) against discrimination claims.[129]

Voluntary Mediation

The EEOC refers about 10% of its charges to a voluntary mediation mechanism. This is "an informal process in which a neutral third party assists the opposing parties to reach a voluntary, negotiated resolution of a charge of discrimination."[130] If the parties don't reach agreement (or a party rejects participation), the EEOC processes the charge through its usual mechanisms.[131]

Faced with an offer to mediate, the employer has three options: Agree to mediate the charge; make a settlement offer without mediation; or prepare a "position statement" for the EEOC. If the employer does not mediate or make an offer, the position statement is required. It should include a forceful defense. Include information relating to the company's business and the charging party's position; a description of any rules or policies and procedures that are applicable; and the chronology of the offense that led to the adverse action.[132]

Mandatory Arbitration of Discrimination Claims

Many employers, to avoid EEO litigation, require applicants and employees to agree to arbitrate such claims. The U.S. Supreme Court's decisions (in *Gilmer* v. *Interstate/Johnson Lane Corp*. and similar cases) make it clear that "employment discrimination plaintiffs [employees] may be compelled to arbitrate their claims under some circumstances."[133] Given this, employers "may wish to consider

Figure 2.4

Questions to Ask When Receiving Notice EEOC Filed a Bias Claim

Sources: Kenneth Sovereign, *Personnel Law* (Upper Saddle River, NJ: Prentice Hall, 1999), pp. 36–37; "EEOC Investigations—What an Employer Should Know," www.eeoc.gov/employers/investigations.html, accessed May 6, 2007; and Equal Employment Opportunity Commission, "What You Can Expect After a Charge is Filed," www.eeoc.gov/employers/process.cfm, accessed January 25, 2017.

1. Exactly what is the charge, and is your company covered by the relevant statutes?
2. Did the employee file the charge on time, and was it processed timely by EEOC?
3. What protected group does employee belong to?
4. Is the claim disparate impact or disparate treatment?
5. Are there obvious bases on which you can challenge and/or rebut the claim? For example, would you have taken the action if the person was not in a protected group?
6. For a sexual harassment claim, are there offensive comments, calendars, posters, and so on, on display in the company?
7. In considering defending against this claim, how effective will the supervisors who took the allegedly discriminatory actions be as witnesses? Get opinion from legal counsel regarding chances of prevailing.

inserting a mandatory arbitration clause (traditionally called an alternative dispute resolution [ADR] program) in their employment applications or handbooks."[134] To protect such a process against appeal, it should include steps to protect against arbitrator bias, allow the arbitrator to offer a claimant broad relief (including reinstatement), and allow for a reasonable amount of prehearing fact finding.

ADR plans are popular, although the EEOC generally prefers mediation for handling bias claims.[135] U.S. federal agencies themselves must have ADR programs.[136]

Figure 2.5 sums up guidelines employers should follow in addressing EEOC charges.

Figure 2.5

Management Guidelines for Addressing EEOC Claims

Sources: "Tips for Employers on Dealing with EEOC Investigations," *BNA Fair Employment Practices*, October 31, 1996, p. 130; "Conducting Effective Investigations of Employee Bias Complaints," *BNA Fair Employment Practices*, July 13, 1995, p. 81; *Commerce Clearing House, Ideas and Trends*, January 23, 1987, pp. 14–15; http://eeoc.gov/employers/investigations.html, accessed October 4, 2009; www.eeoc.gov/employers/process.cfm, accessed January 25, 2017.

During the EEOC Investigation:

Conduct your own investigation to get the facts.

Ensure the EEOC's file contains information *demonstrating lack of merit* of the charge.

Limit the information supplied to those issues raised in the charge itself.

Get as much information as possible about the *charging party's claim.*

Meet with the employee who made the complaint to clarify all the relevant issues. (For example, what happened? Who was involved?)

Remember that *the EEOC can only ask (not compel) employers* to submit documents and ask for testimony of witnesses under oath.

Give the EEOC a *position statement.* It should contain words to the effect that "the company has a policy against discrimination and would not discriminate in the manner charged in the complaint." Support this with documentation.

During the Fact-Finding Conference:

Because the only official record is the notes the EEOC investigator takes, *keep your own records.*

Bring an *attorney.*

Make sure you are *fully informed* of the charges and facts of the case.

Before appearing, make sure *witnesses (especially supervisors) are aware* of the legal significance of the facts they will present.

During the EEOC Determination and Attempted Conciliation:

If there is a finding of cause, *review it carefully,* and point out inaccuracies in writing to the EEOC.

Use this letter to try again to convince the parties that the charge is *without merit.*

Conciliate prudently. If you have properly investigated the case, there may be no real advantage in settling at this stage.

Remember: It is likely that *no suit will be filed* by the EEOC.

LEARNING OBJECTIVE 5
List five strategies for successfully increasing diversity of the workforce.

diversity
Having a workforce comprising two or more groups of employees with various racial, ethnic, gender, cultural, national origin, handicap, age, and religious backgrounds.

gender-role stereotypes
The tendency to associate women with certain (frequently nonmanagerial) jobs.

Diversity Management and Affirmative Action

Diversity means being diverse or varied, and at work means having a workforce comprised of two or more groups of employees with various racial, ethnic, gender, cultural, national origin, handicap, age, and religious backgrounds.[137] Today, because many American workplaces are already diverse, the focus increasingly is on managing diversity at work.[138]

Diversity's Barriers and Benefits

The difficulty is that diversity can trigger problems that undermine collegiality and cooperation. These include the following:

- *Stereotyping* means someone ascribes specific behavioral traits to individuals based on the person's apparent membership in a group, such as, "older people can't work hard."[139]

  Stereotyping probably helps explain the continuing (relative) dearth of females in top management jobs. Cheryl Sandberg, Facebook's Chief Operating Officer, argues that many people hold unconscious assumptions (stereotypes) about women and men; one is that men are expected to be assertive while women should be collaborative. So, when a woman does push for more for herself, she's viewed as "pushy" or "bossy," whereas a man is simply viewed as doing his job.[140] Put another way, women confront **gender-role stereotypes**, the tendency to associate women with certain (frequently nonmanagerial) jobs.[141] The problem doesn't seem to have improved much recently. About the same percentage of millennial women (23%) as nonmillennial women (26%) think being a woman held them back at work; only 4% of millennial men (and 7% of nonmillennial men) believe the same.[142]

- *Prejudice* is a bias toward prejudging someone based on that person's traits, as in "we won't hire him because he's old." Some people's biases are subconscious. To test this, for example, a manager might ask, "Do I typically hire the same type of person?" and "To whom do I generally assign the most challenging jobs?"

With strong top-management support, IBM created several minority task forces focusing on groups such as women and Native Americans.
Source: JOANNE HO-YOUNG LEE/Newscom.

discrimination
Taking specific actions toward or against the person based on the person's group.

- *Discrimination* is prejudice in action. **Discrimination** means taking specific actions toward or against the person based on the person's group.[143] In the United States, it is generally illegal to discriminate at work based on a person's age, race, color, gender, disability, or country of national origin. But in practice, it does exist. For example, a "glass ceiling," enforced by an "old boys' network" (friendships built in places like golf clubs), effectively prevents some women from reaching top management. Similarly, insofar as it reflects national origin or religious discrimination, discrimination against Muslim employees is prohibited under Title VII.[144]
- *Tokenism* occurs when a company appoints a small group of women or minorities to high-profile positions, rather than more aggressively seeking full representation for that group.[145]
- *Ethnocentrism* is the tendency to view members of other social groups less favorably than one's own. For example, in one study, managers attributed the performance of some minorities less to their abilities and more to help they received from others. The same managers attributed the performance of *non*minorities to their own abilities.[146]

Managing Diversity

Because diversity is a fact of life today, making diversity "work" for the company requires *managing diversity*—in other words, taking steps to maximize diversity's potential advantages by heading off problems like prejudice and bias.[147] The main aim here is usually to make employees more sensitive to and better able to adapt to cultural differences.

The problem is that many "diversity" programs aren't just ineffective but may backfire. Some programs fail, for instance, because even positively-inclined employees may object to being "forced" to participate in a mandatory diversity training program. For example, in one study, a mandatory-attendance diversity training program for managers actually seemed to lead to less diversity (among Asian Americans and black women).[148] Other initiatives give employers a false sense of security. One study found that diversity initiatives such as establishing diversity committees and appointing chief diversity officers lulled company decision makers into thinking their workplace was fair and inclusive when it was not.[149] Perhaps most obviously, many employees welcome employers' efforts to make the workplace more inclusive, but others will resist.[150]

Some firms like McDonald's Corp. therefore don't call their diversity programs a "program" at all; McDonald's says diversity management should be an ongoing effort. For example, employee attendance at McDonald's Intercultural Learning Lab facilitates dialogue and communications among employees.[151]

Top-Down Diversity Management Programs In general, though, effective diversity management efforts start at the top, and (according to a diversity management expert) five activities characterize them:

Provide strong leadership. Companies with exemplary reputations in managing diversity typically have CEOs who champion diversity. For example, they role model the behaviors required. One study concluded that the top managers who excelled at creating inclusive organizations were those who were personally passionate about encouraging diversity.[152]

Assess the situation. Common tools for measuring a company's diversity include equal employment hiring and retention metrics, employee attitude surveys, management and employee evaluations, and focus groups.[153]

Provide diversity training and education. Diversity management usually requires diversity training. This aims to sensitize all employees to value cultural differences, to build self-esteem, and to create a more hospitable work environment.

Change culture and management systems. Reinforce the desired values and behaviors. For example, change the performance appraisal process by appraising supervisors based partly on their success in reducing intergroup conflicts.

Evaluate the diversity management program. For example, use attitude surveys to monitor employees' attitudes toward diversity.

Diversity through Engagement As a rule, it seems best to design the diversity effort to elicit the active and willing participation of all participants (such as through voluntary attendance). One study found that such programs did not seem to trigger participants' defenses and had more positive results on diversity. Other effective diversity efforts included college recruitment targeting women, mentoring programs, and creating diversity task forces.[154]

For example, at software company SAP, the Chief Learning Officer discovered that although participants rated highly SAP's diversity training program, the program itself seemed to produce only limited results (for instance, in terms of women in leadership positions). She therefore replaced this program with a year-long leadership development program she called the "Leadership Excellence Acceleration Program" (LEAP). Every year, LEAP gathers together high-performing female employees. For a year they then engage in exercises such as action assignments and listening to speakers.[155] SAP also offers female employees a global business network of 8,000 female employees, and SAP's board recently committed to boosting the leadership positions held by SAP women to 25% (from 23%).[156] SAP's efforts seem to be successful, in terms of its female employees moving into management positions.[157]

Equal Employment Opportunity versus Affirmative Action

Equal employment opportunity aims to ensure that anyone, regardless of race, color, disability, sex, religion, national origin, or age, has an equal chance for a job based on his or her qualifications. **Affirmative action** goes beyond equal employment opportunity. It requires that employers make an extra effort to hire and promote those in a protected group. Affirmative action thus requires taking actions to eliminate the present effects of past discrimination. For example:

- Issue a written policy indicating that the employer is an equal employment opportunity employer, committed to affirmative action.
- Appoint a top official to direct the program.
- Survey present minority and female employment to determine where affirmative action is desirable.[158]
- Develop goals and timetables.
- Develop and implement specific recruitment, selection, training, and promotion programs to achieve these goals.
- Establish internal audit and reporting systems to evaluate these programs' progress.

Reverse Discrimination

Reverse discrimination means discriminating against *non*minority applicants and employees. Many court cases addressed these issues, but until recently, few consistent guidelines emerged.

In one of the first such cases, *Bakke* v. *Regents of the University of California* (1978), the University of California at Davis Medical School denied admission to white student Allen Bakke, allegedly because of the school's affirmative action quota system, which required that a specific number of openings go to minority applicants. In a 5-to-4 vote, the U.S. Supreme Court struck down the policy that made race the only factor in considering applications for a certain number of class openings and thus allowed Bakke's admission.

Bakke was followed by many other cases. In 2009, the U.S. Supreme Court ruled in an important reverse discrimination suit brought by Connecticut firefighters. In *Ricci* v. *DeStefano*, 19 white firefighters and one Hispanic firefighter said the city of New Haven should have promoted them based on their successful test scores. The city argued that certifying the tests would have left them vulnerable to lawsuits from minorities for violating Title VII.[159] The Court ruled in favor of the (predominantly white) plaintiffs. In New Haven's desire to avoid making promotions that might appear to adversely impact minorities, Justice Kennedy wrote that "The city rejected the test results solely because the higher scoring candidates were white." The consensus of observers was that the decision would make it much harder for employers to ignore the results obtained by valid tests, even if the results disproportionately impact minorities.[160] In 2017 an applicant sued Harvard University, charging discrimination against Asians. The bottom line seems to be that employers should bolster the external recruitment and internal development of better-qualified minority and female employees, "while basing employment decisions on legitimate criteria."[161]

Review

MyLab Management

If your instructor is using MyLab Management, go to **www.pearson.com/mylab/ management** to complete the problems marked with this icon ⭐.

SUMMARY

1. Legislation barring employment discrimination includes Title VII of the 1964 Civil Rights Act (as amended), which bars discrimination because of race, color, religion, sex, or national origin; various executive orders; federal guidelines (covering procedures for validating employee selection tools, etc.); the Equal Pay Act of 1963; the Age Discrimination in Employment Act of 1967, and the ADA. In addition, various Court decisions (such as *Griggs* v. *Duke Power Company*) and state and local laws bar various aspects of discrimination. The EEOC was created by Title VII of the Civil Rights Act. The Civil Rights Act of 1991 had the effect of revising several Supreme Court equal employment decisions and "rolling back the clock."

2. A person who believes he or she has been discriminated against by a personnel procedure must prove either that he or she was subjected to unlawful disparate treatment (intentional discrimination) or disparate impact (unintentional discrimination) on members of his or her protected class. There are two basic defenses: the bona fide occupational qualification (BFOQ) defense and the business necessity defense.

3. A manager should avoid various specific discriminatory human resource management practices. For example, in *recruitment*, an employer usually should not rely on word-of-mouth advertising or give false or misleading information to minority group members. In *selection*, an employer should avoid using any educational or other requirements where (1) it can be shown that minority-group members are less likely to possess the qualification and (2) such requirement is also not job related.

4. In practice, a discrimination charge to the EEOC is often first referred to a local agency. When the EEOC finds reasonable cause to believe that discrimination occurred, it may suggest the parties try to work out a conciliation. EEOC investigators can only make recommendations.

5. Making diversity "work" for the company requires *managing diversity*—in other words, maximizing diversity's potential advantages while minimizing the potential barriers—such as prejudices and bias. The main aim is to make employees more sensitive to and better able to adapt to individual cultural differences.

Key Terms

Equal Pay Act of 1963   28
Title VII of the 1964 Civil Rights Act   29
Equal Employment Opportunity Commission
  (EEOC)   29
Office of Federal Contract Compliance Programs
  (OFCCP)   29
Age Discrimination in Employment Act (ADEA) of
  1967   29
Vocational Rehabilitation Act of 1973   30
Pregnancy Discrimination Act (PDA)   30
Griggs v. *Duke Power Company*   30
protected class   31
Civil Rights Act of 1991 (CRA 1991)   31

disparate impact   31
disparate treatment   31
Americans with Disabilities Act (ADA)   32
sexual harassment   36
adverse impact   41
bona fide occupational qualification (BFOQ)   44
business necessity   45
diversity   50
discrimination   51
gender-role stereotypes   51
affirmative action   52
reverse discrimination   52

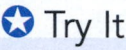 Try It

How would you do applying the concepts and skills you learned in this chapter? If your professor has chosen to assign this, go to **www.pearson.com/mylab/management** and complete the HR and diversity simulation to find out.

Discussion Questions

2-1. Present a summary of what employers can and cannot legally do with respect to recruitment, selection, and promotion and layoff practices.
2-2. Explain the Equal Employment Opportunity Commission enforcement process.
2-3. List five strategies for successfully increasing diversity of the workforce.
2-4. What is Title VII? What does it state?

2-5. What important precedents were set by the *Griggs* v. *Duke Power Company* case? The *Albemarle* v. *Moody* case?
2-6. What is adverse impact? How can it be proven?
2-7. Explain the defenses and exceptions to discriminatory practice allegations.
2-8. What is the difference between affirmative action and equal employment opportunity?

Individual and Group Activities

2-9. Working individually or in groups, respond to the following three scenarios based on what you learned in this chapter. Under what conditions (if any) do you think the following constitute sexual harassment? (a) A female manager fires a male employee because he refuses her requests for sexual favors. (b) A male manager refers to female employees as "sweetie" or "baby." (c) A female employee overhears two male employees exchanging sexually oriented jokes.
2-10. Working individually or in groups, discuss how you would set up an affirmative action program.

2-11. Working individually or in groups, use online sources to compile examples of actual EEOC claims that have used each of the methods we discussed (such as the standard deviation rule) for showing adverse impact.
2-12. Working individually or in groups, write a paper entitled "What the Manager Should Know about How the EEOC Handles a Person's Discrimination Charge."
2-13. Assume you are the manager of a small restaurant. You are responsible for hiring employees, supervising them, and recommending them for promotion. Working individually or in groups, compile a list of potentially discriminatory management practices you should avoid.

2-14. For this activity, you will need the documents titled (1) "HRCI PHR® and SPHR® Certification Body of Knowledge," and (2) "About the Society for Human Resource Management (SHRM) Body of Competency & Knowledge® Model and Certification Exams." Your instructor can obtain these two documents from the Pearson Instructor Resource Center and pass them on to you. These two documents list the knowledge someone studying for the HRCI or SHRM certification exam needs to have in each area of human resource management (such as in Strategic Management, and Workforce Planning). In groups of several students, do four things: (1) review the HRCI and/or SHRM documents; (2) identify the material in this chapter that relates to HRCI's or SHRM's required knowledge lists; (3) write four multiple-choice exam questions on this material that you believe would be suitable for inclusion in the HRCI exam and/or the SHRM exam; and, (4) if time permits, have someone from your team post your team's questions in front of the class, so that students in all teams can answer the exam questions created by the other teams.

MyLab Management

If your instructor is using MyLab Management, go **www.pearson.com/mylab/ management** for Auto-graded writing questions as well as the following Assisted-graded writing questions:

2-15. Summarize the basic equal employment opportunity laws regarding age, race, sex, national origin, religion, and handicap discrimination.

2-16. Explain the basic defenses against discrimination allegations.

APPLICATION EXERCISES

HR IN ACTION CASE INCIDENT 1

An Accusation of Sexual Harassment in Pro Sports

The jury in a sexual harassment suit brought by a former high-ranking New York Knicks basketball team executive awarded her over $11 million in punitive damages. They did so after hearing testimony during what the *New York Times* called a "sordid four-week trial." Officials of the Madison Square Garden (which owns the Knicks) said they would appeal the verdict. However, even if they were to win on appeal (which one University of Richmond Law School professor said was unlikely), the case still exposed the organization and its managers to a great deal of unfavorable publicity.

The federal suit pitted Anucha Browne Sanders, the Knicks' senior vice president of marketing and business operations (and former Northwestern University basketball star), against the team's owner, Madison Square Garden, and its president, Isiah Thomas. The suit charged them with sex discrimination and retaliation. Ms. Browne Sanders accused Mr. Thomas of verbally abusing and sexually harassing her over a two-year period, and says the Garden fired her about a month after she complained to top management about the harassment. "My pleas and complaints about Mr. Thomas's illegal and offensive actions fell on deaf ears," she said. At the trial, the Garden cited numerous explanations for the dismissal, saying she had "failed to fulfill professional responsibilities." At a news conference, Browne Sanders said that Thomas "refused to stop his demeaning and repulsive behavior and the Garden refused to intercede." For his part, Mr. Thomas vigorously insisted he was innocent, and said, "I will not allow her or anybody, man or woman, to use me as a pawn for their financial gain." According to one report of the trial, her claims of harassment and verbal abuse had little corroboration from witnesses, but neither did the Garden's claims that her performance had been subpar. After the jury decision came in favor of the plaintiff, Browne Sanders's lawyers said, "This [decision] confirms what we've been saying all along, that [Browne Sanders] was sexually abused and fired for complaining about it." The Garden's statement said, in part, that "We look forward to presenting our arguments to an appeals court and believe they will agree that no sexual harassment took place."

Questions

2-17. Do you think Ms. Browne Sanders had the basis for a sexual harassment suit? Why or why not?

2-18. From what you know of this case, do you think the jury arrived at the correct decision? If not, why not? If so, why?

2-19. Based on the few facts that you have, what steps, if any, could Garden management have taken to protect themselves from liability in this matter?

2-20. Aside from the appeal, what would you do now if you were the Garden's top management?

2-21. "The allegations against the Madison Square Garden in this case raise ethical questions with regard to the employer's actions." Explain whether you agree or disagree with this statement, and why.

Sources: "Jury Awards $11.6 Million to Former Executive of Pro Basketball Team in Harassment Case," *BNA Bulletin to Management,* October 9, 2007, p. 323; Richard Sandomir, "Jury Finds Knicks and Coach Harassed a Former Executive," *New York Times,* www.nytimes.com/2007/10/03/sports/basketball/03garden.html?em&ex=1191556800&en=41d47437f805290d&ei=5087%0A, accessed November 13, 2007; "Thomas Defiant in Face of Harassment Claims," www.espn.com, accessed November 13, 2007.

HR IN ACTION CASE INCIDENT 2
Carter Cleaning Company

A Question of Discrimination

One of the first problems Jennifer faced at her father's Carter Cleaning Centers concerned the inadequacies of the firm's current HR management practices and procedures.

One problem that particularly concerned her was the lack of attention to equal employment matters. Virtually all hiring was handled independently by each store manager, and the managers themselves had received no training regarding such fundamental matters as the types of questions that should not be asked of job applicants. It was therefore not unusual—in fact, it was routine—for female applicants to be asked questions such as, "Who's going to take care of your children while you are at work?" and for minority applicants to be asked questions about arrest records and credit histories. Nonminority applicants—three store managers were white males and three were white females, by the way—were not asked these questions, as Jennifer discerned from her interviews with the managers. Based on discussions with her father, Jennifer deduced that part of the reason for the laid-back attitude toward equal employment stemmed from (1) her father's lack of sophistication regarding the legal requirements and (2) the fact that, as Jack Carter put it, "Virtually all our workers are women or minority members anyway, so no one can really come in here and accuse us of being discriminatory, can they?"

Jennifer decided to mull that question over, but before she could, she was faced with two serious equal rights

problems. Two women in one of her stores privately confided to her that their manager was making unwelcome sexual advances toward them, and one claimed he had threatened to fire her unless she "socialized" with him after hours. And during a fact-finding trip to another store, an older man—he was 73 years old—complained of the fact that although he had almost 50 years of experience in the business, he was being paid less than people half his age who were doing the very same job. Jennifer's review of the stores resulted in the following questions.

Questions

2-22. Is it true, as Jack Carter claims, that "we can't be accused of being discriminatory because we hire mostly women and minorities anyway"?

2-23. How should Jennifer and her company address the sexual harassment charges and problems?

2-24. How should she and her company address the possible problems of age discrimination?

2-25. Given the fact that each of its stores has only a handful of employees, is her company in fact covered by equal rights legislation?

2-26. And finally, aside from the specific problems, what other human resource management matters (application forms, training, and so on) have to be reviewed given the need to bring them into compliance with equal rights laws?

Experiential Exercise

The Interplay of Ethics and Equal Employment

If one accepts the proposition that equal employment is at least partly an ethical matter, then we should expect that real employers recognize and emphasize that fact, for instance, on their websites. Some do. For example, the Duke Energy Company (which, when

known as Duke Power many years ago, lost one of the first and most famous equal employment cases) posted the following on its website:

Equal Employment Opportunity: Duke Energy's Code of Business Ethics: Duke Energy seeks and values diversity. The dignity of each person is respected, and everyone's contributions are recognized. We expect Duke Energy employees to act with mutual respect and cooperation toward one another. We do not tolerate discrimination in the workplace.

We comply with laws concerning discrimination and equal opportunity that specifically prohibit discrimination on the basis of certain differences. We will recruit, select, train and compensate based on merit, experience and other work-related criteria.

Our Responsibilities: Duke Energy employees are expected to treat others with respect on the job and comply with equal employment opportunity laws, including those related to discrimination and harassment.

Duke Energy employees must not:

- Use any differences protected by law as a factor in hiring, firing, or promotion decisions.
- Use any differences protected by law when determining terms or conditions of employment, such as work assignments, employee development opportunities, vacation, or overtime.
- Retaliate against a person who makes a complaint of discrimination in good faith, reports suspected unethical conduct, violations of laws, regulations, or company policies, or participates in an investigation.

Source: www.duke-energy.com/corporate-governance/code-of-business-ethics/equal-employment-opportunity.asp, accessed May 28, 2010. © Duke Energy Corporation. All Rights Reserved.

Purpose: Ethical decision making is an important HR-related personal competency. The purpose of this exercise is to increase your understanding of how ethics and equal employment are interrelated.

Required Understanding: Be thoroughly familiar with the material presented in this chapter.

How to Set Up the Exercise/Instructions:

2-27. Divide the class into groups of several students.
2-28. Each group should use the Internet to identify and access at least five companies that emphasize how ethics and equal employment are interrelated.
2-29. Next, each group should develop answers to the following questions:
   a. Based on your Internet research, how much importance do employers seem to place on emphasizing the ethical aspects of equal employment?
   b. What seem to be the main themes these employers emphasize with respect to ethics and equal employment?
   c. Given what you've learned, explain how you would emphasize the ethical aspects of equal employment if you were creating an equal employment training program for new supervisors.

3

Human Resource Strategy and Performance

OVERVIEW:
In this chapter, we will cover . . .

- The Strategic Management Process
- Strategic Human Resource Management
- HR Metrics and Benchmarking
- Building High-Performance Work Systems
- Employee Engagement and Performance
- Employee Engagement Guide For Managers: How Kia Motors (UK) Improved Performance with an HR Strategy Aimed at Boosting Employee Engagement

MyLab Management

⭐ Improve Your Grade!
When you see this icon, visit **www.pearson.com/mylab/management** for activities that are applied, personalized, and offer immediate feedback.

LEARNING OBJECTIVES

When you finish studying this chapter, you should be able to:

1. Explain, with examples, each of the steps in the strategic management process.

2. Define strategic human resource management, and give an example of strategic human resource management in practice.

3. Explain, with examples, why metrics are important for managing human resources.

4. Answer the question "What are high-performance work systems?" and give examples of how they differ from non-high-performance ones.

5. Answer the question (with examples) "Why is employee engagement important?"

6. Describe how you would execute a program to improve employee engagement.

⭐ Learn It

If your professor has chosen to assign this, go to **www.pearson.com/mylab/management** to see what you should particularly focus on and to take the Chapter 3 Warm Up.

INTRODUCTION

It was with great optimism that Angelo opened his first Angelo's Pizza Store, but the optimism didn't last long. Customers flooded the store for several days after he opened, drawn, no doubt, by the advertised claim that "We offer only the best, at reasonable prices." But after two weeks, his "meals served" had dropped to the point where he could barely pay the rent. Customers on sites like Yelp were dinging him with comments such as "My waiter acted like he was doing me a favor taking my order," and "If you want to be aggravated while you eat, this is the place for you." Angelo suspected he had a "personnel" problem but wasn't sure what to do. In brief, he felt that his employees just didn't care.

Source: Paul Vasarhelyi/123RF.

LEARNING OBJECTIVE 1
Explain, with examples, each of the steps in the strategic management process.

strategic plan
The company's plan for how it will match its internal strengths and weaknesses with its external opportunities and threats to maintain a competitive position.

The Strategic Management Process

Angelo, like any employer, needs human resource policies that make sense in terms of supporting the company's strategic plan—which he sums up as "to offer only the best, at reasonable prices." As we'll see in this chapter, a **strategic plan** is "the company's overall plan for how it will match its internal strengths and weaknesses with its external opportunities and threats to maintain a competitive position." Based on this plan, the human resource manager formulates human resource policies and practices that aim to produce the employee competencies and skills the company needs to achieve its strategic goals. The accompanying HR Practices around the Globe feature shows how one company did this.

◼ HR Practices Around the Globe

The Shanghai Portman's New Human Resource Management Strategy

When the Ritz-Carlton Company took over managing the Portman Hotel in Shanghai, China, the hotel's new management reviewed the Portman's strengths and weaknesses, and its fast-improving local competitors. They decided that to compete, they had to improve the hotel's level of service. Achieving that in turn meant formulating new human resource management policies, practices, and plans for hiring, training, and rewarding hotel employees. Their aim was to use these new HR practices to produce the employee skills and behaviors that the Portman would need to achieve its strategy of excelling in service. Their HR strategy involved taking these steps:

- *Strategically*, they set the goal of making the Shanghai Portman outstanding by offering superior customer service.
- To achieve this, Shanghai Portman employees would have to exhibit new *skills* and *behaviors*, for instance, in terms of how they treated and responded to guests.
- To produce these employee skills and behaviors, management formulated new human resource management plans, policies, and procedures. For example, they introduced the Ritz-Carlton Company's *human resource system* to the Portman: "Our selection [now] focuses on talent and personal values because these are things that can't be taught . . . it's about caring for and respecting others."[1]

Management's efforts paid off. Their new human resource policies, practices, and plans helped to produce the employee behaviors required to improve the Portman's level of service, thus attracting new guests. Travel publications were soon calling it the "best employer in Asia," and "best business hotel in China." Profits soared, in no small part due to effective strategic human resource management.

⭐ Talk About It – 1

If your professor has chosen to assign this, go to **www.pearson.com/mylab/management** to discuss the following question. Asian culture is different from that in the United States. For example, team incentives tend to be more attractive to people in Asia than are individual incentives. How do you think these cultural differences would have affected how the hotel's new management selected, trained, appraised, and compensated Portman employees?

At the Shanghai Portman Hotel, management's new human resource plans and practices produced the employee behaviors required to improve the Portman's level of service, thus attracting new guests and improving the hotel's profitability.

Source: FEATURECHINA/XIANG SHEREN/Newscom.

Whether it's a pizza store or a fine hotel, managers can't really design their human resource policies and practices without understanding the role these policies and practices are to play in achieving their companies' strategic goals. This chapter looks at how managers design strategic and human resource policies, practices, and plans, and how they evaluate the results of those plans. Because strategic planning is part of planning, we'll start with an overview of the basic management planning process.

The Basic Management Planning Process

Management planning involves five steps: setting *goals*, making basic planning *forecasts*, reviewing alternative *courses of action*, *evaluating* which options are best, and then choosing and *implementing* your plan. A *plan* is a device that shows the course of action for getting from where you are to the goal. Planning is therefore always "goal directed" (such as, "Double sales revenue to $16 million in fiscal year 2019").

In companies, managers traditionally view the goals from the top of the firm down to front-line employees as a chain or *hierarchy of goals*. Figure 3.1 illustrates this. At the top, the president sets long-term or "strategic" goals (such as "double sales revenue to $16 million in fiscal year 2019"). His or her vice presidents then set goals that flow from and make sense in terms of accomplishing the president's goal. Then the vice presidents' subordinates set their own goals, and so on down the chain of command.[2]

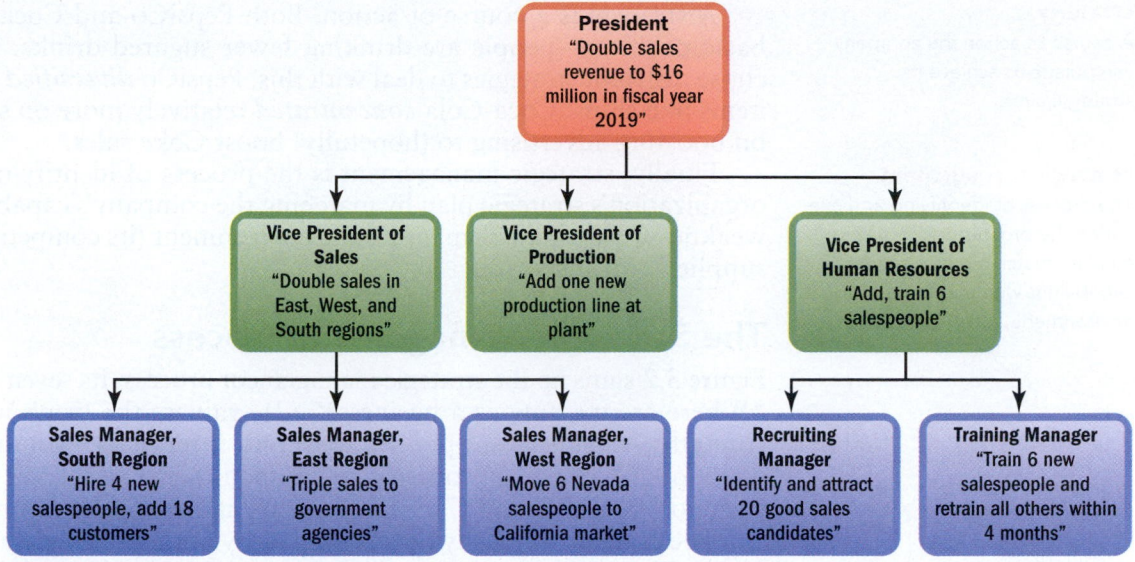

Figure 3.1

Sample Hierarchy of Goals Diagram for a Company

Policies and Procedures Policies and procedures provide the day-to-day guidance employees need to do their jobs in a manner that is consistent with the company's plans and goals. *Policies* set broad guidelines delineating how employees should proceed. For example, "It is the policy of this company to comply with all laws, regulations, and principles of ethical conduct. Each employee must observe this policy." *Procedures* spell out what to do if a specific situation arises. For example,

> Any employee who has reason to believe this policy has been violated must report this belief to the employee's immediate supervisor. If that is not practical, the employee should file a written report with the Director of Human Resources.[3]

Employers write their own policies and procedures, or adapt ones from existing sources (or both). For example, most employers have an employee manual listing the company's policies and procedures regarding various HR matters. A Google search would produce vendors (for instance, please go to www.bizmanualz.com/, and then click HR Policies & Employee Manual).[4] These sites offer prepackaged HR policies manuals covering policies and procedures for appraisal, compensation, equal employment, and other human resource matters.

What Is Strategic Planning?

Setting goals for the company usually starts at the top, by formulating an overall strategic plan for the company. As noted, a strategic plan is the company's overall plan for how it will match its internal strengths and weaknesses with its external opportunities and threats to maintain a competitive position. The person doing the strategic planning asks, "Where are we now as a business, where do we want to be, and how should we get there?" He or she then formulates a strategic plan to take the company from where it is now to where he or she wants it to be. For example, deciding whether Mom and Pop's Supermarket will compete with Enormous Markets head-to-head by building similar superstores or instead will stay as a few small local gourmet markets is a strategic-planning problem.

strategy
A course of action the company can pursue to achieve its strategic aims.

strategic management
The process of identifying and executing the organization's strategic plan, by matching the company's capabilities with the demands of its environment.

vision statement
A general statement of the firm's intended direction that shows, in broad terms, "what we want to become."

A **strategy** is a course of action. Both PepsiCo and Coca-Cola face the same basic problem—people are drinking fewer sugared drinks. However, they each chose different strategies to deal with this. PepsiCo *diversified* by selling more food items like chips. Coca-Cola *concentrated* relatively more on sweet beverages, and on boosting advertising to (hopefully) boost Coke sales.

Finally, **strategic management** is the process of identifying and executing the organization's strategic plan by matching the company's capabilities (strengths and weaknesses) with the demands of its environment (its competitors, customers, and suppliers, for instance).

The Strategic Management Process

Figure 3.2 sums up the strategic management process. Its seven steps include (1) ask, "Where are we now as a business?" (2) evaluate the firm's internal and external strengths, weaknesses, opportunities, and threats; (3) formulate a new business direction; (4) decide on strategic goals; and (5) choose specific strategies or courses of action. Steps (6) and (7) are to implement and then evaluate the strategic plan.

The manager typically begins (step 1) by asking, "Where are we now as a business?" Here he or she defines the company's current business. Specifically, "What products do we sell, where do we sell them, and how do our products or services differ from our competitors'?" For example, the Coca-Cola Company sells mostly sweetened beverages such as Coke and Sprite, while PepsiCo sells drinks but also foods such as Quaker Oats and Frito-Lay chips.

The second step is to ask, "*Are we in the right business* given our strengths and weaknesses and the challenges that we face?" To answer this, managers "audit," or examine, both the firm's environment and the firm's internal strengths and weaknesses. For example, the *environmental scan worksheet* in Figure 3.3 is a guide for compiling information about the company's environment. As you can see, this includes the economic, competitive, and political trends that may affect the company. The *SWOT chart* in Figure 3.4 (page 65) is widely used. Managers use it to compile and organize the company strengths, weaknesses, opportunities, and threats. The manager's aim is to create a strategic plan that makes sense in terms of the company's strengths, weaknesses, opportunities, and threats.

Next, based on this analysis (in other words, on the environmental scan and SWOT), the task in step 3 is to decide *what should our new business be*, in terms of what we sell, where we will sell it, and how our products or services differ from competitors' products and services? Some managers express the essence of their new business with a *vision statement*. A **vision statement** is a general statement of the firm's intended direction; it shows, in broad terms, "what we want to

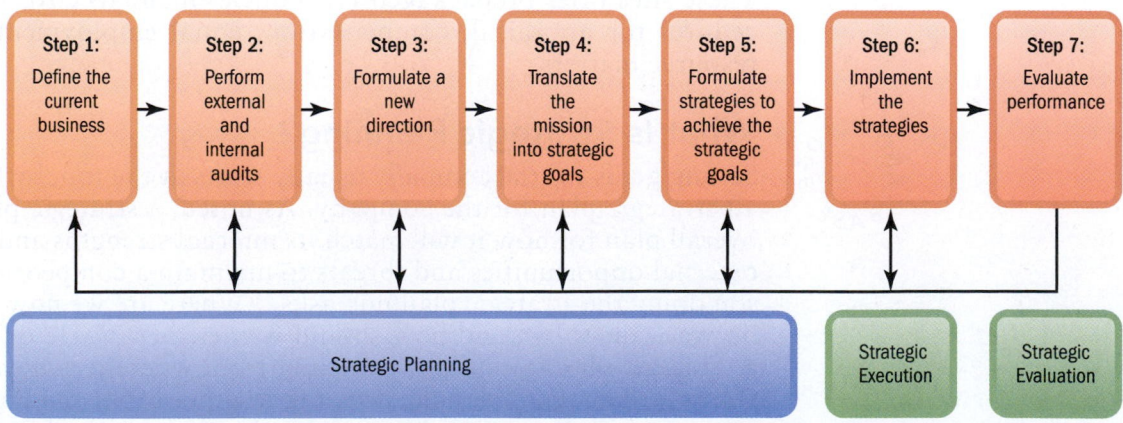

Figure 3.2
The Strategic Management Process

Economic Trends
(such as recession, inflation, employment, monetary policies)

_____
_____
_____
_____

Competitive and Market Trends
(such as market/customer trends, entry/exit of competitors, new products from competitors)

_____
_____
_____
_____

Political Trends
(such as legislation and regulation/deregulation)

_____
_____
_____
_____

Technological Trends
(such as introduction of new production/distribution technologies, rate of product obsolescence, trends in availability of supplies and raw materials)

_____
_____
_____
_____

Social Trends
(such as demographic trends, mobility, education, evolving values)

_____
_____
_____
_____

Geographic Trends
(such as opening/closing of new markets, factors affecting current plant/office facilities location decisions)

_____
_____
_____
_____

Figure 3.3
Worksheet for Environmental Scanning

become."[5] PepsiCo's vision is "Performance with Purpose." CEO Indra Nooyi says her company's executives choose which businesses to be in based on Performance with Purpose's focus on human sustainability, environmental sustainability, and talent sustainability.[6] For example, that vision prompted PepsiCo to add the healthy Quaker Oats and Gatorade to its lineup of products.

mission statement
Summarizes what the company's main tasks are today.

Some companies also have mission statements. The company's **mission statement** summarizes what the company's main tasks are today. Several years ago, Ford adopted what was for several years a powerful Ford mission statement—making "Quality Job One."

In any case, the manager's next step (step 4) is to translate step 3's desired new direction into *strategic goals*. At Ford, for example, what exactly did making

Potential Strengths	Potential Opportunities
• Market leadership	• New overseas markets
• Strong research and development	• Failing trade barriers
• High-quality products	• Competitors failing
• Cost advantages	• Diversification
• Patents	• Economy rebounding
Potential Weaknesses	**Potential Threats**
• Large inventories	• Market saturation
• Excess capacity for market	• Threat of takeover
• Management turnover	• Low-cost foreign competition
• Weak market image	• Slower market growth
• Lack of management depth	• Growing government regulation

Figure 3.4
SWOT Matrix, with Generic Examples

"Quality Job One" mean for each department in terms of how they would boost quality? The answer was laid out in goals such as "no more than 1 initial defect per 10,000 cars."

Next (step 5), the manager *chooses strategies*—courses of action—that will enable the company to achieve its strategic goals. For example, how should Ford pursue its goal of no more than 1 initial defect per 10,000 cars? Perhaps open two new high-tech plants, and put in place new, rigorous employee selection, training, and performance-appraisal procedures.

Step 6, *strategy execution*, means putting the strategies into action. This means actually hiring (or firing) people, building (or closing) plants, and adding (or eliminating) products and product lines.

Finally, in step 7, the manager *evaluates* the results. Things don't always turn out as planned. All managers should periodically assess the progress of their strategic decisions.

Types of Strategies

In practice, managers often distinguish between *companywide* strategic plans, business unit (or *competitive*) strategic plans, and *functional* (or departmental) strategic plans.

The company's top management (see Figure 3.5) uses corporate strategy to answer the question, "How many and what kind of businesses should we be in?" The **corporate-level strategy** identifies the portfolio of businesses that, in total, comprise the company and how these businesses relate to each other.

corporate-level strategy
Type of strategy that identifies the portfolio of businesses that, in total, comprise the company and the ways in which these businesses relate to each other.

- For example, with a *concentration* (single-business) corporate strategy, the company offers one product or product line, usually in one market. WD-40 Company (which makes a spray hardware lubricant) is one example.
- A *diversification* corporate strategy means the firm will expand by adding new product lines. PepsiCo is diversified. For example, over the years, Pepsi Co added Frito-Lay chips and Quaker Oats.
- A *vertical integration* strategy means the firm expands by, perhaps, producing its own raw materials, or selling its products direct. Thus, Apple opened its own Apple stores.
- With a *consolidation* strategy, the company reduces its size.
- With *geographic expansion*, the company grows by entering new territorial markets, for instance, by taking the business abroad.

Once the manager decides what businesses to be in, each business needs a basis on which to compete. For example, within PepsiCo, each of its businesses (such as

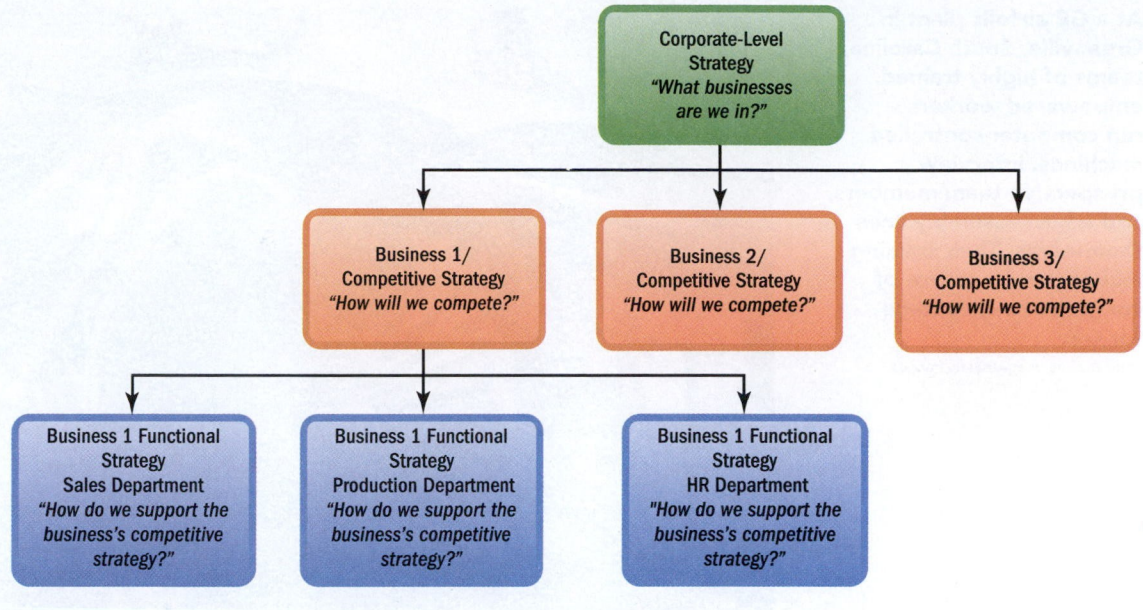

Figure 3.5

Type of Strategy at Each Company Level

Pepsi and Frito-Lay) should have a *business-level/competitive strategy* (again, see Figure 3.5). The **competitive strategy** identifies how to build and strengthen the business's competitive position in the marketplace.[7] It answers the question, for instance, "How should Pizza Hut compete with Papa John's?" or "How should Walmart compete with Target?"

Managers build their competitive strategies around their businesses' competitive advantages. **Competitive advantage** means any factors that allow a company to differentiate its product or service from those of its competitors to increase market share. The competitive advantage needn't be something tangible like high-tech machines. For example, at a GE air foils plant in Greenville, South Carolina, teams of highly trained empowered workers run computer-controlled machines, interview prospective team members, and adjust assembly lines themselves.[8] For GE, the workers' knowledge, skills, and dedication (their "human capital") produce the quality that makes GE an aerospace leader. Similarly, here is how a former vice president of human resources at the Toyota Motor Manufacturing facility in Georgetown, Kentucky, described the importance of human capital as a competitive advantage:

> People are behind our success. Machines don't have new ideas, solve problems, or grasp opportunities. Only people who are involved in thinking can make a difference . . . Every auto plant in the United States has basically the same machinery. But how people are utilized and involved varies widely from one company to another. The workforce gives any company its true competitive edge.[9]

Managers use three *standard competitive strategies* to achieve competitive advantage:

- *Cost leadership* means becoming the low-cost leader in an industry. Walmart is a classic example.
- *Differentiation* is a second possible competitive strategy. In a differentiation strategy, the firm seeks to be unique in its industry along dimensions that are widely valued by buyers.[10] Thus, Volvo stresses the safety of its cars, Uber stresses fast, seamless pickups, and GE stresses the reliability of its Greenville plant's aircraft parts.
- *Focusers* carve out a market niche (like Ferrari). They offer a product or service that their customers cannot get from generalist competitors (such as Toyota).

At a GE airfoils plant in Greenville, South Carolina, teams of highly trained, empowered workers run computer-controlled machines, interview prospective team members, and adjust assembly lines themselves. Their training makes them a source of competitive advantage for GE.

Source: Juice Images/Getty Images.

functional strategy
A department's functional strategy identifies what the department must do in terms of specific departmental policies and practices to help the business accomplish its competitive goals.

Functional strategies are the third type of strategy. They identify what each of the business's departments (such as finance, sales, and HR) must do to help the business accomplish its competitive goals. As an example, the Shanghai Portman Hotel wants to differentiate itself with exceptional service. Therefore, its human resource managers put in place policies and practices that will enable the hotel to select and train employees who are exceptionally customer oriented.

Managers' Roles in Strategic Planning

Devising a strategic plan is top management's responsibility. However, top executives rarely formulate strategic plans without the input of lower-level managers. Few people know as much about the firm's competitive pressures, vendor capabilities, product and industry trends, and employee capabilities and concerns than do the company's department managers.

For example, the human resource manager is in a good position to supply "competitive intelligence"—information on what competitors are doing. Details regarding competitors' incentive plans, employee opinion surveys that elicit information about customer complaints, and information about pending legislation such as labor laws are examples. Human resource managers should also be the masters of information about their own firms' employees' strengths and weaknesses.[11]

In practice, devising the firm's overall strategic plan involves frequent meetings and discussions among and between top and lower-level managers. The top managers then use the information from these interactions to hammer out their strategic plan.

LEARNING OBJECTIVE 2
Define strategic human resource management, and give an example of strategic human resource management in practice.

Strategic Human Resource Management

We've seen that once a business decides how it will compete, it turns to formulating functional (departmental) strategies to support its competitive aims. One of those departments is human resource management, and its functional strategies are human resource management strategies.

What Is Strategic Human Resource Management?

Every company needs its human resource management policies and practices to make sense in terms of its broad strategic aims. For example, a high-end hotel like the Shanghai Portman will have different employee selection, training, and pay policies than will a small roadside motel because the Shanghai's customers expect service commensurate with the higher fees they're paying. **Strategic human resource management** means formulating and executing human resource policies and practices that produce the employee competencies and behaviors the company needs to achieve its strategic aims.

The basic idea behind strategic human resource management is this: In formulating human resource management policies and activities, the aim should be to produce the employee skills and behaviors that the company needs to achieve its strategic goals. Accenture, a major global consulting company, puts it this way: HR strategy involves "[C]reating an HR vision and roadmap that supports strategic business outcomes while delivering high-value talent and HR services that drive an improved employee and manager experience."[12]

Figure 3.6 graphically outlines this idea. First, management formulates *strategic plans* and goals. In turn, executing these plans and achieving these goals depends on having the right mix of *employee competencies* and *behaviors*. And finally, to produce these required employee competencies and behaviors, the human resource manager must put in place the right mix of recruitment, selection, training, and other *HR strategies*, *policies*, and *practices*.[13]

strategic human resource management

Formulating and executing human resource policies and practices that produce the employee competencies and behaviors the company needs to achieve its strategic aims.

Figure 3.6

The HR Strategy Model

Note: This figure opens Parts 2–5 of this book and says this: The company's HR policies and practices should produce the employee competencies and behaviors that the company needs to achieve its strategic goals.

The Shanghai Portman Hotel was one example of strategic human resource management in action: *Strategically*, they set the goal of having superior customer service; to achieve this, employees had to exhibit new *skills* and *behaviors*, such as in how they treated guests, and to produce these employee skills and behaviors, management introduced new human resource management plans, policies, and procedures, such as the Ritz-Carlton Company's human resource system. The accompanying HR in Practice feature presents another strategic human resource management example.

■ HR In Practice

The Zappos "WOW" Way

When your strategy involves selling shoes and clothes online to people who can't try them on, you need employees who are energized and enjoy what they're doing—they want employees to deliver "wow" through service (http://about.zappos.com/our-unique-culture/zappos-core-values).[14] That's why Zappos' founders knew they needed special methods for hiring, developing, and retaining employees, and that's just what they created. As their website (http://about.zappos.com/meet-zappos-family/zap-poscom-inc/human-resources) says, *"This ain't your mama's HR! Recruiting, benefits, and employee relations keep this cruise ship afloat with fun, inventive ways of getting employees motivated and educated about the Zappos Family of companies, their benefits, and the other fun stuff going on around here!"*[15]

Although they may not appeal to everyone, these "inventive, fun techniques" include interviewing job applicants in what looks like the set of a talk show, asking employees to submit their own designs for Steve Madden shoes, and (during their annual "Bald & Blue Day") having some employees volunteer to shave their heads or dye their hair blue.[16] And, by the way, if you're not happy working at Zappos, the company will pay you to leave—it wants no one there who doesn't truly want to be there.

Again, that may not be for everyone, but it works for Zappos. It knows that selling online successfully calls for employees who are energized and who really enjoy what they're doing. Management uses these special HR practices to cultivate just that sort of energized and fun environment, and judging from the firm's success they seem to be working.

✪ Talk About It – **2**

If your professor has chosen to assign this, go to **www.pearson.com/mylab/management** to discuss the following question. Why do you think Zappos' top managers believe it is so important for employees to provide a "WOW" factor in their business?

✪ Watch It

How does a company actually go about developing a human resource strategy? If your professor has chosen to assign this, go to **www.pearson.com/mylab/management** to watch the video Joie de Vivre Hospitality Strategic Management and then answer the questions to show what you'd do if you ran this company.

■ HR and the Gig Economy

Integrating HR into the Employer's Gig Worker Strategy

Formulating an HR strategy for a gig economy company obviously presents some interesting challenges. After all, why do you need much of an HR department at all when most of your workers, strictly speaking, aren't even employees of your company?[17]

In fact, when it comes to hiring contingent or contractor employees, in many companies today HR hardly gets involved. In small firms, line managers do most hiring of freelancers, often through online marketplaces like Upwork.com. Here the HR manager may just get involved in administrative tasks like getting the person on payroll, (although less-experienced line managers in small firms may ask HR to actually do the recruitment and selection). In many large firms, HR doesn't process contingent workers at all; instead the company contracts them through a formal procurement process, much as the company procures equipment. The bottom line is that many times, a line manager simply hires a gig employee and gets the person paid, and this all takes place without the HR department. That's not necessarily an optimal situation. For example, it makes it more difficult to keep track of the company's gig workers, assess them, engage them, and communicate with them.

Employers and human resource managers can do at least two things to involve HR more in the gig worker staffing process. One is for human resource managers to be more proactive about getting their departments more involved. For example, explain how they can help integrate the contingent workers with the firm's long-term full-time employee staffing needs. The second is to rely more on new technologies from vendors such as SAP and ADP. They are introducing new platforms that, for example, enable HR departments to seamlessly get contingent workers on the payroll, distinguish between salaried and contingent workers, and make it easier for the firm's recruiters to help with recruiting contingent workers.

⭐ Talk About It – 3

If your professor has chosen to assign this, go to **www.pearson.com/mylab/ management** to discuss the following question. Based on your experience, what would you tell an employer are the pros and cons of getting HR involved in the gig worker hiring process?

Sustainability and Strategic Human Resource Management

Today's emphasis on *sustainability* has important consequences for human resource management. *Strategic human resource management* means having human resource policies and practices that produce the employee skills and behaviors that are necessary to achieve the company's strategic goals, and these include sustainability goals.

For example, PepsiCo aims to deliver "Performance with Purpose." This means achieving financial performance while also achieving human sustainability, environmental sustainability, and talent sustainability.[18] PepsiCo's human resource managers can help the company achieve these goals.[19] For example, they can use its *workforce planning* processes to help determine how many and what sorts of "green" jobs the company will need to recruit for. They can work with top management to institute *flexible work arrangements* that help sustain the environment by reducing commuting. They can use *incentive systems* that motivate employees to achieve PepsiCo's sustainability goals.[20] The bottom line is that HR policies and practices can support a firm's sustainability strategy and goals.

Strategic Human Resource Management Tools

Managers use several tools to translate the company's broad strategic goals into specific human resource management policies and practices. Three important tools are the strategy map, the HR scorecard, and the digital dashboard.

strategy map
A strategic planning tool that shows the "big picture" of how each department's performance contributes to achieving the company's overall strategic goals.

Strategy Map The **strategy map** summarizes how each department's performance contributes to achieving the company's overall strategic goals. It helps the manager and each employee visualize and understand the role his or her department plays in achieving the company's strategic plan. Management gurus sometimes say that the map clarifies employees' "line of sight," by linking their efforts with the company's ultimate goals.[21]

Figure 3.7 presents a strategy map example for Southwest Airlines. The top-level interest is in achieving its strategic financial goals. Then the strategy map shows the chain of activities that help Southwest Airlines achieve these goals. Southwest has a low-cost leader strategy. So, for example, to boost revenues and profitability, Southwest must fly fewer planes (to keep costs down), maintain low prices, and maintain on-time flights. In turn (further down the strategy map), on-time flights and low prices require fast turnaround. This, in turn, requires motivated ground and flight crews. The strategy map thereby helps each department understand what it needs to do to support Southwest's low-cost strategy.[22] For example, what steps must Southwest's human resource team take to boost the motivation and dedication of its ground crews?

HR scorecard

A process for assigning financial and nonfinancial goals or metrics to the human resource management–related chain of activities required for achieving the company's strategic aims and for monitoring results.

The HR Scorecard Many employers quantify and computerize the strategy map's activities, via an HR scorecard. The **HR scorecard** is not a scorecard. It refers to *a process for assigning financial and nonfinancial goals or metrics* to the human resource management–related strategy map chain of activities required for achieving the company's strategic aims.[23] The idea is to take the strategy map and to quantify it. ("Metrics" for Southwest might include airplane turnaround time, percent of on-time flights, and ground crew productivity.)

Figure 3.7

Strategy Map for Southwest Airlines

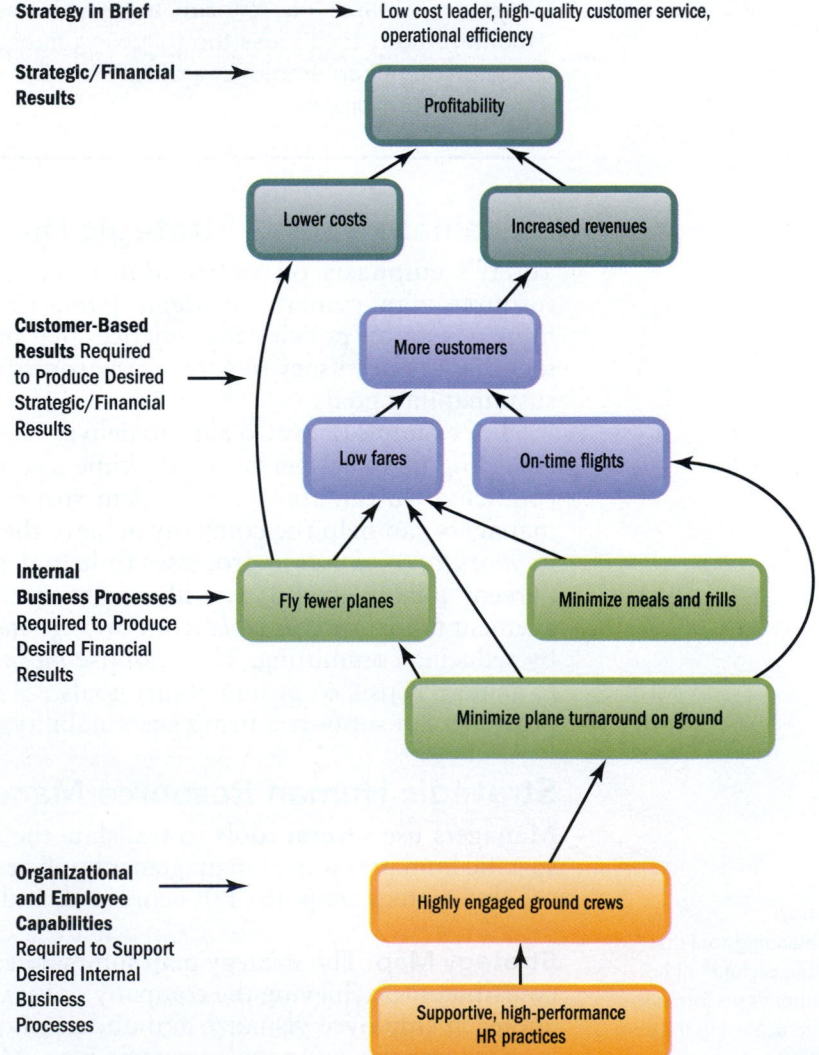

Strategy Map	HR Scorecard	Digital Dashboard
Graphical tool that summarizes the chain of activities that contribute to a company's success, and so shows employees the "big picture" of how their performance contributes to achieving the company's overall strategic goals.	A process for assigning financial and nonfinancial goals or metrics to the human resource management–related chain of activities required for achieving the company's strategic aims and for monitoring results.	Presents the manager with desktop graphs and charts, so he or she gets a picture of where the company has been and where it's going, in terms of each activity in the strategy map.

Figure 3.8

Three Important Strategic HR Tools

Managers use special scorecard software to facilitate this. This computerized scorecard process helps the manager quantify the relationships between (1) the HR activities (amount of testing, training, and so forth), (2) the resulting employee behaviors (customer service, for instance), and (3) the resulting firm-wide strategic outcomes and performance (such as customer satisfaction and profitability).[24]

digital dashboard

Presents the manager with desktop graphs and charts, thus presenting a computerized picture of where the company stands on all the metrics from the HR Scorecard process.

Digital Dashboards The saying "a picture is worth a thousand words" explains the purpose of the digital dashboard. A **digital dashboard** presents the manager with desktop graphs and charts, showing a computerized picture of how the company is doing on all the metrics from the HR Scorecard process. For example, a top Southwest Airlines manager's dashboard might display real-time trends for various strategy map activities, such as aircraft turnaround time, market share, annual passengers to date, and on-time flights. This enables the manager to take corrective action. For example, if ground crews are turning planes around slower today, financial results tomorrow may decline unless the manager takes action.

Figure 3.8 summarizes the three strategic planning tools.

LEARNING OBJECTIVE 3
Explain, with examples, why metrics are important for managing human resources.

HR Metrics and Benchmarking

We've seen that strategic human resource management means formulating human resource policies and practices that produce the employee competencies and behaviors that the company needs to achieve its strategic goals. Being able to measure what you are doing is an essential part of this process. For example, it would have been futile for the Shanghai Portman's management to set "better customer service" as a goal, if they couldn't measure customer service.[25]

Types of Metrics

human resource metric

The quantitative gauge of a human resource management activity such as employee turnover, hours of training per employee, or qualified applicants per position.

Human resource managers use many measures (or "**human resource metrics**"). For example, there is (on average) one human resource employee per 100 company employees for firms with 100–249 employees. The HR employee-to-employee ratio drops to about 0.79 for firms with 1,000–2,499 employees and to 0.72 for firms with more than 7,500 employees.[26] Figure 3.9 illustrates other human resource management metrics, such as employee tenure, cost per hire, and annual overall turnover rate.[27]

Benchmarking

Measuring how one is doing (for instance, in terms of employee turnover or productivity) is rarely enough for deciding what to change. Instead, one must know *"How are we doing?" in relation to something.* For example, are our accident rates rising or falling? Similarly, you may want to *benchmark* your results—compare high-performing companies to your own, to understand what makes them better.[28]

Organizational Data
- Revenue
- Revenue per FTE
- Net Income Before Taxes
- Net Income Before Taxes per FTE
- Positions Included within the Organization's Succession Plan

HR Department Data
- Total HR Staff
- HR-to-Employee Ratio
- Percentage of HR Staff in Supervisory Roles
- Percentage of HR Staff in Professional/Technical Roles
- Percentage of HR Staff in Administrative Support Roles
- Reporting Structure for the Head of HR
- Types of HR Positions Organizations Expect to Hire in 2011

HR Expense Data
- HR Expenses
- HR Expense to Operating Expense Ratio
- HR Expense to FTE Ratio

Compensation Data
- Annual Salary Increase
- Salaries as a Percentage of Operating Expense
- Target Bonus for Non-Executives
- Target Bonus for Executives

Tuition/Education Data
- Maximum Reimbursement Allowed for Tuition/Education Expenses per Year
- Percentage of Employees Participating in Tuition/Education Reimbursement Programs

Employment Data
- Number of Positions Filled
- Time-to-Fill
- Cost-Per-Hire
- Employee Tenure
- Annual Overall Turnover Rate
- Annual Voluntary Turnover Rate
- Annual Involuntary Turnover Rate

Expectations for Revenue and Organizational Hiring
- Percentage of Organizations Expecting Changes in Revenue in 2011 compared to 2010
- Percentage of Organizations Expecting Changes in Hiring in 2011 compared to 2010

Metrics for More Profitable Organizations
- Total HR Staff
- HR-to-Employee Ratio
- HR Expenses
- HR Expense to Operating Expense Ratio
- HR Expense to FTE Ratio
- Annual Salary Increase
- Target Bonus for Non-Executives
- Target Bonus for Executives
- Maximum Reimbursement Allowed for Tuition/Education Expenses per Year
- Percentage of Employees Participating in Tuition/Education Reimbursement Programs
- Time-to-Fill
- Cost-Per-Hire
- Annual Overall Turnover Rate

Figure 3.9

Metrics for the SHRM® 2011–2012 Customized Human Capital Benchmarking Report

Source: Reprinted with permission from the Society for Human Resource Management. All rights reserved.

The Society for Human Resource Management's (SHRM's) benchmarking service enables employers to compare their own HR metrics with those of other companies. The employer can request comparable (benchmark) figures not just by industry, but by employer size, company revenue, and geographic region (see http://shrm.org/research/benchmarks/).

Figure 3.10 illustrates one of SHRM's many sets of comparable benchmark measures. It shows how much employers are spending for tuition reimbursement programs.

Strategy and Strategy-Based Metrics

Benchmarking provides only one perspective on how your company's human resource management system is performing.[29] It shows how your human resource management system's performance compares to the competition. However it may *not* show the extent to which your firm's HR practices are supporting its strategic goals. For example, if the strategy calls for doubling profits by improving customer service, to what extent are your new training practices helping to improve customer service?

Figure 3.10

SHRM Customized Human Capital Benchmarking Report

Source: "HR Expense Date," from *SHRM Customized Human Capital Benchmarking Report*. Reprinted with permission from the Society for Human Resource Management. All rights reserved. www.shrm.org/Research/benchmarks/Documents/sample_human_capital_report.pdf.

strategy-based metrics

Metrics that specifically focus on measuring the activities that contribute to achieving a company's strategic aims.

Tuition/Education Data					
	n	25th Percentile	Median	75th Percentile	Average
Maximum reimbursement allowed for tuition/education expenses per year	32	$1,000	$5,000	$7,500	$6,000
Percentage of employees participating in tuition/education reimbursement programs	32	1.0%	3.0%	5.0%	4.0%

Managers use *strategy-based metrics* to answer such questions. **Strategy-based metrics** measure the activities that contribute to achieving a company's strategic aims.[30] Thus, for the Shanghai Portman, the strategic HR metrics might include 100% employee testing, 80% guest returns, 40% incentive pay as a percent of total salaries, and sales up 50%. Then, if new HR practices such as increased training and better incentives have their intended effects, other strategic metrics like guest returns and guest compliments should also rise.

Workforce/Talent Analytics and Data Mining

Data, workforce, or talent analytics, used by many employers, means utilizing special software applications to analyze human resources data and metrics and to draw conclusions from it.[31] For example, a talent analytics team at Google analyzed data on employee backgrounds, capabilities, and performance. The team was able to identify the factors (such as an employee feeling underutilized) likely to lead to the employee leaving. In a similar project, Google analyzed data on things like employee survey feedback and performance appraisal to identify the attributes of successful Google managers. Microsoft identified correlations among the schools and companies that the employees arrived from and the employees' subsequent performance. This enabled Microsoft to improve its recruitment and selection practices.[32] Software company SAS's employee retention program sifts through employee data on traits like skills, tenure, performance, education, and friendships. Their program can predict which high-value employees are more likely to quit in the near future.[33] Alliant Techsystems created a "flight risk model" to calculate the probability an employee would leave. This enabled it to predict high turnover and to take corrective action.[34]

Data Mining Such efforts often employ data mining techniques. Data mining is "the set of activities used to find new, hidden, or unexpected patterns in data."[35] Department stores often use data mining. For example, Macy's data mining reveals which customers come in to redeem "20% off" coupons, and what they buy. Data mining systems can use tools like statistical analysis to sift through huge amounts of employee data to identify correlations; these can then be used to improve an employer's employee selection and other practices.

Managers use talent analytics to discover patterns and to make predictions. The accompanying HR as a Profit Center presents examples.

■ HR as a Profit Center

Using Workforce/Talent Analytics

Data/talent analytics tools enable employers to analyze together employee data (like employee demographics, training, and performance ratings) from traditional sources such as employee records, as well as data from new sources (like company internal social media sites, GPS tracking, and e-mail activity).[36] Talent analytics can produce strik-ing profitability results. For example, Best Buy used talent analytics to determine that a 0.1% increase in employee engagement led to a more than $100,000 rise in a Best Buy store annual operating income.[37] Employers are using talent analytics to answer questions like these:[38]

Analytical HR. For example, "Which units, departments, or individuals need attention?" Lockheed Martin collects performance data to identify units needing improvement.

Human capital investment analysis. For example, "Which actions have the greatest impact on my business?" By monitoring employee satisfaction levels, Cisco was able to improve its employee retention rate from 65% to 85%, saving the company nearly $50 million in recruitment, selection, and training costs.

Talent value model. For example, "Why do employees choose to stay with—or leave—my company?" For example, Google was able to anticipate when an employee felt underutilized and was preparing to quit, thus reducing turnover costs.

Talent supply chain. For example, retail companies use special analytical models to predict daily store volume and release hourly employees early.

⭐ Talk About It – **4**

If your professor has chosen to assign this, go to **www.pearson.com/mylab/ management** to discuss the following questions. Could Best Buy or some of these other companies have made the same discoveries without using sophisticated computerized tools? How?

The accompanying HR as a Profit Center feature explains that Best Buy used talent analytics to determine that a 0.1% increase in employee engagement led to a more than $100,000 rise in a Best Buy store annual operating income.

Source: Andriy Blokhin/Shutterstock.

Using HR Audits

HR audit
An analysis by which an organization measures where it currently stands and determines what it has to accomplish to improve its HR function.

Human resource managers often collect data on matters such as employee turnover and safety via *human resource audits*. To paraphrase one practitioner, the employer conducts an **HR Audit** to determine the HR function's current effectiveness and to ascertain what steps need to be taken to improve it. [39] The HR audit generally involves reviewing the company's human resource function (recruiting, testing, training, and so on), usually using a checklist, as well as ensuring that the firm is adhering to regulations, laws, and company policies. [40]

In conducting the HR audit, managers often benchmark their results to comparable companies. Typical things audited include the following:[41]

1. Roles and head count (including job descriptions and employees categorized by exempt/nonexempt and full- or part-time)
2. Compliance with federal, state, local employment–related legislation
3. Recruitment and selection (including use of selection tools, background checks, and so on)
4. Compensation (policies, incentives, survey procedures, and so on)
5. Employee relations (union agreements, disciplinary procedures, employee recognition)
6. Mandated benefits (Social Security, unemployment insurance, workers' compensation, and so on)
7. Group benefits (insurance, time off, flexible benefits, and so on)
8. Payroll (such as legal compliance)
9. Documentation and record keeping (For example, do our files contain information including résumés and applications, offer letters, job descriptions, performance evaluations, benefit enrollment forms, payroll change notices, and documentation related to personnel actions such as employee handbook acknowledgments?[42])
10. Training and development (new employee orientation, workforce development, technical and safety, career planning, and so on)
11. Employee communications (employee handbook, newsletter, recognition programs)
12. Termination and transition policies and practices

Evidence-Based HR and the Scientific Way of Doing Things

In this chapter, we've seen that decision making based on an objective review of the situation is important. Managers have a name for this: *Evidence-based human resource management* means using data, facts, analytics, scientific rigor, critical evaluation, and critically evaluated research/case studies to support human resource management proposals, decisions, practices, and conclusions.[43]

You may sense that being evidence based is similar to being scientific, and if so, you are correct. One *Harvard Business Review* article even argues that managers must become more scientific and to "think like scientists" when making business decisions.[44]

But how can managers think like scientists? First, in gathering evidence, scientists (or managers) need to be *objective*, or there's no way to trust their conclusions. For example, a medical school disciplined several of its professors. These doctors had failed to reveal that they were on the payroll of the drug company that supplied the drugs, the results of which the doctors were studying. Who could trust their objectivity—or their conclusions?

Being scientific also requires *experimentation*. An experiment is a test the manager sets up in such a way as to ensure that he or she understands the reasons for the results obtained. For example, in their *Harvard Business Review* article, "A Step-by-Step Guide to Smart Business Experiments," the authors argue that, if you want to judge a new incentive plan's impact on corporate profits, don't start by implementing the plan with all employees. Instead, implement it with an

For managers the point of being "scientific" is to make better decisions by forcing the managers to gather the facts. For example, "Is our employee sales incentive plan really boosting appliance sales?"
Source: Bloomberg/Getty Images.

"experimental" group (which gets the incentive plan) *and* with a "control" group (a group that does *not* get the incentive plan). Doing so will help you gauge if any performance improvement stemmed from the incentive, or from some other cause (such as a new companywide training program).[45] And, it will enable you to *predict* how changing the incentive plan will affect performance. Objectivity, experimentation, and prediction are at the heart of what it means to be scientific.

For managers, the point of being "scientific" is to make better decisions by forcing you to gather the facts. The problem is that what's "intuitively obvious" can be misleading. "Is this sales incentive plan really boosting sales?" "We've spent $40,000 in the past five years on our tuition-refund plan; what (if anything) did we get out of it?" What's the evidence? The HR Tools feature presents examples.

■ HR Tools for Line Managers and Small Businesses

An insurance firm was considering cutting costs by buying out senior underwriters, most of whom were earning very high salaries. But after analyzing the data, HR noticed that these underwriters also brought in a disproportionate share of the company's revenue. In fact, reviewing data on things such as employee salaries and productivity showed that it would be much more profitable to eliminate some low-pay call-center employees, replacing them with even less-expensive employees.

As another example, the chemical company BASF Corp. analyzed data on the relationship among stress, health, and productivity in its 15,000 U.S. headquarters staff. Based on that analysis, the company instituted health programs that it calculated would more than pay for themselves in increased productivity by reducing stress.[46]

✪ Talk About It – 5

If your professor has chosen to assign this, go to **www.pearson.com/mylab/management** to discuss the following questions. If it is apparently so easy to do what BASF did to size up the potential benefits of health programs, why do you think more employers do not do so? How would you use this approach if you were managing a 10-person retail shop?

LEARNING OBJECTIVE 4
Answer the question "What are high-performance work systems?" and give examples of how they differ from non-high-performance ones.

high-performance work system

A set of human resource management policies and practices that promote organizational effectiveness.

Building High-Performance Work Systems

Being able to measure, benchmark, and scientifically analyze human resource management practices makes it possible for the manager to identify and then to put in place high-performance work practices.

A **high-performance work system** (HPWS) is a set of human resource management policies and practices that together produce superior employee performance.[47] One study looked at 17 manufacturing plants, some of which adopted high-performance work system practices. The high-performance plants *paid more* (median wages of $16 per hour compared with $13 per hour for all plants), *trained more*, used *more sophisticated recruitment* and *hiring practices* (tests and validated interviews, for instance), and used *more self-managing work teams*.[48] Those with the high-performance HR practices also performed significantly better than did those without such practices.[49]

High-Performance Human Resource Policies and Practices

Studies show that high-performance work systems' policies and practices do differ from less productive ones. For example (see Table 3.1), in terms of HR practices, high-performing companies recruit more job candidates, use more selection tests, and spend many more hours training employees. Table 3.1 actually illustrates three things.

First, it shows *examples of* human resource metrics, such as hours of training per employee, or qualified applicants per position.[50] (In Table 3.1, the metric for "Number of qualified applicants per position" is 37 in the high-performing companies.) Managers use such metrics to assess their companies' performance and to compare one company's performance with another's.[51]

Table 3.1 Examples Selected from Several Studies of How Recruitment, Selection, Training, Appraisal, Pay, and Other Practices Differ in High-Performance and Low-Performance Companies

	Lower-Performance Companies' HR Practice Averages (e.g., company performance in terms of sales/employee, innovation, and employee retention)*	Higher-Performance Companies' HR Practice Averages (e.g., company performance in terms of sales/employee, innovation, and employee retention)*
Recruitment: Average number of qualified applicants per position	8	37
Selection: Average percentage of employees hired based on a validated *selection* test	4%	30%
Training: Average number of hours of *training* for new employees	35 Hours	117 Hours
Appraisal: Average percentage of employees receiving a regular *performance appraisal*	41%	95%
Pay Practices: Average percentage of the workforce eligible for *incentive pay*	28%	84%
Use of Teams: Average percentage of the workforce routinely working in all teams, semiautonomous, cross-functional, or project teams	11%	42%
Self-Directed Teams: Percent of companies with *semiautonomous or autonomous* work teams	9%	70%

Table 3.1 (Continued)

	Lower-Performance Companies' HR Practice Averages (e.g., company performance in terms of sales/employee, innovation, and employee retention)*	Higher-Performance Companies' HR Practice Averages (e.g., company performance in terms of sales/employee, innovation, and employee retention)*
Operational Information Sharing: Employees receive relevant operating performance information	62%	82%
Financial Information Sharing: Employees receive relevant financial performance information	43%	66%

*Findings rounded.

Source: Based on "Comparison of HR Practices in High-Performance and Low-Performance Companies," by B. E. Becker et al., from *The HR Scorecard: Linking People, Strategy and Performance* (Boston: Harvard Business School Press, 2001); Barry Macy, Gerard Farias, Jean-Francois Rosa, and Curt Moore, "Built to Change: High-Performance Work Systems and Self-Directed Work Teams—A Longitudinal Field Study," *Research in Organizational Change and Development*, 16, pp. 339–418, 2007; James Gathrie, Wenchuan Liu, Patrick Flood, and Sarah MacCurtain, "High Performance Work Systems, Workforce Productivity, and Innovation: A Comparison of MNCs and Indigenous Firms," The Learning, Innovation and Knowledge (LINK) Research Centre Working Paper Series, WP 04-08, 2008; Richard A. Posthuma, Michael C. Campion, and Malika Masimova, "A High Performance Work Practices Taxonomy: Integrating the Literature and Directing Future Research," *Journal of Management*, 39, no. 5, July 2013, pp. 1184–1220.

Second, it illustrates *what employers must do* to have high-performance systems. For example, high-performing companies have more than four times the number of qualified applicants per job than do low performers. They also hire based on validated selection tests and extensively train employees.

Third, Table 3.1 shows that high-performance work practices usually *aspire to encourage employee involvement and self-management*. In other words, an aim of the high-performance recruiting, screening, training, and other human resources practices is to nurture an involved, informed, empowered, engaged, and self-motivated workforce.[52] Employees who are highly involved in managing their work processes tend to be more engaged employees as well.[53]

LEARNING OBJECTIVE 5
Answer the question (with examples) "Why is employee engagement important?"

Employee Engagement and Performance

Employee engagement refers to being psychologically involved in, connected to, and committed to getting one's jobs done. Engaged employees "experience a high level of connectivity with their work tasks," and therefore work hard to accomplish their task-related goals.[54] Engaged employees do their jobs as if they own the company.

Why Is Employee Engagement Important?

Employee engagement is important because it drives performance and productivity. For example, based on a Gallup survey, business units with the highest levels of employee engagement have an 83% chance of performing above the company median; those with the lowest employee engagement have only a 17% chance.[55] Gallup distinguishes between engaged, disengaged, and actively disengaged employees (the latter are actively *counterproductive* at work). Gallup found that organizations that had about nine *engaged* employees for every one *actively disengaged* employee had about one and one-half times the earnings per share of their competitors.[56] According to one review of the evidence, employee engagement is correlated with employees' customer service productivity, and improvements in employee engagement were associated with significant increases in sales, product quality, productivity, safety incidents at work, retention and absenteeism, and revenue growth.[57] One consulting firm estimates that a 5% increase in employee engagement correlates to a 0.7% increase in operating margins.[58] Companies with highly engaged employees are also less likely to be unionized.[59] In one survey, highly engaged employees lost only about 7.5 days of productivity per year, compared to about 14 days for disengaged employees.[60] A survey by consultants Watson Wyatt Worldwide concluded that companies with highly engaged employees have 26% higher revenue per employee.[61] A *Harvard Business Review* article notes that for optimal customer service (for instance, in retail establishments), "Employees should be engaged by providing them with reasons and methods to satisfy customers and then rewarded for appropriate behavior."[62] That's why employers such as Starwood Hotels measure not just engagement but engagement's consequences, such as customer satisfaction, financial results, absenteeism, safety, sales, turnover, and profitability.[63]

The Employee Engagement Problem

The problem is that, depending on the study, only about 21–30% of employees nationally are engaged.[64] Gallup distinguishes among engaged employees "who work with passion and feel a profound connection to their company," not-engaged employees who are essentially "checked out," and actively disengaged employees who "act out their unhappiness" by undermining what their engaged coworkers are accomplishing.[65] Gallup recently found that about 30% of employees were engaged, 50% were not engaged, and 20% were actively disengaged.

What Can Managers Do to Improve Employee Engagement?

Managers improve employee engagement by taking concrete steps to do so. We'll look more closely at what exactly these steps are in a moment, but one important activity is *providing supportive supervision* (for instance Gallup found that managers who focus on their employees' strengths can "practically eliminate active disengagement," while "bosses from hell" will kill employee engagement).[66] Other surveys like one by consultants Towers Watson indicate that other practical managerial actions that can foster employee engagement include making sure employees (1) *understand* how their departments contribute to the company's success, (2) see how their *own efforts contribute* to achieving the company's goals, and (3) get a *sense of accomplishment* from working at the firm.[67] Employees who are highly *involved*—as when working in self-managing teams—also tend to be engaged employees.[68] Employers should also *hold managers responsible* for employee engagement. For example, WD-40 Company periodically surveys employee engagement, and managers then meet with their employees to discuss how to improve the results.[69]

We'll use special Employee Engagement Guide for Managers sections in this and the following chapters to show how managers use human resource activities such as recruiting and selection to improve employee engagement.

How to Measure Employee Engagement

Gallup (www.gallup.com), Towers Watson (go to www.towerswatson.com/en-US, then click Solutions, and then Surveys), and other vendors offer comprehensive employee engagement survey services. Beyond that, monitoring employee engagement needn't be complicated. With about 180,000 employees worldwide, the consulting firm Accenture uses a three-part "shorthand" method it calls "say, stay, and strive." First, Accenture assesses how positively the employee speaks about the company and recommends it to others. Second, it looks at who stays with the company, and why. Third, it looks at "strive." For instance, "do employees take an active role in the overall success of the organization by moving beyond just doing tasks to going above and beyond?"[70]

Employee Engagement Guide For Managers
How Kia Motors (UK) Improved Performance with an HR Strategy Aimed at Boosting Employee Engagement

Kia Motors today is a successful automobile manufacturer employing tens of thousands of employees around the world, and one famous for its 10-year warranty and for the quality and value of its products. However, Kia was not always so successful. In July 1997, Kia was under bankruptcy protection and having difficulty servicing its $10.6 billion of debt.[71] In 1998, Hyundai Motorcar Company of Korea purchased 51% of Kia. That triggered a multiyear program aimed at improving Kia's operating performance. Today, Hyundai only owns about one-third of Kia Motors, although Kia is still a close-knit part of Hyundai Motor Group.

The Challenges

After several years of improving operating conditions under Hyundai Motor Group, Kia (as well as most auto manufacturers around the world) ran into strong headwinds as credit tightened and consumers cut spending around 2006. Looking at the situation in 2006–2007, Kia's chairman, writing in the company's annual report said,

> In today's automobile industry, competition is so severe that even the bold at heart, if well-informed, would be hesitant to confidently predict future victors in the car market. Japanese automobile companies are unrelenting in their measures against us, while latecomers, such as China, are speeding up to catch up with us as far as they can. Stagnation and the world economic growth, coupled with exchange-rate risks and other major threats, present unfavorable economic conditions for any global player.[72]

In the face of these challenges, the chairman went on to lay out what Kia's strategy for dealing with this intense global competition would be. As he said:

> We intend to base future growth on raising our competencies as a global maker in all areas including production, sales, marketing, branding, as well as before and after servicing. We will also concentrate on our global quality management we have driven so far. We will first strengthen our basic competitiveness in terms of production costs and final products. Second, we will exclude all the unnecessary elements from the management through advanced systems to groundwork the base of stable profit making. Third, we will efficiently invest in new future businesses with our specialized R&D and global production bases.[73]

Also in 2006–2007, Kia Motor's UK subsidiary (Kia UK), which employed about 2,500 people, faced particularly dire circumstances; these included rapidly falling sales, increased financial losses, and low levels of employee engagement. Employee turnover was 31%. The direct cost to the company from the 31% turnover alone was estimated at about 600,000 British pounds (about $1 million) in 2006 (due to higher than necessary recruitment, legal, and employee dismissal costs).[74]

The New Human Resource Management Strategy

Gary Tomlinson, Kia UK's newly appointed head of HR, believed that Kia UK's low employee engagement was probably both a cause and an effect of the unit's poor performance. In fact, a survey of Kia UK employees had identified numerous personnel issues including possibly poor morale and communications. He knew Kia UK needed a new HR strategy to address this. He also knew that this strategy should support the parent company's strategy of basing "future growth on raising our competencies as a global maker in all areas including production, sales, marketing, branding, as well as before and after servicing."

Tomlinson (with the support of Kia UK's top management) wisely decided to develop, as he put it, "an employee engagement strategy to improve employee morale and address the high levels of employee turnover."[75] In brief, the idea was that, by (1) putting in place new HR policies and practices aimed at improving employee engagement, he could (2) change Kia UK employees' behavior (improve performance and reduce turnover, for instance) and thereby (3) support the parent company's stated strategy of "raising our competencies as a global maker in all areas." The accompanying Management Skills feature shows what he actually did to boost employee engagement.

BUILDING YOUR MANAGEMENT SKILLS
How to Execute an Employee Engagement Strategy

Actually executing Kia UK's employee engagement HR strategy involved six steps (and these provide a roadmap for any such endeavor). First, Kia UK set *measurable objectives* for the program. These objectives included improving by at least 10% survey feedback scores for line managers' behaviors, in terms of communication, the quality of appraisal feedback they gave their direct reports, the recognition of work done, and the respect between manager and employee.[76] Other objectives included reducing employee turnover employment costs (e.g., recruitment costs) by at least 10% per year.

Second, Kia UK held an extensive *leadership development* program. For example, they sent all managers for training to improve their management skills. They then tested the new skills with "360-degree" assessment tools (these basically meant having managers' bosses, peers, and subordinates rate the managers' new leadership skills).

Third, Kia UK instituted new *employee recognition programs*. These included, for instance, giving "Outstanding Awards" to selected employees quarterly, and "Kia thank you" cards for jobs well done.[77]

Fourth, Kia UK *improved internal communications*. For example, they instituted quarterly employee briefings, more extensive use of performance appraisals, and launched a new corporate intranet called Kia Vision (this provided key business information and other useful communiqués to all employees). Based on employee feedback, Kia UK also decided, as part of the enhanced communications, to institute an *employee forum*. This consisted of one representative from each department; the forum in effect empowered and involved employees by enabling them to express opinions, suggestions, and concerns about their jobs.

Fifth, they instituted a new *employee development program*. This involved using the company's appraisal process to identify employees' training needs. Kia then created training plans for each employee. They based these plans on Kia's needs and on the employee's stated career aspirations.

Sixth, Kia UK made a number of changes to its *compensation and other policies*. For instance, they eliminated bonuses and substituted fixed-rate percentage-based salary increases. They also rewrote the entire employee handbook and all HR policies and procedures "to ensure they were aligned with [Kia UK's new] cultural values."[78]

The Results

The results of the new employee engagement program were impressive. Employee surveys of employee engagement and of line managers' communications and other behaviors improved markedly; employee turnover fell from 31% in 2006 to 15% in 2007, to 5% in 2008, and to below 2% by the end of 2009; and recruitment and turnover costs fell by more than 400,000 British pounds within two years, a 71% reduction.[79]

Earlier we said that *strategic human resource management* means putting in place the HR policies and practices that will produce the employee competencies and behaviors that the company needs to achieve its strategic goals. Kia UK's employee engagement program illustrates how one company actually did this. (Do you think Angelo, from the chapter opener, could apply any of this to improve his service? What should he do?)

Review

MyLab Management

If your instructor is using MyLab Management, go to **www.pearson.com/mylab/ management** to complete the problems marked with this icon ⭐.

Summary

1. Managers' personnel and other decisions should be consistent with the goals that cascade down from the firm's overall strategic plan. Those goals form a hierarchy, stemming from the president's overall strategic goals and filtering down to what each individual manager needs to do to support that overall company goal. The management planning process includes setting an objective, making forecasts, determining what your alternatives are, evaluating your alternatives, and implementing and evaluating your plan.

2. Each function or department in the business needs its own functional strategy; strategic human resource management means formulating and executing human resource policies and practices that produce the employee competencies and behaviors the company needs to achieve its strategic aims. Human resource strategies are the human resource management policies and practices managers use to support their strategic aims. Important strategic human resource management tools include the strategy map, the HR scorecard, and digital dashboards.

3. The manager will want to gather and analyze data prior to making decisions. A high-performance work system is a set of human resource management policies and practices that promote organizational effectiveness. Human resource metrics (quantitative measures of human resource management activities such as employee turnover) are critical in creating high-performance human resource policies and practices.

4. A high-performance work system is a set of human resource management policies and practices that together produce superior employee performance.

5. Employee engagement is important because it drives performance and productivity. For example, based on one survey, business units with the highest levels of employee engagement have an 83% chance of performing above the company median; those with the lowest employee engagement have only a 17% chance.

6. Executing Kia UK's employee engagement HR strategy involved six steps. These were: set *measurable objectives* for the program; provide *leadership development,* for example, send all managers for training to improve their management skills; institute new *employee recognition programs,* for instance, giving "Outstanding Awards" to selected employees quarterly; develop *improved internal communications*, for instance, begin quarterly employee briefings; institute a new *employee development program*, for instance, using the company's appraisal process to identify employees' training needs and to create training plans for each employee; and change the *compensation* and *other policies* to ensure they are aligned with the new cultural values.

Key Terms

strategic plan 62
strategy 62
strategic management 62
vision statement 62
mission statement 63
corporate-level strategy 64
competitive strategy 65
competitive advantage 65
functional strategies 66

strategic human resource management 67
strategy map 69
HR scorecard 70
digital dashboard 71
strategy-based metrics 73
HR audit 75
high-performance work system 77
human resource metric 77

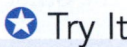 Try It

How would you apply the concepts and skills you learned in this chapter? If your professor has chosen to assign this, go to **www.pearson.com/mylab/management** and complete the strategic management simulation.

Discussion Questions

3-1. Give an example of hierarchical planning in an organization.

3-2. Define and give at least two examples of the cost leadership competitive strategy and the differentiation competitive strategy.

3-3. What is a high-performance work system? Provide several specific examples of the typical practices in a high-performance work system.

3-4. Explain why strategic planning is important to all managers.

3-5. Explain with examples each of the seven steps in the strategic planning process.

3-6. List with examples the main generic types of corporate strategies and competitive strategies.

3-7. Define strategic human resource management, and give an example of strategic human resource management in practice.

Individual and Group Activities

3-8. With three or four other students, form a strategic management group for your college or university. Your assignment is to develop the outline of a strategic plan for the college or university. This should include such things as mission and vision statements; strategic goals; and corporate, competitive, and functional strategies. In preparing your plan, make sure to show the main strengths, weaknesses, opportunities, and threats the college faces, and which prompted you to develop your particular strategic plans.

3-9. Using the Internet or library resources, analyze the annual reports of five companies. Bring to class examples of how those companies say they are using their HR processes to help them achieve their strategic goals.

3-10. Interview an HR manager, and write a short report entitled "The Strategic Roles of the HR Manager at XYZ Company."

3-11. Using the Internet or library resources, bring to class and discuss at least two examples of how companies are using an HR scorecard to help create HR systems that support the company's strategic aims. Do all managers seem to mean the same thing when they refer to HR scorecards? How do they differ?

3-12. Possibly in teams of several students, choose a company for which you will develop an outline of a strategic HR plan. What seem to be this company's main strategic aims? What is the firm's competitive strategy? What would the strategic map for this company look like? How would you summarize your recommended strategic HR policies for this company?

CHAPTER 3

3-13. For this activity, you will need the appendices titled "HRCI PHR® and SPHR® Certification Body of Knowledge" and "About the Society for Human Resource Management (SHRM) Body of Competency & Knowledge® Model and Certification Exams." Your instructor can obtain these appendices from the Pearson Instructor Resource Center and pass them onto you. These appendices list the knowledge someone studying for the HRCI or SHRM certification exam needs to have in each area of human resource management (such as in Strategic Management, and Workforce Planning). In groups of several students, do four things: (1) review Appendix A and/or B; (2) identify the material in this chapter that relates to the Appendix A and/or B required knowledge lists; (3) write four multiple-choice exam questions on this material that you believe would be suitable for inclusion in the HRCI exam and/or the SHRM exam; and, (4) if time permits, have someone from your team post your team's questions in front of the class, so that students in all teams can answer the exam questions created by the other teams.

MyLab Management

If your instructor is using MyLab Management, go to **www.pearson.com/mylab/management** for Auto-graded writing questions as well as the following Assisted-graded writing questions:

3-14. What is the difference between a strategy, a vision, and a mission? Give one example of each.

3-15. Explain how human resource management can be instrumental in helping a company create a competitive advantage.

APPLICATION EXERCISES

HR IN ACTION CASE INCIDENT 1
Siemens Builds a Strategy-Oriented HR System

Siemens is a 150-year-old German company, but it's not the company it was even a few years ago. Until recently, Siemens focused on producing electrical products. Today, the firm has diversified into software, engineering, and services. It is also global, with more than 400,000 employees working in 190 countries. In other words, Siemens became a world leader by pursuing a corporate strategy that emphasized diversifying into high-tech products and services, and doing so on a global basis.

With a corporate strategy like that, human resource management plays a big role at Siemens. Sophisticated engineering and services require more focus on employee selection, training, and compensation than in the average firm, and globalization requires delivering these HR services globally. Siemens sums up the basic themes of its HR strategy in several points. These include the following:

1. **A living company is a learning company.** The high-tech nature of Siemens's business means that employees must be able to learn on a continuing basis. Siemens uses its system of combined classroom and hands-on apprenticeship training around the world to help facilitate this. It also offers employees extensive continuing education and management development.

2. **Global teamwork is the key to developing and using all the potential of the firm's human resources.** Because it is so important for employees throughout Siemens to feel free to work together and interact, employees have to understand the whole process, not just bits and pieces. To support this, Siemens provides extensive training and development. It also ensures that all employees feel they're part of a strong, unifying corporate identity. For example, HR uses cross-border, cross-cultural experiences as prerequisites for career advances.

3. **A climate of mutual respect is the basis of all relationships—within the company and with society.** Siemens contends that the wealth of nationalities, cultures, languages, and outlooks represented by its employees is one of its most valuable assets. It therefore engages in numerous HR activities aimed at building openness, transparency, and fairness, and supporting diversity.

Questions

3-16. Based on the information in this case, provide examples for Siemens of at least four strategically required organizational outcomes (for example, customer service), and four required workforce competencies and behaviors.

3-17. Identify at least four strategically relevant HR policies and activities that Siemens has instituted to help human resource management contribute to achieving Siemens's strategic goals.

3-18. Provide a brief illustrative outline of a strategy map for Siemens.

HR IN ACTION CASE INCIDENT 2

Carter Cleaning Company

The High-Performance Work System

As a recent graduate and as a person who keeps up with the business press, Jennifer is familiar with the benefits of programs such as total quality management and high-performance work systems.

Jack has actually installed a total quality program of sorts at Carter, and it has been in place for about five years. This program takes the form of employee meetings. Jack holds employee meetings periodically, but particularly when there is a serious problem in a store—such as poor-quality work or machine breakdowns. When problems like these arise, he meets with all the employees in that store. Hourly employees get extra pay for these meetings. The meetings have been useful in helping Jack to identify and rectify several problems. For example, in one store, all the fine white blouses were coming out looking dingy. It turned out that the cleaner/spotter had been ignoring the company rule that required cleaning ("boiling down") the perchloroethylene cleaning fluid before washing items like these. As a result, these fine white blouses were being washed in cleaning fluid that had residue from other, earlier washes.

Jennifer now wonders whether these employee meetings should be expanded to give the employees a bigger role in managing the Carter stores' quality. "We can't be everywhere watching everything all the time," she said. "Yes, but these people earn only about $8 to $15 per hour. Will they really want to act like mini-managers?" Jack replied.

Questions

3-19. Would you recommend that the Carters expand their quality program? If so, specifically what form should it take?

3-20. Assume the Carters want to institute a high-performance work system as a test program in one of their stores. Write a one-page outline summarizing important HR practices you think they should focus on.

Experiential Exercise

Developing an HR Strategy for Starbucks

Several years ago, Starbucks was facing serious challenges. Sales per store were stagnant or declining, and its growth rate and profitability were down. Many believed that its introduction of breakfast foods had diverted its "baristas" from their traditional jobs as coffee-preparation experts. McDonald's and Dunkin' Donuts were introducing lower-priced but still high-grade coffees. Starbucks's former CEO stepped back into the company's top job. You need to help him formulate a new direction for his company.

Purpose: The purpose of this exercise is to give you experience in developing an HR strategy; in this case, by developing one for Starbucks.

Required Understanding: You should be thoroughly familiar with the material in this chapter.

How to Set Up the Exercise/Instructions: Set up groups of three or four students for this exercise. You are probably already quite familiar with what it's like to have a cup of coffee or tea in a Starbucks coffee shop, but if not, spend some time in one prior to this exercise. Meet in groups and develop an outline for an HR strategy for Starbucks Corp. Your outline should include four basic elements: a basic business/competitive strategy for Starbucks; workforce requirements (in terms of employee competencies and behaviors) this strategy requires; specific HR policies and the activities necessary to produce these workforce requirements; and suggestions for metrics to measure the success of the HR strategy.

PART

2

STAFFING: WORKFORCE PLANNING AND EMPLOYMENT

Company's Strategic Goals

Employee Competencies and Behaviors Required for Company to Achieve These Strategic Goals

2 Planning, Recruitment, and Selection

1 Strategic and Legal Environment

3 Training and Development

HR Policies and Practices Required to Produce Employee Competencies and Behaviors

5 Employee and Labor Relations

4 Compensation and Total Rewards

WHERE WE ARE NOW

Part 1, Introduction explained what human resource management is, the basic equal employment laws that govern personnel practices, and the meaning and methods of Strategic Human Resource Management.

Now we turn to actually managing human resources. Doing so usually starts with defining each worker's job and then recruiting and selecting new employees. *In Part 2, Staffing: Workforce Planning and Employment, we will therefore cover*

- Chapter 4, Job Analysis and Talent Management;
- Chapter 5, Personnel Planning and Recruiting; and
- Chapter 6, Selecting Employees.

The concepts and techniques we'll study here in Part 2 play a central role in strategic human resource management. As the accompanying HR Strategy Model shows, Strategic Human Resource Management means *formulating and executing human resource policies and practices that produce the employee competencies and behaviors the company needs to achieve its strategic aims.* We will see here in Part 2 that producing those required employee competencies and behaviors requires first putting in place practices for defining what each job entails (job analysis). Then the manager recruits high-potential applicants and selects the best. Then in Part 3, we will turn to training and developing these employees.

Job Analysis and Talent Management

OVERVIEW:
In this chapter, we will cover . . .

- The Talent Management Process
- The Basics of Job Analysis
- Methods for Collecting Job Analysis Information
- Writing Job Descriptions
- Writing Job Specifications
- Employee Engagement Guide for Managers
- Using Competencies Models

MyLab Management

⭐ Improve Your Grade!
When you see this icon, visit **www.pearson.com/mylab/management** for activities that are applied, personalized, and offer immediate feedback.

LEARNING OBJECTIVES

When you finish studying this chapter, you should be able to:

1. Define talent management, and explain why it is important.
2. Discuss the process of job analysis, including why it is important.
3. Explain how to use at least three methods of collecting job analysis information, including interviews, questionnaires, and observation.
4. Explain how you would write a job description.
5. Explain how to write a job specification.
6. List some human traits and behaviors you would want an employee to bring to a job if employee engagement is important to doing the job well.
7. Explain how to write competency-based models.

⭐ Learn It

If your professor has chosen to assign this, go to **www.pearson.com/mylab/management** to see what you should particularly focus on and to take the Chapter 4 Warm Up.

INTRODUCTION

Meg was pleased when her boss promoted her to accounting supervisor for Andean Research LLC, a 90-person company that solves pollution control problems. Four people reported to Meg in her new position: an accountant/internal auditor; two accounting clerks for accounts payable and for accounts receivable; and one payroll clerk. About one month into her new job, Meg discovered that the past month's payroll reports were wrong. Apparently, the clerk who was supposed to compare the actual payroll data to the IRS reports wasn't doing his job. How could the payroll clerk not know he had to do this? "You'd better get your people organized," said the president. We'll see what she did.

Source: Hero Images/Getty Images.

The Talent Management Process

For many people, Chapters 4–11 represent the heart of human resource management, specifically recruitment, selection, training, appraisal, career planning, and compensation. Managers traditionally view these activities as a series of steps:

1. Decide what positions to fill, through job analysis, personnel planning, and forecasting.
2. Build a pool of job applicants, by recruiting internal or external candidates.
3. Obtain application forms and perhaps have initial screening interviews.
4. Use selection tools like tests, interviews, background checks, and physical exams to identify viable candidates.
5. Decide to whom to make an offer.
6. Orient, train, and develop employees so they have the competencies to do their jobs.
7. Appraise employees to assess how they're doing.
8. Compensate employees to maintain their motivation.

This stepwise view makes sense. For example, an employer needs job candidates before selecting whom to hire.

The problem with the stepwise view is twofold. First, the process usually isn't really stepwise. For example, managers don't just train employees (step 6) and then appraise how they're doing (step 7). Instead (to use our example), the appraisal may well also loop back to shape the employee's subsequent training. So, first, rather than view these eight HR activities as stepwise, it is best to view them holistically—because the steps interactively affect each other and work together. The second problem is that focusing just on each step may cause the manager to miss, as it were, the forest for the trees. It's not just each step but the *results you obtain* by applying them together that's important. So, second, it's important to remember that each and every step should be focused on having the right people in the right jobs for some specific organizational result (such as, say, improving customer service).

Recognizing all this, the trend today is to view these eight activities not stepwise but as part of a coordinated *talent management* effort.[1] In simplest terms, talent management aims to get the right workers ("talent") on the right jobs at the right time. We will define **talent management** as *the holistic, integrated, and results and goal-oriented process of planning, recruiting, selecting, developing, managing, and compensating employees.* What does this involve in practice? The manager who takes a talent management approach tends to do the following:

talent management
The holistic, integrated, and results and goal-oriented process of planning, recruiting, selecting, developing, managing, and compensating employees.

1. He or she *starts with the results* and asks, "What recruiting, testing, training, or pay action should I take to produce the employee competencies we need *to achieve our company's goals?*"
2. He or she treats HR activities such as recruiting and training as *holistic and interrelated.* For example, the manager knows that having employees with the right skills depends as much on recruiting and training as on applicant testing.
3. Because talent management is holistic and integrated, the manager will endeavor to use the same "profile" of required human skills, knowledge, and behaviors ("competencies") for formulating a job's recruitment plans as for making selection, training, appraisal, and compensation decisions for it.
4. And, the manager will take steps to coordinate/integrate talent management functions such as recruiting and training, for example, by making sure he or she is using the same skills profile to recruit as to select, train, and appraise employees for a particular job. Doing so often involves the use of special talent management software.

Improving Performance through HRIS

Talent Management Software Many employers use talent management software systems to coordinate their talent-related activities. For example, Oracle says its Talent Management suite helps the manager to hire the best talent, provide real-time evaluations of workforce performance, and "[a]lign and develop your workforce with your talent management goals."[2] SilkRoad Technology's Talent Management Solution includes applicant tracking, onboarding, performance management, and compensation support. It helps the manager to ". . . recruit, manage, and retain your best employees."[3]

organization chart
A chart that shows the organization-wide distribution of work, with titles of each position and interconnecting lines that show who reports to and communicates with whom.

The Basics of Job Analysis

Talent management starts with understanding what jobs need to be filled and the human traits and competencies employees need to do those jobs effectively.

What Is Job Analysis?

Organizations consist of positions that have to be staffed. The **organization chart** (see Figure 4.1) shows the *title* of each supervisor's position and, by means of connecting lines, *who is accountable to whom,* who has *authority* for each area, and who is

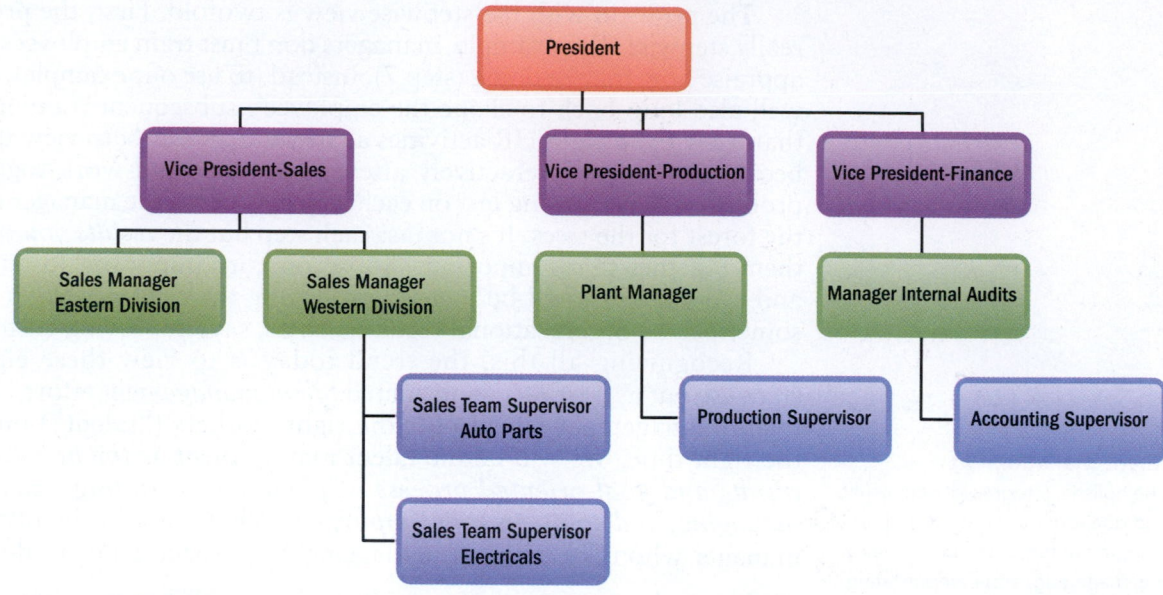

Figure 4.1
Organization Chart

job analysis

The procedure for determining the duties and skill requirements of a job and the kind of person who should be hired for it.

job descriptions

A list of a job's duties, responsibilities, reporting relationships, working conditions, and supervisory responsibilities—one product of a job analysis.

job specifications

A list of a job's "human requirements," that is, the requisite education, skills, personality, and so on—another product of a job analysis.

expected to *communicate* with whom. **Job analysis** is the procedure through which you determine the duties of the company's positions and the characteristics of the people to hire for them.[4] Job analysis produces information for writing **job descriptions** (a list of what the job entails) and **job (or "person") specifications** (what kind of people to hire for the job). Virtually every personnel-related action—interviewing applicants, and training and appraising employees, for instance—requires knowing what the job entails and what human traits one needs to do the job well.[5]

The supervisor or human resources specialist normally collects one or more of the following types of information via the job analysis:

- **Work activities.** Information about the job's actual work activities, such as cleaning, selling, teaching, or painting. This list may also include how, why, and when the worker performs each activity.
- **Human behaviors.** Information about human behaviors the job requires, like sensing, communicating, lifting weights, or walking long distances.
- **Machines, tools, equipment, and work aids.** For instance, tools used, materials processed, and knowledge applied (such as finance or law).
- **Performance standards.** Information about the job's performance standards (in terms of quantity or quality levels for each job duty, for instance).
- **Job context.** Information about such matters as physical working conditions, work schedule, incentives, and, for instance, the number of people with whom the employee would normally interact.
- **Human requirements.** Information such as knowledge or skills (education, training, work experience) and required personal attributes (aptitudes, personality, interests).

Uses of Job Analysis Information

Job analysis is essential. As summarized in Figure 4.2, the information produced by the job analysis is the basis for several HR activities that managers engage in almost every day. Specifically:

Recruitment and Selection: The job analysis produces information about what duties the job entails and what human characteristics are required to perform

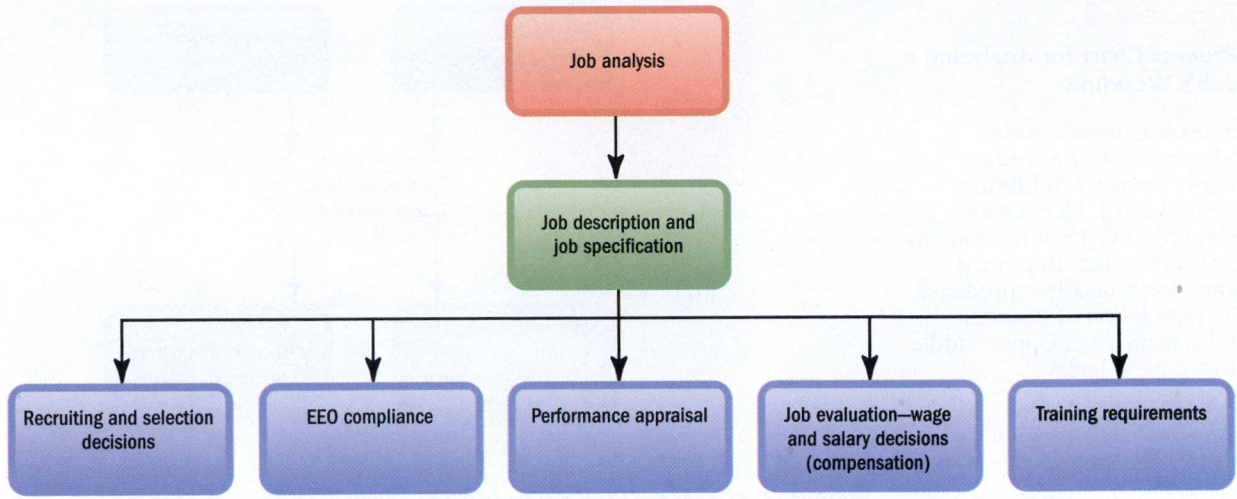

Figure 4.2
Uses of Job Analysis Information

these activities, and thus helps managers decide what sort of people to recruit and hire.

EEO Compliance: For example, to comply with the Americans with Disabilities Act, employers should know each job's essential job functions—which in turn requires a job analysis.

Training: The job description lists the job's specific duties and requisite skills—thus pinpointing what training the job requires.

Performance Appraisal: A performance appraisal compares each employee's actual performance with his or her duties and performance standards. Managers use job analysis to learn what these duties and standards are.

Compensation: Compensation levels usually depend on the job's required skill and education level, safety hazards, degree of responsibility, and so on—all factors you assess through job analysis.

Steps in Job Analysis

The typical job analysis involves six main steps:

Step 1: Identify the use to which the information will be put because this will determine how you collect the information. Some data collection techniques—like interviewing the employee—are good for writing job descriptions. Other techniques, like the position analysis questionnaire we describe later, provide numerical ratings you can use to compare jobs for compensation purposes.

Step 2: Review relevant background information about the job, such as organization charts and process charts.[6] For example, the *organization chart* shows where the job fits in the organization. A **process chart** provides a detailed picture of the job's work flow. In the process chart in Figure 4.3, the quality control clerk should review components coming from suppliers, check components going to the plant managers, and give information regarding the components' quality to these managers. Finally, an existing *job description* may provide a starting point for revising the job description. We'll look at work flow in more detail next.

process chart
A workflow chart that shows the flow of inputs to and outputs from a particular job.

Figure 4.3

Process Chart for Analyzing a Job's Workflow

Source: *Compensation Management: Rewarding Performance*, 6th Edition, by Richard J. Henderson. Copyright © 1994 by Pearson Education, Inc. Reprinted and electronically reproduced by permission of Pearson Education, Inc., Upper Saddle River, New Jersey.

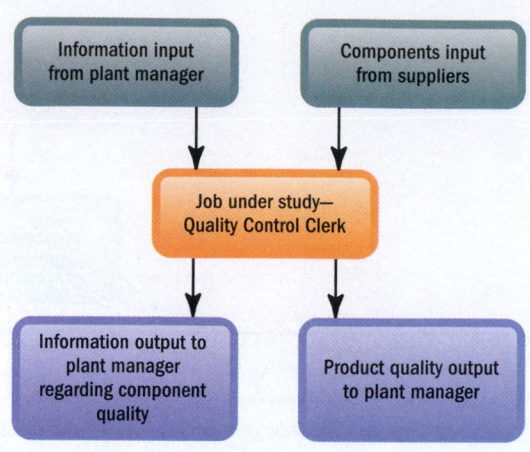

workflow analysis

A detailed study of the flow of work from job to job in a work process.

WORKFLOW ANALYSIS Reviewing the organization chart, process chart, and job description helps the manager understand what a job's duties and demands are now. However, it does *not* answer questions like "Does how this job relates to other jobs make sense?" or "Should this job even exist?" or "Should we redesign how this job is done?" To answer such questions, the manager may conduct a *workflow analysis*. **Workflow analysis** is a detailed study of the flow of work from job to job in one identifiable work process (such as processing a mortgage application). In turn, this analysis may lead to changing or "reengineering" the job. The accompanying HR as a Profit Center feature illustrates workflow analysis.

■ HR as a Profit Center

Boosting Productivity through Work Redesign

The Atlantic American insurance company conducted a workflow analysis to identify inefficiencies in how it processes insurance claims. As the firm's HR director said, "We followed the life of a claim to where it arrived in the mail and where it eventually ended up" in order to find ways to improve the process.[7]

The workflow analysis prompted several performance-boosting redesigns of the insurance claim jobs. The firm reduced from four to one the number of people opening mail, replacing three people with a machine that does it automatically. A new date stamping machine lets staff stamp 20 pages at a time rather than 1. A new software program adds bar codes to each claim automatically, rather than manually. The new system lowered costs.

✪ Talk About It– **1**

If your professor has chosen to assign this, go to **www.pearson.com/mylab/ management** to discuss the following questions. Based on your experience, what would the workflow look like for the process a dry-cleaning store uses to accept and chronicle a new order of clothes from a customer? How might this process be improved?

business process reengineering

Redesigning business processes, usually by combining steps, so that small multifunction process teams using information technology do the jobs formerly done by a sequence of departments.

To aid in conducting a workflow analysis, the manager may use a *flow process chart*; this lists each step of the process. The manager may convert this step-by-step flow process chart into a diagrammatic process chart. This shows, with arrows and circles, each step in the process.

BUSINESS PROCESS REENGINEERING The workflow analysis at American Atlantic led to a reengineering of its claims processing operation. **Business process reengineering**

means redesigning business processes, usually by combining steps so that small multifunction teams using information technology do the jobs formerly done by a sequence of departments. The basic reengineering process is to:

1. identify a business process to be redesigned (such as processing an insurance claim);
2. measure the performance of the existing processes;
3. identify opportunities to improve these processes;
4. redesign and implement a new way of doing the work; and
5. assign ownership of sets of formerly separate tasks to an individual or a team who uses computers to support the new arrangement.

As at Atlantic American, reengineering usually requires *redesigning* individual jobs. For example, Atlantic's "date stamping" workers must now learn the new date-stamping machine. In turn, job redesign may lead to job enlargement, rotation, or enrichment.

JOB REDESIGN Early economists enthusiastically described why specialized jobs were more efficient (as in, "practice makes perfect"). Today, most agree that specialized jobs can backfire, for instance by sapping morale. Experts typically suggest three ways to redesign specialized jobs to make them more challenging.

job enlargement

Assigning workers additional same-level activities.

job rotation

Systematically moving workers from one job to another.

job enrichment

Redesigning jobs in a way that increases the opportunities for the worker to experience feelings of responsibility, achievement, growth, and recognition.

Job enlargement means assigning workers additional same-level activities. Thus, the worker who previously only bolted the seat to the legs might attach the back too. **Job rotation** means systematically moving workers from one job to another.

Psychologist Frederick Herzberg argued that the best way to motivate workers is through job enrichment. **Job enrichment** means redesigning jobs in a way that increases the opportunities for the worker to experience feelings of responsibility, achievement, growth, and recognition—and therefore more motivation. At Atlantic American, managers enriched jobs by, for instance, putting a team in charge of processing an entire claim.[8] This assumedly empowers the workers—for instance, by giving them the skills and authority to inspect the work, instead of having supervisors do that. Herzberg said empowered employees would do their jobs well because they wanted to, and quality and productivity would rise. That philosophy, in one form or another, is the theoretical basis for the team-based self-managing jobs in many companies around the world today. Now lets return to the main steps in job analysis.

Step 3: With a job to analyze, the manager then generally selects a sample of positions to focus on. For example, to analyze an assembler's job, it is probably unnecessary to analyze the jobs of all the firm's 200 assembly workers; instead, a sample of 10 jobs will do.

Step 4: Analyze the job. The manager then turns to actually analyzing the job, using one or more of the methods we describe in the next section.

Step 5: After actually analyzing the job, verify the information with the worker and with his or her immediate supervisor. The aims here are to confirm that the information (for instance, on the job's duties) is factually correct and complete, and to help gain the worker's and supervisor's acceptance.

Step 6: Develop a job description and job specification. The *job description* lists the duties, activities, and responsibilities of the job, as well as its important features, such as working conditions. The *job specification* summarizes the personal qualities, traits, skills, and background required for getting the job done.

Methods for Collecting Job Analysis Information

There are various methods (interviews or questionnaires, for instance) for actually collecting job information, and you should use those that best fit your purpose. For example, an interview might be best for creating a list of job duties, while the "position analysis questionnaire" is better for quantifying each job's worth for pay purposes.

In larger firms, the job analysis should be a joint effort by the human resource manager, worker, and worker's supervisor. The human resource manager might observe the worker doing the job and have both the supervisor and worker fill out job questionnaires. Then he or she lists the job's duties and required human traits. The supervisor and worker then verify the HR manager's list of job duties.

Actually collecting the job analysis information is straightforward: greet each worker; briefly explain the job analysis process and the participants' roles in this process; spend about 15 minutes interviewing the employee to get agreement on a basic summary of the job; identify the job's broad areas of responsibility, such as "calling on potential clients"; and then identify specific duties/tasks within each area using one of the following standard job analysis methods.[9] Make sure the worker understands the questions and the process.

The Interview

Managers may conduct *individual* interviews with each employee, *group* interviews with groups of employees who have the same job, and/or *supervisor* interviews with one or more supervisors who know the job. Use group interviews when a large number of employees are performing similar or identical work because this can be a quick and inexpensive way to gather information. As a rule, the workers' immediate supervisor attends the group session; if not, you can interview him or her separately.

The worker should understand the reason for the interview. There's a tendency for workers to view such interviews as "efficiency evaluations" and to hesitate to describe their jobs accurately.

Typical Questions Typical interview questions include the following:

What is the job being performed?

What exactly are the major duties of your position?

What physical locations do you work in?

What are the education, experience, skill, and (where applicable) certification and licensing requirements?

What are the job's responsibilities and duties?

What are the basic accountabilities or performance standards that typify your work?

What are your responsibilities?

What are the environmental and working conditions involved?

What are the job's physical demands? The emotional and mental demands?

Are you exposed to any hazards or unusual working conditions?

Structured Interviews Many managers use questionnaires to structure and guide the interview, as in Figure 4.4. These include questions regarding matters like the general purpose of the job; supervisory responsibilities; job duties; and education, experience, and skills required.

Such structured lists are not just for interviews. Job analysts who collect information by personally observing the work or by using questionnaires—two methods explained later—can also use structured lists.[10] The Skills feature elaborates.

Job analysts may conduct _individual_ interviews with each employee, _group_ interviews with groups of employees, and/or _supervisor_ interviews with one or more supervisors who know the job.

Source: Antonio Diaz/123RF.

BUILDING YOUR MANAGEMENT SKILLS
Interviewing Guidelines

There are several things to keep in mind when conducting a job analysis interview. First, the job analyst and supervisor should work together. Identify workers who know the most about the job, and who might be expected to be the most objective in describing their duties and responsibilities.

Second, establish rapport quickly with the interviewee; know the person's name; speak in easily understood language; briefly review the purpose of the interview; and explain how the person was chosen for the interview. Distortion of information can be a problem.[11] Job analysis often precedes changing a job's pay rate. Employees therefore may exaggerate some responsibilities.

Third, if possible, follow a structured guide or checklist, one that lists questions and provides space for answers. This ensures that you'll identify crucial questions ahead of time, and that all interviewers cover the same ground. However, also ask, "Was there anything we didn't cover with our questions?"

Fourth, when duties are not performed in a regular manner—for instance, when the worker doesn't perform the same job repeatedly—you should ask the worker to list his or her duties in order of importance and frequency of occurrence. This will ensure that crucial activities that occur infrequently—like a nurse's occasional emergency-room duties—aren't overlooked.

Finally, review and verify the data with the worker and his or her supervisor.

Questionnaires

Having employees fill out questionnaires to describe their job duties and responsibilities is another good way to obtain job analysis information.

Some questionnaires are structured checklists. Here each employee gets an inventory of perhaps hundreds of specific tasks (such as "change and splice wire"). He or she must indicate if he or she performs each task and, if so, how much time is spent on each. At the other extreme, the questionnaire may simply ask, "Describe the major duties of your job."

Figure 4.4

Job Analysis Questionnaire for Developing Job Descriptions

Sources: Adapted from: www .tsu.edu/PDFFiles/Human%20 Resources/HR%20Forms/ JAQ%20FORM_rev%20 100809%20a.pdf; www .delawarepersonnel.com/class/ forms/jaq/jaq.shtml; www .uh.edu/human-resources/ forms/JAQ.doc; www.tnstate .edu/hr/documents/.../Job%20 Analysis%20Questionnaire .doc. All accessed July 24, 2013. *Copyright Gary Dessler PhD.

JOB ANALYSIS QUESTIONNAIRE*

PURPOSE AND INSTRUCTIONS

Because no one knows the job as well as the person doing it, we are asking you to complete this form. The purpose is to obtain current information on your job based on a review of job duties and responsibilities. We are not asking you about your job performance; only what your job requires you to do.

EMPLOYEE DATA (PLEASE PRINT):

Your Name: _____   Today's date _____

Employee ID: _____

Location/Department: _____

Your Job Title: _____   Job Code: _____

How long have you been in your current position: _____

Work Telephone Number: _____

Supervisor's Name: _____   Supervisor's Title: _____

SUMMARY OF DUTIES/RESPONSIBILITIES

Give a brief description of the main function/purpose of your job. This statement should be a brief summary of the responsibilities listed in the next section.

_____

_____

_____

Listing of Job Duties

What do you do on your job? Please list your job's specific duties/responsibilities in the space below. In doing so:

   Please list the most important duties/responsibilities first. Write a separate statement for each duty/responsibility.

   At the end of each statement, please indicate the approximate percent of your workday (25%, 7%, etc.) you spend on that duty.

   Please place an asterisk (*) next to the duties that you consider to be absolutely essential to this job.

_____

_____

_____

_____

_____

(Add additional duties as necessary)

Are there duties you are now performing that are not now in your job description? If so, please list them on back of this page.

(Continued)

Figure 4.4
(*Continued*)

Minimum Level of Education (or Equivalent Experience) This Job Requires

What is the minimum level of education necessary to perform your job? Select only one please:

1. Elementary education
2. Some high school
3. A high school diploma or equivalent (G.E.D.)
4. A formal vocational training program (approximately one year), an apprenticeship, or some formal college education
5. An associate's degree (AA, AS)
6. A bachelor's degree (BA, BS)
7. A master's degree (MA, MS, MBA, MPA)
8. A doctorate degree (Ph.D., MD, JD, EED)
9. Are you required to be licensed or certified to perform your work?

[ ] Yes [ ] No List type _____

Required Training on Job

What is the level of on-the-job or classroom training someone requires to do your job? Please select one choice below:

1. No additional training required.
2. A day or two
3. A week
4. A month
5. Several months
6. One year
7. Two years or more

SUPERVISORY RESPONSIBILITIES

Do you supervise others as part of your job? If so, please briefly describe the nature of your supervisory responsibilities.

PHYSICAL JOB DEMANDS

Please briefly describe this job's main physical demands. For example, does it involve: Sitting? Walking? Standing? Lifting? Detailed repetitive motions? Climbing? Etc.

Working Conditions: Environmental and Safety Job Demands

Please list this job's working conditions, such as: air-conditioned office work; outdoor or indoor extreme heat or cold; wet; noise; job hazards; working in elevated conditions; etc.

EMPLOYEE COMMENTS

Is there any other information that would be important in understanding your job? If so, please give us your comments below.

SUPERVISOR'S REVIEW

Based on your understanding of the job as it currently exists, please review the employee's response and provide your own comments in the space below. **Please do not change the employee's responses.**

In practice, the best questionnaires fall in between. As in Figure 4.4, a typical job analysis questionnaire might include several open-ended questions (such as "What do you do on your job?") as well as structured questions (concerning, for instance, education required).

A questionnaire is a quick and efficient way to obtain information from a large number of employees; it's less costly than interviewing hundreds of workers, for instance. However, developing the questionnaire and testing it (perhaps by making sure the workers understand the questions) can be time consuming. And, as with interviews, employees may distort their answers.

Observation

Direct observation is especially useful when jobs consist mainly of observable physical activities—assembly-line worker and accounting clerk are examples. However, observation is usually not appropriate when the job entails a lot of mental activity (lawyer, design engineer). Nor is it useful if the employee only occasionally engages in important activities, such as a nurse who handles emergencies. *Reactivity*—the worker changing what he or she normally does because you are watching—is another problem.

Managers often use direct observation and interviewing together. One approach is to observe the worker on the job during a complete work cycle. (The *cycle* is the time it takes to complete the job; it could be a minute for an assembly-line worker or an hour, a day, or longer for complex jobs.) Here you take notes of all the job activities. Then, ask the person to clarify open points and to explain any unobserved activities he or she performs.

Participant Diary/Logs

diary/log
Daily listings made by workers of every activity in which they engage, along with the time each activity takes.

Another method is to ask workers to keep a **diary/log**; here, for every activity engaged in, the employee records the activity (along with the time) in a log.

Some firms give employees pocket dictating machines and pagers. Then randomly during the day they page the workers, who dictate what they are doing at that time.

Quantitative Job Analysis Techniques: The Position Analysis Questionnaire (PAQ)

position analysis questionnaire (PAQ)
A questionnaire used to collect quantifiable data concerning the duties and responsibilities of various jobs.

Qualitative methods like interviews and questionnaires are not always suitable. For example, if your aim is to compare jobs for pay purposes, a mere listing of duties may not suffice. You may need to say that, in effect, "Job A is twice as challenging as Job B, and so is worth twice the pay." For this, quantitative job ratings are useful.

The **position analysis questionnaire (PAQ)** is one popular quantitative job analysis tool, consisting of a questionnaire containing 194 items.[12] The 194 items each belong to one of five PAQ basic activities: (1) having decision-making/communication/social responsibilities, (2) performing skilled activities, (3) being physically active, (4) operating vehicles/equipment, and (5) processing information. For example, two items an employee may (or may not) use within the basic activity "processing information" would be "written materials," and "pictorial material." The job analyst decides if each of the 194 items plays a role in the person's job, and, if so, to what extent. For example, he or she might rate "written materials" a 4. Because the scale ranges from 1 to 5, a 4 suggests that written materials (such as books and reports) do play a significant role in this job. The job's final PAQ "score" shows the job's rating on each of the five basic activities on a 1 (very infrequent use) to 5 (very substantial use) scale. The analyst can use an online version of the PAQ (see www.paq.com) for each job he or she is analyzing.

The PAQ is particularly useful for assigning jobs to job classes for pay purposes. With ratings for each job's decision making, skilled activity, physical activity, vehicle/equipment operation, and information-processing characteristics, you can quantitatively compare jobs relative to one another,[13] and then classify jobs for pay purposes.[14]

Electronic Job Analysis Methods[15]

Employers increasingly rely on electronic or online job analysis methods. For example, rather than collecting information about a job through direct interviews or questionnaires, the analyst uses online systems to send job questionnaires to job experts (often job incumbents) in remote company locations. The job analyst may also convene, perhaps via Facetime or Skype, the job experts to discuss and finalize the knowledge, skills, abilities, and other characteristics required for doing the job and its tasks.[16]

Conducting the job analysis this way is often an obvious choice.[17] Most simply, the human resource department can distribute standardized job analysis questionnaires to geographically disbursed employees digitally, with instructions to complete the forms and return them by a particular date. Ensure the instructions are clear, and first test the process.

✪ Watch It

If the professor has chosen to assign this, go to **www.pearson.com/mylab/ management** to see how an actual company uses job analysis, and to watch the video Weather Channel Talent Management and then answer the questions to show what you'd do in this situation.

LEARNING OBJECTIVE **4**
Explain how you would write a job description.

Writing Job Descriptions

The most important product of job analysis is the job description. A job description is a written statement of what the worker actually does, how he or she does it, and what the job's working conditions are. This information is in turn used to write a job specification; this lists the knowledge, abilities, and skills required to perform the job satisfactorily.[18]

There is no standard format for writing a job description. However, most descriptions contain sections that cover:

1. Job identification
2. Job summary
3. Responsibilities and duties
4. Authority of incumbent
5. Standards of performance
6. Working conditions
7. Job specification

Figures 4.5 and 4.6 (on pages 100–101, 104) present two sample forms of job descriptions.

Job Identification

As in Figure 4.5, the job identification section (on top) contains several types of information.[19] The *job title* specifies the name of the job, such as "supervisor of data processing operations," or "inventory control clerk." The Fair Labor

Standards Act (FLSA) status section identifies the job as exempt or nonexempt. (The FLSA exempts certain positions from the act's overtime and minimum wage provisions.) *Date* is the date the job description was actually approved.

There may also be a space to indicate who approved the description and for the immediate supervisor's title, and perhaps one showing the job's location (facility/

JOB TITLE: Telesales Representative	JOB CODE: 100001
RECOMMENDED SALARY GRADE:	EXEMPT/NONEXEMPT STATUS: Nonexempt
JOB FAMILY: Sales	EEOC: Sales Workers
DIVISION: Higher Education	REPORTS TO: District Sales Manager
DEPARTMENT: In-House Sales	LOCATION: Boston
	DATE: May 18, 2017

SUMMARY (Write a brief summary of job.)

The person in this position is responsible for selling college textbooks, software, and multimedia products to professors, via incoming and outgoing telephone calls, and to carry out selling strategies to meet sales goals in assigned territories of smaller colleges and universities. In addition, the individual in this position will be responsible for generating a designated amount of editorial leads and communicating to the publishing groups product feedback and market trends observed in the assigned territory.

SCOPE AND IMPACT OF JOB
Dollar responsibilities (budget and/or revenue)

The person in this position is responsible for generating approximately $2 million in revenue, for meeting operating expense budget of approximately $4000, and a sampling budget of approximately 10,000 units.

Supervisory responsibilities (direct and indirect)

None

Other

REQUIRED KNOWLEDGE AND EXPERIENCE (Knowledge and experience necessary to do job)
Related work experience

Prior sales or publishing experience preferred. One year of company experience in a customer service or marketing function with broad knowledge of company products and services is desirable.

Formal education or equivalent

Bachelor's degree with strong academic performance or work equivalent experience.

Skills

Must have strong organizational and persuasive skills. Must have excellent verbal and written communications skills and must be PC proficient.

Other

Limited travel required (approx 5%)

(Continued)

Figure 4.5

Sample Job Description, Pearson Education

Source: Reprinted and electronically reproduced by permission of Pearson Education, Inc., Upper Saddle River, New Jersey.

PRIMARY RESPONSIBILITIES (List in order of importance and list amount of time spent on task.)

<u>Driving Sales (60%)</u>

- Achieve quantitative sales goal for assigned territory of smaller colleges and universities.
- Determine sales priorities and strategies for territory and develop a plan for implementing those strategies.
- Conduct 15–20 professor interviews per day during the academic sales year that accomplishes those priorities.
- Conduct product presentations (including texts, software, and Web site); effectively articulate author's central vision of key titles; conduct sales interviews using the PSS model; conduct walk-through of books and technology.
- Employ telephone selling techniques and strategies.
- Sample products to appropriate faculty, making strategic use of assigned sampling budgets.
- Close class test adoptions for first edition products.
- Negotiate custom publishing and special packaging agreements within company guidelines.
- Initiate and conduct in-person faculty presentations and selling trips as appropriate to maximize sales with the strategic use of travel budget. Also use internal resources to support the territory sales goals.
- Plan and execute in-territory special selling events and book-fairs.
- Develop and implement in-territory promotional campaigns and targeted email campaigns.

<u>Publishing (editorial/marketing) 25%</u>

- Report, track, and sign editorial projects.
- Gather and communicate significant market feedback and information to publishing groups.

<u>Territory Management 15%</u>

- Track and report all pending and closed business in assigned database.
- Maintain records of customer sales interviews and adoption situations in assigned database.
- Manage operating budget strategically.
- Submit territory itineraries, sales plans, and sales forecasts as assigned.
- Provide superior customer service and maintain professional bookstore relations in assigned territory.

<u>Decision-Making Responsibilities for This Position:</u>

Determine the strategic use of assigned sampling budget to most effectively generate sales revenue to exceed sales goals.
Determine the priority of customer and account contacts to achieve maximum sales potential.
Determine where in-person presentations and special selling events would be most effective to generate the most sales.

Submitted By: Jim Smith, District Sales Manager	Date: May 18, 2017
Approval:	Date:
Human Resources:	Date:
Corporate Compensation:	Date:

Figure 4.5
(*Continued*)

division and department). There might also be spaces here for the job's grade/level (programmer II, programmer III, and so on,) and for information on salary and/or pay scale.

What's in a Name (or in a Job Title)? Some of the job titles you'll find on social media are quite creative. For example, Pinterest calls its designers Pixel Pushers, and its interns Pinterns.[20]

At first glance such titles might seem frivolous, but they may in fact be useful. Researchers conducted several studies (including one in a hospital) to determine if job titles affected employee morale. They asked workers to rewrite their job titles (thus someone specializing in infectious diseases became a "germ slayer").[21] The researchers concluded that employees who are involved with retitling their jobs and who have more descriptive job titles tend to be more satisfied and to feel more recognized.

The U.S. Navy recently discovered that the hard way. Probably from the beginnings of the Navy, each sailor traditionally had a descriptive job title, such as "electrician's mate first class." In part to strip its job titles of gender specific labels containing "man" or "men," the Navy decided to simply group all sailors with the same pay rate together, with the same (bland) job title, such as "petty officer first class."[22] An uproar ensued. A petition with over 100,000 signatures got to the White House. The Navy soon returned to its traditional job titles.

Job Summary

The job summary should summarize the essence of the job and include only its major functions or activities. Thus (in Figure 4.5), the telesales rep "... is responsible for selling college textbooks. . . . " For the job of mailroom supervisor, "the mailroom supervisor receives, sorts, and delivers all incoming mail properly, and he or she handles all outgoing mail including the accurate and timely posting of such mail."[23]

Some experts state unequivocally that "one item frequently found that should never be included in a job description is a 'cop-out clause' like 'other duties, as assigned,' "[24] because this leaves open the nature of the job. State in the summary that the employee is expected to carry out his or her duties efficiently, attentively, and conscientiously.

Relationships

There may be a "relationships" statement (not in Figure 4.5) that shows the jobholder's relationships with others. For example, a human resource manager's statement might say:[25]

Reports to: Vice president of employee relations

Supervises: Human resource clerk, test administrator, labor relations director, and one secretary

Works with: All department managers and executive management

Outside the company: Employment agencies, executive recruiting firms, union representatives, state and federal employment offices, and various vendors[26]

Responsibilities and Duties

This is the heart of the job description. It should present a list of the job's significant responsibilities and duties. As in Figure 4.5, list each of the job's major duties separately, and describe it in a few sentences. In the figure, for instance, the job's duties include "achieve quantitative sales goal . . . " and "determine sales priorities. . . . " Typical duties for other jobs might include making accurate postings to accounts payable, maintaining favorable purchase price variances, and repairing production-line tools and equipment. This section may also define the jobholder's authority limits, such as to approve purchase requests up to $5,000.

BUILDING YOUR MANAGEMENT SKILLS
Determining the Job's Duties

Standard Occupational Classification (SOC)
Classifies all workers into one of 23 major groups of jobs that are subdivided into minor groups of jobs and detailed occupations.

Of course the crucial question here is, "How do I determine what the job's duties are and should be?" The answer first is, from the *job analysis*; this should reveal what the employees on each job are doing now.

Second, there are governmental sources of standardized job description information. For example, the U.S. Department of Labor did much of the early work developing job analysis.[27] It compiled its results in what was for many years the bible of job descriptions, the *Dictionary of Occupational Titles*. This mammoth book contained detailed information on virtually every job in America. We'll see that Internet-based tools such as O*NET online have largely replaced the *Dictionary*. (We present an example later in this section.) Another option is the government's **Standard Occupational Classification** (SOC; www.bls.gov/soc/socguide.htm). This classifies all workers into one of 23 major groups of jobs, such as "Management Occupations" and "Healthcare Occupations." These in turn contain 96 minor groups of jobs, which in turn include 821 detailed occupations, such as the marketing manager description in Figure 4.6 (on page 104). The manager may also use proprietary online sources of job description information, such as www.jobdescription.com.

Another simple solution is just to Google the job description you want, to see online what others are doing. Thus, someone writing job descriptions for jobs such as marketing manager would readily find relevant online descriptions as follows:

Go to http://hiring.monster.com. Then click Resource Center, then Recruiting and Hiring Advice, then Job descriptions, then Sample job descriptions. Then scroll down to Marketing and Sales Manager Sample Job Description.[28]

Or go to http://www.careerplanner.com/. Then click Job Descriptions, then scroll down to the job description you're interested in.[29]

As an example, Meg, the accounting supervisor from the chapter opener, couldn't see how her payroll clerk could have missed reconciling the actual payroll with the payroll report he sent to the IRS. What duty was missing? How might she make use of online descriptions such as:

Go to http://www.americasjobexchange.com/. Then click resources, then Browse Job Description. Then go to Clerical & Administrative, then to Payroll & Timekeeping Clerk.[30] (Or she could try similar descriptions at careerbuilder.com.) LinkedIn is another option, as in the following Trends feature.

TRENDS SHAPING HR: *Digital and Social Media*

USING LINKEDIN Sometimes the easiest way to unearth job titles and duties is just to use social media like LinkedIn. For example, to paraphrase what someone who recruits for open positions in his company posted on LinkedIn: I hope some of you IT recruiters out there can help me to better understand what I need to put into the job descriptions that I'm writing for the developers and development managers I'm recruiting for. The first of many replies listed 12 tasks including: (1) Do technical skills match the desired job? (2) What technical problems were solved by the job seeker? and (3) Did job seeker know about Cloud Deployment?[31]

Figure 4.6

Marketing Manager Description from DOL Standard Occupational Classification

Source: U.S. Department of Labor, Bureau of Labor Statistics.

**U.S.
Department
of Labor**
Bureau of
Labor Statistics
Standard Occupational Classification

www.bls.gov   **Advanced Search | A-Z Index**

BLS Home | Programs & Surveys | Get Detailed Statistics | Glossary | What's New | Find It! In DOL

11-2021 Marketing Managers

Determine the demand for products and services offered by a firm and its competitors and identify potential customers. Develop pricing strategies with the goal of maximizing the firm's profits or share of the market while ensuring the firm's customers are satisfied. Oversee product development or monitor trends that indicate the need for new products and services.

In any case, writing clear job duties is crucial. For a nurse, for example, one duty might be:[32]

Incorrect: Ensures that patients receive medical attention when needed.

Comment: What the nurse does is ambiguous, and the expected results of the nurse's actions aren't clear.

Correct: Administers minor medical treatments or medication (taking temperatures, treating minor cuts and bruises, giving aspirin or cough syrup) to correct or treat residents' minor health problems using common first aid supplies and using own discretion to determine need following established institutional medical department procedures.

KNOW YOUR EMPLOYMENT LAW
Writing Job Descriptions that Comply with the ADA

The list of job duties is crucial to employers' efforts to comply with the Americans with Disabilities Act (ADA). Under the ADA, the individual must have the requisite skills, educational background, and experience to perform the job's essential functions. The EEOC says, "Essential functions are the basic job duties that an employee must be able to perform, with or without reasonable accommodation."[33] Factors to consider include:

- Whether the position exists to perform that function
- The number of other employees available to perform the function
- The degree of expertise or skill required to perform the function
- Whether employees in the position are actually required to perform the function[34]
- What the degree of expertise or skill required to perform the function is[35]

As an example, answering calls and directing visitors to the proper offices might be essential functions for a receptionist's job. The EEOC says it will consider the employer's judgment about which functions are essential and a written job description prepared before advertising or interviewing for a job as evidence of essential functions. Other evidence includes the actual work experience of present or past employees in the job, the time spent performing a function, and the consequences of not requiring that an employee perform a function. Although the EEOC does not require employers to have job descriptions, it is obviously useful here to have one.

The ADA requires that employers list a job's essential functions.

Source: Blend Images - DreamPictures/ Vstock/Getty Images.

If the disabled individual can't perform the job as currently structured, the employer is required to make a "reasonable accommodation," unless doing so would present an "undue hardship." According to the EEOC, reasonable accommodation may include:

- acquiring or modifying equipment or devices;
- job restructuring;
- part-time or modified work schedules;
- reassignment to a vacant position;
- adjusting or modifying examinations, training materials, or policies;
- providing readers and interpreters; and
- making the workplace readily accessible to and usable by people with disabilities. ■

Standards of Performance and Working Conditions

A "standards of performance" section lists the standards the company expects the employee to achieve for each of the job description's main duties and responsibilities. One way to set standards is to finish the statement, "I will be completely satisfied with your work when. . . . " This sentence, if completed for each listed duty, should result in a usable set of performance standards. For example:

Duty: **Accurately Posting Accounts Payable**

1. Post all invoices received within the same working day.
2. Route all invoices to the proper department managers for approval no later than the day following receipt.
3. Commit an average of no more than three posting errors per month.

The job description may also list the job's working conditions, such as noise level, hazardous conditions, or heat. The following HR Tools feature shows how to use the Internet to create a job description.

■ HR Tools for Line Managers and Small Businesses

Using O*NET

Without their own job analysts or even HR managers, many small business owners face two hurdles when doing job analyses. First, most need a more streamlined approach than those provided by job analysis questionnaires like that in Figure 4.4. Second is the concern that, in writing their job descriptions, they'll overlook duties that subordinates should be assigned. What they need is an encyclopedia listing all the possible positions they might encounter, including a list of the duties normally assigned to these positions.

The small business owner has at least three options. The Standard Occupational Classification, mentioned earlier, provides detailed descriptions of thousands of jobs and their human requirements. Websites like www.jobdescription.com provide customizable descriptions by title and industry. And the Department of Labor's O*NET is a third alternative. We'll focus here on how to write a job description using O*NET (www.onetonline.org/).[36]

O*NET

The U.S. Department of Labor's online occupational information network, called O*NET, is a popular tool. It enables users (not just managers, but workers and job seekers) to see the most important characteristics of various occupations, as well as the experience, education, and knowledge required to do each job well. Both the Standard Occupational Classification and O*NET list the specific duties associated with numerous occupations. O*NET also lists skills, including *basic skills* such as reading and writing, *process skills* such as critical thinking, and *transferable skills* such as persuasion and negotiation.[37] An O*NET job listing also includes information on worker requirements (required knowledge, for instance), occupation requirements (such as compiling, coding, and categorizing data, for instance), and experience requirements (including education and job training). Employers and career planners also use O*NET to check the job's labor market characteristics, such as employment projections and earnings data.[38]

The steps in using O*Net to facilitate writing a job description follow.

Step 1: Decide on a Plan. Ideally, the jobs you need should flow from your departmental or company plans. Do you plan to enter or exit businesses? What do you expect your sales to be in the next few years? What departments will have to be expanded or reduced? What new positions will you need?

Step 2: Develop an Organization Chart. Start with the organization as it is now. Then produce a chart showing how you want it to look in a year or two. Microsoft Office and others offer free tools.[39]

Step 3: Use a Job Analysis Questionnaire. Next, gather information about each job's duties. (You can use job analysis questionnaires, such as those shown in Figure 4.4 and Figure 4.7).

Step 4: Obtain Job Duties from O*NET. The list of job duties you uncovered through the job analysis in step 3 may or may not be complete. We'll therefore use O*NET to compile a more complete list. (Refer to the A, B, and C examples pictured.)

Start by going to www.onetonline.org/[40] (A). Here, click on *Find Occupations*. Assume you want to create job descriptions for a retail salesperson. Key *Retail Sales* in the Industry Keyword drop-down box. This brings you to the Occupations matching "retail sales" page (B).[41]

Clicking on the *Retail Salespersons* summary produces the job summary and specific occupational duties for retail salespersons (C).[42] For a small store, you might want to combine the duties of the "retail salesperson" with those of "first-line supervisors/managers of retail sales workers."

Step 5: List the Job's Human Requirements from O*NET. Next, return to the summary for *Retail Salespersons* (C). Here, click, for example, Knowledge, Skills, and Abilities. Use this information to help develop a job specification for your job. Use this information for recruiting, selecting, and training your employees.

Source: Reprinted by permission of O*NET OnLine.

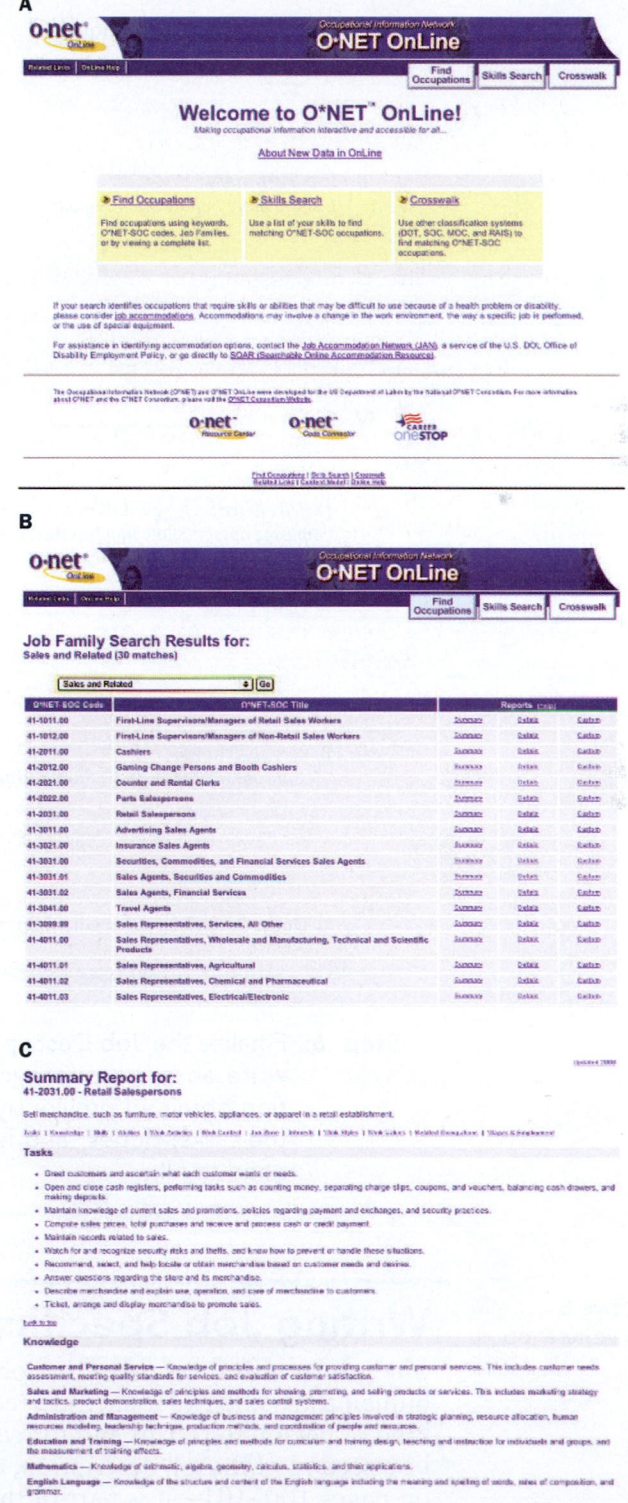

Figure 4.7

**Simple Job Analysis/
Description Questionnaire**
Source: Copyright Gary
Dessler PhD.

**Background Data
for Job Description**

Job Title _____   Department _____

Job Number _____   Written by _____

Today's Date _____   Applicable DOT Codes _____

I. Applicable DOT Definition(s):

II. Job Summary:
(List the more important or regularly performed tasks)

III. Reports To:

IV. Supervises: _____

V. Job Duties: _____
*(Briefly describe, for each duty, what employee does and, if possible, how
employee does it. Show in parentheses at end of each duty the approximate
percentage of time devoted to duty.)*

A. Daily Duties:

B. Periodic Duties:
(Indicate whether weekly, monthly, quarterly, etc.)

C. Duties Performed at Irregular Intervals:

Step 6: Finalize the Job Description. Finally, perhaps using Figure 4.5 as a guide, write an appropriate job summary for the job. Then use the information obtained previously in steps 4 and 5 to create a complete listing of the tasks, duties, and human requirements of each of the jobs you will need to fill.

LEARNING OBJECTIVE 5
Explain how to write a job specification.

Writing Job Specifications

The job specification takes the job description and answers the question, "What human traits and experience are required to do this job effectively?" It shows what kind of person to recruit and for what qualities you should test that person. It may be a section of the job description, or a separate document. Often—as in Figure 4.5 on pages 100–101—it is part of the job description.[43]

Specifications for Trained versus Untrained Personnel

Writing job specifications for trained and experienced employees is relatively straightforward. Here job specifications tend to focus on factors such as length of previous service, quality of relevant training, and previous job performance.

The problems are more complex when you're filling jobs with untrained people (with the intention of training them on the job). Here you must specify qualities such as physical traits, personality, interests, or sensory skills that imply some potential for performing the job or for trainability. Thus, for a job that requires detailed manipulation, you might want someone with excellent finger dexterity. Employers identify the job's human requirements either through a subjective, judgmental approach or through statistical analysis (or both).

Specifications Based on Judgment

Most job specifications simply reflect the educated guesses of people like supervisors and human resource managers. The basic procedure here is to ask, "What does it take in terms of education, intelligence, training, and the like to do this job well?"

How does one make such "educated guesses"? You could simply review the job's duties and deduce from those what human traits and skills the job requires. You can also choose human traits and skills from the competencies listed in online job descriptions like those at www.jobdescription.com. (For example, a typical job description there lists competencies like "Generates creative solutions" and "Manages difficult or emotional customer situations.") O*NET online is another option. Job listings there include lists of required education and other experience and skills.

In any case, use common sense. Don't ignore the behaviors that may apply to almost any job but that might not normally surface through a job analysis. Industriousness is an example. Who wants an employee who doesn't work hard? One researcher collected supervisor ratings and other information from 18,000 employees in 42 different hourly entry-level jobs.[44] "Generic" work behaviors that he found to be important to all jobs included thoroughness, attendance, unruliness (lack of), and schedule flexibility (accepts schedule changes when necessary; offers to stay late when the store is extremely busy).[45]

■ HR and the Gig Economy

Do Gig Workers Need Job Specifications?

Hiring gig workers doesn't mean the employer doesn't need job descriptions and job specifications. With respect to job descriptions, the prudent employer will still want to list at least the main duties it expects the worker to do. And job specifications are surely required, because the employer must ensure that the people doing its work at least fit certain minimum requirements.

For example, both Lyft and Uber list "driver requirements," which are essentially job specifications.[46] Although driver requirements vary somewhat by location, both Uber and Lyft require drivers to be at least 21, have a Social Security number and in-state driver's license (at least one year old), have in-state insurance, and undergo both DMV and national and county-wide background checks. For Uber, the background check also means for the past 7 years no DUI or drug-related offenses, or incidents of driving without insurance or license, or fatal accidents, or history of reckless driving, and no criminal history. And there are other requirements, including that your car pass muster. As a partial list, it must be a four-door sedan, seat four or more (excluding driver), be 2001 or newer, have in-state plates and be currently registered, and pass Uber's vehicle inspection.

✪ Talk About It– 2

If your professor has chosen to assign this, go to **www.pearson.com/mylab/ management** to discuss the following questions. Based on your experience, what other human requirements would you say there are to be a good Uber or Lyft driver? Should the companies add these as requirements? Why?

The job analyst may well distinguish between human characteristics that are essential to doing the job and those that are desirable. The recruiter may then translate these into recruiting ads listing required job qualifications (such as a medical degree) and desirable qualifications (such as experience working abroad.) Similarly, some job analysts classify a job's human requirements in terms of "KSAOs," namely Knowledge (i.e., how to use Excel), Skills (programming), Abilities (mathematical), and Other (conscientiousness).

Job Specifications Based on Statistical Analysis

Basing job specifications on statistical analysis rather than only judgment is the more defensible approach, but it's also more difficult. The aim is to determine statistically the relationship between (1) some *predictor* (human trait such as height, intelligence, or finger dexterity), and (2) some indicator or *criterion* of job effectiveness, such as performance as rated by the supervisor.

This procedure has five steps: (1) Analyze the job, and decide how to measure job performance; (2) select personal traits like finger dexterity that you believe should predict performance; (3) test candidates for these traits; (4) measure these candidates' subsequent job performance; and (5) statistically analyze the relationship between the human trait (finger dexterity) and job performance. Your aim is to determine whether the trait predicts employment.

This is more defensible than the judgmental approach. First, if the trait does not predict performance, why use it? Second, equal rights laws prohibit using traits that you can't prove distinguish between high and low job performers. Hiring standards that discriminate based on sex, race, religion, national origin, or age may have to be shown to predict job performance, as with the five-step approach just listed. Yet in practice, most employers rely on judgmental approaches.

The Job-Requirements Matrix

job-requirements matrix
A more complete description of what the worker does and how and why he or she does it; it clarifies each task's purpose and each duty's required knowledge, skills, abilities, and other characteristics.

Although most employers use job descriptions and specifications to summarize what their jobs entail, the **job-requirements matrix** is also popular.[47] A typical matrix lists the following information, in five columns:

Column 1: Each of the job's four or five *main job duties*

Column 2: The *task statements* for the main tasks associated with each main job duty

Column 3: The relative *importance* of each main job duty

Column 4: The *time spent* on each main job duty

Column 5: The *knowledge, skills, ability*, and *other* human characteristics (KSAO) related to each main job duty[48]

task statement
Written item that shows what the worker does on one particular job task; how the worker does it; the knowledge, skills, and aptitudes required to do it; and the purpose of the task.

The main step in creating a job requirements matrix involves writing the *task statements*. Each **task statement** shows *what* the worker does on each of a job duty's separate job tasks and *how* the worker does it.

Employee Engagement Guide for Managers

Job Specifications and Employee Engagement

As noted earlier, the manager should not ignore, while writing the job specification, desirable on-the-job behaviors that apply to almost any job but that might not normally surface through a job analysis. *Employee engagement* is one such behavior.

In terms of the job specification, the human resource consulting company Development Dimensions International conducted a study of 3,800 employees, and identified several personal characteristics that seemed to predict the likelihood someone would be engaged.[49] These traits included adaptability, passion for work, emotional maturity, positive disposition, self-advocacy, and achievement orientation.

A sensible suggestion is to seek out people who already have track records of being engaged employees. Because past behavior is often the best predictor of future behavior, one good suggestion is that if you want to hire people who are more likely to become engaged employees, ". . . look for examples of engagement in other areas of life."[50] For example, seek out candidates with a demonstrated commitment to serve others, such as nurses and veterans, and voluntary first responders.

The Employee Engagement Manager's Job Description

With the growing importance of employee engagement, many employers are appointing special employee engagement managers. The accompanying composite job description (Figure 4.8), created from actual *Employee Engagement Manager* job descriptions, illustrates such a manager's typical duties and responsibilities. A careful reading of the composite job description highlights the fact that while employee engagement programs may vary from company to company, they share several basic elements. Employee engagement program activities include improving supervisory skills through training, providing appraisal-based employee training plans and training, changing HR policies and procedures to coordinate them with the engagement effort's goals, and improving organizational involvement, communications, and recognition programs.

Figure 4.8

Employee Engagement Manager Job Description

Source: This composite job description is based on "Employee Engagement Manager Position Description," www.mnodn.org/wp-content/uploads/2012/04/U-of-M-Employee-Engagement-Manager.pdf, "Human Resources/Employee Engagement Manager," www.LinkedIn.com, and "Job Title: Director of Employee Engagement," www.hrapply.com/mgmresorts/AppJobView.jsp?link=17240, all accessed April 17, 2014. Copyright Gary Dessler PhD.

JOB DESCRIPTION
Employee Engagement Manager
Position Summary

The Employee Engagement Manager will work with the Director of Human Resources and with our company's other managers to create a companywide employee engagement strategy to support the company's strategic plan. The engagement manager will lead the development and implementation of communication strategies, recognition programs, and other programs with the aim of supporting and improving employee engagement. The employee engagement manager will also work with the company's training managers and others responsible for supervisor training to integrate engagement concepts into existing and future supervisor training to make strong supervision a primary means of increasing engagement. The employment engagement manager will also be responsible for identifying and implementing metrics to measure employee engagement and for developing action plans and objectives to continuously improve employee engagement. The employee engagement manager will also be responsible for developing an employee survey process that enables the company to monitor employee engagement and for working with other managers to ensure effective administration of the survey.

Key Responsibilities

- Create a comprehensive and sustainable employee engagement strategy.
- Work with senior leaders and teams to develop engagement strategies and goals as well as demonstrable links between engagement and their strategic goals.
- Develop a survey process and metrics that will enable the company to track employee engagement programs at a companywide and division level.
- Conduct employee focus groups to complement engagement surveys.
- Serve as subject matter expert on the survey results and create reports to monitor progress to devise action plans to drive positive employee engagement.
- Develop a *train the trainer* program to enable all units to analyze their own employee engagement data and build employee engagement training plans.
- Oversee the overall production of internal communications, including events, newsletters, e-blast, Facebook, etc., for the purpose of communicating critical information to employees.
- Develop employee recognition strategies to include reviewing, evaluating, and making recommendations for departmental recognition programs.

Figure 4.8
(Continued)

- Develop employee involvement programs, for instance in the form of employee participation programs and forums.
- Monitor employee retention and retention strategies.
- Develop, evaluate, and implement new processes to ensure employees are informed of company and all the relevant initiatives, programs, and announcements.
- Work with the other managers to make sure the company's performance appraisal process provides an opportunity for the appraisal to be used as a basis for developing training plans for employees.
- With the company's HR and top managers, review all HR policies and procedures and make recommendations for modifying any if required to better support the engagement program.
- Help all managers understand the links between engagement and outcomes such as turnover, health care cost, grievances, and customer service.

Required Education and Experience

- Masters' degree in business, psychology, or other related subject.
- Minimum of five years in direct human resource work or in a closely related field.
- Minimum two years' experience managing a staff.
- Demonstrated ability to move an agenda or initiative forward.

Preferred Experience

- PHR or SHRM-CP certification.
- Experience interacting with all levels of management and across organizational levels.
- Experience implementing high-impact HR initiatives to support organizational objectives.
- Experience working with detailed information and numerical data.
- Experience in change management to improve efficiency and effectiveness.
- Experience reflecting a demonstrated commitment to serving others.

LEARNING OBJECTIVE 7
Explain how to write competency-based models.

Using Competencies Models

Many people still think of a "job" as a set of specific duties someone carries out for pay, but the concept of job is changing. Companies today are flattening their hierarchies, squeezing out managers, and leaving the remaining workers with more jobs to do. Changes like these tend to blur where one job starts and another ends. In situations like these, relying on a list of job duties that itemizes specific things you expect the worker to do is often impractical.[51]

Many employers are therefore using a newer job analysis approach. Instead of listing the job's duties, they are listing, in *competency models* (or profiles), the knowledge, skills, and experience someone needs to do the job. Such models or profiles (see Figure 4.9) list the competencies employees must be able to exhibit to get their jobs done.[52] For example, in creating its competency model for HR managers, the Society for Human Resource Management describes a competency as a "cluster of highly interrelated attributes" (such as research design knowledge, critical thinking skills, and deductive reasoning abilities) that give rise to the behaviors (such as *critical evaluation*) someone would need to perform a given job (in this case, HR manager) effectively.[53]

The competency model or profile then becomes the guidepost for recruiting, selecting, training, evaluating, and developing employees for each job.[54] For instance, the manager *hires* new employees using tests that measure the profile's list of competencies, *trains* employees with courses that develop these competencies, and *appraises* performance by assessing the worker's competencies. The accompanying HR Practices Around the Globe feature illustrates this.

In many situations today, workers don't have single jobs but change jobs daily with their teammates.

Source: Thomas Niedermueller/Stringer/ Getty Images.

Roles
Line Function
(Within HR)
Staff Function
(Advise, Assist)
Coordinative Function
(Monitor)
Strategic HR Function
(Formulate, Execute)

Areas of Knowledge/Expertise
HR Practices (Recruiting,
Selection, Training, etc.)
Strategic Planning
Employment Law
Finance and Budgeting
General Management

Foundation Competencies

Personal
Competencies
- Behave Ethically
- Exercise Good Judgment Based on Evidence
- Set and Achieve Goals
- Manage Tasks Effectively
- Develop Personally

Interpersonal
Competencies
- Communicate Effectively
- Exercise Leadership
- Negotiate Effectively
- Motivate Others
- Work Productively with Others

HR/Business/
Management
- Institute Effective HR Systems
- Analyze Financial Statements
- Craft Strategies
- Manage Vendors

ILLUSTRATIVE

HUMAN RESOURCE MANAGER

COMPETENCY MODEL/JOB PROFILE

Figure 4.9

HR Manager Competency Model

■ HR Practices Around the Globe

Daimler Alabama Example

Several years ago, Daimler opened a new Alabama Mercedes-Benz factory, built to be a high-tech factory.[55] The plant emphasizes *just-in-time* inventory methods, so inventories stay negligible due to the arrival "just in time" of parts. It also organizes employees into *work teams* and emphasizes that all employees must dedicate themselves to *continuous improvement*.

Such production operations require certain employee competencies (skills and behaviors), such as interpersonal skills and flexibility.

Competencies-based job analysis helped Daimler staff this factory. Guidelines regarding whom to hire and how to train them emphasize the competencies someone needs to do the job (such as "ability to work cooperatively on a team") rather than lists of job duties. Because employees don't have to follow detailed job descriptions showing what "my job" is, they can more easily move from job to job within their teams.

Stressing competencies rather than duties also encourages workers to look beyond their own jobs to find ways to improve things. For instance, one team redesigned the racks that the assembly parts move on, saving assembly workers thousands of steps per year.

Now that the new system, including the competencies-based job analysis, has proved itself in Alabama, Daimler plants in South Africa, Brazil, and Germany now use it.

✪ Talk About It– 3

If your professor has chosen to assign this, go to **www.pearson.com/mylab/management** to discuss the following questions. Are you surprised that Daimler could implement a team-based production system like this in places where the cultures are as disparate as Alabama, Germany, and Brazil? Why? What intercountry cultural differences would you think might have impeded Daimler's efforts?

---

competency-based job analysis

Describing the job in terms of measurable, observable, behavioral competencies (knowledge, skills, and/or behaviors) that an employee doing that job must exhibit to do the job well.

How to Write Competencies Statements

Identifying the job's required competencies is similar to traditional job analysis. For example, you might interview job incumbents and their supervisors and ask open-ended questions regarding job responsibilities and activities.

But instead of compiling lists of job duties, your aim is to finish the statement, "*In order to perform this job competently, the employee should be able to. . . .*" Use your knowledge of the job to answer this, or the worker's or supervisor's insights, or use information from a source such as O*NET, or the Department of Labor's Office of Personnel Management (see www.opm.gov). Then, for each competency write a *competency statement*.

Ideally, the competency statement will include three elements.[56] One is the *name and a brief description* of the competency, such as "Project Management—creating accurate and effective schedules." The second is a *description of the observable behaviors* that represent proficiency in the competency, such as "personally accountable for the project's execution and invested in the success of the project; continuously manage project risks and dependencies by making timely decisions." Third are *proficiency levels*. For example (for project management):[57]

Proficiency Level 1. *Identifies* project risks and dependencies and communicates routinely to stakeholders

Proficiency Level 2. *Develops systems to monitor* risks and dependencies and report changes

Proficiency Level 3. *Anticipates* changing conditions, risks, and dependencies and takes preventive action

BP Example British Petroleum's (BP's) exploration division executives wanted to shift employees from a job duties–oriented "that's-not-my-job" attitude to one that motivated employees to obtain the skills required to accomplish broader responsibilities.[58]

Figure 4.10

Skills Matrix

This is an example of a skills matrix for technical/engineering product development employees. The light blue boxes show the level required for each skill for these product development employees. An accompanying key would provide specific examples for each level of each skill, with difficulty increasing for each skill level starting at Level 1. For example, Level 1 for Technical Expertise/Skills might say, "Has or is in process of acquiring the basic knowledge necessary to do this type of job," while Level 6 might say, "Capable of conducting and supervising highly complex analytical tasks requiring advanced technical know-how and skills."

Source: Copyright Gary Dessler PhD.

	Technical Expertise/Skills	Decision Making and Problem Solving Skills	Interpersonal Skills	Leadership Skills	Commercial Awareness Skills
Level 6	6	6	6	6	6
Level 5	5	5	5	5	5
Level 4	4	4	4	4	4
Level 3	3	3	3	3	3
Level 2	2	2	2	2	2
Level 1	1	1	1	1	1

Their solution was a skills matrix like that in Figure 4.10. They had skills matrices for each job or job family (such as drilling managers). As in Figure 4.10, each matrix listed (1) the types of skills required to do that job such as technical expertise, and (2) the minimum skill required for proficiency at each level. The figure's note shows how to actually use the matrix.

BP's skills matrix approach also supported its talent management efforts. Talent management efforts in this unit could now focus on recruiting, hiring, training, appraising, and rewarding employees based on the set of skills employees need to perform the job in question.

Review

MyLab Management

Go to **www.pearson.com/mylab/management** to complete the problems marked with this icon ⭐.

Summary

1. Employers today often view all the staff–train–reward activities as part of a single integrated *talent management* process. We defined talent management as *the holistic, integrated, and results and goal-oriented process of planning, recruiting, selecting, developing, managing, and compensating employees*. When a manager takes a talent management perspective, he or she should: keep in mind that the talent management tasks are parts of a single, interrelated talent management process; make sure talent management decisions such as staffing and pay are goal-directed; consistently use the same "profile" for formulating recruitment plans for a job as you do for making selection, training, appraisal, and payment decisions for it; and integrate/coordinate all the talent management functions.

2. All managers need to be familiar with the *basics of job analysis*.
   - Job analysis is the procedure through which you determine the duties of the department's positions and the characteristics of the people to hire for them.
   - Job descriptions are a list of what the job entails, while job specifications identify what kind of people to hire for the job.
   - The job analysis involves collecting information on matters such as work activities; required human behaviors; and machines, tools, and equipment used.
   - Managers use job analysis information in recruitment and selection, compensation, training, and performance appraisal.

- The basic steps in job analysis include: deciding the use of the job analysis information, reviewing relevant background information including organization charts, analyzing the job, verifying the information, and developing job descriptions and job specifications.

3. There are various *methods for collecting job analysis information*. These include interviews, questionnaires, observation, participant diary/logs, and quantitative techniques such as position analysis questionnaires. Employers increasingly collect information from employees via the Internet.

4. Managers should be familiar with the process for *writing job descriptions*. Most descriptions contain sections that cover job identification, a job summary, a listing of responsibilities and duties, the job incumbent's authority, and performance standards. The job description may also contain information regarding the job's working conditions and the job specifications. Many employers use Internet sources such as www.jobdescription.com to facilitate writing job descriptions.

5. In *writing job specifications*, distinguish between specifications for trained versus untrained personnel. For trained employees, the process is relatively straightforward because you're looking primarily for traits like experience. For untrained personnel, it's necessary to identify traits that might predict success on the job. Most job specifications come from the educated guesses of people like supervisors and are based mostly on judgment. Some employers use statistical analyses to identify predictors or human traits that are related to success on the job.

6. Human traits and behaviors that may predict the job candidates' likelihood to be engaged and which the manager might therefore want to include in the job specification include adaptability, passion for work, emotional maturity, positive disposition, self-advocacy, achievement orientation, and a work history that includes a demonstrated commitment to serve others.

7. Employers are using **competencies** and profiles in talent management, particularly creating "profiles" for each of their jobs. The profiles list the competencies, personal attributes, knowledge, and experience required to do the job. Each job's profile then becomes the anchor for creating recruitment, selection, training, and evaluation and development plans for each job. **Competency-based job analysis** means describing the job in terms of measurable, observable, behavioral competencies (such as specific skills) that an employee doing the job must exhibit to do the job well. With the job of, say, a team member possibly changing daily, one should identify the skills the employee may need to move among jobs.

Key Terms

talent management   89
organization chart   89
job analysis   90
job descriptions   90
job specifications   90
process chart   91
workflow analysis   92
business process reengineering   92
job enlargement   93

job rotation   93
job enrichment   93
diary/log   98
position analysis questionnaire (PAQ)   98
Standard Occupational Classification (SOC)   103
job-requirements matrix   110
task statement   110
competency-based job analysis   114

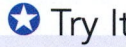 Try It

How would you do applying the concepts and skills you learned in this chapter? If your professor has chosen to assign this, go to **www.pearson.com/mylab/management** and complete the Teams simulation to find out.

Discussion Questions

4-1. Why, in summary, should managers think of staffing, training, appraising, and paying employees as a talent management process?

4-2. What items are typically included in the job description?

4-3. We discussed several methods for collecting job analysis data—questionnaires, the position analysis questionnaire, and so on. Compare and contrast these methods, explaining what each is useful for and listing the pros and cons of each.

4-4. Describe the types of information typically found in a job specification.

4-5. Explain how you would conduct a job analysis.

CHAPTER 4

4-6. Do you think all companies can really do without detailed job descriptions? Why or why not?

4-7. Explain how you would create a job requirements matrix for a job.

4-8. In a company with only 25 employees, is there less need for job descriptions? Why or why not?

Individual and Group Activities

4-9. Working individually or in groups, obtain copies of job descriptions for clerical positions at the college or university where you study, or the firm where you work. What types of information do they contain? Do they give you enough information to explain what the job involves and how to do it? How would you improve on the description?

4-10. Working individually or in groups, use O*NET to develop a job description for your professor in this class. Based on that, use your judgment to develop a job specification. Compare your conclusions with those of other students or groups. Were there any significant differences? What do you think accounted for the differences?

4-11. For this activity, you will need the documents titled (1) "HRCI PHR® and SPHR® Certification Body of Knowledge, and (2) "About the Society for Human Resource Management (SHRM) Body of Competency & Knowledge® Model and Certification

Exams." Your instructor can obtain these two documents from the Pearson Instructor Resource Center and pass them on to you. These two documents list the knowledge someone studying for the HRCI or SHRM certification exam needs to have in each area of human resource management (such as in Strategic Management, and Workforce Planning). In groups of several students, do four things: (1) review the HRCI and/or SHRM documents; (2) identify the material in this chapter that relates to HRCI's or SHRM's required knowledge lists; (3) write four multiple-choice exam questions on this material that you believe would be suitable for inclusion in the HRCI exam and/or the SHRM exam; and, (4) if time permits, have someone from your team post your team's questions in front of the class, so that students in all teams can answer the exam questions created by the other teams.

MyLab Management

Go to **www.pearson.com/mylab/management** for Auto-graded writing questions as well as the following Assisted-graded writing questions:

4-12. Why, in summary, should managers think of staffing, training, appraising, and paying employees as a talent management process?

4-13. Do you think companies can really do without detailed job descriptions? Why or why not?

APPLICATION EXERCISES

HR IN ACTION CASE INCIDENT 1

Optima Air Filter Company: The Flood

In May 2011, Mississippi River flooding hit Vicksburg, Mississippi, and the Optima Air Filter Company. Many employees' homes were devastated. Optima found that it had to hire almost three completely new crews, one for each shift. The problem was that the "old-timers" had known their jobs so well that no one had ever bothered to draw up job descriptions for them. When about 30 new employees began taking their places, there was general confusion about what they should do and how they should do it.

The flood quickly became old news to the firm's out-of-state customers, who wanted filters, not excuses. Phil

Mann, the firm's president, was at his wits' end. He had about 30 new employees, 10 old-timers, and his original factory supervisor, Maybelline. He decided to meet with Linda Lowe, a consultant from the local university's business school. She immediately had the old-timers fill out a job questionnaire that listed all their duties. Arguments ensued almost at once: Both Phil and Maybelline thought the old-timers were exaggerating to make themselves look more important, and the old-timers insisted that the lists faithfully reflected their duties. Meanwhile, the customers clamored for their filters.

Questions

4-14. Should Phil and Linda ignore the old-timers' protests and write the job descriptions as they see fit? Why? Why not? How would you go about resolving the differences?

4-15. How would you have conducted the job analysis? What should Phil do now?

HR IN ACTION CASE INCIDENT 2

Carter Cleaning Company

The Job Description

Based on her review of the stores, Jennifer concluded that one of the first matters she had to attend to involved developing job descriptions for her store managers.

As Jennifer tells it, her lessons regarding job descriptions in her basic management and HR management courses were insufficient to convince her of the pivotal role job descriptions actually play in the smooth functioning of an enterprise. Many times during her first few weeks on the job, Jennifer found herself asking one of her store managers why he was violating what she knew to be recommended company policies and procedures. Repeatedly, the answers were either "Because I didn't know it was my job" or "Because I didn't know that was the way we were supposed to do it." Jennifer knew that a job description, along with a set of standards and procedures that specified what was to be done and how to do it, would go a long way toward alleviating this problem.

In general, the store manager is responsible for directing all store activities in such a way that quality work is produced, customer relations and sales are maximized, and profitability is maintained through effective control of labor, supply, and energy costs. In accomplishing that general aim, a specific store manager's duties and responsibilities include quality control, store appearance and cleanliness, customer relations, bookkeeping and cash management, cost control and productivity, damage control, pricing, inventory control, spotting and cleaning, machine maintenance, purchasing, employee safety, hazardous waste removal, human resource administration, and pest control.

The questions that Jennifer had to address follow.

Questions

4-16. What should be the format and final form of the store manager's job description?

4-17. Is it practical to specify standards and procedures in the body of the job description, or should these be kept separate?

4-18. How should Jennifer go about collecting the information required for the standards, procedures, and job description?

4-19. What, in your opinion, should the store manager's job description look like and contain?

Experiential Exercise

The Instructor's Job Description

Purpose: The purpose of this exercise is to give you experience in developing a job description, by developing one for your instructor.

Required Understanding: You should understand the mechanics of job analysis and be thoroughly familiar with the job analysis questionnaires. (See Figures 4.4 and 4.7.)

How to Set Up the Exercise/Instructions: Set up groups of four to six students for this exercise. As in all exercises in this book, the groups should be separated and should not converse with each other. Half of the groups in the class will develop the job description using the job analysis questionnaire (Figure 4.4), and the other half of the groups will develop it using the job description questionnaire (Figure 4.7). Each student should review his or her questionnaire (as appropriate) before joining his or her group.

4-20. Each group should do a job analysis of the instructor's job: Half of the groups should use the Figure 4.4 job analysis questionnaire for this purpose, and half should use the Figure 4.7 job description questionnaire.

4-21. Based on this information, each group will develop its own job description and job specification for the instructor.

4-22. Next, each group should choose a partner group, one that developed the job description and job specification using the alternate method. (A group that used the job analysis questionnaire should be paired with a group that used the job description questionnaire.)

4-23. Finally, within each of these new combined groups, compare and critique each of the two sets of job descriptions and job specifications. Did each job analysis method provide different types of information? Which seems superior? Does one seem more advantageous for some types of jobs than others?

5

Personnel Planning and Recruiting

OVERVIEW:
In this chapter, we will cover . . .

- Workforce Planning and Forecasting
- Why Effective Recruiting Is Important
- Internal Sources of Candidates
- Employee Engagement Guide for Managers: Internal Recruitment and Promotion-from-Within
- Outside Sources of Candidates
- Recruiting a More Diverse Workforce
- Developing and Using Application Forms

MyLab Management

⭐ Improve Your Grade!
When you see this icon, visit
www.pearson.com/mylab/management for activities that are applied, personalized, and offer immediate feedback.

LEARNING OBJECTIVES

When you finish studying this chapter, you should be able to:

1. Explain the main techniques used in employment planning and forecasting.
2. Answer the question: "Why is effective recruiting important?"
3. Name and describe the main internal sources of candidates.
4. Discuss a workforce planning method you would use to improve employee engagement.
5. List and discuss the main sources of outside candidates.
6. Explain how to recruit a more diverse workforce.
7. Discuss the main issues to address in developing application forms.

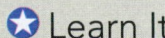 Learn It

If your professor has chosen to assign this, go to **www.pearson.com/mylab/management** to see what you should particularly focus on and to take the Chapter 5 Warm Up.

Source: Dean Drobot/Shutterstock.

INTRODUCTION

Marlene was wondering what to do. As sales manager for Epoch Holdings, she was responsible for leading a sales team to sell real estate and condominium apartments. The problem was that most of the salesperson candidates the HR department sent her simply didn't fill the bill. How could she get some good candidates without violating the company's HR policies? We'll see what she did.

Job analysis identifies the duties and human requirements of each of the company's jobs. The next step is to decide which of these jobs you need to fill, and to recruit and select employees for them.

The recruiting and selecting process can be envisioned as a series of hurdles, illustrated in Figure 5.1. Specifically:

1. Decide what positions you will need to fill, through workforce planning and forecasting.
2. Build a pool of candidates for these jobs, by recruiting internal or external candidates.
3. Have candidates complete application forms and perhaps have initial screening interviews.
4. Use selection tools like tests and background investigations to screen candidates.
5. Decide to whom to make an offer, by having the supervisor and perhaps others interview the candidates.

This chapter focuses on workforce planning and on recruiting employees. Chapter 6 addresses selection tests, background checks, and interviews.

LEARNING OBJECTIVE 1
Explain the main techniques used in employment planning and forecasting.

workforce (or employment or personnel) planning
The process of deciding what positions the firm will have to fill, and how to fill them.

Workforce Planning and Forecasting

Workforce planning is the process of deciding what positions the firm will have to fill and how to fill them. Its aim is to identify and to eliminate the gaps between the employer's forecasted workforce needs and the current employees who might

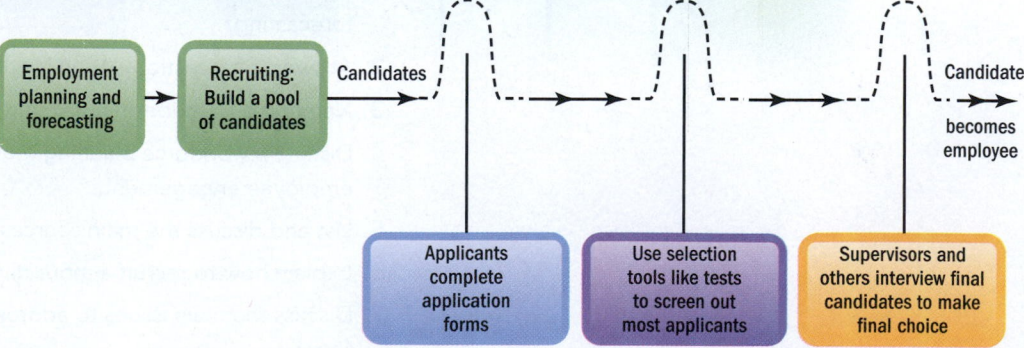

The recruitment and selection process is a series of hurdles aimed at selecting the best candidate for the job.

Figure 5.1

Steps in Recruitment and Selection Process

succession planning
The ongoing process of systematically identifying, assessing, and developing organizational leadership to enhance performance.

be suitable for filling those needs. Workforce planning is also known as *employment* or *personnel planning*. Workforce planning embraces all future positions, from maintenance clerk to CEO. However, most firms call the process of deciding how to fill executive jobs **succession planning**.[1]

Strategy and Workforce Planning

Workforce planning is part of the firm's strategic and business planning processes (see Figure 5.2). Strategically, for example, plans to enter new businesses or to reduce some activities all influence the types of positions to be filled and, therefore, the firm's workforce plans. For example, as IBM transitioned from supplying hardware to software and consulting, it knew many employees' skills would be obsolete.[2] IBM's human resource executives therefore reviewed "What sorts of skills and competencies will we need to execute our strategic plans?"[3] They then put in place development and recruitment plans to address those needs.

Towers Watson Example

One consulting firm's methodology illustrates workforce planning's basic steps.[4]

First, Towers Watson *reviews the client's business plan and workforce data* (for instance, on how revenue influences staffing levels). This helps them understand how projected business changes may influence the client's headcount and skills requirements.

Second, they *forecast and identify what positions the firm will have to fill and potential workforce gaps*; this helps them understand what new future positions they'll have to fill, and what current employees may be promotable into them.

Third, they develop a *workforce strategic plan*; here they prioritize key workforce gaps (such as, what positions will have to be filled, and who do we have who can fill them?) and identify specific (recruitment, training, and other) plans for filling any gaps.

Finally, they implement the plans (for instance, new recruiting and training programs) and use various metrics to monitor the process.

Towers Watson clients can use its special "MAPS" software to facilitate this workforce planning process. MAPS contains dashboards (see the four exhibits on page 122). The manager uses these, for instance, to monitor key recruitment metrics and to conduct a detailed analysis of the current workforce and historical workforce trends.

Figure 5.2
Linking Employer's Strategy to Personnel Plans

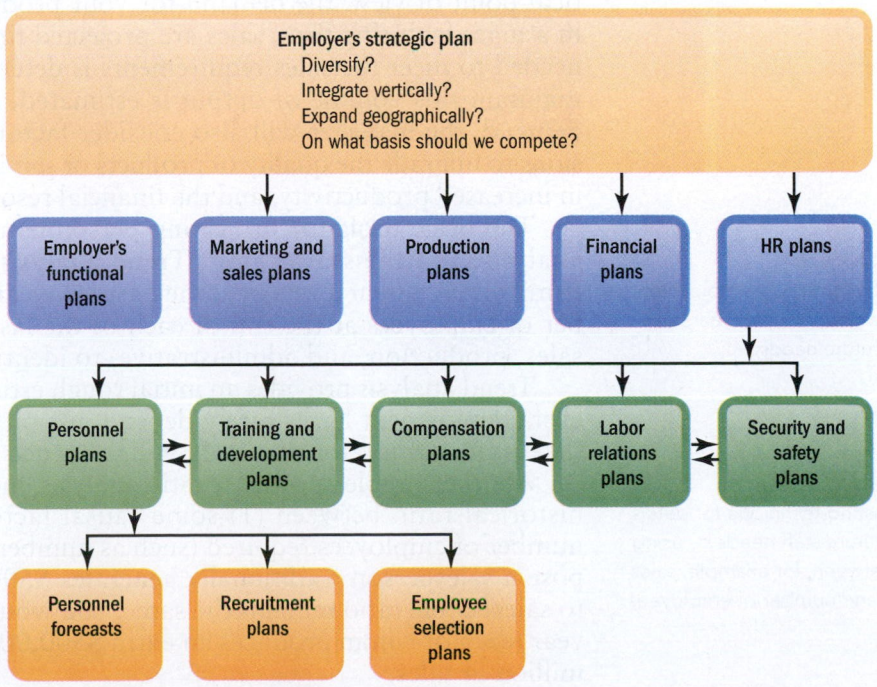

Workforce scan

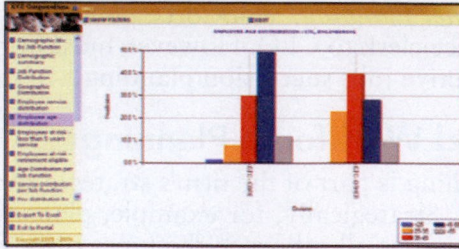

Dashboards

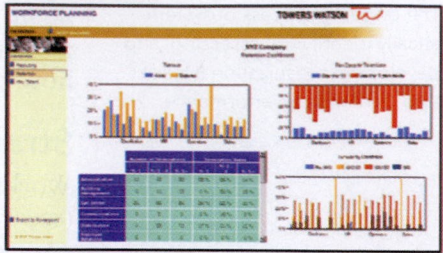

Workforce projection model

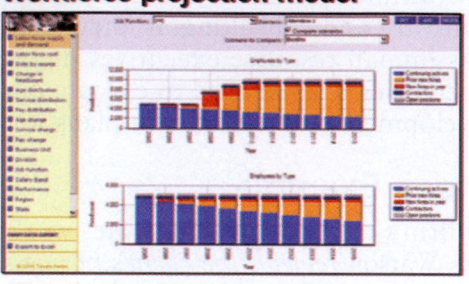

External labour scan

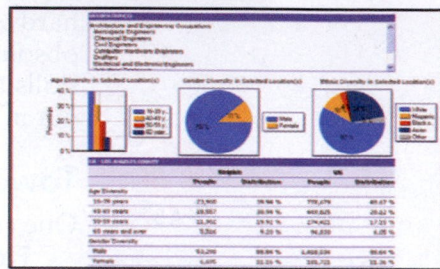

Forecasting Workforce Needs (Labor Demand)

Like any good plans, workforce plans are built on forecasts—basic assumptions about what the future will be. Here the manager will need three forecasts: one for personnel needs (demand), one for the supply of inside candidates, and one for the supply of outside candidates. With these in hand, the manager can identify supply–demand gaps and develop action plans to fill the projected gaps. As an example, when a new staffing director came on board at Valero Energy he reviewed Valero's employee demographics, growth plans, and turnover history. He discovered that projected employment shortfalls were four times what Valero could fill with its current recruitment procedures. He formulated new personnel plans for boosting employee retention and recruiting and screening more candidates.[5] We will start with how to forecast personnel needs/demand.

The basic process here usually starts with forecasting revenues. From a practical point of view, the demand for your product or service is paramount. Thus, in a manufacturing firm, sales are projected first. Then the volume of production needed to meet the sales requirements is determined. Finally, the staff needed to maintain this volume of output is estimated. In addition to production or sales demand, the manager will also consider factors such as projected turnover, decisions to upgrade the quality of products or services, technological changes resulting in increased productivity, and the financial resources available to your department.

The basic tools for projecting personnel needs include trend analysis, ratio analysis, and the scatter plot. **Trend analysis** means studying variations in the firm's employment levels over the past few years. For example, compute the number of employees at the end of each of the last five years in each subgroup (like sales, production, and administrative) to identify trends.

Trend analysis provides an initial rough estimate of future staffing needs. However, employment levels rarely depend just on the passage of time. Other factors (like productivity, for instance), will influence impending workforce needs.

Another simple approach, **ratio analysis**, means making forecasts based on the historical ratio between (1) some causal factor (like sales volume) and (2) the number of employees required (such as number of salespeople). For example, suppose a salesperson traditionally generates $500,000 in sales. If the sales revenue to salespeople ratio remains the same, you would require six new salespeople next year (each of whom produces an extra $500,000) to produce a hoped-for extra $3 million in sales.

trend analysis

Study of a firm's past employment needs over a period of years to predict future needs.

ratio analysis

A forecasting technique for determining future staff needs by using ratios between, for example, sales volume and number of employees needed.

Like trend analysis, ratio analysis assumes that things like productivity remain about the same. If sales productivity were to rise or fall, the ratio of sales to salespeople would change.

scatter plot
A graphical method used to help identify the relationship between two variables.

A **scatter plot** shows graphically how two variables—such as sales and your firm's staffing levels—are related. If they are, then if you can forecast the business activity (like sales), you should also be able to estimate your personnel needs.

For example, suppose a 500-bed hospital expects to expand to 1,200 beds over the next five years. The human resource director wants to forecast how many registered nurses the hospital will need. The human resource director realizes she must determine the relationship between hospital size (in number of beds) and number of nurses required. She calls eight hospitals of various sizes and finds this:

Size of Hospital (Number of Beds)	Number of Registered Nurses
200	240
300	260
400	470
500	500
600	620
700	660
800	820
900	860

Figure 5.3's graph compares hospital size and number of nurses. If the two are related, then the points you plot (from the preceding data) will tend to fall on a straight line, as here. If you carefully draw in a line to minimize the distances between the line and each one of the plotted points, you will be able to estimate the number of nurses needed for each hospital size. Thus, for a 1,200-bed hospital, the human resource director would assume she needs about 1,210 nurses.

Note that although simple, tools like scatter plots have drawbacks.[6]

1. Historical sales/personnel relationships assume that the firm's existing ways of doing things will continue as is.
2. They tend to reward managers for adding employees, irrespective of the company's needs.
3. They tend to institutionalize existing ways of doing things, even in the face of change.

Figure 5.3

Determining the Relationship Between Hospital Size and Number of Nurses

Note: After fitting the line, you can project how many employees you'll need, given your projected volume.

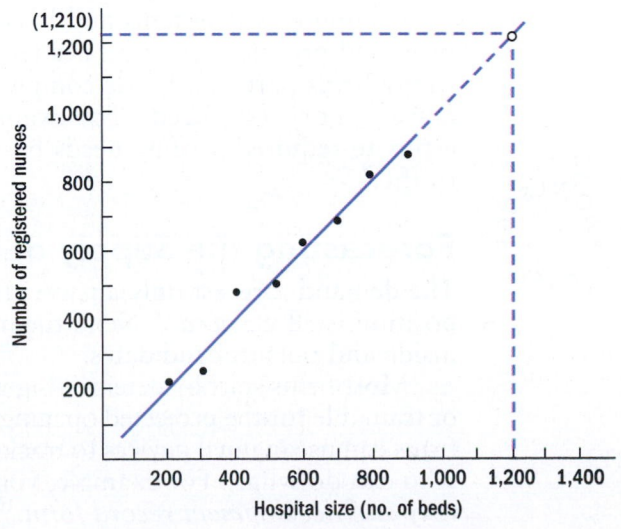

Workforce planning begins with forecasting workforce needs. For example, if a hospital administrator expects to expand a 500-bed hospital to 1,200 beds over the next five years, forecasting how many registered nurses they'll need is critical.

Source: Caiaimage/Robert Daly/Getty Images.

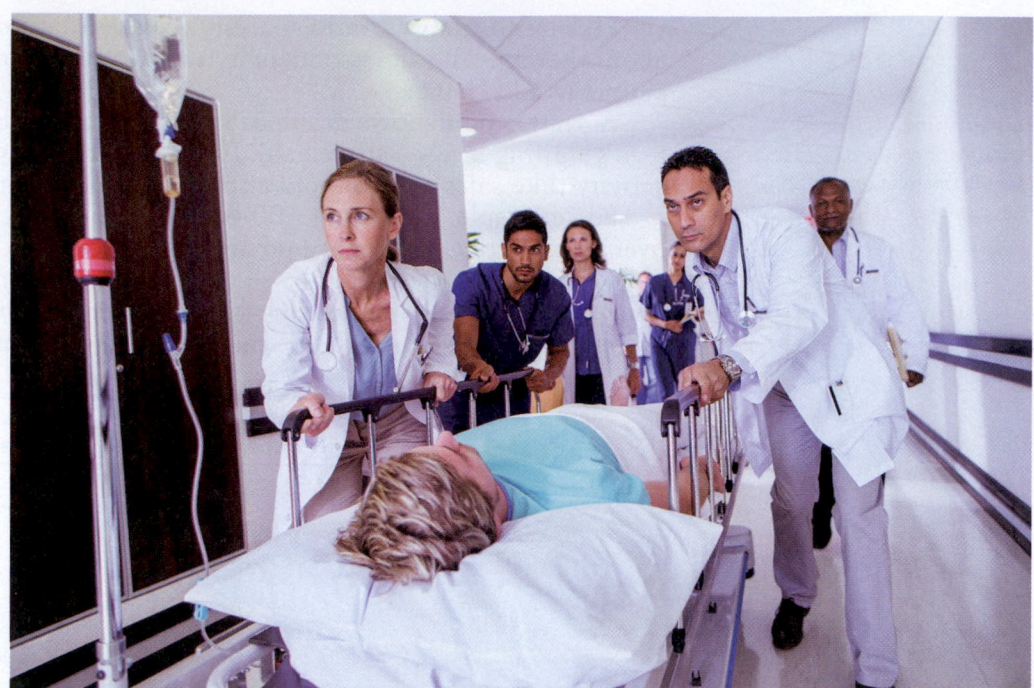

Managerial Judgment Few historical trends, ratios, or relationships will continue unchanged into the future. Judgment is needed to adjust the forecast. Illustrative factors that may modify your initial forecast of personnel requirements include decisions to upgrade quality or enter into new markets; technological changes resulting in increased productivity; and financial resources available, for instance, a looming budget crunch.

Improving Performance through HRIS

Computerized Workforce Forecasts *Computerized forecasts* enable managers to build more variables into their workforce projections.[7] For example, at Chelan County Public Utility District, the development manager built a statistical model encompassing such things as employee age, tenure, turnover rate, and time to train new employees. This helped them identify five occupational "hotspots" among 33 occupational groups at their company. This prompted them to focus more closely on creating plans to retain and hire, for instance, more systems operators.[8]

Computerized systems and Excel spreadsheets quickly translate estimates of projected productivity and sales levels into forecastable personnel requirements. Many firms particularly use computerized employee forecasting systems for estimating short-term needs. For example, labor scheduling systems help retailers estimate required staffing needs based on weather forecasts and estimated store traffic.[9]

Forecasting the Supply of Inside Candidates

The demand forecast only answers the question: "How many employees in what positions will we *need*?" Next, the manager must forecast the *supply* of available inside and outside candidates.

Most firms start by determining which current (inside) employees are qualified or trainable for the projected openings. Department managers or owners of smaller firms can use manual devices to track employee qualifications (or will simply know who can do what). For example, you can create your own *personnel skills inventory and development record form.*[10] For each current employee, list the person's skills, education, company-sponsored courses taken, career and development interests, languages, desired assignments, and other relevant experiences. Computerized versions of *skills inventory* systems are also available.[11]

Personnel replacement charts (Figure 5.4) are another option, particularly for top positions. They show the present performance and promotability for each position's potential replacement. As an alternative, you can develop a **position replacement card**. For this you create a card for each position, showing possible replacements as well as their present performance, promotion potential, and training.

Larger firms can't track the qualifications of hundreds or thousands of employees manually. Therefore they computerize this information, using packaged software systems such as Skill-Base's skills inventory software.[12] Skills inventory systems such as these enable employers to collect and compile employee skills information in real time via online employee surveys. Skills inventory programs help management anticipate staffing and skills shortages, and facilitate workforce planning, recruitment, and training.[13] They typically include items like *work experience codes, product knowledge*, the employee's *level of familiarity* with the employer's product lines or services, the person's *industry experience, formal education*, foreign *language* skills, *relocation* limitations, *career* interests, and *performance* appraisals.

Often the employee, supervisor, and human resource manager will enter information about the employee's background, experience, and skills via the system. Then, when a manager needs a person for a position, he or she uses key words to describe the position's specifications (for instance, in terms of education and skills). The computerized system then produces a list of qualified candidates. As the user of one such system said, it "allows us to track and assess the talent pool and promote people within the company . . . 75% of key openings are fulfilled by internal candidates. The succession module helps us to identify who the next senior managers could be and build development plans to help them achieve their potential."[14]

The Matter of Privacy The employer must control the personal data stored in its data banks, and all managers must be vigilant about protecting employees' privacy, for several reasons.[15] First is the volume and personal nature of information in

personnel replacement charts
Company records showing present performance and promotability of inside candidates for the most important positions.

position replacement card
A card prepared for each position in a company to show possible replacement candidates and their qualifications.

Figure 5.4

Management Replacement Chart Showing Development Needs of Potential Future Divisional Vice Presidents

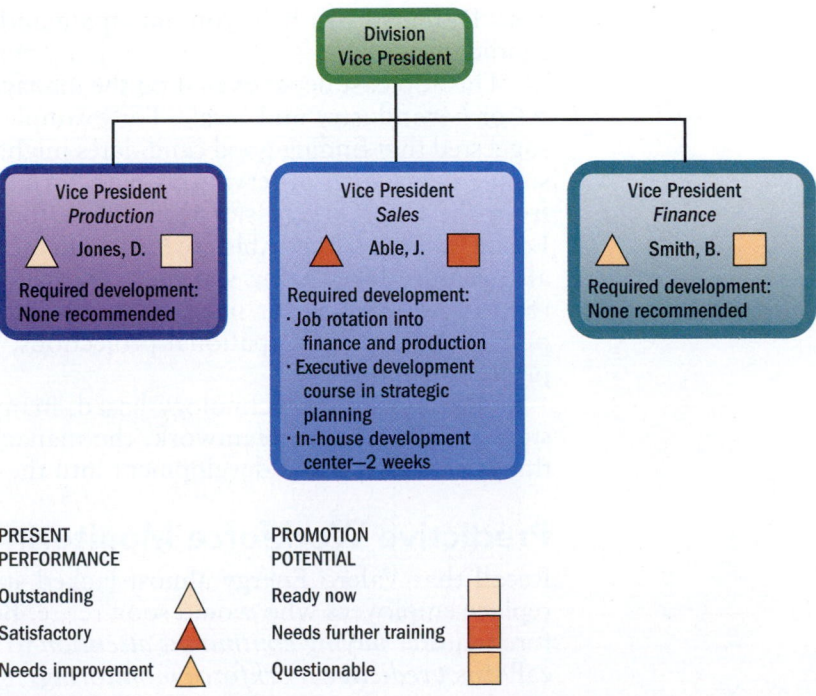

Figure 5.5

Keeping Data Safe

Source: Taken from an interview with Linda Foley, cofounder of the ITRC. Published in "Safeguarding HR Information" by Dan Caterinicchia, in *HR Magazine*, November 2005. Copyright © 2005 by the Society for Human Resource Management, Alexandria, VA.

Since intruders can strike from outside an organization or from within, HR departments can help screen out potential identity thieves by following four basic rules:

- Perform background checks on anyone who is going to have access to personal information.
- If someone with access to personal information is out sick or on leave, don't hire a temporary employee to replace him or her. Instead, bring in a trusted worker from another department.
- Perform random background checks such as random drug tests. Just because someone passed 5 years ago doesn't mean their current situation is the same.
- Limit access to information such as SSNs, health information, and other sensitive data to HR managers who require it to do their jobs.

most employee data banks. Second, laws (such as HIPAA, the Health Insurance Portability and Accountability Act) give employees legal rights regarding access to their information.[16] Third, Internet access makes it relatively easy for more people to access the firm's computerized files.[17] The U.S. Office of Personnel Management lost data on as many as 14 million current and former employees this way.[18] Solutions include the need for password-protected folders.[19] Figure 5.5 summarizes guidelines for keeping employee data safe.

Markov Analysis Employers also use a mathematical process known as *Markov analysis* (or "transition analysis") to forecast availability of internal job candidates. Markov analysis involves creating a matrix that shows the probabilities that employees in the chain of feeder positions for a key job (such as from junior engineer to engineer, to senior engineer, to engineering supervisor, to director of engineering) will move from position to position and therefore be available to fill the key position.

Forecasting the Supply of Outside Candidates

If there will not be enough inside candidates to fill anticipated openings (or you want to go outside for another reason), you will probably focus next on projecting supplies of outside candidates—those not currently employed by your organization. Doing so can help you anticipate and adapt to problems finding qualified candidates.

This forecast depends first on the manager's own sense of what's happening in his or her industry and locale. For example, falling unemployment rates recently suggested that finding good candidates might be getting tougher. The manager then supplements such observations with formal economic projections, for instance, from the U.S. Congressional Budget Office (www.cbo.gov/) and the Bureau of Labor Statistics (www.bls.gov/news.release/ecopro.toc.htm). Your planning may also require forecasting specific occupations. O*NET (discussed in Chapter 4) reports projections for most occupations. The U.S. Bureau of Labor Statistics publishes annual occupational projections, as at www.bls.gov/emp/ep_pub_occ_projections.htm.

With more jobs technology-based, many applicants will lack required skills, such as in math and teamwork; the manager will therefore have to factor such things as training and development into the workforce plan.[20]

Predictive Workforce Monitoring

Recall that Valero Energy almost lacked sufficient time to implement a plan to replace employees who would soon retire. Best talent management practice therefore requires *paying continuous attention* to workforce planning issues. Managers call this *predictive workforce monitoring*.

For example, Intel Corporation's staffing department works with Intel's business heads twice a year to assess workforce needs—both immediate and up to two years in the future.[21] Amerada Hess has an Organizational Capability (OC) group to monitor and predict workforce attrition (such as retirement age, experience, education) and likely talent requirements. The group "considers how each line of business is evolving, examines what jobs at Hess will look like in the future, identifies sources for procuring the best talent, and assists in developing current and newly hired employees."[22] The accompanying HR as a Profit Center feature shows another example. Then the Management Skills feature provides some practical advice.

■ HR as a Profit Center

Predicting Labor Needs

Valero Energy created a "labor supply chain system" for improving the efficiency of its workforce planning, recruiting, and hiring process. It includes a statistical tool that predicts Valero's labor needs based on past trends. And, it includes computer screen "dashboards" that show how components in the staffing chain, such as ads placed on job boards, are performing according to cost, speed, and quality. Before implementing this system, it took 41 pieces of paper to bring on board an employee and more than 120 days to fill a position; each hire cost about $12,000. The new system eliminated most of the paper forms needed to hire an employee, time-to-fill fell below 40 days, and cost per hire dropped to $2,300.[23]

⭐ Talk About It – 1

If your professor has chosen to assign this, go to **www.pearson.com/mylab/ management** to discuss the following: Explain how Valero might use the Towers Watson workforce planning process on pages 121–122 to further improve its processes.

BUILDING YOUR MANAGEMENT SKILLS:
Developing a Workforce Plan

Workforce planning should culminate in a workforce plan. In essence, this plan shows the employer's projected workforce skills gaps, as well as plans for filling these gaps.

Creating the workforce plan will involve several steps. You should first summarize what positions/skills you will need (workforce demand), based on your workforce demand analysis. Next, summarize the internal workforce supply, specifically, current internal candidates for the new positions. Then for each projected position (or group of positions) itemize any personnel and skills gaps (not enough skilled current employees to fill these positions) and your plans for eliminating those gaps. So, at a minimum, the plan should include positions to be filled; personnel replacement charts and/or position replacement cards for these positions; potential internal (and if necessary, external) sources for these positions; the recruitment, training, development, and promotions that moving people into the positions will entail; and the resources that implementing the plan will require, for instance in recruiter fees, estimated training costs, relocation costs, and interview expenses.[24]

The manager will find illustrative workforce plans on the Web (type *sample workforce plan* into the Google search box). One typical plan contains workforce projections, provides discussions of how to close skills gaps, and then presents actual specific recruiting and other workforce plans.[25]

Managers use the narrower term *staffing plan* to specify the personnel required to staff a specific project (such as constructing a new building).[26]

⭐ Watch It

How does a company actually do workforce planning? If your professor has chosen to assign this, go to **www.pearson.com/mylab/management** to watch the video *Gawker Media Personnel Planning and Recruiting*, and then answer the questions to show what you'd do in this situation.

LEARNING OBJECTIVE 2
Answer the question: "Why is effective recruiting important?"

Why Effective Recruiting is Important

Assuming the employer authorizes the manager to fill a position, the next step is to build an applicant pool.[27] **Employee recruiting** means finding and/or attracting applicants for the employer's open positions.

Recruiting is important. If only two candidates apply for two openings, you may have little choice but to hire them. But if 10 or 20 applicants appear, you can use tools like interviews and tests to screen out all but the best. More than twice as many large U.S. employers administer pre-hire screening tests than they did about 15 years ago; that means more rejections and, consequently, the need to attract larger applicant pools.[28]

Effective recruiting is not easy. First, some recruiting methods are superior to others, depending on the job. Second, recruiting depends on nonrecruitment issues such as pay scales.[29] Third, employment law prescribes what you can do.[30] (See the accompanying Know Your Employment Law feature.)

Line and staff cooperation in recruitment is essential. The human resource manager charged with filling a position is seldom very familiar with the job itself. He or she will therefore work with the supervisor to ascertain what the job really entails and its job specifications, as well as informal things like how the team gets along.

employee recruiting
Finding and/or attracting applicants for the employer's open positions.

The Recruiting Yield Pyramid

Filling even a few positions might require recruiting dozens or hundreds of candidates. Managers therefore use a **recruiting yield pyramid**, as shown in Figure 5.6, to gauge the magnitude of the staffing issues it needs to address. In Figure 5.6, the company knows it needs 50 new entry-level accountants next year. From experience, the firm also knows the following:

- The ratio of offers made to actual new hires is 2 to 1.
- The ratio of candidates interviewed to offers made is 3 to 2.
- The ratio of candidates invited for interviews to candidates interviewed is about 4 to 3.
- Finally, the firm knows that of six leads that come in from all its recruiting sources, it typically invites only one applicant for an interview—a 6-to-1 ratio.

Therefore, the firm must generate about 1,200 leads to be able to invite in 200 viable candidates of which it interviews about 150, and so on.

recruiting yield pyramid
The historical arithmetic relationships between recruitment leads and invitees, invitees and interviews, interviews and offers made, and offers made and offers accepted.

Improving Recruitment Effectiveness: Recruiters, Sources, and Branding

Of course, it is not just recruiting but effective recruiting that is important, starting with the recruiters themselves. For example, one classic study involved 41 graduating students from a northeastern university who had applied for job interviews.[31] When asked why they judged some firms as bad fits, 39 mentioned the nature of the job, but 23 said they had been turned off by recruiters. For example, some were dressed sloppily; others were "barely literate;" some were rude; and some made offensive comments.

As with all employees, the employer should carefully select and train recruiters. This should include interpersonal skills training (such as in communicating), as

Figure 5.6

Recruiting Yield Pyramid

New hires — 50
Offers made (2:1) — 100
Candidates interviewed (3:2) — 150
Candidates invited (4:3) — 200
Leads generated (6:1) — 1,200

well as providing basic knowledge about how to recruit, the employer's recruitment process, the pros (and cons) of working for the employer, and about how laws (such as EEO) affect what recruiters can do.

Recruitment Sourcing *Recruitment sourcing* involves determining what your recruitment options are, and then assessing which are best for the job in question. Internal (within company) sources include, for instance, employee referrals and job posting systems. External (outside company) sources range from social media sites like LinkedIn to executive search firms and newspaper ads.

For assessing which source is best for the job, most employers probably still look first at the number of applicants the source produces. However quantity doesn't necessarily mean quality. Therefore other effectiveness metrics would include, for each source, how many of its applicants were hired, how well its applicants performed on the job, how many failed and had to be replaced, and applicants' performance in terms of training, absence, and turnover.[32]

Developing the "Employer Brand" More employers are using marketing techniques to bolster their recruiting; this usually starts with building their "employer brand." Most obviously, it is futile to recruit if the employer's reputation is that it's an awful place to work.

Effective branding therefore requires effective policies. For example, Google's founders decided early on that they wanted their firm to be known as a great place to work. They then translated this into tangible policies regarding employee benefits, compensation, and recruitment and selection practices.[33]

Prospective applicants typically peruse several online reviews while deciding whether to apply.[34] How does the employer want others to see it as a place to work? Branding often focuses on what it's like to work at the company, including company values and the work environment.[35] GE, for instance, stresses innovation (hiring "bright, interesting people working together on new and exciting projects").[36] Others stress that they are environmentally or socially responsible."[37]

KNOW YOUR EMPLOYMENT LAW

Preemployment Activities

As we explained in Chapter 2, numerous federal, state, and local laws and court decisions restrict what employers can and cannot do when recruiting job applicants. For example, employers can't rely on word-of-mouth dissemination of information about job opportunities when its workforce is substantially all white or all members of some other class such as all female or all Hispanic. It is unlawful to give false or misleading information to members of any group, or to fail or to refuse to advise them of work opportunities and the procedures for obtaining them.

In practice, "the key question in all recruitment procedures is whether the method limits qualified applicants from applying."[38] So, for example, gender-specific ads that call for "busboy" or "firemen" would obviously raise red flags.[39] The bottom line: avoid limiting recruitment efforts to just one recruitment method; use multiple sources to reach out as widely as possible; and don't do anything to illegally limit classes of people from applying. ■

Internal Sources of Candidates

Although *recruiting* may bring to mind LinkedIn and classified ads, *internal sources*—in other words, current employees or "hiring from within"—are often the best source of candidates. For example, Cisco Systems uses its proprietary Talent Connection program to seek qualified internal Cisco employees who may not be actively seeking jobs.[40]

Filling open positions with inside candidates has several advantages. First, there is really no substitute for already knowing a candidate's *strengths and weaknesses*. Current employees may also be more *committed* to the company. *Morale* and engagement may rise if employees see their colleagues promoted for loyalty and competence. And inside candidates should require *less orientation* and (perhaps) training than outsiders.

There are other advantages. External hires tend to come in at higher salaries than do those promoted internally, and some apparent "stars" hired from outside may turn out to have excelled more because of the company they came from than from their own skills.

One executive recruiter argues that internal candidates are always better than external ones unless the internal candidates simply can't pass muster. One study concluded that firms that hired their CEOs from inside rather than outside performed better. On the other hand, some firms—particularly those facing challenges, such as McDonald's—have done very well by bringing in outside managers.[41]

Hiring from within can also backfire. *Inbreeding* is a problem if new perspectives are required. The process of posting openings and getting inside applicants can also be a *waste of time* because often the department manager already knows whom he or she wants to hire. Rejected inside applicants may become *discontented*; telling them why you rejected them and what remedial actions they might take is crucial.

There are some practical rules to use in determining whether to go outside or promote from within. If you need specific skills that aren't available in your company, or have to embark on a tough turnaround, or face a situation in which your current succession planning or skills inventory systems are inadequate, it may be best to look outside. But if your company is thriving and you have the skills you need internally, and have a unique and strong company culture, then look within.[42]

Identifying Internal Candidates

In a perfect world, the employer will adhere to formal internal-recruitment policies and practices. These typically rely heavily on job posting and on the firm's skills inventories. **Job posting** means publicizing the open job to employees (usually by posting it on company intranets or bulletin boards). These postings list the job's attributes, such as qualifications, supervisor, work schedule, and pay rate. Qualifications skills inventories may reveal employees who have potential for further training, or who have the right background for the open job. Similarly, an examination of personnel records (including application forms) may uncover employees who are working in jobs below their educational or skill levels and may also reveal persons who have the right background for the open jobs in question.

job posting
Publicizing an open job to employees (often by literally posting it on bulletin boards) and listing its attributes, like qualifications, supervisor, working schedule, and pay rate.

Employee Engagement Guide for Managers
Internal Recruitment and Promotion-from-Within

Many employers encourage internal recruiting, on the reasonable assumption that doing so improves employee engagement. Thus, as IBM shifted from supplying mostly hardware to consulting, it assessed its skills gaps and instituted workforce plans to train current employees for new jobs; this assumedly fostered employee engagement. Other employers, faced with strategic shifts, simply dismiss employees who don't "fit."

FedEx has had strong internal recruiting and promotion-from-within policies almost from its inception. FedEx's commitment to promotion-from-within grew out of founder Frederick Smith's belief that "when people are placed first they will provide the highest possible service, and profits will follow."[43] FedEx weaves together promotion-from-within with other policies—including annual employee attitude surveys, employee recognition and reward programs, a leadership evaluation process, extensive employee communication, and an employee appeals process—to foster employee commitment and engagement.

As at FedEx, effective promotion-from-within requires a method for accessing career records and posting job openings, one that guarantees eligible employees are informed of and considered for openings. FedEx calls its job posting system JCATS (Job Change Applicant Tracking System). Announcements of new job openings via this online system usually take place each Friday. All employees applying for the position get numerical scores based on job performance and length of service. They are then advised whether they were chosen as candidates.

The manager interested in fostering employee engagement can draw several lessons from FedEx's successful promotion-from-within system: show a genuine interest in your employees' career aspirations; provide career-oriented appraisals; see that your employees have access to the training they need to develop themselves; and balance your desire to keep good employees, with the benefits of helping them learn of and apply for other positions in your company.

LEARNING OBJECTIVE 5
List and discuss the main sources of outside candidates.

Outside Sources of Candidates

Employers can't always get all the employees they need from their current staff, and sometimes they just don't want to. If so, they turn to outside candidates. There are many ways to do this.

Informal Recruiting and the Hidden Job Market

Many (or most) job openings aren't publicized at all; jobs are created and become available when employers serendipitously come across the right candidates. The author of *Unlock the Hidden Job Market* estimates that perhaps half of all positions are filled informally (without formal recruiting).[44] Similarly, one survey found that 28% of those surveyed found their most recent job through word-of-mouth.[45]

Recruiting via the Internet[46]

Most employers recruit through their own websites, or use job boards such as Indeed.com. For example, by using Indeed and its smartphone App, users may search for jobs by key word, read job descriptions and salaries, save jobs to a list of favorites, e-mail job links, search for jobs near where they're located, and often directly apply for the job. One particularly useful phone App feature is that it updates the job seeker's job listings: once he or she has checked the new job listings, those jobs won't be listed as "new" the next time they check; they'll just see the latest ones highlighted.

Online Recruiting Tools Online recruiting is getting more sophisticated. In Hungary, the local office of accountants PriceWaterhouseCoopers (PWC) lets prospective applicants use an online simulation it calls Multipoly, to give applicants a better idea of what working for PWC is like. The firm attributes a significant increase in applicants to use of the game.[47] McDonald's Corporation posted employee testimonials on social networking sites to attract applicants.[48] Other employers simply screen through job boards' résumé listings. The *dot-jobs* domain gives job seekers a one-click conduit for finding jobs at the employers who register at www.[].jobs. For example, applicants seeking a job at Disneyland can go to www.Disneyland.jobs. HireVue "lets candidates create video interviews and send them to employers to review, share, and compare with other applicants."[49]

Virtual (fully online) job fairs are another option. Here online visitors see a similar setup to a regular job fair. They can listen to presentations, visit booths, leave résumés and business cards, participate in live chats, and get contact information from recruiters and even hiring managers.[50] Fairs last about 5 hours.

Online Recruitment around the Globe Just about every country has its own recruitment sites, such as Zhaopin.com in China. The popularity of baitoru.com in Japan shows how culture is changing there. After decades in which most workers there had lifetime job security, that system recently has broken down. Today large numbers of Japanese workers are part-time or temporary. They use baitoru.com to find jobs.[51]

Pros and Cons Online recruiting generates more responses quicker and for a longer time at less cost than just about any other method. And, because they are richer and more comprehensive in describing the jobs, Internet-based ads have a stronger effect on applicant attraction than do printed ads.[52]

However online recruiting has two potential problems. First, older people and some minorities are less likely to use the Internet, so online recruiting may inadvertently exclude older applicants (and certain minorities).[53]

The second problem is Internet overload: Employers end up deluged with résumés. Self-screening helps: The Cheesecake Factory posts detailed job duties listings, so those not interested needn't apply. Another approach is to have job seekers complete a short online prescreening questionnaire, then use these to identify those who may proceed in the hiring process.[54] Most employers also use applicant tracking systems, to which we now turn.

Improving Performance through HRIS

applicant tracking systems
Online systems that help employers attract, gather, screen, compile, and manage applicants.

Using Applicant Tracking A deluge of applications means that just about all *Fortune* 500 companies and many others now use applicant tracking software to screen applications.[55] **Applicant tracking systems (ATS)** are online systems that help employers attract, gather, screen, compile, and manage applicants.[56] They also provide other services, including requisitions management (for monitoring the firm's open jobs), applicant data collection (for scanning applicants' data into the system), and reporting (to create various recruiting-related reports such as cost per hire and hire by source).[57] Most systems are from *application service providers* (ASPs). These basically redirect applicants from the employers to the ASP's site where, for instance, they may fill out forms and take tests.[58] Major ASPs include Automatic Data Processing (ADP.com), HRSmart (hrsmart.com), Silkroad Technology (silkroad.com), and Monster (monster.com).[59]

As one example, a bank uses its ATS to bump applicants who don't meet the basic job requirements. It then uses phone interviews or automated video interview systems to whittle the applicant pool. Then its recruiters interview and send the remaining through the final selection process.[60]

ATS tools are improving. For example, application completion rates drop dramatically if applicants have to spend more than 15 minutes finishing the online application, so many ATS vendors streamlined their applications. Most now also give immediate acknowledgment of applications. One ATS vendor lets recruiters fine-tune and send a standardized rejection to applicants who don't make the cut.[61]

Improving Online Recruiting Effectiveness Employers can easily improve their online recruiting results. For example, place employment information one click

Figure 5.7

Ineffective and Effective
Web Ads

Ineffective Ad, Recycled from Magazine to the Web	Effective Online Ad (Space Not an Issue)
Process Engineer Pay: $65k–$85k/year	Do you want to help us make this a better world?
Immediate Need in Florida for a Wastewater Treatment Process Engineer. Must have a min. 4–7 years Industrial Wastewater exp. Reply KimGD@WatersCleanX.com	We are one of the top wastewater treatment companies in the world, with installations from Miami to London to Beijing. We are growing fast and looking for an experienced process engineer to join our team. If you have at least 4–7 years' experience designing processes for wastewater treatment facilities and a dedication to make this a better world, we would like to hear from you. Pay range depending on experience is $65,000–$85,000. Please reply in confidence to KimGD@ WatersCleanX.com

away from their home pages.[62] Let applicants submit their résumés via your website. Give job seekers the option of completing online applications.

Furthermore, effective online ads don't just transfer newspaper ads to the Web. As one specialist put it, "getting recruiters out of the 'shrunken want ad mentality' is a big problem." The ineffective online ad in Figure 5.7 has needless abbreviations and says little about why job seekers should want that job.[63]

Now look at the effective online ad in Figure 5.7. It starts with an attention-grabbing heading and uses the extra space to provide more specific job information. It provides good reasons to work for this company. Many employers include the entire job description.[64] Ideally, the ad should provide a checklist of the job's human requirements for applicants to gauge if the job is a good fit.[65]

The following two Trends features look at other aspects of Online recruiting.

TRENDS SHAPING HR: *Digital and Social Media*

HOW RECRUITERS USE SOCIAL MEDIA If you're seeking a job, sign up with LinkedIn. Accenture predicts that about 80% of new recruits will soon come through prospective employees' social media connections.[66]

Recruiters use social media recruiting in several ways. They dig through social websites and competitors' publications to find passive applicants who may not even be looking for jobs. Many firms use Twitter to announce job openings to job seekers who subscribe to their Twitter feeds.[67] Theladders.com's Pipeline™ networking tool lets recruiters maintain a dialogue with prospective job seekers even before they're interested in seeking a job. Others use Facebook's friend-finding search function, and Twitter, to learn more about prospective and actual candidates. TalentBin searches sites such as Pinterest to find qualified tech workers.[68]

In addition to enabling employers to post jobs on LinkedIn, LinkedIn Recruiter Lite lets them search through LinkedIn's database to find the most relevant profiles (including names, résumés, and profiles) for open positions.[69] Recruiters can then use LinkedIn InMail to send short personalized messages to people they're interested in. And by joining relevant LinkedIn groups, recruiters can discover LinkedIn group members who might be potential hires.[70] Recruiters mine the applicants' sites for feedback from the person's blog comments and likes/dislikes. Recruiters also post job openings on professional associations and other social networks.[71]

Cloud-based applications such as Oracle Talent Acquisition Cloud enable employers to integrate recruiting with applicant tracking and interview management. The Oracle Taleo Social Sourcing Cloud Service is integrated with social media sites like LinkedIn and Facebook. It also notifies the client company's current employees about its open positions and scans their social connections for referral suggestions that they may want to make to friends, or directly to the employer. With the My Staffing Pro applicant tracking system, applicants can apply on Facebook, share job openings, connect with hiring managers, and log in with the social profile.[72]

TRENDS SHAPING HR: *Science in Talent Management*

GOOGLE'S PEOPLE OPERATIONS TEAM When Google's "People Operations" (HR) group's research found that job boards weren't cost effective for them, they created their own in-house recruiting firm. This in-house team uses a proprietary candidate database called gHire. Google's recruiters continually expand and winnow this candidate list by searching social networking and other sites, by searching who's working where, and by reaching out to prospective hires and maintaining dialogues with them, sometimes for years. These in-house recruiters produce hand-picked candidates and account for about half of Google's yearly hires.[73]

Google's career website is another big source of candidates. Applicants apply through it, share examples of their skills with Google employees, and discover what Google employment is like.

Google also actively solicits employee referrals. Google analyzed how to boost employee referrals. It found that higher referral fees weren't the answer (because Googlers loved recommending great candidates). Instead, Google streamlined the selection process, so more referrals got hired. Google uses outside recruiters sparingly for special assignments and dropped job boards several years ago.[74]

Advertising

Digital recruiting is replacing traditional help wanted ads, but print ads are still popular. Here employers should address two issues: the advertising medium and the ad's construction. The best medium—the local paper, *The Wall Street Journal, The Economist,* for instance—depends on the positions for which you're recruiting. For example, the local newspaper can be a good source for local blue-collar help, clerical employees, and lower-level administrative employees. On the other hand, if recruiting for workers with special skills, such as furniture finishers, you'd probably want to advertise in places with many furniture manufacturers, such as the Carolinas. The point is to target your ads where they'll reach your prospective employees.

For specialized employees, advertise in trade and professional journals like *American Psychologist, Sales Management, Chemical Engineering,* and *Women's Wear Daily.* Help wanted ads in *The Wall Street Journal* can be good sources of middle- or senior-management personnel. Most of these print outlets now include online ads with the purchase of print help wanted ads.

Technology lets companies be creative.[75] For example, Electronic Arts (EA) includes information about its internship program on the back of its video game manuals, helping it create a database of more than 200,000 potential job candidates.

Figure 5.8

Help Wanted Ad That Draws Attention

Source: Giombetti Associates, Hampden, MA. Reprinted with permission.

Are You Our Next Key Player?

PLANT CONTROLLER   Northern New Jersey

Are you looking to make an impact? Can you be a strategic business partner and team player, versus a classic, "bean counter"? Our client, a growing **Northern New Jersey** manufacturer with two locations, needs a high-energy, self-initiating, technically competent Plant Controller. Your organizational skills and strong understanding of general, cost, and manufacturing accounting are a must. We are not looking for a delegator, this is a hands-on position. If you have a positive can-do attitude and have what it takes to drive our accounting function, read oh!

Responsibilities and Qualifications:

- Monthly closings, management reporting, product costing, and annual budget.
- Accurate inventory valuations, year-end physical inventory, and internal controls.
- 4-year Accounting degree, with 5–8 years experience in a manufacturing environment.
- Must be proficient in Microsoft Excel and have general computer skills and aptitude.
- Must be analytical and technically competent, with the leadership ability to influence people, situations, and circumstances.

If you have what it takes to be our next key player, tell us in your cover letter, *"Beyond the beans, what is the role of a Plant Controller?"* Only cover letters addressing that question will be considered. Please indicate your general salary requirements in your cover letter and email or fax your resume and cover letter to:

Ross Giombetti
Giombetti Associates
2 Allen Street, P.O. Box 720
Hampden, MA 01036
Email: Rossgiombetti@giombettiassoc.com
Fax: (413) 566-2009

Constructing (Writing) the Ad Experienced advertisers use the guide AIDA (attention, interest, desire, action) to construct ads. First, you must attract attention to the ad. Why does the ad in Figure 5.8 attract attention? The phrase "next key player" helps.

Next, develop interest. For instance, "Are you looking to make an impact?"

Create desire by spotlighting words such as *travel* or *challenge*. As an example, having a graduate school nearby may appeal to engineers and professional people.

Finally, the ad should prompt action, such as "call today."

Job applicants view ads with more specific job information as more attractive and more credible.[76] If the job has big drawbacks, consider a realistic ad. When the New York City Children's Services Administration was having problems with employee retention, it began using these ads: "Wanted: men and women willing to walk into strange buildings in dangerous neighborhoods, [and] be screamed at by unhinged individuals. . . ." Realism reduces applicants, but improves employee retention.[77] Finally, the ad should comply with equal employment laws, avoiding features like "man wanted."

Employment Agencies

There are three main types of employment agencies: (1) public agencies operated by federal, state, or local governments; (2) agencies associated with nonprofit organizations; and (3) privately owned agencies.

Every state has a public, state-run employment service agency. The U.S. Department of Labor supports these agencies, through grants and through other assistance such as a nationwide job bank. The National Job Bank enables agency counselors to advise applicants about available jobs in other states as well.

Some employers have mixed experiences with public agencies. For one thing, applicants for unemployment insurance are required to register and to make themselves available for job interviews. Some of these people are not interested in returning to work, so employers can end up with applicants who have little desire for immediate employment. And fairly or not, employers probably view some of these local agencies as lethargic in their efforts to fill area employers' jobs.

Yet these agencies are useful. Beyond just filling jobs, counselors will visit an employer's work site, review the employer's job requirements, and even assist the employer in writing job descriptions. Most states have turned their local state employment service agencies into "one-stop" shops—neighborhood training/employment/career assessment centers.[78]

Most (nonprofit) professional and technical societies, such as the Institute for Electrical and Electronic Engineers (IEEE), have units that help members find jobs. Public agencies place people such as those who are disabled.

Private employment agencies are important sources of clerical, white-collar, and managerial personnel. They charge fees (set by state law and posted in their offices) for each applicant they place. Most are "fee-paid" jobs, in which the employer pays the fee. Use one if:

1. Your firm doesn't have its own human resources department and feels it can't do a good job recruiting and screening.
2. You must fill a job quickly.
3. There is a perceived need to attract more minority or female applicants.
4. You want to reach currently employed individuals, who might feel more comfortable dealing with intermediaries.
5. You want to reduce the time you're devoting to recruiting.[79]

Yet using employment agencies requires avoiding the potential pitfalls. For example, the employment agency's screening may let poor applicants go directly to the supervisors responsible for hiring, who may in turn naively hire them. Conversely, improper screening at the agency could block potentially successful applicants.

To help avoid problems:

1. Give the agency an accurate and complete job description.
2. Make sure tests, application blanks, and interviews are part of the agency's selection process.

Every state has a public, state-run employment service agency.
Source: Slobo/Getty Images.

3. Periodically review EEOC data on candidates accepted or rejected by your firm, and by the agency.
4. Screen the agency. Check with other managers to find out which agencies have been the most effective at filling the sorts of positions you need filled. Review the Internet and classified ads to discover the agencies that handle the positions you seek to fill.
5. Supplement the agency's reference checking by checking at least the final candidate's references yourself.

■ HR and the Gig Economy

alternative staffing
The use of nontraditional recruitment sources.

Vast numbers of workers today work in the gig economy (also called the sharing, 1099, on-demand, and **alternative-staffing** economy).[80] Gig workers typically work in freelance, contract, temporary, or consultant capacities. By one estimate, they will represent about half of the U.S. workforce in the next few years.[81]

Temporary Workers

Employers increasingly supplement their permanent workforces with contingent or temporary workers. This "temp" or "contingent" workforce isn't limited to clerical or maintenance staff. It includes engineering, science, and management support occupations, such as temporary chief financial officers and chief executive officers.[82]

Employers use temps for many reasons. Employers have long used "temps" to fill in for employees who were out sick or on vacation. But they have other advantages. Flexibility is one concern, with more employers wanting to reduce employment levels quickly if the economic turnaround proves short-lived.[83] Temps' output per hour paid is higher because temps usually don't get paid days off. If the economy sags, it's easier to let temps go. Many firms also use temporary hiring to try out prospective employees.[84] Another factor is the trend toward outsourcing work for short-term projects. For example, Makino outsources the installation of large machines to contract firms, who in turn hire temps for the installations.[85]

Employers can hire temp workers either through direct hires or through temporary staff agencies such as Kelly Services, Manpower Group, Robert Half, and Adecco Group North America. The agency handles the temp's recruiting, screening, and payroll administration. Thus, Nike hired Kelly Services to manage Nike's temp needs.

Direct hiring involves simply hiring workers and placing them on the job. The employer usually pays these people directly, as it does all its employees, but classifies them separately, as casual, seasonal, or temporary employees and often pays few if any benefits.[86]

To make temporary relationships successful, those supervising temps should understand their concerns. In one survey, temporary workers said they were:

1. Treated in a dehumanizing and ultimately discouraging way.
2. Insecure about their employment and pessimistic about the future.
3. Worried about their lack of insurance and pension benefits.
4. Misled about their job assignments and in particular about whether temporary assignments were likely to become full-time.
5. "Underemployed" (particularly those trying to return to the full-time labor market).[87]

When working with temporary agencies, understand their policies. For example, once the supervisor signs the time sheet, it's usually an agreement to pay the agency's fees. What is the policy if the client wants to hire one of the agency's temps as a permanent employee? How does the agency plan to recruit employees? Checking a temporary agency's references and listing with the Better Business Bureau is advisable.[88]

KNOW YOUR EMPLOYMENT LAW
Contract Employees

Several years ago, federal agents rounded up about 250 illegal "contract" cleaning workers in 60 Walmart stores. The raid underscores the need to understand the status of the contract employees who work on your premises handling activities like security or after-hours store cleaning.[89] The fact that they actually work for a temp agency is no excuse. Generally, with certain limited exceptions, employees of temporary staffing firms working in an employer's workplace are considered employees both of the agency and of the employer.[90]

The employer's liability depends on the degree to which its supervisors control the temp employee's activities, so the more the agency does the better. For example, have the staffing agency handle training and negotiate and set pay rates with the temp.

Employers can take other steps. The employer should require the staffing agency to follow the employer's background checking process and to assume the legal risks if the employer and agency are jointly responsible. Carefully track how many temporary employees the employer has. Supervise temporary employees with care if they may have access to your firm's intellectual property and computer systems.[91] Do not treat temporary workers as "employees," for instance in terms of business cards, employee handbooks, or employee ID badges.[92] ∎

Poaching

Apple recently hired someone who was managing Amazon's Fire TV business to run Apple TV. Such "poaching" of current employees from competitors is a popular and potentially useful source of recruits, but also one fraught with potential problems. For example, the target employee (like all employees) almost always has a fiduciary responsibility to the current employer, for instance regarding proprietary employer information. He or she may also have legal obligations. Therefore, proceed with the possibility of litigation in mind. Do not ask for or accept proprietary information about your competitor.

For a target firm, there is no way to become "poaching proof." However, steps such as having employees sign noncompete agreements prohibiting them from joining competitors for a reasonable time or antisolicitation clauses prohibiting them from soliciting current customers may, if crafted wisely, protect the target employer for a time.[93] Both Apple and Google allegedly took a more questionable approach to protect themselves from poaching. According to several lawsuits, those companies (and several other Silicon Valley firms) simply agreed among themselves not to poach each other's employees. Apple and Google agreed to pay a $415 million settlement.[94]

Offshoring and Outsourcing Jobs and the H-1B Visa

Rather than bringing people in to do the company's jobs, outsourcing and offshoring send the jobs out. *Outsourcing* means having outside vendors supply services (such as benefits management or manufacturing) that the company's own employees previously did in-house. *Offshoring* means having outside vendors or employees *abroad* supply services that the company's own employees previously did in-house.

Employees, unions, legislators, and even many business owners feel that "shipping jobs out" (particularly overseas) is ill-advised, and that feeling became more intense with the new Republican administration. That notwithstanding, employers are sending jobs out, and not just blue-collar jobs. For example, U.S. employers shipped about 135,000 IT jobs recently to countries like India.[95]

But doing so creates special personnel challenges. One is the likelihood of cultural misunderstandings (such as between your home-based customers and the employees abroad). Others are security and information privacy concerns; the need to deal with foreign contract, liability, and legal systems issues; and the fact that the offshore employees need special training (for instance, in using pseudonyms like "Jim" without discomfort).

Rising wages in Asia, coupled with reputational issues, a desire to invest more in local communities, and a changing political climate are prompting employers to bring jobs back. Many U.S. employers, including Apple and Microsoft, have shifted some jobs back to the United States.

Particularly with the new Republican administration, employers and legislators are also focusing more on the potential drawbacks of the H-1B visa program. The program originally aimed at helping U.S. employers temporarily hire workers from abroad in specialty occupations. Today, newspaper accounts of major companies bringing in large numbers of foreign workers to be trained by their American counterparts before taking over their jobs has prompted some legislators (and others) to argue that the program is misused.[96] For one thing, they want to strictly limit use of H – 1B visas to highly skilled foreign workers.[97]

Executive Recruiters

Executive recruiters (also known as *headhunters*) are special employment agencies that employers retain to seek out top-management talent for their clients. The percentage of your firm's positions filled by these services might be small. However, these jobs include key executive and top technical positions. The employer always pays the fees.

There are contingent and retained executive recruiters. Members of the Association of Executive Search Consultants usually focus on executive positions paying $150,000 or more and on "*retained* executive search." They are paid regardless of whether the employer hires the executive through the search firm's efforts. *Contingency-based recruiters* tend to handle junior- to middle-level management job searches in the $90,000 to $150,000 range. Top recruiters (all retained) include Heidrick and Struggles, Egon Zehnder International, Russell Reynolds, and Spencer Stuart. Today, recruiter fees are dropping from the usual 30% or more of the executive's first-year pay.

The challenge has always been finding potential candidates. Internet-based databases speed up such searches. Executive recruiters are also creating specialized units aimed at specialized functions (such as sales) or industries (such as oil products).

Recruiters have many contacts and are relatively adept at finding qualified candidates who aren't actively looking to change jobs. They can keep your firm's name confidential and can save top management's time by building an applicant pool. The recruiter's fee might actually turn out to be small when you compare it to the executive time saved.

The big issue is ensuring that the recruiter really understands your needs and then delivers properly vetted candidates. It is essential to explain completely what sort of candidate is required. Some recruiters also may be more interested in persuading you to hire a candidate than in finding one who will really do the job. Some "final candidates" may actually be fillers to make the recruiter's one "real" candidate look better. The Management Skills feature provides some suggestions.

BUILDING YOUR MANAGEMENT SKILLS:
Working with Recruiters

Hiring and working with executive recruiters requires some caution. Guidelines include the following:[98]

1. Make sure the firm can conduct a thorough search. Under their ethics code, a recruiter can't approach the executive talent of a former client for two years after completing a search for that client. Therefore, the recruiter must search from a constantly diminishing pool.[99]
2. Meet the individual who will actually handle your assignment.
3. Make sure to ask how much the search firm charges. Get the agreement in writing.[100]

Continued

4. Make sure the recruiter and you agree on what sort of person to hire for the position.
5. Ask if the recruiter has vetted the final candidates. *Do not be surprised if the answer is, "No, I just get candidates—we don't really screen them."*
6. Therefore *never* rely on any recruiter to do all the reference checking. Let them check the candidates' references, but get notes of these references in writing from the recruiter (if possible). Recheck at least the final candidate's references yourself.
7. Preferably use a recruiter who has a special expertise in your specific industry—he or she may have the best grasp of who's available.

Internal Recruiting More employers today do their own management recruiting.[101] They still call on executive recruiters to conduct top officer (CEO and president) and board member placements and for confidential searches. But firms ranging from GE to PepsiCo now have their own internal recruiting offices handling most of their own management recruiting. (GE reports an internal recruiting staff of about 500 people.) Time Warner reported saving millions of dollars per year using internal recruiting teams.[102] The accompanying HR Tools feature explains what small businesses can do.

◼ HR Tools for Line Managers and Small Businesses

Recruiting 101

There comes a time in the life of most small businesses when it dawns on the owner that new blood is needed to take the company to the next level. Should the owner personally recruit this person?

Although most large firms don't think twice about hiring executive search firms, small-firm owners will understandably hesitate before committing to a fee that could reach $40,000 or more for a $120,000 marketing manager.

However, engaging in a search like this is not like seeking data entry clerks. There's a good chance your ideal candidate isn't reading the want ads. Many applicants may be capable, but you will have to uncover the gem by assessing them. Chances are, you won't know where to place or how to write the ads; or where to search, whom to contact, or how to screen out the laggards who may seem like viable candidates. Even if you do, it will be time consuming and will divert your attention from other duties.

If you decide to do the job yourself, consider retaining an industrial psychologist to spend 4 or 5 hours assessing the problem-solving ability, personality, interests, and energy level of the two or three candidates in whom you are most interested.

Exercise special care when recruiting applicants from competing companies. Always check to see if applicants are bound by noncompete or nondisclosure agreements. And (especially when recruiting other firms' higher-level employees) perhaps check with an attorney before asking certain questions—regarding patents or potential antitrust issues, for instance.[103]

If you're a manager with an open position to fill in a *Fortune* 500 company, even you may find you have a dilemma. You may find that your local HR office will do little recruiting other than, perhaps, placing an ad on an online job board. On the other hand, you probably can't place your own help wanted ads (a problem Marlene faced in this chapter's opening scenario). Instead, contact your colleagues in other firms: use word of mouth to "advertise" your open position within and outside your company.

✪ Talk About It – 2

If your professor has chosen to assign this, go to **www.pearson.com/mylab/ management** to discuss the following question. You own a small chemical engineering company and want to hire a new president. Based on what you read in this chapter, how would you go about doing so, and why?

Referrals and Walk-Ins

Employee referral campaigns are an essential recruiting option. Here the employer posts openings and requests for referrals on its website and bulletin boards. It may offer payments for successful referrals. For example, at Kaiser Permanente, referring someone for one of its "award-eligible positions" can produce bonuses of $3,000 or more.[104] The Container Store trains employees to recruit candidates from among the firm's customers. Many employers use tools like Jobvite Refer to make it easier for their employees to publicize the firm's open positions via their own social media sites.[105]

Referral's big advantage is that it tends to generate "more applicants, more hires, and a higher yield ratio (hires/applicants)."[106] Current employees tend to provide accurate information about their referrals because they're putting their own reputations on the line. A SHRM survey found that of 586 employers, 69% said referral programs are more cost effective than other recruiting practices, and 80% specifically said they are more cost effective than employment agencies.[107]

If morale is low, address that prior to soliciting referrals. Remember that relying on referrals may be discriminatory where a workforce is already homogeneous. And if you don't hire someone's referral, explain the reason to your employee/referrer. Employee referral programs can also backfire when most of a firm's employees are nonminority. Even here, however, employers can use employee referrals to produce more minority candidates, such as by offering bigger bonuses for diversity hires.[108]

Particularly for hourly workers, *walk-ins*—direct applications made at your office—are a big source of applicants. Sometimes, posting a "Help Wanted" sign outside the door may be the most cost-effective way of attracting good local applicants. Treat walk-ins courteously, for both the employer's community reputation and the applicant's self-esteem. Many employers give every walk-in a brief interview, even if it is only to get information on the applicant in case a position should be open in the future. There will also be unsolicited applications from professional and white-collar applicants; answer all inquiries promptly.

Recruitment Process Outsourcers and On-Demand Recruiting Services

Recruitment process outsourcers (RPOs) are special vendors that handle all or most of an employer's recruiting needs. They usually sign short-term contracts with the employer and receive a monthly fee that varies with the amount of actual

Particularly when hiring locally, a "Help Wanted" sign can be an excellent recruiting tool.
Source: Andrey Popov/Shutterstock.

recruiting the employer needs done. This makes it easier for an employer to ramp up or ramp down its recruiting expenses, as compared with paying the relatively fixed costs of an in-house recruitment office.[109]

Today, clients expect recruitment process outsourcers (RPOs) to do more than bring in applicants. They also want them to make the application process more personalized, to identify more passive candidates, and to help them build their employment brand. Large RPOs include Manpower Group Solutions, Allegis Global Solutions, and IBM Recruitment Services.[110]

on-demand recruiting services (ODRS)
Services that provide short-term specialized recruiting to support specific projects without the expense of retaining traditional search firms.

On-demand recruiting services (ODRS) are recruiters who are paid by the hour or project, instead of a percentage fee, to support a specific project. For example, when the human resource manager for a biotech firm had to hire several dozen people with scientific degrees and experience in pharmaceuticals, she used an ODRS firm. A traditional recruiting firm might charge 20% to 30% of each hire's salary. The ODRS firm charged by time, rather than per hire. It handled recruiting and prescreening and left the client with a short list of qualified candidates.[111]

College Recruiting

college recruiting
Sending an employer's representatives to college campuses to prescreen applicants and create an applicant pool from the graduating class.

College recruiting—sending an employer's representatives to college campuses to prescreen applicants and create an applicant pool from the graduating class—is an important source of management trainees and professional and technical employees. One study several years ago concluded that new college graduates filled about 38% of all externally filled jobs requiring a college degree.[112]

Good campus recruiting isn't easy. Schedules must be set, company brochures printed, interviews held, and much time spent on campus. And some recruiters are unprepared, show little interest in the candidate, and act superior. Many don't screen candidates effectively.

Employers should train recruiters in how to interview candidates, how to explain what the company has to offer, and how to put candidates at ease. The recruiter should be personable and have a record of attracting good candidates.[113] GE hires 800 to 1,000 students each year from about 40 schools and uses teams of employees and interns to build GE's brand at each school. Similarly, IBM has 10 people who focus on on-campus recruiting.[114] Shell Oil reduced the list of schools its recruiters visit, using criteria such as quality of academic program, number of students enrolled, and diversity of the student body.[115]

The campus recruiter has two main goals. One is to determine if a candidate is worthy of further consideration. Usual traits to assess include communication

The campus recruiter has two main goals. One is to determine if a candidate is worthy of further consideration. The other is to attract good candidates.
Source: Asiseeit/Getty Images.

skills, education, experience, and technical and interpersonal skills. The other aim is to attract candidates. A sincere and informal attitude, respect for the applicant, and prompt follow-up letters can help sell the employer to the interviewee. And employers who build relationships with opinion leaders such as career counselors and professors have better recruiting results.[116]

Employers generally invite good candidates for an on-site visit. The invitation should be warm but businesslike and provide a choice of dates. A package containing the applicant's schedule as well as other information—such as annual reports and employee benefits—should be waiting for the applicant at the hotel.

Plan the interviews, and adhere to the schedule. Avoid interruptions; give the candidate the undivided attention of each person with whom he or she interviews. Make any offer as soon as possible, preferably at the visit. Frequent follow-ups to "find out how the decision's going" may help to tilt the applicant in your favor.

A study of 96 graduating students provides some insights. Fifty-three percent said "on-site visit opportunities to meet with people in positions similar to those applied for, or with higher-ranking persons" had a positive effect. Fifty-one percent mentioned, "Impressive hotel/dinner arrangements and having well-organized site arrangements." "Disorganized, unprepared interviewer behavior, or uninformed, useless answers" turned off 41%.[117]

Internships Internships can be win–win situations. They can help the student hone business skills, learn more about the employer, and discover career preferences. And employers can use the interns to make useful contributions while evaluating them as possible full-time employees. About 60% of internships turn into job offers.[118]

Others turn into nightmares. Many interns, particularly in industries like high-fashion and media, report long unpaid days doing menial work. *The New York Times* quoted one company's manager as saying "we need to hire a 22—22—22," a 22-year-old willing to work 22 hour days for $22,000 a year.[119]

Courts have laid out several criteria for determining whether someone is an intern or an employee. Criteria include, for example, whether both the intern and employer clearly understand that no compensation is expected; whether the internship provides training similar to that of an educational environment; and whether the internship is tied to the person's formal education program.[120]

Telecommuters

Telecommuters do all or most of their work remotely, often from home, using information technology. As one example, JetBlue uses at-home agents to handle its reservation needs. These "crewmembers" live around Salt Lake City and work from their homes. They use JetBlue-supplied computers and technology and receive JetBlue training.[121]

Military Personnel

Discharged U.S. military personnel are an excellent source of trained and disciplined recruits.[122] Yet all too often they have trouble getting placed. For example, at the time, the unemployment rate for veterans of the second Gulf War was about 10% versus 6.4% for nonveterans. To help remedy this, the federal government offers tax credits to employers who hire veterans, and many employers including Walmart have special programs to recruit veterans.[123] The U.S. Army's Partnership for Youth Success enables someone entering the Army to select a postarmy corporate partner as a way to smooth the way to having a job after leaving the Army.[124] The website www.helmetstohardhats.org/ puts vets together with building trades employers.

Misconceptions about veterans (for instance, that stress disorders influence job performance) are generally not valid.[125] The U.S. Army's Warrior Transition Command website (www.wtc.army.mil/) discusses such misconceptions.

LEARNING OBJECTIVE 6
Explain how to create a more diverse workforce.

Recruiting a More Diverse Workforce

We saw in Chapter 2 that recruiting a diverse workforce isn't just socially responsible. Given the rise in minority, older worker, and women candidates, it's a necessity. Consultants McKinsey and Company found that employers it surveyed that had gender diversity outperformed those that did not by 15%.[126]

The recruiting tools we described to this point are useful for minority applicants, too. However, diversity recruiting requires some special steps.[127] For example, Facebook is said to award its recruiters more points for hiring black, Hispanic, or female engineers.[128] Facebook also has its hiring managers interview at least one person from an underrepresented group for each open position.[129] Pinterest recently set aggressive diversity goals, such as to hire women for 30% of open engineer jobs. It missed that goal, although women still represented 22% of the engineers it hired. Microsoft ties manager bonuses to hiring diverse employees.[130]

Recruiting Women

Given the progress women have made in excelling in professional, managerial, and military occupations, one might assume that employers need no special recruitment efforts to recruit them, but that's not the case. For example, women still face headwinds in certain occupations such as engineering. They also fill proportionately fewer high-level managerial posts and earn only about 70% of what men earn for similar jobs.

The most effective remedy starts with top management.[131] Here the employer emphasizes the importance of recruiting women (as well as men), identifies gaps in the recruitment and retention of women, and puts in place a comprehensive plan to attract women applicants.

The overall aim is to show that the employer is a place in which women want to work. For example, particularly for "nontraditional" jobs (like engineering), use the company website to highlight women now doing those jobs. Emphasize the employer's mentoring program. Offer real workplace flexibility, such as the option of staying on a partner track even while working part-time. Focus a portion of the recruiting effort on women's organizations, women's employment websites, and career fairs at women's colleges. Make sure benefits cover matters such as family planning and prenatal care. Maintain a zero-tolerance sexual harassment policy.

Recruiting Single Parents

Recently, there were about 15 million single-parent families with children under 18 maintained by the mother and about 5 million maintained by the father.[132] Being a single parent isn't easy, and recruiting and keeping them requires understanding the problems they face.[133] (Of course many of these issues also apply to families in which both parents are struggling to make ends meet.) In one survey,

> Many described falling into bed exhausted at midnight without even minimal time for themselves . . . . They often needed personal sick time or excused days off to care for sick children. As one mother noted, "I don't have enough sick days to get sick."[134]

Given such concerns, the first step in attracting and keeping single parents is to make the workplace user friendly.[135] A supportive supervisor can go far toward making the single parent's work–home balancing act more bearable.[136] Many firms have flextime programs that provide some schedule flexibility (such as 1-hour windows at the beginning or end of the day). Unfortunately, for many single parents this may not be enough. CNN has a "Work/Life Balance Calculator" (go to www.cnn.com and type balance calculator into the search box; then choose work/life balance calculator to assess how out of balance one's life may be).[137] We'll discuss other options in Chapter 11: Pay for Performance and Employee Benefits.

Older Workers

When it comes to hiring older workers, employers don't have much choice.[138] The fastest-growing labor force segment is those from 45 to 64 years old. It therefore makes sense for employers to encourage older workers to stay (or to come to work at the company).

The big draw is probably to provide opportunities for flexible (and often shorter) work schedules.[139] At one company, workers over 65 can progressively shorten their work schedules; another uses "mini shifts" to accommodate those interested in working less than full-time. Other suggestions include the following:

- Phased retirement that allows workers to ease out of the workforce. [140]
- Portable jobs for "snowbirds" who wish to live in warmer climates in the winter.
- Part-time projects for retirees.
- Full benefits for part-timers.[141]

As always in recruiting, projecting the right image is crucial. For example, writing the ad so that it sends the message "we're older-worker friendly" is important. The most effective ads emphasize schedule flexibility and accentuate the firm's equal opportunity employment statement, not "giving retirees opportunities to transfer their knowledge" to the new work setting.[142]

Diversity Counts

Older workers are good workers. One study focused on the six stereotypes about older workers: They are less motivated, less willing to participate in training and career development, more resistant to change, less trusting, less healthy, and more vulnerable to work–family imbalance.[143] They found not a negative but a weakly *positive* relationship between age and motivation and job involvement (suggesting that as age goes up motivation actually rises). They did find a weak negative relationship between age and trainability. Age was weakly but positively related to willingness to change, and to being more trusting. Older workers were no more likely than younger ones to have psychological problems or day-to-day physical health problems, but were more likely to have heightened blood pressure and cholesterol levels. Older workers did not experience more work–family imbalance. So there was little support for the common age stereotypes.

What should employers do? First, raise employees', managers', and recruiters' consciousness about incorrect age stereotypes. And provide opportunities for more contacts with older people and for information flows between younger and older workers.[144]

Recruiting Minorities

Similar prescriptions apply to recruiting minorities.[145] First, understand the barriers that prevent minorities from applying, and then take steps to reduce them. For example, some minority applicants won't meet the job's educational or skills standards. Steps here may include programs for remedial training, flexible work options, role models, and redesigned jobs.

Many job seekers check with friends or relatives when job hunting, so encouraging your minority employees to assist in your recruitment efforts makes sense. Diversity recruitment specialists include www.diversity.com and www.2trabajo.com. Firms such as Facebook offer recruiters incentives to bring in minority candidates.

Other firms collaborate with specialist professional organizations. These include the National Black MBA Association (www.nbmbaa.org),[146] the National Society of Hispanic MBAs (www.nshmba.org/), and the Organization of Chinese Americans (www.ocanational.org/).

Some employers have difficulty hiring and assimilating people previously on welfare. Applicants sometimes lack basic work skills, such as reporting for work on time, working in teams, and taking orders. The key to welfare-to-work seems to be the employer's pretraining program. Here, participants get counseling and basic skills training over several weeks.[147]

The Disabled

Bias against disabled applicants may or may not be intentional but surely occurs. In one study, researchers responded to accounting job openings by sending résumés and cover letters from fictitious candidates; all "candidates" were qualified, but some letters revealed a disability. The candidates with expressed disabilities were chosen by recruiters 26% less frequently for follow up than were those with no revealed disability.[148]

The research is quite persuasive that in terms of virtually all work criteria, employees with disabilities are capable workers. Thousands of employers in the United States and elsewhere have found that disabled employees provide an excellent and largely untapped source of competent, efficient labor for jobs ranging from information technology to creative advertising to receptionist.[149]

Employers can do several things to tap this huge potential workforce. The U.S. Department of Labor's Office of Disability Employment Policy offers several programs, including one that helps link disabled college undergraduates who are looking for summer internships with potential employers.[150] All states have local agencies (such as Corporate Connections in Tennessee) that provide placement services and other recruitment and training tools and information for employers seeking to hire the disabled. Employers also must use common sense. For example, employers who only post job openings in the paper may miss potential employees who are visually impaired.[151]

LEARNING OBJECTIVE 7
Discuss the main issues to address in developing application forms.

application form
A form used by employers to compile information regarding an applicant's identity and educational, military, and work history.

Developing and Using Application Forms
Purpose of Application Forms

With a pool of applicants, the prescreening process can begin. The **application form**—a form used by employers to compile information regarding an applicant's identity and educational, military, and work history—is usually the first step in this process (some firms first require a brief, prescreening interview or online test).

A filled-in application provides four types of information. First, you can make judgments on *substantive matters*, such as whether the applicant has the education and experience to do the job. Second, you can draw conclusions about the applicant's *previous progress* and growth, especially important for management candidates. Third, you can draw tentative conclusions about the applicant's *stability* based on previous work record (although years of downsizing suggest the need for caution here). Fourth, you may be able to use the data in the application to *predict* which candidates will succeed on the job.

The Management Skills feature addresses practical guidelines.

BUILDING YOUR MANAGEMENT SKILLS:
HR Tools for Line Managers and Entrepreneurs

Application Guidelines

Ineffective use of the application form can cost the manager dearly. Managers should keep several practical guidelines in mind. In the "Employment History" section, request detailed information on each prior employer, including supervisor's name and e-mail address or phone; this is essential for reference checking. In signing the application, the applicant should certify that falsified statements may be cause for dismissal, that investigation of credit and employment and driving record is authorized, that a medical examination and drug screening tests may be required, and that employment is for no definite period.

Continued

Estimates of how many applicants exaggerate their qualifications (particularly education or experience) range from 40% to 70%.[152] A majority of graduating seniors reportedly believe that employers expect a degree of exaggeration on résumés. Much of this exaggeration occurs on résumés, but may occur on application forms too. Therefore, make sure applicants sign a statement indicating the information is true. The court will almost always support a discharge for falsifying information when applying for work.[153]

Finally, doing a less-than-complete job of filling in the form may reflect poor work habits or subterfuge. Some applicants scribble, "See résumé attached." This is not acceptable. You need the signed, completed form. Some firms no longer ask applicants for résumés at all, but instead request and then use social media links, such as Twitter or LinkedIn accounts.[154]

 Talk About It – **3**

If your professor has chosen to assign this, go to **www.pearson.com/mylab/management** to discuss the following question. Review several employers' online applications. Do they conform to the guidelines in this feature?

Most employers need several application forms. One for technical and managerial personnel may require detailed answers to questions about education and training. One form for factory workers might focus on tools and equipment. Figure 5.9 illustrates one employment application.

As noted, some employers use statistical methods to analyze application information ("biodata") to *predict* employee tenure and performance. In one study, the researchers found that applicants who had longer tenure with previous employers were less likely to quit and also had higher performance within six months after hire.[157] Examples of predictive biodata items might include "quit a job without giving notice," "graduated from college," and "traveled considerably growing up."[158]

Choose biodata items with care. Equal employment law limits the items you'll want to use (avoid age, race, or gender, for instance). And, some applicants will fake biodata answers in an effort to impress the employer.[159]

KNOW YOUR EMPLOYMENT LAW
Application Forms and EEO Law

The application form should comply with equal employment laws. Questions concerning race, religion, age, sex, or national origin are generally not illegal per se under federal laws, but are under certain state laws. However, they are viewed with disfavor by the EEOC, and the burden of proof will always be on the employer to prove the potentially discriminatory items are both related to success or failure on the job and not unfairly discriminatory. Items to be aware of include the following:

Education: A question on the dates of attendance and graduation from various schools is one potential violation, insofar as it may reflect the applicant's age.

Arrest record: The courts have usually held that employers violate Title VII by disqualifying applicants from employment because of an arrest. This item has an adverse impact on minorities, and employers usually can't show it's required as a business necessity.

Notify in case of emergency: It is generally legal to require the name, address, and phone number of a person to notify in case of emergency. However, asking the relationship of this person could indicate the applicant's marital status or lineage.

Membership in organizations: Some forms ask the applicant to list memberships in clubs, organizations, or societies. Employers should include instructions not to include organizations that would reveal race, religion, physical handicaps, marital status, or ancestry.

Figure 5.9

FBI Employment Application

Source: FBI Preliminary Application for Honors Internship Program.

FEDERAL BUREAU OF INVESTIGATION

Preliminary Application for
Honors Internship Program
(Please Type or Print in Ink)

Date: _____

FIELD OFFICE USE ONLY

HP

Div: _____ Program: _____

I. PERSONAL HISTORY

Name in Full (Last, First, Middle, Maiden)	List College(s) attended, Major, Degree (if applicable), Grade Point Average

Birth Date (Month, Day, Year)	Social Security Number: (Optional)
Birth Place:	

Current Address

Street _____ Apt. No. _____   Home Phone _____ Area Code _____ Number _____

City _____ State _____ Zip Code _____   Work Phone _____ Area Code _____ Number _____

Are you: Licensed Driver ☐ Yes ☐ No   U. S. Citizen ☐ Yes ☐ No

Have you served on active duty in the Armed Forces of the United States? ☐ Yes ☐ No	Branch of military service and dates of active duty:	Type of Discharge

How did you learn or become interested in the FBI Honors Internship Program?

Do you have a foreign language background? ☐ Yes ☐ No List proficiency for each language on reverse side.

Have you ever been arrested or charged with any violation including traffic, but excluding parking tickets? ☐ Yes ☐ No If so, list all such matters even if found not guilty, not formally charged, no court appearance, or matter settled by payment of fine or forfeiture of collateral. Include date, place, charge, disposition, details, and police agency on reverse side.

II. EMPLOYMENT HISTORY

Identify your most recent three years FULL-TIME work experience, after high school (excluding summer, part-time and temporary employment).

From	To	Description of Work	Name/Location of Employer

III. PERSONAL DECLARATIONS

Persons with a disability who require an accommodation to complete the application process are required to notify the FBI of their need for the accommodation.

Have you used marijuana during the last three years or more than 15 times? ☐ Yes ☐ No

Have you used any illegal drug(s) or combination of illegal drugs, other than marijuana, more than 5 times or during the last 10 years? ☐ Yes ☐ No

All Information provided by applicants concerning their drug history will be subject to verification by a preemployment polygraph examination.

Do you understand all prospective FBI employees will be required to submit to an urinalysis for drug abuse prior to employment? ☐ Yes ☐ No

I am aware that willfully withholding information or making false statements on this application constitutes a violation of Section 1001, Title 18, U.S. Code and if appointed, will be the basis for dismissal from the Federal Bureau of Investigation. I agree to these conditions and I hereby certify that all statements made by me on this application are true and complete, to the best of my knowledge.

_____

Signature of Applicant as usually written. (**Do Not Use Nickname**)

The Federal Bureau of Investigation is an equal opportunity employer.

Physical handicaps: It is usually illegal to require the listing of an applicant's physical handicaps or past illnesses unless the application blank specifically asks only for those that "may interfere with your job performance." Similarly, it is generally illegal to ask whether the applicant has ever received workers' compensation.

Marital status: In general, the application should not ask whether an applicant is single, married, divorced, separated, or living with anyone, or the names, occupations, and ages of the applicant's spouse or children.

Housing: Asking whether an applicant *owns, rents,* or *leases* a house may also be discriminatory. It can adversely affect minority groups and is difficult to justify on business necessity.

Video résumés: More candidates are submitting video résumés, a practice replete with benefits and threats. About half of employers in one survey thought video résumés might give employers a better feel for the candidate. The danger is that a video résumé makes it more likely that rejected candidates may claim discrimination.[155] To facilitate using video résumés, several websites compile multimedia résumés for applicants.[156]∎

KNOW YOUR EMPLOYMENT LAW
Mandatory Arbitration

Many employers, aware of the high costs of employment litigation, require applicants to agree on their applications to mandatory arbitration should a dispute arise.

Different federal courts have taken different positions on the enforceability of such "mandatory alternative dispute resolution" clauses. They are generally enforceable, with some caveats.

First, it must be a fair process.[160] For example, the agreement should be a signed and dated separate agreement. Use simple wording. Provide for reconsideration and judicial appeal if there is an error of law.[161] The employer must absorb most of the cost of the arbitration process. The process should be reasonably swift. Employees should be eligible to receive the full remedies that they would have had if they had access to the courts.

Mandatory arbitration clauses turn some candidates off. In one study, 389 MBA students read simulated employment brochures. Mandatory employment arbitration had a significantly negative impact on the attractiveness of the company as a place to work.[162]∎

BUILDING YOUR MANAGEMENT SKILLS:
The Human Side of Recruiting

Not too long ago, recruiting or applying for a job were fairly simple processes. The employer might place local newspaper ads or retain an employment agency. The applicant would usually apply directly to the company, or to the agency. The process was (relatively) personal, and the agency might even help good applicants fine-tune their résumés and improve their interview skills.

Things are different today. Most nonreferral recruiting is online. Large numbers of replies to online ads means most employers use automated keyword screening tools (ATSs) to winnow applicants. Some of these tools have no provisions for even acknowledging applications. This leaves many applicants—many of whom may invest hours or days perfecting personalized résumés and applications—in the dark. In one survey, almost 60% of job seekers said they had a poor applicant experience. Of these, the most negative feedback came from those who never even heard back from the companies they applied to.[163]

Such incivility hurts everyone. For the employer, angry or offended applicants won't hesitate to post negative views on websites like Glassdoor, to be read by generations of potential applicants.[164] Many people who have bad hiring experiences with a company are unlikely to buy from it going forward.[165] For job seekers, such incivility can undermine self-esteem and cripple a job search. In one study, recruiter incivility undermined job seekers' "self-efficacy"—basically, the person's confidence in his or her ability to get a job.

What sorts of comments and behaviors qualified as "uncivil" in this study? Comments or actions that were *dismissive* of the applicant's qualifications ("the recruiter looked at my résumé and said they'd never hire someone like me"); *unresponsive* or untimely communication ("they said they'd get back to me and they never did"); *rude* interactions ("after waiting for my interview for 15 minutes, the interviewer just kept checking her watch while I was talking"); *belittling* ("the interviewer talked down to me in a demeaning tone"); *rushing* through the interview; and *dismissive of appearance* ("she criticized me for being underdressed at the job fair").[166] Most employers can and should do better.

Review

MyLab Management

If your instructor is using MyLab Management, go to **www.pearson.com/mylab/management** to complete the problems marked with this icon ⭐.

Summary

1. Recruitment and selection starts with *workforce planning and forecasting*. Workforce planning is the process of deciding what positions the firm will have to fill, and how to fill them. This often starts by forecasting personnel needs, perhaps using trend analysis, ratio analysis, scatter plots, or computerized software packages. The other side of the equation is forecasting the supply of inside candidates. Here employers use manual systems, replacement charts, and computerized skills inventories. Forecasting the supply of outside candidates is important, particularly when unemployment is low and good candidates are more difficult to come by.

2. All managers need to understand why *effective recruiting is important*. Without enough candidates, employers cannot effectively screen the candidates or hire the best. Some employers use a recruiting yield pyramid to estimate how many applicants they need to generate to fill predicted job openings.

3. Filling open positions with *internal sources of candidates* has several advantages. You are familiar with their strengths and weaknesses, and they require less orientation. Finding internal candidates often utilizes job posting. For filling the company's projected top-level positions, succession planning—the ongoing process of systematically identifying, assessing, and developing organizational leadership to enhance performance—is the process of choice.

4. Workforce plans influence *employee engagement*. For example, plans to develop and retain employees and promote-from-within tend to foster engagement, while contrary policies may erode it. Recognizing this, at some companies such as FedEx, internal recruiting and promotion-from-within both play central roles in employee engagement.

5. Employers use a variety of *outside sources of candidates* when recruiting applicants. These include recruiting via the Internet, advertising and employment agencies (including public and nonprofit agencies, and private agencies), temporary agencies and other alternative staffing methods, executive recruiters, college recruiting, referrals and walk-ins, and military personnel.

6. Understanding how to *recruit a more diverse workforce* is important. Whether the target is the single parent, older workers, or minorities, the basic rule is to understand their special needs and to create a set of policies and practices that create a more hospitable environment in which they can work.

7. *Employers develop and use application forms* to collect essential background information about the applicant. The application should enable you to make judgments on substantial matters such as the person's education and to identify the person's job references and supervisors. Of course, it's important to make sure the application complies with equal employment laws, for instance with respect to questions regarding physical handicaps.

Key Terms

workforce (or employment or personnel)
    planning   120
succession planning   121
trend analysis   122
ratio analysis   122
scatter plot   123
personnel replacement charts   125
position replacement card   125

employee recruiting   128
recruiting yield pyramid   128
job posting   130
applicant tracking systems   132
alternative staffing   137
on-demand recruiting services (ODRS)   142
college recruiting   142
application form   146

⭐ Try It

How would you do applying the concepts and skills you learned in this chapter? If your professor has chosen to assign this, go to **www.pearson.com/mylab/management** and complete the Plans & Planning Tools simulation to find out.

Discussion Questions

5-1. What are the pros and cons of five sources of job candidates?

5-2. What are the main types of information that application forms provide?

5-3. What should employers keep in mind when using Internet sites to find job candidates?

5-4. What are the main things you would do to recruit and retain a more diverse workforce?

⭐ 5-5. How would you describe the recruiting "brand" of your current or previous employer, or your university? What would you do to revise that brand?

⭐ 5-6. What metrics would you use to analyze the effectiveness of the recruiting efforts of your current or previous employer? Why did you choose these?

5-7. Choose two tools HR managers use for employment forecasting, and explain how to use them.

5-8. Briefly describe how you would apply talent management principles in improving your employer's workforce planning processes.

Individual and Group Activities

5-9. Bring to class several classified and display ads from the Sunday help wanted ads. Analyze the effectiveness of these ads using the guidelines discussed in this chapter.

5-10. Working individually or in groups, develop a five-year forecast of occupational supply and demand for three occupations such as accountant, nurse, and engineer.

5-11. Working individually or in groups, visit the local office of your state employment agency (or check out their site online). Come back to class prepared to discuss the following questions: What types of jobs seem to be predominantly available through this agency? To what extent do you think this particular agency would be a good source of professional, technical, and/or managerial applicants? What sorts of paperwork are applicants to the state agency required to complete before their applications are processed by the agency? What other services does the office provide? What other opinions did you form about the state agency?

5-12. Working individually or in groups, find at least five employment ads, either on the Internet or in a local newspaper, that suggest that the company is family friendly and should appeal to women, minorities, older workers, and single parents. Discuss what they're doing to be family friendly.

5-13. Working individually or in groups, interview a manager between the ages of 25 and 35

at a local business who manages employees age 40 or older. Ask the manager to describe three or four of his or her most challenging experiences managing older employees.

5-14. For this activity, you will need the documents titled (1) "HRCI PHR® and SPHR® Certification Body of Knowledge, and (2) "About the Society for Human Resource Management (SHRM) Body of Competency & Knowledge® Model and Certification Exams." Your instructor can obtain these two documents from the Pearson Instructor Resource Center and pass them on to you. These two documents list the knowledge someone studying for the HRCI or SHRM certification exam needs to have in each area of human resource management (such as in Strategic Management, and Workforce Planning). In groups of several students, do four things: (1) review the HRCI and/or SHRM documents; (2) identify the material in this chapter that relates to HRCI's or SHRM's required knowledge lists; (3) write four multiple-choice exam questions on this material that you believe would be suitable for inclusion in the HRCI exam and/or the SHRM exam; and, (4) if time permits, have someone from your team post your team's questions in front of the class, so that students in all teams can answer the exam questions created by the other teams.

MyLab Management

If your instructor is using MyLab Management, go to **www.pearson.com/mylab/management** for Auto-graded writing questions as well as the following Assisted-graded writing questions:

5-15. Using specific examples, how do equal employment laws affect what managers can and cannot do with respect to recruiting employees?

5-16. What human resource management tools would you use to identify possible internal candidates for a job opening and to assess the candidates' promotability?

APPLICATION EXERCISES

HR IN ACTION CASE INCIDENT 1

Finding People Who Are Passionate about What They Do

Trilogy Enterprises Inc. of Austin, Texas, is a fast-growing software company and provides software solutions to giant global firms for improving sales and performance. It prides itself on its unique and unorthodox culture. Many of its approaches to business practice are unusual, but in Trilogy's fast-changing and highly competitive environment, they seem to work.

There is no dress code, and employees make their own hours, often very long. They tend to socialize together (the average age is 26), both in the office's well-stocked kitchen and on company-sponsored events and trips to places like local dance clubs and retreats in Las Vegas and Hawaii. An in-house jargon has developed, and the shared history of the firm has taken on the status of legend. Responsibility is heavy and comes early, with a "just do it now" attitude that dispenses with long apprenticeships. New recruits are given a few weeks of intensive training, known as "Trilogy University" and described by participants as "more like boot camp than business school." Information is delivered as if with "a fire hose," and new employees are expected to commit their expertise and vitality to everything they do. The director of college recruiting admits the intense and unconventional firm is not the employer for everybody. "But it's definitely an environment where people who are passionate about what they do can thrive."

The firm employs about 700 such passionate people. Trilogy's managers know the rapid growth they seek depends on having a staff of the best people they can find, quickly trained, and given broad responsibility and freedom as soon as possible. Former CEO Joe Liemandt says, "At a software company, people are everything. You can't build the next great software company, which is what we're trying to do here, unless you're totally committed to that. Of course, the leaders at every company say, 'People are everything.' But they don't act on it."

Trilogy makes finding the right people (it calls them "great people") a companywide mission. Recruiters actively pursue the freshest, if least experienced, people in the job market, scouring college career fairs and computer science departments for talented overachievers with ambition and entrepreneurial instincts. Top managers conduct the first rounds of interviews, letting prospects know they will be pushed to achieve but will be well rewarded. Employees take top recruits and their significant others out on the town when they fly into Austin for the standard, three-day preliminary visit. A typical day might begin with grueling interviews but end with mountain biking, rollerblading, or laser tag. Executives have been known to fly out to meet and woo hot prospects who couldn't make the trip.

One year, Trilogy reviewed 15,000 résumés, conducted 4,000 on-campus interviews, flew 850 prospects in for interviews, and hired 262 college graduates, who account for over a third of its current employees. The cost per hire was $13,000; the recruiting director believes it was worth every penny.

Questions

5-17. Identify some of the established recruiting techniques that apparently underlie Trilogy's unconventional approach to attracting talent.

5-18. What particular elements of Trilogy's culture most likely appeal to the kind of employees it seeks? How does it convey those elements to job prospects?

5-19. Would Trilogy be an appealing employer for you? Why or why not? If not, what would it take for you to accept a job offer from Trilogy?

5-20. What suggestions would you make to Trilogy for improving its recruiting processes?

Sources: Chuck Salter, "Insanity, Inc.," *Fast Company*, January 1999, pp. 101–108; and www.trilogy.com/sections/careers/work, accessed August 24, 2007.

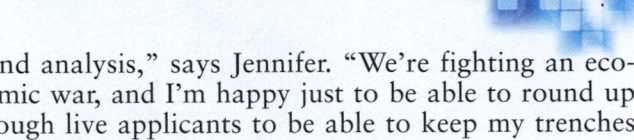

HR IN ACTION CASE INCIDENT 2
Carter Cleaning Company

Getting Better Applicants

If you were to ask Jennifer and her father what the main problem was in running their firm, their answer would be quick and short: hiring good people. Originally begun as a string of coin-operated laundromats requiring virtually no skilled help, the chain grew to six stores, each heavily dependent on skilled managers, cleaner/spotters, and pressers. Employees generally have no more than a high school education (often less), and the market for them is very competitive. Over a typical weekend, literally dozens of want ads for experienced pressers or cleaner/spotters can be found online or in area newspapers. All these people usually are paid around $15 per hour, and they change jobs frequently. Jennifer and her father thus face the continuing task of recruiting and hiring qualified workers out of a pool of individuals they feel are almost nomadic in their propensity to move from area to area and job to job. Turnover in their stores (as in the stores of many of their competitors) often approaches 400%. "Don't talk to me about human resources planning and

trend analysis," says Jennifer. "We're fighting an economic war, and I'm happy just to be able to round up enough live applicants to be able to keep my trenches fully manned."

In light of this problem, Jennifer's father asked her to answer the questions that follow.

Questions

5-21. First, how would you recommend we go about reducing the turnover in our stores?

5-22. Provide a detailed list of recommendations concerning how we should go about increasing our pool of acceptable job applicants so we no longer face the need to hire almost anyone who walks in the door. (Your recommendations regarding the latter should include completely worded online and hard-copy advertisements and recommendations regarding any other recruiting strategies you would suggest we use.)

Experiential Exercise

The Nursing Shortage

Although many people are still unemployed, that is not the case with nurse professionals. Virtually every hospital is aggressively recruiting nurses. Many turn to foreign-trained nurses, for example, by recruiting nurses in the Philippines. Experts expect nurses to be in very short supply for years to come.

Purpose: The purpose of this exercise is to give you experience in creating a recruitment program.

Required Understanding: You should be thoroughly familiar with the contents of this chapter and with the nurse recruitment program of a hospital such as Lenox Hill/Northwell Hospital in New York (see jobs.northwell.edu).

How to Set Up the Exercise/Instructions: Set up groups of four to five students for this exercise. The groups should work separately and should not converse with each other. Each group should address the following tasks:

5-23. Based on information available on the hospital's website, create a hard-copy ad for the hospital to place in the Sunday edition of *The New York Times.* Which (geographic) editions of the *Times* would you use, and why?

5-24. Analyze the hospital's current online nurses' ads. How would you improve on it?

5-25. Prepare in outline form a complete nurses' recruiting program for this hospital, including all recruiting sources your group would use.

6

Selecting Employees

OVERVIEW:
In this chapter, we will cover . . .

- The Basics of Testing and Selecting Employees
- Types of Tests
- Interviewing Candidates
- Using Other Selection Techniques
- Employee Engagement Guide for Managers

MyLab Management

⭐ Improve Your Grade!
When you see this icon, visit
www.pearson.com/mylab/management for
activities that are applied, personalized, and
offer immediate feedback.

LEARNING OBJECTIVES

When you finish studying this chapter, you should be able to:

1. Define basic testing concepts, including validity and reliability.
2. Discuss at least four basic types of personnel tests.
3. Explain the factors and problems that can undermine an interview's usefulness and the techniques for eliminating them.
4. Explain how to do background checks on job candidates.
5. Discuss how to use employee selection methods to raise the level of a company's employee engagement.

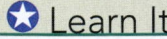 ⭐ Learn It

If your professor has chosen to assign this, go to **www.pearson.com/ mylab/management** to see what you should particularly focus on and to take the Chapter 6 Warm Up.

Source: Jean-Marie Guyon/123RF.

INTRODUCTION

John manages a 12-employee restaurant for an absentee owner who lives about an hour away. Among other things, John is supposed to hire the waitstaff, a job that sounds easier than it is. Last month he hired a fellow who looked good but who proceeded to scream at a customer who complained that his order was wrong. John decides he needs a more organized way to interview prospective waiters. (The owner doesn't want John using selection tests.) We'll see what he did.

<table>
<tr><td>LEARNING OBJECTIVE 1
Define basic testing concepts, including validity and reliability.</td></tr>
</table>

The Basics of Testing and Selecting Employees

Once you have a pool of applicants, the next step is to select the best person for the job. This usually means whittling down the applicant pool by using employee selection tools including tests, interviews, and background checks. The aim of employee selection is to achieve person–job fit. *Person–job fit* means matching the knowledge, skills, abilities, and competencies (KSACs) that are required for performing the job (based on the job analysis) with the applicant's knowledge, skills, abilities, and competencies.

Why Careful Selection Is Important

Effective employee selection is important for several reasons.[1] First is *improved employee and organizational performance*. For example, in one call center, the 90-day attrition rate—employees who left after 90 days—fell from 41% to 12% after applicant testing began.[2] Second, *your own performance* is at stake. Hire employees who lack skills or who are obstructionist, and your own performance will suffer. Third, screening helps reduce *dysfunctional behaviors* at work. By one account, about 30% of all employees say they've stolen from their employers; about 41% of these are managers.[3] The time to screen these people out is before they're hired. Fourth, hiring and training even a clerk can cost $10,000 in fees and supervisory time. That's *money wasted* if the person doesn't work out.[4]

Legal Implications and Negligent Hiring Finally, effective screening is important because of two of the big *legal implications* of inept selection. Violating discrimination laws is one potential legal problem, as we saw in Chapter 2.

Negligent hiring is the second one. Courts will find employers liable when employees with criminal records or other problems use their access to customers' homes or similar opportunities to commit crimes. Hiring workers with such backgrounds without proper safeguards is **negligent hiring**. For example, lawyers sued one large retailer alleging that several of its employees with criminal convictions for sexually related offenses had assaulted young girls at work.[5] Courts may also find the employer negligent if a dangerous employee harms another employee.[6] To protect against negligent hiring claims:

negligent hiring
Hiring workers with criminal records or other such problems without proper safeguards.

- *Carefully scrutinize* all information supplied by the applicant, such as unexplained gaps in employment.
- Get the applicant's *written authorization* for reference checks, and check references.
- *Save all records* and information you obtain about the applicant.
- *Reject applicants* who make false statements of material facts or who have conviction records for offenses directly related and important to the job in question.
- Take *immediate disciplinary action* if problems arise.[7]

Reliability

In this chapter we will discuss the main employee selection tests and tools. Any test or screening tool has two important characteristics: *reliability* and *validity*. We'll start with the former.

reliability
The characteristic that refers to the consistency of scores obtained by the same person when retested with the identical or equivalent tests.

Reliability refers to the test's consistency. It is "the consistency of scores obtained by the same person when retested with the identical tests or with an equivalent form of a test."[8] Test reliability is essential: If a person scored 90 on an intelligence test on Monday and 130 when retested on Tuesday, you wouldn't have much faith in the test.

You can measure reliability in several ways. One is to administer a test to a group of people one day, readminister the same test several days later to the same group, and then correlate the first set of scores with the second (*test-retest reliability estimates*).[9] Or you could administer a test and then administer what experts believe to be an equivalent test later; this would be an *equivalent or alternate form estimate*. The Scholastic Assessment Test (SAT) is an example. Or, compare the test taker's answers to multiple questions on the same test aimed at measuring the same thing. For example, a psychologist includes 10 items on a test believing that they all measure interest in working outdoors. You administer the test and then statistically analyze the degree to which responses to these 10 items vary together. This is an *internal comparison estimate*.

Many things cause a test to be unreliable. These include physical conditions (quiet test conditions one day, noisy the next day); differences in the test taker (healthy one day, sick the next); and differences in the person administering the test (courteous one day, curt the next). Or perhaps the questions do a poor job of sampling the material; test 1 focuses on Chapters 1, 3, 7, while test 2 focuses on Chapters 2, 4, and 8.

Because measuring reliability generally involves comparing two measures that assess the same thing (such as test 1 and test 2), it is typical to judge a test's reliability in terms of a correlation coefficient (in this case, a *reliability coefficient*). This coefficient shows the degree to which the two measures (say, a test score one day and a test score the next day) are related.

Figure 6.1

Correlation Examples

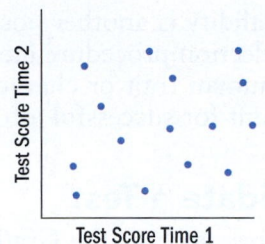
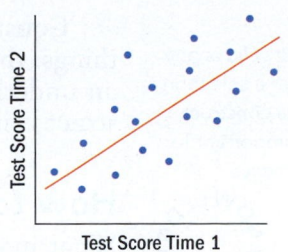

Figure 6.1 illustrates correlation. In both the left and the right scatter plots, the psychologist compared each applicant's test score (on the *x*-axis) with his or her subsequent performance (on the *y*-axis). On the left, the scatter plot points (each point showing one applicant's test score and subsequent performance) are dispersed. There seems to be no correlation between test scores and performance. On the right, the psychologist tried a new test. Here, the resulting points fall in a predictable pattern. This suggests that the applicants' test scores correlate closely with their previous scores.

Validity

Reliability, although indispensable, only tells you that the test is measuring something consistently. *Validity* tells you whether the test is measuring what you think it's supposed to be measuring. **Test validity** answers the question "Does this test measure what it's supposed to measure?" Stated differently, "Validity refers to the confidence one has in the meaning attached to the scores."[10] With respect to employee selection tests, the term *validity* often refers to evidence that the test is job related—in other words, that performance on the test is a *valid predictor* of subsequent performance on the job. A selection test must be valid because, without proof of its validity, there is no logical or legally permissible reason to continue using it to screen job applicants.

test validity

The accuracy with which a test, interview, and so on measures what it purports to measure or fulfills the function it was designed to fill.

Any test is a sample of a person's behavior, but some tests more clearly reflect the behavior you're sampling. For example, a typing test clearly corresponds to an on-the-job behavior—typing. At the other extreme, in the Rorschach test item shown in the accompanying figure, the psychologist asks the person to explain how he or she interprets the somewhat eerie picture. Here it is harder to "prove" that the tests are measuring what they are purported to measure—that they are *valid*.

criterion validity

A type of validity based on showing that scores on the test (*predictors*) are related to job performance (*criterion*).

In employment testing, there are two main ways to demonstrate a test's validity: criterion validity and content validity. **Criterion validity** involves demonstrating statistically a relationship between (1) scores on a selection procedure and (2) job performance of a sample of workers (for example, that those who do well on the test also do well on the job, and that those who do poorly on the test do poorly on the job). In psychological measurement, a predictor is the measurement (in this case, the test score) that you are trying to relate to a criterion, such as job performance (perhaps as measured by performance appraisals). The term *criterion validity* comes from that terminology.

content validity

A test that is *content valid* is one in which the test contains a fair sample of the tasks and skills actually needed for the job in question.

Content validity is a demonstration that the content of a selection procedure is representative of important aspects of performance on the job. For example, employers demonstrate the *content validity* of a test by showing that the test constitutes a fair sample of the job's content. In selecting students for dental school, many schools give applicants chunks of chalk and ask them to carve something that looks like a tooth. If the content you choose for the test is a representative sample of what the person needs to know for the job, then the test is probably content valid. Clumsy dental students need not apply.

A slide from the Rorschach test.

Source: Pdtnc/Fotolia.

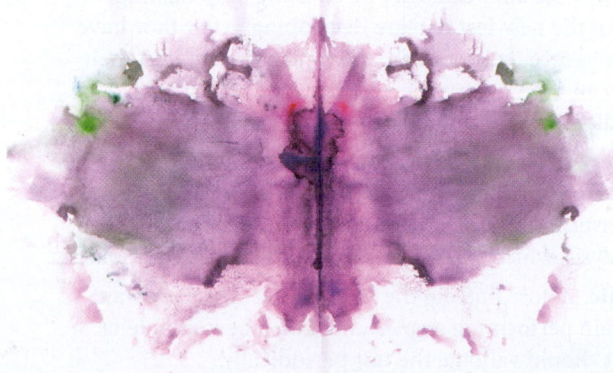

construct validity

A test that is *construct valid* is one that demonstrates that a selection procedure measures a construct and that construct is important for successful job performance.

validity generalization

The degree to which evidence of a measure's validity obtained in one situation can be generalized to another situation without further study.

Construct validity is another possible approach. It means demonstrating two things: that a selection procedure measures a construct (something believed to be an underlying human trait or characteristic, such as honesty); and that the construct is important for successful job performance.

How to Validate a Test

What makes a test such as the Graduate Record Examination (GRE) useful for graduate school admissions directors? What makes a mechanical comprehension test useful for managers hiring machinists? The answer to both questions is usually that people's scores on these tests are predictive of how people perform, for instance in graduate school. For example, the employer would use statistical means to determine the degree of correlation between mechanical comprehension scores and machinists' performance. The validation process (which we outline in Figure 6.2) usually requires the expertise of an industrial psychologist.

For many employers, particularly smaller ones, it's not always cost effective to conduct validity studies for the selection tools they use. These employers must identify tests and other screening tools that have been shown to be valid in other settings (companies) and then bring them in-house in the hopes that they'll be valid there, too.[11]

If the test is valid in one company, to what extent can we generalize those validity findings to our own company? **Validity generalization** "refers to the degree

Figure 6.2

How to Validate a Test

Step 1: Analyze the Job. First, analyze the job descriptions and specifications. Specify the human traits and skills you believe are required for adequate job performance. For example, must an applicant be aggressive? Must the person be able to assemble small, detailed components? These requirements become your predictors. They are the human traits and skills you believe to be predictive of success on the job.

In this first step, you must also define what you mean by "success on the job" because it is this success for which you want predictors. The standards of success are called *criteria*. You could focus on production-related criteria (quantity, quality, and so on), personnel data (absenteeism, length of service, and so on), or judgments (of worker performance by persons such as supervisors). For an assembler's job, *predictors* to use when testing applicants might include manual dexterity and patience. Criteria that you would hope to predict with your test might then include quantity produced per hour and number of rejects produced per hour.

Step 2: Choose the Tests. Next, choose tests that you think measure the attributes (predictors) important for job success. This choice is usually based on experience, previous research, and best guesses, and you usually won't start off with just one test. Instead, you choose several tests, combining them into a test battery aimed at measuring a variety of possible predictors, such as aggressiveness, extroversion, and numeric ability.

Step 3: Administer Tests. Administer the selected test(s) to employees. *Predictive validation* is the most dependable way to validate a test. The test is administered to applicants before they are hired. Then these applicants are hired using only existing selection techniques, not the results of the new test you are developing. After they have been on the job for some time, you measure their performance and compare it to their performance on the earlier test. You can then determine whether their performance on the test could have been used to predict their subsequent job performance.

Step 4: Relate Scores and Criteria. Next, determine whether there is a significant relationship between scores (the predictor) and performance (the criterion). The usual way to do this is to determine the statistical relationship between scores on the test and performance through correlation analysis, which shows the degree of statistical relationship.

Step 5: Cross-Validate and Revalidate. Before putting the test into use, you may want to check it by cross-validating, by again performing steps 3 and 4 on a new sample of employees. At a minimum, an expert should validate the test periodically.

to which evidence of a measure's validity obtained in one situation can be generalized to another situation without further study."[12] Being able to use the test without your own validation study is, of course, the key. Factors to consider include *existing validation evidence* regarding using the test for various specific purposes, the *similarity of the subjects* on whom the test was validated with those in your organization, and the *similarity of the jobs* involved.[13]

utility analysis
The degree to which use of a selection measure improves the quality of individuals selected over what would have happened if the measure had not been used.

It may turn out that the testing is so expensive that it costs more than you save by hiring better employees. Answering the question, "Does it pay to use the test?" requires *utility analysis*. Two selection experts say, "Using dollar and cents terms, [**utility analysis**] shows the degree to which use of a selection measure improves the quality of individuals selected over what would have happened if the measure had not been used."[14] In practice, whether it "pays" to use the test depends on the validity of the selection measure, a dollar measure of job performance, applicants' average test scores, cost of testing an applicant, and the number of applicants tested.[15] The accompanying HR as a Profit Center feature provides an example.

■ HR as a Profit Center

Reducing Turnover at KeyBank

Financial services firm KeyBank needed a better way to screen and select tellers and call-center employees.[16] Analysts calculated it cost KeyBank about $10,000 to select and bring onboard an employee, but they were losing 13% of new tellers and call-center employees in the first 90 days. That turnover number dropped to 4% after KeyBank implemented a virtual job tryout candidate-assessment screening tool. "We calculated a $1.7 million cost savings in teller turnover in one year, simply by making better hiring decisions, reducing training costs, and increasing quality of hires," said the firm's human resources director.

✪ Talk About It – 1

If your professor has chosen to assign this, go to **www.pearson.com/mylab/management** to discuss the following: Choose a position with which you are familiar, such as a counterperson at a McDonald's restaurant, and describe how you would create a selection process for it similar to those in this feature.

KNOW YOUR EMPLOYMENT LAW
Testing and Equal Employment Opportunity

We've seen that various federal, state, and local laws bar discrimination with respect to race, color, age, religion, sex, disability, and national origin. Now, assume that you've used a test and that a rejected minority candidate has demonstrated adverse impact. How might the person have done this? One way is to show that the selection rate (for, say, the applicant's racial group) was less than four-fifths of that for the group with the highest selection rate. Thus, if 90% of white applicants passed the test but only 60% of blacks passed, then (because 60% is less than four-fifths of 90%) adverse impact exists.[17]

The employer would then have at least two alternatives with respect to its testing program. One is to institute a different, valid selection procedure that does not have an adverse impact. The second is to show that the test is valid—in other words, that it is a valid predictor of performance on the job. Ideally, you would do this by conducting your own validation study. In that event, the plaintiff would then have to prove that your explanation for using the test is inadequate.

The employer cannot avoid EEO laws by not using tests. The same burden of proving job relatedness falls on interviews and other techniques (including performance appraisals) that fall on tests. ■

BUILDING YOUR MANAGEMENT SKILLS:
Protecting Employees' Individual Rights and Test Privacy

Managers often find themselves in possession of an applicant's test results. If so, exercise great caution in using that information. Various federal laws restrict promulgating information such as test results for many types of employees, (most notably federal and other government employees). The common law of torts also provides limited protection against disclosing information about employees. The most well-known application here involves defamation (either libel or slander). For example, if an employer or former employer discloses information that is false and defamatory and that causes the employee serious injury, he or she may be able to sue for defamation. Also, under the American Psychological Association's standard for educational and psychological tests (which guide professional psychologists but are not legally enforceable), test takers have the right to the confidentiality of the test results and the right to informed consent regarding the use of these results. They have the right to expect that only people qualified to interpret the scores will have access to them or that sufficient information will accompany the scores to ensure their appropriate interpretation. They have the right to expect that the test is secure; no person taking the test should have prior information concerning the questions or answers. Morally, if not legally, managers should abide by such restrictions.

Also note that even in the best cases, the test score usually accounts for only about 25% of the variation in the measure of performance. Therefore, don't use tests as your sole selection technique; instead, supplement them with other tools like interviews and background checks.

LEARNING OBJECTIVE 2
Discuss at least four basic types of personnel tests.

Types of Tests

Testing is popular at work. For example, Outback Steakhouse wants employees who are social, meticulous, sympathetic, and adaptable. It uses a personality assessment test as part of its preemployment process. Applicants take the test, and the company then compares the results to the profile for Outback Steakhouse employees. Two managers interview those who score high.[18]

As at Outback, employers today are much more focused on hiring quality employees. About 80% of the biggest U.S. employers now use testing.[19] Take the test in Figure 6.3 to see how prone you might be to on-the-job accidents.

We can conveniently classify a test according to whether it measures cognitive (mental) abilities, motor and physical abilities, personality and interests, or achievement. We'll look at these, and at special tests such as assessment centers.[20]

Tests of Cognitive Abilities

Employers often want to assess a candidate's cognitive or mental abilities. For example, you may want to know if a supervisory candidate has the intelligence to do the job's paperwork or a bookkeeper candidate has numeric aptitude.

Intelligence tests, such as IQ tests, are tests of general intellectual abilities. They measure not a single intelligence trait, but rather a range of abilities, including memory, vocabulary, and numeric ability. Psychologists often measure intelligence with individually administered tests such as the Stanford-Binet test or the Wechsler Adult Intelligence Scale. Employers use tests such as the Wonderlic Personnel Test as quick measures of IQ for both individuals and groups of people.[21]

There are also measures of specific mental abilities. Psychologists often call tests in this category *aptitude tests*. For example, because Figure 6.4 tests applicants' mechanical aptitude, it may reflect a person's fit for jobs, such as engineer.

Figure 6.3

Sample Selection Test

Source: Based on a sample selection test from *The New York Times*.

CHECK YES OR NO	YES	NO

1. You like a lot of excitement in your life.

2. An employee who takes it easy at work is cheating on the employer.

3. You are a cautious person.

4. In the past three years you have found yourself in a shouting match at school or work.

5. You like to drive fast just for fun.

Analysis: According to John Kamp, an industrial psychologist, applicants who answered no, yes, yes, no, no to questions 1, 2, 3, 4, and 5 are statistically likely to be absent less often, to have fewer on-the-job injuries, and, if the job involves driving, to have fewer on-the-job driving accidents. Actual scores on the test are based on answers to 130 questions.

Outback Steakhouse has used preemployment testing since just after the company started.

Source: Ken Wolter/Shutterstock.

Tests of Motor and Physical Abilities

There are many motor or physical abilities you might want to measure, such as finger dexterity, strength, and manual dexterity. The Stromberg Dexterity Test is an example. It measures the speed and accuracy of simple judgment as well as the speed of finger, hand, and arm movements.

Measuring Personality

A person's mental and physical abilities alone seldom explain his or her job performance. Other factors, such as motivation and interpersonal skills, are important, too. As one consultant put it, most people are hired based on qualifications, but most are fired for nonperformance. And *nonperformance* (or *performance*) "is usually the result of personal characteristics, such as attitude, motivation,

Figure 6.4

Type of Question Applicant Might Expect on a Test of Mechanical Comprehension

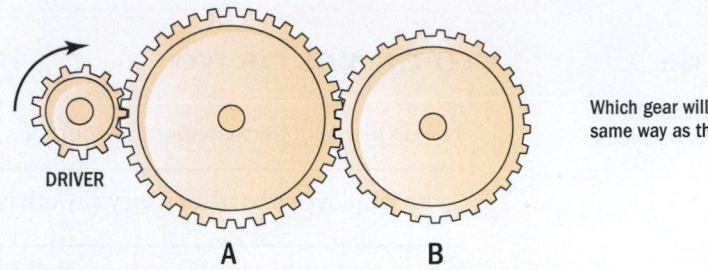

DRIVER

A   B

Which gear will turn the same way as the driver?

and especially, temperament."[22] Employers use personality and interests tests (or "inventories") to measure and predict such intangibles. Thus Acxiom Corporation uses the Birkman Method (www.birkman.com/) personality assessment to help new employees better understand which tasks they perform best.[23]

Personality tests measure basic aspects of an applicant's personality, such as introversion, stability, and motivation. A sample personality inventory item is the following:

It does not make sense to work hard on something if no one will notice.

a. Definitely true
b. Somewhat true
c. Neither true nor false
d. Somewhat false
e. Definitely false[24]

Of course, personality testing isn't limited to employment settings. Online dating services such as eHarmony.com reject those its software judges are unmatchable.

Many personality tests are *projective*, meaning the person taking the test must interpret an ambiguous stimulus such as an inkblot or a clouded picture. The person supposedly projects into the picture his or her own emotions. Thus, a security-oriented person might describe the exhibit on page 157 as "a giant bug coming to get me." Some personality tests are *self-reported*: applicants (rather than psychologists) fill them out. For example, the Minnesota Multiphasic Personality Inventory (MMPI) taps traits like hypochondria and paranoia. Available online, the Myers-Briggs test provides a personality type classification useful for decisions such as career selection and planning.[25] Its DiSC Profile learning instrument enables the user to gain insight into his or her behavioral style.[26]

Personality tests—particularly projective ones—are difficult to evaluate and use. An expert must analyze the test taker's interpretations and reactions and infer from them his or her personality.[27] The usefulness of such tests for selection then assumes that you find a relationship between a measurable personality trait (such as extroversion) and success on the job. Because they are personal in nature, employers should use such tests with caution. Rejected candidates may (legitimately) claim that the results are false, or that they violate the Americans with Disabilities Act (ADA).

interest inventories

Tests that compare one's interests with those of people in various occupations.

Interest inventories compare one's interests with those of people in various occupations. Thus, when a person takes the Strong Interest Inventory, he or she receives a report comparing his or her interests to those of people already in particular occupations.[28] The assumption, which studies support, is that poor vocational fit correlates with counterproductive work behaviors, perhaps because it frustrates the worker.[29]

Personality Test Effectiveness Despite their potential for being difficult to evaluate and use, personality tests can help employers hire effective workers. Industrial psychologists often focus on the "big five" personality dimensions: extroversion, emotional stability, agreeableness, conscientiousness, and openness to experience.[30]

Neuroticism represents a tendency to exhibit poor emotional adjustment and experience negative effects, such as anxiety, insecurity, and hostility. Extroversion represents a tendency to be sociable, assertive, active, and to experience positive effects, such as energy and zeal. Openness to experience is the disposition to be imaginative, nonconforming, unconventional, and autonomous. Agreeableness is the tendency to be trusting, compliant, caring, and gentle. Conscientiousness comprises two related facets: achievement and dependability[31]

For example, in one study of professionals, police officers, managers, sales workers, and skilled/semiskilled workers, conscientiousness showed a consistent relationship with all job performance criteria for all the occupations. Extroversion predicted performance for managers and sales employees.[32]

Industrial psychologists have questioned whether *self-report* personality tests (which applicants fill out themselves) predict performance at all.[33] Overall, the evidence suggests that personality measures do help predict job performance. People can and will give fake responses to personality and integrity tests, but employers can reduce test faking by warning that it may reduce the chance of being hired.[34] But the most important thing is to make sure that any personality tests you use actually do predict performance.[35]

Achievement Tests

An *achievement test* is a measure of what someone has learned. Most tests in school are achievement tests. They measure knowledge in areas such as economics, marketing, or accounting. In addition to job knowledge, achievement tests can measure applicants' abilities; a typing test is one example.[36] The HR Practices Around the Globe feature addresses testing for assignments abroad.

HR Practices Around the Globe

Testing for Assignments Abroad

Living and working abroad requires some special talents. Not everyone can easily adapt to having one's family far away and to dealing with colleagues with different cultural values. Doing so requires high levels of adaptability and interpersonal skills.[37]

Employers often use special inventories such as the Global Competencies Inventory (GCI) here. It focuses on three aspects of adaptability.

- The Perception Management Factor assesses people's tendency to be rigid in their view of cultural differences, to be judgmental about those differences, and to deal with complexity and uncertainty.
- The Relationship Management Factor assesses a person's awareness of the impact he or she is having on others.
- The Self-Management Factor assesses one's mental and emotional health.

⭐ Talk About It – 2

If your professor has chosen to assign this, go to **www.pearson.com/mylab/ management** to discuss the following question. You are trying to decide if you would be a good candidate for a job abroad, but you don't want to take any formal tests. Discuss another indicator you would use to answer the question, "Would I be a good candidate for a job abroad?"

Computerized and Online Testing

Most of the tests in this chapter are available in both computerized and paper form, and studies suggest that paper and computerized version scores are equivalent.[38]

Most selection testing is moving online. For example, Timken Company uses online assessment covering things like math skills for hourly position applicants.[39] Many employers, before reviewing résumés and holding interviews, have applicants first take short online tests. This leaves a smaller pool to undergo the more personal and costly aspects of the selection process.[40] Applicants can take some tests (such as www.iphonetypingtest.com) via their smartphones.[41]

Improving Performance Through HRIS

City Garage Computerized Testing Example Texas-based City Garage knew it had to change how it hired employees.[42] Its old hiring process consisted of a paper-and-pencil application and one interview, followed by a hire/don't hire decision. This was unsatisfactory. For one thing, local shop managers didn't have the time, so "if they had been shorthanded too long, we would hire pretty much anybody who had experience." Furthermore, City Garage differentiates itself with an "open garage" arrangement, where customers interact directly with technicians, so finding mechanics who react positively to customers is essential.

City Garage purchased the Personality Profile Analysis (PPA) online test from Dallas-based Thomas International USA. Now, after a quick application and background check, likely candidates take the 10-minute, 24-question PPA. City Garage staff then enter the answers into the PPA Software system and receive test results in about 2 minutes. These show whether the applicant is high or low in four personality characteristics. It also produces follow-up questions about areas that might cause problems, such as patience. If candidates answer those questions satisfactorily, they're asked back for all-day interviews, after which hiring decisions are made.

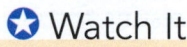 Watch It

How does a company actually do testing? If your professor has chosen to assign this, go to **www.pearson.com/mylab/management** to watch the video Patagonia Employee Testing and Selection, and then answer the questions to show what you'd do in this situation.

In addition to being quicker and less expensive to administer, computerized tests have other benefits. For example, vendors such as PreVisor (www.previsor.com) offer adaptive personality tests. These adapt the next question to each test taker's answers to the previous question. This improves validity and makes it less likely candidates can share test questions (because each candidate gets what amounts to a customized test).[43] For essay tests, a computer program trained to read applicants' essays recently produced scores as reliable as those of a human rater.[44]

talent analytics
Using new number-crunching software to dig through ("mine") existing employee data to better identify what types of people succeed or fail, and therefore whom to hire.

TRENDS SHAPING HR: *Digital and Social Media*

TALENT ANALYTICS Talent analytics uses numbers-crunching data analysis tools including statistical techniques, algorithms, data mining, and problem-solving and is revolutionizing employee selection.[45] It lets employers sift through their employee data to identify patterns and correlations that show what types of people succeed or fail.

For example, department store chain Bon-Ton Stores Inc. had high turnover among its cosmetics sales associates. Bon-Ton chose 450 current cosmetics associates who filled out anonymous surveys aimed at identifying employee traits. By using talent analytics to analyze these and other data, the company identified cosmetics associates' traits that correlated with performance and tenure. Bon-Ton had assumed that the best associates were friendly and enthusiastic about cosmetics. However, the best were actually problem solvers. They take information about what the customer wants and needs and solve the problem.[46] Talent analytics thereby helped Bon-Ton formulate better selection criteria.

Work Samples and Simulations

Work samples and simulations like the situational judgment tests and assessment centers we discuss next can be considered tests. However, they differ from most of the tests we've discussed because they measure job performance directly. Personality and interests inventories, on the other hand, try to predict job performance by measuring traits like extroversion or interests.

Situational Judgment Tests

Situational judgment tests are personnel tests "designed to assess an applicant's judgment regarding a situation encountered in the workplace" and can be quite effective.[47] Here's a sample test question:

> You are a sales associate at Best Buy in Miami, Florida. Many of the customers check the product's feel and price with you, and then buy it at Amazon for a lower price.
>
> Situation 1: A customer comes to you with a printout for a Samsung Galaxy phone from Amazon.com, and proceeds to ask you detailed questions about price, battery life, and how to work the phone, while mentioning that "the price at Amazon is about 25% less than yours." You would:
>
> 1. Tell the customer to go buy the phone at Amazon.
> 2. Tell the customer to wait for 20 minutes while you take care of another customer.
> 3. Explain the advantages of similar phones you have that may better fulfill the buyer's requirements.
> 4. Ask your supervisor to try to sell the customer on buying the Galaxy from Best Buy.

■ HR and the Gig Economy

Selecting Freelance Workers

Many employers today build their staff wholly or in part around freelance workers like short-term self-employed programmers, designers, or marketers. One website design company owner says that if he needs designers for short projects he "just posts" the job online and gets multiple applications within minutes.[48]

Freelancer community websites enable such employers to recruit and select the right freelance team, based on each freelancer's reputation and work product. For example, Upwork.com (see **www.upwork.com/**) reports its members' skills assessments and lists detailed project work experience, making it easier for prospective employers to decide whom to hire. Similarly, the TopCoder.com (see **www.topcoder.com/**) programmer community site helps employers identify top programmers based on the reputations they earned within the community.

★ Talk About It – **3**

If your professor has chosen to assign this, go to **www.pearson.com/mylab/management** to discuss the following questions: Go to one or more sites like these. If you were a programming manager for a company, could you use the site to find and hire a new employee directly? If not, what else might you need?

Management Assessment Centers

management assessment center

A facility in which management candidates are asked to make decisions in hypothetical situations and are scored on their performance.

A **management assessment center** is a two- to three-day simulation in which 10 to 12 candidates perform realistic management tasks (like making presentations) under the observation of experts who appraise each candidate's leadership potential.[49] The center itself may be a plain conference room, but it is often a special room with a one-way mirror to facilitate observation. Typical simulated exercises include the following:

- **The in-basket.** Here the candidate faces an accumulation of reports, memos, notes of incoming phone calls, letters, and other materials. The candidate takes appropriate action on each of these materials.
- **The leaderless group discussion.** A leaderless group receives a discussion question and must arrive at a group decision. The raters then evaluate each group member's interpersonal skills, acceptance by the group, leadership ability, and individual influence.
- **Individual presentations.** A participant's communication skills and persuasiveness are evaluated.

Employers use assessment centers for selection, promotion, and development. Supervisor recommendations usually play a big role in choosing participants. Line managers usually act as assessors and typically arrive at their ratings through consensus.[50] In one study (of 40 police candidates), the researchers concluded: "[A]ssessment center performance shows a unique and substantial contribution to the prediction of future police work success, justifying the usage of such method."[51]

Video-Based Situational Testing

Video-based tests present examinees with scenarios representative of the job, each followed by a multiple-choice question.[52] A scenario might depict an employee handling a situation on the job. At a critical moment, the scenario ends and the video asks the candidate to choose from among several courses of action. Some employers, such as Knack, use video games to determine candidates' creativity and ability to multitask.[53]

The Miniature Job Training and Evaluation Approach

miniature job training and evaluation

A selection procedure in which the employer trains candidates to perform a sample of the job's tasks, and then evaluates their performance.

With **Miniature Job Training and Evaluation,** the employer trains candidates to perform a sample of the job's tasks and then evaluates their performance. It assumes that a person who demonstrates that he or she can learn and perform the sample of tasks will be able to learn and perform the job itself. The accompanying HR in Practice feature presents an actual example.

■ HR in Practice

Selecting Employees at Honda's New Car Plant

When Honda decided to build an auto plant in Lincoln, Alabama, it had to hire thousands of new employees. Working with an Alabama industrial development training agency, Honda began running help wanted ads.

Honda and the Alabama agency first screened the applications by eliminating those who lacked the education or experience and then gave preference to applicants near the plant. About 340 applicants per six-week session received special training at a new facility about 15 miles south of the plant. It included classroom instruction, watching videos of current Honda employees in action, and actually practicing particular jobs. Some candidates who watched the videos simply dropped out when they saw the work's pace and repetitiveness.

The training sessions serve a dual purpose. First, job candidates learn the actual skills they'll need to do the Honda jobs. Second, the training sessions provide an opportunity for special assessors from the Alabama state agency to scrutinize the trainees' work and to rate them. They then invite those who graduate to apply for jobs at the plants. Honda teams, consisting of employees from HR and departmental representatives, do the final screening.[54]

⭐ **Talk About It – 4**

If your professor has chosen to assign this, go to **www.pearson.com/mylab/management** to discuss the following question: What do you think are some of the drawbacks to using this approach?

Computerized Multimedia Candidate Assessment Tools

Employers increasingly use computerized multimedia candidate assessment tools, to deliver virtually to candidates tasks like those Honda uses. The Ford Motor Company uses one for hiring assembly workers. "The company can test everything from how people tighten the bolt, to whether they followed a certain procedure correctly . . . "[55]

■ HR Tools for Line Managers and Small Businesses

Employee Testing and Selection

One of the ironies of being a line manager in even a big company is that, when it comes to screening employees, you're often on your own. Some large firms' HR departments may work with the hiring manager to design and administer screening tools like those we discussed. But in many of these firms, HR departments do little more than some preliminary prescreening (for instance, administering typing tests to clerical applicants) and then follow up with background checks and drug and physical exams.

What should you do if you are, say, a marketing manager and want to screen some of your applicants more formally? It is possible to devise your own test battery, but caution is required. Purchasing and then using packaged tests could be a problem. Doing so may violate company policy, raise validity questions, and even expose your employer to EEO liability.

A preferred approach is to devise and use screening tools, the face validity of which is obvious (face validity means the tool appears to measure what it is intended to measure). The work sampling test we discussed is one example. It's reasonable, for instance, for the marketing manager to ask an advertising applicant to spend an hour designing an ad, or to ask a marketing research applicant to spend a half hour outlining a marketing research program for a hypothetical product. Similarly, a production manager might reasonably ask an inventory control applicant to spend a few minutes using a standard inventory control model to solve an inventory problem.

For small business owners, some tests are so easy to use that they are particularly good for small firms. One is the *Wonderlic Personnel Test*; it measures general mental ability, in about 15 minutes. The tester reads the instructions and then keeps time as the candidate works through the 50 problems on the two inside sheets. The tester scores the test by totaling the number of correct answers. Comparing the person's score with the minimum scores recommended for various occupations shows whether the person achieved the minimally acceptable score for the type of job in question. The *Predictive Index* measures work-related personality traits on a two-sided sheet. For example, there is the "social interest" pattern, for a person who is generally unselfish, congenial, and unassuming. This person would be a good personnel interviewer, for instance. A template makes scoring simple.

⭐ **Talk About It – 5**

If your professor has chosen to assign this, go to **www.pearson.com/mylab/management** to discuss the following: You own a small ladies' dress shop in a mall and want to hire a salesperson. Create a test for doing so.

LEARNING OBJECTIVE 3
Explain the factors
and problems that can
undermine an interview's
usefulness and the
techniques for eliminating
them.

interview
A procedure designed to solicit
information from a person's oral
responses to oral inquiries.

Interviewing Candidates

Although not all employers use tests, it would be very unusual for a manager not to interview a prospective employee. An **interview** is a procedure designed to solicit information from a person's oral responses to oral inquiries. A *selection interview* is "a selection procedure designed to predict future job performance on the basis of applicants' oral responses to oral inquiries."[56]

Types of Selection Interviews

As you may know from your own experience, there are several ways to conduct selection interviews.

Structure First, interviews may vary in the degree to which the interviewer structures or standardizes the interview.[57] In *nonstructured* interviews, the interviewer asks questions as they come to mind, generally with no set format. In more structured or directive interviews, the questions (and perhaps even acceptable answers) are specified in advance, and the answers may be rated for appropriateness. This chapter's Appendix and accompanying Figure 6A.1 (pages 192-194) explains how to create such a form.

Types of Questions Everyone is familiar with typical questions like "What are your strengths?" but the usefulness of such questions is suspect. Situational, behavioral, and knowledge questions are usually more useful. *Situational* questions focus on the candidate's ability to explain what his or her behavior *would be* in a given situation.[58] For example, "How would you react to a subordinate coming to work late three days in a row?"

With *behavioral* questions, you ask interviewees how they behaved *in the past* in some situation. For example, "Did you ever have a situation in which a subordinate came in late? If so, how did you handle the situation?" When Citizen's Banking Corporation in Michigan found that 31 of the 50 people in its call center quit in one year, the center's head switched to behavioral interviews. She no longer tries to predict how candidates will act based on asking them if they want to work with angry clients. Instead, she asks behavioral questions like, "Tell me about a time you were speaking with an irate person, and how you turned the situation around." Only four people left her center in the following year.[59] Vanguard uses a behavioral-based technique they call STAR. The Vanguard manager is told to ask the interviewee about a particular situation (S), or task (T) he or she faced, and to then uncover the actions or behaviors (A) the candidate took, and the result (R) of his or her actions.[60]

Knowledge and background questions probe candidates' job-related knowledge and experience, as in, "What math courses did you take in college?"

"Trick" questions (such as, "What kind of animal would you be?") are becoming more prevalent.[61] Google wants people who fit in with its creative, flexible, open-minded culture.[62] To find out if someone is a fit, Google asks questions like, "A man pushed his car to a hotel and lost his fortune. What happened?"[63] (The answer is at the end of the next paragraph.)

How to Administer Managers can also administer the interview in several ways. In the *one-on-one interview,* two people meet alone and one interviews the other. In a *sequential interview* several people interview the applicant in sequence before a selection decision is made. In a *panel interview* the candidate is interviewed simultaneously by a group (or panel) of interviewers, rather than sequentially. (He was playing Monopoly.)

Some conduct interviews by *video* or *phone*. Phone interviews can be more accurate than face-to-face ones for judging things like interpersonal skills. Perhaps because neither side need worry about things like clothing or handshakes, the phone interview may let both participants focus more on substantive answers. In one study, interviewers tended to evaluate applicants more favorably in telephone versus face-to-face interviews. The interviewers came to about the same conclusions regarding the interviewees whether the interview was face-to-face or by videoconference. Applicants preferred face-to-face interviews.[64]

For better or worse, some employers are using a speed-dating interviewing approach. One employer sent e-mails to all applicants for an advertised position. Of 800 applicants, 400 showed up. Over the next few hours, applicants first mingled with employees, and then (in a so-called speed-dating area) had one-on-one contacts with employees for a few minutes. Based on this, the recruiting team chose 68 candidates for follow-up interviews.[65]

Computer-Based Job Interviews A *computerized selection interview* is one in which a job candidate's oral and/or keyed replies are obtained in response to computerized oral, visual, or written questions and/or situations. Most such interviews present a series of multiple-choice questions regarding background, experience, education, skills, knowledge, and work attitudes. Some confront candidates with realistic scenarios (such as irate customers) to which they must respond.[66]

Diversity Counts

Bias Against Working Mothers Would you hire someone's mother? As absurd as that question seems, managers should be aware of a sad fact: Employers tend to view working mothers negatively.[67] Researchers gave 100 MBA students (34% female, and all of whom worked full-time) copies of a job description summary. The job was assistant vice president of financial affairs. The MBA students also got a "promotion applicant information form" to evaluate for each "applicant." These included researcher-created information such as marital status and supervisor comments. Some "applicants" were mothers.

The student evaluators viewed the mothers as less competent and were less likely to recommend them for the job. As the researchers say, this is consistent with evidence that mothers suffer disadvantages in the workplace, a problem they term "the maternal wall."[68]

In one study, the student evaluators viewed job candidates who were supposedly mothers as less competent and were less likely to recommend them for the job.

Source: Cultura Creative (RF)/Alamy Stock Photo.

How Useful Are Interviews?

Although most employers use interviews, the evidence regarding their validity is mixed.[69] The key is that the interview's usefulness depends on how you conduct the interview itself.[70] The evidence suggests the following:

- For predicting job performance, *situational question interviews* yield a higher mean (average) validity than do behavioral interviews.
- *Structured interviews*, regardless of content, are more valid and reliable than unstructured interviews for predicting job performance.[71]
- *One-on-one interviews* tend to be more valid than panel interviews.[72]

In summary, structured situational interviews (in which you ask the candidates what they would do in a particular situation) conducted one-on-one seem to be the most useful for predicting job performance.

TRENDS SHAPING HR: *Digital and Social Media*

ASYNCHRONOUS ON-DEMAND INTERVIEWS The growing popularity of mobile device–based interviews is disrupting how job interviewing is done. They enable the interviewee to "do" the interview at his or her leisure from wherever the person wants and the hiring manager to review the interview at his or her leisure.[73]

For example, Urban Outfitters needs store employees who share its core values of community, pride, creativity, and respect. But how should it find and attract such applicants, while controlling hiring costs in the competitive retail industry? It switched to "HireVue on-demand interviews" in its 200 retail stores. The HireVue system enabled applicants to watch videos about Urban Outfitters and the job, and then to respond in writing and by video to Urban's interview questions and instructions, at their leisure, "on demand." The hiring managers then reviewed the recorded interviews, usually outside of peak business hours when the stores weren't as busy.

The new system reportedly has been a boon to Urban Outfitters. It reduced screening time by 80%, lets store managers process many more applicants, and is preferred by applicants.[74]

✪ Talk About It – 6

If your professor has chosen to assign this, go to **www.pearson.com/mylab/management** to discuss the following: You have to hire dozens of waitstaff every year for a new restaurant on Miami Beach. Explain how you would use a HireVue interview, including questions and tasks for candidates.

A video interview like the ones described in the preceding Trends feature requires little special preparation for employers, but Career FAQs (www.careerfaqs.com.au) lists things that *interviewees* should keep in mind. It's often the obvious things people overlook (for more on how to take interviews, see the career appendix to chapter 9).[75]

- **Look presentable.** It might seem silly sitting at home wearing a suit, but it could make a difference.
- **Clean up the room.** Do not let the interviewer see clutter.
- **Test first.** As Career FAQs says, "Five minutes before the video interview is not a good time to realize that your Internet is down . . . "

- **Do a dry run.** Record yourself before the interview to see how you're "coming across."
- **Relax.** The golden rule with such interviews is to treat them like face-to-face meetings. Smile, look confident and enthusiastic, make eye contact, and don't shout, but do speak clearly.

How to Avoid Common Interviewing Mistakes

Most people think they're better interviewers than they really are.[76] Actually, several common interviewing mistakes often undermine an interview's usefulness. Avoiding these mistakes improves interviewer performance.[77]

Snap Judgments Interviewers tend to jump to conclusions—make snap judgments—about candidates during the first few minutes of the interview. In fact, this often occurs before the interview begins, based on test scores or résumés. One psychologist interviewed the CEOs of 80 top companies. She concluded that most managers size up the candidate before he or she even says anything, based on things like posture, handshake, and smile.[78] Even structured interviews are usually preceded by a brief discussion, and the impressions the candidate makes here may contaminate even a structured interview's results. [79]

The bottom line for *interviewees*: It's imperative to start off right. For *interviewers*: Keep an open mind until the interview is over.

Negative Emphasis Jumping to conclusions is especially troublesome given three interviewing facts: (1) Interviews are often mostly searches for negative information; (2) interviewers tend to be more influenced by unfavorable than favorable information; and (3) interviewers' impressions are more likely to change from favorable to unfavorable than from unfavorable to favorable.

Again, as an interviewee, remember that you only have one chance to make a good first impression. As an interviewer, the implication is, keep an open mind and consciously guard against unwarranted negative impressions.

Not Knowing the Job Interviewers who don't really know what the job entails and what sort of candidate is best for it usually enter the interview with incorrect stereotypes about the ideal applicant. They then erroneously match interviewees against these incorrect stereotypes. Studies therefore have long shown that more interviewer knowledge about the job translates into better interviews.[80] (What the screeners actually look for may be another matter. A researcher spoke with 120 hiring decision-makers. She found that most of them were looking for "personal chemistry" in terms of things like having backgrounds and hobbies that matched their own.)[81]

Pressure to Hire Being under pressure to hire undermines interview validity. In one study, managers were told that they were behind their recruiting quota. A second group was told they were ahead. Those behind evaluated the same recruits much more highly than did those ahead.[82]

Candidate Order (Contrast) Error Candidate order (or "contrast") error means that the order in which you see applicants affects how you rate them. In one study, researchers asked managers to evaluate a candidate who was "just average" after first evaluating several "unfavorable" candidates. The average candidate was evaluated more favorably than he might otherwise have been, because, in contrast to the unfavorable candidates, the average one looked better than he actually was.[83]

Influence of Nonverbal Behavior Interviewers rate applicants who demonstrate more eye contact, head moving, smiling, and similar nonverbal behaviors higher; such behavior can account for over 80% of the applicant's rating.[84] In one study, vocal cues (such as the interviewee's pitch, speech rates, and pauses) and visual cues (such as physical attractiveness, smile, and body orientation) correlated with evaluators' judgments of interviewee credibility.[85] Similarly, candidate self-promotion is strongly related to the interviewer's perceptions of candidate-job fit.[86] Tattoos and/or piercings result in lower hireability ratings for applicants, particularly for customer facing jobs. [87]

Attractiveness In general, individuals ascribe more favorable traits and more successful life outcomes to attractive people.[88] In one study, researchers asked subjects to evaluate candidates for promotability based on photographs. Men were perceived to be more suitable for hire and more likely to advance than were equally qualified women, and more attractive candidates, especially men, were preferred over less attractive ones.[89] These stereotypes are changing. However, women still account for only about 15% of corporate officers at *Fortune 500* companies.[90]

Research Insight In one study, the researchers manipulated how "candidates" looked, for instance by placing scarlike marks on the cheeks of some applicants but not on others. Managers who interviewed a facially stigmatized applicant "rated the applicant lower [and] recalled less information about the interview" (apparently, staring at the "scars" distracted the interviewers).[91]

Ingratiation Interviewees can boost their chances for job offers through self-promotion and ingratiation, for instance by agreeing with the recruiter's opinions and thus signaling that they share similar beliefs. *Self-promotion* means promoting one's own skills and abilities to create the impression of competence.[92] Self-promotion is the most effective tactic, but faking or lying generally backfires.[93]

Nonverbal Implications The bottom line is that otherwise inferior candidates who "act right" in interviews often get higher ratings than do more competent applicants who lack such skills. Interviewers should thus look beyond the interviewee's behavior. Focus on what the interviewee says. Furthermore (because attributes such as attractiveness, sex, or race are generally irrelevant to job performance), anticipate the potential impact of such biases, and don't let them influence the ratings you give. The Management Skills features shows how to conduct an effective interview.

BUILDING YOUR MANAGEMENT SKILLS:
How to Conduct an Effective Interview

Interview problems like these are so troublesome because managers tend to conduct interviews informally. They ask questions that may have no relevance to the job (such as "What would you say are your main strengths and weaknesses?"), and they make little attempt to standardize how they question each job candidate. The following steps present a more useful approach.

Step 1: **Design the interview.** Before walking into the interview, you should decide what questions to ask, and how you will ask them. Preferably, you should standardize (or "structure") the interview, to ensure consistency from applicant to applicant. The chapter Appendix presents a precise way to do this—to create a structured interview. However,

Continued

there are also less technical ways to increase the interview's standardization.[94] Specifically:

a. First make sure you understand the job and its human requirements.

b. Then compose questions *based on actual job duties from the job description*.[95] Use mostly job knowledge, situational, or behavioral questions. Questions that ask for opinions and attitudes, goals and aspirations, and self-descriptions and self-evaluations encourage self-promotion and let candidates avoid revealing weaknesses. Good examples include (1) *situational* questions like "Suppose you were giving a sales presentation and a difficult technical question arose that you could not answer. What would you do?" (2) *past behavior* questions like "Can you provide an example of a specific instance where you developed a sales presentation that was highly effective?" (3) *background* questions like "What work experiences, training, or other qualifications do you have for working in a teamwork environment?" and (4) *job knowledge* questions like "What factors should you consider when developing a TV advertising campaign?"[96]

c. Use the same questions with all candidates. This boosts reliability and can reduce bias by giving all candidates the same opportunity.

d. *If possible*, use rating scales. For each question, try to have sample ideal, good, fair, and poor answers and a quantitative score for each. Then rate each candidate's answers against this scale.

e. Have several people interview the candidate.

f. *If possible*, create a structured interview form, as in Figure 6A.1 in the Appendix to this chapter.

Step 2: **Review the candidate's background.** Before the interview, review the candidate's application and résumé, and note any vague areas. Review the job specification. Start the interview with a clear picture of an ideal candidate's traits.

Step 3: **Establish rapport.** Start the interview by putting the person at ease. As a rule, all applicants—even drop-ins—should receive friendly, courteous treatment.

Step 4: **Ask questions.** Try to follow your structured interview form or questions you wrote out ahead of time. You'll find many lists of employment interview questions online, for instance at www.glassdoor.com/blog/common-interview-questions/. In asking questions, follow these do's and don'ts:

- **Don't** ask questions that can be answered yes or no.
- **Don't** telegraph the desired answer, for instance, by nodding or smiling when the right answer is given.
- **Don't** interrogate the applicant as if the person were a criminal.
- **Don't** monopolize the interview by rambling, nor let the applicant dominate the interview.
- **Do** ask open-ended questions.
- **Do** listen to the candidate to encourage him or her to express thoughts fully.
- **Do** draw out the applicant's opinions and feelings by repeating the person's last comment as a question (e.g., "You didn't like your last job?").
- **Do** ask for examples.[97] For instance, if the candidate lists strengths or weaknesses, follow up with, "What are specific examples that demonstrate each of your strengths?"

Continued

Step 5: **Close the interview.** Leave time to answer any questions the candidate may have and, if appropriate, to advocate your firm to the candidate. Leave all interviews on a courteous note. Tell the applicant whether there is an interest and, if so, what the next step is. Make rejections diplomatically (for instance, "Thank you but there are other candidates whose experience is closer to our requirements.").

Step 6: **Review the interview.** After the candidate leaves, review your interview notes and fill in the structured interview guide (if any, and if you didn't do so during the interview). Then make your decision.[98]

John, the restaurant manager in this chapter's opening scenario, decides to write several job knowledge, situational, and behavioral questions to ask prospective waitstaff. One behavioral question he came up with was, "Tell me about a time when you had to deal with a particularly obnoxious person; what did you do and how did it work out?" Can you think of other good questions John could ask?

KNOW YOUR EMPLOYMENT LAW
Interviewing Candidates

Recall from Chapter 2 that it's generally not illegal (although it is unwise) to ask, say, a female candidate about marital status or an older-looking applicant "How old are you?" You can usually ask, as long as you show that the employer does not discriminate or that it can defend the question as a BFOQ or business necessity. However, many local laws do bar asking them, and the EEOC disapproves of such practices.

The best approach is to avoid having job candidates file charges in the first place. Avoid red-flag questions. Show applicants that the interview process is fair, that the interviewer treats the interviewee with respect, and that the interviewer is willing to explain the interview process and the rationale for the questions.[99] Emphasize objective/job-related questions, standardize the interview process (so it's the same for all applicants), and use multiple interviewers where possible. ■

Using Competencies Models and Profiles in Employee Interviews

As we explained in Chapter 4, many companies use competencies models (a job's set of desirable competencies, traits, knowledge, and experience) for recruiting, selecting, training, appraising, and compensating the employee. Thus, in its own workforce planning, IBM identified about 500 possible "roles" employees might fill, such as analyst. IBM then created profiles or required skill sets for each role. It rates its employees on these skills, from 0 to 3, and those ratings may then guide promotions, transfers, or training, for instance.

For an example of how to use a job's profile to formulate selection interview questions, see Table 6.1. It shows illustrative competencies, knowledge, traits, and experience for a chemical engineer and related interview questions. The talent management team could then also use the same profile (list of competencies, knowledge, traits, and experience) for guidance in how to recruit, train, appraise, and pay candidates for this position.

Table 6.1 Asking Profile-Oriented Interview Questions

Profile Component	Example	Sample Interview Question
Competency	Able to use computer drafting software	Tell me about a time you used CAD Pro computerized design software.
Knowledge	How extreme heat affects hydrochloric acid (HCl)	Suppose you have an application where HCl is heated to 400 degrees Fahrenheit at 2 atmospheres of pressure; what happens to the HCl?
Trait	Willing to travel abroad at least four months per year visiting facilities	Suppose you had a big affair that you had to attend next week and our company informed you that you had to leave for a job abroad immediately, and stay three weeks. How would you handle that?
Experience	Designed pollution filter for acid-cleaning facility	Tell me about a time when you designed a pollution filter device for an acid-cleaning facility. How did it work? What particular problems did you encounter? How did you address them?

TRENDS SHAPING HR: *Science in Talent Management*

Google takes a scientific, evidence-based approach to its selection (and other HR) practices. The main components in its selection process include work samples, testing, and interviewing.

Almost all of Google's technical hires take work sample tests, such as actually writing algorithms. It combines work samples with tests of cognitive ability (similar to IQ tests) and of conscientiousness. Early in its evolution Google required candidates to take a dozen or more interviews. However Google's own analysis showed that after the first few interviews the amount of useful information it got was minimal. It therefore now generally makes hiring decisions after the fourth interview.

Google interviews emphasize situational and behavioral questions. For specific questions, Google provides its interviewers with access to its "QDroid" system; this e-mails each interviewer specific questions to ask the candidate for the specific job. Google interviewers were once known for trick questions, but the emphasis now is on using validated questions (from the QDroid system). The questions aim to assess the candidate's cognitive ability, leadership (particularly willingness to lead projects), "Googleyness" (values such as fun-loving and conscientious), and role-related knowledge (such as in computer science). Who actually does the interviewing? Here Google believes in the "wisdom of crowds": the interviewing "crowd" includes not just the prospective boss but also prospective subordinates, and representatives of other unrelated departments. Google then averages all the interviewers' ratings on a candidate to get a score. Interviewers get printouts showing how effective they've been as interviewers in terms of candidates hired or not hired. Finally, the hiring committee reviews the file, as does a Google senior manager and the CEO, before an offer is made.[100] Google's interview process is thus analytical, evidence-based, and scientific. ■

LEARNING OBJECTIVE 4
Explain how to do background checks on job candidates.

Using Other Selection Techniques

Testing and interviewing are usually just part of an employer's selection process. Other tools may include background investigations and reference checks, preemployment information services, honesty testing, graphology, and substance abuse screening.

Background Investigations and Reference Checks

One major company was about to announce a new CEO until they discovered he had a wife and two children in one state and a wife and two children in another state.[101] About 80% of HR managers report checking applicants' backgrounds and criminal convictions, and 35% do credit checks.[102] Some employers also do ongoing due diligence background checks for current employees.[103]

There are two key reasons for checking backgrounds. One is to verify the accuracy of facts the applicant provided; the other is to uncover damaging background information such as criminal records. (Note that some enterprising entrepreneurs have created fake job reference services. For a fee, they create fake work histories and references for job seekers.)[104]

What to Verify The most commonly verified background areas are legal eligibility for employment (to comply with immigration laws), dates of prior employment, military service (including discharge status), education, and identification (including date of birth and address). Other items should include county criminal records (current residence, last residence), motor vehicle record, credit, licensing verification, Social Security number, and reference checks.[105] Several states, including Massachusetts and Hawaii, prohibit private employers from asking about criminal records on initial written applications.[106]

The position determines how deeply you search. For example, a credit and education check is more important for hiring an accountant than a groundskeeper. In any case, also periodically check credit ratings of employees who have easy access to company assets, and driving records of those who use company cars.

Collecting Background Information[107] Most employers try to verify directly an applicant's current position, salary, and employment dates with his or her current

Employers sometimes discover after hiring someone that his or her background or training was not what he or she said they were.

Source: Nick White/Getty Images.

employer by phone (assuming that the candidate has cleared doing so). Others call the applicant's current and previous supervisors to try to discover more about the person's motivation, technical competence, and ability to work with others.

Many employers use commercial credit rating companies or employment screening services. These provide information about an applicant's credit standing, indebtedness, reputation, character, lifestyle, and the truthfulness of the person's application data. There are also thousands of online databases and sources for obtaining background information, including sex offender registries; workers' compensation histories; nurse's aide registries; and sources for criminal, employment, and educational histories.[108]

TRENDS SHAPING HR: *Digital and Social Media*

SOCIAL MEDIA BACKGROUND CHECKING Digital tools are changing the background-checking process. Employers are Googling applicants or checking Facebook and LinkedIn, and what they're finding isn't always pretty. One candidate described his interests on Facebook as smoking pot and shooting people. The student may have been kidding, but he didn't get the job.[109] An article called "Funny, They Don't Look Like My References" notes that the new LinkedIn premium service Reference Search lets employers identify people in their own networks who worked for the same company when a job candidate did, and thus use them to get references on the candidate.[110] According to LinkedIn, you just select Reference Search, then enter a company name, candidate's name, and the timeframe, and click search. Employers are integrating such tools with software solutions such as Oracle/Taleo Verify to facilitate obtaining such information and then integrating it into the candidate's dashboard-accessible profile.

The problem is that while Googling is probably safe enough, checking social networking sites raises legal issues.[111] For example, it's probably best to get the candidate's prior approval for social networking searches.[112] And do not use a pretext or fabricate an identity.[113] A Maryland law restricts employer demands for applicant usernames and passwords.[114] And while applicants usually don't list race, age, disability, or ethnic origin on their résumés, their Facebook pages may reveal such information, setting the stage for possible EEOC claims. Or, an overeager supervisor might conduct his or her own Facebook page "background check."[115]

The solution isn't necessarily to prohibit the legitimate use of social media–based applicant and employee information (unless it's illegal, as in Maryland). Instead, the employer should formulate and follow intelligent social media staffing policies and procedures. For example, inform employees and prospective employees ahead of time regarding what information the employer plans to review. Assign one or two specially trained human resource professionals to search social media sites. Prohibit unauthorized employees (such as the prospective supervisor) from accessing such information.[116] Employers should also avoid subterfuge, such as using fictitious login names. Applicants should consider the likelihood that employers may access their sites.

Reference Check Effectiveness Handled correctly, background checks are an inexpensive and straightforward way to verify facts (such as current and previous job titles). Unfortunately, getting candid replies can be tricky. It's not easy for the reference to prove that a bad reference was warranted. The rejected applicant thus has many legal remedies, including suing the reference for defamation. This can understandably inhibit former employers.[117] In one case, a man was awarded $56,000 after being turned down for a job because, among other things, a former employer called him a "character." Furthermore, many supervisors don't want to diminish a former employee's chances for a job. Others give incompetent employees good reviews to get rid of them.

KNOW YOUR EMPLOYMENT LAW
Giving References

Many managers are hesitant to respond candidly to requests for references, and for good reason. Various laws give certain individuals certain rights to knowing the nature and substance of information, for instance in their credit files and files with government agencies.

Furthermore, common law applies to any information the manager supplies. Communication is *defamatory* if it is false and tends to harm the reputation of another by lowering the person in the estimation of the community or by deterring other persons from dealing with him or her. Former employees may even hire reference-checking firms and take legal action for defamatory references.[118]

Truth isn't always a defense. In some states, employees can sue employers for disclosing to a large number of people true but embarrassing private facts about the employee. One case involved a supervisor shouting that the employee's wife had been having sexual relations with certain people. The jury found the employer liable for invasion of the couple's privacy and for intentional infliction of emotional distress.[119]

The bottom line is that most employers and managers restrict who can give references and what they can say. As a rule, only authorized managers should provide information; many centralize the task of responding to reference requests. Other suggestions include: "Don't volunteer information," "Avoid vague statements," and "Do not answer trap questions such as, 'Would you rehire this person?'" In practice, many firms have a policy of not providing any information about former employees except for their dates of employment, last salary, and position titles.[120] ■

BUILDING YOUR MANAGEMENT SKILLS:
How to Obtain More Useful Reference Information

So what is the prospective supervisor or employer to do? Is there any way to obtain better information?

Yes. First, have the candidate sign a release (usually, on the application) authorizing the background check.[121]

Second, always obtain two forms of identification.

Third, ensure that the applicant completed the application fully. Always compare the application to the résumé (people tend to be more creative on their résumés than on their application forms, where they must certify the information).[122] Do not accept an application on which the applicant simply says "see résumé."

Fourth, use a structured reference-checking form as in Figure 6.5. This helps ensure that you don't overlook important questions.

Fifth, persistence and sensitivity to potential red flags can improve results. For example, if the former employer hesitates or seems to qualify his or her answer when you ask, "Would you rehire?" don't just go on to the next question. Instead, try to unearth what the applicant did to make the former employer pause. Because phone references apparently produce more candid assessments, it's probably best to rely more on them. Ask open-ended questions, such as, "How much structure does the applicant need in his/her work?" in order to get the references to talk more about the candidate.[123]

Sixth, use the references offered by the applicant as merely a source for other people who may know of the applicant's performance. Thus, you might ask each reference, "Could you give me the name of another person who might be familiar with the applicant's performance?" In that way, you begin getting

Continued

(Verify that the applicant has provided permission before conducting reference checks.)

Candidate
Name _____

Reference
Name _____

Company
Name _____

Dates of Employment
From: _____ To: _____

Position(s)
Held _____

Salary
History _____

Reason for
Leaving _____

Explain the reason for your call and verify the above information with the supervisor (including the reason for leaving)
_____
_____
_____

1. Please describe the type of work for which the candidate was responsible.
_____
_____
_____

2. How would you describe the applicant's relationships with coworkers, subordinates (if applicable), and with superiors?
_____
_____
_____

3. Did the candidate have a positive or negative work attitude? Please elaborate.
_____
_____
_____

4. How would you describe the quantity and quality of output generated by the former employee?
_____
_____
_____

5. What were his/her strengths on the job?
_____
_____
_____

6. What were his/her weaknesses on the job?
_____
_____
_____

7. What is your overall assessment of the candidate?
_____
_____
_____

8. Would you recommend him/her for this position? Why or why not?
_____
_____
_____

9. Would this individual be eligible for rehire? Why or why not?
_____
_____
_____

Other comments?
_____
_____
_____

Figure 6.5

Reference Checking Form

Source: Reprinted with permission from the Society for Human Resource Management. All rights reserved.

Continued

information from references that may be more objective. Try to contact at least two previous superiors, two peers, and two subordinates.

Finally, automated online reference checking can also improve results. With a system such as Pre-hire 360 (www.skillsurvey.com) the hiring employer inputs the applicant's name and e-mail address. Then the person's preselected references rate the applicant's skills anonymously, using a multi-question survey. The system then compiles these references into a report for the employer.[124]

Using Preemployment Information Services Numerous services offer prehire screening. Large background checking providers include ADP, Hireright, LEXIS-NEXIS Screening Solutions, and Employment Background Investigations.[125] They use databases to access workers' compensation and credit histories and conviction and driving records. For example, retailers use First Advantage Corporation to see if their job candidates have been involved in suspected retail thefts.[126] However, some criminal background information is flawed. Errors include mismatching the subject of the report with someone having the same or similar name.[127]

There are therefore caveats. First, make sure the vendor doesn't violate EEO laws in what it does or asks. Second, ask and ensure that the vendor gets a signed release authorizing the background check, complies with the Fair Credit Reporting Act, and uses only legal data sources. Third, make sure the vendor is providing accurate and complete information on the candidate.[128]

Honesty Testing

Employers can use various tools to assess candidates' and employees' honesty.

Polygraph Tests The *polygraph* (or "*lie detector*") machine measures physiological changes such as increased perspiration. The assumption is that such changes reflect changes in the emotional stress that accompanies lying.

Complaints about offensiveness as well as doubts about the polygraph's accuracy culminated in the Employee Polygraph Protection Act of 1988. With few exceptions, the law prohibits most employers from conducting polygraph examinations of all applicants and most employees.

Paper-and-Pencil Honesty Tests The virtual elimination of the polygraph triggered a burgeoning market for written psychological tests designed to predict job applicants' proneness to dishonesty. Most of these measure attitudes regarding things such as tolerance of others who steal. (See, for example, http://testyourself.psychtests .com/testid/2100.)

Psychologists have some concerns. For example, the tests may be prone to producing a high percentage of false positives and are susceptible to coaching.[129] However, studies tend to support these tests' validity. One study was made of 111 employees hired by a major retail convenience store chain to work at convenience store or gas station outlet counters.[130] The researchers found that scores on an honesty test successfully predicted theft, as measured by termination for theft. The following Skills feature outlines how to spot dishonesty, and then the Profit Center feature illustrates how honesty screening can cut costs.[131]

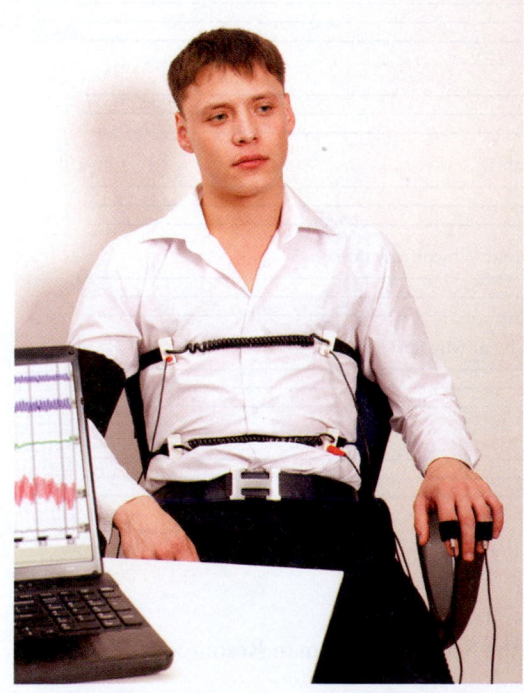

The polygraph (or "lie detector") machine is a device that measures physiological changes such as increased perspiration.

Source: Burmakin Andrey/123RF.

BUILDING YOUR MANAGEMENT SKILLS:
How to Spot Dishonesty

In practice, detecting dishonest candidates involves not just testing but a comprehensive screening procedure. Experts suggest these steps:

- Ask blunt questions.[132] For example, there is probably nothing wrong with asking, "Have you ever stolen anything from an employer?" and "Is any information on your application falsified?"
- Listen carefully, rather than talk. Liars will try to answer direct questions somewhat evasively. For example, ask them if they've ever used drugs and they might say "I don't take drugs."[133]
- Watch for telltale body signals. For example, someone who is not telling the truth may move his or her body slightly away from you.[134] Establish a baseline by seeing how his or her body is positioned when the person is undoubtedly telling the truth. Know that it is *not* true that adult liars won't look you in the eye when they're lying; polished liars may actually do so excessively.[135]
- Include a clause in your application form that gives you the right to background checks, including credit checks and motor vehicle reports, and then check all references.
- Consider using an honesty test.
- Devise a drug-testing program, and give each applicant a copy of the policy.
- Conduct searches and establish a search-and-seizure policy. The policy should state that all lockers, desks, and similar property remain the property of the company and may be inspected. Give each applicant a copy of the policy and require a signed copy.
- Make clear to employees that any failure to follow protocols or falsification of records will result in disciplinary action.[136]
- Use caution. Being rejected for dishonesty carries more stigma than being rejected for, say, poor mechanical comprehension. Furthermore, some states, such as Massachusetts and Rhode Island, limit honesty tests.

Graphology

The use of graphology (handwriting analysis) assumes that the writer's basic personality traits will be expressed in his or her handwriting. Handwriting analysis thus has some resemblance to projective personality tests.

Although some writers estimate that more than 1,000 U.S. companies use handwriting analysis to assess applicants, the validity of handwriting analysis is questionable. One reviewer says, "There is essentially no evidence of a direct link between handwriting analysis and various measures of job performance."[137] Why so many employers use it is thus a matter of debate. Perhaps it's because it seems, to many people, to have face validity.[138]

■ HR as a Profit Center

Using Integrity Tests

At Hospital Management Corporation, an integrity test is the first step in the hiring process, and those who fail go no further. It instituted the test after determining that such tests did weed out applicants with undesirable behaviors. For example, after several months using the test, workers' compensation claims dropped among new hires.[139]

✪ Talk About It – 7

If your professor has chosen to assign this, go to **www.pearson.com/mylab/ management** to discuss the following: Check online, and compile a list of four more examples of how employers report saving money by using integrity tests.

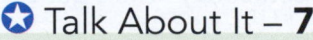

Medical Exams

Medical exams are often the next step in the selection process. Such exams can confirm that the applicant qualifies for the physical requirements of the position and can unearth any medical limitations to take into account in placing the applicant. It can also detect communicable diseases. Under the ADA, a person with a disability can't be rejected for the job if he or she is otherwise qualified and if the person could perform the essential job functions with reasonable accommodation. According to the ADA, a medical exam is permitted during the period *between the job offer and the commencement of work*, if such exams are standard for all applicants for that job.[140]

Drug Screening

Employers generally conduct drug tests. Employers may use: urine testing to test for any illicit drugs; breath alcohol tests to determine amount of alcohol in the blood; blood tests to measure alcohol or drug in the blood at the time of the test; hair analyses to reveal drug history; saliva tests for substances such as marijuana and cocaine; and skin patches to determine drug use.[141]

The most common practice is to test new applicants just before formally hiring them. Many firms also test current employees when there is reason to believe an employee has been using drugs, such as after a work accident. Some firms administer drug tests on a random basis, while others do so when transferring an employee.[142] Most employers that conduct such tests use urine sampling. Numerous vendors provide workplace drug-testing services.[143] Evidence suggests that it's become more difficult recently to find applicants who can pass a drug test.[144]

Problems Drug testing is problematical.[145] Breathalyzers (like those police give roadside to inebriated drivers) do correlate closely with impairment levels. However, urine and blood tests for other drugs only show whether drug residues are present, not impairment, habituation, or addiction.[146] There is also "a swarm of products that promise to help employees (both male and female) beat [urine analysis] drug tests."[147] Hair follicle testing and newer oral fluid samples are less subject to tampering.

Drug testing therefore raises several issues. Without strong evidence linking blood or urine drug levels to impairment, some argue that drug testing violates people's privacy and due process rights and that the procedures themselves are degrading and intrusive. Others argue that workplace drug testing might identify one's use of drugs during leisure hours, but have little or no relevance to the job.[148] It's also not clear that drug testing improves safety or performance. At least one study concluded that other than alcohol, there is no clear evidence that drugs diminish safety or job performance.[149]

Realistic Job Previews

Sometimes, a dose of realism makes the best screening tool. For example, Walmart found that associates who quit within the first 90 days often did so because they preferred to work in another geographic area. The firm then began explicitly explaining and asking about work schedules and work preferences.[150]

Tapping Friends and Acquaintances

Tap the opinions of people you trust who have direct personal knowledge of the candidate. As a former airline CEO said, "[T]he best possible interview is miniscule in value compared to somebody who's got even a couple of months of work experience with somebody."[151]

Making the Selection Decision

Once you've done all your testing and checking, the question arises, "How do you combine all this information and make a selection decision?" Of course, if you're only using one predictor (such as one test score), then the decision is straightforward. For example, an applicant for an engineering position should score at least 30 answers correct on the Wonderlic test to be appointable as an engineer. If your applicant scores lower, you probably wouldn't hire him or her, and if it's higher, you probably would.

But, in reality, things are not so simple. For one thing, you'll probably not make your decision based on a single predictor (in this case, one test score). You'll also want to factor in the person's references, his or her interview and application information (such as school attended), and perhaps the results of other tests. Furthermore, you'll probably have more than one candidate.[152] Will you simply choose the one with the highest Wonderlic score? Probably not. So again, you'll need some way to weigh all the sources of information you have about each candidate.

How do you weigh all the input in reaching a selection decision? You have three basic choices. You could use, first, a clinical (or intuitive or judgmental) approach. Here you intuitively but consciously weigh all the evidence you have about the candidate and make your decision. Second, you could take a statistical or "mechanical" approach. In its purest sense, the mechanical approach involves quantifying all the information you collect about the candidate (including, for example, subjective information from references). You then combine all this quantified information, perhaps then applying a formula that predicts the candidate's likely job success. And third, of course, you could combine the mechanical results you obtained from your formula with judgment. Although it's ideal to use a mechanical/statistical approach, the judgmental approach is usually better than nothing.[153]

Complying with Immigration Law

Under the Immigration Reform and Control Act of 1986, prospective employees must prove that they are eligible to work in the United States. Someone does not have to be a U.S. citizen to be employed under this act. However, employers should ask a candidate who is about to be hired whether he or she is a U.S. citizen or an alien lawfully authorized to work in the United States.

How to Comply There are two ways prospective employees can show their eligibility for employment. One is to show a document such as a U.S. passport or alien registration card containing a photograph that proves *both* identity and employment eligibility. However, many prospective employees do not have either of these documents. Therefore, the other way to verify employment eligibility is to see one document that proves the person's identity, along with a separate document showing the person's employment eligibility, such as a work permit. The applicant fills in the government's I-9 Employment Eligibility Verification form. However, employers run the risk of accepting fraudulent documents. Preemployment screening should therefore include employment verification, criminal record checks, drug screens, and reference checks. You can verify Social Security cards by calling the Social Security Administration.

Many employers now use automated I-9 verification systems with drop-down menus to electronically compile and submit applicants' I-9 data.[154] More employers are also using the federal government's voluntary Online employment verification program, E-Verify, to confirm U.S. work authorization status.[155] E-Verify is mandatory for employers with certain federal contracts. There is no charge to use E-Verify.[156]

The requirement to verify eligibility does not provide any basis to reject an applicant just because he or she is a foreigner, not a U.S. citizen, or an alien residing in the United States. But, the applicant must be able to prove his or her identity and employment eligibility.[157] Employers can avoid accusations of discrimination by verifying all applicants' documents, not just those they think are suspicious.[158]

Improving Performance Through HRIS

Comprehensive Applicant Tracking and Screening Systems The applicant tracking systems we introduced in Chapter 5 do more than track applicants. Most employers also use their applicant tracking systems (ATSs) to prescreen-out applicants who do not meet minimum, nonnegotiable job requirements, like holding a driver's license. Most employers also use them to test and screen applicants online. This includes online skills tests (in arithmetic, for instance), cognitive tests (such as for mechanical comprehension), and even psychological tests.[159]

Developing and Extending the Job Offer

After selecting the candidate to whom an offer is to be made, the employer develops the actual job offer. It will base the offer's financial and other terms on, for instance, the candidate's attractiveness as a prospective employee, the level of the position, and pay rates for similar positions. Next, the employer extends an actual job offer to the candidate verbally. Here the employer's point person (who might be the person to whom the new employee will report, or the human resource director, for instance) discusses the offer's main parameters, for instance in terms of pay rates, benefits, and actual job duties. There may be some negotiations. Then, once agreement is reached, the employer will extend a written job offer.

There are several issues to consider here. Perhaps most important, understand the difference between a *job offer letter* and a *contract*. In a job offer letter, the employer lists the offer's basic information. This typically starts with a welcome sentence. It then includes job-specific information (such as details on salary and pay), benefits information, paid leave information, and terms of employment (including, for instance, successful completion of physical exams).[160] Crucially, there should be a strong statement specifying that the employment relationship is "at will." There is then a closing statement. This again welcomes the employee, mentions who the employer's point person should be if any questions arise, and instructs the candidate to sign the letter if it is acceptable.[161] It is prudent to have an attorney review the offer before extending it.

On the other hand, in hiring for many positions (such as an executive) a *contract* might be in order. In contrast to a letter of offer (which should always be "at will"), it is not unusual for an employment contract to specify a duration (such as three years). Given this, the contract will also describe grounds for termination or resignation and severance provisions. The contract will almost always also include terms regarding confidentiality, nondisclosure requirements, and covenants not to compete (although some job offer *letters* for positions such as engineer may include such provisions as well).[162] In the past, continued employment was often a sufficient quid pro quo for making employees sign noncompete clauses. Today additional remuneration, even $100, is becoming the norm.[163]

Depending on the position, the employment contract (and, occasionally, the offer letter) may include a *relocation provision*. This lays out what the employer is willing to pay the new employee to relocate, for instance in terms of moving expenses. State law generally governs enforcement of individual employment contracts. For some letters of offer and employment contract samples, see, for example, www.jobsearchtech.about.com/, type "job offer letter" in the search box, and click "search."[164]

LEARNING OBJECTIVE 5
Discuss how to use employee selection methods to raise the level of a company's employee engagement.

Employee Engagement Guide for Managers

Engagement refers to being psychologically involved in, connected to, and committed to getting one's job done; how do managers determine if a job candidate has the right traits to become an engaged employee?

For one thing, several measurable traits do distinguish such candidates. For example, consultants Development Dimensions International found that traits including agreeableness, emotional stability, openness to experience, achievement orientation, and self-efficacy ("I can do this.") characterized the more highly engaged employees.[165]

Building Engagement: A Total Selection Program

How do you find such people? A simple first step is probably just to ask the right questions. Before the interview, formulate several behavioral and/or situational questions, such as (for the traits agreeableness and work ethic), "Tell me about a time when you had personal plans, such as to go away for a weekend with friends, and your boss asked you at the last minute to work instead. How exactly did you handle that?"

But in practice, "engagement potential" is just one of several attributes the prospective employer will look for in job candidates. For example, it may want "team players" too. The employer should therefore create a *total selection program* aimed at selecting candidates whose totality of attributes best fit the employer's total requirements.

The program Toyota Motors uses to select employees for auto assembly team jobs illustrates this. Toyota looks for several things in candidates. It wants employees with good interpersonal skills, due to the assembler job's emphasis on teamwork. Toyota's emphasis on *kaizen*—on having the workers improve job processes through worker commitment to top quality—helps explain Toyota's emphasis on reasoning and problem-solving skills and on hiring an intelligent, educated, and engaged workforce.[166] All Toyota workers have at least a high school degree or equivalent, and many plant employees including some assemblers are college educated. Quality is one of Toyota's core values, and so Toyota seeks a history of quality commitment in those it hires. This is one reason it holds group interviews that focus on accomplishments. By asking candidates about what they are proudest of, Toyota gets a better insight into the person's values regarding quality and doing things right. Toyota is also looking for employees who have an eagerness to learn and are willing to try it not just their way, but Toyota's way or the team's way. Toyota's production system relies on consensus decision making, job rotation, and flexible career paths, and these also require open minded, flexible team players, not dogmatists.

The Toyota Way

Toyota's hiring process for assemblers aims to find such candidates. It takes about 20 hours and six phases over several days:[167]

- **Step 1:** an in-depth online application (20–30 minutes)
- **Step 2:** a 2- to 5-hour computer-based assessment
- **Step 3:** a 6- to 8-hour work simulation assessment
- **Step 4:** a face-to-face interview
- **Step 5:** a background check, drug screen, and medical check
- **Step 6:** job offer

For example, in step 1, applicants fill out an application form summarizing their experience and skills and often view a video describing Toyota's work environment and selection system. This gives applicants a realistic preview of work at Toyota and of the hiring process's extensiveness. Many applicants simply drop out at this stage.

Step 2 aims to assess the applicant's technical knowledge and potential. Here applicants take various tests that help identify problem-solving skills and learning potential, as well as occupational preferences. Skilled trade applicants (experienced mechanics, for example) also take tool and die or general maintenance tests.

In step 3, applicants engage in simulated realistic production activities in Toyota's assessment center. This is a separate location where applicants engage in exercises under the observation of Toyota screening experts. The production test assesses how well each candidate does on an actual assembler task. Also here, group discussion exercises help show how individual applicants interact with others in their group and solve problems. For example, in one of the simulations, candidates play the roles of the management and the workers of a firm that makes electrical circuits. During one series of planning and manufacturing scenarios, the team must decide which circuit should be manufactured and how to effectively assign people, materials, and money to produce them. In another typical exercise, participants playing company employees constitute a team responsible for choosing new features for next year's car. Team members first individually rank 12 features based on market appeal and then suggest one feature not included on the list. They must then come to a consensus on the best rank ordering. As one candidate who went through this process said, "There are three workstations in which you will be required to spend 2 hours at each one. You then have to get in a group and problem-solve a special project with them for another hour or so. I left my house at 5 A.M. and did not return until 6:30 P.M.; it was a very long day."[168]

The time and effort applicants invest in their tryouts at Toyota helps guarantee engagement. Toyota seeks engaged, flexible, quality-oriented team players, and those who lack these traits and values tend not to make it through the rigorous screening process. The rigorousness of the process tends to screen out those who aren't as likely to be highly engaged employees.

In summary, high-engagement firms like Toyota use total hiring programs to select employees. While firms do this in various ways, five common themes are obvious from the process at Toyota. First, it knows what it wants. *Value-based hiring* means it clarifies its own values before it embarks on an employee selection program. Whether it is excellence, kaizen/continuous improvement, integrity, or some other indicator, value-based hiring begins with clarifying what your firm's values are and what you're looking for in employees.

Second, high-engagement firms like Toyota commit the time and effort for an *exhaustive screening process.* Eight to ten hours of interviewing even for entry-level employees is not unusual, and firms like Toyota will spend 20 hours or more with someone before deciding to hire. Many are rejected. The ones who make it through tend to be more engaged.

Third, the screening process does not just identify knowledge and technical skills. In addition, the candidate's *values and skills are matched* with the needs of the firm. Teamwork, kaizen, and flexibility are essential values at Toyota. Therefore problem-solving skills, interpersonal skills, and engagement with the firm's commitment to quality are crucial human requirements.

Fourth, hiring at firms like Toyota generally includes *realistic job previews*. These firms are certainly interested in "selling" good candidates. But it's more important to ensure that job candidates know what working for the firm will be like, and even more important that they understand what sorts of values the firm cherishes.

Finally, *self-selection* is an important screening practice at firms like these. In some firms this just means realistic previews. At others, practices such as long probationary periods in entry-level jobs help screen out those who don't fit. At Toyota the screening process itself demands a sacrifice in terms of time and effort—and helps ensure that only engaged employees get through.

Review

MyLab Management

If your instructor is using MyLab Management, go to **www.pearson.com/mylab/management** to complete the problems marked with this icon ⭐.

Summary

1. In this chapter we discuss several techniques for screening and selecting job candidates: The first is testing. Test validity answers the question: "What does this test measure?" Criterion validity means demonstrating that those who do well on the test do well on the job. Content validity is demonstrated by showing that the test constitutes a fair sample of the content of the job. As used by psychologists, the term *reliability* always means "consistency." One way to measure reliability is to administer the same (or equivalent) tests to the same people at two different points in time. Under equal opportunity legislation, an employer may have to prove that his or her tests are predictive of success or failure on the job.

2. There are many types of personnel tests in use, including intelligence tests, tests of physical skills, tests of achievement, aptitude tests, interest inventories, and personality tests. Management assessment centers are screening devices that expose applicants to a series of real-life exercises. Performance is observed and assessed by experts, who then check their assessments by observing the participants when they are back at their jobs. Examples of such real-life exercises include a simulated business game, an in-basket exercise, and group discussions.

3. Several problems can undermine the usefulness of an interview: making premature decisions, letting unfavorable information predominate, not knowing the requirements of the job, being under pressure to hire, not allowing for the candidate order effect, and nonverbal behavior. The five steps in the interview include plan, establish rapport, question the candidate, close the interview, and review the data.

4. Other screening tools include reference checks, background checks, physical exams, and realistic previews. After selecting the candidate to whom an offer is to be made, the employer develops the actual job offer. It will base this offer on, for instance, the candidate's attractiveness as a prospective employee and pay rates for similar positions. Next, the employer extends an actual job offer to the candidate verbally.

5. Candidates with higher potential to be engaged tend to be agreeable, emotionally stable, open to new experiences, achievement oriented, confident about their abilities, more "in control" of the events affecting them, high on self-esteem and self-advocacy, with a strong work ethic and a can-do attitude. The line or supervisory manager can ask behavioral and/or situational questions aimed at identifying such traits. The employer can institute comprehensive total selection programs to identify candidates who fit the job's various requirements. High-engagement firms like Toyota use total hiring programs to select employees. Activities include clarifying the firm's values, committing the time and effort, matching the applicant's values with the firm's, having realistic previews, and encouraging self-selection.

Key Terms

negligent hiring 157
reliability 157
test validity 158
criterion validity 158
content validity 158
construct validity 159
validity generalization 159

utility analysis 160
interest inventories 163
data analytics   158
management assessment center 166
miniature job training and evaluation 167
interview 169
structured situational interview 192

⭐ Try It

How would you do applying the concepts and skills you learned in this chapter? If your professor has chosen to assign this, go to **www.pearson.com/mylab/management** and complete the Individual Behavior simulation to find out.

Discussion Questions

6-1. Explain what is meant by *reliability* and *validity*. What is the difference between them? In what respects are they similar?

⭐ 6-2. Discuss at least four basic types of personnel tests.

6-3. Explain the shortcomings of background investigations, reference checks, and preemployment information services, and how to overcome them.

⭐ 6-4. For what sorts of jobs do you think computerized interviews are most appropriate? Why?

6-5. Briefly discuss and give examples of several common interviewing mistakes. What recommendations would you give for avoiding these interviewing mistakes?

6-6. Compare and contrast a job offer letter and a contract, and discuss the basic components of each.

6-7. Write a short (one-page double-spaced) essay on the topic, "How Equal Employment Law Affects Employee Selection." Please include at least five specific examples.

6-8. You own a small business. How would you go about finding a selection test for a job you want to fill, and what practical and legal issues would you want to keep in mind before choosing a test to use?

Individual and Group Activities

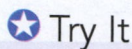

6-9. Working individually or in groups, develop a list of specific selection techniques that you would suggest your dean use to hire the next HR professor at your school. Explain why you chose each selection technique.

6-10. Working individually or in groups, contact the publisher of a standardized test such as the Scholastic Assessment Test, and obtain from it written information regarding the test's validity and reliability. Present a short report in class discussing what the test is supposed to measure and the degree to which you think the test does what it is supposed to do, based on the reported validity and reliability scores.

6-11. Give a short presentation titled, "How to Be Effective as an Interviewer."

6-12. Write a short essay discussing some of the ethical and legal considerations in testing.

6-13. Give some examples of how interest inventories could be used to improve employee selection. In doing so, suggest several examples of occupational interests that you believe might predict success in various occupations, including college professor, accountant, and computer programmer.

6-14. For this activity, you will need the documents titled (1) "HRCI PHR® and SPHR® Certification Body of Knowledge," and (2) "About the Society for Human Resource Management (SHRM) Body of Competency & Knowledge® Model and Certification Exams." Your instructor can obtain these two documents from the Pearson Instructor Resource Center and pass them on to you. These two documents list the knowledge someone studying for the HRCI or SHRM certification exam needs to have in each area of human resource management (such as in Strategic Management, and Workforce Planning). In groups of several students, do four things: (1) review the HRCI and/or SHRM documents; (2) identify the material in this chapter that relates to HRCI's or SHRM's required knowledge lists; (3) write four multiple-choice exam questions on this material that you believe would be suitable for inclusion in the HRCI exam and/or the SHRM exam; and, (4) if time permits, have someone from your team post your team's questions in front of the class, so that students in all teams can answer the exam questions created by the other teams.

MyLab Management

If your instructor is using MyLab Management, go to **www.pearson.com/mylab/management** for Auto-graded writing questions as well as the following Assisted-graded writing questions:

6-15. Explain the factors and problems that can undermine an interview's usefulness and techniques for eliminating them.

6-16. Why is it important to conduct preemployment background investigations? How would you go about doing so?

APPLICATION EXERCISES

HR IN ACTION CASE INCIDENT 1

Ethics and the Out-of-Control Interview

Ethics are "the principles of conduct governing an individual or a group"—they are the principles people use to decide what their conduct should be.[169]

Fairness is important in employee selection. For example, "If prospective employees perceive that the hiring process does not treat people fairly, they may assume that ethical behavior is not important in the company, and that 'official' pronouncements about the importance of ethics can be discounted."[170]

That's one reason why the situation Maria Fernandez ran into is disturbing. Maria is a bright, popular, and well-informed mechanical engineer who graduated with an engineering degree from State University in June 2016. During the spring preceding her graduation, she went out on many job interviews, most of which she thought were conducted courteously and were reasonably useful in giving both her and the prospective employer a good impression of where each of them stood on matters of importance to both of them. It was, therefore, with great anticipation that she looked forward to an interview with the one firm where she most wanted to work: Apex Environmental. She had always had a strong interest in cleaning up the environment and firmly believed she could best use her training and skills in a firm like Apex, where she thought she could have a successful career while making the world a better place.

The interview, however, was a disaster. Maria walked into a room in which a panel of five men—the president of the company, two vice presidents, the marketing director, and another engineer—began throwing questions at her that she felt were aimed primarily at tripping her up rather than finding out what she could offer through her engineering skills. The questions ranged from unnecessarily discourteous ("Why would you take a job as a waitress in college if you're such an intelligent person?") to irrelevant and sexist ("Are you planning on settling down and starting a family anytime soon?"). Then, after the interview, she met with two of the gentlemen individually (including the president), and the discussions focused almost exclusively on her technical expertise. She thought that these later discussions went fairly well.

However, given the apparent aimlessness and even meanspiritedness of the panel interview, she was astonished when several days later she received a job offer from the firm.

The offer forced her to consider several matters. From her point of view, the job itself was perfect—she liked what she would be doing, the industry, and the firm's location. And, in fact, the president had been quite courteous in subsequent discussions, as had been the other members of the management team. She was left wondering whether the panel interview had been intentionally tense to see how she'd stand up under pressure, and, if so, why they would do such a thing.

Questions

6-17. How would you explain the nature of the panel interview Maria had to endure? Specifically, do you think it reflected a well-thought-out interviewing strategy on the part of the firm or carelessness (or worse) on the part of the firm's management? If it was carelessness, what would you do to improve the interview process at Apex Environmental?

6-18. Do you consider the managers' treatment of Maria ethical? Why? If not, what specific steps would you take to make sure the interview process is ethical from now on?

6-19. Would you take the job offer if you were Maria? If you're not sure, is there any additional information that would help you make your decision, and if so, what is it?

6-20. The job of applications engineer for which Maria was applying requires (a) excellent technical skills with respect to mechanical engineering, (b) a commitment to working in the area of pollution control, (c) the ability to deal well and confidently with customers who have engineering problems, (d) a willingness to travel worldwide, and (e) a very intelligent and well-balanced personality. List 10 questions you would ask when interviewing applicants for the job.

HR IN ACTION CASE INCIDENT 2

Honesty Testing at Carter Cleaning Company

Jennifer Carter and her father have what the latter describes as an easy but hard job when it comes to screening job applicants. It is easy because for two important jobs—the people who actually do the pressing and those who do the cleaning-spotting—the applicants are easily screened with about 20 minutes of on-the-job testing. As with typists, as Jennifer points out, "Applicants either know how to press clothes fast enough or how to use cleaning chemicals and machines, or they don't, and we find out very quickly by just trying them out on the job." On the other hand, applicant screening for the stores can also be frustratingly hard because of the nature of some of the other qualities that Jennifer would like to screen for.

Two of the most critical problems facing her company are employee turnover and employee honesty. Jennifer and her father sorely need to implement practices that will reduce the rate of employee turnover. If there is a way to do this through employee testing and screening techniques, Jennifer would like to know about it because of the management time and money that are now being wasted by the never-ending need to recruit and hire new employees. Of even greater concern to Jennifer and her father is the need to institute new practices to screen out those employees who may be predisposed to steal from the company.

Employee theft is an enormous problem for Carter Cleaning Centers, and one that is not just limited to employees who handle the cash. For example, the cleaner-spotter and/or the presser often open the store themselves, without a manager present, to get the day's work started, and it is not unusual to have one or more of these people steal supplies or "run a route." Running a route means that an employee canvasses his or her neighborhood to pick up people's clothes for cleaning and then secretly cleans and presses them in the Carter store, using the company's supplies, gas, and power. It would also not be unusual for an unsupervised person (or his or her supervisor, for that matter) to accept a 1-hour rush order for cleaning or laundering, quickly clean and press the item, and return it to the customer for payment without making out a proper ticket for the item posting the sale. The money, of course, goes into the worker's pocket instead of into the cash register.

The more serious problem concerns the store manager and the counter workers who actually handle the cash. According to Jack Carter, "You would not believe the creativity employees use to get around the management controls we set up to cut down on employee theft." As one extreme example of this felonious creativity, Jack tells the following story: "To cut down on the amount of money my employees were stealing, I had a small sign painted and placed in front of all our cash registers. The sign said: YOUR ENTIRE ORDER FREE IF WE DON'T GIVE YOU A CASH REGISTER RECEIPT WHEN YOU PAY. CALL 552–0235. It was my intention with this sign to force all our cash-handling employees to place their receipts into the cash register where they would be recorded for my accountants. After all, if all the cash that comes in is recorded in the cash register, then we should have a much better handle on stealing in our stores, right? Well, one of our managers found a diabolical way around this. I came into the store one night and noticed that the cash register this particular manager was using just didn't look right, although the sign was dutifully placed in front of it. It turned out that every afternoon at about 5:00 P.M., when the other employees left, this character would pull his own cash register out of a box that he hid underneath our supplies. Customers coming in would notice the sign and of course the fact that he was meticulous in ringing up every sale. But unknown to them and us, for about five months, the sales that came in for about an hour every day went into his cash register, not mine. It took us that long to figure out where our cash for that store was going."

Jennifer would like you to answer the following questions.

Questions

6-21.   What would be the advantages and disadvantages to Jennifer's company of routinely administering honesty tests to all its employees?

6-22.   Specifically, what other screening techniques could the company use to screen out theft-prone and turnover-prone employees, and how exactly could these be used?

6-23.   How should Jennifer's company terminate employees caught stealing, and what kind of procedure should be set up for handling reference calls about these employees when they go to other companies looking for jobs?

Experiential Exercise

The Most Important Person You'll Ever Hire

Purpose: The purpose of this exercise is to give you practice using some of the interview techniques you learned from this chapter.

Required Understanding: You should be familiar with the information presented in this chapter, and read this:

For parents, children are precious. It's therefore interesting that parents who hire nannies to take care of their children usually do little more than ask several interview questions and conduct what is often, at best, a perfunctory reference check. Given the often questionable validity of interviews, and the (often) relative inexperience of the father or mother doing the interviewing, it's not surprising that many of these arrangements end in disappointment. You know from this chapter that it is difficult to conduct a valid interview unless you know exactly what you're looking for and, preferably, also how to structure the interview. Most parents simply aren't trained to do this.

How to Set Up the Exercise/Instructions:

6-24. Set up groups of five or six students. Two students will be the interviewees, while the other students in the group will serve as panel interviewers. The interviewees will develop a form for assessing the interviewers, and the panel interviewers will develop a structured situational interview for a nanny.

6-25. Instructions for the interviewees: The interviewees should leave the room for about 20 minutes. While out of the room, the interviewees should develop an interviewer assessment form based on the information presented in this chapter

regarding factors that can undermine the usefulness of an interview. During the panel interview, the interviewees should assess the interviewers using the interviewer assessment form. After the panel interviewers have conducted the interview, the interviewees should leave the room to discuss their notes. Did the interviewers exhibit any of the factors that can undermine the usefulness of an interview? If so, which ones? What suggestions would you (the interviewees) make to the interviewers on how to improve the usefulness of the interview?

6-26. Instructions for the interviewers: While the interviewees are out of the room, the panel interviewers will have 20 minutes to develop a short, structured situational interview form for a nanny. The panel interview team will interview two candidates for the position. During the panel interview, each interviewer should be taking notes on a copy of the structured situational interview form. After the panel interview, the panel interviewers should discuss their notes. What were your first impressions of each interviewee? Were your impressions similar? Which candidate would you all select for the position, and why?

Chapter 6 Appendix: The Structured Situational Interview

structured situational interview
A series of job-relevant questions with predetermined answers that interviewers ask of all applicants for the job.

There is little doubt that the **structured situational interview**—a series of job-relevant questions with predetermined answers that interviewers ask of all applicants for the job—produces superior results.[171] The basic idea is to write situational (what would you do), behavioral (what did you do), or job knowledge questions, *and* have job experts (like those supervising the job) also write sample answers for these questions, rated from good to poor. The people who interview and rate the applicants then use rating sheets anchored with examples of good or bad answers to rate the interviewees' answers.[172]

In creating structured situational interviews, people familiar with the job develop questions based on the job's required competencies. They then reach consensus on what are and are not acceptable answers. The procedure is as follows.[173]

Step 1: **Job Analysis** Write a job description with a list of job duties and required worker competencies (required knowledge, skills, abilities, and other worker qualifications).

Step 2: **Rate the Job's Main Competencies** Identify the job's main required competencies (such

as "interpersonal skills"). To do so, rate each competency based on its importance to job success. (Alternatively, some managers create questions aimed at assessing the candidate's potential for doing each of the job's main duties. If so, you would write questions related to the job's main duties, such as "What would you do if the machine suddenly began heating up?").

Step 3: **Create Interview Questions** Create interview questions based on required job competencies, with more questions for the important competencies. Recall that *situational questions* pose a hypothetical job situation, such as "What would you do if the machine suddenly began heating up?" *Job knowledge questions* assess knowledge essential to job performance, such as "What is HTML?" *Willingness questions* gauge the applicant's willingness and motivation to meet the job's requirements—to do repetitive physical work or to travel, for instance. *Behavioral questions,* of course, ask candidates how they've handled similar situations.

The people who create the questions often write them in terms of critical incidents. For example, for a supervisory candidate, the interviewer might ask this situational question: "Your spouse and two teenage children are sick in bed with colds. There are no relatives or friends available to look in on them. Your shift starts in three hours. What would you do in this situation?" See Figure 6A.1 for examples.

Step 4: **Create Benchmark Answers** Next, *for each question*, develop ideal (benchmark) answers for good (a 5 rating), marginal (a 3 rating), and poor (a 1 rating). For example, consider

the preceding situational question, where the spouse and children are sick. Three benchmark answers (from low to high) for the example question might be, "I'd stay home—my spouse and family come first." (1); "I'd phone my supervisor and explain my situation." (3); and "Because they only have colds, I'd come to work." (5).

Step 5: **Appoint the Interview Panel and Conduct Interviews** Employers generally conduct structured situational interviews using a panel, rather than one-on-one. The panel

Figure 6A.1

Structured Interview Guide

Source: www.state .gov/documents/ organization.107843 .pdf, and United States Office of Personnel Management. Structured Interviews: Interview Guide and Evaluation Materials for Structured Interviews. United States Department of State.

STEP 1—Create a Structured Interview Guide

Instructions:
First, here in step 1, create a structured interview guide like this one (including a competency definition, a lead question, and benchmark examples and answers, for instance) for each of the job's required competencies:

Competency: Interpersonal Skills

Definition:
Shows understanding, courtesy, tact, empathy, concern; develops and maintains relationships; may deal with people who are difficult, hostile, distressed; relates well to people from varied backgrounds and situations; is sensitive to individual differences.

Lead Questions:
Describe a situation in which you had to deal with people who were upset about a problem. What specific actions did you take? What was the outcome or result?

Benchmark Level	Level Definition	Level Examples
5	Establishes and maintains ongoing working relationships with management, other employees, internal or external stakeholders, or customers. Remains courteous when discussing information or eliciting highly sensitive or controversial information from people who are reluctant to give it. Effectively handles situations involving a high degree of tension or discomfort involving people who are demonstrating a high degree of hostility or distress.	Presents controversial findings tactfully to irate organization senior management officials regarding shortcomings of a newly installed computer system, software programs, and associated equipment.
4		Mediates disputes concerning system design/architecture, the nature and capacity of data management systems, system resources allocations, or other equally controversial/sensitive matters.
3	Cooperates and works well with management, other employees, or customers, on short-term assignments. Remains courteous when discussing information or eliciting moderately sensitive or controversial information from people who are hesitant to give it. Effectively handles situations involving a moderate degree of tension or discomfort involving people who are demonstrating a moderate degree of hostility or distress.	Courteously and tactfully delivers effective instruction to frustrated customers. Provides technical advice to customers and the public on various types of IT such as communication or security systems, data management procedures or analysis.
2		Familiarizes new employees with administrative procedures and office systems.
1	Cooperates and works well with management, other employees, or customers during brief interactions. Remains courteous when discussing information or eliciting non-sensitive or non-controversial information from people who are willing to give it. Effectively handles situations involving little or no tension, discomfort, hostility, or distress.	Responds courteously to customers' general inquiries. Greets and assists visitors attending a meeting within own organization.

Continued

Figure 6A.1
(Continued)

STEP 2—INDIVIDUAL EVALUATION FORM

Instructions:
Next, in step 2, create a form for evaluating each job candidate on each of the job's competencies:

Candidate to be assessed: _____

Date of Interview: _____

Competency: Problem Solving

Definition:
Identifies problems; determines accuracy and relevance of information; uses sound judgment to generate and evaluate alternatives, and to make the recommendations.

Question:
Describe a situation in which you identified a problem and evaluated the alternatives to make a recommendation or decision. What was the problem and who was affected?

Supplementary "Probes":
How did you generate and evaluate your alternatives? What was the outcome?

Describe specific (problem solving) behaviors observed: (Use back of sheet, if necessary)

Level Examples: 1-Low	2	3–Average	4	5–Outstanding
Uses logic to identify alternatives to solve routine problems. Reacts to and solves problems by gathering and applying information from standard materials or sources that provide a limited number of alternatives.		Uses logic to identify alternatives to solve moderately difficult problems. Identifies and solves problems by gathering and applying information from a variety of materials or sources that provide several alternatives.		Uses logic to identify alternatives to solve complex or sensitive problems. Anticipates problems and identifies and evaluates potential sources of information and generates alternatives to solve problems where standards do not exist.

Final Evaluation:	Printed Name:	Signature:

Continued

usually consists of three to six members, preferably the same ones who wrote the questions and answers. It may also include the job's supervisor and/or incumbent, and a human resources representative. The same panel interviews all candidates for the job.[174]

The panel members generally review the job description, questions, and benchmark answers before the interview. One panel member introduces the applicant and asks all questions of all applicants in this and succeeding candidates' interviews (to ensure consistency). However, all panel members record and rate the applicant's answers on the rating scale sheet. They do this by indicating where the candidate's answer to each question falls relative to the ideal poor, marginal, or good answers. At the end of the interview, someone answers any questions the applicant has.[175]

Online programs help interviewers design and organize behaviorally based selection interviews. For example, SelectPro (www.selectpro.net) enables interviewers to create behavior-based selection interviews, custom interview guides, and automated online interviews.

Figure 6A.1
(Continued)

STEP 3—PANEL CONSENSUS EVALUATION FORM
_____

Instructions:
Finally, in step 3, create a panel consensus evaluation form like this one, which the members of the panel who interviewed the candidate will use to evaluate his or her interview performance.

Candidate: _____

Date:_____

Panel Consensus Evaluation Form

Instructions:
Transfer each individual evaluation for each competency onto this form. If all of the individual competency evaluations are within one rating scale point, enter the average of the evaluations in the column labeled Group Evaluation. If more than one point separates any two raters, a consensus discussion must occur with each party justifying his/her evaluation. The lead interviewer or his/her designee should take notes on the consensus discussion in the space provided. Any changes in evaluation should be initialed and a final evaluation entered for each competency.

Competency	Final Individual Rater Evaluations			Group Evaluation
	(1)	(2)	(3)	
Interpersonal Skills				
Self-Management				
Reasoning				
Decision Making				
Problem Solving				
Oral Communication				
Total Score				

Consensus Discussion Notes:

Signature Panel Member 1: _____

Signature Panel Member 2: _____

Signature Panel Member 3: _____

PART

3

TRAINING AND HUMAN RESOURCE DEVELOPMENT

Company's Strategic Goals

Employee Competencies and Behaviors Required for Company to Achieve These Strategic Goals

3 Training and Development

2 Planning, Recruitment, and Selection

4 Compensation and Total Rewards

HR Policies and Practices Required to Produce Employee Competencies and Behaviors

1 Strategic and Legal Environment

5 Employee and Labor Relations

WHERE WE ARE NOW

After selecting and hiring the employee, the employer must orient, train, appraise, and take steps to retain the person. We now therefore turn to methods for training, developing, appraising, and retaining human resources. *In Part 3 we will cover*

- Chapter 7, Training and Developing Employees
- Chapter 8, Performance Management and Appraisal
- Chapter 9, Managing Careers

The concepts and techniques we'll study here in Part 3 play an important role in strategic human resource management. As the accompanying HR Strategy Model shows, strategic human resource management means formulating and executing human resource policies and practices that produce the employee competencies and behaviors the company needs to achieve its strategic aims. Having high-potential employees is not enough; they must also know what to do and how to do it. We will see here in Part 3 accomplishing this requires putting in place HR policies and practices for training, developing, appraising, and retaining employees. Then, in Part 4, we'll turn to compensating employees.

7

Training and Developing Employees

OVERVIEW:
In this chapter, we will cover . . .

- Orienting/Onboarding New Employees
- Employee Engagement Guide for Managers: Onboarding at Toyota
- Overview of the Training Process
- Implementing the Training Program
- Implementing Management Development Programs
- Managing Organizational Change Programs
- Evaluating the Training Effort

MyLab Management

⭐ Improve Your Grade!
When you see this icon, visit **www.pearson.com/mylab/management** for activities that are applied, personalized, and offer immediate feedback.

LEARNING OBJECTIVES

When you finish studying this chapter, you should be able to:

1. Summarize the purpose and process of employee orientation.
2. Give an example of how to design onboarding to improve employee engagement.
3. List and briefly explain each of the five steps in the training process.
4. Explain how to use five training techniques.
5. List and briefly discuss four management development methods.
6. Answer the question, "What is organizational development, and how does it differ from traditional approaches to organizational change?"
7. Explain what to consider in evaluating the effectiveness of a training program.

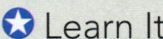 Learn It

If your professor has chosen to assign this, go to **www.pearson.com/mylab/management** to see what you should particularly focus on and to take the Chapter 7 Warm Up.

INTRODUCTION

After working as a head chef in several restaurants, Alex was thrilled to finally get the funding he needed to open his new French restaurant, Alex's Bistro, not far from the new Mid-Town Miami complex close to downtown Miami. For his kitchen staff he hired people with whom he'd worked closely at other restaurants because he knew they knew what to do. Hiring the waitstaff was another thing. He had no personal experience running the "front end" of a restaurant, so he posted a Help Wanted—Waitstaff sign on the window and hired six people who exhibited the conscientiousness and people-orientation that he was looking for. He spent about an hour before opening day explaining details to the waitstaff (such as how to use the computerized order input system) and describing how he wanted them to behave ("supportive and helpful"). Unfortunately, opening day was a disaster. Waiters and waitresses couldn't answer basic questions such as "What's in this dish?" They got almost half the orders wrong, and when they finally did bring the orders to the tables, they didn't remember who ordered what, so the customers ended up passing their dishes around. Later that night, Alex went home and asked his former boss what he thought had gone wrong. "Are you actually telling me you didn't train your waitstaff at all before letting them loose on your customers? That's unbelievable, Al."

Source: Baranq/Shutterstock.

LEARNING OBJECTIVE **1**
Summarize the purpose and process of employee orientation.

Orienting/Onboarding New Employees

Carefully selecting employees doesn't guarantee they'll perform effectively. Even high-potential employees can't do their jobs if they don't know what to do or how to do it. Making sure your employees do know what to do and how to do it is the purpose of orientation and training. The human resources department usually designs the orientation and training programs, but the supervisor does most of the day-to-day orienting and training. Every manager therefore should know how to orient and train employees. We will start with orientation.

The Purposes of Employee Orientation/Onboarding

Employee orientation (often now called *onboarding*) provides new employees with the basic background information (such as computer passwords and company rules) they need to do their jobs; ideally it should also help them start becoming emotionally attached to and engaged in the firm.[1]

The manager therefore aims to accomplish four things when orienting new employees:

1. Make the new employee feel welcome and at home and part of the team.
2. Make sure the new employee has the basic information to function effectively, such as e-mail access, personnel policies and benefits, and expectations in terms of work behavior.
3. Help the new employee understand the organization in a broad sense (its past, present, culture, and strategies and vision of the future).
4. Start socializing the person into the firm's culture and ways of doing things.[2]

The Orientation Process

The length of the orientation program depends on what you cover. Traditional programs take several hours. The human resource specialist (or, in smaller firms, the office manager) usually performs the first part of the orientation by explaining basic matters like working hours, work rules, benefits, and vacations. That person then introduces the new employee to his or her new supervisor.[3] The supervisor continues the orientation by explaining the organization, introducing the person to his or her new colleagues, familiarizing him or her with the workplace, and helping to reduce first-day jitters.

At a minimum, as in Figure 7.1, orientations typically provide information on things like employee benefits, personnel policies, and safety regulations.[4] New employees should receive (and sign for) print or Internet-based employee handbooks covering matters like these. (You'll find a variety of orientation checklists online.)[5] At the other extreme, L'Oréal's onboarding program takes about two years. It includes special training and roundtable discussions, meetings with key insiders, on-the-job learning, individual mentoring, and special site visits.[6]

Ideally, there would be no such thing as a one-day (or less) orientation. The onboarding should begin before the person's first day, with receipt of a welcome note and first-week orientation schedule, as well as instructions about the documents (such as tax documents) needed the first day. On the first day make sure everyone knows the new employee is starting, and preferably arrange for one or more of his or her colleagues to take the new employee to lunch. On subsequent days, the new employee should meet colleagues in other departments. After about two weeks, have someone speak with the new employee to talk through any concerns.[7]

Supervisors should be vigilant. Follow up on and encourage new employees to engage in activities (such as taking breaks with current employees) that will help them to "learn the ropes" and become productive.[8]

Onboarding is not just for lower-level employees. For example, in one survey "poor grasp of how the organization works" was the biggest stumbling block for 69% of new senior executives. Executive onboarding should touch on matters like the firm's operational plans and key business areas, key team members' career histories, key external stakeholders, and briefings on the firm's culture and how it "gets things done."[9]

Orientation Technology Employers use technology to support orientation. For example, IBM uses virtual environments like Second Life to support orientation, particularly for employees abroad. The new employees choose virtual avatars, for instance, to learn how to enroll for benefits.[13] ION Geophysical uses an online onboarding portal solution called RedCarpet. It includes a streaming

UNIVERSITY of CALIFORNIA, SAN DIEGO
MEDICAL CENTER

NEW EMPLOYEE DEPARTMENTAL ORIENTATION CHECKLIST
(Return to Human Resources within 10 days of Hire)

NAME:	HIRE DATE:	SSN:	JOB TITLE:
DEPARTMENT:	NEO DATE:	DEPARTMENTAL ORIENTATION COMPLETED BY:	

TOPIC	DATE REVIEWED	N/A

1. HUMAN RESOURCES INFORMATION
   a. Departmental Attendance Procedures and UCSD Medical Center Work Time & Attendance Policy
   b. Job Description Review
   c. Annual Performance Evaluation and Peer Feedback Process
   d. Probationary Period Information
   e. Appearance/Dress Code Requirements
   f. Annual TB Screening
   g. License and/or Certification Renewals

2. DEPARTMENT INFORMATION
   a. Organizational Structure-Department Core Values Orientation
   b. Department/Unit Area Specific Policies & Procedures
   c. Customer Service Practices
   d. CQI Effort and Projects
   e. Tour and Floor Plan
   f. Equipment/Supplies
      • Keys issued
      • Radio Pager issued
      • Other _____
   g. Mail and Recharge Codes

3. SAFETY INFORMATION
   a. Departmental Safety Plan
   b. Employee Safety/Injury Reporting Procedures
   c. Hazard Communication
   d. Infection Control/Sharps Disposal
   e. Attendance at annual Safety Fair (mandatory)

4. FACILITES INFORMATION
   a. Emergency Power
   b. Mechanical Systems
   c. Water
   d. Medical Gases
   e. Patient Room
      • Bed
      • Headwall
      • Bathroom
      • Nurse Call System

5. SECURITY INFORMATION
   a. Code Triage Assignment
   b. Code Blue Assignment
   c. Code Red – Evacuation Procedure
   d. Code 10 – Bomb Threat Procedure
   e. Departmental Security Measures
   f. UCSD Emergency Number 6111 or 911

This generic checklist may not constitute a complete departmental orientation or assessment. Please attach any additional unit specific orientation material for placement in the employee's HR file

I have been oriented on the items listed above_____

D1999(R7-01)   **WHITE** – HR Records (8912)   **Yellow** – Department Retains

Figure 7.1

New Employee Departmental Orientation Checklist

Source: "New Employee Departmental Orientation Checklist" from http://www.opm.gov/policy-data-oversight/human-capital-management/hiring-reform/sample-employee-checklist.pdf. Used with permission of UC San Diego Medical Center. United States Office of Personnel Management.

video welcome message and photos and profiles of new colleagues.[14] With Workday's iPhone app, employers provide their employees with easy mobile access to their employee directories. Users can search their company's worker directory for names, images, and contact information and call or e-mail coworkers directly.[15]

KNOW YOUR EMPLOYMENT LAW
The Employee Handbook

The employer should carefully review its employee handbook, which courts often view as containing legally binding commitments. Even apparently sensible handbook policies (such as "only authorized overtime is compensated" would probably be illegal (because, for instance, if an employee clocked in 10 minutes early each day you might still have to pay her overtime); it would be better to prohibit unauthorized overtime.[10] The handbook should include a disclaimer stating "nothing in this handbook should be taken as creating a binding contract between employer and employees, and all employment is on an at will basis."[11] Say that statements of company policies, benefits, and regulations do not constitute the terms and conditions of an employment contract, either expressed or implied. Do not insert statements such as "No employee will be fired without just cause" or statements that imply or state that employees have tenure.[12] It's wise to have a lawyer review your handbook, or at least to use a verified source. ■

LEARNING OBJECTIVE 2
Give an example of how to design onboarding to improve employee engagement.

Employee Engagement Guide for Managers: Onboarding at Toyota

In many firms today, orientation goes well beyond providing basic information about things like hours of work.[16] Onboarding at Toyota Motor Manufacturing USA illustrates this. Although it does cover routine topics such as company benefits, its main aim is to engage Toyota's new employees in the firm's ideology of quality, teamwork, personal development, open communication, and mutual respect.[17] It takes about four days:[18]

Day 1: The first day includes an overview of the program, a welcome to the company, and a discussion of the firm's organizational structure and human resource department by the firm's vice president for human resources. He or she devotes about an hour and a half to discussing Toyota history and culture, and about 2 hours to employee benefits. Managers then spend several hours discussing Toyota's commitment to quality and teamwork.

Day 2: A typical second day focuses first on communications, and on the importance of mutual respect, teamwork, and open communication at Toyota. The rest of the day covers topics such as safety, environmental affairs, and the Toyota production system.

Day 3: Given the importance of working in teams at Toyota, this day also begins with 2.5 to 3 hours devoted to communication training, such as "making requests and giving feedback." The rest of the day covers Toyota's problem-solving methods, quality assurance, hazard communications, and safety.

Day 4: Topics today include teamwork training and the Toyota suggestion system. It also covers what work teams are responsible for and how to work together as a team. The afternoon session covers fire prevention and fire extinguishers training. By the end of day 4, new employees should be well on their way toward being steeped in—and engaged in—Toyota's ideology, in particular its mission of quality and its values of teamwork, continuous improvement, and problem solving.[19]

The bottom line is that there's more to orienting employees than introducing them to coworkers. Even without a program like Toyota's, use the onboarding opportunity to start instilling in the new employee the company values and traditions in which you expect the person to become engaged.

training
The process of teaching new or current employees the basic skills they need to perform their jobs.

Overview of the Training Process

Directly after orientation, training should begin. **Training** means giving new or current employees the skills that they need to perform their jobs, such as showing new salespeople how to sell your product.[20] Training might involve having the current jobholder explain the job to the new hire, or multiweek classroom or Internet classes. In one recent year, employers spent about $1,252 per employee on direct training and learning.[21]

Training is important. If even high-potential employees don't know what to do and how to do it, they will improvise or do nothing useful at all. Furthermore, many high achievers begin looking for new jobs within a year of starting, often due to dissatisfaction with inadequate training.[22] Employers also increasingly capitalize on the fact that training fosters engagement. For example, Coca-Cola UK uses employee development plans, training, and leadership development to attract and retain the best employees and inspire their engagement.[23]

KNOW YOUR EMPLOYMENT LAW
Training and the Law

Training decisions can trigger equal employment issues. With respect to discrimination, Title VII of the Civil Rights Act of 1964 and related legislation requires that the employer avoid discriminatory actions *in all aspects* of its human resource management process. Managers face much the same consequences for discriminating against protected individuals when selecting candidates for training programs as they would in selecting candidates for jobs or for promotion. Also, the EEOC stresses that, if feasible, employers "should provide training to all employees to ensure they understand their [sexual harassment] rights and responsibilities." Courts will consider the adequacy of the employer's sexual harassment training to determine whether it exercised reasonable care to prevent harassment. ■

Aligning Strategy and Training

The employer's strategic plans should govern its training goals.[24] In essence, the task is to identify the employee behaviors the firm will require to execute its strategy and then from that deduce what skills and knowledge (what competencies) employees will need. Then, put in place training goals and programs to instill these competencies.[25]

For example, with the health-care landscape in America changing fast, the Walgreens drug chain had to reformulate its strategy. Today it is the second-largest dispenser of flu shots in the United States. Its in-store health clinics provide medical care. It purchased drugstore.com.

These strategic changes affected the skills that Walgreens employees required, and therefore its training and other staffing goals. For example, Walgreens established Walgreens University. It offers more than 400 programs that Walgreens employees can take to build their skills (and even get college credit in pharmacy-related topics). Some programs develop assistant store manager skills, and Walgreens in-store health clinic nurse practitioners can take courses that expand their medical care expertise. The bottom line is that Walgreens reformulated its training (and other) HR policies to produce the employee skills the company needed to support its new strategy.[26]

The ADDIE Five-Step Training Process

The employer should use a rational training process. The gold standard here is still the analysis-design-develop-implement-evaluate (ADDIE) training process model that training experts have used for years.[27] As an example, one training vendor describes its training process as follows:[28]

- *Analyze* the training need.
- *Design* the overall training program.
- *Develop* the course (actually assembling/creating the training materials).
- *Implement* training, by actually training the targeted employee group using methods such as on-the-job or online training.
- *Evaluate* the course's effectiveness.

We'll look at each step next.

Conducting the Training Needs Analysis

The training needs analysis may address the employer's *strategic/longer-term* training needs and/or its *current* training needs.

Strategic Training Needs Analysis Strategic goals (perhaps to enter new lines of business) often mean the firm will have to fill new jobs. *Strategic training needs analysis* identifies the behaviors, skills, and training that employees will need to fill these new future jobs. For example, when Wisconsin-based Signicast Corp. decided to build a new, high-tech plant, the firm's top management knew the plant's employees would need new skills to run the computerized machines. They worked closely with their HR team to formulate hiring policies and training programs to ensure the firm would have the human resources required to populate the new plant.

Current Training Needs Analysis Most training efforts aim to improve current performance—specifically training new employees, and those whose performance is deficient.[29]

How you analyze current training needs depends on whether you're training new or current employees. The main task for *new* employees is to determine what the job entails and to break it down into subtasks, each of which you then teach to the new employee.

Analyzing *current* employees' training needs is more complex because you must also ascertain whether training is the solution. For example, performance may be down due to poor motivation. Managers use *task analysis* to identify new employees' training needs and *performance analysis* to identify current employees' training needs.

task analysis
A detailed study of a job to identify the specific skills required.

Task Analysis: Analyzing New Employees' Training Needs Particularly with lower-level workers, it's customary to hire inexperienced personnel and train them. The aim here is to give them the skills and knowledge they need to do the job. **Task analysis** is a detailed study of the job to determine what specific skills and knowledge the job requires. For task analysis, job descriptions and job specifications are helpful. They list the job's specific duties and skills, which are the basic reference points in determining the training required. Managers also uncover training needs by reviewing performance standards, performing the job, and questioning current job holders and their supervisors.[30]

competency model
A graphic model that consolidates in one diagram a precise overview of the competencies (the knowledge, skills, and behaviors) someone would need to do a job well.

Some managers supplement the job description and specification with a *task analysis record form*. This form (see Table 7.1) consolidates information regarding required tasks and skills. As Table 7.1 illustrates, the form contains six columns of information, such as "Skills or knowledge required."

Using Competency Models A **competency model** is another option. It consolidates in one diagram a precise overview of the competencies someone would need to do the job well. Figure 4.9 (page 113) was one example.

The employer then uses these competencies to design its training program. For example, the Association for Talent Development (ATD) built a competencies model for the job of Training and Development Professional. As one competency

Table 7.1 Sample Task Analysis Record Form

Task List	When and How Often Performed	Quantity and Quality of Performance	Conditions Under Which Performed	Skills or Knowledge Required	Where Best Learned
1. Operate paper cutter	4 times per day		Noisy pressroom: distractions		
1.1. Start motor	4 times per day				On the job
1.2. Set cutting distance		± tolerance of 0.007 in.		Read gauge	On the job
1.3. Place paper on cutting table		Must be completely even to prevent uneven cut		Lift paper correctly	On the job
1.4. Push paper up to cutter				Must be even	On the job
1.5. Grasp safety release with left hand		100% of time, for safety		Essential for safety	On the job, but practice first with no distractions
1.6. Grasp cutter release with right hand				Must keep both hands on releases	On the job, but practice first with no distractions
1.7. Simultaneously pull safety release with left hand and cutter release with right hand				Must keep both hands on releases	On the job, but practice first with no distractions
1.8. Wait for cutter to retract		100% of time, for safety		Must keep both hands on releases	On the job, but practice first with no distractions
1.9. Retract paper				Wait until cutter retracts	On the job, but practice first with no distractions
1.10. Shut off		100% of time, for safety			On the job, but practice first with no distractions
2. Operate printing press					
2.1. Start motor					

Note: Task analysis record form showing some of the tasks and subtasks performed by a printing press operator.

example, the model describes *instructional design* as "designing, creating, and developing formal learning solutions to meet organizational needs; analyzing and selecting the most appropriate strategy, methodologies, and technologies to maximize the learning experience and impact."[31] Training such a trainer would thus require making sure he or she could, once training is complete, exhibit the skills and knowledge (competencies) that enables him or her to design, create, and develop formal learning solutions to meet organizational needs.[32]

Performance Analysis: Analyzing Current Employees' Training Needs For underperforming current employees, you can't assume that training is the solution. Is it lack of training, or something else? **Performance analysis** is the process of

performance analysis
Verifying that there is a performance deficiency and determining whether that deficiency should be corrected through training or through some other means (such as transferring the employee).

verifying that there is a performance deficiency and determining whether the employer should correct such deficiencies through training or some other means (like transferring the employee).

Performance analysis begins with comparing the person's actual performance to what it should be. Doing so helps to confirm that there is a performance deficiency, and (hopefully) helps the manager to identify its cause. Examples of performance deficiencies might be:

I expect each salesperson to make 10 new contracts per week, but John averages only six.

Other plants our size average no more than two serious accidents per month; we're averaging five.

There are several ways to identify how a current employee is doing. These include reviewing:

- Performance appraisals
- Job-related performance data (including productivity, absenteeism and tardiness, grievances, waste, late deliveries, product quality, downtime, repairs, and customer complaints)
- Observations by supervisors or other specialists
- Interviews with the employee or his or her supervisor
- Tests of things like job knowledge, skills, and attendance
- Attitude surveys
- Individual employee daily diaries
- Assessment center results
- Special performance gap analytical software, such as from Saba Software, Inc.

Can't Do/Won't Do Uncovering *why* performance is down is the heart of performance analysis. Here the manager will want to distinguish between can't-do and won't-do problems. First, determine whether it is a *can't-do* problem and, if so, its specific causes. For example: The employees don't know what to do or what your standards are; there are obstacles in the system such as lack of tools or supplies; there are no job aids (such as color-coded wires that show assemblers which wire goes where); you've hired people who haven't the skills to do the job; or there is inadequate training.

Or, it might be a *won't-do* problem. Here employees could do a good job if they wanted to. One expert says, "Perhaps the biggest trap that trainers fall into is [developing] training for problems that training just won't fix."[33] For instance, the better solution might be to change the incentives.[34]

Designing the Training Program

Armed with the needs analysis results, the manager next designs the training program. *Design* means planning the overall training program including training objectives, delivery methods, and program evaluation. Substeps include setting performance objectives, creating a detailed training outline (all training program steps from start to finish), choosing a program delivery method (such as lectures or Web), and verifying the overall program design with management. The design should include summaries of how you plan to set a training environment that motivates your trainees both to learn and to transfer what they learn to the job. It is also here that the manager reviews possible training program content (including workbooks, exercises, and activities) and estimates a budget for the training program.[35] If the program is to use technology, the manager should include a review of the technology he or she plans to use as part of the analysis.[36] Also decide here how to organize the various training content components, choose how to evaluate the program, develop an overall summary plan for the program, and obtain management's approval to move ahead.

We'll look more closely next at several specific design issues, starting with objectives.

Setting Learning Objectives[37] After training needs have been analyzed, measurable training objectives should be set. Training, development, learning, or (more generally) *instructional objectives* should specify in measurable terms what the trainee should be able to do after successfully completing the training program.[38] For example:

> The technical service representative will be able to adjust the color guidelines on this HP Officejet All-in-One printer copier within 10 minutes according to the device's specifications.

The learning objectives should first address the performance deficiencies that you identified via the needs analysis. Thus, if the sales team's sales are 40% too low, the objectives should focus on ensuring they get the knowledge, skills, and attitudes they need to boost sales. But at the same time, the learning objectives must be practical, given the constraints.

One constraint is financial. The employer should want to see and approve a *training budget* for the program. Typical costs include the development costs (of having, say, a human resource specialist working on the program for a week or two), the direct and indirect (overhead) costs of the trainers' time, participant compensation (for the time they're actually being trained), and the cost of evaluating the program.[39] The question isn't just "Can we afford this program?" but "Does it pay to spend this much, given the benefits we'll derive from the program—will it improve performance, and if so by how much?" Therefore, prepare to defend the program on a benefits-versus-costs basis.

There are also other constraints to consider. For example, time constraints may require reducing three or four desirable learning objectives to one or two.

Creating a Motivational Learning Environment Learning requires both ability and motivation, so the training program's design should consider both. In terms of *ability*, the trainee requires (among other things) the necessary reading, writing, and mathematics skills. In setting the learning environment, the manager therefore should address several trainee-ability issues. For example, how will our program accommodate differences in trainee abilities? Do we need to provide remedial training?

Second, the learner must also be motivated. No manager should waste his or her time showing a disinterested employee how to do something (even if he or she has the requisite ability).

Many books exist on how to motivate employees, but several specific observations are pertinent here.[40] The training program's effects will be diminished if trainees return to their jobs to snide comments such as "I hope you liked your little vacation" from colleagues. Therefore, the low-hanging fruit in motivating trainees is to make sure the trainee's peers and supervisor support the training effort. Ideally, particularly for larger programs, top management should visibly support the program. Guidelines follow.

BUILDING YOUR MANAGEMENT SKILLS:
How to Motivate the Trainee: Guidelines

We can summarize useful motivational points as follows.

Make the Learning Meaningful

Learners are more motivated to learn something that has meaning for them. Therefore:

1. At the start of training, provide a bird's-eye view of the material that you are going to present. For example, show why it's important, and provide an overview.[41]

Continued

2. Use familiar examples.
3. Organize the information so you can present it logically, in meaningful units.
4. Use terms and concepts that are already familiar to trainees.
5. Use visual aids.
6. Create a perceived training need in trainees' minds.[42] In one study, pilots who experienced pretraining, accident-related events subsequently learned more from an accident-reduction training program than did those experiencing fewer such events.[43] At least, " . . . sit down and talk with the trainees about why they are enrolled in the class, what they are expected to learn, and how they can use it on the job."[44]

Reinforce the Learning

Provide plenty of feedback. In particular:

1. Trainees learn best when the trainers immediately reinforce correct responses, perhaps with a quick "well done."
2. Incentivize. Some companies, such as Hudson Trail outfitters, an outdoor-gear retailer, offer trainees incentives of outdoor gear for completing each training program segment.[45]
3. Trainees learn best at their own pace. If possible, let them pace themselves.
4. Set goals. In one study, some trainees set goals at the start of the program for the skills they were being taught. After training, they were rated more highly on these skills than were those who hadn't set goals.[46]

Make Skills Transfer Obvious and Easy

Less than 35% of trainees seem to be transferring what they learned in training to their jobs a year after training.[47] Make it easy to transfer new skills and behaviors from the training site to the job site:

1. Maximize the similarity between the training situation and the work situation.
2. Provide enough practice.
3. Label or identify each feature of the machine and/or step in the process.
4. Direct the trainees' attention to important aspects of the job. For example, if you're training a customer service rep to handle calls, explain the different types of calls he or she will encounter.[48]
5. Provide "heads-up" information. For example, supervisors often face stressful conditions. You can reduce the negative impact of such events by letting supervisory trainees know they might occur.[49]
6. Intermingle opportunities for trainees to use their new skills or knowledge ("application tasks") throughout the training episode.[50]
7. Provide follow-up assignments at the close of training, so trainees are reinforced by having to apply back on the job what they've learned.[51]

Developing the Program

Program development means choosing and assembling the actual content the program will present, as well as choosing (or creating) the specific instructional methods (lectures, cases, Web-based, etc.) you will use. Training equipment and materials will include (for example) iPads, workbooks, lectures, PowerPoint slides, cloud-based activities (see Trends feature), and training manuals, for instance.

Some employers create their own training content, but there's also a vast selection of online and offline content. (See, for example, the Association for Talent

Development's Infoline at www.td.org, www.trainerswarehouse.com, and www .gneil.com, among thousands of such suppliers.)[52] Turnkey training packages often include a trainer's guide, self-study book, videos, and other content.

Once you design, approve, and develop the program, management can implement and then evaluate it. *Implement* means actually provide the training, using one or more of the instructional methods (such as lectures) that we discuss next.

✪ Watch It

What do you think of how Wilson Learning conducts its training programs? If your professor has chosen to assign this, go to **www.pearson.com/mylab/management** to watch the video Wilson Learning Training, and then answer the questions to show what you would (or would not) change in their program.

TRENDS SHAPING HR: *Digital and Social Media: Training on the Cloud*

In designing and developing its training program, the employer will have to decide how the program will be delivered. Increasingly, this is occurring via "the cloud." Basically, this refers to placing software programs and services on vendors' remote servers, from which they can then deliver these programs and services seamlessly to employees' digital devices.

Cloud-based training is revolutionizing training. Because both the courses and the overall learning management system are hosted by the vendor, the employer need not concern itself with setting up or updating the programs on its own computers; the vendor manages the software for it. Furthermore the more advanced cloud-based learning systems let trainees access the training software and courses from wherever they are, using a variety of mobile devices. This not only improves convenience, but also facilitates collaboration among employees when, for instance, they're working together on a training-based project. Typical cloud-based learning features include a course library, assessments and quizzes, reports and dashboards (for monitoring training performance), gamification elements (such as points and badges), messaging and notification systems, and a facility for scheduling and delivering both virtual and classroom training.[53] ∎

LEARNING OBJECTIVE 4
Explain how to use five training techniques.

Implementing the Training Program

With objectives set and the program designed and developed, the manager can turn to implementing the training program. This means actually doing the training, using one or more of the following training methods.

On-the-Job Training

On-the-job training (OJT) means having a person learn a job by actually doing it. Every employee, from mailroom clerk to CEO, should get on-the-job training when he or she joins a firm. In many firms, OJT is the only training available.[54]

on-the-job training (OJT)
Training a person to learn a job while working on it.

Types of On-the-Job Training The most familiar on-the-job training is the *coaching or understudy method*. Here, an experienced worker or the trainee's supervisor trains the employee. This may involve simply observing the supervisor, or (preferably) having the supervisor or job expert show the new employee the ropes, step-by-step. Effective coaching is essential. For example in one study of pharmaceuticals sales representatives, supervisors' coaching skills were associated with significant differences in goal attainment between sales districts.[55]

Job rotation, in which an employee (usually a management trainee) moves from job to job at planned intervals, is another OJT technique. *Special assignments* similarly give lower-level executives firsthand experience in working on actual problems.

Do not take the on-the-job training effort for granted. Instead, plan out and structure the OJT experience. Train the trainers themselves (often the employees' supervisors), and provide training materials. They should know, for instance, how to motivate learners. Because low expectations may translate into poor trainee performance, supervisor/trainers should project high expectations. A four-step on-the-job training approach can be useful. First, *prepare the learner,* for instance by putting the person at ease and explaining the job and why he or she is being taught. Second, *present the operation* by going through it at a normal work pace and again more slowly to itemize key points. Third, *try out* the trainee by having the person run through the job several times to enhance his or her skills and speed. Finally, *follow up* by gradually decreasing supervision, correcting errors, and complimenting good work.

Many firms use "peer training" for OJT; for instance, expert employees answer calls at selected times during the day or participate in in-house "radio programs" to answer their peers' call-in questions about technical aspects of doing their jobs.[56] Others use employee teams to analyze the jobs and prepare training materials. The employees, already job experts, reportedly conduct task analyses more quickly and effectively than do training experts.[57]

Apprenticeship Training

Apprenticeship training is a process by which people become skilled workers, usually through a combination of formal learning and long-term on-the-job training, often under the tutelage of a master craftsperson. When steelmaker Dofasco (now part of ArcelorMittal) discovered that many of their employees would be retiring within 5 to 10 years, the company decided to revive its apprenticeship training. New recruits spend about 32 months in an internal apprenticeship training program, learning various jobs under the tutelage of experienced employees.[58]

The U.S. Department of Labor's National Apprenticeship System promotes apprenticeship programs. More than 460,000 apprentices participate in 28,000 programs, and registered programs can receive federal and state contracts and other assistance.[59] Figure 7.2 lists popular recent apprenticeships.

Informal Learning

Surveys estimate that 70% to 80% of what employees learn about their jobs they learn not through formal training but informally.[60] Training experts use the notation "70/20/10" to summarize the idea that as a rule, 70% of job learning occurs

Figure 7.2

Some Popular Apprenticeships

Source: From www.doleta.gov/oa/apprentices.cfm, accessed July 31, 2017.

The U.S. Department of Labor's Registered Apprenticeship program offers access to more than 1,000 occupations, such as the following:

- Able seaman
- Carpenter
- Chef
- Child care development specialist
- Construction craft laborer
- Dental assistant
- Electrician
- Elevator constructor
- Fire medic
- Law enforcement agent
- Over-the-road truck driver
- Pipefitter

informally on or off the job, 20% reflects social interactions (for instance, among employees on the job), and only 10% is actual formal training.[61] A sampling of what would constitute informal training would include participating in forums, coaching other people, attending conferences, searching the Internet for information, working with customers, job rotation, reading books and journals, playing video games, and watching TV.[62]

Employers can facilitate informal learning. For example, one Siemens plant places tools in cafeteria areas to take advantage of the work-related discussions taking place. Even installing whiteboards with markers can facilitate informal learning. Sun Microsystems implemented an informal online learning tool it called Sun Learning eXchange. It eventually contained more than 5,000 informal learning items/suggestions on topics ranging from sales to technical support.[63] Cheesecake Factory employees use VideoCafé, a YouTube-type platform, to let employees share short videos on job-related topics such as food preparation.

Job Instruction Training

job instruction training (JIT)
Listing each job's basic tasks, along with key points, to provide step-by-step training for employees.

Many jobs (or parts of jobs) consist of a sequence of steps best learned step-by-step. Such step-by-step training is called **job instruction training** (JIT). First, list the job's required steps (let's say for using a mechanical paper cutter), each in its proper sequence. Then list a corresponding "key point" (if any) beside each step. The steps in such a *job instruction training sheet* show trainees what to do, and the key points show how it's to be done—and why.

As an example, the steps UPS teaches new drivers include: Shift into the lowest gear or into park; turn off the ignition; apply the parking brake; release the seatbelt with left hand; open the door; place the key on your ring finger.[64]

Lectures

Lecturing is a quick and simple way to present knowledge to large groups of trainees, as when the sales force needs to learn a new product's features.[65] Here are some guidelines for presenting a lecture:[66]

- Don't start out on the wrong foot, for instance, with an irrelevant joke.
- Speak only about what you know well.
- Give your listeners signals. For instance, if you have a list of items, start by saying something like, "There are four reasons why the sales reports are necessary . . . . The first . . . "
- Use anecdotes and stories to show rather than tell.
- Be alert to your audience. Watch body language for negative signals like fidgeting.
- Maintain eye contact with the audience.
- Make sure everyone can hear. Repeat questions that you get from trainees.
- Leave hands hanging naturally at your sides.
- Talk from notes or PowerPoint slides, rather than from a script.
- Don't give a short overview and then spend a 1-hour presentation going point by point through the material. Break the long talk into a series of 10-minute talks, each with its own introduction. Write brief PowerPoint slides, and spend about a minute on each.[67]

Programmed Learning

programmed learning
A systematic method for teaching job skills, involving presenting questions or facts, allowing the person to respond, and giving the learner immediate feedback on the accuracy of his or her answers.

Programmed learning is a step-by-step, self-learning method that consists of three parts:

1. Presenting questions, facts, or problems to the learner
2. Allowing the person to respond
3. Providing feedback on the accuracy of answers, with instructions on what to do next

Generally, programmed learning presents facts and follow-up questions frame by frame. What the next question is often depends on how the learner answers the previous question. The built-in feedback from the answers provides reinforcement.

Programmed learning reduces training time. It also facilitates learning by letting trainees learn at their own pace, get immediate feedback, and reduce their risk of error. Some argue that trainees do not learn much more from programmed learning than from a textbook. Yet studies generally support programmed learning's effectiveness.[68]

Computerized intelligent tutoring systems take programmed learning one step further. They learn what questions and approaches worked and did not work for the learner and then adjust the instructional sequence to the trainee's unique needs.

Behavior Modeling

Behavior modeling involves (1) showing trainees the right (or "model") way of doing something, (2) letting trainees practice that way, and then (3) giving feedback on the trainees' performance. Behavior modeling training is one of the most widely used, well-researched, and highly regarded psychologically based training interventions.[69] The basic procedure is as follows:

1. **Modeling.** First, trainees watch live or video examples showing models behaving effectively in a problem situation. Thus, the video might show a supervisor effectively disciplining a subordinate, if teaching "how to discipline" is the aim of the training program.
2. **Role-playing.** Next, the trainees get roles to play in a simulated situation; here they are to practice the effective behaviors demonstrated by the models.
3. **Social reinforcement.** The trainer provides reinforcement in the form of praise and constructive feedback.
4. **Transfer of training.** Finally, trainees are encouraged to apply their new skills when they are back on their jobs.

Audiovisual-Based Training and Videoconferencing

Although increasingly replaced by online methods, audiovisual-based training techniques like films, PowerPoint, and audiotapes are still popular.[70] Ford uses videos in its dealer training sessions to simulate problems and reactions to various customer complaints, for example.

Videoconferencing involves delivering programs over broadband lines, the Internet, or satellite. For example, Cisco's Unified Video Conferencing (CUVC) product line combines Cisco group collaboration and decision-making software with videoconferencing, video telephone, and realistic "TelePresence" capabilities.[71]

Vestibule Training

With vestibule training, trainees learn on the actual or simulated equipment but are trained off the job (perhaps in a separate room or *vestibule*). Vestibule training is necessary when it's too costly or dangerous to train employees on the job. Putting new assembly-line workers right to work could slow production, for instance, and when safety is a concern—as with pilots—simulated training may be the only practical alternative. Thus UPS uses a life-size learning lab to provide a 40-hour, 5-day realistic training program for driver candidates.[72]

Electronic Performance Support Systems (EPSS)

Electronic performance support systems (EPSS) are computerized tools and displays that automate training, documentation, and phone support.[73] When you contact a Dell service rep, he or she is probably asking questions prompted by an EPSS; it takes you both, step-by-step, through an analytical sequence. Without the EPSS, Dell would have to train its service reps to memorize an unrealistically large number of solutions. Aetna Insurance cut its 13-week instructor-led training course for new call center employees by about two weeks by providing the employees with performance support tools.[74]

job aid
A set of instructions, diagrams, or similar methods available at the job site to guide the worker.

Performance support systems are modern job aids. **Job aids** are sets of instructions, diagrams, or similar methods available at the job site to guide the worker.[75] Job aids work particularly well on complex jobs that require multiple steps, or where it's dangerous to forget a step. For example, airline pilots use job aids (a checklist of things to do prior to takeoff).

Computer-Based Training (CBT)

Computer-based training uses interactive computer-based systems to increase knowledge or skills. For example, employers use CBT to teach employees safe methods for avoiding falls. The system lets trainees replay the lessons and answer questions and is especially effective when paired with actual practice under a trainer.[76]

Computer-based training is increasingly realistic. For example, *interactive multimedia training* integrates text, video, graphics, photos, animation, and sound to create a complex training environment with which the trainee interacts.[77] In training a physician, for instance, such systems let medical students take a hypothetical patient's medical history, conduct an examination, and analyze lab tests. The students can then interpret the sounds and make a diagnosis.

Simulated Learning and Gaming

"Simulated learning" means different things to different people. A survey asked training professionals what experiences qualified as simulated learning experiences. Answers included things like "virtual reality-type games," "step-by-step animated guide," "scenarios with questions and decision trees overlaying animation," and "online role-play with photos and videos."[78]

The U.S. Armed Forces use simulation-based training programs. For example, the army developed video game–type training programs called Full-Spectrum Command and Full-Spectrum Warrior for training troops in urban warfare. They offer realistic "you are there" features and cultivate real-time leadership and decision-making skills.[79]

Many employers use computerized simulations (sometimes called *interactive learning*) to inject realism into their training. Orlando-based Environmental Tectonics Corporation created an Advanced Disaster Management simulation for emergency medical response trainees. One simulated scenario involves a plane crash. So realistic that it's "unsettling," trainees including firefighters and airport officials respond to the simulated crash's sights and sounds via pointing devices and radios.[80] The Cheesecake Factory uses a simulation that shows employees how to build the "perfect hamburger."[81]

Specialist multimedia software houses such as Graphic Media of Portland, Oregon, produce much of the content for these programs. They produce both custom titles and generic programs such as a $999 package for teaching workplace safety.

Virtual reality (VR) puts the trainee in an artificial three-dimensional environment that simulates events and situations experienced on the job.[82] Sensory devices transmit how the trainee is responding to the computer, and the trainee "sees, feels and hears" what is going on, assisted by special goggles and sensory devices.[83] Several National Football League teams use VR to train their quarterbacks in going through plays, and thousands of students have taken virtual field trips via Google's VR pioneer expeditions program.[84] Facebook's purchase of virtual reality glasses maker Oculus VR Inc. highlights virtual reality's growing potential.[85]

Yet training games don't have to be complicated. For example, the trainers at Korea Ginseng Corporation (a leader in the world health-food market) wrote games accessible through app interfaces. Each round of each game is comprised of five multiple-choice quizzes. The more answers the employees get right and the

Virtual reality puts the trainee in an artificial three-dimensional environment that simulates events and situations experienced on the job.
Source: Egor Kotenko/123RF.

quicker they give their answers, the more points they earn. Thus the trainee/players compete against each other, with the top trainees profiled publicly with their names and pictures.[86]

Online/Internet-Based Training

Most employers are moving from classroom-based to online-based learning because of the efficiencies involved. For example, until recently, Utah-based Clearlink's employee training was classroom based. Sales agents often returned to the field without being tested on what they learned, and in general the training was less than effective. Clearlink switched to online learning. Its trainers correspondingly turned from classroom training to creating new online e-learning courses and monitoring training results. The agents were relieved to be able to get their training on demand without interfering with their daily duties. The company estimates it saved almost $800,000 in one recent year due to digitizing their training program.[87]

Employers use online learning to deliver almost all the types of training we've discussed to this point. For example, China's state-owned postal service, China Post, created a new center to manage its online training college, which now delivers about 9,000 hours of training annually, offering over 600 programs.[88] ADP trains new salespeople online, using a Blackboard learning management system similar to one used by college students.[89]

Learning management systems (LMS), often used in online learning, are special software tools that support Internet training by helping employers identify training needs and schedule, deliver, assess, and manage the online training itself. (Blackboard and WebCT are two familiar college-oriented learning management systems.) General Motors uses an LMS to help its dealers in Africa and the Middle East deliver training. The Internet-based LMS includes a course catalog, supervisor-approved self-enrollment, and pre- and post-course tests. The system then automatically schedules the individual's training.[90] Many employers integrate the LMS with the company's talent management systems. That way, skills inventories and succession plans automatically update as employees complete their training.[91]

Online learning doesn't necessarily teach individuals faster or better.[92] But, of course, the need to teach large numbers of students remotely, or to enable trainees to study at their leisure, often makes e-learning attractive.[93] Some employers opt for *blended learning*. Here, trainees use multiple delivery methods (such as manuals, in-class lectures, and online seminars or "webinars") to learn the material.[94] For example, the tool manufacturer Stihl offers prospective tool and die makers online learning combined with hands-on technical training classes.[95] We'll look at some online learning elements.

Learning Portals A *learning portal* is a section of an employer's website that offers employees online access to training courses. Many employers arrange to have an online training vendor make its courses available via the employer's portal. Most often, the employer contracts with application service providers (ASPs). When employees go to their firm's learning portal, they actually access the menu of training courses that the ASP offers for the employer. A Google search for e-learning companies reveals many, such as SkillSoft, Plateau Systems, and Employment Law Learning Technologies.

The Virtual Classroom A **virtual classroom** uses collaboration software to enable multiple remote learners, using their PCs, tablets, or laptops, to participate remotely in live audio and visual discussions, communicate via written text, and learn via content such as PowerPoint slides.

The virtual classroom combines the best of Internet-based learning offered by systems like Blackboard and WebCT with live video and audio. Thus, Elluminate Live! lets learners view video, collaborate with colleagues, and learn with shared PowerPoint slides.[96]

Mobile and Microlearning *Mobile learning* (or "on-demand learning") means delivering learning content, on the learner's demand, via mobile devices like cell phones, laptops, and tablets, wherever and whenever the learner has the time and desire to access it.[97] For example, trainees can take full online courses using dominKnow's (www.dominknow.com) iPhone-optimized Touch Learning Center Portal.[98]

Most large employers distribute internal communications and training via mobile devices.[99] Employees at CompuCom Systems Inc. access instruction manuals through mobile devices; the company subsidizes employee purchases of smart phones or tablets to facilitate this. J.P. Morgan encourages employees to use instant messaging, for instance, to update colleagues about new products quickly. Natural user interfaces such as Apple's Siri facilitate such training.[100]

Employers use mobile learning to deliver training and downloads on topics "from how to close an important sales deal to optimizing organizational change."[101] IBM uses mobile learning to deliver just-in-time information (for instance, about new product features) to its sales force. To facilitate this, its training department often breaks up, say, an hour program into easier-to-use "micro" 10-minute pieces. Such "micro learning" training requires building each learning unit around essential information by "stripping down" the message to its essentials.[102] Also, graphics and videos improve the learning experience.

Employers also use social media, such as LinkedIn, Facebook, and Twitter, and virtual worlds like Second Life to communicate company news and messages and to provide training.[103] For example, British Petroleum (BP) uses Second Life to train new gas station employees. The aim here is to show new gas station employees how to use the safety features of gasoline storage tanks. BP built three-dimensional renderings of the tank systems in Second Life. Trainees use these to "see" underground and observe the effects of using the safety devices.[104]

Web 2.0 learning is learning that utilizes online technologies such as social networks, virtual worlds (such as Second Life), and systems that blend synchronous and asynchronous delivery with blogs, chat rooms, bookmark sharing, and tools such as 3-D simulations.[105] *Collaborative peer forums* require teams of six to eight trainees to virtually "sell" their sales problem and solution to an executive.[106] *Scenario-based e-learning* involves inserting realistic problems or work scenarios that small groups of trainees can discuss into their e-learning lessons. One e-learning vendor includes realistic tasks for employees to address, while others include business cases.[107]

■ HR and the Gig Economy[108]

An Example: On-Demand Microlearning at Uber

If you think that all those Uber drivers simply get hired and go on the road with no formal training, you're wrong. There are hundreds of things those drivers must know about driving for Uber—from how to use the Uber app and driving systems, to how to greet and deal with customers—and Uber needs to train over 30,000 new drivers every week. How do they do it?

Uber's training challenge is actually similar to that of most firms that rely on gig workers. The main problems are (1) the trainees aren't permanent employees but largely just "passing through," so what you invest in their training must be carefully controlled; and (2) the workers are all working on their own schedules, so training must be available when each worker wants it, on demand.

So, the short answer to "how does Uber do it" is that driver training is online, on-demand, and delivered in microparcels. Uber uses a learning management system called MindFlash, which offers its clients around the globe thousands of courses, often focused on training gig workers like Uber's.[109] Among other benefits, the MindFlash system provides real-time reporting of trainees' results, so Uber knows if a driver is ready to go to work.

Building gig-friendly training programs like Uber's has several characteristics. The first and perhaps most crucial is that everyone involved—management, HR, and especially the gig workers themselves—submit detailed "blueprints" of the workers' daily activities, from which workers' (in this case drivers') duties, skills and knowledge, and required training can be ascertained. Then, the courses are split into short digestible microcourses, stored on the vendor's cloud, and delivered on demand to each worker's mobile device when he or she wants it.

Lifelong and Literacy Training Techniques

lifelong learning
Provides employees with continuing learning experiences over their tenure with the firm, with the aims of ensuring they have the opportunity to learn the skills they need to do their jobs and to expand their occupational horizons.

Lifelong learning means providing employees with continuing learning experiences over their tenure with the firm, with the aim of ensuring they have the opportunity to learn the skills they need to do their jobs and to expand their horizons. With people increasingly having to shift jobs and careers, such learning is, for many, a necessity.

Lifelong learning may range from basic remedial skills (for instance, English as a second language) to college. For example, one senior waiter at the Rhapsody restaurant in Chicago received his undergraduate degree and began work toward a master of social work using the lifelong learning account (LiLA) program his employer offers. Employers and employees contribute to LiLA plans (without the tax advantages of 401(k) plans), and the employee can use these funds to better himself or herself.[110]

Literacy Training By one estimate, about one in seven workers can't read their employers' manuals.[111] Yet today's emphasis on teamwork and quality requires that employees read, write, and understand numbers.[112]

Employers often turn to private training firms or community colleges to provide the requisite education. Another simple approach is to have supervisors teach basic skills by giving employees writing and speaking exercises.[113] For example, if an employee needs to use a manual to find out how to change a part, teach that person how to use the index to locate the relevant section. Some call in teachers from a local high school.

Diversity Training

As noted in Chapter 2, diversity training aims to improve cross-cultural sensitivity, with the goal of fostering more harmonious working relationships among a firm's employees. It typically includes improving interpersonal skills, understanding and valuing cultural differences, indoctrinating new workers into the U.S. work ethic, improving English proficiency and basic math skills, and improving bilingual skills for English-speaking employees.[114] For example, IBM has online programs to educate managers regarding diversity, inclusive leadership, and sexual harassment. Training materials include interactive learning modules that enable trainees to practice what they've learned, testimonials from IBM executives, and self-assessment tools.[115]

Most employers opt for an off-the-shelf diversity training program such as Just Be F.A.I.R. from VisionPoint Productions. It includes streaming video, a facilitator discussion guide, participant materials and workbook, and PowerPoint slides. Video vignettes illustrate such things as the potential pitfalls of stereotyping people.[116] The accompanying feature illustrates diversity training.

■ HR in Practice

Diversity Training at ABC Virtual Communications, Inc.

ABC Virtual Communications, Inc. (**www.abcv.com/**) is a provider in Iowa of customized software development and other solutions. It requires many software engineers. Recruiting such employees is difficult anywhere, but particularly in Iowa, where many recent graduates move away.

ABC therefore recruits foreign-born individuals. However, ABC needed a diversity training program that could turn these new employees—and the firm's current employees—into productive colleagues.

New ABC employees, representing 14 countries and 45 ethnic groups, take a mandatory 8-hour orientation overview for new employees on the American Workplace. All ABC employees take an "effective communications" training course. Conversational English and accent reduction classes for employees and their families are available through Rosetta Stone language learning software. The company also partnered with a local community college to create specialized classes for individual needs. At ABC Virtual, a globally diverse workforce was the key to improved performance, and diversity training helps them manage their diversity.[117]

✪ Talk About It – **1**

If your professor has chosen to assign this, go to **www.pearson.com/mylab/management** to discuss the following: List five competencies that you believe such a diversity program should cultivate.

Team Training

Teamwork does not always come naturally. Companies devote many hours to training new employees to listen to each other and to cooperate. For example, a Baltimore Coca-Cola plant suffered from high turnover and absenteeism.[118] The new plant manager decided to address these problems by reorganizing around teams. He then used team training to support and improve team functioning.

Team training focused on technical, interpersonal, and team management issues. In terms of *technical training*, management encouraged team employees to learn each other's jobs, to encourage flexible team assignments. **Cross training**

cross training

Training employees to do different tasks or jobs than their own; doing so facilitates flexibility and job rotation.

means training employees to do different tasks or jobs than their own; doing so facilitates flexibility, as when you expect team members to occasionally share jobs.

Interpersonal problems often undermine team functioning. Team training in this plant therefore included *interpersonal skills* training such as in listening, handling conflict, and negotiating.[119] Effective teams also require team management skills, for instance in problem solving, consensus decision making, and team leadership, and the teams received such training as well.

Many employers use team training to build stronger management teams. The aim is usually to foster trust and cooperation among trainees. One chief financial officer helped organize a retreat for 73 of his firm's financial employees. As he said, "They are very individualistic in their approach to their work . . . . What I have been trying to do is get them to see the power of acting more like a team."[120]

Some simple approaches to team building work fine. For example, Google supports on-site cafeterias, sometimes with free food. Employees tend to eat together and through their interactions learn new ideas and build stronger relationships.[121]

The accompanying Management Skills feature shows how managers can create their own training programs.

BUILDING YOUR MANAGEMENT SKILLS:
HR Tools for Line Managers and Small Businesses

While it would be nice if supervisors in even the largest firms could expect their firms to provide packaged training programs to train the new people they hire, the fact is that many times they cannot. However, you still have many options.

Create Your Own Five-Step Training Program

Remember ADDIE—analyze (is training the problem?), design (including learning objectives, and motivating the trainee), develop (what sources and methods will we use?), implement (train the person), and evaluate.

As a rule, start by *setting training objectives*—be specific about what your employee should be able to do after training. Write a job description—list of the job's duties—if not already available. Write (see Table 7.1, page 203) a *task analysis record form* showing the steps in each of the employee's tasks. Write a *job instruction training form*; here list a key point (such as "carefully read scale") for each step (such as "set cutting distance"). Finally, compile all these in a *training manual*. Also include an introduction to the job and an explanation of how the job relates to other jobs in the company.

Use Private Vendors

The small business owner can tap hundreds of suppliers of prepackaged training solutions. These range from self-study programs from the American Management Association (www.amanet.org) and SHRM (www.shrm.org), to specialized programs. For example, the employer might arrange with www.puresafety .com to have its employees take occupational safety courses. SkillSoft.com is another example.[122] Its courses include software development, business strategy and operations, professional effectiveness, and desktop computer skills. The buyer's guide from the Association for Talent Development (www.td.org/) is a good place to start to find a vendor (check under "Professional Resources").[123]

Check the SBA

The government's Small Business Administration (see www.SBA.gov/) provides a virtual campus that offers online courses, workshops, publications, and learning tools aimed toward supporting entrepreneurs.[124] For example, the small business owner can link under "Small Business Planner" to "Writing Effective Job

Continued

Descriptions," and "The Interview Process: How to Select the Right Person."[125] See their site map at www.sba.gov/sitemap for examples of what they offer.

Check NAM

The National Association of Manufacturers (NAM) is the largest industrial trade organization in the United States. It represents about 14,000 member manufacturers, including 10,000 small and midsized companies.

NAM helps employees maintain and upgrade their work skills and continue their professional development. It offers courses and a skills certification process.[126] There are no long-term contracts to sign. Employers simply pay about $10–$30 per course taken by each employee. The catalog includes OSHA, quality, and technical training as well as courses in areas like customer service.

Facilitate Informal Training

Training expert Stephen Covey says managers can provide some training without establishing formal training programs. His suggestions include the following:[127]

- Offer to cover the tuition for special classes.
- Identify online training opportunities.
- Provide a library of CDs and DVDs for systematic, disciplined learning during commute times.
- Encourage the sharing of best practices among associates.
- When possible, support sending employees to special seminars and association meetings for learning and networking.
- Create a learning ethic by having everyone teach each other what they are learning.

⭐ Talk About It – **2**

If your professor has chosen to assign this, go to **www.pearson.com/mylab/ management** to discuss the following question. What would you suggest now that Alex, from this chapter's opening scenario, do to address the problem in his new restaurant?

LEARNING OBJECTIVE 5
List and briefly discuss four management development methods.

management development
Any attempt to improve current or future management performance by imparting knowledge, changing attitudes, or increasing skills.

Implementing Management Development Programs

Management development is any attempt to improve managerial performance by imparting knowledge, changing attitudes, or increasing skills. It includes in-house programs like courses, coaching, and rotational assignments; professional programs like those from SHRM; online programs from various sources; and university executive MBAs.

Management development is important. For one thing, promotion from within is a major source of management talent, and virtually all promoted managers require some development to prepare for their new jobs. Furthermore, management development facilitates organizational continuity by preparing employees and current managers to smoothly assume higher level positions.

KNOWLEDGE BASE

Strategy's Role in Management Development

Management development programs should reflect the firm's strategic plans.[128] For example, strategies to enter new businesses or expand overseas mean the employer will need managers with the skills to manage these new businesses. Management development programs then impart the knowledge, attitudes, and skills these managers will need to do their jobs.[129]

Some management development programs are companywide and involve all or most new (or potential) managers. Thus, new MBAs may join GE's management development program and rotate through various assignments and educational experiences. The firm may then slot superior candidates onto a "fast track," a development program that prepares them more quickly for senior-level commands.

Other development programs aim to fill specific top positions, such as CEO. For example, GE will spend years developing, testing, and watching potential replacements for its CEO.

Succession Planning

succession planning

The ongoing process of systematically identifying, assessing, and developing organizational leadership to enhance performance.

Management development is often part of the employer's *succession planning process*.[130] **Succession planning** involves developing workforce plans for the company's top positions; it is the ongoing process of systematically identifying, assessing, and developing organizational leadership to enhance performance.[131]

Knowing who is next in line for the firm's top executive positions and having a process in place to develop and select top executives are crucial.[132] First, an organization projection is made.[133] Here, based on the company's strategic and business plans, top management and the human resource director identify the company's future key position needs. The employer anticipates its management needs based on strategic factors like business expansion. Next HR and management review the firm's management skills inventory to identify the management talent now employed.[134] These inventories, you may recall, contain data on things like education and work experience, career preferences, and performance appraisals. At this stage, management replacement charts may be drawn (see Figure 5.4, page 125). These summarize potential candidates for each management slot, as well as each person's development needs. As in Figure 5.4, the development needs for a future division vice president might include activities like job rotation (to obtain more experience in the firm's finance and production division) and executive development programs (to provide training and strategic planning). At this stage, management may decide to recruit one or more outside candidates as well.

Management then turns to providing candidates with the actual developmental experiences. These may include internal training and cross-functional experiences, job rotation, external training, and global/regional assignments.[135]

Finally, succession planning involves assessing all the candidates and selecting those who will actually fill the key positions.[136]

Improving Performance Through HRIS

Succession Systems At Dole Foods, the new president's strategy involved improving financial performance by reducing redundancies and centralizing certain activities, including succession planning.[137] Technology helped Dole do this. Dole contracted with application system providers (ASPs) to handle things like payroll management.[138] For succession management, Dole chose software from Pilat. Pilat keeps all data on its own servers. Dole's managers access the program online using a password. They fill out online résumés for themselves, including career interests, and note special considerations such as geographic restrictions.

The managers also assess themselves on four competencies. Once the manager provides his or her input, the program notifies that manager's boss, who assesses his or her subordinate and indicates whether the person is promotable. This assessment and the online résumés then go automatically to the division head and the divisional HR director. Dole's senior vice president for human resources then uses the information to create career development plans for each manager, including seminars and other programs.

Candidate Assessment and the Nine-Box Grid How do employers choose whom to send through expensive development programs? The assessment center (explained on pages 165–166) is one option.[139]

The Nine-Box Grid is another. It shows *Potential* from low to medium to high on the vertical axis, and *Performance* from low to medium to high across the bottom—a total of nine possible boxes.

The grid can facilitate choosing development candidates. At the extremes, low potentials/low performers would not warrant development, and high potential/high performance stars most assuredly would. Most employers focus their development resources on high performer/high potential stars and secondarily on those rated high potential/moderate performer, or high performer/moderate potential.[140]

We'll look next at some popular management development activities.

Managerial On-the-Job Training

Managerial on-the-job training methods include job rotation, the coaching/understudy approach, and action learning.

job rotation

A management training technique that involves moving a trainee from department to department to broaden his or her experience and to identify strong and weak points.

Job Rotation Job rotation means moving managers among company units to broaden their understanding of the business and to test their abilities. At luxury brand companies like LVMH (which owns Louis Vuitton), rotating employees among luxury brands gives employees what two experts call "extraordinarily rich learning opportunities."[141]

Whether the trainee is a recent college graduate or a senior manager being groomed for further promotion, rotation has several benefits. In addition to exposing the manager to more functions, job rotation helps avoid stagnation by introducing new points of view in each department. It also helps pinpoint the trainee's strong and weak points. Periodic job changing can also improve interdepartmental cooperation, as managers become more understanding of each other's problems. The accompanying HR Practices Around the Globe illustrates this.

◼ HR Practices Around the Globe

Global Job Rotation

At firms like Shell and BP, rotating managers globally is a means through which the firms maintain their flexibility and responsiveness even as they grow to enormous size.

The advantage of global job rotation (rotating managers from, say, Sweden to New York, and from New York to Japan) is that it builds a network of informal ties that ensures superior cross-border communication and mutual understanding as well as tight interunit coordination and control.

Improved communication and understanding stem from the personal relationships forged as managers work in the firm's various locations. These activities can also enhance organizational control. When employees from the firm's global locations are rotated or brought together at, say, Europe's INSEAD for a management-training program, the aim is more than just teaching basic skills. By creating shared values and a consistent view of the firm and its goals, management development activities like these can facilitate communication and ensure that through a sense of shared values and purpose the firm's policies are followed, even with a minimum reliance on more traditional forms of control.[142]

⭐ Talk About It – 3

If your professor has chosen to assign this, go to **www.pearson.com/mylab/management** to discuss the following: Using websites such as **www.sony.net** (click Careers) and **www.mckinsey.com** (insert *how multinationals can attract the talent they need* into their search box), discuss examples of how multinational companies use job rotation and other means to develop their managers.

Coaching/Understudy Approach Here the trainee works directly with a senior manager or with the person he or she is to replace. Normally, the understudy relieves the executive of certain responsibilities, giving the trainee a chance to learn the job.

action learning
A training technique by which management trainees are allowed to work full-time analyzing and solving problems in other departments.

Action Learning **Action learning** programs give managers released time to work analyzing and solving problems in departments other than their own. It is reportedly the fastest-growing leadership development technique today, used by companies ranging from Wells Fargo to Boeing.[143]

Its basics include carefully selected teams of 5 to 25 members, assigning the teams' real-world business problems that extend beyond their usual areas of expertise, and structured learning through coaching and feedback. The employer's senior managers usually choose the projects and decide whether to accept the teams' recommendations.[144] For example, Pacific Gas & Electric Company's (PG&E) Action-Forum Process has three phases:

1. A six- to eight-week *framework* phase, during which the team defines and collects data on an issue;
2. The *action forum*—two to three days at PG&E's learning center, discussing the issue and developing action-plan recommendations; and
3. *Accountability sessions*, where the teams meet with the leadership group at monthly intervals to review progress.

Stretch Assignments Stretch assignments are assignments that "push employees beyond their comfort zone," placing them in jobs and assignments different from and more demanding than those to which they are accustomed.[145] The critical issue is to understand the employee's capabilities: the stretch assignment should be challenging but not overwhelming.

Off-the-Job Management Training and Development Techniques

There are also many off-the-job techniques for training and developing managers.

case study method
A development method in which the manager is presented with a written description of an organizational problem to diagnose and solve.

The Case Study Method As most everyone knows, the **case study method** has trainees solve realistic problems after studying written or video case descriptions. The person then analyzes the case, diagnoses the problem, and presents his or her findings and solutions in a discussion with other trainees.[146]

Integrated case scenarios create long-term, comprehensive case situations. For example, one FBI Academy integrated case scenario starts with "a concerned citizen's telephone call and ends 14 weeks later with a simulated trial. In between is the stuff of a genuine investigation . . . ." Scriptwriters (often employees in the employer's training group) write the scripts. The scripts include background stories, detailed personnel histories, and role-playing instructions; their aim is to develop specific skills, such as interviewing witnesses.[147]

management games
A development technique in which teams of managers compete by making computerized decisions regarding realistic but simulated situations.

Management Games Computerized **management games** enable trainees to learn by making realistic decisions in simulated situations. For example, *Interpret* is a team exercise that "explores team communication, the management of information and the planning and implementation of a strategy. It raises management trainees' communication skills . . . and improves planning and problem-solving skills."[148] Each team might have to decide how much to spend on advertising, how much to produce, and how much inventory to maintain.

Gamification has many benefits. People learn best by being involved, and games gain such involvement. They also help trainees develop their problem-solving skills, and to focus attention on planning rather than just putting out fires. They develop leadership skills and foster cooperation and teamwork. Gamification

Computerized management games enable trainees to learn by making realistic decisions in simulated situations.
Source: Tom Merton/Getty Images.

also reportedly improves learning, engagement, and morale and is fairly easy to achieve. For instance, employers inject point systems, badges, and leaderboards into the training.[149]

Outside Seminars   Numerous companies and universities offer online and traditional classroom management development seminars and conferences. The selection of one- to three-day training programs offered by the American Management Association illustrates what's available. Recently, for instance, their offerings ranged from "developing your emotional intelligence" to "assertiveness training," "assertiveness training for managers," "assertiveness training for women in business," "dynamic listening skills for successful communication," and "fundamentals of cost accounting."[150] Specialized groups, such as SHRM, provide specialized seminars for their profession's members.[151]

University-Related Programs   Many universities provide executive education and continuing education programs in leadership, supervision, and the like. These can range from one- to four-day programs to executive development programs lasting one to four months.

The Advanced Management Program of Harvard's Graduate School of Business Administration illustrates this.[152] In another such program, Hasbro wanted to improve its executives' creativity skills. Dartmouth University's Amos Tuck Business School provided a "custom approach to designing a program that would be built from the ground up to suit Hasbro's specific needs."[153]

role-playing
A training technique in which trainees act out parts in a realistic management situation.

Role-Playing   The aim of **role-playing** is to create a realistic situation and then have the trainees assume the parts (or roles) of specific persons in that situation. Each trainee gets a role, such as:

> You are the head of a crew of telephone maintenance workers, each of whom drives a small service truck to and from the various jobs. Every so often you get a new truck to exchange for an old one, and you have the problem of deciding to which of your crew members you should give the new truck. Often there are hard feelings, so you have a tough time being fair.[154]

When combined with the general instructions and other roles, role-playing can trigger spirited discussions among the trainees. The aim is to develop trainees' skills in areas like leadership and delegating. For example, a supervisor could experiment with both a considerate and an autocratic leadership style, whereas in the real world this isn't so easy.

in-house development center

A company-based method for exposing prospective managers to realistic exercises to develop improved management skills.

Corporate Universities Many firms, particularly larger ones, establish **in-house development centers** (often called *corporate universities*). GE, Caterpillar, and IBM are examples. Employers may collaborate with academic institutions, and with training and development program providers and Internet-based educational portals, to create packages of programs and materials for their centers.[155] Many employers offer virtual—rather than bricks-and-mortar—corporate university program and coursework services.

executive coach

An outside consultant who questions the executive's associates to identify the executive's strengths and weaknesses, and then counsels the executive so he or she can capitalize on those strengths and overcome the weaknesses.

Executive Coaches Many firms retain executive coaches to help develop their top managers' effectiveness. An **executive coach** is an outside consultant who questions the executive's boss, peers, subordinates, and (sometimes) family to identify the executive's strengths and weaknesses and to counsel the executive so he or she can capitalize on those strengths and overcome the weaknesses.[156] Executive coaching can cost $50,000 per executive. Experts recommend using formal assessments prior to coaching, to uncover strengths and weaknesses and to provide more focused coaching.[157]

The coaching field is unregulated, so managers should do their due diligence. Check references, and consult the International Coach Federation, a trade group.

The SHRM Learning System The Society for Human Resource Management (SHRM) encourages HR professionals to qualify for certification by taking examinations. The society offers several preparatory training programs (for instance go to www.shrm.org/, and then click Education). These include self-study, e-learning, and a college/university option that includes classroom interaction with instructors and other learners.[158]

Leadership Development at GE

General Electric is known for its success in developing its executive talent. Their current mix of executive development programs illustrates what they offer:[159]

Leadership programs: These multiyear training programs rotate about 3,000 employees per year through various functions with the aim of enabling people to run a large GE business.

Session C: This is GE's intense multilevel performance appraisal process. The CEO personally reviews GE's top 625 officers every year.

Crotonville: This is GE's corporate training campus in New York and offers a mix of conventional classroom learning and team-based training and cultural trips.

Boca Raton: At this annual meeting of GE's top 625 officers, they network, share their best ideas, and get to understand the company's strategy for the coming year.

The next big thing: Whether it's productivity and quality improvement through "Six Sigma" or "innovation," GE focuses its employees on central themes or initiatives.

Monthly dinners: GE's CEO meets periodically at dinners and breakfasts to learn more about his top executives and to "strengthen his connections with his top team."[160]

Managing Organizational Change Programs

With firms from AT&T and Comcast to Barnes & Noble and Macy's being disrupted by digital competitors, reorganizations are increasingly familiar, but often fail. McKinsey and Company surveyed 1,800 executives to identify why reorganizations fail. Top reasons included *employees resisting the changes, insufficient resources devoted to the effort, individual productivity declining as employees become distracted, leaders resisting the changes,* and *the organization chart changes but the people are still working the same.*[161]

Often, the hardest part is overcoming employee resistance. Individuals, groups, and even entire organizations tend to resist change because they are accustomed to the usual way of doing things or because of perceived threats to their influence, for instance.[162] To deal with such intransigence, some experts suggest that the manager use a process as in the accompanying Management Skills feature to implement the change.[163]

Using Organizational Development

Beyond this process, there are other ways to reduce resistance. Among the many suggestions are that managers impose rewards or sanctions that guide employee behaviors, explain why the change is needed, negotiate with employees, give inspirational speeches, or ask employees to help design the change.[164] Organizational development (OD) taps into the latter. **Organizational development** is a change process through which employees formulate the change that's required and

organizational development
A special approach to organizational change in which employees themselves formulate and implement the change that's required.

BUILDING YOUR MANAGEMENT SKILLS:
How to Bring About a Change at Work

To bring about a desired organizational change at work:

1. **Establish a sense of urgency.** Create a sense of urgency. For example, present employees with a (fictitious) analyst's report describing the firm's imminent demise.
2. **Mobilize commitment** through joint diagnoses of problems. Create a task force to diagnose the problems facing the department or the company. This can help to produce a shared understanding of what they can and must improve.
3. **Create a guiding coalition.** It's never easy to implement big changes alone. Therefore, create a "guiding coalition" of influential people. They'll act as missionaries and implementers.
4. **Develop and communicate a shared vision** of what you see coming from the change. Keep the vision simple (for example, "We will be faster than anyone at satisfying customer needs."), and lead by example.[165]
5. **Help employees make the change.** Eliminate impediments. For example, do current policies or procedures make it difficult to act? Do intransigent managers discourage employees from acting?
6. **Aim first for attainable short-term accomplishments.** Use the credibility from these to make additional changes.[166]
7. **Reinforce the new ways of doing things** with changes to the company's systems and procedures. For example, use new appraisal systems and incentives to reinforce the desired new behaviors.
8. **Monitor and assess progress.** In brief, this involves comparing where the company or department is with where it should be.

implement it, often with the assistance of trained consultants. OD has several distinguishing characteristics:

1. It usually involves *action research*, which means collecting data about a group, department, or organization, and feeding the information back to the employees so they can analyze it and develop hypotheses about what the problems might be.
2. It applies behavioral science knowledge to improve the organization's effectiveness.
3. It changes the organization in a particular direction—toward empowerment, improved problem solving, responsiveness, quality of work, and effectiveness.

For example, according to experts French and Bell, one OD method, *team-building meetings*, begins with the consultant interviewing each of the group members and the leader before the meeting.[167] They are asked what their problems are, how they think the group functions, and what obstacles are keeping the group from performing better. The consultant then categorizes the interview data into themes (such as "inadequate communications") and presents the themes to the group at the start of the meeting. The group ranks the themes in terms of importance, and the most important ones become the agenda for the meeting. The group then explores and discusses the issues, examines the underlying causes of the problems, and begins devising solutions.

Survey research is another OD option. It requires having employees throughout the organization complete attitude surveys. The facilitator then uses those data as a basis for problem analysis and action planning. Surveys are a convenient way to unfreeze a company's management and employees. They provide a comparative, graphic illustration of the fact that the organization does have problems to solve.[168]

Evaluating the Training Effort

Two experts contend that after spending about $560 billion on training in one recent year, employers are getting a poor return on their investment, because it "doesn't lead to better organizational performance . . . ."[169] After trainees complete their training (or perhaps at planned intervals during the training), the program should be evaluated to see how well its objectives have been met.

There are two basic issues to address when evaluating training programs. One is the design of the evaluation study and, in particular, whether to use controlled experimentation. The second is, "What should we measure?"

Designing the Study

In deciding how to design the evaluation study, the basic concern is this: How can we be sure that the training caused the results that we're trying to measure? The *time series design* is one option. Here, as in Figure 7.3, you take a series of performance measures before and after the training program. This can provide some insight into the program's effectiveness.[170] However, you can't be sure that the training (rather than, say, a new companywide pay plan) caused any change.

Controlled experimentation is therefore the evaluation gold standard. A controlled experiment uses a training group and a control group that receives no training. Data (for instance, on quantity of sales or quality of service) are obtained both before and after one group is exposed to training and before and after a corresponding period in the control group. This makes it easier to determine the extent to which any change in the training group's performance resulted from the training, rather than from some organizationwide change like a raise in pay. (The pay raise should have affected employees in both groups equally.)[171]

controlled experimentation
Formal methods for testing the effectiveness of a training program, preferably with before-and-after tests and a control group.

Figure 7.3

Using a Time Series Graph to Assess a Training Program's Effects

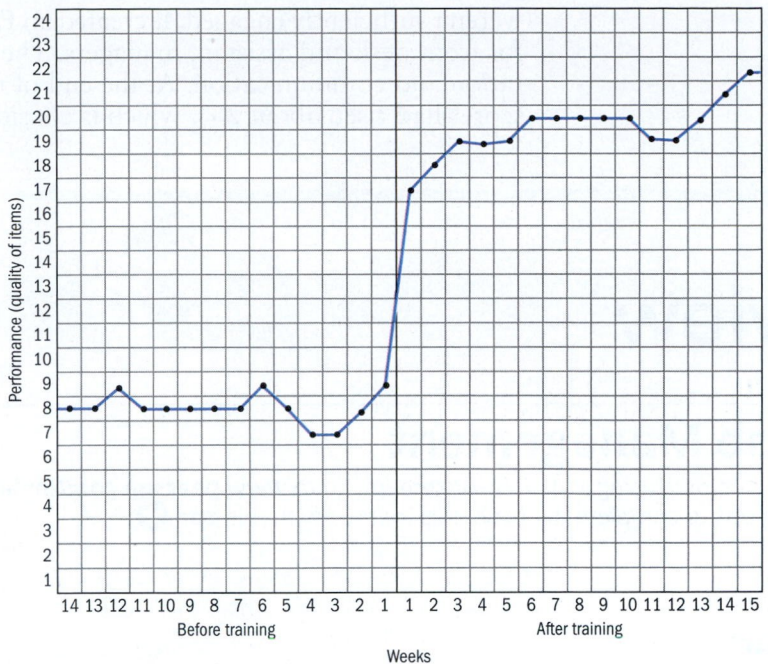

Training Effects to Measure

The widely used Kirkpatrick Model of training evaluation (named for its developer) lists four training effects employers can measure:[172]

1. **Reaction.** Evaluate trainees' reactions to the program. Did they like the program? Did they think it worthwhile?
2. **Learning.** Test the trainees to determine whether they learned the principles, skills, and facts they were supposed to learn.
3. **Behavior.** Ask whether the trainees' on-the-job behavior changed because of the training program. For example, are employees in the store's complaint department more courteous toward disgruntled customers?
4. **Results.** Most important, ask, "What results did we achieve, in terms of the training objectives previously set?" For example, did the number of customer complaints diminish?

Reactions, learning, and behavior are important. But if the training program doesn't produce measurable performance-related results, then it probably hasn't achieved its goals.[173] In one survey of about 500 U.S. organizations, 77% evaluated their training programs by eliciting reactions, 36% evaluated learning, and about 10% to 15% assessed the program's behavior and/or results.[174]

Evaluating these is straightforward. You might assess trainees' *learning* by testing their new knowledge. For *behavioral change,* perhaps assess the effectiveness of a supervisory performance appraisal training program by asking that person's subordinates, "Did your supervisor provide you with examples of good and bad performance when he or she appraised your performance most recently?" Finally, directly assess a training program's *results* by measuring, say, the percentage of phone calls that call center trainees subsequently answered correctly.[175] Sample training evaluation forms are available online, for instance at www.cal.org/caelanetwork/profdev/states/iowa/training-evaluation.pdf. A careful comparison of the training program's costs and benefits can enable the manager to compute the program's return on investment.

A program at MGM Resorts illustrates training evaluation.[176] In the hospitality industry, how likely guests are to return is a crucial metric, and it is measured at MGM by "Net Promoter Scores," or NPS (do past guests promote us?). With MGM's NPS scores not up to par, its training team concluded "guest facing" employees weren't sufficiently engaged. It created an Essentials of Hotel Management Program for front desk and assistant managers. The program emphasized skills like collaboration and communication. At the end of the approximately 1-year program, NPS scores had risen about 2%, which is considered a notable accomplishment.[177]

Review

MyLab Management

If your instructor is using MyLab Management, go to **www.pearson.com/mylab/ management** to complete the problems marked with this icon ⭐.

Summary

1. Getting your new employee on board and up to speed begins with orienting and training him or her. Employee orientation means providing new employees with the information they need to function and helping them start being emotionally attached to the firm. This may simply involve providing them with brief written orientation materials and an employee handbook, but sometimes involves a formal process aimed at instilling in the employee the company's values.

2. There is more to orienting employees than introducing them to their coworkers. Even without a companywide program like Toyota's, use the onboarding opportunity to begin instilling in the new employee the company values and traditions in which you expect the person to become engaged.

3. ADDIE outlines the training process: analyze, develop, design, implement, and evaluate. Before training employees, it's necessary to analyze their training needs and design the training program. In training new employees, employers use task analysis—basically, a detailed study of the job—to determine what skills the job requires. For current employees, performance analysis is required, specifically to verify that there is performance efficiency and to determine if training is the solution. Once you understand the issues, you can design and develop the training program, which entails identifying specific training objectives, clarifying a training budget, and compiling the actual content and technology.

4. Specific training methods include on-the-job training, apprenticeship training, informal learning, job instruction training, lectures, programmed learning, audiovisual-based training, vestibule training, videoconferencing, electronic performance support systems, and computer-based training. Computerized training is increasingly popular, with many packaged programs available. Frequently, programs today are Internet-based, with employees accessing packaged online programs, backed up by learning management systems, through their company's learning portals. Employers also increasingly use mobile learning, for instance, delivering short courses and explanations to employees' iPads.

5. Like all employees, new managers often get on-the-job training, for instance, via job rotation and coaching. In addition, it's usual to supply various off-the-job training and development opportunities—for instance, using the case study method, management games, outside seminars, university-related programs, corporate universities, executive coaches, and (for human resource managers) the SHRM learning system.

6. When facing economic, competitive, or other challenges, managers have to execute organizational change programs. Often, the trickiest part of organizational change is overcoming employees' resistance to it. Steps include establishing a sense of urgency, mobilizing commitment, creating a guiding coalition, developing and communicating a shared vision, helping employees make the change, consolidating gains, reinforcing new ways of doing things, and monitoring and assessing progress. Organizational development involves collecting data about a group and feeding the information back to the employees so they can analyze it and develop solutions.

7. It's important to evaluate the training effort. You can measure reaction, learning, behavior, or results, ideally using a control group that is not exposed to training, in parallel with the group that you're training.

Key Terms

employee orientation 198
training 201
task analysis 202
competency model 202
performance analysis 203
on-the-job training (OJT) 207
apprenticeship training 208
job instruction training (JIT) 209
programmed learning 209
behavior modeling 210
electronic performance support systems (EPSS) 210
job aid 211
virtual classroom 213
Web 2.0 learning 212

lifelong learning 214
cross training 215
management development 217
succession planning 218
job rotation 219
action learning 220
case study method 220
management games 220
role-playing 221
in-house development center 222
executive coach 222
organizational development 223
controlled experimentation 224

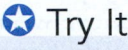 Try It

How would you apply the concepts and skills you learned in this chapter? If your professor has chosen to assign this, go to **www.pearson.com/mylab/management** and complete the Change simulation to find out.

Discussion Questions

7-1. "A well-thought-out orientation program is essential for all new employees, whether they have experience or not." Explain why you agree or disagree with this statement.

7-2. John Santos is an undergraduate business student majoring in accounting. He just failed the first accounting course, Accounting 101. He is understandably upset. How would you use performance analysis to identify what, if any, are John's training needs?

7-3. What are some typical on-the-job training techniques? What do you think are some of the main drawbacks of relying on informal on-the-job training for breaking new employees into their jobs?

7-4. One reason for implementing global training programs is the need to avoid business losses "due to cultural insensitivity." What sort of cultural insensitivity do you think is referred to, and how might that translate into lost business? What sort of training program would you recommend to avoid such cultural insensitivity?

7-5. Describe the pros and cons of five management development methods.

7-6. Do you think job rotation is a good method to use for developing management trainees? Why or why not?

7-7. What is organizational development, and how does it differ from traditional approaches to organizational change?

7-8. List and briefly explain each of the five steps in the training process.

Individual and Group Activities

7-9. You're the supervisor of a group of employees whose task is to assemble disk drives that go into computers. You find that quality is not what it should be and that many of your group's devices have to be brought back and reworked. Your boss says, "You'd better start doing a better job of training your workers."
a. What are some of the staffing factors that could be contributing to this problem?
b. Explain how you would go about assessing whether it is in fact a training problem.

7-10. Choose a task with which you are familiar—mowing the lawn, making a salad, or studying for a test—and develop a job instruction sheet for it.

7-11. Working individually or in groups, develop a short, programmed learning program on the subject "Guidelines for Giving a More Effective Lecture."

7-12. Find a provider of management development seminars. Obtain copies of its recent listings of seminar offerings. At what levels of managers are the offerings aimed? What seem to be the most popular types of development programs? Why do you think that's the case?

7-13. Working individually or in groups, develop several specific examples to illustrate how a professor teaching human resource management could use at least four of the techniques described in this chapter in teaching his or her HR course.

7-14. Working individually or in groups, develop an orientation program for high school graduates entering your university as freshmen.

7-15. For this activity, you will need the documents titled (1) "HRCI PHR® and SPHR® Certification Body of Knowledge," and (2) "About the Society for Human Resource Management (SHRM) Body of Competency & Knowledge® Model and Certification Exams." Your instructor can obtain these two documents from the Pearson Instructor Resource Center and pass them on to you. These two documents list the knowledge someone studying for the HRCI or SHRM certification exam needs to have in each area of human resource management (such as in Strategic Management, and Workforce Planning). In groups of several students, do four things: (1) review the HRCI and/or SHRM documents; (2) identify the material in this chapter that relates to HRCI's or SHRM's required knowledge lists; (3) write four multiple-choice exam questions on this material that you believe would be suitable for inclusion in the HRCI exam and/or the SHRM exam; and, (4) if time permits, have someone from your team post your team's questions in front of the class, so that students in all teams can answer the exam questions created by the other teams.

MyLab Management

If your instructor is using MyLab Management, go to **www.pearson.com/mylab/ management** for Auto-graded writing questions as well as the following Assisted-graded writing questions:

7-16. Explain how you would apply our "motivation points" (pages 205–206) in developing a lecture, say, on orientation and training.

7-17. Your employee is only selling about half the items per week that he or she should be selling. How would you go about determining what the problem is and whether training is the solution?

APPLICATION EXERCISES

HR IN ACTION CASE INCIDENT 1

Reinventing the Wheel at Apex Door Company

Jim Delaney, president of Apex Door, has a problem. No matter how often he tells his employees how to do their jobs, they invariably "decide to do it their way," as he puts it, and arguments ensue between Jim, the employee, and the employee's supervisor. One example is the door-design department, where the designers are expected to work with the architects to design doors that meet the specifications. Although it's not "rocket science," as Jim puts it, the designers invariably make mistakes—such as designing in too much steel, a problem that can cost Apex tens of thousands of wasted dollars, once you consider the number of doors in, say, a 30-story office tower.

The order-processing department is another example. Jim has a very specific and detailed way he wants the order written up, but most of the order clerks don't understand how to use the multipage order form. They simply improvise when it comes to a detailed question such as whether to classify the customer as "industrial" or "commercial."

The current training process is as follows. None of the jobs has a training manual per se, although several have somewhat out-of-date job descriptions. The training for new people is all on the job. Usually, the person leaving the company trains the new person during the one- or two-week overlap period, but if there's no overlap, the new person is trained as well as possible by other employees who have filled in occasionally on the job in the past. The training is the same throughout the company—for machinists, secretaries, assemblers, engineers, and accounting clerks, for example.

Questions

7-18. What do you think of Apex's training process? Could it help to explain why employees "do things their way"? If so, how?

7-19. What role should job descriptions play in training at Apex?

7-20. Explain in detail what you would do to improve the training process at Apex. Make sure to provide specific suggestions.

Source: Copyright © Dr. Gary Dessler.

HR IN ACTION CASE INCIDENT 2

Carter Cleaning Company: The New Training Program

The Carter Cleaning Centers currently have no formal orientation or training policies or procedures, and Jennifer believes this is one reason why the standards to which she and her father would like employees to adhere are generally not followed.

The Carters would prefer that certain practices and procedures be used in dealing with the customers at the front counters. For example, all customers should be greeted with what Jack refers to as a "big hello." Garments they drop off should immediately be inspected for any damage or unusual stains so these can be brought to the customer's attention, lest the customer later return to pick up the garment and erroneously blame the store. The garments are then supposed to be immediately placed together in a nylon sack to separate them from other customers' garments. The ticket also has to be carefully written up, with the customer's name and telephone number and the date precisely and clearly noted on all copies. The counter person is also supposed to take the opportunity to try to sell the customer additional services such as waterproofing, or simply notify the customer that, "Now that people are doing their spring cleaning, we're having a special on drapery cleaning all this month." Finally, as the customer leaves, the counter person is supposed to make a courteous comment like "Have a nice day" or "Drive safely." Each of the other jobs in the stores—pressing, cleaning and spotting, and so forth—similarly contain certain steps, procedures, and most importantly, standards the Carters would prefer to see upheld.

Jennifer thinks the company has had problems because of a lack of adequate employee training and orientation. For example, two new employees became very upset last month when they discovered that they were not paid at the end of the week, on Friday, but instead were paid (as are all Carter employees) on the following Tuesday. The Carters use the extra two days in part to give them time to obtain everyone's hours and compute their pay. The other reason they do it, according to Jack, is that, "Frankly, when we stay a few days behind in paying employees, it helps to ensure that they

at least give us a few days' notice before quitting on us. While we are certainly obligated to pay them anything they earn, we find that psychologically they seem to be less likely to just walk out on us Friday evening and not show up Monday morning if they still haven't gotten their pay from the previous week. This way they at least give us a few days' notice so we can find a replacement."

There are other matters that could be covered during orientation and training, says Jennifer. These include company policy regarding paid holidays, lateness and absences, health benefits (there are none, other than workers' compensation), substance abuse, eating or smoking on the job (both forbidden), and general matters like the maintenance of a clean and safe work area, personal appearance and cleanliness, time sheets, personal telephone calls, and personal e-mail.

Jennifer believes that implementing orientation and training programs would help to ensure that employees know how to do their jobs the right way. And she and her father further believe that it is only when employees understand the right way to do their jobs that there is any hope their jobs will be accomplished the way the Carters want them to be accomplished.

Questions

7-21. Specifically, what should the Carters cover in their new employee orientation program, and how should they convey this information?

7-22. In the HR management course Jennifer took, the book suggested using a job instruction sheet to identify tasks performed by an employee. Should the Carter Cleaning Centers use a form like this for the counter person's job? If so, what should the form look like, say, for a counter person?

7-23. Which specific training techniques should Jennifer use to train her pressers, her cleaner/spotters, her managers, and her counter people? Why should these training techniques be used?

Source: Copyright © Dr. Gary Dessler.

Experiential Exercise

Flying the Friendlier Skies

Purpose: The purpose of this exercise is to give you practice in developing a training program for the job of airline reservation clerk for a major airline.

Required Understanding: You should be fully acquainted with the material in this chapter and should read the following description of an airline reservation clerk's duties:

> Customers contact our airline reservation clerks to obtain flight schedules, prices, and itineraries. The reservation clerks look up the requested information on our airline's online flight schedule systems, which are updated continuously. The reservation clerk must deal courteously and expeditiously with the customer, and be able to find quickly alternative flight arrangements in order to provide the customer with the itinerary that fits his or her needs. Alternative flights and prices must be found quickly, so that the customer is not kept waiting, and so that our reservations operations group maintains its efficiency standards. It is often necessary to look under various routings, since there may be a dozen or more alternative routes between the customer's starting point and destination.

You may assume that we just hired 30 new clerks, and that you must create a three-day training program.

How to Set Up the Exercise/Instructions: Divide the class into teams of five or six students.

Airline reservation clerks obviously need numerous skills to perform their jobs. JetBlue Airlines has asked you to develop quickly the outline of a training program for its new reservation clerks. Please produce the requested outline, making sure to be very specific about what you want to teach the new clerks, and what methods and aids you suggest using to train them.

8

Performance Management and Appraisal Today

MyLab Management

⭐ Improve Your Grade!
When you see this icon, visit **www.pearson.com/mylab/management** for activities that are applied, personalized, and offer immediate feedback.

LEARNING OBJECTIVES

When you finish studying this chapter, you should be able to:

1. Explain the purpose of performance appraisal.
2. Discuss the pros and cons of at least eight traditional performance appraisal methods.
3. Give examples of how to deal with potential appraisal rater error problems.
4. List steps to take in the appraisal interview to improve employee engagement.
5. Explain how you would take a performance management approach to appraisal.

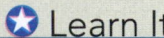 Learn It

If your professor has chosen to assign this, go to **www.pearson.com/mylab/management** to see what you should particularly focus on and to take the Chapter 8 Warm Up.

INTRODUCTION

Gladys had only worked for Ocean Engineering for about six months, but she loved her job as a junior engineer. It was therefore with enthusiasm that she sat down with her supervisor, Phyllis, to get and discuss Gladys's first performance appraisal. Unfortunately, the meeting was a disaster. Phyllis came in armed with a long list of errors that Gladys had supposedly made in the past few months. She followed that up by telling Gladys that she wasn't even doing half the things that the job called for. "Overall," said Phyllis, "I'm rating you a 6.5 out of 10," and then she walked out. Gladys sat there stunned.

Source: PeopleImages/Getty Images.

performance appraisal
Any procedure that involves (1) setting work standards; (2) assessing the employee's actual performance relative to the standards; and (3) providing feedback to the employee with the aim of motivating that person to eliminate performance deficiencies or to continue the performance above par.

Basic Concepts in Performance Appraisal

Most companies have some means of appraising their employees' performance. **Performance appraisal** may be defined as any procedure that involves (1) setting work standards; (2) assessing the employee's actual performance relative to the standards; and (3) providing feedback to the employee with the aim of motivating that person to eliminate performance deficiencies or to continue the performance above par. Therefore, while you may equate filling out appraisal forms as in Figure 8.1 with "performance appraisal," appraisal actually involves more. Effective appraisal also requires that the supervisor set performance standards. And it requires that the employee receives the training, feedback, and incentives required to eliminate performance deficiencies.

Few things managers do are fraught with more peril than appraising subordinates' performance. Employees tend to be overly optimistic about what their ratings will be, and they know that their raises, careers, and peace of mind may hinge on how you rate them. As if that's not enough, few appraisal processes are as fair as employers think. Numerous problems (such as bias and rating everyone "average") undermine the process. However, the perils notwithstanding, performance

Figure 8.1

Online Faculty Evaluation Form

Source: Copyright Gary Dessler, PhD.

Instructions: Thoughtful evaluations help the faculty member better understand and improve his or her teaching practices. For each of the following eight items, please assign a score, giving your highest score of <u>7</u> for Outstanding, a score of <u>4</u> for Average, your lowest score of <u>1</u> for Needs Improvement, and an <u>NA</u> if the question is not applicable:

Evaluation Items

_____ 1. The instructor was prepared for his/her lectures.

_____ 2. The course was consistent with the course objectives.

_____ 3. The instructor was fair in how he/she graded me.

_____ 4. The instructor carefully planned and organized this course.

_____ 5. The instructor was available during his/her posted office hours.

_____ 6. The instructor responded to online inquiries in a timely manner.

_____ 7. In terms of knowledge and/or experience, the instructor was competent to teach this course.

_____ 8. Overall how would you rate this course?

appraisal plays a central role in managing human resources. The challenge is to do the appraisal the right way.

Why Appraise Performance?

There are several reasons to appraise subordinates' performance. First, most employers still base pay, promotion, and retention decisions on the employee's appraisal.[1] Second, appraisals play a central role in *performance management*. (We'll see that performance management means continuously ensuring that each employee's performance makes sense in terms of the company's goals.) Third, the appraisal lets you and the subordinate develop a plan for correcting any deficiencies and to reinforce the things he or she does right. Fourth, appraisals should provide an opportunity to review and recalibrate the employee's career plans in light of his or her exhibited strengths and weaknesses. Finally, supervisors use appraisals to identify employees' training and development needs.

Steps in Performance Appraisal

As we said, performance appraisal contains three steps: (1) setting work standards, (2) assessing the employee's actual performance relative to those standards, and (3) providing feedback to the employee regarding his or her performance. Some managers call these steps the *performance appraisal cycle*, to recognize that the feedback (Step 3) should in turn lead to setting new goals (Step 1).

Defining the Employee's Performance Standards

The job description usually isn't sufficient to clarify what you expect your employee to accomplish; it lists duties, but usually not specific goals. The first step in performance appraisal and management is therefore to let employees know what you expect of them; you do this by setting performance standards. Managers use one or more of three bases—goals, job dimensions or traits, and competencies—to establish ahead of time what these performance standards will be.

First, the manager can assess to what extent *the employee is attaining his or her numerical goals.* Such goals should derive from the company's overall goals. For example, a companywide goal of reducing costs by 10% should translate into goals for how individual employees or teams will cut costs. The HR as a Profit Center feature shows an example.

■ **HR as a Profit Center**

Setting Performance Goals at Ball Corporation

Ball Corporation supplies metal packaging to customers such as food processors and paint manufacturers worldwide.[2] The management team at one Ball plant concluded that it could improve plant performance by instituting an improved process for setting goals and for ensuring that the plant's employees' behaviors were in synch with these goals.[3] The new program began by training plant leaders on how to improve performance and on setting and communicating daily performance goals. They in turn communicated and tracked daily goal attainment by distributing team scorecards to the plant's work teams. Plant employees received special coaching and training to ensure they had the skills required for achieving the goals. According to management, within 12 months the plant increased production by 84 million cans, reduced customer complaints by 50%, and obtained a return-on-investment of more than $3 million.[4]

✪ Talk About It – **1**

If your professor has chosen to assign this, go to **www.pearson.com/mylab/ management** to discuss the following: Explain what performance appraisal behaviors the Ball program included.

Managers often say that effective goals should be "SMART." They are *specific* and clearly state the desired results. They are *measurable* and answer the question "How much?" They are *attainable*. They are *relevant* and clearly derive from what the manager and company want to achieve. And they are *timely*, with deadlines and milestones.[5] Research also provides insights into how to set effective goals. The accompanying HR Tools feature summarizes these findings.

■ **HR Tools for Line Managers and Small Businesses**

How to Set Effective Goals

Studies suggest four guidelines for setting performance goals:

1. Assign specific goals. Employees who receive specific goals usually perform better than those who do not.
2. Assign measurable goals. Put goals in quantitative terms, and include target dates or deadlines. If measurable results will not be available, then "satisfactory completion"—such as "satisfactorily attended workshop"—is the next best thing.
3. Assign challenging but doable goals. Goals should be challenging, but not so difficult that they appear unrealistic.
4. Encourage participation. Should you tell employees what their goals are, or let them participate in setting their goals? The evidence suggests that participatively set goals do not consistently result in higher performance than assigned goals, nor do assigned goals consistently result in higher performance than participative ones. It is only when the participatively set goals are set higher than the assigned ones that the participatively set goals produce higher performance. Because it tends to be easier to set higher standards when your employees participate, participation tends to lead to improved performance.[6]

✪ Talk About It – **2**

If your professor has chosen to assign this, go to **www.pearson.com/mylab/management** to discuss the following. Write a short paragraph that addresses the question: "Why is it not a good idea to simply tell employees to 'do their best' when assigning a task?"

A *second* basis on which to appraise someone is to use a form with *basic job dimensions* or *traits* (such as "Quality," "Quantity," "Communication," or "Teamwork.") For example, the instructor's appraisal form earlier in this chapter (Figure 8.1) includes basic job dimensions (or "criteria") such as, "The instructor is well prepared." The assumption is that "being prepared" is a useful guiding standard for "what should be."

A third option is to appraise employees based *on their mastery of the competencies* (generally the skills, knowledge, and/or personal behaviors) that performing the job requires. For example, we saw in Chapter 4 that BP appraised employees' skills using a skills matrix (see Figure 4.10, page 115). This matrix shows the basic skills to be assessed (such as "technical expertise"), and the minimum level of each skill the job requires (what the minimum skill level "should be").

Who Should Do the Appraising?

The supervisor usually does the actual appraising. Therefore, he or she must be familiar with basic appraisal techniques, understand and avoid problems that can cripple an appraisal, and conduct the appraisal fairly. The HR department usually serves a policy-making and advisory role. For example, they might provide advice and assistance regarding the appraisal tool to use but leave final decisions on appraisal procedures to the company's operating division heads. In other companies, they will prepare detailed forms and procedures that all departments will be expected to use.

In any case, relying only on supervisors' ratings is not always wise. For example, the supervisor may not appreciate how colleagues who interact with the employee rate his or her performance. Furthermore, there is always some danger of bias for or against the employee. If so, managers have several options.

Peer Appraisals With more employees working in teams, appraisal by one's peers—peer appraisal—is popular. The American military requires generals and admirals to be evaluated by their peers (and subordinates).[7] Facebook has employees compile peer reviews every 6 months.[8] Google employees receive annual feedback from both their supervisor and their peers.[9] (We'll discuss automated "crowd" appraisals later in this chapter). At one software firm, employees recognize each other with "wins" and "project completions" at monthly video meetings.[10]

Peer appraisals can be effective. Often no one knows someone's performance and potential as well as do the people one is working with; furthermore, people tend to be motivated to meet their colleagues' expectations.[11] Typically, an employee due for an annual appraisal chooses an appraisal chairperson. The latter then selects one supervisor and three peers to evaluate the employee's work.

Rating Committees Some companies use rating committees. A rating committee is usually composed of the employee's immediate supervisor and three or four other supervisors.[12]

Using multiple raters is advantageous. It can help neutralize bias on the part of individual raters.[13] Different raters also often see different facets of an employee's performance, so ratings by committees let you include these different facets of an employee's performance. It is usually advisable to at least obtain ratings from the supervisor, his or her boss, and perhaps another manager who is familiar with the employee's work.[14] At a minimum, most employers require that the supervisor's boss sign off on any appraisals the supervisor does.

Self-Ratings Some employers obtain employees' self-ratings, usually in conjunction with supervisors' ratings. The basic problem, of course, is that employees usually rate themselves higher than do their supervisors or peers.[15] One study found that, when asked to rate their own job performances, 40% of employees in jobs of all types placed themselves in the top 10%, and virtually all remaining employees rated themselves at least in the top 50%.[16] In another study, subjects' self-ratings

A rating committee is usually composed of the employee's immediate supervisor and three or four other supervisors.
Source: Yuri Arcurs/Getty Images.

actually correlated negatively with their subsequent performance in an assessment center—the higher they appraised themselves, they worse they did in the center.[17]

Appraisal by Subordinates Many employers have subordinates rate their managers, usually for developmental rather than for pay purposes.

Anonymity affects the results. Managers who get feedback from subordinates who identify themselves view the process more positively than do managers who get anonymous feedback. However, subordinates prefer giving anonymous responses, and those who must identify themselves tend to give inflated ratings.[18]

Upward feedback improves performance. In one study, managers who were initially rated poor or moderate "showed significant improvements in [their] upward feedback ratings over the five-year period." And, managers who met with their subordinates to discuss their upward feedback improved more than the managers who did not.[19] Of course, employees no longer need employers for upward evaluation systems—sites like Glassdoor and apps like Memo let employees post their own anonymous comments.[20]

360-degree feedback
The employer collects performance information all around an employee—from his or her supervisors, subordinates, peers, and internal or external customers.

360-Degree Feedback With **360-degree feedback**, the employer collects performance information all around an employee—from his or her supervisors, subordinates, peers, and internal or external customers—generally for developmental rather than pay purposes.[21] The usual process is to have the raters complete online appraisal surveys on the ratee. Computerized systems then compile all this feedback into individualized reports to ratees. The person may then meet with the supervisor to develop a self-improvement plan.

Results are mixed. Participants seem to prefer this approach, but one study concluded that multisource feedback led to "generally small" improvements in subsequent ratings by supervisors, peers, and subordinates.[22] Also, such appraisals are more candid when rewards or promotions are not involved.

There are several ways to improve 360-degree appraisals.[23] Carefully train the people giving and receiving the feedback.[24] Make sure the feedback is productive, unbiased, and development oriented.[25] Reduce the administrative costs associated with collecting feedback by using an Internet-based 360-degree system. Here, typically, the rater logs in and rates the person along such dimensions as "capable and effective."[26]

TRENDS SHAPING HR: *Digital and Social Media*

"CROWD" APPRAISALS More employers are using social media–based appraisals to let most everyone in the company (the "crowd") appraise each other. Workforce Rypple (part of salesforce.com) is one such "social performance management platform."[27] Employees and managers use it to set goals and to provide feedback and recognition.[28] It usually supplements traditional appraisals.

For example, employees at one firm use Rypple comments as an input to its formal employee appraisals.[29] Solar energy company Sunrun also uses Rypple. A spokesman says: "It's great for putting ideas out there, you can unveil objectives to the whole team, ask for opinions and suggestions and then work on them together. We do 360 feedback each week."[30] Employers often combine such ongoing reviews with sites such as Globoforce (www.globoforce.com/), which automate the process of instantaneously rewarding and recognizing colleagues.

LEARNING OBJECTIVE 2
Discuss the pros and cons of at least eight performance appraisal methods.

graphic rating scale
The graphic rating scale is a performance appraisal tool that lists several *job dimensions* and a range of performance values for each. The supervisor rates each subordinate by circling or checking the score that best describes the subordinate's performance for each trait or dimension.

Traditional Appraisal Methods

Employers have traditionally conducted the actual appraisal using one or more of the formal methods we describe in this section.

Graphic Rating Scale Method

The **graphic rating scale** is probably still the most familiar and popular method for appraising performance, and comes in several varieties. The one in Figure 8.2 lists several *job dimensions* (in this case "communication" and "teamwork") and a range of performance values (from "below expectations" to "role model") for each. The supervisor rates each subordinate by circling the score that best describes the subordinate's performance for each trait.

Competency- or *skill-based graphic rating forms* are a second option. For example, Figure 8.3 shows part of the rating form for a pizza chef. Here the employer wants to appraise a pizza chef's job-related skills, one of which is: "Be able to maintain adequate inventory of pizza dough." As another example, a competency (for a nurse supervisor) to be rated in Section I of Figure 8.4 is, "Effectively leads and motivates nurses."[31]

Finally, the graphic rating form might rate (as in Section II of Figure 8.4) how well the employee did with respect to achieving specific *goals.* "Nursing unit experienced zero patient medication errors in period" would be one example.

Alternation Ranking Method

Ranking employees from best to worst on a trait or traits is another popular appraisal method. Because it is usually easier to distinguish between the worst and best employees than to rank them, an alternation ranking method is useful. Here the supervisor uses a form like that in Figure 8.5 to specify the employee who is highest on the trait being measured and also the one who is the lowest. He or she alternates between highest and lowest until all employees to be rated have been ranked.

Sample Performance Rating Form

Employee's Name _____   Level: Entry-level employee

Manager's Name _____

Key Work Responsibilities   Results/Goals to Be Achieved
1. _____   1. _____
2. _____   2. _____
3. _____   3. _____
4. _____   4. _____

Communication

1	2	3	4	5

Below Expectations	Meets Expectations	Role Model
Even with guidance, fails to prepare straight-forward communications, including forms, paperwork, and records, in a timely and accurate manner; products require minimal corrections. Even with guidance, fails to adapt style and materials to communicate straightforward information.	With guidance, prepares straightforward communications, including forms, paperwork, and records, in a timely and accurate manner; products require minimal corrections. With guidance, adapts style and materials to communicate straightforward information.	Independently prepares communications, such as forms, paperwork, and records, in a timely, clear, and accurate manner; products require few, if any, corrections. Independently adapts style and materials to communicate information.

Organizational Know-How

1	2	3	4	5

Below Expectations	Meets Expectations	Role Model
<performance standards appear here>	<performance standards appear here>	<performance standards appear here>

Personal Effectiveness

1	2	3	4	5

Below Expectations	Meets Expectations	Role Model
<performance standards appear here>	<performance standards appear here>	<performance standards appear here>

Teamwork

1	2	3	4	5

Below Expectations	Meets Expectations	Role Model
<performance standards appear here>	<performance standards appear here>	<performance standards appear here>

Achieving Business Results

1	2	3	4	5

Below Expectations	Meets Expectations	Role Model
<performance standards appear here>	<performance standards appear here>	<performance standards appear here>

Figure 8.2

Sample Graphic Rating Form with Behavioral Examples

Source: "Sample Performance Rating Form from Performance Management: A Roadmap for Developing, Implementing and Evaluating Performance Management Systems" by Elaine D. Pulakos from *SHRM Effective Practice Guidelines*. Copyright © 2004 by SHRM Foundation. Reprinted with permission. All rights reserved.

Figure 8.3

One Item from a
Competency-Based Appraisal
Form Assessing Employee
Performance on Specific
Job-Related Skills

POSITION: PIZZA CHEF			
SKILL 1: BE ABLE TO MAINTAIN ADEQUATE INVENTORY OF PIZZA DOUGH		**RATING**	
Each round pizza dough must be between 12 and 14 ounces each, kneaded at least 2 minutes before being placed in the temperature and humidity-controlled cooler, and kept there for at least 5 hours prior to use. There should be enough, but no more for each day's demand.	Needs improvement	Satisfactory	Excellent

Paired Comparison Method

With the paired comparison method, every subordinate to be rated is paired with and compared to every other subordinate on each trait. For example, suppose there are five employees to be rated. With this method, a chart such as that in Figure 8.6 shows all possible pairs of employees for each trait. Then, for each trait, the supervisor indicates (with a plus or minus) who is the better employee of the pair. Next, the number of times an employee is rated better is added up. In Figure 8.6, employee Maria ranked highest (has the most plus marks) for "quality of work," and Art ranked highest for "creativity."

Forced Distribution Method

With the forced distribution method, the manager places predetermined percentages of subordinates in performance categories, as when a professor "grades on a curve." Many *Fortune* 500 firms use some version of this. At Lending Tree, the top 15% appraisees are "1s," the middle 75% are "2s," and the bottom 10% are "3s" and the "first to go."[32] Forced distribution's advantages are that it (1) prevents supervisors from rating most employees "satisfactory" or "high," and (2) makes top and bottom performers stand out.

Although widely used, some balk at forced distribution ratings. As most students know, forced distribution grading is unforgiving. With forced distribution, either you're in the top 10% or you're not. And, if you're in the bottom 10%, you get an F, no questions asked. Your professor has little wiggle room. Some writers refer unkindly to forced ranking as "Rank and Yank."[33]

A research review of forced distribution ratings concluded that in the short term they do motivate effort and may produce higher performance. But in the longer term they're counterproductive because they leave many employees feeling that their appraisals were unjust, and that they were engaged in dysfunctional competition with other employees.[34] Inequities can arise, for instance, when high-performing teams have to cut their "worst" employees, (who may, in fact, be performing as well as the worst teams' "best" employees).[35]

Given this, employers should be vigilant.[36] Appoint a review committee to review any employee's low ranking. Train raters to be objective. And consider using multiple raters in conjunction with the forced distribution approach.

For many years, Microsoft required its managers to grade employees against one another in what employees called the "stack," ranking them on a scale of 1 to 5.[37] Microsoft recently eliminated "stacking," substituting more frequent and qualitative feedback to employees.

Critical Incident Method

The critical incident method involves keeping an anecdotal record of good or undesirable examples of an employee's work-related behavior and reviewing it with the employee at predetermined times. Employers often compile such incidents

Section I: Competencies: Does this employee exhibit the core competencies the job requires?

Exhibits Leadership Competency

Effectively leads and motivates nurses: Builds a culture that is open and receptive to improved clinical care; Sets clear goals for nurses; Is supportive of nurses; Motivates nurses to achieve their goals.

Generally exceeds expectations	Generally meets expectations	Generally fails to meet expectations
_____	_____	_____

Exhibits Technical Supervisory Competency

Effectively supervises nurses' technical activities: Exhibits the command of technical nursing knowledge and skills required to supervise nurses effectively, such as, assuring that nurses accurately administer medications, treat patients, intervene effectively to patients' expressions of symptoms, and accurately carry out physicians' instructions.

Generally exceeds expectations	Generally meets expectations	Generally fails to meet expectations
_____	_____	_____

Exhibits Managerial Supervisory Competency

Effectively manages unit: Develops annual, monthly, weekly, and daily plans within context of hospital's plans; effectively organizes and assigns nurses' work; maintains required nursing staffing levels and trains nurses; effectively monitors and controls nursing unit performance using hospital-approved metrics.

Generally exceeds expectations	Generally meets expectations	Generally fails to meet expectations
_____	_____	_____

Exhibits Communications Competency

Effectively communicates: Actively listens to and understands what others say; effectively conveys facts and ideas in writing and orally.

Generally exceeds expectations	Generally meets expectations	Generally fails to meet expectations
_____	_____	_____

Exhibits Decision-Making Competency

Effectively recognizes and solves problems and makes decisions: uses data to analyze alternatives and support conclusions; able to solve problems even of moderate to high complexity.

Generally exceeds expectations	Generally meets expectations	Generally fails to meet expectations
_____	_____	_____

Section II: Goals: Did this employee achieve his or her goals for the period you are appraising?

Primary goals employee was to achieve for this period (Note: list specific goals)	Rating 5 Exceeded goal 3 Met goal 1 Did not achieve goal	Explanations and/or examples
Goal 1	5 4 3 2 1	
Goal 2	5 4 3 2 1	
Goal 3	5 4 3 2 1	
Goal 4	5 4 3 2 1	
Goal 5	5 4 3 2 1	

Employee name and signature	Person doing appraisal	Date of appraisal

Figure 8.4

Pearson Pennsylvania Hospital Competencies and Goals-Based Appraisal Form for a Nurse-Supervisor
Source: Copyright Gary Dessler, PhD.

Figure 8.5

Alternation Ranking Method

ALTERNATION RANKING SCALE

Trait: _____

For the trait you are measuring, list all the employees you want to rank. Put the highest-ranking employee's name on line 1. Put the lowest-ranking employee's name on line 20. Then list the next highest ranking on line 2, the next lowest ranking on line 19, and so on. Continue until all names are on the scale.

Highest-ranking employee

1. _____   11. _____
2. _____   12. _____
3. _____   13. _____
4. _____   14. _____
5. _____   15. _____
6. _____   16. _____
7. _____   17. _____
8. _____   18. _____
9. _____   19. _____
10. _____   20. _____

Lowest-ranking employee

to supplement a rating or ranking method. Keeping a running list of critical incidents provides concrete examples of what specifically the subordinates can do to eliminate any performance deficiencies. It also provides opportunities for mid-year corrections if required. Compiling incidents all year also helps reduce supervisors' tendencies to focus unduly on just the last few weeks when appraising subordinates' performance.

Behaviorally Anchored Rating Scales

A behaviorally anchored rating scale (BARS) is an appraisal method that combines critical incidents and quantitative ratings, by anchoring a quantified scale with specific narrative examples of good and poor performance expressed as

Figure 8.6

Paired Comparison Method

Note: + means "better than," − means "worse than." For each chart, add up the number of +'s in each column to get the highest-ranked employee.

FOR THE TRAIT "QUALITY OF WORK"

Employee rated:

As Compared to:	A Art	B Maria	C Chuck	D Diane	E José
A Art		+	+	−	−
B Maria	−		−	−	−
C Chuck	−	+		+	−
D Diane	+	+	−		+
E José	+	+	+	−	

↑ Maria ranks highest here

FOR THE TRAIT "CREATIVITY"

Employee rated:

As Compared to:	A Art	B Maria	C Chuck	D Diane	E José
A Art		−	−	−	−
B Maria	+		−	+	+
C Chuck	+	+		−	+
D Diane	+	−	+		−
E José	+	−	−	+	

↑ Art ranks highest here

Figure 8.7

Behaviorally Anchored Rating
Scale

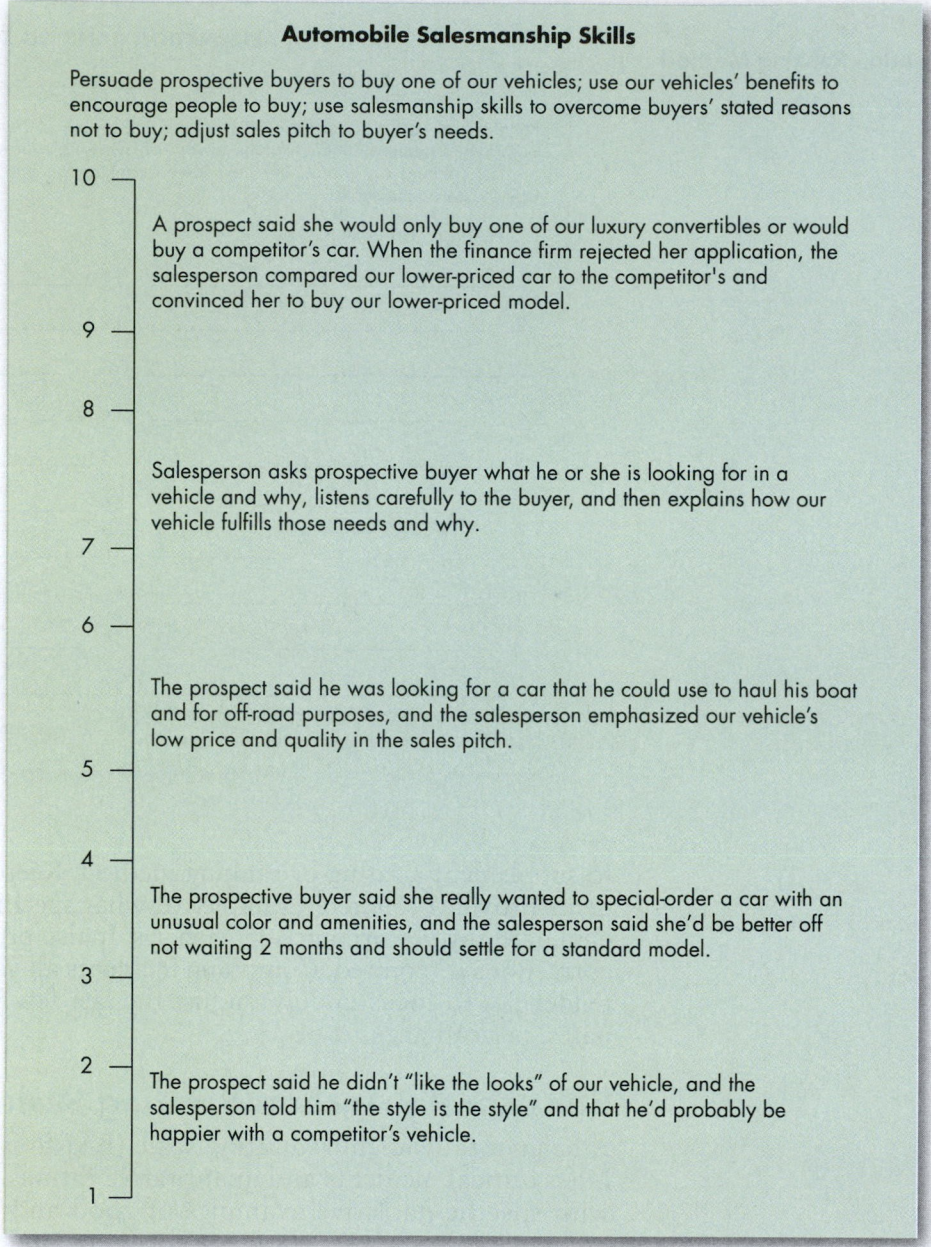

specific behaviors. Figure 8.7 is an example. It shows the behaviorally anchored rating scale for the trait "salesmanship skills" used for an automobile salesperson. Note how the various performance levels, from 10 (high) to 1 (low), are anchored with specific behavioral examples such as "[T]he salesperson told him 'the style is the style' and that he'd probably be happier with a competitor's vehicle."

Appraisal Forms in Practice

In practice, appraisal forms often blend several approaches. For example, Figure 8.2 (page 238) is a graphic rating scale supported with specific examples of good or poor performance. The latter pinpoint what raters should look for. Even without using the more elaborate behaviorally anchored appraisal approach, anchoring a rating scale, as in Figure 8.2, can improve the reliability and validity of the appraisal scale.

The Management by Objectives Method

The term *management by objectives (MBO)* refers to a multistep, companywide, goal-setting and appraisal program. MBO requires the manager to set specific, measurable, organizationally relevant goals with each employee and then periodically discuss the latter's progress toward these goals.[38] The steps are:

1. **Set the organization's goals.** Establish a companywide plan for next year, and set goals.
2. **Set departmental goals.** Department heads and their superiors jointly set goals for their departments.
3. **Discuss departmental goals.** Department heads discuss the department's goals with their subordinates and ask them to develop their own individual goals. They should ask, "How could each employee help the department attain its goals?"
4. **Define expected results (set individual goals).** Department heads and their subordinates set short-term performance targets for each employee.
5. **Conduct performance reviews.** After a period, department heads compare each employee's actual and expected results.
6. **Provide feedback.** Department heads hold periodic performance review meetings with subordinates. Here they discuss the subordinates' performance and make any plans for rectifying or continuing the persons' performance.

Formal MBO programs require numerous time-consuming meetings, and their use has diminished.[39] However, some companies successfully use streamlined versions. For example, Google CEO Larry Page sets companywide "OKRs" (objectives and key results) quarterly. All Google employees then ensure their own goals are more or less in synch with his. All employees' goals are posted on Google's intranet, next to their names.[40]

Computerized and Online Performance Appraisals

More employers today use Web- or PC-supported appraisal tools.

Source: Dragon Images/Shutterstock.

Many employers use Web- or computer-supported appraisal tools. For example, "Employee Appraiser" (see www.halogensoftware.com) presents a menu of evaluation dimensions, including dependability, initiative, communication, decision making, leadership, judgment, and planning and productivity.[41] Within each dimension (such as "communication") are separate performance factors for things like writing, verbal communication, and receptivity to criticism. When the user clicks on a performance factor, he or she is presented with a graphic rating scale. But instead of numerical ratings, Employee Appraiser uses behaviorally anchored examples. Thus, for *verbal communication* there are six choices, ranging from "presents ideas clearly" to "lacks structure." The manager chooses the phrase that most accurately describes the worker. Then Employee Appraiser generates an appraisal with sample text. Successfactors, a subsidiary of SAP, offers an Internet-based employee appraisal solution. It includes performance review forms, 51 competencies for most job types, a built-in writing assistant, and a legal scan.[42]

Virtual Appraisal Games

Dissatisfaction with its current performance appraisal process prompted the technology company Persistent Systems to switch to an *appraisal game*. They had the gaming company eMee create a virtual game that enables employees to evaluate and reward each other. Every employee has a virtual avatar. Employees use them to give real-time feedback to each other, including virtual gifts and points (only immediate supervisors can give reprimands). The system seems to have reduced turnover and improved performance.[43]

Electronic Performance Monitoring

Electronic performance monitoring (EPM) systems use computer technology to enable managers to monitor their employees' rate, accuracy, and time spent working online or just on their computers.[44]

EPM can improve productivity. For example, for repetitive tasks, highly skilled and monitored subjects keyed in more data entries than did highly skilled unmonitored participants. But EPM can also backfire. In this same study, low-skilled highly monitored participants did more poorly than low-skilled, unmonitored participants did. EPM also seems to raise employee stress.[45]

Other employers digitally track workers' performance through wearables. For example, the British retailer Tesco has warehouse workers wear armbands. These track which specific goods each worker is moving and how long the task is taking, and then quantify and report things like how long it takes each worker to fulfil each order.[46]

Talent Management and Differential Employee Appraisal

Talent management emphasizes the importance of linking human resource decisions like pay and promotions to the company's goals. Therefore, some talent management–oriented managers argue that allocating rewards primarily based on the employee's appraisal ratings isn't optimal. Instead, they advocate also directing resources to the company's mission-critical employees, those who are critical to achieving the company's strategic goals.

Figure 8.8 illustrates one way to do this. Accenture uses a 4 × 4 strategic role assessment matrix to plot employees by *Performance* (exceptional, high, medium, low) and *Value to the organization* (mission-critical, core, necessary, nonessential). As an example, consider a chemical engineering company that designs pollution control equipment. Here, the firm's experienced engineers may be "mission-critical," engineer-trainees "core," sales, accounting, (and HR) "necessary," and outsource-able employees such as those in maintenance "nonessential." The company would then tie pay, development, dismissal, and other personnel decisions to each employee's position in the matrix, not just to their performance ratings.

Performance

Value to the organization	Exceptional	High	Average	Low
Mission-critical				
Core				
Necessary				
Nonessential				

- Provide additional rewards and experiences and provide development opportunities to benefit individual and organization
- Provide training and experiences to prepare for mission-critical roles
- Identify as at risk: Provide additional training and performance management attention to improve motivation and performance, and/or to move into necessary or core roles
- Divest/seek alternative sourcing

Figure 8.8

Accenture's Strategic Role Assessment Matrix

Source: "The New Talent Equation" from *Outlook*, June 2009. Copyright © 2009 by Accenture. Reprinted by permission. All rights reserved.

Conversation Days

When employees at Juniper Networks, Inc. expressed concerns about their annual performance reviews and the lack of positive feedback, Juniper changed the process. Instead of once-a-year performance reviews, there are now semiannual "conversation days." The emphasis in these manager–employee conversations is on areas for improvement and growth and on setting stretch goals that align with the employee's career interests. There are no explicit performance ratings. Recently, as we'll see later in this chapter, many other employers similarly began experimenting with substituting periodic conversations for traditional appraisals.

LEARNING OBJECTIVE **3**
Give examples of how to deal with potential appraisal rater error problems.

How to Deal With Rater Error Problems and the Appraisal Interview

The concerns at Juniper Networks illustrate an unpleasant fact about performance appraisals. Ratings often say more about raters than ratees because raters consciously or unconsciously do things that cause rater errors. (Or as one researcher put it, "rater idiosyncratic biases account for the largest percentage of the observed variances in performance ratings."[47]) Employees often therefore (rightfully) view appraisals as unfair, unhelpful, and counterproductive.[48] The solution begins with knowing the problems and how to avoid them, starting (see the Skills feature) with unfairness.

BUILDING YOUR MANAGEMENT SKILLS:
How to Make Sure the Appraisal Is Fair

First, there is no doubt that some managers ignore accuracy and instead use the appraisal process for political purposes (such as encouraging employees with whom they don't get along to quit).[49] The employees' standards should be clear, employees should understand the basis on which you're going to appraise them, and the appraisal should be objective.[50] Give the employee an opportunity to express his or her opinions.

The quality of the supervisor–subordinate interpersonal relationship is also important.[51] Supervisors should engage in continuous and formal performance conversations, diagnose and productively address performance issues, build trust through open relationships, and deliver and react to feedback conversations constructively.[52] Figure 8.9 summarizes best practices for administering fair performance appraisals.

Clarify Standards

Unclear standards is another source of ratings error. For example, the scale in Figure 8.10 may seem objective, but would probably result in dubious appraisals because the traits and degrees of merit are unclear and open to interpretation. For example, different supervisors would probably define "good performance" differently. The best way to rectify this problem is to include descriptive phrases that clearly define each trait and degree of merit.

Avoid Halo Effect Ratings

The halo effect means that the rating you give a subordinate on one trait (such as "gets along with others") influences the way you rate the person on other traits (such as "quantity of work"). Thus, you might rate an unfriendly employee "unsatisfactory" for all traits, rather than just for the trait "gets along with others." Being aware of this problem is a step toward avoiding it.

Figure 8.9

Checklist of Best Practices for Administering Fair Performance Appraisals

Source: Based on Richard Posthuma, "Twenty Best Practices for Just Employee Performance Reviews," *Compensation and Benefits Review*, January/February 2008, pp. 47–54; www. employeeperformance.com/ PerformanceManagement Resources/BestPractices forPerformanceAppraisals. php, accessed July 2010; and www.successfactors.com/ articles/optimizeperformance management, accessed July 2010. Reprinted with permission of the Society for Human Resource Management (www.shrm. com), Alexandria, VA, Publisher of *HR Magazine*, © SHRM.

- The employees should understand on what basis you will appraise them, and the appraisals should be objective. Base the performance review on observable job behaviors or objective performance data, and on the job description.
- Use a standardized performance review procedure for all employees.
- Let the employees know ahead of time how you're going to conduct the reviews.
- Make sure you have had frequent opportunities to observe the employee's job performance.
- Make sure you understand the appraisal procedure to use.
- Consider your personality. Raters who score higher on "conscientiousness" tend to give their peers lower ratings—they are stricter; those more "agreeable" give higher ratings.
- Be consistent. Managers tend to be more lenient when appraising subordinates for things like pay raises than when they're giving, say, career advice.
- Document the appraisal review process and results.
- Discuss the appraisal results with the employee.
- Let the employee provide input regarding your assessment of him or her.
- Indicate what the employee needs to do to improve.
- Have your own supervisor evaluate the appraisal result.
- Include an appeals mechanism.

Avoid the Middle

The "central tendency" problem refers to a tendency to rate all employees as being about average, or in the middle. For example, if the rating scale ranges from 1 to 7, a supervisor may tend to avoid the highs (6 and 7) and lows (1 and 2) and rate most of his or her employees between 3 and 5. Supervisors who do this restrict the range of their appraisals and therefore bestow ratings that don't validly describe their subordinates' actual performance.

Such restrictions make the evaluations less useful for promotion, salary, and counseling purposes. Ranking employees instead of using a graphic rating scale can eliminate this problem. When you rank employees, they can't all be rated average.[53]

Don't Be Lenient or Strict

Conversely, some supervisors rate all their subordinates consistently high or low, a problem referred to as the strictness/leniency problem. Again, one solution is to insist on ranking subordinates because that forces the supervisor to distinguish between high and low performers.

The appraisal you do may be less objective than you realize. One study focused on how personality influenced the peer evaluations students gave their peers. Raters

	Excellent	Good	Fair	Poor
Quality of work				
Quantity of work				
Creativity				
Integrity				

Figure 8.10

A Graphic Rating Scale with Unclear Standards

Note: For example, what exactly is meant by "good," "quantity of work," and so forth?

who scored higher on "conscientiousness" tended to give their peers lower ratings; those scoring higher on "agreeableness" gave higher ratings.[54]

Diversity Counts

Avoid Bias Individual differences among ratees in terms of characteristics like age, race, and gender can affect their ratings, often quite apart from their actual performance. For example, it's often argued that a "glass ceiling" comprised of a lack of access to "old boys' networks" and too few powerful mentors largely explain the relatively few women in top management jobs; however, a recent study suggests a more troubling explanation.

The study concluded that "all else being equal, an evaluator will provide a lower performance evaluation to a female subordinate with stronger competence signals compared to a female subordinate with weaker competent signals."[55] In other words, the better a female employee is, in terms of her actual performance and her educational and work experience, the more likely it is that she'll be rated lower.

Could that be possible? Unfortunately, based on this study, it seems that it is. Not all the evaluators were prone to this negative bias. As the researchers conclude, "only male evaluators who are high on SDO [in other words who are inclined to be socially dominant] and evaluating a high-performing female subordinate appear to be prone."[56] In any case, it would seem that unless employers guard against such bias, they could end up tacitly condoning biased promotion and pay decisions against some of their highest-performing and highest-potential employees. ■

Table 8.1 summarizes how the most popular appraisal methods compare in addressing these problems.

Table 8.1 Important Similarities, Differences, and Advantages and Disadvantages of Appraisal Tools

Tool	Similarities/Differences	Advantages	Disadvantages
Graphic rating scale	These scales both aim at measuring an employee's *absolute* performance based on objective criteria as listed on the scales.	Simple to use; provides a quantitative rating for each employee.	Standards may be unclear; halo effect, central tendency, leniency, bias can also be problems.
BARS		Provides behavioral "anchors." BARS is very accurate.	Difficult to develop.
Alternation ranking	These are both methods for judging the *relative* performance of employees relative to each other, but still based on objective criteria.	Simple to use (but not as simple as graphic rating scales); avoids central tendency and other problems of rating scales.	Can cause disagreements among employees and may be unfair if all employees *are*, in fact, excellent.
Forced distribution method		End up with a predetermined proportion of people in each group.	Appraisal results depend on the adequacy of your original choice of cutoff points (for top 10%, and so on).
Critical incident method	These are both subjective, narrative methods for appraising performance.	Helps clarify what exactly is "right" and "wrong" about the employee's performance; forces supervisor to size up subordinates on an ongoing basis.	Difficult to rate or rank employees relative to one another.
MBO		Tied to agreed-upon performance objectives.	Time consuming.

KNOW YOUR EMPLOYMENT LAW
Appraising Performance

Performance appraisals affect raises, promotions, training opportunities, and other personnel actions. If the manager is inept or biased in making the appraisal, how can one defend the promotion decisions that stem from the appraisal? In one case, a 36-year-old supervisor ranked a 62-year-old subordinate at the bottom of the department's rankings and then terminated him. The U.S. Court of Appeals for the 10th Circuit determined that the discriminatory motives of the younger boss might have influenced the appraisal and termination.[57] Figure 8.11 summarizes steps to ensure your appraisals are legally defensible. ■

The performance appraisal usually culminates in an appraisal interview. Here, you and your subordinate discuss the appraisal and formulate plans to remedy deficiencies. These interviews are potentially uncomfortable because few people like to receive—or give—negative feedback.[58] Adequate preparation and effective implementation are therefore essential. The accompanying Management Skills feature shows how to conduct an effective appraisal interview.

Figure 8.11

Steps to Ensure Your Appraisals Are Legally Defensible

- Base the duties and criteria you appraise on a job analysis.
- At the start of the period, communicate performance standards to employees in writing.
- Using a single overall rating of performance is not acceptable to the courts, which often characterize such systems as vague.[1] Courts generally require combining separate ratings for each performance dimension (quality, quantity, and so on) with some formal weighting system to yield a summary score.
- Include an employee appeals process. Employees should have the opportunity to review and make comments, written or verbal, about their appraisals before they become final, and should have a formal appeals process to appeal their ratings.
- One appraiser should never have absolute authority to determine a personnel action.
- Document all information bearing on a personnel decision in writing. "Without exception, courts condemn informal performance evaluation practices that eschew documentation."[2]
- Train supervisors. If formal rater training is not possible, at least provide raters with written instructions on how to use the rating scale.[3]

[1]James Austin, Peter Villanova, and Hugh Hindman, "Legal Requirements and Technical Guidelines Involved in Implementing Performance Appraisal Systems," in Gerald Ferris and M. Ronald Buckley (eds.), *Human Resources Management*, 3rd ed. (Upper Saddle River, NJ: Prentice Hall, 1996), pp. 271–288.

[2]Austin et al., op. cit., p. 282.

[3]But beware: One problem with training raters to avoid rating errors is that, sometimes, what appears to be an error—such as leniency—isn't an error at all, as when all subordinates really are superior performers. Manuel London, Edward Mone, and John Scott, "Performance Management and Assessment: Methods for Improved Rater Accuracy and Employee Goal Setting," *Human Resource Management* 43, no. 4 (Winter 2004), pp. 319–336; Wayne Cascio and H. John Bernardin, "Implications of Performance Appraisal Litigation for Personnel Decisions," *Personnel Psychology*, Summer 1981, pp. 211–212; Gerald Barrett and Mary Kernan, "Performance Appraisal and Terminations: A Review of Court Decisions Since *Brito v. Zia* with Implications for Personnel Practices," *Personnel Psychology* 40, no. 3 (Autumn 1987), pp. 489–504; Elaine Pulakos, *Performance Management*, SHRM Foundation, 2004.

BUILDING YOUR MANAGEMENT SKILLS:
How to Conduct the Appraisal Interview

Start by preparing for the interview. First, give the employee about a week's notice to review his or her work, read over the job description, analyze problems, and gather questions and comments. Next, study the person's job description, compare performance to the standards, and review the employee's previous appraisals. Finally, find a mutually agreeable time for the interview, and allow enough time for the entire interview. Interviews with lower-level personnel should take no more than an hour. Interviews with management employees often take two or so hours. Be sure the interview is in a private place where you won't be interrupted.

There are four things to keep in mind in actually conducting the interview:

1. **Talk in terms of objective work data.** Use examples such as absences, tardiness, quality records, inspection reports, scrap or waste, orders processed, productivity records, material used or consumed, timeliness of tasks or projects, control or reduction of costs, numbers of errors, costs compared to budgets, customers' comments, product returns, order processing time, inventory level and accuracy, accident reports, and so on.
2. **Don't get personal.** Don't say, "You're too slow in producing those reports." Instead, try to compare the person's performance to a standard. ("These reports should normally be done within 10 days.") Similarly, don't compare the person's performance to that of other people. ("He's quicker than you are.")
3. **Encourage the person to talk.** Stop and listen to what the person is saying; ask open-ended questions such as, "What do you think we can do to improve the situation?" Use a command such as "Go on," or "Tell me more." Restate the person's last point as a question, such as, "You don't think you can get the job done?"
4. **End with an action plan.** Don't get personal, but do make sure the person leaves knowing specifically what he or she is doing right and doing wrong. Give specific examples; make sure the person understands; and get agreement before he or she leaves on how things will be improved, and by when. Develop an action plan showing steps and expected results.

How to Handle a Defensive Subordinate

Defenses are an important and familiar aspect of our lives. For example, when a supervisor tells someone his or her performance is poor, the first reaction is often denial. By denying the fault, the person avoids having to question his or her own competence.

In any event, understanding and dealing with defensiveness is an important appraisal skill. In his book *Effective Psychology for Managers*, psychologist Mortimer Feinberg suggests the following:

1. Recognize that defensive behavior is normal.
2. Never attack a person's defenses. Don't try to "explain someone to themselves" by saying things like, "You know the real reason you're using that excuse is that you can't bear to be blamed for anything." Instead, try to concentrate on the act itself ("sales are down") rather than on the person ("you're not selling enough").
3. Postpone action. Sometimes it is best to do nothing at all. People frequently react to sudden threats by instinctively hiding behind their "masks." But given sufficient time, a more rational reaction takes over.
4. Recognize your own limitations. Don't expect to solve every problem that comes up, especially the human ones. More important, remember that a supervisor should not try to be a psychologist. Offering understanding is one thing; trying to deal with psychological problems is another.

Continued

How to Criticize a Subordinate

When criticism is required, do it in a manner that lets the person maintain his or her dignity and sense of worth. Criticize in private, and do it constructively. Provide examples of critical incidents and specific suggestions of what could be done and why. Avoid once-a-year "critical broadsides" by giving feedback frequently, so that the formal review contains no surprises. Never say the person is "always" wrong (because no one is ever "always" wrong or right). Finally, criticism should be objective and free of any personal biases on your part.

How to Ensure the Interview Leads to Improved Performance

Whether subordinates express satisfaction with their appraisal interview depends on their not feeling threatened during the interview, and on having an opportunity to express their ideas, and having a helpful supervisor conducting the interview.

But, of course, you don't just want subordinates to be satisfied with their appraisal interviews. Your main aim is to get them to improve their performance. Here, clearing up job-related problems with the employee and setting measurable performance targets and a schedule for achieving them—an action plan—are essential. And remember that providing the tools and support the person needs to move ahead is also necessary.[59]

Many employers today emphasize praise over criticism. One tells its managers not to touch on more than two areas that need improvement but instead to emphasize their subordinates' strengths. For example, in one recent year, almost all the *Fortune* 500 companies used the Gallup StrengthsFinder tool (www.gallupstrengthscenter.com) to help employees identify and build on their strengths. To attract, motivate, and retain todays new employees, a less critical approach may be advisable.[60]

How to Handle a Formal Written Warning

There will be times when an employee's performance is so poor that a formal written warning is required. Such warnings serve two purposes: (1) They may serve to shake your employee out of his or her bad habits, and (2) they can help you defend your rating, both to your own boss and (if needed) to the courts. Written warnings should identify the standard by which the employee is judged, make it clear that the employee was aware of the standard, specify any deficiencies relative to the standard, and show the employee had an opportunity to correct his or her performance.[61]

Given this, what do you think you would tell Phyllis (from the chapter's opener) what she did wrong in appraising Gladys and should do differently?

Employee Engagement Guide for Managers: Use the Appraisal Interview to Build Engagement

Research shows that managers can also use the appraisal interview to improve their employees' level of engagement. Here are relevant research findings and their implications.

1. Employees who understand how they and their departments contribute to the company's success are more engaged.[62] Therefore, *take the opportunity to show the employee how his or her efforts contribute to the "big picture"—to his or her teams' and the company's success.*

2. Employees' engagement rises when they experience what the researchers called "psychological meaningfulness" (namely, the perception that one's role in the organization is worthwhile and valuable).[63] *Use the interview to emphasize the meaningfulness to the company of what the employee is doing.*

3. Employees who experience "psychological safety" (namely, the perception that it's safe to bring oneself to a role without fear of damage to self-image, status, or career) were more engaged.[64] Therefore, *be candid and objective but do so supportively and without unnecessarily undermining the employee's self-image.*[65]

4. Use the interview to make sure your employee *has what he or she needs* to do a good job. To paraphrase one writer, effectively enable workers with internal support, resources, and tools.[66]

5. Employees and managers face appraisals with trepidation because appraisals often focus on negatives. Doing so undermines employee engagement. In one survey, for instance, Gallup asked about 1,000 U.S. employees to respond to two statements: "My supervisor focuses on my strengths or positive characteristics" and "My supervisor focuses on my weaknesses or negative characteristics." They found that about three times the number of employees whose *managers focused on strengths* were engaged, compared with those whose managers focused on weaknesses.[67]

6. Involvement in decision making and letting employees voice their ideas and opinions improves employee engagement.[68] Use the interview as an opportunity to *show your employees that you listen to their ideas and value their contributions.*

7. Engagement rises when employees have an opportunity to develop in their careers.[69] Take an opportunity during the interview to discuss the person's evaluation *in the context of where he or she sees himself or herself heading career-wise.*[70]

8. There is "a significant positive association between distributive (what rewards people get) and informational (what information they get) justice dimensions, and employee engagement."[71] Bottom line: *make sure that the interviewee views the appraisal and the rewards or remedial actions as just and fair.*

LEARNING OBJECTIVE 5
Explain how you would take a performance management approach to appraisal.

Performance Management Today

Performance appraisal is fine in theory, but in practice, appraisals don't always go smoothly. Goals aren't set, the "appraisal" is a form from an office supply store, and the yearly feedback, if any, may be agonizing, with both participants fleeing before any coaching takes place. This runs counter to common sense. Employees should know what their goals are, performance feedback should be useful, and if there is a problem, the time to take action is right away, not six months later.

Total Quality Management and Performance Appraisal

Management experts have long argued that most performance appraisals neither motivate employees nor guide their development.[72] Some proponents of the total quality management (TQM) movement even argued for eliminating performance appraisals altogether.[73] *Total quality management* (TQM) programs are organizationwide programs that integrate all functions and processes of the business such that all aspects of the business, including design, planning, production, distribution, and field service, are aimed at maximizing customer satisfaction through continuous improvements.[74] TQM programs are built on a philosophy encapsulated by several principles, such as: cease dependence on inspection to achieve quality; aim for continuous improvement; institute extensive training; drive out fear so that everyone may work effectively; remove barriers that rob employees of their pride of workmanship (in particular, the annual merit rating); and institute a vigorous program of self-improvement.[75] Basically, TQM advocates argue that the organization is a system of interrelated parts, and that employees' performance is more a function of factors like training, communication, tools, and supervision than of their motivation.

What would performance appraisal look like in this kind of company? Visitors to Toyota Motor's Lexington, Kentucky Camry plant would find such a system. Teams of employees monitor their own results, generally without managers' interventions. In frequent meetings, the team members continuously align those results with the work team's standards and with the plant's overall quality and productivity goals. Team members who need coaching and training receive it. Procedures that need changing are changed.

Performance Management Examples

In fact, appraisals today are undoubtedly shifting from traditional ratings-form/annual reviews to less formal more frequent feedback.[76]

For example, after years of using a much-imitated forced ranking scale, GE switched a few years ago to a qualitative system. Supervisors labeled employees as, for example, "role model" or "strong contributor." They also began using a smart phone app GE calls PD@GE to assess employees continuously rather than once a year.[77] GE is now experimenting with moving from the "role model" type categorical employee ratings to entirely narrative ratings/reviews.[78]

IBM Corp. recently introduced a new app-based performance review it calls Checkpoint.[79] The new system facilitates flexibility (such as by allowing employees to change their goals) and allows for more continuous monitoring of performance and feedback.

Other companies including Gap, Adobe Systems, and Microsoft have eliminated numerical performance ratings. Goldman Sachs continues to have annual reviews that are crucial for employees' career progress, but instituted a new system through which employees can also get continuous feedback. Goldman also still compiles 360-degree feedback on its employees. On the other hand, Accenture dropped its annual performance reviews and replaced them with more frequent communication sessions. Morgan Stanley no longer has numerical appraisal ratings, instead emphasizing qualitative feedback.[80]

Even airlines do it. Landing or taking off with the nose of a stretched Boeing 767 just a bit too high can cause the tail to strike the runway, so piloting one requires special care. Until recently, pilots didn't know how they were doing until well after they landed, when they got the report of the in-flight data (or, of course, if the tail touched the runway). Today, right after each takeoff and landing, pilots get an in-flight report showing how their performance (in terms of takeoff angle and speed, for instance) compares with those of the airline's and industry's standards. That enables pilots to adjust their performance before their next takeoff or landing.[81]

"Performance management" doesn't mean a company can't be tough. For many years, Kimberly-Clark Corp. was reportedly known for lifetime employment and for retaining even less than well-performing employees. Recently it embarked on a much stricter performance management system. It includes using continuous online performance management reviews to carefully track employees' performance relative to their goals. Turnover is up dramatically.[82]

What Is Performance Management?

These are all examples of performance management in action. In comparing performance management and performance appraisal, "the distinction is the contrast

performance management
The *continuous* process of identifying, measuring, and developing the performance of individuals and teams and *aligning* their performance with the organization's *goals*.

between a year-end event—the completion of the appraisal form—and a process that starts the year with performance planning and is integral to the way people are managed throughout the year."[83] **Performance management** is the *continuous* process of identifying, measuring, and developing the performance of individuals and teams and *aligning* their performance with the organization's *goals*.[84] We can summarize performance management's six basic elements as follows:[85]

- *Direction sharing* means communicating the company's goals throughout the company and then translating these into doable departmental, team, and individual goals.
- *Goal alignment* means having a method that enables managers and employees to *see* the link between the employees' goals and those of their department and company.
- *Ongoing performance monitoring* usually includes using computerized systems that measure and then e-mail progress and exception reports based on the person's progress toward meeting his or her performance goals.
- *Ongoing feedback* includes both face-to-face and computerized feedback regarding progress toward goals (see the Trends feature).
- *Coaching and developmental support* should be an integral part of the feedback process.
- *Recognition and rewards* provide the consequences needed to keep the employee's goal-directed performance on track.

TRENDS SHAPING HR: *Digital and Social Media*

Many employers use digital technologies including cloud computing and social media to support performance management. For example, with Oracle TBE Performance Management Cloud Service, management would:

- First, *assign financial and nonfinancial goals* to each team's activities, goals that support the company's overall strategic goals. (Thus, an airline might measure ground crew aircraft turnaround time in terms of "improve turnaround time to 26 minutes per plane this year.")
- *Inform all teams and employees* of their goals.
- *Use IT-supported tools* (cloud-based performance management software, HR scorecards, and digital dashboards) to continuously display, monitor, and assess each team's and employee's performance (Figure 8.12). Oracle TBE Performance Management Cloud Service illustrates this.[86] With it, goals are "in the cloud" rather than embedded in documents, so managers needn't wait until the annual or semiannual reviews to revise them. And the system's dashboards enable managers to continuously monitor each team or employee's performance, let employees update progress toward goal achievement, and let employees and managers log comments so the process is real-time and interactive.[87]
- Finally, if exceptions are noted, ensure you've *taken corrective action* before things swing out of control.

⭐ Talk About It – **3**

If your professor has chosen to assign this, go to **www.pearson.com/mylab/ management** to discuss the following: How would you use a scorecard display similar to Figure 8.12 in a performance management system for one of your current (or former) professors?

Figure 8.12

Summary of Performance Management Report

Source: Based on "Personal Goal Management" from the Active Strategy Web site. Copyright © 2012 by ActiveStrategy, Inc.

PERFORMANCE GOAL MANAGEMENT

Report Card | Link | Edit | Options | Copy

Details - 2013 Performance Goal Scorecard				In Progress (01/01/2013 - 12/31/13)
Goals for	Brown, Lisa			Score 4.5

Employee's Individual Performance Goals

Goal	Target	Weight	Score	Date
Achieve 10% Sales Increase	8	45	7.0	June 2013
Improved Customer Satisfaction Rating	4.2	25	4.0	June 2013
Meet Budgetary Constraints	5	15	2.5	June 2013
Improved Leadership Ratings	4.8	15	4.5	June 2013

Departmental Performance Goals

Goal	Target	Weight	Score	Date
Achieve 15% Sales Increase	5	50	3.5	June 2013
Increase Online sales 10%	3.5	25	2.8	June 2013
Meet Budgetary Constraints	5	10	4.2	June 2013
All Employees Cross-Trained on All Products	4.5	15	3.5	June 2013

The Manager's Role in Performance Management

However, technology isn't mandatory for managers who want to take a performance management approach. What is mandatory is the philosophy and on-the-job behaviors. As a philosophy, performance management reflects nonthreatening TQM principles such as cease dependence on inspection to achieve quality, aim for continuous improvement, institute extensive training, and drive out fear so that everyone may work effectively. Behaviors include linking employees' goals to the company's goals, giving employees continuous feedback, providing required resources and coaching, rewarding good performance, and remembering that employees' performance reflects more than just whether they're "motivated."[88]

⭐ Watch It

How does an employee know how they are doing? If your professor has chosen to assign this, go to **www.pearson.com/mylab/management** to watch the video Weather Channel Appraising, and answer the questions to show an example. .

Making Performance Management Practical

Frequent subjective feedback is the heart of performance management, but such programs suffer from one potentially calamitous weakness: at the end of the day, the employer needs some way to differentiate among employees and to make hard-nosed pay raise and promotional decisions. Any performance management process that can't do that is not very practical.

The HR in Practice feature explains how one company put in place a practical performance management process.

■ HR in Practice

Performance Management in Action: Deloitte's New Performance Management Process[89]

The Problem

As at many employers, the managers and employees at the global accounting and consulting company Deloitte suspected that their performance management system could be improved.

There were several concerns. Many questioned whether the system drove improved performance. Traditional performance ratings (they knew from academic research) often said more about the rater's personal idiosyncrasies than about the employees being rated. Furthermore, Deloitte discovered that with 65,000 employees, the company was devoting two *million* hours per year to doing appraisals. And as in many firms, the appraisals themselves focused more on history than on what should be done to improve employees' performance in the future. Management decided to change the process.

The New Goals

The team assigned to create the new performance management process set three goals for the new process: first, it should *recognize employee performance*, particularly in terms of variable compensation; second (particularly because ratings traditionally say more about the raters than the ratees), they wanted to ensure that the new process *clearly reflected employee performance*. Third, they wanted the new process *to energize performance*, particularly in terms of monitoring performance often enough so that employees could adapt and improve their performance as they were working on their assignments.

The New Performance Management Process

In any year, a Deloitte employee may be assigned to one or more teams working on projects (such as an audit), with each team focusing on a particular client company project.

Deloitte's new performance management process has several elements. First, each team member *interacts with his or her team leader periodically* during the course of the assignment, to get frequent feedback on how the employee is doing and advice on how to improve.

Second, at the end of the assignment, rather than having the team leaders present their perceptions or opinions about how the employee performed, the team leader provides an "employee performance snapshot" by reporting on four aspects of how he or she *plans to act* regarding the employee, specifically: (1) From what I know about this person's performance, if it were my money, here is how I would compensate this person; (2) based on what you know about this person's performance, would you want this person on your team again; (3) do you think this person's performance is such that it might harm the customer or the team, and; (4) would you say this person is ready for promotion today?

Finally, toward the end of the year, all of these assignment "snapshots" are *compiled in a year-end evaluation*. That final evaluation, combined with input from a team leader who knows the employee's performance personally (or a group of leaders looking at a larger part of the company's practice) determines what the employee's compensation will be.

■ HR and the Gig Economy

Rating Uber Drivers[90]

The Uber Driver Rating System

Uber's driver rating system rates drivers on three metrics, specifically on how passengers rate the driver, on what percentage of rides the driver accepts, and on how many he or she cancels. When you request a ride, the Uber system pings the nearest driver, who then has 15 seconds to accept. The percentage that the driver accepts is his or her acceptance rate. Uber reportedly wants drivers to maintain at least an 80–90% acceptance rate and no more than a 5% trip cancellation rate. Otherwise, they risk being deactivated (permanently or temporarily).

As most Uber users know, after every ride Uber also prompts the passenger to rate the driver on a 1–5 star scale. In this way, Uber obtains continuous real-time ratings on how their drivers are performing. A driver's rating of the passenger is mandatory, but the passenger's driver rating is optional. A new driver begins with a 5-star rating. Then, as more passengers rate the driver, the driver's average rating will probably change. The driver's rating is generally an average of his or her last 500 trips; cancelled or nonaccepted trips aren't included. For driver ratings, an average below 4.6 reportedly puts the driver in the "danger zone" for possible deactivation. Only about 2–3% of drivers fall in this zone. One or two star ratings often reflect arguments or harassment. Drivers get weekly emails from Uber that include notices if they're activation is in danger.

Potential Rating Problems

As with most ratings systems, the danger is that, at least potentially, the ratings say more about the passenger than about the driver. For example, people not fully familiar with Uber's system may well view a 4-star rating as equivalent to a "B" and not bad at all, when in fact at Uber it's a failing grade. Furthermore, while most employers try to minimize biased or discriminatory appraisals by their employee–supervisors, it's more difficult to guard against such problems when the rater is not an employee (and indeed is probably a stranger). Furthermore, extraneous factors out of the driver's control (such as surge pricing) may prompt passengers to lower the stars they award (although Uber says it guards against this.)

How to Get a Better Driver Rating

In any case, Uber and Uber drivers have listed some of the things drivers can do to get better ratings. Some things to avoid include having an attitude, not knowing your way around, reckless driving, and texting while driving. Some "Do's" for drivers include offer passengers bottled water, open the door, offer to carry bags, keep the car clean—and don't ask for five-star ratings.

⭐ Talk About It – **4**

If your professor has chosen to assign this, go to **www.pearson.com/mylab/ management** to discuss the following. Write a paragraph that addresses the question: "What (based on what I read in this chapter) is good about the Uber driver rating system, and what could Uber do to improve it?"

Review

MyLab Management

If your instructor is using MyLab Management, go to **www.pearson.com/mylab/ management** to complete the problems marked with this icon ⭐.

Summary

1. Performance appraisal means evaluating an employee's current or past performance relative to his or her performance standards. Performance management is the process through which companies ensure that employees are working toward organizational goals and includes defining goals, developing skills, appraising performance, and rewarding the employee. Managers appraise their subordinates' performance to obtain input on which promotion and salary raise decisions can be made, to develop plans for correcting performance deficiencies, and for career-planning purposes. Supervisory ratings are still at the heart of most appraisal processes.

2. The appraisal is generally conducted using one or more popular appraisal methods or tools. These include graphic rating scales, alternation ranking, paired comparison, forced distribution, critical incidents, behaviorally anchored rating scales, MBO, computerized performance appraisals, and electronic performance monitoring.

3. The appraisal process can be improved, first, by eliminating chronic problems that often undermine appraisals and graphic rating scales in particular. These common problems include unclear standards, halo effect, central tendency, leniency or strictness, and bias. An appraisal typically

culminates in an appraisal interview. Adequate preparation, including giving the subordinate notice, reviewing his or her job description and past performance, choosing the right place for the interview, and leaving enough time for it, is essential.

4. The manager can use the appraisal interview to improve the employees' level of engagement. For example, show the employee how his or her efforts contribute to the teams' and the company's success; use the interview to emphasize the meaningfulness to the company of what the

employee is doing; and emphasize support rather than threats.

5. Performance management is the *continuous* process of identifying, measuring, and developing the performance of individuals and teams and *aligning* their performance with the organization's *goals*. It means continuous interactions and feedback to ensure continuous improvement in the employee's and team's capacity and performance. Most important, it requires remembering that your employee's performance usually reflects more than just whether he or she is "motivated."

Key Terms

performance appraisal   232
360-degree feedback   236

graphic rating scale   237
performance management   253

Discussion Questions

8-1. Answer the question, "Who should do the appraising?"

⭐ 8-2. Discuss the pros and cons of at least eight performance appraisal methods.

8-3. Explain how to conduct an appraisal feedback interview.

8-4. Give examples of five potential appraisal problems.

8-5. Explain how to install a performance management program.

8-6. Provide an example of talent management-oriented appraisals.

8-7. Explain how you would use the alternation ranking method, the paired comparison method, and the forced distribution method.

⭐ 8-8. Discuss the pros and cons of using various potential raters to appraise an employee's performance.

Individual and Group Activities

8-9. Working individually or in groups, develop a graphic rating scale for the following jobs: secretary, professor, directory assistance operator.

8-10. Working individually or in groups, describe the advantages and disadvantages of using the forced distribution appraisal method for college professors.

8-11. Working individually or in groups, develop, over the period of a week, a set of critical incidents covering the classroom performance of one of your instructors.

8-12. Working individually or in groups, evaluate the rating scale in Figure 8.1. Discuss ways to improve it.

8-13. Create an Accenture-type grid for your place of work or college, showing how you would segment employees into four groups.

8-14. For this activity, you will need the documents titled (1) "HRCI PHR® and SPHR® Certification Body of Knowledge," and (2) "About the Society for Human Resource Management (SHRM) Body of

Competency & Knowledge® Model and Certification Exams." Your instructor can obtain these two documents from the Pearson Instructor Resource Center and pass them on to you. These two documents list the knowledge someone studying for the HRCI or SHRM certification exam needs to have in each area of human resource management (such as in Strategic Management, and Workforce Planning). In groups of several students, do four things: (1) review the HRCI and/or SHRM documents; (2) identify the material in this chapter that relates to HRCI's or SHRM's required knowledge lists; (3) write four multiple-choice exam questions on this material that you believe would be suitable for inclusion in the HRCI exam and/or the SHRM exam; and, (4) if time permits, have someone from your team post your team's questions in front of the class, so that students in all teams can answer the exam questions created by the other teams.

APPLICATION EXERCISES

HR IN ACTION CASE INCIDENT 1

Appraising the Secretaries at Sweetwater U

Rob Winchester, newly appointed vice president for administrative affairs at Sweetwater State University, faced a tough problem shortly after his university career began. Three weeks after he came on board in September, Sweetwater's president, Rob's boss, told Rob that one of his first tasks was to improve the appraisal system used to evaluate secretarial and clerical performance at Sweetwater U. Apparently the main difficulty was that the performance appraisal was traditionally tied directly to salary increases given at the end of the year. So most administrators were less than accurate when they used the graphic rating forms that were the basis of the clerical staff evaluation. In fact, what usually happened was that each administrator simply rated his or her clerk or secretary as "excellent." This cleared the way for all support staff to receive a maximum pay increase every year.

But the current university budget simply did not include enough money to fund another "maximum" annual increase for every staffer. Furthermore, Sweetwater's president felt that the custom of providing invalid feedback to each secretary on his or her year's performance was not productive, so he had asked the new vice president to revise the system. In October, Rob sent a memo to all administrators telling them that in the future no more than half the secretaries reporting to any particular administrator could be appraised as "excellent." This move, in effect, forced each supervisor to begin ranking his or her secretaries for quality of performance. The vice president's memo met widespread resistance immediately—from administrators, who were afraid that many of their secretaries would begin leaving for more lucrative jobs in private industry; and from secretaries, who felt that the new system was unfair and reduced each secretary's chance of receiving a maximum salary increase. A handful of secretaries had begun quietly picketing outside the president's home on the university campus. The picketing, caustic remarks by disgruntled administrators, and rumors of an impending slowdown by the secretaries (there were about 250 on campus) made Rob Winchester wonder whether he had made the right decision by setting up forced ranking. He knew, however, that there were a few performance appraisal experts in the School of Business, so he decided to set up an appointment with them to discuss the matter.

He met with them the next morning. He explained the situation as he had found it: The present appraisal system had been set up when the university first opened 10 years earlier, and the appraisal form had been developed primarily by a committee of secretaries. Under that system, Sweetwater's administrators filled out forms similar to the one shown in Figure 8.10. This once-a-year appraisal (in March) had run into problems almost immediately because it was apparent from the start that administrators varied widely in their interpretations of job standards, as well as in how conscientiously they filled out the forms and supervised their secretaries. Moreover, at the end of the first year it became obvious to everyone that each secretary's salary increase was tied directly to the March appraisal. For example, those rated "excellent" received the maximum increases, those rated "good" received smaller increases, and those given neither rating received only the standard across-the-board, cost-of-living increase. Because universities in general—and Sweetwater in particular—have paid secretaries somewhat lower salaries than those prevailing in private industry, some secretaries left in a huff that first year. From that time on, most administrators simply rated all secretaries excellent to reduce staff turnover, thus ensuring each a maximum increase. In the process, they also avoided the hard feelings aroused by the significant performance differences otherwise highlighted by administrators.

Two Sweetwater School of Business experts agreed to consider the problem, and in two weeks they came back to the vice president with the following recommendations. First, the form used to rate the secretaries was grossly insufficient. It was unclear what "excellent" or "quality of work" meant, for example. They recommended instead a form like that in Figure 8.2. In addition, they recommended that the vice president rescind his earlier memo and no longer attempt to force university administrators to arbitrarily rate at least half their secretaries as something less than excellent. The two consultants pointed out that this was, in fact, an unfair procedure because it was quite possible that any particular administrator might have staffers who were all or virtually all excellent—or conceivably, although less likely, all below standard. The experts said that the way to get all the administrators to take the appraisal process more seriously was to stop tying it to salary increases. In other words, they recommended that every administrator fill out a form like that in Figure 8.2 for each secretary at least once a year and then use this form as the basis of a counseling session. Salary increases would have to be made on some basis other than the performance appraisal, so that administrators would no longer hesitate to fill out the rating forms honestly.

Rob thanked the two experts and went back to his office to ponder their recommendations. Some of the recommendations (such as substituting the new rating form for the old) seemed to make sense. Nevertheless, he still had serious doubts as to the efficacy of any graphic rating form, particularly if he were to decide in favor of his original forced ranking approach. The experts' second recommendation—to stop tying the appraisals to automatic salary increases—made sense but raised at least one very practical problem: If salary increases were not to be based on performance appraisals, on what were they to be based? He began wondering whether the experts' recommendations weren't simply based on ivory tower theorizing.

Questions

8-17. Do you think that the experts' recommendations will be sufficient to get most of the administrators to fill out the rating forms properly? Why or why not? What additional actions (if any) do you think will be necessary?

8-18. Do you think that Vice President Winchester would be better off dropping graphic rating forms, substituting instead one of the other techniques discussed in this chapter, such as a ranking method? Why?

8-19. What performance appraisal system would you develop for the secretaries if you were Rob Winchester? Defend your answer.

HR IN ACTION CASE INCIDENT 2

Carter Cleaning Company

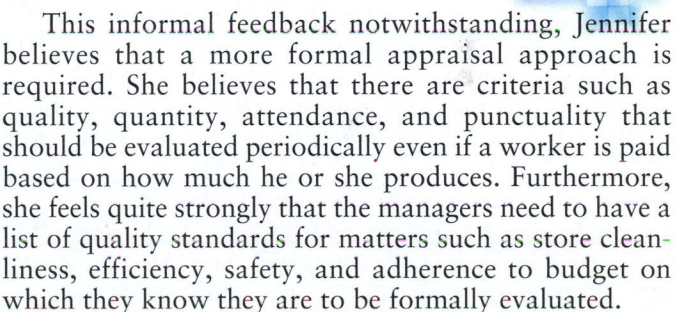

The Performance Appraisal

After spending several weeks on the job, Jennifer was surprised to discover that her father had not formally evaluated any employee's performance for all the years that he had owned the business. Jack's position was that he had "a hundred higher-priority things to attend to," such as boosting sales and lowering costs, and, in any case, many employees didn't stick around long enough to be appraised anyway. Furthermore, contended Jack, manual workers such as those doing the pressing and the cleaning did periodically get positive feedback in terms of praise from Jack for a job well done, or criticism, also from Jack, if things did not look right during one of his swings through the stores. Similarly, Jack was never shy about telling his managers about store problems so that they, too, got some feedback on where they stood.

This informal feedback notwithstanding, Jennifer believes that a more formal appraisal approach is required. She believes that there are criteria such as quality, quantity, attendance, and punctuality that should be evaluated periodically even if a worker is paid based on how much he or she produces. Furthermore, she feels quite strongly that the managers need to have a list of quality standards for matters such as store cleanliness, efficiency, safety, and adherence to budget on which they know they are to be formally evaluated.

Questions

8-20. Is Jennifer right about the need to evaluate the workers formally? The managers? Why or why not?

8-21. Develop a performance appraisal method for the workers and managers in each store.

Experiential Exercise

Setting Goals for and Appraising an Instructor

Purpose: The purpose of this exercise is to give you practice in developing and using a performance appraisal form.

Required Understanding: You are going to develop a performance appraisal form for an instructor and should therefore be thoroughly familiar with the discussion of performance appraisals in this chapter.

How to Set Up the Exercise/Instructions: Divide the class into groups of four or five students.

8-22. First, based on what you now know about performance appraisals, do you think Figure 8.1 is an effective scale for appraising instructors? Why or why not?

8-23. Next, your group should develop its own tool for appraising the performance of an instructor. Decide which of the appraisal tools (graphic rating scales, alternation ranking, and so on) you are going to use, and then design the instrument itself. Apply what you learned in this chapter about goal setting to provide the instructor with practical goals.

8-24. Next, have a spokesperson from each group put his or her group's appraisal tool on the board. How similar are the tools? Do they all measure about the same factors? Which factor appears most often? Which do you think is the most effective tool on the board? Can you think of any way of combining the best points of several of the tools into a new performance appraisal tool?

9

Managing Careers

OVERVIEW:
In this chapter, we will cover . . .

- Career Management
- Improving Mentoring and Coaching Skills
- Employee Engagement Guide for Managers
- Managing Employee Retention and Turnover
- Managing Promotions and Transfers
- Managing Dismissals

MyLab Management

⭐ Improve Your Grade!
When you see this icon, visit **www.pearson.com/mylab/management** for activities that are applied, personalized, and offer immediate feedback.

LEARNING OBJECTIVES

When you finish studying this chapter, you should be able to:

1. Discuss what employers and supervisors can do to support employees' career development needs.

2. List and discuss the four steps in effectively coaching and mentoring an employee.

3. Explain why career development can improve employee engagement.

4. Describe a comprehensive approach to retaining employees.

5. List the main decisions employers should address in reaching promotion decisions.

6. Explain the factors you would consider when dismissing an employee.

⭐ 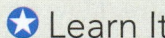 Learn It

If your professor has chosen to assign this, go to **www.pearson.com/mylab/management** to see what you should particularly focus on and to take the Chapter 9 Warm Up.

Source: Pressmaster/Shutterstock.

INTRODUCTION

Paul had been an engineer for a civil engineering firm for 12 years when it began to dawn on him that his career was going nowhere. He wanted to move into management, a desire he'd mentioned many times in the past five years to his boss, Fred, the company's founder and CEO. Fred seemed receptive, but always found a way to change the conversation. Today, at the annual performance appraisal, Paul decided to press the issue and was astounded at what Fred said: "You're a good engineer, Paul, but you do not have what it takes to be a manager. It's up to you whether you go or stay."

LEARNING OBJECTIVE 1
Discuss what employers and supervisors can do to support employees' career development needs.

career
The occupational positions a person has had over many years.

career management
The process for enabling employees to better understand and develop their career skills and interests, and to use these skills and interests more effectively.

career development
The lifelong series of activities that contribute to a person's career exploration, establishment, success, and fulfillment.

career planning
The deliberate process through which someone becomes aware of personal skills, interests, knowledge, motivations, and other characteristics and establishes action plans to attain specific goals.

Career Management

After appraising performance, it's often necessary to address career-related issues and to discuss them with subordinates. We'll address career planning and related topics in this chapter.

Before proceeding, we should define some of the terms we will be using. We may define **career** as the occupational positions a person holds over the years. **Career management** is a process for enabling employees to better understand and develop their career skills and interests and to use these skills and interests most effectively both within the company and after they leave the firm. **Career development** is the lifelong series of activities (such as workshops) that contribute to a person's career exploration, establishment, success, and fulfillment. **Career planning** is the deliberate process through which someone becomes aware of personal skills, interests, knowledge, motivations, and other characteristics; acquires information about opportunities and choices; identifies career-related goals; and establishes action plans to attain specific goals.

Careers Today

People once viewed careers as a sort of upward stairway from job to job, more often than not with one or, at most, a few firms. Today, recessions, mergers, outsourcing, consolidations, and more or less endless downsizings have changed the rules. Many people do still move up. But more often employees find themselves having to reinvent themselves. For example, the sales rep, laid off by a publishing firm that's just merged, may reinvent herself as an account executive at a media-oriented advertising firm.[1] Others aren't employees at all, instead building their careers around portfolios of evolving short term "gig" assignments.

Psychological Contract

One implication is that what employers and employees expect from each other is changing. What the employer and employee expect of each other is part of what psychologists call a *psychological contract*. This is an unwritten agreement between employers and employees that identifies each party's mutual expectations.[2] For example, one unstated expectation is that management will treat employees fairly and provide satisfactory work conditions, hopefully in a long-term relationship.

Employees are expected to respond "by demonstrating a good attitude, following directions, and showing loyalty to the organization."[3]

But with today's tumultuous labor markets, few employers or employees can count on long-term commitments. That undercuts the traditional psychological contract and makes managing one's career even more critical.

The Employee's Role in Career Management

The individual, the manager, and the employer all play roles in the individual's career development. For example, the manager should provide timely and objective performance feedback, offer developmental assignments and support, and participate in career development discussions with the employee. For its part, the employer should provide promotional opportunities, offer career information and career programs, and give employees career options.

Ultimately, however, the employee must accept responsibility for his or her own career; assess interests, skills, and values; seek out career information resources; and generally take those steps required to ensure a happy and fulfilling career. For the employee, career planning means matching one's strengths and weaknesses with occupational opportunities and threats. In other words, the person wants to pursue occupations, jobs, and a career that capitalize on his or her interests, aptitudes, values, and skills. He or she also wants to choose occupations, jobs, and a career that make sense in terms of projected future demand for various occupations. Ideally, he or she should create in his or her mind an ideal future "self" to strive for.[4]

As one example, career-counseling expert John Holland says that personality (including values, motives, and needs) is one important career choice determinant. For example, a person with a strong social orientation might be attracted to careers that entail interpersonal rather than intellectual or physical activities and to occupations such as social work. Holland found six basic personality types or orientations. Individuals can use his Self-Directed Search (SDS) test (available online at www.self-directed-search.com/) to assess their occupational orientations and preferred occupations. The SDS has an excellent reputation, but one study of 24 no-cost online career assessment websites concluded that many suffered from insufficient validation and confidentiality. However, a number of online career assessment instruments such as Career Key (www.careerkey.org) do reportedly provide validated and useful information.[5] O*Net offers a free comprehensive online My Next Move occupations and career assessment system (www.onetcenter.org/mynextmove.html). You will find other useful career tools at http://workday.com, in the following two exercises, and in the more complete discussion in this chapter's appendix.

Exercise 1 One useful exercise for identifying occupational skills is to head a page "The School or Occupational Tasks I Was Best At." Then write a short essay describing the tasks. Provide as much detail as you can about your duties and responsibilities and what you found enjoyable about each task. (It's not necessarily the most enjoyable *job* you've had, but the most enjoyable *task* you've had to perform within your jobs.) Next, do the same for two other tasks you've had. Now scrutinize the three essays. Underline the skills that you mentioned the most often. For example, did you especially enjoy the hours you spent doing research when you worked one summer as an office intern?[6]

Exercise 2 Another exercise may prove enlightening. On a page, answer the question: "If you could have any kind of job, what would it be?" Invent your own job if need be, and don't worry about what you *can* do—just what you want to do.[7]

■ HR and the Gig Economy

The Portfolio Career

Ana is living her dream. After graduating from State University as a marketing major in 2014, she worked in marketing for a big local firm for two years, and then left. Now she earns her living with a "portfolio" of what are essentially six to seven ever-changing part-time and consulting jobs (or gigs). At the moment, she's the part-time marketing manager for two local retail stores, she writes an "Ask Ana" column answering local business peoples' marketing questions for her local paper, she publishes an online blog of the same name, and she teaches two online courses—on retail marketing and on how to freelance—for State U's online college.

"At this point in my life, I love what I'm doing," she says. "I'm my own boss, I pretty much choose when I work, I only accept gigs that I truly want to do, and I can see in real time how I'm impacting the small businesses that I consult for. And every day brings unanticipated opportunities, most of them good." On the other hand, there are downsides. "I don't have a steady income stream (although having six different gigs at least means I'm not dependent on any one source). And I've had to piece together health insurance because I don't get benefits from any of my gigs." Like most people with portfolio careers, this isn't necessarily her long-term choice of career, but for where she is in life now, "I love what I'm doing."

---

portfolio career
a career built around using one's skills to create a livelihood based on multiple income sources.

What Are Portfolio Careers? Like Ana in the Gig Economy feature, more and more people today are embracing **portfolio careers**, in other words, careers built around using one's skills to create a livelihood based on multiple income sources, often from a variety of jobs paying different rates.[8] In Ana's case, she uses her marketing skills for her marketing manager gigs, her writing and marketing skills for her column and blog, and her coaching skills and sociability to excel at teaching her online courses. She earns about $150/hour in her marketing gigs, about $200/week from her column and blog, and $1,800/course for each course she teaches.

Are Portfolio Careers for You? Millions of people support themselves through portfolio careers today, and every one of them probably is doing so for his or her own reasons—from just wanting to be independent, to not being able to find a full-time job, or needing the flexibility for family matters. But there are some questions to ask yourself to see if this is for you:

Do you have what it takes to fly solo? For example, can you tolerate not having a steady full-time job; are you comfortable not having the same job to go to every day; are you good at juggling several different big tasks; and do you have the social and salesmanship skills to get out and beat the pavement to line up what will probably be a continually changing cast of clients?

What can you do? Especially, what saleable skills do you have for which someone will pay you?

Is it practical? Think through who your potential clients are, how much you can actually earn, and what the odds are that you'll be able to put it all together, to help you avoid a rude surprise. Try out your ideas on friends, and talk with them about which ideas seem more likely to succeed. (On the other hand is the saying, "Nothing ventured, nothing gained," so don't be too practical! One benefit of portfolio careers is that they're fluid, so you can make adjustments as you learn.)

The Employer's Role in Career Management

Along with the employee, the person's manager and employer have career management responsibilities. These responsibilities depend partly on how long the employee has been with the firm.

For example, *before hiring*, realistic job interviews can help prospective employees more accurately gauge whether the job is a good fit for them. Especially for recent college graduates, *the first job* can be crucial for building confidence and a more realistic picture of what he or she can and cannot do: providing challenging first jobs and having an experienced mentor who can help the person learn the ropes are important. Some refer to this as preventing **reality shock**, a phenomenon that occurs when a new employee's high expectations and enthusiasm confront the reality of a boring, unchallenging job. Periodic job rotation can help the person develop a more realistic picture of what he or she is good at, and thus the career moves that might be best. The accompanying HR in Practice features illustrates this.

reality shock
Results of a period that may occur at the initial career entry when the new employee's high job expectations confront the reality of a boring or otherwise unattractive work situation.

■ HR in Practice

Intuit's Job Rotation Program

Intuit offers new graduates entrée into its Rotational Development Programs.[9] These are comprehensive, two-year programs in which the new employee first learns about Intuit's products, customers, employees, strategies, and values. Next, the employee completes four six-month rotations, getting experience in a range of Intuit business units and a variety of functions, for instance, product management, marketing, and human resources. All Rotational Development Program participants are paired with an executive advisor, who provides career coaching and professional development mentoring.

⭐ Talk About It – 1

If your professor has chosen to assign this, go to **www.pearson.com/mylab/management** to discuss the following questions. Would such a program interest you? Why?

After the person has been *on the job* for a while, career-oriented appraisals—in which the manager is trained not just to appraise the employee but also to help match the person's strengths and weaknesses with a feasible career path and required development work—is important.

Employer Career Management Methods

Many employers provide employee career development support. For example, American Express opened career counseling centers for its call-center workers. Both Genentech and AFLAC hired career counselors, and are preparing their line managers to give career advice.[10] Google has employees who volunteer as career coaches and mentors for other employees, and whom Google officially designates "career gurus." Recently, over 1,000 Google employees used the gurus.[11]

Career development needn't be complicated. Even just receiving performance feedback from supervisors, getting individual development plans, and having access to training is enough for many employees. Figure 9.1 illustrates a simple employee performance summary/career planning form. Beyond that, job postings, formal mentoring with managers, and individual succession planning for high-potential employees are valuable.[12] Systems are widely available. For example, Halogen Software Company offers an online performance management system (go to www.halogensoftware.com/solutions/performance).[13] This system enables the employer and employee to choose employee development activities that support both the company's staffing needs and the employee's career aspirations.

Employee's Name	Employee's Current Position	Today's Date

I Performance Summary: *Briefly discuss this employee's performance over the past year (or other period), in terms of his or her achievement of assigned goals, effectiveness at interacting with colleagues, and any other criteria you believe are relevant here:*

II Strengths: *Based on your evaluation and experience with and discussions with employee, what would you say are his or her main strengths?*

III Career aspirations and goals: *Based on your experience with and discussions with employee, what would the two of you agree should be this person's career goals over the next 1-3 years and beyond?*

IV Areas for Development: *Based on what you know about this employee, what would the two of you agree are the main areas for development he or she should concentrate on over the next year or two?*

Development Objectives and Activities: *Planned to achieve this person's career goals.*

Development activities	Specific Action Plans	Milestones/Dates
1		
2		
3		
4		
5		

Signatures: Supervisor_____ Employee_____

Figure 9.1

Employee Career Development Plan

Source: Copyright Gary Dessler, PhD.

Other employer methods are popular. A *career planning workshop* is "a planned learning event in which participants are expected to be actively involved, completing career planning exercises and inventories and participating in career skills practice sessions."[14] A typical workshop includes self-assessment exercises (skills, interests, values, and so on), an assessment of important occupational trends, and goal-setting and action-planning segments.

As we explained in Chapter 7, some employers provide 401(k)-type *lifelong learning accounts* for their employees. Both employers and employees contribute, and the employees can tap into these to get career-related education and development. *Career coaches* help employees create five-year plans, showing where their careers with the firm may lead; the employer and employee can then base the latter's development plans on what the employee needs.[15] At Shell China, "career stewards" meet regularly with its "emerging leaders." The HR Tools feature illustrates steps individual managers can take to support their employees' career development.[16]

■ HR Tools for Line Managers and Small Businesses

The Manager's Role in Employee Career Development

It is hard to overstate the impact that a manager can have on his or her employees' career development. With little or no effort than realistic performance reviews and candid skills assessments, a competent supervisor can help the employee get on and stay on the right career track. Conversely, an indifferent supervisor may look back on years of having inhibited his or her employees' progress.

Therefore, responsible supervisors schedule regular performance reviews and, at these reviews, as appropriate, also discuss whether the employee's exhibited skills are consistent with the person's career goals. Even a simple informal career development plan like the one in Figure 9.1 (page 265) can suffice. The aim is for the manager and employee to translate the latter's performance appraisal into development plans.

Small Business Applications

Beyond that, there is much a small business owner can do to facilitate employee career development. For example, we saw in Chapter 7 (Training) that small businesses can provide significant career-related training at nominal or no cost;[17] for example, identify/provide online training opportunities; provide a library of DVD tutorials; send employees to seminars, classes, and association meetings for learning and networking; and encourage them to enroll in professional associations.

Furthermore, being small should enable the owner to be better attuned to his or her employees' strengths, weaknesses, and aspirations and thereby to be more attentive to which jobs they'd like to do; give them an opportunity to train for and move into these jobs. Use an online appraisal system that includes career planning, such as eAppraisal from www.halogensoftware.com.[18]

Finally, one small business writer provides a selection of particularly useful insights for promoting professional development.[19] These include the following:

- Facilitate cross-training. Once an employee masters his or her job, encourage the person to learn the skills of complementary positions. Such cross-training engages employees by developing their repertoire of skills. It also makes good business sense, for instance, making it easier to move employees when someone is out sick.
- Offer professional development opportunities, such as on-site workshops or seminars and lunch-and-learns with guest speakers.
- Facilitate informal or formal mentoring and peer-coaching relationships between staff members.

- And again, consider creating (or at least discussing) a career development plan with each employee as part of the performance appraisal process. Have each employee identify at least one skill or area they would like to work on.

 Talk About It – 2

Provide an example of a time when a manager (or someone else) was particularly helpful in guiding your career progress. What exactly did he or she do? How well do you think Fred, from the chapter opener, handled the matter of Paul's career development? Why?

Diversity Counts

Toward Career Success People with disabilities tend to have less career success than do those without disabilities.[20] Some of this may be self-imposed. For example, some with disabilities may have lower career expectations or may not proactively seek work-related help or the accommodations they are due under EEO law.

However, most such problems aren't self-imposed but reflect erroneous assumptions by managers and coworkers. Though well meaning, they may view those with disabilities as unable to perform certain jobs, negatively evaluate them as "poor occupational fits," and assume that jobs designed for those without disabilities are inappropriate for those with disabilities. It is the managers and coworkers who must rid themselves of such stereotypes.

LEARNING OBJECTIVE 2
List and discuss the four steps in effectively coaching an employee.

KNOWLEDGE BASE

coaching
Educating, instructing, and training subordinates.

mentoring
Advising, counseling, and guiding.

Improving Mentoring and Coaching Skills

Supporting employees' career-development needs invariably requires tapping the manager's training and mentoring skills. **Coaching** means educating, instructing, and training subordinates. **Mentoring** means advising, counseling, and guiding. Coaching focuses on teaching shorter-term job-related skills. Mentoring focuses on helping employees navigate longer-term career-type hazards. Supervisors have always coached and mentored employees. But with more managers leading highly trained employees and self-managing teams, supporting, coaching, and mentoring are fast replacing giving orders for getting things done. The Management Skills feature shows what to do.

Employers understand that coaching and mentoring are important. One survey of training programs found that the top skills taught were "coaching a performance problem" (72%), "communicating performance standards" (69%), "coaching a development opportunity" (69%), and "conducting a performance appraisal" (67%).[21]

BUILDING YOUR MANAGEMENT SKILLS:
How to Be an Effective Coach

> Coaching and mentoring require both analytical and interpersonal skills. They require *analysis* because it's futile to advise someone if you don't know what the problem is. They require *interpersonal skills* because it's equally futile to know the problem if you can't get the person to change.
>
> Some performance situations don't require coaching. For example, if your new employee learns the first time how to do the job, or if your employee's performance review is flawless, you won't need to do much coaching. Otherwise, you're probably going to have to coach the employee.

Coaching does not mean just telling someone what to do. We can best think of coaching in terms of a four-step process: *preparation, planning, active coaching,* and *follow-up.*[22] *Preparation* means understanding the problem, the employee, and the employee's skills. Your aim is to formulate a hypothesis about what the problem is. You'll watch the employee to see what he or she is doing, and observe the workflow and how coworkers interact with the employee. In addition to observation, you may review (as we explained in Chapter 7, Training) objective data on things like productivity, absenteeism, accidents, grievances, product quality, customer complaints, and the employee's previous performance reviews and training.

Planning the solution is next. Perhaps the most powerful way to get someone to change is to obtain his or her enthusiastic agreement on what change is required. This requires reaching agreement on the problem and on what to change. You'll then lay out a change plan in the form of *steps to take, measures of success,* and *date to complete.*

With agreement on a plan, you can start the *actual coaching.* Here you are, in essence, the teacher. Your toolkit will include what you learned about on-the-job training in Chapter 7 (for example, *prepare the learner, present the operation, try out the trainee,* and *follow up*). As one writer says, "an effective coach offers ideas and advice in such a way that the subordinate can hear them, respond to them, and appreciate their value."[23]

Finally, bad habits sometimes reemerge. Therefore *follow up* and reobserve the person's progress periodically.

Figure 9.2 presents a coaching self-evaluation checklist for assessing your coaching skills.

Questions to Ask Yourself	Yes	No
Did you plan the approach you'll take before you started the coaching session?	☐	☐
Do you take your position as a coach seriously?	☐	☐
Do you address the employee's career, not just his or her current performance?	☐	☐
Do you listen for and address the trainee's concerns about the job?	☐	☐
Do you adapt the lessons to the abilities of the trainee?	☐	☐
Do you check for trainee understanding?	☐	☐
Do you make sure the employee has the skills required to do the job, or plans to develop them?	☐	☐
Do you set high but attainable goals?	☐	☐
Do you work with the employee to develop viable alternatives?	☐	☐
Do you give timely and specific positive and negative feedback?	☐	☐
Does your feedback focus on the person's behavior and its consequences?	☐	☐
Do you define the ongoing job performance expectations for the employee?	☐	☐
Do you listen to the trainee's opinions about doing the job?	☐	☐
Do you provide encouragement?	☐	☐

Figure 9.2

Coach's Self-Evaluation Checklist

Source: Based on *Coaching and Mentoring: How to Develop Top Talent and Achieve Stronger Performance,* by Richard Luecke.

Being a Better Mentor

Mentoring traditionally means having experienced senior people advising, counseling, and guiding employees' longer-term career development. An employee who agonizes over which career to pursue might need mentoring.

Mentoring may be formal or informal. Informally, mid- and senior-level managers may voluntarily help less-experienced employees—for instance, by giving them career advice and helping them to navigate office politics. Many employers also have formal mentoring programs. Here the employer pairs protégés with mentors and provides training to help the mentor and protégé better understand their respective responsibilities. Either formal or informal, studies show that having a mentor can significantly enhance one's career satisfaction and success.[24]

Mentoring is both valuable and dangerous. It can be valuable insofar as the mentor may influence, in a positive way, the careers and lives of subordinates and colleagues. The danger lies on the other side of that coin. *Coaching* focuses on daily tasks that you can easily relearn, so the downside is usually limited. *Mentoring* focuses on relatively hard-to-reverse longer-term issues and often touches on the person's psychology (motives, needs, aptitudes, and how one gets along with others, for instance). Because the supervisor is usually not a psychologist or trained career advisor, he or she must be cautious in the mentoring advice he or she gives.

Research on what supervisors can do to be better mentors reveals few surprises. Effective mentors *set high standards*; are willing to *invest the time* and effort the mentoring relationship requires; and actively *steer protégés* into important projects, teams, and jobs.[25] Effective mentoring requires *trust*, and the level of trust reflects the mentor's *professional competence*, *consistency*, *ability to communicate*, and readiness to *share control*.[26]

However, studies suggest that traditional mentoring is less effective for women than it is for men. For example, in one survey of employees who had mentoring relationships, a CEO or other senior executive mentored 78% of the men, compared with 69% of women.[27] Figures like these are prompting employers to assign women to "mentor/sponsors" who have more organizational clout. For example, when Deutsche Bank discovered that several female managing directors had left the firm for better jobs at competitors, it began pairing them with mentor/sponsors from the bank's executive committee. The latter were in a position to advocate the women for promotion.

The Protégé's Responsibilities Effective mentors are important but the protégé is still responsible for making the relationship work. *Choose an appropriate potential mentor*, one who is objective enough to help guide your career. *Make it easier for a potential mentor to agree to your request*, by making it clear what you expect in terms of time and advice. *Be selective* about the work-related issues that you ask about. The mentoring relationship generally should not address personal problems.[28]

Improving Performance Through HRIS

Integrating Talent Management and Career/Succession Planning Various talent management systems enable employers to integrate data from appraisals, career development, training, and succession planning. For example, Halogen eSuccession enables the employer to "identify the skills and competencies required to support your three- to five-year strategic plans and cultivate these in your high-potential employees with career and development planning . . . ."[29] Cornerstone Succession integrates talent profiles, career management, and internal recruiting.[30] Sum-Total Succession Planning supports "a holistic, end-to-end talent management strategy" including:[31]

- **360 feedback.** Competency reviews by peers are input into succession gap analysis.
- **Career development.** As employees map out their career progress, plans can be established that address competency, skill, and behavior gaps.
- **Compensation management.** Financial plans can be tied to future succession plans so that their financial impact can be modeled.
- **Career progression.** Historical information regarding past positions and career progress can be used to guide future succession decisions.
- **Learning management.** Learning paths and courses can be set for projected future positions.
- **Performance management.** Performance reviews can identify consistent high performers and top talent in the organization.
- **Recruiting and hiring.** The Sum-Total system compares current job profiles with succession plans; external candidates can then be recruited as needed.[32]

LEARNING OBJECTIVE 3
Explain why career development can improve employee engagement.

Employee Engagement Guide for Managers
Career Management

The globalization of the world economy has been a boon in many ways. For products and services ranging from cars to computers to air travel, it powered lower prices, better quality, and, in many countries, higher productivity and living standards. However, these advances haven't come without a price. The same cost-efficiencies, belt-tightening, and productivity improvements that globalization produced also triggered workforce dislocations in many places. The desire for efficiencies drove firms to downsize, and to "do more with less." It prompted thousands of mergers, many of which aim specifically to "eliminate redundancies;" in other words, cut headcount. Partly as a reaction to these changes, and to the Great Recession of 2008–2009, the U.S. unemployment rate rocketed up from about 4.5% to over 8%, before moving down to about 4.5% more recently.

The New Psychological Contract

As mentioned earlier, changes like these understandably prompt many employees to ask why they should be loyal to their employers. "Why," they might ask, "should I be loyal to you if you're just going to dump me when you decide to cut costs again?" To paraphrase the author of the book *Pack Your Own Parachute*, many employees today thus tend to think of themselves as free agents, there to do a good job but also to prepare for the next career move to another firm. Yesterday's psychological contract may have been something like, "Do your best and be loyal to us, and we'll take care of your career." Today, it often is "Do your best for us and be loyal to us for as long as you're here, and we'll provide you with the developmental opportunities you'll need to move on and have a successful career." In other words, employers have to think through how they're going to maintain employee engagement in the face of potential downsizings and thereby minimize voluntary departures and maximize employee effort.

Commitment-Oriented Career Development Efforts

The employer's career planning and development process can play a role in achieving this. Many years ago, the psychologist Abraham Maslow suggested that, for most people, what he called the ultimate need is the desire for self-fulfillment, namely the desire to become "actualized" in terms of what he or she is capable of becoming.[33] Ironically, many companies not only don't try to fulfill this need, but they actually thwart it, for instance by offering unchallenging jobs and a dearth of career-growth opportunities.

Not surprisingly, progressive firms such as SAS and Google do things differently. They adopt career development practices that aim to ensure that employees have an opportunity to use and develop their skills at work. To paraphrase the CEO of software giant SAS, his company works hard to create a corporate culture that cares about employees' personal and professional growth.[34] In one survey, about 33% of respondents in high-performing organizations said their organizations' career development programs were effective in raising employee engagement, versus 21% of respondents in poor-performing ones.[35] The bottom line is that the employer's career-related processes should send the signal that the employer cares about the employee's career success and thus deserves the employee's engagement.

In such companies, career development goes beyond career coaching and workshops (although these are important.) As one example, we saw in Chapter 5 that FedEx fosters career growth through its strong internal recruiting and promotion-from-within policies. The centerpiece is its career records and job posting system, which it calls JCATS (Job Change Applicant Tracking System). Announcements of new job openings via JCATS usually take place each Friday. All employees applying for the position get numerical scores based on job performance and length of service. They are then advised whether they were chosen as candidates.

Career-Oriented Appraisals

As another example, managers who use their companies' performance review only to tell the employee how he or she is doing miss an opportunity. The performance appraisal should also provide an opportunity to link the employee's performance, career interests, and developmental needs into a coherent career plan. With *career-oriented appraisals*, the supervisor and employee jointly merge the latter's past performance, career preferences, and developmental needs into a formal career plan.

Such an appraisal system need not be automated, but as noted earlier, several effective online systems are available. For example, Halogen eAppraisal™ enables the manager to identify relevant employee development activities given the employee's competencies and career development plans and/or goals. The employer then organizes development activities around the person's needs.

The JCPenney (Penney's) management career-grid approach provides a classic illustration of what is possible (although management changes several years ago sidelined much of this effort). The company trained its managers to consider the employee's performance, career interests, and Penney's needs, and to develop a career plan including development activities for the employee.

Here is how it worked. Prior to the annual appraisal, the associate and his or her manager reviewed Penney's career grid. The grid itemized all supervisory positions at Penney's (grouped by operation jobs, merchandise jobs, personnel jobs, and general management jobs); it also included specific job titles such as "regional catalog sales manager." The firm also provided thumbnail job descriptions for all the grid's jobs.

The grid also identified typical promotional routes. For example, when considering the next assignment for a management associate, the supervisor could consider not only merchandise positions but also operations and personnel positions. Promotional projections could cross all four groups, as well as one or two job levels. For example, a senior merchandising manager might be projected for promotion to either assistant buyer or general merchandise manager. In sum, the Penney's grid approach shows how employers can use the performance appraisal process to help employees and managers formulate employee career plans built around the employee's strengths, weaknesses, and career preferences.[36]

Other employers use special training and development programs to facilitate career development. The accompanying HR in Practice feature provides an example.

■ HR in Practice

Career Development at Medtronic[37]

Medtronic, which engineers and manufactures advanced medical devices, has an effective career development program. The company offers a wide range of career planning and development support tools aimed at helping employees understand their occupational strengths and weaknesses and reach their potential. These tools include customized development plans; self-assessment and feedback tools; mentoring programs; comprehensive on-site classes covering business, engineering, and science topics; tuition reimbursement scholarships; and online job listings so the employee can seek out new career opportunities within the company.

In addition, new MBA employees can participate in Medtronic's corporate Leadership Development Rotation Program. This is a two- to three-year program. It includes 12- to 18-month assignments in two different geographic locations, providing participants with a broad understanding of Medtronics, combined with in-depth functional experiences. Functional tracks include clinical, corporate development, finance, human resources, information technology, marketing/business development, operations, and regulatory. In addition to their job assignments, participants engage in developmental experiences including peer mentoring programs, functional training, and leadership workshops.

Among other things, program candidates require three to five years of professional and relevant work experience, an MBA (or other master's-level degree as appropriate), and to be mobile and willing to pursue opportunities in various geographic locations.

✪ Talk About It – 3

If your professor has chosen to assign this, go to **www.pearson.com/mylab/management** to discuss the following question. Look more closely at this program (go to **www.Medtronic.com**; then click Careers, and discuss why its programs should positively impact employee engagement.

LEARNING OBJECTIVE 4
Describe a comprehensive approach to retaining employees.

Managing Employee Retention and Turnover

Turnover—the rate at which employees leave a firm—varies widely. For example, in the hotel and food services industry, about half the employees leave voluntarily each year. In contrast, voluntary turnover in education is about 12%.[38]

And that reflects only employees who leave voluntarily, such as for better jobs. It doesn't include *involuntary* separations, such as for poor performance.[39] Combining voluntary and involuntary turnover produces some astounding statistics. For example, the turnover in many restaurants is around 100% per year. Many need to replace just about all their employees every year! The costs of such turnover are high, as the accompanying HR as a Profit Center feature illustrates.[40]

■ HR as a Profit Center

Costs of Turnover

A research team analyzed the tangible and intangible costs of turnover in a call center with 31 agents and 4 supervisors.[41] Tangible costs of an agent's leaving included, for instance, the costs of recruiting, screening, interviewing, and testing applicants, as well as the cost of wages while the new agent was oriented and trained. Intangible costs included the cost of lost productivity for the new agent (who is less productive at first than his or her predecessor), the cost of rework for errors the new agent makes, and the supervisory cost for coaching the new agent. The researchers estimated the cost of an agent leaving at about $21,500. This call center averaged 18.6 vacancies per year (about a 60% turnover rate). Therefore, the researchers estimated the total annual cost of agent turnover at $400,853. Taking steps to cut this turnover rate in, say, half could save this firm about $200,000 per year.[42]

⭐ Talk About It – **4**

If your professor has chosen to assign this, go to **www.pearson.com/mylab/ management** to discuss the following: Discuss three steps you would take to reduce the need to dismiss employees.

Managing Voluntary Turnover

Reducing turnover requires identifying and managing the reasons for both voluntary and involuntary turnover.[43] We address managing voluntary turnover here and managing involuntary turnover later in the chapter.

Managing voluntary turnover requires identifying its causes and then addressing them. Unfortunately, identifying why employees voluntarily leave is easier said than done. People who are dissatisfied with their jobs are more likely to leave, but the sources of dissatisfaction are many and varied.

Consultants collected survey data from 262 U.S. organizations having a minimum of 1,000 employees. In this survey, the five top reasons high-commitment/ top-performing employees gave for leaving (ranked from high to low) were pay, promotional opportunities, work–life balance, career development, and health care benefits. Other reasons employees voluntarily leave include unfairness, not having their voices heard, and a lack of recognition.[44] (Sometimes just asking, "All things considered, how satisfied are you with your job?" is as effective as surveying employees' attitudes toward multiple facets of the job, such as supervision and pay.[45]) Practical considerations also affect turnover. For example, high unemployment reduces voluntary turnover, and some locales have fewer job opportunities (and thus turnover) than do others.

As the text explains, voluntary turnover is just one way that employees withdraw. Withdrawal in general means separating oneself from one's current situation, and at work it may manifest itself in daydreaming, lack of attention to one's job, or other counterproductive behaviors.

Source: Syda Productions/Shutterstock.

Turnover isn't always bad. For example, losing low-performing employees isn't as problematical as losing high-performing ones. Some firms, such as the restaurant chain Applebee's, even incentivize their managers differentially, with higher incentives for reducing turnover among top-performing employees.[46]

Retention Strategies for Reducing Voluntary Turnover

In any case, given the variety of things prompting employees to leave voluntarily, what can one do to manage retention? There is no silver bullet. The manager should understand that retaining employees is a talent management issue and that the best retention strategies are therefore multifunctional. For example, employees who aren't interested in their jobs, sense that they're not suited for their jobs, or who feel undercompensated are more likely to leave. Employers can address such issues only by instituting effective and comprehensive talent management practices. Put another way, turnovers (both voluntary and involuntary) often start with poor selection decisions, compounded by inadequate training, insensitive appraisals, and inequitable pay. Therefore, trying to formulate a "retention strategy" without considering all of one's HR practices is generally futile.[47]

A Comprehensive Approach to Retaining Employees

However, research findings plus survey results and insights from practitioners such as consultants Development Dimensions International (DDI) and Robert Half International do provide insights into the building blocks of a comprehensive retention program.

The logical place to start is by *periodically tracking* the number of employees—and particularly top performers and high potentials—who leave the company.[48] Then, identify the issues. Exit interviews can provide useful insights into potential turnover problems. Many employers administer attitude surveys to monitor employees' feelings about matters such as supervision and pay. Open-door policies and anonymous "hotlines" help management identify and remedy morale problems before they get out of hand. Sometimes, analyzing the situation leads to simple solutions. For example, Walmart discovered it could significantly reduce turnover by providing aggressively realistic previews about the job's demands and work hours. Having identified potential problems, the employer can then take steps like the following to boost employee retention.

The most obvious explanation for why employees quit is often also the correct one: *low pay*. Particularly for high performers and key employees, enhanced pay has been the retention tool of choice for many employers.[49]

However, employees don't just leave for better pay. For example, people who are unsuited for their jobs or who work for abusive supervisors are more likely to leave. Therefore, retention starts with *selecting* the right employees.[50] Selection here refers not just to the worker but also to choosing and monitoring supervisors. For example, FedEx conducts periodic employee attitude surveys to get a continuing sense for how its supervisors are performing.

In addition, inadequate *career prospects* and professional development prompt many employees to leave. Conversely, a training and career development program can provide a strong incentive for staying. One expert says, "Professionals who feel their company cares about their development and progress are much more likely to stay."[51] Periodically discuss with employees their career preferences and prospects at your firm, and help them lay out career paths. Furthermore, "don't wait until performance reviews to remind top employees how valuable they are to your company."[52]

People can't do their jobs if they don't know what to do or what their goals are. Therefore, an important part of retaining employees is *clarifying what your expectations* are regarding their performance.

Psychology is important as well. In addition to pay and benefits, employees need and appreciate *recognition* for a job well done. And companies that are tense and "*political*" may prompt employees to leave, while companies that make them feel comfortable encourage them to stay.

High-performance/involvement work practices seem to improve employee retention. One study focused on call-center employees. Employers that made greater use of high-involvement work practices (for instance, problem-solving groups, increased employee discretion, and self-directed teams) had significantly lower rates of quits, dismissals, and total turnover. So did those that "invested" more in employees (for instance, in promotion opportunities, high relative pay, pensions, and full-time jobs).[53] Conversely, performance pressures (such as intensive performance monitoring) related to significantly higher turnover rates.[54] In one survey conducted by Robert Half and CareerBuilder.com, workers identified "*flexible work arrangements*" and "telecommuting" as the two top benefits that would encourage them to choose one job or another.[55]

Finally, data are important in controlling employee turnover. At Nationwide Mutual Insurance Co., for instance, managers receive monthly "*scorecards*" with turnover data. Alliant Techsystems Inc. uses business analytics to sift through employee data to calculate, in terms of a "flight-risk model," the likelihood that any particular employee will leave.[56] The Trends feature provides more examples

TRENDS SHAPING HR: *Digital and Social Media*

RETENTION AT SAS Digital and social media tools can vastly improve the employee engagement/retention process. Software company SAS's employee-retention program sifts through employee data on traits like skills, tenure, performance, education, and friendships. It can predict which high-value employees are more likely to quit in the near future (allowing SAS to try to head that off).[57] As noted, Alliant Techsystems created a "flight risk model" to calculate the probability an employee would leave and to take corrective action.[58] Based on its analysis of previous survey results, Google's "Googlegeist" survey contains five questions aimed at identifying Googlers who are more likely to leave; if a team's responses fall below 70% favorable, Google takes corrective action.[59] Analytical software from Evolv (now Cornerstone, www.cornerstone-ondemand.com/evolv) can crunch more than 500 million data points on an array of items ranging from unemployment rates to a person's social media usage, to help clients like Xerox improve retention.[60] For example, Evolv discovered that employees with two social media accounts perform much better than those with more or less, and that in call-center work, employees with criminal backgrounds perform better than those never arrested.[61] ■

Job Withdrawal

Voluntary turnover is just one way that employees withdraw. Withdrawal in general means separating oneself from one's current situation—it's often a means of escape for someone who is dissatisfied or fearful. At work, *job withdrawal* refers to "actions intended to place physical or psychological distance between employees and their work environments."[62]

Poor attendance and voluntary turnover are two ways employees withdraw. Other familiar types of job withdrawal can be less obvious if no less corrosive. Some examples include spending time gossiping with colleagues, taking many informal work breaks, and simply not doing parts of the job that the person finds onerous.[63] Other employees stop "showing up" mentally ("psychological withdrawal"), perhaps daydreaming at their desks while productivity suffers.[64] The employee is there, but mentally absent. In fact, the *job withdrawal process* tends to be incremental, often evolving from daydreaming to absences to quitting: "When an employee perceives that temporary withdrawal will not resolve his/her problems, then the employee is apt to choose a more permanent form of withdrawal," such as turnover.[65]

Dealing with Job Withdrawal[66] Because many people have experienced the desire to "get away," it's usually not difficult to empathize with those who feel they must escape. People tend to move toward situations that make them feel good and away from those that make them feel bad. More technically, "negative emotional states make people aware that their current situation is problematic, and this awareness motivates them to take action."[67] People are repelled by situations that produce unpleasant, uncomfortable emotions and are attracted to those that produce pleasant, comfortable ones.[68] The point is that the more negative (or less positive) the person's mood about a situation, the more likely he or she will try to avoid or withdraw from the situation.[69]

The manager can therefore think of withdrawal-reducing strategies in terms of reducing the job's negative effects and/or raising its positive effects. Because potential negatives and positives are virtually limitless, addressing withdrawal again requires a comprehensive human resource management approach. Illustrative potential negatives include, for instance, boring jobs, poor supervision, low pay, bullying, lack of career prospects, and poor working conditions. Potential positives include job enrichment, supportive supervision, equitable pay/family-friendly benefits, disciplinary/appeals processes, career development opportunities, safe and healthy working conditions, and high-morale colleagues.[70] Interviews, surveys, and observation can help identify issues to address.

With more employees taking their jobs home via smart phones and iPads, employee detachment (not withdrawal) isn't always bad. Two researchers found detaching oneself from work improves family life. They advise working out a system for ensuring some quality family time. For example, the employee and his or her partner might "agree on certain rules such as keeping the weekend free of work, or switching off the mobile phone after dinner."[71]

LEARNING OBJECTIVE 5
List the main decisions employers should address in reaching promotion decisions.

Managing Promotions and Transfers

Career planning and mentoring often precede promotion decisions. Most people crave promotions, which usually mean more pay, responsibility, and (often) job satisfaction. For employers, promotions can provide opportunities to reward exceptional performance and to fill open positions with tested and loyal employees. Yet the promotion process isn't always a positive experience. Unfairness or secrecy can poison the process. Furthermore, with more employers downsizing, some "promotions" take the form of more challenging, but not necessarily better-paid, jobs. Several decisions, therefore, loom large in any firm's promotion process.

KNOW YOUR EMPLOYMENT LAW
Establish Clear Guidelines for Managing Promotions

In general, the employer's promotion processes must comply with all the same antidiscrimination laws as do procedures for recruiting and selecting employees or any other HR actions. For example, Title VII of the 1964 Civil Rights Act covers any "terms, conditions, or privileges of employment." Similarly, the Age Discrimination in Employment Act of 1967 made it unlawful to discriminate against older employees or applicants for employment in any manner, including promotion.

The employer should establish safeguards to ensure that the promotion decision doesn't prompt a discrimination claim, or a claim of retaliation, as it often does. For example, the Fifth U.S. Circuit Court of Appeals allowed a woman's claim of retaliation to proceed when she provided evidence that she was turned down for promotion because a supervisor she had previously accused of sexual harassment persuaded her current supervisor not to promote her.[72]

One way to defend against such claims is to make promotion procedures clear and objective. For example, the Eighth U.S. Circuit Court of Appeals held that a company's failure to set objective guidelines and procedures for promoting current employees may suggest employment discrimination.[73] (In this case, the court found that the organization, a community college, did not consistently use the same procedures for hiring and promotions, did not clarify when and under what conditions vacant positions were announced, or whether or not there were application deadlines.) In another case, the employer turned down a 61-year-old employee for a promotion because of his interview performance; the person who interviewed him said he did not "get a real feeling of confidence" from the candidate.[74] In this case, "the court made it clear that while subjective reasons can justify adverse employment decisions, an employer must articulate any clear and reasonably specific factual bases upon which it based its decision." In other words, have objective evidence supporting your subjective assessment for promotion. ■

Promotions are usually good for those promoted, but what of those left behind?[75] Here caution is needed. In one study, military officer training candidates who were *not* promoted were more likely to engage in counterproductive work behaviors (such as verbal and physical acts of aggression, property theft, and sleeping on duty) than were those who were promoted.

Crucial promotion-related decisions include the following.

Decision 1: Is Seniority or Competence the Rule?

Probably the most important decision is whether to base promotion on seniority or competence, or some combination of the two.

Today's focus on competitiveness favors competence. However, this depends on several things. Union agreements sometimes contain clauses that emphasize seniority. Civil service regulations that stress seniority rather than competence often govern promotions in many public-sector organizations.

Decision 2: How Should We Measure Competence?

If the firm opts for competence, it must define and measure competence. Defining and measuring *past* performance is relatively straightforward. But promotions should rest on procedures for predicting the candidate's future performance.

For better or worse, most employers use prior performance as a guide and assume that (based on exemplary prior performance) the person will do well on the new job. Many others use tests or assessment centers, or tools such as the **9-Box Grid** (Chapter 7, page 219), to evaluate promotable employees and identify those with executive potential.

For example, given the public safety issues involved, police departments and the military tend to be very systematic when evaluating candidates for promotion to command positions. For the police, traditional promotional reviews include a written knowledge test, an assessment center, credit for seniority, and a score based on

9-box grid

In workforce planning, this displays three levels of current job performance (exceptional, fully performing, not yet fully performing) across the top, and also shows three levels of likely potential (eligible for promotion, room for growth in current position, not likely to grow beyond current position) down the side.

Most federal and state employment laws contain antiretaliation provisions. One court allowed a claim of retaliation to proceed when a female employee provided evidence that her employer turned her down for a promotion because a supervisor she had previously accused of sexual harassment made comments that persuaded her current supervisor not to promote her.

Source: Sylvain Robin/123RF.

recent performance appraisal ratings. Most include a personnel records review. This includes evaluation of things like supervisory-related education and experience and ratings from multiple sources and behavioral evidence.[76]

Decision 3: Is the Process Formal or Informal?

Many firms have informal promotion processes. They may or may not post open positions, and key managers may use their own "unpublished" criteria to make decisions. Here employees may (reasonably) conclude that factors like "who you know" are more important than performance and that working hard to get ahead—at least in this firm—is futile.

Other employers set formal, published promotion policies and procedures. Employees receive a *formal promotion policy* describing the criteria by which the firm awards promotions. A *job posting policy* states the firm will post open positions and their requirements, and circulates these to all employees. As explained in Chapter 5 (Recruiting), many employers also maintain *employee qualification databanks* and use replacement charts and computerized employee information systems.

Decision 4: Vertical, Horizontal, or Other?

Promotions aren't necessarily upward. For example, how do you motivate employees with the prospect of promotion when your firm is downsizing? And how do you provide promotional opportunities for those, like engineers, who may have little or no interest in managerial roles?

Several options are available. Some firms, such as the exploration division of British Petroleum (BP), create two parallel career paths, one for managers and another for "individual contributors" such as high-performing engineers. At BP, individual contributors can move up to nonsupervisory but senior positions, such as "senior engineer." These jobs have most of the financial rewards attached to management-track positions at that level.

Another option is to move the person horizontally. For instance, move a production employee to human resources, to develop his or her skills and to test and challenge his or her aptitudes. And, in a sense, "promotions" are possible even when leaving the person in the same job. For example, you can usually enrich the job and enhance the opportunity for assuming more responsibility.

Finally, reach out to employees who may have aspired to a promotion but who were not yet ready to be promoted. To paraphrase Google's chief HR officer, doing so is far better than having them quit or withdraw.[77]

Diversity Counts

The Gender Gap Women still don't reach the top of the career ladder in numbers proportionate to their numbers in U.S. industry. Women constitute more than 40% of the workforce, but hold less than 2% of top management positions. Blatant or subtle discrimination may account for much of this. In one study, promoted women had to receive higher performance ratings than promoted men to get promoted, "suggesting that women were held to stricter standards for promotion."[78] Women report greater barriers (such as being excluded from informal networks) than do men and more difficulty getting developmental assignments. Women have to be more proactive than men to get such assignments. Minority women seem particularly at risk. Women of color hold only a small percentage of professional and managerial private-sector positions.[79]

Unfortunately, many career development programs are inconsistent with the needs of minority and nonminority women. For example, many such programs underestimate the role played by family responsibilities in many women's (and men's) lives. Similarly, some programs assume that career paths are continuous; yet the need to stop working for a time to attend to family needs often punctuates the career paths of many people of color and women (and perhaps men).[80] Many refer to this totality of subtle and not-so-subtle barriers to women's career progress as the *glass ceiling*. Employers need to eliminate the barriers that impede women's career progress. Some specific steps include the following.

Eliminate Institutional Barriers: Many practices (such as required late-night meetings) may seem gender-neutral but in fact disproportionately affect women.

Improve Networking and Mentoring: To improve female employees' networking opportunities, Marriott International instituted a series of leadership conferences for women. Speakers offered practical tips for career advancement and shared their experiences. More important, the conferences provided informal opportunities—over lunch, for instance—for the Marriott women to meet and forge business relationships.

Break the Glass Ceiling: Eliminating glass ceiling barriers requires more than an order from the CEO because the problem is usually systemic. As one expert puts it, "The roots of gender discrimination are built into a platform of work practices, cultural norms and images that appear unbiased . . . . People don't even notice them, let alone question them." These range from the late meetings mentioned earlier to golf course memberships.

Adopt Flexible Career Tracks: Inflexible promotional ladders (such as "You must work eight years of 50-hour weeks to apply for partner") can put women—who often have more responsibility for child-raising chores—at a disadvantage. In many large accounting firms, men are therefore more likely than women to have put in the continuous dozen or so years someone normally needs to become eligible for partner. One solution is to institute career tracks (including reduced hours and more flexible year-round work schedules) that enable women to periodically reduce their time at work, but remain on a partner track. For example, when the accounting firm Deloitte noticed it was losing female auditors, it instituted a new flexible/reduced work schedule. This enabled many working mothers who might otherwise have left to stay with the firm.[81]

Managing Transfers

transfer
Reassignments to similar positions in other parts of the firm.

A **transfer** is a move from one job to another, usually with no change in salary or grade. Employers may transfer a worker to vacate a position where he or she is no longer needed, to fill one where he or she is needed, or more generally to find a better fit for the employee. Many firms today boost productivity by consolidating positions. Transfers are a way to give displaced employees a chance for another assignment or, perhaps, some personal growth. Employees seek transfers for many reasons, including more interesting jobs, greater convenience—better hours, location of work, and so on—or to jobs offering greater advancement possibilities. Some promotions and job transfers require the employee to move to a new locale. In this case, the "transfer" is physical. Here the employee may have to consider not just the job but also the effects of the transfer on his or her family.

Managing Retirements

For many employees, years of appraisals and career planning end with retirement.

Retirement planning is a significant long-term issue for employers. In the United States, the number of 25- to 34-year-olds is growing slowly, and the number of 35- to 44-year-olds is declining. So, with many employees in their 50s and 60s moving toward traditional retirement age, a shortage of talented workers caused by retirements is a looming threat; however, many employees have focused less on this longer-term threat than on the need for shorter-term downsizings to cut costs.[82]

Many have wisely chosen to fill their staffing gaps in part with current or soon-to-be retirees. Fortuitously, 78% of employees in one survey said they expect to continue working in some capacity after normal retirement age (64% want to do so part time). Only about a third said they plan to continue work for financial reasons; about 43% said they just wanted to remain active.[83]

The bottom line is that "retirement planning" is no longer just for helping current employees slip into retirement.[84] It can also enable the employer to retain, in some capacity, the skills of those who would normally retire and leave the firm.

A reasonable first step is to conduct numerical analyses of pending retirements. This should include a demographic analysis (including a census of the company's employees), a determination of the average retirement age for the company's employees, and a review of how retirement is going to affect the employer's health care and pension benefits. The employer can then determine the extent of the "retirement problem" and take fact-based workforce planning steps to address it.[85]

Methods Employers seeking to attract and/or retain retirees should take several steps. The general idea is to institute human resource policies that encourage and support older workers.

Not surprisingly, studies show that employees who are more committed and loyal to the employer are more likely to stay beyond their normal retirement age.[86] Such loyalty often starts by creating a culture that honors experience. For example, the CVS pharmacy chain knows that traditional recruiting media such as help-wanted signs might not attract older workers; CVS thus works through the National Council on Aging, city agencies, and community organizations to find new employees. CVS also made it clear that they welcome older workers: "I'm too young to retire. [CVS] is willing to hire older people. They don't look at your age but your experience," said one dedicated older worker.[87] Others modify selection procedures. For example, one British bank stopped using psychometric tests, replacing them with role-playing exercises to gauge how candidates deal with customers.

Employers have various options for retaining older workers. These include offering them part-time positions, hiring them as consultants or temporary workers, offering them flexible work arrangements, encouraging them to work past traditional retirement age, providing training to upgrade skills, and instituting a phased retirement program. The latter lets older workers ease into retirement with gradually reduced work schedules.[88]

LEARNING OBJECTIVE 6
Explain the factors you would consider when dismissing an employee.

Managing Dismissals

Not all employee separations are voluntary. Some career plans and appraisals end not in promotion or graceful retirement but in **dismissal**—involuntary termination of an employee's employment with the firm. The best way to "handle" such involuntary turnover is to avoid it in the first place, when possible. For example, many dismissals start with bad hiring decisions. Using assessment tests, reference and background checks, drug testing, and clearly defined jobs can reduce the need for dismissals.[89]

dismissal
Involuntary termination of an employee's employment with the firm.

KNOW YOUR EMPLOYMENT LAW
Termination at Will

For more than 100 years, the prevailing rule in the United States has been that without an employment contract, either the employer or the employee can **terminate at will** the employment relationship. In other words, the employee could resign for any reason, at will, and the employer could similarly dismiss an employee for any reason, at will. Today, however, dismissed employees increasingly take their cases to court, and in many cases employers are finding that they no longer have a blanket right to fire.

terminate at will
The idea, based in law, that the employment relationship can be terminated at will by either the employer or the employee for any reason.

Termination-at-Will Exceptions

Three main protections against wrongful discharge eroded the termination-at-will doctrine—*statutory exceptions, common law exceptions,* and *public policy exceptions.*

First, *statutory exceptions* include federal and state equal employment and workplace laws that prohibit certain dismissals. For example, Title VII of the Civil Rights Act of 1964 prohibits discharging employees based on race, color, religion, sex, or national origin.[90] Eighteen states and the District of Columbia have laws protecting LGBT workers from termination for sexual orientation, but in 29 states someone can still be terminated based on sexual orientation.[91] For federal employees, the EEOC held that Title VII of the Civil Rights Act of 1964 applies to LGBT individuals.[92]

Second, numerous *common law exceptions* exist. Courts create these exceptions based on precedents. For example, courts have held that employee handbooks promising termination only "for just cause" may create an exception to the at-will rule.[93]

Finally, under the *public policy exception,* courts have held a discharge to be wrongful when it was against a well-established public policy. Thus a public policy exception might prohibit an employer from firing an employee for refusing to break the law. ■

⭐ Watch It

How would an attorney actually guide a client when it comes to dismissals? If your professor has chosen to assign this, go to **www.pearson.com/mylab/management** to watch the video PTC Employee Engagement and then answer the questions to show what you'd do in this situation.

Grounds for Dismissal

There are four bases for dismissal: unsatisfactory performance, misconduct, lack of qualifications for the job, and changed requirements of (or elimination of) the job.

Unsatisfactory performance refers to a persistent failure to perform assigned duties or to meet prescribed standards on the job.[94] Specific reasons include excessive absenteeism; tardiness; a persistent failure to meet normal job requirements; or an adverse attitude toward the company, supervisor, or fellow employees.

Misconduct is deliberate and willful violation of the employer's rules and may include stealing, rowdy behavior, and insubordination.

Lack of qualifications for the job is an employee's inability to do the assigned work, although he or she is diligent. Because this employee may be trying to do the job, it is reasonable to try to salvage him or her—perhaps by assigning the employee to another job.

Changed requirements of the job is an employee's incapability of doing the job after the nature of the job has changed. Similarly, you may have to dismiss an employee when his or her job is eliminated. Again, the employee may be industrious, so it is reasonable to retrain or transfer this person, if possible.

Insubordination, a form of misconduct, is sometimes the grounds for dismissal. The two basic categories of insubordination are unwillingness to carry out the manager's orders, and disrespectful behavior toward the manager. (This assumes that the orders were legitimate, and that the manager did not incite the reaction through his or her own extreme behavior.) Examples of insubordination include:[95]

insubordination
Willful disregard or disobedience of the boss's authority or legitimate orders.

- Direct disregard of the boss's authority
- Direct disobedience of, or refusal to obey, the boss's orders, particularly in front of others
- Deliberate defiance of clearly stated company policies, rules, regulations, and procedures
- Public criticism of the boss
- Blatant disregard of reasonable instructions
- Contemptuous display of disrespect
- Disregard for the chain of command
- Participation in (or leadership of) an effort to undermine and remove the boss from power

Dismissals are never easy. However, the manager can take steps to make them fair.[96]

First, allow the employee to explain why he (or she) did what he did. It could turn out, for instance, that the employee "disobeyed" the order because he or she did not understand it. Similarly, people who get *full explanations* of why and how termination decisions were made "were more likely to perceive their layoff as fair . . . and indicate that they did not wish to take the past employer to court."

Second, have a formal *multistep procedure* (including warning) and an appeal process.

Third, *the person who actually does the dismissing* is important. Employees in one study whose managers informed them of an impending layoff viewed the dismissal fairer than did those told by, say, a human resource manager. Some employers take a less diplomatic approach. About 10% of respondents in one survey said they've used e-mail to fire employees.[97] When JCPenney's former CEO dismissed thousands of employees in 2012, many were fired in groups of a few dozen to over 100 in an auditorium.[98] Use the right person, and do the dismissal humanely.

Fourth, dismissed employees who feel they've been treated unfairly financially are more likely to sue. Many employers use *severance pay* to blunt a dismissal's sting. Figure 9.3 summarizes typical severance policies.

SEVERANCE CALCULATION METHOD	MEDIAN WEEKS OF SEVERANCE		
	EXECUTIVES	MANAGERS	PROFESSIONALS
Fixed	26	6	4
VARIABLE AMOUNT BY EMPLOYMENT TENURE			
1 year	4	2	2
3 years	7	5	5
5 years	10	7	7
10 years	20	12	10
15 years	26	16	15
Maximum	39	26	24

Figure 9.3

Median Weeks of Severance Pay by Job Level

Source: "Severance Pay: Current Trends and Practices," from Culpepper Compensation Surveys & Services, July 2007. Copyright © 2012 Culpepper and Associates, Inc. All Rights Reserved. Reprinted with permission.

Avoiding Wrongful Discharge Suits

Wrongful discharge occurs when an employee's dismissal does not comply with the law or with the contractual arrangement stated or implied by the firm via its employment application forms, employee manuals, or other promises. (In a *constructive discharge* claim, the plaintiff argues that he or she quit, but had no choice because the employer made the situation so intolerable at work.[99]) The time to protect against such suits is before the manager errs and suits are filed.

Protecting against wrongful discharge suits requires two things: following procedural steps, and fairness safeguards. First lay the groundwork to help avoid such suits. Procedural steps include the following:[100]

- Have applicants sign the employment application. Make sure it contains a statement that "the employer can terminate at any time."
- Review your employee manual to delete statements that could undermine your defense in a wrongful discharge case. For example, delete "employees can be terminated only for just cause."
- Have written rules listing infractions that may require discipline and discharge.
- If a rule is broken, get the worker's side of the story in front of witnesses, and preferably get it signed. Then check out the story.
- Be sure that employees get a written appraisal at least annually. If an employee shows evidence of incompetence, give that person a warning. Provide an opportunity to improve.
- Keep careful confidential records of all actions such as employee appraisals, warnings or notices, and so on.
- Finally, ask the questions in Figure 9.4.

Figure 9.4

Avoiding Wrongful Discharge Claims

Source: Personal Law, 4th Edition, by Kenneth L. Sovereign. Copyright © 1999 by Pearson Education, Inc. Reprinted by permission of Pearson Education, Inc., Upper Saddle River, New Jersey; Ashley Pack and Katherine Capito, "8 Questions an Employer Should Ask Before Taking an Adverse Employment Action," September 11, 2012, http://www.dinsmore.com/adverse_employment_action_steps/, accessed May 31, 2017; "Wrongful Termination Checklist," http://employment.findlaw.com/losing-a-job/wrongful-termination-checklist.html, accessed May 1, 2017.

Avoiding Wrongful Discharge Claims: Some Questions to Ask Before Making the Dismissal Final

Avoiding wrongful discharge claims is a complicated matter that involves, for instance, ensuring that the dismissal is fair and that it does not involve issues of discrimination, harassment, retaliation, or breach of contract. Illustrative questions to ask would include:

- Is the employee covered by any type of written agreement, including a collective bargaining agreement?
- Is there any workers' compensation involvement?
- Have reasonable rules and regulations been communicated and enforced?
- Has the employee been given an opportunity to explain any rule violations or to correct poor performance?
- Is there any direct or circumstantial evidence (such as statements) that the employee is being terminated for discriminatory reasons?
- Are similar employees treated differently on the basis of age, gender, race or other protected group category?
- Did an employer make unwelcome sexual advances, request sexual favors, or seek to establish a romantic or sexual relationship?
- Before being fired, did the employee report potential violations in the company to a supervisor, colleagues, your human resources department, or an enforcement agency such as OSHA?
- Is the employee working under a written contract and if so, did it establish permissible reasons for termination or a termination procedure?
- Did the employer, supervisor, or superior make any verbal promises, such as saying the person's job was "guaranteed" or ensuring "tenure" at work?
- How long has the employee been working here and is this his or her first discipline issue?
- Are you sure there have been past warnings?
- Has anyone else committed this offense and been treated differently?

Supervisor Liability

Courts sometimes hold managers personally liable for their supervisory actions.[101] For example, the Fair Labor Standards Act defines *employer* to include "any person acting directly or indirectly in the interest of an employer in relation to any employee." This can mean the individual supervisor.

Steps to Take There are several ways to avoid having personal liability become an issue.

- *Follow company policies and procedures.* An employee may initiate a claim against a supervisor who he or she alleges did not follow policies and procedures.
- Administer the discipline in a manner that does not add to the employee's *emotional hardship* (as would having them publicly collect their belongings and leave the office).
- *Do not act in anger* because doing so undermines the appearance of objectivity.
- Finally, *utilize the HR department* for advice regarding how to handle difficult disciplinary matters. The following Management Skills feature shows how to handle the termination interview.

termination interview
The interview in which an employee is informed of the fact that he or she has been dismissed.

BUILDING YOUR MANAGEMENT SKILLS:
Managing the Termination Interview

Dismissing an employee is one of the most difficult tasks you can face at work.[102] The dismissed employee, even if warned many times in the past, may still react with disbelief or even violence. Guidelines for the **termination interview** itself are as follows:

1. **Plan the interview carefully.** According to experts at Hay Associates, this includes:
   - Make sure the employee keeps the appointment time.
   - Never inform an employee over the phone.
   - Allow 10 minutes as sufficient time for the interview.
   - Use a neutral site, not your own office.
   - Have employee agreements, the human resource file, and a release announcement prepared in advance.
   - Be available at a time after the interview in case questions or problems arise.
   - Have phone numbers ready for medical or security emergencies.
2. **Get to the point.** As soon as the employee enters your office, give the person a moment to get comfortable and then inform him or her of your decision.
3. **Describe the situation.** Briefly, in three or four sentences, explain why the person is being let go. For instance, "Production in your area is down 4%, and we are continuing to have quality problems. We have talked about these problems several times in the past three months, and the solutions are not being followed through on. We have to make a change." Don't personalize the situation by saying things like "Your production is just not up to par." Also, emphasize that the decision is final and irrevocable. Preserving the employee's dignity is crucial.[103]
4. **Listen.** Continue the interview until the person appears to be talking freely and reasonably calmly.
5. **Review the severance package.** Describe severance payments, benefits, access to office support people, and the way references will be handled. However, under no conditions make any promises or benefits beyond those already in the support package.
6. **Identify the next step.** The terminated employee may be disoriented and unsure what to do next. Explain where the employee should go next, upon leaving the interview.

outplacement counseling
A systematic process by which a terminated person is trained and counseled in the techniques of self-appraisal and securing a new position.

Outplacement Counseling With **outplacement counseling**, the employer arranges for an outside firm to provide terminated employees with career planning and job search skills. *Outplacement firms* usually provide the actual outplacement services. Employees (often managers or professionals) who are let go typically have office space and secretarial services they can use at local offices of such firms, plus the counseling services. The outplacement counseling is part of the terminated employee's support or severance package.

Why not just give the person you're dismissing the outplacement fee as additional severance? In general, providing outplacement services seems to have positive effects for both the terminated employee and the employer.[104]

For the Employee What should you do if you get fired or passed over for a position?[105] Most people surrender to the usual stages of shock, denial, and anger. However, the better first step is often to figure out why you lost the job. Doing so isn't easy. Actively explore what (if anything) you did to contribute to the problem. Then objectively consider what you might do differently in the future, keeping in mind that you should view the loss (difficult though this may be) as an opportunity. Then evaluate your new options and be ready to seize the right one.

exit interviews
Interviews conducted by the employer immediately prior to the employee leaving the firm with the aim of better understanding what the employee thinks about the company.

Exit Interview Many employers conduct **exit interviews** with employees leaving the firm. These are usually conducted by an HR professional just prior to the employee leaving, and they elicit information with the aim of giving employers insights into their companies. Exit interview questions include: How were you recruited? Was the job presented correctly and honestly? What was the workplace environment like? What was your supervisor's management style like? What did you like most/least about the company?[106] Other questions would relate to HR (for instance, the employer's hiring and promotion processes), managers' leadership styles and effectiveness, the work itself (including working conditions), competitive benchmarks (such as salaries compared to competitors'), and ideas for improving the company. Women and minorities are more likely to quit early in their employment, so this is an issue for which to watch.[107] Finally, try to make sure that the exiting employee leaves as a supporter of the employer.[108]

The assumption is that because the employee is leaving he or she will be candid. However, that is questionable.[109] Researchers found that at the time of separation, 38% of those leaving blamed salary and benefits, and 4% blamed supervision. Followed up 18 months later, 24% blamed supervision and 12% blamed salary and benefits. Getting to the real issues may thus require digging.

The Exit Process The exit interview is just one part of a rational exit process. The employer should follow a checklist. Ensure, for example, that the employee returns all keys and company equipment, that all computer and database password access is terminated, that proper communications are sent internally (for instance, to other employees if appropriate, and to payroll) and externally, that the employee leaves the premises in a timely fashion, and that if necessary, precautions are followed to ensure security.

By one report, almost 40% of workers who were laid off left a negative employer review on social media. Most prospective employees search such reviews, so it's sensible to make the separation as humane as possible.[110]

More employees today quit without giving notice. Sometimes this is justified. For example, those taking jobs with competitors should no longer have access to the current employer's information. But, more often, quitting without notice reflects a lack of familiarity with the traditional two-week notice standard, or of seeing one's colleagues dismissed in large numbers.[111]

Layoffs and the Plant Closing Law

Nondisciplinary separations may be initiated by either employer or employee. For the *employer*, reduced sales or profits or the desire for more productivity may require layoffs. *Employees* (as we've seen) may leave for better jobs, to retire, or for other reasons. The Worker Adjustment and Retraining Notification Act (WARN Act, or the plant closing law) requires employers of 100 or more employees to give 60 days' notice before closing a facility or starting a layoff of 50 or more people.[112]

A **layoff,** in which the employer sends workers home for a time for lack of work, is usually not a permanent dismissal (although it may turn out to be). Rather, it is a temporary one, which the employer expects will be short term. However, some employers use the term *layoff* as a euphemism for discharge or termination. In the deep recession years of 2008 and 2009 combined, employers carried out a total of about 51,000 mass layoffs, idling over 5 million workers.[113]

The Layoff Process A study illustrates one firm's layoff process. In this company, senior management first met to make strategic decisions about the size and timing of the layoffs. They also debated the relative importance of the skills the firm needed going forward. Supervisors then assessed their subordinates, rating their nonunion employees either A, B, or C (union employees were covered by a union agreement making layoffs dependent on seniority). The supervisors then informed each of their subordinates about his or her A, B, or C rating and told each that those with C grades were designated "surplus" and most likely to be laid off.[114]

Adjusting to Downsizings and Mergers

Downsizing means reducing, usually dramatically, the number of people employed by a firm. The basic idea is to cut costs and raise profitability. Downsizings (some call them "productivity transformation programs"[115]) require careful consideration of several matters.

1. One is to make sure *the right people* are let go; this requires having an effective appraisal system in place.
2. Second is *compliance with all applicable laws,* including WARN.
3. Third is ensuring that the employer executes the dismissals in a manner that is *just and fair.*
4. Fourth is the practical consideration of *security,* for instance, retrieving keys and ensuring that those leaving do not take any prohibited items with them.
5. Fifth is to reduce the remaining *employees' uncertainty* and to address their concerns. This typically involves a postdownsizing announcement and program, including meetings where senior managers field questions from the remaining employees.

Downsizings aren't pleasant but needn't be unfair. Providing advanced notice regarding the layoff can help cushion the otherwise negative effects. So can interpersonal sensitivity (in terms of the manager's demeanor during layoffs).[116] Dismissals and turnover are particularly disruptive in high-performance-work-system-type firms such as Toyota Motor.[117] Therefore, it may be particularly important here to cut costs without reducing the workforce. Options here include pay freezes or cuts, introduce a hiring freeze before reducing the workforce, provide candid communications about the need for the downsizing, give employees an opportunity to express their opinions about the downsizing, and be fair and compassionate in implementing the downsizing.[118]

layoff
A situation in which employees are told there is no work for them but that management intends to recall them when work is again available.

downsizing
Refers to the process of reducing, usually dramatically, the number of people employed by the firm.

Review

MyLab Management

If your instructor is using MyLab Management, go to **www.pearson.com/mylab/ management** to complete the problems marked with this icon ⭐.

Summary

1. Employees are ultimately responsible for their own careers, but employers and managers also have roles in **career management**. These include establishing company-based career centers, offering career planning workshops, providing employee development budgets, and offering online career development programs. Perhaps the simplest is to make the appraisal career oriented, by linking the appraisal feedback to the employee's aspirations and plans.

2. Getting employees to do better requires improving your coaching skills. Ideally, the coaching process involves preparation (in terms of analyzing the issues), planning (development of an improvement plan), active coaching, and follow-up. Effective mentors set high standards, invest the time, steer protégés into important projects, and exhibit professional competence and consistency.

3. Managing voluntary turnover requires identifying its causes and then addressing them. A comprehensive approach to retaining employees should be multifaceted, and include improved selection, a well-thought-out training and career development program, assistance in helping employees lay out potential career plans, providing employees with meaningful work and recognition and rewards, promoting work–life balance, acknowledging employees'

achievements, and providing all this within a supportive company culture.

4. The employer's career planning and development process can play a role in fostering employee engagement. It is through this process that the employer supports the employee's efforts to test and develop viable career goals and to develop the skills and experiences that accomplishing those goals requires. Managed effectively, the employer's career development process should send the signal that the employer cares about the employee's career success.

5. Several decisions loom large in any firm's promotion process: Is seniority or competence the rule? How should we measure competence? Is the process formal or informal? Vertical, horizontal, or other? In general, the employer's promotion processes must comply with all the same antidiscrimination laws as do procedures for recruiting and selecting employees or any other HR actions.

6. Among the reasons for dismissal are unsatisfactory performance, misconduct, lack of qualifications, changed job requirements, and insubordination. In dismissing one or more employees, however, remember that termination at will as a policy has been weakened by exceptions in many states, and that care should be taken to avoid wrongful discharge suits.

Key Terms

career 261
career management 261
career development 261
career planning 261
portfolio career 263
reality shock 264
coaching 268
mentoring 268
9-box matrix 278
transfer 280

dismissal 281
terminate at will 281
insubordination 282
wrongful discharge 283
termination interview 284
outplacement counseling 285
exit interviews 285
layoff 286
downsizing 286

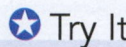 Try It

How would you do in managing your own career? If your professor has chosen to assign this, go to **www.pearson.com/mylab/management**, and complete the career management simulation.

Discussion Questions

9-1. Why is it advisable for an employee retention effort to be comprehensive?

9-2. Explain why employee engagement is important, and how to foster such engagement. What exactly would you as a supervisor do to increase your employees' engagement?

9-3. What is the employee's role in the career development process? The manager's role? The employer's role?

9-4. List and discuss the four steps in effectively coaching an employee. How could (and would) a professional football coach apply these steps?

9-5. Discuss at least four procedural suggestions for managing dismissals effectively.

9-6. Is it advantageous to take a talent management approach to managing employee retention? Why or why not?

9-7. What would you as a supervisor do to avoid someone accusing you of wrongful dismissal?

Individual and Group Activities

9-8. Many rightfully offer IBM as an example of an employer that works hard to improve employee retention and engagement. Browse through the employment pages of IBM.com's website (for instance, go to www.ibm.com; then click at the bottom Careers. In this chapter, we discussed actions employers can take to improve employee retention and engagement. From the information on IBM's web pages, what is IBM doing to support retention and engagement?

9-9. In groups of four or five students, meet with one or two administrators and faculty members in your college or university and, based on this, write a two-page paper on the topic "the faculty promotion process at our college." What do you think of the process? Based on our discussion in this chapter, could you make any suggestions for improving it?

9-10. Working individually or in groups, choose two occupations (such as management consultant, HR manager, or salesperson), and use sources such as O*Net to size up the future demand for this occupation in the next 10 years or so. Does this seem like a good occupation to pursue? Why or why not?

9-11. In groups of four or five students, interview a small business owner or an HR manager with the aim of writing a two-page paper addressing the topic "steps our company is taking to reduce voluntary employee turnover." What is this employer's turnover rate now? How would you suggest it improve its turnover rate?

9-12. Several years ago, a survey of college graduates in the United Kingdom found that although many hadn't found their first jobs, most were already planning "career breaks" and to keep up their hobbies and interests outside work.[119] Part of the problem seems to be that many already see their friends "putting in more than 48 hours a week" at work. Career experts reviewing the results concluded that many of these recent college grads "are not looking for high-pay, high-profile jobs anymore."[120] Instead, they seem to be looking to "compartmentalize" their lives. They want to keep the number of hours they spend at work down, so they can maintain their hobbies and outside interests. If you were mentoring one of these people at work, what three bits of career advice would you give him or her? Why? What (if anything) would you suggest their employers do to accommodate these graduates' stated career wishes?

9-13. Websites occasionally run a story listing what they call the greatest coaches (for example, key "greatest coaches" into Google search).[121] Look at this list, and pick out two of the names. Then research these people online to determine what behaviors they exhibited that seem to account for why they were great coaches. How do these behaviors compare with what this chapter had to say about effective coaching?

9-14. For this activity, you will need the documents titled (1) "HRCI PHR® and SPHR® Certification Body of Knowledge," and (2) "About the Society for Human Resource Management (SHRM) Body of Competency & Knowledge® Model and Certification Exams." Your instructor can obtain these two documents from the Pearson Instructor Resource Center and pass them on to you. These two documents list the knowledge someone studying for the HRCI or SHRM certification exam needs to have in each area of human resource management (such as in Strategic Management, and Workforce Planning). In groups of several students, do four things: (1) review the HRCI and/or SHRM documents; (2) identify the material in this chapter that relates to HRCI's or SHRM's required knowledge lists; (3) write four multiple-choice exam questions on this material that you believe would be suitable for inclusion in the HRCI exam and/or the SHRM exam; and, (4) if time permits, have someone from your team post your team's questions in front of the class, so that students in all teams can answer the exam questions created by the other teams.

MyLab Management

If your instructor is using MyLab Management, go to **www.pearson.com/mylab/management** for Auto-graded writing questions as well as the following Assisted-graded writing questions:

9-15. Why is it important to manage employee dismissals properly?

9-16. What are the main decisions employers should address in reaching promotion decisions?

APPLICATION EXERCISES

HR IN ACTION CASE INCIDENT 1

Google Reacts

On the face of it, Google would seem to be the last company that one would expect to have an employee retention problem. Google usually shows up on "Best Employers to Work For" lists; it's famous for full benefits, from dry-cleaning to free Internet-enabled transportation from San Francisco, to great pensions; it offers great stock options; and as a fast-growing company, it usually has many job applicants. So when its employee turnover began creeping up a few years ago, Google's human resource team had to decide what to do. Part of the problem is that as attractive as Google is to work for, Silicon Valley is filled with attractive employers, from Apple to Facebook. One of Google's first steps was to boost compensation. It gave all 23,000 Google employees a 10% raise, plus a $1,000 tax-free holiday bonus.[122]

But still, Google management knew that pay was just part of the solution. It had to take other steps.

Questions

9-17. Without doing any further research than what you learned in this chapter, what other steps would you suggest Google take to improve employee retention?

9-18. Was there any information in previous chapters of this book that would help illustrate other steps Google took to improve retention?

9-19. Use other Internet sources, including Google.com, to finalize an answer to the question: What other steps should Google take to improve employee retention?

HR IN ACTION CASE INCIDENT 2

Carter Cleaning Company

The Career Planning Program

Career planning has always been a pretty low-priority item for Carter Cleaning because "just getting workers to come to work and then keeping them honest is enough of a problem," as Jack likes to say. Yet Jennifer thought it might not be a bad idea to give some thought to what a career-planning program might involve for Carter. Many of their employees had been with them for years in dead-end jobs, and she frankly felt a little badly for them: "Perhaps we could help them gain a better perspective

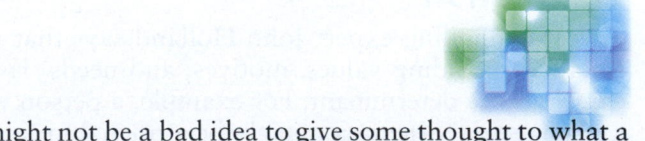

on what they want to do," she thought. And she definitely believed that career support would have an effect on improving Carter's employee retention.

Questions

9-20. What would be the advantages to Carter Cleaning of setting up a career planning program?

9-21. Who should participate in the program? All employees? Selected employees?

9-22. Outline and describe the career development program you would propose for the cleaners, pressers, counter people, and managers at the Carter Cleaning Centers.

Experiential Exercise

Where Am I Going . . . and Why?

Purpose: The purpose of this exercise is to provide you with experience in analyzing your career preferences.

Required Understanding: Students should be thoroughly familiar with the section "The Employee's Role in Career Management" in this chapter, as well as using O*Net (which we discussed in Chapter 4) and this chapter's appendix.

How to Set Up the Exercise/Instructions: Using O*Net and our section titled "The Employee's Role in Career Management," and this chapter's appendix, analyze your career-related inclinations (you can also take the self-directed search for about $10

at www.self-directed-search.com). Based on this analysis, answer the following questions (if you wish, you may do this analysis in teams of three or four students).

9-23. What does your research suggest to you about what would be your preferable occupational options?

9-24. What are the prospects for these occupations?

9-25. Given these prospects and your own occupational inclinations, outline a brief, one-page career plan for yourself, including current occupational inclinations, career goals, and an action plan listing four or five development steps you will need to take to get from where you are now career-wise to where you want to be, based on your career goals.

Chapter 9 Appendix: Managing Your Career and Finding a Job

Making Career Choices

Many people don't put much thought into their careers. Some choose majors based on class scheduling preferences, favorite professors, or unstated psychological motives. Others stumble into jobs because "that's all that was available." If there was ever anything that cried out for fact-based decisions, it is choosing your career. The first and essential step here is to learn as much as possible about your interests, aptitudes, and skills.

Identify Your Occupational Orientation

Career-counseling expert John Holland says that personality (including values, motives, and needs) is one career choice determinant. For example, a person with a strong social orientation might be attracted to careers that entail interpersonal rather than intellectual or physical activities and to occupations such as social work.

Based on research with his Vocational Preference Test (VPT), Holland found six basic personality types or orientations (see www.self-directed-search.com).[123]

1. **Realistic orientation.** These people are attracted to occupations that involve physical activities requiring skill, strength, and coordination. Examples include forestry, farming, and agriculture.

2. **Investigative orientation.** Investigative people are attracted to careers that involve cognitive activities (thinking, organizing, understanding) rather than affective activities (feeling, acting, or interpersonal and emotional tasks). Examples include biologist, chemist, and college professor.

3. **Social orientation.** These people are attracted to careers that involve interpersonal rather than intellectual or physical activities. Examples include clinical psychology, foreign service, and social work.

4. **Conventional orientation.** A conventional orientation favors careers that involve structured, rule-regulated activities, as well as careers in which it

is expected that the employee subordinate his or her personal needs to those of the organization. Examples include accountants and bankers.

5. **Enterprising orientation.** Verbal activities aimed at influencing others characterize enterprising personalities. Examples include managers, lawyers, and public relations executives.

6. **Artistic orientation.** People here are attracted to careers that involve self-expression, artistic creation, expression of emotions, and individualistic activities. Examples include artists, advertising executives, and musicians.

Most people have more than one occupational orientation (they might be social, realistic, and investigative, for example), and Holland believes that the more similar or compatible these orientations are, the less internal conflict or indecision a person will face in making a career choice. To help illustrate this, Holland suggests placing each orientation in one corner of a hexagon, as in Figure 9A.1. As you can see, the model has six corners, each of which represents one personal orientation (for example, enterprising). According to Holland's research, the closer two orientations are in this figure, the more compatible they are. If your number-one and number-two orientations fall side by side, you will have an easier time choosing a career. You can take Holland's SDS online for a small fee (see www.self-directed-search.com).

Identify Your Skills

You may have a conventional orientation, but whether you have *the skills* to be an accountant, banker, or credit manager will largely determine which occupation you ultimately choose. Therefore, you have to identify your skills. We presented some exercises for this earlier in this chapter, on page 262.

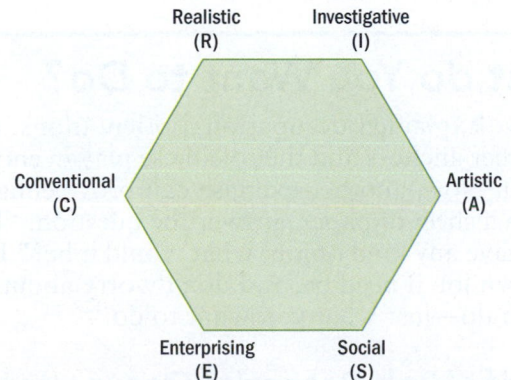

Figure 9A.1

Choosing an Occupational Orientation

Aptitudes and Special Talents

For career planning purposes, a person's aptitudes are usually measured with a test battery such as the general aptitude test battery (GATB), which most state one-stop career centers make available. This instrument measures various aptitudes including intelligence and mathematical ability. You can also use specialized tests, such as for mechanical comprehension. Holland's Self-Directed Search will also provide some insights into your aptitudes, as will O*NET.[124]

O*NET

O*NET offers a free, online My Next Move occupation and career assessment system (www.onetcenter.org/mynextmove.html). It includes *O*NET Interest Profiler*, a tool that offers customized career suggestions on over 900 different careers based on a person's interests and level of education and work experience. Users obtain important information including skills, tasks, salaries, and employment outlook for occupations.[125]

Identify Your Career Anchors

Edgar Schein says that career planning is a continuing process of discovery—one in which a person slowly develops a clearer occupational self-concept in terms of what his or her talents, abilities, motives, needs, attitudes, and values are. Schein also says that as you learn more about yourself, it becomes apparent that you have a dominant *career anchor*, a concern or value that you will not give up if a [career] choice has to be made.

Career anchors, as their name implies, are the pivots around which a person's career swings; a person becomes conscious of them because of learning, through experience, about his or her talents and abilities, motives and needs, and attitudes and values. Based on his research at the Massachusetts Institute of Technology, Schein believes that career anchors are difficult to predict because they are evolutionary and a product of a process of discovery. Some people may never find out what their career anchors are until they have to make a major choice—such as whether to take the promotion to the headquarters staff or strike out on their own by starting a business. It is at this point that all the person's past work experiences, interests, aptitudes, and orientations converge into a meaningful pattern that helps show what (career anchor) is the most important factor in driving the person's career choices. Based on his study of MIT graduates, Schein identified five career anchors.[126]

Technical/Functional Competence People who had a strong technical/functional career anchor tended to avoid decisions that would drive them toward general management. Instead, they made decisions that would enable them to remain and grow in their chosen technical or functional fields.

Managerial Competence Other people showed a strong motivation to become managers, and their career experience enabled them to believe they had the skills and values required. A management position of high responsibility is their ultimate goal. When pressed to explain why they believed they had the skills necessary to gain such positions, many in Schein's research sample answered that they were qualified because of what they saw as their competencies in a combination of three areas: (1) *analytical competence* (ability to identify, analyze, and solve problems under conditions of incomplete information and uncertainty); (2) *interpersonal competence* (ability to influence, supervise, lead, manipulate, and control people at all levels), and; (3) *emotional competence* (the capacity to be stimulated by emotional and interpersonal crises rather than exhausted or debilitated by them, and the capacity to bear high levels of responsibility without becoming paralyzed).

Creativity Some of the graduates had become successful entrepreneurs. To Schein, these people seemed to have a need "to build or create something that was entirely their own product—a product or process that bears their name, a company of their own, or a personal fortune that reflects their accomplishments." For example, one graduate had become a successful purchaser, restorer, and renter of townhouses.

Autonomy and Independence Some seemed driven by the need to be on their own, free of the dependence that can arise when a person elects to work in a large organization where promotions, transfers, and salary decisions make them subordinate to others. Many of these graduates also had a strong technical/functional orientation. Instead of pursuing this orientation in an organization, they had decided to become consultants, working either alone or as part of a relatively small firm. Others had become professors of business, freelance writers, and proprietors of a small retail business.

Security A few of the graduates were mostly concerned with long-run career stability and job security. For those interested in *geographic security*, maintaining a stable, secure career in familiar surroundings was generally more important than pursuing superior career choices, if choosing the latter meant injecting instability or insecurity into their lives by forcing them to pull up roots and move to another city. For others, security meant *organizational security*. They might today opt for government jobs, where tenure still tends to be a way of life. They were much more willing to let their employers decide what their careers should be.

Assessing Career Anchors

To help you identify career anchors, take a few sheets of blank paper, and write out your answers to the following questions:[127]

1. What was your major area of concentration (if any) in high school? Why did you choose that area? How did you feel about it?
2. What is (or was) your major area of concentration in college? Why did you choose that area? How did you feel about it?
3. What was your first job after school? (Include military if relevant.) What were you looking for in your first job?
4. What were your ambitions or long-range goals when you started your career? Have they changed? When? Why?
5. What was your first major change of job or company? What were you looking for in your next job?
6. What was your next major change of job, company, or career? Why did you initiate or accept it? What were you looking for? (Do this for each of your major changes of job, company, or career.)
7. As you look back over your career, identify some times you have especially enjoyed. What was it about those times that you enjoyed?
8. As you look back, identify some times you have not especially enjoyed. What was it about those times you did not enjoy?
9. Have you ever refused a job move or promotion? Why?
10. Now review all your answers carefully, as well as the descriptions for the five career anchors (technical/functional competence, managerial competence, creativity and independence, autonomy, security). Based on your answers to the questions, rate, for yourself, each of the anchors from 1 to 5, where 1 equals low importance and 5 equals high importance.

Technical/functional competence _____
Managerial competence _____
Creativity and independence _____
Autonomy _____
Security _____

What do You Want to Do?

We have explained occupational orientations, skills, and career anchors and the role these play in choosing a career. Now, another exercise can prove enlightening. On a sheet of paper, answer the question: "If you could have any kind of job, what would it be?" Invent your own job if need be, and don't worry about what you can do—just what you want to do.[128]

Identify High-Potential Occupations

Learning about your skills and interests is only half the job of choosing an occupation. You also have to identify those occupations that are right (given your occupational orientations, skills, career anchors, and occupational preferences) as well as those that will be in high demand in the years to come.

[1]The most efficient way to learn about, compare, and contrast occupations is through the Internet. The U.S. Department of Labor's online *Occupational Outlook Handbook* (https://www.bls.gov/ooh/l) is updated each year and provides detailed descriptions and information on hundreds of occupations. O*NET similarly provides occupational demand updates. The New York State Department of Labor (www.career-zone.ny.gov/views/careerzone/index.jsf) similarly provides excellent information on careers categorized in clusters, such as Arts and Humanities, Business and Information Systems, and Engineering and Technology. Figure 9A.2 lists some other sites to turn to both for occupational information and for information on searching for a job.

The states' one-stop career centers are another good source. In them, job seekers can now apply for unemployment benefits, register with the state job service, talk to career counselors, use computers to write résumés and access the Internet, take tests, and use career libraries, which offer books and videos on various employment topics. In some, job hunters can even make use of free Internet access and telephones, scanners, and photocopiers to facilitate job searches.

Finding the Right Job

You have identified your occupational orientation, skills, and career anchors and have picked out the occupation you want and made plans for a career. Your next step is to find a job that you want in the company and locale in which you want to work.

Before leaving a current job, however, make sure leaving is what you want. Many people change jobs or occupations when a smaller change would suffice. Dissatisfied at work, they assume it must be the job or the occupation. But, why decide to switch from being a lawyer to a teacher, when it's not the profession but that law firm's 80-hour workweek that's the problem?

For example, if, after thinking it through, you are satisfied with your occupation and where you work, but not with your job as it's organized now, try reconfiguring it. For instance, consider alternative work arrangements such as flexible hours or telecommuting; delegate or eliminate the job functions you least prefer; or seek out a "stretch assignment" that will let you work on something more challenging.[129]

Job Search Techniques

Most people seek jobs in a manner that's almost exactly opposite to the approach that experts deem best. For example, surveys of human resource professionals show that about 70% believe the best way to get a job is through referrals, but less than 10% of job seekers see referrals as their best option; instead they rely on job boards, which rank low with HR professionals. Therefore, use social media such as LinkedIn and Facebook to help build your network and to publicize your availability to potential job referrers.[130]

Personal Contacts

Generally, the best way to seek job leads and interviews is to rely on personal contacts such as friends and relatives.[131] So, let as many responsible people as possible know that you are looking for a job and what kind of job you want. (Beware, though, if you are currently employed and don't want your job search getting back to your current boss. If that is the case, then tell a few close friends to be discreet in seeking a job for you.)

Social Media and HR

In one survey, about 90% of HR professionals surveyed said it was "very important" or "somewhat

SELECTED ONLINE SOURCES OF OCCUPATIONAL INFORMATION

- All Star Jobs
- CampusCareerCenter
- CareerBliss.com
- CareerOneSto
- CareerExplorer
- CareerOverview
- CityTownInfo
- College Central Network
- CollegeGrad.com
- Construct My Future (information about construction careers)
- Cool Works
- EducationPlanner
- eMedicalAssistants
- Explore Health Careers
- Green Jobs Ready
- hotjobs.com
- International Jobs
- Job Search Intelligence
- MyArtsCareer
- Occupational Outlook Handbook
- Professional Development for Teachers
- Quintessential Careers
- ResumeINDEX
- SalaryList
- Science Buddies—Careers
- Simply Hired
- Snag a Job

FIGURE 9A.2

Selected Online Sources of Occupational Information

Source: http://mappingyourfuture.org/planyourcareer/careerresources.htm, accessed June 13, 2013.

important" for job seekers to be on LinkedIn, about 83% said the same for the job hunter's professional or association site, and about 60% cited Facebook.[132]

Employers scour social media for recruits, and job seekers should make their names stand out. For example, job seekers enhance their professional reputations by creating a Twitter presence. Those "Liking" a company on Facebook may receive early notice of job openings. Spend a few minutes every day on LinkedIn making new connections, and share links and advice with those in your LinkedIn network.[133] Join LinkedIn industry groups to build visibility. Make sure your résumé is in PDF format and readable on a smart phone screen. To bring yourself to recruiters' attention, follow up on comments they make on their blogs or on industry websites. Some job searchers are using social résumés. *Social résumés* provide snapshots of who the job searcher is by combining text material, photos, and samples of a person's work in infographic résumés posted on social media such as Twitter, LinkedIn, and blogs.[134]

Finally, remember that prospective employers may Google you before extending the offer and perhaps ask for access to your Facebook and LinkedIn pages.

Online Job Boards and Employer Websites

Most large job search sites such as Monster.com have local-area search capabilities. Useful open-job aggregator sites include Indeed.com and SimplyHired.com. Idealist.com is good for nonprofit jobs, and USAJobs for federal jobs.[135] Indeed.com will post on your app local job listings like the ones you are seeking, identify the date listed, and those which you haven't viewed yet.

Use *The Wall Street Journal*'s career website (www.careerjournal.com/) to search for jobs by occupation and location. Most big-city newspapers also have their own (or links to) online local job listings. In addition to job boards like Monster and specialized ones (like www.theladder.com), virtually all large companies, industries, and crafts have their own specialized sites. For example, Financial Executives International (www.fei.org) make it easy for industry employers and prospective employees to match their needs. Remember to use mobile services, for instance, accessing jobs via Indeed's app.

Answering Advertisements

Most experts agree that answering ads is a low-probability way to get a job, and it becomes increasingly less useful as the level of job increases. Automated applicant tracking services now crunch through thousands of résumés in seconds, making it even harder to stand out by answering ads. (This applies especially to answering online ads). Nevertheless, good sources of classified ads for professionals and managers include

the *The New York Times*, *The Wall Street Journal*, and specialized journals in your field that list job openings. All these sources also post the positions online, of course.

Many employers don't accept application letters. For those who do, create the right impression; check the typing, style, grammar, neatness, and so forth. Check your résumé to make sure it is geared to the job for which you are applying. In your cover letter, be sure to have a paragraph or so in which you specifically address why your background and accomplishments are appropriate to the advertised position; you must respond clearly to the company's identified needs.

Be very careful in replying to "blind" ads. Some executive search firms and companies will run ads even when no position exists just to gauge the market, and there is always the chance that you blunder into responding to your own firm.

Employment Agencies

Agencies are especially good at placing people in jobs paying up to about $90,000, but they can be useful for higher-paying jobs as well. The employer usually pays the fees for professional and management jobs. Review jobs going back several weeks on job boards like Indeed and perhaps a few back issues of your paper's Sunday classified ads to identify agencies that handle the positions you want. Approach three or four initially, preferably in response to specific ads, and avoid signing any contract that gives an agency the exclusive right to place you.

Executive Recruiters

We've seen that employers retain executive recruiters to seek out top talent for their clients; employers always pay any fees. Send your résumé and a cover letter summarizing your objective in precise terms, including job title and the size of company desired, work-related accomplishments, current salary, and salary requirements. However, beware; some firms today call themselves executive search or career consultants but do no searches. Sometimes also called "Executive Marketing Consultants," they may charge a hefty fee to help you manage your search. Remember that with an executive search firm, the candidate *never* pays a fee.

Career Counselors

Career counselors will not help you find a job per se; rather, they specialize in aptitude testing and career counseling. They are listed under "Career Counseling" or "Vocational Guidance." Their services usually cost $500 or so and include some psychological testing and interviews with an experienced career counselor. Check the firm's services, prices, and history as well as the credentials of the person you will be dealing with.

Employers' Websites

Most companies list job openings on their websites. Answering any recruitment ads requires some special résumé preparations, as we'll see next.

Writing Your Résumé

Your résumé can determine whether you get a job interview. Of course, do not produce a slipshod résumé: Avoid overcrowded pages, difficult-to-read copies, typographical errors, and other problems of this sort. Produce a new résumé *for each job* you are applying for, gearing your job objective and accomplishments to the job you want and/or to the job ad to which you're responding. Here are some résumé pointers, as offered by employment counselor Richard Payne and other experts.[136]

Introductory Information Start your résumé with your name, home and e-mail address, LinkedIn address, and home or cell phone number.

Job Objective Next, state your job objective. This should summarize in one sentence the specific position you want, where you want to do it (type and size of company), and a special reason an employer might have for wanting you to fill the job. For example, "Marketing manager in a medium-size e-commerce company in a situation in which strong creative skills would be valuable."

Job Scope For each of your previous jobs, write a paragraph that shows job title, whom you reported to directly and indirectly, who reported to you, how many people reported to you, the operational and human resource budgets you controlled, and what your job entailed (in one sentence).

Your Accomplishments This is the heart of your résumé. It shows for each of your previous jobs: (1) a concrete action you took and why you took it and (2) the specific result of your action—the "payoff." For example, "As production supervisor, I introduced a new process to replace costly hand soldering of component parts. The new process reduced assembly time per unit from 30 to 10 minutes and reduced labor costs by over 60%." Use several of these statements for each job.

Length Keep your résumé to two pages or less. As a rule, list education, military service (if any), and personal background (hobbies, interests, associations) on the last page *if* you've been out of school and working for several years.

Make Your Résumé Scannable For most job applications today, you must have a scannable résumé, one that is electronically readable by applicant tracking systems. Make sure to present your qualifications using powerful key words appropriate to the job or jobs for which you are applying. For example, a trainer might use phrases such as: *computer-based training*, *interactive video*, and *group facilitator*.

Online Bios

LinkedIn and many employers require their professionals and managers to post brief biographies on their websites. They are often for potential clients, but can attract recruiters too. Tips for writing such bios include the following:[137]

Fill it with details. The more information you enter, the more likely a person seeking someone with your background will find you.

Avoid touchy subjects. For example, religion and politics.

Look the part. Your profile may require posting photos. If so, dress in professional attire.

Make it search friendly. Make sure your profile contains the key words you think someone searching for someone with your background and expertise would be looking for, such as *manager*, *supervisor*, or *engineer*.

Use abbreviations. For example, someone searching the site might more readily punch in "MBA" than "Masters in Business Administration."

Say it with numbers. Describe specifically how your work has contributed to your current employer's and past employer's bottom lines.

Proofread. Carefully proofread your online profile, as you would your résumé.

A Caveat

Date your résumé (in case it lands on your boss's desk two years from now). Also insert a disclaimer forbidding unauthorized transmission by headhunters.

Handling the Interview

Now you have an interview scheduled with the person who is responsible for hiring for the job you want. What must you do to excel? Here are some suggestions.

Prepare

Before the interview, learn all you can about the employer, the job, and the people doing the recruiting. Search the Internet to find out what is happening in the employer's industry. Know that you may be asked to have a "job tryout," in which you'll have to actually show how well you can do facets of the job.[138]

First Impressions

Interviewers usually jump to conclusions about candidates during the first few minutes of the interview. Therefore, interviewees really do have just one chance to make a good first impression. Appropriate clothing, good grooming and posture, eye contact, a firm handshake, and energy are important.

Uncovering the Interviewer's Needs

Spend as little time as possible briefly answering your interviewer's first questions, and instead get the person to describe his or her needs. Once you know the problems he or she wants solved, describe your own accomplishments in terms of the interviewer's needs. For example, "One of the problem areas you've described is similar to a problem I once faced." Then state that problem, describe your solution, and reveal the results.[139]

Nonverbal Behavior and Impression Management

As an applicant, your *non*verbal behavior will have a big impact on your rating. In one study, 52 human resource specialists watched videotaped job interviews. Here *the applicants' verbal content was identical*, but their nonverbal behavior differed. Researchers told one group of applicants to exhibit minimal eye contact, a low energy level, and low voice modulation. Those in a second group demonstrated the opposite behavior. Twenty-three of the 26 personnel specialists who saw the **high-eye-contact, high-energy-level candidate** would have invited him or her for a second interview. *None* who saw the low-eye-contact, low-energy-level candidate would have recommended a second interview.

Similarly, self-promotion is strongly related to the interviewer's perceptions of candidate–job fit. **Self-promotion means promoting one's own skills and abilities** to create the impression of competence. Another study found that some interviewees used "ingratiation" to persuade interviewers to like them. For instance, they praised the interviewers or agreed with their opinions, thus **signalling they shared similar beliefs**. Psychologists call techniques like ingratiation and self-promotion "impression management."

Today's hiring process is longer than it was even a few years ago. It now takes about 23 days to make a hiring decision, and sometimes much longer. Some candidates check with recruiters to determine their status, which can be a turn off. Something more subtle, like sending a link to an article touching on something you discussed with the recruiter, is usually better.[140]

COMPENSATION AND TOTAL REWARDS

Company's Strategic Goals

Employee Competencies and Behaviors Required for Company to Achieve These Strategic Goals

4 Compensation and Total Rewards

3 Training and Development

5 Employee and Labor Relations

HR Policies and Practices Required to Produce Employee Competencies and Behaviors

2 Planning, Recruitment, and Selection

1 Strategic and Legal Environment

WHERE WE ARE NOW

Part 3, Training and Human Resource Development, explained how to orient, train, appraise, engage, and retain employees. After training and appraising the employee, he or she of course expects to be paid. Now we therefore turn to creating equitable pay plans and to putting in place employee benefits and motivational incentive pay plans.

In Part 4, we will cover

- Chapter 10, Developing Compensation Plans
- Chapter 11, Pay for Performance and Employee Benefits

The concepts and techniques we'll study here in Part 4, Compensation and Total Rewards, play an essential role in strategic human resource management. As the accompanying HR Strategy Model shows, Strategic Human Resource Management means *formulating and executing human resource policies and practices that produce the employee competencies and behaviors the company needs to achieve its strategic aims.* Employing carefully selected and trained employees is not enough; they must also be motivated to do their jobs. We will see here in Part 4 that producing that motivation requires putting in place HR policies and practices that provide employees with equitable and motivational wages, benefits, and pay-for-performance plans. Then, in Part 5, we'll turn to methods for maintaining positive employee relations.

10

Developing Compensation Plans

OVERVIEW:
In this chapter, we will cover . . .

- The Basic Factors in Determining Pay Rates
- Job Evaluation Methods
- Pricing Managerial and Professional Jobs
- Contemporary Topics in Compensation
- Employee Engagement Guide for Managers

MyLab Management

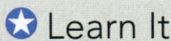 Improve Your Grade!
When you see this icon, visit
www.pearson.com/mylab/management for activities that are applied, personalized, and offer immediate feedback.

LEARNING OBJECTIVES

When you finish studying this chapter, you should be able to:

1. List the basic factors determining pay rates.
2. Define and give an example of how to conduct a job evaluation and set pay rates.
3. Explain how to price managerial and professional jobs.
4. Explain the difference between competency-based and traditional pay plans.
5. Explain the importance of total rewards for improving employee engagement.

⭐ Learn It

If your professor has chosen to assign this, go to **www.pearson.com/mylab/management** to see what you should particularly focus on and to take the Chapter 10 Warm Up.

Source: imagesbavaria/123RF.

INTRODUCTION

Patty owns a small (15 employee) software consulting business just outside Chicago. Her clients include mostly small businesses such as diners and retail shops that need Patty's assistance in installing software to do things such as track inventory. Her staff includes six software consultants (she's the seventh), four sales engineering people charged with developing new business, one secretary/receptionist, one office manager, one accounting clerk, and one office clerk. After five years of setting pay rates just by hiring people based on what other employers in the area were paying for comparable positions, Patty found that her pay plan was causing problems. For example, Moe, one sales engineer, said to her recently, "Patty, I bring in a lot of business for our company, and don't understand why I'm only paid about what Janet the office manager earns—isn't my job worth a lot more?" Patty said she'd get back to him.

---

employee compensation
All forms of pay or rewards going to employees and arising from their employment.

direct financial payments
Pay in the form of wages, salaries, incentives, commissions, and bonuses.

indirect financial payments
Pay in the form of financial benefits such as insurance.

The Basic Factors in Determining Pay Rates

Employee compensation includes all forms of pay going to employees and arising from their employment. It has two main components, **direct financial payments** (wages, salaries, incentives, commissions, and bonuses) and **indirect financial payments** (financial benefits like employer-paid insurance and vacations).

In turn, there are two basic ways to make direct financial payments to employees: based on increments of time or based on performance. Time-based pay is still the foundation of most employers' pay plans. Blue-collar and clerical workers receive hourly or daily wages, for instance. Others, like managers or Web designers, tend to be salaried and paid weekly, monthly, or yearly.

The second direct payment option is to pay for performance. For example, piecework ties compensation to the amount of production (or number of "pieces") the worker turns out. Sales commissions are another performance-based (in this case, sales-based) compensation. Other employers devise pay plans that combine time-based pay plus incentives.

In this chapter, we explain how to formulate plans for paying employees a time-based wage or salary. Chapter 11 addresses performance-based financial incentives, benefits, and total rewards.

Several factors determine the design of any pay plan: company strategy and policy, equity, legal, and union.

Aligning Total Rewards with Strategy

The compensation plan should first advance the firm's strategic aims—management should produce an *aligned reward strategy*. This means creating a total pay package that produces the employee behaviors the firm needs to support and achieve its competitive strategy.[1] We will see that many employers also formulate a *total rewards strategy*. Total rewards encompass the traditional pay, incentives, and benefits, but also things such as more challenging jobs (job design), career

Table 10.1 Do Our Compensation Policies Support Our Strategic Aims?

- What are our strategic aims?
- What employee behaviors and skills do we need to achieve our strategic aims?
- What compensation policies and practices—salary, incentive plans, and benefits—will help produce the employee behaviors we need to achieve our strategic aims?

development, and recognition. Table 10.1 lists illustrative questions to ask when crafting a strategy-oriented pay policy.

Equity and Its Impact on Pay Rates

In studies at Emory University, researchers studied how monkeys reacted to inequitable pay. They trained monkeys to trade pebbles for food. Some got grapes in return for pebbles; others got cucumber slices. Those receiving the sweeter grapes willingly handed in their pebbles. But if a monkey receiving a cucumber slice saw others get grapes, it slammed down the pebble.[2] Perhaps the moral is that even lower primates want fair treatment when it comes to pay.

Equity Theory of Motivation Higher up the primate line, *the equity theory of motivation* postulates that people are strongly motivated to maintain a balance between what they perceive as their contributions and their rewards. Equity theory states that if a person perceives an inequity, a tension will develop in the person's mind, motivating the person to reduce the tension and perceived inequity. Research tends to support equity theory.[3] For example, one study found that retail buyer turnover is significantly lower when the buyers believe they're fairly treated pay-wise.[4] Overpaying people relative to what they think they're worth can backfire too, perhaps "due to feelings of guilt or discomfort."[5]

With respect to compensation, managers should address four forms of equity: *external*, *internal*, *individual*, and *procedural*.[6]

- *External equity* refers to how a job's pay rate in one company compares to the job's pay rate in other companies.
- *Internal equity* refers to how fair a particular job's pay rate is when compared to other jobs within the same company.
- *Individual equity* refers to the fairness of an individual's pay as compared with what his or her coworkers are earning for the same or very similar jobs within the company, based on performance.
- *Procedural equity* refers to the "perceived fairness of the processes and procedures used to make decisions regarding the allocation of pay."[7]

Addressing Equity Issues Managers use various means to address these four equity issues. For example, they use salary surveys (surveys of what other employers are paying) to monitor and maintain external equity. They use job analysis and comparisons of each job ("job evaluation") to maintain internal equity. They use performance appraisal and incentive pay to maintain individual equity. And they use communications, grievance mechanisms, and employee participation to help ensure that employees view the pay process as procedurally fair. Some firms administer surveys to monitor employees' pay satisfaction. Questions typically include, "How satisfied are you with your pay?" and "What factors do you believe are used when your pay is determined?"[8]

To head off discussions that might prompt feelings of internal inequity, some firms maintain secrecy over pay rates, with mixed results.[9] The research concerning pay secrecy is inconclusive, and most employers don't have open pay policies.[10] However, the federal government recently mandated pay transparency for all businesses who have contracts to do business with it.[11] And of course, for external equity, online pay sites like Salary.com preclude secrecy.

Legal Considerations in Compensation

Employers do not have free rein in designing pay plans. Various laws specify things like minimum wages, overtime rates, and benefits.[12] The 1931 **Davis-Bacon Act** lets the secretary of labor set wage rates for laborers and mechanics employed by contractors working for the federal government. The 1936 **Walsh-Healey Public Contract Act** sets basic labor standards for employees working on any government contract that amounts to more than $10,000. It contains minimum wage, maximum hour, and safety and health provisions, and requires time-and-a-half pay for any hours worked over 40 hours a week (for instance, 1.5 times the person's usual hourly pay for those hours worked over 40 hours). **Title VII of the 1964 Civil Rights Act** makes it unlawful for employers to discriminate against any individual with respect to hiring, compensation, terms, conditions, or privileges of employment because of race, color, religion, sex, or national origin.[13]

The 1938 Fair Labor Standards Act The **Fair Labor Standards Act (FLSA)**, originally passed in 1938 and since amended many times, contains minimum wage, maximum hours, overtime pay, equal pay, record-keeping, and child labor provisions that are familiar to most working people.[14] It covers virtually all U.S. workers engaged in the production and/or sale of goods for interstate and foreign commerce. It also covers most agricultural workers. States' fair labor standards laws cover most employers not covered by the FLSA.

One familiar provision governs *overtime pay*. It says employers must pay overtime at a rate of at least one-and-a-half times normal pay for any hours worked over 40 in a workweek. Thus, if a covered worker works 44 hours in one week, he or she must be paid for 4 of those hours at a rate equal to one-and-a-half times the hourly or weekly base rate.[15] For example, if the person earns $12 an hour for a 40-hour week, he or she would receive $18 per hour ($12 times 1.5) for each of the 4 overtime hours worked, or a total of $72 for the extra 4 hours. If the employee instead receives time off for the overtime hours, the employer must also compute the number of hours granted off at the one-and-a-half-times rate. So the person would get 6 hours off for the 4 hours of overtime, in lieu of overtime pay. LinkedIn paid $5.8 million in overtime violation damages to 359 former and current employees.[16]

Employers need to monitor when employees clock in and out, lest the employees accumulate extra minutes, obligating the employer for extra overtime pay.[17] A Department of Labor smartphone app (go to www.dol.gov and key *timesheet app* into the search box[18]) lets employees independently track their work hours.[19] Newer time clocks have touch screens and reduce "buddy punching" with instant photos and biometric sensors.[20]

The FLSA also sets a *minimum wage*. This sets a floor for employees covered by the act (and usually bumps up wages for practically all workers when Congress raises the minimum). The minimum wage was $7.25 in 2017. Many states have their own minimum wage. For example, the minimum wage as of 2017 is $10.00 in California and $11.00 in Massachusetts.[21] New York State is debating raising its minimum wage to $15 per hour. Various cities have set their own (higher) minimum wages.[22] Under new federal rules, workers on federal contracts earn a minimum of $10.10 per hour.[23]

FLSA *child labor provisions* prohibit employing minors between 16 and 18 years old in hazardous occupations and carefully restrict employment of those under 16.

Exempt/Nonexempt Specific categories of employees are *exempt* from the FLSA or certain provisions of the act and particularly from the act's overtime provisions—they are "exempt employees." A person's exemption depends on his or

Davis-Bacon Act (1931)

A law that sets wage rates for laborers employed by contractors working for the federal government.

Walsh-Healey Public Contract Act (1936)

A law that requires minimum wage and working conditions for employees working on any government contract amounting to more than $10,000.

Title VII of the 1964 Civil Rights Act

This act makes it unlawful for employers to discriminate against any individual with respect to hiring, compensation, terms, conditions, or privileges of employment because of race, color, religion, sex, or national origin.

Fair Labor Standards Act (FLSA; 1938)

This act provides for minimum wages, maximum hours, overtime pay, and child labor protection. The law, amended many times, covers most employees.

Figure 10.1

Some Typical Exempt, Nonexempt Job Titles

Source: Based on www.flsa. com/coverage.html, accessed August 5, 2011; and www.dol. gov/elaws/esa/flsa/screen75. asp, accessed October 15, 2012.

Exempt	Nonexempt
Lawyers	Paralegals
Medical doctors	Accounting clerks
Dentists	Bookkeepers
Engineers (with degrees)	Licensed practical nurses
Teachers	Clerical employees
Scientists	Most secretaries (although some, such as
Registered nurses	the CEO's secretary, might be exempt)
General managers	Lab technicians
Pharmacists	
Administrative employees*	

*The administrative exemption is designed for relatively high-level employees whose main job is to "keep the business running." Some examples of administrative functions, whose high-level employees are typically exempt, include labor relations and human resources employees, payroll and finance (including budgeting and benefits management), records maintenance, accounting and tax, marketing and advertising (as differentiated from direct sales), quality control, public relations, legal and regulatory compliance, and some computer-related jobs (such as Internet and database administration).

her responsibilities, duties, and salary. Bona fide executive, administrative (like office managers), and professional employees (like architects) are generally exempt from the minimum wage and overtime requirements of the act.[24] A white-collar worker earning more than $100,000 and performing any one exempt administrative, executive, or professional duty is automatically ineligible for overtime pay. Other employees can generally earn up to $23,660 per year and still automatically get overtime pay (so most employees earning less than $455 per week are nonexempt and earn overtime).[25] Figure 10.1 lists some examples of typically exempt and nonexempt jobs.

In 2016, the Obama administration changed overtime rule exemptions.[26] They said that instead of the salary threshold of $23,660 per year (below which basically anyone working was eligible for overtime pay) the new threshold was $47,476; essentially anyone earning under $47,476 had to be paid overtime.

In November 2016 a federal judge halted implementation of the new overtime rule. As of 2017 the new Republican administration was still considering how to proceed. Employers who had already taken steps to adjust their pay policies to the Obama rule (for instance Walmart raised supervisors' pay to over $47,476) were mostly sticking with their decisions; however labor lawyers were advising other employers to just maintain the status quo until revised rules were announced. Many experts believed that a revised cutoff level of about $35,000 (instead of the Obama rule's $47,476) was likely.[27]

If an employee is exempt from the FLSA's minimum wage provisions, then he or she is also exempt from its overtime pay provisions. However, certain employees are *always* exempt from overtime pay provisions, for example, agricultural employees, live-in household employees, taxi drivers, and motion picture theater employees.[28]

Identifying exemptions is tricky.[29] As noted, some jobs—for example, top managers and lawyers—are clearly exempt. Others—such as office workers earning less than $23,660 (or $47,476) per year—are clearly nonexempt. Unfortunately, beyond the obvious jobs, it's advisable to analyze the job before classifying it as exempt or nonexempt. For example, even supervisors are filing wage and hour suits, saying they don't really supervise two or more employees.[30] Figure 10.2 presents a procedure for making this decision. In all but the clearest situations, carefully review the job description.[31]

Inequity and the Minimum Wage[32] Jamie Dimon, Chairman and CEO of JP Morgan Chase & Company, recently wrote an article for *The New York Times*; he argued that years of wage stagnation had led to income inequality. As an example,

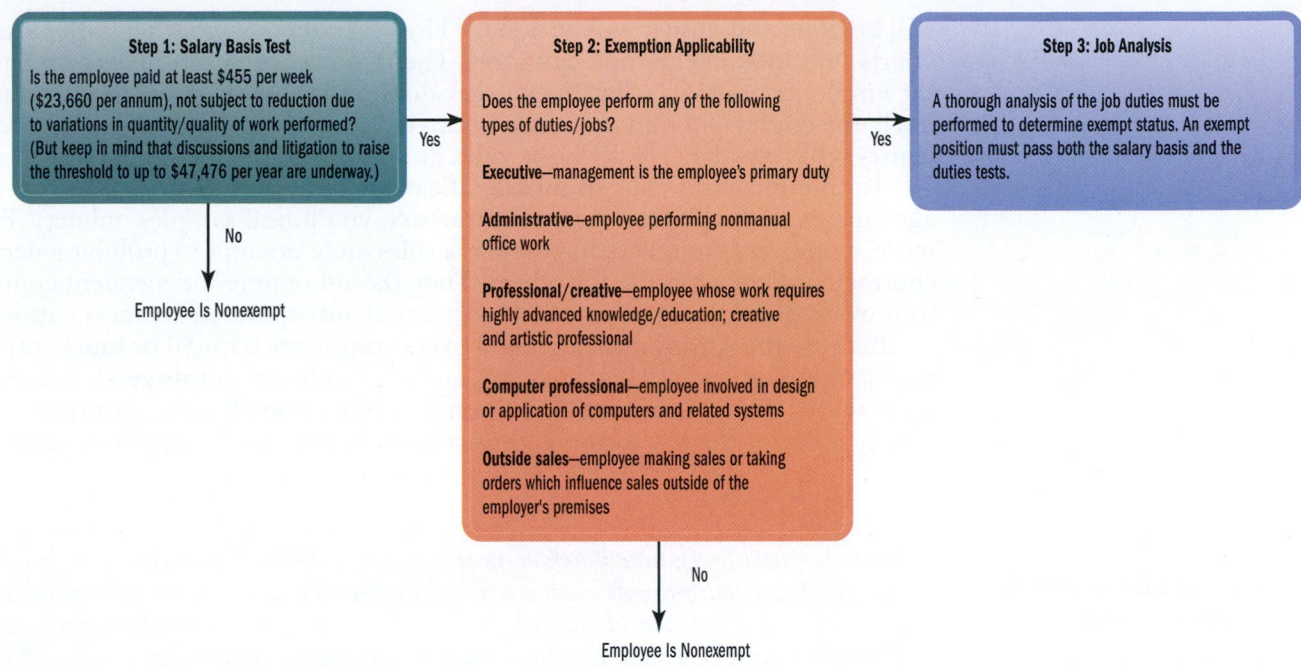

Step 1: Salary Basis Test

Is the employee paid at least $455 per week ($23,660 per annum), not subject to reduction due to variations in quantity/quality of work performed? (But keep in mind that discussions and litigation to raise the threshold to up to $47,476 per year are underway.)

Yes →

Step 2: Exemption Applicability

Does the employee perform any of the following types of duties/jobs?

Executive—management is the employee's primary duty

Administrative—employee performing nonmanual office work

Professional/creative—employee whose work requires highly advanced knowledge/education; creative and artistic professional

Computer professional—employee involved in design or application of computers and related systems

Outside sales—employee making sales or taking orders which influence sales outside of the employer's premises

Yes →

Step 3: Job Analysis

A thorough analysis of the job duties must be performed to determine exempt status. An exempt position must pass both the salary basis and the duties tests.

↓ No

Employee Is Nonexempt

↓ No

Employee Is Nonexempt

Figure 10.2

Who Is Exempt? Who Is Not Exempt?

wages and salaries rose 33% from 1999 to 2007 and only 13% from 2007 to 2014.[33] Several 2016 presidential candidates made similar arguments. Salary inequities are worsened by a tendency for more raises to go to "star" performers, many of whom demand raises in return for not accepting competing jobs.[34] And in the United States, the average CEO earns about 350 times what the average worker does.[35]

Many municipalities and employers are thus moving to raise the local minimum wage or to pay higher entry-level wages. The San José, California City Council recently voted to raise the local minimum to $15. Walmart said it would unilaterally pay all its U.S. hourly workers at least $10 per hour. McDonald's said it would raise its minimum wage to at least one dollar more than the local municipalities' minimum wage in all company-owned stores. Tyson raised its minimum factory wage to $10 per hour.

Not everyone agrees that a higher minimum wage is good. For example, some economists argue that higher minimum wages reduce the chances that traditionally low-wage workers (like younger people) will get hired. But an increasing number of people—including executives at firms like Walmart—seem to agree that income inequality needs to be addressed.

 KNOW YOUR EMPLOYMENT LAW

The Independent Contractor

Whether someone is an employee or an *independent contractor* is a continuing legal concern for employers.[36] Why claim that someone is an independent contractor? Because the FLSA's overtime and most other requirements do not apply, and the employer need not pay unemployment compensation; payroll taxes; Social Security taxes; city, state, and federal income taxes; or compulsory workers' compensation for that worker.

The problem is that many so-called independent contractor relationships aren't independent contractor relationships. In general, someone is an independent contractor if the employer controls or directs only the result of the work and not what will be done and how it will be done.[37] However, there is no single rule or test: the courts will look at the total situation. The major consideration is this: The more the employer controls what the worker does and how he or she does it, the more likely the courts will find the worker is an employee. Figure 10.3 lists some factors courts will consider. The IRS lists rules at its website.[38]

To minimize the risks of misclassification, employers should execute written agreements with all independent contractors; you'll find samples online.[39] Furthermore, employers should not impose work rules on or attempt to prohibit independent contractors from working for others. They should require independent contractors to provide their own tools and to be separately incorporated business entities.[40]

Because the Affordable Care Act covers employers with 50 or more employees, government agencies are looking more closely at employers' independent contractors. To minimize problems, some employers are having staffing companies supply more of their workforce, thus staying below the 50-employee limit.[41] ■

Figure 10.3

Independent Contractor or Employee Checklist

Source: Adapted from information in IRS, Employer's Supplemental Tax Guide, https://www.irs.gov/pub/irs-pdf/p15a.pdf accessed June 6, 2017.

The main question is, how much control does the employer exert over the person at work? Facts that provide evidence of the degree of control/independence fall into three categories: behavioral control, financial control, and relationship of the parties. Affirmative answers below generally suggest "independent contractor."

Behavioral control: Does the business direct and control how the worker does the task, such as:	Independent Contractor	Employee
1. When and where to do the work.		
2. What tools or equipment to use.		
3. What workers to hire or to assist with the work.		
4. Where to purchase supplies and services.		
5. Whether the business has retained the right to control the details of a worker's performance or instead has given up that right.		
Financial control: Does the business control the business/financial aspects of the worker's job, such as:		
6. The extent to which the worker has unreimbursed business expenses.		
7. The extent of the worker's investment.		
8. The extent to which the worker makes his or her services available to other businesses in the relevant market.		
9. Whether the worker is not generally guaranteed a regular wage amount for an hourly, weekly, or other period of time.		
10. The extent to which the worker can realize a profit or loss.		
Questions regarding the parties' relationship include:		
11. Whether the business does not provide the worker with employee-type benefits, such as insurance, a pension plan, vacation pay, or sick pay.		
12. Whether there's no expectation that the relationship will continue indefinitely, rather than for a specific project or period.		

■ HR and the Gig Economy

Are Gig Workers Employees or Independent Contractors?

A few years ago, Uber and Lyft drivers filed suit in California, demanding to be recognized as employees rather than independent contractors. Uber and Lyft contend they're independent contractors in control of what they do for the company: for instance, they can work (or not) as much as they want, start and stop when they want, and use their own cars.

But the answer is not so clear cut. Although it's true that there is much independent about what the drivers do, the drivers' lawyers say that Lyft and Uber control what the drivers do at work. For example algorithms and systems control what ride the drivers can accept or decline, the routes they take, how much they can earn, and even how they're evaluated (evidence was presented to show that below an average rating of about 4.5 stars, a driver was in danger of deactivation).

These cases settled out of court. Uber agreed to pay about $100 million to drivers in certain states and to let them solicit tips; however, the settlement left the drivers as independent contractors.

Still, these suits are a sign of what's to come in how independent contractors are defined in the gig economy. Even in traditional workplaces there was some ambiguity about how to distinguish between independent contractors and employees. Today, gig workers are often free to come and go as they please and to quit any time, but at work computer algorithms tightly control their efforts. It's therefore increasingly difficult to distinguish between employees and independent contractors. The EEOC's strategic enforcement plan for 2017 – 2021 aims to ensure that gig workers are classified correctly and receive the appropriate statutory protections.[42] Expect more lawsuits.

⭐ Talk About It – **1**

If your professor assigned this, go to **www.pearson.com/mylab/management** and answer the following question: How would you itemize the arguments for and arguments against making Lyft and Uber drivers independent contractors?

Equal Pay Act (1963)
An amendment to the Fair Labor Standards Act designed to require equal pay for women doing the same work as men.

1963 Equal Pay Act The **Equal Pay Act**, an amendment to the Fair Labor Standards Act, states that employees of one sex may not be paid wages at a rate lower than that paid to employees of the opposite sex for doing roughly equivalent work. Specifically, if the work requires equal skills, effort, and responsibility, and involves similar working conditions, employees of both sexes must receive equal pay, unless the differences in pay stem from a seniority system, a merit system, the quantity or quality of production, or "any factor other than sex."

Employee Retirement Income Security Act (ERISA)
The law that provides government protection of pensions for all employees with company pension plans. It also regulates vesting rights (employees who leave before retirement may claim compensation from the pension plan).

1974 Employee Retirement Income Security Act The **Employee Retirement Income Security Act (ERISA)** provided for the creation of government-run, employer-financed corporations to protect employees against the failure of their employers' pension plans. In addition, it sets regulations regarding vesting rights (*vesting* refers to the equity or ownership the employees build up in their pension plans should their employment terminate before retirement). ERISA also regulates *portability rights* (the transfer of an employee's vested rights from one organization to another). It also contains employer fiduciary standards to prevent dishonesty in pension plan funding.

Other Legislation Affecting Compensation Various other laws influence compensation decisions. For example, the Age Discrimination in Employment Act prohibits age discrimination against employees who are 40 years of age and older in all aspects of employment, including compensation.[43] The Americans with Disabilities Act prohibits discrimination against qualified persons with disabilities in all aspects of employment, including compensation. The Family and Medical Leave Act entitles eligible employees, both men and women, to take up to 12 weeks of unpaid, job-protected leave for the birth of a child or for the care of a child, spouse, or parent. And various executive orders require federal government contractors or subcontractors to not discriminate and to take affirmative action in compensation.

Each state has its own *workers' compensation laws*. Among other things, these aim to provide prompt, sure, and reasonable income to victims of work-related accidents. The Social Security Act of 1935 (as amended) provides for unemployment compensation for workers unemployed through no fault of their own, generally for up to 26 weeks, and for retirement benefits. (We'll discuss Social Security benefits in Chapter 11.) The federal wage garnishment law limits the amount of an employee's earnings that employers can withhold (garnish) per week and protects the worker from discharge due to garnishment.

Union Influences on Compensation Decisions

Unions and labor relations laws also influence pay plan design. The National Labor Relations Act of 1935 (Wagner Act) granted employees the right to unionize, and to bargain collectively. Historically, the wage rate has been the main issue in collective bargaining. However, unions also negotiate other pay-related issues, including time off with pay and health care benefits.

The Wagner Act created the National Labor Relations Board (NLRB) to oversee employer practices and ensure that employees receive their rights. For example, the NLRB says that employers must give the union a written explanation of the employer's "wage curves"—the graph that relates job to pay rate. The union is also entitled to know its members' salaries.[44]

Pay Policies

The employer's compensation strategy will manifest itself in *pay policies*. For example, a top hospital might have a policy of paying nurses 20% above the

Historically, the wage rate has been the main issue in collective bargaining. However, unions also negotiate other pay-related issues, including time off with pay, income security, cost-of-living adjustments, and health care benefits.

Source: A Lot of People/Shutterstock.

prevailing market wage. Pay policies can influence the employer's performance and profitability, as the accompanying HR as a Profit Center illustrates.

Managers need to formulate pay policies covering various issues. One is whether to emphasize *seniority* or *performance*. For example, it takes 18 years (seniority) for a U.S. federal employee to progress from step 1 to step 9 of the government's pay scale. Seniority-based pay may be advantageous to the extent that seniority is an objective standard. On the downside, top performers may get the same raises as poor ones.

How to distinguish between *high and low performers* is another policy issue. For example, for many years, Payless ShoeSource was paternal in giving raises—it paid everyone about the same. However, after its market share dropped, management decided to differentiate more aggressively between top performers and others.[45] Other pay policies may cover things like overtime pay, probationary pay, leaves for military service, jury duty, and holidays.

■ HR as a Profit Center

Wegmans Foods

Strategic compensation management means formulating a total rewards package that produces the employee skills and behaviors that the company needs to achieve its strategic goals.

Wegmans exemplifies this. It competes in the retail food sector, where profit margins are thin and where online competitors and giants like Walmart drive costs and prices down. The usual reaction is to cut employee benefits and costs.[46] Wegmans instead offers above-market rates and great benefits. It views its workforce as an integral part of achieving Wegmans' strategic aims of *optimizing service while controlling costs by improving systems and productivity*. For example, one dairy department employee designed a new way to organize the cooler, thus improving ordering and inventory control.[47]

Such pay policies probably help explain Wegmans' exceptional profitability. For example, Wegmans' employee turnover (38% for part-timers, 6–7% for full-timers) is well below the industry's overall average of about 47%.[48] Its stores (which at about 120,000 square feet are larger than competitors') average about $950,000 a week in sales (compared to a national average of $361,564), or about $49 million in sales annually, compared with a typical Walmart store's grocery sales of $23.5 million.[49] As Wegmans' human resource head has said, good employees ensure higher productivity, and that translates into better bottom-line results.[50]

★ Talk About It–**2**

If your professor has chosen to assign this, go to **www.pearson.com/mylab/management** to discuss the following question. If Wegmans does so well with a high-pay policy, why don't more employers do this as well?

Geography How to account for geographic cost of living differences is another big pay policy issue. For example, the average base pay for an office supervisor ranges from $49,980 in Florida to $60,980 in New York.[51]

Employers handle cost-of-living differentials for transferees in several ways. For example, one employer pays a differential of $6,000 per year to people earning $35,000 to $45,000 whom it transfers from Atlanta to Minneapolis. Others simply raise the employee's base salary. The problem is more complicated when sending employees overseas, as the following feature explains.[52]

■ HR Practices Around the Globe

Compensating Expatriate Employees

The question of cost-of-living differentials has particular significance to multinational firms, for which things like housing and education costs vary widely.

How should multinationals compensate expatriate employees—those it sends overseas? Two basic international compensation policies are popular: home-based and host-based plans.[53]

With a *home-based salary plan*, an international transferee's base salary reflects his or her home country's salary. The employer then adds allowances for cost-of-living differences—housing and schooling costs, for instance. This is a reasonable approach for short-term assignments and avoids having to change the employee's base salary every time he or she moves.

In the *host-based plan*, the firm ties the international transferee's base salary to the host country's salary structure. In other words, the manager from New York who is sent to France would have his or her base salary changed to the prevailing base salary for that position in France, rather than keep the New York base salary. The firm usually tacks on cost-of-living, housing, schooling, and other allowances here as well.

Most multinational enterprises set expatriates' salaries according to the *home-based salary plan*. (Thus, a French manager assigned to Kiev by a U.S. multinational will generally have a base salary that reflects the salary structure in the manager's home country, in this case, France.) In addition, the person typically gets allowances including cost-of-living, relocation, housing, education, and hardship allowances (for more challenging countries). The employer also usually pays any extra taxes the manager is liable for over and above those he or she would have to pay in the home country.

✪ Talk About It–3

If your professor has chosen to assign this, go to **www.pearson.com/mylab/management** to discuss the following question. Why do you think most employers opt for the home-based salary plan?

LEARNING OBJECTIVE 2
Define and give an example of how to conduct a job evaluation and set pay rates.

Job Evaluation Methods

Employers use two basic methods for setting pay rates: *market-based approaches* and *job evaluation methods*. Many firms, particularly smaller ones, simply use a *market-based* approach. This involves conducting formal or informal salary surveys to determine what others in the relevant labor markets are paying for particular jobs. The employer then uses this information to price its own jobs.

In contrast, *job evaluation methods* involve determining the "worth" to the employer of each of its jobs and then pricing these jobs. This process helps produce a pay plan in which each job's pay is equitable based on what other employers are paying for these jobs *and* based on each job's value to the employer.[54] We'll concentrate here on the job evaluation approach.

What Is Job Evaluation?

job evaluation

A systematic comparison done to determine the worth of one job relative to another.

Job evaluation is a formal and systematic comparison of jobs to determine the worth of one job relative to another. Job evaluation aims to determine a job's relative worth. Job evaluation eventually results in a *wage* or *salary structure* or hierarchy (this shows the pay rate for various jobs or groups of jobs).[55] The basic principle of job evaluation is this: Jobs that require greater qualifications, more responsibilities, and more complex job duties should receive more pay than jobs with lesser requirements.

market-competitive pay plan
A pay system in which the employer's actual pay rates are competitive with those in the relevant labor market.

salary survey
A survey aimed at determining prevailing wage rates. A good salary survey provides specific wage rates for specific jobs. Formal written questionnaire surveys are the most comprehensive, but telephone surveys and Internet and newspaper help-wanted ads are also sources of information.

The basic job evaluation procedure is to compare jobs in relation to one another—for example, in terms of each job's required effort, job complexity, and skills. Suppose you know (based on your job evaluation) the relative worth of the key jobs in your firm. You then conduct a salary survey to see what others are paying for similar jobs. By combining the information from the job evaluation and from the salary survey, you are on your way to being able to create a **market-competitive pay plan**—one where your pay rates are equitable both internally (based on each job's relative value) and externally (in other words, when compared with what other employers are paying).

Salary Surveys

Salary surveys—surveys of what others are paying—play a big role in pricing jobs.[56] Whether the manager is using a market-based approach or a job evaluation method to price jobs, he or she will need a salary survey.

Managers use salary surveys in three ways. First, they use survey data to price benchmark jobs. Benchmark jobs are the anchor jobs around which they slot their other jobs, based on each job's relative worth to the firm. Second, managers typically price some or all of their positions directly in the marketplace (rather than relative to the firm's benchmark jobs), based on a survey of what comparable firms are paying for comparable jobs. Third, surveys also collect data on benefits like insurance, sick leave, and vacations for decisions regarding employee benefits.

Informal phone or Internet surveys are good for checking specific issues, such as when a bank wants to confirm the salary at which to advertise a newly open teller's job. Some large employers can afford to send out their own *formal* surveys to collect compensation information from other employers. These ask about things like number of employees, overtime policies, starting salaries, and paid vacations.

COMMERCIAL, PROFESSIONAL, AND GOVERNMENT SALARY SURVEYS Many employers use surveys published by consulting firms, professional associations, or government agencies. For example, the U.S. Department of Labor's Bureau of Labor Statistics' (BLS) *National Compensation Survey (NCS)* provides comprehensive reports of occupational earnings, compensation cost trends, and benefits (www.bls.gov/bls/wages.htm).

Detailed occupational earnings are available from the national compensation survey for over 800 occupations in the United States, calculated with data from employers in all industry sectors in every state and the District of Columbia (http://stats.bls.gov/oes/current/oes_nat.htm). The *Current Employment Statistics Survey* is a monthly survey of the payroll records of business establishments that provides data on earnings of production and nonsupervisory workers at the national level. This provides information about earnings as well as production bonuses, commissions, and cost-of-living increases. The *National Compensation Survey—Benefits* provides information on the share of workers who participate in specified benefits, such as health care, retirement plans, and paid vacations. These data also show the details of those benefits, such as amounts of paid leave. Internationally, the BLS reports comparative hourly compensation costs in local currencies and U.S. dollars for production workers and all employees in manufacturing in its international labor comparisons tables.

Private consulting and/or executive recruiting companies like Hay Associates, Towers Watson Global Data Services, and Aon (www.aon.com) publish data covering compensation for top and middle management and members of boards of directors. Professional organizations like the Society for Human Resource Management and the Financial Executives Institute publish surveys of compensation practices among members of their associations.[57]

USING THE INTERNET TO DO COMPENSATION SURVEYS Internet-based options make it easy for anyone to access published compensation survey information. Table 10.2 shows some popular salary survey websites.

Many of these sites, such as Salary.com, provide national salary levels for jobs that the site then arithmetically adjusts to each locale based on cost-of-living formulas. To get a real-time picture of what employers in your area are actually paying for, say, accounting clerks, it's useful to access the online Internet sites of one or two of your local newspapers. For example, the *South Florida Sun-Sentinel* (and many papers) uses a site called careerbuilder.com. It lists just about all the job opportunities listed in the newspaper by category and, in many instances, their wage rates (www.careerbuilder.com/).

Compensable Factors

Compensable factors play a central role in job evaluation.

The manager can use two basic approaches to compare the worth of several jobs. First, you can take an intuitive approach. You might decide that one job is more important than another is and not dig any deeper. As an alternative, you could compare the jobs by focusing on certain basic factors the jobs have in common (such as each job's required effort and skills). Compensation management specialists call these **compensable factors**. They are the factors that establish how the jobs compare to one another and that determine the pay for each job.

Some employers develop their own compensable factors. However, most use factors popularized by packaged job evaluation systems or by federal legislation. For example, the Equal Pay Act uses four compensable factors—skills, effort, responsibility, and working conditions. The method popularized by the Hay Group consulting firm emphasizes three factors: know-how, problem solving, and accountability.[58] Walmart uses knowledge, problem-solving skills, and accountability requirements.

Again, compensable factors play a central role in job evaluation. You usually compare each job with the firm's other jobs using the same compensable factors (for instance, how much skill does each job require?). However, the compensable factors you use depend on the job and the job evaluation method. For example, "decision making" might make sense for a manager's job, but not for a cleaner's job.[59]

Preparing for the Job Evaluation

Job evaluation is a judgmental process and demands close cooperation among supervisors, HR specialists, and employees and union representatives. The main steps include identifying the need for the program, getting cooperation, and then

compensable factor

A fundamental, compensable element of a job, such as skills, effort, responsibility, and working conditions.

Table 10.2 Some Pay Data Websites

Sponsor	Internet Address	What It Provides	Downside
Salary.com	Salary.com	Salary by job and zip code, plus job and description, for hundreds of jobs	Adapts national averages by applying local cost-of-living differences
U.S. Office of Personnel Management	www.opm.gov/oca/09Tables/index.asp	Salaries and wages for U.S. government jobs, by location	Limited to U.S. government jobs
Job Star	http://jobstar.org/tools/salary/sal-prof.php	Profession-specific salary surveys	Necessary to review numerous salary surveys for each profession
cnnmoney.com	cnnmoney.com	Input your current salary and city; for comparable salary in destination city	Based on national averages adapted to cost-of-living differences

choosing an evaluation committee. The committee then performs the actual evaluation.

Identifying the need for job evaluation is usually easy. For example, dissatisfaction reflected in high turnover, work stoppages, or arguments may result from paying employees different rates for similar jobs. Managers may express uneasiness with an informal way of assigning pay rates.

Employees may fear that a systematic evaluation of their jobs may reduce their pay rates, so *getting employees to cooperate* in the evaluation is important. For example, you can tell employees that because of the impending job evaluation program, pay rate decisions will no longer be made just by management whim, and that no current employee's rate will be adversely affected because of the job evaluation.

The *job evaluation committee* usually consists of about five members, most of whom are employees. Management has the right to serve on such committees, but employees may view this with suspicion. However, a human resource specialist can usually be justified to provide expert assistance. Union representation is possible but unlikely.[60] Once appointed, each committee member should receive a manual explaining how to conduct the job evaluation.

The evaluation committee performs three main functions. First, it usually identifies 10 or 15 key **benchmark jobs.** These will be the first jobs they'll evaluate and will serve as the anchors or benchmarks against which the relative importance or value of all other jobs is compared. Next, the committee may select compensable factors (although the human resources department will usually choose these). Finally, the committee performs its most important function—actually *evaluating the worth of each job.* For this, the committee will probably use one of the following methods: ranking, job classification, or point method.

Job Evaluation Methods: Ranking

The simplest job evaluation method ranks each job relative to all other jobs, usually based on some overall factor like "job difficulty." There are several steps in the job **ranking method.** The following Building Your Management Skills takes you through the steps, and also helps to illustrate a simple way to develop a pay plan for a small company.

benchmark job
A job that is used to anchor the employer's pay scale and around which other jobs are arranged in order of relative worth.

ranking method
The simplest method of job evaluation that involves ranking each job relative to all other jobs, usually based on overall difficulty.

Members of the job evaluation committee first usually identify 10 or 15 key benchmark jobs. These will be the first jobs they and their committee colleagues will evaluate.
Source: Image Source Plus/Alamy Stock Photo.

BUILDING YOUR MANAGEMENT SKILLS:
How to Create a Pay Scale for a Company by Using the Job Ranking Job Evaluation Method

Creating a pay scale for a company by using the job ranking job evaluation method consists of the following steps:

1. **Obtain job information.** Job analysis is the first step. Here job descriptions for each job are prepared, and the information they contain about the job's duties is usually the basis for ranking jobs. (Sometimes job specifications are also prepared. However, the ranking method usually ranks jobs based on the whole job, rather than on several compensable factors. Therefore, job specifications, which tend to list job demands in terms of compensable factors such as problem solving, decision making, and skills, are not as important with this method as they are for other job evaluation methods.)

2. **Select and group jobs.** It is usually not practical to make a single ranking for all jobs in an organization. The usual procedure is to rank jobs by department or in clusters (such as factory workers or clerical workers). This eliminates the need for direct comparison of, say, factory jobs and clerical jobs.

3. **Select compensable factors.** In the ranking method, it is common to use just one factor (such as job difficulty) and to rank jobs based on the whole job. Regardless of the number of factors you choose, it's advisable to explain the definition of the factor(s) to the evaluators carefully so that they all evaluate the jobs consistently.

4. **Rank jobs.** One way to rank jobs is to give each rater a set of index cards, each of which contains a brief description of a job. Then they arrange these cards from lowest to highest. Some managers use an "alternation ranking method" for making the procedure more accurate. Here you take the cards, first choosing the highest and the lowest, then the next highest and next lowest, and so forth, until you've ranked all the cards. Table 10.3 illustrates a job ranking. Jobs in this small health-care facility rank from orderly up to office manager. The corresponding current pay scales are shown in the column following the job titles. (After ranking, it is possible to slot additional jobs between those already ranked and to assign an appropriate wage rate. This enables us to compare each job's rank with its current pay, to see if what we are currently paying is *internally* equitable; we may adjust a job's pay up or down, based on this). Online programs (for example, go to www.hr-guide.com, click under Job Evaluation, Ranking, and then click Interactive Ranking Program) can help you rank (and check the rankings of) your positions.[61]

5. **Combine ratings.** Note that several raters usually rank the jobs independently. Then the rating committee (or the employer) can simply average the raters' rankings.

6. **Compare current pay with what others are paying based on salary survey.** Next, we show on the same table (in the middle column) what others in the community are paying for similar jobs, based on a salary survey that we conduct. This helps us ensure that our pay will be *externally* equitable.

7. **Assign a new pay scale.** Finally, we compare what we are currently paying for each job with what others are paying and decide (in this case) to adjust our pay scale by raising what we pay for each job. The last column therefore shows our new pay scale.

Table 10.3 Job Ranking at Jackson Hospital

Ranking Order	Our Current Annual Pay Scale	What Others Pay: Salary Survey Pay	Our Final Assigned Pay
1. Office manager	$43,000	$45,000	$44,000
2. Chief nurse	42,500	43,000	42,750
3. Bookkeeper	34,000	36,000	35,000
4. Nurse	32,500	33,000	32,750
5. Cook	31,000	32,000	31,500
6. Nurse's aide	28,500	30,500	29,500
7. Orderly	25,500	27,000	27,000

Note: After ranking, it becomes possible to slot additional jobs (based on overall job difficulty, for instance) between those already ranked and to assign each an appropriate wage rate.

Ranking is the simplest job evaluation method, as well as the easiest to explain. It also usually takes less time than other methods, but has a few weaknesses. For example, "job number 4" may in fact be five times "more valuable" than "job number 5," but with the ranking method all you know is that one job ranks higher than the other. Ranking is usually more appropriate for small employers that can't afford to use a more elaborate system. For them it is a simple way to create a market-competitive pay scale, one that is equitable both internally and externally.

The *factor comparison method* is a special ranking method. It requires ranking each job several times—once for each compensable factor (such as education required, experience, and complexity). It is seldom used today.

Job Evaluation Methods: Job Classification

Job classification (or job grading) is a simple, widely used job evaluation method in which raters categorize jobs into groups; all the jobs in each group are of roughly the same value for pay purposes. We call the groups **classes** if they contain similar jobs, or **grades** if they contain jobs that are similar in difficulty but otherwise different. Thus, in the federal government's pay grade system, a "press secretary" and a "fire chief" might both be graded "GS-10" (GS stands for "General Schedule"). On the other hand, in its job class system, the state of Florida might classify all "secretary IIs" in one class, all "maintenance engineers" in another, and so forth.

In practice, there are several ways to categorize jobs. One is to write class or grade descriptions or summaries (similar to job descriptions) and place jobs into classes or grades based on how well they fit these descriptions. A second is to write a set of compensable factor–based rules for each class (for instance, how much independent judgment, skill, and physical effort does the class of jobs require?). Then categorize the jobs according to these rules.

The usual procedure is to choose compensable factors and then develop class or grade descriptions that describe each class (or grade) in terms of the amount or level of the factors in those jobs. For example, the U.S. government's classification system uses the following compensable factors: (1) difficulty and variety of work, (2) supervision received and exercised, (3) judgment exercised, (4) originality required, (5) nature and purpose of interpersonal work relationships, (6) responsibility, (7) experience, and (8) knowledge required. Based on these compensable factors, raters write a **grade definition** like that in Figure 10.4. This one shows one grade description (GS-7) for the federal government's pay grade system. Then the evaluation committee reviews all job descriptions and slots each job into its appropriate grade, by comparing each job description to the rules in each grade description. For instance, the federal government system classifies the positions automotive mechanic, welder, electrician, and machinist in grade GS-10.

The classification method has several advantages. The main one is that most employers usually end up grouping jobs into classes or grades anyway, regardless

job classification (or grading) method
A method for categorizing jobs into groups.

classes
Grouping jobs based on a set of rules for each group or class, such as amount of independent judgment, skill, physical effort, and so forth, required. Classes usually contain similar jobs.

grades
A job classification system like the class system, although grades often contain dissimilar jobs, such as secretaries, mechanics, and firefighters. Grade descriptions are written based on compensable factors listed in classification systems.

grade definition
Written descriptions of the level of, say, responsibility and knowledge required by jobs in each grade. Similar jobs can then be combined into grades or classes.

Figure 10.4

Example of a Grade Level Definition

Source: "Grade Level Guide for Clerical and Assistance Work" from U.S. Office of Personnel Management, June 1989.

Grade	Nature of Assignment	Level of Responsibility
GS-7	Performs specialized duties in a defined functional or program area involving a wide variety of problems or situations; develops information, identifies interrelationships, and takes actions consistent with objectives of the function or program served.	Work is assigned in terms of objectives, priorities, and deadlines; the employee works independently in resolving most conflicts; completed work is evaluated for conformance to policy; guidelines, such as regulations, precedent cases, and policy statements require considerable interpretation and adaptation.

of the evaluation method they use. They do this to avoid having to price separately dozens or hundreds of jobs. Of course, the job classification automatically groups the employer's jobs into classes. The disadvantages are that it is difficult to write the class or grade descriptions, and considerable judgment is required to apply them. Yet many employers use this method with success.

Job Evaluation Methods: Point Method

point method

The job evaluation method in which a number of compensable factors are identified and then the degree to which each of these factors is present on the job is determined.

The overall aim of the **point method** is to determine the degree to which the jobs being evaluated contain selected compensable factors. It involves identifying several compensable factors for the jobs, as well as the degree to which each factor is present in each job. Assume there are five degrees of the compensable factor "responsibility" a job could contain. Further, assume you assign a different number of points to each degree of each compensable factor. Once the evaluation committee determines the degree to which each compensable factor (like "responsibility" and "effort") is present in a job, it can calculate a total point value for the job by adding up the corresponding degree points for each factor. The result is a quantitative point rating for each job. The point method of job evaluation is the most popular job evaluation method.[62] The appendix to this chapter presents a step-by-step example of how to use the point method to create a market-competitive pay plan.

"Packaged" Point Plans Several groups (such as the Hay Group, the National Electrical Manufacturer's Association, and the National Trade Association) have developed standardized point plan systems. Many thousands of employers use these systems. They contain ready-made factor and degree definitions and point assessments for a wide range of jobs. Employers can often use them with little or no modification.

Computerized Job Evaluations

Using job evaluation methods such as the point method can be time consuming. Many employers therefore turn to computerized systems.

Most such systems have two main components.[63] First is a structured questionnaire with items such as "enter total number of employees who report to this position." Second are statistical models. These allow the computerized system to price jobs more or less automatically, by assigning points based on the questionnaire responses.

Wage Curves

wage curve

Shows the relationship between the value of the job and the average wage paid for this job.

Wage curves are useful when using the point method (or some other job evaluation methods). The **wage curve** shows the pay rates paid for jobs, relative to the points or rankings assigned to each job by the job evaluation. Figure 10.5 is an example. Note that it shows pay rates for jobs on the vertical axis and point values for these jobs along the horizontal axis. The purpose of the wage curve is to show the relationships between (1) the value of the job (expressed in points) as determined by

Figure 10.5

Plotting a Wage Curve

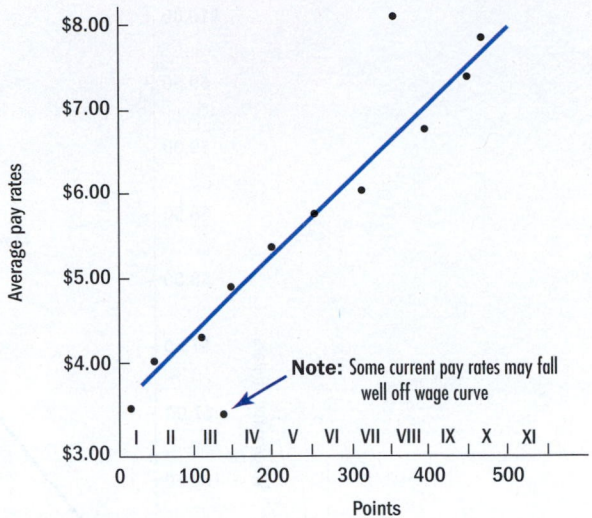

one of the job evaluation methods and (2) the pay rates for the job. The manager can compare (on one graph or on two separate graphs) an "internal" wage curve showing what the company currently pays for its jobs, with an "external" wage curve that shows what others pay for these jobs. The manager then decides whether to adjust the pay for each job or pay grade. He or she can also use the curve to see if a particular job's pay falls off the wage curve, which is a signal that the job is paid too high or too low.

Pay Grades

pay (or wage) grade
A pay grade is comprised of jobs of approximately equal difficulty.

Employers typically group similar jobs (in terms of points) into grades for pay purposes. Then, instead of having to deal with hundreds of job rates, you might only have to focus on, say, pay rates for 10 or 12 pay grades.[64] A **pay (or wage) grade** is comprised of jobs of approximately equal difficulty or importance as determined by job evaluation. If you used the point method of job evaluation, the pay grade consists of jobs falling within a range of points. If the ranking method was used, the grade consists of a specific number of ranks. If you use the classification system, then your jobs are already categorized into classes (or grades).

Rate Ranges and the Wage Structure

pay (or rate) ranges
A series of steps or levels within a pay grade, usually based on years of service.

Most employers do not pay just one rate for all jobs in a particular pay grade. For example, GE Medical won't pay all its accounting clerks, from beginners to long tenure, at the same rate, even though they may all be in the same pay grade. Instead, employers develop vertical pay or "rate" ranges for each of the pay grades (or pay classes). These **pay or rate ranges** often appear as vertical boxes within each grade, showing minimum, maximum, and midpoint pay rates for that grade, as in Figure 10.6. (Specialists call Figure 10.6 a *wage structure.* Figure 10.6 graphically depicts the wage structure for a company, including the range of pay rates—in this case, per hour—paid for each pay grade.)

Alternatively, you may depict the pay range for each class or grade as steps in a table, as in Table 10.4. Thus Table 10.4 shows the steps and pay rates for most federal government grades. As of the time of this pay schedule, for instance, employees in positions classified in grade GS-10 could be paid annual salaries between $ 47,630 and $ 61,922, depending on the level or step at which they were hired into the grade, the amount of time they were in the grade, and any merit increases they've received. The accompanying HR Tools feature illustrates how to create a workable pay plan.

Figure 10.6
Wage Structure

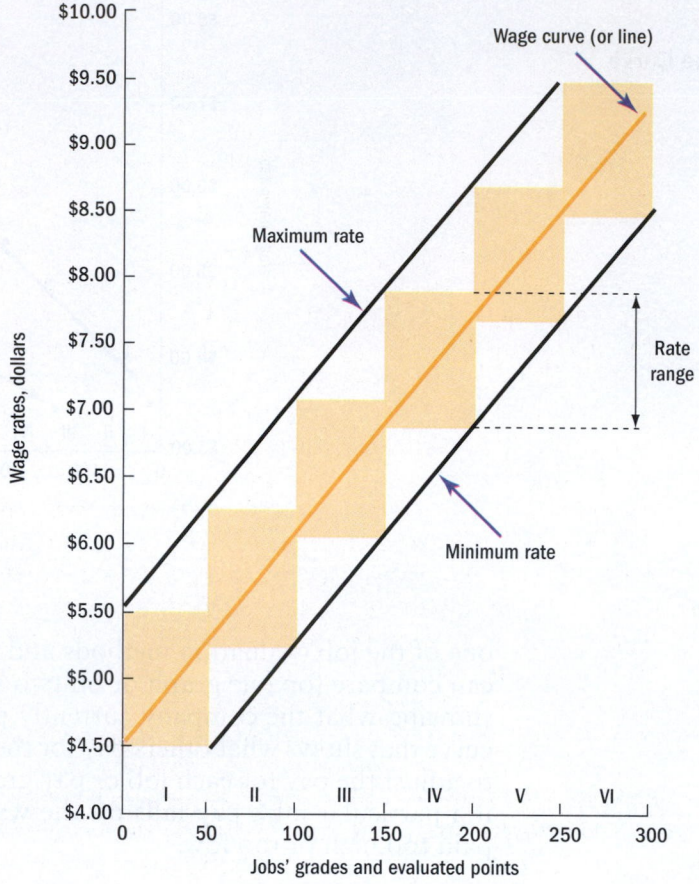

Table 10.4 US Government Annual Rates by Grade and Step

Grade	Step 1	Step 2	Step 3	Step 4	Step 5	Step 6	Step 7	Step 8	Step 9	Step 10	Within Grade Amounts
1	$18,526	$19,146	$19,762	$20,375	$20,991	$21,351	$21,960	$22,575	$22,599	$23,171	VARIES
2	20,829	21,325	22,015	22,599	22,853	23,525	24,197	24,869	25,541	26,213	VARIES
3	22,727	23,485	23,243	25,001	25,759	26,517	27,275	28,033	28,791	29,549	758
4	25,514	26,364	27,214	28,064	28,914	29,764	30,614	31,464	32,314	33,164	850
5	28,545	29,497	30,449	31,401	32,353	33,305	34,257	34,209	36,161	37,113	952
6	31,819	32,880	33,941	35,002	36,063	37,124	38,185	39,246	40,307	41,368	1,061
7	35,359	36,538	37,717	38,896	40,075	41,254	42,433	43,612	44,791	45,970	1,179
8	39,159	40,464	41,769	43,074	44,379	45,684	46,989	48,294	49,599	50,904	1,305
9	43,251	44,693	46,135	47,577	49,019	50,461	51,903	53,345	54,787	56,229	1,442
10	47,630	49,218	50,806	52,394	53,982	55,570	57,158	58,746	60,334	61,922	1,588
11	52,329	54,073	55,817	57,561	59,305	61,049	62,793	64,537	66,281	68,025	1,744
12	62,722	64,813	66,904	68,995	71,086	73,177	75,268	77,359	79,450	81,541	2,091
13	74,584	77,070	79,556	82,042	84,528	87,014	89,500	91,986	94,472	96,958	2,486
14	88,136	91,074	94,012	96,950	99,888	102,826	105,764	108,702	111,640	114,578	2,938
15	103,672	107,128	110,584	114,040	117,496	120,952	124,408	127,864	131,320	134,776	3,456

Source: From Salary table 2015-gs Incorporating the 1% general schedule increase Effective january 2015, from https://www. opm.gov/policy-data-oversight/pay-leave/salaries-wages/salary-tables/pdf/2017/GS.pdf.

■ HR Tools for Line Managers and Small Businesses

Developing a Workable Pay Plan

Developing a pay plan is as important in a small firm as in a large one. Pay that is too high wastes money; too low triggers turnover; and internally inequitable causes endless badgering by employees demanding raises.

Market rates come first. Sites like LinkedIn and Salary.com will show localized average pay rates for jobs in your geographic area. The Sunday newspaper classified ads (on and offline) will yield useful information on wages offered for jobs similar to those you are trying to price. State Job Service "One Stop" offices can provide a wealth of information, as they compile extensive information on pay ranges and averages for many of the jobs listed on O*NET. Employment agencies, always anxious to establish ties with employers, will provide good data. Local college and university career centers will reveal prevailing pay rates for many jobs. Professional associations (such as the careers link for civil engineers at **www.asce.org**/) are good sources of professionals' pay rates.

Smaller firms are making use of the Internet in other ways. StockHouse Media Corp (**www.stockhouse.com**/) is an international provider of online financial content and community development products with employees around the world. It uses the Internet for determining salaries for all the firm's personnel. For example, the HR manager uses e-mail to request salary data from professional groups like the Society for Human Resource Management and surfs the Internet to monitor rates and trends by periodically checking job boards, company websites, and industry associations.[65]

If you employ more than 20 employees or so, conduct at least a basic job evaluation. You will need job descriptions; these will be the source of data regarding the nature and worth of each job. Checking websites like O*NET or JobDescription.com can be useful here.

You may find it easier to split your employees into clusters—say, managerial/professional, office/clerical, and plant personnel. For each of the three clusters, choose one or more compensable factors. Then rank each job in that cluster based on a ranking job evaluation (as explained earlier, in the Building Your Management Skills feature on page 312).

For each job, you may want to create a pay range. In general, you might choose as the midpoint of that range the average pay rate you set for each job. Then produce a range of about 30% around this average, broken into five steps. (Thus, orderlies might earn from $8.00 to $12.60 per hour, in five steps.)

Required compensation policies will include amount of holiday and vacation pay (as we explain in Chapter 11), overtime pay policy, method of pay (weekly, biweekly, monthly), garnishments, and time card or sign-in sheet procedures. For sources of sample policies, see, for example, our HR systems discussion on pages 497–499.

⭐ Talk About It–**4**

If your professor has chosen to assign this, go to **www.pearson.com/mylab/ management** to discuss the following questions. What type of job evaluation method would you use in a company like Patty's (see the chapter opener) with 15 employees? Why? What exactly would you suggest she do now?

LEARNING OBJECTIVE 3
Explain how to price managerial and professional jobs.

Pricing Managerial and Professional Jobs

Developing compensation plans for managers or professionals is similar in many respects to developing plans for any employee. The basic aim is the same: to attract, motivate, and retain good employees. And job evaluation is about as applicable to managerial and professional jobs (below the top executive levels) as to production and clerical ones.

There are differences, though. Managerial jobs tend to stress harder-to-quantify factors like judgment and problem solving more than do production and clerical jobs.

There is also more emphasis on paying managers and professionals based on their performance or on what they can do, rather than on static job demands like working conditions. And one must compete in the marketplace for executives who sometimes have the pay of rock stars. So, job evaluation, although still important, usually plays a secondary role to issues like bonuses, incentives, market rates, and benefits.

Compensating Executives and Managers

Compensation for a company's top executives usually consists of four main elements.[66] *Base pay* includes the person's fixed salary as well as, often, guaranteed bonuses such as "10% of pay at the end of the fourth fiscal quarter, regardless of whether or not the company makes a profit." The CEO of Oracle earned just over $96 million in one recent year, and the CEO of Walt Disney Corporation $37.1 million.[67] *Short-term incentives* are usually cash or stock bonuses for achieving short-term goals, such as year-to-year increases in sales revenue. *Long-term incentives* aim to encourage the executive to take actions that drive up the value of the company's stock and include things like stock options; these generally give the executive the right to purchase stock at a specific price for a specific period. Finally, *executive benefits and perks* include things such as supplemental executive retirement pension plans, supplemental life insurance, and health insurance without a deductible or coinsurance. With so many complicated elements, employers must also be alert to executive compensation tax and securities law implications.

What Determines Executive Pay?

For top executive jobs (especially the CEO), job evaluation typically has little relevance. The traditional wisdom is that company size and performance significantly affect top managers' salaries. Yet studies from the early 2000s showed that size and performance explained only about 30% of CEO pay: "In reality, CEO pay is set by the board taking into account a variety of factors such as the business strategy, corporate trends, and most importantly where they want to be in a short and long term."[68] Whatever it is that accounts for CEO pay, it's often not company performance. In one survey, the best-performing CEOs receive the lowest average compensation, while those in low-performing companies were paid relatively well.[69] In practice, CEOs may have considerable influence over the boards of directors who theoretically set their pay. So, their pay sometimes doesn't reflect strictly arm's-length negotiations.[70]

Shareholder activism and government oversight have tightened the restrictions on what companies pay top executives. For example, the banking giant HSBC shelved plans to raise its CEO's pay after shareholders rejected the proposals.[71]

Managerial Job Evaluation Many employers use job evaluation for pricing managerial jobs (at least, below the top jobs). The basic approach is to classify all executive and management positions into a series of grades, each with a salary range.

As with nonmanagerial jobs, one alternative is to rank the executive and management positions in relation to each other, grouping those of equal value. However, firms also use the job classification and point evaluation methods. They use compensable factors like position scope, complexity, and difficulty. Job analysis, salary surveys, and the fine-tuning of salary levels around wage curves also play roles.

Computer-aided job evaluation can streamline the job evaluation process. CEO pay is set by the board taking into account a variety of factors such as the business strategy, corporate trends, and most important, where they want to be in the short and long term.

Source: Edhar Yuralaits/123RF.

Compensating Professional Employees

In compensating professionals, employers should first ensure that each employee is actually a "professional" under the law. The Fair Labor Standards Act "provides an exemption from both minimum wage and overtime pay for employees employed as bona fide executive, administrative, professional and outside sales employees."[72] However, calling someone a professional doesn't make him or her so. In addition to earning at least $455 per week, the person's main duty must "be the performance of work requiring advanced knowledge," and "the advanced knowledge must be customarily acquired by a prolonged course of specialized intellectual instruction."[73] One company hired a high school graduate as an exempt "Product design specialist II," earning $62,000 per year. The job required 12 years of relevant experience, but no particular education. The court ruled the job was nonexempt.[74]

What to compensate is another problem. Jobs like engineer and scientist emphasize compensable factors such as creativity and problem solving, factors not easily measured or compared.[75] Furthermore, how do you measure performance? For example, the success of an engineer's invention depends on how well the firm markets it. Employers can use job evaluation for professionals. Compensable factors here may include problem solving, creativity, job scope, and technical knowledge and expertise.

Yet in practice, firms rarely rely on just job evaluation for pricing professional jobs. Factors like creativity are hard to measure, and other issues often influence professionals' job decisions. Competing for engineers in Silicon Valley illustrates the problem. Google recently raised its employees' salaries by 10% in the face of defections by even their highest-paid professionals, such as the head of its Chrome OS team.[76] Many of these Google professionals, although well paid by national standards, still felt underpaid. Some undoubtedly moved to jobs they hoped would have more challenges. Many also probably felt that the best way to hit it big in terms of pay was to join a younger, faster-growing firm with stock options.

Most employers therefore use a market-pricing approach. They price professional jobs in the marketplace as best they can, to establish the values for benchmark jobs. Then they slot these benchmark jobs and their other professional jobs into a salary structure. Each professional discipline usually ends up having four to six grade levels, each with a broad salary range. This helps employers remain competitive when bidding for professionals who literally have global employment possibilities.[77]

Improving Performance Through HRIS

Payroll Administration Administering the payroll system—keeping track of each employee's worker status, wage rate, dependents, benefits, overtime, tax status, and so on; computing each paycheck; and then directing the actual printing of checks or direct deposits—is a time-consuming task, one complicated by the need to comply with many federal, state, and local wage, hour, and other laws.

Many employers perform this function in-house, usually with a payroll processing software package. Intuit's *Basic Payroll* lets the employer, "[e]nter hours worked and get instant paycheck calculations, including earnings, payroll taxes, and deductions. Then print paychecks yourself. *Basic Payroll* calculates federal and state payroll taxes for you, so you can easily e-pay federal taxes and write a check for state taxes."[78] Kronos's *Workforce Payroll* automates the payroll process, and offers self-service features. For example, *Workforce Payroll* will "[l]et your employees see pay stubs and earning histories, make changes to direct deposit and W-4 forms, print W-2s, and even check out how changes to their deductions will affect their paychecks."[79]

On the other hand, many employers outsource payroll administration to vendors such as ADP. These vendors offer a range of payroll processing options. For instance, smaller employers may opt to email their payroll data to the vendor's specialists, while larger ones may have this data processed automatically online. Don't just consider the relative cost of outsourcing the function, but also the desirability of integrating the employer's internal systems with the vendor's, streamlining tax compliance and filings, and increasing employee self-service.[80]

competency-based pay
Where the company pays for the employee's range, depth, and types of skills and knowledge, rather than for the job title he or she holds.

Contemporary Topics in Compensation

How employers pay employees is evolving. In this section, we'll look at five important contemporary compensation topics, competency-based pay, broadbanding, talent management, comparable worth, and board oversight.

Competency-Based Pay

Some question whether job evaluations' aim to slot jobs into narrow cubbyholes ("Machinist I," "Machinist II," and so on) might not actually be counterproductive in high-performance work systems. Systems like these depend on flexible, multiskilled job assignments and on teamwork. There's thus no place here for employees to say "That's not my job." **Competency-based pay** (and broadbanding, explained later) aims to avoid that problem.[81] With competency- or skill-based pay, you pay the employee for the skills and knowledge he or she is capable of using rather than for the responsibilities or title of the job currently held.[82] Experts variously call this competence-, knowledge-, or skill-based pay. With competency-based pay, an employee in a class I job who could (but may not have to at the moment) do class II work gets paid as a class II worker, not a class I. *Competencies* are demonstrable personal characteristics such as knowledge, skills, and behaviors. Why pay employees based on the skill levels they achieve, rather than based on the jobs they're assigned to? With more companies organizing around teams, you want to encourage employees to get the skills required to rotate among jobs.

Competency- or skill-based pay programs generally contain five elements. The employer *defines* specific required skills and chooses a *method* for basing the person's pay on his or her skills. A *training* system lets employees acquire skills. There is a formal competency *testing* system. And, the work is *designed* so that employees can easily move among jobs of varying skill levels. In practice, competency-based pay usually comes down to pay for knowledge or skill-based pay.[83] As an example, review Chapter 4's Figure 4.10 (on p. 115). For this job, BP lists the minimum level for each skill (such as Technical Expertise and Problem Solving) someone holding this job must attain. As an employee achieves each level of each skill, he or she would assumedly receive a bump in pay. (For another example, see the accompanying HR in Practice feature.)

■ HR in Practice

JLG's Skill-Based Pay Program

JLG Industries supplies access equipment such as aerial work platforms and mast booms.[84] The firm instituted a skill-based pay program to reward employees for the number of basic skills they can perform rather than for the jobs to which they are assigned.[85] JLG integrated the skill pay program into its existing payroll system, and supported it with a computerized reporting system.

As an employee acquires and masters a new skill, JLG increases his or her pay on a scheduled basis. Pay increases are directly proportional to employee "value" based on skill acquisition. Pay adjustment increments are $0.30 per hour and can be in addition to regularly scheduled merit increases. Qualified employees are eligible to receive a skill-based wage adjustment at three times. The first increase is available at the completion of an initial six-month probationary employment period. An additional skill-based adjustment may come in conjunction with the employee's annual merit review. Other skill-based adjustments are allowed yearly and six months after the annual merit review.

JLG assigns all hourly production and maintenance workers to a particular Job Family. A Job Family consists of a group of employees performing similar activities and requiring similar skills. *Each Job Family has a set of required skills*, including certain job-related skills as well as skills related to quality and safety.

To determine if an employee is qualified for a skill-based pay raise, a comparison is made between the employee's current wage rate and the target rate within the Job Family to which the employee is assigned. Target pay rates are based on the degree of mastery of the complete skill set required for a Job Family. If the current wage rate is equal to or greater than the target rate, no pay adjustment is made. If the current rate is below the target rate, a skill-based adjustment is authorized for employees who mastered the Job Family's skills.

✪ Talk About It – 5

If your professor has chosen to assign this, go to **www.pearson.com/mylab/ management** to discuss the following: Review our discussion of competencies in Chapter 4; then write three competency statements for one job you believe they would have at a company such as JLG. A useful competency statement includes three elements: the *name and a brief description* of the competency, a *description of the observable behaviors* that represent proficiency in the competency, and *proficiency levels*.

Broadbanding

Most firms end up with pay plans that slot jobs into classes or grades, each with its own vertical pay rate range. For example, the U.S. government's pay plan consists of 18 main grades (GS-1 to GS-18), each with its own pay range. For an employee whose job falls in one of these grades, the pay range for that grade dictates his or her minimum and maximum salary.

The question is, "How wide should the salary grades be, in terms of the number of job evaluation points they include?" (For example, might the U.S. government want to collapse its 18 salary grades into six or seven broader bands?) There is a downside to having (say, 18) narrow grades. For instance, if you want someone whose job is in grade 2 to fill in for a time in a job that happens to be in grade 1, it's difficult to reassign that person without lowering his or her salary. Similarly, if you want the person to learn about a job that happens to be in grade 3, the employee might object to the reassignment without a corresponding raise to grade 3 pay. Traditional grade pay plans thus may foster inflexibility.

broadbanding
Consolidating salary grades and ranges into just a few wide levels or "bands," each of which contains a relatively wide range of jobs and salary levels.

That is why some firms are broadbanding their pay plans.[86] **Broadbanding** means collapsing salary grades into just a few wide levels or bands, each of which contains a relatively wide range of jobs and pay levels. Figure 10.7 illustrates this. Here we consolidated the company's previous six pay grades into two broad grades or "broadbands."

A company may create broadbands for all its jobs, or for specific groups such as professionals. The pay rate range of each broadband is relatively large because it ranges from the minimum pay of the lowest grade the firm merged into the broadband up to the maximum pay of the highest merged grade. Thus, for example, instead of having 10 salary grades, each of which contains a salary range of $15,000, the firm might collapse the 10 grades into three broadbands, each with a set of jobs such that the difference between the lowest- and highest-paid jobs might be $40,000 or more. There is thus a much wider range of pay rates. You can move an employee from job to job within the broadband more easily, without worrying

Figure 10.7

Broadbanded Structure and
How It Relates to Traditional
Pay Grades and Ranges

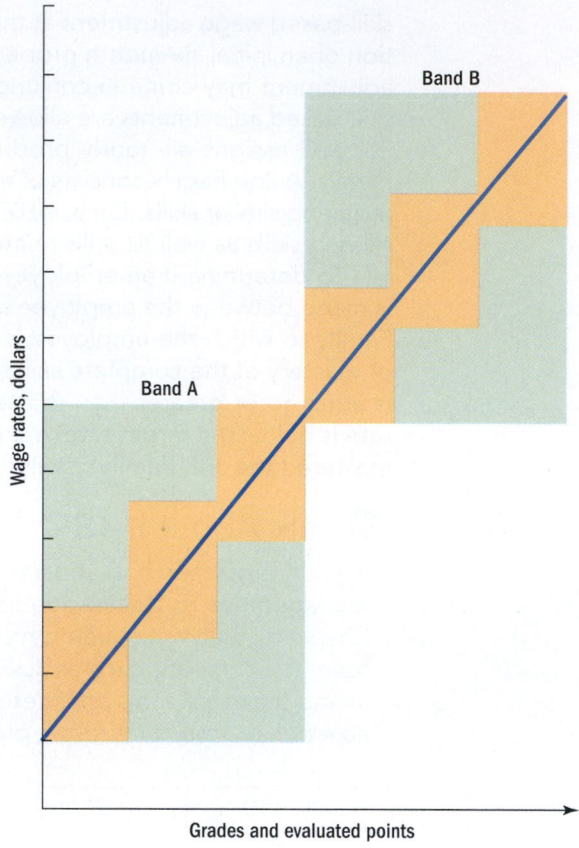

about the employee's moving outside the relatively narrow rate range associated
with a traditional narrow pay grade.

Pros and Cons   The basic advantage is that broadbanding injects greater flexibility
into employee assignments.[87] For example, "the employee who needs to spend
time in a lower-level job to develop a certain skill set can receive higher-than-usual
pay for the work, a circumstance considered impossible under traditional pay
systems."[88]

On the other hand, broadbanding can be unsettling. Some people prefer the
security of knowing exactly what their jobs and job titles are, and for them, moving
often from job to job can be unsettling.[89]

Comparable Worth

comparable worth

The concept by which women who
are usually paid less than men
can claim that men in comparable
rather than in strictly equal jobs are
paid more.

Comparable worth refers to the requirement to pay men and women equal wages
for jobs that are of *comparable* (rather than strictly *equal*) value to the employer.
Thus, comparable worth may mean comparing quite dissimilar jobs, such as nurses
to truck mechanics or secretaries to technicians. The question "comparable worth"
seeks to address is this: Should you pay women who are performing jobs *equal* to
men's or just *comparable* to men's the same as men? If it's only for equal jobs, then
the tendency may be to limit women's pay to that of the other, lower-paid jobs in
which women tend to predominate.

County of Washington v. *Gunther* (1981) was a pivotal case for comparable
worth. It involved Washington County, Oregon prison matrons who claimed sex
discrimination. The county had evaluated roughly comparable but nonequal men's
jobs as having 5% more "job content" (based on a point evaluation system) than
the women's jobs, but paid the men 35% more.[90] Why should there be such a pay

discrepancy for roughly comparable jobs? Washington County finally agreed to pay 35,000 employees in female-dominated jobs almost $500 million in pay raises over seven years to settle the suit.

Comparable worth has implications for job evaluation. Virtually every comparable worth case that reached a court involved the point method of job evaluation. By assigning points to dissimilar jobs, point plans facilitate comparability ratings among different jobs. Should employers still use point-type plans? Perhaps the wisest approach is for employers to price their jobs as they see fit (with or without point plans). However, ensure that women have equal access to all jobs. In other words, eliminate sex-segregated jobs.

Diversity Counts

The Pay Gap All this notwithstanding, women in the United States earn only about 81% as much as men.[91] In general, education may reduce the wage gap somewhat.[92] This "pay gap," bad as it is, is still a small improvement: women earned only about 62% of what men earned in 1979, for instance.[93]

The problem is that big gaps remain. For example, new female medical doctors earn about $17,000 per year less than their male counterparts do.[94] Even the progress that women have made in pay can be a little misleading. Thus women disproportionately are in lower-paying occupations and fields.[95]

Reasons put forward for such male–female gaps range from the outdated notion that employers view women as having less leverage, to the fact that professional men change jobs more often (gaining more raises in the process) and that women tend to end up in departments that pay less.[96] In any case, "the gap" is a problem employers should recognize and address, and some states are already doing so.[97]

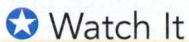 Watch It

How do companies actually adjust salaries and raises? If your professor has chosen to assign this, go to **www.pearson.com/mylab/management** to watch the video Focus Pointe Compensation and then answer the questions to show what you'd do in this situation.

Board Oversight of Executive Pay

There are various reasons for boards clamping down on executive pay.[98] For one thing, the Sarbanes-Oxley Act makes executives personally liable, under certain conditions, for corporate financial oversight lapses. The Dodd-Frank Law of 2010 requires that American companies give shareholders a "say on pay." Law firms are filing class-action suits demanding information from companies about their senior executive pay decisions.[99] In any event, lawyers specializing in executive pay suggest that boards of directors (board compensation committees usually make executive pay decisions in large firms)[100] ask themselves these questions:

- Has our compensation committee thoroughly identified its duties and processes?
- Is our compensation committee using the appropriate compensation advisors?
- Are there particular executive compensation issues that our committee should address?[101]
- Do our procedures demonstrate diligence and independence? (This demands careful deliberations and records.)
- Is our committee appropriately communicating its decisions? How will shareholders react?[102]

LEARNING OBJECTIVE 5
Explain the importance of total rewards for improving employee engagement.

Employee Engagement Guide For Managers

Total Rewards Programs

Total rewards is an increasingly important concept in compensation management. People bring to their jobs many needs—for challenging work and for respect and appreciation, for instance—not all of which are satisfied by pay or bonuses. "'Total rewards' encompasses not only compensation and benefits but also personal and professional growth opportunities and a motivating work environment."[103] It includes not just traditional financial rewards (wages and incentives plus benefits and perks) but also nonfinancial and intangible rewards such as recognition, the nature of the job/quality of work, career development opportunities,[104] good relationships with managers and colleagues, organizational justice, trust in employees, feeling of being valued and involved, opportunities for promotion,[105] and a great work climate.[106] Total rewards also include recognition programs and redesigned jobs (discussed in Chapter 4), telecommuting programs, health and well-being programs, and training and career development.

Noncash recognition/appreciation rewards such as gift cards, merchandise, and recognition are part of such compensation.[107] For example, a West Virginia DuPont plant installed an online system that enabled employees to award each other recognition; 95% were soon using it.[108] International Fitness Holdings lets employees use a Facebook-type application to recognize peers by posting messages and sending private e-mails.[109] Employers contract with sites like Globoforce.com to provide online recognition systems.

Total Rewards and Employee Engagement

When it comes to employee engagement, both material and nonmaterial rewards—total rewards—seem essential.[110] For example, one study found that base pay and benefits alone had a weak relationship with the organization's ability to foster employee engagement.[111] However, intangible rewards such as the nature of the job/quality of work and career development opportunities had a high or very high impact on engagement and performance, when combined with base salary and short-term incentives or bonuses.[112]

Many high-engagement employers do make total rewards part of their human resource strategies. For example, Toyota lays out its human resource values in what it calls "The Toyota Way." These values include "mutual trust and respect between labor and management," "stable employment that avoids layoffs and terminations to the maximum extent," "helping employees to develop their technical skills," and "support for production staff combining work with childcare, career design support, and raising of corporate awareness." Disney emphasizes providing its employees/cast members with a total rewards package that includes pay plus various benefits and career development opportunities.[113]

Many of the "Best Companies to Work For" pay well but also emphasize intangible rewards. These intangible rewards include, for example, "the vice chair at NetApp calling 10 to 20 employees a day who had gotten caught 'doing something right,'" "Whole Foods [taking] transparency to a whole new level, giving employees votes on new hires, field trips to visit suppliers and visibility into everyone's salaries,"[114] and stimulating work and empowering management at the software company SAS.[115]

Finally, periodically list all rewards—financial and nonfinancial—the company offers, and note their importance to the employees' overall well-being.[116]

Review

MyLab Management

If your instructor is using MyLab Management, go to **www.pearson.com/mylab/ management** to complete the problems marked with this icon ⭐.

Summary

1. In establishing strategic pay plans, managers first need to understand some basic factors in determining pay rates. Employee compensation includes both direct financial payments and indirect financial statements. The factors determining the design of any pay plan include legal, union, company strategy/policy, and equity. Legal considerations include, most important, the Fair Labor Standards Act, which governs matters such as minimum wages and overtime pay. Specific categories of employees are exempt from the act or certain provisions of the act, particularly its overtime provisions. The Equal Pay Act of 1963 and the Employee Retirement Income Security Act are other important laws.

2. The process of establishing pay rates while ensuring external, internal, and procedural equity consists of several activities: conducting a salary survey, determining the worth of each job, doing a job evaluation, grouping jobs comprised of approximately equal difficulty and pricing each pay grade with wage curves, and fine-tuning pay rates.
   - Job evaluation is a systematic comparison done to determine the worth of one job relative to another based on compensable factors.
   - Popular job evaluation methods include ranking, job classification, the point method, and factor comparison. With ranking, for instance, you conduct a job analysis, group jobs by department, and have raters rank jobs.

3. Pricing managerial and professional jobs involves some special issues. Managerial pay typically consists of base pay, short-term incentives, long-term incentives, and executive benefits and, particularly at the top levels, doesn't lend itself to job evaluation but rather to understanding the job's complexity, the employer's ability to pay, and the need to be competitive in attracting top talent.

4. We addressed several important special topics in compensation. Broadbanding means consolidating several rates and ranges into a few wide levels or "bands," each of which contains a relatively wide range of jobs in salary levels. Comparable worth refers to the requirement to pay men and women equal pay for jobs that are comparable rather than strictly equal value to the employee. Board oversight of executive pay has become an important issue, and boards of directors should use qualified advisers and exercise diligence and independence in formulating executive pay plans.

5. Research shows that if employee engagement is the aim, it makes sense to emphasize total rewards, not just base pay. Total rewards encompass traditional compensation components, but also things such as recognition and redesigned, more challenging jobs. For example, one study found that intangible rewards such as organization climate, the nature of the job/quality of work, and career development opportunities had a high or very high impact on engagement and performance, when combined with base salary and short-term incentives or bonuses.

Key Terms

employee compensation   299
direct financial payments   299
indirect financial payments   299
Davis-Bacon Act (1931)   301

Walsh-Healey Public Contract Act (1936)   301
Title VII of the 1964 Civil Rights Act   301
Fair Labor Standards Act (FLSA; 1938)   301
Equal Pay Act (1963)   305

⭐ Try It

How would you use pay or other components of a total rewards program to solve a "motivation problem" in a company? If your professor has chosen to assign this, go to **www.pearson.com/mylab/management** and complete the motivation simulation to find out.

Discussion Questions

10-1. What is the difference between exempt and nonexempt jobs?

10-2. What is the relationship between compensable factors and job specifications?

10-3. Compare and contrast the following methods of job evaluation: ranking, classification, factor comparison, and point method.

⭐10-4. What are the pros and cons of broadbanding, and would you recommend your current employer (or some other firm you're familiar with) use it? Why or why not?

⭐10-5. After Walmart raised its minimum starting pay to $10 an hour, some longer-term employees (like one earning $12 per hour) complained that the strictly entry-level increase was unfair to them. And when the head of a company called Gravity Payments decided to pay all his employees at least $70,000 a year, some longer tenure employees complained that it was unfair to raise new peoples' salaries and not theirs.[117] How should Walmart and Gravity address these complaints?

10-6. Define and give an example of how to conduct a job evaluation.

10-7. Explain in detail how to establish a market-competitive pay plan.

10-8. Explain how to price managerial and professional jobs.

Individual and Group Activities

10-9. Working individually or in groups, conduct salary surveys for the following positions: entry-level accountant and entry-level chemical engineer. What sources did you use, and what conclusions did you reach? If you were the HR manager for a local engineering firm, what would you recommend that you pay for each job?

10-10. Working individually or in groups, develop compensation policies for the teller position at a local bank. Assume that there are four tellers: two were hired in May and the other two were hired in December. The compensation policies should address the following: appraisals, raises, holidays, vacation pay, overtime pay, method of pay, garnishments, and time cards.

10-11. Working individually or in groups, access relevant websites to determine what equitable pay ranges are for these jobs: chemical engineer, marketing manager, and HR manager, all with a bachelor's degree and 5 years' experience. Do so for the following cities: New York, New York; San Francisco, California; Houston, Texas; Denver, Colorado; Miami, Florida; Atlanta, Georgia; Chicago, Illinois; Birmingham, Alabama; Detroit, Michigan; and Washington, DC. For each position in each city, what are the pay ranges and the average pay? Does geographic location impact the salaries of the different positions? If so, how?

10-12. Some of America's executives have come under fire because their pay seemed to some to be excessive, given their firms' performances. However, big institutional investors are no longer sitting back and not complaining. For example, pension manager TIAA-CREF is talking to 50 companies about executive pay. Do you think they are right to make a fuss? Why?

10-13. How do you think politicians in the United States should address the problem of income inequality?

10-14. For this activity, you will need the documents titled (1) "HRCI PHR® and SPHR® Certification Body of Knowledge," and (2) "About the Society for Human Resource Management (SHRM) Body of Competency & Knowledge® Model and

Certification Exams." Your instructor can obtain these two documents from the Pearson Instructor Resource Center and pass them on to you. These two documents list the knowledge someone studying for the HRCI or SHRM certification exam needs to have in each area of human resource management (such as in Strategic Management, and Workforce Planning). In groups of several students, do four things: (1) review the HRCI and/or SHRM documents; (2) identify the material in this chapter that relates to HRCI's or SHRM's required knowledge lists; (3) write four multiple-choice exam questions on this material that you believe would be suitable for inclusion in the HRCI exam and/or the SHRM exam; and, (4) if time permits, have someone from your team post your team's questions in front of the class, so that students in all teams can answer the exam questions created by the other teams.

MyLab Management

If your instructor is using MyLab Management, go to **www.pearson.com/mylab/management** for Auto-graded writing questions as well as the following Assisted-graded writing questions:

10-15. Should the job evaluation depend on an appraisal of the jobholder's performance? Why? Why not?

10-16. Do small companies need to develop a pay plan? Why or why not?

APPLICATION EXERCISES

HR IN ACTION CASE INCIDENT 1

Salary Inequities at AstraZeneca

More than 50 years after passage of the Equal Pay Act, women in America still earn about 81 cents for every dollar earned by a man. That adds up to a loss for the average female worker of about $380,000 over a lifetime.

A few years ago, the U.S. Department of Labor's Office of Federal Contract Compliance Programs (OFCCP) entered into an agreement with AstraZeneca, a large international pharmaceuticals firm, for the company to pay some of its female sales associates a total of $250,000.[118] AstraZeneca had a contract valued at over $2 billion with the U.S. Department of Veterans Affairs to provide drugs to hospitals around the country. That made it subject to Executive Order 11246, which aims to ensure that employees of U.S. contractors and subcontractors with federal contracts pay their employees fairly without regard to sex, race, color, religion, and national origin.

After conducting a compliance review, the OFCCP concluded that AstraZeneca violated Executive Order 11246 by failing to ensure certain women employees were paid fairly. According to the OFCCP lawsuit, AstraZeneca's Philadelphia Business Center had routinely paid some of its female "primary care" and "specialty care" level III pharmaceutical sales specialists an average of $1,700 less than men with the same positions. Because of the company's pay secrecy policies, many of the women didn't know they were being paid less. In addition to the financial settlement, AstraZeneca and OFCCP will review records of the firm's female employees in 14 states. If they find additional statistical evidence of wage discrimination, the company must remedy it.

Questions

AstraZeneca has brought you in as a compensation consultant. Here are the questions they would like you to answer for them:

10-17. Although the case with OFCCP is closed, we wonder if there are any less-discriminatory explanations possible for why our women sales reps on average earned less than men. If so, what are they?

10-18. Our company now uses a point method to evaluate jobs for pay purposes, and each resulting job class also has a rate range associated with it. Sales associates are now paid a salary, not based on incentive pay. List three specific things we can do to ensure that a similar problem (inequitable pay based on gender) does not arise again, assuming they continue using the point plan.

10-19. What sort of compensation plan would you recommend for us, and why?

HR IN ACTION CASE INCIDENT 2

Carter Cleaning Company

The New Pay Plan

Carter Cleaning Centers does not have a formal wage structure nor does it have rate ranges or use compensable factors. Wage rates are based mostly on those prevailing in the surrounding community and are tempered with an attempt on the part of Jack Carter to maintain some semblance of equity between what workers with different responsibilities in the stores are paid.

Carter does not make any formal surveys when determining what his company should pay. He peruses the want ads almost every day and conducts informal surveys among his friends in the local chapter of the laundry and cleaners trade association. While Jack has taken a "seat-of-the-pants" approach to paying employees, his salary schedule has been guided by several basic pay policies. Although many of his colleagues adhere to a policy of paying minimum rates, Jack has always followed a policy of paying his employees about 10% above what he feels are the prevailing rates, a policy that he believes reduces turnover while fostering employee loyalty. Of somewhat more concern to Jennifer is her father's informal policy of paying men about 20% more than women for the same job. Her father's explanation is, "They're stronger and can work harder for longer hours, and besides, they all have families to support."

Questions

10-20. Is the company at the point where it should be setting up a formal salary structure based on a complete job evaluation? Why?

10-21. Is Jack Carter's policy of paying 10% more than the prevailing rates a sound one, and how could that be determined?

10-22. Similarly, is Carter's male–female differential wise? If not, why not?

10-23. Specifically, what would you suggest Jennifer do now with respect to her company's pay plan?

Experiential Exercise

Ranking the College's Administrators

Purpose: The purpose of this exercise is to give you experience in performing a job evaluation using the ranking method.

Required Understanding: You should be thoroughly familiar with the ranking method of job evaluation and obtain job descriptions for your college's dean, department chairperson, director of admissions, library director, registrar, and your professor.

How to Set Up the Exercise/Instructions: Divide the class into groups of four or five students. The groups will perform a job evaluation of the positions of dean, department chairperson, and professor using the ranking method.

10-24. Perform a job evaluation by ranking the jobs. You may use one or more compensable factors.

10-25. If time permits, a spokesperson from each group can put his or her group's rankings on the board. Did the groups end up with about the same results? How did they differ? Why do you think they differed?

Chapter 10 Appendix: How to Create a Market-Competitive Pay Plan Using the Point Plan Job Evaluation Method

As we said, many firms simply price their jobs based on what other employers are paying—they use a market-based approach. However, most employers also base their pay plans on job evaluations. In a *market-competitive pay plan*, a job's compensation reflects the job's value in the company, as well as what other employers are paying for similar jobs in the marketplace. Because the point method (or "point-factor method") is so popular, we'll use it as the centerpiece of our step-by-step example for creating a market-competitive pay plan.[119] The 16 steps in creating a market-competitive pay plan begin with choosing benchmark jobs.

1. Choose Benchmark Jobs

Particularly when an employer has dozens or hundreds of different jobs, it's impractical and unnecessary to evaluate each of them separately. Therefore, the first step in the point method is to select benchmark jobs. Benchmark jobs are representative of the entire range of jobs the employer needs to evaluate. Like "accounting clerk," they should be common among employers (thus making it easier to survey what competitors are paying for similar jobs).[120]

2. Select Compensable Factors

The choice of compensable factors depends on tradition (as noted, the Equal Pay Act of 1963 uses four compensable factors: skill, effort, responsibility, and working conditions) and on strategic and practical considerations. For example, if your firm's competitive advantage is quality, you might substitute "responsibility for quality" for working conditions, or simply add it as a fifth factor.[121] Similarly, using "working conditions" makes little practical sense for evaluating executive jobs.

The employer should carefully define each factor. This is to ensure that the evaluation committee members will each apply the factors with consistency. Figure 10A.1 shows (on top) one such definition, in this case, for the factor job complexity. The human resource specialist often draws up the definitions.

3. Assign Weights to Compensable Factors

Having selected compensable factors, the next step is to determine the relative importance (or weighting) of each factor (for instance, how much more important is "skill" than "effort"?). This is important because for each cluster of jobs, some factors are bound to be more important than others. Thus, for executive jobs the "mental requirements" factor would carry far more weight than would "physical requirements." To assign weights, we assume we have a total 100 percentage points to allocate for each job. Then (as an illustration) assign percentage weights of 60% for the factor job complexity, 30% for effort, and 10% for working conditions.[122]

4. Convert Percentages to Points for Each Factor

Next, we want to convert the percentage weights assigned to each compensable factor into point values for each factor (this is, after all, the point method). It is traditional to assume we are working with a total number of 1,000 points (although one could use some other figure). To convert percentages to points for each compensable factor, *multiply the percentage weight for each compensable factor (from the previous step) by 1,000.*[123] This will tell you the *maximum number of points* for each compensable factor. Doing so in this case would translate into 1,000 × 0.60 or 600 possible points for job complexity, 1,000 × 0.30 or 300 points for effort, and 1,000 × 0.10 or 100 points for working conditions.

Figure 10A.1

Illustrative Point Values and Degree Definitions for the Factor Job Complexity

Source: Copyright Gary Dessler, PhD.

Factor Definition: What Is Job Complexity? Job complexity generally refers to the amount of judgment, initiative, ingenuity, and complex data analysis that doing the job requires. To what extent does the person doing this job confront unfamiliar problems, deal with complex decisions, and have to exercise discretion?

Degree	Points	Job Complexity Degree Definitions: What to Look for in the Job
First	120	Here the job is routine and consists of repetitive operations requiring little or no choice of action and the automatic application of easily understood rules and procedures. For example, a filing clerk.
Second	240	Here the employee follows detailed instructions but may have to make limited decisions based on previously prescribed instructions which lay out prescribed alternatives. For example, a billing clerk or a receptionist.
Third	360	Here the employee again follows detailed instructions but because the number of matters to consider is more varied, the employee needs to exhibit initiative and independent judgment, under direct supervision. For example, a nurse's aide.
Fourth	480	Here the employee can generally follow standard practices but the presence of nonroutine problems requires that the employee be able to use initiative and judgment to analyze and evaluate situations, possibly modifying the standard procedures to adjust to the new situations. For example, a nurse.
Fifth	600	On this job, the employee needs to use independent judgment and plan and perform complex work under only general supervision, often working independently toward achieving overall results. For example, medical intern.

5. Define Each Factor's Degrees

Next, split each factor into degrees and define (write degree definitions for) each degree so that raters may judge the amount or degree of a factor existing in a job. Thus, for a factor such as "job complexity," you might choose to have five degrees, ranging from "here the job is routine" to "uses independent judgment." (Our definitions for each degree are shown in Figure 10A.1 under "Job Complexity Degree Definitions: What to Look for in the Job.") The number of degrees usually does not exceed five or six, and the actual number depends mostly on judgment. Thus, if all employees work either in a quiet, air-conditioned office or in a noisy, hot factory, then two degrees would probably suffice for the factor "working conditions." You need not have the same number of degrees for each factor, and you should limit degrees to the number necessary to distinguish among jobs.

6. Determine for Each Factor its Factor Degrees' Points

The evaluation committee must be able to determine the number of points each job is worth. To do this, the committee must be able to examine each job and (from each factor's degree definitions) determine what degree of each compensable factor that job has. For them to do this, we must first assign points to *each degree of each compensable factor*. For example, in our illustration, we have five possible degrees of job complexity, and the job complexity compensable factor is worth up to 600 points maximum. In our case, we simply decide that the first degree level of job complexity is worth 120 (or one-fifth of 600) points, the second degree level is worth 240 points, the third degree level is worth 360 points, the fourth degree level is worth 480 points, and the fifth degree is worth the maximum 600 points (see Figure 10A.1).[124] Do this for each factor (as in Table 10A.1).

Table 10A.1 Points Assigned to Factors and to Their Degrees (Revised)

Factors	First-Degree Points	Second-Degree Points	Third-Degree Points	Fourth-Degree Points	Fifth-Degree Points
Job complexity (Total maximum points equal 600)	120	240	360	480	600
Effort (Total maximum points equal 300)	60	120	180	240	300
Working conditions (Total maximum points equal 100 points)	20	40	60	80	100

7. Review Job Descriptions and Job Specifications

The heart of job evaluation involves determining the amount or degree to which the job contains the selected compensable factors such as effort, job complexity, and working conditions. The team conducting the job evaluation will frequently do so by first reviewing each job's job description and job specification. As we explained in Chapter 4 (Job Analysis), it is through the job analysis that the manager identifies the job's duties and responsibilities and writes the job description and job specification. Ideally, the job analysis should therefore have included information about the compensable factors (such as job complexity) around which the employer plans to build its compensation plan.[125]

8. Evaluate the Jobs

Steps 1–7 provide us with the information (for instance, points and degrees) on which we can evaluate the jobs. The committee now gathers the job descriptions and job specifications for the benchmark jobs they will focus on.

Then, from their review of each job description and job specification, the committee *determines the degree to which each compensable factor is present in each job*. Thus for, say, a job of master mechanic, the team might conclude (after studying the job description and job specification) that the master mechanic's job deserves the third degree level of *job complexity* points, the first degree level of *effort*, and the first degree level of *working conditions*.

Knowing the job complexity, effort, and working conditions degrees for each job, *and knowing the number of points we previously assigned to each degree* of each compensable factor, we can now determine how many job complexity, effort, and working conditions points each benchmark job

should contain. (We know the degree level for each factor for each job, so we merely check the corresponding points [see Table 10A-1] that we previously assigned to each of these degrees.)

Finally, we add up these degree points for each job to determine each job's total number of points.[126] The master mechanic job gets $360 + 60 + 20 = 440$ points from Table 10A-1. This enables us to list a hierarchy of jobs based on each job's points. We can soon turn to assigning wage rates to each job (step 9). But first, we should define market-competitive pay plan and wage curve.

What Is A Market-Competitive Pay Plan? What should the pay rate be for each job? Of course, jobs with more points should command higher pay. The question is what pay rate to use? Our company's current "internal" pay rates? Or pay rates based on what the "external" market is paying?[127]

With a **market-competitive pay plan**, the employer's actual pay rates are competitive with those in the relevant labor market, as well as equitable internally.[128] Put simply, the basic approach is to compare what the employer is *currently* paying for each job ("internal pay") with what the market is paying for the same or similar job ("external pay"), and then to combine this information to produce a market-competitive pay plan.

Use Wage Curves We saw earlier that the wage curve typically shows the pay rates paid for jobs, relative to the points or rankings assigned to each job by the job evaluation. Figure 10A.2 presents an example. Note again that it shows pay rates for jobs on the vertical axis and point values for these jobs along the horizontal axis. The purpose of the wage curve is to show the relationships between (1) the value of the job (expressed in points) as determined by one of the job evaluation methods and (2) the pay rates for the job. (We'll see that many employers may combine jobs into classes or grades. Here the wage curve would show the relationship between average pay rates for each grade and each grade's average point value.) The pay rates on the wage curve

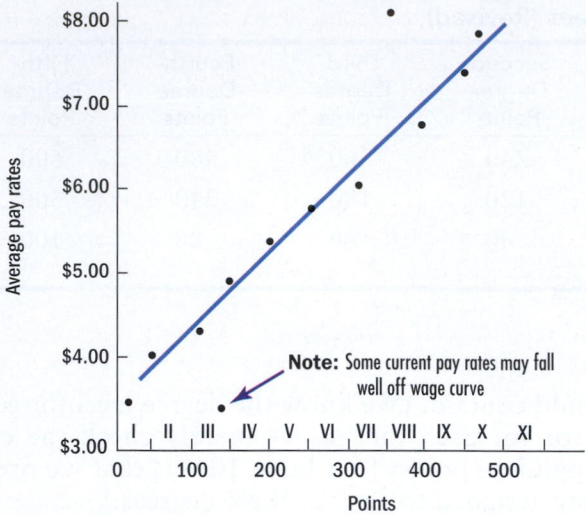

Figure 10A.2

Plotting a Wage Curve

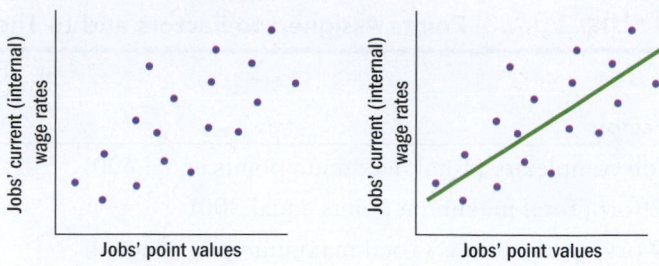

Figure 10A.3

The Current/Internal Wage Curve

are traditionally those now paid by the employer. However, if there is reason to believe the current pay rates are out of step with the market rates for these jobs, the employer will have to adjust them. One way to do this is to compare a wage curve that shows the jobs' *current* wage rates relative to the jobs' points, with a second curve that shows *market* wage rates relative to points. We do this as follows.

9. Draw the Current (Internal) Wage Curve

First, to study how each job's points relates to its current pay rate, we start by drawing an *internal wage curve*. Plotting each job's points and the wage rate the employer is now paying for each job (or wage rates, if there are several for each job) produces a scatter plot as in Figure 10A.3 (left). We now draw a wage curve (on the right) through these plots that shows how point values relate to current wage rates. We can draw this wage line by just estimating a line that best fits the plotted points (by minimizing the distances between the plots and the curve). Or we can use regression, a statistical technique. Using the latter will produce a current/internal wage curve that best fits the plotted points. In any case, we show the results in Figure 10A.3 (right).[129]

10. Conduct a Market Analysis: Salary Surveys

Next, we must compile the information needed to draw an *external wage curve* for our jobs, based on what other employers are paying for similar jobs. We saw earlier in this chapter how to conduct salary surveys—surveys of what others are paying.[130]

11. Draw the Market (External) Wage Curve

The current/internal wage curve from step 9 is helpful. For example, showing, as it does, how a job's current pay rate compares with its points helps the employer identify jobs for which pay rates are currently too high or too low, relative to others in the company. (For example, if a job's current wage rate is well above the internal wage curve, it suggests that the present wage rate for that job is inequitably high, given the number of points we've assigned to that job.)

What the current (internal) wage curve does *not* reveal is whether our pay rates are too high, too low, or just right, relative to what other firms are paying. For this, we need to draw a *market* or *external wage* curve.

To draw the market/external wage curve, we produce a scatter plot and wage curve as in Figure 10A.4 (left and right). However, instead of using our firm's current wage rates, we use market wage rates (obtained from salary surveys). The market/external wage curve compares our jobs' points with market pay rates for our jobs.

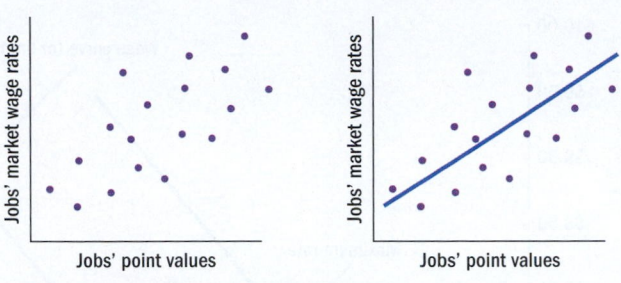

Figure 10A.4

The Market/External Wage Curve

decision by management. Strategic considerations influence this decision. Do our strategic aspirations suggest we should pay more, the same, or less than competitors? For example, we might decide to move our current internal wage curve up (and thereby give everyone a raise) or down (and thereby perhaps withhold pay increases for some time), or adjust the slope of the internal wage curve to increase what we pay for some jobs and decrease what we pay for others. In any case, the wage curve we end up with (the orange line in Figure 10A.6) should now be equitable internally (in terms of the point value of each job) and equitable externally (in terms of what other firms are paying).[132]

12. Compare and Adjust Current and Market Wage Rates for Jobs

How different are the market rates others are paying for our jobs and the current rates we are now paying for our jobs? To determine this, we can draw both the current/internal and market/external wage curves on one graph, as in Figure 10A.5. The market wage curve might be higher than our current wage curve (suggesting that our current pay rates may be too low) or below our current wage curve (suggesting that our current wage rates might be too high). Or perhaps market wage rates are higher for some of our jobs and lower for others.[131]

Based on comparing the current/internal wage curve and market/external wage curve in Figure 10A.5, we must decide whether to adjust the current pay rates for our jobs, and if so, how. This calls for a policy

13. Develop Pay Grades

We saw that employers typically group similar jobs (in terms of points) into grades for pay purposes. Then, instead of having to deal with hundreds of job rates, you might only have to focus on, say, pay rates for 10 or 12 pay grades. It is standard to establish grades of equal point spread. (In other words, each grade might include all those jobs falling between 50 and 100 points, 100 and 150 points, 150 and 200 points, etc.) Because each grade is the same width, the main issue involves determining how many grades to have. There doesn't seem to be any optimal number, although 10 to 16 grades for a given job cluster (shop jobs, clerical jobs, etc.) seems to be common. You need more pay grades if there are, say, 1,000 jobs to be graded than if there are only 100.

14. Establish Rate Ranges

Most employers do not pay just one rate for all jobs in a particular pay grade. For example, GE Medical won't want to pay all its accounting clerks, from beginners to long tenure, at the same rate, even though they may all be in the same pay grade. Instead, employers develop vertical pay (or "rate") ranges for each of the horizontal pay grades (or pay classes). These **pay (or rate) ranges** often appear as vertical boxes within each grade, showing minimum, maximum, and midpoint pay rates for that grade, as in Figure 10A.6. (Specialists call this graph a *wage structure*. Figure 10A.6 graphically depicts the range of pay rates—in this case, per hour—paid for each pay grade.)

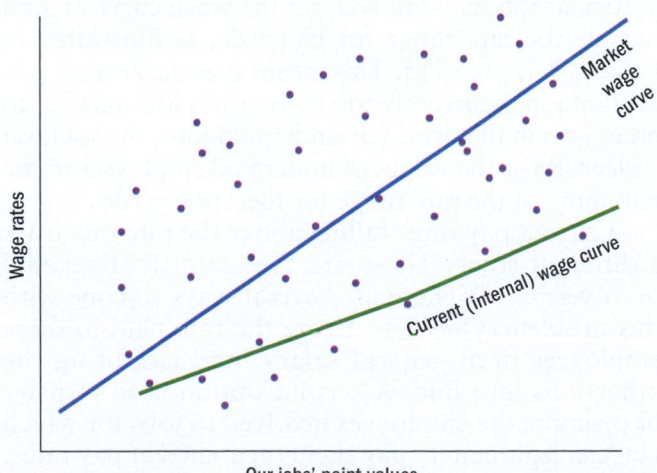

Figure 10A.5

Plotting Both the Market and Internal Wage Curves

Developing Rate Ranges

As in Figure 10A.6, the wage curve usually anchors the average pay rate for each vertical pay range. The firm might then arbitrarily decide on a maximum and minimum rate for each grade, such as 15% above and below the wage curve. As an alternative, some employers allow the pay range for each grade to become taller (they include more pay rates) for the higher pay ranges, reflecting the greater demands and performance variability inherent in more complex jobs. As in Figure 10A.6, most employers structure their rate ranges to overlap a bit, so an employee in one grade who has more experience or seniority may earn more than would someone in an entry-level position in the next higher pay grade.[133]

There are several reasons to use pay ranges for each pay grade. First, it lets the employer take a more flexible stance in the labor market. For example, it makes it easier to attract experienced, higher-paid employees into a pay grade at the top of the range because the starting salary for the pay grade's lowest step may be too low to attract them. Pay ranges also let companies provide for performance differences between employees within the same grade or between those with different seniorities.

Compensation experts sometimes use *compa ratios*. The **compa ratio** equals an employee's pay rate divided by the pay range midpoint for his or her pay grade. A compa ratio of 1 means the employee is being paid exactly at the pay range midpoint. If the compa ratio is above 1, then the person's pay rate exceeds the midpoint pay for the job. If it is below, then the pay rate is less than the midpoint. The compa ratio can help reveal how many jobs in each pay grade are paid above and below competitive pay rates.[134]

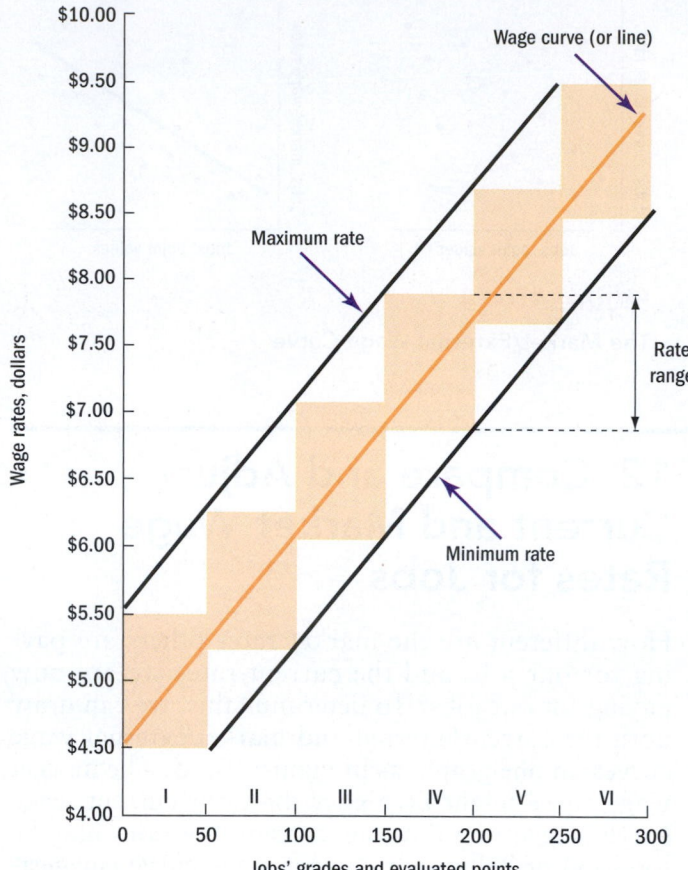

Figure 10A.6
Wage Structure

15. Address Remaining Jobs

To this point, we have focused our job evaluation on a limited number of benchmark jobs, as is traditional. We now want to add our remaining jobs to the wage structure. We can do this in two ways. We can evaluate each of the remaining jobs using the same process we just went through. Or we can simply slot the remaining jobs into the wage structure where we feel they belong, without formally evaluating and assigning points to these jobs. Jobs similar enough to our benchmark jobs we can easily slot into the wage structure. Jobs we're not sure about should undergo the same job evaluation process; we assign points to them and precisely slot them into the wage structure.[135]

16. Correct Out-Of-Line Rates

Finally, the wage rate the firm is now paying for a particular job may fall well off the wage curve or well outside the rate range for its grade, as illustrated in Figure 10.5, page 315. This means that the average pay for that job is currently too high or too low, relative to other jobs in the firm. For underpaid jobs, the solution is clear: Raise the wages of underpaid employees to the minimum of the rate range for their pay grade.

Current pay rates falling above the rate range are a different story. These are "red circle," "flagged," or "overrates." There are several ways to cope with this problem. One is to freeze the rate paid to these employees until general salary increases bring the other jobs into line. A second option is to transfer or promote the employees involved to jobs for which you can legitimately pay them their current pay rates. The third option is to freeze the rate for six months, during which time you try to transfer or promote the overpaid employees. If you cannot, then cut the rate you pay these employees to the maximum in the pay range for their pay grade.

11

Pay for Performance and Employee Benefits

OVERVIEW:
In this chapter, we will cover . . .

- Individual Employee Incentive Plans
- Team and Organizationwide Incentive Plans
- Benefits and Services: The Benefits Picture Today
- Pay For Time Not Worked and Insurance Benefits
- Retirement and Other Benefits
- Personal Services and Family-Friendly Benefits
- Employee Engagement Guide For Managers: Costco's Compensation Plan

LEARNING OBJECTIVES

When you finish studying this chapter, you should be able to:

1. Discuss the main incentives for individual employees.
2. Name and define the most popular organizationwide incentive plans.
3. Define employee benefits.
4. List and discuss the main pay for time not worked and insurance benefits.
5. Describe the main retirement benefits.
6. List and discuss the popular personal services and family-friendly benefits.
7. Explain how to use benefits to improve engagement, productivity, and performance.

MyLab Management

⭐ Improve Your Grade!
When you see this icon, visit **www.pearson.com/mylab/management** for activities that are applied, personalized, and offer immediate feedback.

⭐ Learn It

If your professor has chosen to assign this, go to **www.pearson.com/mylab/management** to see what you should particularly focus on and to take the Chapter 11 Warm Up.

Source: Laflor/Getty Images.

INTRODUCTION

Mal seemed to have everything you'd want in a travel agent. He was smart, good with numbers, sociable, and loved traveling. Lisa thought he'd make a great agent in her Chicago travel agency, so she hired him. Three weeks later, she regretted her choice. Twice last week Mal failed to follow up when clients called, and Thursday Lisa found him sleeping at his desk. "What do I have to do to light a fire under this guy?" she asked Paul, her husband and business partner.

The salary and wage plans we discussed in Chapter 10 represent just part of most employers' total compensation packages. Most today also offer incentive pay, such as year-end bonuses. And virtually all offer benefits such as insurance plans. We'll look at incentives and benefits in this chapter, starting with incentives for individual employees.

financial incentives
Financial rewards paid to workers whose production exceeds some predetermined standard.

productivity
The ratio of outputs (goods and services) divided by the inputs (resources such as labor and capital).

variable pay
Any plan that ties pay to productivity or profitability, usually as one-time lump payments.

KNOWLEDGE BASE

piecework
A system of pay based on the number of items processed by each individual worker in a unit of time, such as items per hour or items per day.

straight piecework
An incentive plan in which a person is paid a sum for each item he or she makes or sells, with a strict proportionality between results and rewards.

KNOWLEDGE BASE

standard hour plan
A plan by which a worker is paid a basic hourly rate but is paid an extra percentage of his or her rate for production exceeding the standard per hour or per day. Similar to piecework payment but based on a percent premium.

Individual Employee Incentive Plans

Frederick Taylor popularized **financial incentives**—financial rewards paid to workers whose production exceeds some predetermined standard—in the late 1800s. As a supervisor at the Midvale Steel Company, Taylor was concerned with what he called "systematic soldiering"—the tendency of employees to produce at the minimum acceptable level. Some workers then had the energy to run home and work on their houses after a 12-hour day. Taylor knew that if he could harness this energy at work, Midvale would be much more productive. **Productivity** "is the ratio of outputs (goods and services) divided by the inputs (resources such as labor and capital)."[1] In pursuing higher productivity, Taylor turned to devising improved financial incentives.

Today's employers use many incentives. All incentive plans are *pay-for-performance* plans because they tie workers' pay to performance.[2] **Variable pay** usually means incentive plans that tie *a group's* pay to company profitability (although some experts use *variable pay* to include incentive plans for individual employees);[3] *profit-sharing plans* are one example.

Individual Incentive Plans: Piecework Plans

Piecework is the oldest and most popular individual incentive plan. Here you pay the worker a sum (called a *piece rate*) for each unit he or she produces. (Of course, the worker must make at least the minimum wage, so the plan should guarantee at least that.) The crucial issue is the production standard. Industrial engineers often set this—for instance, in terms of a standard number of units per hour. But in practice, most employers set the piece rates more informally.

Straight piecework entails a strict proportionality between results and rewards regardless of output. The **standard hour plan** allows for sharing exceptional productivity gains between employer and worker; here the worker receives extra income (such as more per piece) for some above-normal production.[4]

Incentives and the Law

There are legal considerations with piecework and other incentive plans. For example, under the Fair Labor Standards Act, if the incentive is in the form of a prize or cash award, the employer generally must *include the value of that award* when calculating the worker's overtime pay for that pay period.[5] Suppose an employee who earns $10 per hour for 40 hours also got an incentive payment of $60 last week. Then his actual hourly pay last week was $460/40 or

$11.50 per hour. If so, the employee would have to be paid one-and-one-half times $11.50 (not times $10) for any overtime hours worked.

Certain bonuses are excludable from overtime pay calculations. For example, discretionary Christmas and gift bonuses that are not based on hours worked, or are so substantial that employees don't consider them a part of their wages, do not have to be included.

Merit Pay as an Incentive

merit pay (merit raise)
Any salary increase awarded to an employee based on his or her individual performance.

Merit pay, or a **merit raise**, is any salary increase the firm awards to an individual employee based on his or her individual performance. It is different from a bonus in that it usually becomes part of the employee's base salary, whereas a bonus is a one-time payment. The term *merit pay* is more often used for white-collar employees, particularly professional, office, and clerical employees.

Merit pay is the subject of much debate. Advocates argue that just awarding pay raises across the board (without regard to individual merit) may actually detract from performance, by showing employees they'll be rewarded regardless of their performance. Detractors argue, for instance, that because many appraisals are unfair, so too is the merit pay you base them on.[6] Merit plan effectiveness depends on differentiating among employees. Base pay increases by U.S. employers for their highest-ranked employees recently were 5.6%, compared with only 0.6% for the lowest-rated employees.[7]

One version ties merit awards to both individual and organizational performance. In Table 11.1, an outstanding performer would receive 70% of his or her maximum lump-sum award even if the organization's performance were marginal. However, employees with marginal or unacceptable performance would get no lump-sum awards even when the firm's performance was outstanding.

Incentives for Professional Employees

Professional employees are those whose work involves the application of learned knowledge to the solution of the employer's problems, such as lawyers and engineers.

Making incentive pay decisions for professional employees is challenging. For one thing, firms usually pay professionals well anyway. For another, they're already driven to produce high-caliber work.

However, it is unrealistic to assume that people like Google engineers work only for professional gratification. So, for example, Google pays higher incentives to engineers working on important projects.[8] And of course, such professionals also receive potentially millionaire-making stock option grants.

Dual-career ladders are another way to manage professionals' pay. At many employers, a bigger salary requires rerouting from engineering to management, but not all professionals want this. Therefore, many employers have one path for managers and another for technical experts, allowing the latter to earn higher pay without switching to management.[9]

Table 11.1 Merit Award Determination Matrix (an Example)

The Employee's Performance Rating (Weight = 0.50)	The Company's Performance (Weight = 0.50)				
	Outstanding	Excellent	Good	Marginal	Unacceptable
Outstanding	1.00	0.90	0.80	0.70	0.00
Excellent	0.90	0.80	0.70	0.60	0.00
Good	0.80	0.70	0.60	0.50	0.00
Marginal	—	—	—	—	—
Unacceptable	—	—	—	—	—

Note: To determine the dollar value of each employee's award: (1) multiply the employee's annual, straight-time wage or salary as of June 30 times his or her maximum incentive award (as determined by management or the board—such as, "10% of each employee's pay") and (2) multiply the resultant product by the appropriate percentage figure from this table. For example, if an employee had an annual salary of $40,000 on June 30 and a maximum incentive award of 7%, and if her performance and the organization's performance were both "excellent," the employee's award would be $2,240: ($40,000 × 0.07 × 0.80 = $2,240).

Nonfinancial and Recognition-Based Awards

As mentioned in Chapter 10, employers often supplement financial incentives with various nonfinancial and recognition-based awards. The term *recognition program* usually refers to formal programs, such as employee-of-the-month programs. *Social recognition program* generally refers to informal manager–employee exchanges such as praise, approval, or expressions of appreciation for a job well done. *Performance feedback* means providing quantitative or qualitative information on task performance so as to change or maintain performance; showing workers a graph of how their performance is trending is an example.[10]

TRENDS SHAPING HR: *Digital and Social Media*[11]

RECOGNITION APPS Employers are bulking up their recognition programs with digital support. For example, Intuit shifted its employee recognition, years of service, patent awards, and wellness awards programs to Globoforce, an online awards vendor. This "allowed us to build efficiencies and improved effectiveness" into the programs, says Intuit's vice president of performance, rewards, and workplace.[12] Apps also enable employees to praise each other.[13] For example, one lets employees "give recognition by picking out a badge and typing in a quick note to thank the people who matter most . . . ." [14] Others let users post the positive feedback they receive to their LinkedIn profiles.

One survey of 235 managers found that the most-used rewards to motivate employees (top–down, from most used to least) were:[15]

- Employee recognition
- Gift certificates
- Special events
- Cash rewards
- Merchandise incentives
- E-mail/print communications
- Training programs
- Work/life benefits
- Variable pay
- Group travel
- Individual travel
- Sweepstakes

The HR Tools feature elaborates.

Making incentive pay decisions for professional employees is challenging. For one thing, firms usually pay professionals well anyway. For another, they're already driven to produce high-caliber work.

Source: Hero Images/Getty Images.

■ HR Tools for Line Managers and Small Businesses:

Goals and Recognition

The individual line manager should not rely just on the employer's financial incentive plans for motivating subordinates; there are simply too many opportunities to motivate employees every day to let those opportunities pass. What to do?

First, the best option for motivating an employee is also the simplest—*make sure the employee has a doable goal* and that he or she agrees with it. It makes little sense to try to motivate employees with financial incentives if they don't know their goals or don't agree with them.

Figure 11.1

Social Recognition and Related Positive Reinforcement Managers Can Use

Source: Bob Nelson, *1001 Ways to Reward Employees*, New York: Workman Pub., 1994, p. 19; Sunny C. L. Fong and Margaret A. Shaffer, "The Dimensionality and Determinants of Pay Satisfaction: A Cross-Cultural Investigation of a Group Incentive Plan," *International Journal of Human Resource Management*, 14, no. 4, June 2003, p. 559.

- Challenging work assignments
- Freedom to choose own work activity
- Having fun built into work
- More of preferred task
- Role as boss's stand-in when he or she is away
- Role in presentations to top management
- Job rotation
- Encouragement of learning and continuous improvement
- Being provided with ample encouragement
- Being allowed to set own goals
- Compliments
- Expression of appreciation in front of others
- Note of thanks
- Employee-of-the-month award
- Special commendation
- Bigger desk
- Bigger office or cubicle

Second, *recognizing an employee's contribution* is a powerful motivation tool. Studies show that recognition has a positive impact on performance, either alone or in combination with financial rewards. For example, in one study, combining financial rewards with recognition produced a 30% performance improvement in service firms, almost twice the effect of using each reward alone.

Third, use *social recognition* (such as compliments) as positive reinforcement on a day-to-day basis. Figure 11.1 presents a list.[16]

⭐ Talk About It–**1**

If your professor has chosen to assign this, go to **www.pearson.com/mylab/management** to discuss the following question. You have decided to verify that recognition does in fact improve performance. To that end, you will use an honest observation to praise someone's performance today. What was the effect of your experiment?

Job Design

Job design (which we discussed more fully in Chapter 4) can affect employee motivation and retention. A study concluded that job design is a primary driver of employee engagement. A study by Towers Watson concluded that challenging work ranked as the seventh most important driver for attracting employees.[17] Job design is thus a useful part of an employer's total rewards program.

The HR in Practice feature illustrates how employers combine incentives to boost profits.

■ HR in Practice

Using Financial and Nonfinancial Incentives in a Fast-Food Chain

Researchers studied the impact of financial and nonfinancial incentives on performance in 21 stores of a Midwest fast-food franchise.[18] Each store had about 25 workers and two managers. The researchers trained the managers to identify measurable employee behaviors that were currently deficient but that could influence store performance. Example behaviors included "keeping both hands moving at the drive-through window" and "repeating the customer's order back to him or her."[19] Then the researchers instituted financial and nonfinancial incentive plans to incentivize these behaviors. They measured store performance in terms of gross profitability (revenue minus expenses), drive-through time, and employee turnover.

Financial Incentives

Some employees in some of the stores received financial incentives for exhibiting the desired behaviors. The financial incentives consisted of lump-sum bonuses in the workers' paychecks. For example, if the manager observed a work team exhibiting up to 50 behaviors (such as "working during idle time") during the observation period, he or she added $25 to the paychecks of all store employees that period; 50 to 100 behaviors added $50 per paycheck, and more than 100 behaviors added $75 per paycheck. Payouts eventually rose over time as the employees learned to enact the behaviors they were to exhibit.

Nonfinancial Incentives

The researchers trained the managers in some stores to use nonfinancial incentives such as feedback and recognition. For example, for *performance feedback*, managers maintained charts showing the drive-through times at the end of each day. They placed the charts by the time clocks. Thus, these store employees could keep track of their store's performance on measures like drive-through times. The researchers also trained managers to administer *recognition* to employees. For instance, "I noticed that today the drive-through times were really good."[20]

Results

The programs were both successful. Both the financial and nonfinancial incentives improved employee and store performance.[21] For example, store profits rose 30% for those units where managers used financial rewards. Store profits rose 36% for those units where managers used nonfinancial rewards. During the same nine-month period, drive-through times decreased 19% for the financial incentives group, and 25% for the nonfinancial incentives groups. Turnover improved 13% for the financial incentives group and 10% for the nonfinancial incentives group.

Implications for managers include:

- The employee or employees must have specific challenging goals.[22]
- The link between the effort and getting the incentive should be clear.
- Make sure that motivation (rather than, say, poor employee selection) is impeding the behaviors you want to incentivize.
- Employees must have the skills and training to do the job.
- Employers should support the incentive plan with performance feedback, so employees continuously see how they are doing.
- The manager should gather evidence on the effects of the incentive plan over time; make sure it's indeed influencing performance as you intended.[23]
- Combine financial with nonfinancial incentives such as recognition.

⭐ Talk About It–**2**

If your professor has chosen to assign this, go to **www.pearson.com/mylab/management** to discuss the following question. Lisa and Paul (from the chapter opener) have asked you to design an incentive plan for Mal. How would you apply what you learned in this feature to do so?

Incentives for Salespeople

Sales compensation plans may focus on salary, commissions, or some combination.[24]

Salary Plan Some firms pay salespeople fixed salaries (perhaps with occasional incentives in the form of bonuses, sales contest prizes, and the like).[25] Straight salaries make sense when the main task involves prospecting (finding new clients) or account servicing (such as participating in trade shows). A Buick–GMC dealership in Lincolnton, North Carolina, offers straight salary as an option to salespeople who sell an average of at least eight vehicles a month (plus a small "retention bonus" per car sold).[26]

The straight salary approach also makes it easier to switch territories or to reassign salespeople, and it can foster sales staff loyalty. The main disadvantage is that it may not motivate high performers.[27]

Commission Plan Straight commission plans pay salespeople only for results. Such plans tend to attract high-performing salespeople who see that effort produces rewards. Sales costs are proportionate to sales rather than fixed, and the company's fixed sales costs are thus lower. It's a plan that's easy to understand and compute. Alternatives include quota bonuses (for meeting particular quotas), straight commissions, management by objectives programs (pay is based on specific metrics), and ranking programs (these reward high achievers but pay little or no bonuses to the lowest-performing salespeople).[28]

However, problems abound. For example, in poorly designed plans, salespeople may focus on making the sale and neglect duties such as pushing hard-to-sell items.[29] Also, in most firms, a significant portion of the sales in one year reflects a "carryover" (sales that would repeat even without any efforts by the sales force) from the prior year. Why pay the sales force a commission on all the current year's sales if some of those sales aren't "new" sales from the current year?[30] The following feature presents practical guidelines.

BUILDING YOUR MANAGEMENT SKILLS:
How to Build an Effective Sales Incentive Plan

How do managers actually design sales incentive plans? The bottom line is that most companies pay salespeople a combination of salary and commissions, with (on average) an incentive mix of about 70% base salary/30% incentive. This cushions the salesperson's downside risk (of earning nothing), while limiting the risk that the commissions could get out of hand from the firm's point of view.[31]

But getting the best performance from the sales force involves more than the right commissions/sales mix. To maximize the salesperson's efforts, keep the following guidelines in mind:[32]

- Salespeople in high-performing companies receive *38% of their total cash compensation* in the form of sales incentive pay (compared with 27% at low-performing companies).
- Salespeople in high-performing companies are *twice as likely to receive stock, stock options*, or other equity pay as their counterparts at low-performing companies (36% versus 18%).
- Salespeople in high-performing companies spend *264 more hours per year on high-value sales activities* (e.g., prospecting, making sales presentations, and closing) than salespeople at low-performing companies.
- Salespeople in high-performing companies spend *40% more time each year with their best potential customers*—qualified leads and prospects they know—than salespeople at low-performing companies.
- Salespeople in high-performing companies spend nearly 25% *less time on administration* (such as filling out sales forms), allowing them to allocate more time to core sales activities, such as prospecting leads and closing sales.

Incentives' Unintended Consequences Wells Fargo and Co. provided a textbook example of ill-designed incentive plans. Its incentive plan drove retail bank employees to hit high sales goals. For example, it required retail bank employees to sell eight banking products per customer.[33] An annual report mentions "cross sell"

20 times; the company calls its retail bank branches "stores."[34] Wells employees opened accounts for customers without the customer's permission. At ethics workshops, Wells employees were told not to create fake bank accounts without clients' knowledge. But the employees knew they had to meet their sales goals, so they did it anyway.[35] Fines, lawsuits, and the CEO's exit were the results.

> **TRENDS SHAPING HR:** *Digital and Social Media*
>
> **TRACKING SALES COMMISSIONS** Many employers use *enterprise incentive management* (EIM) software to track and control sales commissions.[36] For example, Oracle Sales Cloud EIM enables management to easily create scorecard metrics such as number of prospecting calls and sales contracts, and to monitor these in real time on the system's dashboards.[37] Users can also gamify the sales incentive process with Oracle Sales Cloud, by creating rewards such as points or badges based on each salesperson's performance.

Incentives for Managers and Executives

An executive's reward package elements—base salary, short- and long-term incentives, and perks—should align with each other and with the company's strategic aims. The employer should first ask, "What is our strategy and what are our strategic goals?" Then decide what long-term behaviors (boosting sales, cutting costs, and so on) the executives must exhibit to achieve the firm's strategic goals. Then shape each component of the executive compensation package (base salary, short- and long-term incentives, and perks) and group them into a balanced plan that makes sense in terms of motivating the executive to achieve these aims. The rule is this: each pay component should help focus the manager's attention on the behaviors required to achieve the company's strategic goals.[38] Using multiple, strategy-based performance criteria is best. These include financial performance, number of strategic goals met, performance assessment by the board, employee productivity measures, and employee morale surveys.

One expert estimates that the typical CEO's salary accounts for about one-fifth of his or her pay. A bonus based on explicit performance standards accounts for another fifth, and long-term incentive awards such as stock options and long-term performance plans account for the remaining three-fifths.[39]

Sarbanes-Oxley Congress passed the Sarbanes-Oxley Act of 2002 to inject more responsibility into executives' and board members' decisions. It makes them personally liable for violating their fiduciary responsibilities to their shareholders. The act also requires CEOs and CFOs of a public company to repay any bonuses, incentives, or equity-based compensation received from the company during the 12-month period following the issuance of a financial statement that the company must restate due to material noncompliance stemming from misconduct.[40]

Short-Term Managerial Incentives and the Annual Bonus

Employers are shifting from long-term incentives to put more emphasis on short-term performance and incentives.[41] Most firms have **annual bonus** plans for motivating managers' short-term performance. Such short-term incentives can easily produce plus or minus adjustments of 25% or more to total pay. Four factors influence one's bonus: eligibility, fund size, individual performance, and formula.

annual bonus
Plans that are designed to motivate short-term performance of managers and which are tied to company profitability.

Eligibility Employers traditionally based annual bonus eligibility on job level/title, base salary, and/or officer status. Some simply based eligibility on job level or job title, or salary.[42] Recently, however, more employers are offering executives as well as employees below the executive level single annual incentive plans "in which both executives and other employees participate."[43]

Fund Size How does one determine how big the annual bonus fund should be? Most employers (33% in a recent survey) traditionally use the Sum of Targets approach.[44] Specifically, they estimate the likely bonus for each eligible ("target") employee and total these up to arrive at the bonus pool's size.

However, more employers (32%) are funding the short-term bonus fund based on financial results. For example, if profits were $200,000, the management bonus fund might be 20% of $200,000, or $40,000. Most employers use more than one financial measure, with sales, earnings per share, and cash flow the most popular.[45]

Individual Performance and Formula Deciding the actual individual award involves rating the person's performance and then applying a predetermined bonus formula. Most often, the employer sets a target bonus (as well as maximum bonus, perhaps double the target bonus) for each eligible position. The actual award the manager gets then reflects his or her performance. Other firms tie short-term bonuses to both organizational and individual performance. Thus, a manager might be eligible for an individual performance bonus of up to $10,000, but receive only $2,000 at the end of the year, based on his or her individual performance. But the person might also receive a second bonus of $3,000, based on the firm's profits for the year. One drawback here is that marginal performers still get bonuses. One way to avoid this is to make the bonus a product of both individual and corporate performance. For example (see Table 11.2), multiply the target bonus by 1.00, 0.80, or zero, depending on the person's performance (and assuming excellent company performance). Then managers whose performance is poor receive no bonus.

Executives' Strategic Long-Term Incentives

The employer wants to avoid managers boosting short-term profits by, for instance, delaying required maintenance. They therefore use long-term incentives to inject a long-term perspective into executives' decisions. Popular long-term incentives include cash, stock options, stock, stock appreciation rights, and phantom stock. PepsiCo's CEO was paid $26.4 million for 2015, including a base salary of $1.6 million, stock awards of $6.25 million and a performance-based cash bonus of $13.9 million, a $4.26 million adjustment to her pension, plus perks such as air travel.[46]

stock option
The right to purchase a stated number of shares of a company stock at today's price at some time in the future.

Stock Options A **stock option** is the right to purchase a specific number of shares of company stock at a specific price during a specific period. The executive thus hopes to profit by exercising his or her option in the future but at today's price. This assumes the stock will go up.[47] When stock markets dropped, many employers, including Intel and Google, modified option plans to increase the likely payout.[48]

Table 11.2 Multiplier Approach to Determining Annual Bonus

Individual Performance (Based on Appraisal, Weight = 0.50)	Company Performance (Based on Sales Targets, Weight = 0.50)			
	Excellent	Good	Fair	Poor
Excellent	1.00	0.90	0.80	0.70
Good	0.80	0.70	0.60	0.50
Fair	0.00	0.00	0.00	0.00
Poor	0.00	0.00	0.00	0.00

Note: To determine the dollar amount of a manager's award, multiply the maximum possible (target) bonus by the appropriate factor in the matrix.

The main problem with stock options is that they often reward even managers who have lackluster performance. A study of CEOs of Standard & Poor's 1,500 companies found that 57% received pay increases although company performance didn't improve.[49] Options may also encourage executives to take perilous risks in pursuit of higher (at least short-term) profits.[50]

Other Stock Plans The trend is toward tying rewards more explicitly to performance. For example, instead of stock options, more firms grant various types of performance shares such as *performance-contingent restricted stock*; the executive receives his or her shares only if he or she meets the preset performance targets.[51] With *restricted stock plans*, the firm usually awards rights to the shares without cost to the executive but the employee is restricted from acquiring (and selling) the shares for, say, five years. The employer's aim is to retain the employee's services during that time.[52]

Stock appreciation rights (SARs) permit the recipient to exercise the stock option (by buying the stock) or to take any appreciation in the stock price in cash, stock, or some combination of these. Under *phantom stock plans*, executives receive not shares but "units" that are similar to shares of company stock. Then at some future time, they receive value (usually in cash) equal to the appreciation of the "phantom" stock they own.[53] Companies also provide incentives to persuade executives not to leave the firm. **Golden parachutes** are extraordinary payments companies make to executives in connection with a change in ownership or control of a company. For example, a company's golden parachute clause might state that, with a change in ownership of the firm, the executive would receive a one-time payment of $2 million.[54]

golden parachute
A payment companies make in connection with a change in ownership or control of a company.

⭐ Watch It

How does a company actually go about creating an incentive plan? If your professor has chosen to assign this, go to **www.pearson.com/mylab/management** to watch the video Joie de Vivre Hospitality Pay for Performance and Financial Incentives and then answer the questions to show what you would do in this situation.

LEARNING OBJECTIVE 2
Name and define the most popular organizationwide incentive plans.

Team and Organizationwide Incentive Plans

We've focused on individual employee incentives. We look now at incentives for teams and for all employees companywide.

How to Design Team Incentives

team- (or group-) incentive plan
A plan in which a production standard is set for a specific work group, and its members are paid incentives if the group exceeds the production standard.

Firms also need incentive plans that encourage teamwork and focus team members on performance. **Team- (or group-) incentive plans** pay incentives to the team based on the team's performance.

The main question is how to reward the team's performance, and the wrong choice can prove lethal. Levi Strauss installed a team incentive plan that rewarded the team as a whole for its output, neglecting the fact that some employees worked harder than others. The faster ones soon slowed down, production declined, and Levi's closed its U.S. factories.

Yet the usual approach is still to tie rewards to some overall standard of team performance, such as "total labor hours per car."[55] In one firm, if the team reached 100% of its goal, the employees would share in about 5% of the improvement (in labor costs saved). The firm divided the 5% pool by the number of employees to compute the value of a "share." If the firm achieved less than 100% of its goal, the bonus pool was less. The results of this plan—in terms of changing employee attitudes and focusing teams on strategic goals—were reportedly "extraordinary."[56]

organizationwide incentive plan

Plans in which all or most employees can participate, and that generally tie the reward to some measure of companywide performance.

profit-sharing plan

A plan whereby employees share in the company's profits.

Organizationwide incentive plans are plans in which all or most employees can participate, and which generally tie the reward to some measure of companywide performance. Plans include profit sharing, Scanlon/gainsharing plans, and employee stock ownership (ESOP) plans.

Profit-Sharing Plans

Profit-sharing plans are plans in which all or most employees receive a share of the firm's annual profits.[57] With *current profit-sharing* or cash plans, employees share in a portion of the employer's profits quarterly or annually. In cash plans, the firm simply distributes a percentage of profits (usually 15% to 20%) as profit shares to employees at regular intervals. The Home Depot instituted a cash program for its store workers. It started paying store associates a bonus if their stores meet certain financial goals. In one year, The Home Depot distributed a total of $90 million under that companywide incentive plan.[58]

With *deferred profit-sharing* plans, the employer puts cash awards into trust accounts for the employees' retirement.[59] The employer generally allocates the awards based on a percentage of the employee's salary, or some measure of the employee's contribution to company profits.[60] Employees' income taxes on the distributions are deferred until the employee retires or withdraws from the plan.

gainsharing plan

An incentive plan that engages employees in a common effort to achieve productivity objectives and share the gains.

Gainsharing Plans

Gainsharing is an incentive plan that engages many or all employees in a common effort to achieve a company's productivity objectives, with any resulting cost savings (gains) shared among employees and the company.[61] Gainsharing plans include the Scanlon plan, and the Lincoln, Rucker, and Improshare plans. In general, all emphasize labor–management cooperation, an emphasis on ensuring that employees are trained to do their jobs, and by their use of a formula to distribute gains to employees.

The basic difference among these plans is the formula employers use to determine employee bonuses. In one version of the *Lincoln incentive system*, first instituted at the Lincoln Electric Company of Ohio, employees work on a guaranteed piecework basis. The company distributes total annual profits (less taxes, 6% dividends to stockholders, and a reserve) each year among employees based on their merit rating. Results—from various efforts in hospitals, as well as manufacturing plants—suggest that gainsharing plans can improve productivity and patient care and reduce grievances.[62] For example, some hospitals pay physicians a share of any cost savings attributable in part to the physicians' efforts.[63]

At-Risk Pay Plans

Base pay and benefits represent the lion's share of labor costs, and neither usually vary much, even when sales plummet.[64] So-called variable pay plans are one way around this. For example, in an **earnings-at-risk pay plan**, employees agree to put some portion (say, 10%) of their normal pay at risk (forego it) if they don't meet their goals,

Firms increasingly rely on teams to manage their work. They therefore need incentive plans that encourage teamwork and focus team members' attention on performance.

Source: Monty Rakusen/Getty Images.

earnings-at-risk pay plan
Plan that puts some portion of employees' normal pay at risk if they don't meet their goals, in return for possibly obtaining a much larger bonus if they exceed their goals.

KNOWLEDGE BASE ✓

employee stock ownership plan (ESOP)
A qualified, tax deductible stock bonus plan in which employers contribute stock to a trust for eventual use by employees.

in return for possibly obtaining a much larger bonus if they exceed their goals. For example, put part of the employees' pay "at risk" by replacing 10% of each worker's wages with a 10% bonus if the company meets its goals plus an additional 3% bonus if it exceeds these goals.

Employee Stock Ownership Plans

Employee stock ownership plans (ESOPs) are companywide plans in which the employer contributes shares of its own stock (or cash to be used to purchase such stock) to a trust established to purchase shares of the firm's stock for employees. The firm generally makes these contributions annually in proportion to total employee compensation, with a limit of 15% of compensation. The trust holds the stock in individual employee accounts and distributes it to employees on retirement (or other separation), assuming the person has worked long enough to earn ownership of the stock.

The company receives a tax deduction equal to the fair market value of the shares it transfers to the trustee and can claim an income tax deduction for dividends paid on ESOP-owned stock. Employees, as noted, aren't taxed until they receive a distribution from the trust, usually at retirement. The Employee Retirement Income Security Act (ERISA) allows a firm to borrow against employee stock held in trust and then repay the loan in pretax rather than after-tax dollars, another tax incentive for using such plans.[65]

Some companies offer "broad-based stock option plans" in which all or most employees can participate. The basic thinking is that sharing ownership in the company with employees makes motivational and practical sense. However with current tax laws, companies must show the options as an expense when awarded, reducing their attractiveness as a "costless" reward. Therefore, many employers such as Microsoft award stock instead of options.[66]

LEARNING OBJECTIVE 3
Define employee benefits.

benefits
Indirect financial and nonfinancial payments employees receive for continuing their employment with the company.

Benefits and Services: The Benefits Picture Today

"What are your benefits?" is the first thing many applicants ask. **Benefits**—indirect financial and nonfinancial payments that employees receive for continuing their employment with the company—are an important part of just about everyone's compensation.[67] They include things like health and life insurance, pensions, time off with pay, and child-care assistance. Figure 11.2 summarizes benefits as a percentage of employee compensation.

Figure 11.2

Relative Importance of Employer Benefits Costs for Employee Compensation, December 2016

Source: "Relative Importance of Employer Costs for Employee Compensation," December 2016, https://www.bls.gov/news.release/pdf/ecec.pdf, accessed April 21, 2017.

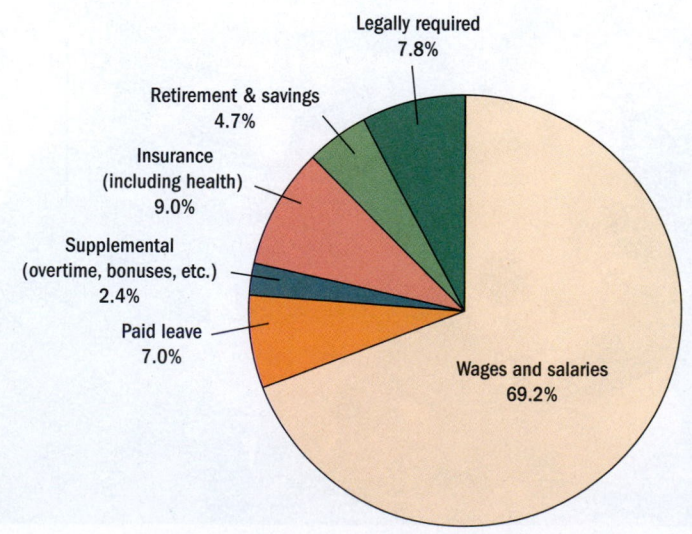

Table 11.3 Some Required and Discretionary Benefits

Benefits Required by Federal or Most State Law	Benefits Discretionary on Part of Employer*
Social Security	Disability, health, and life insurance
Unemployment insurance	Pensions
Workers' compensation	Paid time off for vacations, holidays, sick leave, personal leave, jury duty, etc.
Leaves under Family Medical Leave Act	Employee assistance and counseling programs; "family friendly" benefits for child care, elder care, flexible work schedules, etc.; executive perquisites

*Although not required under federal law, all these benefits are regulated in some way by federal law, as explained in this chapter.

Federal laws mandate some benefits (such as Social Security), while other benefits are at the employer's discretion (see Table 11.3). However, federal law impacts even discretionary benefits such as vacation leave. And employers must also adhere to the laws of the states in which they do business.[68]

supplemental pay benefits
Benefits for time not worked such as unemployment insurance, vacation and holiday pay, and sick pay.

unemployment insurance (or compensation)
Provides benefits if a person is unable to work through some fault other than his or her own.

Pay for Time Not Worked and Insurance Benefits

Employers typically offer various pay for time not worked (also called **supplemental pay**) benefits, as well as insurance benefits. We'll start with the former.

Common pay for time not worked includes, for instance, unemployment insurance, holidays, and sick leave.

Unemployment Insurance

All states have **unemployment insurance (or compensation)** laws. These provide benefits if a person is unable to work through no fault of his or her own. The benefits derive from a tax on employers that can range from 0.1% to 5% of taxable payroll in most states. An employer's unemployment tax rate reflects its rate of employee terminations. While following federal guidelines, states have their own unemployment laws. Unemployment tax rates are rising in many states. For example, prior to the 2007–2009 recession, Maryland's unemployment insurance tax rate was 0.3% or lower. The rate averages 0.3 % to 7.5 % per employee, depending on the employer's claim history.[69] The Skills feature explains how to control unemployment claims.

BUILDING YOUR MANAGEMENT SKILLS:
How to Control Unemployment Claims

Unemployment insurance laws do not require that everyone dismissed receive unemployment benefits—only those dismissed *through no fault of their own.* The manager therefore plays a big role in controlling unemployment claims. First, keep a list of written warnings to support the fact that you repeatedly told the employee to remedy his or her behavior.

Second, use the checklist in Table 11.4 to help demonstrate that the dismissal resulted from the person's own misbehavior.

Table 11.4 Unemployment Insurance Cost-Control Checklist

- Keep documented history of lateness, absence, and warning notices.
- Warn chronically late employees before discharging them.
- Have rule that three days' absence without calling in is reason for automatic discharge.
- Request doctor's note on return to work after absence.
- Make written approval for personal leave mandatory.
- Stipulate date for return to work from leave.
- Obtain a signed resignation statement.
- Mail job abandonment letter if employee fails to return on time.
- Document all instances of poor performance.
- Require supervisors to document the steps taken to remedy the situation.
- Document employee's refusal of advice and direction.
- Require all employees to sign a statement acknowledging acceptance of firm's policies and rules.
- File the protest against a former employee's unemployment claim on time (usually within 10 days).
- Use proper terminology on claim form, and attach documented evidence regarding separation.
- Attend hearings and appeal unwarranted claims.
- Check every claim against the individual's personnel file.
- Routinely conduct exit interviews to produce information for protesting unemployment claims.

Vacations and Holidays

Most firms offer vacation leave benefits. About 90% of full-time workers and 40% of part-timers get paid holidays, an average of eight paid holidays off.[70] Common U.S. paid holidays include New Year's Day, Memorial Day, Independence Day, Labor Day, Thanksgiving Day, and Christmas Day.[71] On average, American workers get about 9 days of vacation leave after 1 year's employment, about 14 days after 5 years, and 17 after 10 years.[72]

Employers have to make several holiday- and vacation-related policy decisions. They must decide, of course, how many days off employees will get and which days (if any) will be the paid holidays. Other vacation policy decisions include, for instance, will employees get their regular base pay while on vacation, or vacation pay based on average earnings (which may include overtime)? And, will the firm pay employees for a holiday if they don't come to work the day before and the day after the holiday?

More firms are moving to a flexible vacation policy. For example, IBM gives each of its employees at least three weeks' vacation, but it doesn't formally track the vacation each takes. Employees simply make informal vacation arrangements with their direct supervisors.[73]

Wage surveys and websites like www.hrtools.com provide sample vacation policies for inclusion in the firm's employee manual.

 KNOW YOUR EMPLOYMENT LAW
Some Legal Aspects of Vacations and Holidays

Although federal law does not require vacation benefits, the employer must still formulate vacation policy with care. As an example, many employers' vacation policies say vacation pay accrues, say, on a biweekly basis. These employers obligate themselves to pay employees pro rata vacation pay when they leave the firm. But if the employer's vacation policy requires that a new employee pass his or her first employment anniversary *before becoming entitled* to a vacation, the employee gets no vacation pay if he or she leaves during that first year. ■

Sick Leave

sick leave
Provides pay to an employee when he or she is out of work because of illness.

Sick leave provides pay to employees when they're out of work due to illness. Most sick leave policies grant full pay for a specified number of sick days—usually up to about 12 per year. The days usually accumulate at the rate of, say, one day per month of service.

The problem is that while many employees use their sick days only when sick, others use it whether sick or not. In one survey, personal illnesses accounted for only about 45% of unscheduled sick leave absences. Family issues (27%), personal needs (13%), and a mentality of "entitlement" (9%) were other reasons cited.[74]

TRENDS SHAPING HR: *Digital and Social Media*

WHEN FRIENDS BACKFIRE Social media sites can get sick leave workers in trouble. In one case, an employee took a sick day, saying that chronic pain prevented her from coming to work. Unfortunately, she posted pictures of herself drinking at a festival the day she was supposed to be home sick. One of her Facebook "friends" got the photo and showed it to a company supervisor. The company fired her for absence, and an appeals court upheld the employer's decision.[75]

Employers use several tactics to reduce excessive sick leave absences. Some repurchase unused sick leave at the end of the year by paying their employees a sum for each sick leave day not used. The problem is that legitimately sick employees may come to work. At Marriott, employees can trade the value of some sick days for other benefits. Other employers aggressively investigate all absences, for instance, calling the absent employees at their homes.[76]

Many employers use *pooled paid leave plans* (or *"banks"*) or paid time off (PTO) plans.[77] Such plans lump together sick leave, vacation, and personal days into a single leave pool. For example, one hospital previously granted new employees 25 days off per year (10 vacation days, 3 personal days, and 12 sick days). Employees used, on average, 5 of those 12 sick days (as well as all vacations and personal days).[78] The pooled paid leave plan allowed new employees to accrue 18 days to use as they saw fit. ("Catastrophic leaves" were handled separately.) The pooled plan reduced absences.[79]

How many paid days off the employee gets in a PTO plan generally depends on tenure. It ranges from about 13 days off for new employees to 26 days for those with 20 years or more with the employer.[80]

Some employers centralize their absence management programs ("integrated absence management"). Proactively managing absences this way begins with analysis. For instance, how many people are on leave; how much the employer is spending to replace absent workers; and what units seem to have the attendance problems.[81] Then put in place solutions such as rigorous absence claims reviews. The accompanying HR as a Profit Center feature expands on this.

■ HR as a Profit Center

Cutting Absences at the Driver and Vehicle Licensing Agency

When she became director of the United Kingdom's Driver and Vehicle Licensing Agency, its new director saw she had to address its sickness absence rate.[82] The rate had peaked at 14 days out per employee in 2005, at a cost of about $20 million per year (£10.3 million).

The new director organized a sick leave initiative.[83] The agency set a goal of reducing absences by 30% by 2010. Agency directors received absence-reduction goals and their progress was tracked. The agency introduced new policies to make it easier for employees to swap work shifts and introduced a guaranteed leave day policy. The average annual sickness absence rate was soon down to 7.5 days per employee. Improved attendance probably contributed to a 7% productivity increase in 2009–2010. This translates into savings of about $48 million dollars (£24.4 million).

> ⭐ **Talk About It – 3**
>
> If your professor has chosen to assign this, go to **www.pearson.com/mylab/management** to discuss the following question. A note on this agency in Wikipedia refers to the extraordinarily high (average three weeks per year) sick leave in this agency around 2007.[84] What sorts of inaction on the part of previous managers could help explain such poor attendance?

Parental Leaves and the Family and Medical Leave Act

Parental leave is an important benefit. About half of workers are women, and about 80% will become pregnant during their work lives. Both parents work full-time in almost half of all two-parent families. Furthermore, many people head single-parent households. As one stressed-out parent said, "You basically just always feel like you're doing a horrible job at everything."[85] Furthermore, many employers are offering generous new-parent paid leaves. For example, Netflix offers 52 weeks of both paid maternity leave and paternity leave. eBay offers 24 weeks and 12 weeks respectively, and Johnson & Johnson offers 17 weeks and 12 weeks. [86]

Several laws apply. Under the Pregnancy Discrimination Act, employers must treat women applying for pregnancy leave as they would any other employee requesting a leave under the employer's policies. The Family and Medical Leave Act of 1993 (FMLA) stipulates that:[87]

1. Private employers of 50 or more employees must provide eligible employees (women or men) up to 12 weeks of unpaid leave for their own serious illness; the birth or adoption of a child; or the care of a seriously ill child, spouse, or parent.
2. Employers may require employees to take any unused paid sick leave or annual leave as part of the 12-week leave provided in the law.
3. Employees taking leave are entitled to receive health benefits while they are on FMLA leave, under the same terms and conditions as on the job.
4. Employers must guarantee most employees the right to return to their previous or equivalent position with no loss of benefits at the end of the leave.

Other laws apply to sick leaves. Under the Americans with Disabilities Act (ADA), a qualified employee with a disability may be eligible for a leave if such a leave is necessary to reasonably accommodate the employee. Under various state workers' compensation laws, employees may be eligible for leave in connection with work-related injuries.[88] President Obama issued an executive order requiring federal contractors to provide their employees with mandatory sick leave; initially, at least, it appeared that the Trump administration would let that rule stand.[89]

KNOW YOUR EMPLOYMENT LAW
Parental Leave Legal Issues

Managers who want to avoid granting unnecessary FMLA leaves need to understand the FMLA. For example, to be eligible for leave under the FMLA, the employee must have worked for the employer for at least a total of 12 months and have worked (not just been paid, as someone might be if on leave) for 1,250 or more hours in the past 12 consecutive months.[90] If these do not apply, no leave is required.

Employers need procedures for all leaves of absence (including those awarded under the FMLA). These include:

- Give no employee a leave until the reason for the leave is clear.
- If the leave is for medical or family reasons, the employer should obtain medical certification from the medical practitioner.
- Use a standard form to record both the employee's expected return date and the fact that, without an authorized extension, the firm may terminate his or her employment. ■

Although the Family and Medical Leave Act provides for leave, it mandates only unpaid leave. Therefore, several states implemented their own paid family leave laws. For example, New York's law initially mandates eight weeks of leave at 50% of the employee's average salary.[91] Recently, more experts have been discussing the need for federal parental paid leave legislation.[92] On average, employers provide 31 days of leave for adoptions, 41 days for maternity leave, and 22 days for paternity leave.[93] In its parental benefits, Facebook also provides new child bonuses (up to $7,000), monetary assistance for adoption, day-care reimbursement, and backup child services.[94]

Severance Pay

severance pay
A one-time payment some employers provide when terminating an employee.

Many employers provide **severance pay**, a one-time separation payment when terminating an employee. Severance pay makes sense. It is humanitarian and good public relations. Furthermore, most managers expect employees to give notice if they plan to quit, so it seems equitable to provide severance pay when dismissing an employee. Reducing the chances of litigation from disgruntled former employees is another reason. Severance pay plans also help reassure employees who stay on after a downsizing that they'll receive some financial help if they're let go.

Most organizations have severance policies. About 95% of employees dismissed in downsizings got severance pay, but only about a third of employers offer severance when terminating for poor performance. It is uncommon to pay when employees quit. The number of maximum weeks of severance pay tends to vary by position. In one survey, about 45% of officers and senior executives got 52 weeks or more, 42% of professionals got 14–26 weeks, and 39% of administrative staff got 14–26 weeks. At the lower levels few pay no severance, but for officers and senior executives 13%–19% got no severance.[95] If the employer obligates itself (for instance, in its employee handbook) to pay severance, then its "voluntary" plan must comply with additional rules under ERISA.[96]

Supplemental Unemployment Benefits

supplemental unemployment benefits
Provide for a "guaranteed annual income" in certain industries where employers must shut down to change machinery or due to reduced work. These benefits are paid by the company and supplement unemployment benefits.

In industries such as automaking, shutdowns to reduce inventories or change machinery are common, and laid-off or furloughed employees must depend on unemployment insurance. As the name implies, **supplemental unemployment benefits** are cash payments that supplement the employee's unemployment compensation, to help the person maintain his or her standard of living while out of work.

Insurance Benefits

Employers also provide various required or voluntary insurance benefits, such as workers' compensation and health insurance.

Workers' Compensation

workers' compensation
Provides income and medical benefits to work-related accident victims or their dependents regardless of fault.

Workers' compensation laws aim to provide sure, prompt income and medical benefits to work-related accident victims or their dependents, regardless of fault.

Every state has its own workers' compensation law and commission, and some run their own insurance programs. However, most require employers to carry workers' compensation insurance with private, state-approved insurance companies. Neither the state nor the federal government contributes any funds for workers' compensation.

In the event of a worker's death or disablement, the person's dependents receive a cash benefit based on prior earnings—usually one-half to two-thirds the worker's average weekly wage, per week of employment. Most states have a time limit—such as 500 weeks—for which benefits can be paid. If the injury causes a specific loss (such as an arm), the employee may receive additional benefits based on a statutory list of losses. In addition to these cash benefits, employers must furnish necessary medical, surgical, and hospital services. ADA provisions generally prohibit employers from inquiring about an applicant's workers' compensation history. Furthermore, failing to let an employee who is on injury-related workers' compensation return to work, or not accommodating him or her, could lead to lawsuits under ADA.

For workers' compensation to cover an injury or work-related illness, the worker must only prove that it arose while on the job. It does not matter if the worker was at fault. For example, suppose you instruct all employees to wear safety goggles when at their machines. One worker does not and experiences an eye injury on the job. The company must still provide workers' compensation benefits.

Controlling Workers' Compensation Costs   It is important to control workers' compensation claims and costs. The employer's insurance company usually pays the claim, but the costs of the employer's premiums reflect the amount of claims.

There are several ways to reduce claims. Screen out accident-prone workers. Reduce accident-causing conditions in your facilities. And reduce the accidents and health problems that trigger these claims—for instance, by instituting effective safety and health programs. Furthermore, although many workers' compensation claims are legitimate, some are not. Red flags include vague accident details, lack of witnesses, and late reporting.[97]

Case management is popular. It refers to having people such as registered nurses assigned on a case-by-case basis to monitoring and coordinating the care an employee is receiving.[98]

Moving aggressively to support the injured employee and to get him or her back to work quickly is important. Many firms have rehabilitation programs, such as physical therapy, to help get claim recipients back to work. The involvement of an attorney and the duration of the claim both influence the worker's claim cost.[99]

Hospitalization, Health, and Disability Insurance

Hospitalization, health, and disability insurance helps protect employees against hospitalization costs and the loss of income arising from off-the-job accidents or illness.[100] Many employers purchase insurance from life insurance companies, casualty insurance companies, or Blue Cross (for hospital expenses) and Blue Shield (for physician expenses) organizations. Others contract with health maintenance organizations or preferred provider organizations. The employer and employee usually both contribute to the plan. Health insurance costs rose about 4% in one recent year, to a total of $15,745 for family coverage.[101] Table 11.5 lists some popular health-related benefits.

Most employer health plans provide at least basic hospitalization and surgical and medical insurance for all eligible employees at group rates. Insurance is generally available to all employees—including new nonprobationary ones—regardless of health or physical condition. Most basic plans pay for hospital room and board, surgery charges, and medical expenses (such as doctors' visits to the hospital). Some also provide "major medical" coverage to meet the medical expenses resulting from serious illnesses.

Table 11.5 Percentage of Employers Offering Selected Health Benefits

2015 Health Care and Welfare Benefits	
Dental insurance	96%
Prescription drug coverage	96%
Mental health coverage	91%
Mail-order prescription program	87%
Vision insurance	87%
Accidental death and dismemberment insurance (AD&D)	85%
Preferred provider organization (PPO)	85%
Contraceptive coverage	83%
Chiropractic coverage	81%
Long-term disability insurance	80%
Employee assistance program (EAP)	79%
Short-term disability insurance	74%
Medical flexible spending accounts	69%

Source: *2015 Employee Benefits*, SHRM, https://www.shrm.org/hr-today/trends-and-forecasting/research-and-surveys/Documents/2015-Employee-Benefits.pdf, accessed April 23, 2017.

Most employers' health plans also cover health-related expenses like doctors' visits, eye care, and dental services. Other plans pay for general and diagnostic visits to the doctor's office, vision care, hearing aids, and prescription drugs. *Disability insurance* provides income protection for salary loss due to illness or accident. Payments usually start when normal sick leave payments end. Disability benefits usually range from 50% to 75% of the employee's base pay if he or she is disabled.

Some employers offer membership in a **health maintenance organization (HMO)** as a hospital/medical insurance option. The HMO is a medical organization consisting of specialists, often operating out of a health care center. The HMO receives a fixed annual fee per employee from the employer (or employer and employee), regardless of whether it provides that person service.

Unlike HMOs, **preferred provider organizations (PPOs)** let employees select providers (such as doctors) from a relatively wide list and see them in their offices, often without gatekeeper doctor approval. The providers agree to certain controls, for example, on testing. Employers are shifting to PPOs.[102]

Mental Health Benefits Mental illnesses represent about 24% of all reported disabilities, more than injuries, respiratory diseases, cardiovascular diseases, and cancer combined.[103] Statistically, millennials are more likely to report being depressed. One expert suggests this might be partly because, while highly educated, they face a relative dearth of good jobs.[104]

Mental health costs are rising. Reasons include widespread drug and alcohol problems and an increase in states that require employers to offer minimum mental health benefits. The Mental Health Parity Act sets minimum mental health care benefits.[105]

health maintenance organization (HMO)

A prepaid health care system that generally provides routine round-the-clock medical services as well as preventive medicine in a clinic-type arrangement for employees, who pay a nominal fee in addition to the fixed annual fee the employer pays.

preferred provider organizations (PPOs)

Groups of health care providers that contract with employers, insurance companies, or third-party payers to provide medical care services at a reduced fee.

KNOW YOUR EMPLOYMENT LAW

The Evolving Patient Protection and Affordable Care Act of 2010

Under the Patient Protection and Affordable Care Act ("Obamacare"), employers with at least 50 full-time-equivalent employees must offer minimum levels of affordable health care coverage or pay a penalty. To be eligible, an employee must work at least 30 hours per week or a total of 130 hours in a calendar month.[106] The bill was signed into law by President Obama in 2010, and employers face a number of other deadlines under the act.[107] By 2018, employers with health care plans that cost more than the threshold the law sets (for instance, $27,500 for family coverage) have to pay a 40% tax on the amount of coverage over $27,500. Individual and group health plans that already provide dependent coverage must expand eligibility up to age 26.[108] Employers with 50 or more employees must either offer full-time employees coverage or risk paying an excise tax.[109] At one extreme, employers might offer a certain minimum level of insurance affordable to at least 95% of its full-time employees and dependents; or at the other extreme, not offer minimum essential coverage and pay a penalty of $167 per month for each full-time employee.

Under the law, each state (or, when necessary, the federal government) may run public health insurance exchanges—in effect, marketplaces for buying insurance. In part to discourage employers from dropping their health care plans and sending employees to the health exchanges, the law imposes fines of $2,000 per worker on any employer with more than 50 workers who doesn't offer a health insurance plan.

Because employers have to pay a 40% surcharge beginning in 2018 on health insurance plans exceeding $27,500 for a family (or $10,200 for an individual), many employers are moving to reduce their health care benefits, for instance by increasing employee copays and deductibles.[110] To avoid penalties that could reach $2,000 per employee, some employers are directing employees who qualify for Medicaid to sign up for it, instead of employer-supplied insurance.[111] Some employers are considering eliminating their health plans, or turning more full-time workers into part-timers working less than 30 hours per week.[112] About 43% of employers surveyed say their workers will have to pay more for their health care plans.[113] Other employers calculate that it may be cheaper to pay the penalty than supply the insurance.[114]

The Evolving Law   The Affordable Care Act (ACA) did not please everyone, and many Republican legislators in particular objected to it. For example, they say it entangles the federal government excessively in citizen's personal health matters, and that it provides excessive monetary subsidies to support the act's provisions. (Indeed, without a change, Obamacare premiums were projected to rise quickly).[115] Many insurance companies were leaving the exchanges by 2017.

An early Republican proposal in 2017 would have changed or eliminated many of the Affordable Care Act's core provisions, by allowing individual states to waive compliance with them. For example, before the Affordable Care Act, people with health problems often paid more for health insurance than did healthy people, and the Republicans' proposals would basically let insurers return to that system. It would also reduce federal funding for Medicaid programs and for parts of the Affordable Care Act that helped many middle-income people buy health insurance coverage.[116]

Congress's initial attempts to replace "Obamacare" failed to obtain sufficient support. With uncertainty surrounding the Affordable Care Act, many insurers were unsure they could continue to provide coverage.[117] (One early uncertainty was whether the administration might withhold the federal subsidies to insurance companies to insure people who couldn't afford their own insurance.)[118] However many employers were proceeding on the assumption that they would have to comply with the ACA.[119]

COBRA   The Consolidated Omnibus Budget Reconciliation Act (COBRA) requires most private employers to continue to make health benefits available to separated employees and their families for a time, generally 18 months after separation.[120] The former employee must pay for the coverage. Most important, you don't

Figure 11.3

Illustrative COBRA Compliance Checklist

Adapted from: www.cobra-plus.com/wp-content/themes/cobra-plus/images/constant/COBRAetup.pdf; COBRA Checklist, www.shrm.org/resourcesand tools/; COBRA record keeping checklist, BLR-Business and Legal Resources; and COBRA compliance checklist, http://brscobra.com/cobra-checklist, all accessed August 1, 2017. Copyright Gary Dessler PhD

Cobra to do list would include, for example:	✓ If Done
Complete COBRA services agreement with vendor.	☐
Complete COBRA census: who is covered, with their ages.	☐
Maintain records of those covered by group health plan.	☐
Notify all employees of their rights under COBRA.	☐
Monitor COBRA election periods.	☐
Document notification to qualified individuals if they are not eligible to continue coverage.	☐
Monitor COBRA election periods.	☐
Document all notifications (7 years).	☐
Receive signed COBRA election form.	☐
Maintain log of all inquiries received re COBRA.	☐
Track eligible individuals' COBRA payments.	☐
Notify insurers of cancellation of coverage.	☐
Notify qualified beneficiaries if they are not eligible for continued COBRA coverage.	☐
Mail COBRA qualifying event notice and election form to former employee.	☐
Maintain current addresses of those on COBRA.	☐
Maintain records of qualified COBRA beneficiaries.	☐
Terminate COBRA coverage.	☐

want separated employees to leave and be injured and then claim you never told them they could have continued their insurance. Therefore, new employees *must* acknowledge receiving an explanation of their COBRA rights. And, all separated employees should sign a form acknowledging that they received and understand those rights. (See Figure 11.3 for a checklist.)

Other Laws Other federal laws are pertinent. For example, among other things, the Employee Retirement Income Security Act (ERISA) of 1974 sets minimum standards for most voluntarily established pension and health plans in private industry.[121] The Newborn Mother's Protection Act of 1996 prohibits employers' health plans from using incentives to encourage employees to leave the hospital after childbirth after less than the legislatively determined minimum stay. Employers that provide health care services must follow the privacy rules of the Health Insurance Portability and Accountability Act (HIPAA) of 1974.[122] Employers must provide the same health care benefits to employees over the age of 65 that they do to younger workers, even though the older workers are eligible for federal Medicare health insurance.[123] ∎

Tools for Employer Health Care Cost Control

Employers are endeavoring to rein in health care costs.[124] First, it makes little sense to initiate cost cuts when employers are paying thousands or millions of dollars in erroneous claims. One survey found that although the industry standard for percentage of claims dollars paid in error was 1%, the *actual* percentage of claims dollars paid in error was 3.4%. So, setting standards for errors and then auditing all claims is crucial.[125] Beyond that, deductibles and copays are the low-hanging fruit in health care cost control. For example, at least 20% of employees were in high-deductible plans recently.[126]

Employers are taking other cost-control steps. *Consumer-driven health plans (CDHPs)* are high-deductible plans that give employees access to, for instance, a health savings account. (The Medicare Modernization Act of 2003 allows employers to establish tax-free health savings accounts [HSAs].)[127] After the employer, employee, or both deposit pretax (and thus tax-sheltered) pay in the employees' HSAs, employees or their families can use their HSA funds to pay for "low-dollar" (not catastrophic) medical expenses.[128] More employers are offering "mini" medical insurance plans with annual caps of about $2,000–$10,000 per year and correspondingly lower premiums.[129]

Some employers offer *defined contribution health insurance plans*. Like 401(k) pension plans, these defined contribution health insurance plans tie each employee's health care benefits to what he or she and the employer contributes, rather than providing health care benefits (for instance, hospital care limits) that are defined in advance.[130] Many employers are moving Medicare-eligible retirees from their company health insurance plans into private individual exchanges, thereby reducing their own administrative obligations while offering retirees more choices for less money.[131] The insurance exchanges are run by companies that include Mercer, Towers Watson, and Aon Hewitt.

Other employers are hiring "patient advocates," for instance, registered nurses who review employees' medications and (with the consultation of independent physicians) recommend reduced medication regimes.[132] Small firms are joining *benefits purchasing alliances,* banding together to purchase health care benefits. Other employers encourage *medical tourism*, which means asking employees to have non-urgent medical procedures abroad, where costs are lower.[133] About 19% of almost 600 employers surveyed had some form of health care plan *spousal exclusion policies*, such as excluding a spouse when similar coverage was available from the spouse's employer.[134] Employers are demanding insurers use *accountable care organizations* (ACO), special vendors who help insurers, health care providers, and others with the goal of improving costs and outcomes.[135] About 34% of employers with over 500 employees offer some type of on-site or nearby health clinics.[136] Also *make sure employees know the costs* of their medical benefits.[137] For example, periodically send a statement to each employee listing the employer's costs for each health benefit.

Outsourcing is important.[138] In one survey, 94% outsourced management of flexible spending accounts, 89% outsourced defined contribution plans, 72% outsourced defined benefit plans, and 68% outsourced the auditing of dependents.[139] The accompanying Profit Center feature shows how one employer cut costs.

◼ HR as a Profit Center

The Doctor Is on the Phone

With more than 12,000 employees in its health plan, Rent A Center was looking for a better way to get its employees the medical advice they required, while also reducing health plan costs. The company signed an agreement with Teladoc, Inc. Teladoc's doctors provide medical consultations over the phone. In the first 16 months the new telemedicine program was in effect, Rent A Center saved more than $770,000 in doctor and hospital visits and in employee productivity that would have been lost.

The program seems to be win–win. The Teladoc consultation is free to employees, compared to a $20 office copayment, and the doctors are available 24 hours per day, usually within 30 minutes. If necessary, they call in antibiotics prescriptions. And for Rent A Center, there's that extra $770,000 in their bottom line.[140]

⭐ Talk About It–4

If your professor has chosen to assign this, go to **www.pearson.com/mylab/management** to discuss the following questions. Would you recommend this program to your employer? Why?

Wellness Programs Employers' top health care priorities in one report were, "Offer incentives or disincentives to motivate sustained health care behavior change;" "Promote a culture of health in the workplace (e.g., healthy cafeteria, flexible schedules to allow time for physical activity);" and "Move to rewarding improved health results or outcomes."[141] In one study "employers who undertook prevention programs aimed at cardiovascular disease . . . reported an average 28% reduction in sick leave, [and] a 26% reduction in direct health care costs."[142]

Many employers therefore offer various preventive or wellness benefits services.[143] Some *link each employee's health care premiums* to his or her healthy behaviors.[144] *Clinical prevention* programs include things like mammograms and routine checkups. Walgreens owns companies that provide *on-site health care services* such as mammograms for employers.[145] *Health promotion and disease prevention* programs include seminars and incentives aimed at improving unhealthy behaviors.[146] Other wellness programs include obesity management, stress management, senior health improvement, and tobacco cessation programs.[147] Incentives, for instance, $50–$100, can boost wellness program participation, but may backfire.[148] Whirlpool gives nonsmoker discounts on health care premiums worth about $500. It suspended 39 workers it caught smoking outside the plant after claiming on their benefits enrollment forms that they were nonsmokers.

As a rule, experts advise against "punishing" employees for not participating in an employer's wellness programs (for instance one university had a monthly $100 nonparticipation fee). Similarly, financial incentives seem to be of limited value. What does work, to paraphrase one expert, is encouraging self-motivation, for instance through education and opportunities for wellness activities.[149] Corporate wellness program providers include vendors like Corporate Wellness Partners, Interactive Health, and Fitbit Inc.

Long-Term Care

With baby boomers in their 60s, long-term care insurance—for things like nursing assistance to former employees in their old age—is a key benefit. The Health Insurance Portability and Accountability Act of 1996 lets employers and employees deduct the cost of long-term care insurance premiums from their annual income taxes, making this more attractive.[150] Other insurance benefits for long-term care include adult day care, assisted living, and custodial care.

Life Insurance

group life insurance
Provides lower rates for the employer or employee and includes all employees, including new employees, regardless of health or physical condition.

In addition to hospitalization and medical benefits, most employers provide **group life insurance** plans. Employees can usually obtain lower rates in a group plan. And group plans usually accept all employees—including new, nonprobationary ones—regardless of health or physical condition.

In general, there are three key personnel life insurance policies to address: the benefits-paid schedule (the amount of life insurance benefits is usually tied to the employee's annual earnings), supplemental benefits (continued life insurance coverage after retirement, for instance), and financing (the amount and percentage the employee contributes).

Accidental death and dismemberment coverage provides a lump-sum benefit in addition to life insurance benefits when death is accidental, and benefits in case of accidental loss of limbs or sight.

Benefits for Part-Time and Contingent Workers

About 19 million people work part-time (less than 35 hours a week). Most firms provide holiday, sick leave, and vacation benefits to part-timers, and about 30% offer some form of health care benefits to them.[151] As noted, the Patient Protection and Affordable Care Act mandates such coverage.

■ HR and the Gig Economy

Gig Worker Benefits

Employers that want to offer gig workers benefits are often reluctant to do so. The problem is how to provide gig workers with benefits while maintaining their status as independent contractors not also entitled to things like payroll tax contributions.

The head of one such company, Handy (whose independent contractors go to people's homes to clean or make repairs), is trying to do something about it.[152] He is working with New York legislators to create legislation that would make it easier for employers to fund things like sick leave and portable benefits for his independent contractors, while keeping them as independent contractors.[153] Uber partners with Stride Health, a health care insurance marketplace that helps Uber drivers arrange for insurance they (not Uber) pay for themselves.[154] Several states, including Washington, California, New York, and New Jersey, as well as the federal government, have introduced gig worker benefits legislation.[155]

■ HR Tools for Line Managers and Small Businesses

Benefits and Employee Leasing

Many businesses—particularly smaller ones—don't have the resources or employee base to offer many of the benefits we've discussed in this chapter. That's one reason they turn to "employee leasing."

In brief, employee leasing firms (also called *professional employer organizations* or *staff leasing firms*) assume all or most of the employer's human resources chores. In doing so, they also become the employer of record for the employer's employees, by transferring them all to the employee leasing firm's payroll. The leasing firm thus becomes the employees' legal employer and usually handles employee-related activities such as recruiting, hiring (with client firms' supervisors' approvals), and paying taxes (Social Security payments, unemployment insurance, and so on).

Insurance and benefits are usually the big attraction. Even group rates for life or health insurance can be high when only 20 or 30 employees are involved. That's where leasing comes in. Remember that the leasing firm is now the legal employer. The employees are thus part of a larger insurable group, along with other employers' former employees. The small business owner may get insurance it couldn't otherwise afford.

As in dealing with all vendors, the manager should have a detailed agreement with the employee leasing firm. Define what the services will be; include priorities, responsibilities, and warranties.[156] Understand that if the leasing firm merges into another firm, the new parent may require you to change your systems once the contract period expires.[157]

✪ Talk About It–5

If your professor has chosen to assign this, go to **www.pearson.com/mylab/management** to discuss the following: Explain how you believe you'd react to having your employer switch you to a leasing firm, and why.

Retirement and Other Benefits

Social Security

When it comes to retirement, people often think first of Social Security. **Social Security** actually provides three types of benefits. The *retirement benefits* provide an income if you retire at age 62 or thereafter and are insured under the Social Security Act. The *survivor's* or *death benefits* provide monthly payments to your dependents regardless of your age at death, if insured under the act. Finally, there are *disability payments*. These provide monthly payments to employees who become disabled totally (and to their dependents) if they meet certain requirements. The Social Security system also administers the Medicare program, which provides health services to people age 65 or older. "Full retirement age" for nondiscounted Social Security benefits traditionally was 65—the usual age for retirement. It is now 67 for those born in 1960 or later.[158]

A tax on the employee's wages funds Social Security (technically, "Federal Old Age and Survivor's Insurance"). As of 2017, the maximum amount of earnings subject to Social Security tax was $127,200; the employer pays 7.65% and the employee 7.65%.[159]

Social Security
Federal program that provides three types of benefits: retirement income at the age of 62 and thereafter; survivor's or death benefits payable to the employee's dependents regardless of age at time of death; and disability benefits payable to disabled employees and their dependents. These benefits are payable only if the employee is insured under the Social Security Act.

Pension Plans

Pension plans provide income to individuals in their retirement, and just over half of full-time workers participate in some type of pension plan at work.

We can classify pension plans in three basic ways: contributory versus noncontributory plans, qualified versus nonqualified plans, and defined contribution versus defined benefit plans.[160] The employee contributes to the contributory pension plan, while the employer makes all contributions to the noncontributory pension plan. Employers derive certain tax benefits (such as tax deductions) for contributing to qualified pension plans (they are "qualified" for preferred tax treatment by the IRS); nonqualified pension plans get less favorable tax treatment.[161]

With **defined benefit plans**, the employee's pension is specified or "defined" ahead of time. Here the person knows ahead of time the pension benefits he or she will receive. There is usually a formula that ties the person's pension to (1) a percentage of (2) the person's preretirement pay (for example, to an average of his or her last five years of employment), multiplied by (3) the number of years he or she worked for the company. Due to tax law changes and other reasons, defined benefit plans now represent a minority of pension benefit plans.[162] However, due to the economic crisis, even younger employees now express a strong preference for defined benefit plans.[163]

Defined contribution plans specify ("define") what contribution the employee and employer will make to the employee's retirement or savings fund. Here the contribution is defined, not the pension. With a *defined benefit* plan, the employee can compute what his or her retirement benefits will be on retirement. With a *defined contribution* plan, the person only knows for sure what he or she is contributing to the pension plan; the actual pension will depend on the amounts contributed to the fund *and* on the success of the retirement fund's investment earnings. Defined contribution plans are popular among employers today due to their relative ease of administration, favorable tax treatment, and other factors. And **portability**—making it easier for employees who leave the firm prior to retirement to take their accumulated pension funds with them—is easier with defined contribution plans.[164]

pension plans
Plans that provide a fixed sum when employees reach a predetermined retirement age or when they can no longer work due to disability.

defined benefit pension plan
A plan that contains a formula for determining retirement benefits.

defined contribution pension plan
A plan in which the employer's contribution to employees' retirement savings funds is specified.

portability
Making it easier for employees who leave the firm prior to retirement to take their accumulated pension funds with them.

401(k) plan
A defined contribution plan based on section 401(k) of the Internal Revenue Code.

401(k) Plans The most popular defined contribution plans are based on section 401(k) of the Internal Revenue Code and called **401(k) plans**. The employee authorizes the employer to deduct a sum from his or her paycheck before taxes and to invest it in the savings in his or her 401(k). The deduction is pretax, so the employee pays no tax on those dollars until after he or she retires—or removes the money from the 401(k) plan. The person can decide to deduct any amount up to the legal IRS maximum (now about $15,000). The employer arranges, usually with an investment company such as Fidelity Investments, to administer the 401(k) plan and to make investment options available to the plan.[165]

Employers must choose their 401(k) providers with care. The employer has a fiduciary responsibility to its employees; it must monitor the fund and its administration.[166]

savings and thrift plan

Plan in which employees contribute a portion of their earnings to a fund; the employer usually matches this contribution in whole or in part.

Other Plans The 401(k) plan is one example of a **savings and thrift plan**.[167] In any savings and thrift plan, employees contribute a portion of their earnings to a fund, and the employer usually matches this contribution completely or in part. An **employee stock ownership plan (ESOP)** is a qualified, tax-deductible defined contribution plan in which employers contribute stock to a trust for eventual use by employees who retire.

employee stock ownership plan (ESOP)

A qualified, tax-deductible stock bonus plan in which employers contribute stock to a trust for eventual use by employees.

One problem with *defined benefits* plans is that to get your maximum pension, you generally must stay with your employer until retirement—the formula, recall, includes years with the employer. With *defined contribution* plans, your pension is more portable—you can leave with it at any time, perhaps rolling it into your next employer's pension plan. Without delving into all the details, **cash balance plans** are a hybrid; they have defined benefit plans' more predictable benefits with defined contribution plans' portability advantages.[168] The employer contributes a percentage of employees' current pay to the employees' pension plans every year, and employees earn interest on this amount.[169]

cash balance plans

Defined benefit plans under which the employer contributes a percentage of employees' current pay to employees' pension plans every year, and employees earn interest on this amount.

KNOW YOUR EMPLOYMENT LAW
Pension Planning and the Law

As a rule, it is impossible to formulate a plan without expert help.[170]

The **Employee Retirement Income Security Act (ERISA) of 1975** is the basic law. It requires that employers have written pension plan documents and adhere to guidelines, such as regarding who is eligible for the employer's plan.[171] ERISA protects the employer's pension or health plans' assets by requiring that those who control the plans act responsibly, in the interest of participants and beneficiaries. Employers (and employees) want their pension contributions to be "qualified," or tax deductible, so they must adhere to the pertinent *income tax codes*. Under *labor relations laws*, the employer must let its unions participate in pension plan administration. The Job Creation and Worker Assistance Act provides guidelines regarding what rates of return employers should use in computing their pension plan values. ■

Employee Retirement Income Security Act (ERISA) of 1975

Signed into law by President Ford in 1974 to require that pension rights be vested and protected by a government agency, the PBGC.

PBGC Thousands of benefits plans are underfunded.[172] ERISA established the **Pension Benefits Guarantee Corporation (PBGC)** to oversee and insure a pension if a plan terminates without sufficient funds. However, the PBGC guarantees only defined benefit plans, not defined contribution plans. And it will only pay a pension of up to $64,432 per year for someone 65 years of age with a plan terminating as of 2017.[173]

Pension Benefits Guarantee Corporation (PBGC)

Established under ERISA to ensure that pensions meet vesting obligations; also insures pensions should a plan terminate without sufficient funds to meet its vested obligations.

Vesting *Vested funds* are the money employer and employee have placed in the latter's pension fund that cannot be forfeited for any reason. The *employees'* contributions are always theirs. Under ERISA, *employers* can choose one of two minimum vesting schedules (employers can allow funds to vest faster if they wish). With *cliff vesting*, the period for acquiring a nonforfeitable right to employer matching contributions (if any) is three years. With the second (*graded vesting*) option, pension plan participants must receive nonforfeitable rights to the matching contributions as follows: 20% after two years, and then 20% for each succeeding year, with a 100% nonforfeitable right by the end of six years.

Pensions and Early Retirement

early retirement window
A type of offering by which employees are encouraged to retire early, the incentive being liberal pension benefits plus perhaps a cash payment.

To trim their workforces or for other reasons, some employers encourage employees to retire early. Many such plans take the form of **early retirement window** arrangements for specific employees (often age 50). The "window" means that for a limited time, the employees can retire early. The financial incentive is generally a combination of improved pension benefits plus a cash payment.

Early retirement programs can backfire. When Verizon Communications offered enhanced pension benefits to encourage what it hoped would be 12,000 employees to retire, more than 21,000 took the plan. Verizon had to replace 16,000 managers.[174]

Discrimination is the other potential problem. Unless structured properly, older employees can challenge early retirement programs as de facto ways for forcing them to retire against their will.

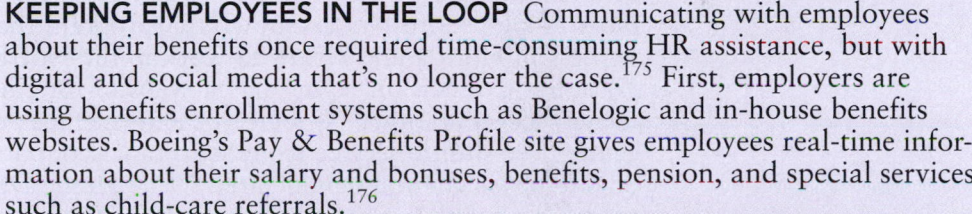

TRENDS SHAPING HR: *Digital and Social Media*

KEEPING EMPLOYEES IN THE LOOP Communicating with employees about their benefits once required time-consuming HR assistance, but with digital and social media that's no longer the case.[175] First, employers are using benefits enrollment systems such as Benelogic and in-house benefits websites. Boeing's Pay & Benefits Profile site gives employees real-time information about their salary and bonuses, benefits, pension, and special services such as child-care referrals.[176]

Others are using their Twitter feeds to keep employees up-to-date. Some use their company blogs to communicate employee perks and benefits, or their Facebook and LinkedIn pages to publicize their benefits to a wider audience. Siemens created an intranet-based social media site for its 13,000 UK employees. Among other things, Siemens uses it to keep its employees up-to-date about its latest benefits offerings, to run real-time employee surveys about Siemens benefits, and to remind employees about its various benefits.

To facilitate employee benefits self-management, other employers use mobile apps. For example, clients of Discovery Benefits Inc., a benefits administrator, reportedly logged in through its app about 25,000 times in one recent year, saving Discovery the time it would have spent dealing with call-ins.[177]

LEARNING OBJECTIVE 6
List and discuss the popular personal services and family-friendly benefits.

Personal Services and Family-Friendly Benefits

Time off, insurance, and retirement benefits account for the lion's share of benefits costs, but most employers also provide various personal services benefits.

Personal Services

"Personal services" benefits include employee assistance, educational subsidies, credit unions, and social and recreational opportunities.[178]

employee assistance program (EAP)
A formal employer program for providing employees with counseling and/or treatment programs for problems such as alcoholism, gambling, or stress.

Employee assistance programs (EAPs) provide advisory services, such as mental health counseling, personal legal and financial services, child- and elder-care referrals, and adoption assistance.[179] More than 60% of larger firms offer such programs. One study found that personal mental health was the most common problem addressed by EAPs, followed by family problems.[180] Most employers contract for the services with vendors such as Magellan Health Services and CIGNA Behavioral Health.[181]

In any case, everyone involved, including supervisors, secretaries, and support staff, must understand the importance of *confidentiality*. Also, ensure files are locked, access is limited and monitored, and identifying information is minimized. *Be aware of legal issues*. For example, in most states counselors must disclose suspicions of child abuse to state agencies. And ensure vendors fulfill *professional and state licensing requirements*.

Google, perennially one of the "100 best companies to work for," is famous for its personal services benefits. Google arranges with local vendors to provide on-Google site programs such as ATMs, mobile libraries, bike repair, car wash and oil change, dry cleaning, haircuts and salons, and organic grocery delivery.[182] Their on-site availability boosts employees' efficiency by reducing the need for them to seek services off-site.[183]

Other Job-Related Benefits

Employers provide various other job-related benefits.[184] More employers offer *elder-care services*. With more millennials caring for their baby boom parents, companies including Facebook, Deloitte, and Vanguard Group are instituting paid time off benefits to care for sick relatives.[185] CVS Caremark, seeking to retain older employees, offers a "snowbird" program that lets pharmacists spend their winters in Florida and return to work in the Northeast when it's warmer.[186] The National Council on Aging has a website for finding benefit programs: www .benefitscheckup.org.[187] Google's benefits include adoption assistance, a child-care center, free shuttle service from San Francisco, backup child-care assistance, and on-site physician and dental care.[188] The Home Depot offers a "nose to tail coverage" pet health insurance program. PriceWaterhouseCoopers helps its employees pay off student loans, and Yahoo transports its employees from home to office.[189]

Diversity Counts

Domestic Partner Benefits With *domestic partner benefits*, employees' same-sex or opposite-sex domestic partners are eligible to receive the same benefits (health care and so forth) as the husband, wife, or legal dependent of the firm's employees. For instance, Northrop Grumman Corp. extends domestic partner benefits to the salaried workers at its Newport News shipyard.

The Defense of Marriage Act provided that employers may not treat same-sex domestic partners the same as employees' spouses for purposes of federal law. However, in 2013, the U.S. Supreme Court struck down part of the Defense of Marriage Act. Under that ruling, gay couples married in states where it is legal must receive the same federal health, tax, Social Security, and other benefits heterosexual couples receive.[190] In 2013, the U.S. Labor Secretary announced that the spousal leave provisions of the Family and Medical Leave Act apply to married gay couples.[191] The U.S. Supreme Court has held that same-sex couples can marry nationwide.[192]

Family-Friendly/Work–Life Benefits

family-friendly (or work–life) benefits
Benefits such as child care and fitness facilities that make it easier for employees to balance their work and family responsibilities.

There are more households where both adults work, more one-parent households, more women in the workforce, and more workers older than age 55. Such facts have led many employers to bolster their **family-friendly (or work–life) benefits**.[193]

Subsidized Child Care For example, employers that want to reduce the distractions associated with finding reliable child care can help in various ways. Some

Employers that want to reduce the distractions associated with finding reliable child care can help in various ways. Some investigate day-care facilities.

Source: Rioblanco/123RF.

investigate day-care facilities and recommend certain ones to employees. Others, such as Google, set up company-sponsored and subsidized day-care facilities.

Sick Child Benefits To reduce unexpected absences, more employers are offering emergency child-care benefits, for example, when a young child's regular babysitter is a no-show. For many millennials, benefits like child care reportedly often trump higher pay. Netflix recently told employees they can take a year off for child care.[194]

Family-Friendly Benefits and the Bottom Line It's not easy to assess the "profitability" of such programs.[195] Many employers are reviewing (and often reducing) these benefits. Even Google, long known for benefits that blow most other employers away (free buses from the city, on-campus day care, and restaurants) has cut back a bit of late.

Executive Perquisites

Executive perquisites (perks, for short) usually go to only top executives. Perks can range from substantial (company planes) to relatively insignificant (private bathrooms). Others include *management loans* (which typically enable senior officers to exercise their stock options); *financial counseling*; and *relocation benefits*, often including subsidized mortgages, purchase of the executive's current house, and payment for the actual move. Publicly traded companies must itemize all executives' perks (if they total more than $100,000).

Flexible/Customized Benefits Programs

Employees prefer choice in their benefits plans. A recent survey by MetLife found that over 70% of employees surveyed said that benefits customized to their needs increased their loyalty to their employers, and were important when considering new jobs. [196]

flexible benefits plan/ cafeteria benefits plan

Individualized plans allowed by employers to accommodate employee preferences for benefits.

Employers traditionally refer to such plans as *cafeteria benefits plans*. (Pay specialists use **flexible benefits plan** and **cafeteria benefits plan** synonymously.) In such plans, the employer typically gives each employee a benefits fund budget and lets the person spend it how he or she prefers, subject to two constraints. First, the employer limits the total cost for each employee's benefits package. Second, each employee's benefits plan must include required items—for example, Social Security and workers' compensation. Employees can often make midyear changes to their plans if, for instance, their dependent care costs rise.[197] IRS regulations regulate such plans and require formal written policies, including benefits and procedures for choosing them.[198]

Cafeteria plans come in several varieties. For example, to give employees more flexibility in the benefits they use, about 70% of employers offer *flexible spending accounts* for medical and other expenses. This option lets employees pay for certain benefits expenses with pretax dollars (so the IRS, in effect, subsidizes some of the employee's expense).

Demographics tends to drive employees' benefits choices. For example, older employees may focus more on pensions, parents more on childcare, and family members more on critical illness benefits. Vendors such as Aon often work with employers to provide online platforms that make it easier for employees to make and adjust their benefits choices. [199]

Flexible Work Schedules Particularly in tight labor markets like Silicon Valley, flexible work scheduling enables employers to be competitive when recruiting top employees. [200] And with workers everywhere increasingly tackling work e-mails after hours, many want more flexible work schedules. In one survey, about 70% of surveyed employees called flexible work hours "very important." [201] Some say that inadequate schedule flexibility helps explain the gender pay gap and the fact that women have fewer top jobs. A new job search company (www.saywerk.com) hopes to change this. It negotiates with employers to provide flexible schedules for any jobs listed on its site. [202]

flextime
A plan whereby employees' workdays are built around a core of mid-day hours, such as 11:00 a.m. to 2:00 p.m.

Flextime is a plan whereby employees' workdays are built around a core of mid-day hours, such as 11:00 a.m. to 2:00 p.m. [203] Workers usually each determine their own starting and stopping hours, such as 8:00 a.m. to 4:00 p.m. In practice, the flextime usually gives an employee about 1 hour of leeway before 9:00 a.m. or after 5:00 p.m.

compressed workweek
Schedule in which employee works fewer but longer days each week.

Other employees such as airline pilots and hospital nurses don't work conventional five-day, 40-hour workweeks. Workers like these typically have **compressed workweek** schedules. They work fewer days each week, but each day they work longer hours, such as four-day workweeks with 10-hour days. [204]

For many employees the ultimate flextime schedule is not having to come to work at all. Gothenburg Sweden recently studied the effects of giving workers a five-day six-hour (instead of eight-hour) workday schedule. Most employees were very happy and more productive with their shorter workdays. The problem was it was too expensive. For the two-year study, the employer (a municipal retirement home) had to hire 17 new employees to cover the hours that the other employees were not working; this cost over $700,000 extra per year, too much to continue. [205] On the other hand, the head of Tower Paddle Boards in California decided that his company's culture was out of sync with its surfing brand, so he reduced his employees' work hours from eight hours to five. (Employees don't get a lunch hour, so the actual reduction is 2 hours, not 3). Employees have the same pay and job obligations, so they basically have to work faster and smarter, something they're apparently eager to do for a shortened workday. [206]

workplace flexibility
Arming employees with the information technology tools they need to get their jobs done wherever they are.

Workplace flexibility means providing the information technology tools (such as iPads) employees need to get their jobs done wherever they are by "telecommuting." [207] (See the accompanying HR as a Profit Center example.) On the other hand, Yahoo famously said it needed its employees "working side by side" and brought them back to the office from telecommuting. [208]

■ HR as a Profit Center

NES Rentals Holdings, Inc.

As at many employers, cost control is part of NES Rentals Holdings, Inc.'s strategy. NES supplies construction equipment, such as aerial lifts. [209] The question is: How can it cut employee costs while maintaining its great reputation?

NES sent its employees home. Today, three-fourths of the company's Chicago office customer support, collections, finance, and other back-office workers work from home ("telecommute") at least part of the week. [210] Productivity is up 20% and employee turnover is down. NES is also leasing less space. It estimates its total savings from its new telecommuting benefit at about $350,000 annually. Introducing an employee benefit turned out to be a smart way to support NES's strategy. [211]

⭐ Talk About It—6

If your professor has chosen to assign this, go to **www.mymanagementlab.com** to discuss the following question. Why do you think telecommuting worked for NES when it apparently had to be curtailed at Yahoo?

job sharing

Allows two or more people to share a single full-time job.

work sharing

Refers to a temporary reduction in work hours by a group of employees during economic downturns as a way to prevent layoffs.

Other Flexible Work Arrangements Job sharing allows two or more people to share a single full-time job, for example with one working mornings and the other afternoons. **Work sharing** refers to a temporary reduction in work hours by a group of employees during economic downturns as a way to prevent layoffs. Thus, 400 employees may all agree to work (and be paid for) only 35 hours per week, to avoid a layoff of 30 workers.

The accompanying HR Tools feature illustrates benefits small businesses can offer.

■ HR Tools For Line Managers and Small Businesses

"Costless" Small-Business–Friendly Benefits

Even without larger firms' resources, small-business owners can offer employees benefits that large employers often can't match. For example:[212]

- **Give extra time off.** For example, Friday afternoons off in the summer.
- **Offer compressed workweeks.** In the summer, offer compressed workweeks that let employees take longer weekends.
- **Give bonuses at critical times.** Small business owners are more likely to know what's happening in the lives of their employees. Use this knowledge to provide special bonuses, for instance, for a new baby.
- **Offer flexibility.** For example, "if an employee is having a personal problem, help him or her create a work schedule that allows the person to solve problems without feeling like they're going to be in trouble."[213]
- **Feed them.** Particularly after a difficult workweek or when, say, a big sale occurs, provide free meals occasionally, perhaps by taking your employees to lunch.
- **Make them feel like owners.** Endeavor to give your employees input into major decisions, let them work directly with clients, get them client feedback, share company performance data with them. Perhaps let them share in the company's financial success.
- **Make sure they have what they need to do their jobs.** Having highly motivated employees is only half the challenge. Also ensure they have the tools they need to do their jobs—for instance, the necessary training, procedures, computers, and so on.
- **Constantly recognize a job well done.** Capitalize on your day-to-day interactions with employees to "never miss an opportunity to give your employees the recognition they deserve."[214]

Simple Retirement Benefits

About 75% of large firms offer retirement benefits, while about 35% of small ones do.[215]

There are several special ways for small firms to provide employee retirement plans. The Pension Protection Act of 2006 provides for a new type of retirement benefit that combines traditional defined benefit and 401(k) (defined contribution) plans.[216] Available only to employers with less than 500 employees, it exempts employers from the complex pension rules to which large employers must adhere.[217]

Probably the easiest way for small businesses to provide retirement benefits is through a SIMPLE IRA plan. With the SIMPLE (for Savings Incentive Match Plan for

Employees) IRA, employers must (and employees may) make contributions to traditional employee IRAs. These plans are for employers or small businesses with 100 or fewer employees and no other retirement plan. The owner contacts an eligible financial institution and fills out several IRS forms. Banks, mutual funds, and insurance companies that issue annuity contracts are generally eligible.[218] The plan has very low administrative costs. Employer contributions are tax deductible. Each employee is always 100% vested.[219] A typical employer contribution might match employee contributions dollar for dollar up to 3% of pay. The financial institution usually handles the IRS paperwork and reporting.

⭐ Talk About It – 7

If your professor has chosen to assign this, go to **www.pearson.com/mylab/ management** to discuss the following: You own a small frozen yogurt shop and have five employees. Based on this feature and anything else you want to draw on from this chapter, give six specific examples of "costless" benefits or incentives you would use.

LEARNING OBJECTIVE 7
Explain how to use benefits to improve engagement, productivity, and performance.

Employee Engagement Guide For Managers
Costco's Compensation Plan

Hard as it is to compete with Walmart's low costs and prices, Costco's per store sales beat those of Walmart's Sam's Club. How does Costco stay ahead? Instead of keeping benefits and pay low like Walmart, Costco pays employees more. For example, Costco pays about 90% of its employees' health insurance costs.[220] This seems to produce higher employee engagement, productivity, and customer service.[221]

Costco doesn't use surveys to measure employee engagement; instead it tracks engagement by its "by-products," such as turnover and productivity.[222] By those criteria, Costco's engagement strategy seems to be working. Its sales per employee are about $500,000 a year versus $340,000 at Sam's Club.[223] Costco's turnover is far below the retail industry average, and employee retention is higher.[224] As Costco's CEO says, "I just think people need to make a living wage with health benefits."[225] Other large retail chains with excellent customer service, like Nordstrom and The Container Store, are also doing well financially, in part by treating their employees well.[226]

Costco treats its employees well, indeed. It pays its employees on average about $21 per hour, not including overtime, almost triple the $7.25 federal minimum wage.[227] That compares with Walmart's average wage for full-time employees in the United States of $12.67 an hour.[228] Costco's *starting* pay is $11.50 per hour, again far above the minimum wage.[229]

Costco's employee benefits are also highly competitive, particularly relative to the typically sparse offerings in the retail industry.[230] Costco not only offers a full range of employee benefits, but extends these benefits to employees' spouses, children, and domestic partners. Costco's employee benefits package includes the following:[231]

Health care: Full-time eligible employees may choose from two health care options, including one in which they may choose their own medical services, physicians, and facilities.

Dental care: These include two dental plans, a "core" dental plan, and a premium dental plan allowing more freedom of choice.

Pharmacy program: Most Costco warehouses have in-house pharmacies, and benefit-eligible employees have copays as little as $5 for generic drugs.

Vision program: Most Costco warehouses also have in-house optical centers, and the vision program pays up to $60 per eye exam, plus annual allowances for purchasing glasses and contact lenses.

401(k) plan: Costco matches employee contributions $0.50 on the dollar for the first $1,000 each year, to a maximum company match of $500 a year for most employees.

Dependent care assistance plan: All eligible Costco employees can derive tax savings under this plan by paying for child care and adult care with pretax dollars.

Care network: Costco employees and their families, from the first day of employment, can tap into this external network of professional counsellors, who are trained to help employees solve personal, work, or family challenges.

Voluntary short-term disability: In states where disability coverage isn't mandated, hourly employees who pass their 90-day probationary period after working at least 3 hours a week are automatically enrolled in short-term disability insurance.

Long-term disability: Costco provides long-term disability coverage at no cost for benefit-eligible employees.

Life insurance: Costco provides basic life insurance and accidental death and dismemberment policies at no cost for eligible employees.

To help employees get the most from these plans, they can go to www.costcobenefits.com/, for instance, to find physicians and other services in their areas. Costco also has an open-door policy that enables employees to get any concerns directly to top managers.[232] It's little wonder why its employee engagement—reflected in productivity and turnover—is excellent.

Review

MyLab Management

If your instructor is using MyLab Management, go to **www.pearson.com/mylab/management** to complete the problems marked with this icon ⭐.

Summary

1. Several incentive plans are particularly suited for individual employee incentives and recognition programs. With piecework, a person is paid a sum for each item he or she makes. Merit pay is a salary increase awarded to an employee based on his or her individual performance. Nonfinancial and recognition-based awards include employee recognition, gift certificates, and individual travel. Many employers use enterprise incentive management systems to automate their incentive plans. Incentives for salespeople are typically sales commissions. Most firms have annual bonus plans aimed at motivating managers' short-term performance. The actual award often depends on individual performance and organizational performance. Long-term incentives include stock options, "golden parachutes," and stock appreciation rights.

2. Team and organizationwide incentive plans are important. With team incentive plans, the main question is whether to reward members based on individual or team performance; both have pros and cons. Organizationwide incentive plans are plans in which all or most employees can participate. These include profit-sharing plans in which employees share in the company's profits; gainsharing plans engage employees in a common effort to achieve productivity objectives and thereby share in gains. Employee stock ownership plans are companywide plans in which the employer contributes shares of its own stock to a trust established to purchase shares of the firm's stock for employees.

3. *Benefits* are indirect financial and nonfinancial payments employees receive for continuing their employment with the company and include

health and life insurance, pensions, time off with pay, and child-care assistance.

4. Employers provide pay for time not worked and insurance benefits. Unemployment insurance provides benefits if a person is unable to work due to some fault other than his or her own. Sick pay provides pay to an employee when he or she is out of work because of illness. Cost-reduction tactics include repurchasing unused sick leave, or paid leave plans that lump sick leave, vacation, and holidays into one leave pool. The Family and Medical Leave Act requires larger employers to provide up to 12 weeks of unpaid leave for family-related issues. Severance pay is a one-time payment some employers provide when terminating an employee. Workers' compensation laws aim to provide sure, prompt medical benefits to work-related accident victims or their dependents, regardless of fault. Most employer health plans provide at least basic hospitalization and surgical and medical insurance for eligible employees. When an employee is terminated or terminates his or her employment, it is essential to make the person aware of his or her COBRA rights.

5. Regarding retirement, Social Security is a federal program that provides retirement income at the age of 62 and thereafter, as well as other benefits. Many employers make available pension plans; these provide an income when employees reach retirement age or can no longer work due to disability. Defined benefit plans contain a formula for determining retirement benefits, while defined contribution plans are plans in which the contribution to employees' retirement savings plans is specified. 401(k) plans are examples. The Employee Retirement Income Security Act of 1975 requires that employers have written pension plan documents and established the Pension Benefits Guarantee Corporation to oversee employers' pension plans. Key pension policy issues include membership requirements and testing.

6. Most employers also provide personal services and family-friendly benefits. These include credit unions, employee assistance programs, and subsidized child care and elder care. Flexible benefits or cafeteria benefits plans are individual plans that accommodate employee preferences for benefits. Some employers turn to employee leasing companies to capitalize on the advantage of the leasing firm's large employee base to get better employee benefits for their employees. Employers also are implementing flexible work schedules, including flextime, compressed workweeks, and other flexible work arrangements such as job sharing.

7. Costco's HR strategy is to deflect Walmart's low wages by paying employees more, thereby producing more employee engagement, higher productivity, and better customer service. As one example, Costco pays about 90% of the health insurance costs of its employees.

Key Terms

financial incentives   336
productivity   336
variable pay   336
piecework   336
straight piecework   336
standard hour plan   336
merit pay (merit raise)   337
annual bonus   342
stock option   343
golden parachute   344
team- (or group-) incentive plan   344
organizationwide incentive plan   345
profit-sharing plan   345
gainsharing plan   345
earnings-at-risk pay plan   346
employee stock ownership plan (ESOP)   346
benefits   346
supplemental pay benefits   347
unemployment insurance (or compensation)   347
sick leave   349

severance pay   351
supplemental unemployment benefits   351
workers' compensation   351
health maintenance organization (HMO)   353
preferred provider organizations (PPOs)   353
group life insurance   357
Social Security   359
pension plans   359
defined benefit pension plan   359
defined contribution pension plan   359
portability   359
401(k) plan   359
savings and thrift plan   360
employee stock ownership plan (ESOP)   360
cash balance plans   360
Employee Retirement Income Security Act (ERISA) of 1975   360
Pension Benefits Guarantee Corporation (PBGC)   360
early retirement window   361

employee assistance program (EAP) 362
family-friendly (or work–life) benefits 362
flexible benefits plan/cafeteria benefits plan 363
flextime 364

compressed workweek 364
workplace flexibility 364
job sharing 365
work sharing 365

Discussion Questions

11-1. Compare and contrast six types of incentive plans.

⭐**11-2.** What is merit pay? Do you think it's a good idea to award employees merit raises? Why or why not?

⭐**11-3.** You are applying for a job as a manager and are at the point of negotiating salary and benefits. What questions would you ask your prospective employer concerning benefits? Describe the benefits package you would try to negotiate for yourself.

11-4. What is unemployment insurance? Is an organization required to pay unemployment benefits to all dismissed employees? Explain how you would go about minimizing your organization's unemployment insurance tax.

11-5. Explain how ERISA protects employees' pension rights.

11-6. What is "portability"? Why do you think it is (or isn't) important to a recent college graduate?

11-7. What are the main provisions of the FMLA?

11-8. Describe the main retirement benefits.

Individual and Group Activities

11-9. Working individually or in groups, create an incentive plan for the following positions: chemical engineer, plant manager, used car salesperson. What factors did you have to consider in reaching your conclusions?

11-10. A state university system in the Southeast instituted a Teacher Incentive Program (TIP) for its faculty. Faculty committees within each university's colleges were told to award $5,000 raises (not bonuses) to about 40% of their faculty members based on how good a job they did teaching undergraduates and how many courses they taught per year. What are the potential advantages and pitfalls of such an incentive program? How well do you think it was accepted by the faculty? Do you think it had the desired effect?

11-11. Working individually or in groups, research the unemployment insurance rate and laws of your state. Write a summary detailing your state's unemployment laws. Assuming Company X has a 30% rate of annual personnel terminations, calculate Company X's unemployment tax rate in your state.

11-12. Assume you run a small business. Working individually or in groups, visit the website www.dol.gov/elaws. See the Small Business Retirement Savings Advisor. Write a one-page summary explaining (1) the various retirement savings programs available to small business employers, and (2) which retirement savings program you would choose for your small business and why.

11-13. You are the HR consultant to a small business with about 40 employees. The owner has asked you to prepare a one-page summary listing (1) the mandatory benefits the employer must provide, and (2) a strategy for figuring out what nonmandatory benefits the employer should also offer.

11-14. For this activity, you will need the documents titled (1) "HRCI PHR® and SPHR® Certification Body of Knowledge," and (2) "About the Society for Human Resource Management (SHRM) Body of Competency & Knowledge® Model and Certification Exams." Your instructor can obtain these two documents from the Pearson Instructor Resource Center and pass them on to you. These two documents list the knowledge someone studying for the HRCI or SHRM certification exam needs to have in each area of human resource management (such as in Strategic Management, and Workforce Planning). In groups of several students, do four things: (1) review the HRCI and/or SHRM documents; (2) identify the material in this chapter that relates to HRCI's or SHRM's required knowledge lists; (3) write four multiple-choice exam questions on this material that you believe would be suitable for inclusion in the HRCI exam and/or the SHRM exam; and, (4) if time permits, have someone from your team post your team's questions in front of the class, so that students in all teams can answer the exam questions created by the other teams.

MyLab Management

If your instructor is using MyLab Management, go to **www.pearson.com/mylab/management** for Auto-graded writing questions as well as the following Assisted-graded writing questions:

11-15. Describe the nature of some important management incentives.

11-16. In this chapter, we listed a number of guidelines for instituting a pay-for-performance plan. Do you think these points make sense? Why or why not?

APPLICATION EXERCISES

HR IN ACTION CASE INCIDENT 1

Striking for Benefits

Several years ago, the strike by Southern California grocery workers against the state's major supermarket chains was getting worse. Because so many workers were striking (70,000), and because of the issues involved, unions and employers across the country were closely following the negotiations. Indeed, grocery union contracts were set to expire in several cities, and many believed the California settlement—assuming one was reached—would set a pattern.

The main issue was employee benefits, and specifically, how much (if any) of the employees' health care costs the employees should pay themselves. Based on their existing contract, Southern California grocery workers had unusually good health benefits. For example, they paid nothing toward their health insurance premiums and paid only $10 copayments for doctor visits. However, supporting these excellent health benefits cost the big Southern California grocery chains over $4 per hour per worker.

The big grocery chains were not proposing cutting health care insurance benefits for their existing employees. Instead, they proposed putting any new employees hired after the new contract went into effect into a separate insurance pool and contributing $1.35 per hour for their health insurance coverage. That meant new employees' health insurance would cost each new employee perhaps $10 per week. And, if that $10 per week weren't enough to cover the cost of health care, then the employees would have to pay more, or do without some of their benefits.

It was a difficult situation for all the parties involved. For the grocery chain employers, skyrocketing health care costs were undermining their competitiveness; the current employees feared any step down the slippery slope that might eventually mean cutting their own health benefits. The unions didn't welcome a situation in which they'd end up representing two classes of employees, one (the existing employees) who had excellent health insurance benefits, and another (newly hired employees) whose benefits were relatively meager, and who might therefore be unhappy from the moment they joined the union.

Questions

11-17. Assume you are mediating this dispute. Discuss five creative solutions you would suggest for how the grocers could reduce the health insurance benefits and the cost of their total benefits package without making any employees pay more.

11-18. From the grocery chains' point of view, what is the downside of having two classes of employees, one of which has superior health insurance benefits? How would you suggest they handle the problem?

11-19. Similarly, from the point of view of the union, what are the downsides of having to represent two classes of employees, and how would you suggest handling the situation?

Source: Based on "Settlement Nears for Southern California Grocery Strike," by James F. Peltz and Melinda Fulmer from *Los Angeles Times*, February 26, 2004.

HR IN ACTION CASE INCIDENT 2

Carter Cleaning Company

The Incentive Plan

The question of whether to pay Carter Cleaning employees an hourly wage or an incentive of some kind has always intrigued Jack Carter.

His basic policy has been to pay employees an hourly wage, except that his managers do receive an end-of-year bonus depending, as Jack puts it, "on whether their stores do well or not that year."

However, he is considering using an incentive plan in one store. Jack knows that a presser should press about 25 "tops" (jackets, dresses, blouses) per hour. Most of his pressers do not attain this ideal standard, though. In one instance, a presser named Walt was paid $8 per hour, and Jack noticed that regardless of the amount of work he had to do, Walt always ended up going home at about 3:00 p.m., so he earned about $300 at the end of the week. If it was a holiday week, for instance, and there were a lot of clothes to press, he might average 22 to 23 tops per hour (someone else did pants) and so he'd earn perhaps $300 and still finish each day in time to leave by 3:00 p.m. so he could pick up his children at school. But when things were very slow in the store, his productivity would drop to perhaps 12 to 15 pieces an hour, so that at the end of the week he'd end up earning perhaps $280, and in fact, not go home much earlier than he did when it was busy.

Jack spoke with Walt several times, and while Walt always promised to try to do better, it gradually became apparent to Jack that Walt was simply going to earn his $300 per week no matter what. Though Walt never told him so directly, it dawned on Jack that Walt had a family to support and was not about to earn less than his "target" wage, regardless of how busy or slow the store was. The problem was that the longer Walt kept pressing each day, the longer the steam boilers and compressors had to be kept on to power his machines, and the fuel charges alone ran close to $6 per hour. Jack clearly needed some way short of firing Walt to solve the problem, since the fuel bills were eating up his profits.

His solution was to tell Walt that, instead of an hourly $8 wage, he would henceforth pay him $0.33 per item pressed. That way, said Jack to himself, if Walt presses 25 items per hour at $0.33, he will in effect get a small raise. He'll get more items pressed per hour and will therefore be able to shut the machines down earlier.

On the whole, the experiment worked well. Walt generally presses 25 to 35 pieces per hour now. He gets to leave earlier and, with the small increase in pay, he generally earns his target wage. Two problems have arisen, though. The quality of Walt's work has dipped a bit, plus his manager has to spend a minute or two each hour counting the number of pieces Walt pressed that hour. Otherwise, Jack is fairly pleased with the results of his incentive plan, and he's wondering whether to extend it to other employees and other stores.

Questions

11-20. Should this plan be extended to pressers in the other stores?

11-21. Should other employees (cleaner/spotters, counter people) be put on a similar plan? Why or why not? If so, how, exactly?

11-22. Is there another incentive plan you think would work better for the pressers? Describe it.

11-23. A store manager's job is to keep total wages to no more than 30% of sales and to maintain the fuel bill and the supply bill at about 9% of sales each. Managers can also directly affect sales by ensuring courteous customer service and by ensuring that the work is done properly. What suggestions would you make to Jennifer and her father for an incentive plan for store managers?

Experiential Exercise

Revising the Benefits Package

Purpose: The purpose of this exercise is to provide practice in developing a benefits package for a small business.

Required Understanding: Be very familiar with the material presented in this chapter. In addition, review Chapter 10 to reacquaint yourself with sources of compensation survey information, and come to class prepared to share with your group the benefits package for the small business in which you work or in which someone with whom you're familiar works.

How to Set Up the Exercise/Instructions: Divide the class into groups of four or five students. Your assignment is as follows: Maria Cortes runs a small personnel recruiting office in Miami and has decided to start offering an expanded benefits package to her 24 employees. At the current time, the only benefits are seven paid holidays per year and five sick days per year. In her company, there are two other managers, as well as 17 full-time recruiters and five secretarial staff members. In the time allotted, your group should create a benefits package in keeping with the size and requirements of this firm.

EMPLOYEE AND LABOR RELATIONS

Company's Strategic Goals

↓

Employee Competencies and Behaviors Required for Company to Achieve These Strategic Goals

↓

5 — Employee and Labor Relations

1 — Strategic and Legal Environment

2 — Planning, Recruitment, and Selection

3 — Training and Development

4 — Compensation and Total Rewards

HR Policies and Practices Required to Produce Employee Competencies and Behaviors

WHERE WE ARE NOW

Part 4 Compensation and Total Rewards explained how to provide employees with the equitable wages, salaries, benefits, and incentives that will hopefully motivate them to perform effectively and to stay with the firm. However, effective performance requires more than money. Now, in Part 5, we therefore turn to methods for creating a safe, fulfilling, and respectful work environment, including positive employee relations, fair and ethical treatment, productive union relations, and employee safety programs. In Part 5, Employee and Labor Relations, we will therefore cover

- Chapter 12, Maintaining Positive Employee Relations
- Chapter 13, Labor Relations and Collective Bargaining
- Chapter 14, Improving Occupational Safety, Health, and Risk Management

The concepts and techniques we'll study here in Part 5, Employee and Labor Relations, play an important role in strategic human resource management. As the accompanying HR Strategy Model shows, Strategic Human Resource Management means formulating and executing human resource policies and practices that produce the employee competencies and behaviors the company needs to achieve its strategic aims. Producing those required employee competencies and behaviors requires that the employer also provide employees with a safe, fulfilling, and respectful work environment. We'll therefore focus in Part 5 on how managers put in place the HR policies and practices that produce positive employee relations and a safe work environment.

12
Maintaining Positive Employee Relations

OVERVIEW:
In this chapter, we will cover . . .

- Employee Relations
- Employee Relations Programs For Building and Maintaining Positive Employee Relations
- The Ethical Organization
- Managing Employee Discipline
- Employee Engagement Guide For Managers

MyLab Management

⭐ Improve Your Grade!
When you see this icon, visit **www.pearson.com/mylab/management** for activities that are applied, personalized, and offer immediate feedback.

LEARNING OBJECTIVES

When you finish studying this chapter, you should be able to:

1. Define employee relations.
2. Discuss at least four methods for managing employee relations.
3. Explain what is meant by ethical behavior.
4. Explain what is meant by fair disciplinary practices.
5. Answer the question, "How do companies become 'Best Companies to Work For'?"

 Learn It

If your professor has chosen to assign this, go to **www.pearson.com/mylab/management** to see what you should particularly focus on and to take the Chapter 12 Warm Up.

INTRODUCTION

Enrique had worked as a waiter at a well-known all-night restaurant in the Coney Island section of Brooklyn, New York for several years. He enjoyed the job, but not the commute. Unless he left the restaurant promptly at 1:00 a.m., he'd miss his Q train connection to his home in Queens. Then, what should be a 45-minute train and bus ride would take him 2 1/2 hours. One night, two noisy out-of-town men sat down at one of his tables at about 12:45 a.m. When he explained he'd have to leave in 15 minutes, they objected loudly. Enrique's supervisor came over and told him he'd just have to stay until they finished their meal. That could keep him working until 2:00 A.M. Enrique followed his supervisor back to the kitchen and told him, "Let someone else take over; you know I have to get home." His supervisor smiled and said, "Enrique, if you don't like your job here, I know many people who would."

Source: Franek Strzeszewski/Getty Images.

LEARNING OBJECTIVE 1
Define employee relations.

Employee Relations

It's obvious to anyone who has worked for even a few days that some companies are better to work for than are others. Some companies we've touched on in this book—Wegmans, SAS, and Google, for instance—show up repeatedly on "Best Companies to Work For" lists, while others seem to always have labor problems and negative press. This commonsense observation reflects the fact that some companies do have better employee relations than do others.

Employee relations is the management activity that involves establishing and maintaining the positive employee–employer relationships that contribute to satisfactory productivity, motivation, morale, and discipline, and to maintaining a positive, productive, and cohesive work environment.[1] Whether you're recruiting employees, asking employees to work overtime, managing union organizing campaigns, or doing some other task, it obviously makes sense to have employees "on your side." Many employers therefore endeavor to build positive employee relations, on the sensible assumption that doing so beats building negative ones. Managing employee relations is usually assigned to HR and is a topic human resource management certification tests address.

employee relations
The activity that involves establishing and maintaining the positive employee–employer relationships that contribute to satisfactory productivity, motivation, morale, and discipline, and to maintaining a positive, productive, and cohesive work environment.

LEARNING OBJECTIVE 2
Discuss at least four methods for managing employee relations.

Employee Relations Programs For Building and Maintaining Positive Employee Relations

HR activities such as effective training, fair appraisals, and competitive pay and benefits (all of which we discussed in previous chapters) can go far toward building positive employee relations. However, most employers also institute special "employee relations programs." These programs include employee *fair treatment programs*, programs for improving employee relations through *improved communications*, *employee recognition/relations programs*, *employee involvement programs*, and having *fair and predictable disciplinary procedures*. We'll begin with how to ensure fair treatment.

Ensuring Fair Treatment

Unfair treatment at work is demoralizing. It reduces morale, poisons trust, increases stress, and negatively impacts employee relations and performance.[2] Employees of abusive supervisors are more likely to quit and to report lower job and life satisfaction and higher stress.[3] The effects on employees of such abusiveness are particularly pronounced where the abusive supervisors seem to have support from higher-ups.[4] Even when someone witnesses abusive supervision vicariously—for instance, by seeing a coworker being abused—it triggers adverse reactions, including further unethical behavior.[5] At work, **fair treatment** reflects concrete actions such as "employees are treated with respect," and "employees are treated fairly" (see Figure 12.1).[6]

fair treatment
Reflects concrete actions, such as "employees are treated with respect," and "employees are treated fairly."

Figure 12.1

Perceptions of Fair Interpersonal Treatment Scale

Source: "The Perceptions of Fair Interpersonal Treatment Scale: Development and Validation of a Measure of Interpersonal Treatment in the Workplace" by Michelle A. Donovan, *Journal of Applied Psychology*, 1998, Volume 83(5).

What is your organization like most of the time? Circle Yes if the item describes your organization, No if it does not describe your organization, and ? if you cannot decide.

IN THIS ORGANIZATION:

1. Employees are praised for good work	Yes	?	No
2. Supervisors yell at employees (R)	Yes	?	No
3. Supervisors play favorites (R)	Yes	?	No
4. Employees are trusted	Yes	?	No
5. Employees' complaints are dealt with effectively	Yes	?	No
6. Employees are treated like children (R)	Yes	?	No
7. Employees are treated with respect	Yes	?	No
8. Employees' questions and problems are responded to quickly	Yes	?	No
9. Employees are lied to (R)	Yes	?	No
10. Employees' suggestions are ignored (R)	Yes	?	No
11. Supervisors swear at employees (R)	Yes	?	No
12. Employees' hard work is appreciated	Yes	?	No
13. Supervisors threaten to fire or lay off employees (R)	Yes	?	No
14. Employees are treated fairly	Yes	?	No
15. Coworkers help each other out	Yes	?	No
16. Coworkers argue with each other (R)	Yes	?	No
17. Coworkers put each other down (R)	Yes	?	No
18. Coworkers treat each other with respect	Yes	?	No

Note: R = the item is reverse scored

There are many reasons why managers should be fair, including the golden rule. What may not be so obvious is that unfairness can backfire. For example, victims of unfairness exhibit more workplace deviance, such as theft and sabotage.[7] They also suffer a range of ill effects including poor health, strain, and psychological conditions.[8] Unfairness leads to increased tensions between the employee and his or her family or partner.[9] Abusive supervisors undermine their subordinates' effectiveness and may prompt them to act destructively.[10] In terms of employee relations, employees' perceptions of fairness correlate with enhanced employee commitment; enhanced satisfaction with the organization, jobs, and leaders; and enhanced organizational citizenship behaviors.[11]

A study illustrates the effects of unfairness. College instructors first completed surveys concerning the extent to which they saw their colleges as treating them with *procedural* and *distributive* justice. (**Procedural justice** refers to justice in the allocation of rewards or discipline, in terms of the procedures being even-handed and fair; **distributive justice** refers to a system distributing rewards and discipline in which *the actual results* or outcomes are even-handed and fair.) Procedural justice items included, for example, "In general, the department/college's procedures allow for requests for clarification or for additional information about a decision." Distributive justice items included, "I am fairly rewarded considering the responsibilities I have."

Then the instructors completed organizational commitment questionnaires, with items such as "I am proud to tell others that I am part of this department/college." Their students then completed surveys, with items such as "The instructor was sympathetic to my needs" and "The instructor treated me fairly."

The results were impressive. Instructors who perceived high distributive and procedural justice were more committed. Furthermore, these instructors' students reported higher levels of instructor effort, prosocial behaviors, and fairness, and had more positive reactions to their instructors.[12] So in this case, treating professors badly backfired on the university. Treating others fairly produced improved employee commitment and results.

The accompanying HR Practices Around the Globe feature shows how one employer in China improved the fairness with which it treated employees.

▉ HR Practices Around the Globe

The Foxconn Plant in Shenzhen, China

The phrase *social responsibility* tends to trigger images of charitable contributions and helping the homeless, but it actually refers to much more. For example, it refers to the honesty of the company's ads; to the quality of the parts it builds into its products; and to the honesty, ethics, fairness, and "rightness" of its dealings with customers, suppliers, and, of course, employees. The basic *social responsibility* question is always whether the company is serving all its constituencies (or "stakeholders") fairly and honestly. Corporate **social responsibility** thus refers to the extent to which companies should and do channel resources toward improving one or more segments of society other than just the firm's owners or stockholders.[13]

A worker uprising at Apple's Foxconn iPhone assembly plant in Shenzhen, China shows that workers around the globe want their employers to treat them in a fair and socially responsible manner.

After the uprising over pay and work rules at the Foxconn plant, Apple asked the plant's owner to have the Fair Labor Association (FLA) survey the plant's workers. The FLA found "tons of issues."[14] For example, employees faced "overly strict" product-quality demands without adequate training: "Every job is tagged to time, there are targets on how many things must be completed within an hour," said Xie Xiaogang, 22, who worked at Foxconn's Shenzhen plant. "In this environment, many people cannot take it."[15] Heavy overtime work requirements and having to work through a holiday week were other examples.

---

procedural justice
Refers to just procedures in the allocation of rewards or discipline, in terms of the actual procedures being even-handed and fair.

distributive justice
Refers to a system of distributing rewards and discipline in which the actual results or outcomes are even-handed and fair.

social responsibility
Refers to the extent to which companies should and do channel resources toward improving one or more segments of society other than the firm's owners or stockholders.

Hon Hai, the Foxconn plant's owner, soon changed its plant human resource practices, for instance, raising salaries and cutting mandatory overtime. Those changes were among 284 made by Foxconn after the audits uncovered violations of Chinese regulations.[16] The changes show that fair treatment is a global obligation.

⭐ Talk About It—**1**

If your professor has chosen to assign this, go to **www.pearson.com/mylab/ management** to discuss the following question. How would you explain the fact that workers in such diverse cultures as America and China seem to crave fair treatment?

Bullying Some workplace unfairness is subtle. For example, unstated policies requiring law firm associates to work seven days per week may unfairly eliminate working mothers from partner tracks. Other unfairness is blatant. For example, one survey of 1,000 U.S. employees concluded that about 45% said they had worked for abusive bosses.[17]

Unfortunately, bullying and abusiveness—singling out someone to harass and mistreat—is a serious problem. The U.S. government (www.stopbullying.gov/) says bullying involves three things:

- *Imbalance of power.* People who bully use their power to control or harm, and the people being bullied may have a hard time defending themselves.
- *Intent to cause harm.* Actions done by accident are not bullying; the bully has a goal to cause harm.
- *Repetition.* Incidents of bullying happen to the same person over and over by the same person or group, and that bullying can take many forms, such as:
  - *Verbal*: name-calling, teasing
  - *Social*: spreading rumors, leaving people out on purpose, breaking up friendships
  - *Physical*: hitting, punching, shoving
  - *Cyberbullying*: using the Internet, mobile phones, or other digital technologies to harm others

Undoubtedly, the perpetrator is to blame for bullying. However, how some people behave do make them more likely victims.[18] Those "more likely" include submissive

People who bully use their power to control or harm, and the people being bullied may have a hard time defending themselves.

Source: Purestock/Getty Images.

victims (who seem more anxious, cautious, quiet, and sensitive), provocative victims (who show more aggressive behavior), and victims low in self-determination (who seem to leave it to others to make decisions for them). High performers can earn colleagues' envy and thus suffer victimization.[19] Victims of abusive supervision will often suffer in silence because they fear retribution.[20] Building team cohesion through team-building training, social gatherings, and friendly inter-team competition can head off such envy and victimization.[21]

The employer and the manager are responsible for ensuring that the employee is treated fairly and with respect, and that its employees treat each other respectfully.[22] Techniques for minimizing unfairness (discussed in previous chapters) include hiring competent and well-balanced employees and supervisors, ensuring equitable pay, instituting fair performance appraisal systems, and having policies requiring fair treatment of all employees. Communications systems and employee involvement programs (discussed next) can also reduce unfairness and improve employee relations.

Improving Employee Relations Through Communications Programs

Many employers use communications programs to bolster their employee relations efforts. They do this, first, on the reasonable assumption that employees feel better about their employers when they're "kept in the loop" about what is happening. For example, one university's website says, "We believe in keeping our employees fully informed about our policies, procedures, practices and benefits."[23] This employer uses an *open-door policy* to encourage communication between employees and managers, an *employee handbook* covering basic employment information, and "the opportunity to keep abreast of University events and other information of interest through the *website, e-mail,* and *hard copy memoranda.*"[24]

To paraphrase one writer, no one likes getting complaints, but actively soliciting complaints is important for employers who want to find out what's bothering employees, and to short-circuit inequitable treatment and maintain positive employee relations.[25] Options include hosting employee *focus groups*, making available *ombudsman* and *suggestion boxes*, and implementing telephone and Web-based *hotlines*.

Some use hotline providers. A vendor sets up the hot lines for the employer, receives the employees' comments, and provides ongoing feedback to the employer about employees' concerns, as well as periodic summaries and trends. *Exit interviews* provide another opportunity to sample one's employee relations.[26] And supervisors can use open-door policies and "management by walking around" to informally ask employees "how things are going."

Using Organizational Climate Surveys   Employee attitude, morale, or climate surveys often play a part in employee relations efforts. Employers use the surveys to "take the pulse" of their employees' attitudes toward organizational issues such as leadership, safety, fairness, and pay, and to thereby get a sense of whether their employee relations need improvement. The dividing lines between attitude surveys, satisfaction or morale surveys, and climate surveys are somewhat arbitrary; several experts define **organizational climate** as the perceptions a company's employees share about the firm's psychological environment, for instance in terms of things like concern for employees' well-being, supervisory behavior, flexibility, appreciation, ethics, empowerment, political behaviors, and rewards.[27]

Many such surveys are available off the shelf. For instance, one SHRM sample survey has employees use a scale from 1 ("to a very little extent") to 5 ("to a very great extent") to answer questions such as, "Overall, how satisfied are you with your supervisor?", "Overall, how satisfied are you with your job?", and "Does doing your job well lead to things like recognition and respect from those you work with?"[28] Many employers use online surveys from firms like Know Your Company

organizational climate
The perceptions a company's employees share about the firm's psychological environment, for instance, in terms of things like concern for employees' well-being, supervisory behavior, flexibility, appreciation, ethics, empowerment, political behaviors, and rewards.

(http://knowyourcompany.com).[29] Google conducts an annual "Googlegeist" survey focusing on matters such as engagement and willingness to leave.[30] Other employers create specialized surveys. For example, we'll look at the FedEx Survey Feedback Action (SFA) program at the end of this chapter.

Develop Employee Recognition/Relations Programs

In addition to using two-way communications tools like climate surveys to help improve employee relations, employers use other methods.

Most notable are employee recognition and award programs like those we touched on in Chapters 10 and 11. For example, one trade journal notes how one employer, the Murray Supply Co., held a special dinner for all its employees, at which it gave out special awards for things like safe driving, tenure with the company, branch employee of the year, and companywide employee of the year.[31] As here, employers often distribute such awards with much fanfare at special events such as awards dinners. One SHRM survey found that 76% of organizations surveyed had such employee recognition programs, and another 5% planned to implement one within the next year.[32]

Instituting recognition and service award programs requires planning.[33] For example, instituting a *service award program* requires reviewing the tenure of existing employees and establishing meaningful award periods (one year, five years, etc.). It also requires establishing a budget, selecting awards, having a procedure for monitoring what awards to actually award, having a process for giving awards (such as special dinners or staff meetings), and periodically assessing program success. Similarly, instituting a *recognition program* requires developing criteria for recognition (such as customer service, cost savings, etc.), creating forms and procedures for submitting and reviewing nominations, selecting meaningful recognition awards, and establishing a process for actually awarding the recognition awards.

Use Employee Involvement Programs

Employee relations also tend to improve when employees get involved with the company in positive ways, and so *employee involvement* is another useful employee relations strategy.

Getting employees involved in discussing and solving organizational issues provides several benefits. Employees often know more about how to improve their work processes than anyone, so asking them is often the simplest way to boost performance. Getting them involved in addressing some issue will also hopefully boost their sense of ownership of the process. It may also signal to them that their opinions are valued, thereby contributing to better employee relations.

Employers use various means to encourage employee involvement. Some organize focus groups. A *focus group* is a small sample of employees who are presented with a specific question or issue and who interactively express their opinions and attitudes on that issue with the focus group's assigned facilitator.

TRENDS SHAPING HR: *Digital and Social Media*

SOCIAL MEDIA AND EMPLOYEE INVOLVEMENT Many employers use *social media* such as the photo-sharing website Pinterest to encourage involvement.[34] One survey found that just over half of employers use social media tools to communicate with employees and to help develop a sense of community.[35] For example, Red Door Interactive used a Pinterest-based project it called "San Diego Office Inspiration." This encouraged employees to contribute interior design and decor ideas for its new offices.[36]

suggestion teams

Temporary teams whose members work on specific analytical assignments, such as how to cut costs or raise productivity.

problem-solving teams

Teams that identify and research work processes and develop solutions to work-related problems.

quality circle

A special type of formal problem-solving team, usually composed of 6 to 12 specially trained employees who meet once a week to solve problems affecting their work area.

self-managing/self-directed work team

A small (usually 8 to 10 members) group of carefully selected, trained, and empowered employees who basically run themselves with little or no outside supervision, usually for the purpose of accomplishing a specific task or mission.

Using Employee Involvement Teams Employers also use teams to gain employees' involvement in organizational issues. **Suggestion teams** are temporary teams whose members work on specific assignments, such as how to cut costs or raise productivity. One employer, an airline, split employees such as baggage handlers and ground crew into separate teams, linking team members via its website for brainstorming and voting on ideas.[37] Some employers formalize this process by appointing semipermanent **problem-solving teams**. These teams identify and research work processes and develop solutions to work-related problems.[38] They usually consist of the supervisor and five to eight employees from a common work area.[39]

A **quality circle** is a special type of formal problem-solving team, usually composed of 6 to 12 specially trained employees who meet weekly to solve problems affecting their work area.[40] The team first gets training in problem-analysis techniques (including basic statistics). Then it applies the problem-analysis process (problem identification, problem selection, problem analysis, solution recommendations, and solution review by top management) to solve problems in its work area.[41]

In many facilities, specially trained teams of self-managing employees do their jobs with little or no oversight from supervisors. For many, such teams epitomize employee involvement. A **self-managing/self-directed work team** is a small (usually 8 to 10 members) group of carefully selected, trained, and empowered employees who basically run themselves with little or no outside supervision, usually for the purpose of accomplishing a specific task or mission.[42] The "specific task or mission" might be an Acura dashboard installed or a fully processed insurance claim. In any case, such teams have two distinguishing features. They are selected, trained, and empowered to supervise and do virtually all of their own work, and their work results in a specific item or service.

For example, the GE aircraft engine plant in Durham, North Carolina is a self-managing team-based facility. The plant's workers work in teams, all of which report to the factory manager.[43] In such teams, employees "train one another, formulate and track their own budgets, make capital investment proposals as needed, handle quality control and inspection, develop their own quantitative standards, improve every process and product, and create prototypes of possible new products."[44] As the vice president of another company said about organizing his firm around teams, "People on the floor were talking about world markets, customer needs, competitors' products, making process improvements—all the things managers are supposed to think about."[45]

Using Suggestion Systems Employee suggestion systems can produce significant savings and, through involvement and awards, improved employee relations. For example, one study several years ago of 47 companies concluded that the firms had saved more than $624 million in one year from their suggestion programs; more than 250,000 suggestions were submitted, of which employers adopted over 93,000 ideas.[46] Furthermore, employees like these programs. In one survey, 54% of the 497 employees surveyed said they made more than 20 suggestions per year, while another 24% said they made between 10 and 20 suggestions per year.[47] The accompanying HR in Practice feature provides an example.

■ HR in Practice

The Cost-Effective Suggestion System[48]

A Lockheed Martin unit in Oswego, New York developed what it called its "Cost-Effectiveness Plus" suggestion program to encourage and recognize employees for streamlining processes. With the Cost-Effectiveness Plus program, employees electronically submit their ideas. These are then evaluated and approved by the local manager and the program's coordinator (and by higher management when necessary). This particular program reportedly saves this facility about $77,000 per implemented idea, or more than $100 million each year.

Today's suggestion systems are more sophisticated than the "suggestion boxes" of years ago.[49] The main improvements are in how the manager formalizes and communicates the suggestion process. The head of one company that designs and installs suggestion systems lists the essential elements of an effective employee suggestion system as follows:[50]

- Senior staff support
- A simple, easy process for submitting suggestions
- A strong process for evaluating and implementing suggestions
- An effective program for publicizing and communicating the program
- A program focus on key organizational goals

⭐ Talk About It – 2

If your professor has chosen to assign this, go to **www.pearson.com/mylab/management** to discuss the following: Based on this, write a one-page outline describing an employee suggestion system for a small department store.

■ HR and the Gig Economy

Getting Gig Workers Involved[51]

Can an employer do anything to make short-term gig workers who are "just passing through" feel engaged in its activities? The answer, it seems, is "yes."

First, understand that (like everyone), gig workers each come to the job with his or her own set of needs. Most important, some gig workers are more "hobbyists," while others are in it full-time to support themselves and their families.

For example, one researcher interviewed Uber and Lyft drivers. He found that how the drivers reacted to things like pay cuts depended on why the drivers were driving. Many were not primarily driving for the money, but for social interaction and to relax from their full-time jobs. (For example, one full-time psychotherapist who earned over $100 per hour as a therapist wasn't too upset by Uber pay cuts. He was just happy to have a chance to unwind from 40 hours per week of helping people deal with their problems). Most such "hobbyist" drivers weren't financially dependent on driving. On the other hand, drivers who *were* more financially dependent on driving were understandably quite upset by the cuts.

In any case, here are several suggestions for improving gig-worker employee relations:

- Don't treat gig workers like they're disposable. Even if it's a short gig, communicate with the worker and get to know him or her. Recognize their contributions.
- Make signing on as frictionless as possible. Many gig workers are looking for part-time flexible gigs, and they want to work, not do paperwork.
- Research shows that most employers put little or no time into onboarding gig workers, which is a mistake: even an abbreviated onboarding-welcoming process is better than nothing. Put some time into giving them a brief background on your company and project, and on making them feel part (but clearly an independent-contractor part) of your business.
- Although it's important legally to make it clear that they are independent contractors, to the extent possible share company news and seek feedback from your gig workers, and include them in intracompany communications and, to the extent possible, in company social and educational events.

<table>
</table>

LEARNING OBJECTIVE 3
Explain what is meant by ethical behavior.

The Ethical Organization

People face ethical choices every day. Is it wrong to use a company credit card for personal purchases? Is a $50 gift to a client unacceptable? Compare your answers by doing the quiz in Figure 12.2.

Most everyone reading this book rightfully views themselves as an ethical person, so why include ethics in a human resource management book? For three reasons: First, ethics is not theoretical. Instead, it greases the wheels that make businesses work. Managers who promise raises but don't deliver, salespeople who say "The order's coming" when it's not, production managers who take kickbacks from suppliers—they all corrode the trust that day-to-day business transactions depend on.

Second, it is hard to even imagine an *un*ethical company with good employee relations.

Third, ethical dilemmas are part of human resource management. For example, your team shouldn't start work on the new machine until all the safety measures are checked, but your boss is pressing you to start: What should you do? One survey found that 6 of the 10 most serious ethical work issues—workplace safety,

---

The spread of technology into the workshop has raised a variety of new ethical questions and many old ones still linger. Compare your answers with those of other Americans surveyed, on page 401.

Office Technology

1. Is it wrong to use company e-mail for personal reasons?
☐ Yes   ☐ No

2. Is it wrong to use office equipment to help your children or spouse do schoolwork?
☐ Yes   ☐ No

3. Is it wrong to play computer games on office equipment during the workday?
☐ Yes   ☐ No

4. Is it wrong to use office equipment to do Internet shopping?
☐ Yes   ☐ No

5. Is it unethical to blame an error you made on a technological glitch?
☐ Yes   ☐ No

6. Is it unethical to visit pornographic Web sites using office equipment?
☐ Yes   ☐ No

Gifts and Entertainment

7. What's the value at which a gift from a supplier or client becomes troubling?
☐ $25   ☐ $50   ☐ $100

8. Is a $50 gift to a boss unacceptable?
☐ Yes   ☐ No

9. Is a $50 gift *from* the boss unacceptable?
☐ Yes   ☐ No

10. Of gifts from suppliers: Is it OK to take a $200 pair of football tickets?
☐ Yes   ☐ No

11. Is it OK to take a $120 pair of theater tickets?
☐ Yes   ☐ No

12. Is it OK to take a $100 holiday food basket?
☐ Yes   ☐ No

13. Is it OK to take a $25 gift certificate?
☐ Yes   ☐ No

14. Can you accept a $75 prize won at a raffle at a supplier's conference?
☐ Yes   ☐ No

Truth and Lies

15. Due to on-the-job pressure, have you ever abused or lied about sick days?
☐ Yes   ☐ No

16. Due to on-the-job pressure, have you ever taken credit for someone else's work or idea?
☐ Yes   ☐ No

Figure 12.2
The Wall Street Journal Workplace Ethics Quiz

Source: Ethics and Compliance Officer Association, Waltham, MA and the Ethical Leadership Group, Global Compliance's Expert Advisors, Wilmette, IL. (Printed in *The Wall Street Journal*, October 21, 1999, pp. B1–B4). © 1999 by Ethics and Compliance Officer Association. Reprinted by permission. All rights reserved.

employee records security, employee theft, affirmative action, comparable work, and employee privacy rights—were HR-related.[52] Another found that 54% of human resource professionals surveyed had observed misconduct ranging from violations of Title VII to violations of the Occupational Safety and Health Act.[53]

ethics
The study of standards of conduct and moral judgment; also the standards of right conduct.

Ethics are "the principles of conduct governing an individual or a group"—the principles people use to decide what their conduct should be.[54] Of course, not all conduct involves ethics.[55] For example, buying an iPad usually isn't an ethical decision. Instead, ethical decisions are rooted in *morality*. Morality refers to society's accepted standards of behavior. To be more precise, morality (and therefore ethical decisions) always involves the most fundamental questions of what is right and wrong, such as stealing, murder, and how to treat other people.

Ethics and Employee Rights

Societies don't rely on employers' ethics or sense of fairness or morality to ensure that they do what's right. Societies also institute various laws and procedures for enforcing these laws. These laws lay out what employers can and cannot do, for instance, in terms of discriminating based on race. In so doing, these laws also carve out explicit rights for employees. For example, Title VII of the Civil Rights Act gives employees the right to bring legal charges against an employer who they believe discriminated against them due to race.

Employee rights is thus part and parcel of all the employment laws we discuss in this book. For example, the National Labor Relations Act established the right of employees to engage in collective bargaining. And the Fair Labor Standards Act gave employees the right to a minimum wage and overtime pay.

The bottom line is that although ethics, fairness, and morality certainly help determine how employers treat their employees, remember that the enforceable rights embedded in employment law also govern what employers and employees can do.

What Shapes Ethical Behavior at Work?

Why do people do bad things? It's complicated. However one review of over 30 years of ethics research concluded that three factors combine to determine the ethical choices we make.[56] The authors titled their paper "Bad Apples, Bad Cases, and Bad Barrels." This title highlighted their conclusion that when

"Bad apples" (people who are inclined to make unethical choices) must deal with

"Bad cases" (ethical situations that are ripe for unethical choices) while working in

"Bad barrels" (company environments that foster or condone unethical choices), . . . then this mixture combines to determine whether someone acts ethically.

Here's a closer look at what they found.

The Person (What Makes Bad Apples?)

First, because people bring to their jobs their own ideas of what is morally right and wrong, each person must shoulder much of the credit (or blame) for his or her ethical choices.

For example, researchers surveyed CEOs to study their intentions to engage in two questionable practices: soliciting a competitor's technological secrets and making illegal payments to foreign officials. The researchers concluded that the CEOs' personal predispositions more strongly affected their decisions than did outside pressures or characteristics of their firms.[57] The most principled people, with the highest level of "cognitive moral development," think through the implications of their decisions and apply ethical principles. How would you rate your own ethics? Figure 12.2 (page 382) presented a short self-assessment survey (you'll find typical survey takers' answers on page 401). Furthermore, employees who identify more strongly with the organization are also more likely to engage in unethical actions to support it, so strong loyalty isn't always a blessing.[58] Similarly, employees who worry about being excluded from a group may support the group's unethical behavior just to stay in the group.[59]

Which Ethical Situations Make for Ethically Dangerous (Bad Cases) Situations?

But, it's not just the person but the type of decision that's important. For example, these researchers found that "smaller" ethical dilemmas prompt more bad choices. What determines "small"? Basically, how much harm can befall victims of the choice, or the number of people potentially affected. People seemed more likely to "do the wrong thing" in "less serious" situations, in other words. That obviously doesn't mean that some people don't do bad things when huge consequences are involved; it just means that people seem to cut more ethical corners when small things are involved. The problem is that one thing often leads to another; people start by doing small bad things and then "graduate" to larger ones.[60]

What Are the "Bad Barrels"?—The Outside Factors That Mold Ethical Choices

Finally, the study concluded that some companies produce more poisonous social environments ("outside factors" or "barrels") than do others; these bad environments in turn trigger unethical choices.[61] For example, companies that encouraged an "everyone for him or herself" culture were more likely to suffer from unethical choices. Those that encouraged employees to consider the well-being of everyone had more ethical choices. Most important, a company whose managers put in place "a strong ethical culture that clearly communicates the range of acceptable and unacceptable behavior" was associated with fewer unethical decisions in the workplace.[62]

Steps Managers Take to Create More Ethical Environments

Given this, here are some steps managers can take to create more ethical environments.

Reduce Job-Related Pressures If people did unethical things at work solely for personal gain, it perhaps would be understandable (though inexcusable). The scary thing is that it's often not personal interests but the pressures of the job. As one former executive said at his trial, "I took these actions, knowing they were wrong, in a misguided attempt to preserve the company to allow it to withstand what I believed were temporary financial difficulties."[63]

A study illustrates this. It asked employees to list their reasons for taking unethical actions at work.[64] For most of these employees, "meeting schedule pressures," "meeting overly aggressive financial or business objectives," and "helping the company survive" were the three top causes. "Advancing my own career or financial interests" ranked about last.[65] Reducing such "outside" pressures helps head off ethical lapses.

"Walk the Talk" It's hard to resist even subtle pressure from one's boss. So it's not surprising that according to one report, "the level of misconduct at work dropped dramatically when employees said their supervisors exhibited ethical behavior."[66] Examples of how supervisors lead subordinates astray ethically include:

- Tell staffers to do whatever is necessary to achieve results.
- Overload top performers to ensure that work gets done.

- Look the other way when wrongdoing occurs.
- Take credit for others' work or shift blame.[67]

Some managers also urge employees to apply a quick "ethics test" to evaluate whether what they're about to do fits the company's code of conduct. For example, Raytheon Co. asks employees who face ethical dilemmas to ask:

Is the action legal?

Is it right?

Who will be affected?

Does it fit Raytheon's values?

How will it "feel" afterward?

How will it look in the newspaper?

Will it reflect poorly on the company?[68]

Have Ethics Policies and Codes Managers use ethics policies and codes to signal that their companies are serious about ethics. For example, IBM's code of ethics says, in part:

> Neither you nor any member of your family may, directly or through others, solicit or accept from anyone money, a gift, or any amenity that could influence or could reasonably give the appearance of influencing IBM's business relationship with that person or organization. If you or your family members receive a gift (including money), even if the gift was unsolicited, you must notify your manager and take appropriate measures, which may include returning or disposing of what you received.[69]

Enforce the Rules Having rules without enforcing them is futile. Managers' statements and encouragement can reduce unethical employee behavior, but knowing that one's behavior is actually being monitored and the rules enforced is what has the biggest impact.[70] *Ethics audits* monitor things like conflicts of interest, giving and receiving gifts, employee discrimination, and access to company information.[71] One study found that fraud controls such as whistleblower hotlines, surprise audits, fraud training for employees, and mandatory vacations can each reduce internal theft by around 50%.[72] Firms, such as Lockheed Martin Corp., also appoint chief ethics officers.[73]

Encourage Whistleblowers Some companies encourage employees to use hotlines and other means to "blow the whistle" on the company when they discover fraud. Several U.S. laws, including Dodd Frank, the False Claims Act, the U.S. Financial Institutions Reform, Recovery, and Enforcement Act, and U.S. federal sentencing guidelines address whistleblowing.[74] Under the U.S. Securities and Exchange Commission's whistleblower program, whistleblowing awards aren't just limited to company employees. Consultants, independent contractors, vendors, and sometimes even internal audit and compliance personnel, working in the United States or abroad, are also eligible.

Foster the Right Culture[75] Managing people and shaping their behavior depends on shaping the values they use as behavioral guides. For example, if management really believes "honesty is the best policy," the actions it takes should reflect this value. Managers therefore have to think through how to send the right signals to their employees—in other words, create the right culture. **Organizational culture** is the "characteristic values, traditions, and behaviors a company's employees share." A *value* is a basic belief about what is right or wrong, or about what you should or shouldn't do. ("Honesty is the best policy" would be a value.) Creating a culture involves:

organizational culture

The characteristic values, traditions, and behaviors a company's employees share.

- *Clarifying expectations.* First, make clear what values you want subordinates to follow. For example, the IBM ethics statement makes it clear the company takes ethics seriously.
- *Using signs and symbols. Symbolism*—what the manager actually does—ultimately does the most to create and sustain the company's culture. As we said earlier, managers need to "walk the talk." They can't say "don't fudge the financials" and then do so themselves.
- *Providing physical support.* The physical signs of the manager's values—the firm's incentive plan, appraisal system, and disciplinary procedures, for instance—send strong signals regarding what employees should and should not do. For example, does the firm reward ethical behavior or penalize it?[76]

The accompanying HR Tools feature applies this to the small business.

■ HR Tools for Line Managers and Small Businesses

Small Business Ethics

When people think of unethical corporate behavior, big companies are usually in the headlines. Yet small and midsize enterprises are prone to the same unethical corporate behavior as big firms.

For example, one study of 20 small to midsize firms found that bribery, corrupt dealings, payoffs to local gangsters, and a general tone of dishonesty were all "business as usual" at many of these firms.[77] Some were clever about their corrupt dealings. When doing business abroad, one U.S. business tried to keep its hands clean by forming a "strategic alliance" with a local firm. The latter then did the dirty work, for example, handling the local bribes, while the U.S. firm's managers looked the other way.

There are several reasons why smaller firms should be particularly alert to unethical behavior. Small firms don't have the resources for ethics officers, ethics hotlines, or the ethics training that big firms have. Furthermore, having an unethical accountant in a billion-dollar firm embezzle $10 million is a nuisance. Having the sales manager of a $10 million firm walk off with $1 million cash could be the end.

Small business owners can take several steps to establish an effective ethics program. First, size up your company's current ethics-related activities.[78] Even a self-audit based on guidelines like those in this chapter (the availability of an ethics code, ethics training, internal controls to monitor ethical behavior, and so on) can be worthwhile. Second, create a code of conduct (Googling "code of conduct" will reveal thousands of examples) and make it clear that you take it seriously. Third, train your people. Training needn't be complicated. For example, one expert suggests having your managers develop scenarios, relevant to your business, illustrating which behaviors are ethical and which are not; then meet to discuss these. Fourth, make it easier to solicit feedback from your employees, so that they can more easily provide you with suspicions of unethical behavior. ("Open door" polices and anonymous suggestion boxes are examples.) And, perhaps most important, walk the talk. In a small business, the owner or CEO is so visible that employees will take their ethical signals from him or her.

⭐ Talk About It–3

If your professor has chosen to assign this, go to **www.pearson.com/mylab/management** to discuss the following: Create a 50-word ethics code for a small business like the one that Enrique, from the chapter opener, works at in Brooklyn. Then, explain how the owner might use an ethics code to help avoid the situation with Enrique from ever happening again.

Hire Ethical People One writer says, "The simplest way to tune up an organization, ethically speaking, is to hire more ethical people."[79] Start by using recruitment materials that emphasize your firm's commitment to ethics. Then use honesty tests, background checks, and interview questions (such as "Have you ever observed someone stretching the rules at work? What did you do about it?") to screen out those who may be problematic.[80] Finally, treat job applicants fairly. "If prospective employees perceive that the hiring process does not treat people fairly, they may assume that ethical behavior is not important in the company."[81]

Use Ethics Training Ethics training is basically mandatory. Since 1991, federal sentencing guidelines have prescribed reduced penalties for employers accused of misconduct who implement codes of conduct and ethics training.[82] The Sarbanes–Oxley Act of 2002 makes ethics training even more important.

Ethics training usually involves showing employees how to recognize ethical dilemmas, how to apply codes of conduct to resolve problems, and how to use personnel activities like disciplinary practices in ethical ways.[83] The training should emphasize the moral underpinnings of the ethical choice and the company's deep commitment to integrity and ethics. Include participation by top managers in the program to emphasize that commitment.[84]

Some employers are switching from packaged ethics training to more company-relevant customized programs. For example, Yahoo! had a vendor produce an animated package containing ethical scenarios set in Yahoo! company offices around the world. The 45-minute program covers Yahoo!'s code of conduct as well as issues like the Foreign Corrupt Practices Act.[85] Online ethics training tools include *Business Ethics for Managers* from SkillSoft (www.skillsoft.com).[86]

Use Rewards and Discipline Employees expect you to punish unethical conduct and to reward ethical conduct.[87] The employer should discipline executives, not just underlings, who misbehave.[88]

Institute Employee Privacy Policies[89]

Most employees probably view employers' invasions of their privacy as unethical. At work, employee privacy violations include *intrusion* (such as locker room and e-mail surveillance), *publication* of private matters, *disclosure* of medical records, and *appropriation* of an employee's name or likeness for commercial purposes.[90] In practice, background checks, monitoring off-duty conduct and lifestyle, drug testing, workplace searches, and workplace monitoring trigger most privacy violations.[91]

Workplace privacy is a growing challenge due to the proliferation of online and "smart" devices.[92] For example, a New Jersey court found one employer liable when one of its employees used his company computer at work to distribute child pornography.[93] Another employer gave employees iPods to use and found they were now clogging the firm's servers with illegal music downloads.[94] Security is a problem: One "4-gigabyte MP3 player, such as the first generation of iPod Mini . . . can take home a lot of corporate data," said one employer (a process some graphically describe as "podslurping").[95]

KNOW YOUR EMPLOYMENT LAW
Electronic Monitoring

Electronic Communications Privacy Act (ECPA)
The ECPA is a federal law intended to help restrict interception and monitoring of oral and wire communications.

What can the employer do to balance privacy concerns with its need to protect itself? There are two main restrictions on workplace monitoring: the **Electronic Communications Privacy Act (ECPA)**, and *common-law protections* against invasion of privacy (protections that have evolved from court decisions, for instance,

Figure 12.3

Sample E-Mail Monitoring
Acknowledgment Statement

I understand that XYZ Company periodically monitors any e-mail communications created, sent, or retrieved using this company's e-mail system. Therefore I understand that my e-mail communications may be read by individuals other than the intended recipient. I also understand that XYZ Company periodically monitors telephone communications, for example to improve customer service quality.

_____   _____
Signature   Date

_____   _____
Print Name   Department

decisions against defaming employees by publicizing personal matters about them without their permission). The ECPA is a federal law intended to help restrict interception and monitoring of oral and wire communications. It contains two exceptions. The "business purpose exception" permits employers to monitor communications if they can show a legitimate business reason for doing so. The second, "consent exception," lets employers monitor communications if they have their employees' consent to do so.[96]

Electronic eavesdropping is thus legal—up to a point. For example, federal law and most state laws allow employers to monitor employees' phone calls in the ordinary course of business. However, they must stop listening when it becomes clear the conversation is personal. You can also intercept e-mail to protect the property rights of the e-mail provider. However, court cases suggest employers may have fewer rights to monitor e-mail than previously assumed.[97]

To be safe, employers issue e-mail and online usage policies, which warn employees that those systems should be used for business only. Employers also have employees sign e-mail and telephone monitoring acknowledgment statements like that in Figure 12.3. Many employees probably assume that their communications using the corporate e-mail system are open to review, but that e-mails they send via the employer's system but using personal e-mail accounts such as Gmail aren't. However, that's not necessarily true. An attorney should review the company's e-mail policy, but, at a minimum, make it clear that employees should have no expectation of privacy in their e-mail and Internet usage.[98] Also emphasize that all messages sent and received on the employer's e-mail system are company property and not confidential.[99] Recommended employee monitoring best practices include not targeting a legally protected class, not monitoring in nonwork areas, being consistent in how you monitor and discipline employees, and getting legal advice before establishing the monitoring system.[100]

Videotaped workplace monitoring requires more caution. The employer should disclose that it is monitoring, and employees should acknowledge that in writing. Continuous video surveillance of employees in an office setting may not be a problem. However cameras are illegal under federal law in restrooms or clothing changing rooms.[101] A Boston employer had to pay over $200,000 to five workers it secretly videotaped in an employee locker room.[102] ▪

In one survey, 41% of employers with more than 20,000 employees had someone reading employee e-mails.[103] Ninety-six percent block access to adult websites and 61% to game sites.[104] Some check employees' personal blogs or Facebook sites to see if they're publicizing work-related matters.[105] But such broad monitoring can be a dilemma for employers, as the HR as a Profit Center feature illustrates.

■ HR as a Profit Center

Monitoring and Profits

Monitoring today obviously goes far beyond listening in on phone lines. New York's Bronx Lebanon Hospital uses biometric scanners to ensure that employees who clock in really are who they say they are.[106] Iris scanning tends to be the most accurate authorization device. Some organizations like the Federal Aviation Administration use it to control employees' access to its network information systems.[107] UPS uses GPS to monitor their truckers' whereabouts—and therefore productivity.[108] One restaurant in Dallas digitally monitors most everything waiters do, for instance, every ticket, dish, and drink that they process.[109] This makes it easier to track employee theft and also helps identify exceptionally conscientious waiters.

Such monitoring raises privacy issues.[110] But it can also boost profits. For example, when one employer noticed that employees were piling up overtime claims, they installed new software and discovered many employees were spending hours shopping online instead of working. To keep productivity up, the British grocery chain Tesco has some distribution center employees wear "Motorola arm-mounted terminals" (armbands) that keep track of how quickly employees are unloading and scanning goods.[111]

Physicians often say that "every medicine contains a little poison" because anything, even aspirin, becomes dangerous if misused. For employers, the dilemma is to obtain the profit advantages of monitoring, while minimizing the ethical and privacy issues that using it raises.

✪ Talk About It–4

If your professor has chosen to assign this, go to **www.pearson.com/mylab/management** to discuss the following questions. How would you feel if your employer told you to wear an armband monitor? Why? How would you react?

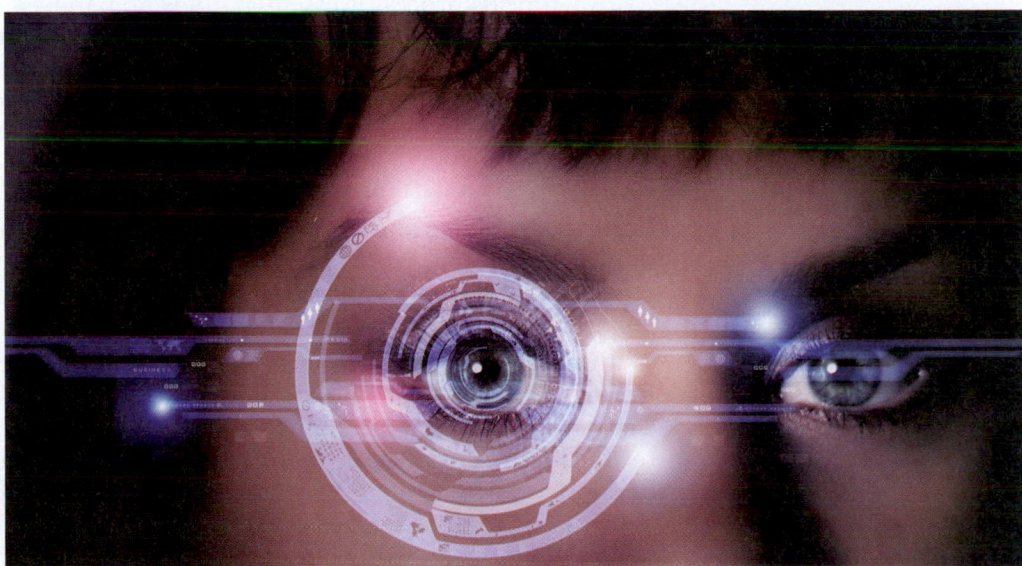

More employers are using iris scanning to verify employee identity.

Source: Sergey Nivens/123RF.

LEARNING OBJECTIVE 4
Explain what is meant by fair disciplinary practices.

Managing Employee Discipline

As we said earlier in this chapter, positive employee relations are best built on trust, and few personnel practices are more unethical or will undermine trust and employee relations more than will unfair, arbitrary disciplinary actions. The purpose of discipline is to encourage employees to adhere to rules and regulations. Discipline is necessary when an employee violates one of the rules.[112]

The Three Pillars of Fair Discipline

The manager builds a fair discipline process on three pillars: rules and regulations, a system of progressive penalties, and an appeals process.[113]

Rules and Regulations   An acceptable disciplinary process begins with a set of clear disciplinary rules and regulations. The rules should cover issues such as theft, destruction of company property, drinking on the job, and insubordination. Examples of rules include the following:

> *Poor performance is not acceptable.* Each employee is expected to perform his or her work properly and efficiently and to meet established standards of quality.
>
> *Alcohol and drugs do not mix with work.* The use of either during working hours and reporting for work under the influence of either are both strictly prohibited.

The purpose of the rules is to inform employees ahead of time what is and is not acceptable behavior. Tell employees, preferably in writing, what is not permitted. The employee orientation handbook should contain the rules and regulations.

Penalties   A system of progressive penalties is the second pillar of effective discipline. The severity of the penalty should depend on the offense and the number of times it has occurred. For example, most companies issue warnings for the first unexcused lateness. However, for a fourth offense, discharge is usual.

Appeals Process   Third, an appeals process should be part of the disciplinary process. The aim is to ensure that supervisors mete out discipline fairly. FedEx's *guaranteed fair treatment* multistep program illustrates this. We'll look at it in a moment.

An appeals process is essential but is no panacea. The employer can sometimes mitigate the effects of unfair discipline by catching it during an appeal. However, some supervisory behavior may be impossible to overcome. For example, actions that attack the employee's personal identity are difficult to remedy.[114]

Diversity Counts

Comparing Males and Females in a Discipline Situation   What several researchers sadly call the "Evil Woman Thesis" argues that when a woman doesn't act the way other men and women expect she should act, they treat her more harshly than they might if a man acted unexpectedly.[115]

Although such a thesis might seem ridiculous, the research seems to support it. In one study, 360 business school students reviewed a labor arbitration case. The case involved two employees, one male and one female, with similar work records and tenure with their employers. Both were discharged for violation of company rules related to alcohol and drugs. The case portrays one worker's behavior as a more serious breach of company rules: The more culpable worker (a male in half the study and a female in the other half) had brought the intoxicant to work. The students had to express their agreement with two alternative approaches (tough or not-so-tough) to settling the dispute that arose after the discharge.

Both the male and female students recommended harsher treatment for the "culpable" female employee in the case than they did for the "culpable" man. As the researchers conclude, "women, as decision makers, appear to be as willing as men to impose harsher discipline on women than upon men." One solution is knowing how to discipline, as explained in the following Skills feature.

BUILDING YOUR MANAGEMENT SKILLS:
How to Discipline an Employee

Even if you're a manager in a *Fortune* 500 company, you may find yourself without company guidelines when you have to discipline an employee for violating company rules. An error could trigger a costly appeal or even litigation. To help head off errors, fair discipline guidelines would include:[116]

- Make sure the evidence supports the charge of employee wrongdoing. Arbitrators often cite "the employer's evidence did not support the charge of employee wrongdoing" when reinstating discharged employees.
- Protect the employees' due process rights. Arbitrators normally reverse discharges and suspensions when the process that led to them is obviously unfair or violates due process.[117] For example, did the person have a chance to defend himself or herself?
- Warn the employee of the disciplinary consequences of his or her alleged misconduct. Have the employee sign a form as in Figure 12.4.
- The rule that allegedly was violated should be "reasonably related" to the efficient and safe operation of the particular work environment.

Apex Telecommunications Corporation
Report of Disciplinary Action and Warning

Employee's Name_____

Employee's Department_____

Date of Misconduct_____   Today's Date_____

Description of Incident and misconduct (including witnesses, if any)_____
_____
_____

Witnesses to Incident_____
_____
_____

If the misconduct violated an Apex Co. policy or rule, state the policy or rule_____
_____
_____

Employee's explanation for misconduct, if any_____
_____
_____

Disciplinary action taken, if any_____
_____
_____

The employee was warned today that if misconduct such as this reoccurs at any time during the next_____
weeks, he or she may be subject to the following disciplinary action _____
_____
_____
_____

_____   _____
Supervisor's signature   Employee's signature

_____   _____
Print name   Print name

Figure 12.4
Report of Employee Discipline

(Continued)

- Fairly and adequately investigate and confirm the matter before administering discipline.
- Apply applicable rules, orders, or penalties *without discrimination*.
- Maintain the employee's right to counsel. For example, all union employees generally have the right to bring a representative to an interview that they reasonably believe might lead to discipline.
- Don't rob your subordinate of his or her dignity, for instance by disciplining the person in public.
- Listen to what the person has to say.
- Remember the burden of proof is on you. In U.S. society, a person is considered innocent until proven guilty.
- Get the facts. Don't base your decision on hearsay evidence or on your general impression.
- Don't act while angry.
- Adhere to your company's disciplinary appeals process. Some firms also use an ombudsperson, neutral counselors to whom employees who believe they were treated unfairly can turn for advice.[118]

Discipline Without Punishment

Traditional discipline processes have two main drawbacks. First, no one likes being punished. Second, punishment tends to gain short-term compliance, but not long-term cooperation.

Discipline without punishment (or alternative or *nonpunitive discipline*) aims to avoid these drawbacks by reducing the punitive nature of the discipline. Steps include:[119]

1. *Issue an oral reminder for a first infraction.*
2. *Should another incident arise within six weeks, issue a formal written reminder, and place a copy in the employee's personnel file.* Also, hold a second private discussion with the employee.
3. *Give a paid, one-day "decision-making leave."* If another incident occurs in the next six weeks or so, tell the employee to take a one-day leave with pay, and to consider whether he or she wants to abide by the company's rules. When the employee returns to work, he or she meets with you and gives you a decision.
4. *If no further incidents occur in the next year or so, purge the one-day paid suspension from the person's file.* If the behavior is repeated, the next step is dismissal.

The process would not apply to exceptional circumstances. Criminal behavior or in-plant fighting might be grounds for immediate dismissal, for instance.

LEARNING OBJECTIVE 5
Answer the question, "How do companies become 'Best Companies to Work For'?"

Employee Engagement Guide For Managers

How Companies Become "Best Companies to Work For"

We began this chapter by noting that some companies are better to work for than are others, and we therefore focused on programs managers use to cultivate the positive employee relations that contribute to being a best place to work. This final section zeroes in on three companies that are known in part for actually being the best places to work.

The "Best Companies to Work For"

Each year, several organizations publish "Best Companies to Work For" lists, the most notable of which is probably "*Fortune* Magazine's 100 Best Companies to

Work For®."[120] Based on an extensive multinational survey of employees by the Great Place to Work® Institute (www.greatplacetowork.com), the survey seeks to identify the best companies to work for based on how the employees working in them actually feel about working there. The Institute defines a great workplace "as one where employees trust the people they work for, have pride in the work they do, and enjoy the people they work with."[121] They say that the companies on their great companies list "have the highest levels of trust, strongest evidence of employee engagement and demonstrate the best applied management practices and programs" as defined by the institute's proprietary models.[122] We'll look at three recent "*Fortune* Magazine's 100 Best Companies to Work For"—SAS, Google, and FedEx.[123]

SAS: Great Benefits, Trust, and Work–Life Balance

SAS, headquartered in Cary, North Carolina, is a leader in providing business analytics software and services to companies that include 90 of the top 100 companies on the *Fortune* global 500 list.[124] Founded in the 1970s, the company is privately owned and has long been known for its extensive benefits and for supporting its employees' work–life balance. It has annual revenues of over $2.3 billion and a worldwide workforce of over 14,000 people, about half of whom work at the company's North Carolina campus.[125]

When most people think about SAS employee relations, the first thing that comes to mind is the firm's extraordinary employee benefits. To paraphrase SAS's CEO, the firm's employees are happier and healthier because SAS' extensive benefits remove unnecessary distractions and stress.[126] Benefits include three to four weeks per year paid vacations; paid sick days; flexible work schedules; 11 paid holidays; competitive pay; company paid life insurance and accidental death and dismemberment insurance; retirement plans; medical, dental, and vision plans including on-site health care centers (at their Cary and Austin, Texas sites); an on-site recreation and fitness center; employee assistance programs; domestic partner benefits; paid paternity leave; and subsidized on-site child-care centers in Cary (based on seniority).[127]

In a larger sense, such benefits symbolize SAS's approach to employee relations. Many employers claim to "put employees first," but SAS has long done so. For example, as the 2008–2009 "Great Recession" was gaining speed, most employers were laying off employees. In January 2009, SAS's founder and CEO, Dr. Jim Goodnight, held a special global employee webcast. He announced that none of SAS's 13,000 worldwide employees would lose their jobs.[128] (SAS has reportedly never laid off an employee.)[129] SAS fosters trust in other ways, for instance by having the Great Place to Work Institute independently survey SAS workers on matters such as open communication, respect, career paths, and being treated as a human being.[130]

What does all this do for SAS? As one long-term employee put it, "I just can't imagine leaving SAS, and I felt that way for a very long time . . . if somebody offered to double my salary, I wouldn't even think about it."[131] Employee turnover, about 20% in software companies, is about 3% at SAS.[132] One person who has studied SAS estimates that the lower turnover alone saves SAS $60–$80 million a year.[133] And, of course, the effect on engagement, morale, and productivity is probably priceless.

Google: Happiness and People Analytics

When founders Larry Page and Sergey Brin began building Google, they wanted it to be a great place to work, so they turned to SAS. They met with SAS executives and sent a team there to study what made SAS a "Best Company to Work For."[134]

It's therefore probably not surprising that Google is one of the few employers whose benefits equal or exceed those at SAS. In addition to health care benefits and flexible work hours (and the possibility of making millions on stock options), its benefits include on-site dry cleaners, bowling alleys, cafés, transportation to and from campus, and nap pods.[135] As Google puts it, "It's all about removing barriers so Googlers can focus on the things they love, both inside and outside of work. We're constantly searching for unique ways to improve the health and happiness of our Googlers."[136]

Aside from its benefits, what sets Google apart is its scientific approach to deciding how to "improve the health and happiness" of Google employees.[137] At Google, maintaining positive employee relations isn't left to chance, but is highly analytical (one writer calls Google "The Happiness Machine").[138] Google calls its human resource department "People Operations" ("POPS"). Within "POPS," Google hired social scientists to create its People & Innovation Lab, with a Google "people analytics team" charged with finding out how to make Googlers happy.[139]

Google thus "monitors its employees' well-being to a degree that can seem absurd to those who work outside [Google's headquarters in] Mountain View [California]."[140] The social scientists run small experiments, for instance to determine if successful middle managers have certain skills, and what's the best way to remind people to contribute to their 401(k)s.[141] Once, the analytics team found new mothers were leaving at twice Google's average departure rate.[142] The study led to a redesigned maternity leave plan that includes five months off at full pay and full benefits. The new plan cut female Googler turnover in half.[143] To support its analytical approach, Google "solicits employee feedback on everything from how they prefer to be compensated, to the design of new bicycles used throughout the expansive headquarters campus."[144] So, it's little wonder why Googlers are happy.

FedEx: Guaranteed Fair Treatment

FedEx has been one of the "*Fortune* Magazine's 100 Best Companies to Work For" for 12 of the past 15 years. Several things—excellent benefits, competitive salaries, and (as we discussed in Chapter 5) a focus on promoting from within (as embodied by its Job Change Applicant Tracking System [JCATS]) help to explain this. For example, FedEx's corporate vice president for human resources began in customer service about 35 years ago and has had "many different careers," all "under the FedEx umbrella."[145] However, it may be FedEx's emphasis on building trust through communications that most sets it apart.

Survey Feedback Action (SFA) The FedEx survey feedback action (SFA) program is one example. SFA includes an anonymous survey that lets employees express feelings about the company and their managers and to some extent about service, pay, and benefits. Each manager can then use the results as a blueprint for improving workgroup commitment.[146]

SFA has three phases. First, the survey itself is an anonymous questionnaire given each year to every employee. The questions are designed to gather information about what helps and hinders employees in their work environment. Sample items include: "I can tell my manager what I think;" "My manager listens to my concerns;" "Upper management listens to ideas from my level;" "FedEx does a good job for our customers;" and "I'm paid fairly for this kind of work."

A workgroup's survey results are compiled and sent to the manager. To ensure anonymity, the smaller units don't receive their own results. Instead their results are combined with those of several other similar work units until a department head of 20 or 25 people obtains the overall group results.

The second phase is a feedback session between the manager and his or her workgroup. The goal here is to identify specific problems, examine causes for these problems, and devise plans to correct the problems. Managers ask probing questions. For example, suppose the low-scoring survey item was, "I feel free to tell my manager what I think." Managers are trained to ask their groups questions such as, "What do I do that makes my employees feel that I'm not interested?"

The feedback meeting should lead to a third, "action plan" phase. The action plan is a list of actions that the manager will take to address employees' concerns

An important part of SFA is a feedback session between the manager and his or her workgroup. The goal is to identify problems, examine causes, and devise plans to correct the problems.
Source: FangXiaNuo/Getty Images.

and boost results. It includes four main items: What is the concern? What's your analysis? What's the cause? and What should be done?

The FedEx Guaranteed Fair Treatment Process Many firms today (and virtually all unionized ones) have grievance processes. A grievance procedure helps ensure that every employee's grievance is heard and treated fairly, and unionized firms do not hold a monopoly on such fair treatment. Even in nonunionized firms, formal grievance procedures can help ensure that labor–management peace prevails.

FedEx's Guaranteed Fair Treatment Process (GFTP) is a sort of turbocharged grievance process because it goes beyond most grievance processes in several ways, most notably in that an appeal can go to the CEO. The effect is twofold: complaints don't get a chance to accumulate, and all managers think twice before acting unfairly because their actions may come to their boss's attention.[147] GFTP is available to all permanent FedEx employees. It covers concerns regarding matters such as disputed performance reviews, disciplinary actions and terminations affecting the individual complainant, and promotions or job changes for which employees feel they received inadequate consideration.[148]

Guaranteed Fair Treatment Process packets, available through HR, include a fact sheet listing the complainant's name and work history; a GFTP tracking sheet to keep track of the complaint at each step; instructions (for instance, in terms of applicable policies and procedures); a write-up from the HR department; and space for key documents (termination letters, and so on). There is also space for backup information including witness statements, medical statements, and training records. The employee must try to resolve the problem with his or her supervisor before filing a GFTP appeal.

STEPS GFTP contains three steps.[149] In step one, *management review*, the complainant submits a written complaint to a member of management (manager, senior manager, or managing director) within seven calendar days of the occurrence of the eligible issue. Then the manager, senior manager, and managing director of the employee's group review all relevant information; hold a telephone conference and/or meeting with the complainant; make a decision to either uphold, modify, or overturn management action; and communicate their decision in writing to the complainant and the department personnel represented.

If turned down in step one, then in step two, *officer complaint*, the complainant submits a written complaint to an officer (VP or senior vice president) of the division within seven calendar days of the step one decision. The vice president and senior vice president review all relevant information; conduct additional investigations, when necessary; make a decision to either uphold, overturn, or modify management action, or initiate a board of review; and communicate their decision in writing to the complainant with copies to the department's personnel representative and the complainant's management.

Finally, in step three, *executive appeals review*, the complainant submits a written complaint within seven calendar days of the step two decision to the employee relations department. This department investigates and prepares a GFTP case file for the appeals board executive review. The appeals board—the CEO, the COO, the chief HR officer, and senior vice presidents—then reviews all relevant information; makes a decision to either uphold, overturn, or initiate a board of review or to take other appropriate action; and generally does this within 14 calendar days of receipt of the complaint. Barring the formation of a separate board of review, the executive appeals board's decision is final.

A five-member *board of review* (if any) is used when there is a question of fact regarding the complaint. Two members are chosen by the complaining employee from a list of names submitted by the board chair. Three are selected by the board chair from a list of names submitted by the employee. Board chairpersons are chosen from the ranks of management at the director level or above.

A "Best Company" Human Resource Philosophy

SAS, Google, and FedEx are different from each other, and from other companies, and so there's no guarantee that what works for them will work for other firms. For example, SAS is privately owned. Its owners can therefore more easily absorb the short-term profit fluctuations that great benefits and no layoffs engender than can most other companies. Google has grown fast through a series of smart strategic moves, and when the economy turns down, its managers generally still have to focus more on retaining great employees than on laying them off. FedEx, still a "Best Company to Work For," has run into some labor relations problems recently, for instance litigation by drivers who don't want to be independent contractors.

However, at a minimum, there are several things that any manager intent on building positive employee relations can learn from studying any of these three companies. For example, their managers work hard to cultivate trust and to ensure—for instance by monitoring employees' attitudes and by instituting open-door and guaranteed fair treatment type grievance processes—that employees are treated fairly. And, in numerous ways (such as in their recognition programs, involvement programs, ethical standards, and climate surveys and other two-way communications programs), they all exhibit a deep and evident respect for their employees and to "putting employees first."

But perhaps the single most important thing a manager can glean from these three companies is the human resource philosophy on which they built their human resource management practices. In Chapter 1, we said that people's actions are always based in part on the basic assumptions they make, and that this is especially true in regard to human resource management. The basic assumptions you make about people—Can they be trusted? Do they dislike work? Why do they act as they do? How should they be treated?—together comprise your philosophy of human resource management. And every personnel decision you make—the people you hire, the training you provide, your leadership style, and the like—reflects (for better or worse) this basic philosophy.

One of the things molding your own philosophy is that of your organization's top management. While it may or may not be stated, it is usually communicated by their actions and permeates every level and department. Google's founders want their employees to be happy, and they've worked since Google's founding to make sure that they are. FedEx founder and CEO Frederick Smith is famous for (among many other things) his P-S-P mantra, namely that when you treat your People well, they will provide great Service, and Profits will follow (a mantra, as we've seen in this book, that it put into action through its Survey Feedback Action and Guaranteed Fair Treatment programs, promotion from within policy, Job Change Applicant Tracking System (JCATS), leadership evaluation process, extensive communications, and pay for performance programs).[150] Similarly, the founder and CEO of SAS has said, "We've worked hard to create a corporate culture that is based on trust between our employees and the company . . . a culture that rewards innovation, encourages employees to try new things and yet doesn't penalize them for taking chances, and a culture that cares about employees' personal and professional growth."[151] Such HR philosophies may well be the "magic sauce" that explains why great companies to work for are great.

Review

MyLab Management

If your instructor is using MyLab Management, go to **www.pearson.com/mylab/management** to complete the problems marked with this icon ⭐.

Summary

1. Employee relations is the activity that involves establishing and maintaining the positive employee–employer relationships that contribute to satisfactory productivity, motivation, morale, and discipline, and to maintaining a positive, productive, and cohesive work environment.

2. Managers and HR management can take steps to build positive employee relations. Unfair treatment reduces morale, increases stress, and has negative effects on employees and should be weeded out. Managers also use communications programs, recognition programs, and employee involvement programs to build positive employee relations.

3. Ethics refers to the principles of conduct governing an individual or a group and specifically to the standards you use to decide what your conduct should be. Numerous factors shape ethical behavior at work. These include individual factors, organizational factors, the boss's influence, ethics policies and codes, and the organization's culture. HR management can influence ethics and fair treatment at work in numerous ways. Having a fair and open selection process, establishing special ethics training programs, and rewarding (or disciplining) ethical (or unethical) work-related behavior are some examples.

4. The basic aim of discipline without punishment is to gain an employee's acceptance of the rules by reducing the punitive nature of the discipline itself. A fair and just discipline process is based on three prerequisites: rules and regulations, a system of progressive penalties, and an appeals process. A number of discipline guidelines are important, including that discipline should be in line with the way management usually responds to similar incidents, that management must adequately investigate the matter before administering discipline, and that managers should not rob a subordinate of his or her dignity.

5. There are several things that any manager intent on building positive employee relations can draw from studying "Best Companies to Work For" such as SAS, Google, and FedEx. Their managers work relentlessly to cultivate trust and to ensure that employees are treated fairly. In numerous ways they all exhibit a deep and evident respect for their employees and to "putting employees first." The human resource philosophy on which they seem to have built their human resource management practices emphasizes trust, respect, and caring about their employees' personal and professional growth.

Key Terms

employee relations   374
fair treatment   375
procedural justice   376
distributive justice   376
social responsibility   376
organizational climate   378
suggestion teams   380

problem-solving teams   380
quality circle   380
self-managing/self-directed work team   380
ethics   383
organizational culture   385
Electronic Communications Privacy Act
    (ECPA)   387

⭐ Try It

How would you go about applying the concepts and skills you learned in this chapter? If your professor has chosen to assign this, go to **www.pearson.com/mylab/management** and complete the Management and Ethics simulation to find out.

Discussion Questions

12-1. Discuss important factors that shape ethical behavior at work.

12-2. Discuss at least four specific ways in which HR management can influence ethical behavior at work.

12-3. Give examples of four fair disciplinary practices.

⭐12-4. Describe the similarities and differences between a program such as FedEx's Guaranteed Fair Treatment Process and your college or university's student grievance process.

12-5. Explain how you would ensure fairness in disciplining, discussing particularly the prerequisites to disciplining, disciplining guidelines, and the discipline without punishment approach.

⭐12-6. What techniques would you use as alternatives to traditional discipline? What do such alternatives have to do with "organizational justice"? Why do you think alternatives like these are important, given industry's current need for highly committed employees?

12-7. Discuss at least four specific HR tools managers use to influence ethical behavior at work.

12-8. Define *employee relations* and discuss at least four methods for managing it.

Individual and Group Activities

12-9. Working individually or in groups, interview managers or administrators at your employer or college to determine the extent to which the employer or college endeavors to build two-way communication, and the specific types of programs used. Do the managers think they are effective? What do the employees (or faculty members) think of the programs in use at the employer or college?

12-10. Working individually or in groups, obtain copies of the student handbook for your local college, and determine to what extent there is a formal process through which students can air grievances. Based on your contacts with students and others, has it been an effective grievance process? Why or why not?

12-11. Working individually or in groups, determine the nature of the academic discipline process in your college. Do you think it is effective? Based on what you read in this chapter, would you recommend any modifications?

12-12. You need to select a nanny for your or a relative's child, and want someone ethical. Working individually or in groups, what would you do to help ensure that you ended up hiring someone ethical?

12-13. Choose two companies, one (such as software firm SAS) that you believe is known for outstanding employee relations, and one that is known for less-harmonious employee relations. Using any sources available, write a two-page report laying out the factors that you think explain the differences between the two companies' approaches to employee relations.

12-14. For this activity, you will need the documents titled (1) "HRCI PHR® and SPHR® Certification Body of Knowledge," and (2) "About the Society for Human Resource Management (SHRM) Body of Competency & Knowledge® Model and Certification Exams." Your instructor can obtain these two documents from the Pearson Instructor Resource Center and pass them on to you. These two documents list the knowledge someone studying for the HRCI or SHRM certification exam needs to have in each area of human resource management (such as in Strategic Management, and Workforce Planning). In groups of several students, do four things: (1) review the HRCI and/or SHRM documents; (2) identify the material in this chapter that relates to HRCI's or SHRM's required knowledge lists; (3) write four multiple-choice exam questions on this material that you believe would be suitable for inclusion in the HRCI exam and/or the SHRM exam; and, (4) if time permits, have someone from your team post your team's questions in front of the class, so that students in all teams can answer the exam questions created by the other teams.

MyLab Management

If your instructor is using MyLab Management, go to **www.pearson.com/mylab/management** for Auto-graded writing questions as well as the following Assisted-graded writing questions:

12-15. Explain what is meant by ethical behavior.

12-16. What is *employee relations*? Why is it important, and what would you do to improve the employee relations in a company where relations were bad?

APPLICATION EXERCISES

HR IN ACTION CASE INCIDENT 1

Enron, Ethics, and Organizational Culture

For many people, Enron Corp. still ranks as one of history's classic examples of ethics run amok. Even 10 years after the fact, courts (including the U.S. Supreme Court) were debating the fates of one of Enron's top executives. During the 1990s and early 2000s, Enron was in the business of wholesaling natural gas and electricity. Rather than actually owning the gas or electric, Enron made its money as the intermediary (wholesaler) between suppliers and customers. Without getting into all the details, the nature of Enron's business and the fact that Enron didn't actually own the assets meant that its accounting procedures were unusual. For example, the profit statements and balance sheets listing the firm's assets and liabilities were unusually difficult to understand.

As most people know by now, it turned out that the lack of accounting transparency enabled the company's managers to make Enron's financial performance look much better than it actually was. Outside experts began questioning Enron's financial statements in 2001. In fairly short order, Enron's house of cards collapsed, and several of its top executives were convicted of things like manipulating Enron's reported assets and profitability. Many investors (including former Enron employees) lost all or most of their investments in Enron.

It's probably always easier to understand ethical breakdowns like this in retrospect, rather than to predict they are going to happen. However, in Enron's case, the breakdown is perhaps more perplexing than usual. As one writer said,

> Enron had all the elements usually found in comprehensive ethics and compliance programs: a code of ethics, a reporting system, as well as a training video on vision and values led by [the company's top executives].[152]

Experts subsequently put forth many explanations for how a company that was apparently so ethical on its face could actually have been making so many bad ethical decisions without other managers (and the board of directors) noticing. The explanations ranged from a "deliberate concealment of information by officers" to more psychological explanations such as employees not wanting to contradict their bosses, and the "surprising role of irrationality in decision making."[153]

But perhaps the most persuasive explanation of how an apparently ethical company could go so wrong concerns organizational culture. Basically, the reasoning here is that it's not the rules but what employees feel they should do that determines ethical behavior. For example (speaking in general, not specifically about Enron), the executive director of the Ethics Officer Association put it this way:

> [W]e're a legalistic society, and we've created a lot of laws. We assume that if you just knew what those laws meant that you would behave properly. Well, guess what? You can't write enough laws to tell us what to do at all times every day of the week in every part of the world. We've got to develop the critical thinking and critical reasoning skills of our people because most of the ethical issues that we deal with are in the ethical gray areas. Virtually every regulatory body in the last year has come out with language that has said in addition to law compliance, businesses are also going to be accountable to ethics standards and a corporate culture that embraces them.[154]

How can one tell or measure when a company has an "ethical culture"? Key attributes of a healthy ethical culture include:

- Employees feel a sense of responsibility and accountability for their actions and for the actions of others.[155]

- Employees freely raise issues and concerns without fear of retaliation.
- Managers model the behaviors they demand of others.
- Managers communicate the importance of integrity when making difficult decisions.

Questions

12-17. Based on what you read in this chapter, summarize in one page or less how you would explain Enron's ethical meltdown.

12-18. It is said that when one securities analyst tried to confront Enron's CEO about the firm's unusual accounting statements, the CEO publicly used vulgar language to describe the analyst, and that Enron employees subsequently thought doing so was humorous. If true, what does that say about Enron's ethical culture?

12-19. This case and this chapter both had something to say about how organizational culture influences ethical behavior. What role do you think culture played at Enron? Give five specific examples of things Enron's CEO could have done to create a healthy ethical culture.

HR IN ACTION CASE INCIDENT 2

Carter Cleaning Company

Guaranteeing Fair Treatment

Being in the laundry and cleaning business, the Carters have always felt strongly about not allowing employees to smoke, eat, or drink in their stores. Jennifer was therefore surprised to walk into a store and find two employees eating lunch at the front counter. There was a large pizza in its box, and the two of them were sipping colas and eating slices of pizza and submarine sandwiches off paper plates. Not only did it look messy, but there were also grease and soda spills on the counter and the store smelled from onions and pepperoni, even with the four-foot-wide exhaust fan pulling air out through the roof. In addition to being a turnoff to customers, the mess on the counter increased the possibility that a customer's order might actually become soiled in the store.

Although this was a serious matter, neither Jennifer nor her father felt that what the counter people were

doing was grounds for immediate dismissal, partly because the store manager had apparently condoned their actions. The problem was, they didn't know what to do. It seemed to them that the matter called for more than just a warning but less than dismissal.

Questions

12-20. What would you do if you were Jennifer, and why?

12-21. Should a disciplinary system be established at Carter Cleaning?

12-22. If so, what should it cover, and how would you suggest it deal with a situation such as the one with the errant counter people?

12-23. How would you deal with the store manager?

Experiential Exercise

The Discipline Dilemma

Purpose: The purpose of this exercise is to provide you with some experience in analyzing and handling employee relations and disciplinary situations.

Required Understanding: Students should be thoroughly familiar with the information provided in the following paragraph, and with our discussions in this chapter.

You are a midlevel manager working for the U.S. federal government. One of your subordinates has a long record of being difficult to deal with. In the most recent incident, after being warned on several occasions not to come in late, he again showed up 15 minutes late. You want to discipline this person. However, after reviewing the information on adverse actions and on related matters at www.opm.gov/er/, it's not clear to you whether you can discipline this person.

How to Set Up the Exercise/Instructions: Divide the class into groups of four or five students. Each group should answer the following questions:

12-24. Based on what the site says about adverse actions and performance-based actions, are you in a strong position to discipline or dismiss this employee or not?

12-25. What appeals processes are open to this person?

12-26. What employee relations-building techniques that we discussed in this chapter does the OPM use, according to its website?

Ethics Quiz Answers

Quiz is on page 382.

1. 34% said personal e-mail on company computers is wrong.
2. 37% said using office equipment for schoolwork is wrong.
3. 49% said playing computer games at work is wrong.
4. 54% said Internet shopping at work is wrong.
5. 61% said it's unethical to blame your error on technology.
6. 87% said it's unethical to visit pornographic sites at work.
7. 33% said $25 is the amount at which a gift from a supplier or client becomes troubling, while 33% said $50, and 33% said $100.
8. 35% said a $50 gift to the boss is unacceptable.
9. 12% said a $50 gift from the boss is unacceptable.
10. 70% said it's unacceptable to take the $200 football tickets.
11. 70% said it's unacceptable to take the $120 theater tickets.
12. 35% said it's unacceptable to take the $100 food basket.
13. 45% said it's unacceptable to take the $25 gift certificate.
14. 40% said it's unacceptable to take the $75 raffle prize.
15. 11% reported they lie about sick days.
16. 4% reported they take credit for the work or ideas of others.

13

Labor Relations and Collective Bargaining

OVERVIEW:
In this chapter, we will cover . . .

- The Labor Movement
- Employee Engagement Guide for Managers: Employee Engagement and Unionization
- Unions and the Law
- The Union Drive and Election
- The Collective Bargaining Process
- What's Next for Unions?

MyManagement Lab

⭐ Improve Your Grade!
When you see this icon, visit **www.pearson.com/mylab/management** for activities that are applied, personalized, and offer immediate feedback.

LEARNING OBJECTIVES

When you finish studying this chapter, you should be able to:

1. Briefly describe the U.S. labor movement.
2. Explain how employee engagement may affect unionization.
3. Discuss the nature of the major federal labor relations laws.
4. Describe the process of a union drive and election.
5. Discuss the main steps in the collective bargaining process.
6. Explain why union membership dropped and what the prospects are for the union movement.

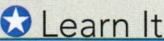 ⭐ Learn It

If your professor has chosen to assign this, go to **www.pearson.com/mylab/management** to see what you should particularly focus on and to take the Chapter 13 Warm Up.

Source: Rawpixel.com/Shutterstock.

INTRODUCTION

Melinda wasn't sure what to do. As the office manager for Avril Electronics, she thought that everyone in the office really liked working there. So when Jim came up to her and said he wanted to start a union at Avril, her first reaction was to tell him he'd better not. "I don't know, Jim. We're like a family here, and we don't need or want anyone working here who isn't happy."

LEARNING OBJECTIVE 1
Briefly describe the U.S. labor movement.

The Labor Movement

Today, almost 15 million U.S. workers belong to unions—about 11.1% of the total number of men and women working in America—and another 1.5 million are covered by union agreements but don't report being union members.[1] Almost 36% of public-sector workers belong to unions, including heavily unionized occupations such as teachers, police officers, and firefighters. In some private-sector industries such as utilities (22.3% unionization), transportation and warehousing (19.6%), and telecommunications (14.8%), it can still be hard to get jobs without joining unions. And unions today are successfully organizing "new media" firms like salon.com, Gawker Media, and Vice Media. (Soon after one Vice Media cofounder bought an expensive new home, its writers voted to join the Writers Guild of America, East.)[2] Unionization also varies widely by state, from a high of 24.6% in New York down to 1.9% in North Carolina.[3] So, unions are still a force in America.

Furthermore, don't assume that unions are always bad for employers. For example, perhaps by professionalizing the staff and systematizing company practices, unionization may actually improve performance. In one study, heart attack mortality among patients in hospitals with unionized registered nurses were 5% to 9% lower than in nonunion hospitals.[4]

We'll look at unions and dealing with them in this chapter.

Why Do Workers Organize?

Experts have spent much time trying to figure out why workers unionize, but there's no simple answer. Money certainly enters into it. For example, recent median weekly wages for union workers was $980, versus $776 for nonunion workers.[5] Union workers also generally receive more benefits—about $14.50 per hour in benefits compared with about $7.50 per hour for nonunion workers.[6]

But it's not just about money. The urge to unionize often seems to boil down to the belief on the part of workers that it is only through unity that they can get their fair share of the "pie" and also protect themselves from the arbitrary whims of management. The bottom line is that low morale, fear of job loss, and poor communication (in other words, poor employee relations) also foster unionization. One labor relations lawyer put it this way, "The one major thing unions offer is making you a 'for cause' instead of an 'at will' employee, which guarantees a hearing and arbitration if you're fired."[7] For example, a butcher hired by Walmart said his new supervisor told him he might be able to move up to supervisor. The butcher bought a car to commute, partly because he hoped to be promoted. But after he hurt his back at work, his supervisor never mentioned the promotion again. Feeling cheated, the butcher asked the Grocery Workers Union to send an organizer. The store's meat cutters voted to unionize. Walmart soon announced it would switch to prepackaged meats, and that its stores no longer needed butchers.[8] (See the Gig Economy feature for another example.)

■ HR and the Gig Economy

Will Uber Drivers Organize?

For many gig workers, feeling that they're at the employer's mercy may be the biggest downside of gig work. For example, low user ratings can lead to Uber summarily deactivating drivers, often with no appeal available. Would unionizing help?

Many Uber drivers think so. In New York City, for instance, pressure from drivers for more representation apparently prompted Uber to create a union-like entity known as the Independent Drivers Guild (IDG), in conjunction with the International Association of Machinists and Aerospace Workers union.[9] The IDG isn't really a union under the law. For instance, Uber itself funds the Guild, Uber drivers are independent contractors not employees, they didn't vote to have the Guild represent them, and the Guild itself agreed not to instigate strikes or to push for forming a union prior to 2021. On the other hand, the IDG has established a mechanism through which Uber drivers can appeal deactivations (staffed by other drivers and overseen by the American Arbitration Association) and also provides other types of driver assistance.[10]

★ Talk About It–1

If your professor has chosen to assign this, go to **www.pearson.com/mylab/management** to discuss the following questions. Based on your experience, do you think drivers like those for Uber, Via, and Lyft need union representation? Why?

LEARNING OBJECTIVE 2
Explain how employee engagement may affect unionization.

Employee Engagement Guide for Managers: Employee Engagement And Unionization

Why else do workers unionize? *Modern Survey* conducted a study that measured items such as employees' interest in being represented by a union, confidence in senior management, and employee engagement. It concluded that 50% of "actively disengaged" employees would vote "yes" to unionization, while only 20% of such disengaged employees would vote "no union." It concludes that "paying attention to employee engagement levels within your organization helps to foster positive relationships between employees and management and decreases the likelihood of a workforce seeking union representation."[11]

Gallup conducts its own surveys that complements these conclusions. For example, among the over 500 organizations in which Gallup measures employee engagement, 45% of *nonunion* employees were engaged, while fewer—38%—of unionized employees were engaged.[12]

Findings like these don't prove that engaged employees are less likely to support a unionization effort in their companies, or that unionized employees are less engaged. The findings are correlational, so they only show that when employee engagement goes up unionization goes down. It could be that the same management policies (such as guaranteed fair treatment systems) affect both employee engagement and nonunionization. But on the whole, such findings do suggest that the same sorts of policies (such as good benefits, building trust, and guaranteeing fair treatment) that improve employee engagement may also reduce the likelihood of being unionized.

What Do Unions Want?

We can generalize by saying that unions have two sets of aims, one for union security and one for improved wages, hours, working conditions, and benefits for their members.

Union Security   First and probably foremost, unions seek to establish security for themselves. They fight hard for the right to represent a firm's workers and to be the *exclusive* bargaining agent for all employees in the unit. (As such, they negotiate contracts for all employees, including those who are not members of the union.) Five types of union security are possible:

1. **Closed shop.**[13] The company can hire only current union members. Congress outlawed closed shops in interstate commerce in 1947, but they still exist in some states for particular industries (such as printing). They account for less than 5% of union contracts.
2. **Union shop.** The company can hire nonunion people, but they must join the union after a prescribed period and pay dues. (If not, they can be fired.) This category accounts for about 73% of union contracts. Unions and employers also tend to negotiate versions of the union shop—for instance, letting older workers quit the union when the contract ends.
3. **Agency shop.** Employees who do not belong to the union still must pay the union an amount equal to union dues (on the assumption that the union's efforts benefit *all* the workers).[14]
4. **Preferential shop.** Union members get preference in hiring, but the employer can still hire nonunion members.
5. **Maintenance of membership arrangement.** Employees do not have to belong to the union. However, union members employed by the firm must maintain membership in the union for the contract period. These account for about 4% of union agreements.

Not all states give unions the right to require union membership as a condition of employment. **Right to work** "is a term used to describe state statutory or constitutional provisions banning the requirement of union membership as a condition of employment."[15] Section 14(b) of the Taft-Hartley Act (an early labor relations act that we'll discuss later) permits states to forbid the negotiation of compulsory union membership provisions, not just for firms engaged in interstate commerce but also for those in intrastate commerce. Right-to-work laws don't outlaw unions. They do outlaw (within those states) any form of *union security*. This understandably inhibits union formation in those states. Recently, there were 23 right-to-work

closed shop
A form of union security in which the company can hire only union members. This was outlawed in 1947 for interstate commerce, but still exists in some industries (such as printing).

union shop
A form of union security in which the company can hire nonunion people but they must join the union after a prescribed period of time and pay dues. (If they do not, they can be fired.)

agency shop
A form of union security in which employees who do not belong to the union must still pay union dues on the assumption that union efforts benefit all workers.

preferential shop
Union members get preference in hiring, but the employer can still hire nonunion members.

maintenance of membership arrangement
Employees do not have to belong to the union. However, union members employed by the firm must maintain membership in the union for the contract period.

right to work
The public policy in a number of states that prohibits union security of any kind.

states.[16] After Oklahoma became the 22nd state to pass right-to-work legislation, Oklahoma's union membership dropped dramatically in the next three years.[17] Right to work adversely affects union membership levels.[18]

Improved Wages, Hours, Working Conditions, and Benefits for Members Once their security is ensured, unions fight to better the lot of their members—to improve their wages, hours, and working conditions, for example. The typical labor agreement also gives the union a role in other HR activities, including recruiting, selecting, compensating, promoting, training, and discharging employees.

The AFL-CIO and the SEIU

The American Federation of Labor and Congress of Industrial Organizations (AFL-CIO) is a voluntary federation of about 56 national and international labor unions in the United States. The separate AFL and CIO merged many years ago. For some people in the United States, the AFL-CIO is still synonymous with the word *union*.

There are three layers in the structure of the AFL-CIO and most other U.S. unions. The worker joins the local union, to which he or she pays dues. The local is in turn a single chapter in the national union. For example, if you were a teacher in Detroit, you would belong to the local union there, which is one of hundreds of local chapters of the American Federation of Teachers, their national union (most unions actually call themselves international unions). The third layer in the structure is the national federation, in this case, the AFL-CIO.

Union federation membership is in flux. The Service Employees International Union (SEIU) is a fast-growing federation of more than 2.2 million members. It includes the largest health care union, with more than 1.1 million members, including registered nurses (RNs), licensed practical nurses (LPNs), and doctors. It also includes the second-largest public employees union, with more than 1 million local and state government workers.[19] Several years ago, six big unions, including SEIU and the International Brotherhood of Teamsters, left the AFL-CIO and established their own federation, called the Change to Win Coalition. Together, the departing unions represented over one-quarter of the AFL-CIO's membership and budget. Change to Win plans to be more aggressive about organizing workers than they say the AFL-CIO was.[20] (The UNITE HERE union then left Change to Win, possibly slowing Change to Win's momentum.)

Some people think of the federation (such as the AFL-CIO or the SEIU) as the most important part of the labor movement, but it is not. Thus, the president of the teachers' union wields more power in that capacity than in his capacity as a vice president of the AFL-CIO. Yet as a practical matter, the presidents of the AFL-CIO or SEIU do have considerable political influence.

LEARNING OBJECTIVE 3
Discuss the nature of the major federal labor relations laws.

Unions and The Law

Until about 1930, there were no special labor laws. Employers didn't have to engage in collective bargaining with employees and were virtually unrestrained in how they treated unions. "Yellow dog" contracts, whereby management could require nonunion membership as a condition for employment, were widely enforced. Most union weapons—even strikes—were illegal.

This one-sided situation lasted in the United States from the Revolution to the Great Depression (around 1930). Since then, in response to changing public attitudes, values, and economic conditions, labor law has gone through three clear changes: from "strong encouragement" of unions, to "modified encouragement coupled with regulation," to "detailed regulation of internal union affairs."[21]

Period of Strong Encouragement: The Norris-LaGuardia Act (1932) and the National Labor Relations Act (1935)

Norris-LaGuardia Act
This law marked the beginning of the era of strong encouragement of unions and guaranteed to each employee the right to bargain collectively "free from interference, restraint, or coercion."

Wagner Act
A law that banned certain types of unfair labor practices and provided for secret-ballot elections and majority rule for determining whether or not a firm's employees want to unionize.

National Labor Relations Board (NLRB)
The agency created by the Wagner Act to investigate unfair labor practice charges and to provide for secret-ballot elections and majority rule in determining whether or not a firm's employees want a union.

The **Norris-LaGuardia Act** set the stage for an era in which government encouraged union activity. The act guaranteed to each employee the right to bargain collectively "free from interference, restraint, or coercion." It declared yellow dog contracts unenforceable. It limited the courts' abilities to issue injunctions for activities such as peaceful picketing and payment of strike benefits.[22]

Yet this act did little to restrain employers from fighting labor organizations. Therefore, the National Labor Relations (or **Wagner**) Act was passed in 1935 to add teeth to the Norris-LaGuardia Act. It did this by banning certain unfair labor practices, providing for secret-ballot elections and majority rule for determining whether a firm's employees were to unionize, and creating the **National Labor Relations Board (NLRB)** for enforcing these two provisions.

In addition to activities like overseeing union elections, the NLRB periodically issues interpretive rulings. For example, about 6 million employees fall under the "contingent" or "alternative" employee umbrella today. The NLRB therefore ruled that temporary employees could join the unions of permanent employees in the companies where their employment agencies assign them to work.[23] As another example, several years ago the NLRB ruled that unions could file election petitions and other documents via e-mail rather than by mail, and required employers to give unions their employees' e-mail addresses. This cut the average time it took to hold elections from about five weeks to three and gave employers less time to persuade their employees to vote "no union." [24] (Actually, the word *union* doesn't appear in the National Labor Relations Act, which just refers to "labor organizations." In fact, many unions, such as the Fraternal Order of Police, don't include "union" in their names.)[25]

Unfair Employer Labor Practices The Wagner Act deemed as "statutory wrongs" (but not crimes) five unfair labor practices used by employers:

1. It is unfair for employers to "interfere with, restrain, or coerce employees" in exercising their legally sanctioned right of self-organization.
2. It is an unfair practice for company representatives to dominate or interfere with either the formation or the administration of labor unions. Among other management actions found to be unfair under practices 1 and 2 are bribing employees, using company spy systems, moving a business to avoid unionization, and blacklisting union sympathizers.
3. Employers are prohibited from discriminating in any way against employees for their legal union activities.
4. Employers are forbidden to discharge or discriminate against employees simply because the latter file unfair practice charges against the company.
5. Finally, it is an unfair labor practice for employers to refuse to bargain collectively with their employees' duly chosen representatives.[26]

An unfair labor practice charge may be filed with the NLRB (using its standard online form[27]). The board then investigates the charge. Possible actions include dismissal of the complaint, request for an injunction against the employer, and an order that the employer cease and desist.

From 1935 to 1947 Union membership increased quickly after passage of the Wagner Act in 1935. Other factors such as an improving economy and aggressive union leadership contributed to this as well. But by the mid-1940s, the tide was turning. Largely because of a series of massive postwar strikes, public policy began to shift against what many viewed as the union excesses of the times.

Period of Modified Encouragement Coupled with Regulation: The Taft-Hartley Act (1947)

Taft-Hartley Act
A law prohibiting union unfair labor practices and enumerating the rights of employees as union members. It also enumerates the rights of employers.

The **Taft-Hartley Act** (or Labor Management Relations Act) reflected the public's less-enthusiastic attitudes toward unions. It amended the Wagner Act with provisions aimed at limiting unions in four ways: by prohibiting unfair union labor practices, by enumerating the rights of employees as union members, by enumerating the rights of employers, and by allowing the president of the United States to temporarily bar national emergency strikes.

Unfair Union Labor Practices The Taft-Hartley Act enumerated several labor practices that unions were prohibited from engaging in:

1. Unions were banned from restraining or coercing employees from exercising their guaranteed bargaining rights.
2. It is an unfair labor practice for a union to cause an employer to discriminate in any way against an employee in order to encourage or discourage his or her membership in a union.
3. It is an unfair labor practice for a union to refuse to bargain in good faith with the employer about wages, hours, and other employment conditions.

Rights of Employees The Taft-Hartley Act also protected the rights of employees against their unions. For example, many people felt that compulsory unionism violated the basic U.S. right of freedom of association. The new *right-to-work laws* sprang up in 19 states (mainly in the South and Southwest); as noted, these outlawed labor contracts that made union membership a condition for keeping one's job.

In general, the National Labor Relations Act does not restrain unions from unfair labor practices to the extent that it does employers. Unions may not restrain or coerce employees. However, "violent or otherwise threatening behavior or clearly coercive or intimidating union activities are necessary before the NLRB will find an unfair labor practice."[28] Examples here would include physical assaults or threats of violence, economic reprisals, and mass picketing that restrains the lawful entry or leaving of a work site. In one typical case, *Pattern Makers* v. *National Labor Relations Board,* the U.S. Supreme Court found the union guilty of an unfair labor practice when it tried to fine some members for resigning from the union and returning to work during a strike.[29]

Rights of Employers The Taft-Hartley Act also explicitly gave employers certain rights. For example, it gave them full freedom to express their views concerning union organization. Thus, a manager can tell his or her employees that in his or her opinion unions are worthless, dangerous to the economy, and immoral. Employers can set forth the union's record concerning violence and corruption, if appropriate. The only major restraint is that there can be no threat of reprisal or force or promise of benefit.[30] The employer also cannot meet with employees on company time within 24 hours of an election or suggest to employees that they vote against the union while they are at home or in the employer's office, although he or she can do so while in their work area or where they normally gather.

national emergency strikes
Strikes that might "imperil the national health and safety."

National Emergency Strikes The Taft-Hartley Act also allows the U.S. president to intervene in **national emergency strikes**, which are strikes (for example, on the part of steel firm employees) that might imperil national health and safety. The president may appoint a board of inquiry and, based on its report, apply for an injunction restraining the strike for 60 days. If no settlement is reached during that time, the injunction can be extended for another 20 days. During this period, employees are polled in a secret ballot to ascertain their willingness to accept the employer's last offer.

Period of Detailed Regulation of Internal Union Affairs: The Landrum-Griffin Act (1959)

Landrum-Griffin Act
A law aimed at protecting union members from possible wrongdoing on the part of their unions.

In the 1950s, senate investigations revealed unsavory practices on the part of some unions, and the result was the **Landrum-Griffin Act** (officially, the Labor Management Reporting and Disclosure Act). An overriding aim was to protect union members from possible wrongdoing on the part of their unions. It was also an amendment to the Wagner Act.

The Landrum-Griffin Act contains a bill of rights for union members. Among other things, this provides for certain rights in the nomination of candidates for union office. It also affirms a member's right to sue his or her union. And, it ensures that no member can be fined or suspended without due process (including a list of charges and a fair hearing).

The act also laid out rules regarding union elections. For example, national and international unions must elect officers at least once every five years, using some type of secret-ballot mechanism.

The senate investigators also discovered flagrant examples of employer wrongdoing. The Landrum-Griffin Act therefore also greatly expanded the list of unlawful employer actions. For example, companies can no longer pay their own employees to entice them not to join the union. The pendulum therefore again shifted a bit back toward strengthening unions.

Labor Law Today As we'll see toward the end of this chapter, it isn't quite clear whether the pressures toward a more encouraging or a more discouraging climate for labor law will prevail for the next few years. On the one hand, unions are pushing for new legislation that would substantially improve unions' efforts. On the other hand, economic realities (shrinking state budgets and increased competitive pressures, for instance) and a new Republican administration may (or may not) dampen union efforts.[31]

LEARNING OBJECTIVE 4
Describe the process of a union drive and election.

The Union Drive and Election

It is through the union drive and election that a union tries to be recognized to represent employees. This process has five basic steps: initial contact, authorization cards, hearing, campaign, and election.[32]

Step 1: Initial Contact

During the initial contact stage, the union determines the employees' interest in organizing, and establishes an organizing committee.

The initiative for the first contact between the employees and the union may come from the employees, from a union already representing other employees of the firm, or from a union representing workers elsewhere. Sometimes a union effort starts with a disgruntled employee contacting the local union to learn how to organize his or her place of work. Sometimes, though, the campaign starts when a union decides it wants to expand to representing other employees in the firm or industry, or when the company looks like an easy one to organize. (For instance, the Teamsters union, which was already firmly in place at UPS, began an intensive organizing campaign at FedEx.) In any case, there is an initial contact between a union representative and a few employees.

When an employer becomes a target, a union official usually assigns a representative to assess employee interest. The representative visits the firm to determine whether enough employees are interested to make a union campaign worthwhile. He or she also identifies employees who would make good leaders in the organizing campaign and calls them together to create an organizing committee. The

The Teamsters union—already firmly in place at UPS—began an intensive organizing campaign at FedEx.

Source: Kurhan/Shutterstock.

objective is to "educate the committee about the benefits of forming a union, the law and procedures involved in forming a local union, and the issues management is likely to raise during a campaign."[33]

The union must follow certain procedures when contacting employees. The law allows union organizers to solicit employees for membership as long as it doesn't endanger the performance or safety of the employees. Therefore, much of the contact occurs off the job. Organizers can also safely contact employees on company grounds during off hours (such as break time). Under some conditions, union representatives may solicit employees at their workstations, but this is rare. In practice, there will be much informal organizing at the workplace as employees debate organizing. In any case, this initial contact stage may be deceptively quiet. In some instances the first inkling management has of the union is the distribution of a handbill soliciting union membership.[34]

Labor Relations Consultants Both management and unions may use outside advisors. The use by management of consultants (whom unions often disparagingly refer to as *union busters*) has grown considerably. This so-called union avoidance industry includes the consultants, law firms, industry psychologists, and strike management firms that employers often turn to when the union comes to call.[35] One study found management consultants involved in 75% of the elections they surveyed.[36]

One expert says an employer's main goal shouldn't be to win representation elections, but to avoid them altogether. He says doing so means taking fast action when the first signs of union activity appear. His advice in a nutshell: Don't just ignore the union's efforts while it spreads pro-union rumors, such as "If we had a union, we wouldn't have to work so much overtime." Retain an attorney and react at once.[37]

union salting

A union organizing tactic by which workers who are employed by a union as undercover union organizers are hired by unwitting employers.

Union Salting Unions are also not without creative ways to win elections, one of which is union salting. The National Labor Relations Board defines **union salting** as "placing of union members on nonunion job sites for the purpose of organizing." Critics claim that "salts" also often interfere with business operations and harass employees.[38] A U.S. Supreme Court decision, *NLRB* v. *Town and Country Electric,* held the tactic to be legal.

Public pressure is another tactic. For example, in one case, the Service Employees International Union (SEIU) sought to pressure the small contractors who provided janitorial services in large office buildings to let their workers organize. Rather than just pressuring the small contractors, the SEIU brought media and political pressure to bear on the large real estate companies that owned the office buildings. The real estate firms soon pressured their contractors to let their workers organize.[39] The following Trends feature explains another union tool.

TRENDS SHAPING HR: *Digital and Social Media*

UNIONS GO DIGITAL When it comes to organizing just about any sort of campaign, communication is king, a fact that hasn't been lost on unions. For example, in one survey, 49% of unions said they used Facebook to communicate with members and employees, 23% used Twitter, and 13% used You-Tube.[40] About 92% of unions have a website, while just over 78% use e-mail newsletters.[41] The group trying to organize Starbucks workers (the *Starbucks Workers' Union*) started their own website (www.starbucksunion.org). It includes notes like "Our hard work has made record profits for Starbucks. It's time to unite for our fair share."[42] In one recent campaign, the employer restricted the use of its electronic systems (including e-mail) to "business purposes only." The union filed objections. The NLRB held that nonmanagement employees who normally have access to an employer's e-mail system as part of their jobs may use the system to communicate about union matters when not working, such as during lunch or break times.[43]

Labor–management attorneys often counsel employers to institute policies that restrict employees' use of social media. Such policies typically state, for instance, that employees should not use such media during work time, and that disparaging comments about the employer or its employees are prohibited.[44]

However, such policy restrictions may violate employees' rights under the National Labor Relations Act (such as to take "concerted activity" by discussing working conditions with coworkers).[45] At least one labor–management attorney advises against publishing any such social media policy at all, lest the employer run afoul of NLRB rules.[46]

Step 2: Authorization Cards

authorization cards

In order to petition for a union election, the union must show that at least 30% of employees may be interested in being unionized. Employees indicate this interest by signing authorization cards.

For the union to petition the NLRB for the right to hold an election, it must show that a sizable number of employees may be interested in being organized. The next step is thus for union organizers to try to get the employees to sign **authorization cards** (Figure 13.1). Among other things, these usually authorize the union to seek a representation election and state that the employee has applied to join the union. Before the union can petition an election, 30% of the eligible employees in an appropriate bargaining unit must sign.

During this stage, both union and management typically use propaganda. The union claims it can improve working conditions, raise wages, increase benefits, and generally get the workers better deals. Management need not be silent; it can attack the union on ethical and moral grounds and cite the cost of union membership, for example. Management can also explain its record, express facts and opinions, and explain to its employees the law applicable to organizing campaigns.

However, neither side can threaten, bribe, or coerce employees. Further, an employer may not make promises of benefits to employees or make unilateral changes in terms and conditions of employment that were not planned to be implemented prior to the onset of union organizing activity. Managers also should know that looking through signed authorization cards could be construed as spying on those who signed, which is an unfair labor practice.

Figure 13.1

Sample Authorization Card

SAMPLE UNION of AMERICA
Authorization for Representation

I hereby authorize Local 409 of the SAMPLE union to be my exclusive representative for the purposes of collective bargaining with my employer. I understand that my signature on this card may be used to obtain certification of Local 409 as our exclusive bargaining representative without an election.

This card will verify that I have applied for union membership and that effective _____ I hereby authorize you to deduct each pay period from my earnings an amount equal to the regular current rate of monthly union dues and initiation fee.

Employer: _____ **Worksite:** _____

Date: _____ **Name:** _____

Street Address: _____ **City:** _____ **Zip Code:** _____

Home Phone: _____ **Cell Phone:** _____ **Home E-Mail:** _____

Department: _____

Job Title/Classification: _____

Signature: _____

You must print and mail in this authorization card for it to be recognized. Only original cards are valid and should be submitted. Mail to:

SAMPLE UNION of America, Local 409

301 Sample Way

Miami, FL 33101

During this stage, unions can picket the company, subject to three constraints: The union must file a petition for an election within 30 days after the start of picketing, the firm cannot already be lawfully recognizing another union, and there cannot have been a valid NLRB election during the past 12 months. The union would file a petition using NLRB Form 502.

Step 3: The Hearing

After the authorization cards are collected, one of three things can occur. The employer may choose not to contest union recognition, in which case no hearing is needed, and a *consent election* is held immediately. The employer may choose not to contest the union's *right to an election* (and/or the scope of the bargaining unit, or which employees are eligible to vote in the election), in which case no hearing is needed, and the parties can stipulate an election. Or, the employer may contest the union's right, in which case it can insist on a *hearing* to determine those issues. An employer's decision about whether to insist on a hearing is a strategic one based on the facts of each case, and whether it feels it needs more time to try to persuade a majority of its employees not to elect a union to represent them.

Most companies contest the union's right to represent their employees: They claim that a significant number of their employees do not really want the union. It is at this point that the NLRB gets involved. The NLRB is usually contacted by the union, which requests a hearing. Based on this, the regional director of the NLRB sends a hearing officer to investigate. (For example, did 30% or more of the employees in an appropriate bargaining unit sign the authorization cards?) The examiner sends both management and the union a notice of representation hearing that states the time and place of the hearing.

The **bargaining unit** is one decision to come out of the hearing; it is the group of employees that the union will be authorized to represent and bargain for collectively.

bargaining unit
The group of employees the union will be authorized to represent.

Finally, if the results of the hearing are favorable for the union, the NLRB directs that an election be held. It issues a Decision and Direction of Election notice to that effect and sends NLRB Form 666 ("Notice to Employees") to the employer to post, notifying employees of their rights under federal labor relations law.

Step 4: The Campaign

During the campaign that precedes the election, the union and employer appeal to employees for their votes. The union emphasizes that it will prevent unfairness, set up a grievance/seniority system, and improve unsatisfactory wages. Union strength, they'll say, will give employees a voice in determining wages and working conditions. Management emphasizes that improvements such as those the union promises don't require unionization, and that wages are equal to or better than they would be with a union contract. Management also emphasizes the financial cost of union dues; the fact that the union is an "outsider;" and that if the union wins, a strike may follow.[47] It can even attack the union on ethical and moral grounds. But neither side can threaten, bribe, or coerce employees. [48]

The Supervisor's Role in the Campaign A few years ago, Target won a unionization election at its Valley Stream, New York store, but a federal judge overturned it and required a new election. Among other things, the judge found that Target managers had violated labor law by telling employees they couldn't wear union buttons or distribute flyers and by threatening to discipline workers who discussed union matters.[49] In another case, a plant superintendent prohibited distribution of union literature in the lunchroom. Because solicitation of off-duty workers in nonwork areas is generally legal, the company subsequently allowed the union to post and distribute union literature in the plant's nonworking areas. However, the NLRB still ruled that the initial act of prohibiting distribution of the literature was an unfair labor practice. The NLRB used the superintendent's action as one reason to invalidate an election that the company won.[50] A supervisor allegedly did something similar in 2017 at Nissan Motors' Jackson, Mississippi, plant. The bottom line is that supervisors must know what they can and can't do to legally hamper organizing activities, lest they commit unfair labor practices. (Certain "supervisors" can't be excluded from the bargaining unit. The employer could trigger an unfair labor practice charge if it tries to use those people to assist in its campaign.)[51]

The Management Skills feature lays out guidelines.

BUILDING YOUR MANAGEMENT SKILLS:
What Supervisors Can and Cannot Do

What may the supervisor do? Remember what you can and can't do during the campaign with the acronyms TIPS and FORE.[52]
Use TIPS to remember what *not* to do:

T—Threaten. Do not threaten or imply the company will take adverse action of any kind for supporting the union.[53] Do not threaten to terminate employees because of their union activities, and don't threaten to close the facility if the union wins the election.

I—Interrogate. Don't interrogate or ask employees their position concerning unions, or how they are going to vote in an election.

P—Promise. Don't promise employees a pay increase, special favors, better benefits, or promotions.

S—Spy. Don't spy at any union activities or attend a union meeting, even if invited.

Continued

Use FORE to remember what the supervisor *may do* to discourage unionization:

F—Facts. Do tell employees that by signing the authorization card the union may become their legal representative in matters regarding wages and hours, and do tell them that by signing a union authorization card it does not mean they must vote for the union.

O—Opinion. You may tell employees that management doesn't believe in third-party representation, and that management believes in having an open-door policy to air grievances.

R—Rules. Provide factually correct advice such as telling employees that the law permits the company to permanently replace them if there's a strike, and that the union can't make the company agree to anything it does not want to during negotiations.

E—Experience. The supervisor may share personal experiences he or she may have had with a union.[54]

KNOW YOUR EMPLOYMENT LAW
Rules Regarding Literature and Solicitation

To avoid legal problems, employers need rules governing distribution of literature and solicitation of workers, and should train supervisors in how to apply them.[55] For example:

- Nonemployees can always be barred from soliciting employees during their work time—that is, when the employee is on duty and not on a break.
- Employers can usually stop employees from soliciting other employees for any purpose if one or both employees are on paid-duty time and not on a break.
- Most employers (not including retail stores, shopping centers, and certain other employers) can bar nonemployees from the building's interiors and work areas as a right of private property owners.

Such restrictions are valid only if the employer does not discriminate. For example, if company policy permits employees to collect money for baby gifts or to engage in other solicitation during their working time, the employer will not be able to prohibit them from union soliciting during work time. ■

There are many more ways to commit unfair labor practices than just keeping union organizers off your private property. For example, one employer decided to have a cookout and paid day off two days before a union representation election. The NLRB held that this was too much of a coincidence and called a second election. The union had lost the first vote but won the second.[56] Figure 13.2 illustrates what the employer and union generally cannot do during campaigns.

The accompanying HR Tools feature focuses on how smaller companies should address these matters.

■ HR Tools for Line Managers and Small Businesses

What to Do when the Union Comes Calling

Unions are not just a big-company phenomenon, and the small business owner who ignores the first signs of union activity (or responds in an illegal manner to them) is asking for trouble.

Just about every business, regardless of size, is covered by labor law. For example, a retail store would have to have sales below $500,000 a year, and not be involved in interstate commerce, to not be unionize-able.

Small business owners should keep several things in mind. For one thing, (to head off organizing at work) make sure your employee manual contains a "nonsolicitation" policy; it should say that no solicitation will be allowed when employees are working. (That includes *any* solicitation, including, for instance, for charities, and you should enforce it.) Also remember that you can't prohibit your employees from meeting with union representatives during lunch or breaks or any time when they're not working for you. Be careful that you do not look at the authorization cards if the union representative hands them to you after they're collected; if you look at them, you may have to accept the union!

Similarly (as we listed earlier in the Building Management Skills guidelines) do *not* interfere with your employees' rights, or discriminate against those employees who support the union. For example (again, see our guidelines), don't threaten employees with loss of jobs if they vote for the union, spy on union gatherings, discharge employees who urge other employees to join the union, or demote employees whom you find circulating a union petition.[57]

⭐ Talk About It–**2**

If your professor has chosen to assign this, go to **www.pearson.com/mylab/management** to discuss the following questions. What would you do as the owner of a company that has, say, seven employees and $750,000 sales per year to head off your employees even wanting to unionize? What do you think of how Melinda (in the chapter opener) responded to Jim?

Figure 13.2

NLRA Union Campaign Violations

Source: National Labor Relations Board, www.nlrb.gov/.

Examples of Employer Conduct that Violates the NLRA:

- Threatening employees with loss of jobs or benefits if they join or vote for a union or engage in protected concerted activity (such as two or more employees together asking their employer to improve working conditions and pay)
- Threatening to close the plant if employees unionize
- Promising benefits to employees to discourage their union support
- Transferring, laying off, terminating, assigning employees more difficult work tasks, or otherwise punishing employees because they engaged in union or protected concerted activity
- Transferring, laying off, terminating, assigning employees more difficult work tasks, or otherwise punishing employees because they filed unfair labor practice charges or participated in an investigation by NLRB

Examples of Labor Organization Conduct that Violates the NLRA:

- Threatening employees with loss of jobs unless they support the union
- Seeking the suspension, discharge, or other punishment of an employee for not being a union member even if the employee has paid or offered to pay a lawful initiation fee and periodic fees thereafter
- Refusing to process a grievance because an employee has criticized union officials or because an employee is not a member of the union in states where union security clauses are not permitted
- Fining employees who have validly resigned from the union for engaging in protected concerted activities following their resignation or for crossing an unlawful picket line
- Engaging in picket line misconduct, such as threatening, assaulting, or barring nonstrikers from the employer's premises
- Striking over issues unrelated to employment terms and conditions or coercively enmeshing neutrals into a labor dispute

Figure 13.3

Sample NLRB Ballot

Source: National Labor Relations Board, www.nlrb.gov/.

UNITED STATES OF AMERICA

National Labor Relations Board

OFFICIAL SECRET BALLOT

FOR CERTAIN EMPLOYEES OF

Do you wish to be represented for purposes of collective bargaining by —

MARK AN "S" IN THE SQUARE OF YOUR CHOICE

YES ☐   NO ☐

DO NOT SIGN THIS BALLOT. Fold and drop in ballot box.
If you spoil this ballot return it to the Board Agent for a new one.

Step 5: The Election

The election itself can be held within 30 to 60 days after the NLRB issues its Decision and Direction of Election. The election is by secret ballot. The NLRB provides the ballots (see Figure 13.3), as well as the voting booth and ballot box. It also counts the votes and certifies the results of the election. Historically, the more workers who vote, the less likely the union is to win. This is probably because more workers who are not strong union supporters end up voting.

The union becomes the employees' representative if it wins the election, and "winning" means getting a majority *of the votes cast*, not a majority of the workers in the bargaining unit. The union typically wins just over half of such elections. In one recent year, the NLRB conducted 1,628 elections, of which unions won 1,128 or about 66.8%.[58]

Winning an election and signing an agreement don't necessarily mean that the union is in the company to stay. The same law that grants employees the right to unionize also gives them a way to terminate legally (decertify) their union's right to represent them. There were 180 such **decertification** elections in one recent year, of which unions won about 39%.[59] In terms of how they're conducted by union and management, decertification campaigns are similar to certification campaigns.[60]

decertification

In labor law, the process that enables employees to terminate legally (decertify) their union's right to represent them.

How to Lose an NLRB Election

According to expert Matthew Goodfellow, there is no sure way employers can win elections, but several sure ways to lose one.[61]

Reason 1. Asleep at the switch. In one study, in 68% of the companies that lost to the union, executives were caught unaware. In these companies, turnover and absenteeism had increased, productivity was erratic, and safety was poor. Grievance procedures were rare. But ironically, when the first reports of authorization cards began trickling in, management usually responded with letters describing the company as "one big family."[62]

Reason 2. Appointing a committee. Of the losing companies, 36% formed a committee to manage the campaign. The problems here are that: (1) Promptness is essential in an election situation, and committees move slowly. (2) Most committee members are NLRB neophytes, whose views reflect hope rather than experience. (3) A committee's decision is usually a compromise decision, not necessarily the most effective one. This expert suggests giving full responsibility to one decisive executive. A human resource director and a consultant or advisor with broad experience in labor relations should assist this person.

Reason 3. Concentrating on money and benefits. In 54% of the elections studied, the company lost because top management concentrated on money and benefits. As Goodfellow says:

> Employees may want more money, but quite often, if they feel the company treats them fairly, decently, and honestly, they are satisfied with reasonable, competitive rates and benefits. It is only when they feel ignored, uncared for, and disregarded that money becomes a major issue to express their dissatisfaction.[63]

Reason 4. Delegating too much to divisions. For companies with plants scattered around the country, unionizing one plant tends to lead to unionizing others. The solution is, don't abdicate all personnel and industrial relations decisions to plant managers.[64] Dealing effectively with unions—monitoring employees' attitudes, reacting properly when the union appears, and so on—requires centralized guidance from the main office and its human resources staff.

The HR Practices Around the Globe feature illustrates international aspects of dealing with unions.

■ HR Practices Around the Globe

France Comes to the Workers' Aid

Employers planning to expand abroad should ponder the recent experience of drug maker Sanofi SA, in France. Because of the relatively high cost of running its research facility in southwestern France, Sanofi told its researchers there that it intended to close their facility.[65] Employees began staging weekly protests, supported by the French government, which opposes profitable companies slashing jobs. After nine months, the company was still waiting for a government report on the situation so it could finish negotiating with its unions and try to get some of them other jobs elsewhere. As one Sanofi manager said, "In France, the politics, the labor laws are extremely different than in any other regions . . . anything you want to do differently gets to be a confrontational issue."[66]

★ Talk About It–**3**

If your professor has chosen to assign this, go to **www.pearson.com/mylab/management** to discuss the following question. With government policies like this, how do you think French companies remain competitive with those, say, in the United States?

LEARNING OBJECTIVE 5
Discuss the main steps in the collective bargaining process.

The Collective Bargaining Process

What Is Collective Bargaining?

When and if the union is recognized as a company's employees' representative, a day is set for bargaining. Representatives of management and the union meet to negotiate a labor contract that contains agreements on specific provisions covering wages, hours, and working conditions.

collective bargaining
The process through which representatives of management and the union meet to negotiate a labor agreement.

What exactly is **collective bargaining**? According to the Wagner Act:

> For the purpose of (this act) to bargain collectively is the performance of the mutual obligation of the employer and the representative of the employees to meet at reasonable times and confer in good faith with respect to wages, hours, and terms and conditions of employment, or the negotiation of an agreement, or any question arising thereunder, and the execution of a written contract incorporating any agreement reached if requested by either party, but such obligation does not compel either party to agree to a proposal or require the making of a concession.

In plain language, this means that both management and labor are required by law to negotiate wages, hours, and terms and conditions of employment "in good faith." We'll see that court decisions have clarified the specific provisions that are negotiable.

What Is Good-Faith Bargaining?

good-faith bargaining
A term that means both parties are communicating and negotiating and that proposals are being matched with counterproposals, with both parties making every reasonable effort to arrive at agreements. It does not mean that either party is compelled to agree to a proposal.

Good-faith bargaining means that proposals are matched with counterproposals and that both parties make every reasonable effort to arrive at an agreement. It does not mean that either party is compelled to agree to a proposal. Nor does it require that either party make any specific concessions (although in practice, some may be necessary). In practice, good-faith bargaining includes things like the duty to meet and confer with the representative of the employees (or employer) and the duty to supply, on request, information that is "relevant and necessary" to allow the employees' representative to bargain intelligently.[67]

In assessing whether a party has violated its good-faith obligations, it is the *totality of conduct* by each of the parties that is of prime importance to the NLRB and the courts.[68] Examples of a violation of the requirements for good-faith bargaining may include the following:

1. **Surface bargaining.** This involves going through the motions of bargaining without any real intention of completing a formal agreement.
2. **Proposals and demands.** The advancement of proposals is a positive factor in determining overall good faith.
3. **Withholding information.** The NLRB and courts expect management to furnish information on matters such as wages, hours, and other terms of employment that union negotiators request and legitimately require.[69]
4. **Dilatory tactics.** The law requires that the parties meet and "confer at reasonable times and intervals." It does not require management to meet at the time and place dictated just by the union.[70] However, inordinately delaying the meeting or refusing to meet with the other party may reflect bad-faith bargaining.
5. **Concessions.** The law does not require either party to make concessions. However, being willing to compromise during negotiations is a crucial ingredient of good-faith bargaining.
6. **Unilateral changes in conditions.** This is a strong indication that the employer is not bargaining with the required intent of reaching an agreement.

The Negotiating Team

Both union and management send a negotiating team to the bargaining table, and both teams usually go into the bargaining sessions having done their homework. Union representatives have sounded out union members on their desires and conferred with union representatives of related unions.

Similarly, management compiles pay and benefit data, including comparisons to local pay rates and rates paid for similar jobs in the industry. Management also carefully "costs" the current labor contract and determines the increased cost—total, per employee and per hour—of the union's demands (see the HR as a Profit Center feature). It also tries to identify probable union demands and to size up the ones more important to the union. It uses information from grievances and feedback from supervisors to determine ahead of time what the union's demands might be and thus prepare counteroffers and arguments.

■ HR as a Profit Center

Costing the Contract

Collective bargaining experts emphasize the need to cost the union's demands carefully. One says,

> The mistake I see most often is [HR professionals who] enter the negotiations without understanding the financial impact of things they put on the table. For example, the union wants three extra vacation days. That doesn't sound like a lot, except that in some states, if an employee leaves, you have to pay them for unused vacation time. [So] now your employer has to carry that liability on their books at all times.[71]

✪ Talk About It – 4

If your professor has chosen to assign this, go to **www.mymanagementlab.com** to discuss the following questions. What do you think are the top three workforce-related expenses that most employers should focus on? How would you check this?

---

voluntary (permissible) bargaining items
Items in collective bargaining for which bargaining is neither illegal nor mandatory—neither party can be compelled to negotiate over those items.

illegal bargaining items
Items in collective bargaining that are forbidden by law; for example, the clause agreeing to hire "union members exclusively" would be illegal in a right-to-work state.

mandatory bargaining items
Items in collective bargaining that a party must bargain over if they are introduced by the other party—for example, pay.

Even professional hockey, baseball, basketball, and football players, all relatively well-paid, have gone on strike for better wages and benefits.
Source: Thomas Barwick/Getty Images.

Bargaining Items

Labor law sets out *voluntary illegal*, and *mandatory*, items that are subject to collective bargaining.

Voluntary (or permissible) bargaining items are neither mandatory nor illegal; they become a part of negotiations only through the joint agreement of both management and union. Neither party can be compelled against its wishes to negotiate over voluntary items. An employee cannot hold up signing a contract because the other party refuses to bargain on a voluntary item.

Illegal bargaining items are forbidden by law. The clause agreeing to hire "union members exclusively" would be illegal in a right-to-work state, for example.

About 70 **mandatory bargaining items** exist, some of which we present in Figure 13.4. These include wages, hours, rest periods, layoffs, transfers, benefits, and severance pay.

Bargaining Stages[72]

Bargaining typically goes through several stages.[73] First, each side presents its demands. At this stage, both parties are usually quite far apart on some issues. Indeed, labor negotiators use the term *blue-skying* to refer to demands (such as swimming pools and 17 paid holidays, including Valentine's Day) that negotiators have been known to propose. Next, each side trades off some of its demands to gain others, a process called *trading points*. Third are the subcommittee studies: The parties form joint subcommittees or study groups to try to work out reasonable alternatives. Fourth, the parties reach an informal settlement, and each group goes back to its sponsor. Union representatives check informally with their superiors and the union members; management representatives check with top management. Finally, when everything is in order, the parties fine-tune, proofread, and sign a formal agreement. The Management Skills feature lists negotiating guidelines.

MANDATORY	PERMISSIBLE	ILLEGAL
Rates of pay	Indemnity bonds	Closed shop
Wages	Management rights as to union affairs	Separation of employees based on race
Hours of employment	Pension benefits of retired employees	Discriminatory treatment
Overtime pay		
Shift differentials	Scope of the bargaining unit	
Holidays	Including supervisors in the contract	
Vacations		
Severance pay	Additional parties to the contract such as the international union	
Pensions		
Insurance benefits		
Profit-sharing plans	Use of union label	
Christmas bonuses	Settlement of unfair labor charges	
Company housing, meals, and discounts	Prices in cafeteria	
Employee security	Continuance of past contract	
Job performance		
Union security	Membership of bargaining team	
Management–union relationship		
Drug testing of employees	Employment of strikebreakers	

Figure 13.4
Bargaining Items

BUILDING YOUR MANAGEMENT SKILLS:
How to Negotiate

Hammering out a satisfactory labor agreement requires negotiating skills. Experienced negotiators use *leverage, desire, time, competition, information, credibility,* and *judgment* to improve their bargaining positions. *Leverage* means using factors that help or hinder the negotiator, usually by putting the other side under pressure.[74] Things you can leverage include *necessity, desire, competition,* and *time.*[75] For example, if the union knows that an employer needs to fill a big order fast (time), the latter is at a disadvantage. Being able to walk away (or to look like you can) wins the best terms. Having information about the other side and about the situation is always advantageous.

Some contract terms (such as reduced pension benefits) may be crucial to you. However, the manager who makes his or her *desires* too obvious undercuts his or her position; good negotiators keep their cards "close to their vests." *Competition* is important too. There is no more convincing ploy than subtly hinting you've got an alternative (like shifting services abroad). *Time* (and particularly your deadlines) can also tilt things for or against you. Because the other side will be trying to decide if you're bluffing, bulking up your *credibility* is important.

Finally, good negotiators need *judgment,* namely the ability to "strike the right balance between gaining advantages and reaching compromises, in the

Continued

substance as well as in the style of [their] negotiating technique."[76] The following sums up some other negotiating guidelines.[77]

- *Set clear objectives* for every bargaining item, and understand on what grounds the objectives are established.
- *Do not hurry.*
- When in doubt, *caucus* with your associates.
- Be *well prepared* with firm data supporting your position.
- Always strive to maintain some *flexibility*.
- Don't just concern yourself with what the other party says and does; *find out why*.
- Respect the importance of *face-saving* for the other party.
- Constantly be alert to the other party's *real intentions*.
- Be a good *listener*.
- Build a reputation for *being fair but firm*.
- Learn to *control your emotions*.
- Be sure as you make each bargaining move that you know its *relationship* to all other moves.
- Measure each move against your *objectives*.
- Pay close attention to the *wording* of every clause renegotiated; words and phrases are often sources of grievances.
- Remember that collective bargaining negotiations are, by nature, part of a *compromise* process.
- Consider the impact of present negotiations on those in *future years*.
- Don't be so open, honest, and straightforward that you start making excessive concessions.[78]

Impasses, Mediation, and Strikes

Signing the agreement assumes that there are no insurmountable disagreements. If there are, the parties may instead declare an impasse. For example, after reaching agreement with its unions on many issues after several months of bargaining, the Polk County (Florida) School District recently declared an impasse. It said that although it had negotiated "in good faith" with its two unions, it could not come to agreement on several thorny issues including wages, transfers, and teacher evaluations.[79]

An impasse (or stalemate) usually occurs because one party demands more than the other offers. Sometimes an impasse can be resolved through a *third party*, a disinterested person such as a mediator or arbitrator. If the impasse is not resolved in this way, the union might call a work stoppage, or *strike*, to pressure management.

Opposing parties use three types of third-party interventions to overcome an impasse: mediation, fact-finding, and arbitration. With **mediation**, a neutral third party tries to assist the principals in reaching agreement. The mediator usually holds meetings with each party to determine each party's position and to find common ground.

The mediator communicates assessments of the likelihood of a strike, the possible settlement packages available, and the like. The mediator generally does not have the authority to insist on a concession. However, he or she probably will make his or her position on some issue clear.

In certain situations (as in a national emergency dispute in which the president of the United States determines that a strike would be a national emergency), a fact-finder may be appointed. A **fact-finder** is a neutral party. He or she studies the issues and makes a public recommendation of what a reasonable settlement ought to be.

mediation
Labor relations intervention in which a neutral third party tries to assist the principals in reaching agreement.

fact-finder
In labor relations, a neutral party who studies the issues in a dispute and makes a public recommendation for a reasonable settlement.

arbitration
The most definitive type of third-party intervention, in which the arbitrator often has the power to determine and dictate the settlement terms.

Arbitration is the most definitive type of third-party intervention because the arbitrator may have the power to decide and dictate settlement terms. Unlike mediation and fact-finding, arbitration can guarantee a solution to an impasse. With *binding arbitration*, both parties are committed to accepting the arbitrator's award. With *nonbinding arbitration*, they are not. Arbitration may also be voluntary or compulsory (in other words, imposed by a government agency). In the United States, voluntary binding arbitration is the most prevalent.

Arbitration may not always be as impartial as it's thought to be. Researchers studied 391 arbitrated cases in baseball over about 20 years. Arbitrator awards favored teams 61% of the time. They concluded that (at least in baseball) "self-interested behavior by arbitrators" might lead to bias against players, and particularly against players of African American and Latin ancestry.[80]

Various public and professional agencies make arbitrators and mediators available. For example, both the American Arbitration Association (AAA) and the U.S. Office of Arbitration Services, part of the U.S. Office of Mediation and Conciliation Service (www.fmcs.gov/internet/), maintain a roster of arbitrators qualified to hear and decide disputes. Employers or unions use a form (see www.fmcs.gov/resources/forms-applications/arbitration/) to request arbitrator or mediator services from them.

Alternative dispute resolution—mostly informal tactics such as the mediator asking if the parties want to take a break, or would set the issue at hand aside temporarily, or if they would each explain their perspectives on the issue—is also popular for heading off or dealing with an impasse.[81]

economic strike
A strike that results from a failure to agree on the terms of a contract that involve wages, benefits, and other conditions of employment.

unfair labor practice strike
A strike aimed at protesting illegal conduct by the employer.

wildcat strike
An unauthorized strike occurring during the term of a contract.

sympathy strike
A strike that takes place when one union strikes in support of another's strike.

Strikes An impasse may trigger a strike, which is a withdrawal of labor. There are four main types of strikes. An **economic strike** results from a failure to agree on the terms of a contract—from an impasse, in other words. An **unfair labor practice strike** protests illegal conduct by the employer. A **wildcat strike** is an unauthorized strike occurring during the term of a contract. A **sympathy strike** occurs when one union strikes in support of the strike of another.

Strikes needn't be an inevitable result of the bargaining process. Instead, studies show that they are often avoidable, but occur because of mistakes during bargaining. Mistakes include discrepancies between union leaders' and rank-and-file members' expectations and misperceptions regarding each side's bargaining goals.[82]

The likelihood of and severity of a strike depends partly on the parties' willingness to "take a strike."[83] For instance, several years ago major league baseball owners were willing to let players strike and to lose a whole season because they had "consistently agreed that the players had been ruining the game by getting too much money and that only a hard line against such excesses" would stop that.[84]

Picketing is one of the first activities occurring during a strike. The purpose of picketing is to inform the public about the existence of the labor dispute and often to encourage others to refrain from doing business with the employer against whom the employees are striking.

Employers can make several responses when they become the object of a strike. One is to halt their operations until the strike is over. A second is to contract out work during the duration of the strike in order to blunt the effects of the strike on the employer. A third alternative is for the employer to continue operations, perhaps using supervisors and other nonstriking workers to fill in for the striking workers. A fourth alternative is to hire replacements for the strikers. In an economic strike, such replacements can be deemed permanent and would not have to be let go to make room for strikers who decided to return to work. If the strike were an unfair labor practice strike, the strikers would be entitled to return to their jobs if the employer makes an unconditional offer for them to do so. When one airline began giving permanent jobs to 1,500 substitute workers it hired to replace striking mechanics several years ago, the strike basically fell apart.[85]

An economic strike results from a failure to agree on the terms of a contract—from an impasse, in other words.

Source: Jim Jurica/Getty Images.

boycott

The combined refusal by employees and other interested parties to buy or use the employer's products.

lockout

A refusal by the employer to provide opportunities to work.

Diminished union influence plus competitive pressures now prompt more employers to replace (or consider replacing) strikers with permanent replacement workers. When the United Steel Workers struck refineries recently, BP quickly began training replacement workers.[86]

Some employers make preparations with special strike security companies to provide security during the strike.[87]

Other Ways to Deal with Impasses and Strikes

Management and labor both use other methods to try to break impasses and strikes. The union, for example, may resort to a *corporate campaign* (also called an *advocacy* or *comprehensive campaign*). This is an organized effort by the union to exert pressure on the employer by pressuring the company's other unions, shareholders, directors, customers, creditors, and government agencies, often directly. For example, a member of the company's board of directors might find that the union has organized its members to **boycott**—stop doing business with—the director's own business. Thus, as part of its campaign to organize hourly factory workers at foreign-owned car plants in the United States, the UAW picketed U.S. Hyundai, Daimler, Toyota, and Nissan dealerships.[88]

Inside games are union efforts to convince employees to impede or to disrupt production. They might do this, for example, by slowing the work pace, refusing to work overtime, holding sickouts, or refusing to do work without receiving detailed instructions from supervisors (even though such instruction had not previously been required).

Employers can try to break an impasse with *lockouts*. A **lockout** is a refusal by the employer to provide opportunities to work. The company (often literally) locks out employees and prohibits them from doing their jobs (and thus from being paid). Faced with a new contract that might slash their wages by 50%, Canadian Auto Workers Union employees from a local Caterpillar plant found themselves locked out after six months of negotiations failed to produce a settlement.[89]

The NLRB views a lockout as an unfair labor practice only when the employer acts for a prohibited purpose. It is not a prohibited purpose to try to bring about a settlement of negotiations on terms favorable to the employer. However, employers are usually reluctant to cease operations when employees are willing to continue working (even though there may be an impasse at the bargaining table).

Employers exert pressure in other ways. When Boeing's union resisted accepting new labor concessions at its assembly facility in Washington, Boeing began actively discussing moving the planned assembly of its new Boeing 777X jet to South Carolina. Boeing's Washington state workers subsequently approved the new agreement.[90]

During the impasse, both employers and unions can seek *injunctive relief* if they believe the other side is taking actions that could irreparably harm the other party. To obtain such relief, the NLRB must show the district court that an unfair labor practice—such as interfering with the union organizing campaign—if left unremedied, will irreparably harm the other party's statutory rights. Such relief is requested after the NLRB issues an unfair labor practices complaint. The *injunctive relief* is a judicial order calling for a cessation of certain actions deemed injurious.[91]

The Contract Agreement

The contract agreement itself may be 20 or 30 pages long or longer. The main sections of a typical contract cover subjects such as:

1. Management rights
2. Union security and automatic payroll dues deduction
3. Grievance procedures
4. Arbitration of grievances
5. Disciplinary procedures
6. Compensation rates
7. Hours of work and overtime
8. Benefits such as vacation, holidays, insurance, and pension
9. Health and safety provisions
10. Employee security seniority provisions
11. Contract expiration date

⭐ Watch It

What is it like to actually work with the union? If your professor has chosen to assign this, go to **www.pearson.com/mylab/management** to watch the video UPS Union Management, and then answer the questions to show what you would do in this situation.

Contract Administration: Dealing with Grievances

Signing the labor agreement is not the end of the process because questions will always arise about what various clauses really mean. The *grievance process* is the process or steps that the employer and union agreed to follow to ascertain whether some action violated the collective bargaining agreement. The grievance process should not renegotiate contracts. Instead, the aim is to clarify what those contract points really mean, in the context of addressing grievances regarding things like time off, disciplinary action, and pay. When the Cleveland Browns' head coach fined one of his players $1,701 for not paying for a $3 bottle of water several years ago, players quickly filed grievances with the NFL.[92]

Employees will use just about any issue involving wages, hours, or conditions of employment as the basis of a grievance. Discipline cases and seniority problems (including promotions, transfers, and layoffs) would probably top the list. Others include grievances growing out of job evaluations and work assignments, overtime, vacations, incentive plans, and holidays.

Unions may use the grievance process to pressure employers. For example, postal workers in Roanoke, Virginia filed 1,800 grievances in several months at the Postal Service's mail-processing facility (the usual rate is about 800 grievances per year). They apparently were responding to job changes, including transfers triggered by efforts to further automate processes.[93]

The Grievance Process Whatever the source of the grievance, many firms today (and virtually all unionized ones) do give employees some means through which to air and settle their grievances.

Grievance procedures are typically multistep processes. (FedEx's Guaranteed Fair Treatment Process, discussed in Chapter 12, is one example.) A typical first step might be to file a form that usually includes information on the grievant's name, signature, department, and the date, as well as a statement of the grievance and the remedy sought. Step two might require the grievant to try to work out an agreement with his or her supervisor, perhaps with a union officer or colleague present. Appeals may then go to the supervisor's boss, then that person's boss, and perhaps finally to an arbitrator.

It is generally best, but not always possible, to develop a work environment in which grievances don't occur at all. Doing so depends on being able to recognize, diagnose, and correct the underlying causes of potential employee dissatisfaction before they become grievances. Typical causes include allegedly unfair appraisals, inequitable wages, or poor communications. Yet, in practice, grievances can be minimized, not eradicated. The following Management Skills feature presents important guidelines.

BUILDING YOUR MANAGEMENT SKILLS:
Guidelines for Handling a Grievance[94]

One expert has developed a list of supervisor do's and don'ts as useful guides in handling grievances.[95] Some critical ones include the following:

Do

- Investigate and handle every case as though it may eventually result in an arbitration hearing.
- Talk with the employee about his or her grievance; give the person a full hearing.
- Require the union to identify specific contractual provisions allegedly violated.
- Comply with the contractual time limits for handling the grievance.
- Visit the work area of the grievance.
- Determine whether there were any witnesses.
- Examine the grievant's personnel record.
- Fully examine prior grievance records.
- Treat the union representative as your equal.
- Hold your grievance discussion privately.
- Fully inform your own supervisor of grievance matters.

Don't

- Discuss the case with the union steward alone—the grievant should be there.
- Make arrangements with individual employees that are inconsistent with the labor agreement.
- Hold back the remedy if the company is wrong.
- Admit to the binding effect of a past practice.
- Relinquish to the union your rights as a manager.
- Settle grievances on the basis of what is "fair." Instead, stick to the labor agreement.
- Bargain over items not covered by the contract.
- Treat as subject to arbitration claims demanding the discipline or discharge of managers.
- Give long written grievance answers.
- Trade a grievance settlement for a grievance withdrawal (or try to make up for a bad decision in one grievance by bending over backward in another).
- Deny grievances on the premise that your "hands have been tied by management."
- Agree to informal amendments in the contract.

LEARNING OBJECTIVE 6
Explain why union membership dropped and what the prospects are for the union movement.

What's Next for Unions?

For years, construction trade unions in New York placed a huge inflatable rat balloon in front of construction sites that they were targeting, but they rarely do that anymore. As the business manager for one local plumbers union put it, "Our philosophy for the past 15 years hasn't created any more market share for us. We have been viewed as troublemakers . . . . Now we are going to use [public relations] to dispel those perceptions."[96]

Why the Union Decline?

Union membership has gradually declined in America, from about 20% of the workforce in 1983 (when 17.8 million workers belonged to unions) to about 11.1 % (almost 15 million workers) in 2016.[97]

Several factors contributed to this decline. Unions traditionally appealed mostly to blue-collar workers, and the proportion of blue-collar jobs has dropped while service-sector and white-collar jobs have increased. (Why? A proliferation of free trade agreements prompted intense global competition and increased pressures to cut costs and boost productivity, which many firms reacted to by sending jobs overseas. Robotization and automation displaced still more blue-collar workers.) The poor economy after the 2007–2008 recession triggered budget cuts in both the public and private sectors, prompting anti-union public policy attitudes and the loss of about one million public-sector union jobs. And bankruptcies often end with courts imposing less-favorable contract terms on union employees.[98] For example, a bankruptcy court judge gave Patriot Coal Corp. the right to drastically reduce pay and benefits for thousands of miners, retirees, and dependents.[99] The net effect has been the permanent layoff of hundreds of thousands of union members.

What Are Unions Doing About It?

Unions are becoming more aggressive. For example, unions would like to pass the *Employee Free Choice Act*. This would make it easier for employees to unionize. Instead of secret-ballot elections, the act would institute a "card check" system. Here the union would win recognition when a majority of workers signed authorization cards saying they want the union. The act would also require binding arbitration to set a first contract's terms if the company and union can't negotiate an agreement within 120 days.[100] Unions are also using *class-action lawsuits* to support employees in nonunionized companies to pressure employers.[101] And, unions are cooperating more with so-called "alternative labor groups," which advocate for improved worker benefits and working conditions, but are not unions themselves.[102]

Finally, unions are becoming more proactive in coordinating their efforts.[103] For example, to support its efforts to unionize autoworkers in the United States, the UAW enlisted thousands of union members in Brazil to picket Nissan dealerships there.[104] And when Daimler said it was going to phase out producing its "C" cars in Germany and begin producing them in the United States, its German union, IG Metall, began cooperating with the UAW to unionize Daimler's American plants (please see the HR in Practice feature at the end of this chapter).[105]

Recent Trends in Labor Laws Former president Obama's administration was on balance supportive of unions. For example, one NLRB ruling made it easier for unions to organize by letting them focus on small "micro" groups within the employer's workforce.[106] Also favoring unions, a few years ago the NLRB published its Final Rule permitting what many call "quickie" union elections. By allowing unions to call elections in as little as 13 days after filing a representation petition, this new rule is expected by labor experts to make it more difficult for employers to present their argument against the union.[107] The NLRB also lengthened the amount of time that employees who organized under a card check process (see earlier discussion) had to wait to start a decertification process. And after being exempted for many years from having to disclose their participation with each other in a union campaign, employers and their union campaign-related consultants and attorneys now must report their relationship.[108] In 2017, President Trump appointed a Republican labor law attorney for a vacancy on the NLRB; experts assume the board will soon move to reverse some of the Obama-era board decisions.[109]

Cooperative Labor–Management Relations

News reports tend to highlight adversarial labor–management relations, but the history of labor–management relations is also sprinkled with instances of cooperation.

For example, more than 50 years ago, General Motors and Toyota created a joint venture they called New United Motor Manufacturing Inc. (NUMMI). NUMMI reopened a former GM plant (in what today produces Tesla automobiles) in Fremont, California. The plant had suffered from such poisonous labor relations that GM had to close it. The new partners hoped to merge GM's marketing expertise with Toyota's famous team-based management system.[110] NUMMI and the UAW agreed that management and labor would work together as a team, give workers a voice in decision making, and build the highest-quality cars at the lowest cost. The plant was soon very successful (although the parties eventually ended their joint venture).

Since then, many labor–management agreements have included so-called cooperative agreements and clauses. These express commitments to adhere to one or more cooperative themes, such as a statement of commitment to cooperate, setting up committees to review mutual concerns that arise, and even guarantees of employment security.

What management strategy should an employer follow to foster union–management cooperation?

There is little doubt, as one study says, that unions "that have a cooperative relationship with management can play an important role in overcoming barriers to the effective adoption of practices that have been linked to organizational competitiveness."[111] But as the same study argues, employers who want to capitalize on that potential must change how they think, by avoiding adversarial labor relations and instead emphasizing a cooperative partnership.[112] Here a strategy that emphasizes the fairness and trust we discussed earlier and in Chapter 12 is probably helpful. The HR in Practice feature describes an example.

■ HR in Practice

Labor–Management Cooperation and Works Councils in America

When the United Auto Workers lost an effort to unionize the Volkswagen plant outside Chattanooga, Tennessee, the vote of 712 to 626 against joining the UAW surprised even Volkswagen management.

One reason for the surprise was that Volkswagen actually supported unionizing the plant. Part of the reason Volkswagen supported unionization is because it said it wanted to bring to Chattanooga the works councils that it uses successfully in Germany. A *works council* is an employee committee that elects representatives who work with management to establish policies on things like work hours and dismissal procedures.[113] The works councils meet monthly with managers to discuss topics ranging from no-smoking policies to layoffs.[114] (*Codetermination* is also the rule in Germany and several other countries. **Codetermination** means employees have the legal right to a voice in setting company policies. Workers elect their own representatives to the supervisory board of the employer.[115]) As the CEO of Volkswagen Chattanooga said, works councils are the "key to our success and productivity."[116]

Volkswagen still hopes to bring works councils to its Chattanooga plant, but U.S. labor law may stand in the way, unless the plant's workers vote for a union. Many years ago, some employers tried to neutralize legitimate unions by setting up company-backed "faux unions," a practice Congress soon outlawed. Although works councils are legitimate in many areas, most experts believe that having nonunion employee representatives bargaining on matters such as pay and dismissals won't pass muster with American labor law.

codetermination
Employees have the legal right to a voice in setting company policies. Workers elect their own representatives to the supervisory board of the employer.

⭐ Talk About It—**5**

If your professor has chosen to assign this, go to **www.pearson.com/mylab/ management** to discuss the following question. What do you think accounts for the fact that German labor relations seem to be so much more cooperative than in America?

CHAPTER 13

Review

MyLab Management

If your instructor is using MyLab Management, go to **www.pearson.com/mylab/ management** to complete the problems marked with this icon ⭐.

Summary

1. The labor movement is important. About 14.8 million U.S. workers belong to unions. In addition to improved wages and working conditions, unions seek security when organizing. There are five possible arrangements, including the closed shop, union shop, agency shop, preferential shop, and maintenance of membership.

2. Findings suggest that engaged employees are less likely to support a unionization effort in their companies, and that unionized employees are less engaged. On the whole, the findings suggest that whatever improves employee engagement may also reduce the likelihood of being unionized.

3. The Norris-LaGuardia Act and the Wagner Act marked a shift in labor law from repression to strong encouragement of union activity. They did this by banning certain types of unfair labor practices, by providing for secret-ballot elections, and by creating the NLRB. The Taft-Hartley Act enumerated the rights of employees with respect to their unions, enumerated the rights of employers, and allowed the U.S. president to temporarily bar national emergency strikes. Among other things, it also enumerated certain union unfair labor practices. For example, it banned unions from restraining or coercing employees from exercising their guaranteed bargaining rights. The Landrum-Griffin Act, among other things, affirms a member's right to sue his or her union.

4. There are five steps in a union drive and election: the initial contact, authorization cards, a hearing with the NLRB, the campaign, and the election itself. Remember that the union need only win a majority of the votes cast, *not* a majority of the workers in the bargaining unit.

5. Bargaining collectively in good faith is the next step if and when the union wins the election. Good faith means that both parties communicate and negotiate, and that proposals are matched with counterproposals. Some hints on bargaining include do not hurry, be prepared, find out why, and be a good listener. An impasse occurs when the parties aren't able to move further toward settlement. Third-party involvement—namely, arbitration, fact-finding, or mediation—is one alternative. Sometimes, though, a strike occurs. Responding to the strike involves such steps as shutting the facility, contracting out work, or possibly replacing the workers. Boycotts and lockouts are two other anti-impasse weapons sometimes used by labor and management.

6. Unions are not sitting idly by, watching their numbers dwindle. For example, unions are pushing to pass the Employee Free Choice Act. Employers that want to capitalize on the potential of improved labor–management relations might change how they think, by avoiding adversarial industrial relations and instead emphasizing a cooperative partnership.

Key Terms

closed shop   405
union shop   405
agency shop   405
preferential shop   405
maintenance of membership arrangement   405
right to work   405
Norris-LaGuardia Act   407
Wagner Act   407
National Labor Relations Board (NLRB)   407
Taft-Hartley Act   408
national emergency strikes   408
Landrum-Griffin Act   409
union salting   410
authorization cards   411
bargaining unit   412
decertification   416

collective bargaining   418
good-faith bargaining   418
voluntary (permissible) bargaining items   419
illegal bargaining items   419
mandatory bargaining items   419
mediation   421
fact-finder   421
arbitration   422
economic strike   422
unfair labor practice strike   422
wildcat strike   422
sympathy strike   422
boycott   423
lockout   423
codetermination   427

Discussion Questions

13-1. Briefly describe the history and structure of the U.S. union movement.

⭐13-2. Discuss the nature of the major federal labor relations laws.

⭐13-3. Discuss the main steps in the collective bargaining process.

13-4. Explain why union membership dropped, and what the prospects are for the union movement.

13-5. Why do employees join unions? What are the advantages and disadvantages of being a union member?

13-6. What actions might make employers lose elections?

13-7. Describe important tactics you would expect the union to use during the union drive and election.

13-8. What is meant by good-faith bargaining? Using examples, explain when bargaining is not in good faith.

13-9. Define impasse, mediation, and strike, and explain the techniques that are used to overcome an impasse.

Individual and Group Activities

13-10. You are the manager of a small manufacturing plant. The union contract covering most of your employees is about to expire. Working individually or in groups, discuss how to prepare for union contract negotiations.

13-11. Working individually or in groups, use Internet resources to find situations where company management and the union reached an impasse at some point during their negotiation process, but eventually resolved the impasse. Describe the issues on both sides that led to the impasse. How did they move past the impasse? What were the final outcomes?

13-12. Several years ago, 8,000 Amtrak workers agreed not to disrupt service by walking out, at least not until a court hearing was held. Amtrak had asked the courts for a temporary restraining order, and the Transport Workers Union of America was actually pleased to postpone its walkout. The workers were apparently not upset at Amtrak, but at Congress, for failing to provide enough funding for Amtrak. What, if anything, can an employer do when employees threaten to go on strike, not because of what the employer did, but because of what a third party—in this case, Congress—has done or not done? What laws would prevent the union from going on strike in this case?

CHAPTER 13

13-13. The Kaiser Permanente Health System is often held out as an employer with very good labor relations. What can you discern from websites such as www.kaiserpermanentejobs.org (then click Who we are) that might explain such a reputation?

13-14. What does www.seiu.org/ tell you about this union's aims and how it intends to achieve them?

13-15. For this activity, you will need the documents titled (1) "HRCI PHR® and SPHR® Certification Body of Knowledge," and (2) "About the Society for Human Resource Management (SHRM) Body of Competency & Knowledge® Model and Certification Exams." Your instructor can obtain these two documents from the Pearson Instructor Resource Center and pass them on to you.

These two documents list the knowledge someone studying for the HRCI or SHRM certification exam needs to have in each area of human resource management (such as in Strategic Management, and Workforce Planning). In groups of several students, do four things: (1) review the HRCI and/or SHRM documents; (2) identify the material in this chapter that relates to HRCI's or SHRM's required knowledge lists; (3) write four multiple-choice exam questions on this material that you believe would be suitable for inclusion in the HRCI exam and/or the SHRM exam; and, (4) if time permits, have someone from your team post your team's questions in front of the class, so that students in all teams can answer the exam questions created by the other teams.

MyManagement Lab

If your instructor is using MyLab Management, go to **mymanagementlab.com** for Auto-graded writing questions as well as the following Assisted-graded writing questions:

13-16. Explain in detail each step in a union drive and election.

13-17. Briefly illustrate how labor law has gone through a cycle of repression and encouragement.

APPLICATION EXERCISES

HR IN ACTION CASE INCIDENT 1

Negotiating with the Writers Guild of America

The talks between the Writers Guild of America (WGA) and the Alliance of Motion Picture & Television Producers (producers) started off tense a decade ago, and then got tenser. In their first meeting, the two sides got nothing done. As the then-*Law & Order* producer Dick Wolf said, "Everyone in the room is concerned about this."[117]

The two sides were far apart on just about all the issues. However, the biggest issue was how to split revenue from new media, such as when television shows move on to DVDs or the Internet. The producers said they wanted a profit-splitting system rather than the current residual system. Under the residual system, writers continue to receive "residuals," or income from shows they write, every time they're shown (such as when *Seinfeld* appears in reruns, years after the last original show was shot). Writers Guild executives did their homework. They argued, for instance, that the projections showed producers' revenues from advertising and subscription fees jumped by about 40% in just a few years.[118] Writers wanted part of that.

The situation grew tenser. After the first few meetings, one producers' representative said, "We can see after the dogfight whose position will win out. The open question there, of course, is whether each of us take several lumps at the table, reaches an agreement then licks their wounds later—none the worse for wear—or whether we inflict more lasting damage through work stoppages that benefit no one before we come to an agreement."[119] Even after meeting six times, it seemed that "the parties' only apparent area of agreement is that no real bargaining has yet to occur."[120]

In October 2007, the Writers Guild asked its members for strike authorization, and the producers were claiming that the Guild was just trying to delay negotiations until the current contract expired (at the end of October). As the president of the television producers association said, "We have had six across-the-table sessions and there was only silence and stonewalling from the WGA leadership . . . . We have attempted to engage on major issues, but no dialogue has been forthcoming from the WGA leadership . . . . The WGA leadership apparently has no intention to bargain in good faith."[121] As evidence, the producers claimed that the WGA negotiating committee left one meeting after less than an hour at the bargaining table.

Both sides knew timing in these negotiations was very important. During the fall and spring, television series production is in full swing. So, a strike now by the writers would have a bigger impact than waiting until, say, the summer to strike. Perhaps not surprisingly, by January 2008 some movement was discernible. In a separate set of negotiations, the Directors Guild of America reached an agreement with the producers that addressed many of the issues that the writers were focusing on, such as how to divide up the new media income.[122] In February 2008, the WGA and producers finally reached agreement. The new contract was "the direct result of renewed negotiations between the two sides, which culminated Friday with a marathon session including top WGA officials and the heads of the Walt Disney Co. and News Corp."[123]

Questions

13-18. The producers said the WGA wasn't bargaining in good faith. What did they mean by that, and do you think the evidence is sufficient to support the claim?

13-19. The WGA did eventually strike. What tactics could the producers have used to fight back once the strike began? What tactics do you think the WGA used?

13-20. This was basically a conflict between professional and creative people (the WGA) and TV and movie producers. Do you think the conflict was therefore different in any way than are the conflicts between, say, the autoworkers or Teamsters unions against auto and trucking companies? Why?

13-21. What role did negotiating skills seem to play in the WGA–producers negotiations? Provide examples.

HR IN ACTION CASE INCIDENT 2

Carter Cleaning Company

The Grievance

On visiting one of Carter Cleaning Company's stores, Jennifer was surprised to be taken aside by a long-term Carter employee, who met her as she was parking her car. "Murray (the store manager) told me I was suspended for two days without pay because I came in late last Thursday," said George. "I'm really upset, but around here the store manager's word seems to be law, and it sometimes seems like the only way anyone can file a grievance is by meeting you or your father like this in the parking lot." Jennifer was very disturbed by this revelation and promised the employee she would look into it and discuss the situation with her father. In the car heading back to headquarters, she began mulling over what Carter Cleaning Company's alternatives might be.

Questions

13-22. Do you think it is important for Carter Cleaning Company to have a formal grievance process? Why or why not?

13-23. Based on what you know about the Carter Cleaning Company, outline the steps in what you think would be the ideal grievance process for this company.

13-24. In addition to the grievance process, can you think of anything else that Carter Cleaning Company might do to make sure that grievances and gripes like this one get expressed and also get heard by top management?

Experiential Exercise

The Organizing Campaign at Sam's Cupcake Shop

Purpose: The purpose of this exercise is to give you practice in dealing with some of the elements of a union-organizing campaign.[124]

Required Understanding: You should be familiar with the material covered in this chapter, as well as the following incident, "The Organizing Campaign at Sam's Cupcake Shop."

Incident: Sam's Cupcake Shop sells baked goods (croissants, cupcakes, rolls, cakes, etc.) and serves light meals such as breakfast and salads through its chain of ten small retail stores in the borough of Manhattan, in New York City. Each store is staffed with about 9 employees (plus one manager), some of whom do the cooking and some of whom staff the counter and sell the food items. As with Sam's other four stores, the Sam's Cupcake Shop on First Avenue is staffed primarily with recent (legal) immigrants to America, all of whom are paid at or just above the minimum wage. It was no secret that at least one New York City agency was pressing (in 2015) for food service owners to raise the minimum wage for food service employees to $15 per hour.[125] However everything at the First Avenue store seemed to be going smoothly, but that apparent tranquility ended abruptly about a month ago. That was the day that Anesha, the First Avenue store's manager, called Taylor Brooke, Sam's Cupcake's human resource manager, to tell her that they had "an employee problem."

The problem, Anesha said, is that she'd heard from a few employees that the Service Employees International Union was trying to organize Sam's Cupcake Shop' employees. Taylor's first reaction was one of caution, particularly because food service employees are historically difficult to organize—"they don't stay in their jobs long enough to unionize them," to paraphrase one union leader.[126] However, being a conscientious person, Anesha said she had already taken what she called "sensible steps" to blunt the unionization

effort. She had, first, explained to her employees that if costs went up because they unionized, then "we'd probably have to close this shop."[127] She said she also promised employees benefits (such as better work schedules) if they "ignored" the union and told them they were prohibited from discussing union matters during work time.

The more Anesha talked, the more concerned Taylor became, not with the union but with the possible consequences of Anesha's efforts.

How to Set Up the Exercise/Instructions: Divide the class into groups of four or five students. Assume that you are labor relations consultants retained by Sam's Cupcake Shop to identify the problems and issues involved and to advise Taylor about what to do next. Each group will spend about 45 minutes discussing the issues and outlining those issues as well as an action plan for Taylor. What should he do now? If time permits, a spokesperson from each group should list on the board the issues involved and the group's recommendations.

14

Improving Occupational Safety, Health, and Risk Management

OVERVIEW:
In this chapter, we will cover . . .

- Employee Safety and Health: An Introduction
- What Causes Accidents?
- How to Prevent Accidents
- Employee Engagement Guide for Managers
- Workplace Health: Problems and Remedies
- Occupational Security and Risk Management

MyLab Management

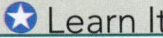 Improve Your Grade!
When you see this icon, visit
www.pearson.com/mylab/management for
activities that are applied, personalized, and
offer immediate feedback.

LEARNING OBJECTIVES

When you finish studying this chapter, you should be able to:

1. Discuss OSHA and how it operates.
2. Explain in detail three basic causes of accidents.
3. Explain how to prevent accidents at work.
4. Describe how one company uses employee engagement to improve workplace safety.
5. Discuss major health problems at work and how to remedy them.
6. Discuss the main elements in an occupational security and risk management program.

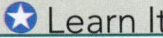 Learn It

If your professor has chosen to assign this, go to **www.pearson.com/mylab/ management** to see what you should particularly focus on and to take the Chapter 14 Warm Up.

Source: Kali9/Getty Images.

LEARNING OBJECTIVE 1
Discuss OSHA and how it operates.

INTRODUCTION

Janet felt awful. She'd been store manager of the QuickClean Dry-cleaning store for three years, and no one had ever had a serious accident. But today Moe the cleaner-spotter was cleaning a garment, and the cleaning chemical sprayed in his eyes; they had to rush him to the emergency room. Janet had to figure out how to make sure something like that didn't happen again.

Employee Safety and Health: An Introduction

Why Safety Is Important

Several years ago while filming *Star Wars: The Force Awakens*, a hydraulic door on the Millennium Falcon spaceship slammed Harrison Ford with the weight of a small car. It put him out of commission for several weeks, but thankfully didn't injure him seriously.[1]

Safety and accident prevention concern managers for several reasons, one of which is the staggering number of workplace accidents. In one recent year, 4,836 U.S. workers died in workplace incidents,[2] and workplace accidents caused about 2.9 million occupational injuries and illnesses.[3] There are about one million workplace hand injuries annually, from cuts to amputations.[4] Such figures probably underestimate injuries and illnesses by two or three times.[5] And, they ignore the hardships the accidents cause to the employee and his or her loved ones.[6] More than 80% of the workers in one survey ranked workplace safety as more important than minimum wages, sick days, and maternity leave.[7] Safety also affects costs and profits, as the accompanying HR as a Profit Center feature illustrates.

■ HR as a Profit Center

Improving Safety Boosts Profits

Many people assume that economizing on safety cuts costs, but that's not really the case. Poor safety and the injuries and illnesses it causes actually drive up medical expenses, workers' compensation, and lost productivity.[8] Poor safety practices even raise wage rates: wage rates are higher on riskier jobs, other things equal.[9]

For example, one study found a 9.4% drop in injury claims and a 26% average savings on workers' compensation costs over four years in companies inspected by California's occupational safety and health agency.[10] A survey of chief financial officers concluded that for every one dollar invested in injury prevention, the employer earns two dollars. Forty percent of the chief financial officers said "productivity" was the top benefit of effective workplace safety.[11] One forest products company saved over $1 million by investing only about $50,000 in safety improvements and employee training. In the United States, work-related hearing loss costs employers about $242 million a year in workers' compensation claims alone, costs that are probably avoidable through earmuffs, earplugs, and training.[12] So ironically, one of the easiest ways to cut costs and boost profits is to improve safety.

✪ Talk About It–**1**

If your professor has chosen to assign this, go to **www.pearson.com/mylab/management** to discuss the following question. Assuming this is true, why do so many employers apparently cut corners on safety?

Management's Role in Safety

Several years ago an energy company's CEO was convicted in relation to the deaths of 29 workers in a coal mine.[13] His conviction highlights the fact that the people at the top—the CEO, president, and board members—must set the tone for occupational safety.[14]

Telling supervisors to "watch for spills" and employees to "work safely" is futile unless everyone knows management is serious about safety.[15] For example, DuPont's accident rate has long been lower than that of the chemical industry as a whole. This is partly due to an organizational commitment to safety, which is evident in the following description:

> One of the best examples I know of in setting the highest possible priority for safety takes place at a DuPont Plant in Germany. Each morning at the DuPont Polyester and Nylon Plant, the director and his assistants meet at 8:45 to review the past 24 hours. The first matter they discuss is not production, but safety. Only after they have examined reports of accidents and near misses and satisfied themselves that corrective action has been taken do they move on to look at output, quality, and cost matters.[16]

The employer should institutionalize its commitment with a safety policy, publicize it, and give safety matters high priority.[17] Georgia-Pacific reduced its workers' compensation costs by requiring that managers halve accidents or forfeit 30% of their bonuses. ABB Inc. requires top executives to make safety observation tours of the company's facilities, sites, and projects at least quarterly.[18] (Possibly because they provide more apprenticeship training and make it easier to report dangers, unionized facilities tend to have fewer accidents than nonunionized ones.)[19]

The first-line supervisor also plays a vital role in safety, as the HR Tools feature illustrates.

■ HR Tools for Line Managers and Small Businesses

The Supervisor's Role in Accident Prevention

After inspecting a work site where workers were installing sewer pipes in a 4-foot trench, the Occupational Safety and Health Administration (OSHA) inspector cited the employer for violating the OSHA rule requiring employers to have a "stairway, ladder, ramp or other safe means of egress."[20] In the event the trench caved in, workers needed a quick way out.

As in most such cases, the employer had the primary responsibility for safety, but the local supervisor was responsible for day-to-day inspections. Here, the supervisor did not properly do his daily inspection. The trench collapsed, injuring workers (and, secondarily, costing his company many thousands of dollars).

Whether you're the manager in the IT department of a *Fortune* 500 company or managing a dry cleaning store, daily safety inspections should be part of your routine. As one safety recommendation put it, "a daily walk-through of your workplace—whether you are working in outdoor construction, indoor manufacturing, or any place that poses safety challenges—is an essential part of your work."[21]

What to look for depends on the workplace. For example, construction sites and dry cleaning stores have hazards all their own. But in general you can use a checklist of unsafe conditions such as the one in Figure 14.4 (pages 441–443) to spot problems.

✪ Talk About It–**2**

If your professor has chosen to assign this, go to **www.pearson.com/mylab/ management** to discuss the following question. Please stop what you are doing and look around the immediate area where you are now: List four potential safety hazards. How could Janet (from the chapter opener) use Figure 14.4 now?

A Manager's Briefing on Occupational Law

Congress passed the **Occupational Safety and Health Act of 1970**[22] "to assure so far as possible every working man and woman in the nation safe and healthful working conditions and to preserve our human resources." The act covers most employers. The main employers it doesn't cover are self-employed persons, farms employing only the employer's immediate family members, and certain workplaces protected by other federal agencies or statutes. The act covers federal agencies. It usually doesn't apply to state and local governments in their role as employers.

The act created the **Occupational Safety and Health Administration (OSHA)** within the Department of Labor. OSHA's basic purpose is to administer the act and to set and enforce the safety and health standards that apply to almost all workers in the United States. OSHA has about 2,200 inspectors working from branch offices throughout the country.[23] With a limited number of inspectors, OSHA recently has focused on "fair and effective enforcement," combined with outreach, education and compliance assistance, and various OSHA–employer cooperative programs (such as its Voluntary Protection Programs).[24]

OSHA Standards and Record Keeping OSHA operates under the "general duty clause" that each employer

> shall furnish to each of his [or her] employees employment and a place of employment which are free from recognized hazards that are causing or are likely to cause death or serious physical harm to his [or her] employees.

To carry out this basic mission, OSHA is responsible for promulgating enforceable standards. The standards cover just about every conceivable hazard, in detail. (Company safety officials also rely on detailed safety standards from the International Safety Equipment Association [INSEA] and from the American National Standards Institute [ANSI]).[25] Figure 14.1 shows part of the OSHA standard governing scaffold handrails. Such specificity is not excessive. For example, even choosing a ladder requires expertise. One must consider its weight rating, material (most industrial applications require fiberglass ladders for nonconductivity), and length or height (to allow workers to reach the work without climbing on the top rung).[26]

Under OSHA, employers with 11 or more employees must maintain a record of, and report, occupational injuries and occupational illnesses.[27] An *occupational illness* is any abnormal condition or disorder caused by exposure to environmental factors associated with employment. This includes illnesses caused by inhalation, absorption, ingestion, or direct contact with toxic substances or harmful agents.

As summarized in Figure 14.2, employers must report all occupational illnesses.[28] They must also report most occupational injuries, specifically those that result in medical treatment (other than first aid), loss of consciousness, restriction of work (one or more lost workdays), restriction of motion, or transfer to another job.[29] If an on-the-job accident results in the death of an employee or in the hospitalization of five or more employees, all employers, regardless of size, must report the accident to OSHA.[30] If even one employee is hospitalized due to a work-related incident, the employer must notify OSHA within 24 hours.[31]

Figure 14.1

OSHA Standards Example

Source: Occupational Safety and Health Administration (OSHA).

> Guardrails not less than 2" × 4" or the equivalent and not less than 36" or more than 42" high, with a midrail, when required, of a 1" × 4" lumber or equivalent, and toeboards, shall be installed at all open sides on all scaffolds more than 10 feet above the ground or floor. Toeboards shall be a minimum of 4" in height. Wire mesh shall be installed in accordance with paragraph [a] [17] of this section.

Figure 14.2

What Accidents Must Be Reported under the Occupational Safety and Health Act?

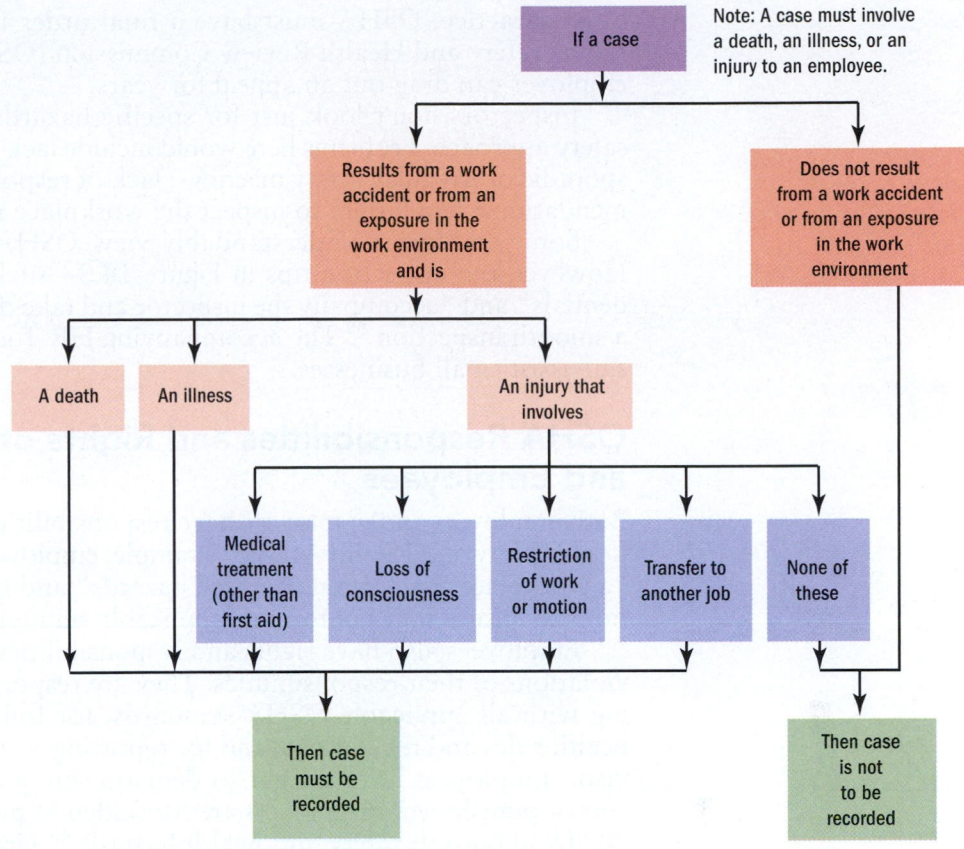

OSHA Inspections and Citations

OSHA enforces its standards through inspections and (if necessary) citations. The inspection is usually unannounced. OSHA may not conduct warrantless inspections without an employer's consent.[32]

Inspection Priorities OSHA makes extensive use of inspections, taking a "worst-first" approach to setting priorities. Priorities include, from highest to lowest, imminent dangers, catastrophes and fatal accidents, employee complaints, high-hazard industries inspections, and follow-up inspections.[33] In one recent year, OSHA conducted about 40,600 inspections[34] and accepted more than 3,000 whistle-blower cases.[35] Because its inspectors can't visit all employers' sites, OSHA publicly posts employers' safety and health data in an effort to encourage safer practices.[36]

The Inspection OSHA inspectors look for violations of all types, but some potential problem areas—such as scaffolding, fall protection, and inadequate hazard communications—grab more of their attention.

After the inspector submits the report to the local OSHA office, the area director determines what citations, if any, to issue. The **citations** inform the employer and employees of the regulations and standards violated and of the time set for rectifying the problem.

citations
Summons informing employers and employees of the regulations and standards that have been violated in the workplace.

Penalties OSHA can also impose penalties. In general, OSHA calculates these based on the violation's gravity, but it also usually considers factors like the size of the business, the firm's compliance history, and the employer's good faith. Penalties generally range from $5,000 up to $70,000 for willful or repeat serious violations (although they can be in the millions). The OSHA area director may enter into settlement agreements. Therefore, many cases are settled before litigation: OSHA then issues the citation and agreed-on penalties simultaneously.[37]

In practice, OSHA must have a final order from the independent Occupational Safety and Health Review Commission (OSHRC) to enforce a penalty. An employer can drag out an appeal for years.

Inspectors don't look just for specific hazards but also for a comprehensive safety approach. Problems here would include lack of a systematic safety approach; sporadic or irregular safety meetings; lack of responsiveness to safety audit recommendations; and failure to inspect the workplace regularly.[38]

Some employers understandably view OSHA inspections with trepidation. However, the inspection tips in Figure 14.3—such as "check the inspector's credentials" and "accompany the inspector and take detailed notes"—can help ensure a smooth inspection.[39] The accompanying HR Tools feature explains how OSHA can assist small businesses.

OSHA Responsibilities and Rights of Employers and Employees

Both employers and employees have responsibilities and rights under the Occupational Safety and Health Act. For example, employers are responsible for providing "a workplace free from recognized hazards" and for examining workplace conditions to ensure they conform to applicable standards.

Employees also have rights and responsibilities, but OSHA can't cite them for violations of their responsibilities. They are responsible, for example, for complying with all applicable OSHA standards, for following all employer safety and health rules and regulations, and for reporting hazardous conditions to the supervisor. Employees have a right to demand safety and health on the job without fear of punishment. Employers are forbidden to punish workers who complain to OSHA about job safety and health hazards.[40] However, they must still make "a diligent effort to discourage, by discipline if necessary, violations of safety rules by employees."[41]

Figure 14.3

OSHA Inspection Tips

Initial Contact

- Refer the inspector to your OSHA coordinator.
- Check the inspector's credentials.
- Ask why he or she is inspecting. Is it a complaint? Programmed visit? Fatality or accident follow-up? Imminent danger investigation?
- If the inspection is the result of a complaint, the inspector won't identify the complainant, but you are entitled to know whether the person is a current employee.
- Notify your OSHA counsel, who should review all requests from the inspector for documents and information. Your counsel also should review the documents and information you provide to the inspector.

Opening Conference

- Establish the focus and scope of the planned inspection: Does the inspector want to inspect the premises or simply study your records?
- Discuss the procedures for protecting trade-secret areas, conducting employee interviews, and producing documents.
- Show the inspector that you have safety programs in place. He or she may not go to the work floor if paperwork is complete and up-to-date.

Walk-Around Inspection

- Accompany the inspector and take detailed notes.
- If the inspector takes a photo or video, you should too.
- Ask the inspector for duplicates of all physical samples and copies of all test results.
- Be helpful and cooperative, but don't volunteer information.
- To the extent possible, immediately correct any violation the inspector identifies.

■ HR Tools for Line Managers and Small Businesses

Free On-Site Safety and Health Services

Small businesses have unique safety challenges. Without HR or safety departments, they often don't know where to turn for safety advice.[42]

OSHA provides free on-site safety and health services for small businesses. This service uses safety experts from state agencies and provides consultations, usually at the employer's workplace. According to OSHA, this consultation program is completely separate from the OSHA inspection effort, and no citations are issued or penalties proposed.

The employer triggers the process by requesting a voluntary consultation. There is then an opening conference with a safety expert, a walk-through, and a closing conference to discuss the consultant's observations. The consultant provides a detailed report. The employer's only obligation is to commit to correcting serious job safety and health hazards in a timely manner.

OSHA also has a website called "OSHA's $afety Pays Program." Use its pull-down window and choose a potential injury or illness such as "Burns." After entering some other data (such as potential number of injuries), this tool will reveal the estimated cost of the specific occupational injury or illness, and the estimated impact on your company's profits.

⭐ Talk About It–3

If your professor has chosen to assign this, go to **www.pearson.com/mylab/ management** to discuss the following: Write a short description on this theme: "How a small business owner can make use of OSHA's $afety Pays website."

Dealing with Employee Resistance Although employees are responsible to comply with OSHA standards, they often resist; the employer usually remains liable for any penalties. According to the Occupational Safety and Health Review Commission, employers must make "a diligent effort to discourage, by discipline if necessary, violations of safety rules by employees."[43] Cited for a workplace injury, the employer may claim employee misconduct. However, the key is to provide documented evidence that the employee was properly trained to do the job correctly but did not.[44] But the only sure way to eliminate liability is to make sure that no accidents occur.

LEARNING OBJECTIVE 2
Explain in detail three basic causes of accidents.

What Causes Accidents?

There are three basic causes of workplace accidents: chance occurrences, unsafe conditions, and employees' unsafe acts. Chance occurrences (such as walking past a tree just when a branch falls) are more or less beyond management's control. We will therefore focus on unsafe conditions and unsafe acts.

Unsafe Working Conditions

Unsafe conditions are one main cause of accidents. These include:

- Faulty scaffolds
- Improperly guarded equipment
- Frayed wiring
- Unsafe storage, such as overloading
- Improper illumination
- Improper ventilation

The basic remedy here is to eliminate or minimize the unsafe conditions. OSHA standards address potential problems like these. The manager can also use a checklist of unsafe conditions, as in Figure 14.4 on pages 441–443. The *Environmental Health and Safety (EHS) Today* magazine website (http://ehstoday.com/) is another good source for safety, health, and industrial hygiene information.

Although accidents can occur anywhere, there are some high-danger zones. Many industrial accidents occur around forklift trucks, wheelbarrows, and other handling and lifting areas. The most serious accidents usually occur near metal and woodworking machines and saws, or around transmission machinery such as gears, pulleys, and flywheels. Construction accounts for a disproportionate share of accidents, with falls the major problem.[45]

Safety Climate   Not all causes of accidents are obvious. Sometimes the workplace suffers from a toxic "safety climate," in other words, from a set of mostly psychological factors that set the stage for employees to act unsafely.

One early study focused on the fatal accidents suffered by British oil workers in the North Sea.[46] Employees who are under stress, a strong pressure to quickly complete the work, and, generally, a poor safety climate—for instance, supervisors who never mention safety—were some of the not-so-obvious working conditions that led to oil rig accidents.

The participants in another study were nurses working in 42 large U.S. hospitals. The researchers measured safety climate with items like "the nurse manager on this unit emphasizes safety." The results revealed that "safety climate predicted medication errors, nurse back injuries, urinary tract infections, [and] patient satisfaction."[47]

Other Working Condition Factors   Work schedules and fatigue also affect accident rates. Accident rates usually don't increase much during the first five or six hours of the workday, but after six hours, they accelerate. This is due partly to fatigue and partly to the fact that accidents occur more often during night shifts. With reduced headcounts, employee fatigue is rising.[48]

Accidents also occur more frequently in plants with a high seasonal layoff rate, hostility among employees, and blighted living conditions. Temporary stress

People usually cause accidents, and no one has a surefire way to eliminate an unsafe act.
Source: Carlos E. Santa Maria/Shutterstock.

Figure 14.4

Supervisor's Safety Checklist

Source: Office of the Chief Information Officer, United States Department of Commerce, http://ocio.os.doc .gov/s/groups/public/@doc/@ os/@ocio/@oitpp/documents/ content/dev01_002574.pdf, accessed October 15, 2013.

FORM **CD-574**
(9/02)

U.S. Department of Commerce
Office Safety Inspection Checklist for
Supervisors and Program Managers

Name:	Division:
Location:	Date:
Signature:	

This checklist is intended as a guide to assist supervisors and program managers in conducting safety and health inspections of their work areas. It includes questions relating to general office safety, ergonomics, fire prevention, and electrical safety. Questions which receive a "**NO**" answer require corrective action. If you have questions or need assistance with resolving any problems, please contact your safety office. More information on office safety is available through the Department of Commerce Safety Office website at http://ohrm.doc.gov/safetyprogram/safety.htm.

Work Environment

Yes	No	N/A	
○	○	⊙	Are all work areas clean, sanitary, and orderly?
○	○	⊙	Is there adequate lighting?
○	○	⊙	Do noise levels appear high?
○	○	⊙	Is ventilation adequate?

Walking / Working Surfaces

Yes	No	N/A	
○	○	⊙	Are aisles and passages free of stored material that may present trip hazards?
○	○	⊙	Are tile floors in places like kitchens and bathrooms free of water and slippery substances?
○	○	⊙	Are carpet and throw rugs free of tears or trip hazards?
○	○	⊙	Are hand rails provided on all fixed stairways?
○	○	⊙	Are treads provided with anti-slip surfaces?
○	○	⊙	Are step ladders provided for reaching overhead storage areas and are materials stored safely?
○	○	⊙	Are file drawers kept closed when not in use?
○	○	⊙	Are passenger and freight elevators inspected annually and are the inspection certificates available for review on-site?
○	○	⊙	Are pits and floor openings covered or otherwise guarded?
○	○	⊙	Are standard guardrails provided wherever aisle or walkway surfaces are elevated more than 48 inches above any adjacent floor or the ground?
○	○	⊙	Is any furniture unsafe or defective?
○	○	⊙	Are objects covering heating and air conditioning vents?

Ergonomics

Yes	No	N/A	
○	○	⊙	Are employees advised of proper lifting techniques?
○	○	⊙	Are workstations configured to prevent common ergonomic problems? (Chair height allows employees' feet to rest flat on the ground with thighs parallel to the floor, top of computer screen is at or slightly below eye level, keyboard is at elbow height. Additional information on proper configuration of workstations is available through the Commerce Safety website at http://ohrm.doc.gov/safetyprogram/safety.htm)
○	○	⊙	Are mechanical aids and equipment, such as; lifting devices, carts, dollies provided where needed?
○	○	⊙	Are employees surveyed annually on their ergonomic concerns?

Figure 14.4
(Continued)

FORM CD-574
(9/02)

Emergency Information (Postings)

Yes	No	N/A	
○	○	⊙	Are established emergency phone numbers posted where they can be readily found in case of an emergency?
○	○	⊙	Are employees trained on emergency procedures?
○	○	⊙	Are fire evacuation procedures/diagrams posted?
○	○	⊙	Is emergency information posted in every area where you store hazardous waste?
○	○	⊙	Is established facility emergency information posted near a telephone?
○	○	⊙	Are the OSHA poster, and other required posters displayed conspicuously?
○	○	⊙	Are adequate first aid supplies available and properly maintained?
○	○	⊙	Are an adequate number of first aid trained personnel available to respond to injuries and illnesses until medical assistance arrives?
○	○	⊙	Is a copy of the facility fire prevention and emergency action plan available on site?
○	○	⊙	Are safety hazard warning signs/caution signs provided to warn employees of pertinent hazards?

Fire Prevention

Yes	No	N/A	
○	○	⊙	Are flammable liquids, such as gasoline, kept in approved safety cans and stored in flammable cabinets?
○	○	⊙	Are portable fire extinguishers distributed properly (less than 75 feet travel distance for combustibles and 50 feet for flammables)?
○	○	⊙	Are employees trained on the use of portable fire extinguishers?
○	○	⊙	Are portable fire extinguishers visually inspected monthly and serviced annually?
○	○	⊙	Is the area around portable fire extinguishers free of obstructions and properly labeled ?
○	○	⊙	Is heat-producing equipment used in a well ventilated area?
○	○	⊙	Are fire alarm pull stations clearly marked and unobstructed?
○	○	⊙	Is proper clearance maintained below sprinkler heads (i.e., 18" clear)?

Emergency Exits

Yes	No	N/A	
○	○	⊙	Are doors, passageways or stairways that are neither exits nor access to exits and which could be mistaken for exits, appropriately marked "NOT AN EXIT," "TO BASEMENT," "STOREROOM," etc.?
○	○	⊙	Are a sufficient number of exits provided?
○	○	⊙	Are exits kept free of obstructions or locking devices which could impede immediate escape?
○	○	⊙	Are exits properly marked and illuminated?
○	○	⊙	Are the directions to exits, when not immediately apparent, marked with visible signs?
○	○	⊙	Can emergency exit doors be opened from the direction of exit travel without the use of a key or any special knowledge or effort when the building is occupied?
○	○	⊙	Are exits arranged such that it is not possible to travel toward a fire hazard when exiting the facility?

Figure 14.4

(Continued)

FORM **CD-574**
(9/02)

Electrical Systems
(Please have your facility maintenance person or electrician accompany you during this part of the inspection)

Yes	No	N/A	
○	○	◉	Are all cord and cable connections intact and secure?
○	○	◉	Are electrical outlets free of overloads?
○	○	◉	Is fixed wiring used instead of flexible/extension cords?
○	○	◉	Is the area around electrical panels and breakers free of obstructions?
○	○	◉	Are high-voltage electrical service rooms kept locked?
○	○	◉	Are electrical cords routed such that they are free of sharp objects and clearly visible?
○	○	◉	Are all electrical cords grounded?
○	○	◉	Are electrical cords in good condition (free of splices, frays, etc.)?
○	○	◉	Are electrical appliances approved (Underwriters Laboratory, Inc. (UL), etc)?
○	○	◉	Are electric fans provided with guards of not over one-half inch, preventing finger exposures?
○	○	◉	Are space heaters UL listed and equipped with shutoffs that activate if the heater tips over?
○	○	◉	Are space heaters located away from combustibles and properly ventilated?
○	○	◉	In your electrical rooms are all electrical raceways and enclosures securely fastened in place?
○	○	◉	Are clamps or other securing means provided on flexible cords or cables at plugs, receptacles, tools, equipment, etc., and is the cord jacket securely held in place?
○	○	◉	Is sufficient access and working space provided and maintained about all electrical equipment to permit ready and safe operations and maintenance? (This space is 3 feet for less than 600 volts, 4 feet for more than 600 volts)

FORM **CD-574**
(9/02)

Material Storage

Yes	No	N/A	
○	○	◉	Are storage racks and shelves capable of supporting the intended load and materials stored safely?
○	○	◉	Are storage racks secured from falling?
○	○	◉	Are office equipment stored in a stable manner, not capable of falling?

factors such as high workplace temperature, poor illumination, and a congested workplace also relate to accident rates.

Unsafe Acts

In practice, it's impossible to eliminate accidents just by reducing unsafe conditions. People usually cause accidents, and no one has a surefire way to eliminate *unsafe acts* such as:

- Throwing materials
- Operating or working at unsafe speeds
- Making safety devices inoperative by removing them
- Lifting improperly

There is no one explanation for why an employee may behave in an unsafe manner. Sometimes, as noted, the working conditions may set the stage for unsafe acts. For instance, stressed-out oil rig employees may behave unsafely even if they know better. Sometimes, employees aren't trained adequately in safe work methods; some companies don't supply employees with the right safe procedures, and employees may then develop their own (often bad) work habits.[49]

What Traits Characterize "Accident-Prone" People?

It may seem intuitively obvious that some people are simply accident prone, but the research is mixed.[50] On closer inspection, some apparently accident-prone people were just unlucky, or may have been more meticulous about reporting their accidents.[51]

However, there is evidence that people with specific traits may indeed be accident prone. For example, people who are impulsive, extremely extroverted, and less conscientious (less fastidious and dependable) have more accidents.[52] One study found that agreeableness was negatively associated with unsafe behaviors.[53]

Furthermore, the person who is accident prone on one job may not be so on a different job. Driving is one example. Personality traits that correlate with filing vehicular insurance claims include *entitlement* ("bad drivers think there's no reason they should not speed or run lights"); *impatience* ("drivers with high claim frequency were 'always in a hurry'"); *aggressiveness* ("always the first to want to move when the red light turns green"); and *distractibility* ("easily and frequently distracted by cell phones, eating, drinking, and so on"). A study in Thailand similarly found that drivers who are *competitive* and prone to *anger* are particularly risky drivers.[54]

LEARNING OBJECTIVE 3
Explain how to prevent accidents at work.

How to Prevent Accidents

In practice, accident prevention boils down to: (1) reducing unsafe conditions and (2) reducing unsafe acts. In large firms, the chief safety officer (often called the "environmental health and safety officer") is responsible for this.[55] In smaller firms, managers (including those from human resources, plant management, and first-line managers) share these responsibilities.

Reduce Unsafe Conditions

Reducing unsafe conditions is always an employer's first line of defense in accident prevention. Safety engineers should first design jobs to remove or reduce physical hazards. For example, slippery floors in commercial kitchens often cause slips and falls. Employers work with safety engineers to "engineer out" potentially hazardous conditions like these, for instance, by placing nonslip mats in kitchens, or guardrails around moving machines. For machinery, for example, employees can use emergency stop devices like the one shown in the photo below to cut power to machines.[56] *Lockout/tagout* is a formal procedure to disable equipment, such as power saws, to avoid unexpected releases of electrical or other energy. It involves disarming the device and affixing a "disabled" tag to the equipment.[57] With more employees working alongside robots, safety standards are evolving. For example, industrial robots are designed with safety stops so humans can "hand" them parts without the robot arm hitting them, and with speed and separation monitoring to ensure the robot maintains the required distance from its operator.[58]

The manager can use checklists such as that in Figure 14.4 to identify hazardous conditions.

Job Hazard Analysis A Yale University science student was injured critically when her hair was caught in a spinning lathe. **Job hazard analysis** is a systematic

For machinery, for example, employees can use emergency stop devices to cut power to hazardous machines.

Source: Martin Balija/EyeEm/Getty Images.

job hazard analysis

A systematic approach to identifying and eliminating hazards before they occur, and focuses on the relationship between the worker, the task, the tools, and the work environment and ends by reducing the potential risks to acceptable levels.

operational safety reviews

Reviews conducted by agencies to ascertain whether units under their jurisdiction are complying with all the applicable safety laws, regulations, orders, and rules.

approach to identifying and eliminating hazards before they occur. According to OSHA, job hazard analysis "focuses on the relationship between the worker, the task, the tools, and the work environment" and ends by reducing the potential risks to acceptable levels.[59]

Consider a safety analyst looking at the Yale science lab, with the aim of identifying potential hazards. Performing a job hazard analysis here might involve looking at the situation and asking these questions:

- **What can go wrong?** A student's hair or clothing could touch the lathe, a rotating object that "catches" it and pulls it into the machine.
- **What are the consequences?** The student could receive a severe injury as his or her body part or hair is drawn into the spinning lathe.
- **How could it happen?** The accident could happen as a result of the student leaning too close to the lathe while working at the bench, or walking too close to the lathe, or bending to reach for something that fell close to the lathe.
- **What are other contributing factors?** Speed is one contributing factor. The problem would occur so quickly that the student couldn't take evasive action once the lathe ensnarled the hair.

The job hazard analysis should provide the basis for creating countermeasures. Given the speed with which any such accident would occur, it's unlikely that training by itself would suffice. Instead, the lathe area should be ensconced in its own protective casing and changes made to ensure that the lathe can't spin unless the student takes action via a foot pedal to keep power on.

Operational Safety Reviews After a nuclear power plant in northern Japan exploded in 2011, many wondered if the International Atomic Energy Agency (IAEA) had conducted the necessary operational safety review. **Operational safety reviews** are conducted by agencies to ascertain whether units under their jurisdiction are complying with all the applicable safety laws, regulations, orders, and rules. For example, under IAEA's Operational Safety Review Program, "international teams of experts conduct in-depth reviews of operational safety performance at a nuclear power plant."[60]

Provide Personal Protective Equipment

Prevent Blindness America estimates that each year, more than 700,000 Americans injure their eyes at work, and that employers could avoid 90% of these injuries with safety eyewear.[61]

After taking steps to eliminate unsafe conditions, management can turn its attention to providing workers with personal protective equipment (PPE). Note, though, that reducing unsafe conditions (such as enclosing noisy equipment) is always the first line of defense. Then use administrative controls (such as job rotation to reduce long-term exposure to the hazard). Only then turn to PPE.[62]

Getting employees to wear personal protective equipment is famously difficult.[63] In addition to providing reliable protection, protective gear should fit properly; be easy to care for, maintain, and repair; be flexible and lightweight; provide comfort and reduce heat stress; have rugged construction; and be relatively easy to put on and remove.[64] Similarly, cold weather means employers must help protect their outdoor workers.[65] This should include, among other things, monitoring temperature and wind chill conditions, making sure workers have adequate cold-weather apparel, monitoring workers for signs of frostbite, and providing adequate indoor breaks.[66]

TRENDS SHAPING HR: *Digital and Social Media*

LOCATION BEACONS Beacons—tiny devices that continuously transmit radio signals identifying themselves—are used in many ways. For example, beacons in seats at ballparks enable fans with smart phones to get to their seats.

Beacons are also becoming increasingly useful for reducing accidents. Employers are using beacons indoors to help employers keep track of their employees, particularly if they're in distress. Other employers use them to prompt employees to take specific actions—such as when they are too close to a danger zone. And by placing beacons on vehicles such as forklifts, it becomes possible to automatically warn the operator and others in the vicinity if the forklift is maneuvering into a dangerous situation.[67]

Diversity Counts

Protecting Vulnerable Workers In designing safe and healthy environments, employers should pay special attention to vulnerable workers, such as young, immigrant, aging, and women workers.[68] For example, as the CEO of one safety engineering company said, "For decades, women essentially were ignored when it came to designing eye and face protection." Today, more products are available in smaller sizes.[69]

Employers should pay special attention to workers age 17 and under, most of whom are new to working. Although 14- and 15-year-olds can generally only legally perform tasks like cashiering and office work, 16- and 17-year-olds may work in jobs like cooking and construction. In one recent year, almost 556 16- and 17-year-olds were injured at work.[70]

Similarly, with more workers postponing retirement, older workers are doing more manufacturing jobs.[71] They can do these jobs effectively. However, there are numerous potential physical changes associated with aging, including loss of strength, loss of muscular flexibility, and reduced reaction time.[72] This means that employers should make special provisions such as designing jobs to reduce heavy lifting and boosting lighting levels.[73] The fatality rate for older workers is about three times that of younger workers.[74]

Propaganda such as safety posters can help reduce unsafe acts. In an early study, their use apparently increased safe behavior by more than 20%.

Source: Lucian Milasan/123RF.

Reduce Unsafe Acts

Human misbehavior can short-circuit even the best safety efforts. Sometimes the misbehavior is intentional, like disconnecting a safety switch, but often it's not. For example, not noticing that a floor is wet often causes accidents.[75] And, ironically, "making a job safer with machine guards or PPE lowers people's risk perceptions and thus can lead to an increase in at-risk behavior."[76]

Unfortunately, just telling employees to "pay attention" is usually not enough. The manager should take specific steps as follows.

Screen to Reduce Unsafe Acts

Psychologists have had success in screening out individuals who might be accident prone for some specific job. The basic technique is to identify the human trait (such as visual skill) that might relate to accidents on the specific job. Then determine whether scores on this trait predict accidents on the job. For example, screening prospective delivery drivers for traits like impatience and aggressiveness might be sensible.[77]

Provide Safety Training

Safety training reduces unsafe acts, especially for new employees. You should instruct employees in safe practices and procedures, warn them of potential hazards, and work on developing a safety-conscious attitude. Safety "propaganda" posters can help too.[78]

OSHA's standards require more than training. Employees must demonstrate that they actually learned what to do. (For example, OSHA's respiratory standard requires that each employee demonstrate how to inspect, put on, and remove respirator seals.)[79] Note, though, that the main aim of safety training is not to meet OSHA training standards but to reduce accidents. The "least engaging" (and therefore assumedly least effective) training uses lectures, films, reading materials, and video-based training. The most engaging uses behavioral modeling, simulation, and hands-on training.[80]

Internet-Based Safety Improvement Solutions Employers use the Internet to support their safety training. For example, PureSafety (https://ulworkplace.puresafety.com/) enables firms to create their own training websites, complete with a "message from the safety director."[81] Once an employer installs the website, it can populate the site with courses from companies that supply health and safety courses via https://ulworkplace.puresafety.com/. OSHA, NIOSH (the National Institute of Occupational Safety and Health), and numerous private vendors also provide online safety training solutions.[82]

When the University of California system wanted to deliver mandated safety training to its 50,000 employees on 10 different campuses, it developed an online program. The two-hour custom online lab safety fundamentals course covers OSHA regulations as well as interactive exercises and feedback opportunities for participants.[83]

Use Posters, Incentives, and Positive Reinforcement

Employers also use various tools to motivate worker safety.[84] Safety posters are one, but are no substitute for comprehensive safety programs. Employers should combine the posters with other tools (like screening and training), and change the posters often. Posters should be visible, legible, and well-lit.[85]

Incentive programs are also useful.[86] Management at Tesoro Corporation's Golden Eagle refinery in California instituted one such plan. Employees earn "WINGS" (an acronym for Willing Involvement Nurtures Greater Safety) points for engaging in one or more specific safety activities, such as taking emergency response training. Employees can each earn up to $20 per month by accumulating points.[87] The HR in Practice feature shows another example.

As of 2016, OSHA rules prohibited employers from using incentive programs that have the effect of penalizing workers for reporting accidents or injuries.[88]

One option is to emphasize nonfinancial incentives, like recognition.[89] In any case, the incentive program needs to be part of a comprehensive safety program.[90] The accompanying HR in Practice feature describes an actual positive reinforcement safety program.

■ HR in Practice

Using Positive Reinforcement

Many employers use *positive reinforcement programs* to improve safety. Such programs provide workers with continuing positive feedback, usually in the form of graphical performance reports and supervisory support, to shape the workers' safety-related behavior.

Researchers introduced one program in a wholesale bakery.[91] The new safety program included training and positive reinforcement. The researchers set and communicated a reasonable safety goal (in terms of observed incidents performed safely). Next, employees participated in a 30-minute training session by viewing pairs of slides depicting scenes that the researchers staged in the plant. One slide, for example, showed the supervisor climbing over a conveyor; the parallel slide showed the supervisor walking around the conveyor. After viewing an unsafe act, employees had to describe, "What's unsafe here?" Then the researchers demonstrated the same incident again, but performed in a safe manner, and explicitly stated the safe-conduct rule ("go around, not over or under, conveyors").

At the conclusion of the training phase, supervisors showed employees a graph with their pretraining safety record (in terms of observed incidents performed safely) plotted. Supervisors then encouraged workers to consider increasing their performance to the new safety goal for their own protection, to decrease costs, and to help the plant get out of its last place safety ranking. Then the researchers posted the graph and a list of safety rules.

Whenever observers walked through the plant collecting safety data, they posted on the graph the percentage of incidents they had seen performed safely by the group as a whole, thus providing the workers with positive feedback. Workers could compare their current safety performance with both their previous performance and their assigned goal. In addition, supervisors praised workers when they performed selected incidents safely. Safety in the plant subsequently improved markedly.

⭐ Talk About It–**4**

If your professor has chosen to assign this, go to **www.pearson.com/mylab/management** to discuss the following: List six more unsafe incidents you believe might occur in a bakery and a "safe manner" for dealing with each.

Foster a Culture of Safety

Employers and supervisors should create a safety-conscious culture by showing that they take safety seriously. One study measured safety culture with questions like "my supervisor says a good word whenever he sees the job done according to the safety rules" and "my supervisor approaches workers during work to discuss safety issues." The workers here perceived that their supervisors were committed to safety. In turn, these perceptions apparently influenced the workers to work safely in the months following the survey.[92]

According to one safety expert, a workplace with a safety-oriented culture exhibits:

1. *Teamwork*, in the form of management and employees both involved in safety;
2. Highly visible and interactive *communication and collaboration* on safety matters;
3. A *shared vision* of safety excellence (specifically, an overriding attitude that all accidents and injuries are preventable);
4. *Assignment* of critical safety functions to specific individuals or teams, and;
5. A *continuous effort* toward identifying and correcting workplace safety problems and hazards.[93]

Establish a Safety Policy and Set Specific Loss Control Goals

The company's written safety policy should emphasize that accident prevention is of the utmost importance at your firm, and that the firm will do everything practical to eliminate or reduce accidents and injuries. Then set specific safety goals, for instance in terms of frequency of lost-time injuries per number of full-time employees.

TRENDS SHAPING HR: *Digital and Social Media*

CONDUCTING SAFETY AND HEALTH AUDITS AND INSPECTIONS Employers enable employee-generated safety audits by using mobile digital tools. For example, managers and employees use the iAuditor Safety Audit and Checklist App,[94] available via iTunes, to facilitate safety audits. It contains numerous safety checklists and tools.[95] As another example, AssessNET is cloud-based safety software that lets employers remotely manage risk assessments, accident records, and safety audits from their desktops and mobile devices. [96] It gives them quick access to safety records, lets them quickly report hazards, and alerts management of safety incidents.[97]

With such tools, security-related metrics might include injury and illness rates, workers' compensation cost per employee, at-risk behavior reduction, and safety training exercises.[98] To ensure that audits result in improvements, *trend the audit data* (for instance, to see if accident rates are rising or falling or steady), and *track the corrective actions* through to completion.[99]

Conduct Regular Safety and Health Inspections

Routinely inspect all premises for possible safety and health problems using checklists such as those in Figure 14.4 (pages 441–443) as aids. Similarly, investigate all accidents and "near misses," and have a system in place for letting employees notify management about hazardous conditions (see preceding Trends feature).[100]

The term *safety audit* means two things: It refers to the actual safety inspection using a checklist as in Figure 14.4. It also refers to the employer's review and analysis of its safety-related data—for instance, regarding accidents, workers' compensation claims, and days lost due to injuries. Other metrics include, for example, injury and illness rates, workers' compensation cost per employee, and the percentage of conformance to safety-critical behaviors.[101] Effective safety management means identifying crucial metrics like these and then monitoring them.

Most safety experts believe unsafe acts account for most accidents and that the way to address this is to identify and rectify the unsafe acts that employees are committing on their jobs. *Behavior-based safety* means observing the employee's unsafe (and safe) on-the-job behaviors and rectifying (through training and/or feedback) the unsafe ones. The process usually begins with having a safety expert and/or safety committee compile a checklist of safe and unsafe behaviors for each job. Then periodically have supervisors or others (1) observe each employee's on-the-job behavior, (2) complete the checklist of safe and unsafe behaviors, and then (3) reinforce the safe ones and rectify the unsafe ones.[102]

Employers also use safety awareness programs to improve employee safety behavior. A **safety awareness program** enables trained supervisors to orient new workers regarding common safety hazards and simple prevention methods. For example, the Roadway Safety Awareness Program covers trucker safety issues such as stopping distances required at various speeds (see the screen grab, page 450).

Organize a Safety Committee

Employee safety committees can improve workplace safety. For example, when airborne sawdust became a problem at a Boise Cascade facility, plant management appointed an employee safety committee. The committee took on the role of safety watchdog and trained its members in hazard identification. After talking to employees who worked with the woodchips where the sawdust originated, the committee members discovered the sawdust became airborne as the workers transferred the woodchips from one belt to another. They corrected the problem quickly.[103] The HR in Practice feature shows how one company puts these ideas into practice.

Figure 14.5 on page 450 summarizes these and other safety steps.[104]

safety awareness program
Program that enables trained supervisors to orient new workers arriving at a job site regarding common safety hazards and simple prevention methods.

The Roadway Safety Awareness Program covers trucker safety issues such as stopping distances required at various speeds.

Source: National Work Zone Information Clearinghouse, a project of the American Road & Transportation Builders Association—Transportation Development Foundation.

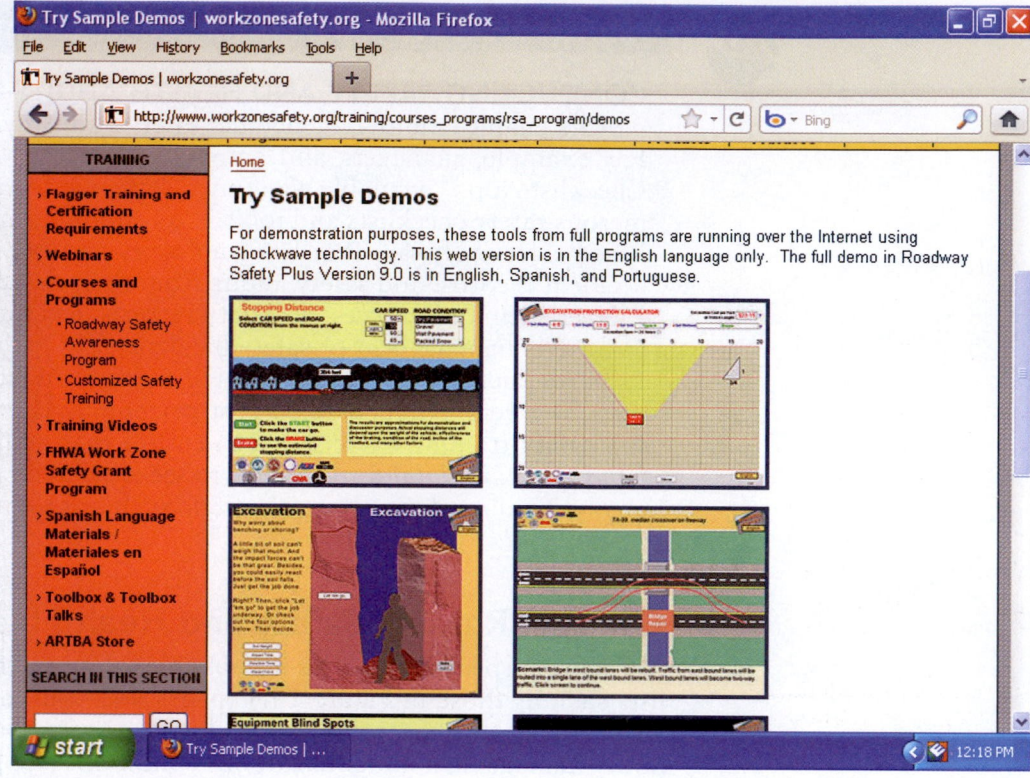

Figure 14.5

Steps the Manager Can Take to Reduce Accidents

- Reduce unsafe conditions.
- Reduce unsafe acts.
- Use posters and other propaganda.
- Provide safety training.
- Perform a job hazard analysis.
- Conduct operational safety reviews.
- Encourage behavior-based safety.
- Foster a culture of safety.
- Use positive reinforcement.
- Emphasize top-management commitment.
- Emphasize safety.
- Establish a safety policy.
- Set specific loss control goals.
- Conduct safety and health inspections regularly.
- Conduct safety awareness programs.
- Establish texting policies.
- Move Beyond Zero Defects.

■ HR in Practice

Safety at Saudi Petrol Chemical

The industrial safety and security manager for the Saudi Petrol Chemical Co., in Jubail City, Saudi Arabia, says his company's excellent safety record results from the fact that "our employees are champions of safety."[105] Employees are involved in every part of the safety process. They serve on safety committees, develop and lead daily and monthly safety meetings, and conduct job safety analyses, for instance.

Safety begins with the company's top management. Senior management representatives serve on the company's Management Health and Safety Committee. This committee meets monthly to review incident reports, establish health and safety goals, review safety statistics, and endorse and sponsor safety programs.

The firm cultivates its "safety first" culture from the day a new employee arrives at work. For example, new employees are encouraged to participate in the safety process during orientation. Then (about six weeks later) they attend a one-day orientation where company officials emphasize the importance of the company's health, safety, and environmental policies and programs. Employees also participate in monthly departmental training sessions to discuss departmental safety issues and safety suggestions. They work with their departmental committees to conduct monthly safety audits, to review and document departmental job safety, and to submit safety suggestions. Employees are required to report every safety incident and near miss, and more than 600 reports are submitted each year.

⭐ Talk About It–5

If your professor has chosen to assign this, go to **www.pearson.com/mylab/ management** to discuss the following: Answer this: "Based on what I read so far in this chapter, here is why I think this facility has a good safety record."

LEARNING OBJECTIVE **4**
Describe how one company uses employee engagement to improve workplace safety.

Employee Engagement Guide for Managers

Milliken & Company—World-Class Safety through Employee Engagement

Milliken & Company, founded in 1865, designs, manufactures, and markets chemicals, floor coverings, protective fabrics, and textiles. The company has about 7,000 employees in more than 39 facilities worldwide. The privately owned Milliken has received widespread recognition for the quality of its innovative products, for its high employee engagement, and for its employee engagement-based occupational safety program; it's also the only company to consistently rank as a "most ethical company" for 15 years running.[106] A survey of Milliken's employees found an 80% positive engagement level.[107] Its extraordinarily low workplace illness and injury rates mean it's one of the safest companies in which to work.[108]

Involvement-Based Employee Engagement

The centerpiece of Milliken's safety process is its *involvement-based employee engagement* program. For example, employees staff the safety steering and safety subcommittee system, submit "opportunity for improvement" suggestions weekly, review each of these suggestions, and provide feedback on every suggestion.[109] The safety process depends on *cascading goals* deriving from federal, state, and Milliken-based safety guidelines. These goals are translated through weekly meetings into specific metrics (for instance, "accidents per employee hour worked") to be achieved by each plant's subcommittees. Each safety subcommittee then performs weekly *audits*, to ensure compliance and to ensure the plant's safety activities are continuously improved.

The Milliken safety program quantifies each employee's involvement, for instance, in terms of serving on safety subcommittees, being a safety subject matter expert, or conducting safety audits.[110] Also to help win engagement, the program *empowers* employees, for instance, by training each to do his or her "safety job" (such as being knowledgeable about OSHA safety regulations). All plant employees are also trained to give and receive peer-to-peer safety comments. Each is authorized to act on what he or she observes by providing "constructive feedback" or "appreciative feedback" when observing another employee doing something safely (or not). Each employee is also trained to use Milliken's safety tracking mechanism. This tool helps employees make sure that safety suggestions, safety audit findings, or other safety agenda items are tracked and finalized, by giving each item a number, date, and the name of the responsible Milliken employee.[111]

Members of each plant's employee safety steering committee investigate all safety incidents to help discover the causes.[112] Milliken recognizes employees' safety efforts in formal celebratory events throughout the year, such as having "cheerleaders" provide safety cheers as engineers enter the plant.[113]

LEARNING OBJECTIVE 5
Discuss major health problems at work and how to remedy them.

Workplace Health: Problems and Remedies

Most workplace hazards aren't obvious ones like unguarded equipment or slippery floors. Many are unseen hazards (like chemicals) that the company produces as part of its production processes. Others, like drug abuse, the employees may create for themselves. Typical workplace exposure hazards include chemicals and other hazardous materials such as asbestos, as well as alcohol abuse, stressful jobs, ergonomic hazards (such as uncomfortable equipment), infectious diseases, smoking, and biohazards (such as mold and anthrax).[114]

Chemicals, Air Quality, and Industrial Hygiene

OSHA standards list exposure limits for about 600 chemicals such as benzene. Hazardous substances like these require air sampling and other precautionary measures.

Managing such exposure hazards comes under the area of *industrial hygiene* and involves recognition, evaluation, and control. First, the facility's health and safety officers must *recognize* possible exposure hazards. This typically involves activities like conducting plant/facility walk-around surveys.

Having identified a possible hazard, the *evaluation* phase involves determining how severe it is. This requires measuring the exposure, comparing the measured exposure to some benchmark, and determining whether the risk is within tolerances.[115]

Finally, the hazard *control* phase involves eliminating or reducing the hazard. Personal protective gear is the *last* option. Before these, the employer must install engineering controls (such as ventilation) and administrative controls (including training); this is mandatory under OSHA regulations.[116]

As an example, there are four major sources of occupational respiratory diseases: asbestos, silica, lead, and carbon dioxide. Of these, asbestos is a major concern, in part due to publicity surrounding huge lawsuits alleging asbestos-related diseases.

OSHA standards require several actions with respect to asbestos. Companies must monitor the air whenever an employer expects the level of asbestos to rise to one-half the allowable limit (0.1 fiber per cubic centimeter). Engineering

OSHA standards list exposure limits for about 600 chemicals. Hazardous substances like these require air sampling and other precautionary measures.
Source: Shank_ali/Getty Images.

controls—walls, special filters, and so forth—are required to maintain an asbestos level that complies with OSHA standards. Respirators can be used only if they are then still required to achieve compliance.

Ironically, one of the downsides of environmentally "green" office buildings is that sealed buildings can produce poor *air quality* and illnesses such as itchy eyes and trouble breathing (some call this "sick building syndrome"). The problem is that emissions from printers and photocopiers and other chemical pollutants, left unmonitored, can reduce air quality.[117] The solution is continuous monitoring.

KNOW YOUR EMPLOYMENT LAW
Hazard Communication

In, say, a dry cleaning store, it might not be apparent just by looking at it that the clear cleaning chemical hydrofluoric acid will eat through glass and blind an unsuspecting worker. Under OSHA's regulations, employers must communicate the presence and nature of hazards like this to which workers might be exposed. OSHA's *hazard communication standard* states that "in order to ensure chemical safety in the workplace, information about the identities and hazards of the chemicals must be available and understandable to workers. OSHA's hazard communication standard (HCS) requires the development and dissemination of such information." OSHA says chemical manufacturers and importers must label and provide hazard safety data sheets to their customers. In turn, all employers must have labels and safety data sheets available for their exposed workers and train workers to handle the chemicals appropriately.[118]

More generally, the employer should make provisions for communicating the full range of safety and security matters, including, for instance, safety policies, facilities security procedures, violence reduction policies and procedures, and how it plans to deal with natural or human-made disasters.[119] ∎

■ HR and the Gig Economy

Temp Employee Safety[120]

Temp workers in the United States account for a disproportionate number of workplace fatalities, as much as five times more than one might expect, by some estimates.

Several things explain this disparity. Temp or gig workers (many of whom are independent contractors) do lack some familiar legal employment protections (for example, independent contractors generally don't get unemployment insurance or workers' compensation).[121] Such lack of legal protection may prompt some host employers to be less attentive to temps' safety training (perhaps on the mistaken assumption that they're not responsible for supplying it). Temp workers may also lack the colleagues at work who might otherwise guide them in safety matters. And some experts contend that temp workers often get the "dirtiest, most hazardous" jobs to do.

However, although such workers do lack some legal employment protections, they *are* covered by occupational health and safety laws: host companies have the same safety and health obligations to them as to their own employees. So, for example, OSHA says the hiring company has the primary responsibility for providing temp workers with site-specific hazard communications information and training and that such training must be identical to that the host employer gives its own employees. Its other site-specific responsibilities include ensuring appropriate labelling of chemical containers, providing access to Safety Data Sheets (SDS), and providing appropriate personal protective equipment (PPE). Many host employers hire temps through staffing agencies. According to OSHA, such staffing agencies must, for example, provide generic hazard communications and should visit the host's facility to review the adequacy of that company's hazard safety processes.

The bottom line is that the host company is responsible for providing all temps with adequate site-specific safety training. Major matters to address include Hazard Communications; Lockout/Tagout; Powered Industrial Trucks; Machine Guarding; Respiratory Protection; Occupational Noise Exposure; Electrical, Wiring Methods; Electrical, General Requirements; Personal Protective Equipment (PPE); and Guarding Floor and Wall Openings and Holes.

Alcoholism and Substance Abuse

Alcoholism and substance abuse are problems at work. About two-thirds of people with an alcohol disorder work full-time.[122] Some estimate that almost 13 million workers use drugs illicitly.[123] About 15% of the U.S. workforce (just over 19 million workers) "has either been hung over at work, been drinking shortly before showing up for work, or been drinking or impaired while on the job at least once during the previous year."[124] Breathalyzer tests detected alcohol in 16% of emergency room patients injured at work.[125] Employee alcoholism may cost U.S. employees about $226 billion per year, for instance in higher absenteeism and accidents.[126]

Dealing with substance abuse often begins with *substance abuse testing*.[127] It's unusual to find employers who don't at least test job candidates for substance abuse before formally hiring them. And many states have mandatory random drug testing for high-hazard workers. For example, New Jersey now requires random drug testing of electrical workers.[128]

There is debate about whether drug tests reduce workplace accidents. One study, conducted in three hotels, concluded that pre-employment drug testing seemed to have little effect on workplace accidents. However, a combination of pre-employment and random ongoing testing was associated with a significant reduction in workplace accidents.[129]

Dealing with Substance Abuse Ideally, a drug-free workplace program includes five components:[130]

1. A drug-free workplace policy
2. Supervisor training
3. Employee education
4. Employee assistance
5. Drug testing

The policy should state, at a minimum, "The use, possession, transfer, or sale of illegal drugs by employees is prohibited." It should also explain the policy's rationale and the disciplinary consequences for violating it. Supervisors should be trained to monitor employees' performance, and to stay alert to drug-related performance problems.

Tools Several tools are available to screen for alcohol or drug abuse. The most widely used self-reporting screening instruments for alcoholism are the 4-item CAGE and the 25-item Michigan Alcoholism Screening Test (MAST). The former asks questions like these: Have you ever (1) attempted to Cut back on alcohol, (2) been Annoyed by comments about your drinking, (3) felt Guilty about drinking, (4) had an Eye-opener first thing in the morning to steady your nerves?[131]

As in Table 14.1, alcohol-related symptoms range from tardiness in the earliest stages of alcohol abuse to prolonged, unpredictable absences in its later stages.[132]

A combination of pre-employment and ongoing random testing is best. Pre-employment drug testing discourages those on drugs from applying for or coming to work for employers who do testing. (One study found that over 30% of regular drug users employed full-time said they were less likely to work for a company that conducted pre-employment screening.[133]) Some applicants or employees may try

Table 14.1 Observable Behavior Patterns Indicating Possible Alcohol-Related Problems

Alcoholism Stage	Some Possible Signs of Alcoholism Problems	Some Possible Alcoholism Performance Issues
Early	Late arrival at work Untrue statements Early departure from work	Reduced job efficiency Misses deadlines
Middle	Frequent absences, especially Mondays Colleagues' mention of erratic behavior Mood swings Anxiety Late returns from lunch Frequent multiday absences	Accidents Warnings from boss Noticeably reduced performance
Advanced	Personal neglect Unsteady gait Violent outbursts Blackouts and frequent forgetfulness Possible drinking on job	Frequent falls, accidents Strong disciplinary actions Basically incompetent performance

Source: Gopal Patel and John Adkins Jr., "The Employer's Role in Alcoholism Assistance," *Personnel Journal*, 62, no. 7, July 1983, p. 570; Mary Anne Enoch and David Goldman, "Problem Drinking and Alcoholism: Diagnosis and Treatment," *American Family Physician*, February 1, 2002, www.aafp.org/afp/20020201/441.html, accessed July 20, 2008; Ken Pidd et al., "Alcohol and Work: Patterns of Use, Workplace Culture, and Safety," www.nisu.flinders.edu.au/pubs/reports/2006/injcat82.pdf, accessed July 20, 2008; https://www.ncadd.org/about-addiction/addiction-update/drugs-and-alcohol-in-the-workplace, accessed April 12, 2017.

to evade the test, for instance, by purchasing "clean" specimens. Several states—including New Jersey, North Carolina, Virginia, Oregon, South Carolina, Pennsylvania, Louisiana, Texas, and Nebraska—have laws making drug-test fraud a crime.[134] The newer oral fluid drug test eliminates the "clean specimen" problem and is much less expensive to administer.[135]

Job Stress and Burnout

Problems like alcoholism and drug abuse sometimes stem from *job stress*.[136] Northwestern National Mutual Life found that one-fourth of all employees it surveyed viewed their jobs as the number one stressor in their lives.[137]

Many external factors can trigger stress. These include work schedule, pace of work, job security, route to and from work, workplace noise, and the number and nature of customers.[138] Many service workers (especially in retail stores and fast food) have unpredictable work schedules, often set at the last minute by their employer. This raises stress and reduces employee health.[139]

However, no two people react the same because personal factors also influence stress.[140] For example, people who are **workaholics** and who feel driven to always be on time and meet deadlines normally put themselves under more stress than do others.

Job stress has serious consequences for employer and employee. The human consequences include anxiety, depression, anger, and various physical consequences, such as cardiovascular disease, headaches, accidents, and possibly even early-onset Alzheimer's disease.[141] A Danish study found that nurses working under excessive pressure had double the risk for heart attacks.[142] Stress also has serious consequences for the employer. A study of 46,000 employees concluded that healthcare costs of high-stress workers were 46% higher than those of their less-stressed coworkers.[143] Yet not all stress is dysfunctional. Some people, for example, are more productive as a deadline approaches.

Reducing Your Own Job Stress A person can do several things to alleviate stress. These include commonsense remedies like getting more sleep, eating better, finding

workaholics
People who feel driven to always be on time and meet deadlines and so normally place themselves under greater stress than do others.

a more suitable job, getting counseling, and planning each day's activities. Various experts suggest the following to reduce job stress:[144]

Build pleasant, cooperative relationships with as many of your colleagues as you can.

Work to resolve conflicts with other people.

Find time every day for detachment and relaxation.

Get away from your office from time to time for a change of scene and a change of mind.[145]

Write down the problems that concern you, and what you're going to do about each.

Participate in something you don't find stressful, such as sports, social events, or hobbies.

Create realistic goals and deadlines for yourself, and set regular progress reviews.

Prepare a list of tasks, and rank them in order of priority. Throughout the day, review your list, and work on tasks in priority order.

Ask for help from a parent, friend, counselor, doctor, or pastor. Talk with them about the stress you feel and problems you face.

Take care of yourself:

- Eat a healthy, well-balanced diet.
- Exercise on a regular basis.
- Get plenty of sleep.
- Give yourself a break if you feel stressed out.

Meditation works for some. Choose a quiet place with soft light, sit comfortably, and then meditate by focusing your thoughts, for instance, by counting breaths or by visualizing a calming location such as a beach. When your mind wanders, come back to focusing on your breathing or the beach.[146]

What the Employer Can Do The employer can also help reduce job stress. Indeed, one's relationship with his or her immediate supervisor is an important factor in one's peace of mind at work.

One British firm follows a three-tiered approach to managing workplace stress.[147] First is *primary prevention,* which focuses on ensuring that things like job designs are correct. Second is *intervention,* including individual employee assessment, and attitude surveys to find sources of stress such as personal conflicts on the job. Third is *rehabilitation* through employee assistance programs and counseling. One hospital introduced an on-site concierge service to help its employees.[148] Several years ago, World Bank employees were experiencing high stress levels. Several times a week, trainers from a Buddhist meditation instruction company ran meditation classes at the bank. Employees generally felt the classes were useful.[149] Employers recognize that employee wellness programs can reduce such problems and are broadening theirs to include stress and depression.[150]

burnout
The total depletion of physical and mental resources caused by excessive striving to reach an unrealistic work-related goal.

Burnout Burnout is closely associated with job stress. Experts define *burnout* as the total depletion of physical and mental resources caused by excessive striving to reach an unrealistic work-related goal. Some experts say burnout consists of three components, *exhaustion* (profound fatigue), *cynicism* (a loss of engagement in what you do), and *inefficacy* (feelings of incompetence).[151] Burnout doesn't just spontaneously appear. Instead, it builds gradually, leading to irritability, discouragement, entrapment, and resentment.[152]

What can a burnout candidate do? First, watch for warning signs such as tiredness, lack of focus, and depressed mood.[153] In his book *How to Beat the High Cost of Success,* Dr. Herbert Freudenberger suggests the following:[154]

- **Break your patterns.** Survey how you spend your time. The more well-rounded your life, the better protected you are against burnout.
- **Get away from it all periodically.** Schedule occasional periods during which you escape your usual routine.
- **Reassess your goals in terms of their intrinsic worth.** Are the goals you've set for yourself attainable? Are they worth the sacrifices?
- **Think about your work.** Could you do as good a job without being so intense?

Another way to reduce burnout is to put your job aside once you go home. In one study, researchers measured psychological detachment from work during nonwork time with items such as "during after-work hours, I forget about work."[155] Lack of psychological detachment from work while off the job (not leaving your job behind once home) predicted higher emotional exhaustion one year later. Similarly, take your vacation: one survey found that only about 47% of workers used all their paid vacation days recently, down from 60% a few years ago.[156] Also, stay active. A recent study concluded that "the increase in job burnout and depression was strongest among employees who did not engage in physical activity and weakest to the point of non-significance among those engaging in high physical activity."[157]

Depression *Employee depression* is a serious problem at work. Experts estimate that depression results in about 68 million lost workdays in the United States annually and may cost U.S. businesses $23 billion or more per year just in absenteeism and lost productivity.[158] Depressed people also tend to have worse safety records.[159]

Employers should work harder to ensure that depressed employees utilize support services. Depression is an illness. It makes no more sense to tell a depressed person to "snap out of it" than it does to tell a heart patient to "stop acting tired." One survey found that although about two-thirds of large firms offered employee assistance programs covering depression, only about 14% of employees with depression said they ever used one.[160] Training managers to recognize signs of depression—persistent sad moods, too little sleep, reduced appetite, difficulty in concentrating, and loss of interest in activities once enjoyed, for instance—and then making assistance more readily available can help.

Sitting Studies suggest that people who sit a lot are in poorer health and need to get up and walk around about 30 or 40 times a day; that's why several apps, including the iPhone health app reminds users to get up and walk around hourly.[161] Some use slow treadmills (up to 3-4 miles/hour) while working.[162]

Computer Monitor and Ergonomic Health Problems and How to Avoid Them

Even with advances in computer monitor technology, there's still a risk of computer-related health problems. Problems include short-term eye burning, itching, and tearing, as well as eyestrain and eye soreness. Backaches and neck aches are also widespread. Computer users may also suffer from carpal tunnel syndrome, caused by repetitive use of the hands and arms at uncomfortable angles.[163] According to the U.S. National Institutes of Health, *repetitive motion disorders* include disorders such as carpal tunnel syndrome, bursitis, and tendonitis. They result from excessive repetitions of an activity or motion, or from unnatural motions such as twisting the arm or wrist, or incorrect posture. It usually affects people who perform repetitive tasks such as assembly-line work or computer work. Employers can reduce the problem, for instance, with programs to help workers adjust their pace of work.[164]

OSHA provides an e-Tool for designing computer workstations.[165] Some of its prescriptions include place the monitor directly in front of you, ensure it is at arm's length, and look away from the monitor every 20 minutes and focus on something at least 20 feet away.[166] NIOSH does provide general recommendations. These include the following:

1. Have employees take a 3- to 5-minute break from working at the computer every 20 to 40 minutes, and use the time for other tasks, like making copies.
2. Design maximum flexibility into the workstation so it can be adapted to the individual operator and so that he or she doesn't stay in one position for long.
3. Reduce glare with devices such as recessed or indirect lighting.[167]
4. Give workers a preplacement vision exam to ensure properly corrected vision.
5. Allow users to position their wrists at the same level as the elbow.
6. Put the screen at or just below the user's eye level, at a distance of 18 to 30 inches from the eyes.
7. Instruct users to let the wrists rest lightly on a pad for support.
8. Instruct users to put the feet flat on the floor, or provide a footrest.[168]

Infectious Diseases

With many employees traveling to and from international destinations, monitoring and controlling infectious diseases has become an important safety issue.[169]

Employers can take steps to prevent the entry or spread of infectious diseases. These steps include the following:

1. Closely monitor the Centers for Disease Control and Prevention (CDC) travel alerts. Access this information at www.cdc.gov.
2. Provide daily medical screenings for employees returning from infected areas.
3. Deny access for 10 days to employees or visitors who have had contact with suspected infected individuals.
4. Tell employees to stay home if they have a fever or respiratory system symptoms.
5. Clean work areas and surfaces regularly. Make sanitizers containing alcohol easily available.
6. Stagger breaks. Offer several lunch periods to reduce overcrowding.

Workplace Smoking

To some extent, the problem of workplace smoking is becoming moot: Many states and municipalities now ban indoor smoking in public areas (see www .smokefreeworld.com/usa.shtml for a list).[170] Yet smoking continues to be a problem for employees and employers. Costs derive from higher health and fire insurance, as well as increased absenteeism and reduced productivity (which occurs when, for instance, a smoker takes a 10-minute break to smoke a cigarette outside).

In general, you can probably deny a job to a smoker as long as you don't use smoking as a surrogate for prohibited discrimination. A "no-smokers-hired" policy does not seem to violate the Americans with Disabilities Act (because smoking is not considered a disability), and in general, "employers' adoption of a no-smokers-hired policy is not illegal under federal law."[171] However, 17 states and the District of Columbia ban discriminating against smokers.[172] Most employers these days ban indoor smoking, often designating small outdoor areas for smokers. NIOSH suggests prohibiting both tobacco smoke and e-cigarette emissions from the workplace.[173] Although marijuana use is still illegal by federal law, it is legal in about 26 states, some of which have instituted safety standards to protect cannabis industry workers. [174]

⭐ Watch It

To see how one organization addresses safety issues, if your professor has chosen to assign this, go to **www.pearson.com/mylab/management** to watch the video City of Los Angeles Safety and then answer the questions to show what you would do.

Occupational Security and Risk Management

Workplace *safety* relates to risks of injury or illness to employees. Workplace *security* relates to protecting employees from internal and external security risks such as criminal acts by outside perpetrators and terrorism.[175] According to SHRM, workplace security plans should address tasks such as establishing a formal security function, protecting the firm's intellectual property (for instance, through noncompete agreements), protecting against cyber threats, developing crisis management plans, establishing theft and fraud prevention procedures, preventing workplace violence, and installing facility security systems.[176]

Most employers have security arrangements.[177] SHRM found that about 85% of responding organizations now have some type of formal disaster plan.[178] Many firms also instituted special handling procedures for suspicious mail packages and hold regular emergency evacuation drills.

Enterprise Risk Management

The plans you make reflect the risks you want to mitigate. Companies face a variety of risks, only some of which are direct risks to employees' health and safety. Potential risks include, for instance, natural disaster risks, financial risks, and risks to the firm's computer systems. However, *human capital risks* would also rank high. These include safety risks like those we discussed in this chapter (such as health hazards) as well as, for instance, risks from unionization and from inadequate staffing plans.[179]

Identifying security and other corporate risks falls within the domain of *enterprise risk management,* which means identifying risks and planning to and actually mitigating these risks. Thus, as part of its risk management, Walmart asks questions such as, "What are the risks? What will we do about them?"[180] Reducing occupational violence and enhancing facility security are two examples.

Preventing and Dealing with Violence at Work

In April 2017, a former employee returned to an Equinox health club in Coral Gables, Florida, and killed the managers who had just fired him for workplace violence.

Violence against employees is a huge problem.[181] In one recent year, there were 400 workplace homicides and about 2 million worker victims of workplace violence.[182] Customers, not coworkers, are more often the perpetrators.[183] One report called bullying the "silent epidemic" of the workplace, "where abusive behavior, threats, and intimidation often go unreported."[184] Sadly, many assaults involve a current or former partner or spouse.[185] According to one survey, 29% of workers who knew about or experienced workplace violence said nothing about it.[186]

Workplace violence is predictable and avoidable. *Risk Management Magazine* estimates that about 86% of past workplace violence incidents were anticipated by coworkers, who had brought them to management's attention prior to the incidents actually occurring. Yet management usually did little or nothing.[187]

Men have more fatal occupational injuries than do women, but the proportion of women who are victims of assault is much higher. The Gender-Motivated Violence Act (part of the Violence against Women Act) imposes liabilities on employers whose female employees become violence victims.[188] Of all females murdered at work, more than three-fourths are victims of random criminal violence carried out by an assailant unknown to the victim. Family members, coworkers, or acquaintances commit the remaining acts. Tangible security improvements including better lighting, cash-drop boxes, and similar steps can help. Women (and men) should have access to domestic crisis hotlines, such as www.ndvh.org, and to employee assistance programs.

Human resource managers can take several steps to reduce workplace violence. *Heightened security measures* are the first line of defense, whether the violence derives from coworkers, customers, or outsiders. According to OSHA, measures should include those in Figure 14.6.

Improve Employee Screening With about 30% of workplace attacks committed by coworkers, screening out potentially violent applicants is the employer's next line of defense.

Personal and situational factors correlate with workplace aggression. Men, and individuals scoring higher on "trait anger" (the predisposition to respond to situations with hostility) are more likely to exhibit workplace aggression. In terms of the situation, interpersonal injustice and poor leadership predict aggression against supervisors.[189]

Employers can screen out potentially violent workers before they're hired. Obtain an employment application, and check the applicant's employment history, education, and references.[190] Sample interview questions include "What frustrates you?" and "Who was your worst supervisor, and why?"[191] Certain background circumstances, such as the following, may call for a more in-depth background checking:[192]

- An unexplained gap in employment
- Incomplete or false information on the résumé or application
- A negative, unfavorable, or false reference
- Prior insubordinate or violent behavior on the job[193]
- A criminal history involving harassing or violent behavior
- A prior termination for cause with a suspicious (or no) explanation
- History of drug or alcohol abuse
- Strong indications of instability in the individual's work or personal life as indicated, for example, by frequent job changes or geographic moves
- Lost licenses or accreditations[194]

Use Workplace Violence Training You can also train supervisors to identify the clues that typify potentially violent current employees. Common clues include the following:[195]

- An act of violence on or off the job
- Erratic behavior evidencing a loss of perception or awareness of actions
- Overly confrontational or antisocial behavior
- Sexually aggressive behavior
- Isolationist or loner tendencies
- Insubordinate behavior with a threat of violence
- Tendency to overreact to criticism
- Exaggerated interest in war, guns, violence, mass murders, catastrophes, and so on

Figure 14.6

How to Heighten Security in Your Workplace

- Improve external lighting.
- Use drop safes to minimize cash on hand.
- Post signs noting that only a limited amount of cash is on hand.
- Install silent alarms and surveillance cameras.
- Increase the number of staff on duty.
- Provide staff training in conflict resolution and nonviolent response.
- Close establishments during high-risk hours late at night and early in the morning.
- Issue a weapons policy; for instance, "firearms or other dangerous or deadly weapons cannot be brought onto the facility either openly or concealed."*

*See "Creating a Safer Workplace: Simple Steps Bring Results," *Safety Now*, September 2002, pp. 1–2. See also L. Claussen, "Disgruntled and Dangerous," *Safety & Health* 180, no. 1 (July 2009), pp. 44–47.

- Commission of a serious breach of security
- Possession of weapons, guns, knives, or like items in the workplace
- Violation of privacy rights of others, such as searching desks or stalking
- Chronic complaining and the raising of frequent, unreasonable grievances
- A retributory or get-even attitude

The U.S. Postal Service took steps to reduce workplace assaults. The steps include more background checks, drug testing, a 90-day probationary period for new hires, more stringent security (including a hotline that lets employees report threats), and training for managers to create a healthier culture.[196] The Management Skills feature lists useful guidelines for firing high-risk employees..

BUILDING YOUR MANAGEMENT SKILLS:
Guidelines for Firing a High-Risk Employee

When firing a high-risk employee:

- Plan all aspects of the meeting, including its time, location, the people to be present, and the agenda.
- Involve security enforcement personnel.
- Advise the employee that he or she is no longer permitted onto the employer's property.
- Conduct the meeting in a room with a door leading to the outside of the building.
- Keep the termination brief and to the point.
- Make sure he or she returns all company-owned property at the meeting.
- Don't let the person return to his or her workstation.
- Conduct the meeting early in the week and early in the morning so he or she has time to meet with employment counselors or support groups.
- Offer as generous a severance package as possible.
- Protect the employee's dignity by not advertising the event.[197]

Setting Up a Basic Security Program

As noted, workplace *security* relates to protecting employees *from internal and external security risks* (such as robberies and terrorism). This often starts with facilities security.

As one corporate security summary put it, "workplace security involves more than . . . installing an alarm system."[198] Ideally, a comprehensive corporate anti-crime program should start with the following:[199]

- **Company philosophy and policy on crime**—Make sure employees understand that the employer has a zero-tolerance policy with respect to workers who commit any crimes.
- **Investigations of job applicants**—Always conduct full background checks.
- **Crime awareness training**—Make it clear during training and orientation that the employer is tough on workplace crime.
- **Crisis management**—Establish and communicate what to do in the event of a bomb threat, fire, or other emergency.

In simplest terms, instituting a basic facility security program requires analyzing the current *level* of risk, and then installing *mechanical*, *natural*, and *organizational* security systems.[200]

In terms of the facility's *current level of risk*, start with the obvious. For example, what is the neighborhood like? Does your facility (such as the office building you're in) house other businesses or individuals that might bring unsafe activities to your doorstep? As part of this initial threat assessment, also review these six matters:

1. **Reception area access**, including need for a "panic button;"
2. **Interior security**, including secure restrooms and better identification of exits;
3. **Authorities' involvement**, in particular, emergency procedures developed with local law enforcement;
4. **Mail handling**, including screening and opening mail;
5. **Evacuation**, including evacuation procedures and training, and;
6. **Backup systems**, such as storing data off site.

Having assessed the potential current level of risk, the employer then turns to improving natural, mechanical, and organizational security.[201] *Natural security* means capitalizing on the facility's natural or architectural features to minimize security problems. For example, do too many entrances now hamper controlling facility access? *Mechanical security* is the utilization of security systems such as locks, intrusion alarms, access control systems, and surveillance systems to reduce the need for continuous human surveillance.[202] Mail rooms use scanners to check incoming mail. Biometric scanners that read thumb or palm prints or retina or vocal patterns make it easier to enforce plant security.[203]

Finally, *organizational security* means using good management to improve security. For example, it means properly screening, training, and motivating security staff and lobby attendants. Also ensure that the security staff has written orders that define their duties, especially in fire, elevator entrapment, spills, medical emergencies, hostile intrusions, suspicious packages, civil disturbances, and workplace violence.[204] HR information can be a "gold mine" for hackers and requires effective defenses.[205]

Mechanical security is the utilization of security systems such as locks, intrusion alarms, access control systems, and surveillance systems to reduce the need for continuous human surveillance.

Source: Titikul_B/Shutterstock.

Terrorism

The employer can take steps to protect its employees and physical assets from a terrorist attack. These steps, now familiar at many workplaces, include the following:

- Screen the identities of everyone entering the premises.
- Check mail carefully.
- Identify ahead of time a lean "crisis organization" that can run the company on an interim basis after a terrorist threat.
- Identify in advance under what conditions you will close the company down, as well as what the shutdown process will be.
- Institute a process to put the crisis management team together.
- Prepare evacuation plans, and make sure exits are well marked and unblocked.
- Designate an employee who will communicate with families and off-site employees.
- Identify an upwind, off-site location near your facility to use as a staging area for all evacuated personnel.
- Designate in advance several employees who will do headcounts at the evacuation staging area.
- Establish an emergency text-messaging policy and procedure to notify affected individuals that an emergency may exist.[206]

The HR Practices Around the Globe feature elaborates on this.

■ HR Practices Around the Globe

Dealing with Terrorism Abroad

Terrorism abroad is a serious issue. Even stationing employees in assumedly safe countries is no guarantee there won't be problems. For example, when protests erupted in Egypt several years ago, Medex Global Solutions evacuated more than 500 of its clients' people from Egypt; Medex had already been advising their clients about likely political unrest.[207]

Employers thus increasingly institute comprehensive safety plans abroad, such as evacuation plans to get employees to safety. Many employers purchase intelligence services for monitoring potential terrorist threats abroad. The head of one intelligence firm estimates such services at costing $6,000–$10,000 per year.[208]

Business Travel

Keeping business travelers safe is a specialty all its own, but suggestions here include:[209]

- Provide expatriates with training about the place they're going to, so they're more oriented.
- Tell them not to draw attention to the fact they're Americans—by wearing T-shirts with American names, for instance.
- Have travelers arrive at airports as close to departure time as possible and wait in areas away from the main flow of traffic.
- Equip the expatriate's car and home with security systems.
- Tell employees to vary their departure and arrival times and take different routes.
- Keep employees current on crime and other problems by regularly checking, for example, the State Department's travel advisories and warnings at http://travel.state.gov/.[210] Click on "Travel Alerts" and "Country Information."
- Advise employees to act confident at all times. Body language can attract perpetrators, and those who look like victims often become victimized.[211]

✪ Talk About It–6

If your professor has chosen to assign this, go to **www.pearson.com/mylab/management** to discuss the following questions. Have you traveled abroad and violated any of these rules? Which? Would you do things differently now, knowing what you know?

Emergency Plans and Business Continuity

The possibility of emergencies means that employers need facility continuity and emergency plans.[212] Such plans should cover *early detection of a problem*, *methods for communicating the emergency externally*, and *communications plans for initiating an evacuation*. Ideally, an initial alarm should come first. The employer should then follow the initial alarm with an announcement providing specific information about the emergency and letting employees know what action they should take. Many use social networks or text messaging.[213] To help the organization prepare for potential disasters, the HR department should develop a plan and identify key responsibilities, make sure all employees are aware of the plan, and train employees regularly.[214] OSHA provides an evacuation planning E-tool.[215]

One should also have plans for dealing with health issues.[216] Thus, in the case of a cardiac arrest emergency, early CPR and the use of an automated external defibrillator are essential. These devices should be available and one or more local employees trained in their use.[217]

Plans are also required for *business continuity* in the event of a disaster. The employer can designate a secure area of the company website for employee communications, listing such things as expected hours of operation, facilities opening schedules, and alternative work locations.[218] Disaster plans should include establishing a command center and identification of employees considered essential in the event of a disaster, including responsibilities for each. The SBA provides business continuity information at www.preparemybusiness.org.

Social media such as Twitter are obvious choices for quickly communicating emergency information to large numbers of dispersed individuals. When a tornado hit Bridgeport Connecticut, a few years ago, the city's administrators used Twitter to let citizens know about things like power outages and blocked roads. [219]

Review

MyLab Management

If your instructor is using MyLab Management, go to **www.pearson.com/mylab/management** to complete the problems marked with this icon ⭐.

Summary

1. The purpose of OSHA is to ensure every working person a safe and healthful workplace. OSHA standards are complete and detailed and are enforced through a system of workplace inspections. OSHA inspectors can issue citations and recommend penalties to their area directors.

2. There are three basic causes of accidents: chance occurrences, unsafe conditions, and unsafe acts on the part of employees. In addition, three other work-related factors—the job itself, the work schedule, and the psychological climate—also contribute to accidents.

3. There are several approaches to preventing accidents. One is to reduce unsafe conditions. The other approach is to reduce unsafe acts—for example, through selection and placement, training, positive reinforcement, propaganda, and top-management commitment.

4. The centerpiece of Milliken's safety process is its *involvement-based employee engagement* program. Milliken's safety processes are led almost entirely by Milliken's employees. For example, they staff the steering and safety subcommittee system, submit "opportunity for improvement" suggestions weekly, review each of these suggestions, and provide feedback on every suggestion.

5. Alcoholism, drug addiction, stress, and emotional illness are four important and growing health problems among employees. Alcoholism is a particularly serious problem that can drastically lower the effectiveness of your organization. Techniques including disciplining, discharge, in-house counseling, and referrals to an outside agency are used to deal with these problems.

6. Basic facility security relies on natural security, mechanical security, and organizational security.

Key Terms

Occupational Safety and Health Act of 1970   436
Occupational Safety and Health Administration (OSHA)   436
citations   437
job hazard analysis   445

operational safety reviews   445
safety awareness program   449
workaholic   455
burnout   456

Discussion Questions

⭐ 14-1. Discuss OSHA and how it operates.

14-2. Explain in detail three basic causes of accidents.

⭐ 14-3. Discuss major health problems at work and how to remedy them.

⭐ 14-4. Discuss the basic facts about OSHA—its purpose, standards, inspection, and rights and responsibilities.

14-5. Explain the supervisor's role in safety.

14-6. Explain what causes unsafe acts.

14-7. Explain how an employee could reduce stress at work.

Individual and Group Activities

14-8. Working individually or in groups, answer the question, "Is there such a thing as an accident-prone person?" Develop your answer using examples of actual people you know who seemed to be accident prone in some endeavor.

14-9. Working individually or in groups, compile a list of the factors at work or in school that create dysfunctional stress for you. What methods do you use for dealing with the stress?

14-10. An issue of the journal *Occupational Hazards* presented some information about what happens when OSHA refers criminal complaints about willful violations of OSHA standards to the U.S. Department of Justice (DOJ). In one 20-year period, OSHA referred 119 fatal cases allegedly involving willful violations of OSHA to the DOJ for criminal prosecution. The DOJ declined to pursue 57% of them, and some were dropped for other reasons. Of the remaining 51 cases, the DOJ settled 63% with pretrial settlements involving no prison time. So, counting acquittals, of the 119 cases OSHA referred to the DOJ, only 9 resulted in prison time for at least one of the defendants. "The Department of Justice is a disgrace," charged the founder of an organization for family members of workers killed on the job. One possible explanation for this low conviction rate is that the crime in cases like these is generally a misdemeanor, not a felony, and the DOJ generally tries to focus its attention on felony cases. What implications does this have for how employers should manage their safety programs? Why?

14-11. A 315-foot-tall, 2-million-pound crane collapsed on a construction site in East Toledo, Ohio, killing four ironworkers. Do you think accidents like this are avoidable? If so, what steps would you suggest the general contractor take to avoid a repeat?

14-12. In groups of three or four students, spend 15 minutes walking around the building in which your class is held or where you are now, listing possible natural, mechanical, and organizational security measures you'd suggest to the building's owner.

14-13. For this activity, you will need the documents titled (1) "HRCI PHR® and SPHR® Certification Body of Knowledge," and (2) "About the Society for Human Resource Management (SHRM) Body of Competency & Knowledge® Model and Certification Exams." Your instructor can obtain these two documents from the Pearson Instructor Resource Center and pass them on to you. These two documents list the knowledge someone studying for the HRCI or SHRM certification exam needs to have in each area of human resource management (such as in Strategic Management, and Workforce Planning). In groups of several students, do four things: (1) review the HRCI and/or SHRM documents; (2) identify the material in this chapter that relates to HRCI's or SHRM's required knowledge lists; (3) write four multiple-choice exam questions on this material that you believe would be suitable for inclusion in the HRCI exam and/or the SHRM exam; and, (4) if time permits, have someone from your team post your team's questions in front of the class, so thats can answer the exam questions created by the other teams.

MyLab Management

If your instructor is using MyLab Management, go to **www.pearson.com/mylab/management** for Auto-graded writing questions as well as the following Assisted-graded writing questions:

14-14. Explain how to prevent accidents at work.

14-15. How would you go about providing a safer work environment for your employees?

APPLICATION EXERCISES

HR IN ACTION CASE INCIDENT 1

The Office Safety and Health Program

LearnInMotion is a firm that delivers employee training, both online and via delivery of DVDs. At first glance, such a firm is probably one of the last places you'd expect to find potential safety and health hazards—or so the owners, Jennifer and Mel, thought. There's no danger of moving machinery, no high-pressure lines, no cutting or heavy lifting, and certainly no forklift trucks. However, there are safety and health problems.

In terms of accident-causing conditions, for instance, the one thing such companies have is lots of cables and wires. WiFi not withstanding, there are cables connecting the computers to each other and to the servers, and in many cases, separate cables running from some computers to separate printers. There are 10 wireless telephones in the office, the bases of which are connected to 15-foot phone lines that always seem to be snaking around chairs and tables.

When the installation specialists wired the office (for electricity, high-speed cable, phone lines, burglar alarms, and computers), they estimated they used well over 5 miles of cables of one sort or another. Most of these are hidden in the walls or ceilings, but many of them snake their way from desk to desk, and under and over doorways. Several employees have tried to reduce the nuisance of having to trip over wires whenever they get up by putting their plastic chair pads over the wires closest to them. However, that still leaves many wires unprotected. In other cases, they brought in their own packing tape and tried to tape down the wires in those spaces where they're particularly troublesome, such as across doorways.

The cables and wires are only one of the more obvious potential accident-causing conditions. The firm's programmer had tried to repair the main server while the unit was still electrically alive. To this day, they're not sure exactly where he stuck the screwdriver, but the result was that he was "blown across the room," as Mel puts it. Carpal tunnel syndrome is another risk, as are eyestrain and strained backs.

One recent accident particularly scared them. The firm uses independent contractors to deliver the firm's book- and CD/DVD-based courses in New York and two other cities. A delivery person was riding his bike at the intersection of Second Avenue and East 64th Street in New York when he was struck by a car. Luckily, he was not hurt, but the bike's front wheel was wrecked, and the close call got Mel and Jennifer thinking about their lack of a safety program.

And it's not just the physical conditions. They also have some concerns about potential health problems such as job stress and burnout. Although the business may be (relatively) safe with respect to physical conditions, it is also relatively stressful in terms of the demands it makes in hours and deadlines. It is not at all unusual for employees to get to work by 7:30 or 8:00 in the morning and to work through until 11:00 or 12:00 at night. Just getting the company's new service operational required five of LearnInMotion's employees to work 70-hour workweeks for three weeks.

The bottom line is that both Jennifer and Mel feel they need to do something about implementing a health and safety plan. Now they want you to help them actually do it. Here's what they want you to do for them.

Questions

14-16. Based on your knowledge of health and safety matters and your actual observations of operations that are similar to ours, make a list of the potential hazardous conditions employees and others face at LearnInMotion. What should we do to reduce the potential severity of the top five hazards?

14-17. Would it be advisable for us to set up a procedure for screening out stress-prone or accident-prone individuals? Why? If so, how should we screen them?

14-18. Write a short position paper on what we should do to get all our employees to behave more safely at work.

14-19. Based on what you know and on what other dot-coms are doing, write a short position paper on what we can do to reduce the potential problems of stress and burnout in our company.

HR IN ACTION CASE INCIDENT 2
Carter Cleaning Company

Motivating Safe Behavior

Employees' safety and health are very important in the laundry and cleaning business. Each facility is a small production plant in which machines, powered by high-pressure steam and compressed air, work at high temperatures washing, cleaning, and pressing garments, often under very hot, slippery conditions. Chemical vapors are continually produced, and caustic chemicals are used in the cleaning process. High-temperature stills are almost continually "cooking down" cleaning solvents to remove impurities so that the solvents can be reused. If a mistake is made in this process—like injecting too much steam into the still—a boil-over occurs, in which boiling chemical solvent erupts out of the still and over the floor, and on anyone who happens to be standing in its way.

As a result of these hazards and the fact that these stores continually produce chemically hazardous waste, several government agencies (including OSHA and the EPA) have strict guidelines regarding management of these plants. For example, posters must be placed in each store, notifying employees of their right to be told what hazardous chemicals they are dealing with and what the proper method for handling each chemical is. Special waste-management firms must be used to pick up and properly dispose of the hazardous waste.

A chronic problem the Carters (and most other laundry owners) have is the unwillingness on the part of the cleaning-spotting workers to wear safety goggles. Not all the chemicals they use require safety goggles, but some—like the hydrofluorous acid used to remove rust stains from garments—are very dangerous. The latter is kept in special plastic containers because it dissolves glass. The problem is that safety goggles are somewhat uncomfortable, and they become smudged easily and thus reduce visibility. As a result, Jack has found it almost impossible to get these employees to wear their goggles.

Questions

14-20. How should the firm go about identifying hazardous conditions that should be rectified? Use data and checklists, such as in Figure 14.4, to list at least 10 possible dry cleaning store hazardous conditions.

14-21. Would it be advisable for the firm to set up a procedure for screening out accident-prone individuals? How should it do so?

14-22. In general, how would you suggest the Carters get all employees to behave more safely at work?

14-23. Describe in detail how you would use motivation to get those who should be wearing goggles to do so.

Experiential Exercise

How Safe Is My University?

Purpose: The purpose of this exercise is to give you practice in identifying unsafe conditions.

Required Understanding: You should be familiar with material covered in this chapter, particularly that on unsafe conditions and that in Figure 14.4.

How to Set Up the Exercise/Instructions: Divide the class into groups of four. Assume that each group is a safety committee retained by your college or university's safety engineer to identify and report on any possible unsafe conditions in and around the school building. Each group will spend about 45 minutes in and around the building you are now in for the purpose of identifying and listing possible unsafe conditions. (Make use of Figure 14.4.)

Return to the class in about 45 minutes. A spokesperson for each group should list on the board the unsafe conditions you think you have identified. How many were there? Do you think these also violate OSHA standards? How would you go about checking?

WHERE WE ARE NOW

Parts 1 through 5 explained the basics of human resource management, in particular how to recruit, select, train, appraise, and compensate employees and provide them with positive employee relations and a safe work environment. In Part 6, Special Issues in Human Resource Management, we turn to how to manage human resources in two special situations—when managing HR globally, and in small entrepreneurial businesses. In Part 6, we will therefore cover

- Module A, Managing HR Globally
- Module B, Managing HR in Small and Entrepreneurial Firms

Managing HR Globally

OVERVIEW:
In this module, we will cover . . .

- HR and the Internationalization of Business
- International Employee Selection Issues
- Training and Maintaining International Employees
- Managing HR Globally: How to Put a Global HR System into Practice

MyLab Management

⭐ Improve Your Grade!
When you see this icon, visit
www.pearson.com/mylab/management
for activities that are applied, personalized, and offer immediate feedback.

LEARNING OBJECTIVES

When you finish studying this chapter, you should be able to:

1. Explain how intercountry differences influence human resource management.
2. Answer the question, "How does selecting someone to be an expatriate manager differ from selecting one to work domestically?"
3. Discuss the basics of an effective employee repatriation program.
4. List the main points in developing, making acceptable, and implementing a global HRM program.

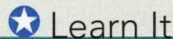 Learn It

If your professor has chosen to assign this, go to **www.pearson.com/mylab/management** to see what you should particularly focus on and to take the Module A Warm Up.

HR and the Internationalization of Business

You don't have to dig very far to see how important international business is. For example, the total sum of U.S. imports and exports rose by about nine times in the past 30 years, to about $5 trillion recently.[1] That growth has been great for all sorts of businesses, but also confronts managers with special challenges. For one thing, managers have to formulate and execute their marketing, product, and production plans worldwide. Ford Motor, for instance, has a "One Ford" strategy aimed at offering similar Ford cars internationally.

Similarly, "going global" means employers must address international human resource management issues. For example, "Should we staff our offices in Europe with local or U.S. managers?" And, "How should we appraise and pay our Asia employees?"[2]

The Human Resource Challenges of International Business

Dealing with such global human resource challenges isn't easy, because the employer faces an array of political, social, legal, and cultural differences among countries.

Companies operating only within the United States generally have the luxury of dealing with a relatively limited set of economic, cultural, and legal variables. Different states and municipalities do have their own laws affecting HR. However, a basic federal framework helps produce a fairly predictable set of legal guidelines regarding things like employment discrimination, labor relations, and safety and health. Similarly, political risks within the United States are minimal. *Political risks* "are any governmental action or politically motivated event that could adversely affect the long-run profitability or value of the firm."[3] For example, Venezuela's president moved to nationalize a GM plant.

A company operating multiple units abroad isn't blessed with such homogeneity. For example, even with the increasingly standardized European Union, minimum mandated holidays range from none in the United Kingdom to five weeks per year in Luxembourg. The point is that the need to adapt personnel policies and procedures to the differences among countries complicates human resource management in multinational companies.

Similarly, what works in one country may not work in another: An incentive plan may work in the United States, but backfire in some Eastern Europe countries, where workers need a predictable weekly wage to buy necessities. Employee recruitment processes that work well in the United States may not work in China, where special rules sometimes restrict changing jobs. But despite such intercountry differences, the employer needs to create, for each country's local facility and for the company as a whole, effective human resource practices. Distance adds to the challenge. For example, how should Starbucks' chief HR officer in Seattle keep track of Starbucks' top managers' performance overseas? The accompanying HR in Practice Box feature illustrates the challenges involved.

■ HR in Practice

Unionizing Walmart Stores in China

Walmart Stores' competitive strategy is to be retailing's low-cost leader, and avoiding unions has been one of its main tactics for keeping down costs.[4] It believes unions probably would drive up its labor costs and impede its ability to make personnel changes the company views as desirable.

With its powerful, government-backed All-China Federation of Trade Unions, China's cultural, political, and labor relations and legal systems are (literally) a world away from what Walmart dealt with in America. Several years ago, the union formed its first Walmart union in China.[5] It didn't take long for Walmart China to experience the difference unions can make. The company offered 54 local midlevel managers three options—transferring to outlets in other cities, accepting demotions, or leaving the company.[6] Not wanting to change, the China managers sprang into action. One led 11 colleagues to the local federation of trade unions for assistance. Whatever they did, it worked. Walmart apparently halted its planned reshuffle. Walmart had to adjust its HR strategy for China.

⭐ Talk About It—**1**

If your professor has chosen to assign this, go to **www.pearson.com/mylab/management** to discuss the following question. What other nonunion surprises do you think Walmart should be planning for in its HR practices in China?

What Is International Human Resource Management?

international human resource management (IHRM)

The human resource management concepts and techniques employers use to manage the human resource challenges of their international operations.

Employers rely on **international human resource management (IHRM)** to deal with global HR challenges like these.[7] We can define IHRM as the human resource management concepts and techniques employers use to manage the human resource challenges of their international operations. IHRM generally focuses on tasks such as selecting, training, compensating, and managing employees who are assigned abroad ("expatriates"), selecting, training, and compensating the company's "local" employees abroad, and comparing, applying, and managing human resource management practices across different countries.[8]

How Intercountry Differences Affect Human Resource Management

As we said, the challenges of international human resource management don't just stem from the distances involved (though this is important). The bigger issue is dealing with the cultural, political, legal, and economic differences among countries.

Cultural Factors   For one thing, countries differ widely in their cultures—in the basic values that their citizens share, and in how these values manifest themselves in the nation's arts, social programs, and ways of doing things. Cultural differences mean people abroad react differently to the same or similar situations. For example, when one Michelin manager does appraisals in France, he doesn't mention what's right because employees know what they've done right. He focuses instead on what's wrong.[9] That approach would surprise many U.S. employees, where there's a tendency for managers to sugarcoat what's wrong.

Studies by Professor Geert Hofstede illustrate international cultural differences. Hofstede says societies differ in five values, which he calls *power distance*, *individualism*, *"masculinity,"* *uncertainty avoidance*, and *long-term orientation*. For example, power distance represents the degree to which less powerful people accept the unequal distribution of power in society.[10] He concluded that acceptance of such inequality was higher in some countries (such as Mexico) than in others (such as Sweden).[11] In turn, such differences manifest themselves in different behaviors. To see how your country's culture compares with others, go to www.geert-hofstede.com/hofstede_dimensions.php.

Cultural differences such as these help shape human resource policies. For example, in one study, power distance (acceptance of the unequal distribution of power) correlated positively with the gap between the CEO's and other workers' pay.[12]

Legal Factors   Employers expanding abroad must be familiar with the labor law systems in the countries they're entering. For example, in India, companies with more than 100 workers must get government permission to fire anyone.[13] In Brazil, firing someone without "just cause" could trigger a fine of 4% of the total amount

Cultural differences mean people abroad react differently to the same or similar situations.
Source: Robert Kneschke/Shutterstock.

the worker ever earned.[14] As another example, "employment at will" is basically nonexistent in European law, so recruiting and hiring abroad can be treacherous. One firm hired someone as an independent contractor, only to find later that they owed the person hundreds of thousands of dollars in back taxes and penalties for misclassifying the person.[15]

Economic Systems Similarly, differences in *economic systems* translate into differences in intercountry HR practices. Economists distinguish among market, planned, and mixed economies. In market economies (such as the United States), governments play a relatively restrained role in deciding things such as what will be produced and sold. In planned economies (such as North Korea), the government decides and plans what to produce and sell, at what price. In mixed economies (such as China), many industries are still under direct government control, while others make pricing and production decisions based on market demand.

Labor costs also vary widely. For example, hourly compensation costs (in U.S. dollars) for production workers range from $2 in the Philippines to $35.5 in the United States, to $64.2 in Norway.[16] And compared to the usual two or three weeks of U.S. vacation, workers in France can expect two and a half days of paid holiday per full month of service per year.

Example: Europe To appreciate the employment effects of cultural, economic, and legal differences like these, consider Europe. Over the past five decades, the separate countries of the former European Community (EC) unified into a common market for goods, services, capital, and even labor called the European Union (EU). Generally speaking, this means that products and even labor can move from country to country with few impediments.

Companies doing business in Europe (including U.S.-based companies like Ford) must adjust their human resource policies and practices to both EU directives and to country-specific employment laws. The directives' *objectives* are binding on all member countries (although each member country can implement the directives as it chooses). For example, the *confirmation of employment* directive requires employers to provide employees with written terms and conditions of their employment. However, these terms vary from country to country.[17] In England, a written statement is required, including things like rate of pay, date employment began, and hours of work. Germany doesn't require a written contract, but it's customary to have one. Similarly, most EU countries have minimum wage systems. Some set national limits. Others allow employers and unions to work out their own minimum wages.

LEARNING OBJECTIVE 2
Answer the question, "How does selecting someone to be an expatriate manager differ from selecting one to work domestically?"

International Employee Selection Issues

Increasingly today, international human resource management focuses on how employers should manage their global HR functions, for instance, in terms of applying home office appraisal and compensation practices abroad. However, *filling the employer's international jobs* has traditionally been the heart of international human resource management. The process involves identifying and selecting the people who will fill the positions abroad and then placing them in those positions.

International Staffing: Home or Local?

In general, we can classify an international company's employees as *expatriates, home-country nationals, locals (host-country nationals),* or *third-country nationals.*[18] **Expatriates** are noncitizens of the countries in which they are working. Expatriates may also be **home-country nationals**, which means citizens of the country in which the company is headquartered. **Locals** (also known as *host-country nationals*) work for the company abroad and are citizens of the countries where they are working. **Third-country nationals** are citizens of a country other than the parent or the host country—for example, a French executive working in the Shanghai branch of a U.S. multinational bank.[19] (Of course, not all expatriates are sent abroad by employers; many recent graduates, academics, volunteer workers, doctors, and business professionals decide to move and live abroad and to find employment there.)[20]

expatriates
Employees a company posts abroad, and who are noncitizens of the country in which they are working.

home-country nationals
Citizens of the country in which the multinational company has its headquarters.

locals
Employees who work for the company abroad and are citizens of the countries where they are working, also known as "host-country nationals."

third-country nationals
Citizens of a country other than the parent or host country.

Why Local? Most hires will be "locals," for good reason. Within the United States, it can be challenging bringing workers in from abroad, so using U.S. locals may be a necessity.

And abroad, cost is a big incentive for "hiring local." It costs a lot to send expatriates abroad. Agilent Technologies estimated that it cost about three times the expatriate's annual salary to keep the person abroad for one year. But when Agilent hired an outside firm to handle its expatriate program, it discovered that the costs were much higher. Agilent then reduced the expats it sent abroad.[21] Yet cost may also work in the opposite direction. For example, difficulties attracting management trainees to work in relatively low-wage hospitality jobs in the United States prompts some hotels to hire people from abroad to fill these jobs. Finally, the host country's government and citizens may view the multinational as a "better citizen" if it uses local management talent.

Why Expats? There are also good reasons to use expatriates—either home-country or third-country nationals—for positions abroad. Employers often can't find local candidates with the required technical qualifications. As noted earlier, companies also view a successful stint abroad as a required step in developing top managers. Control is important too. The assumption is that home-country managers are already steeped in the firm's policies and culture and thus more likely to implement headquarters' instructions and ways of doing things.

In any case, the trend is to use locals. Posting expatriates abroad is expensive, security problems give potential expats pause, returning expats often leave for other employers, colleges are producing top-quality candidates abroad, and the recent recession made the cost of posting employees abroad even more unattractive.

One survey found that about 47% of U.S. multinationals are maintaining the size of their expat workforces; 18% were increasing it, and 35% were decreasing the number of expatriates.[22] However, about half the global companies in one survey were doubling the number of expats they send to countries like China.[23] The HR team needs to control expat expenses, as the accompanying HR as a Profit Center explains.

■ HR as a Profit Center

Reducing Expatriate Costs

Given the expense of sending employees abroad for overseas assignments, the employer's human resource team must help control expatriate costs. Employers use several alternatives to reduce or avoid the expenses of the typical 1-5 year expat assignment.[24] First, companies are upping the numbers of short-term assignments they make. This lets them use lower-cost short-term assignments to replace some long-term assignments that require supporting expats (and their families) abroad for extended periods. Fifty percent of the companies surveyed are also replacing some expatriate postings with local hires. With an eye on cutting costs, many employers were also reviewing their firms' policies regarding things like housing, education, home leave, and expatriate allowances and premiums (cost-of-living allowances, etc.).[25]

✪ Talk About It–2

If your professor has chosen to assign this, go to **www.pearson.com/mylab/management** to discuss the following questions. Might not some of these policies make it harder to get employees to move abroad? Why?

Other Solutions The choice isn't just expatriate versus local. For example, one survey found that about 78% of employers had some form of "localization" policy. This is a policy of transferring a home-country national employee to a foreign subsidiary as a "permanent transferee."[26] For example, U.S. IBM employees originally from India eventually filled many of the 5,000 jobs that IBM shifted from the United States to India. They elected to move back to India, albeit at local, India pay rates.

As we explained in Chapter 5, *offshoring* (having local employees abroad do jobs that the firm's domestic employees previously did in-house) is another option. However, doing so entangles the employer in numerous human resource decisions. IBM Business Consulting Services surveyed employers to see what roles HR was actually playing in these decisions.[27] Here, HR helps top management:[28]

- To understand the *local labor markets*, for example, in terms of their size, education levels, and language skills.
- To understand how the firm's current *reputation* may affect outsourcing to this locale.
- To decide how much the firm should *integrate the local workforce* into the parent firm's corporate organization. For example, engineering employees might best become employees. Call center employees might remain independent contractors or employees of vendor firms.
- To deal with skill shortages.[29] This often requires attracting employees from other local firms using signing bonuses, higher wages, and improved employee retention policies (such as improved promotion opportunities).
- To identify what *"levers"* reduce attrition. These levers include more training and development, better compensation and benefits, and improved career opportunities.

virtual transnational teams
Groups of geographically dispersed coworkers who interact using a combination of telecommunications and information technologies to accomplish an organizational task.

Some companies run multicountry projects by using "transnational" teams composed of employees whose locations and activities span several countries.[30] Thus a European beverage manufacturer formed a 13-member "European Production Task Force," with members from its facilities in five countries. Its task was to analyze how many factories the firm should operate in Europe, and where to place them.[31] Often such teams meet and work in virtual environments. **Virtual transnational teams** are groups of geographically dispersed coworkers who interact using information technologies to accomplish an organizational task.

In a Skype and FaceTime world, virtual teams are practical and popular. Collaborative software systems such as Microsoft NetMeeting,[32] Cisco WebEx,[33] and GoToMeeting[34] enable virtual teams to hold live project reviews and discussions, share documents and exhibits, and store the sessions on the project's website. Cloud-based tools such as Huddle[35] allow team members to "attend" using mobile devices. Large-screen tools such as Cisco Immersive TelePresence[36] can make it seem as if team members are together in the same room.

Some of the problems involved in managing virtual teams are more subtle. For example, if most team members reside in one country, the other team members may assume that the real power is also in that country. Here the manager should stress that the team is a single entity with a unified goal, and that it shares a common purpose.[37]

Values and International Staffing Policy

It's not just facts such as technical skills or attrition rates that influence whether employers use expats, locals, or offshore solutions. In addition, the top executives' values play a role. Some executives are just more "expat-oriented."

ethnocentric
A management philosophy that leads to the creation of home market–oriented staffing decisions.

polycentric
A management philosophy oriented toward staffing positions with local talent.

geocentric
A staffing policy that seeks the best people for key jobs throughout the organization, regardless of nationality.

Experts sometimes classify people's values as **ethnocentric**, **polycentric**, or **geocentric**, and these values translate into corresponding corporate behaviors and policies.[38] In a firm whose top managers tend to be *ethnocentric*, "the prevailing attitude is that home-country attitudes, management style, knowledge, evaluation criteria, and managers are superior to anything the host country might have to offer."[39] In the *polycentric* corporation, "there is a conscious belief that only host-country managers can ever really understand the culture and behavior of the host-country market; therefore, the foreign subsidiary should be managed by local people."[40] *Geocentric* executives believe they must scour the firm's management staff on a global basis, on the assumption that the best manager for a specific position anywhere may be found in any of the countries in which the firm operates.

These values in turn translate into three broad international staffing policies. With an *ethnocentric* staffing policy, the firm tends to fill key management jobs with home (parent-country) nationals. A *polycentric*-oriented firm would staff its foreign subsidiaries with host-country nationals, and its home office with parent-country nationals. A *geocentric* staffing policy guides the firm to choose the best people regardless of nationality.

Ethics Codes In terms of values, employers also need to ensure that their employees abroad are adhering to the firm's ethics codes. Sometimes the main concern is establishing global standards for adhering to U.S. laws with cross-border impacts. Here employers set policies on things like discrimination, harassment, bribery, and Sarbanes-Oxley. One company paid $10 million to settle accusations that it had bribed Chinese and South Korean officials to get $54 million in government contracts.[41] For other firms, the main concern may be enforcing codes of conduct for avoiding, for instance, sweatshop conditions.

Special Tools for Selecting International Managers

In most respects, screening managers for jobs abroad is similar to screening them for domestic jobs. Candidates need the technical knowledge and skills to do the job and the required intelligence and people skills. Testing (as discussed in Chapter 6) is widely used.

However, foreign assignments are different. The expatriate and his or her family will have to cope with and adapt to colleagues whose culture may be very different from their own. And, there's the stress of being in a foreign land. Despite this, one study concluded, "Traditionally, most selection of expatriates appears to be done solely on the basis of successful records of job performance in the home country."[42] Whether the candidate could adapt to a new culture is often secondary.

Preferably, international assignee selection should therefore include *realistic previews* and *adaptability screening procedures*.[43] Even in the most familiar countries there will be language barriers, bouts of homesickness, and the need for children to adapt to new friends. Realistic previews about the problems as well as about the country's cultural benefits are thus an important part of screening. The rule should always be to "spell it all out" ahead of time.[44]

Similarly, with adaptability high on the list of what makes expats succeed, adaptability screening should be part of the screening process. Employers often use psychologists for this. Adaptability screening aims to assess the assignee's (and spouse's) probable success in handling the foreign transfer and to alert them to issues (such as the impact on children) the move may involve. Here, companies often look for overseas candidates whose work and nonwork experience, education, and language skills already demonstrate living and working with different cultures. Even several summers spent traveling overseas or in foreign study programs might provide some basis to believe the candidate can adjust abroad.

Success abroad also requires an "international mind-set," sometimes measured with the Global Mindset Inventory. Sample questions include "Knows how to work well with people from different parts of the world?" And "Enjoys exploring different parts of the world?"[45]

Diversity Counts: Sending Women Managers Abroad

Although women represent about 50% of middle management in U.S. companies, they represent only about 20% of managers sent abroad.[46] That's up from about 15% in 2005, but still low.[47] What accounts for this?

Many of the misperceptions that have impeded women's progress over the years still exist.[48] Line managers make these assignments, and many assume that women don't want to work abroad, are reluctant to move their families abroad, or can't get their spouses to move.[49] In fact, this survey found, women do want international assignments, they are not less inclined to move their families, and their male spouses are not necessarily reluctant. (One survey asked female expatriates why they took international assignments. "Career development" was the most cited reason. Other reasons included "cultural understanding," "gaining experience," "doing something different," "personal goals," and "development learning.")[50]

Safety is another issue. Employers tend to assume that women abroad are more likely to become crime victims. However, most surveyed women expats said that safety was no more an issue with women than it was with men.[51]

Fear of cultural prejudices against women is another common issue. In some cultures, women do have to follow different rules than do men, for instance, in terms of attire. But as one expat said, "Even in the more harsh cultures, once they recognize that the women can do the job, once your competence has been demonstrated, it becomes less of a problem."[52]

Employers take several steps to overcome misperceptions like these and to identify more women to assign abroad. For example, *formalize a process* for identifying employees who are willing to take assignments abroad. (At Gillette, for instance, supervisors use the performance review to identify the subordinate's career interests, including assignments abroad.) *Train managers* to understand how employees really feel about going abroad, and what the real safety and cultural issues are. Let successful female expats *help recruit* prospective female expats. And provide the expat's spouse with *employment assistance*.[53]

TRENDS SHAPING HR: *Digital and Social Media: Job Boards Abroad*

Although a few U.S.-based job boards (like Indeed and Monster) are global, most countries have their own major job boards. For instance, there is www.51job.com in China, www.careerone.com.au in Australia and New Zealand, and www.laborum.cl in Latin America.[54]

How to Avoid Failed International Assignments

As a rule, "expatriates typically experience a gradual increase in work adjustment over time."[55] However, many such assignments do fail, usually culminating in an early unplanned return. Determining why the foreign assignments of technically qualified expats fail is a cottage industry itself, but two factors loom large—the expat him or herself, and family pressures.

Sometimes the employer simply chooses the wrong person. In particular, successful expatriate employees tend not only to have the necessary technical skills but to be extroverted, agreeable, and emotionally stable individuals.[56] One study found three characteristics—extroversion, agreeableness, and emotional stability—were inversely related to the expatriate's desire to terminate the assignment. Not surprisingly, sociable, outgoing, conscientious people seem more likely to fit into new cultural settings.[57] Furthermore, people who want expatriate careers try harder to adjust to such a life.[58] And expatriates who are more satisfied with their jobs abroad are more likely to adapt to the foreign assignment.[59] Studies also suggest that it's not how different culturally the host country is from the person's home country that causes problems; it's the person's ability to adapt.[60] Some people are so culturally at ease that they do fine transferred anywhere; others will fail anywhere.[61]

However, it is usually not technical or personality factors but family and personal ones that undermine international assignees. As one writer says:[62]

> The selection process is fundamentally flawed . . . . Expatriate assignments rarely fail because the person cannot accommodate to the technical demands of the job . . . . They fail because of family and personal issues and lack of cultural skills that haven't been part of the process.[63]

It's usually not technical or cultural factors but family and personal ones that undermine international assignees.

Source: Maksym Topchii/123RF.

The solution here is to provide realistic previews of what to expect abroad, careful *screening* (of both the prospective expat and his or her spouse), and improved *orientation* (discussions with recent returnees about the challenges of the foreign posting, for instance). Other suggestions include: *shorten the length* of the assignment;[64] and form "*global buddy*" programs, wherein local managers and their spouses assist new expatriates and their families with advice on things such as office politics, norms of behavior, and emergency medical assistance.[65] Most expatriates and their families make use of medical care while abroad; their main concern isn't the cost, but rather the quality of healthcare.[66]

LEARNING OBJECTIVE 3
Discuss the basics of
an effective employee
repatriation program.

Training and Maintaining International Employees

Orienting and Training Employees on International Assignment

When it comes to the orientation and training required for expatriate success overseas, the practices of most U.S. employers reflect more talk than substance. Executives tend to agree that international assignees do best when they receive the special training (in things like language and culture) that they require. Fewer actually provide it.

Many vendors offer packaged cross-cultural predeparture training programs. Most programs use lectures, simulations, videos, and readings. One program aims to provide the trainee with (1) the basics of the new country's history, politics, business norms, education system, and demographics; (2) an understanding of how cultural values affect perceptions, values, and communications; and (3) examples of why moving to a new country can be difficult, and how to manage these challenges.[67] Another aims to boost self-awareness and cross-cultural understanding and to reduce stress and provide coping strategies.[68] Language training is the most basic and obvious training for employees about to go abroad. After buying Sprint Nextel, for instance, Japan's Softbank Mobile offered its employees a $10,000 incentive to excel on a test of English.[69]

Some employers use returning managers as resources. Bosch holds regular seminars, where newly arrived returnees impart their experience to managers and their families going abroad.

Training Employees Abroad Extending the parent company's training to its local employees abroad is increasingly important. In one study (involving a Middle Eastern emerging market), training was the HR function that most consistently impacted organizational performance.[70] Starbucks brings new management trainees from abroad to its Seattle, Washington, headquarters. This gives them "a taste of the West Coast lifestyle and the company's informal culture," as well as the technical knowledge required to manage their local stores.[71] Other firms arrange for classroom programs such as those at the London Business School. Figure MA.1 illustrates some corporate programs to develop global managers.

Performance Appraisal of International Managers

Several things complicate appraising an expatriate's performance. Cultural differences are one. For example, a candid exchange is often the norm in the United States, but sometimes less so in Asia, where "face" is a concern.

Figure MA.1

Corporate Programs to Develop Global Managers

Source: *International Organizational Behavior,* 2nd ed., by Anne Marie Francesco and Barry Gold. Copyright © 2005 by Pearson Education, Inc. Reprinted and electronically reproduced by Pearson Education, Inc., Upper Saddle River, New Jersey.

- Asea Brown Boveri (ABB) rotates about 500 managers around the world to different countries every 2 to 3 years to develop a management cadre of "transpatriates" to support their strategic aims.
- PepsiCo has an orientation program for its foreign managers, which brings them to the United States for 1-year assignments.
- At British Telecom, existing expatriate workers talk to prospective assignees about the cultural factors to expect.
- Honda of America Manufacturing gives its U.S. supervisors and managers extensive preparation in Japanese language, culture, and lifestyle and then sends them to the parent company in Tokyo for up to 3 years.
- General Electric gives their engineers and managers regular language and cross-cultural training so that they are equipped to conduct business with people around the world.

Furthermore, who does the appraisal? Local managers must have some input, but again, as in China, cultural differences may distort the appraisals. On the other hand, home-office managers may be so out of touch that they can't provide useful appraisals. In one survey, managers knew that having appraisers from both the host and home countries produced the best appraisals. But, in practice, most employers didn't do this. Instead, they had raters from the host or the home countries do them.[72] In terms of their basic values and ways of doing things, the "cultural distance" is much wider between some countries (such as Japan and South Africa) than others (such as the United States and Great Britain). Such cultural differences can particularly distort multisource appraisal feedback from peers and subordinates. Therefore, one study concludes that "peer and subordinate ratings should be used for feedback related to development and only supervisor ratings should be used to make HR administrative decisions such as performance appraisal and merit pay."[73]

Other suggestions for improving the expatriate appraisal process include: weigh the evaluation more toward the on-site manager's appraisal than the home-office manager's; and if the home-office manager does the actual written appraisal, have him or her use a former expatriate from the same overseas location for advice.

International Compensation

As discussed in Chapter 10 (Compensation), the usual way to formulate expatriate pay is to equalize purchasing power across countries, a technique known as the *balance sheet* approach.[74] The basic idea is that each expatriate should enjoy the same standard of living he or she would have at home.

In practice, this usually boils down to building the expatriate's total compensation around five or six separate components. Table MA.1 illustrates the balance sheet approach. In this case, the manager's annual earnings are $160,000, and she faces a U.S. income tax rate of 28%. (Multiple-nation taxation can be a problem. Respondents often list "tax compliance" as the top challenge in sending employees abroad.[75]) Other costs are based on the index of living costs abroad, published in the "U.S. Department of State Indexes of Living Costs Abroad, Quarters Allowances, and Hardship Differentials," available via the www.state.gov website.[76] The HR in Practice feature shows one example.

To help the expatriate manage his or her home and foreign financial obligations, most employers use a *split pay* approach; they pay, say, half a person's actual pay in home-country currency and half in the local currency.[77] For compensating *host country* nationals, employers tend to use a similar process to what they use at home, namely methods like job grading to create equitable pay plans adjusted for local market conditions.[78]

Determining pay rates abroad isn't easy. Although there is a wealth of compensation survey data available in the United States, such data are not as easy to come by overseas. Some multinationals therefore conduct their own local annual compensation surveys. For example, Kraft has conducted one of total compensation in Europe. However, most employers abroad do probably purchase one or more of various international salary surveys such as the Call Centre Remuneration Report/Australia, from Aon Hewitt, or the International Salary Survey Database/United Arab Emirates, from Executive Resources Limited.[79]

Table MA.1 The Balance Sheet Approach (Assumes U.S. Base Salary of $160,000)

Annual Expense	Chicago, U.S.	Shanghai, China (US $ Equivalent)	Allowance
Housing and utilities	$35,000	$ 44,800	$ 9,800
Goods and services	6,000	7,680	1,680
Taxes	44,800	57,344	12,544
Discretionary income	10,000	12,800	2,800
Total	$95,800	$122,624	$26,824

■ **HR in Practice**

Expat Pay at CEMEX

Expats working for the company CEMEX (a multinational building supplies company) get foreign service premium equal to a 10% increase in salary. Some get a hardship premium, depending on the country; it ranges from zero in a relatively comfortable posting to, for example, 30% in Bangladesh. The company pays for their housing and for their children's schooling up to college. There's home leave—a ticket back to their home country for the entire family once a year. There are language lessons for the spouse. And CEMEX grosses up the pay of all expats, to take out the potential effects of local tax law. Say there is a CEMEX executive earning $150,000. This person would cost close to $300,000 as an expat.[80]

⭐ Talk About It–**3**

If your professor has chosen to assign this, go to **www.pearson.com/mylab/ management** to discuss the following question. Reading between the lines here, what does CEMEX seem to be doing right as far as minimizing the risks that their foreign assignments will fail?

Incentives While training and appraising expatriates may vary widely among multinationals, there is relative unanimity with setting clear links between performance and compensation.[81] However, the employer also needs to tie the incentives to local realities. For example, in Eastern Europe, workers spend a large share of their disposable income on basics like food and utilities. They therefore require a higher proportion of more predictable base salary than do workers in, say, the United States.[82] However, in Japan, a worker might expect to receive perhaps half (or more) of his or her total annual compensation near year-end, as a sort of profit-sharing bonus. In Asia, including China, incentives, even for production workers, are popular.

Safety and Fair Treatment Abroad

Employee safety abroad is an important issue for several reasons. For one thing, providing safety and fair treatment shouldn't stop at a country's borders. The United States has often taken the lead in occupational safety. However, other countries have such laws, with which all employers must comply. In any case, it's hard to make a legitimate case for being less safety conscious or fair with workers abroad than you are with those at home.

Increased terrorism worldwide is causing more employers to use special travel safety tools to track and communicate with workers in real time.[83] For example, International SOS provides its clients with online and smart phone tools. These let the client quickly notify employees traveling abroad of potential problems and what to do about them. The following feature elaborates.

■ **HR Practices Around the Globe**

Business Travel

Keeping business travelers safe is a specialty all its own, but suggestions here include the following:[84]

- Provide expatriates with training about the place they're going to, so they're more oriented.
- Tell them not to draw attention to the fact they're Americans—by wearing T-shirts with American names, for instance.
- Have travelers arrive at airports as close to departure time as possible and wait in areas away from the main flow of traffic.

- Equip the expatriate's car and home with security systems.
- Tell employees to vary their departure and arrival times and take different routes.
- Keep employees current on crime and other problems by regularly checking, for example, the State Department's travel advisories and warnings at **http://travel.state.gov**.[85] Click on "Travel Alerts" and "Country Information."
- Advise employees to act confident at all times. Body language can attract perpetrators, and those who look like victims often become victimized.[86]

Repatriation: Problems and Solutions

A three-year assignment abroad for one employee with a base salary of about $150,000 may cost the employer $1 million, once extra living costs, transportation, and family benefits are included;[87] yet about 40% to 60% of them will probably quit within three years of returning home.[88] Given the investment, it obviously makes sense to keep them with the firm. However, one survey found that only about 31% of employers surveyed had formal repatriation programs for executives.[89] About a quarter of employers don't even know if their recently returned expats quit within 11 months of returning.[90]

Formal repatriation programs are useful. For instance, one study found that about 4% of returning employees resigned if their firms had formal repatriation programs, while about 21% left if their firms had no such programs.[91]

Steps in Repatriation The guiding principle of repatriation is this: Make sure the expatriate and his or her family don't feel that the company has forgotten them. For example, one firm has a three-part repatriation program.[92]

First, the firm matches the expat and his or her family with a psychologist trained in repatriation issues. The psychologist meets with the family before they go abroad. The psychologist discusses the challenges they will face abroad, assesses with them how well they think they will adapt to their new culture, and stays in touch with them throughout their assignment.

Second, the program makes sure that the employee always feels that he or she is still "in the home-office loop." For example, the expat gets a mentor and travels back to the home office periodically for meetings.

Third, once it's time for the expat employee and his or her family to return home, there's a formal repatriation service. About six months before the overseas assignment ends, the psychologist and an HR representative meet with the expat and the family to start preparing them for return. For example, they help plan the employee's next career move, help the person update his or her résumé, and begin putting the person in contact with supervisors back home.[93]

At the end of the day, probably the simplest thing employers can do is value expats' experience. As one returnee put it: "My company was, in my view, somewhat indifferent to my experience in China as evidenced by a lack of monetary reward, positive increase, or leverage to my career in any way." Such feelings prompt former expats to look elsewhere.[94] Having a system that facilitates keeping track of employees as they move from position to position in a global organization is essential. One reason for returnees' high attrition rates is that employers simply lose track of their returnees' new skills and competencies.[95]

⭐ Watch It

How does a company actually go about managing its international human resource management function? If your professor has chosen to assign this, go to **www.pearson.com/mylab/management** to watch the video titled Global HR Management (Joby), and then answer the questions to show what you would do in this situation.

Managing HR Locally: How to Put a Global HR System into Practice

With employers increasingly relying on local rather than expatriate employees, applying one's selection, training, appraisal, pay, and other human resource practices abroad is a priority. Is it realistic for a company to try to institute a standardized human resource management system in its facilities around the world?

A study suggests that the answer is "yes." The results show that employers may have to defer to local managers on some specific human resource management policy issues. However, they also suggest that big intercountry differences in HR practice are often not required or even advisable. The important thing is *how* you implement the global human resource management system.

In this study, the researchers interviewed human resource personnel from six global companies—Agilent, Dow, IBM, Motorola, Procter & Gamble (P&G), and Shell Oil Co.—as well as international human resources consultants.[96] The study's overall conclusion was that employers who successfully implement global HR systems do so by applying several best practices. The basic idea is to *develop* systems that are *acceptable* to employees in units around the world, and ones that the employers can *implement* more effectively. Figure MA.2 summarizes this. We'll look at each.

Developing a More Effective Global HR System

First, these employers engage in two best practices in *developing* their worldwide human resource policies and practices.

- **Form global HR networks.** To head off resistance, human resource managers around the world should feel that they're part of the firm's global HR team.[97] Treat the local human resource managers as equal partners. For instance, best practice firms formed global teams to help develop the new human resources systems.
- **Remember that it's more important to standardize ends than means.** For example, IBM uses a more or less standardized recruitment and selection process worldwide. However, "details such as who conducts the interview (hiring manager vs. recruiter) . . . differ by country."[98]

Figure MA.2

Best Practices for Creating Global HR Systems

Implement the international HR system and practices, for instance, by allocating adequate resources

Develop the international HR System, such as by forming global networks

Take steps to ensure the system is **acceptable** to those who must implement it, such as by investigating pressures to differentiate practices

Making the Global HR System More Acceptable

Next, employers engage in three best practices so that the global human resource systems they develop will be *acceptable* to local managers around the world. These are:

- **Remember that truly global organizations find it easier to install global systems.** For example, truly global companies require their managers to work on global teams and recruit the employees they hire globally. As one manager put it, "If you're truly global, then you are hiring here [in the United States] people who are going to immediately go and work in the Hague, and vice versa."[99] This global mind-set makes it easier for managers everywhere to accept the wisdom of having a standardized human resource management system.
- **Investigate pressures to differentiate and determine their legitimacy.** Local managers will insist, "You can't do that here because we are different culturally." These researchers found that these "differences" are usually not persuasive. For example, when Dow wanted to implement an online recruitment and selection tool abroad, the local hiring managers said that their managers would not use it. After investigating the supposed cultural roadblocks, Dow successfully implemented the new system.[100]
- **Try to work within the context of a strong corporate culture.** For example, because of how P&G recruits, selects, trains, and rewards them, its managers have a strong sense of shared values. For instance, new recruits quickly learn to think in terms of "we" instead of "I." They learn to value thoroughness, consistency, and a methodical approach. Having such global unanimity in values makes it easier to implement standardized human resource practices worldwide.

Implementing the Global HR System

Finally, two best practices helped ensure success in actually *implementing* the globally consistent human resource policies and practices.

- **"You can't communicate enough."** "There's a need for constant contact [by HR] with the decision makers in each country, as well as the people who will be implementing and using the system."[101]
- **Dedicate adequate resources.** For example, don't require the local human resource management offices to implement new job analysis procedures unless the head office provides adequate resources for these additional activities.

Review

MyLab Management

If your instructor is using MyLab Management, go to **www.pearson.com/mylab/ management** to complete the problems marked with this icon ⭐.

Summary

1. *International business* is important to almost every business today, so firms are increasingly managed globally. Intercountry differences affect HR processes. Cultural factors such as assertiveness suggest differences in values, attitudes, and therefore behaviors and reactions of people from country to country. Economic and labor cost factors help determine whether HR's emphasis should be on efficiency or some other approach. Industrial relations and specifically the relationship among the workers, the union, and the employer influence the nature of a company's specific HR policies from country to country.

2. *Selecting managers* for expatriate assignments means screening them for traits that predict success in adapting to new environments. Such traits include adaptability and flexibility, self-orientation, job knowledge and motivation, relational skills, and family situation. Adaptability

screening focusing on the family's probable success in handling the foreign assignment can be an especially important step in the selection process.

3. *Training* for expat managers typically focuses on cultural differences, on how attitudes influence behavior, and on factual knowledge about the target country. The most common approach to expatriate pay is to equalize purchasing power across countries, known as the "balance sheet" approach. Repatriation problems are common, but you can minimize them. Suggestions include using repatriation agreements, assigning a sponsor, and keeping the expatriate plugged in to home-office business.

4. To successfully implement *global HR systems*, the basic idea is to *develop* systems that are *acceptable* to employees in units around the world, and ones that the employers can *implement* more effectively.

MODULE A

Key Terms

international human resource management (IHRM)   470
expatriates   472
home-country nationals   472
locals   472

third-country nationals   472
virtual transnational teams   474
ethnocentric   474
polycentric   474
geocentric   474

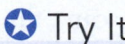 Try It

How would you do applying the concepts and skills you learned in this chapter? If your professor has chosen to assign this, go to **www.pearson.com/mylab/management** and complete the Managing in a Global Environment simulation to find out.

Discussion Questions

A-1. List the HR challenges faced by an international business.

A-2. List and describe the basic steps in training employees whom the employer is about to transfer abroad.

A-3. Explain the main things to keep in mind when designing and implementing a global HR system.

⭐A-4. Give several examples of how each intercountry difference that affects HR managers may specifically affect an HR manager.

⭐A-5. What special training do overseas candidates need? In what ways is such training similar to and different from traditional diversity training?

A-6. How does appraising an expatriate's performance differ from appraising that of a home-office manager? How would you avoid some of the unique problems of appraising the expatriate's performance?

MyLab Management

If your instructor is using MyLab Management, go to **www.pearson.com/mylab/ management** for Auto-graded writing questions as well as the following Assisted-graded writing questions:

A-7. Illustrate how intercountry differences affect HR.

A-8. Explain why foreign assignments fail and what to do to minimize the problems.

APPLICATION EXERCISES

HR IN ACTION CASE INCIDENT 1

"Boss, I Think We Have a Problem"

Central Steel Door Corp. has been in business for about 20 years, successfully selling a line of steel industrial-grade doors, as well as the hardware and fittings required for them. Focusing mostly in the United States and Canada, the company had gradually increased its presence from the New York City area, first into New England and then down the Atlantic Coast, then through the Midwest and West, and finally into Canada. The company's basic expansion strategy was always the same: Choose an area, open a distribution center, hire a regional sales manager, then let that regional sales manager help staff the distribution center and hire local sales reps.

Unfortunately, the company's traditional success in finding sales help has not extended to its overseas operations. With the expansion of the European Union, Mel Fisher, president of Central Steel Door, decided to expand his company abroad, into Europe. However, the expansion has not gone smoothly. He tried for three weeks to find a sales manager by advertising in the *International Herald Tribune*, which is read by businesspeople in Europe and by Americans living and working in Europe. Although the ads placed in the *Tribune* also ran for about a month on the *Tribune*'s website, Fisher so far has received only five applications. One came from a possibly viable candidate, whereas four came from candidates whom Fisher refers to as "lost souls"—people who seem to have spent most of their time traveling restlessly from country to country, sipping espresso in sidewalk cafés. When asked what he had done for the last three years, one told Fisher he'd been on a "walkabout."

Other aspects of his international HR activities have been equally problematic. Fisher alienated two of his U.S. sales managers by sending them to Europe to temporarily run the European operations, but neglected to work out a compensation package to cover their relatively high living expenses in Germany and Belgium. One ended up staying the better part of the year, and Fisher was rudely surprised to be informed by the Belgian government that his sales manager owed thousands of dollars in local taxes. The managers had hired about 10 local people to staff each of the two distribution centers. However, without full-time local European sales managers, the level of sales was disappointing, so Fisher decided to fire about half the distribution center employees. That's when he got an emergency phone call from his temporary sales manager in Germany: "I've just been told that all these employees should have had written employment agreements and that in any case we can't fire anyone without at least one year's notice, and the local authorities here are really up in arms. Boss, I think we have a problem."

Questions

A-9. Based on the chapter and the case incident, compile a list of 10 international HR mistakes Fisher has made so far.

A-10. How would you have gone about hiring a European sales manager? Why?

A-11. What would you do now if you were Mel Fisher?

B

Managing Human Resources in Small and Entrepreneurial Firms

OVERVIEW:
In this module, we will cover . . .

- The Small Business Challenge
- Using Internet and Government Tools to Support the HR Effort
- Leveraging Small Size: Familiarity, Flexibility, Fairness, Informality, and HRM
- Managing HR Systems, Procedures, and Paperwork

MyLab Management

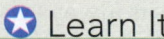 Improve Your Grade!
When you see this icon, visit **www.pearson.com/mylab/management** for activities that are applied, personalized, and offer immediate feedback.

LEARNING OBJECTIVES

When you finish studying this module, you should be able to:

1. Explain why HRM is important to small businesses and how small business HRM is different from that in large businesses.
2. Give four examples of how entrepreneurs can use Internet and government tools to support the HR effort.
3. List five ways entrepreneurs can use their small size to improve their HR processes.
4. Describe how you would create a start-up human resource system for a new small business.

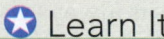 Learn It

If your professor has chosen to assign this, go to **www.pearson.com/mylab/ management** to see what you should particularly focus on and to take the Module B Warm Up.

LEARNING OBJECTIVE 1
Explain why HRM is
important to small
businesses and how
small business HRM is
different from that in large
businesses.

The Small Business Challenge

In terms of the U.S. economy, the phrase *small business* is a misnomer. About half the people working in the United States today work for small firms.[1] Small businesses as a group also account for most of the 650,000 or so new businesses created every year,[2] as well as for most of the country's business growth (small firms grow faster than big ones). And small firms create most of the new jobs in the United States.[3]

Statistically speaking, therefore, most people graduating from colleges probably do or will work for small businesses—those with less than 200 or so employees. Anyone interested in human resource management thus needs to understand how managing human resources in small firms is different from doing so in huge multinationals.

How Small Business Human Resource Management Is Different

Managing human resources in small firms is different for four main reasons: *size*, *priorities*, *informality*, and the nature of the *entrepreneur*.

Size For one thing, it would be very unusual to find a very small business with a dedicated human resource management professional. The rule of thumb is that it's not until a company reaches about 100 employees that it can afford an HR specialist. That's not to say that small businesses don't have HR tasks. Even five- or six-person retail shops must recruit, select, train, and compensate employees. It's just that in such situations, it's usually the owner and (sometimes) his or her assistant that does all the HR paperwork and tasks. SHRM found that even firms with under 100 employees often spend the equivalent of two-or-so people's time each year on human resource management issues.[4] But, that time usually comes out of the owner's very long workday.

Priorities It's not just size but their priorities that drive many entrepreneurs to expend more time and resources on non-HR issues. After studying small e-commerce firms in the United Kingdom, one researcher concluded that, as important as human resource management is, it wasn't a high priority for these firms:

> Given their shortage of resources in terms of time, money, people and expertise, a typical SME [small and medium-sized enterprise] manager's organizational imperatives are perceived elsewhere, in finance, production and marketing, with HR of diminished relative importance.[5]

Informality One effect of this is that human resource management activities tend to be more informal in smaller firms. For example, one study analyzed training practices in about 900 small companies.[6] Training tended to be informal, with an emphasis, for instance, on methods like coworker and supervisory on-the-job training. One researcher says that the need for small businesses to adapt quickly to competitive challenges often means handling matters like raises, appraisals, and time off "on an informal, reactive basis."[7]

The Entrepreneur *Entrepreneurs* are people who create businesses under risky conditions, and starting new businesses is always risky. Hence, entrepreneurs need to be dedicated and visionary. Researchers therefore believe that small firms' relative informality partly stems from entrepreneurs' unique personalities. Entrepreneurs tend (among other things) to be somewhat controlling: They want to impose their personal stamp on the company (and on its HR practices).[8]

Implications These four differences often mean that smaller businesses face several special human resource management–related risks.[9]

- First, their relatively rudimentary human resource practices may put them at a *competitive disadvantage*. Thus a small business owner not using online prescreening may be incurring unnecessary costs and probably deriving inferior results than (larger) competitors.
- Second, the firm lacks *specialized HR expertise*. It may have at most one or two dedicated human resource management people responsible for the full range of HR functions. This makes them more likely to miss problems in specific areas, such as equal employment law.
- Third, the small business owner may not be fully complying with *compensation regulations and laws*. These include (as examples) how to pay compensatory time for overtime hours worked, and distinguishing between employees and independent contractors.
- Fourth, paperwork duplication means *data entry errors*. For small businesses, many of which don't use human resource information systems, employee data (name, address, marital status, and so on) often appear on multiple human resource management forms (medical enrollment forms, W-4 forms, and so on). Any change requires manually changing all forms. This is time-consuming and inefficient and can precipitate errors.

Why HRM Is Important to Small Businesses

Turmoil ensued when social media postings from one employee in a start-up software firm accused another of harassment. The point is that although most start-ups assume that HR is the last thing they need, most actually do need such expertise from the start. To paraphrase one expert, it's a mistake to assume that all you need is an employee handbook; start-ups need a rational HR system.[10]

In fact, small firms with effective HR practices do better than those without them.[11] For example, researchers studied 168 family-owned, fast-growth small and medium-sized enterprises (SMEs). They concluded that successful high-growth SMEs placed greater importance on training and development, performance appraisals, recruitment packages, maintaining morale, and setting competitive compensation levels than did low-performing firms: "These findings suggest that these human resource activities do in fact have a positive impact on performance [in smaller businesses]."[12] And for many small firms, effective human resource management is required for getting and keeping big customers. For example, to comply with international ISO-9000 quality standards, many large customers check that their small vendors follow the necessary HR standards.[13] The accompanying HR as a Profit Center feature illustrates how HR can help a small business.

We'll look in this module at methods small business managers can use to improve their human resource management practices, starting with using Internet and government tools.

■ HR as a Profit Center

The Dealership

Carlos Ledezma runs a successful car dealership. His strategy for the dealership is to boost profits by building repeat business from customers who like dealing with friendly, long-term employees, and that's what he's done.[14] To achieve that, he put in place a customer-oriented human resource management strategy. He tests each employment candidate to make sure the job is the right fit. There's a weeklong new-employee orientation, to introduce them to their jobs and to the firm's mission and culture. Then he gives each new employee a senior employee to shadow for 90 days.[15] For the first 90 days, Ledezma gives each of these mentors $50 to $100 for each vehicle the trainee sells. In one recent year, Ledezma spent $150,000 on training.

Ledezma's HR strategy pays off in profits that are well above the industry average. Customers like dealing with dedicated, competent, long-term employees. Employee turnover is about 28%, and the average employee stays about eight years, both much better than average.

⭐ Talk About It – 1

If your professor has chosen to assign this, go to **www.pearson.com/mylab/management** to discuss the following: Write a short note on this topic: "What Carlos Ledezma is doing right with respect to HR management, based on what I've read about HR in the other chapters of this book."

LEARNING OBJECTIVE 2
Give four examples of how entrepreneurs can use Internet and government tools to support the HR effort.

Using Internet and Government Tools to Support the HR Effort

City Garage is an expanding auto servicing company in Texas.[16] One way they distinguish themselves is by letting customers interact directly with its mechanics in what it calls its "open service area,"[17] City Garage needs mechanics who are comfortable interacting with customers in this format. The old hiring process was a paper-and-pencil application and one interview. The process ate up management time and was ineffective. The solution was to purchase the Personality Profile Analysis (PPA) online test from Thomas International USA. Now, after a quick application and background check, candidates take the 10-minute, 24-question PPA. City Garage staff then enter the answers into the PPA Software system and receive test results almost at once. These show whether the applicant is right for the job, based on four personality characteristics.

Like City Garage, no small business need cede the "HR advantage" to big competitors. Knowledgeable small business managers can level the terrain by using Internet-based HR resources, including free online resources from the U.S. government. We'll look at how.

City Garage's managers knew they would never implement their firm's growth strategy without changing how they tested and hired employees.

Source: Jetta Productions/Getty Images.

Complying with Employment Laws

As one example, complying with federal (and state and local) employment law is a thorny issue for entrepreneurs. For example, the small business owner may want to know, "What can I ask a job candidate?" "Must I pay this person overtime?" and "Must I report this injury?"

Addressing such issues starts with deciding which federal employment laws apply to the company. For example, Title VII of the Civil Rights Act of 1964 applies to employers with 15 or more employees, while the Age Discrimination in Employment

Figure MB.1

FirstStep Employment Law Advisor

Source: U.S. Department of Labor, www.dol.gov/elaws/firststep, accessed September 21, 2017.

Act of 1967 applies to those with 20 or more.[18] Small business owners will find the legal answers they need online at federal agencies' websites like the following.

The DOL The U.S. Department of Labor's (DOL) "*FirstStep* Employment Law Advisor" (see http://webapps.dol.gov/elaws/firststep/) helps small businesses determine which laws apply to their business.[19] First, as in Figure MB.1, click "Begin FirstStep-Employment Law Overview Advisor Now"). The elaw wizard then takes the owner through questions such as "What best describes the nature of your business or organization?" and "What is the maximum number of employees your business or organization employs or will employ during the calendar year?"

Proceeding through the wizard, the small business owner arrives at a "results" page. This says, "Based on the information you provided in response to the questions in the Advisor, the following employment laws administered by the Department of Labor (DOL) may apply to your business or organization."[20] For a typical small firm, these laws might include the Consumer Credit Protection Act, Employee Polygraph Protection Act, Fair Labor Standards Act, Immigration and Nationality Act, Occupational Safety and Health Act, Uniformed Services Employment and Reemployment Rights Act, and Whistleblower Act.

A linked DOL site (www.dol.gov/whd/flsa/index.htm) provides information on the Fair Labor Standards Act (FLSA).[21] It also contains several specific related links. Each provides practical guidance on questions such as when to pay

Figure MB.2

Sample DOL elaws Advisors

Source: U.S. Department of Labor, http://webapps.dol.gov/elaws/, accessed September 21, 2017.

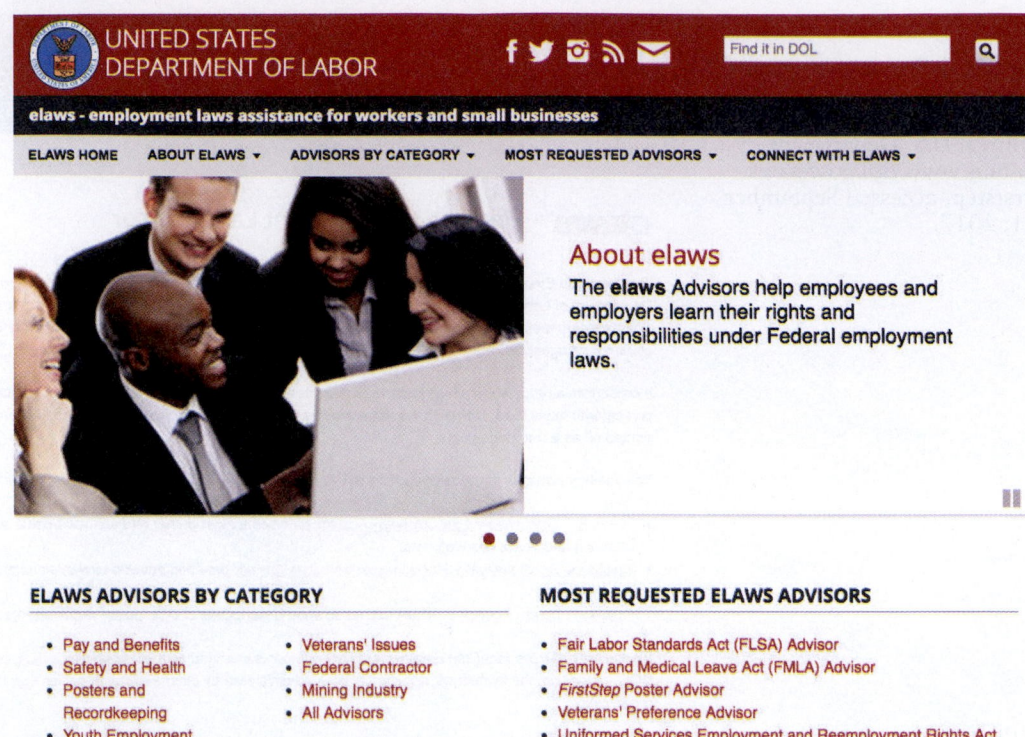

overtime. Figure MB.2 presents, from the website http://webapps.dol.gov/elaws/, a list of elaws Advisors.[22] As we explained in Chapter 2, the website of the U.S. Equal Employment Opportunity Commission (**EEOC**; www.EEOC.gov/employers/) contains important information regarding matters such as how a small business can resolve a charge without undergoing an investigation or facing a lawsuit.

OSHA The DOL's Occupational Safety and Health Administration site (www.OSHA.gov/) similarly supplies small business guidance. (See Figure MB.3.[23]) OSHA's site provides, among other things, easy access to the *OSHA Small Business Handbook*. This contains practical information, including industry-specific safety and accident checklists.

Employment Planning, Recruiting, and Selection

Internet resources can make small business owners as effective as their large competitors at writing job descriptions and building applicant pools. As we saw in Chapter 4 (pp. 100–101), the Department of Labor's O*NET (http://online.onetcenter.org) illustrates this.[24] Its online wizard enables business owners to create accurate and professional job descriptions and job specifications quickly. Similarly, small business owners use the online recruiting tools we discussed in Chapter 5. For example, they post positions on job boards such as CareerBuilder.com, on the sites of professional associations, or on the sites of local newspapers. The accompanying Trends feature elaborates.

Figure MB.3

OSHA Small Business Website

Source: U.S. Department of Labor, https://www.osha.gov/dcsp/smallbusiness/index.html.

TRENDS SHAPING HR: *Digital And Social Media*[25]

RECRUITMENT AND SELECTION TOOLS Many small businesses use social media to recruit applicants. For example, LinkedIn lets employers post job openings and facilitates business networking. One recruiter reportedly looks for LinkedIn members with compelling summaries, excellent recommendations, and memberships in industry groups. On Twitter, recruiters see if a potential candidate has an appropriate username and photos. But also check Twitter for things like the person's status updates and retweets, to see (for instance) if he or she shares useful information. Small business recruiters should also focus on the social media that makes sense for them. For example, if you're looking for a Facebook marketing expert, look on Facebook. Or look for a photographer on Instagram. And on Facebook and LinkedIn, focus recruiting efforts on industry groups that make sense for your company. Check to see how your competitors use social media, and which communities they use.

Employment Selection

Some tests are so easy to use, they are particularly good for smaller firms. One example is the *Wonderlic Personnel Test*, which measures general mental ability. With questions somewhat similar to the SAT, it takes less than 15 minutes to administer the four-page booklet. The tester reads the instructions, and then keeps time as the candidate works through the 50 problems. The tester scores the test by totaling the number of correct answers. Comparing the person's score with the minimum scores recommended for various occupations shows whether the candidate achieved the minimally acceptable score for the job in question.

The *Predictive Index* is another example. It measures work-related personality traits, drives, and behaviors—in particular, dominance, extroversion, patience, and blame avoidance. A template makes scoring simple. The Predictive Index program includes 15 standard benchmark personality patterns. For example, there is the "social interest" pattern, for a person who is generally unselfish, congenial, persuasive, patient, and unassuming. This person would be a good personnel interviewer, for instance.

Many vendors, including Wonderlic and the Predictive Index, offer online applicant testing and screening services. Wonderlic's service (which costs about $8,500 per year for a small firm) first provides job analyses for the employer's jobs. Wonderlic then provides a website that the small business applicants can log into to take one or several selection tests (including the Wonderlic Personnel Test).

The following are suggestions from *Inc.* magazine for supercharging a small business's recruiting and screening processes.

- **Keep it in the industry.** Use online job boards that target a particular industry or city to minimize irrelevant applicants.[26] For example, Jobing.com maintains city-specific job sites in over 19 states.[27] Beyond.com hosts more than 15,000 industry-specific communities.
- **Automate the process.** Automated applicant processing systems are inexpensive enough for small employers. For example, systems from Taleo, NuView Systems, and Accolo accept résumés and help automate the screening process. NuView, which costs about $6 to $15 per month per user, asks applicants questions and bumps out those without, for instance, the required education.[28]
- **Test online.** Use online tests, for instance, to test an applicant's proficiency at QuickBooks, or even at selling over the phone. Vendors include (as a small sample) IBM's Kenexa, eskill.com/, selectivehiring.com, and berkeassessment.com.[29]
- **Poll your inner circle.** Tap friends and employees for recommendations, and use social networking sites such as LinkedIn. One employer says, "I get people vouching for each applicant, so I don't have to spend hours sorting through résumés."[30]
- **Send a recording.** InterviewStream records online video interviews for about $30 to $60.[31] It sends the candidate an e-mail invitation with a link. When he or she clicks the link, a video interviewer asks the company's prerecorded questions. Hiring managers can review the videos at their leisure.[32]

COMPLYING WITH THE LAW Given the time pressures facing most small business owners, confirming the validity of tests one buys online or through office supply stores is probably the exception, not the rule. Many test providers will assist the employer in establishing a testing procedure. For example, as noted, Wonderlic will review your job descriptions as part of its process. Tests you order should contain validity information.

Employment Training

Small companies can't compete with the training resources of giants like General Electric. However, as explained in Chapter 7 (Training), online training can provide, at a relatively low cost, employee training that used to be beyond most small employers' reach. These (see Chapter 7) range from private vendors (such as www.PureSafety.com and www.skillsoft.com) to the small business administration (www.sba.gov/sitemap) and the National Association of Manufacturers (NAM).

The buyer's guide from the Association for Talent Development (www.td.org/) is a good place to start to find a vendor (check under Resources). [33]

Employment Appraisal and Compensation

Small employers have easy access to computerized and online appraisal and compensation services. For example, Oracle Corporation's ePerformance[34] facilitates performance management by enabling managers to formalize the employee's goals and then assess progress toward meeting those goals. The eAppraisal system from Halogen Software[35] is another example.

Similarly, lack of easy access to salary surveys once hindered smaller businesses from fine-tuning their pay scales. Today, sites like www.salary.com make it easy to determine local pay rates.

Employment Safety and Health

Safety is an important issue for small employers. One European study found that the majority of all the workplace accidents and serious workplace accidents occur in firms with less than 50 employees.[36] (This is not surprising because so many people work for smaller businesses.) As explained earlier in this chapter and in Chapter 14, OHSA provides several free services for small employers.[37] These include free on-site safety and health services for small businesses, and its *Sharp* program, through which OSHA certifies that small employers have achieved commendable levels of safety awareness.[38]

LEARNING OBJECTIVE 3
List five ways entrepreneurs can use their small size to improve their HR processes.

Leveraging Small Size: Familiarity, Flexibility, Fairness, Informality, and HRM

Because small businesses need to capitalize on their strengths, they should capitalize on their smallness when dealing with employees. Smallness should translate into personal *familiarity* with each employee's strengths, needs, and family situation. And it should translate into the luxury of being able to be relatively *flexible* and *informal* in the human resource management policies and practices the company follows. Smaller businesses must quickly adapt to competitive challenges. This often means that raises, appraisals, and time off tend to be administered "on an informal, reactive basis with a short time horizon."[39] However, being informal and flexible does not necessarily mean ineffective.

Simple, Informal Employee Selection Procedures

For example, there are many simple ways in which the small business manager can improve employee selection. Using the effective interviewing process (Building Your Management Skills, Chapter 6, pages 168–169) is one. Work-sampling tests are another. As explained in Chapter 6, a work-sampling test means having the candidates perform actual samples of the job in question. The process is simple. Break down the job's main duties into component tasks such as writing an ad. Then have the candidate do a sample task.

Flexibility in Training

Small companies are also typically more informal about training and development. For example, one study of 191 small and 201 large firms in Europe found that many of the small firms didn't systematically monitor their managers' skill needs, and fewer than 50% (as opposed to 70% of large firms) had career-development programs.[40]

Four-Step Training Process Limited resources or not, small businesses can and do have effective training procedures. For example, a simple but effective four-step training process follows.

Step 1: **Write a job description.** A detailed job description is the heart of a training program. List the tasks of each job, along with a summary of the steps in each task.

Step 2: **Develop a task analysis record form.** Next, summarize the job's steps with a *Task Analysis Record Form*. This form (see Table 7-1, page 203) consolidates information regarding required tasks and required skills. As Table 7-1 illustrates, the form contains six columns of information, such as "Skills or knowledge required." For example, in the first column, list *specific tasks*. Include what is to be performed in terms of each of the main tasks and the steps involved in each task. In the third column, list *performance standards* (in terms of quantity, quality, accuracy, and so on).

Step 3: **Develop a Job Instruction Sheet.** Next, develop a *Job Instruction Sheet* for the job. As in Table MB.1, a *Job Instruction Sheet* again shows the steps in each task, but this time also key points for each.

Step 4: **Prepare the training program for the job.** At a minimum, the job's training manual should include the job description, Task Analysis Record Form, and Job Instruction Sheet, all compiled in a training manual. Perhaps also include a brief overview/introduction to the job and a graphical and/or written explanation of how the job fits with other jobs in the plant or office.

You also have to decide what training media to use. A simple but effective on-the-job training program using current employees or supervisors as trainers requires only the written materials we just listed. However, some situations may require producing or purchasing special training media. Vendors like those we discussed in Chapter 7 and earlier in this chapter provide packaged multimedia training programs.

Informal Training Methods Training expert Stephen Covey says small businesses can provide training without actually establishing expensive formal training programs. His suggestions include the following:[41]

- Offer to cover the tuition for special classes.
- Identify online training opportunities.

Table MB.1 Sample Job Instruction Sheet

Steps in Task	Key Points to Keep in Mind
1. Start motor.	None.
2. Set cutting distance.	Carefully read scale—to prevent wrong-sized cut.
3. Place paper on cutting table.	Make sure paper is even—to prevent uneven cut.
4. Push paper up to cutter.	Make sure paper is tight—to prevent uneven cut.
5. Grasp safety release with left hand.	Do not release left hand—to prevent hand from being caught in cutter.
6. Grasp cutter release with right hand.	Do not release right hand—to prevent hand from being caught in cutter.
7. Simultaneously pull cutter and safety releases.	Keep both hands on corresponding releases—avoid hands being on cutting table.
8. Wait for cutter to retract.	Keep both hands on releases—to avoid having hands on cutting table.
9. Retract paper.	Make sure cutter is retracted; keep both hands away from releases.
10. Shut off motor.	Make sure "on" light is off.

- Provide a library of CDs and DVDs for systematic, disciplined learning during commute times.
- Encourage the sharing of best practices among associates.
- When possible, send people to special seminars and association meetings for learning and networking.
- Create a learning ethic by having everyone teach each other what they are learning.

Flexibility in Benefits and Rewards

Studies suggest that large firms offer more *extensive* benefits packages than do smaller ones.[42] However, many small firms overcome this by offering more flexibility: "They've discovered how to turn tiny into tight-knit, earning employees' trust by keeping them in the loop on company news and financials, and their loyalty by providing frequent feedback on performance."[43] For example, at ID Media, with 90 employees, the CEO gives all new employees a welcome breakfast on their first day. "It shows she wanted to meet us and get our opinions," says one new employee.[44]

A Culture of Flexibility The study also found that small companies, because owners personally interact with all employees each day, did a better job of fostering a "culture of flexibility." Most important, this meant that "supervisors are more supportive and understanding when work/life issues emerge."[45] Ward's Furniture in Long Beach, California, exemplifies this. Many of Ward's 17 employees have been with the firm for 10 to 20 years. Brad Ward, an owner, attributes this in part to his firm's willingness to adapt to its workers' needs. For example, workers can share job responsibilities and work part-time from home. As a result, Ward's Furniture is a good example of using small size to capitalize on work-life benefits such as extra time off, compressed workweeks, schedule flexibility, and recognition for employees.

An easy way for small businesses to provide retirement benefits is through a SIMPLE IRA plan[46] (discussed in Chapter 10). With the SIMPLE (for Savings Incentive Match Plan for Employees) IRA, employers must (and employees may) make contributions to traditional employee IRAs. These plans are for employers or small businesses with 100 or fewer employees and no other retirement plan.

At Ward's Furniture, workers can share job responsibilities, and some work part-time from home.

Source: Kzenon/123RF.

Fairness and the Family Business

Most small businesses are "family businesses" because the owner and, often, one or more managers and employees are family members.

Being a nonfamily employee here isn't easy. The tendency to treat family and nonfamily employees differently can undermine perceptions of fairness.[47] Reducing such "fairness" problems involves several steps, including the following:[48]

- **Set the ground rules.** One family business consultant says,

During the hiring process the applicant should be informed as to whether . . . there will be potential for promotion. At a minimum, make the expectations clear, regarding matters such as the level of authority the person can expect to attain.[49]

- **Treat people fairly.** Most employees in a family business understand that they won't be treated exactly the same as family members. However, they expect to be treated fairly. This means avoiding "any appearance that family members are benefiting unfairly from the sacrifice of others."[50] For that reason, family members in many family businesses avoid ostentatious purchases like expensive cars.
- **Confront family issues.** Discord among family members distracts and demoralizes other employees. Family members must confront and work out their differences.
- **Erase privilege.** Family members "should avoid any behavior that would lead people to the conclusion that they are demanding special treatment in terms of assignments or responsibilities."[51] They should come in earlier, work harder, and stay later than other employees. Endeavor to show that family members earned their promotions.

Using Professional Employer Organizations

Many small business owners look at the issues involved with managing personnel and decide to outsource most of their human resource functions to vendors.[52] These vendors (as explained in Chapter 11) go by the names *professional employer organizations (PEOs)*, *human resource outsourcers (HROs)*, or sometimes *employee or staff leasing firms*. Figure MB.4 summarizes guidelines small business owners can use for finding and working with PEOs.

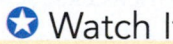 Watch It

How does a small company actually carry out its human resource management tasks? If your professor has chosen to assign this, go to **www.pearson.com/mylab/management** to watch the video Managing Human Resources in Entrepreneurial Firms (Black Bird Guitars), and then answer the questions to show what you'd do in this situation.

Figure MB.4

Guidelines for Finding and Working with PEOs

Source: Based on Robert Beck and J. Starkman, "How to Find a PEO That Will Get the Job Done," *National Underwriter*, 110, no. 39, October 16, 2006, pp. 39, 45; Lyle DeWitt, "Advantages of Human Resource Outsourcing," *CPA Journal*, 75, no. 6, June 2005, p. 13; www.peo.com/dnn/, accessed April 28, 2008; Layne Davlin, "Human Resource Solutions for the Franchisee," *Franchising World*, 39, no. 10, October 2007, p.27; www.workforce.com/ext/resources/archive_mediafiles/White%20Paper-%20What%20is%20a%20PEO-.pdf?1372871757, accessed September 16, 2014.

Employers should choose and manage the PEO relationship carefully. Some guidelines for doing so include:

- *Know ahead of time* exactly what human resource concerns your company wants to address.
- *Review the services* of all PEO firms you're considering. Determine which can meet all your requirements.
- *Determine if the PEO is accredited.* There is no rating system. However, the Employer Services Assurance Corporation of Little Rock, Arkansas (www.Esacorp.org), imposes higher financial, auditing, and operating standards on its members.
- *Check* the provider's bank, credit, insurance, and professional *references*.
- Understand how the *employee benefits will be funded.* Is it fully insured or partially self-funded?
- *Review the service agreement* carefully. Are the respective parties' responsibilities and liabilities clear? *Understand how you will be charged.*
- Investigate *how long the PEO has been in business.*
- *Check out the prospective PEO's staff.* Do they seem to have the expertise to deliver on its promises?
- Ask, *how will the firm deliver its services*? In person? By phone? Via the Web?
- Ask about *upfront fees* and how these are determined.
- *Periodically get proof that payroll taxes and insurance premiums are being paid properly* and that any legal issues are handled correctly.

LEARNING OBJECTIVE 4
Describe how you would create a start-up human resource system for a new small business.

Managing HR Systems, Procedures, and Paperwork

Introduction

Consider the paperwork required to run a five-person retail shop. Just to start, recruiting and hiring an employee might require an employment application, an interviewing checklist, various verifications—of education and immigration status, for instance—and a reference checklist. You then might need an employment agreement, confidentiality and noncompetition agreements, and an employer indemnity agreement. To process that new employee, you might need a background verification, a new employee checklist, and forms for withholding tax and to obtain new employee data. And to keep track of the employee once on board, you'd need—just to start—a personnel data sheet, daily and weekly time records, an hourly employee's weekly time sheet, and an expense report. Then come all the performance appraisal forms, a disciplinary notice, an employee orientation record, separation notice, and employment reference response.

With just one or two employees, you might keep track of everything in your head, or just write a separate memo for each HR action, and place it in a folder for each worker. But with more than a few employees, you'll need a human resource system comprising standardized forms. Then, as the company grows, most employers begin to computerize various parts of the HR system—payroll or appraising, for instance.

Basic Components of Manual HR Systems

Very small employers (say, with 10 employees or less) often start with a manual human resource management system. From a practical point of view, this generally means obtaining and organizing a set of standardized personnel forms covering each important aspect of the HR process—recruitment, selection, training, appraisal, compensation, safety—as well as some means for organizing all this information for each of your employees.

Basic Forms The number of forms you would conceivably need even for a small firm is quite large, as the illustrative list in Table MB.2 shows. One simple way to obtain the basic component forms of a manual HR system is from websites (such as www.hr.com/en/free_forms/) or books or CDs that provide compilations of HR forms.[53] The forms you want can then be adapted from these sources for your particular situation. Office supply stores (such as Office Depot and Staples) also sell packages of personnel forms. For example, Office Depot sells packages of various personnel forms such as: Application, Employment Interview, Reference Check, Employee Record, Performance Evaluation, Warning Notice, Exit Interview, and Vacation Request, plus a Lawsuit-Prevention Guide.[54] Also available is a package of Employee Record Folders. Use the folders to maintain a file on each individual employee; on the outside of the pocket is printed a form for recording information such as name, start date, company benefits, and so on.

Other Sources Several direct-mail catalog companies similarly offer a variety of HR materials. For example, HRdirect (www.hrdirect.com) offers packages of personnel forms.[55] These include, for instance, Short- and Long-Form Employee Applications, Applicant Interviews, Employee Performance Reviews, Job Descriptions, Exit Interviews, and Absentee Calendars and Reports. There are also various legal-compliance forms, including standardized Harassment Policy and FMLA Notice forms, as well as posters (for instance, covering legally required postings for matters such as the Americans with Disabilities Act and Occupational Safety and Health Act) available.

Table MB.2 Some Important Employment Forms

New Employee Forms	Current Employee Forms	Employee Separation Forms
Application	Employee Status	Retirement Checklist
New Employee Checklist	Change Request	Termination Checklist
Employment Interview	Employee Record	COBRA Acknowledgment
Reference Check	Performance Evaluation	Unemployment Claim
Telephone Reference Report	Warning Notice	Employee Exit Interview
Employee Manual Acknowledgment	Vacation Request	
Employment Agreement	Probation Notice	
Employment Application Disclaimer	Job Description	
Employee Secrecy Agreement	Probationary Evaluation	
	Direct Deposit Acknowledgment	
	Absence Report	
	Disciplinary Notice	
	Grievance Form	
	Expense Report	
	401(k) Choices Acknowledgment	
	Injury Report	

Automating Individual HR Tasks

As the small business grows, it becomes difficult to rely on manual HR systems. For a company with 40 or 50 employees or more, the amount of management time devoted to things like attendance history and performance appraisals can swell into weeks. It is therefore at about this point that most small- to medium-sized firms begin computerizing individual human resource management tasks.

Packaged Systems Here again, there are many resources available. For example, various websites contain categorical lists of HR software vendors.[56] These vendors provide software solutions for virtually all personnel tasks, ranging from benefits management to compensation, compliance, employee relations, outsourcing, payroll, and time and attendance systems.

The G. Neil Company sells software packages for monitoring attendance, employee record keeping, writing employee policy handbooks, and conducting computerized employee appraisals. www.HRdirect.com, www.effortlesshr.com, and others offer solutions for writing employee policy manuals, maintaining employee records (including name, address, marital status, number of dependents, emergency contact and phone numbers, hire date, and job history), writing performance reviews, creating job descriptions, tracking attendance and hours worked for each employee, employee scheduling, writing organizational charts, managing payroll, conducting employee surveys, scheduling and tracking employee training activities, and managing OSHA compliance, often cloud-based.[57] Websites such as www.capterra.com/ list HR software available from vendors such as Zenefits, Halogen TalentSpace, Fairsail HRIS, and Cezanne HR.[58]

Human Resource Information Systems (HRIS)

As companies grow, they often turn to integrated *human resource information systems (HRIS)*. We can define an *HRIS* as interrelated components working together to collect, process, store, and disseminate information to support decision making, coordination, control, analysis, and visualization of an organization's human resource management activities.[59] Because the HRIS's software components (record keeping, payroll, appraisal, and so forth) are integrated (able to "talk with each other"), they enable the employer to streamline its HR function. For example, a typical HRIS would electronically route salary increases, transfers, and other e-forms through the organization to the proper managers for approval. As one person signs off, it's routed to the next. If anyone forgets to process a document, a smart agent issues reminders until the task is completed.

HRIS Vendors

Many vendors offer HRIS packages, many cloud-based (see accompanying Trends feature). Vendors include, for example, Oracle Corporation, SAP America, Inc., Automatic Data Processing, Inc., Business Information Technology, Inc., Human Resource Microsystems, and Lawson Software.

HR and Intranets

Employers often install intranet-based HR information systems. For example, LG&E Energy Corporation uses its intranet for benefits communication. Employees can access the benefits homepage and (among other things) review the company's 401(k) plan investment options, get answers to frequently asked questions about the company's medical and dental plans, and report changes in family status. Other uses for human resource intranets include, for instance: automate job postings and applicant tracking, set up training registration, provide electronic pay stubs, publish an electronic employee handbook, and let employees update their personal profiles and access their accounts, such as 401(k)s.

TRENDS SHAPING HR: *Digital and Social Media*

HR ON THE CLOUD Most suppliers of human resource management systems, such as ADP, Ceridian, Kronos, Oracle, and SAP, offer totally cloud-based systems. For small business owners particularly, the advantages of cloud systems are that the vendors can easily update them with the latest system features—saving the small business owner much time and expense—and that the owner and employees can easily access the information from wherever they are.[60]

BambooHR illustrates an HR system especially designed for small- and medium-sized businesses (www.bamboohr.com).[61] For example, bambooHR enables authorized managers and employees to securely and remotely access company information on matters like time off and personal information and to produce reports and/or follow trends on the system's customizable dashboards. It offers applicant tracking, onboarding processes, time-off tracking, and employee database management. Furthermore, it can be seamlessly integrated with the small business's payroll systems, applicant tracking systems, benefits enrollment systems, and performance review systems.[62]

Many such systems integrate with employees' mobile devices. For example, in many firms, HR professionals still assist employees in signing up for benefits. Others increasingly outsource those tasks to cloud-based services offered by firms like Zenefits. A new employee simply uses his or her laptop or smartphone to access the Zenefits website. He or she can then input personal information, sign documents via a touchscreen, and register for benefits such as flexible spending accounts.[63]

Review

MyLab Management

If your instructor is using MyLab Management, go to **www.pearson.com/mylab/ management** to complete the problems marked with this icon ⭐.

Summary

1. Managing human resources in small firms is different for four main reasons: size, priorities, informality, and the nature of the entrepreneur. These create several risks. Small business owners run the risk that their human resource practices will put them at a competitive disadvantage; there is a lack of specialized HR expertise; the smaller firm is probably not adequately addressing potential workplace litigation; the small business owner may not be fully complying with compensation regulations and laws; duplication and paperwork lead to inefficiencies and errors.

2. The U.S. Department of Labor's *FirstStep* Employment Law Advisor helps employers (and particularly small businesses) determine which laws apply to their business. The DOL's site also provides information on the Fair Labor Standards Act (FLSA). It contains several "elaws Advisors." The U.S. Equal Employment Opportunity Commission's (EEOC) website provides important information regarding EEOC matters, such as Title VII. The DOL's Occupational Safety and Health Administration site similarly provides, among other things, the *OSHA Handbook for Small Businesses*. Internet resources can make small business owners more effective in HRM. For example, the Department of Labor's O*NET is effective for creating job descriptions. Small businesses can use the online recruiting tools we discussed in Chapter 5.

3. In dealing with employees, small firms should capitalize on their smallness. Smallness should translate into personal *familiarity* with each employee's strengths, needs, and family situation. And it should translate into being relatively flexible and informal in the human resource management policies and practices the company follows. Even without the deep pockets of larger firms, small firms can offer employees work–life benefits that large employers usually can't match. Small firms also rely on more informal employee selection, recruitment, and training practices.

4. Even small businesses need HR forms. Very small employers start with a manual human resource management system. This generally means obtaining and organizing a set of standardized personnel forms covering each aspect of HR—recruitment, selection, training, appraisal, compensation, and safety—as well as some means for organizing all this information. Office Depot and several direct-mail catalog companies offer HR materials. As the company grows, most small- to medium-sized firms begin computerizing individual HR tasks. For example, the G. Neil Company sells off-the-shelf software packages for monitoring attendance, employee record keeping, writing job descriptions, writing employee policy handbooks, and conducting computerized employee appraisals.

 Try It

How would you do applying the concepts and skills you learned in this chapter? If your professor has chosen to assign this, go to **www.pearson.com/mylab/management** and complete the Entrepreneurship simulation to find out.

Discussion Questions

B-1. Explain why HRM is important to small businesses.

B-2. Explain and give at least four examples of how small business owners can use Internet and government tools to support the HR effort.

B-3. Explain and give at least five examples of ways small business owners can use small size—familiarity, flexibility, and informality—to improve their HR processes.

⭐ **B-4.** Discuss what you would do to find, retain, and deal with, on an ongoing basis, a professional employee organization.

B-5. What is "The Small Business Challenge" in managing HR in a small business?

B-6. Briefly describe two simple examples of how small firms can provide retirement plans for their employees.

MyLab Management

If your instructor is using MyLab Management, go to **www.pearson.com/mylab/management** for Auto-graded writing questions as well as the following Assisted-graded writing questions:

B-7. How and why is HR in small businesses different than in large firms?

B-8. Describe with examples how you would create a start-up paper-based human resource system for a new small business.

APPLICATION EXERCISES

HR IN ACTION CASE INCIDENT 1

Carter Cleaning Company: The New Pay Plan

Carter Cleaning Company does not have a formal wage structure nor does it have rate ranges or use compensable factors. Wage rates are based mostly on those prevailing in the surrounding community and are tempered with an attempt on the part of Jack Carter to maintain some semblance of equity between what workers with different responsibilities in the stores are paid.

Needless to say, Carter does not make any formal surveys when determining what his company should pay. He peruses the want ads almost every day and conducts informal surveys among his friends in the local chapter of the laundry and cleaners trade association. Although Jack has taken a "seat-of-the-pants" approach to paying employees, his salary schedule has been guided by several basic pay policies. Many of his dry cleaner colleagues adhere to a policy of paying absolutely minimum rates, but Jack has always followed a policy of paying his employees about 10% above what he feels are the prevailing rates, a policy that he believes reduces turnover while fostering employee loyalty. Of somewhat more concern to Jennifer is her father's informal policy

of paying men about 20% more than women for the same job. Her father's explanation is, "They're stronger and can work harder for longer hours, and besides, they all have families to support."

Questions

B-9. Is the company at the point where it should be setting up a formal salary structure based on a complete job evaluation? Why?

B-10. How exactly could Carter use free online sources like O*NET to help create the necessary salary structure?

B-11. Do you think paying 10% more than the prevailing rates is a sound idea, and how would Jack determine that?

B-12. How could Jack Carter use online government sources to determine if his policy of a male–female differential pay rate is wise and, if not, why not?

B-13. Specifically, what would you suggest Jennifer do now with respect to her company's pay plan?

Comprehensive Cases

Bandag Automotive*

Jim Bandag took over his family's auto supply business in 2012, after helping his father, who founded the business, run it for about 10 years. Based in Illinois, Bandag employs about 300 people, and distributes auto supplies (replacement mufflers, bulbs, engine parts, and so on) through two divisions, one that supplies service stations and repair shops, and a second that sells retail auto supplies through five "Bandag Automotive" auto supply stores.

Jim's father, and now Jim, have always endeavored to keep Bandag's organization chart as simple as possible. The company has a full-time controller, managers for each of the five stores, a manager who oversees the distribution division, and Jim Bandag's executive assistant. Jim (along with his father, working part-time) handles marketing and sales.

Jim's executive assistant administers the firm's day-to-day human resource management tasks, but the company outsources most HR activities to others, including an employment agency that does its recruiting and screening, a benefits firm that administers its 401(k) plan, and a payroll service that handles its paychecks. Bandag's human resource management systems consist almost entirely of standardized HR forms purchased from an HR supplies company. These include forms such as application and performance appraisal forms, as well as an "honesty" test Bandag uses to screen the staff that works in the five stores. The company performs informal salary surveys to see what other companies in the area are paying for similar positions, and use these results for awarding annual merit increases (which in fact are more accurately cost-of-living adjustments).

Jim's father took a fairly paternal approach to the business. He often walked around speaking with his employees, finding out what their problems were, and even helping them out with an occasional loan—for instance, when he discovered that one of their children was sick, or for part of a new home down payment. Jim, on the other hand, tends to be more abrupt, and does not enjoy the same warm relationship with the employees as did his father. Jim is not unfair or dictatorial. He's just very focused on improving Bandag's financial performance, and so all his decisions, including his HR-related decisions, generally come down to cutting costs. For example, his knee-jerk reaction is usually to offer fewer days off rather than more, fewer benefits rather than more, and to be less flexible when an employee needs, for instance, a few extra days off because a child is sick.

It's therefore perhaps not surprising that over the past few years Bandag's sales and profits have increased markedly, but that the firm has found itself increasingly enmeshed in HR/equal employment–type issues. Indeed, Jim now finds himself spending a day or two a week addressing HR problems. For example, Henry Jaques, an employee at one of the stores, came to Jim's executive assistant and told her he was "irate" about his recent firing and was probably going to sue. Henry's store manager stated on his last performance appraisal that Henry did the technical aspects of his job well, but that he had "serious problems interacting with his coworkers." He was continually arguing with them, and complaining to the store manager about working conditions. The store manager had told Jim that he had to fire Henry because he was making "the whole place poisonous," and that (although he felt sorry because he'd heard rumors that Henry suffered from some mental illness) he felt he had to go. Jim approved the dismissal.

Gavin was another problem. Gavin had worked for Bandag for 10 years, the last two as manager of one of the company's five stores. Right after Jim Bandag took over, Gavin told him he had to take a Family and Medical Leave Act medical leave to have hip surgery, and Jim approved the leave. When Gavin returned from leave, Jim told him that his position had been eliminated. Bandag had decided to close his store and open a new, larger store across from a shopping center about a mile away,

*© Gary Dessler, PhD.

and had appointed a new manager in Gavin's absence. However, the company did give Gavin a (nonmanagerial) position in the new store as a counter salesperson, at the same salary and with the same benefits as he had before. Even so, "This job is not similar to my old one," Gavin insisted. "It doesn't have nearly as much prestige." His contention is that the FMLA requires that the company bring him back in the same or equivalent position, and that this means a supervisory position, similar to what he had before he went on leave. Jim said no, and they seem to be heading toward litigation.

In another sign of the times at Bandag, the company's controller, Miriam, who had been with the company for about six years, went on pregnancy leave for 12 weeks in 2012 (also under the FMLA), and then received an additional three weeks' leave under Bandag's extended illness days program. Four weeks after she came back, she asked Jim Bandag if she could arrange to work fewer hours per week, and spend about a day per week working out of her home. He refused, and about two months later fired her. Jim Bandag said, "I'm sorry, it's not anything to do with your pregnancy-related requests, but we've got ample reasons to discharge you—your monthly budgets have been several days late, and we've got proof you may have forged documents." She replied, "I don't care what you say your reasons are; you're really firing me because of my pregnancy, and that's illegal."

Jim felt he was on safe ground as far as defending the company for these actions, although he didn't look forward to spending the time and money that he knew it would take to fight each. However, what he learned over lunch from a colleague undermined his confidence about another case that Jim had been sure would be a "slam dunk" for his company. Jim was explaining to his friend that one of Bandag's truck maintenance service people had applied for a job driving one of Bandag's distribution department trucks, and that Jim had turned him down because the worker was deaf. Jim (whose wife has occasionally said of him, "No one has ever accused Jim of being politically correct") was mentioning to his friend the apparent absurdity of a deaf person asking to be a truck delivery person. His friend, who happens to work for UPS, pointed out that the U.S. Court of Appeals for the Ninth Circuit had recently decided that UPS had violated the Americans with Disabilities Act by refusing to consider deaf workers for jobs driving the company's smaller vehicles.

Although Jim's father is semiretired, the sudden uptick in the frequency of such EEO-type issues troubled him, particularly after so many years of labor peace. However, he's not sure what to do about it. Having handed over the reins of the company to his son, he was loath to inject himself back into the company's operational decision making. On the other hand, he was afraid that in the short run these issues were going to drain a great deal of Jim's time and resources, and that in the long run they might be a sign of things to come, with problems like these eventually overwhelming Bandag Automotive. He comes to you, who he knows consults in human resource management, and asks you the following questions.

Questions

1. Given Bandag Automotive's size, and anything else you know about it, should we reorganize the human resource management function, and if so, why and how?

2. What, if anything, would you do to change and/or improve upon the current HR systems, forms, and practices that we now use?

3. Do you think that the employee whom Jim fired for creating what the manager called a poisonous relationship has a legitimate claim against us, and if so, why and what should we do about it?

4. Is it true that we really had to put Gavin back into an equivalent position, or was it adequate to just bring him back into a job at the same salary, bonuses, and benefits as he had before his leave?

5. Miriam, the controller, is basically claiming that the company is retaliating against her for being pregnant, and that the fact that we raised performance issues was just a smokescreen. Do you think the EEOC and/or courts would agree with her, and, in any case, what should we do now?

6. An employee who is deaf has asked us to be one of our delivery people and we turned him down. He's now threatening to sue. What should we do, and why?

7. In the previous 10 years, we've had only one equal employment complaint, and now in the last few years we've had four or five. What should I do about it? Why?

Based generally on actual facts, but Bandag is a fictitious company. Bandag source notes: "The Problem Employee: Discipline or Accommodation?" *Monday Business Briefing*, March 8, 2005; "Employee Says Change in Duties after Leave Violates FMLA," *BNA Bulletin to Management*, January 16, 2007, p. 24; "Manager Fired Days after Announcing Pregnancy," *BNA Bulletin to Management*, January 2, 2007, p. 8; "Ninth Circuit Rules UPS Violated ADA by Barring Deaf Workers from Driving Jobs," *BNA Bulletin to Management*, October 17, 2006, p. 329.

Angelo's PIZZA*

Angelo Camero was brought up in the Bronx, New York, and basically always wanted to be in the pizza store business. As a youngster, he would sometimes

---

*© Gary Dessler, PhD.

spend hours at the local pizza store, watching the owner knead the pizza dough, flatten it into a large circular crust, fling it up, and then spread on tomato sauce in larger and larger loops. After graduating from college as a marketing major, he made a beeline back to the Bronx, where he opened his first Angelo's Pizza store, emphasizing its clean, bright interior; its crisp green, red, and white sign; and his all-natural, fresh ingredients. Within five years, Angelo's store was a success, and he had opened three other stores and was considering franchising his concept.

Eager as he was to expand, his four years in business school had taught him the difference between being an entrepreneur and being a manager. As an entrepreneur/small business owner, he knew he had the distinct advantage of being able to personally run the whole operation himself. With just one store and a handful of employees, he could make every decision and watch the cash register, check in the new supplies, oversee the takeout, and personally supervise the service.

When he expanded to three stores, things started getting challenging. He hired managers for the two new stores (both of whom had worked for him at his first store for several years) and gave them only minimal "how to run a store"–type training, on the assumption that, having worked with him for several years, they already knew pretty much everything they needed to know about running a store. However, he was already experiencing human resource management problems, and he knew there was no way he could expand the number of stores he owned, or (certainly) contemplate franchising his idea, unless he had a system in place that he could clone in each new store to provide the managers (or the franchisees) with the necessary management knowledge and expertise to run their stores. Angelo had no training program in place for teaching his store managers how to run their stores. He simply (erroneously, as it turned out) assumed that by working with him they would learn how to do things on the job. Since Angelo had no system in place, the new managers were, in a way, starting off below zero when it came to how to manage a store.

There were several issues that particularly concerned Angelo. Finding and hiring good employees was number one. He'd read the new National Small Business Poll from the National Federation of Independent Business Education Foundation. It found that 71% of small business owners believed that finding qualified employees was "hard." Furthermore, "the search for qualified employees will grow more difficult as demographic and education factors" continue to make it more difficult to find employees. Similarly, reading the *Kiplinger Letter* one day, he noticed that just about every type of business couldn't find enough good employees to hire. Small firms were particularly

in jeopardy; the *Letter* said that giant firms can outsource many (particularly entry-level) jobs abroad, and larger companies can also afford to pay better benefits and to train their employees. Small firms rarely have the resources or the economies of scale to allow outsourcing or to install the big training programs that would enable them to take untrained new employees and turn them into skilled ones.

Although finding enough employees was his biggest problem, finding enough honest ones scared him even more. Angelo recalled from one of his business school courses that companies in the United States are losing a total of well over $400 billion a year in employee theft. As a rough approximation, that works out to about $9 per employee per day and about $12,000 lost annually for a typical company. Furthermore, it was small companies like Angelo's that were particularly in the crosshairs, because companies with fewer than 100 employees are particularly prone to employee theft. Why are small firms particularly vulnerable? Perhaps they lack experience dealing with the problem. More importantly: Small firms are more likely to have a single person doing several jobs, such as ordering supplies and paying the delivery person. This undercuts the checks and balances managers often strive for to control theft. Furthermore, the risk of stealing goes up dramatically when the business is largely based on cash. In a pizza store, many people come in and buy just one or two slices and a cola for lunch, and almost all pay with cash, not credit cards.

And, Angelo was not just worried about someone stealing cash. They can steal your whole business idea, something he learned from painful experience. He had been planning to open a store in what he thought would be a particularly good location, and was thinking of having one of his current employees manage the store. Instead, it turned out that this employee was, in a manner of speaking, stealing Angelo's brain: what Angelo knew about customers, suppliers, where to buy pizza dough, where to buy tomato sauce, how much everything should cost, how to furnish the store, where to buy ovens, store layout—everything. This employee soon quit and opened up his own pizza store, not far from where Angelo had planned to open his new store.

That he was having trouble hiring good employees, there was no doubt. The restaurant business is particularly brutal when it comes to turnover. Many restaurants turn over their employees at a rate of 200% to 300% per year—so every year, each position might have a series of two to three employees filling it. As Angelo said, "I was losing two to three employees a month," adding, "We're a high-volume store, and while we should have about six employees per store [to fill all the hours in a week], we were down to only three or four, so my managers and I were really under the gun."

The problem was bad at the hourly employee level: "We were churning a lot at the hourly level," said Angelo. "Applicants would come in, my managers or I would hire them and not spend much time training them, and the good ones would leave in frustration after a few weeks, while often it was the bad ones who'd stay behind." But in the last two years, Angelo's three company-owned stores also went through a total of three store managers—"They were just blowing through the door," as Angelo put it, in part because, without good employees, their workday was brutal. As a rule, when a small business owner or manager can't find enough employees (or an employee doesn't show up for work), about 80% of the time the owner or manager does the job himself or herself. So, these managers often ended up working seven days a week, 10 to 12 hours a day, and many just burned out in the end. One night, working three jobs himself with customers leaving in anger, Angelo decided he'd never just hire someone because he was desperate again, but would start doing his hiring more rationally.

Angelo knew he should have a more formal screening process. As he said, "If there's been a lesson learned, it's much better to spend time up front screening out candidates who don't fit than to hire them and have to put up with their ineffectiveness." He also knew that he could identify many of the traits that his employees needed. For example, he knew that not everyone has the temperament to be a waiter (he has a small pizza/Italian restaurant in the back of his main store). As Angelo said, "I've seen personalities that were off the charts in assertiveness or overly introverted, traits that obviously don't make a good fit for a waiter or waitress."

As a local business, Angelo recruits by placing help wanted ads in two local newspapers, and he's been "shocked" at some of the responses and experiences he's had in response to the ads. Many of the applicants left voicemail messages (Angelo or the other workers in the store were too busy to answer), and some applicants Angelo "just axed" on the assumption that people without good telephone manners wouldn't have very good manners in the store, either. He also quickly learned that he had to throw out a very wide net, even if hiring only one or two people. Many people, as noted, he eliminated from consideration because of the messages they left, and about half the people he scheduled to come in for interviews didn't show up. He'd taken courses in human resource management, so (as he said) "I should know better," but he hired people based almost exclusively on a single interview (he occasionally made a feeble attempt to check references). In total, his HR approach was obviously not working. It wasn't producing enough good recruits, and the people he did hire were often problematic.

What was he looking for? Service-oriented courteous people, for one. For example, he'd hired one employee who used profanity several times, including once in front of a customer. On that employee's third day, Angelo had to tell her, "I think Angelo's isn't the right place for you," and he fired her. As Angelo said, "I felt bad, but also knew that everything I have is on the line for this business, so I wasn't going to let anyone run this business down." Angelo wants reliable people (who'll show up on time), honest people, and people who are flexible about switching jobs and hours as required. He calls his management style "trust and track." "I coach them and give them goals, and then carefully track results."

Angelo's Pizza business has only the most rudimentary human resource management system. Angelo bought several application forms at a local Office Depot, and rarely uses other forms of any sort. He uses his personal accountant for reviewing the company's books, and Angelo himself computes each employee's paycheck at the end of the week and writes the checks. Training is entirely on-the-job. Angelo personally trained each of his employees. For those employees who go on to be store managers, he assumes that they are training their own employees the way that Angelo trained them (for better or worse, as it turns out). Angelo pays "a bit above" prevailing wage rates (judging by other help wanted ads), but probably not enough to make a significant difference in the quality of employees whom he attracts. If you asked Angelo what his reputation is as an employer, Angelo, being a candid and forthright person, would probably tell you that he is a supportive but hard-nosed employer who treats people fairly, but whose business reputation may suffer from disorganization stemming from inadequate organization and training. He approaches you to ask you several questions.

Questions

8. My strategy is to (hopefully) expand the number of stores and eventually franchise, while focusing on serving only high-quality fresh ingredients. What are three specific human resource management implications of my strategy (including specific policies and practices)?

9. Identify and briefly discuss five specific human resource management errors that I'm currently making.

10. Develop a structured interview form that we can use for hiring (1) store managers, (2) wait staff, and (3) counter people/pizza makers.

11. Based on what you know about Angelo's, and what you know from having visited pizza restaurants, write a one-page outline showing specifically how you think Angelo's should go about selecting employees.

Based generally on actual facts, but Angelo's Pizza is a fictitious company. Angelo's Pizza source notes: Dino Berta, "People Problems: Keep Hiring from Becoming a Crying Game," *Nation's Business News*, 36, no. 20, May 20, 2002, pp. 72–74; Ellen Lyon, "Hiring, Personnel Problems Can Challenge Entrepreneurs," *Patriot-News*, October 12, 2004; Rose Robin Pedone, "Businesses' $400 Billion Theft Problem," *Long Island Business News*, 27, July 6, 1998, pp. 1B–2B; "Survey Shows Small-Business Problems with Hiring, Internet," *Providence Business News*, 16, September 10, 2001, pp. 1B; "Finding Good Workers Is Posing a Big Problem as Hiring Picks Up," *Kiplinger Letter*, 81, February 13, 2004; Ian Mount, "A Pizzeria Owner Learns the Value of Watching the Books," *New York Times*, October 25, 2012, p. B8.

Google*

Fortune magazine named Google the best of the 100 best companies to work for, and there is little doubt why. Among the benefits it offers are free shuttles equipped with Wi-Fi to pick up and drop off employees from San Francisco Bay Area locations, unlimited sick days, annual all-expense-paid ski trips, free gourmet meals, five on-site free doctors, $2,000 bonuses for referring a new hire, free flu shots, a giant lap pool, on-site oil changes, on-site car washes, volleyball courts, TGIF parties, free on-site washers and dryers (with free detergent), Ping-Pong and foosball tables, and free famous people lectures. For many people, it's the gourmet meals and snacks that make Google stand out. For example, human resources director Stacey Sullivan loves the Irish oatmeal with fresh berries at the company's Plymouth Rock Cafe, near Google's "people operations" group. "I sometimes dream about it," she says. Engineer Jan Fitzpatrick loves the raw bar at Google's Tapis restaurant, down the road on the Google campus. Then, of course, there are the stock options—each new employee gets about 1,200 options to buy Google shares (recently worth about $480 per share). In fact, dozens of early Google employees ("Googlers") are already multimillionaires thanks to Google stock. The recession that began around 2008 did prompt Google and other firms to cut back on some of these benefits (cafeteria hours are shorter today, for instance), but Google still pretty much leads the benefits pack.

For their part, Googlers share certain traits. They tend to be brilliant, team oriented (teamwork is the norm, especially for big projects), and driven. *Fortune* describes them as people who "almost universally" see themselves as the most interesting people on the planet, and who are happy-go-lucky on the outside, but type A—highly intense and goal directed—on the inside. They're also super-hardworking (which makes sense, since it's not unusual for engineers to be in the

hallways at 3 A.M. debating some new mathematical solution to a Google search problem). They're so team oriented that when working on projects, it's not unusual for Google team members to give up their larger, more spacious offices and to crowd into a small conference room, where they can "get things done." Historically, Googlers generally graduate with great grades from the best universities, including Stanford, Harvard, and MIT. For many years, Google wouldn't even consider hiring someone with less than a 3.7 average—while also probing deeply into the why behind any B grades. Google also doesn't hire lone wolves, but wants people who work together and people who also have diverse interests (narrow interests or skills are a turnoff at Google). Google also wants people with growth potential. The company is expanding so fast that it needs to hire people who are capable of being promoted five or six times—it's only, the company says, by hiring such overqualified people that it can be sure that the employees will be able to keep up as Google and their own departments expand.

The starting salaries are highly competitive. Experienced engineers start at about $130,000 a year (plus about 1,200 shares of stock options, as noted), and new MBAs can expect between $80,000 and $120,000 per year (with smaller option grants). Most recently, Google had about 10,000 staff members, up from its beginnings with just three employees in a rented garage.

Of course, in a company that's grown from 3 employees to 10,000 and from zero value to hundreds of billions of dollars, it may be quibbling to talk about "problems," but there's no doubt that such rapid growth does confront Google's management, and particularly its "people operations" group, with some big challenges. Let's look at these.

For one, Google, as noted earlier, is a 24-hour operation, and with engineers and others frequently pulling all-nighters to complete their projects, the company needs to provide a package of services and financial benefits that supports that kind of lifestyle, and that helps its employees maintain an acceptable work–life balance.

As another challenge, Google's enormous financial success is a two-edged sword. Although Google usually wins the recruitment race when it comes to competing for new employees against competitors like Microsoft or Yahoo!, Google does need some way to stem a rising tide of retirements. Most Googlers are still in their 20s and 30s, but many have become so wealthy from their Google stock options that they can afford to retire. One 27-year-old engineer received a million-dollar founder's award for her work on the program for searching desktop computers, and wouldn't think of leaving "except to start her own company." Similarly, a former engineering vice president retired (with his

Google stock profits) to pursue his love of astronomy. The engineer who dreamed up Gmail recently retired (at the age of 30).

Another challenge is that the work involves not only long hours but can also be very tense. Google is a very numbers-oriented environment. For example, consider a typical weekly Google user interface design meeting. Marisa Meyer, the company's vice president of search products and user experience, runs the meeting, where her employees work out the look and feel of Google's products. Seated around a conference table are about a dozen Googlers, tapping on laptops. During the 2-hour meeting, Meyer needs to evaluate various design proposals, ranging from minor tweaks to a new product's entire layout. She's previously given each presentation an allotted amount of time, and a large digital clock on the wall ticks off the seconds. The presenters must quickly present their ideas, but also handle questions such as "what do users do if the tab is moved from the side of the page to the top?" Furthermore, it's all about the numbers—no one at Google would ever say, for instance, "the tab looks better in red"—you need to prove your point. Presenters must come armed with usability experiment results, showing, for instance, that a certain percentage preferred red or some other color. While the presenters are answering these questions as quickly as possible, the digital clock is ticking, and when it hits the allotted time, the presentation must end, and the next team steps up to present. It is a tough and tense environment, and Googlers must have done their homework.

Growth can also undermine the "outlaw band that's changing the world" culture that fostered the services that made Google famous. Even cofounder Sergi Brin agrees that Google risks becoming less "zany" as it grows. To paraphrase one of its top managers, the hard part of any business is keeping that original innovative, small business feel even as the company grows.

Creating the right culture is especially challenging now that Google is truly global. For example, Google works hard to provide the same financial and service benefits every place it does business around the world, but it can't exactly match its benefits in every country because of international laws and international taxation issues. Offering the same benefits everywhere is more important than it might initially appear. All those benefits make life easier for Google staff, and help them achieve a work–life balance. Achieving the right work–life balance is the centerpiece of Google's culture, but this also becomes more challenging as the company grows. On the one hand, Google does expect all of its employees to work super hard; on the other hand, it realizes that it needs to help them maintain some sort of balance. As one manager says, Google acknowledges "that we work hard but that work is not everything."

Recruitment is another challenge. While Google certainly doesn't lack applicants, attracting the right applicants is crucial if Google is to continue to grow successfully. Working at Google requires a special set of traits, and screening employees is easier if it recruits the right people to begin with. For instance, Google needs to attract people who are super-bright, love to work, have fun, can handle the stress, and who also have outside interests and flexibility.

As the company grows internationally, it also faces the considerable challenge of recruiting and building staff overseas. For example, Google now is introducing a new vertical market–based structure across Europe to attract more business advertisers to its search engine. (By vertical market–based structure, Google means focusing on key vertical industry sectors such as travel, retail, automotive, and technology.) To build these industry groupings abroad from scratch, Google promoted its former head of its U.S. financial services group to be the vertical markets director for Europe; he moved there recently. Google is thus looking for heads for each of its vertical industry groups for all of its key European territories. Each of these vertical market heads will have to educate their market sectors (retailing, travel, and so on) so Google can attract new advertisers. Google already has offices across Europe, and its London office had tripled in size to 100 staff in just two years.

However, probably the biggest challenge Google faces is gearing up its employee selection system, now that the company must hire thousands of people per year. When Google started in business, job candidates typically suffered through a dozen or more in-person interviews, and the standards were so high that even applicants with years of great work experience often got turned down if they had just average college grades. But recently, even Google's cofounders have acknowledged to security analysts that setting such an extraordinarily high bar for hiring was holding back Google's expansion. For Google's first few years, one of the company's cofounders interviewed nearly every job candidate before he or she was hired, and even today one of them still reviews the qualifications of everyone before he or she gets a final offer.

The experience of one candidate illustrates what Google is up against. A 24-year-old was interviewed for a corporate communications job at Google. Google first made contact with the candidate in May, and then, after two phone interviews, invited him to headquarters. There he had separate interviews with about six people and was treated to lunch in a Google cafeteria. They also had him turn in several "homework" assignments, including a personal statement and a marketing plan. In August, Google invited the candidate back for a second round, which it said would involve another four or five interviews. In the meantime, he decided he'd rather work at a start-up, and accepted another job at a new Web-based instant messaging provider.

Google's new head of human resources, a former GE executive, says that Google is trying to strike the right balance between letting Google and the candidate get to know each other while also moving quickly. To that end, Google recently administered a survey to all Google's current employees in an effort to identify the traits that correlate with success at Google. In the survey, employees responded to questions relating to about 300 variables, including their performance on standardized tests, how old they were when they first used a computer, and how many foreign languages they speak. The Google survey team then went back and compared the answers against the 30 or 40 job performance factors they keep for each employee. They thereby identified clusters of traits that Google might better focus on during the hiring process. Google is also moving from the free-form interviews it used in the past to a more structured process.

Questions

12. What do you think of the idea of Google correlating personal traits from the employees' answers on the survey to their performance, and then using that as the basis for screening job candidates? In other words, is it or is it not a good idea? Please explain your answer.

13. The benefits that Google pays obviously represent an enormous expense. Based on what you know about Google and on what you read in this text, how would you defend all these benefits if you're making a presentation to the security analysts who were analyzing Google's performance?

14. If you wanted to hire the brightest people around, how would you go about recruiting and selecting them?

15. To support its growth and expansion strategy, Google wants (among other traits) people who are super-bright and who work hard, often round-the-clock, and who are flexible and maintain a decent work–life balance. List five specific HR policies or practices that you think Google has implemented or should implement to support its strategy, and explain your answer.

16. What sorts of factors do you think Google will have to take into consideration as it tries transferring its culture and reward systems and way of doing business to its operations abroad?

17. Given the sorts of values and culture Google cherishes, briefly describe four specific activities you suggest it pursue during new-employee orientation.

Source: Notes for Google: "Google Brings Vertical Structure to Europe," *New Media Age*, August 4, 2005, p. 2; Debbie Lovewell, "Employer Profile—Google: Searching for Talent," *Employee Benefits*, October 10, 2005, p. 66; "Google Looking for Gourmet Chefs," *Internet Week*, August 4, 2005; Douglas Merrill, "Google's 'Googley' Culture Kept Alive by Tech," *eWeek*, April 11, 2006; Robert Hof, "Google Gives Employees Another Option," *BusinessWeek Online*, December 13, 2005; Kevin Delaney, "Google Adjusts Hiring Process as Needs Grow," *Wall Street Journal*, October 23, 2006, pp. B1, B8; Adam Lishinsky, "Search and Enjoy," *Fortune*, January 22, 2007, pp. 70–82; www.nypost.com/seven/10302008/business/frugal_google_cuts_perks_136011.htm, accessed July 12, 2009; Adam Bryant, "The Quest to Build a Better Boss," *New York Times*, March 13, 2011, pp. 1, 7; Mark C. Crowley, "Not A Happy Accident: How Google Deliberately Designs Workplace Satisfaction", www.fastcompany.com/3007268/where-are-they-now/not-happy-accident-how-google-deliberately-designs-workplace-satisfaction, accessed September 16, 2014.

Muffler Magic*

Muffler Magic is a fast-growing chain of 25 automobile service centers in Nevada. Originally started 20 years ago as a muffler repair shop by Ronald Brown, the chain expanded rapidly to new locations, and as it did so Muffler Magic also expanded the services it provided, from muffler replacement to oil changes, brake jobs, and engine repair. Today, one can bring an automobile to a Muffler Magic shop for basically any type of service, from tires to mufflers to engine repair.

Auto service is a tough business. The shop owner is basically dependent upon the quality of the service people he or she hires and retains, and the most qualified mechanics find it easy to pick up and leave for a job paying a bit more at a competitor down the road. It's also a business in which productivity is very important. The single largest expense is usually the cost of labor. Auto service dealers generally don't just make up the prices that they charge customers for various repairs; instead, they charge based on standardized industry rates for jobs like changing spark plugs or repairing a leaky radiator. Therefore, if someone brings a car in for a new alternator and the standard number of hours for changing the alternator is an hour, but it takes the mechanic 2 hours, the service center's owner may end up making less profit on the transaction.

Quality is a persistent problem as well. For example, "rework" has recently been a problem at Muffler Magic. A customer recently brought her car to a Muffler Magic to have the car's brake pads replaced,

*© Gary Dessler, PhD.

which the service center did for her. Unfortunately, when she left she drove only about two blocks before she discovered that she had no brake power at all. It was simply fortuitous that she was going so slowly she was able to stop her car by slowly rolling up against a parking bumper. It subsequently turned out that the mechanic who replaced the brake pads had failed to properly tighten a fitting on the hydraulic brake tubes and the brake fluid had run out, leaving the car with no braking power. In a similar problem the month before that, a (different) mechanic replaced a fan belt, but forgot to refill the radiator with fluid; that customer's car overheated before he got four blocks away, and Muffler Magic had to replace the whole engine. Of course problems like these not only diminish the profitability of the company's profits, but, repeated many times over, have the potential for ruining Muffler Magic's word-of-mouth reputation.

Organizationally, Muffler Magic employs about 300 people, and Ron runs his company with eight managers, including himself as president, a controller, a purchasing director, a marketing director, and the human resource manager. He also has three regional managers to whom the eight or nine service center managers in each area of Nevada report. Over the past two years, as the company has opened new service centers, company-wide profits have diminished rather than increased. In part, these diminishing profits probably reflect the fact that Ron Brown has found it increasingly difficult to manage his growing operation. ("Your reach is exceeding your grasp" is how Ron's wife puts it.)

The company has only the most basic HR systems in place. It uses an application form that the human resource manager modified from one that he downloaded from the Web, and the standard employee status change request forms, sign-on forms, I-9 forms, and so on, that it purchased from a human resource management supply house. Training is entirely on-the-job. Muffler Magic expects the experienced technicians that it hires to come to the job fully trained; to that end, the service center managers generally ask candidates for these jobs basic behavioral questions that hopefully provide a window into these applicants' skills. However, most of the other technicians hired to do jobs like rotating tires, fixing brake pads, and replacing mufflers are untrained and inexperienced. They are to be trained by either the service center manager or by more experienced technicians, on-the-job.

Ron Brown faces several HR-type problems. One, as he says, is that he faces the "tyranny of the immediate" when it comes to hiring employees. Although it's fine to say that he should be carefully screening each employee and checking his or her references and work ethic, from a practical point of view, with 25 centers to run, the centers' managers usually just hire anyone who seems to be breathing, as long as he or she can answer some basic interview questions about auto repair, such as, "What do you think the problem is if a 2001 Camry is overheating, and what would you do about it?"

Employee safety is also a problem. An automobile service center may not be the most dangerous type of workplace, but it is potentially dangerous. Employees are dealing with sharp tools, greasy floors, greasy tools, extremely hot temperatures (for instance, on mufflers and engines), and fast-moving engine parts including fan blades. There are some basic things that a service manager can do to ensure more safety, such as insisting that all oil spills be cleaned up immediately. However, from a practical point of view, there are few ways to get around many of the problems—such as when the technician must check out an engine while it is running.

With Muffler Magic's profits going down instead of up, Brown's human resource manager has taken the position that the main problem is financial. As he says, "You get what you pay for" when it comes to employees, and if you compensate technicians better than your competitors do, then you get better technicians, ones who do their jobs better and stay longer with the company—and then profits will rise. So, the HR manager scheduled a meeting between himself, Ron Brown, and a professor of business who teaches compensation management at a local university. The HR manager has asked this professor to spend about a week looking at each of the service centers, analyzing the situation, and coming up with a compensation plan that will address Muffler Magic's quality and productivity problems. At this meeting, the professor makes three basic recommendations for changing the company's compensation policies.

Number one, she says that she has found that Muffler Magic suffers from what she calls "presenteeism"—in other words, employees drag themselves into work even when they're sick, because the company does not pay them if they are out; the company offers no sick days. In just a few days the professor couldn't properly quantify how much Muffler Magic is losing to presenteeism. However, from what she could see at each shop, there are typically one or two technicians working with various maladies like the cold or flu, and it seemed to her that each of these people was probably really only working about half of the time (although they were getting paid for the whole day). So, for 25 service centers per week, Muffler Magic could well be losing 125 or 130 personnel days per week of work. The professor suggests that Muffler Magic start allowing everyone to take three paid sick days per year, a reasonable suggestion. However, as Ron Brown points out, "Right now, we're only losing about half a day's pay for each employee who comes in and who works unproductively; with your suggestion, won't we lose the whole day?" The professor says she'll ponder that one.

Second, the professor recommends putting the technicians on a skill-for-pay plan. Basically, she suggests the following. Give each technician a letter grade (A through E) based upon that technician's particular skill level and abilities. An "A" technician is a team leader and needs to show that he or she has excellent diagnostic troubleshooting skills, and the ability to supervise and direct other technicians. At the other extreme, an "E" technician would typically be a new apprentice with little technical training. The other technicians fall in between those two levels, based on their individual skills and abilities.

In the professor's system, the "A" technician or team leader would assign and supervise all work done within his or her area but generally not do any mechanical repairs himself or herself. The team leader does the diagnostic troubleshooting, supervises and trains the other technicians, and test drives the car before it goes back to the customer. Under this plan, every technician receives a guaranteed hourly wage within a certain range, for instance:

> A tech = $25–$30 an hour
> B tech = $20–$25 an hour
> C tech = $15–$20 an hour
> D tech = $10–$15 an hour
> E tech = $8–$10 an hour

Third, to directly address the productivity issue, the professor recommends that each service manager calculate each technician-team's productivity at the end of each day and at the end of each week. She suggests posting the running productivity total conspicuously for daily viewing. Then, the technicians as a group get weekly cash bonuses based upon their productivity. To calculate productivity, the professor recommends dividing the total labor hours billed by the total labor hours paid to technicians; in other words, total labor hours billed *divided by* total hours paid to technicians.

Having done some homework, the professor says that the national average for labor productivity is currently about 60%, and that only the best-run service centers achieve 85% or greater. By her rough calculations, Muffler Magic was attaining about industry average (about 60%—in other words, they were billing for only about 60 hours for each 100 hours that they actually had to pay technicians to do the jobs). (Of course, this was not entirely the technicians' fault. Technicians get time off for breaks and for lunch, and if a particular service center simply didn't have enough business on a particular day or during a particular week, then several technicians may well sit around idly waiting for the next car to come in.) The professor recommends setting a labor efficiency goal of 80% and posting each team's daily productivity results in the workplace to provide them with additional feedback. She

recommends that if at the end of a week the team is able to boost its productivity ratio from the current 60% to 80%, then that team would get an additional 10% weekly pay bonus. After that, for every 5% boost of increased productivity above 80%, technicians would receive an additional 5% weekly bonus. So, if a technician's normal weekly pay is $400, that employee would receive an extra $40 at the end of the week when his team moves from 60% productivity to 80% productivity.

After the meeting, Ron Brown thanked the professor for her recommendations and told her he would think about it and get back to her. After the meeting, on the drive home, Ron was pondering what to do. He had to decide whether to institute the professor's sick leave policy, and whether to implement the professor's incentive and compensation plan. Before implementing anything, however, he wanted to make sure he understood the context in which he was making his decision. For example, did Muffler Magic really have an incentive pay problem, or were the problems more broad? Furthermore, how, if at all, would the professor's incentive plan impact the quality of the work that the teams were doing? And should the company really start paying for sick days? Ron Brown had a lot to think about.

Questions

18. Write a one-page summary outline listing three or four recommendations you would make with respect to each HR function (recruiting, selection, training, and so on) that you think Ron Brown should be addressing with his HR manager.

19. Develop a 10-question structured interview form Ron Brown's service center managers can use to interview experienced technicians.

20. If you were Ron Brown, would you implement the professor's recommendation addressing the presenteeism problem—in other words, start paying for sick days? Why or why not?

21. If you were advising Ron Brown, would you recommend that he implement the professor's skill-based pay and incentive pay plan as is? Why? Would you implement it with modifications? If you would modify it, please be specific about what you think those modifications should be, and why.

Based generally on actual facts, but Muffler Magic is a fictitious company. This case is based largely on information in Drew Paras, "The Pay Factor: Technicians' Salaries Can Be the Largest Expense in a Server Shop, as Well as the Biggest Headache. Here's How One Shop Owner Tackled the Problem," *Motor Age*, November 2003, pp. 76–79; see also Jennifer Pellet, "Health Care Crisis," *Chief Executive*, June 2004, pp. 56–61; "Firms Press to Quantify, Control Presenteeism," *Employee Benefits*, December 1, 2002.

Bp Texas City*

When British Petroleum's (BP) Horizon oil rig exploded in the Gulf of Mexico in 2010, it triggered tragic reminders for experts in the safety community. In March 2005, an explosion and fire at BP's Texas City, Texas, refinery killed 15 people and injured 500 people in the worst U.S. industrial accident in more than 10 years. That disaster triggered three investigations: one internal investigation by BP, one by the U.S. Chemical Safety Board, and an independent investigation chaired by former U.S. Secretary of State James Baker and an 11-member panel that was organized at BP's request.

To put the results of these three investigations into context, it's useful to understand that under its current management, BP had pursued, for the past 10 or so years before the Texas City explosion, a strategy emphasizing cost-cutting and profitability. The basic conclusion of the investigations was that cost-cutting helped compromise safety at the Texas City refinery. It's useful to consider each investigation's findings.

The Chemical Safety Board's (CSB) investigation, according to Carol Merritt, the board's chair, showed that "BP's global management was aware of problems with maintenance, spending, and infrastructure well before March 2005." Apparently, faced with numerous earlier accidents, BP did make some safety improvements. However, it focused primarily on emphasizing personal employee safety behaviors and procedural compliance, and thereby reducing safety accident rates. The problem (according to the CSB) was that "catastrophic safety risks remained." For example, according to the CSB, "unsafe and antiquated equipment designs were left in place, and unacceptable deficiencies in preventive maintenance were tolerated." Basically, the CSB found that BP's budget cuts led to a progressive deterioration of safety at the Texas City refinery. Said Merritt, "In an aging facility like Texas City, it is not responsible to cut budgets related to safety and maintenance without thoroughly examining the impact on the risk of a catastrophic accident."

Looking at specifics, the CSB said that a 2004 internal audit of 35 BP business units, including Texas City (BP's largest refinery), found significant safety gaps they all had in common, including, for instance, a lack of leadership competence, and "systemic underlying issues" such as a widespread tolerance of noncompliance with basic safety rules and poor monitoring of safety management systems and processes. Ironically, the CSB found that BP's accident prevention effort at Texas City had achieved a 70% reduction in worker injuries in the year before the explosion. Unfortunately, this simply meant that individual employees were having fewer accidents. The larger, more fundamental problem was that the potentially explosive situation inherent in the depreciating machinery remained.

The CSB found that the Texas City explosion followed a pattern of years of major accidents at the facility. In fact, there had apparently been an average of one employee death every 16 months at the plant for the last 30 years. The CSB found that the equipment directly involved in the most recent explosion was an obsolete design already phased out in most refineries and chemical plants, and that key pieces of its instrumentation were not working. There had also been previous instances where flammable vapors were released from the same unit in the 10 years prior to the explosion. In 2003, an external audit had referred to the Texas City refinery's infrastructure and assets as "poor" and found what it referred to as a "checkbook mentality," one in which budgets were not sufficient to manage all the risks. In particular, the CSB found that BP had implemented a 25% cut on fixed costs between 1998 and 2000 and that this adversely impacted maintenance expenditures and net expenditures, and refinery infrastructure. Going on, the CSB found that in 2004, there were three major accidents at the refinery that killed three workers.

BP's own internal report concluded that the problems at Texas City were not of recent origin, and instead were years in the making. It said BP was taking steps to address them. Its investigation found "no evidence of anyone consciously or intentionally taking actions or making decisions that put others at risk." Said BP's report, "The underlying reasons for the behaviors and actions displayed during the incident are complex, and the team has spent much time trying to understand them—it is evident that they were many years in the making and will require concerted and committed actions to address." BP's report concluded that there were five underlying causes for the massive explosion:

- A working environment had eroded to one characterized by resistance to change, and a lack of trust.
- Safety, performance, and risk reduction priorities had not been set and consistently reinforced by management.
- Changes in the "complex organization" led to a lack of clear accountabilities and poor communication.
- A poor level of hazard awareness and understanding of safety resulted in workers accepting levels of risk that were considerably higher than at comparable installations.
- Adequate early warning systems for problems were lacking, and there were no independent means of understanding the deteriorating standards at the plant.

*© Gary Dessler, PhD.

The report from the BP-initiated but independent 11-person panel chaired by former U.S. Secretary of State James Baker contained specific conclusions and recommendations. The Baker panel looked at BP's corporate safety oversight, the corporate safety culture, and the process safety management systems at BP at the Texas City plant as well as at BP's other refineries.

Basically, the Baker panel concluded that BP had not provided effective safety process leadership and had not established safety as a core value at the five refineries it looked at (including Texas City).

Like the CSB, the Baker panel found that BP had emphasized personal safety in recent years and had in fact improved personal safety performance, but had not emphasized the overall safety process, thereby mistakenly interpreting "improving personal injury rates as an indication of acceptable process safety performance at its U.S. refineries." In fact, the Baker panel went on, by focusing on these somewhat misleading improving personal injury rates, BP created a false sense of confidence that it was properly addressing process safety risks. It also found that the safety culture at Texas City did not have the positive, trusting, open environment that a proper safety culture required. The Baker panel's other findings included the following.

- BP did not always ensure that adequate resources were effectively allocated to support or sustain a high level of process safety performance.
- BP's refinery personnel are "overloaded" by corporate initiatives.
- Operators and maintenance personnel work high rates of overtime.
- BP tended to have a short-term focus and its decentralized management system and entrepreneurial culture delegated substantial discretion to refinery plant managers "without clearly defining process safety expectations, responsibilities, or accountabilities."
- There was no common, unifying process safety culture among the five refineries.
- The company's corporate safety management system did not make sure there was timely compliance with internal process safety standards and programs.
- BP's executive management either did not receive refinery-specific information that showed that process safety deficiencies existed at some of the plants, or did not effectively respond to any information it did receive.[1]
- These findings and the following suggestions are based on "BP Safety Report Finds Company's Process Safety Culture Ineffective," *Global Refining & Fuels Report*, January 17, 2007.

The Baker panel made several safety recommendations for BP, including the following.

1. The company's corporate management must provide leadership on process safety.
2. The company should establish a process safety management system that identifies, reduces, and manages the process safety risks of the refineries.
3. The company should make sure its employees have an appropriate level of process safety knowledge and expertise.
4. The company should involve "relevant stakeholders" in developing a positive, trusting, and open process safety culture at each refinery.
5. BP should clearly define expectations and strengthen accountability for process safety performance.
6. BP should better coordinate its process safety support for the refining line organization.
7. BP should develop an integrated set of leading and lagging performance indicators for effectively monitoring process safety performance.
8. BP should establish and implement an effective system to audit process safety performance.
9. The company's board should monitor the implementation of the panel's recommendations and the ongoing process safety performance of the refineries.
10. BP should transform itself into a recognized industry leader in process safety management.

In making its recommendations, the panel singled out the company's chief executive at the time, Lord Browne, by saying, "In hindsight, the panel believes if Browne had demonstrated comparable leadership on and commitment to process safety [as he did for responding to climate change] that would have resulted in a higher level of safety at refineries."

Overall, the Baker panel found that BP's top management had not provided "effective leadership" on safety. It found that the failings went to the very top of the organization, to the company's chief executive, and to several of his top lieutenants. The Baker panel emphasized the importance of top management commitment, saying, for instance, that "it is imperative that BP leadership set the process safety tone at the top of the organization and establish appropriate expectations regarding process safety performance." It also said BP "has not provided effective leadership in making certain its management and U.S. refining workforce understand what is expected of them regarding process safety performance."

Lord Browne, the chief executive, stepped down about a year after the explosion. About the same time, some BP shareholders were calling for the company's executives and board directors to have their bonuses more closely tied to the company's safety and environmental performance in the wake of Texas City. In October 2009, OSHA announced it was filing the largest fine in its history for this accident, for $87 million, against BP. One year later, BP's Horizon oil rig in the Gulf of Mexico exploded, taking 11 lives. In September 2014, the U.S. District judge presiding over negligence claims in the ensuing case found BP guilty of gross negligence, basically reckless and extreme behavior; the company will appeal his ruling.

Questions

22. The text defines ethics as "the principles of conduct governing an individual or a group," and specifically as the standards one uses to decide what his or her conduct should be. To what extent do you believe that what happened at BP is as much a breakdown in the company's ethical systems as it is in its safety systems, and how would you defend your conclusion?

23. Are the Occupational Safety and Health Administration's standards, policies, and rules aimed at addressing problems like the ones that apparently existed at the Texas City plant? If so, how would you explain the fact that problems like these could have continued for so many years?

24. Since there were apparently at least three deaths in the year prior to the major explosion, and an average of about one employee death per 16 months for the previous 10 years, how would you account for the fact that mandatory OSHA inspections missed these glaring sources of potential catastrophic events?

25. The text lists numerous suggestions for "how to prevent accidents." Based on what you know about the Texas City explosion, what do you say Texas City tells you about the most important three steps an employer can take to prevent accidents?

26. Based on what you learned in Chapter 14, would you make any additional recommendations to BP over and above those recommendations made by the Baker panel and the CSB? If so, what would those recommendations be?

27. Explain specifically how strategic human resource management at BP seems to have supported the company's broader strategic aims. What does this say about the advisability of always linking human resource strategy to a company's strategic aims?

Source: Notes for BP Texas City: Sheila McNulty, "BP Knew of Safety Problems, Says Report," *Financial Times*, October 31, 2006, p. 1 "CBS: Documents Show BP Was Aware of Texas City Safety Problems," *World Refining & Fuels Today*, October 30, 2006; "BP Safety Report Finds Company's Process Safety Culture Ineffective," *Global Refining & Fuels Report*, January 17, 2007; "BP Safety Record Under Attack," *Europe Intelligence Wire*, January 17, 2007; Mark Hofmann, "BP Slammed for Poor Leadership on Safety, Oil Firm Agrees to Act on Review Panel's Recommendations," *Business Intelligence*, January 22, 2007, p. 3 "Call for Bonuses to Include Link with Safety Performance," *Guardian*, January 18, 2007, p. 24 www.bp.com/genericarticle.do?categoryId=9005029&contentId=7015905, accessed July 12, 2009; Steven Greenhouse, "BP Faces Record Fine for '05 Blast," *New York Times*, October 30, 2009, pp. 1, 6; Kyle W. Morrison, "Blame to Go Around," *Safety & Health*, 183, no. 3, March 2011, p. 40 Ed Crooks, "BP Had Tools to End Spill Sooner, Court Told," www.ft.com/cms/s/0/40d7b076-2ae8-11e3-8fb8-00144feab7de.html?ftcamp=published_links%2Frss%2Fhome_uk%2Ffeed%2F%2Fproduct#axzz2gZshHFOc, accessed October 2, 2013; Daniel Gilbert and Justin Scheck, "Judge Hammers BP for Gulf Disaster", *The Wall Street Journal*, September 5, 2014, pp. B1, B2.

Glossary

360-degree feedback The employer collects performance information all around an employee—from his or her supervisors, subordinates, peers, and internal or external customers.

401(k) plan A defined contribution plan based on section 401(k) of the Internal Revenue Code.

9-box matrix In workforce planning, this displays three levels of current job performance (exceptional, fully performing, not yet fully performing) across the top, and also shows three levels of likely potential (eligible for promotion, room for growth in current position, not likely to grow beyond current position) down the side.

action learning A training technique by which management trainees are allowed to work full-time analyzing and solving problems in other departments.

adverse impact The overall impact of employer practices that result in significantly higher percentages of members of minorities and other protected groups being rejected for employment, placement, or promotion.

affirmative action Making an extra effort to hire and promote those in protected groups, particularly when those groups are underrepresented.

Age Discrimination in Employment Act (ADEA) of 1967 The act prohibiting arbitrary age discrimination and specifically protecting individuals over 40 years old.

agency shop A form of union security in which employees who do not belong to the union must still pay union dues on the assumption that union efforts benefit all workers.

alternative staffing The use of nontraditional recruitment sources.

Americans with Disabilities Act (ADA) The act requiring employers to make reasonable accommodations for disabled employees; it prohibits discrimination against disabled persons.

annual bonus Plans that are designed to motivate short-term performance of managers and which are tied to company profitability.

applicant tracking systems Online systems that help employers attract, gather, screen, compile, and manage applicants.

application form A form used by employers to compile information regarding an applicant's identity and educational, military, and work history.

apprenticeship training A structured process by which people become skilled workers through a combination of classroom instruction and on-the-job training.

arbitration The most definitive type of third-party intervention, in which the arbitrator often has the power to determine and dictate the settlement terms.

authority The right to make decisions, direct others' work, and give orders.

authorization cards In order to petition for a union election, the union must show that at least 30% of employees may be interested in being unionized. Employees indicate this interest by signing authorization cards.

bargaining unit The group of employees the union will be authorized to represent.

behavior modeling A training technique in which trainees are first shown good management techniques in a film, are asked to play roles in a simulated situation, and are then given feedback and praise by their supervisor.

benchmark job A job that is used to anchor the employer's pay scale and around which other jobs are arranged in order of relative worth.

benefits Indirect financial and nonfinancial payments employees receive for continuing their employment with the company.

bona fide occupational qualification (BFOQ) Requirement that an employee be of a certain religion, sex, or national origin where that is reasonably necessary to the organization's normal operation. Specified by the 1964 Civil Rights Act.

boycott The combined refusal by employees and other interested parties to buy or use the employer's products.

broadbanding Consolidating salary grades and ranges into just a few wide levels or "bands," each of which contains a relatively wide range of jobs and salary levels.

burnout The total depletion of physical and mental resources caused by excessive striving to reach an unrealistic work-related goal.

business necessity Justification for an otherwise discriminatory employment practice, provided there is an overriding legitimate business purpose.

business process reengineering Redesigning business processes, usually by combining steps, so that small multifunction process teams using information technology do the jobs formerly done by a sequence of departments.

career The occupational positions a person has had over many years.

career development The lifelong series of activities that contribute to a person's career exploration, establishment, success, and fulfillment.

career management The process for enabling employees to better understand and develop their career skills and interests, and to use these skills and interests more effectively.

career planning The deliberate process through which someone becomes aware of personal skills, interests, knowledge, motivations, and other characteristics and establishes action plans to attain specific goals.

case study method A development method in which the manager is presented with a written description of an organizational problem to diagnose and solve.

cash balance plans Defined benefit plans under which the employer contributes a percentage of employees' current pay to employees' pension plans every year, and employees earn interest on this amount.

citations Summons informing employers and employees of the regulations and standards that have been violated in the workplace.

Civil Rights Act of 1991 (CRA 1991) The act that places burden of proof back on employers and permits compensatory and punitive damages.

classes Grouping jobs based on a set of rules for each group or class, such as amount of independent judgment, skill, physical effort, and so forth, required. Classes usually contain similar jobs.

closed shop A form of union security in which the company can hire only union members. This was outlawed in 1947 for interstate commerce, but still exists in some industries (such as printing).

coaching Educating, instructing, and training subordinates.

codetermination Employees have the legal right to a voice in setting company policies. Workers elect their own representatives to the supervisory board of the employer.

collective bargaining The process through which representatives of management and the union meet to negotiate a labor agreement.

college recruiting Sending an employer's representatives to college campuses to prescreen applicants and create an applicant pool from the graduating class.

comparable worth The concept by which women who are usually paid less than men can claim that men in comparable rather than in strictly equal jobs are paid more.

compa ratio Equals an employee's pay rate divided by the pay range midpoint for his or her pay grade.

compensable factor A fundamental, compensable element of a job, such as skills, effort, responsibility, and working conditions.

competency-based job analysis Describing the job in terms of measurable, observable, behavioral competencies (knowledge, skills, and/or behaviors) that an employee doing that job must exhibit to do the job well.

competency-based pay Where the company pays for the employee's range, depth, and types of skills and knowledge, rather than for the job title he or she holds.

competency model A graphic model that consolidates in one diagram a precise overview of the competencies (the knowledge, skills, and behaviors) someone would need to do a job well.

competitive advantage Any factors that allow an organization to differentiate its product or service from those of its competitors to increase market share.

competitive strategy A strategy that identifies how to build and strengthen the business's long-term competitive position in the marketplace.

compressed workweek Schedule in which employee works fewer but longer days each week.

construct validity A test that is *construct valid* is one that demonstrates that a selection procedure measures a construct and that construct is important for successful job performance.

content validity A test that is *content valid* is one in which the test contains a fair sample of the tasks and skills actually needed for the job in question.

controlled experimentation Formal methods for testing the effectiveness of a training program, preferably with before-and-after tests and a control group.

corporate-level strategy Type of strategy that identifies the portfolio of businesses that, in total, comprise the company and the ways in which these businesses relate to each other.

criterion validity A type of validity based on showing that scores on the test (*predictors*) are related to job performance (*criterion*).

cross training Training employees to do different tasks or jobs than their own; doing so facilitates flexibility and job rotation.

Davis-Bacon Act (1931) A law that sets wage rates for laborers employed by contractors working for the federal government.

decertification In labor law, the process that enables employees to terminate legally (decertify) their union's right to represent them.

defined benefit pension plan A plan that contains a formula for determining retirement benefits.

defined contribution pension plan A plan in which the employer's contribution to employees' retirement savings funds is specified.

diary/log Daily listings made by workers of every activity in which they engage along with the time each activity takes.

digital dashboard Presents the manager with desktop graphs and charts, and so a computerized picture of where the company stands on all those metrics from the HR Scorecard process.

direct financial payments Pay in the form of wages, salaries, incentives, commissions, and bonuses.

discrimination Taking specific actions toward or against the person based on the person's group.

dismissal Involuntary termination of an employee's employment with the firm.

disparate impact An unintentional disparity between the proportion of a protected group applying for a position and the proportion getting the job.

disparate treatment An intentional disparity between the proportion of a protected group and the proportion getting the job.

distributive justice Refers to a system of distributing rewards and discipline in which the actual results or outcomes are evenhanded and fair.

diversity Having a workforce comprising two or more groups of employees with various racial, ethnic, gender, cultural, national origin, handicap, age, and religious backgrounds.

downsizing Refers to the process of reducing, usually dramatically, the number of people employed by the firm.

early retirement window A type of offering by which employees are encouraged to retire early, the incentive being liberal pension benefits plus perhaps a cash payment.

earnings-at-risk pay plan Plan that puts some portion of employees' normal pay at risk if they don't meet their goals, in return for possibly obtaining a much larger bonus if they exceed their goals.

economic strike A strike that results from a failure to agree on the terms of a contract that involve wages, benefits, and other conditions of employment.

Electronic Communications Privacy Act (ECPA) The ECPA is a federal law intended to help restrict interception and monitoring of oral and wire communications.

electronic performance support systems (EPSS) Sets of computerized tools and displays that automate training, documentation, and phone support; integrate this automation into applications; and provide support that's faster, cheaper, and more effective than traditional methods.

employee assistance program (EAP) A formal employer program for providing employees with counseling and/or treatment programs for problems such as alcoholism, gambling, or stress.

employee compensation All forms of pay or rewards going to employees and arising from their employment.

employee orientation A procedure for providing new employees with basic background information about the firm.

employee recruiting Finding and/or attracting applicants for the employer's open positions.

employee relations The activity that involves establishing and maintaining the positive employee–employer relationships that contribute to satisfactory productivity, motivation, morale, and discipline and to maintaining a positive, productive, and cohesive work environment.

Employee Retirement Income Security Act (ERISA) of 1975 Signed into law by President Ford in 1974 to require that pension rights be vested and protected by a government agency, the PBGC.

Employee Retirement Income Security Act (ERISA) The law that provides government protection of pensions for all employees with company pension plans. It also regulates vesting rights (employees who leave before retirement may claim compensation from the pension plan).

employee stock ownership plan (ESOP) A qualified, tax deductible stock bonus plan in which employers contribute stock to a trust for eventual use by employees.

employment engagement The extent to which an organization's employees are psychologically involved in, connected to, and committed to getting one's jobs done.

Equal Employment Opportunity Commission (EEOC) The commission, created by Title VII, empowered to investigate job discrimination complaints and sue on behalf of complainants.

Equal Pay Act (1963) An amendment to the Fair Labor Standards Act designed to require equal pay for women doing the same work as men.

Equal Pay Act of 1963 The act requiring equal pay for equal work, regardless of sex.

ethics The principles of conduct governing an individual or a group; specifically, the standards you use to decide what your conduct should be.

ethics The study of standards of conduct and moral judgment; also the standards of right conduct.

ethnocentric A management philosophy that leads to the creation of home market–oriented staffing decisions.

executive coach An outside consultant who questions the executive's associates to identify the executive's strengths and weaknesses, and then counsels the executive so he or she can capitalize on those strengths and overcome the weaknesses.

exit interviews Interviews conducted by the employer immediately prior to the employee leaving the firm with the aim of better understanding what the employee thinks about the company.

expatriates Employees a company posts abroad, and who are noncitizens of the country in which they are working.

fact-finder In labor relations, a neutral party who studies the issues in a dispute and makes a public recommendation for a reasonable settlement.

Fair Labor Standards Act (FLSA; 1938) This act provides for minimum wages, maximum hours, overtime pay, and child labor protection. The law, amended many times, covers most employees.

fair treatment Reflects concrete actions, such as "employees are treated with respect," and "employees are treated fairly."

family-friendly (or work–life) benefits Benefits such as child care and fitness facilities that make it easier for employees to balance their work and family responsibilities.

financial incentives Financial rewards paid to workers whose production exceeds some predetermined standard.

flexible benefits plan/cafeteria benefits plan Individualized plans allowed by employers to accommodate employee preferences for benefits.

flextime A plan whereby employees' workdays are built around a core of mid-day hours, such as 11:00 a.m. to 2:00 p.m.

functional strategy A department's functional strategy identifies what the department must do in terms of specific departmental policies and practices to help the business accomplish its competitive goals.

gainsharing plan An incentive plan that engages employees in a common effort to achieve productivity objectives and share the gains.

gender-role stereotypes The tendency to associate women with certain (frequently nonmanagerial) jobs.

geocentric A staffing policy that seeks the best people for key jobs throughout the organization, regardless of nationality.

gig workers The large and growing workforce comprised of contract, temp, freelance, independent contractor, "on-demand," or simply "gig" workers.

golden parachute A payment companies make in connection with a change in ownership or control of a company.

good-faith bargaining A term that means both parties are communicating and negotiating and that proposals are being matched with counterproposals, with both parties making every reasonable effort to arrive at agreements. It does not mean that either party is compelled to agree to a proposal.

grade definition Written descriptions of the level of, say, responsibility and knowledge required by jobs in each grade. Similar jobs can then be combined into grades or classes.

grades A job classification system like the class system, although grades often contain dissimilar jobs, such as secretaries, mechanics, and firefighters. Grade descriptions are written based on compensable factors listed in classification systems.

graphic rating scale The graphic rating scale is a performance appraisal tool that lists several *job dimensions* and a range of performance values for each. The supervisor rates each subordinate by circling or checking the score that best describes the subordinate's performance for each trait or dimension.

Griggs v. Duke Power Company Supreme Court case in which the plaintiff argued that his employer's requirement that coal handlers be high school graduates was unfairly discriminatory. In finding for the plaintiff, the Court ruled that discrimination need not be overt to be illegal, that employment practices must be related to job performance, and that the burden of proof is on the employer to show that hiring standards are job related.

group life insurance Provides lower rates for the employer or employee and includes all employees, including new employees, regardless of health or physical condition.

health maintenance organization (HMO) A prepaid health care system that generally provides routine round-the-clock medical services as well as preventive medicine in a clinic-type arrangement for employees, who pay a nominal fee in addition to the fixed annual fee the employer pays.

high-performance work system A set of human resource management policies and practices that promote organizational effectiveness.

home-country nationals Citizens of the country in which the multinational company has its headquarters.

HR audit An analysis by which an organization measures where it currently stands and determines what it has to accomplish to improve its HR function.

HR scorecard A process for assigning financial and non-financial goals or metrics to the human resource management-related chain of activities required for achieving the company's strategic aims and for monitoring results.

human resource management (HRM) The process of acquiring, training, appraising, and compensating employees, and of attending to their labor relations, health and safety, and fairness concerns.

human resource metric The quantitative gauge of a human resource management activity such as employee turnover, hours of training per employee, or qualified applicants per position.

illegal bargaining items Items in collective bargaining that are forbidden by law; for example, the clause agreeing to hire "union members exclusively" would be illegal in a right-to-work state.

in-house development center A company-based method for exposing prospective managers to realistic exercises to develop improved management skills.

indirect financial payments Pay in the form of financial benefits such as insurance.

insubordination Willful disregard or disobedience of the boss's authority or legitimate orders.

interest inventories Tests that compare one's interests with those of people in various occupations.

international human resource management (IHRM) The human resource management concepts and techniques employers use to manage the human resource challenges of their international operations.

interview A procedure designed to solicit information from a person's oral responses to oral inquiries.

job aid A set of instructions, diagrams, or similar methods available at the job site to guide the worker.

job analysis The procedure for determining the duties and skill requirements of a job and the kind of person who should be hired for it.

job classification (or grading) method A method for categorizing jobs into groups.

job descriptions A list of a job's duties, responsibilities, reporting relationships, working conditions, and supervisory responsibilities—one product of a job analysis.

job enlargement Assigning workers additional same-level activities.

job enrichment Redesigning jobs in a way that increases the opportunities for the worker to experience feelings of responsibility, achievement, growth, and recognition.

job evaluation A systematic comparison done to determine the worth of one job relative to another.

job hazard analysis A systematic approach to identifying and eliminating hazards before they occur, and focuses on the relationship between the worker, the task, the tools, and the work environment and ends by reducing the potential risks to acceptable levels.

job instruction training (JIT) Listing each job's basic tasks, along with key points, to provide step-by-step training for employees.

job posting Publicizing an open job to employees (often by literally posting it on bulletin boards) and listing its attributes, like qualifications, supervisor, working schedule, and pay rate.

job-requirements matrix A more complete description of what the worker does and how and why he or she does it; it clarifies each task's purpose and each duty's required knowledge, skills, abilities, and other characteristics.

job rotation A management training technique that involves moving a trainee from department to department to broaden his or her experience and to identify strong and weak points.

job rotation Systematically moving workers from one job to another.

job sharing Allows two or more people to share a single full-time job.

job specifications A list of a job's "human requirements," that is, the requisite education, skills, personality, and so on—another product of a job analysis.

Landrum-Griffin Act A law aimed at protecting union members from possible wrongdoing on the part of their unions.

layoff A situation in which employees are told there is no work for them but that management intends to recall them when work is again available.

lifelong learning Provides employees with continuing learning experiences over their tenure with the firm, with the aims of ensuring they have the opportunity to learn the skills they need to do their jobs and to expand their occupational horizons.

line manager A manager who is authorized to direct the work of subordinates and is responsible for accomplishing the organization's tasks.

locals Employees who work for the company abroad and are citizens of the countries where they are working, also known as "host-country nationals."

lockout A refusal by the employer to provide opportunities to work.

maintenance of membership arrangement Employees do not have to belong to the union. However, union members employed by the firm must maintain membership in the union for the contract period.

management assessment center A facility in which management candidates are asked to make decisions in hypothetical situations and are scored on their performance.

management development Any attempt to improve current or future management performance by imparting knowledge, changing attitudes, or increasing skills.

management games A development technique in which teams of managers compete by making computerized decisions regarding realistic but simulated situations.

management process The five basic functions of planning, organizing, staffing, leading, and controlling.

manager Someone who is responsible for accomplishing the organization's goals, and who does so by managing the efforts of the organization's people.

managing To perform five basic functions: planning, organizing, staffing, leading, and controlling.

mandatory bargaining items Items in collective bargaining that a party must bargain over if they are introduced by the other party—for example, pay.

market-competitive pay plan A pay system in which the employer's actual pay rates are competitive with those in the relevant labor market.

mediation Labor relations intervention in which a neutral third party tries to assist the principals in reaching agreement.

mentoring Advising, counseling, and guiding.

merit pay (merit raise) Any salary increase awarded to an employee based on his or her individual performance.

miniature job training and evaluation A selection procedure in which the employer trains candidates to perform a sample of the job's tasks, and then evaluates their performance.

mission statement Summarizes what the company's main tasks are today.

national emergency strikes Strikes that might "imperil the national health and safety."

National Labor Relations Board (NLRB) The agency created by the Wagner Act to investigate unfair labor practice charges and to provide for secret-ballot elections and majority rule in determining whether or not a firm's employees want a union.

negligent hiring Hiring workers with criminal records or other such problems without proper safeguards.

Norris-LaGuardia Act This law marked the beginning of the era of strong encouragement of unions and guaranteed to each employee the right to bargain collectively "free from interference, restraint, or coercion."

Occupational Safety and Health Act of 1970 The law passed by Congress in 1970 "to assure so far as possible every working man and woman in the nation safe and healthful working conditions and to preserve our human resources."

Occupational Safety and Health Administration (OSHA) The agency created within the Department of Labor to set safety and health standards for almost all workers in the United States.

Office of Federal Contract Compliance Programs (OFCCP) The office responsible for implementing the executive orders and ensuring compliance of federal contractors.

on-demand recruiting services (ODRS) Services that provide short-term specialized recruiting to support specific projects without the expense of retaining traditional search firms.

on-the-job training (OJT) Training a person to learn a job while working on it.

operational safety reviews Reviews conducted by agencies to ascertain whether units under their jurisdiction are complying with all the applicable safety laws, regulations, orders, and rules.

organization A group consisting of people with formally assigned roles who work together to achieve the organization's goals.

organizational climate The perceptions a company's employees share about the firm's psychological environment, for instance in terms of things like concern for employees' well-being, supervisory behavior, flexibility, appreciation, ethics, empowerment, political behaviors, and rewards.

organizational culture The characteristic values, traditions, and behaviors a company's employees share.

organizational development A special approach to organizational change in which employees themselves formulate and implement the change that's required.

organization chart A chart that shows the organization-wide distribution of work, with titles of each position and interconnecting lines that show who reports to and communicates with whom.

organizationwide incentive plan Plans in which all or most employees can participate, and that generally tie the reward to some measure of companywide performance.

outplacement counseling A systematic process by which a terminated person is trained and counseled in the techniques of self-appraisal and securing a new position.

pay (or rate) ranges A series of steps or levels within a pay grade, usually based on years of service.

pay (or wage) grade A pay grade is comprised of jobs of approximately equal difficulty.

Pension Benefits Guarantee Corporation (PBGC) Established under ERISA to ensure that pensions meet vesting obligations; also insures pensions should a plan terminate without sufficient funds to meet its vested obligations.

pension plans Plans that provide a fixed sum when employees reach a predetermined retirement age or when they can no longer work due to disability.

performance analysis Verifying that there is a performance deficiency and determining whether that deficiency should be corrected through training or through some other means (such as transferring the employee).

performance appraisal Any procedure that involves (1) setting work standards; (2) assessing the employee's actual performance relative to the standards; and (3) providing feedback to the employee with the aim of motivating that person to eliminate performance deficiencies or to continue the performance above par.

performance management The *continuous* process of identifying, measuring, and developing the performance of individuals and teams and *aligning* their performance with the organization's *goals*.

personnel replacement charts Company records showing present performance and promotability of inside candidates for the most important positions.

piecework A system of pay based on the number of items processed by each individual worker in a unit of time, such as items per hour or items per day.

point method The job evaluation method in which a number of compensable factors are identified and then the degree to which each of these factors is present on the job is determined.

polycentric A management philosophy -oriented toward staffing positions with local talent.

portability Making it easier for employees who leave the firm prior to retirement to take their accumulated pension funds with them.

portfolio careers A career built around using one's skills to create a livelihood based on multiple income sources.

position analysis questionnaire (PAQ) A questionnaire used to collect quantifiable data concerning the duties and responsibilities of various jobs.

position replacement card A card prepared for each position in a company to show possible replacement candidates and their qualifications.

preferential shop Union members get preference in hiring, but the employer can still hire nonunion members.

preferred provider organizations (PPOs) Groups of health care providers that contract with employers, insurance companies, or third-party payers to provide medical care services at a reduced fee.

Pregnancy Discrimination Act (PDA) An amendment to Title VII of the Civil Rights Act that prohibits sex discrimination based on "pregnancy, childbirth, or related medical conditions."

problem-solving teams Teams that identify and research work processes and develop solutions to work-related problems.

procedural justice Refers to just procedures in the allocation of rewards or discipline, in terms of the actual procedures being evenhanded and fair.

process chart A workflow chart that shows the flow of inputs to and outputs from a particular job.

productivity The ratio of outputs (goods and services) divided by the inputs (resources such as labor and capital).

profit-sharing plan A plan whereby employees share in the company's profits.

programmed learning A systematic method for teaching job skills, involving presenting questions or facts, allowing the person to respond, and giving the learner immediate feedback on the accuracy of his or her answers.

protected class Persons such as minorities and women protected by equal opportunity laws, including Title VII.

quality circle A special type of formal problem-solving team, usually composed of 6 to 12 specially trained employees who meet once a week to solve problems affecting their work area.

ranking method The simplest method of job evaluation that involves ranking each job relative to all other jobs, usually based on overall difficulty.

ratio analysis A forecasting technique for determining future staff needs by using ratios between, for example, sales volume and number of employees needed.

reality shock Results of a period that may occur at the initial career entry when the new employee's high job expectations confront the reality of a boring or otherwise unattractive work situation.

recruiting yield pyramid The historical arithmetic relationships between recruitment leads and invitees, invitees and interviews, interviews and offers made, and offers made and offers accepted.

reliability The characteristic that refers to the consistency of scores obtained by the same person when retested with the identical or equivalent tests.

reverse discrimination Discriminating against *non*minority applicants and employees.

right to work The public policy in a number of states that prohibits union security of any kind.

role-playing A training technique in which trainees act out parts in a realistic management situation.

safety awareness program Program that enables trained supervisors to orient new workers arriving at a job site regarding common safety hazards and simple prevention methods.

salary survey A survey aimed at determining prevailing wage rates. A good salary survey provides specific wage rates for specific jobs. Formal written questionnaire surveys are the most comprehensive, but telephone surveys and Internet and newspaper help-wanted ads are also sources of information.

savings and thrift plan Plan in which employees contribute a portion of their earnings to a fund; the employer usually matches this contribution in whole or in part.

scatter plot A graphical method used to help identify the relationship between two variables.

self-managing/self-directed work team A small (usually 8 to 10 members) group of carefully selected, trained, and empowered employees who basically run themselves with little or no outside supervision, usually for the purpose of accomplishing a specific task or mission.

severance pay A one-time payment some employers provide when terminating an employee.

sexual harassment Harassment on the basis of sex that has the purpose or effect of substantially interfering with a person's work performance or creating an intimidating, hostile, or offensive work environment.

sick leave Provides pay to an employee when he or she is out of work because of illness.

social responsibility Refers to the extent to which companies should and do channel resources toward improving one or more segments of society other than the firm's owners or stockholders.

Social Security Federal program that provides three types of benefits: retirement income at the age of 62 and thereafter; survivor's or death benefits payable to the employee's dependents regardless of age at time of death; and disability benefits payable to disabled employees and their dependents. These benefits are payable only if the employee is insured under the Social Security Act.

staff manager A manager who assists and advises line managers.

standard hour plan A plan by which a worker is paid a basic hourly rate but is paid an extra percentage of his or her rate for production exceeding the standard per hour or per day. Similar to piecework payment but based on a percent premium.

Standard Occupational Classification (SOC) Classifies all workers into one of 23 major groups of jobs that are subdivided into minor groups of jobs and detailed occupations.

stock option The right to purchase a stated number of shares of a company stock at today's price at some time in the future.

straight piecework An incentive plan in which a person is paid a sum for each item he or she makes or sells, with a strict proportionality between results and rewards.

strategic human resource management Formulating and executing human resource policies and practices that produce the employee competencies and behaviors the company needs to achieve its strategic aims.

strategic management The process of identifying and executing the organization's strategic plan, by matching the company's capabilities with the demands of its environment.

strategic plan The company's plan for how it will match its internal strengths and weaknesses with its external opportunities and threats to maintain a competitive position.

strategy A course of action the company can pursue to achieve its strategic aims.

strategy map A strategic planning tool that shows the "big picture" of how each department's performance contributes to achieving the company's overall strategic goals.

strategy-based metrics Metrics that specifically focus on measuring the activities that contribute to achieving a company's strategic aims.

structured situational interview A series of job-relevant questions with predetermined answers that interviewers ask of all applicants for the job.

succession planning The ongoing process of systematically identifying, assessing, and developing organizational leadership to enhance performance.

suggestion teams Temporary teams whose members work on specific analytical assignments, such as how to cut costs or raise productivity.

supplemental pay benefits Benefits for time not worked such as unemployment insurance, vacation and holiday pay, and sick pay.

supplemental unemployment benefits Provide for a "guaranteed annual income" in certain industries where employers must shut down to change machinery or due to reduced work. These benefits are paid by the company and supplement unemployment benefits.

sympathy strike A strike that takes place when one union strikes in support of another's strike.

Taft-Hartley Act A law prohibiting union unfair labor practices and enumerating the rights of employees as union members. It also enumerates the rights of employers.

talent analytics Using new number-crunching software to dig through ("mine") existing employee data to better identify what types of people succeed or fail, and therefore whom to hire.

talent management The holistic, integrated and results and goal-oriented process of planning, recruiting, selecting, developing, managing, and compensating employees.

task analysis A detailed study of a job to identify the specific skills required.

task statement Written item that shows what the worker does on one particular job task; how the worker does it; the knowledge, skills, and aptitudes required to do it; and the purpose of the task.

team- (or group-) incentive plan A plan in which a production standard is set for a specific work group, and its members are paid incentives if the group exceeds the production standard.

terminate at will The idea, based in law, that the employment relationship can be terminated at will by either the employer or the employee for any reason.

termination interview The interview in which an employee is informed of the fact that he or she has been dismissed.

test validity The accuracy with which a test, interview, and so on measures what it purports to measure or fulfills the function it was designed to fill.

third-country nationals Citizens of a country other than the parent or host country.

Title VII of the 1964 Civil Rights Act The section of the act that says an employer cannot discriminate on the basis of race, color, religion, sex, or national origin with respect to employment.

Title VII of the 1964 Civil Rights Act This act makes it unlawful for employers to discriminate against any individual with respect to hiring, compensation, terms, conditions, or privileges of employment because of race, color, religion, sex, or national origin.

training The process of teaching new or current employees the basic skills they need to perform their jobs.

transfer Reassignments to similar positions in other parts of the firm.

trend analysis Study of a firm's past employment needs over a period of years to predict future needs.

unemployment insurance (or compensation) Provides benefits if a person is unable to work through some fault other than his or her own.

unfair labor practice strike A strike aimed at protesting illegal conduct by the employer.

union salting A union organizing tactic by which workers who are employed by a union as undercover union organizers are hired by unwitting employers.

union shop A form of union security in which the company can hire nonunion people but they must join the union after a prescribed period of time and pay dues. (If they do not, they can be fired.)

utility analysis The degree to which use of a selection measure improves the quality of individuals selected over what would have happened if the measure had not been used.

validity generalization The degree to which evidence of a measure's validity obtained in one situation can be generalized to another situation without further study.

variable pay Any plan that ties pay to productivity or profitability, usually as one-time lump payments.

virtual classroom Teaching method that uses special collaboration software to enable multiple remote learners, using their PCs or laptops, to participate in live audio and visual discussions, communicate via written text, and learn via content such as PowerPoint slides.

virtual transnational teams Groups of geographically dispersed coworkers who interact using a combination of telecommunications and information technologies to accomplish an organizational task.

vision statement A general statement of the firm's intended direction that shows, in broad terms, "what we want to become."

Vocational Rehabilitation Act of 1973 The act requiring certain federal contractors to take affirmative action for disabled persons.

voluntary (permissible) bargaining items Items in collective bargaining for which bargaining is neither illegal nor mandatory—neither party can be compelled to negotiate over those items.

wage curve Shows the relationship between the value of the job and the average wage paid for this job.

Wagner Act A law that banned certain types of unfair labor practices and provided for secret-ballot elections and majority rule for determining whether or not a firm's employees want to unionize.

Walsh-Healey Public Contract Act (1936) A law that requires minimum wage and working conditions for employees working on any government contract amounting to more than $10,000.

Web 2.0 learning Learning that utilizes online technologies such as social networks, virtual worlds (such as Second Life), and systems that blend synchronous and asynchronous delivery with blogs, chat rooms, bookmark sharing, and tools such as 3-D simulations.

wildcat strike An unauthorized strike occurring during the term of a contract.

work sharing Refers to a temporary reduction in work hours by a group of employees during economic downturns as a way to prevent layoffs.

workaholic People who feel driven to always be on time and meet deadlines and so normally place themselves under greater stress than do others.

workers' compensation Provides income and medical benefits to work-related accident victims or their dependents regardless of fault.

workflow analysis A detailed study of the flow of work from job to job in a work process.

workforce (or employment or personnel) planning The process of deciding what positions the firm will have to fill, and how to fill them.

workplace flexibility Arming employees with the information technology tools they need to get their jobs done wherever they are.

wrongful discharge An employee dismissal that does not comply with the law or does not comply with the contractual arrangement stated or implied by the firm via its employment application forms, employee manuals, or other promises.

REFERENCES

Chapter 1

1 For some insights into TJX managers' training and responsibilities, see for example, http://www.tjx.com/responsibility/our-workplace/career-development.html, https://www.indeed.com/job/tj-maxxmarshalls-store-leadership-pathway-san-diego-ca-a35deb81991a78eb, and http://www.tjx.com/responsibility/our-workplace/recruitment.html, all accessed April 30, 2017.

2 See, as just one example, Seongmin Ryu and Sunghoon Kim, "First-Line Managers' Involvement and HR Effectiveness: The Case of South Korea," *Human Resource Management*, November–December 2013, 52, no. 6, pp. 947–966.

3 Fred K. Foulkes, "The Expanding Role of the Personnel Function," *Harvard Business Review*, March–April 1975. See also www.bls.gov/oco/ocos021.htm, accessed October 3, 2011.

4 HR professionals also, for instance, track metrics (such as productivity data), document performance issues of marginal employees, and evaluate training programs to ascertain their value to the firm. Tamara Lytle, "Be Prepared: Recessions Are Inevitable," *HR Magazine*, pages 60–64, March 2017.

5 Steve Bates, "No Experience Necessary? Many Companies Are Putting Non-HR Executives in Charge of HR with Mixed Results," *HR Magazine*, 46, no. 11 (November 2001), pp. 34-41. See also Adrienne Fox, "Do Assignments outside HR Pay Off?" *HR Magazine*, November 2011, p. 32. One study concluded that the best path to the CEO's office involves getting experience in as many of the business's functions as possible. Neil Irwin, "A Winding Path to the Top," *The New York Times*, September 11, 2016, pp. B1, B4.

6 "Why Chief Human Resources Officers Make Great CEOs," *Harvard Business Review*, December 2014, p. 31.

7 "A Profile of Human Resource Executives," *BNA Bulletin to Management*, June 21, 2001, p. S5; "Today's HR Executives: How Career Paths Have Changed—and Stayed the Same," http://knowledge.wharton.upenn.edu/article/todays-hr-executives-how-career-paths-have-changed-and-stayed-the-same/, accessed July 25, 2014.

8 Historically, most US employees worked for employers with fewer than 100 workers. However, around 2005 that changed. Today, more employees work for larger employers (2,500 or more) than for small ones. Theo Francis, "Why You Work for Giant Company," *The Wall Street Journal*, April 7, 2017, p. A-10.

9 See, for example, https://www.bls.gov/bdm/entrepreneurship/entrepreneurship.htm, accessed April 17, 2017.

10 "Human Resource Activities, Budgets & Staffs, 1999–2000," *BNA Bulletin to Management*, 51, no. 25, June 29, 2000, pp. S1–S6. Also see for example, Rick Suttle, "Major Categories of HR Management Activities," http://smallbusiness.chron.com/seven-major-categories-hr-management-activities-37354.html; "Line Manager Involvement in HRM: An Inside View," https://www.researchgate.net/publication/241902483_Line_Manager_Involvement_in_HRM_An_Inside_View; Juan López-Cotarelo, "HR Discretion: Understanding Line Managers' Role in Human Resource Management," https://www2.warwick.ac.uk/fac/soc/wbs/research/irru/publications/recentconf/juan_-_edw_-_lest.pdf; Jurgita Šiugžzdinien, "Line Manager Involvement in Human Resource Development," VIEŠOJI POLITIKA IR ADMINISTRAVIMAS, November 25, 2008, https://www.mruni.eu/upload/iblock/ce7/4_j.siugzdiniene.pdf, all accessed April 17, 2017.

11 For another perspective on this see, for example, Chris Brewster, Michael Brooks, and Paul Gollan, "The Institutional Antecedents of the Assignment of HRM Responsibilities to Line Managers," *Human Resource Management*, July–August 2015, 54 no. 4, pp. 57–597.

12 According to *Workforce* magazine, the five companies with the best human resource management functions include (from first to fifth) American Express Inc., Google Inc., Accenture, USAA, and AT&T Inc. "Workforce 100," 2016, *Workforce*, June 2016, pp. 24–29.

13 Some firms have recently worked on eliminating their traditional human resource departments, with generally mixed results. See, for example, Todd Henneman, "Is HR at Its Breaking Point?" *Workforce Management*, March 22, 2013, pp. 29–33.

14 "Technology to Play Role in Updating HR Delivery Services, Report Finds," *Bloomberg BNA Bulletin to Management*, September 4, 2012, p. 281. See also Meg McSherry Breslin, "Strategic Move? Report Examines Future of HR," *Workforce Management*, November 2012, p. 14.

15 www.bls.gov/news.release/ecopro.t01.htm, accessed July 29, 2012.

16 "Percent Growth in Labor Force, Projected 1990–2020," www.bls.gov/news.release/ecopro.t01.htm, accessed July 29, 2012.

17 "Talent Management Leads in Top HR Concerns," *Compensation & Benefits Review*, May/June 2007, p. 12; www.bls.gov/news.release/ecopro.t01.htm, accessed May 12, 2015.

18 https://insight.kellogg.northwestern.edu/article/how-to-revamp-the-visa-program-for-highly-skilled-workers, accessed April 16, 2017.

19 http://www.latimes.com/business/technology/la-fi-tn-silicon-valley-h1b-changes-20170404-story.html, accessed April 16, 2017.

20 Jane Perlez, "Coddled Recruits Are Hindering China's Army," *The New York Times*, February 18, 2015, p. 85.

21 Lindsay Gellman, "Bosses Try to Decode Millennials," *The Wall Street Journal*, May 18, 2016, pp. B1, B7.

22 CNBC, "For a Workplace Productivity Boost, Ban These 10 Websites, http://www.cnbc.com/2016/08/06/for-a-workplace-productivity-boost-ban-these-10-websites.html?slide=1, accessed August 6, 2016.

23 Dan Schawbel, "Meet the Next Wave of Workers Who Are Taking over Your Office," www.CNBC.com/2016/8/31/after-millennials-comes-gen-z, accessed August 31, 2016.

24 https://www.bls.gov/emp/ep_table_201.htm, accessed April 16, 2017.

25 See "Charting the Projections: 2010–2020," *Occupational Outlook Quarterly*, Winter 2011; www.bls.gov/ooq/2011/winter/winter2011ooq.pdf, www.bls.gov/emp/optd/optd003.pdf, accessed July 29, 2012.

26 https://www.elance.com/php/landing/main/login.php?redirect=http%3A%2F%2Fwww.elance.com%2Fmyelance, accessed April 16, 2017.

27 www.elance.com/p/lpg/freelancing/?rid=1TN5N&utm_source=bing&utm_medium=cpc&utm_campaign=c-bBrand-Exact&utm_term=elance%20odesk&ad={creative}&bmt=e&adpos={adposition}, accessed May 12, 2015. Note that the owner of Elance and its related company oDesk recently merged with and rebranded itself as Upwork, www.upwork.com, accessed May 12, 2015. Temporary office space companies such as WeWork help facilitate the growth of the gig economy by providing easy, flexible workspace for independent contractors such as consultants, as well as for more and more giant firms like GE and KPMG, who need flexible office space for regular and contract workers. Rachel Feintzeig, "We Work Courts Big-Time Clients," *The Wall Street Journal*, August 16, 2016, p. B2.

28 Genevieve Douglas, "HR Must Focus on Building Organizations for the Future," *Bloomberg BNA Bulletin to Management*, March 21, 2017.

29 Farhad Manjoo, "Uber's Business Model Could Change Your Work," *The New York Times*, January 29, 2015, pp. B1, B8.

30 Accenture, "Top Trends That Will Reshape the Future of HR," www.accenture.com/us-en/Pages/insight-future-of-HR.aspx, accessed March 6, 2015.

31 Lauren Weber and Rachel Silverman, "On-Demand Workers: 'We Are Not Robots,'" *The Wall Street Journal*, January 28, 2015, pp. B1, B7.

32 Lauren Weber, "The End of Employees," *The Wall Street Journal*, February 3, 2017, pp. A1, A-10.

33 See for example, Genevieve Douglas, "Freelancers Can Solve Hiring Obstacles but Bring Risks," *Bloomberg BNA Bulletin to Management*, March 14, 2017.

34 Manjoo, "Uber's Business Model Could Change Your Work," p. B8.

35 www.census.gov/foreign-trade/statistics/historical/gands.pdf, accessed June 30, 2015.

36 "Study Predicts 4.1 Million Service Jobs Offshored by 2008," *BNA Bulletin to Management*, August 2, 2005, p. 247; and Patrick Thibodeau, "Offshoring Shrinks Number of IT Jobs, Study Says," *Computerworld*, March 21, 2012, www.computerworld.com/s/article/9225376/Offshoring_shrinks_number_of_IT_jobs_study_says_, accessed October 5, 2012.

37 Rich Miller et al., "Backlash to World Economic Order Clouds Outlook and IMF Talks," www.Bloomberg.com/news/articles/2016–10–04, accessed October 4, 2016.

38 www.bls.gov/opub/ted/2006/may/wk2/art01.htm, accessed April 18, 2009.

39 Ibid.

40 Rich Miller, "Yellen Fed Resigns Itself to Diminished Growth Expectations," *Bloomberg*, May 2, 2014, www.bloomberg.com/news/2014-05-02/yellen-s-fed-resigned-to-diminished-growth-expectations.html, accessed May 2, 2014.

41 Peter Coy, "This Economist Foresees 15 Years of Labor Shortages," *Bloomberg BusinessWeek*, March 21, 2014, www.businessweek.com/printer/articles/191219-this-economist-foresees-15-years-of-labor-shortages, accessed April 30, 2014.

42 Bureau of Labor Statistics, "Working in the 21st Century," https://www.bls.gov/opub/working/page1b.htm, accessed April 16, 2017.

43 Ibid.

44 Anthony Abbatiello, "The Digital Override," *Workforce*, May 2014, pp. 36–39. See also, Laime Vaitkus, "Technology Will Disrupt Jobs and Hiring but Reduce Bias," *Bloomberg BNA Bulletin to Management*, January 31, 2017

45 Martin Berman–Gorvine, "HR Not Immune from Changes Automation Will Bring," *Bloomberg BNA Bulletin to Management*, March 14, 2017.

46 Accenture, "Top Trends That Will Reshape the Future of HR."

47 Josh Bersin, "Transformative Tech: A Disruptive Year Ahead," *HR Magazine*, pages 29–37, February 2017.

48 Josh Bersin, "Big Data in Human Resources: Talent Analytics (People Analytics) Comes of Age," www.forbes.com/sites/joshbersin /2013/02/17/bigdata-in-human-resources-talent -analytics-comes-of-age, accessed March 29, 2015.

49 See "A Third Industrial Revolution," *The Economist*, April 21, 2012, pp. 1–20; and Jeffrey Immelt, "The CEO of General Electric on Sparking an American Manufacturing Renewal," *Harvard Business Review*, March 2012, pp. 43–46.

50 Russell Crook, et al., "Does Human Capital Matter? A Meta-Analysis of the relationship between human capital and firm performance," *Journal of Applied Psychology*, 96, no. 3, (2011), pp. 443–456.

51 Peter Drucker, "The Coming of the New Organization," *Harvard Business Review*, January–February 1988, p. 47. See also James Guthrie et al., "Correlates and Consequences of High Involvement Work Practices: The Role of Competitive Strategy," *International Journal of Human Resource Management*, February 2002, pp. 183–197.

52 "Human Resources Wharton," www .knowledge.wharton.upe.edu, accessed January 8, 2006.

53 See, for example, Anthea Zacharatos et al., "High-Performance Work Systems and Occupational Safety," *Journal of Applied Psychology*, 90, no. 1, 2005, pp. 77–93. See also Jennifer Schramm, "Effective HR Practices Drive Profit," *HR Magazine*, November 2012, p. 88.

54 For a book describing the history of human resource management, see, for example, SHRM, *A History of Human Resources*, www.shrmstore .shrm.org/a-history-of-human-resources.html, accessed October 4, 2012.

55 "Human Capital Critical to Success," *Management Review*, November 1998, p. 9. See also "HR 2018: Top Predictions," *Workforce Management*, 87, no. 20, December 15, 2008, pp. 20–21, and Edward Lawler III, "Celebrating 50 Years: HR: Time for a Reset?" *Human Resource Management*, 50, no. 2, March–April 2011, pp. 171–173.

56 See, for example, D. L. Stone, D. I. Deadrick, J. M. Lukaszewski, and R. Johnson, "The Influence of Technology on the Future of Human Resource Management," *Human Resource Management Review* 25, no. 2 (June 2015), pp. 216–231.

57 Abbatiello, "The Digital Override."

58 Tim Good, Catherine Farley, Himanshu Tambe, and Susan Cantrell, "Trends Reshaping the Future of HR: Digital Radically Disrupts HR," Accenture 2015.

59 Ibid. Some companies today think they're better off without an HR department, but the results are decidedly mixed. Lauren Weber and Rachel Feintzeig, "Is It a Dream or a Drag? Companies Without HR," *The Wall Street Journal*, April 9, 2014, pp. B1, B7.

60 This is based on "The Future of Business: Human Resources, How HR Leaders Are Reinventing Their Roles in Transforming Business," *The Economist Intelligence Unit*, 2014.

61 Ibid.

62 There seems to be room for improvement. One study found that only 5% of HR heads rated their employers' programs as "excellent" and 34% as "good". "Less Than Half Of HR Leaders Rate Programs, Talent Excellent or Good, Deloitte Reports," *Bloomberg BNA Bulletin to Management*, March 17, 2015, p. 83.

63 Robert Grossman, "IBM's HR Takes a Risk," *HR Magazine*, April 1, 2007.

64 Chris Brewster et al., "What Determines the Size of the HR Function? A Cross National Analysis," *Human Resource Management*, 45, no. 1, Spring 2006, pp. 3–21.

65 See, for example, www.personneltoday .com/blogs/hcglobal-human-capital -management/2009/02/theres-no-such-thing-as -eviden.html, accessed April 18, 2009.

66 The evidence-based movement began in medicine. In 1996, in an editorial published by the *British Medical Journal*, David Sackett, MD, defined *evidence-based medicine* as "use of the best-available evidence in making decisions about patient care" and urged his colleagues to adopt its tenets. "Evidence-Based Training™: Turning Research into Results for Pharmaceutical Sales Training," An AXIOM White Paper © 2006 AXIOM Professional Health Learning LLC. All rights reserved.

67 "Super-Human Resources Practices Result in Better Overall Performance, Report Says," *BNA Bulletin to Management*, August 26, 2004, pp. 273–274. See also Wendy Boswell, "Aligning Employees with the Organization's Strategic Objectives: Out of Line of Sight, Out of Mind," *International Journal of Human Resource Management*, 17, no. 9, September 2006, pp. 1014–1041; and Patrice Laroche and Marc Salesina, "The Effects of Union and Nonunion Forms of Employee Representation on High-Performance Work Systems: New Evidence from French Micro Data," *Human Resource Management*, January–February 2017, 56, no. 1, pp. 173–189.

68 Susan Wells, "From HR to the Top," *HR Magazine*, June 2003, p. 49. See also "HR Will Have More Opportunities to Demonstrate Value in 2012," *Bloomberg BNA Bulletin to Management*, January 17, 2012, p. 22.

69 Nelson Schwartz, "Good Jobs, Goodbye," *The New York Times*, pp. B1, B4, March 20, 2016.

70 Julia Preston, "Special Visas Help Copycats Take US Jobs," *The New York Times*, September 30, 2015, p. 1.

71 "Wealth Without Workers, Workers Without Wealth," *The Economist*, October 4, 2014, p. 14. And the more the machine learning algorithm explores more and more data, the more accurate it becomes. Sarah Gail, "Machine Learning, 2.0," *Workforce*, November 2015, p. 10. See also "Globalization, Robots, and the Future of Work," *Harvard Business Review*, October 2016, pp. 75–79.

72 William Lazonick, "Profits Without Prosperity," *Harvard Business Review*, September 2014, p. 47.

73 Josh Barrow, "China's Effect on US Labor Gets a Closer Academic Look," January 28, 2016, p. A3.

74 http://www.cnn.com/2016/10/01/politics/hillary -clinton-millennial-voters-audio-bernie-sanders /index.html, accessed September 23, 2016.

75 Michael Christian, Adela Garza, and Jerel Slaughter, "Work Engagement: A Quantitative Review and Test of Its Relations with Task and Contextual Performance," *Personnel Psychology* 60, no. 4 (2011), pp. 89–136.

76 Adrienne Fox, "Raising Engagement," *HR Magazine*, May 2010, pp. 35–40.

77 Except as noted, this is based on Kathryn Tyler, "Prepare for Impact," *HR Magazine* 56, no. 3, (March 2011), pp. 53–56.

78 www.gallup.com/strategicconsulting /163007/state-american-workplace .aspx; Bruce Louis Rich et al., "Job Engagement: Antecedents and Effects on Job Performance," *Academy of Management Journal* 53, no. 3 (2010), pp. 617–635; "Special Report: Employee Engagement—Losing Lifeblood," *Workforce Management*, July 2011, pp. 24–27.

79 "Five Ways to Improve Employee Engagement Now," *Gallup Business Journal*. Gallup.com, accessed April 7, 2014.

80 Ibid. Some say engagement can backfire. To get their jobs done, some overloaded employees, at the pain of getting penalized, work long days and weekends and stay tethered to their jobs round-the-clock through their smart phones. One study found that workers react to situations like these in one of three ways. Some employees are accepting and do what the employer demands of them. Some are "passing" and appeared to be doing what they're supposed to do but are actually finding ways to reduce their loads by getting around the system. Other simply "reveal" that they have other commitments, and tell their employers that they're unwilling to abandon those commitments by working around the clock. Erin Reid and Lakshmi Ramarajan, "Managing the High-Intensity Workplace," *Harvard Business Review*, June 2016, pp. 85–90.

81 However, at least one survey found that employers don't usually give the HR department exclusive control over activities like organizational development and succession planning, and that 54% of employers surveyed have the HR head report directly to the organizations CEO or president. *Bloomberg BNA Bulletin to Management*, October 13, 2015, pp. 321–322.

82 Lindsey Riddell, "Mayer Boosts Yahoo Parental Leave, Escalates Baby-Benefits Arms Race," www.bizjournals.com/sisco/blog/2013/05/mayer -improves-yahoo-parental-leave.html, accessed May 9, 2013.

83 Sully Taylor, Joyce Osland, and Caroline Egri, "Guest Editors' Introduction: Introduction to HRM's Role in Sustainability: Systems, Strategies, and Practices," *Human Resource Management*, November–December 2012, 51, no. 6, p. 789.

84 www.pepsico.com/Purpose/Performance-with -Purpose/Goals, accessed May 5, 2014.

85 For an excellent discussion of how human resource management practices can support sustainability goals, Cathy Dubois and David Dubois, "Strategic HRM as Social Design for Environmental Sustainability Organization," *Human Resource Management* 51, no. 6 (November–December 2012), pp. 816-818.

86 www.pepsico.com/Purpose/Performance-with -Purpose/Goals, accessed May 5, 2014.

87 "Meatpacking Case Highlights HR's Liability," *Workforce Management*, September 20, 2008, p. 6.

88 Kevin Wooten, "Ethical Dilemmas in Human Resource Management," *Human Resource Management Review*, 11, 2001, p. 161. See also Ann Pomeroy, "The Ethics Squeeze," *HR Magazine* 51, no. 3, March 2006, pp. 48-55.

89 In addition, the "HR Open Standards Consortium Inc." announced a certification program for HR tech professionals. Samuel Greengard, "The Debate over HR Credentials," *Workforce*, June 2016, p. 42.

90 SHRM and HRCI provide sample practice questions. See, for example, https://www.hrci .org/how-to-get-certified/preparation-overview /hrci-practice-exams, accessed April 16, 2017.

91 https://www.shrm.org/certification/about /about shrmcertification/pages/shrm-cp.aspx, accessed April 16, 2017.

92 See, for example, "When the Jobs Inspector Calls," *The Economist*, March 31, 2012, p. 73; and Paul Mozur, "Foxconn Workers: Keep Our Overtime," *The Wall Street Journal*, December 18, 2012, pp. B1-B2.

93 Fred Foulkes and Henry Morgan, "Organizing and Staffing the Personnel Function," *Harvard Business Review*, May-June 1977.

94 "Working at SAS: An Ideal Environment for New Ideas," SAS website, April 20, 2012. Copyright © 2011 by SAS Institute, Inc. Reprinted with permission. All rights reserved.

Chapter 2

1 This is based on Joshua Brustein "Studies Show Racial and Gender Discrimination Throughout the Gig Economy," https://www.bloomberg.com/news/articles/2016-11-22/studies-show-racial-and-gender-discrimination-throughout-the-gig-economy, November 22, 2016; Marta Moakley, "EEOC Targets Gig Economy, Workplace Discrimination in Strategic Enforcement Plan," XpertHR Legal Editor, October 25, 2016, http://www.xperthr.com/news/eeoc-targets-gig-economy-workplace-discrimination-in-strategic-enforcement-plan/23960/; Will Knight, "Is the Gig Economy Rigged?" *MIT Technology Review,* November 17, 2016, https://www.technologyreview.com/s/602832/is-the-gig-economy-rigged/). Such discrimination seems to work both ways. For example, one of these studies found that Boston Uber drivers cancelled trips more often when prospective riders had African-American sounding names.

2 "Employers Eyeing More Bias Training, Accommodation Work after Abercrombie," *Bloomberg BNA Bulletin to Management,* June 9, 2015, page 177.

3 For example, see "Wells Fargo to Pay $3.5 Million to Resolve Black Brokers' Claims," *Bloomberg BNA Bulletin to Management,* January 10, 2017.

4 Betsy Morris, "How Corporate America Is Betraying Women," *Fortune,* January 10, 2005, pp. 64–70.

5 Note that private employers are not bound by the U.S. Constitution.

6 Based on or quoted from *Principles of Employment Discrimination Law, International Association of Official Human Rights Agencies,* Washington, DC. See also Bruce Feldacker, *Labor Guide to Labor Law* (Upper Saddle River, NJ: Prentice Hall, 2000); and "EEOC Attorneys Highlight How Employers Can Better Their Nondiscrimination Practices," *BNA Bulletin to Management,* July 20, 2008, p. 233 and www.eeoc.gov, accessed August 4, 2013. Employment discrimination law is a changing field, and the appropriateness of the rules, guidelines, and conclusions in this chapter and book may also be affected by factors unique to the employer's operation. They should be reviewed by the employer's attorney before implementation.

7 James Higgins, "A Manager's Guide to the Equal Employment Opportunity Laws," *Personnel Journal,* 55, no. 8, August 1976, p. 406.

8 The Equal Employment Opportunity Act of 1972, Subcommittee on Labor or the Committee of Labor and Public Welfare, United States Senate, March 1972, p. 3. In general, it is not discrimination, but unfair discrimination against a person merely because of that person's race, age, sex, national origin, or religion that is forbidden by federal statutes. In the federal government's *Uniform Employee Selection Guidelines,* unfair discrimination is defined as follows: "Unfairness is demonstrated through a showing that members of a particular interest group perform better or poorer on the job than their scores on the selection procedure (test, etc.) would indicate through comparison with how members of the other groups performed." For a discussion of the meaning of fairness, see James Ledvinka, "The Statistical Definition of Fairness in the Federal Selection Guidelines and Its Implications for Minority Employment," *Personnel Psychology,* 32, August 1979, pp. 551–562. In summary, a selection device (such as a test) may discriminate—for example, between low performers and high performers. However, unfair discrimination—discrimination that is based solely on the person's race, age, sex, national origin, or religion—is illegal.

9 "Restructured, Beefed-Up OFCCP May Shift Policy Emphasis, Attorney Says," *BNA Bulletin to Management,* August 18, 2009, p. 257; See also "OFCCP Remains Focused on Pay Equity, Dated Tool, Assistance, Director Shiu Says," *Bloomberg BNA Bulletin to Management,* August 6, 2013, p. 249. Some courts have found OFCCP demands for information to be excessive. When the Labor Department recently demanded pay information back to Google's formation, as well as names and contact for about 20,000 of its workers, Google sued; in 2017, an administrative law judge ruled that for now it didn't have to give the OFCCP that information. See Chris Opfer, "Google Faced the Labor Department, and Google Won," *Bloomberg BNA Bulletin to Management,* April 4, 2017.

10 Note that the U.S. Supreme Court (in *General Dynamics Land Systems Inc.* v. *Cline, 2004*) held that the ADEA does *not* protect younger workers from being treated worse than older ones. "High Court: ADEA Does Not Protect Younger Workers Treated Worse Than Their Elders," *BNA Bulletin to Management,* 55, no. 10, March 4, 2004, pp. 73–80. The U.S. Supreme Court recently held that the plaintiff must show that age was the determining factor in the employer's personnel action. See "Justices, 5–4, Reject Burden Shifting," *BNA Bulletin to Management,* June 23, 2009, p. 199.

11 www.eeoc.gov/laws/statutes/adea.cfm, accessed October 3, 2011.

12 "High Court: ADEA Does Not Protect Younger Workers Treated Worse Than Their Elders," *BNA Bulletin to Management,* 55, no. 10, March 4, 2004, pp. 73–80. See also D. Aaron Lacy, "You Are Not Quite as Old as You Think: Making the Case for Reverse Age Discrimination Under the ADEA," *Berkeley Journal of Employment and Labor Law,* 26, no. 2, 2005, pp. 363–403; Nancy Ursel and Marjorie Armstrong-Stassen, "How Age Discrimination in Employment Affects Stockholders," *Journal of Labor Research,* 17, no. 1, Winter 2006, pp. 89–99; www.eeoc.gov/laws/statutes/adea.cfm, accessed October 3, 2011; and Patrick Dorrian, "Older Workers Can Sue for Age Bias Even if Comparators Are 40 – Plus," *Bloomberg BNA Bulletin to Management,* January 17, 2017.

13 "Staples Must Pay Fired Older Workers $16M for Age Bias," *Bloomberg BNA Bulletin to Management,* June 7, 2016, p. 181.

14 Another recent lawsuit was filed against RJ Reynolds Tobacco Company. The plaintiff was 49 years old when he first applied, and the company never replied to him. His attorneys subsequently told him that the employer's résumé screening guidelines allegedly bump out older candidates "Applicant Can Use Disparate Impact Theory for Age Claim," *Bloomberg BNA Bulletin to Management,* December 8, 2015, p 389.

15 John Kohl, Milton Mayfield, and Jacqueline Mayfield, "Recent Trends in Pregnancy Discrimination Law," *Business Horizons,* 48, no. 5, September 2005, pp. 421–429.

16 Lisa Nagele-Piazza, "Pregnant Worker Awarded 550,000 K in Discrimination Suit," *HR Magazine,* October 2016, p. 14.

17 "Pregnancy Claims Rising; Consistent Procedures Paramount," *BNA Bulletin to Management,* November 23, 2010, p. 375.

18 www.uniformguidelines.com/uniformguidelines.html, accessed November 23, 2007.

19 Ibid.

20 "OFCCP Publicly Releases Updated Federal Contract Compliance Manual," *Bloomberg BNA Bulletin to Management,* August 27, 2013, p. 273. The OFCCP recently updated its sex discrimination rules for federal contractors. "Revised OFCCP Sex Bias Rules Include Pay, Pregnancy, Transgender, Other Protections," *Bloomberg BNA Bulletin to Management,* June 21, 2016, p. 193.

21 *Griggs* v. *Duke Power Company,* 3FEP cases 175.

22 IOFEP cases 1181.

23 For example, in *Price Waterhouse* v. *Hopkins,* the Court ruled that an employer's unlawful actions may not be discriminatory if *lawful* actions (such as not promoting the employee due to inferior performance) would have resulted in the same personnel decision.

24 Bruce Feldacker, *Labor Guide to Labor Law* (Upper Saddle River, NJ: Prentice Hall, 2000), p. 513.

25 "The Eleventh Circuit Explains Disparate Impact, Disparate Treatment," *BNA Fair Employment Practices,* August 17, 2000, p. 102. See also Kenneth York, "Disparate Results in Adverse Impact Tests: The 4/5ths Rule and the Chi Square Test," *Public Personnel Management,* 31, no. 2, Summer 2002, pp. 253–262. A recent analysis based on mathematical simulations concluded that employee selection effectiveness in general, and the potential weaknesses of applying the 4/5 rule in particular, can be ameliorated by formulating and using a multistage selection strategy, for instance basing the initial screen, say for conscientiousness, on paper-and-pencil tests, and then one or two subsequent screens on other selection procedures including interviews. See David Finch et al., "Multistage Selection Strategies: Simulating the Effects on Adverse Impact and Expected Performance for Various Predictor, Nations," *Journal of Applied Psychology,* 94, no. 2, 2009, pp. 318–340.

26 "The Eleventh Circuit Explains Disparate Impact, Disparate Treatment," *BNA Fair Employment Practices,* August 17, 2000, p. 102. See also Kenneth York, "Disparate Results in Adverse Impact Tests: The 4/5ths Rule and the Chi Square Test," *Public Personnel Management,* 31, no. 2, Summer 2002, pp. 253–262; and "Burden of Proof under the Employment Non-Discrimination Act," www.civilrights.org/lgbt/enda/burden-of-proof.html, accessed August 8, 2011.

27 Again, though, if the "employer shows that it would have taken the same action even absent the discriminatory motive, the complaining employee will not be entitled to reinstatement, back pay, or damages," www.eeoc.gov/policy/docs/caregiving.html#mixed, accessed September 24, 2011.

28 "ADA: Simple Common Sense Principles," *BNA Fair Employment Practices,* June 4, 1992, p. 63; and www.eeoc.gov/facts/ada17.html, accessed September 24, 2011.

29 Elliot H. Shaller and Dean Rosen, "A Guide to the EEOC's Final Regulations on the Americans with Disabilities Act," *Employee Relations Law Journal,* 17, no. 3, Winter 1991–1992, pp. 405–430; and www.eeoc.gov/ada, accessed November 20, 2007.

30 Shaller and Rosen, "A Guide to the EEOC's Final Regulations," p. 408. Other specific examples include "epilepsy, diabetes, cancer, HIV infection, and bipolar disorder," www1.eeoc.gov//laws/regulations/adaaa_fact_sheet, accessed October 3, 2011.

31 Shaller and Rosen, "A Guide to the EEOC's Final Regulations," p. 409. Thus one court recently held that a worker currently engaging in illegal

use of drugs was "not a qualified individual with a disability" under the ADA. "Drug Addict Lacks ADA Protection, Quarter Firms," *BNA Bulletin to Management*, April 26, 2011, p. 133.

32 James McDonald Jr., "The Americans with Difficult Personalities Act," *Employee Relations Law Journal*, 25, no. 4, Spring 2000, pp. 93–107; and Betsy Bates, "Mental Health Problems Predominate in ADA Claims," *Clinical Psychiatry News*, May 2003, at http://findarticles.com/p/articles/mi_hb4345/is_5_31/ai_n29006702, accessed September 24, 2011. For a detailed discussion of dealing with this issue, see www.eeoc.gov/facts/intellectual_disabilities.html, accessed September 2, 2011.

33 "EEOC Guidance on Dealing with Intellectual Disabilities," *Workforce Management,* March 2005, p. 16.

34 "Driver Fired after Seizure on Job Lacks ADA Claim," *BNA Bulletin to Management*, January 4, 2011, p. 6.

35 www.ada.gov/reg3a.html#Anchor-Appendix-52467, accessed January 23, 2009. See also Michael Studenka, "A Smart Approach to Accommodating Employees with Disabilities," *HR Magazine*, October 2016, p. 72.

36 For example, many employers have had excellent experience employing them. Nicole LaPorte, "Hiring the Blind, While Making a Green Statement," *The New York Times*, March 25, 2012, p. B3.

37 Martha Frase, "An Underestimated Talent Pool," *HR Magazine*, April 2009, pp. 55–58; and http://www.freedomscientific.com/Products/Blindness/Jaws, accessed January 23, 2017.

38 M. P. McQueen, "Workplace Disabilities Are on the Rise," *The Wall Street Journal*, May 1, 2007, p. A1.

39 "No Sitting for Store Greeter," *BNA Fair Employment Practices*, December 14, 1995, p. 150. For more recent illustrative cases, see "Reasonable Accommodation and the ADA-Courts Draw the Line," Tillinghast Licht at http://library.findlaw.com/2004/Sep/19/133574.html, accessed September 6, 2011.

40 For example, a U.S. circuit court recently found that a depressed former kidney dialysis technician could not claim ADA discrimination after the employer fired him for attendance problems. The court said he could not meet the essential job function of predictably coming to work. "Depressed Worker Lacks ADA Claim, Court Decides," *BNA Bulletin to Management*, December 18, 2007, p. 406. See also www.eeoc.gov/press/5-10-01-b.html, accessed January 8, 2008.

41 *Toyota Motor Manufacturing of Kentucky, Inc. v. Williams.* 534 U.S. 184 (2002).

42 "Supreme Court Says Manual Task Limitation Needs Both Daily Living, Workplace Impact," *BNA Fair Employment Practices*, January 17, 2002, p. 8.

43 "EEOC Issued Its Final Regulations for ADA Amendments Act," *Workforce Management*, June 2011, p. 12.

44 Lawrence Postol, "ADAAA Will Result in Renewed Emphasis on Reasonable Accommodations," *Society for Human Resource Management Legal Report*, January 2009, pp. 1–3.

45 Susan Wells, "Counting on Workers with Disabilities," *HR Magazine*, April 2008, p. 45.

46 Mark Lengnick-Hall et al., "Overlooked and Underutilized: People with Disabilities Are an Untapped Human Resource," *Human Resource Management*, 47, no. 2, Summer 2008, pp. 255–273; and https://www.walgreens.com/topic/sr/sr_talent_raises_productivity.jsp, accessed January 23, 2017.

47 "Wachovia Violated USERRA by Failing to Reinstate Reservist to Comparable Job," *BNA Bulletin to Management*, September 20, 2011, p. 297.

48 www.eeoc.gov/press/2-25-09.html, accessed April 3, 2009; Susan Hauser, "Sincerely Yours, Gina," *Workforce Management*, July 2011, pp. 16–18.

49 James Ledvinka and Robert Gatewood, "EEO Issues with Preemployment Inquiries," *Personnel Administrator*, 22, no. 2, February 1997, pp. 22–26.

50 Joanne Deshenaux and Dori Meinert, "States, Cities Go Beyond Federal Government," *HR Magazine*, February 2013, pp. 28–32. On the other hand, many states have religious freedom requirements that could have the effect of enabling some employers to seek religious exemptions from certain state workplace antidiscrimination requirements and laws. See for example Jay-Anne Casuga, "Religious Freedom, Bias Protections: Something's Got to Give," *Bloomberg BNA Bulletin to Management*, March 21, 2017.

51 Quoted or paraphrased from www.eeoc.gov/laws/types/index.cfm; www.eeoc.gov/laws/types/religion.cfm; www.eeoc.gov/eeoc/internal_eeo/index.cfm; and www.eeoc.gov/federal/otherprotections.cfm, all accessed May 9, 2013.

52 A federal appeals court recently ruled that Title VII does not prohibit discrimination based on sexual orientation. "Title VII Doesn't Reach Sex Orientation Bias, 7th. Cir. Rules, Contrary to EEOC's Position," *Bloomberg BNA Bulletin to Management*, August 9, 2016, p. 249.

53 Melanie Trottman, "Religious Discrimination Claims on the Rise," *The Wall Street Journal*, October 28, 2013, page B1.

54 "More Muslim Workers Allege Bias to Prayer Breaks," *Bloomberg BNA Bulletin to Management*, May 10, 2016, p. 150.

55 "Employer Should Respond to DOMA with Steps That Offset Risks, Attorneys Say," *Bloomberg BNA Bulletin to Management*, July 2, 2013, pp. 209–210.

56 "DOL Says 'Spouse' and 'Marriage' in ERISA Include Same-Sex Legally Married Couples," *Bloomberg BNA Bulletin to Management*, September 24, 2013, p. 305.

57 "OFCCP Announces Final Rule Protecting LGBT Federal Contractor Workers from Bias," *Bloomberg BNA Bulletin to Management*, December 9, 2014.

58 Kevin McGowan, "Landmark Gay Bias Ruling May Move Issue Closer to High Court," *Bloomberg BNA Bulletin to Management*, April 11, 2017.

59 "OFCCP Announces 'Higher Historic' Final Rules on Contractor Hiring of Veterans, Disabled," *Bloomberg BNA Bulletin to Management*, September 3, 2013, p. 281; Lauren Weber, "Are You Disabled? Now Your Boss Wants to Know," *The Wall Street Journal*, March 19, 2014, p. B1.

60 Adam Liptak, "Justices Back Ban on Race as Factor in College Entry," *The New York Times*, April 23, 2014, pp. A1, A12.

61 Melanie Trottman and Lauren Weber, "Bar Is Raised in Worker Bias Cases," *The Wall Street Journal*, June 25, 2013, p. B1, B8.

62 https://www.eeoc.gov/employers/index.cfm, accessed January 23, 2017.

63 Note also that small businesses often use staffing companies to supply workers, and in some cases, someone employed by and assigned by a staffing agency can sue the employer to which he or she is assigned when he or she is a victim of alleged racial discrimination at the worksite. "Companies Not Safe from Title VII Liability for Claims of Workers from Temp Agencies," *Bloomberg BNA Bulletin to Management*, November 24, 2015, p. 369.

64 Larry Drake and Rachel Moskowitz, "Your Rights in the Workplace," *Occupational Outlook Quarterly*, Summer 1997, pp. 19–29.

65 Richard Wiener et al., "The Fit and Implementation of Sexual Harassment Law to Workplace Evaluations," *Journal of Applied Psychology*, 87, no. 4, 2002, pp. 747–764. Recently, for instance, a U.S. Court of Appeals told a male Walmart employee that he could proceed with his claim that a female supervisor had sexually harassed him. "Man's Harassment Claims Advanced," *BNA Bulletin to Management*, September 6, 2011, p. 285.

66 https://www.eeoc.gov/eeoc/statistics/enforcement/sexual_harassment_new.cfm, accessed January 23, 2017.

67 Jennifer Berdahl and Celia Moore, "Workplace Harassment: Double Jeopardy for Minority Women," *Journal of Applied Psychology*, 91, no. 2, 2006, pp. 426–436.

68 "EEOC: 'Boss's Shoulder Touching Not Sexual Harassment', *Bloomberg BNA Bulletin to Management,* February 11, 2014, p. 45.

69 Patricia Linenberger and Timothy Keaveny, "Sexual Harassment: The Employer's Legal Obligations," *Personnel*, 58, November/December 1981, p. 64 and "Court Examines Workplace Flirtation," http://hr.blr.com/HR-news/Discrimination/Sexual-Harassment/Court-Examines-Workplace-Flirtation, accessed October 2, 2011.

70 Edward Felsenthal, "Justice's Ruling Further Defines Sexual Harassment," *The Wall Street Journal*, March 5, 1998, p. B5.

71 Hilary Gettman and Michele Gelfand, "When the Customer Shouldn't Be King: Antecedents and Consequences of Sexual Harassment by Clients and Customers," *Journal of Applied Psychology*, 92, no. 3, 2007, pp. 757–770.

72 See the discussion in "Examining Unwelcome Conduct in a Sexual Harassment Claim," *BNA Fair Employment Practices*, October 19, 1995, p. 124. In cases where even a single workplace comment is sufficiently severe or is combined with touching or physical assault, courts have supported the job harassment claim. "One Offensive Workplace Comment, Incident Can Support Job Harassment Claim, Liability," *Bloomberg BNA Bulletin to Management*, January 19, 2016, p. 17.

73 "Examining Unwelcome Conduct in a Sexual Harassment Claim," p. 124.

74 For example, a server/bartender filed a sexual harassment claim against Chili's Bar & Grill. She claimed that her former boyfriend, also a restaurant employee, had harassed her. The court ruled that the restaurant's prompt response warranted ruling in favor of it. "Ex-Boyfriend Harassed, but Employer Acted Promptly," *BNA Bulletin to Management*, January 8, 2008, p. 14.

75 See Mindy D. Bergman et al., "The (Un)reasonableness of Reporting: Antecedents and Consequences of Reporting Sexual Harassment," *Journal of Applied Psychology*, 87, no. 2, 2002, pp. 230–242. See also www.eeoc.gov/policy/docs/harassment-facts.html, accessed October 2, 2011.

76 Adapted from *Sexual Harassment Manual for Managers and Supervisors,* published in 1991, by CCH Incorporated, a WoltersKluwer Company; www.eeoc.gov/types/sexual_harrassment.html, accessed May 6, 2007; and www.eeoc.gov/policy/docs/harassment-facts.html, accessed January 25, 2017.

77 One software engineer wrote that when she told her HR department she was being harassed, they allegedly said the alleged offender was a "high performer" and that he probably just made an innocent mistake. Genevieve Douglas, "Uber Sexual Harassment Claims Hold Lessons for HR," *Bloomberg BNA Bulletin to Management*, February 28, 2017.

78 Jennifer Berdahl and Karl Aquino, "Sexual Behavior at Work: Fun or Folly?" *Journal of Applied Psychology*, 94, no. 1, 2009, pp. 34–47.

79 Jessica Guynn, "Sexism a Problem in Silicon Valley, Critics Say," *Miami Herald*, October 29, 2013, p. 10B.

80 Rebecca Thacker and Stephen Gohmann, "Male/Female Differences in Perceptions and Effects of Hostile Environment Sexual Harassment: 'Reasonable' Assumptions?" *Public Personnel Management*, 22, no. 3, Fall 1993, pp. 461–472; Jennifer Berdahl and Karl Aquino, "Sexual Behavior at Work: Fun or Folly?" *Journal of Applied Psychology*, 94, no. 1, 2009, pp. 34–47; Maria Rotundo et al., "A Meta-Analytic Review of Gender Differences in Perceptions of Sexual Harassment," *Journal of Applied Psychology*, 86, no. 5 (2001), pp. 914–922; and Nathan Bowling and Terry Beehr, "Work-place Harassment from the Victim's Perspective: A Theoretical Model and Meta-Analysis," *Journal of Applied Psychology*, 91, no. 5, 2006, pp. 998–1012.

81 Jathan Janove, "Sexual Harassment and the Three Big Surprises," *HR Magazine*, 46, no. 11, November 2001, p. 123ff. California mandates sexual harassment prevention training for supervisors. See "California Clarifies Training Law; Employers Take Note," *BNA Bulletin to Management*, November 20, 2007, p. 375.

82 Ana Campoy and Julian Barnes, "Air Force Combats Sex Misconduct," *The Wall Street Journal*, November 15, 2012, p. A-8; and James Risen, "Air Force Leaders Testify on Culture That Led to Sexual Assaults of Recruits," *The New York Times*, January 24, 2013, p. A-15.

83 Mary Rowe, "Dealing with Sexual Harassment," *Harvard Business Review*, May–June 1981, p. 43; Rose Johnson, "Seven Ways to Deal with Sexual Harassment in the Workplace," http://smallbusiness.chron.com/seven-ways-deal-sexual-harassment-workplace-18095.html, accessed January 25, 2017.

84 As of 2017, the EEOC was testing a new online system to let people submit EEOC inquiries and to schedule appointments, as a way to encourage people who believe they were discriminated against to reach out to the EEOC. Patrick Dorrian, "Federal Job Bias Tool Rolled Out in Five Cities," *Bloomberg BNA Bulletin to Management*, March 21, 2017.

85 Patricia Feltes, Robert Robinson, and Ross Fink, "American Female Ex-Patriots and the Civil Rights Act of 1991: Balancing Legal and Business Interest," *Business Horizons*, March–April 1993, p. 82–85.

86 Ibid., page 84.

87 "Expansion of Employment Laws Abroad Impacts U.S. Employers," *BNA Bulletin to Management*, April 11, 2006, p. 119 Richard Posthuma, Mark Roehling, and Michael Campion, "Applying U.S. Employment Discrimination Laws to International Employers: Advice for Scientists and Practitioners," *Personnel Psychology*, 59, 2006, pp. 705–739.

88 Based on Gregory Baxter, "Over There: Enforcing the 1991 Civil Rights Act Abroad," *Employee Relations Law Journal*, 19, no. 2, August 1993, pp. 257–266; "Enforcement Guidance on Application of Title VII and the Americans with Disabilities Act to Conduct Overseas and to Foreign Employers Discriminating in the United States," https://www.eeoc.gov/policy/docs/extraterritorial-vii-ada.html, *accessed January 25, 2017*.

89 "Employers Should Address Inappropriate Behavior on Social Sites," *Bloomberg BNA Bulletin to Management*, February 19, 2013, p. 62.

90 "Be Careful with Social Media When Vetting Potential Workers," *Bloomberg BNA Bulletin to Management*, June 25, 2013, p. 206.

91 John Moran, *Employment Law* (Upper Saddle River, NJ: Prentice Hall, 1997), p. 166.

92 *Systemic bias* is bias that may result from practices that have a systemic or broad impact on an industry or company. For example, at one company, software engineer applicants with Asian backgrounds were allegedly routinely eliminated via resume screening and telephone interviews. Katie Benner, "US Says Tech Start-Up Had Bias Against Asians," *The New York Times*, p. B3, August 27, 2016. From 2006 to 2015, the EEOC obtained over $530 million in compensation for about 71,000 workers who claimed systemic bias. "EEOC Chair's Report Finds Much Progress in Agency's Efforts Against Systemic Bias," *Bloomberg BNA Bulletin to Management*, July 12, 2016, p. 217.

93 "The Eleventh Circuit Explains Disparate Impact, Disparate Treatment," p. 102.

94 Moran, *Employment Law*, p. 168.

95 John Klinefelter and James Tompkins, "Adverse Impact in Employment Selection," *Public Personnel Management*, May/June 1976, pp. 199–204; and www.eeoc.gov/policy/docs/factemployment_procedures.html, accessed October 2, 2011.

96 Employers use several types of statistics in addressing adverse impact. For a discussion, see Robert Gatewood and Hubert Feild, *Human Resource Selection* (Fort Worth, TX: The Dryden Press, 1994), pp. 40–42, and Jean Phillips and Stanley Gulley, *Strategic Staffing* (Upper Saddle River, NJ: Pearson, 2012), pp. 68–69. For example, *stock statistics* might compare *at a single point in time* (1) the percentage of female engineers the company has as a percentage of its total number of engineers, with (2) the number of trained female engineers in the labor force as a percentage of the total number of trained engineers in the labor force. Here, the question of relevant labor market is important. For example, the relevant labor market if you're hiring unskilled assemblers might be the local labor market within, say, 20 miles from your plant, whereas the relevant labor market for highly skilled engineers might well be national. *Flow statistics* measure proportions of employees, in particular, groups at two points in time: before selection and after selection takes place. For example, when comparing the percentage of minority applicants who applied with the percentage hired, the employer is using flow statistics. An employer's company-wide minority hiring statistics may be defensible companywide but not departmentally. The employer therefore may employ *concentration statistics* to drill down and determine the concentration of minorities versus nonminorities in particular job categories.

97 One study found that using the 4/5ths rule often resulted in false-positive ratings of adverse impact, and that incorporating tests of statistical significance could improve the accuracy of applying the 4/5ths rule. See Philip Roth, Philip Bobko, and Fred Switzer, "Modeling the Behavior of the 4/5ths Rule for Determining Adverse Impact: Reasons for Caution," *Journal of Applied Psychology*, 91, no. 3, 2006, pp. 507–522.

98 The results must be realistic. In this example, hiring two out of five women suggests there is no adverse impact. But suppose we had hired only one woman? Then the difference between those we would be expected to hire (five) and whom we actually hired (one) would rise to four. Hiring just one less woman might then trigger adverse impact issues because twice the standard deviation is also about four. However, realistically, it probably would not trigger such concerns because with such small numbers, one person makes such a difference. The point is that tools like the 4/5ths rule and the standard deviation rule are only rules of thumb. They do not themselves determine if the employer's screening process is discriminatory. This fact may work both for and against the employer. As the Uniform Guidelines (www.uniformguidelines.com/-qandaprint.html) put it, "Regardless of the amount of difference in selection rates, unlawful discrimination may be present, and may be demonstrated through appropriate evidence."

99 The ADEA does not just protect against intentional discrimination (disparate treatment). Under a Supreme Court decision (*Smith* v. *Jackson*, Miss., 2005), it also covers employer practices that seem neutral but that actually bear more heavily on older workers (disparate impact). "Employees Need Not Show Intentional Bias to Bring Claims Under ADEA, High Court Says," *BNA Bulletin to Management*, 56, no. 14, April 5, 2005, p. 105.

100 The Fair Treatment for Experienced Pilots Act raised commercial pilots' mandatory retirement age from 60 to 65 in 2008. Allen Smith, "Congress Gives Older Pilots a Reprieve," *HR Magazine*, February 2008, p. 24.

101 *Usery v. Tamiami Trail Tours*, 12FEP cases 12–33. Alternatively, an employer faced with an age discrimination claim may raise the FOA (factors other than age) defense. Here, it argues that its actions were "reasonable" based on some factor other than age, such as the terminated person's poor performance.

102 James Ledvinka, *Federal Regulation of Personnel and Human Resources Management* (Boston: Kent, 1982), p. 41.

103 www.foxnews.com/story/0,2933,517334,00.html, accessed January 7, 2010.

104 Howard Anderson and Michael Levin-Epstein, *Primer of Equal Employment Opportunity* (Washington, DC: The Bureau of National Affairs, 1982), pp. 13–14.

105 *U.S.* v. *Bethlehem Steel Company*, 3FEP cases 589.

106 *Robinson* v. *Lorillard Corporation*, 3FEP cases 653.

107 *Spurlock* v. *United Airlines*, 5FEP cases 17.

108 Anderson and Levin-Epstein, *Primer of Equal Employment Opportunity*, p. 14.

109 James Ledvinka and Robert Gatewood, "EEO Issues with Preemployment Inquiries," *Personnel Administrator*, 22, no. 2, February 1997, pp. 22–26.

110 Ibid.; www.eeoc.gov/laws/practices/index.cfm, accessed August 2, 2013.

111 Anderson and Levin-Epstein, *Primer of Equal Employment Opportunity*, p. 28.

112 See, for example, Enrica Ruggs, Amber Williams, and Michelle Hebl, "Weight Isn't Selling: The Insidious Effects of Weight Stigmatization in Retail Settings," *Journal of Applied Psychology*, 100, no. 5, 2015, pp. 1483–1496.

113 See, for example, Patrick Dorrian, "EEOC Commissioner Offers Insights on Obesity as a Disability," *BNA Bloomberg Bulletin to Management*, September 17, 2013, pp. 302–303.

114 Jenessa Shapiro et al., "Expectations of Obese Trainees: How Stigmatized Trainee Characteristics Influence Training Effectiveness," *Journal of Applied Psychology*, 92, no. 1, 2007, pp. 239–249. See also Lisa Finkelstein et al., "Bias against Overweight Job Applicants: Further Explanations of When and Why," *Human Resource Management*, 46, no. 2, Summer 2007, pp. 203–222; and Svetlana Shkolnikova, "Weight Discrimination Could Be as Common as Racial Bias," www.usatoday.com/news/health/weightloss/2008-05-20-overweight-bias_N.htm, accessed January 21, 2009.

115 "American Airlines, Worldwide Flight Sued by EEOC over Questioning of Applicants," *BNA Fair Employment Practices*, October 12, 2000, p. 125.

116 "OFCCP Issues Criminal Records Directive, Cautions Contractors on Blanket Exclusions," *Bloomberg BNA Bulletin to Management*, February 12, 2013, p. 49; and "EEOC to Focus on Hiring, Pay and Harassment," *HR Magazine*, February 2013, p. 11.

117 See, for example, www.eeoc.gov/policy/docs /guidanceinquiries.html, accessed June 28, 2009.

118 This is based on Anderson and Levin-Epstein, *Primer of Equal Opportunity*, pp. 93–97.

119 Eric Matusewitch, "Tailor Your Dress Codes," *Personnel Journal*, 68, no. 2, February 1989, pp. 86–91; Matthew Miklave, "Sorting Out a Claim of Bias," *Workforce*, 80, no. 6, June 2001, pp. 102–103, and "Laws and Cases Affecting Appearance," www.boardmanlawfirm .com/perspectives_articles/appearance.php, accessed September 8, 2011.

120 Rita Pyrillis, "Body of Work," *Workforce Management*, November 7, 2010, pp. 20–26.

121 Kenneth Sovereign, *Personnel Law*, 4th ed. (Upper Saddle River, NJ: Prentice Hall, 1999), p. 220.

122 www.eeoc.gov/employers/smallbusiness/faq /what_is_retaliation.cfm, accessed January 24, 2017.

123 https://www.eeoc.gov/eeoc/plan/upload /2016par.pdf, accessed January 24, 2017.

124 https://www.eeoc.gov/employees/upload/charge _status_flow_chart.pdf. Also see, https://www.ftc .gov/sites/default/files/attachments/filing -complaint-discrimination-federal-trade -commission/eeocomplaint-flowchart.pdf all accessed June 7, 2017.

125 In 2007, the U.S. Supreme Court in *Ledbetter* v. *Goodyear Tire & Rubber Company* held that employees claiming Title VII pay discrimination must file their claims within 180 days of when they first receive the allegedly discriminatory pay. In 2009, Congress formulated and the president signed new legislation enabling employees to file claims anytime, as long as the person is still receiving a paycheck.

126 www.eeoc.gov/eeoc/statistics/enforcement /charges.cfm, accessed January 24, 2017.

127 "Attorneys: Employer Should Handle EEOC Discharges Strategically," *Bloomberg BNA Bulletin to Management*, October 15, 2013, p. 334.

128 "EEOC Attorneys Stress the Importance of Cooperation during Investigations," *BNA Bulletin to Management*, March 8, 2011, p. 73.

129 "EPLI Now Established Employer Litigation Strategy," *BNA Bulletin to Management*, November 29, 2011, p. 382.

130 www.eeoc.gov/mediate/facts.html, accessed June 29, 2009.

131 "EEOC's New Nationwide Mediation Plan Offers Option of Informal Settlements," *BNA Fair Employment Practices*, February 18, 1999, p. 21 and www.eeoc.gov/employees/mediation.cfm, accessed October 2, 2011.

132 Timothy Bland, "Sealed without a Kiss," *HR Magazine*, October 2000, pp. 85–92.

133 Stuart Bompey and Michael Pappas, "Is There a Better Way? Compulsory Arbitration of Employment Discrimination Claims after Gilmer," *Employee Relations Law Journal*, 19, no. 3, Winter 1993–1994, pp. 197–216, and www .eeoc.gov/policy/docs/mandarb.html, accessed September 5, 2011. The EEOC says here, for instance, that "the employer imposing mandatory arbitration is free to manipulate the arbitral mechanism to its benefit."

134 See Bompey and Pappas, pp. 210–211.

135 "EEOC Opposes Mandatory Arbitration," *BNA Fair Employment Practices*, July 24, 1997, p. 85; and www.eeoc.gov/employees/mediation .cfm, accessed October 2, 2011.

136 David Nye, "When the Fired Fight Back," *Across-the-Board*, June 1995, pp. 31–34; and www.eeoc.gov/federal/fed_employees/adr.cfm, accessed October 3, 2011.

137 See, for example, Michael Carrell and Everett Mann, "Defining Work Force Diversity in Public Sector Organizations," *Public Personnel Management*, 24, no. 1, Spring 1995, pp. 99–111; Richard Koonce, "Redefining Diversity,"

Training and Development Journal, December 2001, pp. 22–33; Kathryn Canas and Harris Sondak, *Opportunities and Challenges of Workplace Diversity* (Upper Saddle River, NJ: Pearson, 2008), pp. 3–27. Others list race and ethnicity diversity, gender diversity, age diversity, disability diversity, sexual diversity, and cultural and national origin diversity as examples. Lynn Shore et al., "Diversity in Organizations: Where Are We Now and Where Are We Going?" *Human Resource Management Review*, 19, 2009, pp. 117–133.

138 Brian O'Leary and Bart Weathington, "Beyond the Business Case for Diversity in Organizations," *Employee Responsibilities and Rights*, 18, no. 4, December 2006, pp. 283–292; "Diversity Is Used as Business Advantage by Three Fourths of Companies, Survey Says," *BNA Bulletin to Management*, November 7, 2006, p. 355; and Claire Armstrong et al., "The Impact of Diversity and Equality Management on Firm Performance: Beyond High Performance Work Systems," *Human Resource Management*, 49, no. 6, November–December 2010, pp. 977–998.

139 Taylor Cox Jr., *Cultural Diversity in Organizations* (San Francisco, CA: Berrett-Kohler Publishers, Inc., 1993), p. 88 also see Stefanie Johnson et al., "The Strong, Sensitive Type: Effects of Gender Stereotypes and Leadership Prototypes on the Evaluation of Male and Female Leaders," *Organizational Behavior and Human Decision Processes* 106, no. 1 (May 2008), pp. 39–60.

140 Cheryl Sandberg, "Women Are Leaning In—But They Face Pushback," *The Wall Street Journal*, September 27, 2016, p. R2.

141 For example, see Zoe Kinias and Jessica Sim, "Facilitating Women's Success in Business: Interrupting the Process of Stereotype Threat Through Affirmation of Personal Values," *Journal of Applied Psychology*, 101, no. 11, 2016, pp. 1585–1597.

142 Dalia Bazzaz, "Millennial Women Face Familiar Obstacles at Work," *The Wall Street Journal*, September 27, 2016, p. R8.

143 Cox, *Cultural Diversity in Organizations*, p. 64.

144 "Workplace Bias against Muslims Increasingly a Concern for Employers," *BNA Bulletin to Management*, October 26, 2010, p. 337. See also Robert Grossman, "Valuable but Vulnerable," *HR Magazine*, March 2011, pp. 22–27.

145 Cox, *Cultural Diversity in Organizations*, pp. 179–180.

146 J. H. Greenhaus and S. Parasuraman, "Job Performance Attributions and Career Advancement Prospects: An Examination of Gender and Race Affects," *Organizational Behavior and Human Decision Processes*, 55, July 1993, pp. 273–298. Much research here focuses on how ethnocentrism prompts consumers to avoid certain products based on their country of origin. See, for example, T. S. Chan et al., "How Consumer Ethnocentrism and Animosity Impair the Economic Recovery of Emerging Markets." *Journal of Global Marketing*, 23, no. 3, July/August 2010, pp. 208–225.

147 Lisa Nishii and David Mayer, "Do Inclusive Leaders Help to Reduce Turnover in Diverse Groups? The Moderating Role of a Leader–Member Exchange in the Diversity to Turn over Relationship," *Journal of Applied Psychology*, 94, no. 6, 2009, pp. 1412–1426. As another example, leaders who facilitated high levels of power sharing within their groups helped to reduce the frequently observed positive relationship between increased diversity and increased turnover. But, leaders who were inclusive of only a select few followers "may actually exacerbate the relationship between diversity and turnover," p. 1422.

148 Frank Dobbin and Alexandra Kalev, "Why Diversity Programs Fail," *Harvard Business Review*, July–August 2016, p. 59.

149 Mark Phillis, "You Have a Chief Diversity Officer, but Is Your Workplace Inclusive?" *Workforce*, June 2016, pp. 20–21.

150 "As LGBT Rights Stir Controversy in States, Firms Across America Seek LGBT Workers," *Bloomberg BNA Bulletin to Management*, April 5, 2016, p. 105.

151 Susan Hauser, "The Clone Danger," *Workforce Management*, April 2013, p. 40.

152 Boris Groysberg and Katherine Connolly, "Great Leaders Who Make the Mix Work," *Harvard Business Review*, September 2013, pp. 68–76.

153 Patricia Digh, "Creating a New Balance Sheet: The Need for Better Diversity Metrics," *Mosaics* (by Society for Human Resource Management), September/October 1999, p. 1. For diversity management steps, see Taylor Cox, Jr., *Cultural Diversity in Organizations: Theory, Research and Practice* (San Francisco: Berrett-Koehler, 1993), p. 236; see also Richard Bucher, *Diversity Consciousness* (Upper Saddle River, NJ: Prentice Hall, 2004), pp. 109–137.

154 Ibid.

155 Nikki Waller, "How Men and Women See the Workplace Differently," *The Wall Street Journal*, September 27, 2016, pp. R1, R2.

156 Rita Pyrillis, "SAP Feted for Gender Diversity," *Workforce*, April 2016, p. 17.

157 Nikki Waller, "How Men and Women See the Workplace Differently," *The Wall Street Journal*, September 27, 2016, pp. R1, R2.

158 Frank Jossi, "Reporting Race," *HR Magazine*, September 2000, pp. 87–94.

159 http://newsfeedresearcher.com/data/articles_n17 /tests-city-court.html, accessed April 24, 2009.

160 Adam Liptak, "Supreme Court Finds Bias against White Firefighters," *The New York Times*, June 30, 2009, pp. A1, A13.

161 Ibid., p. 560.

Chapter 3

1 See, for example, Evan Offstein, Devi Gnyawali, and Anthony Cobb, "A Strategic Human Resource Perspective of Firm Competitive Behavior," *Human Resource Management Review*, 15, 2005, pp. 305–318.

2 For a good discussion of aligning goals, see, for example, Eric Krell, "Change Within," *HR Magazine*, August 2011, pp. 43–50.

3 James Jenks (1994), *The Hiring, Firing (And Everything in Between) Personnel Forms*.

4 https://www.bizmanualz.com/, accessed January 29, 2017.

5 See, for example, Fred David, *Strategic Management* (Upper Saddle River, NJ: Prentice Hall, 2007), p. 11.

6 Tony Bingham and Pat Galagan, "Doing Good While Doing Well," *Training & Development*, June 2008, p. 33. See also www.pepsico .com/Purpose/Our-Mission-and-Values, accessed July 31, 2014.

7 Paul Nutt, "Making Strategic Choices," *Journal of Management Studies*, January 2002, pp. 67–96.

8 Peter Coy, "A Renaissance in U.S. Manufacturing," *Bloomberg Business-week*, May 9–15, 2011, pp. 11–13.

9 Commerce Clearing House, "HR Role: Maximize the Competitive Advantage of People," *Ideas and Trends in Personnel*, August 5, 1992, p. 121.

10 Michael Porter, *Competitive Strategy* (New York: The Free Press, 1980), p. 14. See also Chris Zook and James Allen, "The Great Repeatable Business Model," *Harvard Business Review*, November 2011, pp. 107–112.

11 For a recent discussion, see, for example, Torben Juul Andersen and Dana Minbaeva, "The Role of Human Resource Management in Strategy Making," *Human Resource Management*, September–October 2013, 52, no. 5, pp. 803–827.

12 https://www.accenture.com/us-en/service-human-resources-hr-service-offering, accessed January 26, 2017.

13 Brian Hults, "Integrate HR with Operating Strategy," *HR Magazine*, October 2011, pp. 54–56.

14 Michael Hargis and Don Bradley III, "Strategic Human Resource Management in Small and Growing Firms: Aligning Valuable Resources," *Academy of Strategic Management Journal*, 10, no. 2, July 2011, pp. 105–126.

15 "Meet the Zappos Family: Human Resources" from Zappos website. Copyright © 1999–2012 by Zappos.com, Inc. Reprinted with permission.

16 www.weknownext.com/workplace/delivering -hr-at-zappos-hr-magazine-june-2011, accessed August 23, 2012; See also, Richard Feloni, "Here's What Happened to Zappos' HR Boss When the Company Got Rid Of Managers and Her Job Became Obsolete," February 12, 2016, http://www.businessinsider.com/zappos-hr-boss -hollie-delaney-talks-about-holacracy-2016-2, ac-cessed January 29, 2017.

17 Kristen McAlister, "Why the Gig Economy Should be Part of Your Talent Strategy," http://www .business.com/human-resources/kristen-mcalister -gig-economy-should-be-part-of-your-talent -strategy/, December 14, 2016, accessed January 29, 2017; "How the Gig Economy and Freelancers are Reshaping HR Departments," http://www.hrmguide.com/recruitment/perfect-work.htm, accessed January 29, 2017; Mark Fef-fer, "Tech Tools Could Bridge Gap Between HR, Gig Workers," https://www.shrm.org/ resourcesandtools/hr-topics/technology/pageshr -and-tech-tools-for-gig-economy.aspx, August 15, 2016, accessed January 29, 2017.

18 www.pepsico.com/Purpose/Performance-with -Purpose/Goals, accessed May 5, 2014.

19 For an excellent discussion of how human resource management practices can support sustainability goals, see Cathy Dubois and David Dubois, "Strategic HRM as Social Design for Environmental Sustainability Organization," *Human Resource Management* 51, no. 6 (November–December 2012), pp. 816–818.

20 www.pepsico.com/Purpose/Performance-with-Purpose/Goals, accessed May 5, 2014.

21 Paul Buller and Glenn McEvoy, "Strategy, Human Resource Management and Performance: Sharpening Line of Sight," *Human Resource Management Review*, 22, 2012, pp. 43–56.

22 Managers can access their companies' strategy maps while on the go. They can use the Active Strategy Company's *ActiveStrategy Enterprise* to create and automate their strategy maps, and to access them through iPhone or similar devices. Available at: www.activestrategy.com /solutions/strategy_mapping.aspx, accessed March 24, 2009.

23 When focusing on HR activities, managers call this an "HR scorecard." When applying the same process broadly to all the company's activi-ties, including, for example, sales, production, and finance, managers call it the "balanced scorecard process."

24 The idea for the HR scorecard derives from a broader measurement tool managers call the "bal-anced scorecard." This does for the company as a whole what the HR scorecard does for HR, sum-marizing instead the impact of various functions including HRM, sales, production, and distribu-tion. The "balanced" in balanced scorecard refers to a balance of goals—financial and nonfinancial.

25 See, for example, "Using HR Performance Met-rics to Optimize Operations and Profits," *PR News-wire*, February 27, 2008; and "How to 'Make Over' Your HR Metrics," *HR Focus*, 84, no. 9, September 2007, p. 3.

26 SHRM Human Capital Benchmarking Study: 2007 Executive Summary.

27 For additional information on HR metrics see, for example, Karen M. Kroll, "Repurposing Metrics for HR: HR Professionals Are Looking Through a People-Focused Lens at the CFO's Metrics on Revenue and Income per FTE," *HR Magazine*, 51, no. 7, July 2006, pp. 64–69; and http://shrm .org/metrics/library_publishedover/measurementsy stemsTOC.asp, accessed February 2, 2008.

28 See, for example, "Benchmarking for Functional HR Metrics," *HR Focus*, 83, no. 11, November 2006, p. 1; and John Sullivan, "The Last Word," *Workforce Management*, November 19, 2007, p. 42. SHRM makes various metrics calculators available to members at www.shrm.org /TemplatesTools/Samples/Metrics/Pages /GeneralHumanResources.aspx, accessed October 6, 2012.

29 See Brian Becker and Mark Huselid, "Measur-ing HR? Benchmarking Is Not the Answer!" *HR Magazine*, 8, no. 12, December 2003. Available at: www.charmed.org, accessed February 2, 2008.

30 Ibid.

31 Ed Frauenheim, "Keeping Score with Analytics Software," *Workforce Management*, 86, no. 10, May 21, 2007, pp. 25–33. See also Andrew McAfee and Eric Brynjolfsson, "Big Data: The Management Revolution," *Harvard Business Review*, October 2012, pp. 61–68. Installing a talent analytics system can be expensive, perhaps $3.5 million including the data warehouse and ad-ditional technology, licenses, and administrators. However, the payoff can be even larger. One study found that the stock prices of companies with ef-fective talent analytics systems outperformed peers by 30%. See Laime Vaitkus, "Money Makes the Case for Workforce Analytics," *Bloomberg BNA Bulletin to Management*, February 14, 2017.

32 Steven Baker, "Data Mining Moves to Human Resources," *Bloomberg Businessweek*, March 12, 2009. Available at: www.BusinessWeek.com /magazine/, accessed April 13, 2011.

33 Ibid. See also "HR Analytics," *Workforce Management*, August 2012, p. 24.

34 Ed Frauenheim, "Numbers Game," *Workforce Management*, 90, no. 3, March 2011, p. 21. See also, "Executive Workplace Analytics," www.aon.com/human-capital-consulting/hrbpo, accessed March 19, 2013.

35 George Marakas, *Decision Support Systems* (Upper Saddle River, NJ: Prentice Hall), 2003, p. 326.

36 Josh Bersin, "Big Data in Human Resources: Talent Analytics (People Analytics) Comes of Age," February 17, 2013, http://www .forbes.com/sites/joshbersin/2013/02/17 /bigdata-in-human-resources-talent-analytics -comes-of-age/ accessed June 20, 2015.

37 Thomas Davenport, Jeanne Harris, and Jeremy Shapiro, "Competing on Talent Analytics," *Harvard Business Review*, October 2010, pp. 52–58.

38 Ibid., p. 54. See also, Cliff Stevenson, "Five Ways High Performance Organizations Use HR Analytics," www.i4cp.com/print /trendwatchers/2012/12/12/five-ways-high -performance-organizations-use-hr-analytics, accessed July 14, 2013.

39 Lin Grensing-Pophal, "HR Audits: Know the Market, Land Assignments," SHRM Consul-tants Forum, December 2004. Available at: www.shrm.org/-hrdisciplines/consultants /Articles/Pages/CMS_010705.aspx, accessed July 7, 2010.

40 "Best Practices for a Human Resources Compli-ance Audit," *Bloomberg BNA Bulletin to Man-agement*, January 21, 2014, pp. 22–24.

41 Lin Grensing-Pophal, "HR Audits: Know the Market, Land Assignments"; and Bill Coy, "Intro-duction to the Human Resources Audit," La Piana Associates, Inc., www.lapiana.org/consulting, accessed May 1, 2008.

42 Dana R. Scott, "Conducting a Human Resources Audit," *New Hampshire Business Review*, Au-gust 2007. See also Eric Krell, "Auditing Your HR Department," *HR Magazine*, September 2011, pp. 101–103.

43 See, for example, www.personneltoday.com /blogs/hcglobal-human-capital-management /2009/02/theres-no-such-thing-as-eviden.html, accessed October 2, 2012.

44 Eric Anderson and Duncan Simester, "A Step-by-Step Guide to Smart Business Experiments," *Harvard Business Review*, March 2011, pp. 98–105.

45 Ibid.

46 Bill Roberts, "How to Put Analytics on Your Side," *HR Magazine*, October 2009, pp. 43–46.

47 See, for example, Samuel Aryee et al., "Impact of High Performance Work Systems on Individual—and Branch—Level Performance: Test of a Multi-level Model of Intermediate Linkages," *Journal of Applied Psychology*, 97, no. 2, 2012, pp. 287–300.

48 www.bls.gov/opub/ted/2006/may/wk2/art01.htm, accessed April 18, 2009; "Super Human Resources Practices Result in Better Overall Performance, Report Says," *BNA Bulletin to Management*, August 26, 2004, pp. 273–274. See also Wendy Boswell, "Aligning Employees with the Organization's Strategic Objectives: Out of Line of Sight, Out of Mind," *International Journal of Human Resource Management*, 17, no. 9, September 2006, pp. 1014–1041. A study found that some employers, which the researchers called cost minimizers, intentionally took a lower-cost approach to human resource practices, with mixed results. See Soo Min Toh et al., "Human Resource Configurations: Investigating Fit with the Organizational Context," *Journal of Applied Psychology*, 93, no. 4, 2008, pp. 864–882.

49 Perhaps not surprisingly, one study found that top managers who (1) did not have strongly employee-centered values and (2) were not con-vinced of the importance of HR investments, were much less likely to approve creation of a high-performance work system. Jeffrey Arthur, et al., "How Top Management HR Beliefs and Values Affect High-Performance Work System Adoption and Implementation Effectiveness," *Human Resource Management*, May—June 2016, volume 55, no 3, pp. 413–435.

50 A recent study used the following dimensions to define high-performance work systems: *au-tonomous job design* (for instance, in terms of employees have the opportunity to decide how to do their work); *internal promotions* (for instance, employees have a real opportunity of being pro-moted); *performance appraisals* (for instance, appraisals are used to plan skill development and training for future promotions); *information sharing* (for instance, there are regular informa-tion sharing meetings); *performance-based pay; employee participation; availability of formal employee training and development; and employ-ment security* (for instance, providing employ-ment security is a priority). Jeffrey Arthur, et al., "How Top Management HR Beliefs and Values Affect High-Performance Work System Adoption and Implementation Effectiveness," *Human Re-source Management*, May—June 2016, volume 55, no 3, pp. 413–435.

51 See for example, www.halogensoftware.com /blog/are-you-using-hr-analytics-and-metrics -effectively, accessed August 27, 2014.

52 See, for example, J. G. Messersmith, "Unlocking the Black Box: Exploring the Link between High-Performance Work Systems and Performance," *Human Resource Management International Digest*, 20, no. 3, 2012, pp. 1118–1132.

53 Alison Konrad, "Engaging Employees through High-Involvement Work Practices," *Ivey Business Journal*, March/April 2006, p. 1.

54 Michael Christian, Adela Garza, and Jerel Slaughter, "Work Engagement: A Quantitative Review and Test of Its Relations with Task and Contextual Performance," *Personnel Psychology*, 60, no. 4, 2011, pp. 89–136.

55 Adrienne Fox, "Raising Engagement," *HR Magazine*, May 2010, pp. 35–40. See also Michael MacKay, et al., "Investigating the Incremental Validity of Employee Engagement in the Prediction of Employee Effectiveness: A Meta-Analytic Path Analysis," *Human Resource Management Review*, volume 27, pp.108–120, 2017.

56 www.gallup.com/strategicconsulting/163007/state-american-workplace.aspx

57 Kevin Kruse, "Why Employee Engagement? (These 28 Research Studies Prove the Benefits)," September 4, 2012, www.Forbes.com.

58 Ibid.

59 "Employee Engagement and Labor Relations," *Gallup Business Journal*: BusinessJournal.Gallup.com, accessed April 10, 2014.

60 "Fatter Bottom Line Results from Sustained Engagement," *Bloomberg BNA Bulletin to Management*, July 30, 2013, p. 243.

61 Except as noted, this is based on Kathryn Tyler, "Prepare for Impact," *HR Magazine*, 56, no. 3, March 2011, pp. 53–56.

62 Rosa Chun and Gary Davies, "Employee Happiness Isn't Enough to Satisfy Customers," *Harvard Business Review*, 87, no. 4, April 2009, p. 19.

63 Kathryn Tyler, "Prepare for Impact," *HR Magazine*, March 2011, pp. 53–56.

64 www.gallup.com/strategicconsulting/163007/state-american-workplace.aspx; Bruce Louis Rich et al., "Job Engagement: Antecedents and Effects on Job Performance," *Academy of Management Journal*, 53, no. 3, 2010, pp. 617–635; "Special Report: Employee Engagement—Losing Lifeblood," *Workforce Management*, July 2011, pp. 24–27.

65 "Five Ways to Improve Employee Engagement Now," *Gallup Business Journal*: businessjournal.gallup.com, accessed April 7, 2014.

66 www.gallup.com/strategicconsulting/163007/state-american-workplace.aspx.

67 Rich et al., "Job Engagement."

68 Konrad, "Engaging Employees through High-Involvement Work Practices."

69 Michael Tucker, "Make Managers Responsible," *HR Magazine*, March 2012, pp. 75–78.

70 Paula Ketter, "What's the Big Deal about Employee Engagement?" *Training & Development*, January 2008, pp. 47–48.

71 "Kia Motors in Big Trouble," *Business Career*, 14, no. 8, August 1997, pp. 12–13.

72 Kia Motors Corporation, 2006 annual report, p. 6.

73 Ibid.

74 Gary Tomlinson, "Building a Culture of High Employee Engagement," *Strategic HR Review*, 9, no. 3, 2010, pp. 25–31.

75 Ibid.

76 Ibid.

77 Ibid.

78 Ibid.

79 Ibid. Note that during these years economic activity in the UK was tumbling, which may account for at least some of the reduced turnover.

Chapter 4

1 See, for example, Toni Hodges DeTuncq and Lynn Schmidt, "Examining Integrated Talent Management," *Training & Development*, September 2013, pp. 31–35.

2 https://go.oracle.com/LP=36875?elqCampaignId=48547&src1=ad:pas:bi:dg:hcm&src2=wwmk160606p00037c0002&SC=sckw=WWMK160606P00037C0002, accessed February 2, 2017.

3 www.silkRoadTech.com, accessed December 10, 2007; http://www.silkroad.com/, accessed February 2, 2017.

4 For a good discussion of job analysis, see James Clifford, "Job Analysis: Why Do It, and How Should It Be Done?" *Public Personnel Management*, 23, no. 2, Summer 1994, pp. 321–340; and "Job Analysis," www.paq.com/index.cfm?FuseAction=bulletins.job analysis, accessed February 3, 2009.

5 One writer calls job analysis, "The hub of virtually all human resource management activities necessary for the successful functioning organizations." See Parbudyal Singh, "Job Analysis for a Changing Workplace," *Human Resource Management Review*, 18, 2008, p. 87.

6 Richard Henderson, *Compensation Management: Rewarding Performance*, Upper Saddle River, NJ: Prentice Hall, 1994, pp. 139–150. See also T. A. Stetz et al., "New Tricks for an Old Dog: Visualizing Job Analysis Results," *Public Personnel Management*, 38, no. 1, Spring 2009, pp. 91–100.

7 Ron Miller, "Streamlining Claims Processing," *eWeek* 23, no. 25, June 19, 2006, pp. 33, 35.

8 J. Richard Hackman et al., "A New Strategy for Job Enrichment," *California Management Review*, 17, no. 4, pp. 57–71.

9 Darin Hartley, "Job Analysis at the Speed of Reality," *Training & Development*, September 2004, pp. 20–22.

10 See Henderson, *Compensation Management*, pp. 148–152.

11 Wayne Cascio, *Applied Psychology in Human Resource Management*, Upper Saddle River, NJ: Prentice Hall, 1998, p. 142. Distortion of information is a potential problem with all self-report methods of gathering information. See, for example, apps.opm.gov/ADT/ContentFiles/AssessmentDecisionGuide071807.pdf, accessed October 1, 2011.

12 http://www.paq.com/, accessed February 2, 2017.

13 We will see that job evaluation is the process through which jobs are compared to one another and their values determined. Although usually viewed as a job analysis technique, the PAQ, in practice, is actually as much or more of a job evaluation technique and is therefore also applicable to our discussion in Chapter 10.

14 Jack Smith and Milton Hakel, "Convergence among Data Sources, Response Bias, and Reliability and Validity of a Structured Job Analysis Questionnaire," *Personnel Psychology*, 32, Winter 1979, pp. 677–692. See also Frederick Morgeson and Stephen Humphrey, "The Work Design Questionnaire (WDQ): Developing and Validating a Comprehensive Measure for Assessing Job Design and the Nature of Work," *Journal of Applied Psychology*, 91, no. 6, 2006, pp. 1321–1339; www.paq.com/index.cfm?FuseAction=bulletins.job analysis, accessed February 3, 2009.

15 This is based on Dianna Stone et al., "Factors Affecting the Effectiveness and Acceptance of Electronic Selection Systems," *Human Resource Management Review*, 23, 2013, pp. 53–54.

16 Ibid.

17 Roni Reiter-Palmon et al., "Development of an O*NET Web-Based Job Analysis and Its Implementation in the U.S. Navy: Lessons Learned," *Human Resource Management Review*, 16, 2006, pp. 294–309.

18 See, for example, Kathryn Tyler, "Job Worth Doing: Update Descriptions," *HR Magazine*, January 2013, pp. 47–49.

19 Regarding this discussion, see Henderson, *Compensation Management*, pp. 175–184. See also Louisa Wah, "The Alphabet Soup of Job Titles," *Management Review*, 87, no. 6, June 1, 1998, pp. 40–43.

20 Ashley Ross, "Job Titles Retailored to Fit," *The New York Times*, September 1, 2013, p. 11.

21 "Creative Job Titles Can Energize Workers," *Harvard Business Review*, May 2016, pp. 24, 25.

22 Ben Kesling and Gordon Lubold, "Navy Restores Traditional Job Titles," *The Wall Street Journal*, December 22, 2016, p. 87.

23 For discussions of writing job descriptions, see James Evered, "How to Write a Good Job Description," *Supervisory Management*, April 1981, pp. 14–19; Roger J. Plachy, "Writing Job Descriptions That Get Results," *Personnel*, October 1987, pp. 56–58; and Jean Phillips and Stanley Gulley, *Strategic Staffing* (Upper Saddle River, NJ: Pearson Education, 2012), pp. 89–95.

24 Evered, "How to Write a Good Job Description," p. 16.

25 Ibid.

26 Ibid.

27 www.paq.com/index.cfm?FuseAction=bulletins.job analysis, accessed February 3, 2009.

28 http://hiring.monster.com/hr/hr-best-practices/recruiting-hiring-advice/job-descriptions/marketing-director-job-description-sample.aspx, accessed February 3, 2017.

29 https://www.careerplanner.com/JobDescSearch-Tool.cfm, accessed February 3, 2017.

30 http://www.americasjobexchange.com/payroll-and-timekeeping-clerk-job-description, accessed February 3, 2017.

31 www.linkedin.com/groups/Best-job-descriptions-40949.S.201279941, accessed March 26, 2013.

32 http://academicaffairs.ucsd.edu/staffhr/classification/task-statements.html, accessed March 27, 2013.

33 www.eeoc.gov/facts/ada17.html, accessed July 17, 2013.

34 Deborah Kearney, *Reasonable Accommodations: Job Descriptions in the Age of ADA, OSHA, and Workers Comp*, New York: Van Nostrand Reinhold, 1994, p. 9. See also Paul Starkman, "The ADA's Essential Job Function Requirements: Just How Essential Does an Essential Job Function Have to Be?" *Employee Relations Law Journal*, 26, no. 4, Spring 2001, pp. 43–102; and Benjamin Wolkinson and Sarah Wolkinson, "The Pregnant Police Officer's Overtime Duties and Forced Leave Policies Under Title VII, the ADA, and FMLA," *Employee Relations Law Journal*, 36, no. 1, Summer 2010, pp. 3–20.

35 Kearney, *Reasonable Accommodations*.

36 O*Net™ is a trademark of the U.S. Department of Labor, Employment, and Training Administration. https://www.onetonline.org/, accessed February 3, 2017.

37 See, for example, Christelle Lapolice et al., "Linking O*NET Descriptors to Occupational Literacy Requirements Using Job Component Validation," *Personnel Psychology*, 61, 2008, pp. 405–441.

38 Mariani, "Replace with a Database."

39 https://support.office.com/en-us/article/Create-an-organization-chart-21ADA00D-82E6-4340-9033-439AC2843C37, accessed February 3, 2017.

40 https://www.onetonline.org/, accessed February 3, 2017.

41 https://www.onetonline.org/find/industry?
    i=44&g=Go, accessed February 3, 2017.

42 https://www.onetonline.org/link/summary
    /41-2031.00, accessed February 3, 2017.

43 Based on Ernest J. McCormick and Joseph Tif-
    fin, *Industrial Psychology*, Upper Saddle River,
    NJ: Prentice Hall, 1974, pp. 56–61.

44 Steven Hunt, "Generic Work Behavior: An
    Investigation into the Dimensions of Entry-
    Level, Hourly Job Performance," *Personnel
    Psychology*, 49, 1996, pp. 51–83.

45 Similarly, in one study of more than 7,000 execu-
    tives, the researchers found that the behaviors top
    leaders exemplify included: takes initiative, practices
    self-development, displays high integrity, drives for
    results, and develops others. "Are the Best People
    Being Promoted?" *Harvard Business Review*,
    September 2013, p. 89.

46 https://www.lyft.com/drive-with-lyft?1v
    =jb_apply&utm_source=perengo&ref
    =DRIVER500BONUS&utm_jobtitle=Lyft%20Dr
    iver&adgroup=SJC&var3=68543f9f6da1825c
    -1485814525700&adname=68543f9f6da1825c
    -1485814525700&scid=2&_sp=68543f9f6da18
    25c.1485814525700; http://www.idrivewithuber
    .com/uber-driver-requirements/, both accessed
    January 30, 2017.

47 Jean Phillips and Stanley Gulley, *Strategic
    Staffing* (Upper Saddle River, NJ: Pearson
    Education, 2012), pp. 96–102.

48 Ibid., p. 102.

49 "Hiring Engaged and Self-Motivated New
    Employees Is Often the Intangible Ingredient
    That Eludes Managers in the Selection Process,"
    http://www.HR.com, February 21, 2006,
    accessed January 21, 2014.

50 Paul Marciano, "How to Hire Engaged
    Employees," http://www.monsterthinking.com,
    accessed June, 20, 2015.

51 Jeffrey Shippmann et al., "The Practice of
    Competency Modeling," *Personnel Psychology*,
    53, no. 3, 2000, p. 703.

52 Michael Campion et al., "Doing Competencies
    Well: Best Practices in Competency Modeling,"
    Personnel Psychology, 64, 2011, pp. 225–262.

53 http://www.shrm.org/certification/Documents
    /SHRM-BoCK-FINAL4.pdf, p. 4, accessed March
    20, 2015.

54 Richard S. Wellins et al., "Nine Best Practices
    for Effective Talent Management," DDI Develop-
    ment Dimensions International, Inc. www
    .ddiworld.com/DDIWorld/media/white-papers
    /ninebestpracticetalentmanagement_wp_ddi
    .pdf?extpdf, accessed August 20, 2011. For a dis-
    cussion of competency modelling, see Campion et
    al., "Doing Competencies Well."

55 Lindsay Chappell, "Mercedes Factories Em-
    brace a New Order," *Automotive News*,
    May 28, 2001. Daimler is now expanding this
    plant; see www.autoblog.com/2009/03/23
    /rumormill--mercedes-benz-expected-to-expand
    -alabama-plant, accessed March 25, 2009; and
    http://mbusi.com/, accessed August 20, 2011.
    The plant currently builds Daimler's newly
    redesigned C-Class car. http://wot.motortrend.
    com/daimler-invests-in-alabama-plant-for-next-c
    -class-99493.html, accessed March 21, 2015.

56 This is adapted from Campion et al., "Doing
    Competencies Well."

57 Ibid.

58 See, for example, Carol Spicer, "Building a
    Competency Model," *HR Magazine*, April 2009,
    pp. 34–36.

Chapter 5

1   "Transforming Talent Management: Pursuing
    New Perspectives," 2013 Talent Management
    Conference & Exposition, Society for Hu-
    man Resource Management, "Preparing for

    Tomorrow's Talent Gap: Five Strategies to Start
    Today" workshop, p. 4. See also "Succession
    Planning Orientation Guide," *Workforce*, Febru-
    ary 2014, pp. 32–34.

2   Spencer Ante and Joann Lublin, "IBM Crafts
    Succession Plan," *The New York Times*, June 13,
    2011, pp. B1, B12.

3   "More Companies Turn to Work-force Planning
    to Boost Productivity and Efficiency," The Con-
    ference Board, press release/news, August 7, 2006;
    Carolyn Hirschman, "Putting Forecasting in Fo-
    cus," *HR Magazine*, March 2007, pp. 44–49.

4   This section is quoted or paraphrased from,
    "Workforce Planning: Translating the Business
    Plan into the People Plan," Towers Watson, www
    .towerswatson.com/en-GB/Insights/IC-Types
    /Survey-Research-Results/2012/11/workforce
    -planning-translating-the-business-plan-into-the
    -people-plan?page=0, accessed March 29, 2013.

5   Hirschman, "Putting Forecasting in Focus,"
    pp. 44–49.

6   Jones Shannon, "Does HR Planning Improve
    Business Results?," *Industrial Management*,
    January/February 2003, p. 16.

7   See, for example, Fay Hansen, "The Long
    View," *Workforce Management*, April 20, 2008,
    pp. 1, 14.

8   Bill Roberts, "Can They Keep Our Lights On?"
    HR Magazine, June 2010, pp. 62–68.

9   For an example of a computerized personnel
    planning system, see Dan Kara, "Automating
    the Service Chain," *Software Magazine*, 20, June
    2000, pp. 3, 42. www.kronos.com/scheduling
    -software/scheduling.aspx, accessed October 2,
    2011.

10 See, for example, www.shrm.org/Templates-
    Tools/hrqa/Pages/Howcanaskillsinventorybeused
    for strategicHRplanning.aspx, accessed February
    6, 2014.

11 http://skillsdbpro.com/SkillsDBPROWeb.html;
    http://skillsdbpro.com/client-list/; and www
    .surveyanalytics.com/skills-inventory.html,
    accessed June 22, 2015.

12 http://www.skills-base.com/, accessed
    February 12, 2015.

13 www.surveyanalytics.com/skills-inventory
    -software.html, accessed June 1, 2011.

14 www.sumtotalsystems.com/datasheets/sumt
    _succession_planning.pdf, accessed June 1, 2011.

15 For a discussion, see, for example, "Pitfalls
    Abound for Employers Lacking Electronic In-
    formation Retention Policies," *BNA Bulletin to
    Management*, January 1, 2008, pp. 1–2.

16 The legislation includes the Federal Privacy Act
    of 1974 (applies to federal workers), the New
    York Personal Privacy Act of 1985, HIPAA
    (regulates use of medical records), and the
    Americans with Disabilities Act.

17 Ibid. See also Bill Roberts, "Risky Business," *HR
    Magazine*, October 2006, pp. 69–72.

18 www.wired.com/2015/06/opm-breach
    -security-privacy-debacle/, accessed August 25,
    2015.

19 "For the Paperless HR Department, Security
    and Accessibility Are Watchwords," *Bloomberg
    BNA Bulletin to Management*, November 12,
    2013, p. 362.

20 www.astd.org/NR/rdonlyres/CBAB6F0D-97FA
    -4B1F-920C-6EBAF98906D1/0
    /BridgingtheSkillsGap.pdf, accessed June 1, 2011.

21 "Next Generation Talent Management,"
    www.hewittassociates.com/_MetaBasicCMAs
    setCache_/Assets/Articles/next_generation.pdf,
    accessed November 9, 2010.

22 Ibid. See also "Boeing Soars over Potential
    Talent Gaps with its Work-force Planning
    Strategies," *Bloomberg BNA, Bulletin to
    Management*, February 19, 2013, p. 57.

23 Ed Frauenheim, "Valero Energy," *Workforce
    Management*, March 13, 2006.

24 Jean Phillips and Stanley Gully, *Strategic Staffing*
    (Boston: Pearson, 2015), pp. 116–181.

25 For example, the workforce plan for Waverly
    Council (www.waverley.nsw.gov.au/__data
    /assets/pdf_file/0018/17640/WaveleyWorkforce
    Plan.pdf) contains workforce projections on pages
    15–24, discussions of how to close skills gaps, and
    then actual specific recruiting and other workforce
    plans on pages 25–34.

26 See images of actual staffing plans at www
    .google.com/search?q=example+of+a+staffing+pl
    an&client=firefoxa&hs=8bm&rls=org.mozilla
    :en-US:official&tbm=isch&tbo=u&source=univ
    &sa=X&ei=zDTxUunwJI3qkQeTrYHACw&ved
    =0CCcQsAQ&biw=1024&bih=557.

27 On the other hand, Facebook and Intuit are do-
    ing "program hiring;" here they hire particularly
    promising candidates, although they don't have
    specific jobs for them. Lindsay Gellman, "When
    a Job Offer Comes Without a Job," *The Wall
    Street Journal*, December 2, 2015, pp. B1, B7.

28 Lauren Weber, "To Get a Job, New Hires
    Are Put to the Test," *The Wall Street Journal*,
    April 15, 2015, pp. A1, A10.

29 Tom Porter, "Effective Techniques to Attract,
    Hire, and Retain 'Top Notch' Employees for
    Your Company," *San Diego Business Journal*,
    21, no. 13, March 27, 2000, p. B36.

30 Jonathan Segal, "Land Executives, Not
    Lawsuits," *HR Magazine*, October 2006,
    pp. 123–130.

31 Sara Rynes, Robert Bretz Jr., and Barry Gerhart,
    "The Importance of Recruitment and Job
    Choice: A Different Way of Looking," *Personnel
    Psychology*, 44, no. 3, September 1991,
    pp. 487–521.

32 Jean Phillips and Stanley Gully, *Strategic
    Staffing*.

33 Samuel Greengard, "Recruit Like a Marketer!"
    Workforce, August 2016, pp. 40–43; see also
    Tony Lee, "Follow the Leaders: 12 Tips from
    Talent Acquisition Pros," *HR Magazine*, July/
    August 2016, pp. 46–51.

34 Genevieve Douglas, "Online Reviews Greatly
    Influence Employer Brands," *Bloomberg BNA
    Bulletin to Management*, February 7, 2017

35 "Recruitment Marketing," available at:
    www.recruiter.com/recruitment_marketing/, ac-
    cessed May 1, 2012.

36 www.ge.com/careers/why_ge.html, accessed May
    1, 2012.

37 Stanley Gully, Jean Phillips, William Castellano,
    Khongji Han, and Andrea Kim, "A Mediated
    Moderation Model of Recruiting Socially and Envi-
    ronmentally Responsible Job Applicants," *Person-
    nel Psychology*, 2013, no. 66, p. 966.

38 Kenneth Sovereign, *Personnel Law* (Upper Sad-
    dle River, NJ: Prentice Hall, 1999), pp. 47–49.

39 Ibid., p. 48.

40 Rachel Emma Silverman and Lauren Weber,
    "An Inside Job: More Firms Opt to Recruit
    from Within," *The Wall Street Journal*, May 30,
    2012, p. B1.

41 Todd Henneman, "The Insiders or the Outsiders?"
    Workforce, March 2014, pp. 29–31, 48.

42 Eric Krell, "Look Outside or Seek Within?" *HR
    Magazine*, January/February 2015, pp. 61–64.

43 www.fedex.com/ma/about/overview/philosophy
    .html.

44 Lauren Weber and Leslie Kwoh, "Beware the
    Phantom Job Listing," *The Wall Street Journal*,
    January 9, 2013, p. B1.

45 "Many Workers Use Social Networking Sites in
    Job Hunt, Edit Own Content, Survey Finds,"
    BNA Bulletin to Management, May 10, 2011,
    p. 147.

46 See, for example, J. De Avila, "Beyond Job Boards: Targeting the Source," *The Wall Street Journal* (Eastern Edition), July 2, 2009, pp. D1, D5; and C. Fernandez-Araoz et al., "The Definitive Guide to Recruiting in Good Times and Bad" [Financial crisis spotlight], *Harvard Business Review*, 87, no. 5, May 2009, pp. 74–84.

47 Dave Zielinski, "The Gamification of Recruitment," *HR Magazine*, November 2015, pp. 59–61.

48 "Innovative HR Programs Cultivate Successful Employees," *Nation's Restaurant News* 41, no. 50, December 17, 2007, p. 74.

49 Sarah Fister Gale, "Social Media Transforms a Recruiting Source Software Industry," *Workforce Management,* workforce.com, June 2013, p. 26. See also Thomas Cottereau, "The Future of Live Video Interviews for Recruitment," *HR Magazine*, November 2014, pp. 48–50. Similarly, Main Line Health, a healthcare network with 10,000 employees, uses web-based video for prescreening applicants, allowing them to respond on their own schedule to prerecorded questions; Main Line recruiters then view these videos and invite selected applicants for in-person interviews. Drew Robb, "For HR, Video Is a Star," *HR Magazine*, February 2016, p. 65.

50 Elizabeth Agnvall, "Job Fairs Go Virtual," *HR Magazine*, July 2007, p. 85; Gary Stern, "Virtual Job Fairs Becoming More of a Reality," *Workforce Management*, February 2011, p. 11.

51 Yuko Takeo and Nao Sano, "A Job Website Thrives in the New Japan," *Bloomberg BusinessWeek*, pp. 41–42.

52 Matthias Baum and Rudiger Kabst, "The Effectiveness of Recruitment Advertisements and Recruitment Websites: Indirect and Interactive Effects on Applicant Attraction," *Human Resource Management* 53, no. 3, May–June 2014, pp. 353–378.

53 "EEOC Issues Much Delayed Definition of 'Applicant,'" *HR Magazine*, April 2004, p. 29; Valerie Hoffman and Greg Davis, "OFCCP's Internet Applicant Definition Requires Overhaul of Recruitment and Hiring Policies," *Society for Human Resources Management Legal Report*, January/February 2006, p. 2.

54 This carries legal risks, particularly if the device disproportionately screens out minority or female applicants. Lisa Harpe, "Designing an Effective Employment Prescreening Program," *Employment Relations Today* 32, no. 3, Fall 2005, pp. 43–51.

55 Lauren Weber, "Your Resume versus Oblivion," *The Wall Street Journal*, January 24, 2012, pp. B1, B6.

56 William Dickmeyer, "Applicant Tracking Reports Make Data Meaningful," *Workforce*, February 2001, pp. 65–67; and, as an example, www.icims.com/prelude/1101/3009?_vsrefdom =google_ppc&gclid=CPHki_nx1KsCFcPt7Qodm kjLDA, accessed October 4, 2011.

57 Paul Gilster, "Channel the Resume Flood with Applicant Tracking Systems," *Workforce*, January 2001, pp. 32–34; William Dickmeyer, "Applicant Tracking Reports Make Data Meaningful," *Workforce*, February 2001, pp. 65–67; and, as an example, www.icims.com/prelude/1101/3009? _vsrefdom=google_ppc&gclid=CPHki_nx1KsCF cPt7QodmkjLDA, accessed October 4, 2011.

58 Note that the U.S. Department of Labor's Office of Federal Contract Compliance programs reviews federal contractors' online application tracking systems to ensure they're providing equal opportunity to qualify prospective applicants with disabilities. "Feds Want a Look at Online Job Sites," *HR Magazine*, November 2008, p. 12.

59 "E-Recruiting Software Providers," *Workforce Management*, June 22, 2009, p. 14.

60 Lauren Weber, "Your Resume versus Oblivion."

61 Dave Zielinski, "Seven Reasons to Love Your ATS," *HR Magazine*, October 2015, pp. 31–36.

62 "Does Your Company's Website Click with Job Seekers?" *Workforce*, August 2000, p. 260.

63 Sarah Gale, "Internet Recruiting: Better, Cheaper, Faster," *Workforce*, December 2001, p. 75.

64 "Help Wanted—and Found," *Fortune*, October 2, 2006, p. 40.

65 James Breaugh, "Employee Recruitment: Current Knowledge and Important Areas for Future Research," *Human Resource Management Review*, 18, 2008, p. 114.

66 Anthony Abbatiello, "The Digital Override," *Workforce*, May 2014, pp. 36–39; "Social Recruiting in 2012, the Ladders.com," Special Advertising Supplement to *Workforce Management*, 2012; and http://cdn.theladders.net/static /recruit-ladder/pdf/WP%20Social%20Recruiting %20in%202012.pdf, accessed July 2, 2014.

67 Jennifer Arnold, "Twittering at Face Booking While They Were," *HR Magazine*, December 2009, p. 54.

68 Ibid.

69 Aliah Wright, "Your Social Media Is Showing," *HR Magazine*, March 2012, p. 16. However, one survey by Glassdoor concluded that about half of those making hiring decisions say their passive recruiting efforts are less effective than they used to be: fewer passive candidates respond to unsolicited e-mails and phone calls than in the past. Sarah Fister Gale, "The New Recruits in the Recruiting," *Workforce*, May 2015, p. 44.

70 https://premium.linkedin.com/ premiumhiring/features, accessed April 6, 2015.

71 Jim Lundy, "Research Note," *Aragon Research* 3, January 31, 2014.

72 http://mystaffingpro.com/, accessed February 12, 2017.

73 Laszlo Bock, *Work Rules!* (New York: Twelve, 2015) pp. 81, 82.

74 Laszlo Bock, Ibid., pp. 79–86.

75 Eric Krell, "Recruiting Outlook: Creative HR for 2003," *Workforce*, December 2002, pp. 40–44.

76 Breaugh, "Employee Recruitment," p. 111.

77 Breaugh, Ibid., p. 113.

78 Find your nearest one-stop center at www .servicelocator.org.

79 Ibid.

80 Taryn Barnes, "Real Gig-Getters," *Workforce*, October 2015, p. 50.

81 Laime Vaitkus, "Gig Economy Begets More Agile Workforce," *Bloomberg BNA Bulletin to Management*, December 13, 2016.

82 One "Wharton MBA and GE alum" manages short-term projects for major companies and served as interim CEO for one firm. See Jodi Greenstone Miller and Matt Miller, "The Best Executive and Professional Jobs May No Longer Be Full-Time Gigs," *Harvard Business Review*, May 2012, p. 51.

83 "As Hiring Falters, More Workers Are Temporary," *The New York Times*, December 20, 2010, pp. A1, A4.

84 John Zappe, "Temp-to-Hire Is Becoming a Full-Time Practice at Firms," *Workforce Management*, June 2005, pp. 82–86.

85 Ibid.

86 Robert Bohner Jr. and Elizabeth Salasko, "Beware the Legal Risks of Hiring Temps," *Workforce*, October 2002, pp. 50–57. See also Fay Hansen, "A Permanent Strategy for Temporary Hires," *Workforce Management*, February 26, 2007, p. 27; and Robert Grossman, "Strategic Temptations," *HR Magazine*, March 2012, pp. 24–34.

87 Daniel Feldman, Helen Doerpinghaus, and William Turnley, "Managing Temporary Workers: A Permanent HRM Challenge," *Organizational Dynamics*, 23, no. 2, Fall 1994, p. 49. See also Kathryn Tyler, "Treat Contingent

Workers with Care," *HR Magazine*, March 2008, p. 75; and www.employment.oregon .gov/EMPLOY/ES/BUS/index.shtml, accessed October 4, 2011.

88 This is based on or quoted from Nancy Howe, "Match Temp Services to Your Needs," *Personnel Journal*, March 1989, pp. 45–51. See also Stephen Miller, "Collaboration Is Key to Effective Outsourcing," *HR Magazine*, 58, 2008, pp. 60–61; and (as an example), www.bbb .org/shreveport/accredited-business -directory/employment-contractors-temporary -help/plain-dealing-la, accessed September 23, 2011.

89 Carolyn Hirschman, "Are Your Contractors Legal?" *HR Magazine*, March 2004, pp. 59–63. One staffing agency allegedly used 39 Filipino nationals to work 16-hour days at country clubs and golf courses, paying them little and allegedly treating them as "slaves." Dori Meinert, "Modern-Day Slavery," *HR Magazine*, May 2012, pp. 22–24.

90 Ibid.

91 Margaret Steen, "More Employers Take on Temps, but Planning Is Paramount," *Workforce Management*, May 2011, p. 14.

92 Heather Jackson and Cary Donham, "Five Things to Know about Working with Staffing Firms," *Workforce Management*, October 2013, p. 47.

93 Harry Davis and Christopher Giampapa, "How to Protect Your Firm from Employee Raiding," *Bloomberg BNA Bulletin to Management*, 66, no. 18, May 5, 2015, pp. 51–52.

94 "Apple and Google Will Pay $415 Million; Intuit and eBay Settle in Separate No Poach Case," *Bloomberg BNA Bulletin to Management*, September 15, 2015, p. 201.

95 Patrick Thibodeau, "Offshoring Shrinks Number of IT Jobs, Study Says," http://www .computerworld.com/article/2502949/it -outsourcing/offshoring-shrinks-number-of-it-jobs -study-says.html, accessed February 13, 2017.

96 See for example, Esther Lander and Andrew Turnbull, "Defending and Avoiding Citizenship Discrimination Claims When Using Staffing Firms with H1-B Visa Holders," *Bloomberg BNA Bulletin to Management*, 67, no. 11, March 15, 2016, pp. 51–54.

97 Eli Stocols and Laura Meckler, "Trump Unveils H-1B Order," *The Wall Street Journal*, April 19, 2017, p. A4; and Vindu Goel, "How 'Hire American' Could Affect the World of Tech Workers," *The New York Times*, April 19, 2017, p. A16.

98 Michelle Martinez, "Working with an Outside Recruiter? Get It in Writing," *HR Magazine*, January 2001, pp. 98–105.

99 See, for example, Stephenie Overman, "Searching for the Top," *HR Magazine*, January 2008, p. 49.

100 Bill Leonard, "Recruiting from the Competition," *HR Magazine*, February 2001, pp. 78–86. See also G. Anders, "Secrets of the Talent Scouts," *The New York Times* (Late New York Edition), March 15, 2009, pp. 1, 7 (Sec 3).

101 One survey estimates that in-house recruiting has increased by 25% between 2008 in 2013. "Searching for Answers," *The Economist*, August 24, 2013, p. 61.

102 Carol Hymowitz and Jeff Green, "These Days, Anybody Can Head-hunt," *Bloomberg Business Week*, January 20 7, 2013, pp. 19–20; Joann Lublin, "More Executive Recruiting Ships in House," *The Wall Street Journal*, October 10, 2012, p. B8. With employers increasingly finding new ways of recruiting top management talent, executive search firms are diversifying. For example, Korn/Ferry is expanding into areas such as employee development. Lauren Weber, "Here's What Boards Want in Executives," *The Wall Street Journal*, December 10, 2014, p. B5.

103 John Wareham, *Secrets of a Corporate Head-hunter* (New York: Playboy Press, 1981), pp. 213–225; Chip McCreary, "Get the Most out of Search Firms," *Workforce*, August 1997, pp. S28–S30.

104 www.kaiserpermanentejobs.org/employee-referral-program.aspx, accessed August 20, 2011.

105 Mark Feffer, "New Connections," *HR Magazine*, April 2015, pp. 46–50.

106 Breaugh, "Employee Recruitment," p. 109.

107 "Tell a Friend: Employee Referral Programs Earn High Marks for Low Recruiting Costs," *BNA Bulletin to Management*, June 28, 2001, p. 201.

108 Rebecca Greenfield, "Hiring an Employee's Buddy Is Fueling a Major Workplace Crisis," *Bloomberg BNA Bulletin to Management*, January 10, 2017.

109 Robert Grossman, "How to Recruit a Recruitment Outsourcer," *HR Magazine*, July 2012, pp. 51–54; and Susan Ladika, "A Lot to Process," *Workforce Management*, July 2012, pp. 16–18.

110 Sarah Fister Gale, "RPO Customers: We Want More of Everything," *Workforce*, January/February 2017, pp. 44–45.

111 Martha Frase-Blunt, "A Recruiting Spigot," *HR Magazine*, April 2003, pp. 71–79.

112 Sara Rynes, Marc Orlitzky, and Robert Bretz Jr., "Experienced Hiring versus College Recruiting: Practices and Emerging Trends," *Personnel Psychology*, 50, 1997, pp. 309–339. See also Lisa Munniksma, "Career Matchmakers: Partnering with Collegiate Career Centers Offers Recruiters Access to Rich Source of Applicants," *HR Magazine*, 50, no. 2, February 2005, p. 93.

113 See, for example, Breaugh, "Employee Recruitment," p. 111.

114 "Recruiters Look to Be Big Man on Campus," *Workforce Management*, September 2010, p. 12.

115 Joe Mullich, "Finding the Schools That Yield the Best Job Applicant ROI," *Workforce Management*, March 2004, pp. 67–68.

116 Greet Van Hoye and Filip Lievens, "Tapping the Grapevine: A Closer Look at Word-of-Mouth as a Recruitment Source," *Journal of Applied Psychology*, 94, no. 2, 2009, pp. 341–352.

117 Wendy Boswell et al., "Individual Job Choice Decisions and the Impact of Job Attributes and Recruitment Practices: A Longitudinal Field Study," *Human Resource Management*, 42, no. 1, Spring 2003, pp. 23–37. See also Breaugh, "Employee Recruitment," p. 115.

118 Hao Zhao Oh and Robert Liden, "Internship: A Recruitment and Selected Perspective," *Journal of Applied Psychology*, 96, no. 1, 2011, pp. 221–229.

119 Teddy Wayne, "The No Limits Job," *The New York Times*, March 3, 2013, Sunday Styles p. 1.

120 Lawrence Peikes and Christine Salmon Wachter, "Court Adopts New Test for Determining Interns, Status," *HR Magazine*, October 2015, p. 73.

121 Martha Frase-Blunt, "Call Centers Come Home," *HR Magazine*, January 2007, pp. 85–90.

122 Dori Meinert, "The Value of Veterans," *HR Magazine*, November 2016, pp. 53–55.

123 Christopher Stone and Dianna Stone, "Factors Affecting Hiring Decisions About Veterans," *Human Resource Management Review* 25, no. 1, 2015, pp. 68–79.

124 Theresa Minton-Eversole, "Mission: Recruitment," *HR Magazine*, January 2009, pp. 43–45.

125 See, for example, Stephanie Castellano, "The Value of Veterans," *Training & Development*, February 2013, p. 16.

126 Rebecca Greenfield, "Hiring an Employee's Buddy Is Fueling a Major Workplace Crisis," *Bloomberg BNA Bulletin to Management*, January 10, 2017.

127 "Internship Programs Help These Recruiters toward Qualified Students with Disabilities," *BNA Bulletin to Management*, July 17, 2003, p. 225.

128 Ellen McGirt, "Google Searches Its Soul," *Fortune*, February 1, 2017, p. 55.

129 Ibid.

130 Ellen Huet, "In the Land of the Blind Hire," *Bloomberg BusinessWeek*, January 23–29, 2017, pp. 27–28.

131 www.recruitingtrends.com/recruiting-women/; http://online.wsj.com/article/SB1000142412788 7323764804578314450063914388.html; www .theresumator.com/blog/how-to-recruit-women -for-your-workforce/; http://blogs.kenan-flagler .unc.edu/2012/06/12/the-new-business-imperative -recruiting-and-retaining-women-in-the- workplace/. All accessed May 9, 2013.

132 https://www.census.gov/prod/2013pubs/ p20-570.pdf, accessed February 13, 2017.

133 Judith Casey and Marcie Pitt-Catsouphes, "Employed Single Mothers: Balancing Job and Home Life," *Employee Assistance Quarterly*, 9, no. 324, 1994, pp. 37–53; www.catalyst .org/publication/252/working-parents, accessed October 3, 2011.

134 Casey and Pitt-Catsouphes, "Employed Single Mothers," p. 42.

135 "Barclaycard Helps Single Parents to Find Employment," *Personnel Today*, November 7, 2006.

136 Caroline Straub, "Antecedents and Organizational Consequences of Family Supportive Supervisor Behavior: A Multilevel Conceptual Framework for Research," *Human Resource Management Review* 22, 2012, pp. 15–26.

137 Susan Glairon, "Single Parents Need More Flexibility at Work, Advocate in Denver Says," *Daily Camera*, February 8, 2002; www.cnn .com/2008/LIVING/worklife/06/04 /balance.calculator, accessed October 5, 2011.

138 Sandra Block and Stephanie Armour, "Many Americans Retire Years before They Want To," *USA Today*, July 26, 2006, http://usatoday.com, accessed December 23, 2007.

139 Alison Wellner, "Tapping a Silver Mine," *HR Magazine*, March 2002, p. 29.

140 Phased retirements are increasingly popular, with various employers letting employees close to retirement reduce their schedules to between 16 and 30 hours weekly. Carol Hymowitz, "American Firms Want to Keep Older Workers a Bit Longer," *Bloomberg BNA Bulletin to Management*, January 3, 2017.

141 Sue Shellenbarger, "Gray Is Good." See also Robert Grossman, "Keep Pace with Older Workers," *HR Magazine*, May 2008, pp. 39–46.

142 Gary Adams and Barbara Rau, "Attracting Retirees to Apply: Desired Organizational Characteristics of Bridge Employment," *Journal of Organizational Behavior*, 26, no. 6, September 2005, pp. 649–660.

143 Thomas Ng and Daniel Feldman, "Evaluating Six Common Stereotypes About Older Workers with Meta-Analytical Data," *Personnel Psychology*, 60, no. 6, 2012, pp. 821–858.

144 Ibid.

145 Abby Ellin, "Supervising the Gray-beards," *The New York Times*, January 16, 2000, p. B16; Derek Avery and Patrick McKay, "Target Practice: An Organizational Impression Management Approach to Attracting Minority and Female Job Applicants," *Personnel Psychology*, 59, 2006, pp. 157–189.

146 www.nbmbaa.org/home.aspx?PageID=637&.

147 Herbert Greenberg, "A Hidden Source of Talent," *HR Magazine*, March 1997, pp. 88–91.

148 Noam Scheiber, "Study Using Fake Job Letters Exposes Bias Against Disabled," *The New York Times*, November 2, 2015, pp. B1, B2.

149 Linda Moore, "Firms Need to Improve Recruitment, Hiring of Disabled Workers, EEO Chief Says," *Knight Ridder/Tribune Business News*, November 5, 2003. See also "Recruiting Disabled More Than Good Deed, Experts Say," *BNA Bulletin to Management*, February 27, 2007, p. 71.

150 "Students with Disabilities Available," *HR Briefing*, June 15, 2002, p. 5.

151 Moore, "Firms Need to Improve Recruitment."

152 This paragraph is based on Jennifer L. Wood, James M. Schmidtke, and Diane L. Decker, "Lying on Job Applications: The Effects of Job Relevance, Commission, and Human Resource Management Experience," *Journal of Business and Psychology*, 22, 2007, pp. 1–9.

153 Kenneth Sovereign, *Personnel Law* (Upper Saddle River, NJ: Pearson, 1999), pp. 51, 132.

154 Rachel Emma Silverman, "No More Resumes, Say Some Firms," *The Wall Street Journal*, January 24, 2012, p. B6.

155 Kathy Gurchiek, "Video Resumes Spark Curiosity, Questions," *HR Magazine*, May 2007, pp. 28–30; "Video Resumes Can Illuminate Applicants' Abilities, but Pose Discrimination Concerns," *BNA Bulletin to Management*, May 20, 2007, pp. 169–170.

156 As of August 20, 2014, these companies included resumebook.tv, and optimalresume.com. Alina Dizik, "Wooing Job Recruiters with Video Resumes," *The Wall Street Journal*, May 20, 2010, p. D4.

157 Murray Barrick and Ryan Zimmerman, "Hiring for Retention and Performance," *Human Resource Management*, 48, no. 2, March/April 2009, pp. 183–206.

158 James Breaugh, "The Use of Biodata for Employee Selection: Test Research and Future Directions," *Human Resource Management Review*, 19, 2009, pp. 219–231. Utilizing biodata items of course presumes that the employer can show that the items predict performance. Biodata items such as "graduated from college" may have an adverse impact on minorities but studies suggest that employers can avoid that problem through judicious choice of biodata items.

159 Fred Mael, Mary Connerley, and Ray Morath, "None of Your Business: Parameters of Biodata Invasiveness," *Personnel Psychology*, 49, 1996, pp. 613–650; and Kenneth Law et al., "Impression Management and Faking in Biodata Scores among Chinese Job-Seekers," *Asia Pacific Journal of Management*, 19, no. 4, December 2002, pp. 541–556.

160 "Supreme Court Denies Circuit City's Bid for Review of Mandatory Arbitration," *BNA Bulletin to Management*, June 6, 2002, p. 177.

161 "Supreme Court Gives the Employers Green Light to Hold Most Employees to Arbitration Pacts," *BNA Bulletin to Management*, March 29, 2001, pp. 97–98.

162 Douglas Mahony et al., "The Effects of Mandatory Employment Arbitration Systems on Applicants' Attraction to Organizations," *Human Resource Management*, 44, no. 4, Winter 2005, pp. 449–470; see also H. John Bernardin et al., "Mandatory and Binding Arbitration: Effects on Employee Attitudes and Recruiting Results," *Human Resource Management*, 50, no. 2, March–April 2011, pp. 175–200.

163 Sarah Fister Gale, "Candidate Experience Tech Is Ticking Them Off," *Workforce*, September/October 2016, p. 10.

164 Ibid.

165 Martin Berman – Gorvine, "Treat Job Candidates Well for Brand-Name Boost," *Bloomberg BNA Bulletin to Management*, April 18, 2017.

166 Abdifatah A. Ali, Ann Marie Ryan, Brent J. Lyons, Mark J. Ehrhart, and Jennifer L. Wessel, "The Long Road to Employment: Incivility Experienced by Job Seekers," *Journal of Applied Psychology*, 101, no. 3, 2016, pp. 333–349.

Chapter 6

1 Indeed, psychologists have called selection and recruitment the "supreme problem." Robert Ployhart et al., "Solving the Supreme Problem: 100 Years of Selection and Recruitment at the Journal of Applied Psychology," *Journal of Applied Psychology*, volume 102, number three, 2017, pp. 291–304.

2 Lauren Weber, "To Get a Job, New Hires Are Put to the Test," *The Wall Street Journal*, April 15, 2015, pp. A1, A10.

3 Kevin Hart, "Not Wanted: Thieves," *HR Magazine*, April 2008, p. 119.

4 Note that in one survey, about 16% of HR professionals said their firms were less rigorous about checking the backgrounds of executive candidates than non-executives. This is a dubious practice, given the high cost of hiring the wrong executive. Genevieve Douglas, "Employers Beware Potential Skeletons in Executives, Closets," *Bloomberg BNA Bulletin to Management*, May 9, 2017.

5 "Wal-Mart to Scrutinize Job Applicants," *CNN Money*, August 12, 2004, available at: http://money.cnn.com/2004/08/12/News /fortune500/walmart_jobs/index.htm, accessed August 8, 2005.

6 Bart Wille et al., "Expanding and Reconceptualizing Aberrant Personality at Work: Validity of Five Factor Model Aberrant Personality Tendencies to Predict Career Outcomes," *Personnel Psychology*, 60, no. 6, 2013, pp. 173–223.

7 Steven Mitchell Sack, "Fifteen Steps to Protecting against the Risk of Negligent Hiring Claims," *Employment Relations Today*, August 1993, pp. 313–320; Fay Hansen, "Taking 'Reasonable' Action to Avoid Negligent Hiring Claims," *Workforce Management*, September 11, 2006, p. 31.

8 Anne Anastasi, *Psychological Patterns* (New York: Macmillan, 1968). See also Kevin Murphy and Charles Davidshofer, *Psychological Testing* (Upper Saddle River, NJ: Prentice Hall, 2001), pp. 108–124.

9 Murphy and Davidshofer, *Psychological Testing*, pp. 116–119.

10 M. Guion, "Changing Views for Personnel Selection Research," *Personnel Psychology*, 40, no. 2, Summer 1987, pp. 199–213. The Standards for Educational and Psychological Testing define validity as "the degree to which accumulated evidence and theories support specific interpretations of test scores entailed by proposed uses of a test." Deborah Whetzel and Michael McDaniel, "Situational Judgment Tests: An Overview of Current Research," *Human Resource Management Review*, 19, 2009, p. 191.

11 The Uniform Guidelines say, "Employers should ensure that tests and selection procedures are not adopted casually by managers who know little about these processes. . . . [N]o test or selection procedure should be implemented without an understanding of its effectiveness and limitations for the organization, its appropriateness for a specific job, and whether it can be appropriately administered and scored."

12 Jean Phillips and Stanley Gully, *Strategic Staffing* (Upper Saddle River, NJ: Pearson Education, 2012), p. 220.

13 Ibid.

14 Robert Gatewood and Hubert Feild, *Human Resource Selection* (Fort Worth, TX: Dryden Press, 1994), p. 243.

15 Bill Leonard, "Wanted: Shorter Time to Hire," *HR Magazine*, November 2011, pp. 49–52.

16 Based on Dave Zielinski, "Effective Assessments," *HR Magazine*, January 2011, pp. 61–64.

17 For a recent discussion, see, for example, Jonathan Cottrell, Daniel Newman, and Glenn Roisman, "Explaining the Black–White Gap in Cognitive Test Scores: Toward a Theory of Adverse Impact," *Journal of Applied Psychology*, 100, no. 6, 2015, pp. 1713–1736.

18 Sarah Gale, "Three Companies Cut Turnover with Tests," *Workforce*, April 2002, pp. 66–69.

19 Weber, "To Get a Job, New Hires Are Put to the Test."

20 SHRM members can use the SHRM testing center to access to hundreds of scientifically scored assessments and tests.

21 See, for example, Paul Agnello, Rachel Ryan, and Kenneth Yusko, "Implications of Modern Intelligence Research for Assessing Intelligence in the Workplace," *Human Resource Management Review* 25, no. 1, 2015, pp. 47–55; and C. A. Scherbaum and H. W. Goldstein, "Intelligence and the Modern World of Work," *Human Resource Management Review* 25, no. 1, March 2015, pp. 1–3.

22 William Wagner, "All Skill, No Finesse," *Workforce*, June 2000, pp. 108–116. See also, for example, James Diefendorff and Kajal Mehta, "The Relations of Motivational Traits with Workplace Deviance," *Journal of Applied Psychology*, 92, no. 4, 2007, pp. 967–977. The relationship between personality and job performance isn't necessarily one-way. One study found that success on the job looped back and influenced workers' personalities. Bart Wille and Filip De Fruyt, "Vocations as a Source of Identity: Reciprocal Relations Between Big Five Personality Traits and RIASEC Characteristics over 15 Years," *Journal of Applied Psychology*, 99, no. 2, 2014, pp. 262–281.

23 Toddi Gutner, "Applicants' Personalities Put to the Test," *The Wall Street Journal*, August 26, 2008, p. D4.

24 Elaine Pulakos, *Selection Assessment Methods* (Alexandria, VA: SHRM Foundation, 2005), p. 9.

25 www.myersbriggsreports.com/?gclid=CK71m6r Eh6ACFVZS2godDEjgkw, accessed August 21, 2014.

26 www.myersbriggsreports.com/?gclid=CK71m6r Eh6ACFVZS2godDEjgkw, accessed August 21, 2014.

27 Projective tests are usually administered individually, an expensive and time-consuming process. Nathan Carter et al., "Projective Testing: Historical Foundations and Uses for Human Resources Management," *Human Resource Management Review*, 20, no. 3, 2013, p. 214.

28 Studies suggest that vocational interests tests can be useful for predicting employee performance and turnover. Chad H. Van Iddeking et al., "Are You Interested? A Meta-Analysis of Relations between Vocational Interests and Employee Performance and Turnover," *Journal of Applied Psychology*, 96, no. 6, 2011, pp. 1167–1194.

29 Dracos Iliescu et al., "Vocational Fit and Counterproductive Work Behaviors: A Self-Regulation Perspective," *Journal of Applied Psychology* 100, no. 1, 2015, pp. 21–39.

30 See, for example, Jesus Salgado, "The Five Factor Model of Personality and Job Performance in the European Community," *Journal of Applied Psychology*, 82, no. 1, 1997, pp. 30–43; Joyce Hogan et al., "Personality Measurement, Faking, and Employee Selection," *Journal of Applied Psychology*, 92, no. 5, 2007, pp. 1270–1285; Lisa Penney and Emily Witt, "A Review of Personality and Performance: Identifying Boundaries,

Contingencies, and Future Research Directions," *Human Resource Management Review*, 20, no. 1, 2011, pp. 297–310.

31 Timothy Judge et al., "Personality and Leadership: A Qualitative and Quantitative Review," *Journal of Applied Psychology*, 87, no. 4, 2002, p. 765.

32 Murray Barrick and Michael Mount, "The Big Five Personality Dimensions and Job Performance: A Meta-Analysis," *Personnel Psychology*, 44, no. 1, Spring 1991, pp. 1–26. See also Robert Schneider, Leatta Hough, and Marvin Dunnette, "Broad-Sided by Broad Traits: How to Sink Science in Five Dimensions or Less," *Journal of Organizational Behavior*, 17, no. 6, November 1996, pp. 639–655; and Paula Caligiuri, "The Big Five Personality Characteristics as Predictors of Expatriate's Desire to Terminate the Assignment and Supervisor-Rated Performance," *Personnel Psychology*, 53, 2000, pp. 67–68.

33 Frederick Morgeson et al., "Reconsidering the Use of Personality Tests in Personnel Selection Contexts," *Personnel Psychology*, 60, 2007, p. 683. Other experts call such concerns "unfounded." Robert Tett and Neil Christiansen, "Personality Tests at the Crossroads: A Response to Morgeson, Campion, Dipboye, Hollenbeck, Murphy, and Schmitt," *Personnel Psychology*, 60, 2007, p. 967. See also Deniz Ones et al., "In Support of Personality Assessment in Organizational Settings," *Personnel Psychology*, 60, 2007, pp. 995–1027. Part of the problem with self-report personality tests is that some applicants will see through to the aim of the test and provide answers they think the employer is looking for (they "fake" the test). The problem here, of course, is that less worthy candidates may actually succeed in earning higher test scores than more worthy candidates. See, Christopher Berry and Paul Sackett, "Faking in Personnel Selection: Trade-Offs in Performance versus Fairness Resulting from Two Cut Score Strategies," *Personnel Psychology*, 62, 2009, pp. 835–863; Edwin A. J. van Hoot and Marise P. Born, "Intentional Response Distortion on Personality Tests: Using Eye Tracking to Understand Response Processes when Thinking," *Journal of Applied Psychology*, 97, no. 2, 2012, pp. 301–316.

34 Mitchell Rothstein and Richard Goffin, "The Use of Personality Measures in Personnel Selection: What Does Current Research Support?" *Human Resource Management Review*, 16, 2006, pp. 155–180.

35 See, for example, W. A. Scroggins et al., "Psychological Testing in Personnel Selection, Part III: The Resurgence of Personality Testing," *Public Personnel Management*, 38, no. 1, Spring 2009, pp. 67–77.

36 Kathryn Tyler, "Put Applicants' Skills to the Test," *HR Magazine*, January 2000, pp. 75–79.

37 Adapted from www.kozaigroup.com /-inventories.php, accessed March 3, 2008; and http://kozaigroup.com/inventories/the-global competencies-inventory-gci/whatis-the-gci/, accessed August 21, 2014.

38 Hal Whiting and Theresa Kline, "Assessment of the Equivalence of Conventional versus Computer Administration of the Test of Workplace Essential Skills," *International Journal of Training and Development*, 10, no. 4, December 2006, pp. 285–290.

39 Ed Frauenheim, "More Companies Go with Online Test to Fill in the Blanks," *Workforce Management*, May 2011, p. 12.

40 John Bateson et al., "When Hiring, First Test, and Then Interview," *Harvard Business Review*, November 2013, p. 34.

41 www.iphonetypingtest.com/, accessed August 19, 2012.

42 Gilbert Nicholson, "Automated Assessments for Better Hires," *Workforce,* December 2000, pp. 102–107.

43 Ed Frauenheim, "Personality Tests Adapt to the Times," *Workforce Management,* February 2010, p. 4.

44 Michael C. Campion, Michael A. Campion, Emily D. Campion, and Matthew Reider, "Initial Investigation into Computer Scoring of Candidate Essays for Personnel Selection," *Journal of Applied Psychology,* 101, no. 7, 2016, pp. 958–975.

45 Based on Joseph Walker, "Meet the New Boss: Big Data," *The Wall Street Journal,* September 20, 2012, p. B1. Also see Josh Bersin, "Big Data in Human Resources: Talent Analytics (People Analytics) Comes of Age," www.forbes.com/sites/joshbersin/2013/02/17/bigdata-in-human-resources-talent-analytics-comes-of-age, accessed March 29, 2015.

46 Bill Roberts, "Hire Intelligence," *HR Magazine,* May 2011, p. 64.

47 Whetzel and McDaniel, "Situational Judgment Tests."

48 Steve Bates, "Freelance Nation," *HR Magazine,* July/August 2015, p. 47.

49 George Thornton III and Alyssa Gibbons, "Validity of Assessment Centers for Personnel Selection," *Human Resource Management Review,* 19, 2009, pp. 169–187. See also Brian Hoffman et al., "Exercises and Dimensions Are the Currency of Assessment Centers," *Personnel Psychology,* 60, no. 4, 2011, pp. 351–395.

50 Annette Spychalski, Miguel Quinones, Barbara Gaugler, and Katja Pohley, "A Survey of Assessment Center Practices in Organizations in the United States," *Personnel Management,* 50, no. 10, Spring 1997, pp. 71–90. See also Winfred Arthur Jr. et al., "A Meta-Analysis of the Criterion Related Validity of Assessment Center Data Dimensions," *Personnel Psychology,* 56, 2003, pp. 124–154.

51 Kobi Dayan et al., "Entry-Level Police Candidate Assessment Center: An Efficient Tool or a Hammer to Kill a Fly?" *Personnel Psychology,* 55, 2002, pp. 827–848. A recent review concluded "the [assessment center method] has a long history of demonstrating strong predictive relationships between AC ratings and criteria . . . such as promotions, performance evaluations, [and] salary progress." George Thornton III and Alyssa Gibbons, "Validity of Assessment Centers for Personnel Selection," *Human Resource Management Review,* 19, 2009, pp. 169–187.

52 J. A. Weekley and C. Jones, "Video-Based Situational Judgment Testing," *Personnel Psychology,* 50(1), p. 26.

53 Catherine Rampell, "Your Next Job Application Could Involve a Video Game," *The New York Times,* January 25, 2014.

54 Robert Grossman, "Made from Scratch," *HR Magazine,* April 2002, pp. 44–53.

55 Except as noted, this is based on Dave Zielinski, "Effective Assessments," *HR Magazine,* January 2011, pp. 61–64.

56 Michael McDaniel et al., "The Validity of Employment Interviews: A Comprehensive Review and Meta-Analysis," *Journal of Applied Psychology,* 79, no. 4, 1994, p. 599. See also Richard Posthuma et al., "Beyond Employment Interview Validity: A Comprehensive Narrative Review of Recent Research and Trends over Time," *Personnel Psychology,* 55, 2002, pp. 1–81.

57 Therese Macan, "The Employment Interview: A Review of Current Studies and Directions for Future Research," *Human Resource Management Review,* 19, 2009, pp. 203–218.

58 McDaniel et al., "The Validity of Employment Interviews," p. 601. See also Allen Huffcutt et al.,

"Comparison of Situational and Behavior Description Interview Questions for Higher Level Positions," *Personnel Psychology,* 54, Autumn 2001, pp. 619–644; Stephen Maurer, "A Practitioner-Based Analysis of Interviewer Job Expertise and Scale Format as Contextual Factors in Situational Interviews," *Personnel Psychology,* 55, 2002, pp. 307–327.

59 Bill Stoneman, "Matching Personalities with Jobs Made Easier with Behavioral Interviews," *American Banker,* 165, no. 229, November 30, 2000, p. 8a.

60 Margery Weinstein, "You're Hired!" *Training,* 48, no. 4, pp. 34–37; http://www.trainingmag.com/article/you%E2%80%99re-hired, accessed July 19, 2013.

61 Jon Wolper, "Keeping Interviews Weird," *TD,* January 2017, p. 16.

62 This is based on William Poundstone, "How to Ace a Google Interview," December 24, 2011, http://online.wsj.com/article/SB10001424052970204552304577112522982505222.html, accessed April 24, 2012.

63 Ibid. To check cultural fit, applicants at one tour company have to remove their shoes and join some of its employees to show off dance moves. Rachel Feintzeig, "Culture Fit Plays Role in Hiring," *The Wall Street Journal,* October 12, 2016, p. B6.

64 Susan Strauss et al., "The Effects of Videoconference, Telephone, and Face-to-Face Media on Interviewer and Applicant Judgments in Employment Interviews," *Journal of Management,* 27, no. 3, 2001, pp. 363–381. If the employer records a video interview with the intention of sharing it with hiring managers who don't participate in the interview, it's advisable to first obtain the candidate's written permission; Matt Bolch, "Lights, Camera . . . Interview!" *HR Magazine,* March 2007, pp. 99–102.

65 Emily Maltby, "To Find the Best Hires, Firms Become Creative," *The Wall Street Journal,* November 17, 2009, p. B6.

66 Douglas Rodgers, "Computer-Aided Interviewing Overcomes First Impressions," *Personnel Journal,* April 1987, pp. 148–152; see also Linda Thornburg, "Computer-Assisted Interviewing Shortens Hiring Cycle," *HR Magazine,* February 1998, p. 73ff; and http://interviewstream.com/demorequest?gclid=COyxjOqd36sCFUbs7QodMziuOw, accessed August 22, 2014.

67 Madeline Heilman and Tyler Okimoto, "Motherhood: A Potential Source of Bias in Employment Decisions," *Journal of Applied Psychology,* 93, no. 1, 2008, pp. 189–198.

68 Ibid., p. 196. See also Michelle Ryan et al., "Think Crisis—Think Female: The Glass Cliff and Contextual Variation in the Think Manager—Think Male Stereotype," *Journal of Applied Psychology,* 96, no. 3, 2011, pp. 470–484.

69 See, for example, M. M. Harris, "Reconsidering the Employment Interview: A Review of Recent Literature and Suggestions for Future Research," *Personnel Psychology,* 42, 1989, pp. 691–726; Richard Posthuma et al., "Beyond Employment Interview Validity: A Comprehensive Narrative Review of Recent Research and Trends over Time," *Personnel Psychology,* 55, no. 1, Spring 2002, pp. 1–81.

70 Timothy Judge et al., "The Employment Interview: A Review of Recent Research and Recommendations for Future Research," *Human Resource Management,* 10, no. 4, 2000, p. 392. There is disagreement regarding the relative superiority of individual versus panel interviews. See, for example, Marlene Dixon et al., "The Panel Interview: A Review of Empirical Research and Guidelines for Practice," *Public Personnel Management,* Fall 2002, pp. 397–428. For an

argument against holding selection interviews, see D. Heath et al., "Hold the Interview," *Fast Company,* 136, June 2009, pp. 51–52.

71 Frank Schmidt and Ryan Zimmerman, "A Counterintuitive Hypothesis about Employment Interview Validity and Some Supporting Evidence," *Journal of Applied Psychology,* 89, no. 3, 2004, pp. 553–561.

72 The validity discussion and these findings are based in McDaniel et al., "The Validity of Employment Interviews," pp. 607–610. See also Robert Dipboye et al., "The Validity of Unstructured Panel Interviews," *Journal of Business & Strategy,* 16, no. 1, Fall 2001, pp. 35–49; and Marlene Dixon et al., "The Panel Interview: A Review of Empirical Research and Guidance," *Public Personnel Management,* 3, no. 3, Fall 2002, pp. 397–428. See also Todd Maurer and Jerry Solamon, "The Science and Practice of a Structured Employment Interview Coaching Program," *Personnel Psychology,* 59, 2006, pp. 433–456.

73 Similarly, Goldman Sachs used to conduct first-round on-campus interviews, but recently changed its process. Now undergraduates seeking summer internships or jobs first take a HireVue online interview using standardized questions. ("Goldman Sachs Is Making a Change to the Way It Hires," http://www.cnbc.com/2016/06/23/goldman-sachs-is-making-a-change-to-the-way-it-hires.html; see also Dahlia Bazzaz, "Job Seekers Face Virtual Interviews," *The Wall Street Journal,* August 17, 2016, p. B6.

74 http://learn.hirevue.com/urbanoutfitters-casestudy, accessed June 25, 2015.

75 These are quoted or adapted from www.careerfaqs.com.au/getthatjob_video_interview.asp, accessed March 2, 2009.

76 Derek Chapman and David Zweig, "Developing a Nomological Network for Interview Structure: Antecedents and Consequences of the Structured Selection Interview," *Personnel Psychology,* 58, 2005, pp. 673–702.

77 Christopher Hartwell and Michael A. Campion, "Getting on the Same Page: The Effect of Normative Feedback Interventions on Structured Interview Ratings," *Journal of Applied Psychology,* 101, no. 6, 2016, pp. 757–778.

78 Anita Chaudhuri, "Beat the Clock: Applying for a Job? A New Study Shows that Interviewers Will Make Up Their Minds about You Within a Minute," *The Guardian,* June 14, 2000, pp. 2–6.

79 Brian Swider, Murray Barrick, and T. Brad Harris, "Initial Impressions: What They Are, What They Are Not, and How They Influence Structured Interview Outcomes," *Journal of Applied Psychology,* 101, no. 5, 2016, pp. 625–638.

80 Don Langdale and Joseph Weitz, "Estimating the Influence of Job Information on Interviewer Agreement," *Journal of Applied Psychology,* 57, 1973, pp. 23–27.

81 Lauren Rivera, "Guess Who Doesn't Fit in at Work," *The New York Times,* May 31, 2015, p. SR 5.

82 R. E. Carlson, "Selection Interview Decisions: The Effects of Interviewer Experience, Relative Quota Situation, and Applicant Sample on Interview Decisions," *Personnel Psychology,* 20, 1967, pp. 259–280.

83 R. E. Carlson, "Effects of Applicant Sample on Ratings of Valid Information in an Employment Setting," *Journal of Applied Psychology,* 54, 1970, pp. 217–222.

84 See, for example, Scott Fleischmann, "The Messages of Body Language in Job Interviews," *Employee Relations,* 18, no. 2, Summer 1991, pp. 161–176. See also James Westphal and Ithai Stern, "Flattery Will Get You Everywhere (Especially if You're a Male Caucasian): How Ingratiation, Board Room Behavior, and a

Demographic Minority Status Affect Additional Board Appointments at U.S. Companies," *Academy of Management Journal*, 50, no. 2, 2007, pp. 267–288. Impression management is a two-way street: interviewers also try to impress applicants. Annika Wilhelmy, "How and Why Do Interviewers Try to Make Impressions on Applicants? A Qualitative Study," *Journal of Applied Psychology*, 101, no. 3, 2016, pp. 313–332.

85 Tim DeGroot and Stephen Motowidlo, "Why Visual and Vocal Interview Cues Can Affect Interviewer's Judgments and Predicted Job Performance," *Journal of Applied Psychology*, December 1999, pp. 968–984.

86 Amy Kristof-Brown et al., "Applicant Impression Management: Dispositional Influences and Consequences for Recruiter Perceptions of Fit and Similarity," *Journal of Management*, 28, no. 1, 2002, pp. 27–46. See also Linda McFarland et al., "Impression Management Use and Effectiveness across Assessment Methods," *Journal of Management*, 29, no. 5, 2003, pp. 641–661.

87 Andrew Timming, Dennis Nickson, Daniel Re, and David Perett, "What Do You Think of My Ink? Assessing the Effects of Body Art on Employment Chances," *Human Resource Management*, 56, no. 1, January–February 2017, pp. 133–149.

88 See, for example, Cynthia Marlowe, Sondra Schneider, and Carnot Nelson, "Gender and Attractiveness Biases in Hiring Decisions: Are More Experienced Managers Less Biased?" *Journal of Applied Psychology*, 81, no. 1, 1996, pp. 11–21. See also Shari Caudron, "Why Job Applicants Hate HR," *Workforce*, June 2002, p. 36.

89 Marlowe et al., "Gender and Attractiveness Biases in Hiring Decisions," p. 18. See also Timothy Judge, Charlice Hurst, and Lauren Simon, "Does It Pay to Be Smart, Attractive, or Confident (Or All Three)? Relationships among General Mental Ability, Physical Attractiveness, Core Self-Evaluations, and Income," *Journal of Applied Psychology*, 94, no. 3, 2009, pp. 742–755.

90 http://money.cnn.com/2015/03/24/investing/female-ceo-pipeline-leadership/index.html, accessed February 17, 2017.

91 Juan Madera and Michele Hebl, "Discrimination against Facially Stigmatized Applicants in Interviews: An Eye Tracking and Face-to-Face Investigation," *Journal of Applied Psychology*, 97, no. 2, pp. 317–330. Another study found that people with a history of cancer are stereotyped as higher in warmth than competence and are more likely to be discriminated against. Larry Martinez, Craig White, Jenessa Shapiro, and Michelle Hebl, "Selection Bias: Stereotypes and Discrimination Related to Having a History of Cancer," *Journal of Applied Psychology*, 101, no. 1, 2016, pp. 122–128. Sometimes the physical attributes employers seek are surprising. Researchers analyzed the faces of CEOs that companies hired after the firms had to restate their earnings; the assumption was that they'd be looking for "trustworthy looking" CEOs. Their research showed that people with narrower facial structures look more trustworthy, and those were indeed the sorts of CEOs the firms hired. David Gomulya, et al., "The Role of Facial Appearance on CEO Selection After Firm Misconduct," *Journal of Applied Psychology*, Vol. 102, no. 4, 2017, pp. 617–635.

92 Chad Higgins and Timothy Judge, "The Effect of Applicant Influence Tactics on Recruiter Perceptions of Fit and Hiring Recommendations: A Field Study," *Journal of Applied Psychology*, 89, no. 4, 2004, pp. 622–632.

93 Brian Swider et al., "Managing and Creating an Image in the Interview: The Role of Interviewee Initial Impressions," *Journal of Applied Psychology*, no. 6, 2011, pp. 1275–1288.

94 Laura Gollub Williamson et al., "Employment Interview on Trial: Linking Interview Structure with Litigation Outcomes," *Journal of Applied Psychology*, 82, no. 6, 1996, p. 901; Michael Campion, David Palmer, and James Campion, "A Review of Structure in the Selection Interview," *Personnel Psychology*, 50, 1997, pp. 655–702.

95 Unless otherwise specified, the following are based on Williamson et al., "Employment Interview on Trial," pp. 901–902.

96 Todd Maurer and Jerry Solamon, "The Science and Practice of a Structured Employment Interview Coaching Program," *Personnel Psychology*, 59, 2006, pp. 433–456.

97 Panel Kaul, "Interviewing Is Your Business," *Association Management*, November 1992, p. 29. See also Nancy Woodward, "Asking for Salary Histories," *HR Magazine*, February 2000, pp. 109–112. Gathering information about specific interview dimensions such as social ability, responsibility, and independence (as is often done with structured interviews) can improve interview accuracy, at least for more complicated jobs. See Andrea Poe, "Graduate Work: Behavioral Interviewing Can Tell You If an Applicant Just Out of College Has Traits Needed for the Job," *HR Magazine*, 48, no. 10, October 2003, pp. 95–96.

98 For a good discussion of how to interview, see, for example, Stephen Bates, "The Art of the Interview," *HR Magazine*, June 2016, pp. 93–96.

99 Richard A. Posthuma, Frederick P. Morgeson, and Michael A. Campion, "Beyond Employment Interview Validity: A Comprehensive Narrative Review of Recent Research and Trends over Time," *Personnel Psychology*, 55, no. 1, March 2002, pp. 1–81.

100 Laszlo Bock, *Work Rules! Insights from Inside Google that Will Transform How You Live and Lead* (New York: Twelve, 2015), pp. 87–127.

101 Lara Walsh, "To Tell the Truth: Catching Tall Tales on Résumés," *Workforce*, December 2014, p. 10.

102 "Are Your Background Checks Balanced? Experts Identify Concerns over Verifications," *BNA Bulletin to Management*, May 13, 2004, p. 153.

103 Roy Maurer, "Making Every Check Count," *HR Magazine*, October 2016, p. 69.

104 "Fake Job Reference Services Add New Wrinkle to Screening," *HR Magazine*, January 2010, p. 9.

105 Carroll Lachnit, "Protecting People and Profits with Background Checks," *Workforce*, February 2002, p. 52. See also Robert Howie and Lawrence Shapero, "Pre-employment Criminal Background Checks: Why Employers Should Look before They Leap," *Employee Relations Law Journal*, Summer 2002, pp. 63–77.

106 Bill Roberts, "Close-up on Screening," *HR Magazine*, February 2011, pp. 23–29.

107 See, for example, A. M. Forsberg et al., "Perceived Fairness of a Background Information Form and a Job Knowledge Test," *Public Personnel Management*, 38, no. 1, Spring 2009, pp. 33–46.

108 Ibid., p. 50ff.

109 Alan Finder, "When a Risqué Online Persona Undermines a Chance for a Job," *The New York Times*, June 11, 2006, p. 1.

110 Natasha Singer, "Funny, They Don't Look Like My References," *The New York Times*, November 9, 2014, p. 4.

111 "Vetting via Internet Is Free, Generally Legal, but Not Necessarily Smart Hiring Strategy," *BNA Bulletin to Management*, February 20, 2007, pp. 57–58.

112 Rita Zeidner, "How Deep Can You Probe?" *HR Magazine*, October 1, 2007, pp. 57–62.

113 "Web Searches on Applicants Are Potentially Perilous for Employers," *BNA Bulletin to Management*, October 14, 2008, p. 335.

114 "Maryland Is First State to Restrict Employer Demands for Employee, Applicant Passwords," *Bloomberg BNA Bulletin to Management*, May 8, 2012, p. 145.

115 "Practitioners Discuss Various Pitfalls of Using Social Media to Vet Job Applicants," *BNA Bulletin to Management*, November 1, 2011, pp. 345–346.

116 Ibid.

117 For example, see Lawrence Dube Jr., "Employment References and the Law," *Personnel Journal*, 65, no. 2, February 1986, pp. 87–91. See also Mickey Veich, "Uncover the Resume Ruse," *Security Management*, October 1994, pp. 75–76; Mary Mayer, "Background Checks in Focus," *HR Magazine*, January 2002, pp. 59–62.

118 Kris Maher, "Reference Checking Firms Flourish, but Complaints about Some Arise," *The Wall Street Journal*, March 5, 2002, p. B8.

119 *Kehr v. Consolidated Freightways of Delaware*, Docket No. 86–2126, July 15, 1987, U.S. Seventh Circuit Court of Appeals. Discussed in *Commerce Clearing House, Ideas and Trends*, October 16, 1987, p. 165.

120 James Bell, James Castagnera, and Jane Patterson Young, "Employment References: Do You Know the Law?" *Personnel Journal*, 63, no. 2, February 1984, pp. 32–36. In order to demonstrate defamation, several elements must be present: (a) the defamatory statement must have been communicated to another party; (b) the statement must be a false statement of fact; (c) injury to reputation must have occurred; and (d) the employer must not be protected under qualified or absolute privilege. For a discussion, see Ann M. Ryan and Marja Lasek, "Negligent Hiring and Defamation: Areas of Liability Related to Pre-Employment Inquiries," *Personnel Psychology*, 44, no. 2, 1991, p. 307. See also James Burns Jr., "Employment References: Is There a Better Way?" *Employee Relations Law Journal*, 23, no. 2, Fall 1997, pp. 157–168. Note however, that *not* disclosing relevant information can be dangerous, too. In one Florida case, a company fired an employee for allegedly bringing a handgun to work. After his next employer fired him for absenteeism, he returned to that company and shot several employees. The injured parties and their relatives sued the previous employer, who had provided the employee with a clean letter of recommendation allegedly because that first employer didn't want to anger the employee over his firing.

121 Diane Cadrain, "Job Detectives Dig Deep for Defamation," *HR Magazine*, 49, no. 10, October 2004, p. 34ff.

122 Carroll Lachnit, "Protecting People and Profits with Background Checks," *Workforce*, February 2002, p. 54; Shari Caudron, "Who Are You Really Hiring?" *Workforce*, November 2002, p. 31.

123 "Getting Applicant Information Difficult but Still Necessary," *BNA Bulletin to Management*, February 5, 1999, p. 63. See also Robert Howie and Lawrence Shapiro, "Pre-Employment Criminal Background Checks: Why Employers Should Look Before They Leap," *Employee Relations Law Journal*, Summer 2002, pp. 63–77.

124 Michelle Goodman, "Reference Checks Go Tech," *Workforce Management*, May 2012, pp. 26–28.

125 "Background Checking Providers," *Workforce Management*, April 2012, p. 22.

126 Stephanie Clifford and Jessica Silver-Greenberg, "Retailers Track Employee Thefts in Vast Databases," *The New York Times*, April 4, 2013, pp. A1, A16.

127 "Employers Often Receive Flawed Information in Criminal Background Screens, Report Says,"

Bloomberg BNA Bulletin to Management, April 24, 2012, p. 131.

128 See, for example, Dori Meinert, "Search and Verify," *HR Magazine*, December 2012, pp. 37–41.

129 Ronald Karren and Larry Zacharias, "Integrity Tests: Critical Issues," *Human Resource Management Review*, 17, 2007, pp. 221–234.

130 John Bernardin and Donna Cooke, "Validity of an Honesty Test in Predicting Theft among Convenience Store Employees," *Academy of Management Journal*, 36, no. 5, 1993, pp. 1097–1108. Management Skills suggestions adapted from "Divining Integrity through Interviews," *BNA Bulletin to Management*, June 4, 1987, p. 184; and "Ideas and Trends," *Commerce Clearing House,* December 29, 1998, pp. 222–223. Note that some suggest that by possibly signaling mental illness, integrity tests may conflict with the Americans with Disabilities Act, but one review concludes that such tests pose little legal risk to employers. Christopher Berry et al., "A Review of Recent Developments in Integrity Test Research," *Personnel Psychology*, 60, 2007, pp. 271–301.

131 Note that a recent meta-analysis concluded that "relations between integrity tests and measures of job performance tend to be rather weak," See Chad H. Van Iddeking et al., "The Criterion-Related Validity of Integrity Tests: An Updated Meta-Analysis," *Journal of Applied Psychology*, 97, no. 3, 2012, pp. 499–530, a point disputed by a panel of test publishers: William G. Harris et al., "Test Publishers' Perspective on "An Updated Meta-Analysis: Comment on Van Iddeking, Ross, Raymark, and Odle-Dusseau," *Journal of Applied Psychology*, 97, no. 3, 2012, pp. 531–536.

132 Based on "Divining Integrity through Interviews," *BNA Bulletin to Management,* June 4, 1987, and "Ideas and Trends," *Commerce Clearing House*, December 29, 1998, pp. 222–223.

133 Ibid.

134 www.clearfit.com/resource-center/hiring-process/how-to-spot-someone-lying-in-an-interview/, accessed February 19, 2014.

135 www.forbes.com/sites/carolkinseygoman/2013/05/20/7-tips-for-spotting-liars-at-work/, accessed February 19, 2014.

136 Christopher S. Frings, "Testing for Honesty," *Medical Laboratory Observer*, 35, no. 12, December 2003, p. 27(1).

137 Steven L. Thomas and Steve Vaught, "The Write Stuff: What the Evidence Says about Using Handwriting Analysis in Hiring," *Advanced Management Journal*, 66, no. 4, August 2001, pp. 31–35.

138 Ibid.; Murphy and Davidshofer, *Psychological Testing*, pp. 438–439.

139 Bill Roberts, "Your Cheating Heart," *HR Magazine*, June 2011, pp. 55–57.

140 See Bridget A. Styers and Kenneth S. Shultz, "Perceived Reasonableness of Employment Testing Accommodations for Persons with Disabilities," *Public Personnel Management*, 38, no. 3, Fall 2009, pp. 71–91.

141 Rita Zeidner, "Putting Drug Screening to the Test," *HR Magazine,* November 2010, p. 26.

142 Peter Cholakis, "How to Implement a Successful Drug Testing Program," *Risk Management*, 52, no. 11, November 2005, pp. 24–28; Elaine Davis and Stacie Hueller, "Strengthening the Case for Workplace Drug Testing: The Growing Problem of Methamphetamines," *Advanced Management Journal*, 71, no. 3, Summer 2006, pp. 4–10.

143 For example, www.questdiagnostics.com/home/companies/employer/drug-screening/testing-reasons/pre-employment.html, accessed August 22, 2014.

144 Jackie Calmes, "One Step Short of Hired," *The New York Times*, May 18, 2016, pp. B1, B3; Lauren Weber, "Tests Show More American Workers Using Drugs," *The Wall Street Journal,* May 17, 2017.

145 Scott MacDonald et al., "The Limitations of Drug Screening in the Workplace," *International Labor Review*, 132, no. 1, 1993, p. 100.

146 Ibid., p. 103.

147 Diane Cadrain, "Are Your Employees' Drug Tests Accurate?" *HR Magazine,* January 2003, pp. 40–45. See also Ari Nattle, "Drug Testing Impaired," *Traffic World*, 271, no. 45, November 12, 2007, p. 18.

148 MacDonald et al., "The Limitations of Drug Screening in the Workplace," pp. 105–106.

149 Lewis Maltby, "Drug Testing: A Bad Investment," *Business Ethics*, 15, no. 2, March 2001, p. 7.

150 Coleman Peterson, "Employee Retention: The Secrets behind WalMart's Successful Hiring Policies," *Human Resource Management*, 44, no. 1, Spring 2005, pp. 85–88.

151 Lawrence Kellner, "Corner Office," *The New York Times,* September 27, 2009.

152 There may be other complications as well. For example, you may want to decide which of several possible potential jobs is best for your candidate.

153 See, for example, Frank Landy and Don Trumbo, *Psychology of Work Behavior* (Homewood, IL: Dorsey Press, 1976), pp. 131–169. There are many other possibilities. See, for example, Gatewood and Feild, *Human Resource Selection*, pp. 278–279.

154 Davis Zielinski, "Automating I-9 Verification," *HR Magazine*, May 2011, p. 57; see also "Administrative Judges Push Back on Sanctions for I-9 Violations," *Bloomberg BNA Bulletin to Management*, October 29, 2013, p. 350; Max Mihelich, "Formal I-9 Gets an Update," *Workforce Management*, June 2013, p. 16; and Matthew Orso and Susan Rodriguez, "The Compliance Risks of I-9 Software," *HR Magazine*, September 2016, pp. 83–84.

155 "Conflicting State E-Verify Laws Troubling for Employers," *BNA Bulletin to Management*, November 4, 2008, p. 359. Identity theft—undocumented workers stealing and using an authorized worker's identity—remains a problem, even with E-Verify. "Identity Theft Remains Top Challenge for E-Verify," *BNA Bulletin to Management*, April 19, 2011, p. 121. In 2017, the Republican administration said it was moving toward requiring use of E-verify by all employers. Laura Francis, "Mandatory E-Verify, More Enforcement Spending in Trump Budget," *Bloomberg BNA Bulletin to Management*, March 21, 2017.

156 www.dhs.gov/files/programs/gc_1185221678150.shtm, accessed February 21, 2010. Many small-business owners, in particular, find that the new system makes it much more difficult to fill open positions. Angus Loten, Sarah Needleman, and Adam Janofsky, "Small Business Has a Beef with the Verify," *The Wall Street Journal*, July 25, 2013, p. B6.

157 "New Tools Will Aid Employers during Verification Process," *BNA Bulletin to Management,* March 15, 2011.

158 Russell Gerbman, "License to Work," *HR Magazine,* June 2000, pp. 151–160. The employment and training administration agency of the U.S. Department of Labor installed a system called iCERT to make it easier for employers to receive labor condition applications for the H-1B program. "EPA Announces Electronic Portal to Receive Applications for H1B, Perm Certifications," *BNA Bulletin to Management,* April 21, 2009, p. 123.

159 Note that unproctored Internet tests raise serious questions in employment settings. Nancy Tippins et al., "Unproctored Internet Testing in Employment Settings," *Personnel Psychology*, 59, 2006, pp. 189–225.

160 For letter of offer and employment contract samples, see, for example, http://office.microsoft.com/en-us/templates/results.aspx?ctags=CT010147171, accessed May 18, 2017.

161 For information and guidance, see www.Shrm.org/templatetools/how-to-guides.

162 See www.Shrm.org/templatetools/toolkits.

163 Peter Steinmeyer and Scarlet Freeman, "Too Restrictive? Courts Taking Closer Look at Noncompete Clauses," *Workforce*, August 2016, pp. 18–19.

164 https://www.thebalance.com/job-offer-letter-sample-2071614, accessed February 18, 2017.

165 http://www.ddiworld.com/DDI/media/monographs/employeeengagement_mg_ddi.pdf?ext=.pdf, accessed February 18, 2017.

166 See, for example, Gary Dessler, *Winning Commitment* (New York: McGraw-Hill, 1993).

167 "Toyota Looking for 1,500 Outstanding Mississippians from All Backgrounds," http://www.cdfms.org/cdf/press-releases/sept-2010/toyota-looking-for-1,500-outstanding-mississippians-from-all-backgrounds#.WRB6T_nyu70.

168 "Toyota Hiring Process," www.indeed.com/forum/cmp/Toyota/Toyota-Hiring-Process/t31886, accessed August 22, 2014.

169 Manuel Velasquez, *Business Ethics: Concepts and Cases* (Upper Saddle River, NJ: Prentice Hall, 1992), p. 9. See also O. C. Ferrell, John Fraedrich, and Linog Ferrell, *Business Ethics* (Boston: Houghton Mifflin, 2008).

170 Gary Weaver and Linda Trevino, "The Role of Human Resources in Ethics/Compliance Management: A Fairness Perspective," *Human Resource Management Review*, 11, 2001, p. 123. See also Linda Andrews, "The Nexus of Ethics," *HR Magazine*, August 2005, pp. 53–58.

171 This section is based on Elliot Pursell et al., "Structured Interviewing: Avoiding Selection Problems," *Personnel Journal*, 59, November 1980, pp. 907–912; and G. Latham et al., "The Situational Interview," *Journal of Applied Psychology*, 65, 1980, pp. 422–427. See also Jeff Weekley and Joseph Gier, "Reliability and Validity of the Situational Interview for a Sales Position," *Journal of Applied Psychology*, August 1987, pp. 484–487; and Therese Macan, "The Employment Interview: A Review of Current Studies and Directions for Future Research," *Human Resource Management Review*, 19, 2009, pp. 203–218.

172 P. Taylor and B. Small, "Asking Applicants What They Would Do versus What They Did Do: A Meta-Analytic Comparison of Situational and Past-Behavior Employment Interview Questions," *Journal of Occupational and Organizational Psychology*, 75, no. 3, September 2002, pp. 277–295. Structured employment interviews using either situational questions or behavioral questions tend to yield high validities. However, structured interviews with situational question formats yield the higher ratings. This may be because interviewers get more consistent (reliable) responses with situational questions (which force all applicants to apply the same scenario) than they do with behavioral questions (which require each applicant to find applicable experiences). However, there is some evidence that for higher-level positions, situational question–based interviews are inferior to behavioral question–based ones, possibly because the situations are "just too simple to allow any real differentiation among candidates for higher-level positions." Alan Huffcutt et al., "Comparison of Situational and Behavioral Description Interview Questions for Higher-Level Positions," *Personnel Psychology*, 54, no. 3, 2001, p. 619.

173 See also Phillip Lowry, "The Structured Interview: An Alternative to the Assessment Center?" *Public Personnel Management*, 23, no. 2, Summer 1994, pp. 201–215; Steven Maurer, "The Potential of the Situational Interview: Existing Research and Unresolved Issues," *Human Resource Management Review*, 7, no. 2, Summer 1997, pp. 185–201; and Todd Maurer and Jerry Solamon, "The Science and Practice of a Structured Employment Interview Coaching Program," *Personnel Psychology*, 59, no. 2, Summer 2006, pp. 433–456.

174 Elliott D. Pursell, Michael A. Campion, and Sarah R. Gaylord, "Structured Interviewing: Avoiding Selection Problems," *Personnel Journal*, November 1980, pp. 907–912.

175 From a speech by industrial psychologist Paul Green and contained in *BNA Bulletin to Management*, June 20, 1985, pp. 2–3. For additional practical guidance, see, for example, www.state.gov/documents/organization/107843.pdf, accessed October 10, 2012.

Chapter 7

1 Marjorie Derven, "Management Onboarding," *T&D*, April 2008, pp. 49–52. See also, www.roberthalf.com/onboarding, accessed August 23, 2014.

2 Sabrina Hicks, "Successful Orientation Programs," *T&D*, April 2000, p. 59. See also Laurie Friedman, "Are You Losing Potential New Hires at Hello?" *Training & Development*, November 2006, pp. 25–27; and Jon Wolper, "Get on Board with Onboarding," *Training and Development*, January 2017, pp. 18–20.

3 Supervisors should know that new employees typically begin work motivated to learn about their new supervisors and to ignore negative traits and find something positive about them. Trevor Fouke and David Long, "Impressed by Impression Management: New, Reactions to Ingratiated Supervisors," *Journal of Applied Psychology*, 101, no. 10, 2016, pp. 1487–1497.

4 See, for example, John Kammeyer-Mueller and Connie Wanberg, "Unwrapping the Organizational Entry Process: Disentangling Multiple Antecedents and Their Pathways to Adjustments," *Journal of Applied Psychology*, 88, no. 5, 2003, pp. 779–794.

5 www.shrm.org/templatestools/samples/hrforms/articles/pages/1cms_002153.aspx, http://hrweb.berkeley.edu/guides/managing-hr/recruiting-staff/new-employee/checklist, and www.go2hr.ca/articles/new-hire-orientation-checklist, all accessed March 30, 2015.

6 www.right.com/thought-leadership/research/shrm-foundations-effective-practice-guidelines-series-onboardingnew-employees-maximizing-success-sponsored-by-right-management.pdf, accessed August 23, 2014.

7 "The First 90 Days: Help New Employees Start out on the Right Foot," *HR Magazine*, December 2015/January 2016, p. 27.

8 Ibid. See also Sushil S. Nifadekar and Talya N. Bauer, "Breach of Belongingness: New, Relationship Conflict, Information, and Task-Related Outcomes During Organizational Socialization," *Journal of Applied Psychology*, 101, no. 1, 2016, pp. 1–13.

9 Martin Byford, et al., "Onboarding Isn't Enough," *Harvard Business Review*, May-June 2017, pp. 78–86.

10 John Hyman, "The Hands-on Handbook," *Workforce*, November 2015, p. 20.

11 "Drug Rep Claims Handbook Protection from Retaliation," *BNA Bulletin to Management*, December 18, 2012, p. 8.

12 Employers should also adjust their employee handbook contents to the realities of social media. For example, the National Labor Relations Board might take issue with a handbook policy prohibiting employees from badmouthing their employer in social media, arguing that doing so constrains employees' rights to complain about working conditions to coworkers. Steve Taylor, "Employee Handbook Updates for 2013," *HR Magazine*, February 2013, p. 14. See also Stephen Bates, "Top 10 Employee Handbook Update for 2016," *HR Magazine*, February 2016, pp. 40–45.

13 Ed Frauenheim, "IBM Learning Programs Get a 'Second Life,'" *Workforce Management*, December 11, 2006, p. 6. See also J. T. Arnold, "Gaming Technology Used to Orient New Hires," *HR Magazine*, 2009 (HR Trend-book supp), pp. 36, 38.

14 Jennifer Taylor Arnold, "Ramping Up on Boarding," *HR Magazine*, May 2010, pp. 75–78.

15 www.workday.com/company/news/workdaymobility.php, accessed March 24, 2009.

16 For example, IBM's "assimilation process" has three main steps: *affirming* (which includes things like welcoming the new employee and assigning a coach); *beginning* (ensuring that during the new employee's first 30 days he or she is met in person, meets the team, is introduced on the company's intranet onboarding platform, and learns his or her roles and responsibilities); and *connecting* (which lasts about a year and includes having an "ask coach" make sure the employee is on track and understands IBM's procedures). www.right.com/thought-leadership/research/shrm-foundations-effective-practice-guidelines-series-onboarding-new-employees-maximizing-success-sponsored-by-right-management.pdf.

17 See, for example, Gary Dessler, *Winning Commitment: How to Build and Keep a Competitive Workforce*, New York: McGraw-Hill, 1993, and Gary Dessler, "How to Earn Your Employees' Commitment," *Academy of Management Executive*, 13, no. 2, 1999, pp. 58–67.

18 Ibid., and see www.autonews.com/article/20050718/SUB/507180713/toyota-seeks-efficiency-training-for-all; http://thetoyotaway.org/excerpts.html; www.toyotageorgetown.com/tps1.asp; http://sloanreview.mit.edu/article/what-really-happened-to-toyota/; www.glassdoor.com/Reviews/Employee-Review-Toyota-Tsusho-America-RVW3553588.htm; all accessed February 28, 2014.

19 Although long respected for its commitment to these principles—and to the high-quality cars that its employee engagement produced—Toyota ran into problems a few years ago. In pursuing a new faster-growth strategy, Toyota's famed employee selection and onboarding/training program may have faltered, possibly leading to some employee morale and vehicle quality problems. Soon under new top management, the company seems to have returned to its quality roots. www.autonews.com/article/20050718/SUB/507180713/toyota-seeks-efficiency-training-for-all; http://thetoyotaway.org/excerpts.html; www.toyota-georgetown.com/tps1.asp; http://sloanreview.mit.edu/article/what-really-happened-to-toyota/; www.glassdoor.com/Reviews/Employee-Review-Toyota-Tsusho-America-RVW3553588.htm; all accessed February 28, 2014.

20 For a discussion of the evolution of training and development, see Bradford Bell et al., "100 Years of Training and Development Research: What We Know And Where We Should Go," *Journal of Applied Psychology*, volume 102, no. 3, 2017, pp. 305–323.

21 Maria Ho, "Investment in Learning Increases for Fourth Straight Year," *Training and Development*, November 2016, pp. 31–32.

22 "Lack of Training Fuels Desire to Job Search," *Training & Development*, January 2013, p. 23.

23 Go to www.coca-cola.co.uk, then click "About Us" and "Employment—Our People."

24 Rita Smith, "Aligning Learning with Business Strategy," *Training & Development*, November 2008, pp. 41–43.

25 Christine Ellis and Sarah Gale, "A Seat at the Table," *Training*, March 2001, pp. 90–96.

26 Paul Harris, "The Value Add of Learning," *TD*, October 2014, pp. 53–55. Similarly, with AT&T's traditional landline phone evaporating, they are moving into Internet and cloud-based businesses. This in turn meant AT&T needed employees with new skill sets. To ensure that AT&T had the employee skills it needed, the company established a program it called Workforce 2020. The program consolidated 250 AT&T job roles down to 80 and specified the skills each role required. The company also identified performance metrics for evaluating employees on those skills, raised its performance expectations for all employees, and redesigned compensation, putting more emphasis on incentives. It also initiated new training and development programs, to help employees fill their skill gaps. John Donovan and Cathy Benko, "AT&T's Talent Overhaul," Harvard Business Review, October 2016, pp. 69–73.

27 W. Clayton Allen, "Overview and Evolution of the ADDIE Training System," *Advances in Developing Human Resources*, 8, no. 4, November 2006, pp. 430–441.

28 www.intulogy.com/process//, accessed April 20, 2011.

29 See, for example, Beth McGoldrick and Deborah Tobey, "Assess Needs First, Train Second," *Training and Development*, September 2016, pp. 60–66.

30 P. Nick Blanchard and James Thacker, *Effective Training: Systems, Strategies, and Practices* (Upper Saddle River, NJ: Prentice Hall, 1999), pp. 138–139. See also Matthew Casey and Dennis Doverspike, "Training Needs Analysis and Evaluation for New Technologies through the Use of Problem-Based Inquiry," *Performance Improvement Quarterly*, 18, no. 1, 2005, pp. 110–124; and Judy Murray, "Get to the Root of the Problem," *TD*, February 2017, pp. 26–29.

31 Justin Arneson et al., "Training and Development Competencies: We Define to Create Competitive Advantage," *T&D*, January 2013, p. 45.

32 See also, for example, Jennifer Salopek, "The Power of the Pyramid," *Training & Development*, May 2009, pp. 70–73.

33 Tom Barron, "When Things Go Haywire," *T&D*, February 1999, pp. 25–27; see also, for example, Bill Stetar, "Training: It's Not Always the Answer," *Quality Progress*, March 2005, pp. 44–49, http://performancetechnology.com/ptg_pdfs/qp0305stetar.pdf, accessed October 11, 2012.

34 For example, a department head asked the training group at BB&T Bank to design a new training program to improve the department's productivity. The training group examined the situation. They found ". . . zero correlation between how the division's personnel perform on their assessments and their actual success as wealth advisors." The solution here wasn't instituting a training program, but rather other activities such as revising the incentive plan and performance appraisal system. Paul Harris, "Less Is More," *Training & Development*, October 2013, p. 40.

35 Employers increasingly utilize learning content management systems (LCMS) to compile an author-training content. See, for example, Bill Perry, "Customized Content at Your Fingertips," *Training and Development*, June 2009, pp. 29–30.

36 Blanchard and Thacker, *Effective Training*, pp. 26–94, 153–199, 285–316; see also Bruno Neal, " e-ADDIE!," *T&D*, 65, no. 3, March 2011, pp. 76–77.

37 Jay Bahlis, "Blueprint for Planning Learning," *T&D*, March 2008, pp. 64–67. See also Nick Van Dam, "Inside the Learning Brain," *Training & Development*, April 2013, pp. 30–34.

38 Blanchard and Thacker, *Effective Training*, p. 8; and G. Sadri, "Boosting Performance through Self-Efficacy," *T&D* 65, no. 6, June 2011, pp. 30–31.

39 There are algorithms for estimating training program costs, for instance, in terms of labor hours and direct costs. Emily Baumann and Greta Ballentine, "Estimate Training Resources with Precision," *TD*, February 2014, pp. 20–22.

40 Blanchard and Thacker, *Effective Training*, pp. 30–31.

41 Ibid., p. 90.

42 Kenneth Wexley and Gary Latham, *Developing and Training Human Resources in Organizations* (Upper Saddle River, NJ: Prentice Hall, 2002), p. 305.

43 Ibid.

44 Kathryn Tyler, "Focus on Training," *HR Magazine*, May 2000, pp. 94–102.

45 Eric Krell, "Get Sold on Training Incentives," *HR Magazine*, February 2013, p. 57.

46 Alan Saks and Monica Belcourt, "An Investigation of Training Activities and Transfer of Training in Organizations," *Human Resource Management*, 45, no. 4, Winter 2006, pp. 629–648. The percentage of managers transferring behaviors from training to the job may be as low as 10% to 20%. See George Vellios, "On the Level," *T&D*, December 2008, pp. 26–29. See also K. Lee, "Implement Training Successfully," *Training*, 46, no. 5, June 2009, p. 16.

47 Saks and Belcourt, op. cit. See also, Stefanie Johnson, "Go for the Goal(s): Relationship between Goal Setting and Transfer of Training Following Leadership Development," *Academy of Management Learning & Education*, 11, no. 4, 2012, pp. 555–569.

48 Janice A. Cannon-Bowers et al., "Framework for Understanding Pre-Practice Conditions and Their Impact on Learning," *Personnel Psychology*, 51, 1998, pp. 291–320; see also J. S. Goodman et al., "Feedback Specificity, Information Processing, and Transfer of Training," *Organizational Behavior and Human Decision Processes*, 115, no. 2, July 2011, pp. 253–267.

49 Ibid., p. 305.

50 Sebastian Bailey, "Seven Tricks to Make Learning Stick," *Training and Development*, April 2016, pp. 63–66.

51 Ibid., and see Kendra Lee, "Reinforce Training," *Training*, 48, no. 3, May/June 2011, p. 24.

52 Large training providers include Element K, Geo Learning, learn.com, Outsmart, Plateau, Saba People Systems, and Sum-Total Systems. "Training Providers," *Workforce Management*, January 2011, p. 8.

53 www.litmos.com/learning–management–system; www.talentlms.com; http://money.CNN.com/2014/09/03/technology/enterprise/what-is-the-cloud, both accessed March 31, 2015.

54 Wexley and Latham, *Developing and Training Human Resources in Organizations*, pp. 78–79.

55 Jason Dahling, Samantha Taylor, Samantha Chau, and Stephen Dwight, "Does Coaching Matter? A Multilevel Model Linking Managerial Coaching Skill and Frequency to Sales Goal Attainment," *Personnel Psychology*, 69, 2016, pp. 863–894.

56 See, for example, www.aps-online.net/consulting/structured_ojt.htm, accessed June 1, 2011; and Kathryn Tyler, "15 Ways to Train on the Job," *HR Magazine*, 53, no. 9, September 2008, pp. 105–108.

57 The preceding four steps in on-the-job training are based on William Berliner and William McLarney, *Management Practice and Training* (Burr Ridge, IL: Irwin, 1974), pp. 442–443. For the discussion of employee task analysis, see "Eight Steps to Better On-the-Job Training," *HR Focus*, 80, no. 7, July 2003, pp. 11, 13–14.

58 Cindy Waxer, "Steelmaker Revives Apprentice Program to Address Graying Workforce, Forge Next Leaders," *Workforce Management*, January 30, 2006, p. 40.

59 Kermit Kaleba, "New Changes to Apprenticeship Program Could Be Forthcoming," *T&D*, February 2008, p. 14.

60 Robert Weintraub and Jennifer Martineau, "The Just-in-Time Imperative," *T&D*, June 2002, p. 52; Andrew Paradise, "Informal Learning: Overlooked or Overhyped?" *T&D*, July 2008, pp. 52–53. In one survey, about one-third of respondents said they did not earmark training dollars for informal learning.

61 Ibraiz Tarique, *Seven Trends in Corporate Training and Development* (Upper Saddle River, NJ: Pearson, 2014), p. 67. See also Elaine-Biech, "The 90% Solution," *Training and Development*, December 2016, pp. 58–63.

62 Tarique, *Seven Trends in Corporate Training and Development*, p. 71.

63 Aparna Nancherla, "Knowledge Delivered in Any Other Form Is . . . Perhaps Sweeter," *T&D*, May 2009, pp. 54–60.

64 Nadira Hira, "The Making of a UPS Driver," *Fortune*, November 12, 2007, p. 120.

65 Arthur Winfred Jr. et al., "Effectiveness of Training in Organizations: A Meta-Analysis of Design and Evaluation Features," *Journal of Applied Psychology*, 88, no. 2, 2003, pp. 234–245.

66 Donald Michalak and Edwin G. Yager, *Making the Training Process Work* (New York: Harper & Row, 1979), pp. 108–111. See also Richard Wiegand, "Can All Your Trainees Hear You?" *Training & Development Journal*, 41, no. 8, August 1987, pp. 38–43; and "Dos and Don'ts at the Podium," *Journal of Accountancy*, 200, no. 3, September 2005.

67 Jacqueline Schmidt and Joseph Miller, "The Five-Minute Rule for Presentations," *T&D*, March 2000, pp. 16–17; and "Dos and Don'ts at the Podium."

68 G. N. Nash, J. P. Muczyk, and F. L. Vettori, "The Role and Practical Effectiveness of Programmed Instruction," *Personnel Psychology*, 24, 1971, pp. 397–418; Duane Schultz and Sydney Ellen Schultz, *Psychology and Work Today* (Upper Saddle River, NJ: Prentice Hall, 1998), pp. 181–183; N. Izzet Kurbanoglu, Yavuz Taskesenligil, and Mustafa Sozbilir, "Programmed Instruction Revisited: A Study on Teaching Stereochemistry," *Chemistry Education Research and Practice*, 7, no. 1, 2006, pp. 13–21.

69 Paul Taylor et al., "A Meta-Analytic Review of Behavior-Modeling Training," *Journal of Applied Psychology*, 90, no. 4, 2005, pp. 692–719.

70 Wexley and Latham, *Developing and Training Human Resources in Organizations*, pp. 131–133. See also Teri O. Grady and Mike Matthews, "Video . . . Through the Eyes of the Trainee," *Training*, 24, no. 7, July 1987, pp. 57–62; "New ARTBA PPE Video and Laborers' Night Work Suggestions Highlight Construction Safety Advances," *EHS Today*, 2, no. 7, July 2009, p. 51.

71 www.radvision.com/Support/cisco.htm, accessed June 1, 2011.

72 Paula Ketter, "What Can Training Do for Brown?" *T&D*, May 2008, pp. 30–36.

73 Craig Marion, "What Is the EPSS Movement and What Does It Mean to Information Designers?" http://www.smnweb.com/e-hr/letture/perform/EPSS%20Movement.htm, August 20, 1999, accessed June 28, 2015.

74 Josh Bersin and Karen O'Leonard, "Performance Support Systems," *T&D*, April 2005, p. 68.

75 Blanchard and Thacker, *Effective Training*, p. 163.

76 Dina Berta, "Computer-Based Training Clicks with Both Franchisees and Their Employees," *Nation's Restaurant News*, July 9, 2001, pp. 1, 18; and, "Is Online Fall Protection Training Effective?" *EHS Today*, 3, no. 7, July 2010.

77 Blanchard and Thacker, *Effective Training*, p. 247; see also Michael Laff, "Simulations: Slowly Proving Their Worth," *T&D*, June 2007, pp. 30–34.

78 Laff, "Simulations."

79 Paul Harris, "Simulation: The Game Is On," *T&D*, October 2003, p. 49. See also Jenni Jarventaus, "Virtual Threat, Real Sweat," *T&D*, May 2007, pp. 72–78. More employers are extending simulations to creating training games for employees. As in well-known entertainment games like Angry Birds, the advantages from a learning standpoint of using games include constant feedback on how you're doing, "accrued grading" in which you move ahead challenge by challenge, competition and cooperation, and the "freedom to fail," particularly to learn from one's own mistakes. Sebastian Deterding, "Gameful Design for Learning," *Training & Development*, July 2013, pp. 61–63. See also Karl Kapp and Sharon Boller, "Gametime," *TD*, January 2017, pp. 37–41.

80 Jarventaus, "Virtual Threat, Real Sweat."

81 Drew Robb, "Let the Games Begin," *HR Magazine*, September 2012, p. 96.

82 Blanchard and Thacker, *Effective Training*, p. 248.

83 Ibid., p. 249. See also Kim Kleps, "Virtual Sales Training Scores a Hit," *T&D*, December 2006, pp. 63–64.

84 Anders Gronstedt, "From Immersion to Presence," *TD*, June 2016, pp. 55–56.

85 www.reuters.com/article/2014/03/26/us-facebook-acquisition-idUSBREA2O1WX20140326, accessed June 28, 2015. See also Jennifer Hofmann, "Are You Virtually Competent?" *TD*, April 2015, pp. 54–59.

86 Gi Hun Yang and Jae Young Lee, "Learning While Playing," *TD*, May 2016, pp. 46–52.

87 Cammie Cable, "Sales Up, Costs Down," *TD*,, June 2016, pp. 68–69.

88 Pat Galagan, "Made Fast in China," *Training & Development*, January 2013, p. 30.

89 Kevin Alansky, "Blackboard Pays Off for ADP," *T + D* 65, no. 6 (June 2011), pp. 68–69; see also Barbara Carnes, "The Ties That Bind," *Training & Development*, January 2013, pp. 38–40.

90 John Zonneveld, "GM Dealer Training Goes Global," *Training & Development*, December 2006, pp. 47–51. See also "What's Next for the LMS?" *Training & Development*, September 2011, p. 16.

91 "The Next Generation of Corporate Learning," *Training & Development*, June 2003, p. 47.

92 Ibid.

93 For a list of guidelines for using e-learning, see, for example, Mark Simon, "E-Learning No How," *Training & Development*, January 2009, pp. 34–39. See also Sarah Gilbert, "E-learning Design with Ease," *TD*, July 2014, pp. 70–71.

94 "The Next Generation of Corporate Learning," *Training & Development*, June 2004, p. 47 Jennifer Hofmann and Nanatte Miner, "Real Blended Learning Stands Up," *Training & Development*, September 2008, pp. 28–31; J. Hofmann, "Top 10 Challenges of Blended Learning," *Training* (Minneapolis, Minn.) 48, no. 2 (March/April 2011), pp. 12–13; and Lee Salz, "Use Webinars for Training and Revenue," *Training* 48, no. 2 (March/April 2011), p. 14.

95   Tony Bingham and Pat Galagan, "Training Powers Up That Steele," *Training & Development*, January 2014, p. 31.

96   Traci Sitzmann et al., "The Comparative Effectiveness of Web-Based and Classroom Instruction: A Meta-Analysis," *Personnel Psychology* 59 (2006), pp. 623–664. See also, https://sas.elluminate.com/site/internal/home, accessed March 7, 2017.

97   Jennifer Taylor Arnold, "Learning On-the-Fly," *HR Magazine*, September 2007, p. 137; see also M. Donahue, "Mobile Learning Is the Next Generation in Training," *Hotel Management* 226, no. 4 (April 4, 2011), p. 17; and Geoff Holle, "Using Mobile Technology to Support Talent Development," *TD*, January 2017, pp. 22–24.

98   www.dominknow.com, accessed March 9, 2017.

99   Bill Roberts, "From IT Learning to Mobile Learning," *HR Magazine*, August 2012, pp. 61–65.

100 Chris Pirie, "Technology Plus Learning Equals Inspiration," *Training & Development*, December 2012, pp. 39–46.

101 Elizabeth Agnvall, "Just-in-Time Training," *HR Magazine*, May 2006, pp. 67–78.

102 Ann Paul, "Micro Learning 101," *HR Magazine*, May 2016, pp. 37–41. See also, Megan Cole, "Talent Development Pros Predict Spike in Micro-Learning," *TD*, May 2017, p. 9.

103 Catherine Skrzypinski, "Social Media Changes Employee Expectations Regarding Communication," *HR Magazine*, January 2013, p. 14; see also Dan Steer, "Improve Formal Learning with Social Media," *Training & Development*, December 2012, pp. 31–33.

104 Pat Galagan, "Second That," *Training & Development*, February 2008, pp. 34–37.

105 Paraphrased from Manuel London and M. J. Hall, "Unlocking the Value of Web 2.0 Technologies for Training and Development: The Shift from Instructor-Controlled, Adaptive Learning to Learner-Driven, Generative Learning," *Human Resource Management* 50, no. 6 (November–December 2011), p. 761.

106 This is based on ibid., pp. 763–765.

107 Ruth Clark, "Accelerate Expertise with Scenario-Based e-Learning," *TD*, August 2016, pp. 51–55.

108 Karen McCandless, "How to Train Your Staff in the Gig Economy," May 19, 2016, https://lab.getapp.com/how-to-train-your-staff-in-the-gig-economy/; Margery Weinstein, "Training Challenges in Today's 'Gig Economy,'" July 24, 2015, https://trainingmag.com/training-challenges-today%E2%80%99s-%E2%80%9Cgig-economy%E2%80%9D; "How the Gig Economy Is Revolutionizing Restaurant Training Programs." https://www.hotschedules.com/blog/how-the-gig-economy-is-revolutionizing-restaurant-training-programs. All accessed March 7, 2017.

109 https://www.mindflash.com/, accessed March 9, 2017.

110 Susan Ladika, "When Learning Lasts a Lifetime," *HR Magazine*, May 2008, p. 57.

111 https://www.panopto.com/blog/1-in-7-workers-cant-read-your-manual-whats-a-trainer-to-do/, accessed March 7, 2017.

112 Paula Ketter, "The Hidden Disability," *T&D*, June 2006, pp. 34–40.

113 Rita Zeidner, "One Workforce—Many Languages," *HR Magazine*, January 2009, pp. 33–37.

114 Matthew Reis, "Do-It-Yourself Diversity," *Training & Development*, March 2004, pp. 80–81.

115 www.prismdiversity.com/resources/diversity_training.html, accessed August 24, 2014.

116 Jennifer Salopek, "Trends: Lost in Translation," *T&D*, December 2003, p. 15 www.visionpoint.com/training-solutions/title/just-be-fair-basic-diversity-training, accessed June 17, 2011; http://sollah.com/training-solutions/just-be-fair-basic-diversity-training/, accessed March 7, 2017.

117 Paraphrased from "Best Practice: Workforce Diversity Training," The Manufacturing Practices Center of Excellence, www.brmpcoe.org/bestpracticea/internal/abev/abcv_15.html.

118 Blanchard and Thacker, *Effective Training*, pp. 403–405.

119 Ibid., p. 404.

120 Douglas Shuit, "Sound of the Retreat," *Workforce Management*, September 2003, p. 40.

121 "Collaboration Teambuilding in the Cafeteria," *Harvard Business Review*, December 2015, pp. 24–25.

122 http://www.skillsoft.com/business-solutions/, accessed March 7, 2017.

123 https://www.td.org/Professional-Resources, accessed March 7, 2017.

124 Ibid.

125 https://www.sba.gov/tools/sba-learning-center/search/training, accessed March 7, 2017.

126 www.themanufacturinginstitute.org/Skills-Certification/Right-Skills-Now/Right-Skills-Now.aspx, accessed August 24, 2014.

127 From Stephen Covey, "Small Business, Big Opportunity," *Training*, 43, no. 11, November 2006, p. 44.

128 For a discussion of leadership development tools, see John Beeson, "Building Bench Strength: A Tool Kit for Executive Development," *Business Horizons*, 47, no. 6, November 2004, pp. 3–9. See also Rita Smith and Beth Bledsoe, "Grooming Leaders for Growth," *T&D*, August 2006, pp. 47–50.

129 Paula Caligiuri, "Developing Global Leaders," *Human Resource Management Review*, 16, 2006, pp. 219–228.

130 Ibid.

131 Whereas *succession planning* aims to identify and develop employees to fill specific slots, talent management is a broader activity. *Talent management* involves identifying, recruiting, hiring, and developing high-potential employees to ensure the company has the right people in the right roles at the right time. Soonhee Kim, "Linking Employee Assessments to Succession Planning," *Public Personnel Management*, 32, no. 4, Winter 2003, pp. 533–547. See also Michael Laff, "Talent Management: From Hire to Retire," *T&D*, November 2006, pp. 42–48. Most surveyed members of corporate boards said they spend too little time on CEO succession. Joann Lublin and Theo Francis, "Boards Often Fumbled CEO Changes," *The Wall Street Journal*, January 9, 2016, p. B1.

132 Stephen Bates, "Putting a Spotlight on CEO Succession," *HR Magazine*, December 2015/January 2016, pp. 53–55.

133 See, for example, David Day, "Developing Leadership Talent," *SHRM Foundation*, www.shrm.org/about/foundation/research/Documents/Developing%20Lead%20Talent-%20FINAL.pdf, accessed October 4, 2011.

134 Quoted in Susan Wells, "Who's Next," *HR Magazine*, November 2003, p. 43. See also Christee Atwood, "Implementing Your Succession Plan," *T&D*, November 2007, pp. 54–57; and David Day, "Developing Leadership Talent."

135 See "Succession Management: Identifying and Developing Leaders," *BNA Bulletin to Management*, 21, no. 12, December 2003, p. 15; and David Day, "Developing Leadership Talent."

136 Soonhee Kim, "Linking Employee Assessments to Succession Planning," *Public Personnel Management*, Winter 2003.

137 Bill Roberts, "Matching Talent with Tasks," *HR Magazine*, November 2002, pp. 91–96.

138 www.sumtotalsystems.com/datasheets/sumt_succession_planning.pdf, accessed June 1, 2011; http://www.pilat.com/hcm/, accessed March 7, 2017.

139 But see Duncan Jackson et al., "Everything That You Have Ever Been Told About Assessment Center Ratings Is Confounded," *Journal of Applied Psychology*, 101, no. 7, 2016, pp. 976–994.

140 Gail Johnson Morris and Kim Rogers, "High Potentials Are Still Your Best Bet," *T&D*, February 2013, pp. 58–62.

141 Andrew Shipilov and Frederic Godart, "Luxury's Talent Factories," *Harvard Business Review*, June 2015, p. 101.

142 See Paul Evans, Yves Doz, and Andre Laurent, *Human Resource Management in International Firms* (New York: St. Martin's Press, 1990), pp. 122–124; www.sony.net/SonyInfo/csr_report/employees/training/index3.html; accessed March 4, 2014; and www.mckinsey.com/insights/organization/how_multinationals_can_attract_the_talent_they_need, accessed March 4, 2014.

143 Michael Marquardt, "Action Learning Around the World," *TD*, February 2015, pp. 45–49.

144 "Thrown into Deep End, Workers Surface as Leaders," *BNA Bulletin to Management*, July 11, 2002, p. 223. See also Michelle Peters, "Accomplish Two for One with Action Learning," *T&D*, February 2013, pp. 52–54.

145 Ibraiz Tarique, *Seven Trends in Corporate Training and Development* (Upper Saddle River, NJ: Pearson, 2014), p. 114.

146 A good case, says one Harvard Business School expert is "the vehicle by which a chunk of reality is brought into the classroom." Marsha Dollarhide and Darrell Van Hutten, "On the Case," *Training & Development*, April 2013, p. 36.

147 Chris Whitcomb, "Scenario-Based Training at the FBI," *Training & Development*, June 1999, pp. 42–46. See also Michael Laff, "Serious Gaming: The Trainer's New Best Friend," *Training & Development*, January 2007, pp. 52–57.

148 http://teamcommunication.blogspot.com/, accessed July 6, 2014.

149 Carol Leaman, "Boost Basic Job Skills Training," *Training & Development*, August 2014, pp. 34–39.

150 American Management Association, www.amanet.org/, accessed July 6, 2014.

151 For information on the SHRM learning system, see www.shrm.org/Education/educationalproducts/learning/Pages/default.aspx?utm_campaignLearningSystem_All_2012&utm_mediummailing&utm_sourcebrochure, accessed July 21, 2013.

152 For a list of Harvard programs, https://www.exed.hbs.edu/Pages/default.aspx, accessed May 18, 2017.

153 Ann Pomeroy, "Head of the Class," *HR Magazine*, January 2005, p. 57. See also Michael Laff, "Centralized Training Leads to Nontraditional Universities," *Training & Development*, January 2007, pp. 27–29; and Ralph Miller and David Abdow, "Executive Education That Works," *T&D*, December 2012, pp. 28–30.

154 Norman Maier, Allen Solem, and Ayesha Maier, *The Role-Play Technique* (San Diego, CA: University Associates, 1975), pp. 2–3. See also Karen Griggs, "A Role-Play for Revising Style and Applying Management Theories," *Business Communication Quarterly*, 68, no. 1, March 2005, pp. 60–65.

155 Martha Peak, "Go Corporate U!" *Management Review*, 86, no. 2, February 1997, pp. 33–37; and Jessica Li and Amy Lui Abel, "Prioritizing and Maximizing the Impact of Corporate Universities," *T&D* 65, no. 5, May 2011, pp. 54–57.

156 "Executive Coaching: Corporate Therapy," *The Economist*, November 15, 2003, p. 61. See also Steve Gladis, "Executive Coaching Builds Steam in Organizations," *T&D*, December 2007, pp. 59–61.

157 "As Corporate Coaching Goes Mainstream, Key Prerequisite Overlooked: Assessment," *BNA Bulletin to Management*, May 16, 2006, p. 153.

158 For information on the SHRM learning system, see www.shrm.org/Education /educationalproducts/learning/Pages/default .aspx?utm_campaignLearningSystem_All_2012 &utm_mediummailing&utm_sourcebrochure, accessed July 21, 2013.

159 This is based on Diane Brady, "Can GE Still Manage?" *Bloomberg Business Week*, April 25, 2010, p. 29; see also, http://talent.gecareers .com/university/leadership-programs, accessed March 7, 2017.

160 Brady, "Can GE Still Manage?"

161 Stephen Heidari-Robinson and Suzanne Heywood, "Getting Reorgs Right," *Harvard Business Review*, November 2016, pp. 85–89.

162 See, for example, John Austin, "Mapping Out a Game Plan for Change," *HR Magazine*, April 2009, pp. 39–42.

163 The steps are based on Michael Beer, Russell Eisenstat, and Bert Spector, "Why Change Programs Don't Produce Change," *Harvard Business Review*, November–December 1990, pp. 158–166; Thomas Cummings and Christopher Worley, *Organization Development and Change*, Minneapolis, MN: West Publishing Company, 1993; John P. Kotter, "Leading Change: Why Transformation Efforts Fail," *Harvard Business Review*, March–April 1995, pp. 59–66; and John P. Kotter, *Leading Change* (Boston: Harvard Business School Press, 1996). Change doesn't necessarily have to be painful. See, for example, Eric Abrahamson, "Change without Pain," *Harvard Business Review*, July–August 2000, pp. 75–79; and David Herold et al., "Beyond Change Management: A Multilevel Investigation of Contextual and Personal Influences on Employees' Commitment to Change," *Journal of Applied Psychology*, 92, no. 4, 2007, p. 949.

164 Kotter, "Leading Change," p. 85.

165 Beer, Eisenstat, and Spector, Why Change Programs Don't Produce Change," p. 164.

166 Stacie Furst and Daniel Cable, "Employee Resistance to Organizational Change: Managerial Influence Tactics and Leader Member Exchange," *Journal of Applied Psychology*, 3, no. 2, 2008, p. 453.

167 Wendell French and Cecil Bell Jr., *Organization Development* (Upper Saddle River, NJ: Prentice Hall, 1995), pp. 171–193. For examples of actual team-building programs see, for example, www .teambuildinginc.com/, and www.teamcraft.com/, both accessed August 24, 2014.

168 Benjamin Schneider, Steven Ashworth, A. Catherine Higgs, and Linda Carr, "Design Validity, and Use of Strategically Focused Employee Attitude Surveys," *Personnel Psychology*, 49, 1996, pp. 695–705.

169 Michael Beer, Magnus Finnstrom, and Derek Schrader, "Why Leadership Training Fails—and What to Do About It," *Harvard Business Review*, October 2016, pp. 49–56.

170 Wexley and Latham, *Developing and Training Human Resources in Organizations*, p. 153.

171 See, for example, Jack Phillips and Patti Phillips, "Moving from Evidence to Proof," *T&D* 65, no. 8, August 2011, pp. 34–39 for a discussion of a process for gathering training assessment data.

172 James Kirkpatrick and Wendy Kirkpatrick, "Evaluation Blunders & Missteps to Avoid," *Training and Development*, November 2016, p. 39.

173 One review concluded that the relationship of training to human resource outcomes and organizational performance is positive, but that training "is only very weakly related to financial outcomes. Given this, managers may want to assess training results not just in terms of employee behavior and performance, but company financial performance as well." See Phyllis Tharenou et al., "A Review and Critique of Research on Training and Organizational Level Outcomes," *Human Resource Management Review*, 17, 2007, pp. 251–273.

174 Wexley and Latham, *Developing and Training Human Resources in Organizations*, p. 128.

175 In one study, for instance, training teams of hospital workers reduced preventable errors and patient harm. Ashley Hughes et al., "Saving Lives: A Meta-Analysis of Team Training in Healthcare," *Journal of Applied Psychology*, 101, no. 9, 2016, pp. 1266–1304.

176 Jennifer Salopek, "Showstopping Learning," *T&D*, October 2014, pp. 56–59.

177 Ibid.

Chapter 8

1 Experts debate the pros and cons of tying appraisals to pay decisions. One side argues that doing so distorts the appraisals, while some studies conclude the opposite. Mary Jo Ducharme et al., "Exploring the Links between Performance Appraisals and Pay Satisfaction," *Compensation and Benefits Review*, September/October 2005, pp. 46–52. See also Robert Morgan, "Making the Most of Performance Management Systems," *Compensation and Benefits Review*, September/October 2006, pp. 22–27.

2 www.ball.com/, accessed August 28, 2014.

3 "Aligning People and Processes for Performance Improvement," *T&D* 65, no. 3, March 2011, p. 80.

4 Ibid.

5 "Get SMART about Setting Goals," *Asia Africa Intelligence Wire*, May 22, 2005.

6 See, for example, E. A. Locke and G. P. Latham, "Building a Practically Useful Theory of Goal Setting and Task Motivation. A 35-Year Odyssey," *American Psychologist*, 57, no. 9, 2002, pp. 705–717. Letting employees help set their performance measures (in terms of what is measured, and how it's measured when they're appraised) is associated with improved job performance. Bianca Groen et al., "High Job Performance Through Codeveloping Performance Measures with Employees," *Human Resource Management*, 56, no. 1, January–February 2017, pp. 111–132.

7 Thom Shanker, "Conduct at Issue as Subordinates Review Officers," *The New York Times*, April 14, 2013, pp. A1, A4.

8 www.quora.com/What-does-Facebooks -performance-review-process-look-like, accessed April 2, 2015.

9 Laszlo Bock, *Work Rules!* (New York: Twelve, 2015), p. 171.

10 Martin Berman–Gorvine, "Coworker Recognition Programs Yield Employers Great Returns," *Bloomberg BNA Bulletin to Management*, January 10, 2017.

11 Vanessa Druskat and Steven Wolf, "Effects and Timing of Developmental Peer Appraisals in Self-Managing Work-Groups," *Journal of Applied Psychology*, 84, no. 1, 1999, pp. 58–74.

12 See, for example, Brian Hoffman and David Woehr, "Disentangling the Meaning of Multisource Performance Rating Source and Dimension Factors," *Personnel Psychology*, 62, 2009, pp. 735–765.

13 As one study concluded, "Far from being a source of non-meaningful error variance, the discrepancies among ratings from multiple perspectives can in fact capture meaningful variance in multilevel managerial performance." In Sue Oh and Christopher Berry, "The Five Factor Model of Personality and Managerial Performance: Validity Gains through the Use of 360° Performance Ratings," *Journal of Applied Psychology*, 94, no. 6, 2009, p. 1510.

14 For example, Kevin Murphy et al., "Raters Who Pursue Different Goals Give Different Ratings," *Journal of Applied Psychology*, 89, no. 1, 2004, pp. 158–164.

15 Such findings may be culturally related. One study compared self and supervisor ratings in "other-oriented" cultures (as in Asia, where values tend to emphasize teams). It found that self and supervisor ratings were related. M. Audrey Korsgaard et al., "The Effect of Other Orientation on Self: Supervisor Rating Agreement," *Journal of Organizational Behavior*, 25, no. 7, November 2004, pp. 873–891. See also Heike Heidemeier and Klaus Mosar, "Self–Other Agreement in Job Performance Ratings: A Meta-Analytic Test of a Process Model," *Journal of Applied Psychology*, 94, no. 2, 2009, pp. 353–370.

16 Forest Jourden and Chip Heath, "The Evaluation Gap in Performance Perceptions: Illusory Perceptions of Groups and Individuals," *Journal of Applied Psychology*, 81, no. 4, August 1996, pp. 369–379. See also Sheri Ostroff, "Understanding Self–Other Agreement: A Look at Rater and Ratee Characteristics, Context, and Outcomes," *Personnel Psychology*, 57, no. 2, Summer 2004, pp. 333–375.

17 Paul Atkins and Robert Wood, "Self versus Others' Ratings as Predictors of Assessment Center Ratings: Validation Evidence for 360-Degree Feedback Programs," *Personnel Psychology*, 55, no. 4, Winter 2002, pp. 871–904.

18 David Antonioni, "The Effects of Feedback Accountability on Upward Appraisal Ratings," *Personnel Psychology*, 47, 1994, pp. 349–355; Similarly, raters who are also periodically assessed by their ratees tend to give their ratees higher performance ratings. Michael Harari and Cort Rudolph, "The Effect of Greater Accountability on Performance Ratings: A Meta -Analytic Review," *Human Resource Management Review*, Volume 27, 2017, pp. 121–133.

19 Alan Walker and James Smither, "A Five-Year Study of Upward Feedback: What Managers Do with Their Results Matters," *Personnel Psychology*, 52, 1999, pp. 393–423.

20 Lindsay Gellman, "Memo Lets Workers Vent Anonymously About the Boss," *The Wall Street Journal*, January 21, 2015, p. B7.

21 See, for example, "360-Degree Feedback on the Rise Survey Finds," *BNA Bulletin to Management*, January 23, 1997, p. 31; Leanne Atwater et al., "Multi-source Feedback: Lessons Learned and Implications for Practice," *Human Resource Management*, 46, no. 2, Summer 2007, p. 285. However, employers also use 360-degree feedback for performance appraisals, rather than just development. See, for example, Tracy Maylett, "360° Feedback Revisited: The Transition from Development to Appraisal," *Compensation & Benefits Review*, September/October 2009, pp. 52–59.

22 James Smither et al., "Does Performance Improve Following Multi-Score Feedback? A Theoretical Model, Meta-Analysis, and Review of Empirical Findings," *Personnel Psychology*, 58, 2005, pp. 33–36.

23 Christine Hagan et al., "Predicting Assessment Center Performance with 360-Degree, Top-Down, and Customer-Based Competency Assessments," *Human Resource Management*, 45, no. 3, Fall 2006, pp. 357–390.

24 Bruce Pfau, "Does a 360-Degree Feedback Negatively Affect the Company Performance?" *HR Magazine*, June 2002, pp. 55–59.

25 Jim Meade, "Visual 360: A Performance Appraisal System That's 'Fun,'" *HR*

Magazine, July 1999, pp. 118–119; www .halogensoftware.com/landing/free-trial/360 -multiraterfeedback?source=msn&c=Search -e360&kw=360%2520evaluations, accessed August 28, 2014.

26. http://www.sumtotalsystems.com/ solutions/talent/360-degree-feedback/, accessed May 20, 2017.

27. Leena Rao, "Salesforce Debuts 'Rypple-Powered Work.com' to Help Companies Manage Talent, Partners with Facebook," September 19, 2012, http://techcrunch.com/2012/09/19/salesforce -debuts-rypple-powered-work-com-to-help -companies-manage-talent/, accessed April 5, 2013.

28. Rao, op. cit.

29. Rachel Silverman and Leslie Kwoh, "Performance Reviews Facebook Style," *The Wall Street Journal,* August 1, 2012, p. B6.

30. Jenny Hill, "Could Social Media Revolutionise the Performance Appraisal Process?" www .hrmagazine.co.uk/hro/features/1073216/could -social-media-revolutionise-performance -appraisal-process, accessed April 5, 2013.

31. Howard Risher, "Getting Serious about Performance Management," *Compensation & Benefits Review,* November/December 2005, pp. 18–26.

32. Leslie Kwoh, "Rank and Yank Retains Vocal Fans," *The Wall Street Journal,* January 31, 2012, p. B12.

33. Steve Bates, "Forced Ranking: Why Grading Employees on a Scale Relative to Each Other Forces a Hard Look at Finding Keepers, Losers May Become Weepers," *HR Magazine,* 48, no. 6, June 2003, p. 62.

34. Sue Moon, Steven Scullen, and Gary Latham, "Precarious Curve Ahead: The Effects of Forced Distribution Rating Systems on Job Performance," *Human Resource Management Review,* 26, 2016, pp. 166–179.

35. "Survey Says Problems with Forced Ranking Include Lower Morale and Costly Turnover," *BNA Bulletin to Management,* September 16, 2004, p. 297. For example, to paraphrase one executive at Adobe Systems, the company hired the best employees, and then in rating them against each other, basically said that some of them weren't so good after all. Perhaps not surprisingly, voluntary turnover often spiked after the yearly reviews. Dori Meinert, "Reinventing Reviews," *HR Magazine,* April 2015, p. 37.

36. "Straight Talk about Grading Employees on a Curve," *BNA Bulletin to Management,* November 1, 2001, p. 351.

37. Shira Ovide and Rachel Feintzeig, "Microsoft Abandons Dreaded 'Stack,'" *The Wall Street Journal,* November 13, 2013, p. B1.

38. Many managers see management-by-objectives as out of date. For one thing, goal setting is no panacea—for instance, people tend to focus on their goals, which can lead them to neglect important activities that the MBO program doesn't measure. See Howard Risher, "Individual Performance Goals Can Be Problematic," *Compensation & Benefits Review,* 45, no. 2, March/April 2013, pp. 63–66.

39. Ibid.

40. Bock, *Work Rules!,* p. 155.

41. www.employeeappraiser.com/index.php, accessed January 10, 2008.

42. www.successfactors.com/en_us/lp/ppc /employee-appraisal-software.html?Campaign _CRM=CRM-XJ14-HCM-1DG_GPPCPA& CmpLeadSource=Search%20Engine &source=Google_ppc&kw=Employee %20Appraisals%20Software&ad- %E2%80%90id=48484314803&adgroup =Google&gclid=CN2P2c233cQCFZEdgQodVn UA9w, accessed April 4, 2015.

43. "Game Changing Performance Management: A Software Company Makes a Game out of Yearly Performance Appraisals," *Training & Development,* 68, no. 1, January 2014, p. 80.

44. See, for example, Stoney Alder and Maureen Ambrose, "Towards Understanding Fairness Judgments Associated with Computer Performance Monitoring: An Integration of the Feedback, Justice, and Monitoring Research," *Human Resource Management Review,* 15, no. 1, March 2005, pp. 43–67.

45. See, for example, John Aiello and Y. Shao, "Computerized Performance Monitoring," paper presented at the Seventh Conference of the Society for Industrial and Organizational Psychology, Montreal, Quebec, Canada, May 1992; for a recent analysis of EPM, see Katherine J. S. Rogers, Michael J. Smith, and Pascale C. Sainfort, "Electronic Performance Monitoring, Job Design, and Psychological Stress," paper available at www .igi-global.com/chapter/electronic-performance -monitoring-job-design/45284, accessed October 12, 2012.

46. H. James Wilson, "Wearables in the Workplace," *Harvard Business Review,* September 2013, pp. 23–25.

47. Gary Greguras et al., "A Field Study of the Effects of Rating Purpose on the Quality of Multiscore Ratings," *Personnel Psychology,* 56, 2003, pp. 1–21.

48. "Communicating beyond the Ratings Can Be Difficult," *Work-force Management,* April 24, 2006, p. 35; Rita Pyrielis, "The Reviews Are In," *Workforce Management,* May 2011, pp. 20–25.

49. M. Ronald Buckley et al., "Ethical Issues in Human Resources Systems," *Human Resource Management Review,* 11, 2001, pp. 11, 29. See also Ann Pomeroy, "The Ethics Squeeze," *HR Magazine,* March 2006, pp. 48–55.

50. G. R Weaver and L. K. Treviño, "The Role of Human Resources in Ethics/Compliance Management: A Fairness Perspective," *Human Resource Management Review,* 2001, pp. 113–134. Also see, Julie McCarthy et al., "Progression Through the Ranks: Assessing Employee Reactions to High Stakes Employment Testing," *Personnel Psychology* 62, 2009, p. 826.

51. This is based on Howard Risher, "Getting Performance Management on Track," *Compensation & Benefits Review,* 43, no. 5, 2011, pp. 273–281.

52. E. Pulakos and R. O'Leary, "Why Is Performance Management Broken?" *Industrial and Organizational Psychology,* 4, 2011, pp. 146–164.

53. See, for example, Jochen Reb and Gary Greguras, "Understanding Performance Ratings: Dynamic Performance, Attributions, and Rating Purpose," *Journal of Applied Psychology,* 95, no. 1, 2010, pp. 213–220.

54. H. John Bernardin et al., "Conscientiousness and Agreeableness as Predictors of Rating Leniency," *Journal of Applied Psychology,* 85, no. 2, 2000, pp. 232–234.

55. M. Ena Inesi, and Daniel M. Cable, "When Accomplishments Come Back to Haunt You: The Negative Effect of Competence Signals on Women's Performance Evaluations," *Personnel Psychology,* 68, 2015, pp. 615–657.

56. Ibid., p. 647.

57. "Flawed Ranking System Revives Worker's Bias Claim," *BNA Bulletin to Management,* June 28, 2005, p. 206.

58. Donald Fedor and Charles Parsons, "What Is Effective Performance Feedback?" in Gerald Ferris and M. Ronald Buckley, *Human Resources Management,* 3rd ed. (Upper Saddle River, NJ: Prentice Hall, 1996), pp. 265–270. See also Jeffrey A. Daniels and Lisa M. Larson, "The Impact of Performance Feedback on Counseling Self-Efficacy and Counselor Anxiety," *Counselor Education and Supervision,* 41, no. 2, December 2001, pp. 120–130.

59. Annette Simmons, "When Performance Reviews Fail," *Training and Development,* 57, no. 9, September 2003, pp. 47–53.

60. Rachel Feintzeig, "You're Awesome! Firms Scrap Negative Feedback," *Wall Street Journal,* February 11, 2015, pp. B1, B5.

61. Brian Cawley et al., "Participation in the Performance Appraisal Process and Employee Reactions: A Meta-Analytic Review of Field Investigations," *The Journal of Applied Psychology,* 83, no. 4, 1998, pp. 615–633.

62. "Working Today: Understanding What Drives Employee Engagement," from the 2003 TowersPerrin Talent Report. Copyright TowersPerrin.

63. Jamie Gruman and Alan Saks, "Performance Management and Employee Engagement," *Human Resource Management Review,* 21, no. 2, 2011, p. 123.

64. Ibid.

65. Ibid.

66. "Sustainable Employee Engagement," *Training & Development,* 67, no. 2, February 2013, p. 20.

67. "Driving Engagement by Focusing on Strengths," *Gallup Business Journal:* http:// BusinessJournal.Gallup.com/content/124214 /driving-engagement, accessed March 8, 2014.

68. D. Robinson, S. Perryman, and S. Hayday, "The Drivers of Employee Engagement," Institute for Employment Studies, April 2004.

69. Ibid.

70. Ibid.

71. Vishal Gupta, Sushil Kumar, "Impact of Performance Appraisal Justice on Employee Engagement: A Study of Indian Professionals," *Employee Relations,* 35, no. 1, pp. 61–78.

72. Edward Lawler, "Performance Management: The Next Generation," *Compensation & Benefits Review,* May–June 1994, p. 16.

73. See, for example, Greg Boudreau, "Response: What TQM Says about Performance Appraisal," *Compensation & Benefits Review,* June 1994, pp. 20–24.

74. Based in part on Joel D. Ross, *Total Quality Management: Text, Cases, and Readings* (Delray Beach, FL: St. Lucie Press, 1993), p. 1.

75. Ibid., pp. 2–3, 35–36.

76. Peter Cappelli and Anna Tavis, "The Performance Management Revolution," *Harvard Business Review,* October 2016, p. 61; see also "Performance Feedback Getting More Frequent," *Bloomberg BNA Bulletin to Management,* August 2, 2016, p. 246.

77. "GE Scraps Employee Rating Scale as It Rethinks Annual Reviews," *Bloomberg BNA Bulletin to Management,* August 9, 2016, p. 251.

78. Rachel Silverman, "GE Tries to Reinvent the Employee Review, Encouraging Risks," *The Wall Street Journal,* June 8, 2016, pp. B1, B6.

79. Bravetta Hassell, "IBM's New Checkpoint Reflects Employee Preferences," *Workforce,* April 2016, p. 12.

80. Liz Hoffman, "Goldman Makes Feedback Shift," *The Wall Street Journal,* April 22–23rd, 2017, page B1, B2.

81. Andy Pasztor, "Airlines Quicken Data Flow to Pilots," *The Wall Street Journal,* May 19, 2017, p. B3.

82. Lauren Weber, "Nowhere to Hide for Deadwood Workers," *The Wall Street Journal,* August 22, 2016, pp. A1, A10.

83. Howard Risher, "Getting Serious About Performance Management," *Compensation & Benefits Review,* November/December, 2005, p. 19. See also Marie-Helene Budworth, "Performance Management: Where Do We Go from Here?" *Human Resource Management Review,* 20, no. 1, 2011, pp. 81–84.

84 Peter Glendinning, "Performance Management: Pariah or Messiah," *Public Personnel Management*, 31, no. 2, Summer 2002, pp. 161–178. See also Herman Aguinis, *Performance Management* (Upper Saddle River, NJ: Prentice Hall 2007), p. 2; "Performance Management Orientation Guide," *Workforce Management*, July 2012, pp. 20–22; and Angelo Kinicki, Kathryn Jacobson, Suzanne Peterson, and Gregory Prussia, "Development and Validation of the Performance Management Behavior Questionnaire," *Personnel Psychology*, 60, no. 6, 2013, p. 4.

85 These are quoted or paraphrased from Risher, "Getting Serious about Performance Management," p. 19.

86 https://go.oracle.com/LP=3174?elqCampaignId=6310&src1=ad:pas:go:dg:tal&src2=wwmk14 054343mpp012&SC=sckw=WWMK14054343 MPP012, accessed April 4, 2015.

87 For more details, see www.oracle.cocm/taleo-tbe.

88 Howard Risher, "Getting Serious about Performance Management," *Compensation & Benefits Review*, November/December 2005, p. 45.

89 Based on Martin Buckingham and Ashley Goodall, "Reinventing Performance Management," *Harvard Business Review*, April 2015, pp. 40–50.

90 Based on Jon Younger and Norm Smallwood, "Performance Management in the Gig Economy," *Harvard Business Review*, January 11, 2016, https://hbr.org/2016/01/performance-management-in-the-gig-economy; Cath Everett, "What Does the Gig Economy Mean for HR?" *Personnel Today*, February 15, 2016, http://www.personneltoday.com/hr/gig-economy-what-it-means-for-hr/; Philip McCabe, "The 'Gig Economy': How Does HR Need to Adapt to This New Breed of Employee?" *HR Zone*, July 28, 2016, http://www.hrzone.com/engage/employees/the-gig-economy-how-does-hr-need-to-adapt-to-this-new-breed-of-employee, all accessed March 11, 2017.

Chapter 9

1 For example, see Phyllis Moen and Patricia Roehling, *The Career Mystique*, Boulder, CO: Rowman & Littlefield, 2005; and Geoff Williams, "3 Steps to Reinventing Your Career," *U.S. News & World Report*, June 5, 2013, http://money.usnews.com/money/personal-finance/articles/2013/06/05/3-steps-to-reinventing-your-career, accessed September 2, 2014.

2 Stephen Robbins and Timothy Judge, *Organizational Behavior* (Upper Saddle River, NJ: Pearson Education, 2011), p. 285.

3 Ibid., p. 284.

4 Karoline Strauss et al., "Future Work Selves: How Salient Hoped-For Identities Motivate Proactive Career Behaviors," *Journal of Applied Psychology*, 97, no. 3, pp. 580–598.

5 Edward Levinson et al., "A Critical Evaluation of the Web-Based Version of the Career Key," *Career Development Quarterly*, 50, no. 1, September 1, 2002, pp. 26–36; https://www.careerkey.org/choose-a-career/hollands-theory-of-career-choice.html accessed March 5, 2017.

6 Richard Bolles, *What Color Is Your Parachute?* (Berkeley, CA: Ten Speed Press, 2003), pp. 5–6; published annually, the 2017 edition is published by Ten Speed Press in Berkeley, California.

7 This example is based on Richard Bolles, *The Three Boxes of Life* (Berkeley, CA: Ten Speed Press, 1976). Richard Bolles updates his famous career book *What Color Is Your Parachute?* annually. It contains this and many other career exercises.

8 Steven Lindner, "New Government Rule This Year Making Millions of Part-Timers Eligible for Overtime May Boost Opportunities for Portfolio Careerists," June 13, 2016, http://www.nydailynews.com/life-style/millennials-portfolio-careers-multiple-jobs-increasing-article-1.2671919; "Portfolio Careers: Is the Latest Work Trend Right for You?," https://www.forbes.com/sites/learnvest/2013/02/27/portfolio-careers-is-the-latest-work-trend-right-for-you/#640b029a7688; Ian Christie, "Pursue a Portfolio Career," www.monster.com; all accessed March 23, 2017.

9 http:/careers.intuit.com/university/new-grads, accessed March 12, 2013.

10 Rachel Silverman, "Workers Get Help Climbing the Career Ladder," *The Wall Street Journal,* January 14, 2015, p. B6.

11 Laszlo Bock, *Work Rules!* (New York: Twelve, 2015), pp. 217–218.

12 Yehuda Baruch, "Career Development in Organizations and Beyond: Balancing Traditional and Contemporary Viewpoints," *Human Resource Management Review*, 16, 2006, p. 131.

13 www.halogensoftware.com, accessed March 23, 2017.

14 Fred Otte and Peggy Hutcheson, *Helping Employees Manage Careers* (Upper Saddle River, NJ: Prentice Hall, 1992), p. 143.

15 David Foote, "Wanna Keep Your Staff Happy? Think Career," *Computerworld*, October 9, 2000, p. 38. For an example, the U.S. Homeland Security Department's TSA has a career coaching/planning program. See http://tsacareercoaching.tsa.dhs.gov/, accessed May 25, 2017.

16 Julekha Dash, "Coaching to Aid IT Careers, Retention," *Computerworld*, March 20, 2000, p. 52.

17 Stephen Covey, "Small Business, Big Opportunity," *Training*, 43, no. 11, November 2006, p. 40.

18 www.halogensoftware.com, accessed March 23, 2017.

19 This is based on Sarita Harbour, "Ways to Promote Professional Development in the Workplace," http://smallbusiness.chron.com/ways-promote-professional-development-workplace-45524.html, accessed March 27, 2014.

20 Mukta Kulkarni and K. V. Gopakumar, "Career Management Strategies of People with Disabilities," *Human Resource Management* 53, no. 3 (May–June 2014), pp. 445–466.

21 Ann Pace, "Coaching Gains Ground," *Training & Development*, 62, no. 7, July 21, 2008, http://findarticles.com/p/articles/mi_m4467/is_200807/ai_n27996020/, accessed July 28, 2009.

22 This is based on Richard Luecke, *Coaching and Mentoring* (Boston: Harvard Business School Press, 2004), pp. 8–9.

23 Ibid., p. 9.

24 Michael Doody, "A Mentor Is a Key to Career Success," *Health-Care Financial Management*, 57, no. 2, February 2003, pp. 92–94.

25 Luecke, *Coaching and Mentoring*, pp. 100–101.

26 Ferda Erdem and Janset Özen Aytemur, "Mentoring—A Relationship Based on Trust: Qualitative Research," *Public Personnel Management*, 37, no. 1, Spring 2008, pp. 55–65.

27 Herminia Ibarra, Nancy Carter, and Christine Silva, "Why Men Still Get More Promotions Than Women," *Harvard Business Review*, September 2010, pp. 80–85.

28 "Preparing Future Leaders in Health-Care," *Leaders*, c/o Witt/Kieffer, 2015 Spring Road, Suite 510, Oak Brook, IL 60523.

29 www.halogensoftware.com/products/halogen-esuccession/, accessed August 27, 2012.

30 www.cornerstoneondemand.com/leadership-development-and-succession, accessed August 27, 2012.

31 Quoted from www.sumtotalsystems.com/products/career-succession-planning.html, accessed August 28, 2011.

32 Ibid.

33 Abraham Maslow, "A Theory of Human Motivation," *Psychological Review*, 50, 1943, pp. 370–396.

34 "Working at SAS: An Ideal Environment for New Ideas," SAS website, April 20, 2012. Copyright © 2011 by SAS Institute, Inc. Reprinted with permission. All rights reserved.

35 *Connecting the Dots: Comprehensive Career Development as a Catalyst for Employee Engagement*, 2011, Human Capital Institute.

36 This is based on Gary Dessler, *Winning Commitment* (New York: McGraw-Hill, 1993), Chapter 10. See also, www.glassdoor.com/Reviews/J-CPenney-Reviews-E361.htm, http://jobs.jcp.com/viewalljobs/, and http://www.glassdoor.com/Reviews/Employee-Review-J-CPenney-RVW479729.htm, all accessed July 7, 2014.

37 www.Medtronic.com/careers/develop-your-potential/, accessed March 12, 2013; www.medtronic.com/us-en/about-3/medtronic-plc-facts.html?cmpid=mdt_plc_2015_US_about_3_story_panel_featured_company_facts_cta_text_link_learn_more, accessed April 10, 2015; https://jobs.medtronic.com/, accessed May 25, 2017.

38 See, for example, www.nobscot.com/survey/index.cfm and www.bls.gov/jlt/, accessed April 21, 2011; and Adrienne Fox, "Drive Turnover Down," *HR Magazine*, July 2012, p. 24.

39 Jean Phillips and Stanley Gulley, *Strategic Staffing* (Upper Saddle River, NJ: Pearson Education, 2012).

40 The following example is based on Barbara Hillmer, Steve Hillmer, and Gale McRoberts, "The Real Costs of Turnover: Lessons from a Call Center," *Human Resource Planning*, 27, no. 3, 2004, pp. 34–41.

41 Ibid.

42 A separate study found that turnover probably impacts outcomes such as customer satisfaction and service quality more quickly and more significantly than it impacts secondary outcomes such as productivity and financial performance. Julie Hancock, David Allen, and Craig Soelberg, "Collective Turnover: An Expanded Meta-Analytic Exploration And Comparison," *Human Resource Management Review*, V 27, 2017, pages 61–86.

43 Tae–Youn Park and Jason Shaw, "Turnover Rates and Organizational Performance: A Meta-Analysis," *Journal of Applied Psychology*, 98, no. 2, 2013, pp. 268–309.

44 Phillips and Gulley, *Strategic Staffing*, p. 329.

45 www.worldatwork.org/waw/adimLink?id=17180, accessed April 27, 2011; see also, Robbins and Judge, *Organizational Behavior*, p. 81.

46 Phillips and Gulley, *Strategic Staffing*, p. 328.

47 See, for example, Rosemary Batt and Alexander Colvin, "An Employment Systems Approach to Turnover: Human Resources Practices, Quits, Dismissals, and Performance," *Academy of Management Journal*, 54, no. 4, 2011, pp. 695–717.

48 Fox, "Drive Turnover Down," pp. 23–27. SHRM recommends computing turnover as follows: "First calculate turnover for each month by dividing the number of separations during the month by the average number of employees during the month and multiplying by 100 (# of separations during month ÷ average # of employees during the month × 100). Then calculate the annual turnover rate by adding the 12 months of turnover percentages together." SHRM, "Executive Brief: Differences in Employee Turnover across Key Industries," http://SHRM.org, accessed August 30, 2012.

49 "Employers Using Cash to Retain Key Talent," *Bloomberg BNA Bulletin to Management*, June 26, 2012, p. 202.

50 Max Messmer, "Employee Retention: Why It Matters Now," *CPA Magazine*, June/July 2009, p. 28 "The Employee Retention Challenge,"

Development Dimensions International, 2009. See also Claudio Fernandez-Araoz, Boris Groysberg, and Nitin Nohria, "How to Hang on to Your High Potentials," *Harvard Business Review*, October 2011, pp. 76–83; and Eric Krell, "Five Ways to Manage High Turnover," *HR Magazine*, April 2012, pp. 63–65.

51 Messmer, "Employee Retention."

52 Ibid.

53 Batt and Colvin, "An Employment Systems Approach to Turnover."

54 Ibid.

55 Ibid.

56 Ed Frauenheim, "Numbers Game," *Workforce Management*, March 2011, pp. 20–21.

57 Stephen Baker, "Data Mining Moves to Human Resources" *BloombergBusiness*, March 11, 2009. See also "HR Analytics," *Workforce Management*, August 2012, p. 24.

58 Frauenheim, "Numbers Game," p. 21.

59 Bock, *Work Rules!*, p. 142.

60 "The World's Top 10 Most Innovative Companies in Big Data," www.fastcompany.com/most-innovative-companies/2014/industry/big-data, accessed April 24, 2015.

61 Ibid.

62 David Wilson, "Comparative Effects of Race/Ethnicity and Employee Engagement on Withdrawal Behavior," *Journal of Managerial Issues*, 21, no. 2, Summer 2009, pp. 165–166, 195–215.

63 Paul Eder and Robert Eisenberger, "Perceived Organizational Support: Reducing the Negative Influence of Coworker Withdrawal Behavior," *Journal of Management*, 34, no. 1, February 2008, pp. 55–68.

64 Wilson, "Comparative Effects of Race/Ethnicity and Employee Engagement."

65 Lisa Hope Pelled and Katherine R. Xin, "Down and Out: An Investigation of the Relationship between Mood and Employee Withdrawal Behavior," *Journal of Management*, 25, no. 6, 1999, pp. 875–895.

66 Ibid.

67 Pelled and Xin, "Down and Out."

68 Ibid.

69 For an examination of this, see ibid.

70 See, for example, Margaret Shaffer and David Harrison, "Expatriates' Psychological Withdrawal from International Assignments: Work, Nonwork, and Family Influences," *Personnel Psychology*, 51, no. 1, Spring 1998, pp. 87–118; Karl Pajo, Alan Coetzer, and Nigel Guenole, "Formal Development Opportunities and Withdrawal Behaviors by Employees in Small and Medium-Sized Enterprises," *Journal of Small Business Management*, 48, no. 3, July 2010, pp. 281–301; and Eder and Eisenberger, "Perceived Organizational Support," pp. 55–68.

71 Verena Hahn and Christian Dormann, "The Role of Partners and Children for Employees' Psychological Detachment from Work and Well-Being," *Journal of Applied Psychology*, 98, no. 1, 2013, pp. 26–36.

72 *Gee v. Pincipi*, 5th Cir., number 01-50159, April 18, 2002, "Alleged Harasser's Comments Tainted Promotion Decision," www.shrm.org, accessed March 2, 2004.

73 Maria Danaher, "Unclear Promotion Procedures Smack of Discrimination," www.shrm.org, accessed March 2, 2004.

74 Elaine Herskowitz, "The Perils of Subjective Hiring and Promotion Criteria," www.shrm.org, accessed January 1, 2009.

75 Saul Fine, Judith Goldenberg, and Yair Noam, "Beware of Those Left Behind: Counterproductive Work Behaviors among Non-Promoted Employees and the Moderating Effect of Integrity," *Journal of Applied Psychology*, 101, no. 12, 2016, pp. 1721–1729.

76 George Thornton III and David Morris, "The Application of Assessment Center Technology to the Evaluation of Personnel Records," *Public Personnel Management*, 30, no. 1, Spring 2001, p. 55. See also, http://www.gachiefs.com/index.php/assessment-for-promotion/, and http://www.copsandfiretesting.com/cops-psychological-evaluation/, both accessed May 25, 2017.

77 Bock, *Work Rules!*, p. 358.

78 Karen Lyness and Madeline Heilman, "When Fit Is Fundamental: Performance Evaluations and Promotions of Upper-Level Female and Male Managers," *Journal of Applied Psychology*, 91, no. 4, 2006, pp. 777–785.

79 "Minority Women Surveyed on Career Growth Factors," *Community Banker*, 9, no. 3, March 2000, p. 44; Valerie Purdie-Vaughns, "Why so few black women are senior managers in 2015," Apr 22, 2015, http://fortune.com/2015/04/22/black-women-leadership-study/, accessed May 25, 2017.

80 In Ellen Cook et al., "Career Development of Women of Color and White Women: Assumptions, Conceptualization, and Interventions from an Ecological Perspective," *Career Development Quarterly*, 50, no. 4, June 2002, pp. 291–306.

81 Robin Shay, "Don't Get Caught in the Legal Wringer When Dealing with Difficult to Manage Employees," www.shrm.org; http://moss07.shrm.org/Publications/hrmagazine/EditorialContent/Pages/0702toc.aspx, accessed July 28, 2009.

82 Ken Dychtwald et al., "It's Time to Retire Retirement," *Harvard Business Review*, March 2004, p. 49.

83 "Employees Plan to Work Past Retirement, but Not Necessarily for Financial Reasons," *BNA Bulletin to Management*, February 19, 2004, pp. 57–58. See also Mo Wang, "Profiling Retirees in the Retirement Transition and Adjustment Process: Examining the Longitudinal Change Patterns of Retirees' Psychological Well-Being," *Journal of Applied Psychology*, 92, no. 2, 2007, pp. 455–474.

84 See, for example, Matt Bolch, "Bidding Adieu," *HR Magazine*, June 2006, pp. 123–127; and Claudia Deutsch, "A Longer Goodbye," *The New York Times*, April 20, 2008, pp. H1, H10.

85 Luis Fleites and Lou Valentino, "The Case for Phased Retirement," *Compensation & Benefits Review*, March/April 2007, pp. 42–46.

86 Andrew Luchak et al., "When Do Committed Employees Retire? The Effects of Organizational Commitment on Retirement Plans under a Defined Benefit Pension Plan," *Human Resource Management*, 47, no. 3, Fall 2008, pp. 581–599.

87 Dychtwald et al., "It's Time to Retire Retirement," p. 52.

88 Eric Krell, "Ways to Phased Retirement," *HR Magazine*, October 2010, p. 90.

89 Andrea Poe, "Make Foresight 20/20," *HR Magazine*, February 20, 2000, pp. 74–80. See also Nancy Hatch Woodward, "Smoother Separations," *HR Magazine*, June 2007, pp. 94–97.

90 Robert Lanza and Morton Warren, "United States: Employment at Will Prevails Despite Exceptions to the Rule," *Society for Human Resource Management Legal Report*, October/November 2005, pp. 1–8.

91 Max Mihelich, "The Changing Landscape of LGBT Discrimination Laws," *Workforce*, October 2014, pp. 22–24.

92 "Facts about Discrimination in Federal Government Employment Based on Marital Status, Political Affiliation, Status as a Parent, Sexual Orientation, or Transgender (Gender Identity) Status," www.eeoc.gov/federal/otherprotections.cfm, accessed July 9, 2015. See also, http://employment.findlaw.com/employment-discrimination/sexual-orientation-discrimination-in-the-workplace.html, accessed July 9, 2015.

93 Ibid.

94 Joseph Famularo, *Handbook of Modern Personnel Administration* (New York: McGraw Hill, 1982), pp. 65.3–65.5. See also Carolyn Hirschman, "Off Duty, Out of Work," *HR Magazine*, www.shrm.org/hrmagazine/articles/0203/0203hirschman.asp, accessed January 10, 2008.

95 Kenneth Sovereign, *Personnel Law* (Upper Saddle River, NJ: Prentice Hall, 1999), p. 148; "Disciplinary Issues: What Constitutes Insubordination?" www.shrm.org/TemplatesTools/hrqa/Pages/CMS_020144.aspx, accessed September 11, 2013.

96 Connie R. Wanberg, Mark B. Gavin, and Larry W. Bunce, "Perceived Fairness of Layoffs among Individuals Who Have Been Laid Off: A Longitudinal Study," *Personnel Psychology*, 52, no. 1, March 1999, pp. 59–84; Brian Klass and Gregory Dell'Omo, "Managerial Use of Dismissal: Organizational Level Determinants," *Personnel Psychology*, 50, 1997, pp. 927–953; Woodward, "Smoother Separations," pp. 94–97.

97 "E-Mail Used for Layoffs, Humiliation," *BNA Bulletin to Management*, October 2, 2007, p. 315.

98 Donna Mattioli et al., "Penney Wounded by Deep Staff Cuts," *The Wall Street Journal*, April 15, 2013.

99 Paul Falcon, "Give Employees the (Gentle) Hook," *HR Magazine*, April 2001, pp. 121–128, and see John Gallagher, "Do I Have a Case for Constructive Discharge?," https://www.lexisnexis.com/legalnewsroom/labor-employment/b/top-blogs/archive/2011/10/10/do-i-have-a-case-for-constructive-discharge.aspx, accessed May 25, 2017.

100 James Coil III and Charles Rice, "Three Steps to Creating Effective Employee Releases," *Employment Relations Today*, Spring 1994, pp. 91–94; Richard Bayer, "Termination with Dignity," *Business Horizons*, 43, no. 5, September 2000, pp. 4–10; Betty Sosnin, "Orderly Departures," *HR Magazine*, 50, no. 11, November 2005, pp. 74–78; "Severance Pay: Not Always the Norm," *HR Magazine*, May 2008, p. 28; "Strategies In Drafting Effective Separation Agreements," http://apps.americanbar.org/labor/lel-annualcle/08/materials/data/papers/171.pdf, accessed May 25, 2017.

101 Edward Isler et al., "Personal Liability and Employee Discipline," *Society for Human Resource Management Legal Report*, September/October 2000, pp. 1–4.

102 Based on Coil III and Rice, "Three Steps to Creating Effective Employee Releases." See also Martha Frase-Blunt, "Making Exit Interviews Work," *HR Magazine*, August 2004, pp. 9–11.

103 William J. Morin and Lyle York, *Outplacement Techniques* (New York: AMACOM, 1982), pp. 101–131; F. Leigh Branham, "How to Evaluate Executive Outplacement Services," *Personnel Journal*, 62, April 1983, pp. 323–326; Sylvia Milne, "The Termination Interview," *Canadian Manager*, Spring 1994, pp. 15–16; Matthew S. Wood and Steven J. Karau, "Preserving Employee Dignity during the Termination Interview: An Empirical Examination," *Journal of Business Ethics*, 86, no. 4, 2009, pp. 519–534, and "Termination: Exit Interview Questions," https://www.shrm.org/resourcesandtools/tools-and-samples/hr-forms/pages/1cms_015225.aspx, accessed May 25, 2017.

104 Bram Lowsky, "Inside Outplacement," *Workforce*, June 2014, pp. 36–39, 48.

105 Mitchell Lee Marks et al., "Rebounding from Career Setbacks," *Harvard Business Review*, October 2014, pp. 105–108.

106 Marlene Piturro, "Alternatives to Downsizing," *Management Review*, October 1999, pp. 37–42;

"How Safe Is Your Job?" *Money*, December 1, 2001, p. 130.

107 Peter Hom et al., "Challenging Conventional Wisdom about Who Quits: Revelations from Corporate America," *Journal of Applied Psychology*, 93, no. 1, 2008, pp. 1–34.

108 Everett Spain and Boris Groysberg, "Making Exit Interviews Count," *Harvard Business Review*, April 2016, pp. 88–94.

109 Joseph Zarandona and Michael Camuso, "A Study of Exit Interviews: Does the Last Word Count?" *Personnel*, 62, no. 3, March 1981, pp. 47–48. For another point of view, see "Firms Can Profit from Data Obtained from Exit Interviews," *Knight-Ridder/Tribune Business News*, February 13, 2001, Item 0104 4446.

110 "Careful How You Fire Employees; You May Be Damaging Your Brand," *Bloomberg BNA Bulletin to Management*, August 7, 2015, p. 211.

111 Sue Shellenbarger, "Two Weeks' Notice? More Say, 'I'm Quitting Today,'" *The Wall Street Journal*, June 22, 2016, pp. B1, D2.

112 See Rodney Sorensen and Stephen Robinson, "What Employers Can Do to Stay Out of Legal Trouble When Forced to Implement Layoffs," *Compensation & Benefits Review*, January/February 2009, pp. 25–32.

113 "Mass Layoffs at Lowest Level since July 2008, BLS Says," *BNA Bulletin to Management*, January 12, 2010, p. 13.

114 Leon Grunberg, Sarah Moore, and Edward Greenberg, "Managers' Reactions to Implementing Layoffs: Relationship to Health Problems and Withdrawal Behaviors," *Human Resource Management*, 45, no. 2, Summer 2006, pp. 159–178.

115 "Calling a Layoff a Layoff," *Workforce Management*, April 21, 2008, p. 41.

116 "Communication Can Reduce Problems, Litigation after Layoffs, Attorneys Say," *BNA Bulletin to Management*, April 14, 2003, p. 129.

117 Roderick Iverson and Christopher Zatzick, "The Effects of Downsizing on Labor Productivity: The Value on Showing Consideration for Employees' Morale and Welfare and High Performance Work Systems," *Human Resource Management*, 50, no. 1, January/February 2011, pp. 29–44.

118 Ibid., p. 40.

119 "New Trend in Career Hunt," *Europe Intelligence Wire*, February 10, 2004.

120 Ibid.

121 See, for example, http://aol.sportingnews.com/ncaabasketball/story/2009-07-29/sporting-news-50-greatest-coaches-all-time, accessed July 7, 2014.

122 http://abclocal.go.com/kgo/story?section=news/business&id=7775524, accessed June 1, 2011.

123 John Holland, *Making Vocational Choices: A Theory of Careers* (Upper Saddle River, NJ: Prentice Hall, 1973); and see, https://www.careerkey.org/choose-a-career/hollands-theory-of-career-choice.html accessed March 5, 2017.

124 Holland, *Making Vocational Choices*, p. 5.

125 Quoted or paraphrased from www.onetcenter.org/mynextmove.html, accessed March 24, 2017.

126 This is based on Edgar Schein, *Career Dynamics* (Reading, MA; Addison Wesley, 1978), pp. 128–129; and Edgar Schein, "Career Anchors Revisited: Implications for Career Development in the 21st Century," *Academy of Management Executive*, 10, no. 4, 1996, pp. 80–88.

127 Ibid. For a test of Schein's career anchor concept, see Yvon Martineau et al., "Multiple Career Anchors of Québec Engineers: Impact on Career Path and Success," *Relations Industrielles/Industrial Relations*, 60, no. 3, Summer 2005, pp. 455–482.

128 This example is based on Bolles, *The Three Boxes of Life*. See also Bolles, *What Color Is Your Parachute?*

129 Deb Koen, "Revitalize Your Career," *Training and Development*, January 2003, pp. 59–60. Being out of work for a while can be more corrosive than you might realize. One study followed a group of workers, some of whom became unemployed in the ensuing years. The chilling finding is that compared to those who remained employed, the unemployed workers' personalities seemed to change. In before-and-after testing, the long-term unemployed showed reduced levels of agreeableness, conscientiousness, and openness (those who lost their jobs and became reemployed experienced only limited changes in these personality traits). Christopher Boyce, Alex Wood, Michael Daly, and Constantine Sedikides, "Personality Change Following Unemployment," *Journal of Applied Psychology*, 100, no. 4, 2015, pp. 991–1011.

130 Jon Wolper, "The Power of Referrals," *TD*, July 2016, p. 10.

131 See for example, John Wareham, "How to Make a Headhunter Call You," *Across-the-Board*, 32, no. 1, January 1995, pp. 49–50, and Deborah Wright Brown and Alison Konrad, "Job Seeking in a Turbulent Environment: Social Networks and the Importance of Cross-Industry Ties to an Industry Change," *Human Relations*, 54, no. 8, August 2001, p. 1018. This is also the recommendation of Richard Bolles, whose *What Color Is Your Parachute* has long been a number-one selling career management guide: http://www.jobhuntersbible.com/ accessed March 25, 2017.

132 Jennifer Schramm, "Are You on #Social Media?" *HR Magazine*, December 2015/January 2016, p. 57.

133 Based on Phyllis Korkke, "How to Say 'Look at Me!' to an Online Recruiter," *The New York Times*, January 20, 2013, p. 8; and Eilene Zimmerman, "Recruiting a Recruiter for Your Next Job," *The New York Times*, April 7, 2013, p. 10.

134 Sheryl Jean, "Say Goodbye to Paper, Hello to Social Resume," *Miami Herald*, March 4, 2013, p. 19.

135 Susan Adams, "The 10 Best Websites for Your Career," *Forbes*, www.forbes.com/sites/susanadams/2012/09/14/the-10-best-websites-for-your-career, accessed April 10, 2015.

136 A classic but still very useful job search guide available: Richard Payne, *How to Get a Better Job Quicker* (New York: Mentor, 1987), pp. 54–87.

137 Sara Needleman, "Posting a Job Profile Online? Keep It Polished," August 29, 2006, *The Wall Street Journal*, p. B7.

138 Rachel Silverman, Lauren Weber, Lindsay Gelman, and Rachel Feintzeig, "New Year, New Job? Read This First," *The Wall Street Journal*, January 2, 2015, p. B1.

139 See Payne, *How to Get a Better Job Quicker*.

140 Sue Shellenbarger, "The Six-Month Job Interview," *The Wall Street Journal*, January 20, 2016, pp. B1, B3.

Chapter 10

1 Richard Henderson, *Compensation Management* (Reston, VA: Reston Publishing, 1980), pp. 101–127; Stacey L. Kaplan, "Total Rewards in Action: Developing a Total Rewards Strategy," *Benefits & Compensation Digest*, 42, no. 8, August 2005.

2 Nicholas Wade, "Play Fair: Your Life May Depend on It," *The New York Times*, September 12, 2003, p. 12.

3 Robert Bretz and Stephen Thomas, "Perceived Inequity, Motivation, and Final Offer Arbitration in Major League Baseball," *Journal of Applied Psychology*, June 1992, pp. 280–282; Reginald Bell, "Addressing Employees' Feelings of Inequity: Capitalizing on Equity Theory in Modern Management," *Supervision*, 72, no. 5, May 2011, pp. 3–6.

4 James DeConinck and Duane Bachmann, "An Analysis of Turnover among Retail Buyers," *Journal of Business Research*, 58, no. 7, July 2005, pp. 874–882.

5 Michael Harris et al., "Keeping Up with the Joneses: A Field Study of the Relationships among Upward, Lateral, and Downward Comparisons and Pay-Level Satisfaction," *Journal of Applied Psychology*, 93, no. 3, 2008, pp. 665–673.

6 David Terpstra and Andre Honoree, "The Relative Importance of External, Internal, Individual, and Procedural Equity to Pay Satisfaction," *Compensation & Benefits Review*, November/December 2003, pp. 67–74.

7 Ibid., p. 68.

8 Millicent Nelson et al., "Pay Me More: What Companies Need to Know about Employee Pay Satisfaction," *Compensation & Benefits Review*, March/April 2008, pp. 35–42.

9 Pay inequities manifest in unexpected ways. In one study, the researchers studied the impact of keeping pay rates secret, rather than publicizing them on individual employee's test performance. They found that individuals with lower levels of tolerance for inequity reacted particularly harshly to pay secrecy in terms of weaker individual test performance. Peter Bamberger and Elena Belogolovsky, "The Impact of Pay Secrecy on Individual Test Performance," *Personnel Psychology*, 60, no. 3, 2010, pp. 965–996.

10 Frank Giancola, "What the Research Says About the Effects of Open Pay Policies on Employees' Pay Satisfaction and Job Performance," *Compensation & Benefits Review*, 46, no. 3, May/June 2014, pp. 161–168.

11 Debra Friedman, "Pay Transparency: The New Way of Doing Business," *Compensation & Benefits Review*, 46, 2014, pp. 292–294; Google, which has a contract with the Interior Department to provide cloud computing services, was recently asked by the Department of Labor to provide pay information on its employees. Chris Opfer, "Google Faces Labor Department Lawsuit over Pay Data," *Bloomberg BNA Bulletin to Management*, January 10, 2017.

12 Henderson, *Compensation Management*; see also Barry Gerhart and Sara Rynes, *Compensation: Theory, Evidence, and Strategic Implications* (Thousand Oaks, CA: Sage, 2003); Joseph Martocchio, *Strategic Compensation* (Upper Saddle River, NJ: Prentice Hall, 2006), pp. 67–94.

13 In a famous case, *Ledbetter v. Goodyear Tire & Rubber Co.*, the U.S. Supreme Court notably restricted the amount of time (to 180 or 300 days) after each allegedly discriminatory pay decision under Title VII to file or forever lose the claim. Congress subsequently passed and President Obama signed a new law significantly expanding the amount of time to file such claims. See, for example, "Following *Ledbetter* Ruling, Issue of Workers Sharing Pay Information Takes Center Stage," *BNA Bulletin to Management*, July 17, 2007, p. 225.

14 The recently approved Genetic Information Nondiscrimination Act amended the Fair Labor Standards Act to increase penalties for the death or serious injury of employees under age 18. Allen Smith, "Penalties for Child Labor Violations Increase," *HR Magazine*, July 2008, p. 19.

15 Technology is changing what "the work day" means, and perhaps when to pay overtime. Recently, for instance, about 45% of workers said they already do work outside of office

hours, and about 49% say they handle work e-mails after work. "Technology, Flexible Work Options Are Retiring the Traditional 9-to-5 Job," *Bloomberg BNA Bulletin to Management*, August 2, 2016, p. 243.

16 "LinkedIn to Pay $5.8 Million in Overtime, Damages to 359 Employees in Four States," *Bloomberg BNA Bulletin to Management*, August 12, 2014, p. 251.

17 One company, Healthcare Management Group, estimates that "clock creep"—employees regularly clocking in a bit earlier—costs as much as $250,000 per year in overtime. The company remedied the situation by installing an automated time and attendance system. These systems help provide real-time labor data to line managers and automatically update timing systems for changes such as daylight-savings time. Jennifer Arnold, "Reining in Overtime Costs," *HR Magazine*, April 2009, pp. 74–76; Dave Zielinski, "On the Clock," *HR Magazine*, April 2012, pp. 67–68.

18 www.dol.gov/dol/apps/timesheet.htm, accessed March 26, 2017.

19 James Coleman, "App Provides Reminder to Ensure Recordkeeping Is in Order," *BNA Bulletin to Management*, June 14, 2011, p. 191.

20 Zielinski, "On the Clock," pp. 67–68. "Time stealing" is a serious problem. One study concluded that about 21% of hourly employees may be stealing company time, mostly by punching in and out earlier or later than scheduled. To deal with this problem, employers are increasingly utilizing biometric technology to track attendance. For example, in one company, the time clock uses a facial recognition device to identify who is actually punching in or out. Sarah Fister Gale, "Employers Punching in Biometric Technology to Track Attendance," *Workforce Management*, May 2013, p. 14.

21 https://www.dol.gov/whd/minwage/america.htm#California, accessed March 26, 2017.

22 www.nbcnews.com/feature/in-plain-sight/minimum-wage-hikes-where-voters-gave-themselves-raise-n241616, accessed April 12, 2015.

23 "The DOL Releases Proposed Rule Setting $10.10 as Minimum Wage for Federal Contractors," *Bloomberg BNA Bulletin to Management*, June 17, 2014, pp. 185–186.

24 For a description of exemption requirements, see Jeffrey Friedman, "The Fair Labor Standards Act Today: A Primer," *Compensation*, January/February 2002, pp. 51–54. See also www.shrm.org/-issues/FLSA, accessed August 12, 2007; and www.dol.gov/whd/flsa/, accessed September 3, 2014.

25 http://webapps.dol.gov/elaws/whd/flsa/overtime/info.htm, accessed March 26, 2017.

26 "DOL Issues Final Overtime Rule Doubling Exemption Threshold to $47,476," *Bloomberg BNA Bulletin to Management*, May 24, 2016, pp. 161–168; Noam Scheiber, "White House Moves to Make Millions Eligible for Overtime," *The New York Times*, May 18, 2016, pp. A1, B6; Rachel Silverman and Rachel Feintzeig, "Workers May Need to Clock Back In," *The Wall Street Journal*, October 7, 2015, p. B8; Ben Penn, "Employers Wrestle with Whether to Cancel Overtime Rule Plans," *Bloomberg BNA, Bulletin to Management*, November 29, 2016.

27 Ben Penn, "Overtime Rule Under Trump Enters Repeal and Replace Talks," *Bloomberg BNA Bulletin to Management*, March 7, 2017; Martin Berman – Gorvine, "With Overtime Rule in Limbo, Caution Is Urged for Employers," *Bloomberg BNA Bulletin to Management*, February 7, 2017.

28 If there's doubt about exemption eligibility, it's best to check with the local Department of Labor Wage and Hour office. See, for example, "Attorneys Say FLSA Draws a Fine Line Between Exempt/Nonexempt Employees," *BNA Bulletin to Management*, July 5, 2005, p. 219; Tim Watson and Barry Miller, "Tightening a White Collar Exemption," *HR Magazine*, December 2010, p. 95.

29 For instance, the U.S. Supreme Court held that pharmaceutical company sales reps who encourage doctors to prescribe their firms' medicines are FLSA-exempt outside sales persons. "Justices 5–4 Reject Labor Department View, Find Pharmaceutical Sales Reps FLSA-Exempt." *Bloomberg BNA Bulletin to Management*, June 19, 2012, p. 193.

30 Diane Cadrain, "Guard against FLSA Claims," *HR Magazine*, April 2008, pp. 97–100.

31 See, for example, Friedman, "The Fair Labor Standards Act Today," p. 53; Andre Honoree, "The New Fair Labor Standards Act Regulations and the Sales Force: Who Is Entitled to Overtime Pay?" *Compensation & Benefits Review*, January/February 2006, p. 31; www.shrm.org/issues/FLSA, accessed August 12, 2007; www.dol.gov/whd/flsa/, accessed September 3, 2014.

32 See Peter Coy, "Is a $15 Minimum Wage Too High?" *Bloomberg Business Week*, August 10–August 23, 2015, pp. 14–16; Jacob Bunge, "Tyson to Raise Wages for Chicken Plant Staff," *The Wall Street Journal*, October 24, 2015, p. B4 "Walmart to Raise Hourly Workers Paid to Nine Dollars Per Hour, Increasing to $10 in 2016," *Bloomberg BNA Bulletin to Management*, February 24, 2015, p. 57; "McDonald's Plans to Boost Pay, Offer Vacation to Non-Franchise Workers," *Bloomberg BNA Bulletin to Management*, April 7, 2015, p. 107; and Joyce Cutler, "San Jose Is Latest Silicon Valley City to Okay $15 Minimum Wage," *Bloomberg BNA Bulletin to Management*, November 22, 2016.

33 Howard Risher, "A Closer Look at Total Compensation," *Compensation & Benefits Review*, 46, no. 5–6, 2014, pp. 251–253.

34 Nelson Schwartz, "Gap Widening as Top Workers Reap the Raises," *The New York Times*, July 25, 2015, pp. A1, A3.

35 In Germany, the gap is about 140 times, in Spain, 120 times, in Britain, about 90 times, in Japan, about 80, and in Denmark, about 50 times. ("Paycheck," *The Economist*, August 6, 2016, p. 53. See also, Andrea Vittorio, "CEOs Earned 347 Times what US Workers Make, Tracker Shows, *BNA Bulletin to Management*, May 16, 2017.

36 Several state legislatures moved to tighten regulations regarding misclassifying workers as independent contractors, some going so far as adding criminal penalties for violations. "Misclassification Cases Draw More Attention, Attorneys Say," *BNA Bulletin to Management*, December 15, 2009, p. 399. The U.S. Department of Labor is working with state agencies to challenge independent contractor worker misclassifications. "DOL, State Agencies, and Litigants Proceed with Challenges to Worker Misclassification," *BNA Bulletin to Management*, August 14, 2012, p. 257.

37 www.irs.gov/Businesses/Small-Businesses-&-Self-Employed/Independent-Contractor-Defined, accessed March 19, 2014.

38 http://www.irs.gov/Businesses/Small-Businesses-&-Self-Employed/Independent-Contractor-Self-Employed-or-Employee, accessed July 13, 2015.

39 See, for instance, www.uschambersmallbusinessnation.com/toolkits/tool/indcon_m.

40 This is based on Matthew Simpson, "Five Steps to Reduce the Risks of Miscalculation," *BNA Bulletin to Management*, February 21, 2012, p. 63.

41 Conrad De Aenlle, "Employee or Contractor? Healthcare Law Raises Stakes," *The New York Times*, February 15, 2015, p. BU 11. Under the Obama administration, the DOL became more aggressive against employers who misclassified employees as independent contractors. Keith Covington and John Rodgers, "The DOL Weighs in on Worker Misclassification," *Bloomberg BNA Bulletin to Management*, September 15, 2015, pp. S1–S4.

42 Patrick Dorrian, "Gig Workers and Job Related Bias: Are Protections on the Way?" Bloomberg BNA Bulletin to Management, January 3, 2017.

43 Robert Nobile, "How Discrimination Laws Affect Compensation," *Compensation & Benefits Review*, July/August 1996, pp. 38–42; www.eeoc.gov/policy/docs/compensation.html, accessed March 26, 2017.

44 See, for example, Barry Hirsch and Edward Schumacher, "Unions, Wages, and Skills," *Journal of Human Resources*, 33, no. 1, Winter 1998, p. 115; see also www.bls.gov/opub/cwc/cm20030124ar01p1.htm, accessed October 9, 2011; www.eeoc.gov/policy/docs/compensation.html, accessed March 26, 2017.

45 Jessica Marquez, "Raising the Performance Bar," *Workforce Management*, April 24, 2006, pp. 31–32.

46 Elayne Robertson Demby, "Two Stores Refused to Join the Race to the Bottom for Benefits and Wages," *Workforce Management*, February 2004, pp. 57–59; www.wegmans.com, accessed June 1, 2011.

47 Ibid.

48 Ibid.

49 Ibid.

50 Ibid.

51 www.bls.gov/oes/current/oes431011.htm, accessed July 27, 2013. Salaries in some specialties (such as engineering) and in some geographic areas (such as Silicon Valley) have become astronomical; firms like Amazon, Google, and Facebook compete to hire more engineers, and most are supplementing those big salaries with stock options grants. "Money Honeys," *The Economist*, November 5, 2016, p. 53.

52 Bobby Watson Jr. and Gangaram Singh, "Global Pay Systems: Compensation in Support of Multinational Strategy," *Compensation & Benefits Review*, January/February 2005, pp. 33–36.

53 Ibid.

54 See, for example, Joseph Martocchio, *Strategic Compensation* (Upper Saddle River, NJ: Pearson Education, 2011), p. 140; John Kilgour, "Job Evaluation Revisited: The Point-Factor Method," *Compensation & Benefits Review*, July/August 2008, pp. 37–46; and www.shrm.org/TemplatesTools/Toolkits/Pages/PerformingJobEvaluations.aspx, accessed April 5, 2014.

55 Martocchio, *Strategic Compensation*, p. 138. See also Nona Tobin, "Can Technology Ease the Pain of Salary Surveys?" *Public Personnel Management*, 31, no. 1, Spring 2002, pp. 65–78.

56 Henderson, *Compensation Management*, pp. 260–269. See also "Web Access Transforms Compensation Surveys," *Workforce Management*, April 24, 2006, p. 34.

57 For more information on these surveys, see the company's brochure, "Domestic Survey References," Towers Watson Data Services, 218 Route 17 North, Rochelle Park, NJ 07662. See www.watsonwyatt.com/search/publications.asp?ArticleID?21432, accessed October 29, 2009.

58 www.haygroup.com/ww/services/index.aspx?ID=11, accessed August 31, 2012.

59 You may have noticed that job analysis as discussed in Chapter 4 can be a useful source of information on compensable factors, as well as on job descriptions and job specifications. For example, a quantitative job analysis technique like the position analysis questionnaire generates quantitative information on the degree to which the following five basic factors are present in

each job: having decision-making, communication, or social responsibilities; performing skilled activities; being physically active; operating vehicles or equipment; and processing information. As a result, a job analysis technique like the PAQ is actually as (or some say, more) appropriate as a job evaluation technique (than for job analysis) in that jobs can be quantitatively compared to one another on those five dimensions and their relative worth thus ascertained. Another point worth noting is that you may find that a single set of compensable factors is not adequate for describing all your jobs. This is another reason why many managers therefore divide their jobs into job clusters. For example, you might have a separate job cluster for factory workers, for clerical workers, and for managerial personnel. You would then probably have a somewhat different set of compensable factors for each job cluster.

60 Michael Carrell and Christina Heavrin, *Labor Relations and Collective Bargaining* (Upper Saddle River, NJ: Prentice Hall, 2004), pp. 300–303.

61 www.hr-guide.com/data/G909.htm, accessed July 10, 2014.

62 John Kilgour, "Job Evaluation Revisited: The Point-Factor Method," *Compensation & Benefits Review*, July/August 2008, p. 40.

63 See, for example, http://pristina.usembassy.gov/uploads/images/TPAyt1xR9zbj_JQ2iG1tpw/caje1.pdf.

64 David W. Belcher, *Compensation Administration* (Englewood Cliffs, NJ: Prentice Hall, 1974), pp. 257–276; and Nicola Sullivan, "Serco Introduces Pay Grade Structure for Senior Staff," *Employee Benefits*, July 2010, p. 5.

65 Susan Marks, "Can the Internet Help You Hit the Salary Mark?" *Workforce*, January 2001, pp. 86–93.

66 Mark Meltzer and Howard Goldsmith, "Executive Compensation for Growth Companies," *Compensation & Benefits Review*, November/December 1997, pp. 41–50; Martocchio, *Strategic Compensation*, pp. 421–428. See also "Realities of Executive Compensation— 2006/2007 Report on Executive Pay and Stock Options," www.watsonwyatt.com/research/resrender.asp?id=2006-US-0085&page=1, accessed May 20, 2007.

67 "At the Top of Their Industries," *The New York Times*, April 7, 2013, p. B.8.

68 James Reda, "Executive Pay Today and Tomorrow," *Corporate Board*, 22, no. 126, January 2001, p. 18. See also, Mark Farmer and George Alexandrou, "CEO Compensation and Relative Company Performance Evaluation: UK Evidence," *Compensation & Benefits Review*, 45, no. 2, 2013, pp. 88–96.

69 Theo Francis and Joann Lublin, "Divide Persists Between Pay, Performance," *The Wall Street Journal*, June 3, 2016, pp. B1, B5.

70 For example, one book argues that executives of large companies use their power to have themselves compensated in ways that are not sufficiently related to performance. Lucian Bebchuk and Jesse Fried, *Pay without Performance: The Unfulfilled Promise of Executive Compensation* (Boston: Harvard University Press, 2004).

71 http://uk.reuters.com/article/2010/02/23/uk-hsbc-idUKTRE61M6FT20100223, accessed June 23, 2011.

72 www.dol.gov/whd/regs/compliance/fairpay/fs17d_professional.pdf, accessed June 1, 2011.

73 Ibid.

74 Roger S. Achille, "FLSA Requires Education for Professional Exemption," www.shrm.org/LegalIssues/FederalResources/Pages/2ndFLSAProfessionalExemption.aspx, accessed August 28, 2011.

75 See, for example, Martocchio, *Strategic Compensation*; and Patricia Zingheim and Jay Schuster, "Designing Pay and Rewards in Professional Services Companies," *Compensation & Benefits Review*, January/February 2007, pp. 55–62.

76 Farhad Manjoo, "Engineers to the Valley: Pay Up," *Fast Company*, 153, no. 38, March 2011.

77 Dimitris Manolopoulos, "What Motivates Research and Development Professionals? Evidence from Decentralized Laboratories in Greece," *International Journal of Human Resource Management*, 17, no. 4, April 2006, pp. 616–647.

78 www.bing.com/shopping/quickbooks-basic-payroll-2012-complete-package/p/F0EBDFF1F6F276B60004?q=payroll?software&lpf=0&lpq=payroll%2bsoftware&FORM=ENCA&lppc=16, accessed May 20, 2012.

79 www.kronos.com/HR/Payroll-Software/Payroll-Software.aspx, accessed May 20, 2012.

80 www.shrm.org/HRdisciplines/pages/CMS_012013.aspx, accessed May 20, 2012.

81 See, for example, Robert Heneman and Peter LeBlanc, "Development of and Approach for Valuing Knowledge Work," *Compensation & Benefits Review*, July/August 2002, p. 47.

82 Gerald Ledford Jr., "Paying for the Skills, Knowledge, and Competencies of Knowledge Workers," *Compensation & Benefits Review*, July/August 1995, p. 56; see also P. K. Zingheim et al.," Competencies and Rewards: Substance or Just Style?" *Compensation and Benefits Review*, 35, no. 5, September/October 2003, pp. 40–44.

83 Martocchio, *Strategic Compensation*, p. 168.

84 www.jlg.com/en-US/Industries.html, accessed April 9, 2013.

85 Quoted or paraphrased from JLG Industries, Inc., "Information: Skill-Based Pay Program," www.bmpcoe.org/bestpractices/internal/jlg/jlg_14.html, accessed April 9, 2013.

86 See, for example, www.shrm.org/hrdisciplines/compensation/articles/pages/salarystructures.aspx, accessed September 27, 2013.

87 David Hofrichter, "Broadbanding: A 'Second Generation' Approach," *Compensation & Benefits Review*, September/October 1993, pp. 53–58. See also "The Future of Salary Management," *Compensation & Benefits Review*, July/August 2001, pp. 7–12, and "The Best Salary Grading System for Your Company," *J. J. Keller's HR Advantage*, November 22, 2010.

88 Hofrichter, "Broadbanding," p. 55.

89 Dawne Shand, "Broadbanding the IT Worker," *Computerworld*, 34, no. 41, October 9, 2000.

90 *County of Washington v. Gunther*, U.S. Supreme Court, no. 80–426, June 8, 1981.

91 Laura Fitzpatrick, "Why Do Women Still Earn Less Than Men?" www.time.com/time/nation/article/0,8599,1983185,00.html, accessed September 4, 2014. See also Rebecca Greenfield, "Young Women Aren't Closing the Great American Gender Pay Gap," *Bloomberg BNA Bulletin to Management*, April 11, 2017.

92 Christopher Dougherty, "Why Are the Returns to Schooling Higher for Women than for Men?" *Journal of Human Resources*, 40, no. 4, Fall 2005, pp. 969–988.

93 Kurt Stanberry and Forrest Aven, "Equal Pay for Equal Work: Why Women Still Lag Behind after the 50th Anniversary of the U.S. Equal Pay Act," *Compensation & Benefits Review*, 45, no. 4, 2013, pp. 193–199.

94 Rachel Silverman, "Women Doctors Face Pay Disparity," *The Wall Street Journal*, February 8, 2011, p. D4.

95 Stanberry and Aven, "Equal Pay for Equal Work," pp. 193–199.

96 "Women Still Earned Less than Men, BLS Data Show," *BNA Bulletin to Management*, June 8, 2000, p. 72. See also E. Frazier, "Raises for Women Executives Match Those for Men, but Pay Gap Persists," *Chronicle of Philanthropy*, 20, no. 24, October 2, 2008, p. 33. "Open pay" has taken on new importance recently, as a tool for reducing the male-female pay gender gap. Alan Berkowitz et al., "What Employers Should Know About Federal and State Pay Transparency Laws," *Bloomberg BNA Bulletin to Management*, January 3, 2017.

97 The California Fair Pay Act went into effect January 1, 2016, and aims to minimize the gender pay gap. Michelle Rafter, "Wagering on Equal Wages," *Workforce*, February 2016, pp. 33–35, 48.

98 Mark Poerio and Eric Keller, "Executive Compensation 2005: Many Forces, One Direction," *Compensation & Benefits Review*, May/June 2005, pp. 34–40.

99 "The Say-on-Pay Payday," *The Economist*, February 16, 2013, p. 65.

100 Society for Human Resource Management, "Changing Leadership Strategies," *Workplace Visions*, no. 1, 2008, p. 3.

101 For a discussion of some of the issues that go into hammering out an executive employment agreement, see, for example, Jonathan Cohen and Laura Clark, "Is the Executive Employment Agreement Dead?" *Compensation & Benefits Review*, July/August 2007, pp. 50–55.

102 Ibid. See also Brent Longnecker and James Krueger, "The Next Wave of Compensation Disclosure," *Compensation & Benefits Review*, January/February 2007, pp. 50–54.

103 Robert L. Heneman, "Implementing Total Rewards Strategies," www.shrm.org/hrdisciplines/benefits/Documents/07RewardsStratReport.pdf, accessed March 24, 2014.

104 Dow Scott and Tom McMullen, "The Impact of Rewards Programs on Employee Engagement," *WorldatWork: Survey of Rewards and Employee Engagement*, June 2010; www.worldatwork.org.

105 Duncan Brown and Peter Reilly, "Reward and Engagement: The New Realities," *Compensation & Benefits Review*, 45, no. 3, 2013, pp. 145–157.

106 Tom McMullen, "Eight Recommendations to Improve Employee Engagement," *Journal of Compensation and Benefits*, July/August 2013, p. 23.

107 Melissa Van Dyke and Mike Ryan, "Changing the Compensation Conversation on the Growing Utility of Non-Cash Rewards and Recognition," *Compensation & Benefits Review*, 44, no. 5, 2013, pp. 276–279.

108 Meg Breslin, "Solid Rewards Program Can Be Rewarding for Businesses," *Workforce Management*, January 2013, p. 8.

109 Dave Zielinski, "Giving Praise," *HR Magazine*, October 2012, p. 77.

110 Scott and McMullen, "The Impact Rewards Programs on Employee Engagement."

111 Ibid.

112 Although variable pay for performance and pay for acquiring needed skills seem to improve performance, it's not clear, as compensation experts put it, that "programs such as pet insurance and working at home add anything to the business success of our organization." See Jay Schuster and Patricia Zingheim, "Recalibrating Best Practice," *Compensation & Benefits Review*, 45, no. 3, 2013, pp. 134–135.

113 http://disneycareers.com/en/working-here/total-rewards/, accessed March 24, 2014.

114 This is based on George Bradt, "How the Best Big Companies to Work for Drive Appreciation, Access and Rewards," www.forbes.com/sites/georgebradt/2014/03/12/how-the-best-fortune-500-companies-to-work-for-drive-appreciation-access-rewards-2/, accessed March 24, 2014.

115 www.sas.com/en_us/careers.html, accessed March 24, 2014.

116 McMullen, "Eight Recommendations to Improve Employee Engagement."

117 Sharon Pettypiece, "Unintended Consequences of Walmart's Raise: Unhappy Workers," *Bloomberg Business*, August 6, 2015; Patricia Cohen, "The Raise that Roared," *The New York Times*, August 2, 2015, pp. 1, 4.

118 This case is based on www.nature.com/scitable /forums/women-in-science/astro-zeneca-settles -women-s-pay-inequality-20334719; www.dol .gov/opa/media/press/ofccp/OFCCP20110829 .htm; http://social.dol.gov/blog/astrazeneca -what-we-learned/, all accessed August 31, 2012.

119 For a discussion, see Roger Plachy, "The Point Factor Job Evaluation System: A Step-by-Step Guide, Part I," *Compensation & Benefits Review*, July/August 1987, pp. 12–27; Roger Plachy, "The Case for Effective Point-Factor Job Evaluation, Viewpoint I," *Compensation & Benefits Review*, March/April 1987, pp. 45–48; Roger Plachy, "The Point-Factor Job Evaluation System: A Step-by-Step Guide, Part II," *Compensation & Benefits Review*, September/ October 1987, pp. 9–24; and particularly John Kilgour, "Job Evaluation Revisited: The Point-Factor Method," *Compensation & Benefits Review*, July/August 2008, pp. 37–46.

120 Martocchio, *Strategic Compensation*, p. 141.

121 Kilgour, "Job Evaluation Revisited," pp. 37–46.

122 Ibid.

123 Ibid.

124 Ibid.

125 Ibid.

126 Ibid.

127 Ibid. Of course, the level of economic activity influences compensation expectations. Fay Hansen, "Currents in Compensation and Benefits," *Compensation & Benefits Review*, 42, no. 6, 2010, p. 435.

128 Martocchio, *Strategic Compensation*, p. 151.

129 Kilgour, "Job Evaluation Revisited," pp. 37–46.

130 Henderson, *Compensation Management*, pp. 260–269. See also "Web Access Transforms Compensation Surveys," *Workforce Management*, April 24, 2006, p. 34.

131 Kilgour, "Job Evaluation Revisited," pp. 37–46.

132 Ibid.

133 Martocchio, *Strategic Compensation*, p. 185.

134 Ibid., p. 189.

135 Kilgour, "Job Evaluation Revisited," pp. 37–46.

Chapter 11

1 Jay Heizer and Barry Render, *Operations Management* (Upper Saddle River, NJ: Pearson, 2001), p. 15.

2 See, for example, Mary Ducharme and Mark Podolsky, "Variable Pay: Its Impact on Motivation and Organization Performance," *International Journal of Human Resources Development and Management*, 6, May 9, 2006, p. 68.

3 Ibid.

4 Richard Henderson, *Compensation Management* (Upper Saddle River, NJ: Prentice Hall, 2000), p. 463.

5 See, for example, Diane Cadrain, "Cash versus Non-Cash Rewards," *HR Magazine*, April 2003, pp. 81–87.

6 Eric R. Schulz and Denise Marie Tanguay, "Merit Pay in a Public Higher Education Institution: Questions of Impact and Attitudes," *Public Personnel Management*, 35, no. 1, Spring 2006, pp. 71–78; Thomas S. Dee and Benjamin J. Keys, "Does Merit Pay Reward Good Teachers? Evidence from a Randomized Experiment," *Journal of Policy Analysis & Management*, 23, no. 3, Summer 2004, pp. 471–488. See also Sanghee Park and Michael Sturman, "How and What

You Pay Matters: The Relative Effectiveness of Merit Pay, Bonuses, and Long-Term Incentives on Future Job Performance," *Compensation & Benefits Review*, 44, no. 2, 2012, pp. 80–85.

7 Fay Hansen, "Wage and Salary Trends," *Compensation & Benefits Review*, 40, no. 5, November/December 2008, p. 5. One study concluded that merit raises are effective and have larger incentive effects than either bonuses or long-term incentives. Sanghee Park and Michael Sturman, "Evaluating Form and Functionality of Pay-for-Performance Plans: The Relative Incentive and Award Effects of Merit Pay, Bonuses, and Long-Term Incentives," *Human Resource Management*, 55, no. 4, July–August 2016, pp. 697–719.

8 Steve Yegge, quoted in http://glinden.blogspot .com/2006/09/management-and-incentives-at -google.html, accessed June 1, 2011.

9 Brian Skelton, "Dual-Career Tracks: Rewarding and Maintaining Technical Expertise," www.todaysengineer.org/2003/May/dual-ladder .asp, accessed September 8, 2014.

10 Suzanne Peterson and Fred Luthans, "The Impact of Financial and Nonfinancial Incentives on Business Unit Outcomes over Time," *Journal of Applied Psychology*, 91, no. 1, 2006, pp. 156–165.

11 "WorkSimple 'Praise' App Boosts Employee Recognition," *T+D*, January 2012, p. 21, *Academic OneFile*, accessed March 17, 2013.

12 Michelle V. Rafter, "Back in a Giving Mood," *Workforce Management* 88, no. 10, September 14, 2009, pp. 25–29.

13 Like those at http://blog.intuit.com/employees/6 -mobile-apps-for-recognizing-and-rewarding -employees, accessed April 23, 2017.

14 Ibid.

15 Charlotte Huff, "Recognition That Resonates," *Workforce Management*, September 11, 2006, pp. 25–29. See also Scott Jeffrey and Victoria Schaffer, "The Motivational Properties of Tangible Incentives," *Compensation & Benefits Review*, May/June 2007, pp. 44–50. One survey of executives concluded that three nonfinancial incentives—praise and commendation from immediate managers, attention from leaders, and opportunities to lead project or task forces—all ranked higher in motivational effectiveness than did financial incentives including stock options. Daniel Morrell, "Employee Perceptions and the Motivation of Non-Monetary Incentives," *Compensation & Benefits Review*, 43, no. 5, September/October 2011, pp. 318–323.

16 Bob Nelson, *1001 Ways to Reward Employees* (New York: Workman Pub., 1994), p. 19. See also Sunny C. L. Fong and Margaret A. Shaffer, "The Dimensionality and Determinants of Pay Satisfaction: A Cross-Cultural Investigation of a Group Incentive Plan," *International Journal of Human Resource Management*, 14, no. 4, June 2003, p. 559(22).

17 www.deloitte.com/assets/DcomUnitedStates /Local%20Assets/Documents/us_consulting _2010StrategicSalesCompensationSur-vey_072910 .pdf, accessed September 8, 2014.

18 Peterson and Luthans, "The Impact of Financial and Nonfinancial Incentives on Business Unit Outcomes over Time."

19 Ibid., p. 159.

20 Ibid.

21 Ibid., p. 162. See also "Delivering Incentive Compensation Plans That Work," *Financial Executive*, 25, no. 7, September 2009, pp. 52–54, and "Survey Finds Many Employers Not Satisfied with Their Pay-for-Performance Programs," *BNA Bulletin to Management*, January 7, 2014, p. 3.

22 A Kleingeld et al., "The Effect of Goal Setting on Group Performance: A Meta-Analysis,"

Journal of Applied Psychology, 96, no. 6, 2011, pp. 1289–1304.

23 Theodore Weinberger, "Evaluating the Effectiveness of an Incentive Plan Design within Company Constraints," *Compensation & Benefits Review*, November/December 2005, pp. 27–33; Howard Risher, "Adding Merit to Pay for Performance," *Compensation & Benefits Review*, November/December 2008, pp. 22–29.

24 www.deloitte.com/assets/DcomUnitedStates /Local%20Assets/Documents/us_consulting _2010StrategicSalesCompensationSurvey_072910 .pdf, accessed September 8, 2014. See also Pankaj Madhani, "Managing Salesforce Compensation: A Lifecycle Perspective," *Compensation & Benefits Review*, 44, no. 6, pp. 315–326.

25 Straight salary by itself is not, of course, an incentive compensation plan as we use the term in this chapter.

26 Donna Harris, "Dealers Rethink How They Pay Salespeople," *Automotive News*, June 14, 2010, www.autonews.com/article/20100614/RETAIL0 7/306149932?CSAuthResp=1%3A3735483632 70147%3A423310%3A4129%3A24%3Aappro ved%3A06E323F6579E1FCB5665B3CC4B7C6 C0B&=, accessed September 8, 2014.

27 Songjun Luo, "Does Your Sales Incentive Plan Pay for Performance?" *Compensation & Benefits Review*, January/February 2003, pp. 18–24.

28 Scott Ladd, "May the Sales Force Be with You," *HR Magazine*, September 2010, p. 105.

29 Luo, "Does Your Sales Incentive Plan Pay for Performance?" pp. 18–24. See also James M. Pappas and Karen E. Flaherty, "The Moderating Role of Individual-Difference Variables in Compensation Research," *Journal of Managerial Psychology*, 21, no. 1, January 2006, pp. 19–35; and T. B. Lopez, C. D. Hopkins, and M. A. Raymond, "Reward Preferences of Salespeople: How Do Commissions Rate?" *Journal of Personal Selling & Sales Management*, 26, no. 4, Fall 2006, pp. 381–390.

30 Pankaj Madhani, "Reallocating Fixed and Variable Pay in Sales Organizations: A Sales Carryover Perspective," *Compensation & Benefits Review*, 43, no. 6, December 5, 2011, pp. 346–360.

31 Bill O'Connell, "Dead Solid Perfect: Achieving Sales Compensation Alignment," *Compensation & Benefits Review*, March/April 1996, pp. 46–47. See also C. Albrecht, "Moving to a Global Sales Incentive Compensation Plan," *Compensation & Benefits Review*, 41, no. 4, July/August 2009, p. 52.

32 "Driving Profitable Sales Growth: 2006/2007 Report on Sales Effectiveness," www .watsonwyatt.com/research/resrender.asp?id =2006-US-0060&page=1, accessed May 20, 2007.

33 Emily Glazer, "Wells Revamps Pay After Scandal," *The Wall Street Journal*, January 7–8, 2017, pp. B1, B2.

34 Emily Glazer, "Wells Fargo Tripped by Its Sales Culture," *The Wall Street Journal*, September 17–18, 2016, pp. A1, 88.

35 Michael Corkery and Stacy Cowley, "Warned About Excesses, Then Prodded to Sell," *The New York Times*, September 17, 2016, pp. A1, B3. Merrill Lynch recently implemented a new incentive plan for its brokers. Each broker must now refer at least two customers to other parts of Bank of America, such as its retail bank, or suffer pay cuts. Michael Wursthorn, "Merrill to Brokers: More Referrals or Pay Cut," *The Wall Street Journal*, December 8, 2016, page B1. Incentive plans can have other consequences. One study found that earning their bonuses caused managers to pressure and stress out their subordinates. Dionne Poehler and Joseph Schmidt, "Does Pay-for-Performance Drain

the Employment Relationship? The Effects of Manager Bonus Eligibility on Nonmanagement Employee Turnover," *Personnel Psychology*, 69, 2016, pp. 395–429.

36 www.vuesoftware.com/Product/Compensation _Management.aspx, accessed September 8, 2014.

37 Oracle Fusion Incentive Compensation Data Sheet, http://www.oracle.com/us/products /applications/fusion/hcm-workforce compensation-1543936.pdf, accessed July 14, 2015.

38 Mark Meltzer and Howard Goldsmith, "Executive Compensation for Growth Companies," *Compensation Benefits Review*, November 1997, 29, no. 6, pp. 41–50. See also Jennifer Wynter-Palmer, "Is the Use of Short-Term Incentives Good Organization Strategy?" *Compensation & Benefits Review*, 44, no. 5, 2013, pp. 254–265.

39 Richard Ericson, "Benchmarking for Executive Incentive Pay: The Importance of Performance Standards," *Compensation & Benefits Review*, 43, no. 2, March/April 2011, pp. 92–99. See also Robert J. Greene, "Reward Performance? What Else?" *Compensation & Benefits Review*, 47, no. 3, 2015, pp. 103–106.

40 See "The Impact of Sarbanes-Oxley on Executive Compensation," www.thelenreid.com, accessed December 11, 2003. See also Brent Longnecker and James Krueger, "The Next Wave of Compensation Disclosure," *Compensation & Benefits Review*, January/February 2007, pp. 50–54.

41 James Reda, "Executive Compensation: Balancing Risk, Performance, and Pay," *Financial Executive*, 25, no. 9, November 2009, pp. 46–50. See also "Compensation: The Case Against Long-Term Incentive Plans," *Harvard Business Review*, October 2016, pp. 22–23.

42 Meltzer and Goldsmith, "Executive Compensation for Growth Companies," pp. 44–45; Max Smith and Ben Stradley, "New Research Tracks the Evolution of Annual Incentive Plans," *Executive Compensation*, Towers Watson, 2010, http://Towerswatson.com, accessed August 28, 2011.

43 Ibid.

44 Ibid.

45 Ibid.

46 https://www.bloomberg.com/ncws/articles /2016-03-18/pepsico-ceo-nooyi-s-pay-package -increases-18-to-26-4-million, accessed April 22, 2017.

47 Benjamin Dunford et al., "Underwater Stock Options and Voluntary Executive Turnover: A Multidisciplinary Perspective Integrating Behavioral and Economic Theories," *Personnel Psychology*, 61, 2008, pp. 687–726.

48 Phred Dvorak, "Slump Yields Employee Rewards," *The Wall Street Journal*, October 10, 2008, p. B2; Don Clark and Jerry DiColo, "Intel to Let Workers Exchange Options," *The Wall Street Journal*, March 24, 2009, p. B3.

49 "Study: CEO Compensation Not Tied to Company Performance," *BNA Bulletin to Management*, March 22, 2011, p. 92.

50 William Gerard Sanders and Donald Hambrick, "Swinging for the Fences: The Effects of CEO Stock Options on Company Risk-Taking and Performance," *Academy of Management Journal*, 50, no. 5, 2007, pp. 1055–1078.

51 www.mercer.com/pressrelease/details.jhtml /dynamic/idContent/1263210, accessed January 2, 2007.

52 www.nceo.org/main/article.php/id/43/, accessed June 1, 2011.

53 Menahchem Abudy and Efrat Shust, "Employees' Attitudes toward Equity-Based Compensation," *Compensation & Benefits Review*, 44, no. 5, 2013, pp. 246–253.

54 Under IRS regulations, companies cannot deduct all golden parachute payments made to executives, and the executive must pay a 20% excise tax on the golden parachute payments. "Final Regs Issued for Golden Parachute Payments," *Executive Tax and Management Report*, 66, no. 17, September 2003, p. 1.

55 Other suggestions are as follows: equal payments to all members on the team; differential payments to team members based on their contributions to the team's performance; and differential payments determined by a ratio of each group member's base pay to the total base pay of the group. See Kathryn Bartol and Laura Hagmann, "Team-Based Pay Plans: A Key to Effective Team Work," *Compensation & Benefits Review*, November/December 1992, pp. 24–29. See also K. Merriman, "On the Folly of Rewarding Team Performance, While Hoping for Teamwork," *Compensation & Benefits Review*, 41, no. 1, January/February 2009, pp. 61–66.

56 Richard Seaman, "The Case Study: Rejuvenating an Organization with Team Pay," *Compensation & Benefits Review*, September/October 1997, pp. 25–30. See also Peter Wright, Mark Kroll, Jeffrey A. Krug, and Michael Pettus, "Influences of Top Management Team Incentives on Firm Risk Taking," *Strategic Management Journal*, 28, no. 1, January 2007, pp. 81–89.

57 Alberto Bayo-Moriones and Martin Larraza-Kintana, "Profit Sharing Plans and Effective Commitment: Does the Context Matter?" *Human Resource Management*, 48, no. 2, March/April 2009, pp. 207–224. Rather than simply using revenue or profits, some plans (as at steelmaker Nucor) use "economic profit" (or EP), defined as "share of profits above a threshold level of profitability." Paul Farris et al., "Executive Compensation: Do Economic Profits Matter?" *Compensation & Benefits Review*, 46, no. 5–6, 2014, pp. 276–286.

58 Kaja Whitehouse, "More Companies Offer Packages Linking Pay Plans to Performance," *The Wall Street Journal*, December 13, 2005, p. B4.

59 Under the U.S. tax code, "any arrangement that provides for the deferral of compensation in a year later than the year in which the compensation was earned may be considered a deferred compensation arrangement." Steven Friedman, "2008 Compliance Strategies for Employers in Light of Final 409A Regulations," *Compensation & Benefits Review*, March/April 2008, p. 27.

60 Joseph Martocchio, *Strategic Compensation* (Upper Saddle River, NJ: Prentice Hall, 2006), pp. 163–165.

61 Barry W. Thomas and Madeline Hess Olson, "Gainsharing: The Design Guarantees Success," *Personnel Journal*, May 1998, pp. 73–79; A. C. Gardner, "Goal Setting and Gain-sharing: The Evidence on Effectiveness," *Compensation and Benefits Review*, 43, no. 4, July/August 2011, pp. 236–244.

62 Paraphrased from Woodruff Imber mann, "Boosting Plant Performance with Gainsharing," *Business Horizons*, November/December 1992, p. 77. See also Max Reynolds and Joane Goodroe, "The Return of Gainsharing: Gainsharing Appears to Be Enjoying a Renaissance," *Healthcare Financial Management*, 59, no. 11, November 2005, pp. 114–116; and Dong-One Kim, "The Benefits and Costs of Employee Suggestions under Gainsharing," *Industrial and Labor Relations Review*, 58, no. 4, July 2005, pp. 631–652; hospital gainsharing discussion in Anjana Patel, "Gain-sharing: Past, Present, and Future," *Healthcare Financial Management*, 60, no. 9, September 2006, pp. 124–128, 130.

63 Paul Rossler and C. Patrick Koelling, "The Effect of Gainsharing on Business Performance at a Paper Mill," *National Productivity Review*, Summer 1993, pp. 365–382; hospital gainsharing discussion in Patel, "Gainsharing."

64 Robert Greene, "Variable Compensation: Good Fit to Turbulent Environments," *Compensation & Benefits Review*, 44, no. 6, p. 308.

65 See, for example, www.dol.gov/dol/topic/health -plans/erisa.htm, accessed October 2, 2011.

66 Eric Dash, "Time Warner Stops Granting Stock Options to Most of Staff," *The New York Times*, February 19, 2005, item 128921996.

67 Based on Frederick Hills, Thomas Bergmann, and Vida Scarpello, *Compensation Decision Making* (Fort Worth, TX: The Dryden Press, 1994), p. 424. See also Fay Hansen, "The Cutting Edge of Benefit Cost Control," *Workforce*, March 2003, pp. 36–42; Crain's Benefits Outlook 2009, www.crainsbenefit.com /news/survey-finds-nearly-20-percent-of -employers-plan-to-drop-health-benefits.php, accessed July 28, 2009.

68 "California Domestic Partner Benefits Mandate Carries Likely Impact Beyond State's Borders," *BNA Bulletin to Management*, November 6, 2003, p. 353.

69 http://dllr.state.md.us/employment /uitrustfundpoints.shtml, accessed April 22, 2017.

70 www.bls.gov/opub/perspectives/issue2.pdf, accessed September 8, 2014.

71 Ibid.

72 Ibid.

73 Ken Belson, "At IBM, a Vacation Anytime, or Maybe No Vacation at All," *The New York Times*, August 31, 2007, pp. A1–A18.

74 "National Compensation Survey," p. 116. See also "Spurious Sick-Notes Spiral Upwards," *Safety and Health Practitioner*, 22, no. 6, June 2004, p. 3; "Unscheduled Employee Absences Cost Companies More than Ever," *Compensation & Benefits Review*, March/April 2003, p. 19; and Robert Grossman, "Gone but Not Forgotten," *HR Magazine*, 56, no. 9, September 2011, pp. 34–46. Job absence rates haven't changed appreciably for years; they averaged about 0.8% of scheduled worker days in one recent year. "Employee Absenteeism Through All of 2016 Remains Low by Historical Standards," *Bloomberg BNA Bulletin to Management*, February 28, 2017.

75 "Employee Whose Facebook Photos Suggested Fraud Lacks FMLA Claims, Sixth Circuit Rules," *BNA Bulletin to Management*, November 20, 2012, p. 371.

76 "Making Up for Lost Time: How Employers Can Curb Excessive Un-scheduled Absences," *BNA Human Resources Report*, October 20, 2003, p. 1097. See also W. H. J. Hassink et al., "Do Financial Bonuses Reduce Employee Absenteeism? Evidence from a Lottery," *Industrial and Labor Relations Review*, 62, no. 3, April 2009, pp. 327–342.

77 "SHRM Benefits Survey Finds Growth in Employer Use of Paid Leave Pools," *BNA Bulletin to Management*, March 21, 2002, p. 89.

78 See M. Michael Markowich and Steve Eckberg, "Get Control of the Absentee-Minded," *Personnel Journal*, March 1996, pp. 115–120; "Exploring the Pluses, Minuses, and Myths of Switching to Paid Time Off Banks," *BNA Bulletin to Management*, 55, no. 25, June 17, 2004, pp. 193–194.

79 Most firms don't include federal holidays in their paid time off "banks." Society for Human Resource Management 2009 employee benefits survey, quoted in Martha Frase, "Taking Time Off to the Bank," *HR Magazine*, March 2010, p. 42.

80 Jen Schramm, "A New Generation of Workers Could Upend Traditional Approaches to Paid Leave," *HR Magazine*, December 2016/January 2017, p. 62.

81 Grossman, "Gone but Not Forgotten," p. 44.
82 Judith Whitaker, "How HR Made a Difference," *People Management*, 27, October 28, 2010.
83 Ibid.
84 http://en.wikipedia.org/wiki/Driver_and _Vehicle_Licensing_Agency, accessed April 13, 2013.
85 Claire Miller, "Stressed, Tired, Rushed: Portrait of the Modern Family," *The New York Times*, November 5, 2015, p. A3.
86 Dawn Onley, "Modern Family Leave," *HR Magazine*, March 2017, pp. 39–43. Major League Baseball has had a paternity leave policy for more than six years, and over 150 players have used it. Carmen Castro–Pagan, "MLB Players: Don't Put Me in, Coach, I'm on Paternity Leave," *Bloomberg BNA Bulletin to Management*, May 23, 2017.
87 For recent regulations for administering the Family and Medical Leave Act, see https://www .dol.gov/whd/fmla/, accessed April 23, 2017.
88 For now, Texas is the only state that doesn't require employers to participate in its state workers compensation system; many "opt out," and are self-insured or insured through private insurers. Other states, including Oklahoma and Tennessee, are looking into opt out plans. Joanne Sammer, "Opting Out," *HR Magazine*, September 2016, pp. 75–79.
89 Ben Penn, "Obama Sick Leave Order Survives Under Trump, for Now," *Bloomberg BNA, Bulletin to Management*, April 18, 2017.
90 Based on Dennis Grant, "Managing Employee Leaves: A Legal Primer," *Compensation & Benefits Review*, 35, no. 4, 2003, p. 41. There are several unresolved issues in what "12 months' employment" means. For example, several courts held that an employee *can* count previous periods of employment with the employer to satisfy the 12-month requirement. See Daniel Ritter et al., "Recent Developments under the Family and Medical Leave Act," *Compensation & Benefits Review*, September/October 2007, p. 33.
91 John Herzfeld, "New York Ramping Up for 2018 Paid Family Leave Start," *Bloomberg BNA Bulletin to Management*, February 28, 2017.
92 See, for example, Genevieve Douglas, "Low-Income Workers Need, Want Federal Parental Paid Leave," *Bloomberg BNA Bulletin to Management*, April 4, 2017.
93 Kristen Knebel, "Adoption Benefits Get Boost from Parenting Leave Push," *Bloomberg BNA Bulletin to Management*, October 18, 2016.
94 "Companies Succeed with Varied Approaches to Paid Parental Leave," *Bloomberg BNA Bulletin to Management*, September 20, 2016, p. 297.
95 *Severance and separation policies*, Lee Hecht Harrison, www.lhh.com/~/media /adeccogroup/brands/lhh-brand/ . . ./severance -study.pdf, accessed April 23, 2017.
96 http://www.natlawreview.com/article/does -your-severance-trigger-erisa-why-you-should -care-and-what-you-should-do, accessed April 23, 2017.
97 "Workers' Comp Claims Rise with Layoffs, but Employers Can Identify, Prevent Fraud," *BNA Bulletin to Management*, October 4, 2001, p. 313.
98 "Using Case Management in Workers' Compensation," *BNA Bulletin to Management*, June 6, 1996, p. 181; for other tactics, see, for example, H. Jorgensen, "Overhauling Claims Management," *Risk Management*, 54, no. 7, July 2007, p. 50.
99 "Workers' Comp Research Provides Insight into Curbing Health Care Costs," *EHS Today*, February 2010, p. 18.
100 In one survey, 53% of workers said they would trade some pay for better retirement benefits: "Employees Willing to Trade Pay for More Benefits, Survey Finds," *BNA Bulletin to Management*, March 6, 2012, p. 78.
101 Emily Jane Fox, "Health Insurance Premiums Climb 4% in 2012," http://money.cnn.com /2012/09/11/pf/insurance/health-insurance -premiums/index.html, **accessed April 12,** 2013. See also "Costs This Year Increased at Highest Rate Since 2004, Survey Reveals," *HR Focus* 88, no. 1 January 10, 2011; "Health Costs," http://kff.org/health-costs/, accessed April 20, 2015.
102 "Costs This Year Increased at Highest Rate Since 2004.
103 Society for Human Resource Management, "Mental Health Trends," *Workplace Visions*, no. 2, http://moss07.shrm.org/Research /FutureWorkplaceTrends/Pages/0303.aspx, accessed July 28, 2009.
104 Genevieve Douglas, "Millennials Report Higher Rates of Depression, Need Support," *Bloomberg BNA Bulletin to Management*, February 21, 2017.
105 "Mental-Health Parity Measure Enacted as Part of Financial Rescue Signed by Bush," *Bloomberg BNA Bulletin to Management*, October 7, 2008, p. 321.
106 "IRS Unveils Proposed Rules of 'Shared Responsibility,'" *Bloomberg BNA Bulletin to Management*, January 18, 2013, p. 12. See also Wendy Voss and Jesse Noa, "The ACA's Employer Mandate: What Are the Implications?" *Bloomberg BNA Bulletin to Management*, June 17, 2014, pp. S1–S12.
107 "Deadlines Vary for Implementing Provisions of Health Care Law," *Bloomberg BNA Bulletin to Management*, May 4, 2010, p. 143; "Ruling Means Employers Now Face Various PPACA Deadlines," *Bloomberg BNA Bulletin to Management*, August 10, 2012, p. 222.
108 "Regulation Will Allow Young Adults Up to Age 26 to Retain Dependent Coverage," *Bloomberg BNA Bulletin to Management*, May 18, 2010, p. 153.
109 Patricia Moran, "2015 Healthcare Compliance: A Checklist for Employers," *Bloomberg BNA Bulletin to Management*, February 10, 2015, pp. S1–S4.
110 "Lavish Cadillac Health Plans Dying Out as ACA Tax Looms Three Years Hence," *Bloomberg BNA Bulletin to Management*, January 13, 2015, p. 9.
111 Anna Mathews and Julie Jargon, "Firms Try to Escape Health Penalties," *The Wall Street Journal*, October 22, 2014, pp. A1, A2.
112 Ibid.
113 "The Insured and the Unsure," *The Economist* 6 (January 20, 2013), p. 59.
114 Joanne Sammer, "How to Choose Health Insurance Exchanges," *HR Magazine*, October 2012, pp. 47–52.
115 Sara Hansard, "Obamacare Premiums Estimated to Rise 10 to 20 percent in 2018," *Bloomberg BNA Bulletin to Management*, April 20, 2017.
116 Margot Sanger Katz, "A New Republican Proposal that Evokes the Old Days," *The New York Times*, April 21, 2017, p. A16; Stephanie Armour and Christina Peterson, "GOP Shifts Help Strategy," *The Wall Street Journal*, April 5, 2017, p. A6.
117 Zachary Tracer and Anna Edney, "Obamacare's Insurers Struggle for Stability Amid Trump Threats," *Bloomberg BNA Bulletin to Management*, April 18, 2017.
118 Reed Abelson, "With Subsidies at Stake, Insurers Seek Direction," *The New York Times*, April 19, 2017, p. A19.
119 Rita Pyrillis, "Despite Repeal Efforts, ACA Compliance Moves Forward," *Workforce*, January/February 2017, p. 16.
120 See, for example, Karli Dunkelberger, "Avoiding COBRA's Bite: Three Keys to Compliance," *Compensation & Benefits Review*, March/April 2005, pp. 44–48.
121 www.dol.gov, accessed December 23, 2006.
122 Larri Short and Eileen Kahaner, "Unlocking the Secrets of the New Privacy Rules," *Occupational Hazards*, September 2002, pp. 51–54. See also, http://www.hipaasurvivalguide.com/ hipaa-privacy-rule.php, accessed April 23, 2017.
123 Other relevant laws (covered earlier) include the *Americans with Disabilities Act,* the *Pregnancy Discrimination Act,* and the *Genetic Information Nondiscrimination Act (GINA)* of 2008. Kevin Maroney, "Prognosis Negative? GINA's Interim Incentives Ruling a Concern for Wellness Programs," *Compensation & Benefits Review*, 42, no. 2, 2010, pp. 94–101. Employers including Visa Inc. offer genetic testing for potential problems such as heart disease and diabetes. Rita Pyrillis, "Jeans Fit? Genetic Testing Joins Wellness Options," *Workforce*, December 2015, p. 14.
124 http://insight.aon.com/?elqPURLPage=6567, accessed April 11, 2013.
125 Vanessa Fuhrmanns, "Oops! As Health Plans Become More Complicated, They're Also Subject to a Lot More Costly Mistakes," *The Wall Street Journal*, January 24, 2005, p. R4.
126 Jerry Geisel, "Employers Accelerate Health Care Cost-Shifting," *Business Insurance* 45, no. 21 (May 23, 2011), pp. 3, 21; http://kff.org/report -section/ehbs-2014-summary-of-findings/, accessed July 15, 2015.
127 Christine Keller and Christopher Condeluci, "Tax Relief and Health Care Act Should Prompt Re-Examination of HSAs," *SHRM Legal Report*, July–August 2007, p. 1.
128 In contrast, with health reimbursement arrangements (HRA) only the employer makes contributions. See "Types of Tax Favored Health Accounts," *HR Magazine*, August 2008, p. 76.
129 Martha Frase, "Minimalist Health Coverage," *HR Magazine*, June 2009, pp. 107–112.
130 "To Cut Costs, Employers Considering Defined Contribution Health Insurance Plans," *BNA Bulletin to Management*, November 20, 2011, p. 377.
131 Tamara Lytle, "Strategic Moves," *HR Magazine,* March 2016, pp. 39–42.
132 Sandra Yin, "A New Breed," *American Way,* May 1, 2013, pp. 40–41.
133 Robert Christadore, "Benefits Purchasing Alliances: Creating Stability in an Unstable World," *Compensation & Benefits Review*, September/ October 2001, pp. 49–53; Betty Liddick, "Going the Distance for Health Savings," *HR Magazine,* March 2007, pp. 51–55; J. Wojcik, "Employers Consider Short-Haul Medical Tourism," *Business Insurance*, 43, no. 29, August 24, 2009, pp. 1, 20.
134 David Tobenkin, "Spousal Exclusions on the Rise," *HR Magazine*, November 2011, pp. 55–56.
135 Rebecca Vesely, "A New Remedy Emerges for Spiralling Health Costs," *Workforce Management*, June 2012, p. 14.
136 Susan Ladika, "Some Firms Find In-House Clinics Just What the Doctor Ordered," *Workforce Management,* March 2011, pp. 6–7.
137 Alan Cohen, "Decision-Support in the Benefits Consumer Age," *Compensation & Benefits Review*, March/April 2006, pp. 46–51.
138 "HR Outsourcing: Managing Costs and Maximizing Provider Relations," *BNA, Inc.* 21, no. 11 (Washington, DC: November 2003), p. 10.
139 Bill Roberts, "Outsourcing in Turbulent Times," *HR Magazine*, November 2009, p. 45.
140 Susan Galactica, "There's a Doctor on the Phone? Employers Dial-Up Telemedicine," *Workforce Management*, September 2012, p. 8.

141 http://insight.aon.com/?elqPURLPage?6567, accessed April 11, 2013.

142 Ron Finch, "Preventive Services: Improving the Bottom Line for Employers and Employees," *Compensation & Benefits Review*, March/April 2005, p. 18.

143 "Employer Partners to Launch a Three-Year Wellness Initiative," *BNA Bulletin to Management*, August 7, 2007, p. 255. See also Drew Robb, "Benefits Choices: Educating the Consumer," *HR Magazine*, March 2011, pp. 29–30.

144 Susan Wells, "Wellness Rewards," *HR Magazine*, February 2012, pp. 67–69.

145 "On-Site Clinics Aimed at Cutting Costs, Promoting Wellness," *BNA Bulletin to Management*, March 25, 2008, p. 103. See also Susan Wells, "Navigating the Expanding Wellness Industry," *HR Magazine*, March 2011, pp. 45–50.

146 Ibid. See also Josh Cable, "The Road to Wellness," *Occupational Hazards*, April 2007, pp. 23–27.

147 George DeVries, "The Top 10 Wellness Trends for 2008 and Beyond," *Compensation & Benefits Review*, July/August 2008, pp. 60–63.

148 Susan Wells, "Getting Paid for Staying Well," *HR Magazine*, February 2010, p. 59.

149 Andy Burjek, "Appetites for Carrots and Sticks Shift with Wellness Perks," *Workforce*, March/April 2017, p. 16.

150 Carolyn Hirschman, "Will Employers Take the Lead in Long-Term Care?" *HR Magazine*, March 1997, pp. 59–66. See also A. D. Postal, "Industry Ramps Up Opposition to LTC Program in Senate Health Bill," *National Underwriter* (Life & Health/Financial Services Edition), 113, no. 14, July 20, 2009, pp. 10, 32.

151 *2015 Employee Benefits: An Overview of Employee Benefits Offerings in the U.S.* Society for Human Resource Management, p.13.

152 Josh Eidelson, "Unionize Me," *Bloomberg BusinessWeek*, January 12, 2017, pp. 26–27.

153 See also Jeff Wald, "The Benefits or Lack Thereof of the Gig," *Workforce*, August 2016, pp. 22–25.

154 Mark Feffer, "What Benefits Can Companies Offer Gig Workers?" March 21, 2017, www.shrm.org/resourcesandtools/hr-topics/benefits/pages/What-benefits-can-companies-offer-gig-workers, accessed April 23, 2017.

155 For instance, such as legislation requiring companies to contribute to nonprofit funds that would provide health insurance, retirement and other benefits for gig workers. Tyrone Richardson, "Congress Could Follow Some States to Add Benefits for Gig Workers", *Bloomberg BNA Bulletin To Management*, May 16, 2017

156 Bill Roberts, "Good Vendor Relations," *HR Magazine*, September 2011, p. 110.

157 Ibid.

158 The U.S. Treasury has spent most of the trust fund on other government programs, so that changes (for instance, in terms of reducing benefits, making people wait longer for benefits, or making some people pay more for benefits) will be necessary. John Kilgour, "Social Security in the 21st Century," *Compensation & Benefits Review*, 42, no. 6, 2010, pp. 459–469.

159 https://www.ssa.gov/OACT/COLA/cbb.html, accessed April 22, 2017.

160 Martocchio, *Strategic Compensation*, pp. 245–248; Lin GrensingPophal, "A Pension Formula That Pays Off," *HR Magazine*, February 2003, pp. 58–62.

161 For one recent example of how to do this, see Gail Nichols, "Reviewing and Redesigning Retirement Plans," *Compensation & Benefits Review*, May/June 2008, pp. 40–47.

162 Many employers are considering terminating their plans but most employers are considering instead either ceasing benefits accruals for all participants or just for future participants. Michael Cotter, "The Big Freeze: The Next Phase in the Decline of Defined Benefit Plans," *Compensation & Benefits Review*, March/April 2009, pp. 44–53.

163 Patty Kujawa, "The Young and Not So Restless," *Workforce Management*, May 2012, p. 6. See also, Joanne Sammer, "Are Defined Benefit Plans Dead?" *HR Magazine*, July 2012, pp. 29–32.

164 In any case, CEO retirement packages usually dwarf the average employee's. For example, when Target's CEO stepped down after a huge credit card breach, he walked away with retirement plans worth more than $47 million, plus a $7.2 million severance payment and $4.1 million from vested stock awards. "Target CEO's $47 Million Package Shows Gap with Workers," *Bloomberg BNA Bulletin to Management*, January 13, 2015, p. 12.

165 Jessica Marquez, "More Workers Yanking Money Out of 401(k)s," *Workforce Management*, August 11, 2008, p. 4. As of 2017, an Obama era rule that would require financial advisors to put their clients' interests first was left in place by the courts. Kristen Kenebel, "Advisors Gets Stay of Execution with Fiduciary Rule Delay," *Bloomberg BNA Bulletin to Management*, April 11, 2017.

166 Nancy Pridgen, "The Duty to Monitor Appointed Fiduciaries under ERISA," *Compensation & Benefits Review*, September/October 2007, pp. 46–51; "Individual 401(k) Plan Participant Can Sue Plan Fiduciary for Losses, Justices Rule," *BNA Bulletin to Management*, February 20, 2008, p. 65. A federal judge recently ruled that a Florida construction company's co-owners are liable under ERISA after they allegedly improperly withdrew about $112,000 from the firm's profit sharing plan. Jaclyn Wille, "Owners of Florida Company Liable for $112k Benefit Plan Theft," *Bloomberg BNA Bulletin to Management*, April 18, 2017.

167 Lindsay Wyatt, 401(k) Conversion: It's as Easy as Riding a Bike," *Workforce*, 76, no. 4, April 1997, p. 20.

168 "New Pension Law Plus a Recent Court Ruling Doom Age-Related Suits, Practitioners Say," *BNA Bulletin to Management*, 57, no. 36, September 5, 2006, pp. 281–282; www.dol.gov/ebsa/FAQs/faq_consumer_cashbalanceplans.html, accessed January 9, 2010.

169 Harold Burlingame and Michael Gulotta, "Cash Balance Pension Plan Facilitates Restructuring the Workforce at AT&T," *Compensation & Benefits Review*, November/December 1998, pp. 25–31; Jerry Geisel, "IRS Releases Long-Awaited Cash Balance Guidance," *Pensions & Investments*, 38, no. 22, November 1, 2010, p. 22.

170 Rita Pyrillis, "Picking a PBM for '13'," *Workforce Management*, June 2012, p. 8.

171 This is based on Eric Parmenter, "Employee Benefit Compliance Checklist," *Compensation & Benefits Review*, May/June 2002, pp. 29–38. Also see, "Retirement Plans and ERISA FAQs," https://www.dol.gov/agencies/ebsa/about-ebsa/our-activities/resource-center/faqs/retirement-plans-and-erisa-consumer, accessed April 23, 2017.

172 John Kilgour, "Public Pension Underfunding in California: A Perfect Storm Likely to Sweep the Nation," *Compensation & Benefits Review*, 44, no. 6, 2013, pp. 345–351. With more pension plans going bust, at least one study concludes that "while the numerous PBGC insurance premium increases will allow some short-term respite, the long-run prospects of the PBGC are bleak." John Kilgour, "The Plight of the Pension Benefit Guarantee Corporation," *Compensation & Benefits Review*, 47, no. 1, 2015, pp. 39–49.

173 https://search.pbgc.gov/search/Search?col=pbgc&col=plan&style=pbgc&filter=1&query=maximum+guarantee&form_id=usasearch_box, accessed April 22, 2017.

174 Patrick Kiger, "Early-Retirement Plans Backfire, Driving Up Costs Instead of Cutting Them," *Workforce Management*, January 2004, pp. 66–68.

175 The following is based on www.tlnt.com/2012/04/26/the-5-best-social-media-tools-for-employee-benefits-communication/, www.abenity.com/celebrate/how-to-use-social-media-to-communicate-employee-perks-benefits/, www.benefitspro.com/2013/04/19/social-media-a-tool-to-boost-employee-engagement-p, and www.employeebenefits.co.uk/benefits/communication/siemens-launches-social-media-website/105812.article, all accessed April 20, 2015.

176 Drew Robb, "A Total View of Employee Records," *HR Magazine*, August 2007, pp. 93–96.

177 Michelle Rafter, "Mobile Apps for Benefits Go from Luxury to Necessity," *Workforce Management*, June 2012, p. 3.

178 Carolyn Hirschman, "Employees' Choice," *HR Magazine*, February 2006, pp. 95–99.

179 Joseph O'Connell, "Using Employee Assistance Programs to Avoid Crises," *Long Island Business News*, April 19, 2002, p. 10.

180 See Scott MacDonald et al., "Absenteeism and Other Workplace Indicators of Employee Assistance Program Clients and Matched Controls," *Employee Assistance Quarterly*, 15, no. 3, 2000, pp. 51–58. See also Paul Courtis et al., "Performance Measures in the Employee Assistance Program," *Employee Assistance Quarterly*, 19, no. 3, 2005, pp. 45–58.

181 "EAP Providers," *Workforce Management*, July 14, 2008, p. 16.

182 Laszlo Bock, *Work Rules!* (New York: 12, 2015), p. 274.

183 See "The 100 Best Companies to Work For," *Fortune*, February 6, 2012, p. 117.

184 "Rising Gas Prices Prompting Employers to Consider Varied Computer Benefit Options," *BNA Bulletin to Management*, June 20, 2008, p. 201.

185 Rebecca Greenfield, "Employers Are Finally Starting to Deal with Death and Dying," *Bloomberg BNA Bulletin to Management*, February 14, 2017.

186 Tamera Lionel, "Benefits for Older Workers," *HR Magazine*, March 2012, pp. 53–58.

187 https://www.benefitscheckup.org/#/ accessed April 23, 2017.

188 https://careers.google.com/how-we-care-for-googlers/, accessed April 23, 2017.

189 Susan Milligan, "The Royal Treatment," *HR Magazine*, September 2016, pp. 30–35.

190 http://articles.washingtonpost.com/2013-06-26/politics/40195683_1_gay-couples-edith-windsor-doma, accessed August 1, 2013.

191 "FMLA Protection Extends to Gay Spouses as BOOL Updates Policies Following Windsor," *Bloomberg BNA Bulletin to Management*, August 20, 2013, p. 265.

192 www.cnn.com/2015/06/26/politics/supreme-court-same-sex-marriage-ruling/index.html; www.nytimes.com/2015/06/27/us/supreme-court-same-sex-marriage.html?_r=0, both accessed July 15, 2015.

193 Susan Wells, "Are You Too Family-Friendly?" *HR Magazine*, October 2007, pp. 35–39.

194 Jeff Green and Rick Clough, "GE Considers Scrapping the Annual Raise," https://www.bloomberg.com/news/articles/2016-06-06/ge-studies-scrapping-annual-raise-in-nod-to-shifting-priorities, June 6, 2016.

195 Marcus Butts et al., "How Important Are Work-Family Support Policies? A Meta-Analytic Investigation of Their Effects on Employee Outcomes," *Journal of Applied Psychology*, 98, no. 1, 2013, pp. 1–25.

196 Genevieve Douglas, "Search Continues for Employee Retention Silver Bullet," *Bloomberg BNA Bulletin to Management*, April 11, 2017.

197 Carolyn Hirshman, "Kinder, Simpler Cafeteria Rules," HR Magazine, January 2001, pp. 74–79.

198 "Employers Should Update Cafeteria Plans Now Based on Proposed Regs, Experts Say," BNA Bulletin to Management, September 4, 2007, pp. 281–282. Douglas, "Search Continues for Employee Retention Silver Bullet," op. cit.

199 http://www.aon.com/unitedkingdom/employee-benefits/online-benefits-and-communications/flexible-benefits.jsp.

200 Genevieve Douglas, "Flex Work Increasingly Valuable in Employee Recruitment," Bloomberg BNA Bulletin to Management, May 16, 2017.

201 Genevieve Douglas, "Flexibility Outpacing Time off, Paid in Valued Benefits," Bloomberg BNA Bulletin to Management, February 14, 2017.

202 Claire Miller, "How to Close the Gender Gap: True Job Flexibility," The New York Times, February 7, 2017, p. 83.

203 Elka Maria Torpey, "Flexible Work: Adjusting the When and Where of Your Job," Occupational Outlook Quarterly, Summer 2007, pp. 14–27.

204 In a related change, more employers, including Disney, David's Tea, and Aeropostale, have stopped requiring employees to stay "on call" and stopped scheduling them for work at the last minute. Michael Bologna, "Employee Scheduling," Bloomberg BNA Bulletin to Management, January 3, 2017.

205 Liz Aldernan, "In Sweden, Happiness from Shorter Workday Can't Overcome the Cost," The New York Times, January 7, 2017, p. B2.

206 Teresa Agovino, "Tinkering with Time," HR Magazine, February 2017, pp. 46–52.

207 Farrokh Mamaghani, "Impact of Information Technology on the Workforce of the Future: An Analysis," International Journal of Management, 23, no. 4, 2006, pp. 845–850; Jessica Marquez, "Connecting a Virtual Workforce," Workforce Management, September 20, 2008, pp. 1–3.

208 Martha White, "One Part Gone: Yahoo Says No to Telecommuting," www.CNBC.com/ID/100492123/, accessed February 25, 2013.

209 John Pletz, "Workers, Go Home," Crain's Chicago Business, 34, no. 8, February 21, 2011, pp. 2, 14.

210 Ibid.

211 Ibid.

212 These are from Ty Freyvogel, "Operation Employee Loyalty," Training Media Review, September–October 2007.

213 Ibid.

214 Ibid.

215 Jeffrey Marshall and Ellen Heffes, "Benefits: Smaller-Firm Workers Often Getting Less," Financial Executive, 21, no. 9, November 1, 2005, p. 10.

216 www.dol.gov/ebsa/pdf/ppa2006.pdf, accessed February 18, 2008.

217 Bill Leonard, "New Retirement Plans for Small Employers," HR Magazine, 51, no. 12, December 2006, p. 30.

218 Kristen Falk, "The Easy Retirement Plan for Small-Business Clients," National Underwriter, 111, no. 45, December 3, 2007, pp. 12–13.

219 Ibid.

220 Ibid.

221 http://articles.moneycentral.msn.com/Investing/Extra/CostcoTheAntiWalMart.aspx?page?1, accessed September 15, 2011; and Hamilton Nolan, "The Anti-Wal-Mart," http://gawker.com/costco-the-anti-wal-mart-511739135, accessed August 25, 2013.

222 Garry Kranz, "Special Report on Employee Engagement Losing Lifeblood," Workforce, July 21, 2011, www.workforce.com/articles/special-report-on-employee-engagement-losing-lifeblood, accessed April 10, 2014.

223 http://articles.moneycentral.msn.com/Investing/Extra/CostcoTheAntiWalMart.aspx?page?1, accessed September 15, 2011; and, Hamilton Nolan, "The Anti-Wal-Mart," http://gawker.com/costco-the-anti-wal-mart-511739135, accessed August 7, 2013.

224 Ibid.

225 Ibid.

226 Ibid.

227 Tavia Grant, "How One Company Levels the Pay Slope of Executives and Workers," Globe and Mail, November 16, 2013, www.theGlobeandMail.com/news/national, accessed April 1, 2014.

228 Brad Stone, "Costco CEO Craig Jelinek Leads the Cheapest, Happiest Company in the World," Bloomberg Businessweek, June 7, 2013.

229 Kevin Short, "11 Reasons to Love Costco That Have Nothing to Do with Shopping," November 19, 2013, www.HuffingtonPost.com/2013/11/19/reasons-love-Costco, accessed April 1, 2014.

230 www.Costco.com/benefits.HTML, accessed April 1, 2014.

231 This is based on or quoted from www.Costco.com/benefits.HTML, accessed April 1, 2014.

232 Kranz, "Special Report on Employee Engagement Losing Lifeblood."

Chapter 12

1 "Workforce Compensation and Performance Service, Office of Performance and Compensation Systems Design, Classification Programs Division," July 1999, HRCD-7; "Employee Relations," HR Magazine, 55, no. 7, July 2010, p. SS-4.

2 See, for example, Chris Long et al., "Fairness Monitoring: Linking Managerial Controls and Fairness Judgments in Organizations," Academy of Management Journal, 54, no. 3, 2012, pp. 1045–1068. Furthermore, it's not just how management treats its own employees; employees also take their signals from how it treats external parties such as customers and the general public. Benjamin Dunford, Christine Jackson, Alan Boss, Louis Tay, and R. Wayne Boss, "Be Fair, Your Employees Are Watching: A Relational Response Model of External Third-Party Justice," Personnel Psychology, 68, 2015, pp. 319–352.

3 Bennett Tepper, "Consequences of Abusive Supervision," Academy of Management Journal, 43, no. 2, 2000, pp. 178–190. See also Samuel Aryee et al., "Antecedents and Outcomes of Abusive Supervision: A Test of a Trickle-Down Model," Journal of Applied Psychology, 92, no. 1, 2007, pp. 191–201; and Lingyan Hu and Yan Liu, "Abuse for Status: A Social Dominance Perspective of Abusive Supervision," Human Resource Management Review, volume 27, 2017, pp. 328–337.

4 Mindy Shoss et al., "Blaming the Organization for Abusive Supervision: The Roles of Perceived Organizational Support and Supervisors Organizational Embodiment," Journal of Applied Psychology, 98, no. 1, 2013, pp. 158–168.

5 Sean Hannah et al., "Joint Influences of Individual and Work Unit Abusive Supervision on Ethical Intentions and Behaviors: A Moderated Mediation Model," Journal of Applied Psychology, 98, no. 4, 2013, pp. 579–592.

6 Michelle Donovan et al., "The Perceptions of Fair Interpersonal Treatment Scale: Development and Validation of a Measure of Interpersonal Treatment in the Workplace," Journal of Applied Psychology, 83, no. 5, 1998, pp. 683–692.

7 Bennett Tepper et al., "Abusive Supervision and Subordinates Organization Deviance," Journal of Applied Psychology, 93, no. 4, 2008, pp. 721–732.

8 Jordan Robbins et al., "Perceived Unfairness and Employee Health: A Meta-Analytic Integration," Journal of Applied Psychology, 97, no. 2, 2012, pp. 235–272.

9 Dawn Carlson et al., "The Fallout from Abusive Supervision: An Examination of Subordinates and Their Partners," Personnel Psychology, 60, no. 4, 2011, pp. 937–961.

10 Marie Mitchell and Maureen Ambrose, "Employees Behavioral Reactions to Supervisor Aggression: An Examination of Individual and Situational Factors," Journal of Applied Psychology, 97, no. 6, 2012, pp. 1148–1170.

11 Gary Weaver and Linda Treviño, "The Role of Human Resources in Ethics/Compliance Management: A Fairness Perspective," Human Resource Management Review, 11, 2001, p. 117.

12 Suzanne Masterson, "A Trickle-Down Model of Organizational Justice: Relating Employees' and Customers' Perceptions of and Reactions to Fairness," Journal of Applied Psychology, 86, no. 4, 2001, pp. 594–601. See also Jane O'Reilly, Karl Aquino, and Daniel Skarlicki, "The Lives of Others: Third Parties 'Responses to Others' Injustice," Journal of Applied Psychology, 101, no. 2, 2016, pp. 171–189.

13 Based on Daniel Denison, Corporate Culture and Organizational Effectiveness (New York: Wiley, 1990), p. 155. See also Christian Voegetlin and Michele Greenwood, "Corporate Social Responsibility and Human Resource Management: A Systematic Review and Conceptual Analysis," Human Resource Management Review, 26, 2016, pp. 181–197.

14 "When the Jobs Inspector Calls," The Economist, March 31, 2012, p. 73.

15 Alexandra Ho and Tim Culpan, with assistance from Jun Yang in Seoul, Andrea Wong in Taipei, Tian Ying in Beijing, and Jasmine Wang in Hong Kong, "Foxconn Labor Disputes Disrupt IPhone Output for 2nd Time," Bloomberg News, October 8, 2012, www.bloomberg.com/news/2012-10-07/foxconn-labor-disputes-disrupt-iphone-output-for-2nd-time.html, accessed April 14, 2013. See also, "Foxconn confirms dispute between workers at China factory" https://www.cnet.com/news/foxconn-confirms-dispute-between-workers-at-china-factory/, accessed March 30, 2017.

16 Ho and Culpan, "Foxconn Labor Disputes Disrupt IPhone Output for 2nd Time."

17 Teresa Daniel, "Tough Boss or Workplace Bully?" HR Magazine, June 2009, pp. 83–86.

18 Eugene Kim and Theresa Glomb, "Get Smarty-Pants: Cognitive Ability, Personality, and Victimization," Journal of Applied Psychology, 95, no. 3, 2010, pp. 889–901.

19 Eugene Kim and Teresa Glomb, "Victimization of High Performers: The Roles of Envy and Work Group Identification," Journal of Applied Psychology 9, no. 4 (2014), pp. 619–634.

20 Christian Kiewitz et al, "Suffering in Silence: Investigating the Role of Fear in the Relationship Between Abusive Supervision and Defensive Silence," Journal of Applied Psychology, 101, no. 5, 2016, pp. 731–742; see also Christopher Rosen, et al., "Who Strikes Back? A Daily Investigation of When and Why Incivility Begets Incivility," Journal of Applied Psychology, 101, no. 11, 2016, pp. 1620–1634.

21 Kiewitz, "Suffering in Silence…," op. cit.. In another study, high-performing employees were more likely to become victims of covert victimization, while low performers were more often victims of overt victimization. Jaclyn Jensen, Jana Raver, and Pankaj Patel, "Is It Better to Be Average? High and Low Performance as Predictors of Employee Victimization," Journal of Applied Psychology, 99, no. 2, 2014, pp. 296–309.

22 For example, monitor social media sites for evidence that one employee is harassing another. "Facebook Harassment: Social Websites May Prompt Need for New Policies, Procedures," *BNA Bulletin to Management*, July 20, 2010, p. 225.

23 http://view.fdu.edu/default.aspx?id=3529, accessed September 6, 2012.

24 Ibid.

25 Carolyn Hirschman, "Giving Voice to Employee Concerns: Encouraging Employees to Speak Out Requires Respectful Treatment and Appropriate Action," *HR Magazine*, 53, no. 8, August 2008, pp. 50–54.

26 Tschanen Niederkohr, "Employee Relations: Use the Exit Interview to Gain Valuable Insight," *Aftermarket Business*, 117, no. 11, November 2007, p. 8.

27 J. G. Carr, A. M. Schmidt, J. K. Ford, and R. P. DeShon, "Climate Perceptions Matter: A Meta-Analytic Path Analysis Relating Molar Climate, Cognitive and Affective States, and Individual Level Work Outcomes," *Journal of Applied Psychology*, 88, 2003, pp. 605–619; quoted in Stephen Robbins and Timothy Judge, *Organizational Behavior* (Upper Saddle River, NJ: Prentice Hall, 2011), p. 524; and www.yourerc.com/blog/post/What-is-Organizational-Climate.aspx, accessed September 8, 2014.

28 Survey: Employee Survey Number One, www.shrm.org/templatestools/samples/HRforms, accessed April 11, 2012.

29 Rachel Silverman, "Are You Happy in Your Job? Bosses Push Weekly Surveys," *The Wall Street Journal*, December 3, 2014, pp. B1, B4.

30 Laszlo Bock, *Work Rules!* (New York: 12, 2015), pp. 140–142.

31 Pat Lenius, "Murray Supply Host Recognition Dinner," *Supply House Times*, May 2011, p. 70.

32 SHRM Survey Findings: Employee Recognition Programs, Winter 2012. In collaboration with and commissioned by Globoforce (www.globoforce.com/).

33 This is based on Recognition: Service Award Checklist, www.shrm.org/templatestools/samples/HR-forms, November 5, 2010, accessed April 14, 2012.

34 http://mashable.com/follow/topics/pinterest, accessed April 15, 2012.

35 "Over Half of Employers Use Social Media for Internal Communications, Survey Reveals," *Bloomberg BNA Bulletin to Management*, June 4, 2013, p. 179.

36 http://mashable.com/2012/04/06/pinterest-employee-engagement/, accessed April 15, 2012.

37 Tamara Lytle, "Giving Employees a Say: Getting—and Acting on—Ideas Offered by Employees Can Save Employers Money and Build a Sense of Ownership among Workers," *HR Magazine*, 56, no. 10, October 2011, pp. 69–74.

38 James H. Shonk, *Team-Based Organizations*, (Chicago: Irwin, 1997), pp. 27–33.

39 Ibid., p. 28.

40 John Katzenbach and Douglas Smith, "The Discipline of Teams," *Harvard Business Review*, March/April 1993, pp. 116–118.

41 Everett Adams Jr., "Quality Circle Performance," *Journal of Management*, 17, no. 1, 1991, pp. 25–39.

42 See for example, Jack Orsburn et al., *Self-Directed Teams*, Homewood, Il: Business One Irwin, 1990, p. 8; http://sloanreview.mit.edu/article/how-to-lead-a-selfmanaging-team/, accessed July 14, 2014.

43 Charles Fishman, "Engines of Democracy," *Fast Company*, October 1999, pp. 173–202.

44 Tom Peters, *Liberation Management*, New York: Alfred A. Knopf, 1992, pp. 238–239.

45 Orsburn et al., *Self-Directed Teams*, pp. 22–23. Also see, Charles Fishman, DEngines of

Democracy," September 30, 1999, https://www.fastcompany.com/37815/engines-democracy, accessed March 30, 2017.

46 Susan Wells, "From Ideas to Results: To Get the Most from Your Company's Suggestion System, Move Ideas up the Ladder through a Formal Process," *HR Magazine*, 50, no. 2, February 2005, pp. 54–59.

47 Rebecca Hastings, "Survey: Employees Have Plenty of Suggestions," www.shrm.org/HRdisciplines/employeerelations/articles, February 29, 2012, accessed April 15, 2012.

48 Based on Wells, "From Ideas to Results."

49 Ibid.

50 This is quoted from ibid.

51 Alex Rosenblat, "What Motivates Gig Economy Workers," https://hbr.org/2016/11/what-motivates-gig-economy-workers, accessed March 30, 2017; Mark Feffer, "What Benefits Can Companies Offer Gig Workers?," March 21, 2017, https://www.shrm.org/resourcesandtools/hr-topics/benefits/pages/what-benefits-can-companies-offer-gig-workers.aspx, accessed March 30, 2017; Mukesh Gupta, "Strategies for Employee Engagement in a Gig Economy," http://www.digitalistmag.com/future-of-work/2017/02/03/strategies-for-employee-engagement-in-gig-economy-04887378, accessed March 30, 2017; Jenny Perkins, "Employee Engagement in the Gig Economy," http://www.cirrus-connect.com/blog/employee-engagement-in-the-gig-economy-10875, accessed March 30, 2017.

52 Kevin Wooten, "Ethical Dilemmas in Human Resource Management: An Application of a Multidimensional Framework, A Unifying Taxonomy, and Applicable Codes," *Human Resource Management Review*, 11, 2001, p. 161. See also Sean Valentine et al., "Employee Job Response as a Function of Ethical Context and Perceived Organization Support," *Journal of Business Research*, 59, no. 5, (2006), pp. 582–588.

53 Paul Schumann, "A Moral Principles Framework for Human Resource Management Ethics," *Human Resource Management Review* 11 (2004), p. 94. See also, *2005 National Business Ethics Survey: How Employees Perceive Ethics at Work*, 2005, p. 25. Copyright © 2006, Ethics Resource Center (ERC). In O. C. Ferrell, John Fraedrich, and Linda Ferrell, *Business Ethics* (Boston: Houghton Mifflin, 2008), p. 61.

54 Manuel Velasquez, *Business Ethics: Concepts and Cases* (Upper Saddle River, NJ: Prentice Hall, 1992), p. 9. See also Ferrell, Fraedrich, and Ferrell, *Business Ethics*.

55 For further discussion of ethics and morality, see Tom Beauchamp and Norman Bowie, *Ethical Theory and Business* (Upper Saddle River, NJ: Prentice Hall, 2001), pp. 1–19.

56 Jennifer Kish-Gephart, David Harrison, and Linda Trevino, "Bad Apples, Bad Cases, and Bad Barrels: Meta-Analytic Evidence about Sources of Unethical Decisions at Work," *Journal of Applied Psychology*, 95, no. 1, 2010, pp. 1–31.

57 Ibid.

58 Ibid.

59 Ibid.

60 David Welsh, Deidre Snyder, Michael Christian, and Lisa Ordonez, "The Slippery Slope: How Small Ethical Transgressions Pave the Way for Larger Future Transgressions," *Journal of Applied Psychology* 100, no. 1 (2015), pp. 114–127.

61 Kish-Gephart, Harrison, and Trevino, "Bad Apples, Bad Cases, and Bad Barrels' op. cit., p. 21.

62 Ibid.

63 "Former CEO Joins WorldCom's Indicted," *Miami Herald*, March 3, 2004, p. 4C.

64 Ferrell, Fraedrich, and Ferrell, *Business Ethics*, p. 28; adapted from Rebecca Goodell,

Ethics in American Business: Policies, Programs, and Perceptions (Washington, DC: Ethics Resource Center, 1994), p. 54. For other insights into unethical behavior's causes, see, for example, F. Gino et al., "Nameless + Harmless = Blameless: When Seemingly Irrelevant Factors Influence Judgment of (Un)ethical Behavior," *Organizational Behavior and Human Decision Processes*, 111, no. 2, March 2010, pp. 93–101; and J. Camps et al., "Learning Atmosphere and Ethical Behavior, Does It Make Sense?" *Journal of Business Ethics*, 94, no. 1, June 2010, pp. 129–147.

65 A study suggests that people may not be so selfless. People who were more prone to take unethical actions were also more likely to expect reciprocity. Elizabeth Umphress, John Bingham, and Marie Mitchell, "Unethical Behavior in the Name of the Company: The Moderating Effect of Organizational Identification and Positive Reciprocity Beliefs on Unethical Pro-organizational Behavior," *Journal of Applied Psychology*, 95, no. 4, 2010, pp. 769–770.

66 "Ethics Policies Are Big with Employers, but Workers See Small Impact on the Workplace," *BNA Bulletin to Management*, June 29, 2000, p. 201.

67 Guy Brumback, "Managing above the Bottom Line of Ethics," *Supervisory Management*, December 1993, p. 12. See also E. E. Umphress et al., "The Influence of Distributive Justice on Lying for and Stealing from a Supervisor," *Journal of Business Ethics*, 86, no. 4, June 2009, pp. 507–518; and S. Chen, "The Role of Ethical Leadership versus Institutional Constraints: A Simulation Study of Financial Misreporting by CEOs," *Journal of Business Ethics*, 93, part supplement 1, June 2010, pp. 33–52.

68 Dayton Fandray, "The Ethical Company," *Workforce*, 79, no. 12, December 2000, pp. 74–77.

69 IBM Business Conduct Guidelines, www.ibm.com/investor/pdf/BCG2012.pdf, accessed August 2, 2013.

70 Richard Beatty et al., "HR's Role in Corporate Governance: Present and Prospective," *Human Resource Management*, 42, no. 3, Fall 2003, p. 268.

71 Eric Krell, "How to Conduct an Ethics Audit," *HR Magazine*, April 2010, pp. 48–51.

72 Betsy Shepherd, "Occupational Fraud," *Workforce Management*, April 2012, p. 18.

73 Dale Buss, "Corporate Compasses," *HR Magazine*, June 2004, pp. 127–132.

74 Richard Girgenti, "As Whistleblowing Surges, Internal Reporting Must Keep Up," *Bloomberg BNA Bulletin to Management*, May 19, 2015, p. 158.

75 David Mayer et al., "Who Displays Ethical Leadership, and Why Does It Matter? An Examination of Antecedents and Consequences of Ethical Leadership," *Academy of Management Journal*, 55, no. 1, 2012, p. 167.

76 Sometimes the most straightforward way of changing a company's culture is to move fast to change its top management. For example, see, Jeremy Smerd, "A Stalled Culture Change?" *Workforce Management*, December 14, 2009, pp. 1, 3.

77 "Ethics: It Isn't Just the Big Guys," *The American Intelligence Wire*, July 28, 2003, p. 10.

78 Ibid.

79 J. Krohe Jr., "The Big Business of Business Ethics," *Across the Board*, 34, May 1997, pp. 23–29; Deborah Wells and Marshall Schminke, "Ethical Development and Human Resources Training: An Integrator Framework," *Human Resource Management Review*, 11, 2001, pp. 135–158.

80 "Ethical Issues in the Management of Human Resources," *Human Resource Management Review*, 11, 2001, p. 6 Joel Lefkowitz, "The Constancy of Ethics amidst the Changing World of Work," *Human Resource Management Review*, 16, 2006, pp. 245–268; William Byham,

"Can You Interview for Integrity?" *Across the Board*, 41, no. 2, March/April 2004, pp. 34–38. For a description of how the U.S. Military Academy uses its student admission and socialization processes to promote character development, see Evan Offstein and Ronald Dufresne, "Building Strong Ethics and Promoting Positive Character Development: The Influence of HRM at the United States Military Academy at West Point," *Human Resource Management*, 46, no. 1, Spring 2007, pp. 95–114.

81 Gary Weaver and Linda Treviño, "The Role of Human Resources in Ethics/Compliance Management: A Fairness Perspective," *Human Resource Management Review*, 11, 2001, p. 123. See also Linda Andrews, "The Nexus of Ethics," *HR Magazine*, August 2005, pp. 53–58.

82 Kathryn Tyler, "Do the Right Thing: Ethics Training Programs Help Employees Deal with Ethical Dilemmas," *HR Magazine*, February 2005, pp. 99–102.

83 "Ethical Issues in the Management of Human Resources," p. 6.

84 Weaver and Treviño, "The Role of Human Resources in Ethics/ Compliance Management," p. 123.

85 Ed Finkel, "Yahoo Takes New Road on Ethics Training," *Workforce Management*, July 2010, p. 2.

86 Tom Asacker, "Ethics in the Workplace," *Training & Development*, August 2004, p. 44; www.skillsoft.com/catalog/detail.asp?CourseCode=pd_18_a01_bs_enus, accessed September 8, 2014.

87 Ibid., p. 125.

88 Grossman, "Executive Discipline," pp. 46–51. See also Jean Thilmany, "Supporting Ethical Employees," *HR Magazine*, 52, no. 9, September 2007, pp. 105–106, 108, 110, 112.

89 Milton Zall, "Employee Privacy," *Journal of Property Management*, 66, no. 3, May 2001, p. 16.

90 Morris Attaway, "Privacy in the Workplace on the Web," *Internal Auditor*, 58, no. 1, February 2001, p. 30. See also, Kenny Brown, "What are Employee Privacy Rights?" http://smallbusiness.chron.com/employee-privacy-rights-1239.html, accessed March 30, 2017.

91 Declan Leonard and Angela France, "Workplace Monitoring: Balancing Business Interests with Employee Privacy Rights," *Society for Human Resource Management Legal Report* (May–June 2003), pp. 3–6.

92 "Twitter Is Latest Electronic Tool to Pose Challenges and Opportunities for Employers," *BNA Bulletin to Management*, June 16, 2009, p. 185.

93 "After Employer Found Liable for Worker's Child Porn, Policies May Need to Be Revisited," *BNA Bulletin to Management*, March 21, 2006, p. 89.

94 Kathy Gurchiek, "iPods Can Hit Sour Note in the Office," *HR Magazine*, April 2006; www.highbeam.com/doc/1G1-144992472.html; Dave Zielinski, "Bring Your Own Device," *HR Magazine*, February 2012, pp. 71–74.

95 Ibid.

96 *Vega-Rodriguez v. Puerto Rico Telephone Company*, CA1, #962061, 4/8/97, discussed in "Video Surveillance Withstands Privacy Challenge," *BNA Bulletin to Management*, April 17, 1997, p. 121. Also see, J. Greenwald, "Monitoring Communications? Know Legal Pitfalls," *Business Insurance*, 45, no. 6, February 7, 2011, pp. 1, 17.

97 *Quon v. Arch Wireless Operating Co.*, 529 F.3d 892 (9th Cir. 2008); "Employers Should Re-Examine Policies in Light of Ruling," *BNA Bulletin to Management*, August 12, 2008, p. 263.

98 Dionne Searcey, "Some Courts Raise Bar on Reading Employee E-mail," *The Wall Street Journal*, November 19, 2009, p. A17.

99 "When Can an Employer Access Private E-Mail on Its System?" *BNA Bulletin to Management*, July 14, 2009, p. 224; One employment lawyer says that courts look to whether the employer's process is reasonable when determining if the employer's monitoring practices are acceptable. Electronic monitoring is generally reasonable "where there is a legitimate business purpose, where policies exist to set the privacy expectations of employees, and where employees are informed of the rules and understand the methods used to monitor the workplace." Nicole Kamm, "Bodyguard for Electronic Information," *HR Magazine*, January 2010, pp. 57–58.

100 Lee Michael Katz, "Big Employer Is Watching," *HR Magazine*, June 2015, pp. 67–74.

101 Kenny Brown, "What are Employee Privacy Rights?" http://smallbusiness.chron.com/employee-privacy-rights-1239.html, accessed March 30, 2017.

102 Bill Roberts, "Are You Ready for Biometrics?" *HR Magazine*, March 2003, pp. 95–96.

103 Fredric Leffler and Lauren Palais, "Filter Out Perilous Company E-Mails," *Society for Human Resource Management Legal Report*, August 2008, p. 3.

104 Bill Roberts, "Stay Ahead of the Technology Use Curve," *HR Magazine*, October 2008, pp. 57–61.

105 One attorney notes that problems can arise with the Federal Stored Communications Act if the employer uses illicit or coercive means to access the employee's private social media accounts. *BNA Bulletin to Management*, July 21, 2009, p. 225.

106 "Time Clocks Go High Touch, High Tech to Keep Workers from Gaming the System," *BNA Bulletin to Management*, March 25, 2004, p. 97.

107 Andrea Poe, "Make Foresight 20/20," *HR Magazine*, February 2000, pp. 74–80.

108 Gundars Kaupin et al., "Recommended Employee Location Monitoring Policies," www.shrm.org, accessed January 2, 2007.

109 Steve Lohr, "Unblinking Eyes Track Employees," *The New York Times*, June 22, 2014, pp. 1, 15.

110 Rita Zeidner, "New Face in the C-Suite," *HR Magazine*, January 2010, p. 39.

111 Claire Suddath, "Tesco Monitors Employees with Motorola Armbands," www.BusinessWeek.com/articles/2013-02-13/Tesco monitors_employees-withMotorola-arm-bands, accessed February 14, 2013.

112 Lester Bittel, *What Every Supervisor Should Know* (New York: McGraw-Hill, 1974), p. 308; Paul Falcone, "Fundamentals of Progressive Discipline," *HR Magazine*, February 1997, pp. 90–92; Thomas Salvo, "Practical Tips for Successful Progressive Discipline," SHRM White Paper, July 2004, www.shrm.org/hrresources/whitepapers_published/CMS_009030.asp, accessed January 5, 2008.

113 For fair discipline guidelines, see Bittel, *What Every Supervisor Should Know*, p. 308; Falcone, "Fundamentals of Progressive Discipline," *HR Magazine*, February 1997, pp. 90–92; and "How to Discipline and Fire Employees," www.entrepreneur.com/article/79928, accessed May 3, 2012.

114 David Mayer et al., "When Do Fair Procedures Not Matter? A Test of the Identity Violation Effect," *Journal of Applied Psychology*, 94, no. 1, 2009, pp. 142–161.

115 Grossman, "Executive Discipline,," pp. 46–51; "The Evil Women Theses," based on Sandra Hartman et al., "Males and Females in a Discipline Situation Exploratory Research on Competing Hypotheses," *Journal of Managerial Issues*, 6, no. 1, Spring 1994, pp. 57, 64–68; "A Woman's Place," *The Economist*, 356, no. 8184, August 19, 2000, p. 56.

116 For fair discipline guidelines, see Bittel, *What Every Supervisor Should Know*, p. 308; Falcone, "Fundamentals of Progressive Discipline," pp. 90–92; and "How to Discipline and Fire Employees."

117 George Bohlander, "Why Arbitrators Overturn Managers in Employee Suspension and Discharge Cases," *Journal of Collective Negotiations*, 23, no. 1, 1994, pp. 76–77.

118 "Employers Turn to Corporate Ombuds to Defuse Internal Ticking Time Bombs," *BNA Bulletin to Management*, August 9, 2005, p. 249.

119 Dick Grote, "Discipline without Punishment," *Across the Board*, 38, no. 5, September 2001, pp. 52–57.

120 http://money.cnn.com/magazines/fortune/best-companies/2014/list/. For 2017, Fortune Magazine's "best companies to work for" included (from 1 to 10) Google, Wegmans Food Markets, Boston Consulting Group, Baird, Edward Jones, Genentech, Ultimate Software, Salesforce, Acuity, and Quicken Loans. *Fortune*, March 15, 2017, pp. 84-87.

121 http://www.greatplacetowork.com/best-companies#sthash.ECoNqRRH.dpbs, accessed July 17, 2015.

122 Ibid. Another thing that makes these companies "great places to work" is an emphasis on building a sense of community. For example, when Cisco Systems Inc. promoted one of its own to CEO, the company held a series of "Cisco Rocks" events globally, bringing together employees for huge events that featured music, entertainment, food, and games to honor Cisco's former and new CEOs. Ed Frauenheim, "Community Outreach," *Workforce*, January 2016, pp. 32–35, 49. See also, Martin Berman—Gorvine, "Employee Engagement Starts at the Top," *Bloomberg BNA Bulletin to Management*, January 3, 2017.

123 In *Fortune* magazine's 2017 listing, SAS was number 15, Google 1, and FedEx 99. *Fortune*, March 15, 2017, pp. 84–136.

124 http://www.sas.com/en_us/company-information/great-workplace.html, accessed July 17, 2015.

125 *Fortune*, March 15, 2017, pp. 88.

126 https://www.sas.com/en_us/careers.html accessed March 30, 2017.

127 www.sas.com/content/dam/SAS/en_us/doc/other1/benefits-brochure.pdf; also see, www.sas.com/en_us/news/pressreleases/2014/january/greatworkplace-US-Fortune-2014.html, accessed September 8, 2014.

128 Mark Crowley, "How SAS Became the World's Best Place to Work," www.fastcompany.com/300-4953/how-SAS-became-worlds-best-place-to-work, accessed April 8, 2014.

129 Rebecca Leung, "Working the Good Life," www.CBSnews.com/news/working-the-good-life/.

130 Ibid.

131 Ibid.

132 Ibid.

133 Ibid.

134 Mark Crowley, "Not a Happy Accident: How Google Deliberately Designed Workplace Satisfaction," www.fastcompany.com/300-7268/where-are-they-now/, accessed April 8, 2014.

135 http://US.Greatrated.com/Googlean, accessed April 6, 2014.

136 www.Google.com/about/careers/lifeatGoogle/benefits/, accessed April 7, 2014.

137 See for example, "The 100 Best Companies to Work For," *Fortune*, March 15, 2017, p. 85.

138 Farhad Manjoo, "The Happiness Machine," January 21, 2013; www.slate.com, accessed April 6, 2014.

139 Manjoo, "The Happiness Machine," and Greta Roberts, "Why Google's Employee Engagement Programs Are Bad for Your Business," www.talentanalytics.com/blog/, accessed April 5, 2014.

140 Manjoo, "The Happiness Machine."
141 Ibid.
142 Ibid.
143 Ibid.
144 Mark Crowley, "Not a Happy Accident: How Google Deliberately Designs Workplace Satisfaction."
145 "FedEx Puts People First and Reaps the Benefits of Their Satisfaction." *Fortune*, March 15, 2017, p. 104.
146 This is based on Gary Dessler, *Winning Commitment* (New York: McGraw-Hill, 1993), pp. 37–51; "The Federal Express Employee Handbook," August 7, 1989, p. 89; and "FedEx Attributes Success to People-First Philosophy," www.fedex.com/ma/about/overview/philosophy.html, accessed July 18, 2015.
147 Ibid.
148 Ibid.
149 Ibid.
150 http://www.fedex.com/cz_english/about/overview/philosophy.html, accessed July 14, 2014.
151 "Working at SAS: An Ideal Environment for New Ideas," SAS website, April 20, 2012. Copyright © 2011 by SAS Institute, Inc. Reprinted with permission. All rights reserved.
152 David Gebler, "Is Your Culture a Risk Factor?" *Business and Society Review*, 111, no. 3, Fall 2006.
153 John Cohan, "'I Didn't Know' and 'I Was Only Doing My Job': Has Corporate Governance Careened out of Control? A Case Study of Enron's Information Myopia," *Journal of Business Ethics*, 40, no. 3, October 2002, pp. 275–299.
154 David Gebler, "Is Your Culture a Risk Factor?" op. cit.
155 Ibid.

Chapter 13

1 Steven Greenhouse, "Share of the Workforce in a Union Falls to a 97 Year Low, 11.3%," *The New York Times*, January 24, 2013, p. B1; https://www.bls.gov/news.release/union2.nr0.htm, accessed January 9, 2017.
2 Lukas Alpert, "Labor Unions Move into New Media as Investors Circle," *The Wall Street Journal,* August 30, 2015, p. B6.
3 www.bls.gov/news.release/union2.nr0.htm, accessed July 22, 2015.
4 Michael Ash and Jean Seago, "The Effect of Registered Nurses' Unions on Heart Attack Mortality," *Industrial and Labor Relations Review*, 57, no. 3, April 2004, pp. 422–442.
5 https://stats.bls.gov/cps/cpsaat43.pdf, accessed January 9, 2017.
6 "Union Benefit Costs Prevailing," *Bloomberg BNA Bulletin to Management*, May 14, 2013, p. 156.
7 Robert Grossman, "Unions Follow Suit," *HR Magazine*, May 2005, p. 49.
8 Ann Zimmerman, "Pro-Union Butchers at Wal-Mart Win a Union Battle but Lose War," *The Wall Street Journal*, April 11, 2000, p. A14. See also Steven Greenhouse, "Report Assails Wal-Mart over Unions," *The New York Times*, May 1, 2007, p. C3.
9 Josh Eidelson, "What Do We Want? Uber Union," *Bloomberg Business Week*, October 31, 2016, pp. 33–34. Unions are still far from unanimous about how to handle gig worker unions, but are working with legislatures to find solutions. See for example Chris Opfer, "Gig Worker Organizers Still Looking for a Roadmap," *Bloomberg Labor & Employment On Bloomberg Law*, May 26, 2017.
10 Eidelson, "What Do We Want? Uber Union." Other cities are moving to let drivers from companies like Uber and Lyft organize. For example, the Seattle City Council approved a bill that, if passed, would let drivers form unions, and in California, the California App–Based Drivers Association has pushed for legislation allowing drivers to organize. Nick Wingfield and Mike Isaac, "Seattle Will Allow Uber and Lyft Drivers to Form Unions," *The New York Times*, www.NYTimes.com/2015/12/15/technology/, December 14, 2015, accessed January 8, 2017; Dennis Romero, "Uber Drivers Team Up with Teamsters Union," *LA Weekly*, August 28, 2014, www.LAweekly.com/news/Uber–drivers–team–up–with–Teamsters, accessed January 8, 2017.
11 "Employee Engagement: A New Union Avoidance Strategy," June 28, 2011, www.modernsurvey.com, accessed April 12, 2014.
12 This is based on Jessica Tyler, "Employee Engagement and Labor Relations," *Gallup Business Journal*. http://businessJournal.Gallup.com, accessed April 9, 2014.
13 Arthur Sloane and Fred Witney, *Labor Relations* (Upper Saddle River, NJ: Prentice Hall, 2007), pp. 335–336.
14 In the public sector, a number of states let unions collect "fair share" fees from nonunion members in public sector employee unions. "Handed a Victory," *The Economist*, April 2, 2016, p. 32.
15 Benjamin Taylor and Fred Witney, *Labor Relations Law* (Upper Saddle River, NJ: Prentice Hall, 1992), pp. 170–171.
16 www.dol.gov/whd/state/righttowork.htm, accessed September 11, 2014. Indiana's law applies only to school teachers; without Indiana, there are 22 right-to-work states. However, see also Rhonda Smith and Chris Brown, "Right-To-Work Bills Move Forward in Missouri, New Hampshire," *Bloomberg BNA Bulletin to Management*, January 17, 2017.
17 "Unions Hit Hard by Job Losses, Right to Work," *Daily Oklahoman* (via *Knight Ridder/Tribune Business News*), February 1, 2005. See also www.dol.gov/whd/state/righttowork.htm, accessed September 11, 2014.
18 "Research Inconclusive about Effective Right to Work on Economy," *BNA Bulletin to Management*, January 8, 2013, p. 14.
19 www.seiu.org/our-union/, accessed June 1, 2011.
20 Steven Greenhouse, "4th Union Quits AFL-CIO in a Dispute over Organizing," *The New York Times*, September 15, 2005, p. A14.
21 The following material is based on Sloane and Witney, *Labor Relations*, pp. 83–132. See also http://history.eserver.org/us-labor-law.txt, accessed April 26, 2008, and Michael Carrell and Christina Heavrin, *Labor Relations and Collective Bargaining* 10th ed. (Boston: Pearson, 2013), pp. 58–60.
22 Sloane and Witney, *Labor Relations*, p. 106.
23 Karen Robinson, "Temp Workers Gain Union Access," *HR News, Society for Human Resource Management*, 19, no. 10, October 2000, p. 1.
24 Melanie Trottman, "New Labor Regulation Hastens Union Votes," *The Wall Street Journal*, August 27, 2015, p. A4.
25 Carrell and Heavrin, *Labor Relations and Collective Bargaining*, p. 7. Similarly, workers can "organize" without forming a union. In one case, employees of a car wash formed a workers' committee and sent a letter to their employer requesting better treatment. The employer reacted by terminating their employment. Federal labor law prohibits employers from retaliating against workers who band together to try to improve their working conditions. Under pressure from the NLRB, the employer reinstated the employees, paid their back wages, and improved the workers' treatment and working conditions. Steven Greenhouse, "Workers Organize, but Don't Unionize, to Get Protection Under Labor Law," *The New York Times*, September 7, 2015, pp. B1, B4.
26 See www.nlrb.gov/workplace_rights/nlra_violations.aspx, accessed January 14, 2008.
27 Find the form at www.nlrb.gov/sites/default/files/attachments/basic-page/node-3040/nlrbform501.pdf accessed June 28, 2017.
28 Carrell and Heavrin, *Labor Relations and Collective Bargaining*, p. 180.
29 Ibid., p. 179.
30 Sloane and Witney, *Labor Relations*, pp. 102–106.
31 See, for example, Steven Greenhouse, "High Court to Weigh Union Cases," *The New York Times*, November 11, 2013, pp. B1, B2.
32 For organizing examples from the unions' point of view, see www.twu.org/international/steps, accessed June 29, 2011; www.opeiu.org/NeedAUnion/StepstoCreatingaUnionWorkplace/tabid/71/Default.aspx, accessed June 29, 2011; and particularly http://ufcwone.org/steps-form-union, accessed August 7, 2013. See also www.nlrb.gov/nlrb-process, and www.nlrb.gov/what-we-do/conduct-elections, both accessed August 7, 2013.
33 William Fulmer, "Step by Step through a Union Election," *Harvard Business Review*, 60, July/August 1981, pp. 94–102. For an example of what to expect, see Edward Young and William Levy, "Responding to a Union-Organizing Campaign: Do You and Your Supervisors Know the Legal Boundaries in a Union Campaign?" *Franchising World*, 39, no. 3, March 2007, pp. 45–49.
34 Fulmer, op. cit.
35 John Logan, "The Union Avoidance Industry in the United States," *British Journal of Industrial Relations*, 44, no. 4, December 2006, pp. 651–675.
36 Sloane and Witney, *Labor Relations*, p. 28.
37 Jonathan Segal, "Expose the Union's Underbelly," *HR Magazine*, June 1999, pp. 166–176.
38 "Some Say Salting Leaves Bitter Taste for Employers," *BNA Bulletin to Management*, March 4, 2004, p. 79; www.shrm.org/templatestools/hrqa/pages/whatdoestheterm%E2%80%9Csalting%E2%80%9Dasaunionorganizingtacticmean.aspx, accessed September 8, 2012.
39 "The SEIU's Odd Recipe for Unionizing Fast Food," *Bloomberg Business Week*, July 6–12, 2015, pp. 16–18.
40 www.blogging4jobs.com/wp-content/uploads/2012/02/unions-social-media.png, accessed April 25, 2015.
41 www.bna.com/social-media-new-b17179923064/, accessed April 25, 2015.
42 www.starbucksunion.org, accessed August 7, 2013.
43 www.hreonline.com/HRE/view/story.jhtml?id=534358235, accessed April 25, 2015.
44 "An Employer Prohibits Social Media Use during Workday?" *BNA Bulletin to Management*, October 23, 2012, p. 344.
45 "Nonunion Employers Should Heed Recent NLRB Rulings, Speakers Say," *BNA Bulletin to Management*, December 4, 2012, p. 385.
46 David Rubin, "Get Antisocial," *HR Magazine*, February 2013, pp. 69–70.
47 Fulmer, "Step by Step through a Union Election," p. 94.
48 Is an employer who uses a staffing firm to hire and supervise contract workers a "joint employer" of those workers? For many years NLRB rules held that it was not. The NLRB said that unless a business had direct control over an employee's supervision, it could not be held responsible as a "joint employer" for employment-related matters for those workers. A 2015 decision changed that. The rise in the use

of contract and temporary employees prompted unions (in this case, a Teamsters union local) to ask the NLRB to make both the parent firm as well as the staffing firm joint employers. It did, and required both to meet with the union for collective bargaining. Melanie Trottman, "Ruling Clears Way for Unions," *The Wall Street Journal*, August 28, 2015, pp. A1, A4.

49   Steven Greenhouse, "Union Gets New Election at a Target," *The New York Times*, May 22, 2012, p. B3.

50   Frederick Sullivan, "Limiting Union Organizing Activity through Supervisors," *Personnel*, 55, July/August 1978, pp. 55–65; Richard Peterson, Thomas Lee, and Barbara Finnegan, "Strategies and Tactics in Union-Organizing Campaigns," *Industrial Relations*, 31, no. 2, Spring 1992, pp. 370–381. See also Edward Young and William Levy, "Responding to a Union-Organizing Campaign: Do You and Your Supervisors Know the Legal Boundaries in a Union Campaign?" *Franchising World*, 39, no. 3, March 2007, pp. 45–49; and Janet Walthall, "Unions Increasingly Using Corporate Campaigns," *BNA Bulletin to Management*, February 16, 2010, p. 55.

51   www.hreonline.com/HRE/view/story.jhtml?id=534358235, accessed April 25, 2015.

52   Carrell and Heavrin, *Labor Relations and Collective Bargaining*, p. 166.

53   Ibid., pp. 167–168.

54   Doug Cahn, "Reebok Takes the Sweat Out of Sweatshops," *Business Ethics*, 14, no. 1, January 2000, p. 9 Mei Fong and Kris Maher, "U.S. Labor Chief Moves into China," *The Wall Street Journal Asia*, June 22–24, 2007, p. 1.

55   Jonathan Segal, "Unshackle Your Supervisors to Stay Union Free," *HR Magazine*, June 1998, pp. 62–65. See also www.nlrb.gov/rights-we-protect/employerunion-rights-and-obligations, accessed September 11, 2014.

56   B&D Plastics, Inc., 302 NLRB No. 33, 1971, 137 LRRM 1039; discussed in "No Such Thing as a Free Lunch," *BNA Bulletin to Management*, May 23, 1991, pp. 153–154.

57   This is based on Stephanie Rabiner, "Can My Employees Form a Union?" http://blogs.Findlaw.com/free_enterprise/2011/02/can-myemployees-form-a-union; and "Unionizing Your Small Business," www.IBAmember.com/2134/, accessed April 12, 2014.

58   https://www.bna.com/nlrb-conducted-elections-n57982068022/, accessed January 10, 2017.

59   Ibid.

60   Carrell and Heavrin, *Labor Relations and Collective Bargaining*, pp. 120–121.

61   This section is based on Matthew Goodfellow, "How to Lose an NLRB Election," *Personnel Administrator*, 23, September 1976, pp. 40–44. See also Matthew Goodfellow, "Avoid Unionizing: Chemical Company Union Election Results for 1993," *Chemical Marketing Reporter*, 246, July 18, 1994, p. SR14; Gillian Flynn, "When the Unions Come Calling," *Workforce*, November 2000, pp. 82–87.

62   Ibid.

63   Ibid.

64   Harry Katz, "The Decentralization of Collective Bargaining: A Literature Review and Comparative Analysis," *Industrial and Labor Relations Review*, 47, no. 1, October 1993, p. 11; and F. Traxler, "Bargaining (De)centralization, Macroeconomic Performance and Control over the Employment Relationship," *British Journal of Industrial Relations*, 41, no. 1, March 2003, pp. 1–27.

65   Mimosa Spencer and Jeanne Whalen, "Change France? Sanofi Finds It Can't," *The Wall Street Journal*, April 11, 2013, pp. B1, D5.

66   Ibid., B1. As another example, to get the French government's approval to close one of its plants in France, Peugeot Citroen had to agree to find jobs for the factory's nearly 3,000 workers. Sam Shechner, "Before Factory Shuts, Peugeot Must Find Gigs for Its Workers," *The Wall Street Journal*, September 9, 2013, p. B3.

67   www.nlrb.gov/nlrb/shared_files/-brochures/basicguide.pdf, accessed January 14, 2008; https://www.nlrb.gov/rights-we-protect/whats-law/employers/bargaining-good-faith-employees-union-representative-section, accessed June 29, 2017.

68   Terry Leap, *Collective Bargaining and Labor Relations* (Upper Saddle River, NJ: Prentice Hall, 1995). See also, www.nlrb.gov/rights-we-protect/whats-law/employers/bargaining-good-faith-employees-union-representative-section, accessed June 29, 2017.

69   Leap, *Collective Bargaining and Labor Relations*, pp. 307–309.

70   Ibid., p. 308.

71   Kathryn Tyler, "Good-Faith Bargaining," *HR Magazine*, January 2005, p. 52.

72   Bargaining items based on Reed Richardson, *Collective Bargaining by Objectives* (Upper Saddle River, NJ: Prentice Hall, 1997), pp. 113–115; see also Sloane and Witney, *Labor Relations*, pp. 180–217.

73   Sloane and Witney, *Labor Relations*, pp. 192–220.

74   These are based on James C. Freund, *Smart Negotiating* (New York: Simon & Schuster, 1992), pp. 42–46.

75   Ibid.

76   Ibid., p. 33. Interestingly, one study found that communicating threats is more effective than communicating anger. See Marwan Sinaceur et al., "Hot or Cold: Is Communicating Anger or Threats More Effective in Negotiation?" *Journal of Applied Psychology*, 96, no. 5, 2011, pp. 1019–1032.

77   From Richardson, *Collective Bargaining by Objectives*, p. 150.

78   D. Scott DeRue et al., "When Is Straightforwardness a Liability in Negotiations? The Role of Integrative Potential and Structural Power," *Journal of Applied Psychology*, 94, no. 4, 2009, pp. 1032–1047.

79   Tori Walker, "Polk School District Reaches Impasse with Unions," January 6, 2017, http://www.theledger.com/news/20170106/polk-school-district-reaches-impasse-with-unions, accessed January 10, 2017.

80   John Burger and Steven Walters, "Arbitrator Bias and Self-Interest: Lessons from the Baseball Labor Market," *Journal of Labor Research*, 26, no. 2, Spring 2005, pp. 267–280.

81   Alternative Dispute Resolution (ADR), http://www.va.gov/ADR/Impasse.asp, accessed January 10, 2017.

82   Jonathan Kramer and Thomas Hyclak, "Why Strikes Occur: Evidence from the Capital Markets," *Industrial Relations*, 41, no. 1, January 2002, pp. 80–93.

83   This is based on Sloane and Witney, *Labor Relations*, p. 213.

84   Ibid.

85   Micheline Maynard and Jeremey W. Peters, "Northwest Airlines Threatens to Replace Strikers Permanently," *The New York Times*, August 26, 2005.

86   L. M. Sixel, "Strike Update: BP Training Additional Replacement Workers," http://fuelfix.com/blog/2015/02/18/strike-update-bp-training-additional-replacement-workers/#30249101=0, accessed July 24, 2015.

87   See for example, www.afimac-us.com/what-we-do/labor-disputes-and-plant-closures/strike-security/, accessed April 11, 2014.

88   Matthew Dolan, "UAW Targets Foreign Car Plants in US," *The Wall Street Journal*, December 23, 2010, p. B3. See also Rachel Feintzeig,

"Teamsters Act Tough with Twinkies Maker," *The Wall Street Journal*, February 14, 2012, p. B4.

89   James Hagerty and Caroline Van Hasselt, "Lockout Tests Union's Clout," *The Wall Street Journal*, January 30, 2012, p. B1.

90   Jon Ostrower, "Boeing Considers Nonunion Plant for 777X," *The Wall Street Journal*, October 20, 2013, p. B3; Jon Ostrower, "Boeing Prods Unions on Pact," *The Wall Street Journal*, November 9–10, 2013, p. B3.

91   Sloane and Witney, *Labor Relations*, p. 84.

92   http://sports.espn.go.com/nfl/news/story?id=4508545, accessed November 17, 2009.

93   Duncan Adams, "Worker Grievances Consume Roanoke, VA, Mail Distribution Center," *Knight-Ridder/Tribune Business News*, March 27, 2001, item 1086009.

94   Walter Baer, *Grievance Handling: 101 Guides for Supervisors* (New York: American Management Association, 1970).

95   M. Gene Newport, *Supervisory Management*, (St. Paul, MN: West Group, 1976), p. 273; see also Walter Baer, *Grievance Handling: 101 Guides for Supervisors* (New York: American Management Association, 1970); and Mark Lurie, "The Eight Essential Steps in Grievance Processing," *Dispute Resolution Journal*, 54, no. 4, November 1999, pp. 61–65.

96   Jessica Marquez, "NY Unions Cage Inflatable Rat, Try Teamwork," *Workforce Management*, November 3, 2008, p. 10. See also "With Membership Bottoming Out, What Does the Future Hold for Unions?" *BNA Bulletin to Management*, March 1, 2011, pp. 65–66. The NLRB approved of using theballoons. See http://staffingtalk.com/nlrb-unions-giant-rat-balloons-protests/, accessed January 10, 2017.

97   https://www.bls.gov/news.release/union2.nr0.htm, accessed January 9, 2017.

98   Susan Carey and Jack Nicas, "AMR Will Ask the Judge to Toss Labor Pacts," *The Wall Street Journal*, March 23, 2012, p. B3.

99   Kris Maher and Jacqueline Palank, "Patriot Coal Allowed to Win Union PACs," *The Wall Street Journal*, May 30, 2013, p. B1.

100   Kris Maher, "Specter Won't Support Union-Backed Bill," *The Wall Street Journal*, March 25, 2009, p. A3.

101   "Unions Using Class Actions to Pressure Non-union Companies," *BNA Bulletin to Management*, August 22, 2006, p. 271.

102   "New Labour, Alt–Labour," *The Economist*, September 14, 2013, pp. 33–34.

103   Dean Scott, "Unions Still a Potent Force," *Kiplinger Business Forecasts*, March 26, 2003.

104   Steven Greenhouse, "At a Nissan Plant in Mississippi, a Battle to Shape the UAW's Future," *The New York Times*, October 7, 2013, pp. B1, B3.

105   Neal Boudette, "A New Alliance: UAW in Germany," *The Wall Street Journal*, November 8, 2013, pp. B1, B2.

106   Max Mihelich, "Labor Daze," *Workforce*, April 2014, pp. 22–24, 31.

107   www.littler.com/publication-press/publication/nlrb-issues-its-long-anticipated-quickie-election-rule-making-union-or, accessed April 25, 2015.

108   Ibid.

109   Eric Morath, "Trump to Nominate Attorney William Emanuel to National Labor Relations Board," *The Wall Street Journal*, June 28, 2017, www.wsj.com/articles/trump-to-nominate-attorney-william-emanuel-to-national-labor-relations-board-1498650169, accessed June 28, 2017.

110   Carrell and Heavrin, *Labor Relations and Collective Bargaining*, pp. 62–63.

111 Carol Gill, "Union Impact on the Effective Adoption of High Performance Work Practices," *Human Resource Management Review*, 19, 2009, pp. 39–50.

112 See also Thomas Kochan, "A Jobs Compact for America's Future," *Harvard Business Review*, March 2012, pp. 64–70.

113 Ibid.

114 See, for example, www.fedee.com/ewc1.html, accessed November 4, 2009.

115 This is discussed in Eduard Gaugler, "HR Management: An International Comparison," *Personnel*, 65, no. 8, 1988, p. 28. See also E. Poutsma et al., "The Diffusion of Calculative and Collaborative HRM Practices in European Firms," *Industrial Relations*, 45, no. 4, October 2006, pp. 513–546; and Matthew Yglesias, "Should Workers Be Represented on Corporate Boards?" www.slate.com/blogs /moneybox/2012/10/03/corporate_co _determination_should_workers_be_represented _on_corporate_boards_.html, accessed June 28, 2017.

116 Steven Greenhouse, "Labor Regroups in South after Volkswagen Vote," *The New York Times*, February 17, 2004, p. B3.

117 Chris Purcell, "Rhetoric Flying in WGA Talks," *Television Week*, 26, no. 30, July 23–30, 2007, pp. 3, 35.

118 Ibid.

119 Ibid.

120 James Hibberd, "Guild Talks Break with No Progress," *Television Week*, 26, no. 38, October 8–15, 2007, pp. 1, 30.

121 Ibid.

122 "DGA Deal Sets the Stage for Writers," *Television Week*, 27, no. 3, January 21, 2008, pp. 3, 33.

123 "WGA, Studios Reach Tentative Agreement," *UPI News Track*, February 3, 2008.

124 © Gary Dessler, Ph.D. For information on what employers should *not do*, see https://www .nlrb.gov/rights-we-protect/whats-law /employers/interfering-employee-rights-section -7-8a1, accessed July 26, 2015.

125 http://www.nytimes.com/2015/07/27 /nyregion/proposed-minimum-wage-increase -for-fast-food-employees-divides-low-wage -workers.html?_r=0, accessed July 26, 2015.

126 Ibid.

127 For a discussion of what supervisors should not do, see for example, https://www.nlrb.gov /rights-we-protect/whats-law/employers/interfering -employee-rights-section-7-8a1, accessed July 26, 2015.

Chapter 14

1 "Film Company Fined over Harrison Ford Injury on Star Wars Set," pagesix.com/2016/10/12 /film–company–fine–over–Harrison–ford–injury –on–star–wars.

2 https://www.bls.gov/iif/oshwc/cfoi/cfch0014 .pdf, accessed April 21, 2017.

3 Figures for 2015; https://www.bls.gov/news .release/osh.nr0.htm, accessed April 20, 2017.

4 Solving this problem can be as simple as promulgating a glove standard that workers and their supervisors must adhere to; analyzing injury data to formulate targeted campaigns to reduce safety problems; and filming and promulgating several safety videos that show the proper procedures to use. Sandy Smith, "High Five: Protecting Our Most Important Tool," *EHS Today*, April 2017, pp. 9–10.

5 "BLS Likely Underestimating Injury and Illness Estimates," *Occupational Hazards*, May 2007, p. 17; Tahira Probst et al., "Organizational Injury Rate Underreporting: The Moderating Effect of Organizational Safety Climate," *Journal of Applied Psychology*, 93, no. 5, 2008, pp. 1,147–1,154.

6 For example, workers' compensation typically covers only about 21% of the total cost of a worker's injuries. Various federal, state, and local government programs pay about 16%, private health insurance 13%, and the worker and his or her family pay about 50% of the total costs out of pocket. "Adding Inequality to Injury: The Cost of Failing to Protect Workers on the Job," Occupational Safety & Health Administration, www.dol.gov/OSHA/report/20150304 -inequality.PDF, accessed March 27, 2017.

7 "Workers Rate Safety Most Important Workplace Issue," *EHS Today*, October 2010, p. 17.

8 www.osha.gov/dcsp/products/topics/business-case/, accessed April 16, 2013.

9 Russell Sobel, "Occupational Safety and Profit Maximization: Friends or Foes?" *Journal of Socioeconomics*, 31, no. 10, 2011, pp. 430–434.

10 David Levine et al., "Randomized Government Safety Inspections Reduce Worker Injuries with No Detectable Job Loss," *Science*, 336, May 18, 2012, pp. 907–911.

11 Chief Financial Officer Survey, Liberty Mutual Insurance Co., 2005.

12 Mike Rich, "Preventing Hearing Loss," www .adhesivesmag.com, January 2012, pp. 40–41.

13 Kristen Ferguson, "The Role of Senior Executives and Board Directors in Safety Leadership," *EHS Today,* January 2016, pp. 17–20.

14 See for example, Len Jannaman, "Are Your Top Leaders Engaged in Driving Safety Performance?" *EHS Today*, January 2017, pp. 14–17.

15 One study concluded that "employee perceptions of the extent to which managers and supervisors are committed to workplace safety likely influence employee safety behavior and, subsequently, injuries." Jeremy Beus et al., "Safety Climate and Injuries: An Examination of Theoretical and Empirical Relationships," *Journal of Applied Psychology*, 95, no. 4, 2010, pp. 713–727. See also Sean Tucker et al., "Safety in the C Suite: How Chief Executive Officers Influence Organizational Safety Climate and Employee Injuries," *Journal of Applied Psychology*, 101, no. 9, 2016, pp. 1228–1239.

16 Willie Hammer, *Occupational Safety Management and Engineering* (Upper Saddle River, NJ: Prentice Hall, 1985), pp. 62–63. See also "DuPont's 'STOP' Helps Prevent Workplace Injuries and Incidents," *Asia Africa Intelligence Wire*, May 17, 2004.

17 Sandy Smith, "Louisiana-Pacific Corp. Builds Safety into Everything It Does," *Occupational Hazards*, November 2007, pp. 41–42.

18 Sandy Smith, "ABB Inc. Relies on Leadership and Accountability for Safety Performance," *EHS Today*, November 2012, p. 38.

19 See, for example, Dominique Bravo, "Death on the Construction Site," *The New York Times*, January 17, 2017, p. A21.

20 "Did This Supervisor Do Enough to Protect Trench Workers?" *Safety Compliance Letter*, October 2003, p. 9.

21 Ibid.

22 Based on *All About OSHA*, rev. ed. (Washington, DC: U.S. Department of Labor, 1980); www .osha.gov/Publications/all_about_OSHA.pdf, accessed June 29, 2017.

23 https://www.osha.gov/dep/index.html, accessed April 12, 2017.

24 https://www.osha.gov/dcsp/vpp/index.html, accessed September 11, 2014. Edwin Foulke Jr., "OSHA's Evolving Role in Promoting Occupational Safety and Health," *EHS Today*, November 2008, pp. 44–49; https:// www.osha.gov/dcsp/compliance_assistance /index_programs.html, accessed July 15, 2014; https://www.osha.gov/dcsp/vpp/all_about_vpp .html, accessed April 1, 2017.

25 Stefanie Valentic, "Protecting Those Peepers: A Guide to Eye Wash and Emergency Shower Stations," *EHS Today*, March 2017, p. 21.

26 David Francis, "The Future of Fall Prevention," *EHS Today*, March 2017, pp. 13–16.

27 https://www.osha.gov/dep/index.html, accessed April 12, 2017.

28 "OSHA Hazard Communication Standard Enforcement," *BNA Bulletin to Management*, February 23, 1980, p. 13. See also William Kincaid, "OSHA vs. Excellence in Safety Management," *Occupational Hazards*, December 2002, pp. 34–36.

29 "What Every Employer Needs to Know About OSHA Record Keeping," U.S. Department of Labor, Bureau of Labor Statistics, Washington, DC, report 412–3, p. 3; https://www.osha .gov/recordkeeping/index.html, accessed September 11, 2014.

30 In a survey of about 2,600 employees, roughly one-fourth said they would not intervene if they saw a coworker acting unsafely, for fear the coworker would be defensive or angry. Phillip Ragain et al., "The Causes and Consequences of Employees' Silence," *EHS Today*, July 2011, pp. 36–38.

31 "New OSHA Recordkeeping Rule in Effect with the New Year," *Bloomberg BNA Bulletin to Management*, January 6, 2015, p. 2.

32 "Supreme Court Says OSHA Inspectors Need Warrants," *Engineering News Record*, June 1, 1978, pp. 9–10; W. Scott Railton, "OSHA Gets Tough on Business," *Management Review*, 80, no. 12, December 1991, pp. 28–29; Steve Hollingsworth, "How to Survive an OSHA Inspection," *Occupational Hazards*, March 2004, pp. 31–33.

33 https://www.osha.gov/dep/index.html, accessed April 12, 2017.

34 www.osha.gov/oshstats/commonstats.html, accessed April 18, 2013.

35 "Safety OSHA Has Record Number of Whistle-blower Investigations, 51% Dismissal Rate," *Bloomberg BNA Bulletin to Management*, 66, no. 3, 2015, p. 19.

36 Chris Mancillas, "OSHA's New Injury Data Disclosure Rule—Good Intentions but Questions on Execution," *EHS Today*, September 2016, pp. 28–29. As of 2017, many employers are required to electronically submit workplace injury and illness data, which OSHA may then post publicly. "New Rule Allows OSHA to Cite Employers' Incentive Programs, Post Injury Data Online," *Bloomberg BNA Bulletin to Management*, May 17, 2016, p. 153.

37 www.osha.gov/Publications/osha1099pdf, accessed April 27, 2008; https://www.osha .gov/ooc/citations/Cits329085.pdf, accessed September 11, 2014.

38 Jim Lastowka, "Ten Keys to Avoiding OSHA Liability," *Occupational Hazards*, October 1999, pp. 163–170. See also "Half of All Working Americans Feel Immune to Workplace Injuries," www.mem-ins.com/newsroom/pr71803.htm, accessed August 11, 2009.

39 Robert Grossman, "Handling Inspections: Tips from Insiders," *HR Magazine*, October 1999, pp. 41–50.

40 OSHA issued a guidance memo reminding employers that retaliating against employees for reporting injuries or safety problems is illegal. "New OSHA Enforcement Memo Target Safety Incentive Programs, Retaliation," *Bloomberg BNA Bulletin to Management*, March 27, 2012, p. 99.

41 Arthur Sapper, "The Oft-Missed Step: Documentation of Safety Discipline," *Occupational Hazards*, January 2006, p. 59. See also Arthur Sapper, "Three Decisions Show the Importance of Documenting Safety Discipline," *EHS Today*, October 2016, pp. 23–26.

42   Sean Smith, "OSHA Resources Can Help Small Businesses with Hazards," *Westchester County Business Journal*, August 4, 2003, p. 4."

43   Arthur Sapper, "The Oft-Missed Step."

44   Courtney Malveaux and J. A. Rodriguez Jr., "Can You Claim Employee Misconduct? Take the Legal Test," *EHS Today*, November 2014, pp. 37–41.

45   "Four Ways a Construction Job Can Kill You," *EHS Today*, February 2015, pp. 23–24.

46   For a discussion of this, see David Hofmann and Adam Stetzer, "A Cross-Level Investigation of Factors Influencing Unsafe Behaviors and Accidents," *Personnel Psychology*, 49, 1996, pp. 307–308.

47   David Hofman and Barbara Mark, "An Investigation of the Relationship between Safety Climate and Medication Errors as Well as Other Nurse and Patient Outcomes," *Personnel Psychology*, 50, no. 9, 2006, pp. 847–869.

48   "The Dawning of a New Era," *Workforce Management*, December 2010, p. 3.

49   See, for example, E. Scott Keller, "Should Safe Behavior Become a Habit?" *EHS Today*, July 2013, pp. 31–32; and Esteban Tristan, "Is Your Brain Hardwired for Safety," *EHS Today*, April 2017, pp. 12–15.

50   Duane Schultz and Sydney Schultz, *Psychology and Work Today* (Upper Saddle River, NJ: Prentice Hall, 1998), p. 351.

51   Robert Pater and Robert Russell, "Drop That Accident-Prone Tag: Look for Causes beyond Personal Issues," *Industrial Safety and Hygiene News*, 38, no. 1, January 2004, p. 50; http://www.highbeam.com/doc/1G2-112858417.html, accessed September 10, 2012.

52   Discussed in Douglas Haaland, "Who Is the Safest Bet for the Job? Find Out Why the Guy in the Next Cubicle May Be the Next Accident Waiting to Happen," *Security Management*, 49, no. 2, February 2005, pp. 51–57.

53   Jeremy Beus et al., "A Meta-Analysis of Personality and Workplace Safety: Addressing Unanswered Questions," *Journal of Applied Psychology*, 100, no. 2, 2015, p. 41.

54   "Thai Research Points to Role of Personality in Road Accidents," February 2, 2005; www.driveandstayalive.com/info%20section/news/individual%20news%20articles/x_050204_personality-in-crash-causation_thailand.htm, accessed August 11, 2009; Donald Bashline et al., "Bad Behavior: Personality Tests Can Help Underwriters Identify High-Risk Drivers," *Best's Review*, 105, no. 12, April 2005, pp. 63–64. Research suggests that up to 80% of traffic accidents involve drivers who were not looking at the road. Sandy Smith, "Deadly Distractions: Advice to Stay Safe in Highway Work Zones," *EHS Today*, May 2016, p. 17.

55   Todd Nighswonger, "Threat of Terror Impacts Workplace Safety," *Occupational Hazards*, July 2002, pp. 24–26.

56   Mike Carlson, "Machine Safety Solutions for Protecting Employees and Safeguarding against Machine Hazards," *EHS Today*, July 2009, p. 24.

57   Benjamin Mangan, "Lockout/Tagout Prevents Workplace Injuries and Saves Lives," *Occupational Hazards*, March 2007, pp. 59–60. See also Todd Grover, "Effective Group Lockout Techniques," *EHS Today*, October 2016, pp. 16–17.

58   Ginger Christ, "Collaborative Robots: Safety Within Arm's Reach," *EHS Today*, January 2016, pp. 14–17. Some experts call these worker-friendly collaborative robots "cobots". Thomas Black, "Armed With Don't Hurt Humans Sensors, Robots Hit Small Factories,"

Bloomberg BNA Bulletin to Management, May 16, 2017.

59   www.osha.gov/Publications/osha2071.pdf, accessed April 21, 2011. See also Hannah Addison, "One World Trade Center: Safe at 1776 Feet," *EHS Today*, September 2013, p. 56.

60   www-ns.iaea.org/reviews/op-safety-reviews.asp, accessed April 21, 2011.

61   James Nash, "Beware the Hidden Eye Hazards," *Occupational Hazards*, February 2005, pp. 48–51.

62   "The Complete Guide to Personal Protective Equipment," *Occupational Hazards*, January 1999, pp. 49–60. See also Judy Smithers, "Use OSHA's Compliance Directive to Evaluate Your PPE Program," *EHS Today*, January 2012, pp. 43–45; Derek Baker and Paul Maturen, "The Importance of Total Safety: Building the ABCs of PPE," *EHS Today*, October 2016, pp. 43–45.

64   James Zeigler, "Protective Clothing: Exploring the Wearability Issue," *Occupational Hazards*, September 2000, pp. 81–82; Sandy Smith, "Protective Clothing and the Quest for Improved Performance," *Occupational Hazards*, February 2008, pp. 63–66; Scott Larsen, "Integrated Use of Personal Protective Equipment," *EHS Today*, June 2012, p. 31.

65   Roger Paquette, "Staying Safe and Warm in Cold Weather Environments," *EHS Today*, January 2015, pp. 19–22.

66   Everything must be considered. For example, if the employees work outdoors during the winter, they should dress for the cold. This might include knit hats under their hardhats, ultraviolet eye protection, a brightly covered outer layer to protect against cold and wet, and gloves that both insulate from the cold and protect against hazards such as cuts. "8 Winter Essentials for Outdoor Workers," *EHS Today*, December 2016, p. 11.

67   Raghu Arunachalam and Scott Jubeck, "Beacons in the Internet of Industrial Things: A New Tool to Enhance Worker Safety," *EHS Today*, August 2016, pp. 27–30.

68   Sandy Smith, "Protecting Vulnerable Workers," *Occupational Hazards*, April 2004, pp. 25–28.

69   J. P. Sankpill, "A Clear Vision for Eye and Face Protection," *EHS Today*, November 2010, p. 29.

70   "Teen Workplace Injuries and the Importance of Training," *EHS Today*, July 2015, p. 19.

71   See, for instance, Laura Walter, "Training the Older Worker," *EHS Today*, February 2011, p. 39.

72   Robert Pater, "Boosting Safety with an Aging Workforce," *Occupational Hazards*, March 2006, p. 24.

73   Michael Silverstein, M.D., "Designing the Age-Friendly Workplace," *Occupational Hazards*, December 2007, pp. 29–31.

74   Elizabeth Rogers and William Wiatrowski, "Injuries, Illnesses, and Fatalities among Older Workers," *Monthly Labor Review*, 128, no. 10, October 2005, pp. 24–30. Actually, studies suggest that workers under 25, especially with less experience on the job, are much more likely to have more injuries and more serious injuries than older workers. Steve Ludwig, "How an Aging Workforce Will Affect Your Productivity and Safety (and What You Can Do about It)," *EHS Today*, April 2015, pp. 21–24.

75   Robert Pater and Ron Bowles, "Directing Attention to Boost Safety Performance," *Occupational Hazards*, March 2007, pp. 46–48.

76   E. Scott Geller, "The Thinking and Seeing Components of People-Based Safety," *Occupational Hazards*, December 2006, pp. 38–40. See also David Lynn, "Principle to Practice Safety Transformation," *EHS Today*, June 2015, pp. 37–39.

77   Bashline et al., "Bad Behavior," *Asia and Africa Intelligence Wire*.

78   Safety training draws on a range of training methods, from face-to-face training to online/on-demand training, video training (online videos available on demand), computer-based training, and safety training apps. Jerry DaValle, "Get Lifesaving Training, Whenever, Wherever," *EHS Today*, February 2017, pp. 11, 12.

79   John Rekus, "Is Your Safety Training Program Effective?" *Occupational Hazards*, August 1999, pp. 37–39.

80   Michael Burke et al., "The Dread Factor: How Hazards and Safety Training Influence Learning and Performance," *Journal of Applied Psychology*, 96, no. 1, 2011, pp. 46–70.

81   https://ulworkplace.puresafety.com/Login?ReturnUrl=%2f, accessed April 12, 2017.

82   Laura Walter, "Surfing for Safety," EHS Today, July 1, 2008, pp. 23–29.

83   Dave Zielinski, "Putting Safety Training Online," *HR Magazine*, January 2013, p. 51.

85   Jack Rubinger, "Signs, Labels and Lighting for a Safe and Productive Workplace," *EHS Today*, October 2012, p. 67.

86   See, for example, Josh Cable, "Seven Suggestions for a Successful Safety Incentive Program," *EHS Today*, March 23, 2005: http://ehstoday.com/safety/incentives/ehs_imp_37488, accessed July 24, 2015. See also J. M. Saidler, "Gift Cards Make Safety Motivation Simple," *Occupational Health & Safety*, 78, no. 1, January 2009, pp. 39–40.

87   Don Williamson and Jon Kauffman, "From Tragedy to Triumph: Safety Grows Wings at Golden Eagle," *Occupational Hazards*, February 2006, pp. 17–25; and www.tsocorp.com/TSOCorp/SocialResponsibility/HealthandSafety/HealthandSafety, accessed June 30, 2011.

88   Jon Hyman, "OSHA Buffers Against Retaliation," *Workforce*, January/February 2017, p. 24.

89   James Nash, "Construction Safety: Best Practices in Training Hispanic Workers," *Occupational Hazards*, February 2004, pp. 35–38.

90   Ibid., p. 37.

91   Judi Komaki, Kenneth Barwick, and Lawrence Scott, "A Behavioral Approach to Occupational Safety: Pinpointing and Reinforcing Safe Performance in a Food Manufacturing Plant," *Journal of Applied Psychology*, 63, August 1978, pp. 434–445. See also Anat Arkin, "Incentives to Work Safely," *Personnel Management*, 26, no. 9, September 1994, pp. 48–52; Peter Makin and Valerie Sutherland, "Reducing Accidents Using a Behavioral Approach," *Leadership and Organizational Development Journal*, 15, no. 5, 1994, pp. 5–10; Sandy Smith, "Why Cash Isn't King," *Occupational Hazards*, March 2004, pp. 37–38.

92   Dov Zohar, "A Group Level Model of Safety Climate: Testing the Effect of a Group Climate on Students in Manufacturing Jobs," *Journal of Applied Psychology*, 85, no. 4, 2000, pp. 587–596. See also Steven Yule, Rhona Flin, and Andy Murdy, "The Role of Management and Safety Climate in Preventing Risk-Taking at Work," *International Journal of Risk Assessment and Management*, 7, no. 2, December 20, 2006, p. 137; and Judy Agnew, "Building the Foundation for a Sustainable Safety Culture," *EHS Today*, February 2013, pp. 41–43; Grover Hardin, "Cultivating a Culture of Safety," *EHS Today*, September 2013, pp. 61–63.

93   Quoted from Sandy Smith, "Breakthrough Safety Management," *Occupational Hazards*, June 2004, p. For a discussion of developing a safety climate survey, see also Sara Singer et al., "Workforce Perceptions of Hospital Safety Culture: Development and Validation of the Patient Safety Climate in Healthcare Organizations

Survey," *Health Services Research*, 42, no. 5, October 2007, pp. 19–23.

94. https://itunes.apple.com/us/app/iauditor-safety-audit-checklist/id499999,532?mt=8, accessed May 6, 2015.

95. http://download.cnet.com/iAuditor-Safety-Audit-and-Checklist/3000-2064_4-75728239.html, accessed May 6, 2015.

96. www.digitalmarketplace.service.gov.uk/service/5-g1-0377-007, accessed May 6, 2015.

97. www.assessnet.co.uk, accessed May 6, 2015.

98. John Garber, "Introduction to the Human Resource Discipline of Safety and Security," www.shrm.org/templates_tools/toolkits, accessed May 27, 2012.

99. Mike Powell, "Sustaining Your Safety Sweep Audit Process," *EHS Today*, December 2012, pp. 35–36.

101. Thomas Krause, "Steps in Safety Strategy: Executive Decision Making & Metrics," *EHS Today*, September 2009, p. 24; John Garber, "Introduction to the Human Resource Discipline of Safety and Security," www.shrm.org/templatestools/toolkits, accessed May 27, 2012.

102. Chuck Pettinger, "Behavior-Based Safety 2: The Next Evolution," *EHS Today*, October 2011, pp. 79–82.

103. Katherine Torres, "Making a Safety Committee Work for You," *Occupational Hazards*, 68, no. 10, October 2006, at http://ehstoday.com/safety/best-practices/ehs_imp_39324, accessed September 10, 2012.

104. See also Terry Mathis, "S.T.E.P.S.: Strategic Targets for Excellent Performance and Safety," *EHS Today*, June 2011, pp. 18–20.

105. S. L. Smith, "Sadaf Drives for Safety Excellence," *Occupational Hazards*, November 1998, p. 41. For further discussion, see also Kathy Seabrook, "10 Strategies for Global Safety Management," *Occupational Hazards*, June 1999, pp. 41–43.

106. "World-Class Safety: DuPont and Milliken Share Their Proven Successes," *BLR*, August 23, 2013, http://safety.blr.com/, accessed April 15, 2014.

107. Carey Tebbetts and Robert Allen, "Milliken's Keys to Employee Engagement, Increased Workplace Safety and Productivity," *EHS Today*, January 9, 2013: http://ehstoday.com/safety/millikens-keys-employee-engagement-increased-workplace-safety-and-productivity, accessed July 24, 2015.

108. Ibid

109. Ibid.

110. Ibid.

111. Ibid.

112. Mike Powell, "Harness the Full Power of Your Incident Investigation Process," *EHS Today*, September 2013, p. 71.

113. www.performancesolutionsbymilliken.com, accessed April 15, 2014. As part of its safety program, Milliken partnered with the Occupational Safety and Health Administration and follows the latter's voluntary protection program's (VPP's) guidelines to help it reach its safety goals. "Milliken and Company VPP Star Site Elm Facility Receiving VPP Recognition," www.osha.gov, accessed April 14, 2014. For another example of how employee engagement impacts occupational safety, see "How Employee Engagement Can Improve the Hospital's Health," *Gallup Business Journal*, http://businessjournal.gallup.com, accessed April 14, 2014.

114. This is based on Paul Puncochar, "The Science and Art to Identifying Workplace Hazards," *Occupational Hazards*, September 2003, pp. 50–54.

115. Ibid., p. 52.

116. Where employees may encounter chemical spills, OSHA standards require that emergency eye washers and showers be available for employees to use. Michael Bolden, "Choosing and Maintaining Emergency Eye Washers/Showers," *EHS Today*, January 2010, pp. 39–41.

117. Gareth Evans, "Wireless Monitoring for a Safe Indoor Environment," *EHS Today*, December 2010, pp. 35–39.

118. "Hazard Communication," www.OSHA.gov/dsg/hazcom/index.HTML, accessed May 26, 2012.

119. Garber, "Introduction to the Human Resource Discipline of Safety and Security."

120. Based on, Beverley Sunderland, "Ensuring legal safety for gig economy workers", PeopleManagement, Feb 2017, http://www2.cipd.co.uk/pm/peoplemanagement/b/weblog/archive/2017/02/06/ensuring-legal-safety-for-gig-economy-workers.aspx ; Elizabeth Grossman "Hazards of the gig economy" – Temp workers at greater risk for workplace injury but poorly protected, say labor advocates", Pump Handle, November 4, 2016 http://scienceblogs.com/thepumphandle/2016/11/04/hazards-of-the-gig-economy-temp-workers-at-greater-risk-for-workplace-injury-but-poorly-protected-say-labor-advocates/ ; Roger Marks, "Who's Responsible for Training Temp Workers on GHS?", May 6, 2016, https://www.lion.com/lion-news/may-2016/who-s-responsible-for-training-temp-workers-on-ghs ; Hazard Communication , https://www.osha.gov/Publications/OSHA3860.pdf; "Temporary Worker Safety", https://www.jjkeller.com/learn/temporary-workers ; all accessed April 8, 2017.

121. If hired by a staffing agency, it, not the host hiring company, would probably pay for workers' compensation insurance.

122. Based on the report "Workplace Screening and Brief Intervention: What Employers Can and Should Do about Excessive Alcohol Use," www.ensuringsolutions.org/resources/resources_show.htm?doc_id=673239, accessed August 11, 2009.

123. "Employers Can Play Key Role in Preventing Painkiller Abuse, but Many Remain Reluctant," *BNA Bulletin to Management*, February 15, 2011, p. 49.

124. "15% of Workers Drinking, Drunk, or Hungover While at Work, according to New University Study," *BNA Bulletin to Management*, January 24, 2006, p. 27.

125. https://www.ncadd.org/about-addiction/addiction-update/drugs-and-alcohol-in-the-workplace, accessed April 12, 2017.

126. Samuel Bacharach et al., "Alcohol Consumption and Workplace Absenteeism: The Moderating Effect of Social Support," *Journal of Applied Psychology*, 95, no. 2, 2010, pp. 334–348.

127. See, for example, L. Claussen, "Can You Spot the Meth Addict?" *Safety & Health*, 179, no. 4, April 2009, pp. 48–52.

128. "New Jersey Union Takes on Mandatory Random Drug Tests," *Record* (Hackensack, NJ), January 2, 2008.

129. Frank Lockwood et al., "Drug Testing Programs and Their Impact on Workplace Accidents: A Time Series Analysis," *Journal of Individual Employment Rights*, 8, no. 4, 2000, pp. 295–306; Sally Roberts, "Random Drug Testing Can Help Reduce Accidents for Construction Companies; Drug Abuse Blamed for Heightened Risk in the Work-place," *Business Insurance*, 40, October 23, 2006, p. 6.

130. See for example, http://workplacedrugpolicy.com/program-components.htm; http://www.workingpartners.com/understanding-dfwp/elements-of-dfwp.asp; and http://www.dol.gov/elaws/asp/drugfree/drugs/screen16asp, accessed July 27, 2015.

131. www.dol.gov/asp/programs/drugs/workingpartners/sab/screen.asp, accessed April 27, 2008; www.dol.gov/whd/FOH/ch64/64a2htm, accessed September 11, 2014.

132. Gopal Pati and John Adkins Jr., "The Employer's Role in Alcoholism Assistance," *Personnel Journal*, 62, no. 7, July 1983, p. 570. See also Commerce Clearing House, "How Should Employers Respond to Indications an Employee May Have an Alcohol or Drug Problem?" *Ideas and Trends*, April 6, 1989, pp. 53–57; www.ncadd.org/about-addiction/addiction-update/drugs-and-alcohol-in-the-workplace, accessed April 12, 2017.

133. William Current, "Pre-Employment Drug Testing," *Occupational Hazards*, July 2002, p. 56. See also William Current, "Improving Your Drug Testing ROI," *Occupational Health & Safety*, 73, no. 4, April 2004, pp. 40, 42, 44.

134. Diane Cadrain, "Are Your Employees' Drug Tests Accurate?" *HR Magazine*, January 2003, pp. 41–45.

135. Roberts, "Random Drug Testing Can Help Reduce Accidents for Construction Companies," p. 6.

136. The research is quite clear that work stress increases alcohol use among normal drinkers and this has several implications for employers. Employers and supervisors should take steps to reduce stressful daily work experiences such as interpersonal conflicts at work, role ambiguity, and excessive workloads. Songqi Liu et al., "Daily Work Stress and Alcohol Use: Testing the Cross Level Moderation Effects of Neuroticism and Job Involvement," *Personnel Psychology*, 60, no. 2, 2009, pp. 575–597.

137. www.OSHA.gov, accessed May 28, 2005. See also Martin Berman-Gorvine, "Take Pressure Off Employees to Avoid Burnout," *Bloomberg BNA Bulletin to Management*, January 17, 2017.

138. Ric Sundstrom et al., "Office Noise, Satisfaction, and Performance," *Environment and Behavior*, no. 2, March 1994, pp. 195–222; "Stress: How to Cope with Life's Challenges," *American Family Physician*, 74, no. 8, October 15, 2006.

139. Sarah Ponczek, "Unpredictable Hours Found to Hurt Workers' Well-Being and Income Stability," *Bloomberg BNA Bulletin to Management*, August 27, 2016, p. 307.

140. S. Antoniou, F. Polychroni, and A. N. Vlachakis, "Gender and Age Differences in Occupational Stress and Professional Burnout between Primary and High School Teachers in Greece," *Journal of Managerial Psychology*, 21, no. 7, September 2006, pp. 682–690.

141. Failing to Tackle Stress Could Cost You Dearly," Personnel Today, September 12, 2006; www.sciencedaily.com/releases/2007/06/070604170722.htm, accessed November 3, 2009; "Research Brief: Stress May Accelerate Alzheimer's," GP, September 8, 2006, p. 2.

142. Tara Parker-Pope, "Time to Review Workplace Reviews?" *The New York Times*, May 18, 2010, p. D5. A recent study illustrates the potential fatal effects of one's work environment. The researchers measured *job demands* with questions such as "To what extent do you agree that your job requires working very hard?" They measured *job control* with questions such as "To what extent do you agree that you have a lot of say about what happens on your job?" They studied more than 2300 individuals over seven years. For individuals who said they felt they had little control over how they did their jobs, high job demands were associated with a 15.4% increase in the odds of death compared to low job demands. As the researchers conclude,

" . . . employers of individuals in highly demanding jobs in which employees also have little control should be aware of the increased risk of mortality facing their employees." Eric Gonzalez-Mule and Bethany Cockburn, "Worked to Death: The Relationships of Job Demands and Job Control with Mortality," *Personnel Psychology*, 70, 2017, pp. 73–112.

143 Stress, Depression Cost Employers," *Occupational Hazards*, December 1998, p. 24; Patricia B. Gray, "Hidden Costs of Stress," *Money*, 36, no. 12, December 2007, p. 44.

144 Karl Albrecht, *Stress and the Manager* (Upper Saddle River, NJ: Prentice Hall, 1979), pp. 253–255; "Stress: How to Cope with Life's Challenges," *American Family Physician*, 74, no. 8, October 15, 2006; http://familydoctor.org/familydoctor/en /prevention-wellness/emotional-wellbeing /mental-health/stress-how-to-cope-better-with -lifes-challenges.html, accessed April 11, 2012; www.mayoclinic.com/health/coping-with-stress/SR30/NSECTIONGROUP=2, accessed April 11, 2012; www.cdc.gov/violenceprevention/ pub/coping_with_stress_tips.html, accessed April 11, 2012.

145 Experts argue that there are pros and cons to the open office spaces that many employees today work in. Pros include encouraging collaboration and reducing unproductiveness. Cons include reduced privacy, the pressure to always be performing, and possibly job dissatisfaction. Genevieve Douglas, "Office Space Design May Affect Worker Productivity," *Bloomberg BNA Bulletin to Management*, March 14, 2017.

146 Kathleen Doler "Meditation Gives Your Mind Permanent Working Holiday; Relaxation Can Improve Your Business Decisions and Your Overall Health," *Investors Business Daily*, March 24, 2004, p. 89.

147 "Going Head to Head with Stress," *Personnel Today*, April 26, 2005, p. 1.

148 Kathryn Tyler, "Stress Management," *HR Magazine*, September 2006, pp. 79–82.

149 "Meditation Helps Employees Focus, Relieve Stress," *BNA Bulletin to Management*, February 20, 2007, p. 63. See also "Workplace Yoga, Meditation Can Reduce Stress," *EHS Today*, September 2009, p. 21.

150 George DeVries III, "Innovations in Workplace Wellness: Six New Tools to Enhance Programs and Maximize Employee Health and Productivity," *Compensation & Benefits Review*, 42, no. 1, January/February 2010, pp. 46–51.

151 Monique Valcour, "MANAGING YOURSELF Beating Burnout Strategies To Recognize, Recover From, and Prevent It," *Harvard Business Review*, November 2016, pp. 98–100.

152 Madan Mohan Tripathy, "Burnout Stress Syndrome in Managers," *Management and Labor Studies*, 27, no. 2, April 2002, pp. 89–111. See also Jonathon R. B. Halbesleben and Cheryl Rathert, "Linking Physician Burnout and Patient Outcomes: Exploring the Dyadic Relationship between Physicians and Patients," *Health Care Management Review*, 33, no. 1, January/March 2008, p. 29.

153 Valcour, "Managing Yourself."

154 Herbert Freudenberger, *Burn-Out* (Toronto: Bantam Books, 1980).

155 Sabine Sonnentag et al., "Staying Well and Engaged When Demands Are High: The Role of Psychological Detachment," *Journal of Applied Psychology*, 95, no. 5, 2010, pp. 965–976.

156 Genevieve Douglas, "US Workers Choosing Burnout over Vacation?" *Bloomberg BNA Bulletin to Management*, March 28, 2017.

157 Sharon Toker and Michael Biron, "Job Burnout and Depression: Unravelling Their Temporal Relationship and Considering the Role of Physical Activity," *Journal of Applied Psychology*, 97, no. 3, 2012, p. 699.

158 Todd Nighswonger, "Depression: The Unseen Safety Risk," *Occupational Hazards*, April 2002, pp. 38–42; http://www.huffingtonpost .com/2013/7/25/depression-missed-work-days -absent_n_3651889html, accessed July 27, 2015.

159 Nighswonger, "Depression: The Unseen Safety Risk," p. 40.

160 "Employers Must Move from Awareness to Action in Dealing with Worker Depression," *BNA Bulletin to Management*, April 29, 2004, p. 137.

161 Mike Stearns, "Silence of the Limbs: The Toll of Inactivity on Our Sedentary Workforce," *EHS Today*, August 2016, pp. 11–14. Walking around briefly a few times each hour can have significant health benefits. One expert estimates that an employer will derive between $3 and $7 in savings (for instance, in insurance costs) for each dollar it invests in getting workers to be more active on the job. Tamara Lytle, "Stand up and Get Moving," *HR Magazine*, March 2017, p. 46.

162 Jon Fitch, "EHS Today Takes Workplace Wellness to a Whole New Level," *EHS Today*, January 2017, pp. 21–22.

163 "Risk of Carpal Tunnel Syndrome Not Linked to Heavy Computer Work, Study Says," *BNA Bulletin to Management*, June 28, 2001, p. 203.

164 www.ninds.nih.gov/disorders/repetitive_motion /repetitive_motion.htm, accessed February 28, 2010. Surveys suggest that most office workers do experience back pain, eyestrain or headaches, and various other muscular pains while working. "Office Workers Face Musculoskeletal Mayhem," *EHS Today*, May 2013, p. 10.

165 https://www.osha.gov/SLTC/etools /computerworkstations/index.html, accessed April 9, 2017.

166 Mark Christian et al., "Single and Dual Monitor Computer Set Up: Ergonomic Tips," *EHS Today*, April 2016, pp. 20–22.

167 Anne Chambers, "Computer Vision Syndrome: Relief Is in Sight," *Occupational Hazards*, October 1999, pp. 179–184; www.OSHA .gov/ETOOLS/computerworkstations/index. html, accessed May 28, 2005.

168 Sandra Lotz Fisher, "Are Your Employees Working Ergosmart?" *Personnel Journal*, December 1996, pp. 91–92. See also www.cdc.gov/od/ ohs/Ergonomics/compergo.htm, accessed May 26, 2007.

169 Sandy Smith, "SARS: What Employers Need to Know," *Occupational Hazards*, July 2003, pp. 33–35.

170 See http://en.wikipedia.org/wiki/List_of _smoking_bans#United_States for a list.

171 However, note that some experts believe that in some circumstances the EEOC might see a smoking addiction as similar to use of illegal drugs, and thus possibly covered by the ADA. "Policies to Not Hire Smokers Raise Privacy, Bias Issues," *BNA Bulletin to Management*, December 14, 2010, p. 399.

172 Joan Deschenauxh, "Is a 'Smoker-Free' Workplace Right for You?" *HR Magazine*, July 2011, pp. 43–45.

173 "No Tobacco or E-Cigarettes in the Workplace, NIOSH Says in Updated Recommendations," *Bloomberg BNA Bulletin to Management*, April 14, 2015, p. 113.

174 Bruce Rolfsen, "Hazy Marijuana Laws Stir Confusion over Worker Protection," *Bloomberg BNA Bulletin to Management*, April 18, 2017.

175 Garber, "Introduction to the Human Resource Discipline of Safety and Security."

176 Ibid.

177 This is based on "New Challenges for Health and Safety in the Work-place," *Workplace Visions* (Society for Human Resource Management), no. 3, 2003, pp. 2–4. See also J. L. Nash, "Protecting Chemical Plants from Terrorists: Opposing Views," *Occupational Hazards*, February 2004, pp. 18–20.

178 "Survey Finds Reaction to September 11 Attacks Spurred Companies to Prepare for Disasters," *BNA Bulletin to Management*, November 29, 2005, p. 377.

179 "Study: Don't Silo Human Capital Risk," www .shrm.org/hrdisciplines/ethics/articles, accessed May 27, 2012.

180 Sources of external risk include legal/regulatory, political, and business environment (economy, e-business, etc.). Internal risks sources include financial, strategic, operational (including safety and security), and integrity (embezzlement, theft, fraud, etc.). William Atkinson, "Enterprise Risk Management at Wal-Mart," www.rmmag .com/MGTemplate.cfm?Section=RMMagazine& NavMenuID=128&template=/Magazine /DisplayMagazines.cfm&MGPreview=1&Volume =50&IssueID=205&AID=2209&ShowArticle =1, accessed April 1, 2009.

181 "Workplace Violence Takes a Deadly Toll," *EHS Today*, December 2009, p. 17; "Workplace Violence," www.osha.gov/SLTC/workplaceviolence /, accessed September 11, 2014.

182 https://www.osha.gov/SLTC/workplaceviolence /, accessed April 12, 2017.

183 Jenny Hoobler and Jennifer Swanberg, "The Enemy Is Not Us," *International Personnel Management Association for HR*, 35, no. 3, Fall 2006, pp. 229–246.

184 "Bullies Trigger 'Silent Epidemic' at Work, but Legal Cures Remain Hard to Come By," *BNA Bulletin to Management*, February 24, 2000, p. 57.

185 www.cdc.gov/ncipc/dvp/ipv_factsheet.pdf, accessed August 8, 2013.

186 "Workplace Violence a Far-Reaching Problem for the American Workforce," *EHS Today*, March 2012, p. 20.

187 Paul Viollis and Doug Kane, "At-Risk Terminations: Protecting Employees, Preventing Disaster," *Risk Management Magazine*, 52, no. 5, May 2005, pp. 28–33.

188 Kenneth Diamond, "The Gender-Motivated Violence Act: What Employers Should Know," *Employee Relations Law Journal*, 25, no. 4, Spring 2000, pp. 29–41; "Bush Signs 'Violence against Women Act'; Funding Badly Needed Initiatives to Prevent Domestic & Sexual Violence, Help Victims," *America's Intelligence Wire*, January 5, 2006.

189 M. Sandy Hershcovis et al., "Predicting Workplace Aggression: A Meta-Analysis," *Journal of Applied Psychology*, 92, no. 1, 2007, pp. 228–238.

190 Alfred Feliu, "Workplace Violence and the Duty of Care: The Scope of an Employer's Obligation to Protect against the Violent Employee," *Employee Relations Law Journal*, 20, no. 3, Winter 1994/95, p. 395.

191 Dawn Anfuso, "Deflecting Work-place Violence," *Personnel Journal*, October 1994, pp. 66–77.

192 Feliu, "Workplace Violence and the Duty of Care," p. 395.

193 See, for example, James Thelan, "Is That a Threat?" *HR Magazine*, December 2009, pp. 61–63.

194 Feliu, "Workplace Violence and the Duty of Care."

195 Ibid., pp. 401–402.

196 "Employers Battling Workplace Violence Might Consider Postal Service Plan," *BNA Bulletin to Management*, August 5, 1999, p. 241.

197 Viollis and Kane, "At-Risk Terminations," pp. 28–33.

198 "Focus on Corporate Security," *BNA HR Executive Series*, Fall 2001, p. 4.

199 Ibid.

200 Unless otherwise noted, the following, including the six matters to address, is based on Richard Maurer, "Keeping Your Security Program Active," *Occupational Hazards*, March 2003, pp. 49–52.

201 Maurer, "Keeping Your Security Program Active," p. 50.

202 Ibid.

203 Bill Roberts, "Are You Ready for Biometrics?" *HR Magazine*, March 2003, pp. 95–99.

204 Maurer, "Keeping Your Security Program Active," p. 52.

205 Genevieve Douglas, "HR Must Evolve to Fight Complex Cyber Threats," *Bloomberg BNA Bulletin to Management*, January 10, 2017.

206 Lloyd Newman, "Terrorism: Is Your Company Prepared?" *Business and Economic Review*, 48, no. 2, February 2002, pp. 7–10; Li Yuan et al., "Texting When There's Trouble," *The Wall Street Journal*, April 18, 2007, p. B1.

207 "Unrest in Egypt Highlights Importance of Crisis Management Plans, Experts Say," *BNA Bulletin to Management*, February 8, 2011, pp. 41–42.

208 Fay Hansen, "Skirting Danger," *Workforce Management*, January 19, 2009, pp. 1, 3.

209 These are based on or quoted from Samuel Greengard, "Mission Possible: Protecting Employees Abroad," *Workforce*, August 1997, pp. 30–32. See also Z. Phillips, "Global Firms Consider Additional Cover for Overseas Execs," *Business Insurance*, 43, no. 23, June 15–22, 2009, pp. 4, 22.

210 http://travel.state.gov/content/passports /english/alertswarnings.html, accessed September 11, 2014.

211 Greengard, "Mission Possible," p. 32.

212 Craig Schroll, "Evacuation Planning: A Matter of Life and Death," *Occupational Hazards*, June 2002, pp. 49–51.

213 Maurer, "Keeping Your Security Program Active," p. 52; Yuan et al., "Texting When There's Trouble," p. B1.

214 "HR Plays Key Role in Preparing Organizations for Disasters," *Bloomberg BNA Bulletin to Management*, June 25, 2013, p. 206.

215 www.osha.gov/SLTC/etools/evacuation/evac .html, accessed June 29, 2017.

216 "Swine Flu Tests Employer Emergency Plan; Experts Urge Communicating Best Practices," *BNA Bulletin to Management*, May 5, 2009, pp. 137–144.

217 Sandy Devine, "Are You Ready for a Sudden Cardiac Arrest Emergency?" *EHS Today*, April 2009, pp. 26–29.

218 "Business Continuity: What Is the Best Way to Plan for Disasters That May Affect Our Business, Like the Gulf Oil Spill?" www.SHRM .org/templates_tools, accessed May 27, 2012.

219 *PR Newswire*, April 2, 2013 pNA; "Get Tips on Using Social Media for Disaster Recovery." *Public Manager*, 42, no. 1, Spring 2013, p. 35(3); Joseph Porcelli, "How FEMA Drove 23,000 People to Join its Online Community," *America's Intelligence Wire*, Oct. 28, 2012 pNA; "Officials Take to Social Media to Share Emergency Information: Canadians Tapped into Social Networks, Expect Emergency Responders to Use Social Media: New Red Cross Survey," *CNW Group*, Oct. 9, 2012 pNA.

Module A

1 https://www.census.gov/foreign-trade/statistics /historical/gands.pdf, accessed April 26, 2017.

2 See, for example, Anne Marie Francesco and Barry Allen Gold, *International Organizational Behavior* (Upper Saddle River, NJ: Pearson, 2005); and Helen Deresky, *International Management*, 9th ed. (Hoboken, NJ: Pearson, 2017).

3 Deresky, *International Management*, p. 17.

4 www.hoovers.com/company/Wal-Mart _Stores_Inc/rrjiff-1.html, accessed June 1, 2011. See also, "Unions File New Wal-Mart Labor Complaint Related to Store Closure," http:// www.reuters.com/article/us-wal-mart-stores -workers-unions-idUSKCN0RA2AH20150910, accessed July 28, 2017.

5 "First Wal-Mart Union Begins in China," www .huffingtonpost.com/2008/08/03/first-wal-mart -union-begin_116629.html, accessed June 30, 2011.

6 Based on "Wal-Mart's Reshuffle Plan in China Falters," www.chinadaily.com.cn /china/2009-04/21/content_7699105.htm, accessed June 30, 2011.

7 For example see Chris Brewster, Wolfgang Mayrhofer, and Adam Smale, "Crossing the Streams: HRM in Multinational Enterprises and Comparative HRM," *Human Resource Management Review*, 26, 2016, pp. 285–297.

8 See for example, Deresky, *International Management*, p. 287.

9 Luc Minguet, Eduardo Caride, Takeo Yamaguchi, and Shane Tedjarati "Voices from the Front Lines." *Harvard Business Review*, September 2014, pp. 72-82, 129.

10 www.geert-hofstede.com/, accessed April 26, 2017.

11 See Vas Taras, Bradley Kirkman, and Piers Steel, "Examining the Impact of Culture's Consequences: A Three-Decade, Multilevel, Multi-Analytic Review of Hofstadter's Cultural Value Dimensions," *Journal of Applied Psychology*, 95, no. 3, 2010, pp. 405–439.

12 Tor Grenness, "The Impact of National Culture on CEO Compensation and Salary Gaps between CEOs and Manufacturing Workers," *Compensation and Benefits Review*, 43, no. 2, 2011, pp. 100–108.

13 "In India, 101 Employees Pose Big Problems," *Bloomberg Businessweek*, January 17–23, 2011, p. 13.

14 "Employer Beware," *The Economist*, March 12, 2011, p. 43.

15 Stephenie Overman, "Tapping Talent around the Globe," *HR Magazine*, February 2016, pp. 47–51.

16 2011 figures, https://www.bls.gov/news .release/pdf/ichcc.pdf www.bls.gov/news .release/pdf/ichcc.pdf, accessed Aril 26, 2017.

17 Phillips Taft and Cliff Powell, "The European Pensions and Benefits Environment: A Complex Ecology," *Compensation & Benefits Review*, January/February 2005, pp. 37–50.

18 Francesco and Gold, *International Organizational Behavior*, p. 145.

19 Ibid., p. 106.

20 Vlad Vainan, et al., "Recognizing the Important Role of Self-Initiated Expatriates and Effective Global Talent Management," *Human Resource Management Review*, 25, 2015, pp. 280–286.

21 Leslie Klass, "Fed Up with High Costs, Companies Winnow the Ranks of Career Expats," *Workforce Management*, October 2004, pp. 84–88. See also Susan Ladika, "Lost in Translation," *Workforce Management*, May 2013, pp. 30–33.

22 See "Workforce Trends: Companies Continue to Deploy Ex-Pats," *Compensation & Benefits Review*, 42, no. 1, January/February 2010, p. 6.See also, Jennifer Alsever, "The great expatriate hiring boom," Fortune, May 15, 2013, http://fortune.com/2013/05/15/the -great-expatriate-hiring-boom/, accessed July 28, 2017.

23 "Expatriate Assignments in Growth Markets to Soar," *HR Magazine*, January 2013, p. 20.

24 "Mercer's International Assignments Survey 2010," www.imercer.com/products/2010 /intl-assignments-survey.aspx, accessed June 2, 2011; "Companies Juggle Cost Cutting with Maintaining Competitive Benefits for International Assignments," www.amanet.org /training/articles/Companies-Juggle-cost-cutting -with-Maintaining-Competitive-Benefits-for -International-Assignments.aspx, accessed June 2, 2011; "3 ways to cut down on international assignment costs," https://www.fidi.org/blog/3 -ways-cut-down-international-assignment-costs, accessed July 28, 2017.

25 "Mercer's International Assignments Survey 2010," "Companies Juggle Cost Cutting with Maintaining Competitive Benefits for International Assignments."

26 Timothy Dwyer, "Localization's Hidden Costs," *HR Magazine*, June 2004, pp. 135–144. See also, Matt C. Altro and Jonah Ravel, "The Challenges of Localization with Cross Border Employee Relocation," http://mcacrossborder .com/blog/challenges-of-localization-with-cross -border-employee-relocation, accessed July 28, 2017.

27 The following is based on "Back-Office and Customer Care Centers in Emerging Economies: A Human Capital Perspective," IBM Business Consulting Services, www-935.ibm.com /services/us/imc/pdf/ge510-3967-back-office -asiapac.pdf, accessed September 16, 2014.

28 Ibid., pp. 3, 4.

29 Ibid., pp. 5, 6.

30 Charles Snow, Scott Snell, Sue Canney Davison, and Donald Hambrick, "Use Transnational Teams to Globalize Your Company," *Organizational Dynamics*, Spring 1996, pp. 50–67.

31 Ibid. See also, Tsedal Neeley, "Global Teams That Work," *Harvard Business Review*, October 2015, https://hbr.org/2015/10/global-teams-that -work, accessed July 28, 2017.

32 www.microsoft.com/en-us/download /details.aspx?id=23745, accessed May 6, 2015.

33 https://signup.webex.com/webexmeetings /US/sem_acquisition.html?CPM=KNC -sem&TrackID=1031986&country=US &psearchID=webex%20collaboration %20meeting%20room, accessed May 6, 2015.

34 www1.gotomeeting.com/m/g2msem3.tmpl ?Portal=www.gotomeeting.com&c_name =msns&c_mark=NAPPC&c_kwd=go_to _meeting_software_download-Broad&c_prod =GTM&c_cmp=sf-70150000000add7&c _date=CATnumber&c_cell=CMjwmL3KrcUCFUI Z7AodlRIAgQ&gclid=CMjwmL3KrcUCFUIZ7 AodlRIAgQ&gclsrc=ds, accessed May 6, 2015.

35 www.huddle.com, accessed May 6, 2015.

36 www.cisco.com/c/en/us/products /collaboration-endpoints/immersive-telePresence /index.html, accessed May 6, 2015.

37 Tsedal Neeley, "Global Teams That Work," *Harvard Business Review*, October 2015, pp. 75–85.

38 See Deresky, *International Management*, p. 288.

39 Arvind Phatak, *International Dimensions of Management* (Boston: PWS Kent, 1989), p. 129.

40 Ibid.

41 www.nytimes.com/2011/03/19/business /global/19blue.html, accessed June 30, 2011.

42 Mary G. Tye and Peter Y. Chen, "Selection of Expatriates: Decision-Making Models Used by HR Professionals," *Human Resource Planning*, 28, no. 4, December 2005, pp. 15–20.

43 Paula Caligiuri, Ibraiz Tarique, and Rick Jacobs, "Selection for International Assignments," *Human Resource Management Review*, 19, no. 3, 2009, pp. 251–262.

44 P. Blocklyn, "Developing the International Executive," *Personnel*, March 1989, p. 45. See also Paula M. Caligiuri and Jean M. Phillips, "An

Application of Self-Assessment Realistic Job Previews to Expatriate Assignments," *International Journal of Human Resource Management*, 14, no. 7, November 2003, pp. 1102–1116.

45 Mansour Javidan, Amanda Bullough, and Rebekah Dibble, "Mind the Gap: Gender Differences in Global Leadership Self-Efficacies," *Academy of Management Perspectives*, 30, no. 1, 2016, pp. 59–73.

46 "More Women, Young Workers on the Move," *Workforce Management*, August 20, 2007, p. 9; Andy Smailes and Tina Vasquez, "Women Abroad—How to Get the Most from an International Assignment," *Living Abroad*, January 18, 2013, www.livingabroad.com/women-abroad-how-to-get-the-most-from-an-international-assignment/, accessed July 28, 2015.

47 "More Women"; Smailes and Vasquez, "Women Abroad."

48 For a good discussion of this, see Yochanan Altman and Susan Shortland, "Women and International Assignments: Taking Stock—A 25-Year Review," *Human Resource Management*, 47, no. 2, Summer 2008, pp. 199–216.

49 Kathryn Tyler, "Don't Fence Her In," *HR Magazine*, 46, no. 3, March 2001, pp. 69–77. See also, Elizabeth Roberts, "More Women Using Expat Postings To Fast-Track Their Careers," http://www.telegraph.co.uk/expat/expatlife/12115571/More-women-using-expat-postings-to-fast-track-their-careers.html, accessed July 28, 2017.

50 Susan Shortland, "The Purpose of Expatriation: Why Women Undertake International Assignments," *Human Resource Management*, 55, no. 4, July–August 2016, pp. 655–678.

51 Tyler, "Don't Fence Her In."

52 Ibid. See also Smailes and Vasquez, "Women Abroad."

53 See Nancy Napier and Sully Taylor, "Experiences of Women Professionals Abroad," *International Journal of Human Resource Management*, 13, no. 5, August 2002, pp. 837–851; Iris Fischlmayr, "Female Self-Perception as a Barrier to International Careers?" *International Journal of Human Resource Management*, 13, no. 5, August 2002, pp. 773–783; Wolfgang Mayrhofer and Hugh Scullion, "Female Expatriates in International Business: Evidence from the German Clothing Industry," *International Journal of Human Resource Management*, 13, no. 5, August 2002, pp. 815–836; Altman and Shortland, "Women and International Assignments;" and Susan Shortland, "The Purpose of Expatriation: Why Women Undertake International Assignments," op. cit.

54 Overman, "Tapping Talent around the Globe."

55 Jing Zhu, et al., "Ups and Downs of the Expatriate Experience? Understanding Work Adjustment Trajectories and Career Outcomes," *Journal of Applied Psychology*, 101, no. 4, 2016, p. 549.

56 P. Caligiuri, "The Big Five Personality Characteristics as Predictors of Expatriates' Desire to Terminate the Assignment and Supervisor-Rated Performance," *Personnel Psychology*, 53, no. 1, Spring 2000, pp. 67–88. See also Margaret A. Shaffer et al., "You Can Take It with You: Individual Differences and Expatriate Effectiveness," *Journal of Applied Psychology*, 91, no. 1, January 2006, pp. 109–125.

57 Quoted in Meredith Downes, Iris I. Varner, and Luke Musinski, "Personality Traits as Predictors of Expatriate Effectiveness: A Synthesis and Reconceptualization," *Review of Business*, 27, no. 3, Spring/Summer 2007, p. 16.

58 Jan Selmer, "Expatriation: Corporate Policy, Personal Intentions and International Adjustment," *International Journal of Human Resource Management*, 9, no. 6, December 1998, pp. 997–1007. See also Barbara Myers and

Judith K. Pringle, "Self-Initiated Foreign Experience as Accelerated Development: Influences of Gender," *Journal of World Business*, 40, no. 4, November 2005, pp. 421–431.

59 Hung-Wen Lee and Ching-Hsing, "Determinants of the Adjustment of Expatriate Managers to Foreign Countries: An Empirical Study," *International Journal of Management*, 23, no. 2, 2006, pp. 302–311.

60 Deresky, *International Management*, p. 90.

61 Sunkyu Jun and James Gentry, "An Exploratory Investigation of the Relative Importance of Cultural Similarity and Personal Fit in the Selection and Performance of Expatriates," *Journal of World Business*, 40, no. 1, February 2005, pp. 1–8. See also Jan Selmer, "Cultural Novelty and Adjustment: Western Business Expatriates in China," *International Journal of Human Resource Management*, 17, no. 7, 2006, pp. 1211–1222.

62 Barbara Anderson, "Expatriate Selection: Good Management or Good Luck?" *International Journal of Human Resource Management*, 16, no. 4, April 2005, pp. 567–583.

63 Michael Schell, quoted in Charlene Marmer Solomon, "Success Abroad Depends on More Than Job Skills," *Personnel Journal*, 73, April 1994, p. 52. See also, "The 5 biggest reasons for expatriate failure, https://www.fidi.org/blog/5-biggest-reasons-expatriate-failure, accessed July 28, 2017.

64 Michael Harvey, Milorad M. Novicevic, and Garry Garrison, "Global Virtual Teams: A Human Resource Capital Architecture," *International Journal of Human Resource Management*, 16, no. 9, September 2005, pp. 1583–1599.

65 Eric Krell, "Budding Relationships," *HR Magazine*, 50, no. 6, June 2005, pp. 114–118. See also Jill Elswick, "Worldly Wisdom: Companies Refine Their Approach to Overseas Assignments, Emphasizing Cost-Cutting and Work–Life Support for Expatriates," *Employee Benefit News*, June 15, 2004, Item 0416600B.

66 Rita Pyrillis, "Quality Quandary," *Workforce*, February 2016, p. 17.

67 Paraphrased from www.interchangeinstitute.org/html/cross_cultural.htm, accessed July 1, 2011.

68 Adapted from www.kwintessential.co.uk/cultural-services/articles/expat-cultural-training.html, accessed July 1, 2011. See also www.global-lt.com/en/us/cultural-training/expatriate-training.html#60Countries, accessed July 28, 2015.

69 Sarah Fister Gale, "Now You're Speaking My Language," *Workforce Management*, July 2013, p. 10.

70 Tamer K. Darwish, Satwinder Singh, and Geoffrey Wood, "The Impact of Human Resource Practices on Actual and Perceived Organizational Performance in a Middle Eastern Emerging Market," *Human Resource Management*, 55, no. 2, March–April 2016, pp. 261–281.

71 Ibid., p. 359. See also Laura Rodriguez-Costacamps, "Training Goes Global," *TD*, April 2016, pp. 38–42.

72 Hal Gregersen et al., "Expatriate Performance Appraisal in U.S. Multinational Firms," *Journal of International Business Studies*, 27, no. 4, Winter 1996, pp. 711–739. See also Hsi-An Shih, Yun-Hwa Chiang, and In-Sook Kim, "Expatriate Performance Management from MNEs of Different National Origins," *International Journal of Manpower*, 26, no. 2, February 2005, pp. 157–175; and Francesco and Gold, *International Organizational Behavior*, pp. 152–153.

73 Ellen Ernst Kossek, Jason L. Huang, Matthew M. Piszczek, John W. Fleenor, and Marian

Ruderman, "Rating Expatriate Leader Effectiveness in Multisource Feedback Systems: Cultural Distance and Hierarchical Effects," *Human Resource Management*, 56, no. 1, January–February 2017, p.165.

74 Charles Hill, *International Business* (Burr Ridge, IL: Irwin, 1994), pp. 519–520; Joseph Martocchio, *Strategic Compensation* (Upper Saddle River, NJ: Pearson, 2006), pp. 402–403.

75 "Expatriate Assignments in Growth Markets to Soar," *HR Magazine*, January 2013, p. 20.

76 http://aoprals.state.gov/content.asp?content_id=186&menu_id=81, accessed May 8, 2014.

77 Thomas Shelton, "Global Compensation Strategies: Managing and Administering Split Pay for an Expatriate Workforce," *Compensation & Benefits Review*, January/February 2008, pp. 56–59.

78 Ibid.; Deresky, *International Management*.

79 www.erieri.com/SurveySources/International, accessed July 28, 2015.

80 "Luis Hernandez on Why Ex-Pat Assignments Succeed—or Fail," *Harvard Business Review*, March 2011, p. 73.

81 Deresky, *International Management*, p. 299.

82 Ibid., p. 361.

83 Jane Levere, "Putting Safety First," *The New York Times*, January 27, 2015, p. B4.

84 Based on Samuel Greengard, "Mission Possible: Protecting Employees Abroad," *Workforce*, August 1997, pp. 30–32. See also Z. Phillips, "Global Firms Consider Additional Cover for Overseas Execs," *Business Insurance*, 43, no. 23, June 15–22, 2009, pp. 4, 22.

85 http://travel.state.gov/content/passports/english/alertswarnings.html, accessed September 11, 2014.

86 Greengard, "Mission Possible," p. 32.

87 Carla Joinson, "Save Thousands per Expatriate," *HR Magazine*, July 2002, p. 77. For a discussion of some personality aspects of the issue, see, for example, Jeffrey Herman and Lois Tetrick, "Problem-Focused versus Emotion-Focused Coping Strategies and Repatriation Adjustment," *Human Resource Management*, 48, no. 1, January/February 2009, pp. 69–88.

88 Joinson, "Save Thousands per Expatriate." A survey by accountants KPMG found that only about 4% of the 430 human resource executives surveyed believed they were effectively managing the repatriation process. Tanya Mohn, "The Long Trip Home," *The New York Times*, March 10, 2009, www.nytimes.com/2009/03/10/business/worldbusiness/10iht-10home.20715091.html, accessed October 15, 2013.

89 Ibid.

90 Deresky, *International Management*, p. 320.

91 Quoted in Leslie Klaff, "The Right Way to Bring Expats Home," *Workforce*, July 2002, p. 43.

92 Ibid.

93 Ibid.

94 Maria Kraimer et al., "The Influence of Expatriate and Repatriate Experiences on Career Advancement and Repatriate Retention," *Human Resource Management*, 48, no. 1, January–February 2009, pp. 27–47.

95 "Survey: Practitioners Say Methods at Global Employers Need Overhaul," *Bloomberg BNA Bulletin to Management*, December 17, 2013, p. 406.

96 Ann Marie Ryan, Darin Wiechmann, and Monica Hemingway, "Designing and Implementing Global Staffing Systems: Part 2—Best Practices," *Human Resource Management*, 42, no. 1, Spring 2003, pp. 85–94.

97 Ibid., p. 89.

98 Ibid., p. 90.

99 Ibid., p. 86. See also M. Schoeff, "Adopting an HR Worldview," *Workforce Management*, 87, no. 19, November 17, 2008, p. 8.

100 Ryan, Wiechmann, and Hemingway, "Designing and Implementing Global Staffing Systems," p. 87.

101 Ibid., p. 92.

Module B

1 Historically, most U.S. employees have worked for small employers with fewer than 100 workers. However around 2005 that changed. Today more employees work for larger employers (2,500 or more) then for small ones. Theo Francis, "Why You Work for Giant Company," *The Wall Street Journal*, April 7, 2017, p. A-10.

2 See, for example, https://www.bls.gov /bdm/entrepreneurship/entrepreneurship.htm, accessed April 17, 2017.

3 http://www.nber.org/digest/feb11/w16300.html, accessed May 4, 2017.

4 Studies show that the size of the business impacts human resource activities such as executive compensation, training, staffing, and HR outsourcing. Peter Hausdorf and Dale Duncan, "Firm Size and Internet Recruiting in Canada: A Preliminary Investigation," *Journal of Small-Business Management*, 42, no. 3, July 2004, pp. 325–334.

5 *SHRM Human Capital Benchmarking Study 2009*, Society for Human Resource Management, p. 12. www.shrm.org/research/surveyfindings /articles/documents/09-0620_human_cap _benchmark_full_fnl.pdf, accessed July 17, 2014.

6 Graham Dietz et al., "HRM inside UK E-commerce Firms," *International Small Business Journal*, 24, no. 5, October 2006, pp. 443–470.

7 Bernice Kotey and Cathleen Folker, "Employee Training in SMEs: Effect of Size and Firm Type—Family and Nonfamily," *Journal of Small-Business Management*, 45, no. 2, April 2007, pp. 14–39.

8 Dietz et al., "HRM inside UK E-commerce Firms."

9 Ibid. See also N. Wasserman, "Planning a Start-Up? Seize the Day... Then Expect to Work All Night," *Harvard Business Review*, 87, no. 1, January 2009, p. 27.

10 The following four points are based on Kathy Williams, "Top HR Compliance Issues for Small Businesses," *Strategic Finance*, February 2005, pp. 21–23. See also, Greg Wright, "10 Tips to Help Small Businesses Avoid Costly HR Errors," https://www.shrm.org/resourcesandtools/hr -topics/behavioral-competencies/leadership-and -navigation/pages/hr-tips-for-small-businesses .aspx, accessed July 28, 2017.

11 Evelyn Rusli, "Torment Claims Make GitHub Grow Up," *The Wall Street Journal*, July 18, 2014, pp. B1, B5.

12 Luc Sels et al., "Unraveling the HRM–Performance Link: Value-Creating and Cost-Increasing Effects of Small-Business HRM," *Journal of Management Studies*, 43, no. 2, March 2006, pp. 319–342. For supporting evidence of HR's positive effects on small companies, see also Andre Grip and Inge Sieben, "The Effects of Human Resource Management on Small Firms' Productivity and Employees' Wages," *Applied Economics*, 37, no. 9, May 20, 2005, pp. 1047–1054.

13 Dawn Carlson et al., "The Impact of Human Resource Practices and Compensation Design on Performance: An Analysis of Family-Owned SMEs," *Journal of Small Business Management*, 44, no. 4, October 2006, pp. 531–543. See also Jake Messersmith and James Guthrie, "High Performance Work Systems in Emergent Organizations: Implications for Firm Performance," *Human Resource Management*, 49, no. 2, March/April 2010, pp. 241–264.

14 Dietz et al., "HRM Inside UK E-commerce Firms." See also, Diana Wicks, "Checklist of Audit Questions for ISO Internal Audits of Human Resources," http://smallbusiness.chron .com/checklist-audit-questions-iso-internal -audits-human-resources-12265.html, accessed July 30, 2015.

15 Based on Donna Harris, "Mentors Cut Turnover Costs, Boost Sales Loyalty," *Automotive News*, June 28 2010, www.highbeam .com/doc/1G1-230393240.html.

16 Ibid.

17 Gilbert Nicholson, "Automated Assessments for Better Hires," *Workforce* (December 2000), pp. 102–107. See also www.citygaragedfw.com, accessed May 5, 2015.

18 www.citygaragedfw.com, accessed May 5, 2015.

19 www.EEOC.gov/employers/overview.html, accessed February 10, 2008.

20 http://webapps.dol.gov/elaws/firststep/, accessed May 4, 2017.

21 See for example, http://webapps.dol.gov/elaws /firststep/results.htm?fs=AA0000000C0YYY0 0000NNNNNN00000000NY, accessed May 4, 2017.

22 https://www.dol.gov/whd/flsa/index.htm, accessed May 4, 2017.

23 http://webapps.dol.gov/elaws/, accessed May 4, 2017.

24 https://www.osha.gov/dcsp/smallbusiness /index.html, accessed May 4, 2017.

25 http://online.onetcenter.org, accessed May 4, 2017.

26 "Six Common Mistakes Small Businesses Make When Incorporating Social Media into Their Recruiting Efforts," www.roberthalf.us /SocialMediaRecruitingMistakes; Rieva Lesonsky, "Find the Perfect Hire by Tapping into Social Media," *Employment Trends*, January 30, 2013, http://smallbiztrends.com/2013/01/3-ways-find -perfect-hire-social-media.html; and Emily Bennington, "Social Media Recruitment: Social Media Platforms and Your Next Hire," http://hiring .monster.com/hr/hr-best-practices/small-business /social-media-trends/social-media-recruitment .aspx, all accessed April 20, 2013.

27 Daren Dahl, "Recruiting: Tapping the Talent Pool . . . Without Drowning in Resumes," *Inc.* 31, no. 3 (April 2009), pp. 121–122.

28 Jobing.com, accessed May 4, 2017.

29 Dahl, "Recruiting."

30 For example, https://www.berkeassessment.com/, accessed May 4, 2017.

31 Dahl, "Recruiting."

32 http://interviewstream.com/, accessed May 4, 2017.

33 Ibid.

34 http://webcasts.td.org/sites, accessed May 4, 2017.

35 www.oracle.com/us/products/applications /peoplesoft-enterprise/hcm-resource -library/051027.pdf, accessed July 29, 2015.

36 http://www.halogensoftware.com/, accessed July, 28, 2017.

37 Jan de Kok, "Precautionary Actions within Small-and Medium-Sized Enterprises," *Journal of Small Business Management*, 43, no. 4, October 2005, pp. 498–516.

38 https://www.osha.gov/dcsp/smallbusiness/sharp .html, accessed May 4, 2017.

39 Dietz et al., "HRM inside UK E-Commerce Firms."

40 Colin Gray and Christopher Mabey, "Management Development: Key Differences between Small and Large Businesses in Europe," *International Small Business Journal*, 23, no. 5, October 2005, pp. 467–485.

41 From Stephen Covey, "Small Business, Big Opportunity," *Training*, 43, no. 11, November 2006, p. 40.

42 Gina Ruiz, "Smaller Firms in Vanguard of Flex Practices," *Workforce Management*, 84, no. 13, November 21, 2005, p. 10; Stephen Miller, "Are Small Businesses Shortchanged on Benefits? Surveys of benefits satisfaction at large and small firms show there's more to it than money spent," SHRM May 15, 2015, https://www.shrm.org /resourcesandtools/hr-topics/benefits/pages /shortchanged-benefits.aspx, accessed July 28, 2017.

43 Kira Bindrum, "Little Firms Redefine Culture of Work," *Crain's New York Business*, 25, no. 49, December 7–13, 2009, p. 20.

44 Ibid., pp. 7–13.

45 Ruiz, "Smaller Firms in Vanguard of Flex Practices."

46 See for example, www.irs.gov/Retirement-Plans /Plan-Sponsor/SIMPLE-IRA-Plan, accessed July 30, 2015.

47 Phillip Perry, "Welcome to the Family," *Restaurant Hospitality*, 90, no. 5, May 2006, pp. 73, 74, 76, 78.

48 Ibid.

49 Ibid.

50 Ibid.

51 Ibid.

52 Jane Applegate, "Employee Leasing Can Be a Savior for Small Firms," *Business Courier Serving Cincinnati– Northern Kentucky*, January 28, 2000, p. 23.

53 www.hr.com/en/free_forms, accessed May 4, 2017.

54 www.officedepot.com/a/browse/business -forms-tax-forms-andrecordkeeping /N=5+516208/;jsession id=0000zlVADjXrV18 WJcAFM0Ped0:13ddq0u44, accessed May 4, 2017.

55 www.hrdirect.com, accessed May 4, 2017.

56 For example, http://www.hr-guide.com/HRIS /HRIS_Vendors_Consultants.htm, http://www .softwareadvice.com/hr/, and http://www .capterra.com/human-resource-software/, all accessed May 4, 2014.

57 See for example, www.effortlesshr.com /hr-software/online-employee-management -software/, and www.capterra.com/human -resource-software/, both accessed July 18, 2014.

58 www.capterra.com/human-resource-software/, accessed July 30, 2015.

59 Adapted from Kenneth Laudon and Jane Laudon, *Management Information Systems: New Approaches to Organization and Technology* (Upper Saddle River, NJ: Prentice Hall, 1998), p. G7.

60 www.comparehris.com/BambooHR and www .bamboohr.com/tour.php, both accessed May 4, 2015; Sarah Fister Gale, "Hey, You, Get onto My Cloud . . . ," *Workforce*, August 2014, pp. 44–45.

61 https://www.bamboohr.com/, accessed July, 2017.

62 Ibid.

63 Eric Newcomer, "This Time, It's HR Getting Fired," *Bloomberg BusinessWeek*, May 25–May 31, 2015, pp. 31–33.

NAME INDEX

SUBJECT INDEX